University Casebook Series

October, 1986

ACCOUNTING AND THE LAW, Fourth Edition (1978), with Problems Pamphlet (Successor to Dohr, Phillips, Thompson & Warren)

George C. Thompson, Professor, Columbia University Graduate School of Business.
Robert Whitman, Professor of Law, University of Connecticut.
Ellis L. Phillips, Jr., Member of the New York Bar.
William C. Warren, Professor of Law Emeritus, Columbia University.

ACCOUNTING FOR LAWYERS, MATERIALS ON (1980)

David R. Herwitz, Professor of Law, Harvard University.

ADMINISTRATIVE LAW, Eighth Edition (1987), with 1983 Problems Supplement (Supplement edited in association with Paul R. Verkuil, Dean and Professor of Law, Tulane University)

Walter Gellhorn, University Professor Emeritus, Columbia University.
Clark Byse, Professor of Law, Harvard University.
Peter L. Strauss, Professor of Law, Columbia University.
Todd D. Rakoff, Professor of Law, Harvard University.

ADMIRALTY, Third Edition (1987), with Statute and Rule Supplement

Jo Desha Lucas, Professor of Law, University of Chicago.

ADVOCACY, see also Lawyering Process

AGENCY, see also Enterprise Organization

AGENCY—PARTNERSHIPS, Third Edition (1982)

Abridgement from Conard, Knauss & Siegel's Enterprise Organization, Third Edition.

ANTITRUST: FREE ENTERPRISE AND ECONOMIC ORGANIZATION, Sixth Edition (1983), with 1983 Problems in Antitrust Supplement and 1986 Case Supplement

Louis B. Schwartz, Professor of Law, University of Pennsylvania.
John J. Flynn, Professor of Law, University of Utah.
Harry First, Professor of Law, New York University.

BANKRUPTCY (1985)

Robert L. Jordan, Professor of Law, University of California, Los Angeles.
William D. Warren, Professor of Law, University of California, Los Angeles.

BUSINESS ORGANIZATION, see also Enterprise Organization

BUSINESS PLANNING, Temporary Second Edition (1984)

David R. Herwitz, Professor of Law, Harvard University.

BUSINESS TORTS (1972)

Milton Handler, Professor of Law Emeritus, Columbia University.

CHILDREN IN THE LEGAL SYSTEM (1983)

Walter Wadlington, Professor of Law, University of Virginia.
Charles H. Whitebread, Professor of Law, University of Southern California.
Samuel Davis, Professor of Law, University of Georgia.

CIVIL PROCEDURE, see Procedure

CLINIC, see also Lawyering Process

COMMERCIAL LAW (1983) with 1986 Bankruptcy Supplement

Robert L. Jordan, Professor of Law, University of California, Los Angeles.
William D. Warren, Professor of Law, University of California, Los Angeles.

COMMERCIAL LAW, CASES & MATERIALS ON, Fourth Edition (1985)

E. Allan Farnsworth, Professor of Law, Columbia University.
John Honnold, Professor of Law, University of Pennsylvania.

COMMERCIAL PAPER, Third Edition (1984)

E. Allan Farnsworth, Professor of Law, Columbia University.

COMMERCIAL PAPER (1983) (Reprinted from COMMERCIAL LAW)

Robert L. Jordan, Professor of Law, University of California, Los Angeles.
William D. Warren, Professor of Law, University of California, Los Angeles.

COMMERCIAL PAPER AND BANK DEPOSITS AND COLLECTIONS (1967), with Statutory Supplement

William D. Hawkland, Professor of Law, University of Illinois.

COMMERCIAL TRANSACTIONS—Principles and Policies (1982)

Alan Schwartz, Professor of Law, University of Southern California.
Robert E. Scott, Professor of Law, University of Virginia.

COMPARATIVE LAW, Fourth Edition (1980)

Rudolf B. Schlesinger, Professor of Law, Hastings College of the Law.

COMPETITIVE PROCESS, LEGAL REGULATION OF THE, Third Edition (1986), with 1986 Selected Statutes Supplement

Edmund W. Kitch, Professor of Law, University of Virginia.
Harvey S. Perlman, Dean of the Law School, University of Nebraska.

CONFLICT OF LAWS, Eighth Edition (1984), with 1986 Case Supplement

Willis L. M. Reese, Professor of Law, Columbia University.
Maurice Rosenberg, Professor of Law, Columbia University.

CONSTITUTIONAL LAW, Seventh Edition (1985), with 1986 Supplement

Edward L. Barrett, Jr., Professor of Law, University of California, Davis.
William Cohen, Professor of Law, Stanford University.

CONSTITUTIONAL LAW, CIVIL LIBERTY AND INDIVIDUAL RIGHTS, Second Edition (1982), with 1985 Supplement

William Cohen, Professor of Law, Stanford University.
John Kaplan, Professor of Law, Stanford University.

CONSTITUTIONAL LAW, Eleventh Edition (1985), with 1986 Supplement (Supplement edited in association with Frederick F. Schauer, Professor of Law, University of Michigan)

Gerald Gunther, Professor of Law, Stanford University.

UNIVERSITY CASEBOOK SERIES—Continued

CONSTITUTIONAL LAW, INDIVIDUAL RIGHTS IN, Fourth Edition (1986), (Reprinted from CONSTITUTIONAL LAW, Eleventh Edition), with 1986 Supplement (Supplement edited in association with Frederick F. Schauer, Professor of Law, University of Michigan)

Gerald Gunther, Professor of Law, Stanford University.

CONSUMER TRANSACTIONS (1983), with Selected Statutes and Regulations Supplement and 1987 Case Supplement

Michael M. Greenfield, Professor of Law, Washington University.

CONTRACT LAW AND ITS APPLICATION, Third Edition (1983)

The late Addison Mueller, Professor of Law, University of California, Los Angeles.
Arthur I. Rosett, Professor of Law, University of California, Los Angeles.
Gerald P. Lopez, Professor of Law, University of California, Los Angeles.

CONTRACT LAW, STUDIES IN, Third Edition (1984)

Edward J. Murphy, Professor of Law, University of Notre Dame.
Richard E. Speidel, Professor of Law, Northwestern University.

CONTRACTS, Fourth Edition (1982)

John P. Dawson, Professor of Law Emeritus, Harvard University.
William Burnett Harvey, Professor of Law and Political Science, Boston University.
Stanley D. Henderson, Professor of Law, University of Virginia.

CONTRACTS, Third Edition (1980), with Statutory Supplement

E. Allan Farnsworth, Professor of Law, Columbia University.
William F. Young, Professor of Law, Columbia University.

CONTRACTS, Second Edition (1978), with Statutory and Administrative Law Supplement (1978)

Ian R. Macneil, Professor of Law, Cornell University.

COPYRIGHT, PATENTS AND TRADEMARKS, see also Competitive Process; see also Selected Statutes and International Agreements

COPYRIGHT, PATENT, TRADEMARK AND RELATED STATE DOCTRINES, Second Edition (1981), with 1985 Case Supplement, 1986 Selected Statutes Supplement and 1981 Problem Supplement

Paul Goldstein, Professor of Law, Stanford University.

COPYRIGHT, Unfair Competition, and Other Topics Bearing on the Protection of Literary, Musical, and Artistic Works, Fourth Edition (1985), with 1985 Statutory Supplement

Ralph S. Brown, Jr., Professor of Law, Yale University.
Robert C. Denicola, Professor of Law, University of Nebraska.

CORPORATE ACQUISITIONS, The Law and Finance of (1986)

Ronald J. Gilson, Professor of Law, Stanford University.

CORPORATE FINANCE, Second Edition (1979), with 1984 Supplement

Victor Brudney, Professor of Law, Harvard University.
Marvin A. Chirelstein, Professor of Law, Columbia University.

CORPORATE READJUSTMENTS AND REORGANIZATIONS (1976)

Walter J. Blum, Professor of Law, University of Chicago.
Stanley A. Kaplan, Professor of Law, University of Chicago.

CORPORATION LAW, BASIC, Second Edition (1979), with 1983 Case and Documentary Supplement

Detlev F. Vagts, Professor of Law, Harvard University.

CORPORATIONS, see also Enterprise Organization

CORPORATIONS, Fifth Edition—Unabridged (1980), with 1986 Supplement

The late William L. Cary, Professor of Law, Columbia University.
Melvin Aron Eisenberg, Professor of Law, University of California, Berkeley.

CORPORATIONS, Fifth Edition—Abridged (1980), with 1986 Supplement

The late William L. Cary, Professor of Law, Columbia University.
Melvin Aron Eisenberg, Professor of Law, University of California, Berkeley.

CORPORATIONS, Second Edition (1982), with 1982 Corporation and Partnership Statutes, Rules and Forms

Alfred F. Conard, Professor of Law, University of Michigan.
Robert N. Knauss, Dean of the Law School, University of Houston.
Stanley Siegel, Professor of Law, University of California, Los Angeles.

CORPORATIONS COURSE GAME PLAN (1975)

David R. Herwitz, Professor of Law, Harvard University.

CORRECTIONS, SEE SENTENCING

CREDITORS' RIGHTS, see also Debtor-Creditor Law

CRIMINAL JUSTICE ADMINISTRATION, Third Edition (1986), with 1986 Case Supplement

Frank W. Miller, Professor of Law, Washington University.
Robert O. Dawson, Professor of Law, University of Texas.
George E. Dix, Professor of Law, University of Texas.
Raymond I. Parnas, Professor of Law, University of California, Davis.

CRIMINAL LAW, Third Edition (1983)

Fred E. Inbau, Professor of Law Emeritus, Northwestern University.
James R. Thompson, Professor of Law Emeritus, Northwestern University.
Andre A. Moenssens, Professor of Law, University of Richmond.

CRIMINAL LAW AND APPROACHES TO THE STUDY OF LAW (1986)

John M. Brumbaugh, Professor of Law, University of Maryland.

CRIMINAL LAW, Second Edition (1986)

Peter W. Low, Professor of Law, University of Virginia.
John C. Jeffries, Jr., Professor of Law, University of Virginia.
Richard C. Bonnie, Professor of Law, University of Virginia.

CRIMINAL LAW, Fourth Edition (1986)

Lloyd L. Weinreb, Professor of Law, Harvard University.

CRIMINAL LAW AND PROCEDURE, Sixth Edition (1984)

Rollin M. Perkins, Professor of Law Emeritus, University of California, Hastings College of the Law.
Ronald N. Boyce, Professor of Law, University of Utah.

UNIVERSITY CASEBOOK SERIES—Continued

CRIMINAL PROCEDURE, Second Edition (1980), with 1986 Supplement

Fred E. Inbau, Professor of Law Emeritus, Northwestern University.
James R. Thompson, Professor of Law Emeritus, Northwestern University.
James B. Haddad, Professor of Law, Northwestern University.
James B. Zagel, Chief, Criminal Justice Division, Office of Attorney General of Illinois.
Gary L. Starkman, Assistant U. S. Attorney, Northern District of Illinois.

CRIMINAL PROCESS, Third Edition (1978), with 1986 Supplement

Lloyd L. Weinreb, Professor of Law, Harvard University.

DAMAGES, Second Edition (1952)

Charles T. McCormick, late Professor of Law, University of Texas.
William F. Fritz, late Professor of Law, University of Texas.

DEBTOR–CREDITOR LAW (1984) with 1986 Supplement

Theodore Eisenberg, Professor of Law, Cornell University.

DEBTOR–CREDITOR LAW, Second Edition (1981), with Statutory Supplement

William D. Warren, Dean of the School of Law, University of California, Los Angeles.
William E. Hogan, Professor of Law, New York University.

DECEDENTS' ESTATES (1971)

Max Rheinstein, late Professor of Law Emeritus, University of Chicago.
Mary Ann Glendon, Professor of Law, Boston College.

DECEDENTS' ESTATES AND TRUSTS, Sixth Edition (1982)

John Ritchie, Emeritus. Dean and Wigmore Professor of Law, Northwestern University.
Neill H. Alford, Jr., Professor of Law, University of Virginia.
Richard W. Effland, Professor of Law, Arizona State University.

DOMESTIC RELATIONS, see also Family Law

DOMESTIC RELATIONS, Successor Edition (1984) with 1987 Supplement

Walter Wadlington, Professor of Law, University of Virginia.

ELECTRONIC MASS MEDIA, Second Edition (1979)

William K. Jones, Professor of Law, Columbia University.

EMPLOYMENT DISCRIMINATION, Second Edition (1987)

Joel W. Friedman, Professor of Law, Tulane University.
George M. Strickler, Professor of Law, Tulane University.

ENERGY LAW (1983) with 1986 Case Supplement

Donald N. Zillman, Professor of Law, University of Utah.
Laurence Lattman, Dean of Mines and Engineering, University of Utah.

ENTERPRISE ORGANIZATION, Third Edition (1982), with 1982 Corporation and Partnership Statutes, Rules and Forms Supplement

Alfred F. Conard, Professor of Law, University of Michigan.
Robert L. Knauss, Dean of the Law School, University of Houston.
Stanley Siegel, Professor of Law, University of California, Los Angeles.

ENVIRONMENTAL POLICY LAW 1985 Edition, with 1985 Problems Supplement (Supplement in association with Ronald H. Rosenberg, Professor of Law, College of William and Mary)

Thomas J. Schoenbaum, Professor of Law, University of Georgia.

UNIVERSITY CASEBOOK SERIES—Continued

EQUITY, see also Remedies

EQUITY, RESTITUTION AND DAMAGES, Second Edition (1974)

Robert Childres, late Professor of Law, Northwestern University.
William F. Johnson, Jr., Professor of Law, New York University.

ESTATE PLANNING, Second Edition (1982), with 1985 Case, Text and Documentary Supplement

David Westfall, Professor of Law, Harvard University.

ETHiCS, see Legal Profession, and Professional Responsibility

ETHICS AND PROFESSIONAL RESPONSIBILITY (1981) (Reprinted from THE LAWYERING PROCESS)

Gary Bellow, Professor of Law, Harvard University.
Bea Moulton, Legal Services Corporation.

EVIDENCE, Fifth Edition (1984)

John Kaplan, Professor of Law, Stanford University.
Jon R. Waltz, Professor of Law, Northwestern University.

EVIDENCE, Seventh Edition (1983) with Rules and Statute Supplement (1984)

Jack B. Weinstein, Chief Judge, United States District Court.
John H. Mansfield, Professor of Law, Harvard University.
Norman Abrams, Professor of Law, University of California, Los Angeles.
Margaret Berger, Professor of Law, Brooklyn Law School.

FAMILY LAW, see also Domestic Relations

FAMILY LAW Second Edition (1985)

Judith C. Areen, Professor of Law, Georgetown University.

FAMILY LAW AND CHILDREN IN THE LEGAL SYSTEM, STATUTORY MATERIALS (1981)

Walter Wadlington, Professor of Law, University of Virginia.

FEDERAL COURTS, Seventh Edition (1982), with 1986 Supplement

Charles T. McCormick, late Professor of Law, University of Texas.
James H. Chadbourn, late Professor of Law, Harvard University.
Charles Alan Wright, Professor of Law, University of Texas.

FEDERAL COURTS AND THE FEDERAL SYSTEM, Hart and Wechsler's Second Edition (1973), with 1981 Supplement

Paul M. Bator, Professor of Law, Harvard University.
Paul J. Mishkin, Professor of Law, University of California, Berkeley.
David L. Shapiro, Professor of Law, Harvard University.
Herbert Wechsler, Professor of Law, Columbia University.

FEDERAL PUBLIC LAND AND RESOURCES LAW, Second Edition (1987), with 1984 Statutory Supplement

George C. Coggins, Professor of Law, University of Kansas.
Charles F. Wilkinson, Professor of Law, University of Oregon.

FEDERAL RULES OF CIVIL PROCEDURE, 1986 Edition

FEDERAL TAXATION, see Taxation

FOOD AND DRUG LAW (1980), with Statutory Supplement

Richard A. Merrill, Dean of the School of Law, University of Virginia.
Peter Barton Hutt, Esq.

FUTURE INTERESTS (1958)

Philip Mechem, late Professor of Law Emeritus, University of Pennsylvania.

FUTURE INTERESTS (1970)

Howard R. Williams, Professor of Law, Stanford University.

FUTURE INTERESTS AND ESTATE PLANNING (1961), with 1962 Supplement

W. Barton Leach, late Professor of Law, Harvard University.
James K. Logan, formerly Dean of the Law School, University of Kansas.

GOVERNMENT CONTRACTS, FEDERAL, Successor Edition (1985)

John W. Whelan, Professor of Law, Hastings College of the Law.

GOVERNMENT REGULATION: FREE ENTERPRISE AND ECONOMIC ORGANI-ZATION, Sixth Edition (1985)

Louis B. Schwartz, Professor of Law, University of Pennsylvania.
John J. Flynn, Professor of Law, University of Utah.
Harry First, Professor of Law, New York University.

HINCKLEY JOHN W., TRIAL OF: A Case Study of the Insanity Defense

Peter W. Low, Professor of Law, University of Virginia.
John C. Jeffries, Jr., Professor of Law, University of Virginia.
Richard C. Bonnie, Professor of Law, University of Virginia.

INJUNCTIONS, Second Edition (1984)

Owen M. Fiss, Professor of Law, Yale University.
Doug Rendleman, Professor of Law, College of William and Mary.

INSTITUTIONAL INVESTORS, 1978

David L. Ratner, Professor of Law, Cornell University.

INSURANCE, Second Edition (1985)

William F. Young, Professor of Law, Columbia University.
Eric M. Holmes, Professor of Law, University of Georgia.

INTERNATIONAL LAW, see also Transnational Legal Problems, Transnational Business Problems, and United Nations Law

INTERNATIONAL LAW IN CONTEMPORARY PERSPECTIVE (1981), with Essay Supplement

Myres S. McDougal, Professor of Law, Yale University.
W. Michael Reisman, Professor of Law, Yale University.

INTERNATIONAL LEGAL SYSTEM, Second Edition (1981), with Documentary Supplement

Joseph Modeste Sweeney, Professor of Law, Tulane University.
Covey T. Oliver, Professor of Law, University of Pennsylvania.
Noyes E. Leech, Professor of Law, University of Pennsylvania.

INTRODUCTION TO LAW, see also Legal Method, On Law in Courts, and Dynamics of American Law

INTRODUCTION TO THE STUDY OF LAW (1970)

E. Wayne Thode, late Professor of Law, University of Utah.
Leon Lebowitz, Professor of Law, University of Texas.
Lester J. Mazor, Professor of Law, University of Utah.

JUDICIAL CODE and Rules of Procedure in the Federal Courts with Excerpts from the Criminal Code, 1984 Edition

Henry M. Hart, Jr., late Professor of Law, Harvard University.
Herbert Wechsler, Professor of Law, Columbia University.

JURISPRUDENCE (Temporary Edition Hardbound) (1949)

Lon L. Fuller, Professor of Law Emeritus, Harvard University.

JUVENILE, see also Children

JUVENILE JUSTICE PROCESS, Third Edition (1985)

Frank W. Miller, Professor of Law, Washington University.
Robert O. Dawson, Professor of Law, University of Texas.
George E. Dix, Professor of Law, University of Texas.
Raymond I. Parnas, Professor of Law, University of California, Davis.

LABOR LAW, Tenth Edition (1986), with 1986 Statutory Supplement

Archibald Cox, Professor of Law, Harvard University.
Derek C. Bok, President, Harvard University.
Robert A. Gorman, Professor of Law, University of Pennsylvania.

LABOR LAW, Second Edition (1982), with Statutory Supplement

Clyde W. Summers, Professor of Law, University of Pennsylvania.
Harry H. Wellington, Dean of the Law School, Yale University.
Alan Hyde, Professor of Law, Rutgers University.

LAND FINANCING, Third Edition (1985)

The late Norman Penney, Professor of Law, Cornell University.
Richard F. Broude, Member of the California Bar.
Roger Cunningham, Professor of Law, University of Michigan.

LAW AND MEDICINE (1980)

Walter Wadlington, Professor of Law and Professor of Legal Medicine, University of Virginia.
Jon R. Waltz, Professor of Law, Northwestern University.
Roger B. Dworkin, Professor of Law, Indiana University, and Professor of Biomedical History, University of Washington.

LAW, LANGUAGE AND ETHICS (1972)

William R. Bishin, Professor of Law, University of Southern California.
Christopher D. Stone, Professor of Law, University of Southern California.

LAW, SCIENCE AND MEDICINE (1984), with 1987 Supplement

Judith C. Areen, Professor of Law, Georgetown University.
Patricia A. King, Professor of Law, Georgetown University.
Steven P. Goldberg, Professor of Law, Georgetown University.
Alexander M. Capron, Professor of Law, Georgetown University.

LAWYERING PROCESS (1978), with Civil Problem Supplement and Criminal Problem Supplement

Gary Bellow, Professor of Law, Harvard University.
Bea Moulton, Professor of Law, Arizona State University.

LEGAL METHOD (1980)

Harry W. Jones, Professor of Law Emeritus, Columbia University.
John M. Kernochan, Professor of Law, Columbia University.
Arthur W. Murphy, Professor of Law, Columbia University.

UNIVERSITY CASEBOOK SERIES—Continued

LEGAL METHODS (1969)

Robert N. Covington, Professor of Law, Vanderbilt University.
E. Blythe Stason, late Professor of Law, Vanderbilt University.
John W. Wade, Professor of Law, Vanderbilt University.
Elliott E. Cheatham, late Professor of Law, Vanderbilt University.
Theodore A. Smedley, Professor of Law, Vanderbilt University.

LEGAL PROFESSION, THE, Responsibility and Regulation (1985)

Geoffrey C. Hazard, Jr., Professor of Law, Yale University.
Deborah L. Rhode, Professor of Law, Stanford University.

LEGISLATION, Fourth Edition (1982) (by Fordham)

Horace E. Read, late Vice President, Dalhousie University.
John W. MacDonald, Professor of Law Emeritus, Cornell Law School.
Jefferson B. Fordham, Professor of Law, University of Utah.
William J. Pierce, Professor of Law, University of Michigan.

LEGISLATIVE AND ADMINISTRATIVE PROCESSES, Second Edition (1981)

Hans A. Linde, Judge, Supreme Court of Oregon.
George Bunn, Professor of Law, University of Wisconsin.
Fredericka Paff, Professor of Law, University of Wisconsin.
W. Lawrence Church, Professor of Law, University of Wisconsin.

LOCAL GOVERNMENT LAW, Second Revised Edition (1986)

Jefferson B. Fordham, Professor of Law, University of Utah.

MASS MEDIA LAW, Third Edition (1987)

Marc A. Franklin, Professor of Law, Stanford University.

MENTAL HEALTH PROCESS, Second Edition (1976), with 1981 Supplement

Frank W. Miller, Professor of Law, Washington University.
Robert O. Dawson, Professor of Law, University of Texas.
George E. Dix, Professor of Law, University of Texas.
Raymond I. Parnas, Professor of Law, University of California, Davis.

MUNICIPAL CORPORATIONS, see Local Government Law

NEGOTIABLE INSTRUMENTS, see Commercial Paper

NEGOTIATION (1981) (Reprinted from THE LAWYERING PROCESS)

Gary Bellow, Professor of Law, Harvard Law School.
Bea Moulton, Legal Services Corporation.

NEW YORK PRACTICE, Fourth Edition (1978)

Herbert Peterfreund, Professor of Law, New York University.
Joseph M. McLaughlin, Dean of the Law School, Fordham University.

OIL AND GAS, Fifth Edition (1987)

Howard R. Williams, Professor of Law, Stanford University.
Richard C. Maxwell, Professor of Law, University of California, Los Angeles.
Charles J. Meyers, Dean of the Law School, Stanford University.
Stephen F. Williams, Professor of Law, University of Colorado.

ON LAW IN COURTS (1965)

Paul J. Mishkin, Professor of Law, University of California, Berkeley.
Clarence Morris, Professor of Law Emeritus, University of Pennsylvania.

PATENTS AND ANTITRUST (Pamphlet) (1983)

Milton Handler, Professor of Law Emeritus, Columbia University.
Harlan M. Blake, Professor of Law, Columbia University.
Robert Pitofsky, Professor of Law, Georgetown University.
Harvey J. Goldschmid, Professor of Law, Columbia University.

PERSPECTIVES ON THE LAWYER AS PLANNER (Reprint of Chapters One through Five of Planning by Lawyers) (1978)

Louis M. Brown, Professor of Law, University of Southern California.
Edward A. Dauer, Professor of Law, Yale University.

PLANNING BY LAWYERS, MATERIALS ON A NONADVERSARIAL LEGAL PROCESS (1978)

Louis M. Brown, Professor of Law, University of Southern California.
Edward A. Dauer, Professor of Law, Yale University.

PLEADING AND PROCEDURE, see Procedure, Civil

POLICE FUNCTION, Fourth Edition (1986), with 1986 Case Supplement

Reprint of Chapters 1–10 of Miller, Dawson, Dix and Parnas's CRIMINAL JUSTICE ADMINISTRATION, Third Edition.

PREPARING AND PRESENTING THE CASE (1981) (Reprinted from THE LAWYERING PROCESS)

Gary Bellow, Professor of Law, Harvard Law School.
Bea Moulton, Legal Services Corporation.

PREVENTIVE LAW, see also Planning by Lawyers

PROCEDURE—CIVIL PROCEDURE, Second Edition (1974), with 1979 Supplement

The late James H. Chadbourn, Professor of Law, Harvard University.
A. Leo Levin, Professor of Law, University of Pennsylvania.
Philip Shuchman, Professor of Law, Cornell University.

PROCEDURE—CIVIL PROCEDURE, Fifth Edition (1984), with 1986 Supplement

Richard H. Field, late Professor of Law, Harvard University.
Benjamin Kaplan, Professor of Law Emeritus, Harvard University.
Kevin M. Clermont, Professor of Law, Cornell University.

PROCEDURE—CIVIL PROCEDURE, Fourth Edition (1985)

Maurice Rosenberg, Professor of Law, Columbia University.
Hans Smit, Professor of Law, Columbia University.
Harold L. Korn, Professor of Law, Columbia University.

PROCEDURE—PLEADING AND PROCEDURE: State and Federal, Fifth Edition (1983), with 1986 Supplement

David W. Louisell, late Professor of Law, University of California, Berkeley.
Geoffrey C. Hazard, Jr., Professor of Law, Yale University.
Colin C. Tait, Professor of Law, University of Connecticut.

PROCEDURE—FEDERAL RULES OF CIVIL PROCEDURE, 1986 Edition

PRODUCTS LIABILITY (1980)

Marshall S. Shapo, Professor of Law, Northwestern University.

PRODUCTS LIABILITY AND SAFETY (1980), with 1985 Case and Documentary Supplement

W. Page Keeton, Professor of Law, University of Texas.
David G. Owen, Professor of Law, University of South Carolina.
John E. Montgomery, Professor of Law, University of South Carolina.

PROFESSIONAL RESPONSIBILITY, Third Edition (1984), with 1986 Selected National Standards Supplement

Thomas D. Morgan, Dean of the Law School, Emory University.
Ronald D. Rotunda, Professor of Law, University of Illinois.

PROPERTY, Fifth Edition (1984)

John E. Cribbet, Dean of the Law School, University of Illinois.
Corwin W. Johnson, Professor of Law, University of Texas.

PROPERTY—PERSONAL (1953)

S. Kenneth Skolfield, late Professor of Law Emeritus, Boston University.

PROPERTY—PERSONAL, Third Edition (1954)

Everett Fraser, late Dean of the Law School Emeritus, University of Minnesota.
Third Edition by Charles W. Taintor, late Professor of Law, University of Pittsburgh.

PROPERTY—INTRODUCTION, TO REAL PROPERTY, Third Edition (1954)

Everett Fraser, late Dean of the Law School Emeritus, University of Minnesota.

PROPERTY—REAL AND PERSONAL, Combined Edition (1954)

Everett Fraser, late Dean of the Law School Emeritus, University of Minnesota.
Third Edition of Personal Property by Charles W. Taintor, late Professor of Law, University of Pittsburgh.

PROPERTY—FUNDAMENTALS OF MODERN REAL PROPERTY, Second Edition (1982), with 1985 Supplement

Edward H. Rabin, Professor of Law, University of California, Davis.

PROPERTY—PROBLEMS IN REAL PROPERTY (Pamphlet) (1969)

Edward H. Rabin, Professor of Law, University of California, Davis.

PROPERTY, REAL (1984)

Paul Goldstein, Professor of Law, Stanford University.

PROSECUTION AND ADJUDICATION, Third Edition (1986), with 1986 Case Supplement

Reprint of Chapters 11–26 of Miller, Dawson, Dix and Parnas's CRIMINAL JUSTICE ADMINISTRATION, Third Edition.

PSYCHIATRY AND LAW, see Mental Health, see also Hinckley, Trial of

PUBLIC REGULATION OF DANGEROUS PRODUCTS (paperback) (1980)

Marshall S. Shapo, Professor of Law, Northwestern University.

PUBLIC UTILITY LAW, see Free Enterprise, also Regulated Industries

REAL ESTATE PLANNING (1980), with 1980 Problems, Statutes and New Materials Supplement

Norton L. Steuben, Professor of Law, University of Colorado.

UNIVERSITY CASEBOOK SERIES—Continued

REAL ESTATE TRANSACTIONS, Second Edition (1985), with 1985 Statute, Form and Problem Supplement

Paul Goldstein, Professor of Law, Stanford University.

RECEIVERSHIP AND CORPORATE REORGANIZATION, see Creditors' Rights

REGULATED INDUSTRIES, Second Edition, 1976

William K. Jones, Professor of Law, Columbia University.

REMEDIES (1982), with 1984 Case Supplement

Edward D. Re, Chief Judge, U. S. Court of International Trade.

RESTITUTION, Second Edition (1966)

John W. Wade, Professor of Law, Vanderbilt University.

SALES, Second Edition (1986)

Marion W. Benfield, Jr., Professor of Law, University of Illinois.
William D. Hawkland, Chancellor, Louisiana State Law Center.

SALES AND SALES FINANCING, Fifth Edition (1984)

John Honnold, Professor of Law, University of Pennsylvania.

SALES LAW AND THE CONTRACTING PROCESS (1982)

Reprint of Chapters 1–10 of Schwartz and Scott's Commercial Transactions.

SECURED TRANSACTIONS IN PERSONAL PROPERTY (1983) (Reprinted from COMMERCIAL LAW)

Robert L. Jordan, Professor of Law, University of California, Los Angeles.
William D. Warren, Professor of Law, University of California, Los Angeles.

SECURITIES REGULATION, Fifth Edition (1982), with 1986 Cases and Releases Supplement and 1986 Selected Statutes, Rules and Forms Supplement

Richard W. Jennings, Professor of Law, University of California, Berkeley.
Harold Marsh, Jr., Member of California Bar.

SECURITIES REGULATION (1982), with 1985 Supplement

Larry D. Soderquist, Professor of Law, Vanderbilt University.

SECURITY INTERESTS IN PERSONAL PROPERTY (1984)

Douglas G. Baird, Professor of Law, University of Chicago.
Thomas H. Jackson, Professor of Law, Stanford University.

SECURITY INTERESTS IN PERSONAL PROPERTY (1985) (Reprinted from Sales and Sales Financing, Fifth Edition)

John Honnold, Professor of Law, University of Pennsylvania.

SENTENCING AND THE CORRECTIONAL PROCESS, Second Edition (1976)

Frank W. Miller, Professor of Law, Washington University.
Robert O. Dawson, Professor of Law, University of Texas.
George E. Dix, Professor of Law, University of Texas.
Raymond I. Parnas, Professor of Law, University of California, Davis.

SOCIAL SCIENCE IN LAW, Cases and Materials (1985)

John Monahan, Professor of Law, University of Virginia.
Laurens Walker, Professor of Law, University of Virginia.

UNIVERSITY CASEBOOK SERIES—Continued

SOCIAL WELFARE AND THE INDIVIDUAL (1971)

Robert J. Levy, Professor of Law, University of Minnesota.
Thomas P. Lewis, Dean of the College of Law, University of Kentucky.
Peter W. Martin, Professor of Law, Cornell University.

TAX, POLICY ANALYSIS OF THE FEDERAL INCOME (1976)

William A. Klein, Professor of Law, University of California, Los Angeles.

TAXATION, FEDERAL INCOME, Successor Edition (1985)

Michael J. Graetz, Professor of Law, Yale University.

TAXATION, FEDERAL INCOME, Fifth Edition (1985)

James J. Freeland, Professor of Law, University of Florida.
Stephen A. Lind, Professor of Law, University of Florida.
Richard B. Stephens, Professor of Law Emeritus, University of Florida.

TAXATION, FEDERAL INCOME, Volume I, Personal Income Taxation, Successor Edition (1986), Volume II, Taxation of Partnerships and Corporations, Second Edition (1980), with 1985 Legislative Supplement

Stanley S. Surrey, late Professor of Law, Harvard University.
Paul R. McDaniel, Professor of Law, Boston College Law School.
Hugh J. Ault, Professor of Law, Boston College Law School.
Stanley A. Koppelman, Boston University

TAXATION, FEDERAL WEALTH TRANSFER, Second Edition (1982) with 1985 Legislative Supplement

Stanley S. Surrey, late Professor of Law, Harvard University.
William C. Warren, Professor of Law Emeritus, Columbia University.
Paul R. McDaniel, Professor of Law, Boston College Law School.
Harry L. Gutman, Instructor, Harvard Law School and Boston College Law School.

TAXATION, FUNDAMENTALS OF CORPORATE, Cases and Materials (1985)

Stephen A. Lind, Professor of Law, University of Florida.
Stephen Schwarz, Professor of Law, University of California, Hastings.
Daniel J. Lathrope, Professor of Law, University of California, Hastings.
Joshua Rosenberg, Professor of Law, University of San Francisco.

TAXATION, FUNDAMENTALS OF PARTNERSHIP, Cases and Materials (1985)

Stephen A. Lind, Professor of Law, University of California, Hastings.
Stephen Schwarz, Professor of Law, University of California, Hastings.
Daniel J. Lathrope, Professor of Law, University of California, Hastings.
Joshua Rosenberg, Professor of Law, University of San Francisco.

TAXATION, PROBLEMS IN THE FEDERAL INCOME TAXATION OF PARTNERSHIPS AND CORPORATIONS, Second Edition (1986)

Norton L. Steuben, Professor of Law, University of Colorado.
William J. Turnier, Professor of Law, University of North Carolina.

TAXATION, PROBLEMS IN THE FUNDAMENTALS OF FEDERAL INCOME, Second Edition (1985)

Norton L. Steuben, Professor of Law, University of Colorado.
William J. Turnier, Professor of Law, University of North Carolina.

TAXES AND FINANCE—STATE AND LOCAL (1974)

Oliver Oldman, Professor of Law, Harvard University.
Ferdinand P. Schoettle, Professor of Law, University of Minnesota.

UNIVERSITY CASEBOOK SERIES—Continued

TORT LAW AND ALTERNATIVES, Third Edition (1983)

Marc A. Franklin, Professor of Law, Stanford University.
Robert L. Rabin, Professor of Law, Stanford University.

TORTS, Seventh Edition (1982)

William L. Prosser, late Professor of Law, University of California, Hastings College.
John W. Wade, Professor of Law, Vanderbilt University.
Victor E. Schwartz, Professor of Law, American University.

TORTS, Third Edition (1976)

Harry Shulman, late Dean of the Law School, Yale University.
Fleming James, Jr., Professor of Law Emeritus, Yale University.
Oscar S. Gray, Professor of Law, University of Maryland.

TRADE REGULATION, Second Edition (1983), with 1985 Supplement

Milton Handler, Professor of Law Emeritus, Columbia University.
Harlan M. Blake, Professor of Law, Columbia University.
Robert Pitofsky, Professor of Law, Georgetown University.
Harvey J. Goldschmid, Professor of Law, Columbia University.

TRADE REGULATION, see Antitrust

TRANSNATIONAL BUSINESS PROBLEMS (1986)

Detlev F. Vagts, Professor of Law, Harvard University.

TRANSNATIONAL LEGAL PROBLEMS, Third Edition (1986) with Documentary Supplement

Henry J. Steiner, Professor of Law, Harvard University.
Detlev F. Vagts, Professor of Law, Harvard University.

TRIAL, see also Evidence, Making the Record, Lawyering Process and Preparing and Presenting the Case

TRIAL ADVOCACY (1968)

A. Leo Levin, Professor of Law, University of Pennsylvania.
Harold Cramer, of the Pennsylvania Bar.
Maurice Rosenberg, Professor of Law, Columbia University, Consultant.

TRUSTS, Fifth Edition (1978)

George G. Bogert, late Professor of Law Emeritus, University of Chicago.
Dallin H. Oaks, President, Brigham Young University.

TRUSTS AND SUCCESSION (Palmer's), Fourth Edition (1983)

Richard V. Wellman, Professor of Law, University of Georgia.
Lawrence W. Waggoner, Professor of Law, University of Michigan.
Olin L. Browder, Jr., Professor of Law, University of Michigan.

UNFAIR COMPETITION, see Competitive Process and Business Torts

UNITED NATIONS LAW, Second Edition (1967), with Documentary Supplement (1968)

Louis B. Sohn, Professor of Law, Harvard University.

WATER RESOURCE MANAGEMENT, Second Edition (1980), with 1983 Supplement

Charles J. Meyers, Dean of the Law School, Stanford University.
A. Dan Tarlock, Professor of Law, Indiana University.

UNIVERSITY CASEBOOK SERIES—Continued

WILLS AND ADMINISTRATION, Fifth Edition (1961)
Philip Mechem, late Professor of Law, University of Pennsylvania.
Thomas E. Atkinson, late Professor of Law, New York University.

WORLD LAW, see United Nations Law

MATERIALS FOR A BASIC COURSE

IN

CIVIL PROCEDURE

By

RICHARD H. FIELD

Late Story Professor of Law Emeritus, Harvard University

BENJAMIN KAPLAN

Royall Professor of Law Emeritus, Harvard University

Retired Associate Justice, Supreme Judicial Court
of Massachusetts

and

KEVIN M. CLERMONT

Professor of Law, Cornell University

FIFTH EDITION

Mineola, New York
THE FOUNDATION PRESS, INC.
1984

Library of Congress Cataloging in Publication Data

Field, Richard H.
    Materials for a basic course in civil procedure.

    (University casebook series)
    Includes index.
    1. Civil procedure—United States. I. Kaplan,
Benjamin, 1911-   . II. Clermont, Kevin M. III. Title.
IV. Series.

KF8839.F5   1984   347.73'5   84-6043
                      347.3075

ISBN 0-88277-173-6

F., K. & C. Civ.Proc. 5th Ed. UCB

2nd Reprint—1986

PREFACE

This Fifth Edition represents a thorough rewriting, updating, and overhauling. Nevertheless, the revision also reflects a basic satisfaction with the objectives, with the methods, and generally with the depth and range of coverage that have characterized this casebook since its beginnings. Therefore, I appropriately begin with the words that Professor Field and Justice Kaplan used to describe their trailblazing First Edition:

"Traditional courses in Civil Procedure suffered from being too much concerned with detail and too diffuse. These defects were perhaps due to an overscrupulous regard for the obligations which Procedure was thought to owe to other courses in the curriculum; in all events Procedure often seemed to underplay the fact that it had distinctive missions of its own. And in straining either for omnibus coverage or for the satisfactions that came from historical exposition, the traditional courses dwelt too long on the common law and older code systems and gave less than adequate attention to current practice.

"We have sought to avoid these errors even if we have succeeded only in committing others. A basic course should, we think, lay stress on the fundamental and recurrent problems of litigative procedure as against particular procedural devices. To be sure, the course should insist on the mastery of specifics, but the larger picture should be kept in view. As a second objective, not antithetical but rather intrinsic to the first, the course should give a rounded understanding of a single, modern system of procedure. The choice naturally falls on the Federal system. The common law and older codes may come in by way of comparison and as a reading of the minutes of yesterday's meeting, but the Federal Rules should be a principal theme.

"The belief that the course should deal in a large way with the litigative process has impelled us at various points to deal explicitly with the general attitudes that underlie and characterize current procedural modes. It has also induced us to draw in some elementary materials on proof and division of functions between judge and jury which are usually reserved for the course in Evidence. With the adoption of Federal procedure as a center of study we have been led into a number of problems of Federal jurisdiction and into questions arising when Federal courts apply State law and State courts apply Federal law. No examination of a modern system could fail to concern itself with multi-party litigation which has so far increased in frequency and importance that it demands attention even of beginning students. We therefore deal with the subject of parties. This and some other topics of equitable flavor seem to have proper place in Procedure, and especially so when, as in our school, Equity is abolished as a separate course and distributed on a functional basis to other parts of the curriculum.

"On the side of method, we set much store by the pedagogical device which will be found early in this book in Part One, Topic B, entitled 'Phases of a Lawsuit.' Here we have about 150 pages of text interspersed with cases, statutes and questions, describing and analyzing the conduct of litigation in the Federal courts from the institution of suit through appeal. We have sought here to convey bedrock information and to locate and expose significant questions which provide the basis for much of the rest of the book. This initial survey makes considerable demands on students but it seems to us to have the virtues of giving them a sense of procedure as a whole, of raising at the threshold and keeping steadily before them the fundamental and recurrent problems of adjudication, and of enabling them to proceed thereafter on a more profound level than they might otherwise attain. Perhaps we should add that after this survey we have felt less than the usual scruples of conscience about making some omissions later in the course as pressure of time has compelled it.

"Treating a number of passages in the materials as background reading for students requiring little if any classroom discussion, we have still been unable to cover the whole book in a course given three times a week for a year. We have followed respectable precedent in leaving in rather more than can be comfortably handled, remitting to individual taste and need some choices that we have not had the fortitude to make firmly between ourselves. We regret especially that on no allocation of space which seemed to us reasonable have we been able to provide the kind of bridge we would like to make between court procedure and the procedure of administrative agencies.

"Teachers of Procedure have differed widely about the route to be travelled, but they have not differed much about the ultimate goal. They have sought in their separate ways to turn out lawyers who will not approach a practice question as just an exercise in using the index to the practice act or the rule book, but who will go about the job with a lively awareness of the importance of farsighted procedural strategy, a sense of the total procedural resources of the law, and a feeling of personal responsibility for the fair and efficient running of procedural machinery. We have hoped in this book to help students toward the vital skills and attitudes."

Those words still stand as a statement of our views on what a Civil Procedure course should try to do. Also, we continue to rely on the three increasingly broad surveys of Topics A, B, and C of Part One to give the student a solid and complete grounding in the subject, thereby freeing the teacher to pick and choose among the fundamental and pressing problem areas explored in the subsequent Parts of the current edition.

Each succeeding edition has altered the emphases and refined the techniques, of course. In this latest edition, for example, a renewed attention to the role of the editors' questions signifies a continuing attempt to make all the materials more instructive and accessible, without betraying their original spirit of rigor and challenge.

The law has not stood still, and so the contents of this edition are again new-fashioned. The undeniable effects of passing time imposed the task of rewriting, undertaken with an effort to integrate rather than append new developments. A slowly shifting legal foundation led to a reworking of the pages on such matters as discovery, costs and attorneys' fees, the Erie doctrine, subject-matter jurisdiction, and appeals. More dramatic events in the last few years obviously demanded new treatment, with such developments including the radical amendment of Rule 16, the tumult in territorial jurisdiction, the Supreme Court's strange fascination with res judicata, and the metamorphosis of the class action and the intervention device.

Despite our regard for earlier editions of this casebook, we have not restricted our alterations in coverage to those forced upon us by the courts, rulemakers, and legislators. For example, we rethought and reordered the materials on territorial authority to adjudicate in Part Five. Moreover, we added depth to Part Six by emphasizing the problems with res judicata doctrine, our growing feeling being that to justify treating res judicata by the case method a casebook should examine the discontinuities that the doctrine exhibits and the dissatisfactions that it elicits. Most important, we extended coverage to three of the hottest topics in civil procedure today, reaching (1) alternative dispute-resolution mechanisms, as part of the overview that concludes Part One, (2) case management by judges, as part of the study of pretrial conferences in Part Three, and (3) public law litigation, as part of the rendering of parties that constitutes Part Seven. Indeed, these three new sections considerably account for the greater length of the new edition. But thanks to that structure of the casebook permitting the instructor to select among problem areas according to tastes and needs, this compartmentalized increase in length should not diminish the casebook's teachability.

In summary, the Fifth Edition represents growth along lines consistent with the First Edition's conception of stressing the current and pursuing Procedure's own distinctive and evolving missions. Yet concerned with methodology, we pruned and trained that growth within the casebook's proven structure. Also wary of letting the new growth obscure the basics, we forgot neither the abiding importance of typical litigation in American courts today as a locus of lawmaking nor the supporting role of Procedure in the law-school curriculum as a source of illumination.

———

I use "we" in writing this preface even though Professor Field died in 1978 and Justice Kaplan's absorption in judging has precluded active participation in recent editions. My reason lies in their original conception and their powers to convey it, which give me the sensation of a continuing collaboration that prevails over the bounds of time.

Now for some miscellanea:

We do not advise the student to turn regularly to treatises or law review articles in preparing for class discussion, but we do indicate their availability for research and other special purposes. In our text we make frequent reference to the two major multi-volume works —Federal Practice and Procedure by Professors Wright and Miller and others, and Moore's Federal Practice—which we simply cite respectively by the authors' names and as Moore. We also often cite C. Wright, The Law of Federal Courts (4th ed. 1983), a single-volume hornbook on the jurisdiction and practice of the federal courts, and F. James & G. Hazard, Civil Procedure (2d ed. 1977), a single volume dealing with procedure more generally. We cite other treatises and law review articles on a highly selective basis, usually when we think they are especially useful adjuncts to our cases and text.

We continue our practice of using the original numbers for footnotes by judges in judicial opinions and by authors in quoted materials, when we retain such footnotes; we omit other such footnotes without any statement to that effect. Editors' footnotes are lettered rather than numbered.

In some of the cases the editors' statement of the facts includes information culled from the record or from related cases. We specifically indicate any such supplementation in our version of the case only when the original omission of information by the opinion-writer could conceivably have had some significance.

Over the course of the life of this casebook, thanks are owing to many. At this time, I want to express special personal gratitude to my wife, Pam, who makes my life so much happier and easier and who cheerfully did so much of the work in getting my draft into published form, to Dean Peter Martin of the Cornell Law School for indulging my desires and supporting my efforts during that drafting period, to Ben Kaplan for the enduring benefits of his instruction and advice, and to my father, whom I owe an immeasurable and growing debt for just about everything that came before.

K.M.C.

May 1984

FEDERAL RULES PAMPHLET

The Federal Rules of Civil Procedure (together with the Advisory Committee's notes on the major amendments), many of the Federal Rules of Appellate Procedure, selected provisions of the Constitution of the United States and title 28 of the United States Code, and the Federal Rules of Evidence are integral to this book. They are printed in a separate pamphlet by Foundation Press.

ACKNOWLEDGMENTS

We gratefully acknowledge the permission extended by the following publishers and authors to reprint excerpts from the works indicated: American Bar Association Journal: Joint Conference on Professional Responsibility, Report, 44 A.B.A.J. 1159 (1958) ("Reprinted with permission from American Bar Association Journal"), and ABA Comm. on Professional Ethics and Grievances, Formal Op. 280, 35 A.B.A.J. 876 (1949); Foundation Press, Inc.: L. Fuller, The Problems of Jurisprudence (1949), and J. Maguire, Evidence: Common Sense and Common Law (1947); American Bar Association Reports: Pound, The Causes of Popular Dissatisfaction with the Administration of Justice, 29 A.B.A.Rep. 395 (1906); Princeton University Press: J. Frank, Courts on Trial (1949) ("Reprinted by permission of Princeton University Press"); West Publishing Co.: Schaefer, Is the Adversary System Working in Optimal Fashion?, 70 F.R.D. 159 (1976), Clark, Simplified Pleading, 2 F.R.D. 456 (1943), B. Shipman, Handbook of Common-Law Pleading (3d ed. 1923), and P. Carrington, D. Meador & M. Rosenberg, Justice on Appeal (1976); Notre Dame Lawyer: Barrett, The Adversary System and the Ethics of Advocacy, 37 Notre Dame Law. 479 (1962) ("Reprinted with permission. © by the *Notre Dame Lawyer*, University of Notre Dame.") (We bear responsibility for any errors which have occurred in reprinting or editing.); American Law Institute: Morgan, Foreword to Model Code of Evidence (1942) ("Copyright 1942 by The American Law Institute. Reprinted with the permission of The American Law Institute."), Restatement of Judgments (1942), Restatement (Second) of Conflict of Laws (1969) ("Copyright 1971 by The American Law Institute. Reprinted with the permission of The American Law Institute."), and Restatement (Second) of Judgments (1980) ("Copyright 1982 by The American Law Institute. Reprinted with the permission of The American Law Institute."); Stanford Law Review: Curtis, The Ethics of Advocacy, 4 Stan.L.Rev. 3 (1951) ("Copyright 1951 by the Board of Trustees of the Leland Stanford Junior University"), and Scott, Two Models of the Civil Process, 27 Stan.L.Rev. 937 (1975) ("Copyright 1975 by the Board of Trustees of the Leland Stanford Junior University"); New York University School of Law: Simpson, "The Problem of Trial," in David Dudley Field Centenary Essays 141 (A. Reppy ed. 1949); Yale Law Journal: Smith, Components of Proof in Legal Proceedings, 51 Yale L.J. 537 (1942) ("Reprinted by permission of The Yale Law Journal Company and Fred B. Rothman & Company from *The Yale Law Journal*, Vol. 51, pp. 537, 575"), and Crick, The Final Judgment as a Basis for Appeal, 41 Yale L.J. 539 (1932); Prentice-Hall, Inc.: R. Summers, Law: Its Nature, Functions, and Limits (2d ed. 1972); Harcourt, Brace & Co.: G. Joughin & E. Morgan, The Legacy of Sacco and Vanzetti (1948); Abram Chayes: The Role of the Judge in Public Law Litigation, 89 Harv.L.Rev. 1281

(1976); Columbia University Press: N.Y. County Lawyers' Ass'n Comm. on Professional Ethics, Op. 309 (1933); Marvin E. Frankel: The Search for Truth: An Umpireal View, 123 U.Pa.L.Rev. 1031 (1975); Buffalo Law Review: Kaplan, Civil Procedure—Reflections on the Comparison of Systems, 9 Buffalo L.Rev. 409 (1960); Cambridge University Press: F. Maitland, The Forms of Action at Common Law (1936), F. Maitland, The Constitutional History of England (1908), and F. Maitland, Equity (1909); Harvard Law Review Association: H. Stephen, A Treatise on the Principles of Pleading in Civil Actions (S. Williston ed. 1895), Morgan, Some Observations Concerning Presumptions, 44 Harv.L.Rev. 906 (1931), Morgan, Instructing the Jury upon Presumptions and Burden of Proof, 47 Harv.L.Rev. 59 (1933), Henderson, The Background of the Seventh Amendment, 80 Harv.L.Rev. 289 (1966), and Note, Appealability in the Federal Courts, 75 Harv.L.Rev. 351 (1961); Stevens & Sons, Ltd.: C. Fifoot, History and Sources of the Common Law (1949); Columbia Law Review: Adams, The Origin of English Equity, 16 Colum.L.Rev. 87 (1916); Butterworth & Co.: T. Plucknett, A Concise History of the Common Law (5th ed. 1956); Harvard University Press: J. Ames, Lectures on Legal History (1913); Methuen & Co., Ltd.: W. Holdsworth, A History of English Law (7th ed. 1956); Charles Warren Center, Harvard University: Katz, "The Politics of Law in Colonial America," in Law in American History 257 (1971); University of Michigan Law School: Z. Chafee, Some Problems of Equity (1950); Little, Brown & Company, Inc.: Bowen, "Progress in the Administration of Justice During the Victorian Period," in 1 Select Essays in Anglo-American Legal History 516 (1907), F. James & G. Hazard, Civil Procedure (2d ed. 1977), and F. James, Civil Procedure (1965); Macmillan Co.: The Diary of George Templeton Strong (A. Nevins & M. Thomas eds. 1952); Georgia Law Review: Wright, Procedural Reform: Its Limitations and Its Future, 1 Ga.L.Rev. 563 (1967); Minnesota Law Review: Wolfram, The Constitutional History of the Seventh Amendment, 57 Minn.L.Rev. 639 (1973); Houghton Mifflin Co.: A. Beveridge, The Life of John Marshall (1919); and Michigan Law Review: Reed, Compulsory Joinder of Parties in Civil Actions (pt. 1), 55 Mich.L.Rev. 327 (1957).

Also: Greenwood Press, Inc.: Golding, "On the Adversary System and Justice," in Philosophical Law 98 (R. Bronaugh ed. 1978); West Publishing Co.: Sander, Varieties of Dispute Processing, 70 F.R.D. 111 (1976), and Current Developments in Judicial Administration: Papers Presented at the Plenary Session of the American Association of Law Schools, December, 1977, 80 F.R.D. 147 (1979); Buffalo Law Review: Landsman, The Decline of the Adversary System: How the Rhetoric of Swift and Certain Justice Has Affected Adjudication in American Courts, 29 Buffalo L.Rev. 487 (1980); National Clearinghouse for Legal Services, Inc.: Singer, Nonjudicial Dispute Resolution Mechanisms: The Effects on Justice for the Poor, 13 Clearinghouse Rev. 569 (1979);

ACKNOWLEDGMENTS

American Judicature Society: Luskin, Building a Theory of Case Processing Time, 62 Judicature 115 (1978); Joseph W. Bartlett: The Law Business: A Tired Monopoly (1982); American Bar Foundation Research Journal: Brazil, Improving Judicial Controls over the Pretrial Development of Civil Actions: Model Rules for Case Management and Sanctions, 1981 Am.B.Found.Research J. 873; Harvard Law Review Association: Resnik, Managerial Judges, 96 Harv.L.Rev. 374 (1982) ("Copyright © 1982 by the Harvard Law Review Association."), Chayes, The Supreme Court, 1981 Term—Foreword: Public Law Litigation and the Burger Court, 96 Harv.L.Rev. 4 (1982) ("Copyright © 1982 by the Harvard Law Review Association."), and Miller, Of Frankenstein Monsters and Shining Knights: Myth, Reality, and the "Class Action Problem," 92 Harv.L.Rev. 664 (1979) ("Copyright © 1979 by the Harvard Law Review Association."); American Bar Association: Ebersole, "Discovery and Pretrial Procedures," in The Improvement of the Administration of Justice 137 (F. Klein 6th ed. 1981); Michigan Law Review: Note, A Probabilistic Analysis of the Doctrine of Mutuality of Collateral Estoppel, 76 Mich.L.Rev. 612 (1978); Frank M. Coffin: The Frontier of Remedies: A Call for Exploration, 67 Calif.L.Rev. 983 (1979); Stanford Law Review: Rhode, Class Conflicts in Class Actions, 34 Stan.L.Rev. 1183 (1982) ("Copyright 1982 by the Board of Trustees of the Leland Stanford Junior University"); Harvard Civil Rights—Civil Liberties Law Review: Jones, Litigation Without Representation: The Need for Intervention to Affirm Affirmative Action, 14 Harv.C.R.—C.L.L.Rev. 31 (1979); and U.C. Davis Law Review: Friedenthal, Increased Participation by Non-Parties: The Need for Limitations and Conditions, 13 U.C.D.L.Rev. 259 (1980).

*

SUMMARY OF CONTENTS

	Page
Preface	xix
Acknowledgments	xxiii
Table of Cases	li
Table of Federal Statutes and Rules	lxiii

PART ONE: A FIRST VIEW OF THE SUBJECT

Topic A. General Considerations 1

Topic B. Phases of a Lawsuit 30
Section
1. Disclosing the matters in dispute 31
2. Provisional remedies 92
3. Trial 98
4. Judgment 139
5. Appellate review 154
6. Selecting a proper court: general division of business between state and federal court systems 160
7. Selecting a proper court: limitations resulting from provisions as to venue and service of process 177
8. More complicated litigation: multiple parties and multiple claims 182
9. What law governs a particular action 196

Topic C. Characteristics of a Procedural System 253
Section
1. The adversary system 253
2. Alterations and alternatives 266
3. A comparative look 291

PART TWO: THE UNITARY CIVIL ACTION

Topic A. Introduction—Federal Rule 2 299

Topic B. Evolution of the Common Law 306
Section
1. Emergence of the forms of action at law 306
2. Evolution through logic-chopping (herein chiefly of trespass and case) 317
3. Evolution through fiction (herein chiefly of trover) 333
4. Development of remedies for breach of promise 337
5. The common-law system of pleading 346

Topic C. The Complementary System of Equity 354
Section
1. Development of equity 354
2. Equity matured 364

Page

Topic D. Abolition of the Forms of Action; Merger of Law and
          Equity --- 384
Section
   1. The condition of civil procedure around 1840 ------------- 384
   2. The reform movement ----------------------------------- 391

Topic E. Problems in Administering the Unitary Civil Action --- 399
Section
   1. Use and misuse of old learning ----------------------- 399
   2. "Theory of the pleadings" --------------------------- 408
   3. Change of theory on appeal -------------------------- 411

PART THREE: PLEADINGS, DISCOVERY, AND
PRETRIAL CONFERENCES

Topic A. General Observations --------------------------------- 420
Section
   1. The objectives of modern pleading --------------------- 420
   2. The relation of pleading to proof --------------------- 422

Topic B. The Complaint --------------------------------------- 436
Section
   1. Stating the claim ----------------------------------- 436
   2. Challenging the statement of the claim ---------------- 449
   3. Completing the complaint --------------------------- 454

Topic C. The Responsive Pleading ----------------------------- 456
Section
   1. Form and scope of defenses --------------------------- 456
   2. Counterclaims ------------------------------------- 464
   3. The reply --- 470

Topic D. Discovery --- 472
Section
   1. Scope of discovery ---------------------------------- 472
   2. Supervision of discovery --------------------------- 499

Topic E. Pretrial Conferences -------------------------------- 517

PART FOUR: TRIAL

Topic A. Preliminary Questions About Forensic Proof ---------- 539
Section
   1. Burden of proof ------------------------------------ 539
   2. Standard of proof --------------------------------- 553

Topic B. Directed Verdict ----------------------------------- 567
Section
   1. General observations -------------------------------- 567
   2. Direction against party with burden of proof ---------- 571
   3. Direction for party with burden of proof ------------- 583

SUMMARY OF CONTENTS

Page

Topic C. Verdict --- 594
Section
  1. Division of functions between judge and jury ------------ 594
  2. Instructions --- 595
  3. Validity of verdict ----------------------------------- 601
  4. Type of verdict --------------------------------------- 607
Topic D. New Trial --- 617
Section
  1. Error in course of trial ------------------------------ 617
  2. Jury's error in weighing evidence --------------------- 623
  3. Newly discovered evidence ----------------------------- 634
  4. Appellate review of grant or denial of new trial ------ 636
  5. Interplay of new trial motion with Rule 50 ------------ 650
Topic E. The Constitutional Guarantee of Jury Trial ----------- 665
Section
  1. Constitutional and statutory framework ---------------- 665
  2. "Historical test" ------------------------------------- 667
  3. New directions -- 683

PART FIVE: AUTHORITY TO ADJUDICATE: HEREIN OF JURISDICTION
AND DUE PROCESS

Topic A. Jurisdiction over Subject Matter --------------------- 712
Section
  1. General observations ---------------------------------- 712
  2. Federal questions ------------------------------------- 715
  3. Pendent jurisdiction ---------------------------------- 722
  4. Ancillary jurisdiction -------------------------------- 725
  5. Diversity of citizenship ------------------------------ 739
  6. Jurisdictional amount --------------------------------- 747
  7. Removal --- 755
  8. "Jurisdiction to determine jurisdiction"—power to punish
      disobedience of court order --------------------------- 760
Topic B. Territorial Authority to Adjudicate ------------------ 772
Section
  1. The framework --- 772
  2. Jurisdiction over things—traditional theory ----------- 781
  3. Jurisdiction over persons—theory in evolution --------- 795
  4. A rondel --- 844
  5. Actions in federal court ----------------------------- 893
  6. Venue --- 905
Topic C. Opportunity to Be Heard ------------------------------ 934

PART SIX: FORMER ADJUDICATION

Topic A. General Observations --------------------------------- 956
Topic B. Claim Preclusion ------------------------------------- 961
Section
  1. Dimensions of a claim --------------------------------- 961
  2. Adjudication not on the merits ----------------------- 982
  3. Counterclaim --- 990

xxix

Page

Topic C. Issue Preclusion --1001
Section
  1. Requirements of the rule -----------------------------------1001
  2. Exceptions to the rule -------------------------------------1014

Topic D. Effects on Persons Not Parties --------------------------1032
Section
  1. Persons bound by prior judgment ----------------------------1032
  2. Persons entitled to benefits of prior judgment -------------1037

Topic E. Credit Due to Valid Judgments ---------------------------1073
Section
  1. American judgments ---1073
  2. Judgments of foreign nations -------------------------------1080
  3. Validity ---1082
  4. "Jurisdiction to determine jurisdiction"—jurisdictional find-
      ings as res judicata ---------------------------------------1087

PART SEVEN: PARTIES

Topic A. General Joinder Provisions ----------------------------- 1094
Topic B. Class Actions --- 1114
Section
  1. Representative litigation -----------------------------------1114
  2. Scope of Rule 23 ---1127
  3. Litigating class actions -----------------------------------1144
  4. Terminating class actions ----------------------------------1161
  5. Overview, review, and preview ------------------------------1172

Topic C. Intervention -- 1189
Topic D. Interpleader -- 1200

PART EIGHT: APPEALS

Topic A. General Observations ----------------------------------1213
Topic B. Review of Final Decisions ----------------------------1220
Topic C. Review of Interlocutory Decisions -------------------- 1230
Topic D. Mandamus --- 1242

Index -- 1255

TABLE OF CONTENTS

		Page
Preface		xix
Acknowledgments		xxiii
Table of Cases		li
Table of Federal Statutes and Rules		lxiii

PART ONE: A FIRST VIEW OF THE SUBJECT

	Page
Topic A. General Considerations	1
Nature of civil controversies	1
Nature of procedural rules	3
The substance-procedure distinction	4
Sibbach v. Wilson & Co.	5
On attitudes toward the subject and the course	28
Topic B. Phases of a Lawsuit	30
The focus: procedure in the United States District Courts	30
Selecting a proper court	30
§ 1. Disclosing the matters in dispute	31
(a) Stating the Claim	31
Dividing the burden of allegation	32
How particularized must allegations be?	33
Sierocinski v. E.I. Du Pont De Nemours & Co.	34
Conley v. Gibson	35
Statements of claim in the alternative	36
What is a "claim"?	37
Consistency and truth in pleading	38
(b) Defenses and Objections	38
Types of defenses and objections	38
Manner of presenting defenses and objections	40
Consolidation and waiver of defenses and objections	41
Black, Sivalls & Bryson, Inc. v. Shondell	43
(c) Replying to Defenses	45
(d) Counterclaims	47
Compulsory counterclaims	47
Permissive counterclaims	48
"Transaction or occurrence"	48
Williams v. Robinson	49
Responding to a counterclaim	51
Recoveries on claim and counterclaim	52
(e) Amending the Pleadings	52
Amendments before trial	52
Amendments at or after trial	53
Relation back of amendments	53
Blair v. Durham	53
"Cause of action" and "claim"	56

Topic B. Phases of a Lawsuit—Continued   **Page**
   (f) Discovery _____ 56
     Purposes of discovery _____ 56
     General provisions governing discovery _____ 57
     Depositions upon oral examination _____ 59
       Umphres v. Shell Oil Co. _____ 61
       Brandenberg v. El Al Israel Airlines _____ 62
     Depositions upon written questions _____ 64
     Interrogatories to parties _____ 65
       O'Brien v. International Brotherhood of Electrical
         Workers _____ 66
     Requests for admission _____ 69
     Production of documents and things for inspec-
      tion and other purposes _____ 69
     Physical and mental examination _____ 70
       Schlagenhauf v. Holder _____ 71
     Supplementation of responses _____ 72
     Use of products of discovery in court proceedings ___ 73
       Freed v. Erie Lackawanna Railway _____ 74
     Sanctions for failure to make discovery _____ 75
     General problems _____ 76
   (g) Pretrial Conferences _____ 77
     Identiseal Corp. v. Positive Identification Sys-
      tems, Inc. _____ 79
     Shuber v. S.S. Kresge Co. _____ 82
   (h) Devices for Terminating Litigation Without Trial ___ 84
     Motion for judgment on the pleadings _____ 84
     Motion for summary judgment _____ 85
       American Airlines v. Ulen _____ 86
     Interchangeability of motion for summary judg-
      ment and motion for judgment on the plead-
      ings _____ 92
 § 2. Provisional remedies _____ 92
     Hamilton Watch Co. v. Benrus Watch Co. _____ 95
     Checker Motors Corp. v. Chrysler Corp. _____ 97
 § 3. Trial _____ 98
   (a) The Jury _____ 98
     Right to jury trial _____ 98
     Incidents of jury trial _____ 99
       Colgrove v. Battin _____ 99
     Jury selection _____ 106
   (b) Order and Method of Proof _____ 107
     Burden of proof _____ 107
     Plaintiff's case _____ 107
     Motion at the close of plaintiff's case _____ 108
     Defendant's case _____ 108
     Motion at the close of defendant's case _____ 109
     Rebuttal and rejoinder _____ 109

Topic B.   Phases of a Lawsuit—Continued   **Page**
           (c) The Rules of Evidence ------------------------- 110
               Kinds of evidence ----------------------------- 111
               Relevance ------------------------------------- 112
               Rules excluding relevant evidence ------------- 113
               Competency of witnesses ----------------------- 114
               Privilege ------------------------------------- 117
               Hearsay --------------------------------------- 118
               Exceptions to the hearsay rule ---------------- 120
                   Handel v. New York Rapid Transit Corp. ---- 124
               Multiple hearsay ------------------------------ 128
               The "best evidence" rule ---------------------- 128
               Remote, confusing, and prejudicial evidence --- 128
               Objections to evidence ------------------------ 129
               Ways of combating admissible evidence --------- 130
               Scope and manner of cross-examination --------- 131
           (d) Motions at the Close of All the Evidence ------ 132
           (e) Submission to Jury and Return of Verdict ------ 134
           (f) Motions After Verdict ------------------------- 136
               Motion for judgment notwithstanding the verdict --- 136
               Motion for a new trial ------------------------ 137
               Joinder of motions ---------------------------- 138
   § 4.   Judgment --- 139
           (a) Entry of Judgment ----------------------------- 139
           (b) Kinds of Relief Afforded by Judgment ---------- 139
               Ritter v. Ritter ------------------------------ 141
               Costs --- 142
               Declaratory relief ---------------------------- 144
               American Machine & Metals, Inc. v. De Bothezat
                   Impeller Co. ------------------------------ 145
               International Longshoremen's Local 37 v. Boyd ----- 148
           (c) Enforcement of Judgment ----------------------- 151
               Gabovitch v. Lundy ---------------------------- 152
   § 5.   Appellate review ----------------------------------- 154
           (a) Appeal to the Court of Appeals ---------------- 154
               Avenues of appeal ----------------------------- 154
                   Russell v. Barnes Foundation -------------- 154
               Appellate procedure --------------------------- 156
               Stay of proceedings to enforce a judgment ----- 157
                   Long v. Robinson -------------------------- 157
           (b) Review by the Supreme Court ------------------- 159
   § 6.   Selecting a proper court: general division of business
               between state and federal court systems ------- 160
           (a) The Judicial Power of the States -------------- 160
           (b) The Judicial Power of the United States ------- 161
           (c) How Congress Has Vested Original Jurisdiction
               in the District Courts ------------------------ 162
           (d) The "Federal Question" Provision -------------- 162
               Louisville & Nashville Railroad v. Mottley ----- 163

Topic B.   Phases of a Lawsuit—Continued   Page
           (e) The "Diversity of Citizenship" Provision _____ 166
               Baker v. Keck _____ 166
               Domicile of students _____ 170
               Domicile of wives _____ 171
               "Citizenship" of corporations _____ 171
               Kelly v. United States Steel Corp. _____ 172
               "Citizenship" of unincorporated associations _____ 175
               Desirability of diversity jurisdiction __:_____ 174
           (f) "Removal" Jurisdiction of the District Courts _____ 174
           (g) Possible Review by the Supreme Court of State-Court
               Actions _____ 175
  § 7. Selecting a proper court: limitations resulting from
           provisions as to venue and service of process _____ 177
        (a) Venue Requirements as a Limitation _____ 177
        (b) Service of Process Requirements as a Limitation ___ 179
        (c) Transfer of Cases from One District Court to
            Another _____ 181
        (d) Addendum on Allocation of Court Business
            Among the States _____ 181
  § 8. More complicated litigation: multiple parties and
           multiple claims _____ 182
        Jurisdiction and venue _____ 183
        (a) Permissive Joinder of Parties _____ 185
        (b) Compulsory Joinder of Persons Needed for Just
            Adjudication _____ 186
        (c) Interpleader _____ 188
        (d) Third-Party Practice _____ 189
        (e) Cross-claims _____ 190
        (f) Class Actions _____ 191
            Actions relating to unincorporated associations _____ 194
            Derivative actions by shareholders _____ 194
        (g) Intervention _____ 194
        (h) General Observations _____ 195
  § 9. What law governs a particular action _____ 196
        (a) State Law in Federal Court _____ 196
            The Erie problem _____ 196
                Erie Railroad v. Tompkins _____ 197
                Burden of proof in diversity actions _____ 205
                Klaxon Co. v. Stentor Electric Manufacturing Co. 206
                Guaranty Trust Co. v. York _____ 207
                Ragan v. Merchants Transfer & Warehouse Co. _ 210
                Woods v. Interstate Realty Co. _____ 211
                Cohen v. Beneficial Industrial Loan Corp. _____ 211
                Federal determination of state law _____ 212

TABLE OF CONTENTS

Topic B.   Phases of a Lawsuit—Continued   Page
                Bernhardt v. Polygraphic Co. of America _____ 212
                State determination of state law _____ 216
                Byrd v. Blue Ridge Rural Electric Cooperative __ 217
                Hanna v. Plumer _____ 220
                Szantay v. Beech Aircraft Corp. _____ 231
                Marshall v. Mulrenin _____ 233
                Day & Zimmermann, Inc. v. Challoner _____ 234
                Walker v. Armco Steel Corp. _____ 235
                Masino v. Outboard Marine Corp. _____ 239
              The role of Congress _____ 241
              Federal common law _____ 242
                Clearfield Trust Co. v. United States _____ 242
                United States v. Kimbell Foods, Inc. _____ 244
                Illinois v. City of Milwaukee _____ 247
            (b) Federal Law in State Court _____ 247
              Hinderlider v. La Plata River & Cherry Creek
                Ditch Co. _____ 247
              Dice v. Akron, Canton & Youngstown Railroad _____ 248
              Brown v. Western Railway _____ 250
              Norfolk & Western Railway v. Liepelt _____ 251
Topic C.   Characteristics of a Procedural System _____ 253
    § 1.   The adversary system _____ 253
           L. Fuller, The Problems of Jurisprudence _____ 253
           Joint Conference on Professional Responsibility, Re-
             port _____ 254
           Pound, The Causes of Popular Dissatisfaction with the
             Administration of Justice _____ 258
           J. Frank, Courts on Trial _____ 259
           Schaefer, Is the Adversary System Working in Optimal
             Fashion? _____ 260
           Simpson, "The Problem of Trial" _____ 260
           Scott, Two Models of the Civil Process _____ 261
           Golding, "On the Adversary System and Justice" _____ 262
           Barrett, The Adversary System and the Ethics of
             Advocacy _____ 262
           Morgan, Foreword _____ 263
           Curtis, The Ethics of Advocacy _____ 263
           Smith, Components of Proof in Legal Proceedings _____ 264
           C. Curtis, It's Your Law _____ 264
           R. Summers, Law: Its Nature, Functions, and Limits 265
    § 2.   Alterations and alternatives _____ 266
           (a) Changing the Advocate's Role _____ 266
             New York County Lawyers' Association Committee
               on Professional Ethics, Opinions _____ 266
             Frankel, The Search for Truth: An Umpireal
               View _____ 270

Topic C.   Characteristics of a Procedural System—Continued   **Page**
    (b) Changing the Adjudicator's Role ------------------ 272
        G. Joughin & E. Morgan, The Legacy of Sacco and
        Vanzetti --- 272
        Reserve Mining Co. v. Lord ---------------------- 275
        Webster Eisenlohr, Inc. v. Kalodner -------------- 276
        Chayes, The Role of the Judge in Public Law Liti-
        gation --- 279
    (c) Changing the System ---------------------------- 280
        R. Summers, Law: Its Nature, Functions, and Limits 281
        Sander, Varieties of Dispute Processing ----------- 281
        Landsman, The Decline of the Adversary System:
        How the Rhetoric of Swift and Certain Justice Has
        Affected Adjudication in American Courts ------- 286
        Current Developments in Judicial Administration:
        Papers Presented at the Plenary Session of the
        American Association of Law Schools, December,
        1977 -- 287
        Singer, Nonjudicial Dispute Resolution Mechanisms:
        The Effects on Justice for the Poor ------------- 290
  § 3.   A comparative look ------------------------------- 291
        Kaplan, Civil Procedure—Reflections on the Comparison
        of Systems ------------------------------------- 291

PART TWO: THE UNITARY CIVIL ACTION

Topic A.   Introduction—Federal Rule 2 ----------------------- 299
  Williamson v. Columbia Gas & Electric Corp. --------------- 299
  F. Maitland, The Forms of Action at Common Law ---------- 301
Topic B.   Evolution of the Common Law ---------------------- 306
  § 1.   Emergence of the forms of action at law ------------- 306
    F. Maitland, The Constitutional History of England ---- 306
    F. Maitland, The Forms of Action at Common Law ---- 312
    F. Maitland, The Constitutional History of England ---- 315
    H. Stephen, A Treatise on the Principles of Pleading in
    Civil Actions --- 316
  § 2.   Evolution through logic-chopping (herein chiefly of tres-
    pass and case) --------------------------------------- 317
    (a) Trespass -- 317
        Writ of trespass ----------------------------------- 317
        Anonymous -- 318
    (b) The Rise of Case --------------------------------- 318
        C. Fifoot, History and Sources of the Common Law 318
        Writ of trespass on the case or case ------------- 320
    (c) Drawing the Line Between Trespass and Case ------- 320
        Reynolds v. Clarke -------------------------------- 320
        Scott v. Shepherd --------------------------------- 321

TABLE OF CONTENTS

Topic B. Evolution of the Common Law—Continued   **Page**
    Day v. Edwards ------------------------------------ 325
    Ogle v. Barnes ----------------------------------- 326
    Leame v. Bray ------------------------------------ 326
    Williams v. Holland ------------------------------ 327
    Sharrod v. London & North Western Railway ------ 329
    American cases ----------------------------------- 330
      Adams v. Hemmenway --------------------- 330
      Kelly v. Lett --------------------------------- 330
      Brown v. Kendall ---------------------------- 330
      Dalton v. Favour ---------------------------- 330
      Brokaw v. New Jersey Railroad & Transportation
       Co. ------------------------------------- 331
    (d) The "Possession" Necessary to Maintain Trespass --- 331
 § 3. Evolution through fiction (herein chiefly of trover) ----- 333
    Writ of debt or detinue -------------------------- 333
    Writ of trespass on the case in trover -------------- 334
    Swift v. Moseley --------------------------------- 336
 § 4. Development of remedies for breach of promise ------- 337
    (a) Debt and Covenant and Their Deficiencies -------- 337
    (b) Rise of Special Assumpsit to Fill Lacunae Left by
     Debt and Covenant ---------------------------- 339
     Watkins' Case ------------------------------------ 339
     Declaration in special assumpsit ----------------- 341
    (c) Assumpsit Engulfs Simple Debt ----------------- 342
    (d) Extension of General Assumpsit Beyond the Range of
     Simple Debt ---------------------------------- 343
     Declaration in general assumpsit ----------------- 343
    (e) Relation Between Special and General Assumpsit --- 345
 § 5. The common-law system of pleading ---------------- 346
    1. Reaching a single issue ----------------------- 346
    2. Declaration -------------------------------- 346
    3. Responses to declaration ---------------------- 347
    4. Replication and later pleadings ----------------- 348
    5. Departures --------------------------------- 349
    6. Motions in arrest and n.o.v. ------------------ 349
    7. Demurrer searches the record ------------------ 349
    8. Subsidiary rules of pleading ------------------- 350
    9. Joinder of causes of action ------------------- 351
    Reforms up to the 1830's -------------------------- 351
Topic C. The Complementary System of Equity -------------- 354
 § 1. Development of equity --------------------------- 354
    Adams, The Origin of English Equity -------------- 354
    T. Plucknett, A Concise History of the Common Law -- 356
    Uses --- 358
    Emerging scope of equity jurisdiction -------------- 360
    Courtney v. Glanvil ------------------------------ 361

Topic C.   The Complementary System of Equity—Continued   Page
           Ellesmere on the nature of equity _____ 361
           Judgment of James I _____ 362
           Katz, "The Politics of Law in Colonial America" _____ 363
    § 2.   Equity matured _____ 364
           (a) Scope of Equity Jurisdiction _____ 364
           (b) Equitable Relief Against Penalties; Mortgages _____ 366
           (c) Specific Performance of Contracts _____ 367
               Inadequacy of legal relief _____ 367
               Difficulty of administering equitable relief _____ 368
               Discretionary character of equitable relief _____ 369
                   Carmen v. Fox Film Corp. _____ 370
               Mutuality of remedy _____ 372
           (d) Equitable Intervention for Misconduct and Mistake _ 373
               Fraud _____ 373
               Mistake _____ 373
           (e) Equitable Relief Against Torts _____ 374
               Recaption or protection of personal property _____ 374
               Waste _____ 374
               Trespass _____ 374
               Nuisance _____ 376
               Unfair competition _____ 376
               Labor injunctions _____ 377
               Other types of injunctions _____ 377
           (f) Accounting; Debtor and Creditor Relationships _____ 378
           (g) Complicated Litigation _____ 379
           (h) Discovery _____ 379
           (i) Flexibility of Equity Decrees _____ 379
           (j) The "Clean-Up" Doctrine _____ 380
           (k) Enforcement of Equity Decrees _____ 381
           (l) Equity in the Infant United States _____ 382

Topic D.   Abolition of the Forms of Action; Merger of Law and
           Equity _____ 384
    § 1.   The condition of civil procedure around 1840 _____ 384
           Bowen, "Progress in the Administration of Justice Dur-
               ing the Victorian Period" _____ 384
           The situation in the United States _____ 391
    § 2.   The reform movement _____ 391
           English advances _____ 392
           The Field Code _____ 393
           Federal reform _____ 395

Topic E.   Problems in Administering the Unitary Civil Action ___ 399
    § 1.   Use and misuse of old learning _____ 399
           Avery v. Spicer _____ 399
           Manhattan Egg Co. v. Seaboard Terminal & Refrig-
               eration Co. _____ 403
           Raab v. Bowery Savings Bank _____ 405

Topic E. Problems in Administering the Unitary Civil Action
     —Continued   **Page**

        Classification _____ 407

§ 2. "Theory of the pleadings" _____ 408

§ 3. Change of theory on appeal _____ 411

        Apex Smelting Co. v. Burns _____ 411

        Sears, Roebuck & Co. v. Marhenke _____ 414

        Wall v. Brim _____ 415

        Diemer v. Diemer _____ 416

        Universe Tankships, Inc. v. United States _____ 417

        Altman v. Altman _____ 418

PART THREE: PLEADINGS, DISCOVERY, AND PRETRIAL CONFERENCES

Topic A. General Observations _____ 420

§ 1. The objectives of modern pleading _____ 420

§ 2. The relation of pleading to proof _____ 422

        Manning v. Loew _____ 423

        Variance _____ 424

        California Code of Civil Procedure _____ 426

        Wasik v. Borg _____ 426

        Robbins v. Jordan _____ 428

        Cox v. Fremont County Public Building Authority _____ 430

        Allegations of time and place _____ 431

        Burlington Transp. Co. v. Josephson _____ 432

        Pleading special damages _____ 434

        Niedland v. United States _____ 434

Topic B. The Complaint _____ 436

§ 1. Stating the claim _____ 436

        Degree of specificity required _____ 436

        Pleading facts necessary to constitute cause of action:
          pros and cons _____ 438

        Pleading evidence, ultimate facts, and conclusions _____ 440

        The common counts _____ 442

        Judicial notice of fact and law _____ 443

        Leggett v. Montgomery Ward & Co. _____ 445

        Defensive matter in the complaint _____ 447

        O'Donnell v. Elgin, Joliet & Eastern Railway _____ 448

§ 2. Challenging the statement of the claim _____ 449

        Motion for more definite statement _____ 449

        Motion to strike _____ 450

        Drewett v. Aetna Casualty & Surety Co. _____ 451

        Consequences of the motion to dismiss for failure to
          state a claim _____ 452

§ 3. Completing the complaint _____ 454

TABLE OF CONTENTS

		Page
Topic C.	The Responsive Pleading	456
§ 1.	Form and scope of defenses	456
	Verification of pleadings	456
	New York Civil Practice Law and Rules	456
	Surowitz v. Hilton Hotels Corp.	457
	Denials	459
	Affirmative defenses	461
	Pleading contributory negligence	462
	Gunder v. New York Times Co.	463
	Watertown Milk Producers' Co-operative Ass'n v. Van Camp Packing Co.	464
§ 2.	Counterclaims	464
	Recoupment	464
	Setoff	465
	Counterclaim	466
	Statute of limitations	466
	Azada v. Carson	467
	New York Civil Practice Law and Rules	469
	United States Code, Title 28	469
§ 3.	The reply	470
Topic D.	Discovery	472
§ 1.	Scope of discovery	472
	Hickman v. Taylor	472
	Trial preparation materials: before and after Hickman	481
	Trial preparation materials: the 1970 amendments	484
	Rackers v. Siegfried	485
	Duplan Corp. v. Moulinage et Retorderie de Chavanoz	486
	Peterson v. United States	489
	Ford v. Philips Electronics Instruments Co.	490
	United States v. Nobles	491
	Person's own statement	492
	Expert information	493
	Berkey Photo, Inc. v. Eastman Kodak Co.	495
	Impeachment evidence	496
	Margeson v. Boston & Maine Railroad	496
	Richards of Rockford, Inc. v. Pacific Gas & Electric Co.	498
	FOIA	499
§ 2.	Supervision of discovery	499
	V. O. Machinoimport v. Clark Equipment Co.	501
	Connell v. Biltmore Security Life Insurance Co.	502
	Sullivan v. Southern Pac. Co.	503
	Oliver v. Kalamazoo Board of Education	503
	D'Ippolito v. American Oil Co.	503
	Koster v. Chase Manhattan Bank	504
	Sequence of depositions	510
	Enforcement of discovery orders	511

Topic D. Discovery—Continued   **Page**
          Rubenstein v. Kleven _____ 513
          Appellate review of discovery rulings _____ 514
Topic E. Pretrial Conferences _____ 517
          Jaquette v. Black Hawk County, Iowa _____ 517
          S. Flanders, Case Management and Court Management
             in United States District Courts _____ 518
          Luskin, Building a Theory of Case Processing Time ____ 522
          J. Bartlett, The Law Business: A Tired Monopoly _____ 524
          Brazil, Improving Judicial Controls over the Pretrial De-
             velopment of Civil Actions: Model Rules for Case
             Management and Sanctions _____ 525
          Resnik, Managerial Judges _____ 528
          Ebersole, "Discovery and Pretrial Procedures" _____ 535
          Beary v. City of Rye _____ 536

PART FOUR: TRIAL

Topic A. Preliminary Questions About Forensic Proof _____ 539
  § 1. Burden of proof _____ 539
          Allocation of the persuasion-burden _____ 541
          Texas Department of Community Affairs v. Burdine ___ 543
          Presumptions _____ 548
          Summers v. Tice _____ 553
  § 2. Standard of proof _____ 553
          Reid v. San Pedro, Los Angeles & Salt Lake Railroad 556
          Sargent v. Massachusetts Accident Co. _____ 557
          Stimpson v. Hunter _____ 561
          Cruzan v. New York Central & Hudson River Railroad 561
          Guinan v. Famous Players-Lasky Corp. _____ 562
          Dyer v. MacDougall _____ 563
          Relation of summary judgment to directed verdict _____ 565
Topic B. Directed Verdict _____ 567
  § 1. General observations _____ 567
          Attrition of the right of voluntary dismissal _____ 567
          Preventing unreasonable verdicts _____ 568
          Revising improper verdicts _____ 571
  § 2. Direction against party with burden of proof _____ 571
          Pedrick v. Peoria & Eastern Railroad _____ 572
          Pennsylvania Railroad v. Chamberlain _____ 574
          Lavender v. Kurn _____ 579
          Wilkerson v. McCarthy _____ 579
          Standard in FELA actions _____ 580
          O'Connor v. Pennsylvania Railroad _____ 581
  § 3. Direction for party with burden of proof _____ 583
          Chesapeake & Ohio Railway v. Martin _____ 584
          Powers v. Continental Casualty Co. _____ 585
          Simblest v. Maynard _____ 588
          Standard in diversity actions _____ 592
          Service Auto Supply Co. v. Harte & Co. _____ 592

Page

Topic C. Verdict -- 594
  § 1. Division of functions between judge and jury ---------- 594
  § 2. Instructions -- 595
        Judicial efforts to induce unanimity ----------------- 599
  § 3. Validity of verdict ----------------------------------- 601
        Jorgensen v. York Ice Machinery Corp. ---------------- 601
        Ford Motor Credit Co. v. Amodt ----------------------- 604
        Freid v. McGrath ------------------------------------- 604
        The sealed verdict ----------------------------------- 605
        The problem of surplusage ---------------------------- 606
        The "impossible verdict" ----------------------------- 606
  § 4. Type of verdict --------------------------------------- 607
        Special verdict -------------------------------------- 609
        Columbia Horse & Mule Commission Co. v. American
          Ins. Co. --- 610
        General verdict with interrogatories ----------------- 612
        Mayer v. Petzelt ------------------------------------- 612
        Arkansas Midland Railway v. Canman ------------------- 614
        The split trial -------------------------------------- 615

Topic D. New Trial --- 617
  § 1. Error in course of trial ----------------------------- 617
        Harmless error --------------------------------------- 618
        Rojas v. Richardson ---------------------------------- 619
        Rojas v. Richardson ---------------------------------- 622
        Evidence rulings in nonjury cases -------------------- 622
  § 2. Jury's error in weighing evidence -------------------- 623
        Dimick v. Schiedt ------------------------------------ 625
        Amount of the remittitur ----------------------------- 631
        Gasoline Products Co. v. Champlin Refining Co. ------- 632
        Akermanis v. Sea-Land Service, Inc. ------------------ 634
  § 3. Newly discovered evidence ---------------------------- 634
  § 4. Appellate review of grant or denial of new trial ----- 636
        Fairmount Glass Works v. Cub Fork Coal Co. ----------- 636
        Pettingill v. Fuller --------------------------------- 641
        Grunenthal v. Long Island Rail Road ------------------ 643
        Taylor v. Washington Terminal Co. -------------------- 645
        Donovan v. Penn Shipping Co. ------------------------- 647
        Appellate review of facts in nonjury cases ----------- 648
  § 5. Interplay of new trial motion with Rule 50 ----------- 650
        Montgomery Ward & Co. v. Duncan ---------------------- 652
        Marsh v. Illinois Cent. R. --------------------------- 657
        Cone v. West Virginia Pulp & Paper Co. --------------- 659
        Neely v. Martin K. Eby Construction Co. -------------- 662
        O'Hare v. Merck & Co. -------------------------------- 663

Page

Topic E. The Constitutional Guarantee of Jury Trial _____ 665
   § 1. Constitutional and statutory framework _____ 665
      New York Constitution and statute _____ 665
      Connecticut Constitution and statute _____ 665
      Advisory jury _____ 666
   § 2. "Historical test" _____ 667
      Wolfram, The Constitutional History of the Seventh
         Amendment _____ 668
      New cause of action _____ 670
         Curtis v. Loether _____ 670
      Joinder of legal and equitable causes _____ 674
         Farrell v. City of Ontario _____ 674
         Imperial Shale Brick Co. v. Jewett _____ 675
         Mutuality _____ 676
      Order of trial _____ 677
         Bruckman v. Hollzer _____ 677
         Ralph Blechman, Inc. v. I.B. Kleinert Rubber Co. __ 678
         Judicial discretion _____ 678
      Alternative remedies _____ 679
         Fraser v. Geist _____ 679
      Equitable device _____ 680
         Rankin v. Frebank Co. _____ 680
      Equitable defense to legal claim _____ 680
      Equitable counterclaim to legal claim (or vice versa) ___ 681
         Life insurance fraud cases _____ 681
   § 3. New directions _____ 683
      Beacon Theatres, Inc. v. Westover _____ 683
      Dairy Queen, Inc. v. Wood _____ 691
      Simler v. Conner _____ 697
      Indianhead Truck Line v. Hvidsten Transport, Inc. _____ 698
      Federal doctrine in state courts _____ 699
      Ross v. Bernhard _____ 700
      Johns Hopkins University v. Hutton _____ 706
      In re Boise Cascade Securities Litigation _____ 707
      In re U.S. Financial Securities Litigation _____ 710
      In re Japanese Electronic Products Antitrust Litigation 710

PART FIVE: AUTHORITY TO ADJUDICATE: HEREIN OF JURISDICTION AND DUE PROCESS

Topic A. Jurisdiction over Subject Matter _____ 712
   § 1. General observations _____ 712
   § 2. Federal questions _____ 715
      Bell v. Hood _____ 717
   § 3. Pendent jurisdiction _____ 722
      United Mine Workers v. Gibbs _____ 723

TABLE OF CONTENTS

Topic A.   Jurisdiction over Subject Matter—Continued   **Page**
  § 4.   Ancillary jurisdiction ------------------------------ 725
         Revere Copper & Brass Inc. v. Aetna Casualty & Surety
           Co. -- 726
         Owen Equipment & Erection Co. v. Kroger ------------ 729
         Ortiz v. United States Government ------------------ 738
  § 5.   Diversity of citizenship -------------------------- 739
         Kramer v. Caribbean Mills, Inc. ------------------- 739
         Lester v. McFaddon -------------------------------- 742
  § 6.   Jurisdictional amount ----------------------------- 747
         Saint Paul Mercury Indemnity Co. v. Red Cab Co. ----- 747
         Nelson v. Keefer ---------------------------------- 749
         Snyder v. Harris ---------------------------------- 751
         Zahn v. International Paper Co. -------------------- 754
  § 7.   Removal --- 755
         Shamrock Oil & Gas Corp. v. Sheets ---------------- 755
         American Fire & Casualty Co. v. Finn -------------- 756
         Luebbe v. Presbyterian Hospital ------------------- 759
  § 8.   "Jurisdiction to determine jurisdiction"—power to punish
           disobedience of court order ---------------------- 760
         United States v. United Mine Workers -------------- 760
         Walker v. City of Birmingham ---------------------- 763
         Shuttlesworth v. City of Birmingham --------------- 769
         United States v. Ryan ----------------------------- 770
         Maness v. Meyers ---------------------------------- 770

Topic B.   Territorial Authority to Adjudicate --------------- 772
  § 1.   The framework ------------------------------------- 772
         Pennoyer v. Neff ---------------------------------- 772
         Closson v. Chase ---------------------------------- 780
  § 2.   Jurisdiction over things—traditional theory -------- 781
         (a) Nature of Such Jurisdiction ------------------- 781
             Tyler v. Judges of the Court of Registration ------ 781
             Garfein v. McInnis ---------------------------- 785
             Harris v. Balk -------------------------------- 788
         (b) Procedural Incidents of Such Jurisdiction --------- 791
             Federal actions under 28 U.S.C. § 1655 ---------- 792
             Federal actions under Rule 4(e)(2) ------------- 792
             Jurisdictional amount ------------------------- 793
             Campbell v. Murdock --------------------------- 793
             Limited appearance ---------------------------- 794
  § 3.   Jurisdiction over persons—theory in evolution -------- 795
         (a) Presence as Basis for Jurisdiction ------------ 795
             Darrah v. Watson ------------------------------ 795
             Enforcement of judgments in other states -------- 796
             Grace v. MacArthur ---------------------------- 798
             Wyman v. Newhouse ----------------------------- 798

Topic B. Territorial Authority to Adjudicate—Continued   **Page**
        Fraud and force ------------------------------------ 799
        Immunity from service of process ----------------- 800
     (b) Domicile as Basis for Jurisdiction ---------------- 800
        Milliken v. Meyer ------------------------------- 800
     (c) Consent as Basis for Jurisdiction ----------------- 801
        Hess v. Pawloski -------------------------------- 802
     (d) Acts Done in State as Basis for Jurisdiction ------- 804
        Flexner v. Farson ------------------------------- 804
        Henry L. Doherty & Co. v. Goodman ------------- 805
        Dubin v. City of Philadelphia -------------------- 806
        Adam v. Saenger -------------------------------- 806
        Appearance as defendant ------------------------ 807
        Hess v. Pawloski -------------------------------- 811
     (e) Jurisdiction over Corporations -------------------- 811
        Domestic corporations --------------------------- 811
        Riverside & Dan River Cotton Mills v. Menefee ---- 812
        Problem of foreign corporations: background of the
          International Shoe case ----------------------- 812
        International Shoe Co. v. Washington ------------- 814
        Additional constitutional limitations: commerce
          clause and first amendment ------------------- 824
        Perkins v. Benguet Consolidated Mining Co. ------- 825
        McGee v. International Life Insurance Co. --------- 830
     (f) Jurisdictional Statutes --------------------------- 832
        Illinois Revised Statutes Chapter 110 ------------- 833
        Nelson v. Miller -------------------------------- 833
        Gray v. American Radiator & Standard Sanitary
          Corp. -- 834
        Longines-Wittnauer Watch Co. v. Barnes & Reinecke,
          Inc. --- 835
        Uniform Interstate and International Procedure Act 837
        California Code of Civil Procedure ---------------- 838
        Cook Associates v. Lexington United Corp. -------- 838
   § 4. A rondel --- 844
     (a) Complex Problems of Relationship to the Forum
        State --- 844
        Mullane v. Central Hanover Bank & Trust Co. ----- 844
        Hanson v. Denckla ------------------------------ 847
        Shaffer v. Heitner ------------------------------ 856
        Atkinson v. Superior Court ---------------------- 870
     (b) The Framework—Restructured or Resurrected? ----- 871
        Kulko v. Superior Court ------------------------- 871
        Rush v. Savchuk -------------------------------- 872
        World-Wide Volkswagen Corp. v. Woodson -------- 878
        Insurance Corp. of Ireland v. Compagnie des Bauxites
          de Guinee --------------------------------- 890

Topic B. Territorial Authority to Adjudicate—Continued   **Page**
    § 5. Actions in federal court ------------------------------ 893
         DeJames v. Magnificence Carriers ------------------- 894
         Arrowsmith v. United Press International ------------ 899
         Dijulio v. Digicon, Inc. ---------------------------- 903
    § 6. Venue -- 905
         Federal provisions --------------------------------- 905
         State provisions ----------------------------------- 905
         (a) Local Actions ---------------------------------- 906
             Livingston v. Jefferson ----------------------- 906
             Casey v. Adams ------------------------------- 911
             Ellenwood v. Marietta Chair Co. --------------- 911
             Stone v. United States ------------------------ 911
             Local actions in state courts ------------------ 912
         (b) Transfer of Venue ------------------------------ 912
             The inconvenient forum ----------------------- 912
             The § 1404(a) transfer provision --------------- 914
             Hoffman v. Blaski ---------------------------- 915
             Van Dusen v. Barrack ------------------------- 918
             Goldlawr, Inc. v. Heiman --------------------- 919
             Martin v. Stokes ----------------------------- 920
             Piper Aircraft Co. v. Reyno ------------------- 921

Topic C. Opportunity to Be Heard ------------------------------ 934
    Mullane v. Central Hanover Bank & Trust Co. -------------- 934
    Mennonite Board of Missions v. Adams -------------------- 939
    Basic principles of procedural due process ----------------- 940
    Sniadach v. Family Finance Corp. ------------------------- 942
    Fuentes v. Shevin ------------------------------------- 943
    Mitchell v. W.T. Grant Co. ----------------------------- 943
    North Georgia Finishing, Inc. v. Di-Chem, Inc. ----------- 944
    Scope of Sniadach's progeny ---------------------------- 949
    D.H. Overmyer Co. v. Frick Co. ------------------------- 952

PART SIX: FORMER ADJUDICATION

Topic A. General Observations -------------------------------- 956
    Some basic propositions -------------------------------- 956
    Second action --- 958
    Validity -- 958
    Finality -- 959
    Personal judgment ------------------------------------- 960
    Closing thoughts -------------------------------------- 960

Topic B. Claim Preclusion ------------------------------------ 961
    § 1. Dimensions of a claim ---------------------------- 961
         Williamson v. Columbia Gas & Electric Corp. --------- 961
         Smith v. Kirkpatrick -------------------------------- 965
         O'Brien v. City of Syracuse ------------------------- 967

Topic B.   Claim Preclusion—Continued   Page
           Hennepin Paper Co. v. Fort Wayne Corrugated Paper Co. 969
           Sutcliffe Storage & Warehouse Co. v. United States ____ 971
           Other ways to split a claim ------------------------- 975
           Restatement of Judgments ---------------------------- 975
           Commercial Box & Lumber Co. v. Uniroyal, Inc. ------- 976
           Harrington v. Vandalia-Butler Board of Education ----- 978
    § 2.   Adjudication not on the merits --------------------- 982
           Waterhouse v. Levine -------------------------------- 982
           Keidatz v. Albany ----------------------------------- 983
           Dismissal for insufficiency of complaint ------------ 985
           Rinehart v. Locke ----------------------------------- 987
           Dismissal for failure to prosecute or to obey a court
               order or rule ----------------------------------- 988
           "On the merits" ------------------------------------- 989
           Restatement (Second) of Judgments ------------------- 989
    § 3.   Counterclaim -- 990
           Counterclaim pleaded -------------------------------- 990
           Permissive counterclaim not pleaded ----------------- 990
               Schwabe v. Chantilly, Inc. ---------------------- 991
               Roach v. Teamsters Local Union No. 688 ---------- 993
           Compulsory counterclaim not pleaded ----------------- 995
               Horne v. Woolever ------------------------------- 996
               Dindo v. Whitney -------------------------------- 997
               Insurer-insured conflicts of interest ----------1000

Topic C.   Issue Preclusion ---------------------------------------1001
    § 1.   Requirements of the rule -----------------------------1001
           Little v. Blue Goose Motor Coach Co. ----------------1001
           Dimensions of an issue ------------------------------1003
           Jacobson v. Miller ----------------------------------1004
           Res judicata and the mechanics of settlement --------1006
           Cambria v. Jeffery ----------------------------------1008
           Home Owners Federal Savings & Loan Association v.
               Northwestern Fire & Marine Insurance Co. --------1009
           Alternative determinations --------------------------1009
           Inconsistent judgments ------------------------------1011
           Berlitz Schools of Languages of America v. Everest
               House --1012
    § 2.   Exceptions to the rule --------------------------------1014
           United States v. Moser ------------------------------1014
           Montana v. United States ----------------------------1016
           Courts of limited jurisdiction ----------------------1019
           Unforeseeability of future litigation ---------------1020
           Spilker v. Hankin -----------------------------------1021
           Restatement (Second) of Judgments -------------------1023
           Federated Department Stores v. Moitie ---------------1024
           Exceptions based on posture of party ----------------1031

Page

Topic D. Effects on Persons Not Parties ----------------------1032
   § 1. Persons bound by prior judgment ------------------1032
         Indemnity --1033
         Restatement (Second) of Judgments ----------------1034
         Show-World Center v. Walsh -----------------------1034
         Neenan v. Woodside Astoria Transportation Co. -----1036
   § 2. Persons entitled to benefits of prior judgment --------1037
         Mutuality of estoppel ----------------------------1037
            Coca-Cola Co. v. Pepsi-Cola Co. ---------------1039
            Bernhard v. Bank of America National Trust & Sav-
               ings Association ---------------------------1039
         Decline of mutuality -----------------------------1042
            Blonder-Tongue Laboratories v. University of Illinois
               Foundation ---------------------------------1045
            Parklane Hosiery Co. v. Shore -----------------1048
            Second Restatement's approach -----------------1053
            United States v. Mendoza ----------------------1053
            Note, A Probabilistic Analysis of the Doctrine of
               Mutuality of Collateral Estoppel ------------1056
            Special types of proceedings ------------------1060
            Allen v. McCurry ------------------------------1061
         Beyond collateral estoppel -----------------------1070
            Fagnan v. Great Central Insurance Co. ----------1070

Topic E. Credit Due to Valid Judgments ---------------------1073
   § 1. American judgments ------------------------------1073
         Fauntleroy v. Lum --------------------------------1073
         James v. Grand Trunk Western Railroad -------------1074
         Hart v. American Airlines ------------------------1075
         Kremer v. Chemical Construction Corp. -------------1078
   § 2. Judgments of foreign nations ---------------------1080
         Hilton v. Guyot ----------------------------------1080
         Restatement (Second) of Conflict of Laws ----------1082
   § 3. Validity ---1082
         Bank of Montreal v. Olafsson ---------------------1082
         Marshall v. Lockhead -----------------------------1084
         Britton v. Gannon --------------------------------1085
   § 4. "Jurisdiction to determine jurisdiction"—jurisdictional
         findings as res judicata --------------------------1087
         Baldwin v. Iowa State Traveling Men's Association ----1087
         Chicot County Drainage District v. Baxter State Bank -1089
         Durfee v. Duke -----------------------------------1093

PART SEVEN: PARTIES

Topic A. General Joinder Provisions -------------------------1094
   Shields v. Barrow ------------------------------------1094
   Findings of Hazard and Reed --------------------------1095

TABLE OF CONTENTS

Topic A.   General Joinder Provisions—Continued   **Page**
   Defects in original Rule 19 _____1096
   Provident Tradesmens Bank & Trust Co. v. Patterson _____ 1097
   Haas v. Jefferson National Bank _____ 1106
   Western Union Telegraph Co. v. Pennsylvania _____1109
   Involuntary plaintiff _____ 1111
   Proper parties _____ 1111

Topic B.   Class Actions _____ 1114
  § 1.   Representative litigation _____1114
     Hansberry v. Lee _____1115
     From the old Rule to the new _____1120
     Gonzales v. Cassidy _____1121
  § 2.   Scope of Rule 23 _____1127
     General Telephone Co. v. Falcon _____1127
     Rule 23(a) and (b) _____1134
     In re Northern District of California, Dalkon Shield IUD
       Products Liability Litigation _____1135
  § 3.   Litigating class actions _____1144
     Eisen v. Carlisle & Jacquelin _____1144
     Appealability of order denying or granting class-action
       status _____1155
     Oppenheimer Fund v. Sanders _____1156
  § 4.   Terminating class actions _____1161
     Grunin v. International House of Pancakes _____1161
     Pettway v. American Cast Iron Pipe Co. _____1167
  § 5.   Overview, review, and preview _____1172
     Coffin, The Frontier of Remedies: A Call for
       Exploration _____1172
     Rhode, Class Conflicts in Class Actions _____1173
     Chayes, The Supreme Court, 1981 Term—Foreword:
       Public Law Litigation and the Burger Court _____1179
     Class-action bill _____1182
     Miller, Of Frankenstein Monsters and Shining Knights:
       Myth, Reality, and the "Class Action Problem" _____1185

Topic C.   Intervention _____1189
   Jones, Litigation Without Representation: The Need for In-
     tervention to Affirm Affirmative Action _____1191
   Friedenthal, Increased Participation by Non-Parties: The Need
     for Limitations and Conditions _____1194
   Babcock & Wilcox Co. v. Parsons Corp. _____1196

Topic D.   Interpleader _____1200
   New York Life Insurance Co. v. Dunlevy _____1200
   Federal legislation _____1202
   State Farm Fire & Casualty Co. v. Tashire _____1203
   Jurisdiction and venue requirements _____1209
   The classic limits on interpleader _____1210

Topic D.   Interpleader—Continued   **Page**
  "Broadening the second stage of federal interpleader" 1211
  Law applied in federal interpleader 1212

PART EIGHT: APPEALS

Topic A.   General Observations 1213
  P. Carrington, D. Meador & M. Rosenberg, Justice on Appeal 1213
  F. James & G. Hazard, Civil Procedure 1214
  Old modes of review 1215
  Crick, The Final Judgment as a Basis for Appeal 1217

Topic B.   Review of Final Decisions 1220
  Note, Appealability in the Federal Courts 1220
  Cohen v. Beneficial Industrial Loan Corp. 1221
  Firestone Tire & Rubber Co. v. Risjord 1223
  Duncan v. Merrill Lynch, Pierce, Fenner & Smith, Inc. 1223
  Appealability of contempt orders 1224
  Gillespie v. United States Steel Corp. 1224
  Appealability in multi-claim and multi-party litigation 1227
  Appealability of state decisions 1228

Topic C.   Review of Interlocutory Decisions 1230
  Ettelson v. Metropolitan Life Insurance Co. 1230
  City of Morgantown v. Royal Insurance Co. 1230
  Baltimore Contractors, Inc. v. Bodinger 1231
  Carson v. American Brands, Inc. 1235
  Kraus v. Board of County Road Commissioners 1239

Topic D.   Mandamus 1242
  Roche v. Evaporated Milk Association 1242
  La Buy v. Howes Leather Co. 1242
  Schlagenhauf v. Holder 1244
  Will v. United States 1247
  Will v. Calvert Fire Insurance Co. 1250

Index 1255

TABLE OF CASES

The principal cases are in italic type. Cases cited or discussed are in roman type. References are to Pages.

Adam v. Saenger, 806, 807
Adams v. Hemmenway, 330
Ager v. Jane C. Stormont Hosp. & Training School for Nurses, 495
Ajamian v. Schlanger, 967
Akermanis v. Sea-Land Service, Inc., 634
Albernaz v. City of Fall River, 1045
Albright v. Gates, 739
Albright v. R.J. Reynolds Tobacco Co., 748
Aldinger v. Howard, 725
Allen v. McCurry, 1061
Allen v. Superior Court, 801
Allen v. United States, 600
Allied Chem. Corp. v. Daiflon, Inc., 1252
Alltmont v. United States, 482
Almaguer v. Chicago, Rock Island & Pacific Railroad, 485
Altman v. Altman, 418
Alyeska Pipeline Service Co. v. Wilderness Society, 142
American Airlines v. Ulen, 86
American Auto Ass'n v. Rothman, 460
American Button Co. v. Warsaw Button Co., 1038
American Fire & Casualty Co. v. Finn, 713, 756
American Life Insurance Co. v. Stewart, 699
American Machine & Metals, Inc. v. De Bothezat Impeller Co., 145
American Publishing Co. v. Fisher, 105
American Well Works Co. v. Layne & Bowler Co., 716
Anniston Soil Pipe Co. v. Central Foundry Co., 173
Anonymous, 318
Anonymous v. Anonymous, 836
Apex Smelting v. Burns, 411
Apodaca v. Oregon, 105
Arkansas Midland Railway v. Canman, 614
Armstrong v. Pomerance, 870
Arnstein v. Porter, 566
Arrowsmith v. United Press International, 899
Atkinson v. Superior Court, 870, 871

Atlantis Dev. Corp. v. United States, 1190, 1191
Avery v. Spicer, 399
Azada v. Carson, 467

Babcock & Wilcox Co. v. Parsons Corp., 1196
Bailey v. Meister Brau, Inc., 494
Baker v. Keck, 166
Baki v. B.F. Diamond Construction Co., 494
Baldwin v. Iowa State Traveling Men's Association, 1087
Ballew v. Georgia, 105
Baltimore Contractors, Inc. v. Bodinger, 1231
Baltimore & Carolina Line v. Redman, 651
Baltimore & Ohio Railroad v. Kepner, 914
Bandy v. Westover, 466
Bank of America Nat'l Trust & Sav. Ass'n v. Parnell, 244
Bank of Augusta v. Earle, 812
Bank of Montreal v. Kough, 1081
Bank of Montreal v. Olafsson, 1082
Barnes v. Berkshire Street Railway, 598
Barnett v. H.L. Green Co., 597
Barnhart v. John B. Rogers Producing Co., 914
Barry, Commonwealth v., 596
Basciano v. Reinecke, 658
Bauer Indus., Inc. v. Shannon Luminous Materials Co., 837
Baxter v. Palmigiano, 561
Beacon Theatres, Inc. v. Westover, 681, 683, 1252
Beary v. City of Rye, 536
Becker, People v., 122
Bell v. Hood, 717, 722, 723
Berkey Photo, Inc. v. Eastman Kodak Co., 495
Berlitz Schools of Languages of America v. Everest House, 1012
Bernhard v. Bank of America National Trust & Savings Association, 1039
Bernhardt v. Polygraphic Co. of America, 212

li

Bernstein v. N.V. Nederlandsche-Amerikaansche Stoomvaart-Maatschappij, 450
Bieri v. Fonger, 410
Biggio v. Magee, 1007
Bishop v. Hendricks, 746
Bivens v. Six Unknown Named Agents of Fed. Bureau of Narcotics, 723
Black, Sivalls & Bryson, Inc. v. Shondell, 43, 136
Black & White Taxicab & Transfer Co. v. Brown & Yellow Taxicab & Transfer Co., 742
Blair v. Durham, 53, 55, 233
Blair v. Pitchess, 952
Blazer v. Black, 453
Blonder-Tongue Laboratories v. University of Illinois Foundation, 1045
Boeing Co. v. Shipman, 581, 592
Bogosian v. Gulf Oil Corp., 58
Boise Cascade Securities Litigation, In re, 707
Bolten v. General Motors Corp., 568
Bonell v. General Accident Fire & Life Assur. Corp., 184
Borden Co. v. Sylk, 514
Bosch, Estate of, Commissioner v., 216
Bothwell v. Boston Elevated Railway, 651
Boudreaux v. Puckett, 725
Boyd v. Geary, 462
Brady v. Daly, 677
Brandenberg v. El Al Israel Airlines, 62, 72
Branzburg v. Hayes, 117
Breedlove v. Beech Aircraft Corp., 495
Bremen, The v. Zapata Off-Shore Co., 955
Bridges v. Wixon, 131
Britt v. Arvanitis, 235
Britton v. Atlantic Coast Line Railroad, 452
Britton v. Gannon, 1085
Brokaw v. New Jersey Railroad & Transportation Co., 331
Brooks v. Bay State Abrasive Products, Inc., 600
Brown v. Allen, 160
Brown v. Board of Education, 380
Brown v. Kendall, 330
Brown v. Liberty Loan Corp., 951
Brown v. Western Railway, 250
Bruce v. Odhams Press, 440
Bruckman v. Hollzer, 677, 1252
Bruheim v. Stratton, 410
Bryant v. Harrelson, 454
Bryson v. Northlake Hilton, 824

Buckley v. New York Post Corp., 825
Builders Steel Co. v. Commissioner, 622
Bulkley v. Bulkley, 799
Burch v. Louisiana, 106
Burlington Indus. v. Milliken & Co., 492
Burlington Transp. Co. v. Josephson, 432
Bushell's Case, 571
Byrd v. Blue Ridge Rural Electric Cooperative, 217, 682

Calder v. Jones, 825
Caldwell-Clements, Inc. v. McGraw-Hill Pub. Co., 511
Calero-Toledo v. Pearson Yacht Leasing Co., 951
California Packing Corp. v. Kelly Storage & Distrib. Co., 424
Cambria v. Jeffery, 1008
Camp v. Gress, 905
Campbell v. Murdock, 793
Canfield v. Tobias, 447
Capital Transit Co., United States v., 469
Carmen v. Fox Film Corp., 370
Carson v. American Brands, Inc., 1235
Cascade Natural Gas Corp. v. El Paso Natural Gas Co., 1189
Case v. Abrams, 83
Casey v. Adams, 911
Cauefield v. Fidelity & Casualty Co., 1060
Caulk v. Baltimore & O.R.R., 58
Central Microfilm Serv. Corp. v. Basic/Four Corp., 1252
Checker Motors Corp. v. Chrysler Corp., 97
Chesapeake & Ohio Ry. v. Carmichael, 461
Chesapeake & Ohio Railway v. Martin, 584
Cheshire National Bank v. Jaynes, 795
Chicago & E. Ill. R.R., People ex rel. v. Fleming, 969
Chicot County Drainage District v. Baxter State Bank, 1089
Chisholm v. Georgia, 161
Cities Service Oil Co. v. Dunlap, 205
City of (see name of city)
Clancey v. McBride, 975, 1003
Clay v. Sun Insurance Office Ltd., 216
Clearfield Trust Co. v. United States, 242
Clemens v. Chicago, R.I. & P. Ry., 600
Closson v. Chase, 780
Clower v. Walters, 485
Cobbledick v. United States, 515

Coca-Cola Co. v. Pepsi-Cola Co., 1039, 1043

Cogswell v. New York, New Haven & Hartford Railroad, 676

Cohen v. Beneficial Industrial Loan Corp., 211, 1155, *1221*

Cole v. Maunder, 443

Colgrove v. Battin, 99, 1252

Collett, Ex parte, 914

Collins v. Miller, 1227

Collins, People v., 559

Colonial Times, Inc. v. Gasch, 60

Colorado River Water Conservation District v. United States, 216

Columbia Horse & Mule Commission Co. v. American Ins. Co., 610

Commercial Box & Lumber Co. v. Uniroyal, Inc., 976

Commissioner v. _____ (see opposing party)

Committee for Jones Falls Sewage System v. Train, 247

Commonwealth v. _____ (see opposing party)

Cone v. West Virginia Pulp & Paper Co., 659, 663

Conley v. Gibson, 35, 438

Connecticut Gen. Life Ins. Co. v. Candimat Co., 681

Connell v. Biltmore Security Life Insurance Co., 502

Cook Associates v. Lexington United Corp., 838

Cook, People v., 601

Cooper v. Chitty, 334

Coopers & Lybrand v. Livesay, 1155, 1226

Cornelison v. Chaney, 838

Costello v. United States, 987

Courtney v. Glanvil, 361

Cox v. Fremont County Public Building Authority, 430

Crawford v. Neal, 746

Cream Top Creamery v. Dean Milk Co., 969, 976

Crease v. Barrett, 618

Crescent Mining Co. v. Silver King Mining Co., 375

Croley v. Matson Navigation Co., 565

Cruzan v. New York Central & Hudson River Railroad, 561, 563

Curtis v. Loether, 670, 699

Curtis Publishing Co. v. Butts, 622

D.H. Overmyer Co. v. Frick Co., 952

Dairy Queen, Inc. v. Wood, 691, 699, 1252

Dallas, City of v. Brown, 771

Dalton v. Favour, 330

Darrah v. Watson, 795, 796

Davis v. Farmers Co-operative Equity Co., 824

Davis v. Passman, 723

Davis v. Piper Aircraft Corp., 235

Davis v. Rodgers, 569

Davis v. Yellow Cab Co., 635

Davis Frozen Foods, Inc. v. Norfolk Southern Ry., 592

Day v. Edwards, 325

Day & Zimmermann, Inc. v. Challoner, 234

De Bruce v. Pennsylvania R., 484

Dean Witter Reynolds Inc. v. Fernandez, 1212

Dearborn Nat. Casualty Co. v. Consumers Petroleum Co., 649

Dearden v. Hey, 975

DeJames v. Magnificence Carriers, 894

Denio v. City of Huntington Beach, 1006

Denver & Rio Grande Western Railroad v. Brotherhood of Railroad Trainmen, 178

Dery v. Wyer, 729

Devoe v. Dusey, 1229

Di Frischia v. New York Central Railroad, 713

Dice v. Akron, Canton & Youngstown Railroad, 248

Dickinson v. Petroleum Conversion Corp., 1227

Dickinson, United States v., 56

Diematic Mfg. Corp. v. Packaging Indus., 470

Diemer v. Diemer, 416

Dijulio v. Digicon, Inc., 903

Dimick v. Schiedt, 625

Dindo v. Whitney, 997

D'Ippolito v. American Oil Co., 503

Doan v. Bush, 1006

Dobkin v. Chapman, 941

Doe dem. Lord Teynham v. Tyler, 618

Doering v. Buechler, 622

Donald v. J.J. White Lumber Co., 1011

Donaldson v. United States, 1190

Donnelly Garment Co. v. National Labor Relations Board, 622

Donovan v. City of Dallas, 771

Donovan v. Penn Shipping Co., 592, *647*

Dragor Shipping Corp. v. Union Tank Car Co., 810

liii

Drewett v. Aetna Casualty & Surety Co., 451
Duberstein, Commissioner v., 649
Dubin v. City of Philadelphia, 806
Duke Gardens Foundation v. Universal Restoration, Inc., 494
Duncan v. McDonough, 801
Duncan v. Merrill Lynch, Pierce, Fenner & Smith, 1223
Duplan Corp. v. Deering Milliken, Inc., 492
Duplan Corp. v. Moulinage et Retorderie de Chavanoz, 486
Durant v. Surety Homes Corp., 632
Durfee v. Duke, 1093
Dyer v. MacDougall, 563, 565
Dziegiel v. Town of Westford, 605

Eagle, Star & British Dominions Insurance Co. v. Heller, 1060
Earl of Oxford's Case, 362
Edgar v. Finley, 515
Egan v. American Airlines, 173
Eggleston v. Chicago Journeymen Plumbers' Local Union No. 130, p. 500
Eikel v. States Marine Lines, 1111
Eisen v. Carlisle & Jacquelin, 193, *1144*
Elfman v. Glaser, 986
Ellenwood v. Marietta Chair Co., 911
Elliott Nursery Co. v. Duquesne Light Co., 376
Engl v. Aetna Life Ins. Co., 565
Environmental Research International, Inc. v. Lockwood Greene Engineers, Inc., 825
Erie Railroad v. Tompkins, 197, 210, 1081
Estate of (see name of party)
Ettelson v. Metropolitan Life Ins. Co., 681, 1230
Evans v. Newton, 950
Everett v. Everett, 622
Evergreens v. Nunan, 1020
Evers v. Dwyer, 151
Evra Corp. v. Swiss Bank Corp., 738
Ex parte (see name of party)
Ex rel. (see name of party)

Factors Etc., Inc. v. Pro Arts, Inc., 214
Fagnan v. Great Central Insurance Co., 1070
Fairmount Glass Works v. Cub Fork Coal Co., 636
Fall v. Eastin, 788
Farrell v. City of Ontario, 674, 678
Fauntleroy v. Lum, 1073, 1082

FDIC v. Siraco, 462
Feathers v. McLucas, 835
Federated Department Stores v. Moitie, 1024
Fenton v. Walling, 515
Finberg v. Sullivan, 951
Firestone Tire & Rubber Co. v. Risjord, 1223
Fisher v. Harris, Upham & Co., 500
Flagg Bros. v. Brooks, 950
Fleming, People ex rel. Chicago & E. Ill. R.R. v., 969
Flexner v. Farson, 804, 806, 813
Foley v. Cowan, 424
Foley v. D'Agostino, 441
Follenfant v. Rogers, 456
Forbes v. Wells Beach Casino, Inc., 832
Ford v. Phillips Electronics Instruments Co., 490
Ford Motor Co. v. Busam Motor Sales, Inc., 659
Ford Motor Credit Co. v. Amodt, 604
Formulabs, Inc. v. Hartley Pen Co., 1189
Fort Worth, City of v. Williams, 606
Foster-Milburn Co. v. Knight, 914
Fowler v. Fowler, 275
Fowler v. Lanning, 330
Fox v. Capital Co., 515
Franchise Tax Bd. v. Construction Laborers Vacation Trust, 717
Francis v. Humphrey, 462
Fraser v. Geist, 679, 680
Frechette v. Ravn, 410
Frederick v. Farr, 618
Freed v. Erie Lackawanna Railway, 74, 123
Freeman v. Howe, 725
Freeman v. Wood, 631
Freid v. McGrath, 604
Friedman v. Meyers, 566
Fuentes v. Shevin, 943
Fuhrer v. Fuhrer, 452

Gabovitch v. Lundy, 152
Gagnon v. Dana, 569
Garcia v. Hilton Hotels International, Inc., 436
Gardner v. Westinghouse Broadcasting Co., 1155
Garfein v. McInnis, 785
Garner v. Wolfinbarger, 514
Garrison v. United States, 623
Gas Service Co. v. Coburn, 751
Gasoline Products Co. v. Champlin Refining Co., 632
Gendron v. Hovey, 1008

General Electric Co. v. Marvel Rare Metals Co., 905

General Motors Corp., United States v., 649

General Telephone Co. v. Falcon, 1127, 1133, 1179

Gentle v. Lamb-Weston, Inc., 742

Georgia v. Tennessee Copper Co., 380

Gibson v. Hunter, 568

Giedrewicz v. Donovan, 1038

Giles v. Giles, 583

Gillespie v. United States Steel Corp., 1224

Gilman v. City of Laconia, 622

Glazer v. Glazer, 631

Goldlawr, Inc. v. Heiman, 919

Goldstein v. D'Arcy, 583

Gollner v. Cram, 1019

Gonzales v. Cassidy, 1121, 1196

Gonzalez v. County of Hidalgo, Texas, 955

Good v. Chiles, 461

Good Health Dairy Products Corp. v. Emery, 1038

Goosman v. A. Duie Pyle, Inc., 483

Gordon v. Harper, 335

Gorsalitz v. Olin Mathieson Chemical Corp., 631

Grace v. MacArthur, 798

Grace Lines v. Motley, 605

Grandin Grain & Seed Co. v. United States, 622

Gray v. American Radiator & Standard Sanitary Corp., 834, 837

Great Am. Indem. Co. v. Brown, 635

Griffin v. McCoach, 1212

Grivas v. Parmelee Transp. Co., 568

Grobart v. Society for Establishing Useful Manufactures, 471

Groover, Christie & Merritt v. LoBianco, 514

Grunenthal v. Long Island Rail Road, 643

Grunin v. International House of Pancakes, 1161

Guaranty Trust Co. v. York, 207

Guenther v. Armstrong Rubber Co., 560

Guilford National Bank v. Southern Railway, 483

Guinan v. Famous Players-Lasky Corp., 562

Gulf Oil Corp. v. Gilbert, 912

Gumperz v. Hofmann, 799

Gunder v. New York Times Co., 463

H.E. Miller Oil Co. v. Socony-Vacuum Oil Co., 451

Haas v. Jefferson National Bank, 1106, 1210

Hackney v. Newman Memorial Hosp., 746

Hadley v. Baxendale, 434

Halkin, In re, 510

Hallin v. C.A. Pearson, Inc., 1211

Halpern v. Schwartz, 1010

Hamilton Watch Co. v. Benrus Watch Co., 95, 155

Hammerstein v. Lyne, 170

Handel v. New York Rapid Transit Corp., 124

Hanley v. Donoghue, 444

Hanley v. James McHugh Construction Co., 515

Hanna v. Plumer, 220, 447

Hans v. Louisiana, 161

Hansberry v. Lee, 1115, 1120, 1189

Hanson v. Denckla, 847, 871

Haring v. Prosise, 1060

Harkness v. Hyde, 810

Harrington v. Vandalia-Butler Board of Education, 978

Harris v. Balk, 788

Hart v. American Airlines, 1075

Hatfield v. Bishop Clarkson Memorial Hospital, 217

Helicopteros Nacionales de Colombia, S.A. v. Hall, 829

Hennepin Paper Co. v. Fort Wayne Corrugated Paper Co., 595, *969*

Henry L. Doherty & Co. v. Goodman, 805

Herbert v. Lando, 117

Hess v. Pawloski, 802, 803, 811

Hickman v. Taylor, 58, 472, 481, 482, 483, 484, 516

Hildebrand v. Board of Trustees of Michigan State University, 667

Hilton v. Guyot, 1080, 1081

Himel v. Continental Ill. Nat'l Bank & Trust, 978

Hinderlider v. La Plata River & Cherry Creek Ditch Co., 247

Hirsch v. Glidden Co., 500

Hoffman v. Blaski, 915, 1252

Hoffman v. Palmer, 481

Holt v. Markham, 345

Home Ins. Co. v. Ballenger Corp., 738, 739

Home Ins. Co. v. Davila, 570

Home Owners Federal Savings & Loan Association v. Northwestern Fire & Marine Insurance Co., 1009

Horne v. Woolever, 996, 997, 1008
Hosie v. Chicago & N.W. Ry., 616
Hughes v. Kaiser Jeep Corp., 450
Hughes Tool Co. v. TWA, 512
Hurn v. Oursler, 722, 723
Hyman v. Regenstein, 1021

Iacurci v. Lummus Co., 663
Identiseal Corp. v. Positive Identification Systems, Inc., 79
Illinois v. City of Milwaukee, 247
Imperial Shale Brick Co. v. Jewett, 675
In re (see name of party)
Indianapolis, City of v. Chase Nat'l Bank, 183
Indianhead Truck Line v. Hvidsten Transport, Inc., 698
Industrial Building Materials, Inc. v. Interchemical Corp., 988
Insurance Corp. of Ireland v. Compagnie des Bauxites de Guinee, 890
International Longshoremen's Local 37 v. Boyd, 148, 150
International Shoe Co. v. Washington, 813, *814,* 824

Jackson v. Ashton, 713
Jackson v. Metropolitan Edison Co., 950
Jackson v. National Grange Mut. Liab. Co., 808
Jackson v. Wilson Trucking Corp., 662
Jacobson v. Miller, 1004, 1021
Jacobson v. Mutual Benefit Health & Accident Association, 960
Jaftex Corp. v. Randolph Mills, 899
James v. Grand Trunk Western Railroad, 1074
Japanese Electronic Products Antitrust Litigation, In re, 710
Jaquette v. Black Hawk County, Iowa, 517
Johns Hopkins University v. Hutton, 706
Johns-Manville Sales Corp. v. Chicago Title & Trust Co., 450
Johnson v. Johnson, 555
Johnson v. Louisiana, 105
Johnson v. New York, N.H. & H.R.R., 662
Johnson v. Railway Express Agency, 244
Johnson v. United States, 274, 635
Johnston v. Compagnie Générale Transatlantique, 1081
Jones v. Borden Co., 566
Jones v. Landry, 748
Jonnet v. Dollar Savings Bank, 951

Jorgensen v. York Ice Machinery Corp., 601
Josephson, In re, 914
Joyce v. Seigel, 746

Kalb v. Feuerstein, 1092
Keene Lumber Co. v. Leventhal, 452
Keeton v. Hustler Magazine, Inc., 825
Keidatz v. Albany, 983
Kelly v. Lett, 330
Kelly v. United States Steel Corp., 172
Kiernan v. Van Schaik, 617
Killian v. Ebbinghaus, 1210
Kimbell Foods, Inc., United States v., 244
King's Case, 561
Kirchstein v. American Airlines, 1075
Klaxon Co. v. Stentor Electric Manufacturing Co., 206, 1212
Klingbeil v. Saucerman, 410
Klipstein v. Raschein, 410
Knapp v. Walker, 409
Knighton v. Villian & Fassio, 494
Knoll v. Socony Mobil Oil Co., 1211
Kodekey Electronics, Inc. v. Mechanex Corp., 635
Koeper v. Town of Louisville, 677
Koster v. Chase Manhattan Bank, 504
Kozlowski v. Ferrara, 447
Kramer v. Caribbean Mills, Inc., 739, 742
Kramer v. Kister, 605
Kraus v. Board of County Road Commissioners, 1239
Kremer v. Chemical Construction Corp., 1078
Krock v. Electric Motor & Repair Co., 635
Kukanskis v. Griffith, 950
Kulko v. Superior Court, 871

La Buy v. Howes Leather Co., 1242
Lamine v. Dorrell, 344
Lampe v. Franklin American Trust Co., 554
Landano v. American Airlines, 1075
Lavender v. Kurn, 579
Lawhorn v. Atlantic Ref. Co., 48
Leame v. Bray, 326
Lee Foods Div., Consol. Grocers Corp. v. Bucy, 759
Lehman Brothers v. Schein, 216, 217
Leggett v. Montgomery Ward & Co., 445
Lester v. McFaddon, 742
Letang v. Cooper, 330
Levering & Garrigues Co. v. Morrin, 722

Liberty Oil Co. v. Condon National Bank, 681

Link Aviation, Inc. v. Downs, 1112

Litsinger Sign Co. v. American Sign Co., 444

Little v. Blue Goose Motor Coach Co., 1001

Livanovitch v. Livanovitch, 553

Livingston v. Jefferson, 906, 912

Long v. Robinson, 157

Long, United States v., 460

Longines-Wittnauer Watch Co. v. Barnes & Reinecke, Inc., 835

Louisiana Power & Light Co. v. City of Thibodaux, 216

Louisville & N.R.R. v. Hull, 450

Louisville & Nashville Railroad v. Mottley, 163, 175, 176, 713, 716

Louisville & Nashville Railroad v. Whitley County Court, 636

Loux v. Rhay, 453

Lowe v. Bentley, 467

Luebbe v. Presbyterian Hospital, 759

Lumley v. Wagner, 369

Lummus Co. v. Commonwealth Oil Refining Co., 959

Lykos v. American Home Insurance Co., 592

Lyric Piano Co. v. Purvis, 48

McCargo v. Hedrick, 78

McCarthy v. Palmer, 481

McCourtie v. United States Steel Corp., 611

McDonald v. Mabee, 801

McFaul v. Ramsey, 408

McGee v. International Life Insurance Co., 830, 837

McNeil Construction Co. v. Livingston State Bank, 1113

Mackensworth v. American Trading Transp. Co., 832

Malloy v. Trombley, 1010

Manhattan Egg Co. v. Seaboard Terminal & Refrigeration Co., 344, *403*

Manning v. Loew, 423

Masino v. Outboard Marine Corp., 239

Maxwell v. Dow, 599

Mayer v. Petzelt, 612, 615

Manchester Modes, Inc. v. Schuman, 177

Maness v. Meyers, 770

Manhattan Life Ins. Co. v. Broughton, 746

Mansfield, Coldwater & Lake Michigan Railway v. Swan, 713

Margeson v. Boston & Maine Railroad, 496

Marine Petroleum Co. v. Champlin Petroleum Co., 495

Marsh v. Illinois Cent. R., 657

Marshall v. Baltimore & Ohio Railroad, 171

Marshall v. Lockhead, 1084

Marshall v. Mulrenin, 233, 235

Marshall's U.S. Auto Supply, Inc. v. Cashman, 634

Martin v. Stokes, 920

Martin Realty Co. v. Garver, 606

Meissner v. Papas, 632

Mellon v. Cooper-Jarrett, Inc., 515

Mendoza, United States v., 1053

Mennonite Board of Missions v. Adams, 939

Merit Insurance Co. v. Colao, 462

Mersey Docks & Harbour Board, Ex parte, 1211

Milliken v. Meyer, 800

Mills v. Duryee, 797

Miner v. Bradley, 330, 346

Mitchell v. Hart, 450

Mitchell v. Silverstein, 561

Mitchell v. W.T. Grant Co., 943

Mladinich v. Kohn, 808

Mobile, Jackson & Kansas City Railroad v. Turnipseed, 551

Momand v. Universal Film Exchange, Inc., 656

Montana v. United States, 1016

Montgomery Ward & Co. v. Duncan, 652

Moore v. Justices of the Municipal Court, 956

Moore v. New York Cotton Exchange, 725

Morgan v. McDonough, 378

Morgantown, City of v. Royal Insurance Co., 681, 1230

Morris v. Pennsylvania R., 607

Moser, United States v., 1014, 1015

Moses v. Macferlan, 345, 359

Mulcahy v. Duggan, 48

Mullane v. Central Hanover Bank & Trust Co., 844, 871, *934*

Murphy v. Erwin-Wasey, Inc., 837

Nanty-Glo Boro. v. American Sur. Co., 587

Nash County Bd. of Educ. v. Biltmore Co., 969

National Acceptance Co. of America v. Bathalter, 461

National Equipment Rental, Ltd. v. Szukhent, 955
National Hockey League v. Metropolitan Hockey Club, 512
Neely v. Martin K. Eby Construction Co., 662
Neenan v. Woodside Astoria Transportation Co., 1036
Nelson v. Keefer, 749
Nelson v. Miller, 833
Nemetz v. Aye, 495
New York v. Dairylea Corp., 1239
New York Life Insurance Co. v. Dunlevy, 1200
New York Times Co. v. Connor, 824
New York Times Co. v. United States, 377
Newbury Mfg. Co., United States v., 452
Newport, City of v. Fact Concerts, Inc., 599
Niagara Duplicator Co. v. Shackleford, 501
Niedland v. United States, 434
Nimrod v. Sylvester, 599
Nixon, United States v., 514
Nobles, United States v., 491
Norfolk & Western Railway v. Liepelt, 251
Norman v. McKee, 1223
North Georgia Finishing, Inc. v. Di-Chem, Inc., 944
Northern District of California, Dalkon Shield IUD Products Liability Litigation, In re, 1135
Norwood v. Kirkpatrick, 914

Oberst v. International Harvester Co., 242
O'Brien v. City of Syracuse, 967
O'Brien v. International Brotherhood of Electrical Workers, 66
O'Connor v. Pennsylvania Railroad, 581
O'Donnell v. Elgin, Joliet & Eastern Railway, 448
Ogle v. Barnes, 326
O'Hare v. Merck & Co., 663
Old Wayne Mutual Life Ass'n v. McDonough, 813
Oliver v. Kalamazoo Board of Education, 503
O'Malley v. Chrysler Corp., 514
Oppenheimer Fund v. Sanders, 1156
Orange Theatre Corp. v. Rayherstz Amusement Corp., 809
Orenstein v. United States, 679

Ortiz v. United States Government, 738
Orvis v. Higgins, 648
Osborn v. Bank of the United States, 715
Osserman v. Jacobs, 986
Owen Equipment & Erection Co. v. Kroger, 729
Owens v. Superior Court, 801

Pacific Greyhound Lines v. Zane, 607
Page v. Wright, 713
Palmer v. Hoffman, 206, 461
Park Tower Development Group v. Goldfeld, 500
Parklane Hosiery Co. v. Shore, 1048
Pedrick v. Peoria & Eastern Railroad, 572
Perkins v. Benguet Consolidated Mining Co., 813, 825
Pesce v. Brecher, 1038
Petrol Shipping Corp., In re, 942
Pettway v. American Cast Iron Pipe Co., 1167
Petty v. Tennessee-Missouri Bridge Comm'n, 161
Pennoyer v. Neff, 772
Pennsylvania Fire Ins. Co. v. Gold Issue Mining & Milling Co., 813
Pennsylvania Railroad v. Chamberlain, 574, 580
People v. _____ (see opposing party)
Perry v. W.S. Darley & Co., 494
Peterson v. Feyereisen, 467
Peterson v. United States, 489
Pettingill v. Fuller, 641, 658
Pfizer Inc. v. Lord, 515
Philadelphia & Reading Railway v. McKibbin, 813
Phoenix Mutual Life Insurance Co. v. Conway, 699
Phoenix Mut. Life Ins. Co. v. Reich, 1212
Pinnix v. Griffin, 1038
Piper Aircraft Co. v. Reyno, 921
Poindexter v. Willis, 836
Poland v. Atlantis Credit Corp., 1211
Potts v. Flax, 1134
Powers v. Continental Casualty Co., 585
Pratt v. Western Bridge & Constr. Co., 597
Provident Tradesmens Bank & Trust Co. v. Patterson, 1097, 1196
Prudential Ins. Co. v. Berry, 788
Prudential Ins. Co. v. Saxe, 682

Raab v. Bowery Savings Bank, 405
Rackers v. Siegfried, 485

Ragan v. Merchants Transfer & Warehouse Co., 210
Railroad Co. v. Stout, 594
Railway Express Agency v. Mackay, 599, 600
Ralph Blechman, Inc. v. I.B. Kleinert Rubber Co., 678
Rankin v. Frebank Co., 680, 699
Ratay v. Lincoln Nat'l Life Ins. Co., 599
Ratcliff v. Davies, 335
Ratliff v. Cooper Laboratories, 829
Reeves v. Crownshield, 152
Reid v. Nelson, 580
Reid v. San Pedro, Los Angeles & Salt Lake Railroad, 566
Reitman v. Mulkey, 950
Renfro v. Johnson, 568
Reserve Mining Co. v. Lord, 275, 1252
Revere Copper & Brass Inc. v. Aetna Casualty & Surety Co., 726
Reynolds v. Clarke, 320
Rich v. Finley, 605
Richards of Rockford, Inc. v. Pacific Gas & Electric Co,. 498
Richardson v. Gregory, 424
Ridgeland Box Mfg. Co. v. Sinclair Ref. Co., 742
Rinehart v. Locke, 987
Riordan v. Ferguson, 956
Ritter v. Ritter, 141
Riverside & Dan River Cotton Mills v. Menefee, 812
Roach v. Teamsters Local Union No. 688, p. 993
Robbins v. Jordan, 428
Robyn v. White, 606
Roche v. Evaporated Milk Association, 1242
Rogers v. Long Island Rail Road, 598
Rogers v. Missouri Pacific Railroad, 580
Rojas v. Richardson, 619, 622
Roller v. Holly, 941
Rosa v. American Oil Co., 632
Rosa v. City of Chester, 634
Ross v. Bernhard, 700
Rubenstein v. Kleven, 513
Rudow v. Fogel, 1009
Rush v. Savchuk, 872
Russell v. Barnes Foundation, 154
Ryan, United States v., 516, 770

Safeway Stores v. Reynolds, 492
Saint Paul Mercury Indemnity Co. v. Red Cab Co., 747
Sam Fox Publishing Co. v. United States, 1189

Sampliner v. Motion Picture Patents Co., 570
Sanderson v. Niemann, 1019
Santosky v. Kramer, 555
Sargent v. Massachusetts Accident Co., 557, 561
Savannah, F. & W. Ry. v. Daniels, 595
Sawyer v. United States, 560
Schlagenhauf v. Holder, 70, 71, 515, 1244
Schmidtke v. Conesa, 461
Schwabe v. Chantilly, Inc., 991
Schwartz v. Public Administrator, 1031
Scott v. Scott, 444
Scott v. Shepherd, 321, 651
Scribner v. Cyr, 588
Sea Colony, Inc. v. Continental Insurance Co., 494
Sears, Roebuck & Co. v. Mackey, 1228
Sears, Roebuck & Co. v. Marhenke, 414
Seiffer v. Topsy's Int'l, Inc., 495
Seigal v. Merrick, 1223
Seiwell v. Hines, 573
Sepinski v. Bergstol, 677
Service Auto Supply Co. v. Harte & Co., 592
Shaffer v. Heitner, 856, 871
Shall v. Henry, 452
Shamrock Oil & Gas Corp. v. Sheets, 755
Shannon v. Dow, 573
Shapiro v. Freeman, 500
Sharrod v. London & North Western Railway, 329
Shephard v. United States, 127
Sherman v. Renth, 449
Shields v. Barrow, 187, 1094, 1096
Shoshone Mining Co. v. Rutter, 717
Show-World Center v. Walsh, 1034
Shuber v. S.S. Kresge Co., 82
Shuttlesworth v. City of Birmingham, 769
Sibbach v. Wilson & Co., 5, 26, 58, 70, 207, 516
Sierocinski v. E.I. Du Pont De Nemours & Co., 34, 57, 68, 415
Silliman, United States v., 1020
Silva v. Silva, 1060
Simblest v. Maynard, 588, 592
Simler v. Conner, 697
Simmons v. Continental Casualty Co., 444
Simmons v. Fish, 606, 608, 634
Simon v. Southern Railway, 813
Sipe v. Moyers, 804
Slade's Case, 342, 343
Slocum v. New York Life Insurance Co., 651

Smedra v. Stanek, 120
Smith v. Central Linen Service Co., 492, 493
Smith v. Kansas City Title & Trust Co., 716
Smith v. Kirkpatrick, 965, 975
Smith v. Swormstedt, 1114, 1115
Smoot v. Fox, 568
Snead v. American Export-Isbrandtsen Lines, 498
Sniadach v. Family Finance Corp., 942
Snyder v. Harris, 194, *751*, 1155
Société Internationale pour Participations Industrielles et Commerciales, S.A. v. Rogers, 512
Southeast Guar. Trust Co. v. Rodman & Renshaw, Inc., 837
Southern Railway v. Campbell, 483
Southern Ry. v. Covenia, 443
Southern Railway v. Lanham, 483, 516
Spangler v. Pugh, 425
Spaulding v. Denton, 494
Spencer v. State, 569
Spielman-Fond, Inc. v. Hanson's, Inc., 950
Spilker v. Hankin, 1021
Springville v. Thomas, 105
Stacy v. Kemp, 465
Stampofski v. Steffens, 618
State Farm Fire & Casualty Co. v. Tashire, 183, *1203*
Stebbins v. Nationwide Mut. Ins. Co., 990
Steinberg v. McKay, 568
Stimpson v. Hunter, 561
Stone v. United States, 911
Stone & Downer Co., United States v., 1015
Stooke v. Taylor, 465
Strangborough v. Warner, 341
Subin v. Goldsmith, 565
Sullivan v. Southern Pac. Co., 503
Summers v. Tice, 553
Sunshine Kitchens, Inc. v. Alanthus Corp., 800
Supervisors of Kewaunee County v. Decker, 408, 410
Supreme Tribe of Ben-Hur v. Cauble, 1114
Surowitz v. Hilton Hotels Corp., 457
Sutcliffe Storage & Warehouse Co. v. United States, 971
Svendsen v. Smith's Moving & Trucking Co., 952
Swift v. Moseley, 336
Swift v. Tyson, 196
Szantay v. Beech Aircraft Corp., 231, 902

Tauza v. Susquehanna Coal Co., 813
Taylor v. Hawkinson, 1044
Taylor v. Kentucky, 548
Taylor v. Washington Terminal Co., 645
Teitelbaum Furs, Inc. v. Dominion Insurance Co., 1060
Terlizzi v. Brodie, 799
Texas Department of Community Affairs v. Burdine, 543
Thompson v. Carley, 622
Thompson v. Harry C. Erb, Inc., 453
Thompson v. Washington National Bank, 958
Tkaczyk v. Gallagher, 453
Todd v. Central Petroleum Co., 975, 976
Trbovich v. United Mine Workers, 1190
Trezza v. Dame, 596
Trotter v. Mutual Reserve Fund Life Ass'n, 447
TWA v. Hughes, 512
Tyler v. Judges of the Court of Registration, 781

UAW v. National Caucus of Labor Comms., 60
Umphres v. Shell Oil Co., 61
Union Pac. Ry. v. Botsford, 27
Union Tool Co. v. Wilson, 515
United Mine Workers v. Gibbs, 723
United Mine Workers, United States v., 760
U.S. Financial Securities Litigation, In re, 710
United States v. _____ (see opposing party)
United States Gypsum Co., United States v., 648
United Steelworkers v. R.H. Bouligny, Inc., 173
Universe Tankships, Inc. v. United States, 417

V.O. Machinoimport v. Clark Equipment Co., 501
Vaise v. Delaval, 603
Van Dusen v. Barrack, 918, 1252
Van Scoten v. Albright, 372
Vaughan v. Southern Ry., 747
Virginia Elec. & Power Co. v. Sun Shipbldg. & Dry Dock Co., 495
Virginian Ry. v. Armentrout, 595

Wabash Western Ry. v. Friedman, 425
Walker v. Armco Steel Corp., 235
Walker v. Clements, 466, 467
Walker v. City of Birmingham, 763

Wagner v. Loup River Public Power District, 636
Wall v. Brim, 415
Wangler v. Harvey, 800
Ward v. Macauley, 335
Washington Hospital Center v. Cheeks, 83
Wasik v. Borg, 426
Waterhouse v. Levine, 982
Watertown Milk Producers' Co-operative Ass'n v. Van Camp Packing Co., 464
Watkins' Case, 339
Watson, United States v., 598
Wayman v. Southard, 18
Webster, Commonwealth v., 555
Webster Eisenlohr, Inc. v. Kalodner, 276, 1252
Weinell v. McKeesport Connecting R.R., 601
Welch v. Louisiana Power & Light Co., 233
West v. AT&T, 212
Western & Atlantic Railroad v. Henderson, 551, 552
Western Life Indemnity Co. v. Rupp, 809
Western Petroleum Co. v. Tidal Gasoline Co., 595
Western Union Telegraph Co. v. Pennsylvania, 1109
Wilkerson v. McCarthy, 579, 581, 592
Will v. Calvert Fire Ins. Co., 1250, 1252

Will v. United States, 1247
Willard v. Tayloe, 369
Williams v. Florida, 99
Williams v. Holland, 327
Williams v. Robinson, 49, 739
Williamson v. Columbia Gas & Electric Corp., 299, 338, *961,* 983
Williamson v. Liverpool & London & Globe Ins. Co., 453
Wood v. Gunston, 624
Wood v. Interstate Realty Co., 211, 220, 231
Woodworth v. Fuller, 450
World-Wide Volkswagen Corp. v. Woodson, 878
Wratchford v. S.J. Groves & Sons Co., 557, 581, 592
Wunderlich v. United States, 594
Wyman v. Newhouse, 798
Wyrough & Loser, Inc. v. Pelmor Laboratories, 809

Yazell, United States v., 244
Yellow Cab Co., United States v., 469
York v. Texas, 808
Youngstown Sheet & Tube Co. v. Sawyer, 276

Zahn v. International Paper Co., 194, 754, 1155
Zygmunt v. Avenue Realty Co., 369

*

TABLE OF FEDERAL STATUTES AND RULES

UNITED STATES CODE

5 U.S.C. —Executive Departments and Government Officers and Employees

U.S.C. Sec.	This Work Page
552	499

15 U.S.C.—Commerce and Trade

1671–1677	94

28 U.S.C.—Judiciary and Judicial Code

41	12
133	11
331	20
	397
636(b)	500
1252	154
1253	154
1254	16
	159
	176
1254(2)	159
1257	176
	1228
1291	16
	154
	155
	514
	959
	1155
	1227
	1228
1292(a)	155
	514
1292(a)(1)	155
	1155
	1239
1292(b)	155
	156
	454
	514
	1155
	1241
1295	12
1331	12
	162
	166
	716
	723
1332	162
	166
	170

28 U.S.C.—Judiciary and Judicial Code

U.S.C. Sec.	This Work Page
1332 (Cont'd)	174
	183
	188
1332(a)	12
	14
1332(b)	748
1332(c)	171
	172
	178
1335	12
	174
	183
	188
	1203
1335(b)	1211
1337	162
1337(a)	12
1338	162
1338(a)	12
1338(b)	723
1343	162
1345	244
1359	742
1391	177
	178
	184
1391(a)	177
	178
	188
1391(b)	177
	178
1391(c)	177
	178
	905
1391(d)	178
1392(a)	184
1397	178
	188
	1203
1401	178
	194
1404(a)	181
	914
	919
1406(a)	920
	921
1441	174
	175
	183
	455
	741
	755

TABLE OF FEDERAL STATUTES AND RULES

28 U.S.C.—Judiciary and Judicial Code

U.S.C. Sec.	This Work Page
1441(a)	178
	755
	759
1441(c)	759
1445(a)	175
1446–1450	175
1446(a)	456
1448	902
1631	974
1651(a)	157
	158
1652	197
1653	454
1655	792
	912
	1210
1695	194
1738	797
1861–1869	106
1870	106
1963	797
	798
2071	21
	156
2072	20
	21
	22
	23
	105
	118
	196
	397
2076	21
	110
	118
	397
2103	176
2106	156
	453
	454
	663
2111	618
2201	144
	145
	165
2202	144
2284	148
2361	179
	181
	188
	894
	1203
	1211
2401(b)	469
2403	1189
2412	144
2415	469

29 U.S.C.—Labor

U.S.C. Sec.	This Work Page
213(a)(1)	461
216(b)	461

42 U.S.C.—The Public Health and Welfare

	This Work Page
1983	979
1988	144

45 U.S.C.—Railroads

	This Work Page
51–60	175

46 U.S.C.—Shipping

	This Work Page
688	175

STATUTES AT LARGE

Stat. Year	This Work Page
1789, Sept. 24, P.L. ch. 20, § 11 1 Stat. 73	910
1789, Sept. 29, P.L. ch. 21, § 2 1 Stat. 93	383
1792, May 8, P.L. ch. 36, § 2 1 Stat. 275	383
1875, Mar. 3, P.L. ch. 137, § 1 18 Stat. 470	716
1973, Mar. 30, P.L. 93–12 87 Stat. 9	110
1975, Jan. 2, P.L. 93–595 88 Stat. 1926	110

FEDERAL RULES OF CIVIL PROCEDURE

F.R.C.P. Rule	This Work Page
1	30
	85
	420
2	22
	301
	407
	410
3	14
	31
	179
4	14
	31
	38
	179

TABLE OF FEDERAL STATUTES AND RULES

FEDERAL RULES OF CIVIL PROCEDURE

F.R.C.P. Rule	This Work Page
4 (Cont'd)	180
	181
	188
4(a)	179
4(b)	179
4(c)	179
4(c)(2)(C)	179
4(d)	179
	180
	894
	899
4(d)(1)	179
4(d)(3)	902
4(e)	179
	180
	829
	832
	894
4(e)(2)	792
	795
4(f)	180
	902
4(i)	180
5	40
5(b)	501
6(a)	38
6(b)	38
6(d)	41
6(e)	40
7	48
	52
7(a)	45
	46
	51
	452
7(b)	15
	52
7(b)(1)	40
8	445
8(a)	14
	31
	33
	37
	394
	436
8(a)(1)	454
8(a)(2)	439
	442
8(a)(3)	454
	455
8(b)	15
	38
	39
	40
	460
8(c)	31
	33
	39

FEDERAL RULES OF CIVIL PROCEDURE

F.R.C.P. Rule	This Work Page
8(c) (Cont'd)	42
	107
	432
	461
	462
	1012
8(d)	42
	45
	46
	51
	84
	85
	470
8(e)	31
	40
8(e)(1)	14
	33
	442
	450
8(e)(2)	36
	37
	38
	448
8(f)	31
9(b)	31
	33
	443
9(f)	432
9(g)	434
9(h)	23
10(a)	14
	44
10(b)	14
	448
	449
11	14
	31
	38
	59
	85
	456
	460
	1112
12	38
	43
	51
	177
	809
12(a)	38
	51
	809
12(a)(1)	40
12(b)	40
	41
	42
	809
12(b)(1)	39
	41

lxv

FEDERAL RULES OF CIVIL PROCEDURE

F.R.C.P. Rule	This Work Page
12(b)(1) (Cont'd)	42
	454
	722
12(b)(2)	39
	809
	810
	902
12(b)(2)–(5)	42
12(b)(3)	39
12(b)(4)	39
12(b)(5)	39
12(b)(6)	39
	40
	42
	43
	46
	47
	52
	84
	92
	432
	438
	452
	722
12(b)(7)	42
12(c)	42
	84
	92
12(d)	41
	98
12(e)	39
	41
	43
	438
	449
12(f)	39
	41
	43
	46
	84
	92
	450
12(g)	41
	42
	43
	809
	905
12(h)	41
	809
	905
12(h)(1)(A)	42
	43
12(h)(1)(B)	42
12(h)(2)	42
	46
12(h)(3)	41
	713
13	47

FEDERAL RULES OF CIVIL PROCEDURE

F.R.C.P. Rule	This Work Page
13 (Cont'd)	48
	49
	182
13(a)	47
	48
	49
	191
	466
	682
	738
	755
	1000
13(a)(2)	795
13(b)	47
	48
	466
13(c)	52
13(f)	47
	470
13(g)	190
	191
13(h)	186
	739
13(i)	196
14	180
	182
	189
	190
14(a)	189
	196
	738
14(b)	189
15	52
	55
15(a)	42
	43
	52
	53
	452
15(b)	53
	84
	983
15(c)	53
	470
16	77
	78
	82
	86
	128
	276
16(a)	77
16(b)	78
16(c)	77
	78
16(c)(7)	78
16(d)	78
16(e)	82

FEDERAL RULES OF CIVIL PROCEDURE

F.R.C.P. Rule	This Work Page
16(f)	84
17(a)	1112
	1113
17(b)	231
	1111
17(c)	1111
18	182
18(a)	37
	49
18(b)	378
	403
19	42
	108
	180
	186
	187
	192
	902
	1000
	1144
	1189
	1191
19–24	182
19(a)	186
	1113
19(a)(2)(i)	194
	1189
19(b)	194
	1199
20	185
	186
	188
	192
	195
	1111
	1191
20(b)	196
21	196
	1111
22	188
	1203
22(1)	188
	1209
	1210
	1211
22(2)	188
23	191
	192
	193
	194
	1115
	1120
	1133
	1135
	1182
	1189
	1191
23(a)	192

FEDERAL RULES OF CIVIL PROCEDURE

F.R.C.P. Rule	This Work Page
23(a) (Cont'd)	1115
	1134
23(a)(1)	1115
23(a)(4)	1126
23(b)	192
	1134
23(b)(1)	192
	193
	1134
	1155
23(b)(1)(A)	192
	1134
23(b)(1)(B)	192
	1134
23(b)(2)	192
	193
	1134
	1155
23(b)(3)	192
	193
	1134
	1155
	1160
	1161
	1182
23(c)	196
23(c)(1)	193
	1167
23(c)(2)	193
	1155
23(c)(4)	193
23(d)	193
	1160
23(d)(2)	195
23(d)(3)	195
23(e)	193
	1161
	1167
23.1	191
	194
	456
23.2	191
	194
24	193
	194
24(a)	195
	1189
	1191
	1199
24(a)(1)	1189
24(a)(2)	1189
24(b)	195
	196
	1191
	1199
24(c)	195
26	56
	57

FEDERAL RULES OF CIVIL PROCEDURE

F.R.C.P. Rule	This Work Page
26 (Cont'd)	59
	60
	69
26–37	20
	379
	449
26(a)	57
26(b)(1)	57
	58
	59
	64
	484
	494
26(b)(2)	58
26(b)(3)	58
	484
	489
	492
	493
26(b)(4)	58
	493
	494
	495
26(b)(4)(A)	493
	494
26(b)(4)(B)	494
26(c)	57
	59
	64
	76
	77
	499
	500
	501
26(d)	57
	511
26(e)	72
	75
26(e)(3)	73
26(f)	77
26(g)	59
	512
27	57
27(a)	456
28(a)	59
29	59
30	59
	64
	65
	75
30–37	56
30(a)	59
	511
30(b)(1)	59
30(b)(2)	59
30(b)(4)	60
30(b)(5)	60
30(b)(7)	60

FEDERAL RULES OF CIVIL PROCEDURE

F.R.C.P. Rule	This Work Page
30(c)	59
	60
	65
30(d)	59
	64
	76
	499
	500
30(e)	59
30(f)	59
31	64
	65
	75
32	73
	74
32(a)	73
	86
	127
32(a)(1)(4)	127
32(a)(2)	74
32(a)(3)	127
32(a)(3)(E)	74
32(b)	60
32(d)(3)(A)	60
32(d)(3)(B)	60
33	35
	65
	68
	69
	75
	481
33(a)	65
33(c)	65
34	69
	70
	75
	483
	484
	512
34(a)	70
34(a)(1)	70
35	15
	20
	23
	24
	25
	26
	27
	58
	70
	76
35(a)	15
35(b)(1)	71
35(b)(2)	71
35(b)(3)	70
36	69
	75

FEDERAL RULES OF CIVIL PROCEDURE

F.R.C.P. Rule	This Work Page
36 (Cont'd)	76
36(a)	69
	76
37	15
	17
	23
	75
	512
37(a)	59
	61
	64
	69
	75
	76
	499
	500
	513
37(a)(4)	61
	512
37(b)	76
	511
	513
37(b)(2)	77
37(b)(2)(D)	26
37(c)	69
	76
37(d)	76
37(g)	77
38	98
	666
	674
38(b)	98
38(c)	98
39	98
	679
39(c)	666
40	98
41(a)	682
	1006
41(a)(1)	567
41(a)(2)	567
41(b)	107
	108
	109
	136
	541
	570
	571
	986
	988
	989
	1156
41(d)	568
42	1111
42(a)	196
42(b)	48
	196
43(a)	74

FEDERAL RULES OF CIVIL PROCEDURE

F.R.C.P. Rule	This Work Page
43(a) (Cont'd)	110
43(d)	114
43(e)	41
44.1	445
45	56
45(b)	60
45(d)	59
	60
45(d)(2)	60
	501
45(f)	76
46	129
47	98
47(a)	106
47(b)	106
48	98
	99
	105
49	134
	607
	608
49(a)	134
	609
	612
49(b)	134
	607
	612
	614
50	136
	664
50(a)	107
	108
	109
	132
	138
	570
50(b)	132
	136
	138
	651
	652
50(c)	652
50(c)(1)	139
50(d)	652
	663
51	134
	135
52	134
52(a)	136
	648
	666
52(b)	139
53	500
54	139
54(a)	140
54(b)	155
	1156
	1227

FEDERAL RULES OF CIVIL PROCEDURE

F.R.C.P. Rule	This Work Page
54(b) (Cont'd)	1241
54(c)	139
	454
	680
54(d)	142
55(a)	38
55(b)	38
55(c)	38
	942
55(d)	51
56	84
	85
	92
	438
56(a)	85
56(b)	85
56(c)	86
	92
56(d)	86
56(e)	85
57	139
	144
58	139
59	136
	635
59(a)	617
59(a)(1)	136
	137
59(a)(2)	139
59(b)	137
	635
59(d)	138
	662
59(e)	136
	452
60	136
60(b)	452
	635
60(b)(1)	809
60(b)(2)	635
60(b)(5)	636
	960
60(b)(6)	636
61	138
	618
62	154
62(a)	157
62(b)	157
62(c)	157
62(d)	157
62(e)	157
62(f)	157
62(g)	157
62(h)	157
64	92
	93
	152
65	92

FEDERAL RULES OF CIVIL PROCEDURE

F.R.C.P. Rule	This Work Page
65(a)(1)	94
65(b)	94
	456
65(c)	94
65(d)	94
65(e)	377
66	456
68	143
69	151
69(a)	151
	153
	382
70	382
	786
81	30
81(a)	23
81(c)	175
83	21
	105
84	35
86(a)	19

FEDERAL RULES OF EVIDENCE

F.R.E. Rule	This Work Page
103(a)	618
103(a)(1)	129
103(a)(2)	130
103(b)(2)	130
103(c)	130
103(d)	129
104(a)	111
	594
104(b)	130
104(c)	111
	594
104(e)	111
105	129
201	112
301	552
302	552
401	112
402	112
403	128
407	58
	129
	242
408	129
411	129
501	118
	241
	484
601	115
	116
	118
602	112

FEDERAL RULES OF EVIDENCE

F.R.E. Rule	This Work Page
602 (Cont'd)	116
603	114
	116
605	116
606	116
606(b)	603
607	131
608	130
608(a)(2)	130
608(b)	131
609	114
	115
	130
611(a)	132
611(b)	131
	132
611(c)	132
614	274
701	112
702	111
703	111
704	112
705	111
706	274
801(a)(1)	127
801(a)(2)	127
801(c)	120
801(d)(1)(A)	131
801(d)(2)	123
802	118
	127
803	120
	121
803(1)	127
803(2)	127
803(13)	127
803(16)	128
803(22)	1060
803(24)	128
804	120
	121
804(b)(1)	127
804(b)(2)	122
	127

FEDERAL RULES OF EVIDENCE

F.R.E. Rule	This Work Page
804(b)(3)	122
804(b)(4)	127
804(b)(5)	128
805	128
901(a)	112
901(b)(8)	128
1001	128
1002	128
1003	128
1004	128
1007	128
1101(c)	484

FEDERAL RULES OF APPELLATE PROCEDURE

F.R.A.P. Rule	This Work Page
3	156
4	156
4(a)	157
5	156
7	156
8(a)	157
8(b)	157
10	156
11	156
12	156
12(a)	44
28	156
30	156
31	156
34	156
47	21
	156

SUPREME COURT RULES

Sup.Ct. Rule	This Work Page
17.1	17
	21
	159

MATERIALS FOR A BASIC COURSE

IN

CIVIL PROCEDURE

*

Part One

A FIRST VIEW OF THE SUBJECT

TOPIC A.   GENERAL CONSIDERATIONS

This course treats of "Civil Procedure." For the purpose of putting general boundaries to the course, what meanings do we ascribe to these words? We shall not attempt to define them in any formal way, but shall rather begin at this point to convey a general sense of the meanings we attach to them.

Nature of civil controversies.—The word "civil" is used in the present context in contradistinction to "criminal." The typical criminal case is one that the state initiates for the purpose of securing obedience to its laws by the punishment or correction of a lawbreaker. In a civil case, on the other hand, ordinarily the state is not seeking a sanction against a lawbreaker, nor is it directly concerned as a party in the proceedings. The typical civil case is initiated and carried on by a person who seeks redress for some wrong alleged to have been committed against him by another. The redress he seeks is commonly, although by no means always, the payment of money to him by the wrongdoer.[a] The state establishes and maintains a system of courts to which a person may resort, if he chooses to do so, to obtain such redress.

Predominantly, then, the task of courts in civil cases is to decide specific disputes brought before them by people who cannot or will not follow the usual course of settling their controversies by themselves. True, in deciding a case a court may announce general rules that will guide other people later involved in similar controversies. Much of the law student's work is devoted to the appraisal and use of past decisions, and judicial opinions explaining these decisions, as precedents to aid in predicting how future cases are likely to be decided. These decisions and opinions are tools of the lawyer's trade. They help him, as adviser, to resolve his client's difficulties short of litigation and, as advocate, to further his client's cause when litigation comes. This constant resort to precedents tends, however, to becloud the traditional proposition that the essential purpose of a typi-

[a] What cases suggest themselves where the payment of money would not be a satisfactory form of redress? What other forms of redress might be appropriate? (After considering these questions, see infra p. 139.)

[*Note:* Editors' footnotes throughout this casebook are lettered. Footnotes by the court in judicial opinions and by authors in quoted materials, when retained, will bear the numbers of the originals; others will be omitted without any statement to that effect.]

1

cal lawsuit is to decide a flesh-and-blood dispute between flesh-and-blood people and, where possible, to resolve it once and for all.[b]

What, then, is the nature of the civil disputes with which the courts have to deal?

People living together in organized society are bound by rules governing their day-to-day conduct, imposed in one way or another by the government. These are rules of substance, or substantive law. A rule of substantive law may be embodied in a legislative enactment—an act of Congress, an act of a state legislature, or a municipal ordinance. Often it finds its source in the "common law," the decisions and opinions of the courts.[c] Whatever the source of a rule of substantive law, it may be cast in the form of a proposition such as the following:

> If *B* knowingly strikes *A*, and . . ., then, unless *A* consented, or . . ., *A* is entitled to a judgment of a court that he recover money damages from *B*.

This proposition describes what in law is called a battery. Rules of this sort state the rights and duties among people and disclose the circumstances in which a court may be expected to grant redress to one person against another.

In many cases that come to the courts there is dispute over what the rule of substantive law is. Legislation may be of doubtful meaning, or precedents may not speak with a clear voice. New sets of circumstances arise to pose problems for which neither existing statutes nor the precedents afford a ready answer. A court must nevertheless decide the case before it and will do so with a view to existing rules of substantive law and upon consideration of historical continuity, of custom, of morals, and of other factors.

In other cases the substantive rule will be pretty clear, and the contest will be over what happened. The parties may agree that the pertinent rule of substantive law is the one given schematically above, but they may differ as to whether *B* struck *A*, whether he did so knowingly, or whether *A* consented.

In still other cases there will be a contest both as to what occurred and as to what the applicable rule is. In lawyers' language, such a

[b] There are elaborate rules designed to prevent the relitigation of disputes once disposed of by a court. Reference to these rules, which are clustered under the banner of "res judicata," recurs throughout this book. They are treated in detail in Part Six.

[c] "With the common law, unlike the civil law and its Roman law precursor, the formulation of general principles has not preceded decision. In its origin it is the law of the practitioner rather than the philosopher. Decision has drawn its inspiration and its strength from the very facts which frame the issues for decision. Once made, the decision controls the future judgments of courts in like or analogous cases. General rules, underlying principles, and finally legal doctrine, have successively emerged only as the precedents, accumulated through the centuries, have been seen to follow a pattern, characteristically not without distortion and occasional broken threads, and seldom conforming consistently to principle." Stone, The Common Law in the United States, 50 Harv.L.Rev. 4, 6 (1936).

controversy presents both questions of fact ("What happened?") and questions of law ("What is the substantive rule?").

Nature of procedural rules.—By statutes enacted by the legislature, by general rules promulgated by the courts, and by decisions of the courts having the force of precedent, the government prescribes the procedures by which persons may bring controversies before its courts, and by which they must unfold and conduct those controversies once in the courts. So also there are procedures by which the decisions of the courts are enforced and made effective. This course deals with such procedures, which may be thought of as constituting the mechanics of litigation. (The scope and coverage of procedural rules may be roughly gauged by examining the table of contents of the "Federal Rules of Civil Procedure.")

Litigation could perhaps be conducted without general rules of procedure established in advance. The parties or the court could conceivably determine as an original matter, case by case, the procedures that they consider appropriate to the particular controversy to be resolved. In out-of-court arbitrations, procedures are in fact frequently improvised for the particular case. But this has not been the mode of our law. The conduct of litigation is governed by rules of more or less general application, although there is room within these rules for a certain amount of individualized treatment of cases, and room also for discretion, experimentation, and invention. Of course the rules are subject to change, have been changed from time to time, and will undergo change in the future. In all events, it is mainly by the apparatus of procedural rules and their application by parties and courts that society seeks to ensure that disputes will be handled in a fair and orderly way and as expeditiously and economically as may be practicable.

Rules of procedure provide among other things the means of laying bare what the contest is about. The court, in theory at least, knows nothing of the state of affairs between the contestants until one of them formally presents a grievance to it. The rules of procedure regulate how he shall do this, and also how his adversary shall present his side of the matter, so that the court may judge between them and grant or refuse redress. One aim of the rules is to disclose the real dispute in a minimum of time and with least expense, and thus to avoid the vexatious and wasteful business of dealing with questions on which the parties are actually not in disagreement. Another aim is to confine the parties to the presentation of materials relevant to the real dispute and helpful in its resolution. Yet another is to give neither side an undeserved forensic advantage in persuading the court. Some of the rules look principally to preserving a settled order of proceeding; they could be radically altered without important consequence. In respect to other rules, there are powerful reasons of policy why they should be as they are or should not be as

they are. The competing considerations in such areas of procedure
will absorb much of our attention in this course.

It may be argued that procedural rules ought to be so definite and
clear-cut as always to furnish a sure guide for the behavior of the
parties in court proceedings. Whether or not this would be the ideal
situation, it can be said at the outset that it has not been attained,
and it may be doubted whether it ever could be attained. We must
approach the study of procedure with full awareness that we shall be
bedeviled by many of the same doubts and difficulties about what the
rule is or ought to be that characterize the study of substantive law.

Therefore, although the rules of procedure are designed to isolate
and sharpen the issues in dispute and thus to simplify the controversy, the uncertainties in the procedural rules may serve to inject a further disputatious ingredient into a lawsuit. Procedural problems are
more obtrusive in our law than a beginner is likely to suppose, and
perhaps more obtrusive than they ought to be.[d]

The substance-procedure distinction.—It is perhaps already apparent that there will be difficulties in assigning particular rules to
the category of substance or the category of procedure, difficulties
that will sometimes defy the most careful and circumspect attempts
to delineate the categories. For example, take a "statute of limitations" that lays it down that an action for battery must be commenced within two years after the event. It might be said that this is
a rule of substance, for it expresses a firm condition on the plaintiff's
right to recover. It might be said, on the other hand, that the rule is
one of procedure, for it regulates a step in a lawsuit, the first step,
the time within which it must be commenced. We shall see many
instances, and many more poignant instances, where classification
will be difficult.

But why should we be concerned with mere classification? Certainly difficulties of classification are of small consequence if the aim
is merely the lowly one of assigning subject matter to courses in a
law school, so that if the statute of limitations were conceived to be a
rule of procedure, it would be dealt with in Civil Procedure, but if
conceived to be a rule of substance, it would be dealt with elsewhere.
We shall be casual about course boundaries; if a problem arises in
the heartland of Civil Procedure and takes us beyond that field, we
shall follow it; and we shall often trespass on other courses without
even that excuse. It is, indeed, one of our main tasks to observe how
a legal problem may cut across many conventional departments of
the law.

[d] Compare the following statement:
"It is characteristic of the prevailing ra-
tionalistic systems of legal philosophy
that they minimize the importance of procedure by calling it adjective law, etc.
But the tendency of all modern scientific
and philosophic thought is to weaken the
distinction between substance and attribute . . . and to emphasize the importance of method, process, or procedure." M. Cohen, "The Process of
Judicial Legislation," in Law and the Social Order 112, 128 (1933).

There is, however, another and graver matter. It happens that legislatures and courts constantly use such titles as "civil procedure" or "civil practice"; they also constantly use the words "procedure" and "substance" and cognate words. Moreover, they attach serious consequences to these labels, so the matter of classification may be important.

Our first case, Sibbach v. Wilson & Co., raises a question of the meaning of "practice and procedure" and "substantive rights" as those words appear in the very Act of Congress that originally empowered the Supreme Court of the United States to promulgate the Federal Rules.

SIBBACH v. WILSON & CO.
Supreme Court of the United States, 1941.
312 U.S. 1, 61 S.Ct. 422.

Certiorari to the Circuit Court of Appeals for the Seventh Circuit.

MR. JUSTICE ROBERTS delivered the opinion of the Court.

This case calls for decision as to the validity of Rules 35 and 37 of the Rules of Civil Procedure for District Courts of the United States.

In an action brought by the petitioner [e] in the District Court for Northern Illinois to recover damages for bodily injuries, inflicted in Indiana, respondent answered denying the allegations of the complaint, and moved for an order requiring the petitioner to submit to a physical examination by one or more physicians appointed by the court to determine the nature and extent of her injuries. The court ordered that the petitioner submit to such an examination by a physician so appointed.

Compliance having been refused, the respondent obtained an order to show cause why the petitioner should not be punished for contempt. In response the petitioner challenged the authority of the court to order her to submit to the examination, asserting that the order was void. It appeared that the courts of Indiana, the state where the cause of action arose, hold such an order proper [citing Indiana precedents], whereas the courts of Illinois, the state in which the trial court sat, hold that such an order cannot be made [citing Illinois precedents]. Neither state has any statute governing the matter.

The court adjudged the petitioner guilty of contempt, and directed that she be committed until she should obey the order for examination or otherwise should be legally discharged from custody. The petitioner appealed.

[e] The petitioner is the party who seeks review in the Supreme Court; the respondent is his adversary. In this case they were the plaintiff and the defendant respectively. The name of the petitioner appears first in the caption of the case.

The Circuit Court of Appeals decided that Rule 35, which authorizes an order for a physical examination in such a case, is valid, and affirmed the judgment. The writ of certiorari was granted because of the importance of the question involved.

The Rules of Civil Procedure were promulgated under the authority of the Act of June 19, 1934, which is:

"Be it enacted . . . That the Supreme Court of the United States shall have the power to prescribe, by general rules, for the district courts of the United States and for the courts of the District of Columbia, the forms of process, writs, pleadings, and motions, and the practice and procedure in civil actions at law. Said rules shall neither abridge, enlarge, nor modify the substantive rights of any litigant. They shall take effect six months after their promulgation, and thereafter all laws in conflict therewith shall be of no further force or effect.

"Sec. 2. The court may at any time unite the general rules prescribed by it for cases in equity with those in actions at law so as to secure one form of civil action and procedure for both: *Provided, however,* That in such union of rules the right of trial by jury as at common law and declared by the seventh amendment to the Constitution shall be preserved to the parties inviolate. Such united rules shall not take effect until they shall have been reported to Congress by the Attorney General at the beginning of a regular session thereof and until after the close of such session." [f]

[The Court here quoted the relevant portions of Rules 35 and 37.[g]]

The contention of the petitioner, in final analysis, is that Rules 35 and 37 are not within the mandate of Congress to this court. This is the limit of permissible debate, since argument touching the broader questions of Congressional power and of the obligation of federal courts to apply the substantive law of a state is foreclosed.

Congress has undoubted power to regulate the practice and procedure of federal courts [citing Wayman v. Southard, 23 U.S. (10 Wheat.) 1, 21 (1825), among other cases], and may exercise that pow-

---

[f] The Rules Enabling Act of 1934 has since been amended and now appears as § 2072 of title 28 of the United States Code, which is cited as 28 U.S.C. § 2072.

Title 28 contains most of the statutes dealing with procedure in the courts of the United States, as distinguished from the courts of the states. It was revised and recodified in 1948.

The Rules pamphlet that accompanies this casebook sets out portions of title 28, along with selected provisions of the Constitution of the United States.

[g] Both of these Rules were heavily amended in 1970. Rule 37(b)(2)(iv), which is now Rule 37(b)(2)(D), formerly read: "In lieu of any of the foregoing orders or in addition thereto, an order directing the arrest of any party or agent of a party for disobeying any of such orders except an order to submit to a physical or mental examination." None of the other changes bears on the Sibbach problem.

The original and amended texts appear in the Rules pamphlet. See the section of the Rules pamphlet containing the 1970 amendments and the Advisory Committee's notes thereon.

er by delegating to this or other federal courts authority to make rules not inconsistent with the statutes or constitution of the United States; but it has never essayed to declare the substantive state law, or to abolish or nullify a right recognized by the substantive law of the state where the cause of action arose, save where a right or duty is imposed in a field committed to Congress by the Constitution. On the contrary it has enacted that the state law shall be the rule of decision in the federal courts.[8]

Hence we conclude that the Act of June 19, 1934, was purposely restricted in its operation to matters of pleading and court practice and procedure. Its two provisos or caveats emphasize this restriction. The first is that the court shall not "abridge, enlarge, nor modify substantive rights," in the guise of regulating procedure. The second is that if the rules are to prescribe a single form of action for cases at law and suits in equity, the constitutional right to jury trial inherent in the former must be preserved. There are other limitations upon the authority to prescribe rules which might have been, but were not mentioned in the Act; for instance, the inability of a court, by rule, to extend or restrict the jurisdiction conferred by a statute.

Whatever may be said as to the effect of the Conformity Act[h] while it remained in force, the rules, if they are within the authority granted by Congress, repeal that statute, and the District Court was not bound to follow the Illinois practice respecting an order for physical examination. On the other hand if the right to be exempt from such an order is one of substantive law, the Rules of Decision Act required the District Court, though sitting in Illinois, to apply the law of Indiana, the state where the cause of action arose, and to order the examination. To avoid this dilemma[i] the petitioner admits, and, we think, correctly, that Rules 35 and 37 are rules of procedure. She insists, nevertheless, that by the prohibition against abridging substantive rights, Congress has banned the rules here challenged. In order to reach this result she translates "substantive" into "important" or "substantial" rights. And she urges that if a rule affects such a right, albeit the rule is one of procedure merely, its prescription is not within the statutory grant of power embodied in the Act of June 19, 1934. . . .

[8] [In a footnote here the Court cited the Rules of Decision Act of 1789, now embodied in 28 U.S.C. § 1652. This statute is considered more extensively in connection with Erie R.R. v. Tompkins, infra p. 197.]

[h] The Conformity Act of 1872, old 28 U.S.C. § 724, provided:

"*Conformity to practice in State courts.* The practice, pleadings, and forms and modes of proceedings in civil causes, other than equity and admiralty causes, in the district courts, shall conform, as near as may be, to the practice, pleadings, and forms and modes of proceedings existing at the time in like causes in the courts of record of the State within which such district courts are held, any rule of court to the contrary notwithstanding."

[i] Assume for the present that the petitioner's dilemma was as stated by the Court. Later cases will shed a different light upon the problem.

[After discussing a number of prior decisions relied on by petitioner, the Court continued:]

We are thrown back, then, to the arguments drawn from the language of the Act of June 19, 1934. Is the phrase "substantive rights" confined to rights conferred by law to be protected and enforced in accordance with the adjective law of judicial procedure? It certainly embraces such rights. One of them is the right not to be injured in one's person by another's negligence, to redress infraction of which the present action was brought. The petitioner says the phrase connotes more; that by its use Congress intended that in regulating procedure this court should not deal with important and substantial rights theretofore recognized. Recognized where and by whom? The state courts are divided as to the power in the absence of statute to order a physical examination. In a number such an order is authorized by statute or rule. The rules in question accord with the procedure now in force in Canada and England.

The asserted right, moreover, is no more important than many others enjoyed by litigants in District Courts sitting in the several states, before the Federal Rules of Civil Procedure altered and abolished old rights or privileges and created new ones in connection with the conduct of litigation. The suggestion that the rule offends the important right to freedom from invasion of the person ignores the fact that, as we hold, no invasion of freedom from personal restraint attaches to refusal so to comply with its provisions. If we were to adopt the suggested criterion of the importance of the alleged right we should invite endless litigation and confusion worse confounded. The test must be whether a rule really regulates procedure,—the judicial process for enforcing rights and duties recognized by substantive law and for justly administering remedy and redress for disregard or infraction of them. That the rules in question are such is admitted.

Finally, it is urged that Rules 35 and 37 work a major change of policy and that this was not intended by Congress. Apart from the fact already stated, that the policy of the states in this respect has not been uniform, it is to be noted that the authorization of a comprehensive system of court rules was a departure in policy, and that the new policy envisaged in the enabling act of 1934 was that the whole field of court procedure be regulated in the interest of speedy, fair and exact determination of the truth. The challenged rules comport with this policy. Moreover, in accordance with the Act, the rules were submitted to the Congress so that that body might examine them and veto their going into effect if contrary to the policy of the legislature.

The value of the reservation of the power to examine proposed rules, laws and regulations before they become effective is well understood by Congress. It is frequently, as here, employed to make sure that the action under the delegation squares with the Congressional purpose. Evidently the Congress felt the rule was within the ambit of the statute as no effort was made to eliminate it from the proposed body of rules, although this specific rule was attacked and defended before the committees of the two Houses. . . .

The District Court treated the refusal to comply with its order as a contempt and committed the petitioner therefor. Neither in the Circuit Court of Appeals nor here was this action assigned as error. We think, however, that in the light of the provisions of Rule 37 it was plain error of such a fundamental nature that we should notice it. Section (b)(2)(iv) of Rule 37 exempts from punishment as for contempt the refusal to obey an order that a party submit to a physical or mental examination. The District Court was in error in going counter to this express exemption. The remedies available under the rule in such a case are those enumerated in § (b)(2)(i), (ii) and (iii). For this error we reverse the judgment and remand the cause to the District Court for further proceedings in conformity to this opinion.

Reversed.

[Justice Frankfurter, in an opinion concurred in by Justices Black, Douglas, and Murphy, took issue with the majority's reasoning. He said, among other things, that "it does not seem to me that the answer to our question is to be found by an analytical determination whether the power of examination here claimed is a matter of procedure or a matter of substance, even assuming that the two are mutually exclusive categories with easily ascertainable contents." To be sure, there is no constitutional immunity from the examination here sought; the matter is "amenable to statutory change." Still we should remember that the rule in question affects the "inviolability of a person" having "historic roots in Anglo-American law." Justice Frankfurter went on to say:]

So far as national law is concerned, a drastic change in public policy in a matter deeply touching the sensibilities of people or even their prejudices as to privacy, ought not to be inferred from a general authorization to formulate rules for the more uniform and effective dispatch of business on the civil side of the federal courts. I deem a requirement as to the invasion of the person to stand on a very different footing from questions pertaining to the discovery of documents, pre-trial procedure and other devices for the expeditious, economic and fair conduct of litigation. That disobedience of an order under Rule 35 cannot be visited with punishment as for contempt does not mitigate its intrusion into an historic immunity of the privacy of the person. Of course the Rule is compulsive in that the doors of the federal courts otherwise open may be shut to litigants who do not submit to such a physical examination.

In this view little significance attaches to the fact that the Rules, in accordance with the statute, remained on the table of two Houses of Congress without evoking any objection to Rule 35 and thereby automatically came into force. Plainly the Rules are not acts of Congress and can not be treated as such. Having due regard to the mechanics of legislation and the practical conditions surrounding the business of Congress when the Rules were submitted, to draw any inference of tacit approval from non-action by Congress is to appeal to unreality. And so I conclude that to make the drastic change that Rule 35 sought to introduce would require explicit legislation.

————

In reading any case in this course, the student should seek to visualize the successive steps taken by the parties and the courts. Topic B of this Part, "Phases of a Lawsuit," should facilitate your understanding of the scenario. Briefing of the cases will aid in this process of visualization and comprehension, as is illustrated by the following sample brief and accompanying notes and questions.

Sample Brief	Notes and Questions
Facts: Mrs. Sibbach claimed to have received bodily injuries in Indiana, presumably caused by an employee of Wilson & Co.	(1) In this part of your brief you should state who the parties are and what happened to them before reaching the courthouse. Limit yourself to the legally relevant facts. For example, Hertha J. Sibbach's case actually arose from an automobile accident occurring on September 3, 1937, and involving the defendant's truck. These facts are not relevant and so should be omitted from your brief, just as they were omitted from the Supreme Court opinion itself. Sometimes, however, judicial opinions will include a great many irrelevant facts, and you must sift through them for the essence. Moreover, write the "Facts" (and the other entries) in your own words. Nothing is gained by transcribing the opinion.

In briefing a case, you should follow a logical and set format. As to choice of format, many possibilities are defensible. We choose to begin with the out-of-court facts in the interest of chronology and as an indication of their enormous importance in shaping decision. However, we do not here record the fruits of some abstract historical inquiry. Instead, we record the facts as they are accepted by the court for the purpose of decision. These emerge from the procedural maneuvers in the case, and the condition of the facts depends on the procedural posture of the case at the time of decision. For example, in Sibbach the facts rest upon the plaintiff's allegations. Accordingly, fixing the facts will prove difficult for you, meaning that you cannot write this first part of your brief until you have thought about the rest

Sample Brief	Notes and Questions

of your brief. This warning reflects the view that competent briefing serves as a record of completed reading and study, as well as a stimulus to further reading and study.

Prior Proceedings: Plaintiff Sibbach (*P*) sued the corporate defendant (*D*) in the United States District Court for the Northern District of Illinois, alleging negligence and seeking money damages.

(2) This portion of your brief should be detailed, covering everything that happens from crossing the threshold of the trial court to the moment as of which the opinion before you speaks. This is especially important for this course because detailed briefing here can be very helpful in mastering procedure and also because the "issues" presented by a procedure case always arise here. Yet even in your other courses, attention should be given to this aspect of the brief, because it is often impossible to know precisely what or why a court is deciding without knowing the procedural background of the case. To put it better: "Now a case never reaches a court of review until it has first been through a tribunal of trial—else there would be nothing to review. But the cases, so-called, in your case-books are almost exclusively chosen from courts of review. To understand them, therefore, you must get at least some quick picture of what has gone on before they got there." K. Llewellyn, The Bramble Bush 25–26 (1960).

(3) There is a considerable amount of learning between the lines of the sample brief's first short entry concerning "Prior Proceedings." We shall attempt to sketch it out, previewing material you will soon study and also using some information concerning the case that appears in the record but does not appear in the opinion itself.

First, Sibbach sued in a United States District Court. The ninety-one United States District Courts are the trial courts of the federal system. A district is conterminous with a state or constitutes part of a state; thus, there is a United States District Court for the District of Maine, and United States District Courts for the Southern, Northern, Western, and Eastern Districts of New York. See 28 U.S.C. § 133.[j] On the next higher

---

[j] However, the District of Hawaii includes certain Pacific islands not part of that state, and the District of Wyoming includes those portions of Yellowstone National Park situated in Montana and Idaho.

The District of Columbia is a judicial district, and the District Court for the District of Columbia is a United States District Court. Prior to 1970, it had a combined federal and local jurisdiction. It now exercises only federal jurisdiction

Sample Brief

Notes and Questions

level of the federal court system, twelve United States Courts of Appeals (formerly called Circuit Courts of Appeals) each cover a circuit comprising a number of districts. See 28 U.S.C. § 41.[k] The primary function of the courts of appeals is to hear appeals from decisions of the district courts in their respective circuits. At the summit is the Supreme Court of the United States.

Second, her suit was one of the sort that can be brought in federal court. An essential concept here is that federal courts, unlike many state courts, are courts of limited jurisdiction. This means that federal courts have the power normally to hear only those kinds of cases that are within the constitutional grant of federal judicial power (see article III, section 2 of the Constitution) and that have also been entrusted by congressional enactment to the federal courts. There are two classes of cases that produce the largest numbers of federal lawsuits. The first comprises "federal question" cases—actions arising under the Constitution, laws, or treaties of the United States. There are a good many statutes conferring jurisdiction over specific kinds of cases of this class. See, e.g., 28 U.S.C. §§ 1337(a) and 1338(a). And there is a residual statute conferring jurisdiction over this class in general terms. See 28 U.S.C. § 1331. The second class comprises "diversity" cases—actions where there is diversity of citizenship between the parties, of which the most important category is actions between citizens of different states. See 28 U.S.C. §§ 1332(a) and 1335. A requirement that the matter in controversy exceed $10,000, exclusive of interest and costs, in order that the case be cognizable in a federal district court, applies

like the other United States District Courts; local jurisdiction is vested in local courts.

The Commonwealth of Puerto Rico is also a judicial district, and the District Court for the District of Puerto Rico is a United States District Court (exercising federal jurisdiction).

The Federal Rules are made applicable by statute to the territorial district courts of the Virgin Islands, Guam, and the Northern Mariana Islands (exercising both local and federal jurisdiction).

[k] However, the United States Court of Appeals for the District of Columbia Circuit covers only a single district.

Additionally, there is a thirteenth court of appeals—the United States Court of Appeals for the Federal Circuit—which hears appeals from a number of specialized tribunals and also hears appeals from all the district courts in cases involving certain special areas such as patents or certain claims against the United States. See 28 U.S.C. § 1295.

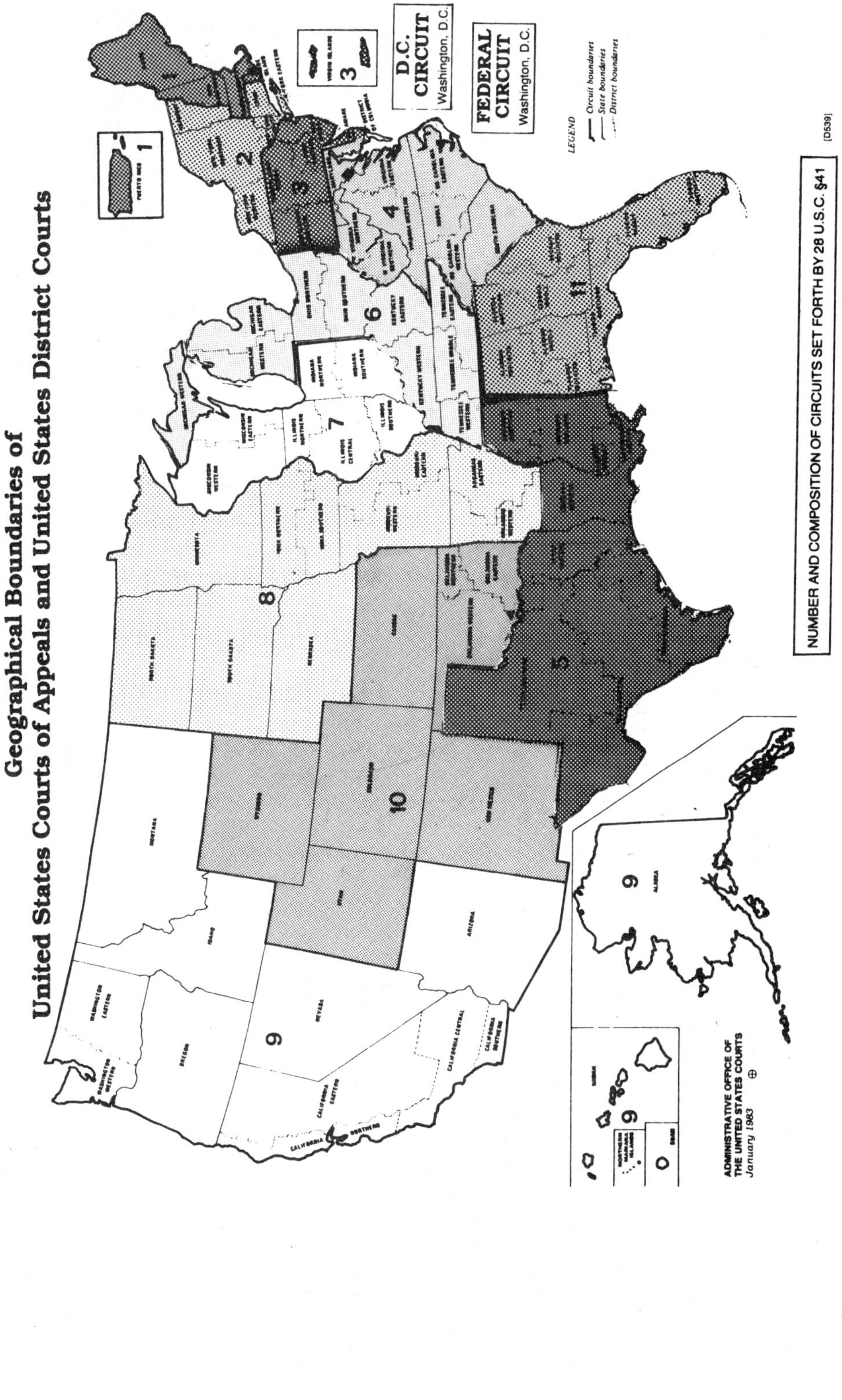

Geographical Boundaries of
United States Courts of Appeals and United States District Courts

NUMBER AND COMPOSITION OF CIRCUITS SET FORTH BY 28 U.S.C. §41

LEGEND

Circuit boundaries
State boundaries
District boundaries

D.C. CIRCUIT
Washington, D.C.

FEDERAL CIRCUIT
Washington, D.C.

ADMINISTRATIVE OFFICE OF
THE UNITED STATES COURTS
January 1983

[D539]

Sample Brief   **Notes and Questions**

to a very few actions in the first class and to most actions in the second class. To come back to the present case, Sibbach based her suit in federal district court on 28 U.S.C. § 1332(a). She could do this because there was diversity of citizenship (*D* was a Delaware corporation, making it a citizen of that state for diversity purposes; *P* was a citizen of Illinois) and her claimed damages exceeded the jurisdictional amount (she claimed $10,000 in damages, but at the time of suit the jurisdictional amount was $3000—the jurisdictional amount was raised to $10,000 in 1958).

Third, when we say that she "sued," we mean that she made her grievance and request for redress known to the court by filing a complaint with the court; this was done on November 24, 1937. See Rules 3, 10(a) and (b), 8(a) and (e)(1), and 11. Following these Rules would yield a result looking much like Form 9 (which is in the Appendix of Forms, following the Federal Rules in the Rules pamphlet), with a heading like that in Form 1, a first paragraph like that in Form 2(a), and a signature section like that in Form 3. See the introductory statement at the beginning of the Appendix of Forms. In fact, Sibbach's complaint was a bit unnecessarily flamboyant, as compared to Form 9. Her complaint alleged in part: "As a direct and proximate result of said acts of negligence of the defendant, the plaintiff Hertha J. Sibbach was greatly cut, wounded, lacerated, and contused in and about the head, body, arms, and legs, and divers bones in plaintiff's body were broken and fractured, and plaintiff became and was and has so remained from thence hitherto sick, sore, lame, diseased, and disordered, and has suffered great pain; all of which injuries are permanent and lasting."

Fourth, it is not enough to file the complaint; the defendant must be notified. This is done by serving the complaint, and a summons issued by the clerk of the court, in conformance with Rule 4. See Form 1.

D answered by denial.

(4) Again, a lot is buried here. Various responses are available to a defendant served with process. In this case, *D* filed an answer containing a denial of the allegations in the

Sample Brief   **Notes and Questions**

complaint. See Rule 8(b). Its answer looked much like the third defense in Form 20, with a suitable heading and signature.

D moved for an order requiring *P* to submit to a Rule 35 physical exam, and the court granted that motion.

(5) *D* proceeded here by motion, as is required by the express terms of Rule 35(a). What is a motion? See Rule 7(b); Form 19.

(6) An order is simply a command of the court. It may be oral or written; it may be rather formal or may be simply the words "so ordered" written at the foot of the motion; it may be accompanied by an opinion explaining the court's reasoning or, as in this case, it may not be. Selected district court opinions are printed, usually either in Federal Supplement or in Federal Rules Decisions.

P refused to comply, so *D* obtained an order to show cause why *P* should not be held in contempt under Rule 37.

(7) An order to show cause serves the same purpose as a motion, but is handled more expeditiously. It is actually an order of the court, usually drafted by the attorney for one side and submitted to the court for signature, directing the other side to appear as specified and present to the court such reasons as it has to offer that some consequence (in this case, a finding of contempt) should not ensue. An order to show cause is usually granted only on a showing of urgency or of special need (as here, where *D* was seeking to force compliance with a court order, for which *D* had already once gone through the slower motion procedure).

(8) Contempt is a willful disregard or disobedience of public authority, such as a court order. There are two types of contempt proceedings, criminal and civil, which differ in purpose and procedure; the difference, it should be noted, is not in the nature of the contemptuous act but in the proceedings consequent thereto—the same contemptuous act might give rise to either or both types of proceedings. For the time being, distinguish the two as follows. Criminal contempt proceedings are intended to serve the interests of society by punishing and deterring deliberate disrespect of public authority; accordingly, an unconditional fine or prison term is the form of sanction. Civil contempt proceedings are intended to help the party who would benefit from the contemnor's obedience; accordingly, the form of sanction is either (a) a compensatory payment to such party or (b) a conditional fine or imprisonment

Sample Brief   **Notes and Questions**

which need not be paid or further suffered by the contemnor if he obeys (thus the maxim that the contemnor "carries the keys to his prison in his own pocket"). In short, the aim of criminal contempt proceedings is to punish and deter, and that of civil contempt proceedings is to compensate or compel.

In response to the order to show cause, *P* argued that the court had no authority to order a physical exam. The court rejected *P* 's argument, found her in contempt, and ordered her imprisoned until she submitted to a physical exam.

(9) What was the court's purpose in ordering *P* imprisoned? Was this a civil or criminal contempt sanction?

P appealed to the United States Court of Appeals for the Seventh Circuit.

(10) In the federal system, the first level of appeal is a matter of right, not judicial discretion. Sibbach had the right, at some time, to appeal to the appropriate court of appeals.

As to the timing of appeal, a party can normally take one appeal at the conclusion of the case. See 28 U.S.C. § 1291. Here, however, *P* took an interlocutory appeal before the case proceeded. Possibly she was not then entitled to appeal, but the question was not raised by the parties or the courts.

There are provisions for staying a lower court's order pending appeal; so chances are that Sibbach never saw the inside of "the common jail of Cook County," to which she had been ordered committed.

The Seventh Circuit affirmed.

(11) The courts of appeals normally act by written decision and opinion, and most of these are printed. They appear in Federal Reporter. In this case, the affirmance can be found in volume 108 of Federal Reporter, Second Series, at page 415. The Seventh Circuit's affirmance was handed down on December 13, 1939. The citation is therefore 108 F.2d 415 (7th Cir.1939).

P petitioned the Supreme Court of the United States for a writ of certiorari, and the writ was granted because her case involved an unsettled, important question of federal law.

(12) There are various routes from a court of appeals to the Supreme Court. See 28 U.S.C. § 1254.

The most common route is by writ of certiorari. Review thereby is not of right, but is discretionary. The party seeking review must petition the Supreme Court for the writ, and hence that party is called the petitioner. The Supreme Court decides whether

Sample Brief	Notes and Questions

to review the case pursuant to United States Supreme Court Rule 17.1, which provides in part: "A review on writ of certiorari . . . will be granted only when there are special and important reasons therefor. The following, while neither controlling nor fully measuring the Court's discretion, indicate the character of reasons that will be considered. . . . When a federal court of appeals has rendered a decision in conflict with the decision of another federal court of appeals on the same matter . . .. When . . . a federal court of appeals has decided an important question of federal law which has not been, but should be, settled by this Court, or has decided a federal question in a way in conflict with applicable decisions of this Court."

You should ask yourself why the Supreme Court bothered to hear this case. What sense does it make to have the Supreme Court review the validity of rules it itself promulgated? Assuming that the Supreme Court would not have promulgated rules it thought invalid, how could this case present "an important question of federal law which has not been, but should be, settled by" the Supreme Court?

At any rate, on April 8, 1940, the Court did grant the writ. Actions by the Supreme Court are reported officially in United States Reports. The grant of the petition for a writ of certiorari in this case appears in volume 309 of United States Reports, at page 650. It also appears in volume 60 of the parallel, unofficial Supreme Court Reporter, at page 809. The citation is therefore 309 U.S. 650 (1940) or, more expansively, 309 U.S. 650, 60 S.Ct. 809 (1940).

Statutes and Rules Involved: Rules Enabling Act; Rules 35 and 37.

(13) This entry in your brief is intended only as a handy reference, so at a glance you can later recall what the case was about. But we shall take this opportunity to give you some historical background on the statute and Rules here involved. For greater detail, reference should be made to C. Wright, The Law of Federal Courts §§ 61–63 (4th ed. 1983).

(14) To understand the Rules Enabling Act, one must go back to the Process Act of 1789. This Act, and the subsequent Process

Notes and Questions

Acts, required the procedural practices in the federal courts to conform in each state to the practices "as are now used or allowed in the supreme courts of the same." Conformity to state procedure was based, in contemporary phraseology, on a fear of an "injurious clashing" with the procedure of the states. What was called for, however, was a *static* conformity; a federal court in, say, 1850 had to apply the state procedure of 1789. Moreover, the problem of new states was not covered; federal courts in the new states were at first free to apply any procedure they wished; later statutes forced the procedure of federal courts in those states to conform to the state procedure of 1828, 1842, or the date of admission, the choice among these base dates depending on when the state in question had been admitted. The situation was even more complicated than this description suggests, because there were exceptions, and exceptions to exceptions. However, the basic idea here is that of static conformity, and this meant that the federal courts had to ignore recent developments and reforms in state procedure and instead follow an outmoded and abandoned version of the state procedure.

This was all reworked by the Conformity Act of 1872, which instituted *dynamic* conformity. From then on, in theory, the same procedure prevailed in state and federal court, and the practitioner could switch courts without relearning his procedure. The first question one might ask is why it took Congress almost a century to make this obvious change. One reason was that it was not until the mid-nineteenth century that state procedural reform started snowballing, leaving the procedure applied in federal courts far behind. Another reason might have been that Congress feared such a change constituted an unconstitutional delegation of rulemaking power to the states, as the Supreme Court itself had suggested in Wayman v. Southard, 23 U.S. (10 Wheat.) 1 (1825); however, after the change in 1872 this question of constitutionality never came up for decision. The second question one might ask is whether dynamic conformity worked. The answer would be that the simplicity of theory was never realized in prac-

Sample Brief   **Notes and Questions**

tice. Instead, the Conformity Act became riddled with exceptions, both judge-made and statutory (note the phrasing "conform, as near as may be" in the Conformity Act itself). Federal courts in the course of a litigation used some state procedure and some home-brewed procedure to create a rampantly confusing federal practice: "To the average lawyer it is Sanskrit; to the experienced federal practitioner it is monopoly; to the author of text books on federal practice it is a golden harvest." Report of the Committee on Uniform Judicial Procedure, 46 A.B.A. Rep. 461, 466 (1921).

It is against this backdrop that the Rules Enabling Act of 1934 can best be viewed. This Act again seems the obvious answer; but it actually represented reformist agitation by the bar and bench dating back to the previous century. Finally, in 1934, reform secured the support of the national administration, and quickly the Rules Enabling Act was enacted. See generally Burbank, The Rules Enabling Act of 1934, 130 U.Pa.L.Rev. 1015 (1982).

Even after that statute passed, it took the Supreme Court a year to act on it; but when the Court eventually did act, it acted in grand style, appointing a highly distinguished Advisory Committee to assist in drafting the rules. The Advisory Committee prepared three drafts for debate and discussion in the legal community. The first draft was circulated in May 1936. The third draft was submitted in November 1937 to the Supreme Court, which promulgated it with minor changes the following month. Congress having taken no action, the Federal Rules of Civil Procedure became effective on September 16, 1938. (For the curious: although as we have seen the Sibbach complaint was filed in 1937 before the Rules were promulgated, the defendant's motion for a physical exam was filed on May 6, 1939, and was thus subject to the new Rules. See Rule 86(a).) Thus ended the long reign of the Conformity Act, which was apparently superseded in toto by the new Rules and which was in any case formally repealed in 1948.

The success of the Federal Rules has been, in Professor Wright's words, "quite phenomenal," creating "a uniform procedure that is

Sample Brief　　　　　　　　　**Notes and Questions**

flexible, simple, clear, and efficient" and that has had a tremendous impact on the development of procedure in other jurisdictions. A less restrained commentator wrote that the Rules were "one of the greatest contributions to the free and unhampered administration of law and justice ever struck off by any group of men since the dawn of civilized law." Carey, In Favor of Uniformity, 3 F.R.D. 507, 507 (1944).

Of course the Rules have not proved perfect, and so they have undergone a continuing review. The old Advisory Committee was discharged in 1956; and in 1958 the Judicial Conference (see 28 U.S.C. § 331), with its own standing committee and advisory committees, took over the advisory function with respect to the Supreme Court's rulemaking power. There were important amendments to the Rules in 1948, 1961, 1963, 1966, 1970, 1980, and 1983.

This background allows you to focus in on the Rules involved in Sibbach. Rules 35 and 37 are part of the so-called discovery Rules, which run from Rule 26 to Rule 37. The discovery Rules were heavily redone in 1970.

(15) This brings us to an important point. When reading an older case, it is important to know how any rule or statute in question read at the time of decision; you have to know this in order to know what the court is referring to and often what it is deciding. For example, the Sibbach Court refers to Rule 37(b)(2)(iv). Today there is no such numbered Rule. You will find the old version of the Rule in the Rules pamphlet.

(16) There is also the converse problem. An old case might quote an obsolete version of a statute or rule. You should look up the current version, and ask yourself how and why it has changed. For example, the Sibbach Court quotes the Rules Enabling Act. This is now 28 U.S.C. § 2072. The original statute has been changed in several important ways.

First, there are now various references in § 2072 to the courts of appeals. This extension of the Supreme Court's rulemaking power came in 1966, and the eventual result thereof was the Federal Rules of Appellate Procedure (portions of which appear in the

Sample Brief   **Notes and Questions**

Rules pamphlet). Prior to the adoption of those Appellate Rules in 1968, each court of appeals had a fairly wide power to make its own rules. (To complete the procedural rulemaking picture, note that under 28 U.S.C. § 2071 the Supreme Court can make its own rules; recall S.Ct. Rule 17.1 above. Note further that all federal courts have the power under § 2071 to promulgate interstitial rules; see Rule 83 and App. Rule 47. See also 28 U.S.C. § 2076.)

Second, there is no longer a reference in § 2072 to the courts of the District of Columbia. That authorization to the Supreme Court to make rules for the local courts of the District of Columbia was never used, although the Federal Rules apply to the District Court for the District of Columbia because it is a United States District Court. Today Congress handles directly the matter of rules for the local courts of the District of Columbia.

Third, the term "at law" is omitted from the current § 2072. This omission is profoundly significant, but to understand it you must appreciate the important distinction between law and equity, two historically distinct systems of courts, of remedies, and of procedures. Again for purposes of introduction, and at the price of over-simplification, law courts in old England typically gave relief only in the form of money damages. Equity courts, on the other hand, typically gave relief only in the form of an order commanding the defendant to do or not to do something, such as to convey land he had promised to sell ("specific performance") or to remove a dam he had wrongfully constructed ("injunction"). The procedures of the two court systems were very different, but one of the more salient differences was that law courts offered trial by jury while equity courts did not.

The equity system was transported to the infant United States. In the federal system, equity and law cases were instituted and litigated separately in different divisions, or sides, of the lower federal courts, although the same judges sat on both sides. The history of federal procedure on the equity side was quite distinct from that of the procedure used on the law side. (The history imparted

Sample Brief   **Notes and Questions**

under (14) above concerned actions at law,
not suits in equity.) Federal equity procedure was never required to conform to state
equity procedure, largely because some of
the newly independent states had not developed any such procedure. Instead, Congress
instructed the federal courts to follow generally the procedure of English equity, but
gave rulemaking power to the Supreme
Court. That power was not exercised until
1822, but from that time on the Supreme
Court promulgated various sets of equity
rules for use in the federal courts. The last
set of these was the modernizing Equity
Rules of 1912, which served as one of the
models for the Federal Rules of Civil Procedure.

As we have already noted, throughout this
long period the Supreme Court, while making rules in equity, was doing nothing with
respect to rulemaking for the separate realm
of actions at law. The Rules Enabling Act
was the legislative response. Section 1
thereof authorized the Supreme Court to do
for law as it had been doing for equity all
along, and section 2 permitted the Supreme
Court to unite the two procedures. The Supreme Court did exercise its section 2 powers; the new Federal Rules united equity
and law, this being the greatest single
achievement of the Rules. See Rule 2. In
summary, it is by reason of this union that
"at law" can now be omitted from § 2072.[l]

Fourth, a related change in § 2072 is the
omission of most of old section 2. This can
be omitted from the current statute because
the union of equity and law has been
achieved.

Fifth, § 2072 now refers to "admiralty and
maritime cases."[m] Again, this reference is
significant, but complex in meaning. We essay only the general statement, itself oversimplified, that these cases comprehend torts
occurring upon, or contracts having to do

---

[l] Yet with regard to other matters—especially the extent of the right to trial by
jury in civil actions—the equity-law distinction remains very important.

[m] The most useful text in this area explains that "the terms 'admiralty' and
'maritime law' are virtually synonymous

in this country today, though the first derives from the connection of our modern
law with the system administered in a
single English court, while the second
makes a wider and more descriptive reference." G. Gilmore & C. Black, The
Law of Admiralty 1 (2d ed. 1975).

Sample Brief	Notes and Questions

Notes and Questions

with commerce or navigation upon, the high seas or the navigable waters of the United States. The history of federal procedure in this realm is analogous to that in equity. Conformity to state practice was never required. Instead, federal courts followed English admiralty practice, with rulemaking power having been given to the Supreme Court. The Court exercised this power by promulgating various sets of admiralty rules, starting in 1844. Finally, in 1966, admiralty and maritime cases were brought within the meaning of "civil action" and within the coverage of the Federal Rules of Civil Procedure, with certain minor special treatment. See Rule 9(h) and the Supplemental Rules (which appear after the Appendix of Forms in the Rules pamphlet). In summary, then, this change in § 2072 reflects the extension of "civil action" to include the realm of admiralty and maritime jurisdiction.

This extension of the Federal Rules leads to the question of what is not covered by those Rules. Most importantly, criminal cases are not so covered. These cases were handled in the federal courts by uncodified procedure until 1946, and since then by the Federal Rules of Criminal Procedure. Several other special kinds of proceedings are not covered by the Federal Rules of Civil Procedure. See Rule 81(a).

Sixth, § 2072 has undergone changes with respect to the mechanism by which rules promulgated by the Court take effect.

Issues:

1. Is Rule 35 valid, as being within the congressional delegation to the Supreme Court expressed in the Rules Enabling Act?

(17) In this part of the brief you should list the precise questions the court is to decide. Often the issues are far from obvious, and so this entry in the brief requires digging and careful analysis on your part.

2. If so, was the sanction imposed by the district court under Rule 37 proper? (N.B.: This second issue was raised by the Supreme Court, not by *P.*)

(18) In appellate cases, the issues normally center on those lower court actions that the appealing party designates as improper in his papers on appeal, i.e., the points assigned as error. The appellate court generally does not "notice" other errors on its own, because ours is a party-propelled adversary system. It is generally for the aggrieved parties, through their lawyers, to specify those lower court actions with which

Sample Brief   **Notes and Questions**

they are dissatisfied, and thus to select the issues to be resolved by the appellate court. What are the reasons behind this policy that allows the parties to shape the issues? If such a policy is generally a good one, why did the Supreme Court by noticing the error here reach out to decide this second issue? [n] That is, why did the Supreme Court consider the propriety of the contempt finding and the commitment order if, as the Supreme Court noted, "[n]either in the Circuit Court of Appeals nor here was this action assigned as error" by Sibbach? What special circumstances were present?

Decisions:

1. Yes (5–4).

(19) Here you should give the decision on each one of the above-listed issues. Also indicate the disposition of the case.

2. No.

(20) Note that the first decision was five to four, with Justice Frankfurter writing for the minority. So this was a very close vote in a very important case, one that was to determine the vitality of the new Federal Rules.

Judgment reversed and case remanded to the district court, because an improper sanction was imposed on *P.*

(21) The case disappeared on remand, there being no further reported lower court action in the case. What do you think happened?

Reasons: Justice Roberts uses deductive reasoning to come to the conclusion that Rule 35 is valid. The major premise of his syllogism is that all rules that deal with procedure are valid, because Congress in the Rules Enabling Act delegated to the Supreme Court the power to make rules throughout the whole realm of procedure; in the Act's limitation on the Court's power, the reference to "substantive rights" is read narrowly to mean only substantive law, i.e., things other than pro-

(22) In this part of your brief you should state the gist of the court's reasoning, probably more briefly than we have. Needless to say, sometimes a great deal of work is necessary in order to perceive the court's reasoning, especially if the opinion is expressed in the form of free association; after all, Justice Roberts himself seemed unable to state his own reasoning simply (but note how Frankfurter immediately grasped, and attacked, Roberts' major premise). When you are setting down the gist of the court's reasoning, another difficult and important task is separating, as well as possible, that reasoning directly involved in and necessary to the decision ("holding") from asides unnecessary to the decision ("dicta").

Why have we not included in the sample brief Roberts' observations on the impor-

---

[n] The Supreme Court's attention was first drawn to this second issue by William D. Mitchell, who was Chairman of the Advisory Committee that had drafted the Federal Rules and who as amicus curiae filed a brief in this case when it reached the Supreme Court.

Sample Brief

cedure. His minor premise is that Rule 35 deals with procedure. So, because all procedural rules are valid, and because Rule 35 is procedural, the conclusion is that Rule 35 is valid. Q.E.D.

Derivation of Roberts' major premise is essentially a problem of divining congressional intent. Roberts offers three arguments in support of his reading of the Rules Enabling Act. First, Congress must have intended that the line demarking the Supreme Court's authority be drawn between substantive law and procedure, because any other division would "invite endless litigation and confusion worse confounded." Second, Congress intended that a comprehensive system of court rules be adopted, and therefore envisaged that "the whole field of court procedure be regulated." Third, the Federal Rules as promulgated by the Court did in fact cover the whole field of procedure, and Congress took no action to "veto their going into effect."

The primary support for Roberts' minor premise is that Sibbach admitted that Rule 35 is procedural. Other support comes from Roberts' definitions of procedure ("the judicial process for enforcing rights

Notes and Questions

tance of the particular right here involved?

Of course, this sample brief is not intended to be definitive. The entry here represents only one way of distilling and analyzing the supposed holding. Do you see other ways?

Sometimes, in uncovering the issues and the court's essential reasoning, it is helpful to reconstruct what the parties were arguing. What precisely was Mrs. Sibbach's dilemma, as stated by the Court? What did she argue in order to avoid the horns of that dilemma? What did the defendant argue in response?

(23) Under Roberts' reading of the Rules Enabling Act, exactly what does the second sentence of section 1 thereof add to the meaning of the Act? What of the canon of statutory construction that "every word and clause must be given effect"?

(24) Do you find Roberts' definitions useful or satisfying?

Sample Brief

and duties recognized by substantive law and for justly administering remedy and redress for disregard or infraction of them") and substantive law ("rights conferred by law to be protected and enforced in accordance with the adjective law of judicial procedure").

As to the second decision, Roberts holds the sanction improper as being simply contrary to the express provisions of the former version of Rule 37(b)(2)(D).

Separate Opinions: Justice Frankfurter likewise argues deductively. His major premise is that only rules affecting unimportant rights are valid, because in his view Congress in the Rules Enabling Act did not intend to empower the Supreme Court to make rules in derogation of important rights. His minor premise is that Rule 35 affects an important right, the inviolability of person. Because all rules affecting important rights are invalid, and because Rule 35 affects an important right, Rule 35 is invalid.

Remarks:

Notes and Questions

(25) Is it really so clear under old Rule 37(b)(2)(iv) that the sanction imposed was improper? Assuming contempt and commitment were not permissible, what kind of order might the district court have properly made in this case?

(26) Here you should sketch out in briefest form the reasoning of the minority. Supporting arguments may be omitted. But think about those arguments. How did Frankfurter support his major premise? his minor premise? Do you agree? Do you see that Frankfurter may very well have been right as to his minor premise, but that the correctness of his minor premise is rendered irrelevant if Roberts' major premise is accepted? Do you also see that Frankfurter's major premise may very well have been closer to congressional intent, but that Roberts' major premise may have been superior from a policy viewpoint? Should such policy notions play a role in a court's decision?

(27) Here you should jot down your comments on and criticisms of the case. You might make a preliminary attempt before class, but this should certainly be supplemented during and after class. There should be special emphasis on the significance of the decision and the validity of the reasoning. For example, what is the significance of Sibbach v. Wilson & Co.? Surely it represents more than a mere "Rule 35 case." What kind of job do you think Justice Roberts did?

What kind of job did Sibbach's lawyer do? Why did he not assign as error the improper

Sample Brief　　　　**Notes and Questions**

sanction? Why, in the first place, did he not sue in Illinois state court, instead of federal court, and thus avoid the whole problem of a physical exam? Possible explanations include mistake, or perhaps this was a test case. Do you see any more subtle explanations?

Does it affect your theorizing to know that, prior to Rule 35, the federal courts had shown hostility to the idea of physical examinations? See, e.g., Union Pac. Ry. v. Botsford, 141 U.S. 250, 11 S.Ct. 1000 (1891). That case was one for negligence, brought by Clara Botsford against a railroad. She complained of head injuries, caused when an upper berth in a sleeping car fell and hit her in the head. Although there were only head injuries, and although the defendant proposed that the physical examination "should be made in manner not to expose the person of the plaintiff in any indelicate manner," the Court denied the defendant's request for a physical examination, observing: "The inviolability of the person is as much invaded by a compulsory stripping and exposure as by a blow. To compel any one, and especially a woman, to lay bare the body, or to submit it to the touch of a stranger, without lawful authority, is an indignity, an assault and a trespass; and no order or process, commanding such an exposure or submission, was ever known to the common law in the administration of justice between individuals, except in a very small number of cases, based upon special reasons, and upon ancient practice, coming down from ruder ages, now mostly obsolete in England, and never, so far as we are aware, introduced into this country." Botsford ended up with $10,000 for her troubles.

Times do change. Currently, among the states, only Mississippi and South Carolina do not provide for physical and mental examinations.

―――――――

We shall have many more occasions to observe how legislatures and courts go about the business of classification, with which the Sibbach case was concerned—and to observe whether a rule is uniformly assigned to the same category, such as substance or procedure, or whether it may be assigned to one category where the consequences

are such-and-such and to another category where the consequences
are thus-and-so.

On attitudes toward the subject and the course.—We shall confine our consideration mainly to procedure in civil cases in *courts*, but
we should observe at the outset that there is a great volume of controversies adjudicated outside the courts. The modes of operation of
tribunals like workers' compensation boards, the National Labor Relations Board, and the Interstate Commerce Commission, to name but
a few of them, will be beyond our scope, except that we shall note
some interrelations between courts and administrative agencies. Nor
shall we do more than touch upon adjudicative procedures within private or public corporations, labor unions, clubs, associations, or
churches, or do much more than describe procedures for arbitration,
mediation, and other alternative dispute-resolution mechanisms.

This notice of exclusion leads to a caveat. The stress laid on court
procedure in the first year of law school sometimes leads to an unhappy insularity or provincialism among some students. They get
the notion that the general style of procedure used in the courts is
the only really viable one for the resolution of controversies and that
other styles, being different and being studied later, are necessarily
inferior. Students are advised to suspend judgment on this matter
until they have examined the other procedures. They may find that
procedure is related to structure, function, and purpose. Although it
is likely that certain fundamentals must be observed in handling any
civil controversy if the handling is to be accurate and fair and efficient, it is also likely that various rules of procedure appropriate to
the regular grist of court business would be quite unsuitable for
resolving a controversy over collective bargaining before the NLRB
or a question of rates before the ICC. It may even be that the courts
have something to learn in the way of procedural finesse from administrative agencies and other bodies that deal with civil controversies.

Another common superstition is that the particular rules making
up the court procedure of one's own time and place are the only ones
that would really work in those courts. A possible corrective for this
kind of intransigence lies in the realization that court procedures
have undergone drastic changes in this country without cataclysm.
Today, significant differences exist among federal and various states'
procedures; other countries, moreover, have procedures very different from our own, and some of them, at least, appear to work well.
A proposal for change certainly deserves consideration on the merits
without any arbitrary assumption that it will be attended by sudden
doom. It is, indeed, part of the purpose of this course to evolve meritorious proposals for change, some of which we shall suggest by
means that include looking at other times and places.

We have talked of "court procedure." Do not let this mode of
expression seduce you into error. One kind of error is to think of
"court" entirely in the abstract as the equivalent of a disembodied

"law" and to assume that procedural steps somehow are taken without any human actors at all. A more common kind of error is to think that it is the court (that is, the judge or his clerks) that alone initiates the procedural steps. The fact is that under the current system, as under the traditional Anglo-American scheme, it is the contending parties through their lawyers who take substantially all the initiative in the court process. The judge's role is predominantly that of deciding what is presented to him by the lawyers by means of their procedural thrusts and parries. All this has lent to the entire court process an air of battle or strife in which the lawyers play the part of combatants and the judge (and jury) the part of umpire. However, modern complex lawsuits, often of considerable social significance, seem destined to demand increased judicial initiative and control. The extent to which the judge currently plays a more active role varies from jurisdiction to jurisdiction and from judge to judge and especially from case to case. We shall consider what his role ought to be.

Just as it is true that court procedure is not self-propelled but is for the most part propelled on the initiative of the lawyers, so it is true that the lawyers may exercise this initiative in a variety of ways. The lawyer at various stages of a lawsuit may have a choice whether to make one or another move. Now we must add the notable fact that success or failure in the lawsuit may well turn on the wisdom, ingenuity, and skill with which the lawyer makes his moves. It is indeed the object of rules of procedure to facilitate the just resolution of controversies; but there is no avoiding the fact that good claims are sometimes lost, and bad claims sometimes won, because of the quality of counsel's use of procedural rules; and it is unlikely that any now foreseeable improvement in the rules themselves could altogether eliminate these miscarriages. It is part of the task of a course in procedure to give you training in the strategy and tactics of controversy so that missteps by you will not contribute to such miscarriages. It will help if you constantly ask as you read the materials: why did the lawyer make this particular move rather than another that was open to him?

TOPIC B.   PHASES OF A LAWSUIT

Our purpose in this Topic is to describe the major phases in the institution and conduct of a lawsuit.   Procedure too often appears to the student to be a maze of unrelated rules to be painfully mastered. We hope in the sketch that follows to give a sense of the subject as a whole and to point out some fundamental problems.   In taking a look at the entire organism before examining the separate parts, we have not been deterred by the knowledge that later amplification will throw a different light on many of the matters here discussed, nor have we always interrupted the narrative with all the qualifications necessary for complete accuracy of statement.

The focus: procedure in the United States District Courts.—Our sketch is focused on the current procedures in civil actions in the United States District Courts, which are regulated to a large extent by the Federal Rules.   See Rules 1 and 81.

Our reasons for selecting these procedures as the basis not only for the sketch but for much of the course will appear more plainly as the course develops.   Some of them may, however, be noted here.   (1) The Federal Rules are a concise corpus, from the study of which the student can see rather quickly in a general way how a going system of procedure functions.   (2) Although the procedural system created by the Rules differs in various respects from the systems of procedure prevailing in the various states, which differ among themselves, it provides a model by reference to which the state systems can later be studied and evaluated.   (3) The Federal Rules' system is generally considered to be a fairly successful representative of modern procedure.   (4) A majority of the state systems are now based in whole or in substantial part on the Federal Rules, and still others adopt particular features of the Rules.[a]   (5) Although the vastly greater percentage of all civil cases in this country are commenced in state courts, the United States District Courts are important courts that handle a large volume of cases, many of which are of major significance.

Selecting a proper court.—The first step in the institution of a lawsuit is to select a proper court to hear the case.   Each state has its own set of courts exerting the judicial power of the state, and there is an overlay of United States courts exerting the judicial power of the nation.   Sometimes there is only one proper court for a particular controversy, but often two or more are available.   Then a choice must be made, and that initially is the plaintiff's.   There are, howev-

[a] It would be useful for the student to examine the procedural statutes and rules of his or her home state, or the state where he or she expects to practice, to see the extent to which they are comparable to the Federal Rules.   There is no state that is wholly unaffected by the federal reform.

er, situations where a suit properly lodged by the plaintiff in one court may be moved to a different one by the defendant at his option.

We shall not now undertake the survey of the judicial systems of the states and the United States that would be necessary in order to determine which court or courts may properly be selected to hear a given case. (Such a survey is deferred to Sections 6 and 7 of this Topic.) Rather we shall assume during the following discussion, except when a question is specially raised, that the case has been properly instituted in a United States District Court—that the case is of a type that such a court is empowered to adjudicate, and that the particular district court has power over the particular case through the filing of a complaint with it (see Rule 3) and the proper service of papers upon the defendant (see Rule 4).

SECTION 1.   DISCLOSING THE MATTERS IN DISPUTE [b]

(a) Stating the Claim [c]

[Rules 8(a), (c), (e), and (f), 9(b), 11; Form 9]

An action is commenced by filing a complaint with the court. Rule 3. What is a complaint, how is it to be written, and what are its purposes?

Rule 8(a) indicates that a complaint shall contain "a short and plain statement of the claim showing that the pleader is entitled to relief." (as well as a statement of the grounds on which the court's jurisdiction depends, and a demand for judgment for the relief to which the pleader deems himself entitled). Here, then, is the first step in laying bare what the controversy is about. By his complaint the plaintiff is to inform his adversary and the court of the basis of his contention that he is entitled to invoke the court's aid in redressing a grievance.

Rule 8(a) by itself, however, does not go far in describing what the form of the complaint should be or just what the complaint should set forth. Other Rules are helpful on these matters; but perhaps the way to begin is to look at Forms 3 to 18, inclusive, which are illustrations of proper complaints in various kinds of lawsuits.

[b] We shall not often interrupt this presentation by contrasting the terminology and provisions of the Federal Rules with those of the common-law practice or state codes of procedure.

However, it may be helpful to the student, who in his or her substantive law courses will encounter cases involving common-law pleading, to read the brief discussion of that subject beginning infra p. 346. And, of course, some provisions of the Federal Rules will become more meaningful when considered in the light of what they superseded.

[c] Immediately under this and later captions we have given references to the most important relevant Federal Rules and Forms. Students are advised to read these Rules and Forms with particular care. Other Rule and Form references in text and questions are less important, but should be examined.

Dividing the burden of allegation.—Examine with special care
Form 9, a "Complaint for Negligence." You will observe that the
plaintiff has here given a somewhat particularized statement within
the compass of a rule of substantive law regarding liability for negligence—a proposition of the type shown schematically in the earlier
example of battery:

If *B* knowingly strikes *A*, and . . ., then, unless *A* consented, or . . ., *A* is entitled to a judgment . . ..

The complaint for negligence does not explicitly state the comparable
substantive rule, but it implicitly invokes it.

Question: (1) Can you phrase schematically the rule of substantive law
that the plaintiff is probably seeking to invoke in the Form 9 complaint?

After putting into words the rule of law that the plaintiff is probably seeking to invoke in the Form 9 complaint, you will notice that he
appears to have limited himself in the complaint to a somewhat particularized statement of the "if" part of the rule; he has not concerned himself with negating the "unless" part. To put the matter
more concretely: assuming that defendant was negligent as alleged,
plaintiff may also have been negligent at the time, which would normally bar his recovery at least in part; yet plaintiff does not in his
complaint assert that he was himself free of negligence, that he was
exercising due care. It thus appears that a plaintiff need not allege
in his complaint all the conditions of defendant's liability. He may
confine himself to the "ifs" and omit any reference to the "unlesses."

But the "if, unless" form of statement is not the only meaningful
one that could be employed. A substantive rule—the conditions under which a court will grant a remedy—can be stated altogether in
"if" fashion, without any "unless" clauses, simply by altering the
form of the statement thus:

If *B* knowingly strikes *A*, and if *A* has not consented, and
 . . ., then *A* is entitled to a judgment . . ..

Why, then, do we use the "if, unless" form? It is a convenient
way to make the point that the burden of allegation is indeed divided
between the parties. The plaintiff is required to assert the matters in
the "if" clauses, and the defendant is required to assert such of the
matters in the "unless" clauses as he proposes to raise. As we shall
see later, a matter that the plaintiff is not required to assert and that
the defendant chooses not to assert is ordinarily not in issue in the
case.

But which matters belong on the "if" side and which on the "unless"? The placing of the dividing line, and the corresponding assignment of the respective burdens of allegation to the parties, cannot be
determined by an exercise of pure logic.[d] Reconsider Form 9. The

---

[d] For the logical involvements of the
scheme here presented, see H.L.A. Hart,
"The Ascription of Responsibilities and
Rights," in Essays on Logic and Language 145 (A. Flew ed. 1951). But see
H.L.A. Hart, Punishment and Responsibility at v & n.1 (1968).

plaintiff might well be required to assert that he was using due care for his own safety when the defendant drove a motor vehicle against him. Indeed, as we shall see, in some state judicial systems the burden is cast on the plaintiff to assert his due care rather than on the defendant to assert the contrary.

Question: (2) What are the considerations that ought to govern the allocation between the parties of the burdens of allegation?

The Federal Rules provide a guide, although not a complete one, to the way in which these burdens are in fact allocated in the United States District Courts. Rule 8(c), entitled "Affirmative Defenses," is a catalogue of certain matters that must be asserted by the defendant in his answer, if he chooses to put them in issue, and need not be asserted by the plaintiff in his complaint. Note that "contributory negligence" of the plaintiff is such an affirmative defense. Beyond Rule 8(c), precedent and form books provide further guidance to the pleader.

All this suggests an idea of what elements the parties are respectively required to plead. Generally, a pleader is well-advised to avoid saying much more than he is required to plead. We shall see later that any excess does risk causing eventual problems—such as putting into issue in the case matters that otherwise would not be or boxing the pleader in—even though the Federal Rules try to minimize most of such risks.

How particularized must allegations be?—We have said that the plaintiff's statement of claim appears to be a somewhat particularized rendering of the "if" part of a rule of law. This leaves at large, however, the question of the degree to which the particularization must be carried. There is no easy or simple answer to this question, but the Rules and Forms throw some light upon it. The statement of the claim is, according to Rule 8(a), to be "short" as well as "plain." And Rule 8(e)(1), applicable to all pleadings, prescribes that each averment of a pleading shall be "simple, concise, and direct." Rule 9, "Pleading Special Matters," gives a number of further directions.

Consider now Rule 9(b), which tells us that in all averments of "fraud or mistake" the circumstances constituting fraud or mistake shall be stated with particularity, but on the other hand "[m]alice, intent, knowledge, and other condition of mind of a person may be averred generally."

Question: (3) What is the reason for the distinction made in Rule 9(b)? Is it not becoming plain that to answer such a question you must first decide what is intended to be accomplished by the pleadings? For example, are the pleadings intended to serve any purpose during the course of the trial?

If you were now asked to draft a complaint in a battery case, would these Rules and illustrative Forms provide enough light to go by? Your client has given you, probably very volubly, a detailed account of what happened. It is your task to cull from this account a properly particularized statement of claim invoking the pertinent rule of substantive law. Should you state in your complaint when and where the attack took place? how your client happened to be there at the time? who witnessed the incident? what were the dimensions of the stick with which the defendant beat your client? the nature and extent of your client's injuries? the conversation between the parties before the attack was made? what the policeman who arrived on the scene said and did?

Question: (4) Does the plaintiff in Form 9 need to plead the amount of his medical expenses?

Surely the plaintiff should be required to assert only relevant matters, but by reference to what is relevancy determined? Doubtless the rule of law sought to be invoked establishes the contours of relevancy, but within those limits how much detail is appropriate? Again we are back to the question of the purposes of the complaint and other pleadings.

SIEROCINSKI v. E.I. DU PONT DE NEMOURS & CO.

United States Circuit Court of Appeals, Third Circuit, 1939.
103 F.2d 843.

Before MARIS, BIDDLE, and BUFFINGTON, CIRCUIT JUDGES.

BIDDLE, CIRCUIT JUDGE. The plaintiff's "statement of claim" (complaint), amended under an order of court granting defendant's motion for a more definite statement under Rule 12(e), Rules of Civil Procedure for District Courts, 28 U.S.C.A. following section 723c, alleged that he was injured by the premature explosion of a dynamite cap. Specifically the plaintiff claimed as negligent acts the manufacturing and distributing of the cap "in such a fashion that it was unable to withstand the crimping which defendant knew it would be subjected to"; and distributing a cap so constructed that it would explode upon being crimped, without warning, the defendant knowing it would be crimped. Judge Kalodner granted the defendant's motion to strike this amended statement, as failing to set forth any specific act of negligence, and dismissed the action. From his order the plaintiff appealed to this court.

The plaintiff, as alleged, was injured while "crimping" a dynamite cap manufactured by the defendant and supplied to him by his employer. "Crimping" is a necessary and anticipated process in using the cap.

Appellée, admitting that a manufacturer is liable for injuries to a person from the use of a defectively manufactured article, argues that it is not put on notice by the complaint as to whether it must meet a claim of warranty, of misrepresentation, of the use of improper ingredients, or of faulty inspection.

But there is a specific averment of negligent manufacture and distribution of the cap in such a fashion as to make it explode when crimped. A plaintiff need not plead evidence. He "sets forth a claim for relief" when he makes "a short and plain statement of the claim showing that the pleader is entitled to relief (Rule 8(a)(2)." The same rule (e)(1), requires that "each averment of a pleading shall be simple, concise, and direct. No technical forms of pleading or motions are required"; and (f) "all pleadings shall be so construed as to do substantial justice". Form 9 in the Appendix of Forms attached to the Rules, "intended to indicate . . . the simplicity and brevity of statement which the rules contemplate [Rule 84]",[e] contains this concise allegation of negligence: "defendant negligently drove a motor vehicle against plaintiff who was then crossing said highway". If defendant needs further information to prepare its defense, it can obtain it by interrogatories (Rule 33).

The judgment is reversed, and the cause remanded for further proceedings.

Question: (5) How convincing are Judge Biddle's arguments drawn from (a) the proposition that the plaintiff need not plead evidence, (b) the style of the Form 9 complaint, and (c) the fact that the defendant might resort to Rule 33?

Upon remand, the Sierocinski case was tried before a judge and jury. The jury brought in a verdict for the plaintiff, the judge denying the defendant's motions for a directed verdict and for judgment notwithstanding the verdict. Judgment was entered for the plaintiff. From this judgment the defendant took an appeal to the circuit court of appeals, which reversed the judgment, 118 F.2d 531 (3d Cir.1941), apparently on the ground that the defendant's motion for a directed verdict should have been granted. The appellate court said: "No proof, . . . either direct or circumstantial, was adduced to support a finding of any of the specific acts of negligence alleged."

Questions: (6) Does this subsequent history demonstrate that the decision on the first appeal was wrong?

(7) After decision on the second appeal, should it be open to the plaintiff to commence a new action, basing his claim on a legal theory not exploited before, for example, on a theory of breach of warranty?

CONLEY v. GIBSON, 355 U.S. 41, 78 S.Ct. 99 (1957). Black members of the Brotherhood of Railway and Steamship Clerks brought suit under the Railway Labor Act to compel the union to represent them in collective bargaining without discrimination because of race.

[e] At the date of this decision, Rule 84 read: "The forms contained in the Appendix of Forms are intended to indicate, subject to the provisions of these rules, the simplicity and brevity of statement which the rules contemplate." Compare the present text of Rule 84, adopted in 1948.

There were in the complaint general allegations that the union had not done so. On motion to dismiss, defendants' main contention was that the National Railroad Adjustment Board had exclusive jurisdiction of the dispute, but defendants also argued that the complaint was defective for failure to state a claim upon which relief could be granted. R12(b)

Ultimately the Supreme Court upheld the jurisdiction of the district court. On the pleading point, the Court said at the outset:

"In appraising the sufficiency of the complaint we follow, of course, the accepted rule that a complaint should not be dismissed for failure to state a claim unless it appears beyond doubt that the plaintiff can prove no set of facts in support of his claim which would entitle him to relief." R12(b)

The Court held that an actionable wrong could conceivably be proven within the scope of the complaint's allegations of discrimination. The Court then dealt with the defendants' contention that dismissal was proper for failure to set forth specific facts to support the general allegations of discrimination, saying:

"The decisive answer to this is that the Federal Rules of Civil Procedure do not require a claimant to set out in detail the facts upon which he bases his claim. To the contrary, all the Rules require is 'a short and plain statement of the claim' that will give the defendant fair notice of what the plaintiff's claim is and the grounds upon which it rests. The illustrative forms appended to the Rules plainly demonstrate this. Such simplified 'notice pleading' is made possible by the liberal opportunity for discovery and the other pretrial procedures established by the Rules to disclose more precisely the basis of both claim and defense and to define more narrowly the disputed facts and issues. Following the simple guide of Rule 8(f) that 'all pleadings shall be so construed as to do substantial justice,' we have no doubt that petitioners' complaint adequately set forth a claim and gave the respondents fair notice of its basis. The Federal Rules reject the approach that pleading is a game of skill in which one misstep by counsel may be decisive to the outcome and accept the principle that the purpose of pleading is to facilitate a proper decision on the merits."

———

Question: (8) What do you think of Professor James's observation that if the test of the first-quoted excerpt from the Conley case is to be applied literally, it would be enough for the plaintiff to recite in his complaint that the defendant had wronged him? See F. James, Civil Procedure 86–87 (1965).

Statements of claim in the alternative.—Rule 8(e)(2) says: "A party may set forth two or more statements of a claim or defense alternately or hypothetically, either in one count or defense or in separate counts or defenses."

As applied to the complaint, the main function of this provision
appears to be to assist a plaintiff who may be genuinely uncertain
about the facts he will be able to prove. The Rule permits the plaintiff to take advantage of whatever pleaded version of the claim he
may eventually establish to the satisfaction of the fact-finder. It
may seem obvious to you that statements of claim in the alternative
should be allowed, but it is worth pointing out that the Rule represents a departure from the practice permitted at common law. Does
this not tell us more about the purposes of federal pleading?

What is a "claim"?—In Rule 8(e)(2), in Rule 8(a), and elsewhere
the word "claim" appears. This word is analogous to the phrase
"cause of action" as it appears in various state codes of procedure,
but it is not to be assumed that "claim" and "cause of action" necessarily mean the same thing. Nor is it to be assumed that either
"claim" or "cause of action" necessarily means the same thing whenever and wherever it is used.

In all events, what does "claim" mean as it appears in Rule
8(e)(2)? We can say at least that the draftsmen of the Rule thought
that a *single claim* may in some cases be stated in different ways.
How far can the statements be varied before they produce not alternative statements of a single claim, but a *number of claims*?

Consider here that the differing statements may all invoke the
same rule of substantive law or may each invoke a distinct rule of
substantive law. Does this have a bearing on whether the statements are alternative statements of a single claim or constitute a
number of distinct claims? Shall we say that a "legal theory" is the
measure of what is a claim?

Moreover, a single, straightforward statement of a transaction or
event may invoke a number of rules of substantive law, each casting
liability on the defendant. Thus, if *B* sells to *A* a machine negligently
constructed, and *A* is injured in the course of operating it by reason
of the defect, *B* may be rendered liable by reference to a rule of tort
law ("negligence") or by reference to a rule of contract law ("warranty"). When *A* sets forth an account of the accident in his complaint,
is he alleging one claim or two? Shall we say broadly that an "episode" or "natural grouping or congeries of events" is the measure of
what is a claim?

The importance of this question—what is the distinction between
alternative statements of a single claim, on the one hand, and multiple claims, on the other hand—is minimized in the present context,
because Rule 18(a) complements Rule 8(e)(2) by permitting a plaintiff
in his complaint to "join, either as independent or as alternate claims,
as many claims . . . as he has against an opposing party."

Nevertheless, here the question is put to call attention to a significant problem that later appears in various guises in other contexts:
what is the meaning of "claim"? of "cause of action"? Again, the

student is warned not to assume from the form of this question that the meaning of these terms is constant irrespective of context.

Consistency and truth in pleading.—Rule 8(e)(2) goes on to say: "A party may also state as many separate claims or defenses as he has regardless of consistency . . . .. All statements shall be made subject to the obligations set forth in Rule 11."

There is in the folklore of the common law the famous Case of the Kettle. The plaintiff claimed damages for a kettle that assertedly the defendant had borrowed and had allowed to become cracked while in his possession. The defendant is supposed to have pleaded (1) that he did not borrow the kettle, (2) that it was never cracked, and (3) that it was cracked when he borrowed it. Would this pleading be permissible today under the Federal Rules?

Note that under Rule 11 pleadings ordinarily need not be verified, that is, they need not be sworn to; but the required signature to a pleading constitutes a certification that there is good ground to support it and that it is not interposed for improper purpose. There are sanctions set forth for violations of the obligations of the Rule.

Questions: (9) Considering the state of knowledge, information, and belief of Sierocinski's lawyer as to the cause of the accident, did he violate his duty under Rule 11 when he instituted that action?

(10) What obligation does Rule 11 impose on an attorney to investigate, before signing the complaint, the motivation and the legal and factual bases for his client's claim? See the section of the Rules pamphlet containing the 1983 amendments and the Advisory Committee's notes thereon.

(11) Would you expect Rule 11 to be effective in regulating professional ethics?

(b) Defenses and Objections

[Rules 8(b), 12; Forms 19, 20]

A defendant who has been served with a summons and complaint pursuant to Rule 4 is allowed within certain time limits [f] to make known his defenses—the grounds upon which he resists the relief demanded against him in the complaint. So also he has opportunity to object to the complaint for vices such as undue vagueness.

Questions: (12) Suppose the defendant does nothing during the prescribed time period. What should the plaintiff do to take advantage of the default? See Rule 55(a) and (b).

(13) What steps may the defendant take to cure such a default? See Rule 55(c). What sort of showing should he be required to make?

Types of defenses and objections.—Let us consider the kinds of defenses and objections that may be available to a defendant. Imag-

---

[f] Ordinarily the time limit is twenty days after service of the summons and complaint. See Rules 12(a) and 6(a). May the parties stipulate, i.e., agree, to enlarge this time? See Rule 6(b).

ine that the defendant faces the complaint of a single plaintiff attempting to state a single claim.

1. In the first place, there may be reasons why the court should not proceed with the case that have no bearing on the intrinsic merits of the plaintiff's claim. The defendant may wish to contend that the case is of a type that cannot be maintained in any federal district court (see Rule 12(b)(1)), that the particular district court selected by the plaintiff as the place of trial—the venue—is wrong (see Rule 12(b)(3)), or that there is another party who ought to be joined before the action goes forward (see Rule 12(b)(7)). The possible bases for such defenses will be considered later (as will the defenses referred to in Rule 12(b)(2), (4), and (5)). *— p. 37*

2. The defendant may take the position that, assuming for the sake of argument the truth of the basic allegations in the complaint, they do not invoke any rule of substantive law that casts liability on the defendant. For example, plaintiff alleges merely that defendant gave him a dirty look, or he follows Form 9 but omits any charge of negligence. Here, in the language of the common-law pleader, is ground for "demurrer" or, in the words of Rule 12(b)(6), a defense of "failure to state a claim upon which relief can be granted." It is plainly desirable that there should be some procedural device for exposing the futility of the plaintiff's claim without further inquiry as to whether his allegations are true. *Not violation of law*

3. Assuming for the sake of argument that the plaintiff's statement of claim does invoke a rule of substantive law casting liability on the defendant, the defendant may wish to challenge the truth of one or more of the allegations corresponding to the "if" clauses in the rule. See Rule 8(b), regarding defense by way of denial. *— p. 33*

4. A further possibility is that, assuming without granting that all of plaintiff's basic allegations are true and do invoke a rule of substantive law casting liability on defendant, there are additional matters that will avoid that liability. In other words, the defendant may wish to activate one or more of the "unless" clauses in the relevant rule of law, such as the plaintiff's contributory negligence, the running of the period of limitations before the commencement of suit, or some other affirmative defense referred to in Rule 8(c).

5. A complaint may be so vague or ambiguous that the defendant "cannot reasonably be required to frame a responsive pleading." In that case it is open to the defendant to object and require the plaintiff to give "a more definite statement." See Rule 12(e) and the Sierocinski case. Or the complaint may be objectionable because it contains "redundant, immaterial, impertinent, or scandalous matter" that causes prejudice to the defendant. In that case Rule 12(f) permits the defendant to have the court strike that matter out.

Question: (14) Is there any other position that a defendant might conceivably want to take?

The defendant may wish to take two or more of the positions outlined above. For example, suppose the plaintiff claims damages for mental anguish suffered by him by reason of the defendant's negligence. Defendant's counsel knows that according to the law of some states there exists a right of action for mental anguish inflicted in the alleged circumstances; that in other states no such right is recognized; and that the courts of the state in which the event occurred have not yet spoken on the question. Further, his investigation of the facts indicates considerable likelihood that the plaintiff cannot prove negligence. Further still, he wishes to challenge the venue, and also to argue that the plaintiff was contributorily negligent. In what manner are these defenses to be presented to the court? Are multiple defenses to be set up successively or simultaneously—and, indeed, may defendant's counsel set up all these defenses or is he limited to some lesser number?

Manner of presenting defenses and objections.—The pattern starts with Rule 12(b). (It is, incidentally, very much at odds with the practice at common law.)

1. It is clear from Rule 12(b) that all defenses to a claim may be raised in the defendant's answer.

Form 20 is an example of an answer. The first defense is that the complaint fails to state a claim. The second is that plaintiff has failed to join a party under Rule 19. The third denies certain allegations of the complaint. The fourth asserts additional matter, namely, the affirmative defense that the applicable period of limitations had expired. Note that defenses, like claims, are stated "in short and plain terms." See Rule 8(b) and (e).

Defendant serves the answer by delivering or mailing a copy to plaintiff's attorney. He also files the answer in court either before or within a reasonable time after service on plaintiff's attorney. See Rules 5 and 6(e). A similar pattern of service and filing normally applies to other papers subsequent to the complaint.

2. Rule 12(b) states that seven enumerated defenses "may at the option of the pleader be made by motion" before answer.[g] Most of these go to matters not affecting the merits of the claim, the exception being Rule 12(b)(6), which treats "failure to state a claim upon which relief can be granted."

"Motion" is not formally defined in the Rules, but Rule 7(b)(1) suggests that it is "[a]n application to the court for an order." (What order does the defendant seek when he presents each of the seven enumerated defenses by motion?) Unless made during a hearing or a trial, which is not the present case, a motion "shall be made in writing, shall state with particularity the grounds therefor, and shall set forth the relief or order sought." Read Form 19, a form of motion,

---

[g] See Rule 12(a)(1), which prescribes when the answer is to be served if such a motion is made by the defendant and later denied by the court.

and see whether you can match the defenses presented in this Form with the terms of Rule 12(b).

Where a moving party wishes to bring up matters of fact in support of his motion, he may do so by affidavits. The opposing party then has an opportunity to file counter-affidavits. The court may either hear and decide the motion on the affidavits or proceed to take oral testimony. See Rules 6(d) and 43(e).

Rule 12(d) provides with respect to the seven enumerated defenses that, whether made in the answer or by motion, they "shall be heard and determined before trial on application of any party, unless the court orders that the hearing and determination thereof be deferred until the trial." Why are these enumerated defenses singled out for preliminary hearing? Consider with respect to each of the enumerated defenses whether it is likely to involve only a question of law to be resolved on briefs and arguments of counsel, or whether it is likely to involve disputed issues of fact. Is the circumstance that a defense will involve only a question of law a sufficient reason for seeking to dispose of it at an early stage before trial? Consider with respect to each of the enumerated defenses whether it is likely to spell the end of the lawsuit.

3. We can deal summarily with the objections under Rule 12(e) and (f) of vagueness or ambiguity or redundancy or the like. These objections are not frequently made, and they should rarely succeed. In the nature of things, they are made by motion before answer.

Consolidation and waiver of defenses and objections.—We shall mention some consequences that attach to the defendant's actions and failures to act at the answer-or-move stage.

---

1. Consider the seven defenses listed in Rule 12(b). The effects of Rule 12(g) and (h) are as follows:

First. If the defendant makes a pre-answer motion based on any of the seven defenses but omits another of those defenses then available to him, he may not make a further pre-answer motion based on the defense omitted. In other words, Rule 12(g) contemplates that the defendant will consolidate defenses in his initial motion if he chooses to make a motion. There is one exception to the consolidation requirement: the defense of lack of subject-matter jurisdiction (Rule 12(b)(1)) may be raised by a second motion—indeed, Rule 12(h)(3) indicates that this defense may be "suggested" at any time and that the court ought to raise it even if the defendant does not.

Example: Defendant moves before answer on the ground of improper venue. The motion is denied. He may not move again before answer to assert the defense of failure of the complaint to state a claim (assuming that was available to him when he first moved).

Second. If the available defense omitted from the pre-answer motion is lack of jurisdiction over the person, improper venue, insufficiency of process, or insufficiency of service of process (Rule 12(b)(2)–(5)), not only may the defense not be made the subject of a second pre-answer motion, but also it is waived, i.e., lost altogether. See Rule 12(h)(1)(A).

Example: Defendant moves before answer on the ground of failure to state a claim. Motion denied. Defendant loses any defense of improper venue (assuming that was available to him when he made his motion).

Third. Defenses under Rule 12(b)(2)–(5), if not waived as just indicated, are nevertheless waived if defendant does not make them by pre-answer motion or include them in his answer or in an amendment thereof permitted to be made under Rule 15(a) as a matter of course, i.e., without applying to the court for permission. See Rule 12(h)(1)(B).

Example: Defendant makes no motion; he answers without making any reference to venue; and the time to amend the answer "of course" expires. The defense of improper venue is no longer open to the defendant.

Fourth. Notwithstanding any omission otherwise to assert the defenses of failure to state a claim upon which relief can be granted and of failure to join a party under Rule 19 (Rule 12(b)(6) and (7)), they are preserved and may be included in the answer or made the subject of a post-answer motion for judgment on the pleadings under Rule 12(c) or presented at the trial. See Rule 12(h)(2).

Questions: (15) What does "available" mean as used in Rule 12(g)?

(16) Why are the defenses enumerated in Rule 12(b)(2)–(5) disfavored as indicated above? Why are those in Rule 12(b)(6) and (7) carefully preserved? Why is the Rule 12(b)(1) defense treated with unique solicitude?

---

2. Other defenses are properly raised by answer. Suppose defendant files an answer. The effects of the Rules are as follows:

First. To the extent that the answer, after any amendment "of course" under Rule 15(a), fails to deny allegations of the complaint, those allegations stand admitted for purposes of the litigation. This follows from Rule 8(d), which states that averments in a pleading to which a responsive pleading is required are admitted when not denied in the responsive pleading.[h]

Second. Any affirmative defenses omitted from the answer, after any amendment "of course," are lost. This is not expressly provided, but follows from the pattern of the Rules. See Rules 12(b) and 8(c).

Example: *A* for consideration releases his claim against *B*, thus giving *B* a perfect defense to *A*'s suit. *A* can nevertheless proceed

[h] There is one exception: averments as to the amount of damage, although not denied in the answer, are not taken as admitted. Why this exception?

with his action and possibly get judgment, if *B* fails to present this defense in his answer or by an amendment "of course."

Third. The waivers just described as to denials and affirmative defenses may, however, be alleviated by amendments of the answer allowed by leave of court under Rule 15(a). But this somewhat uncertain step will entail, like any extra step, extra expense in attorneys' fees.

Questions: (17) Can Rule 15(a) on amendments, either as a matter of course or by leave of court, furnish any escape from the other waivers, for example, a waiver under Rule 12(h)(1)(A)?

(18) Take the case of alleged mental anguish set out supra p. 40 and, on behalf of the defendant, describe the manner and sequence in which you might present your defenses. Mention any strategic or tactical considerations that would affect your choices.

———

3. Objections under Rule 12(e) and (f), dealing with vagueness or ambiguity or redundancy or the like, should be raised in the initial pre-answer motion. An objection under Rule 12(e) may not be interposed if defendant has omitted it from such motion (see Rule 12(g)) or if he has answered (see Rule 12(e)). The same is true of a Rule 12(f) objection to redundancy or the like, although the language "upon the court's own initiative at any time" gives the court discretion to entertain a later request to strike.

Questions: (19) Assume that on Day 1 process is served; on Day 19 defendant serves a 12(f) motion to strike scandalous matter; and on Day 40 the 12(f) motion is granted. How much time does defendant have to serve an answer?

(20) Assume that on Day 1 process is served; on Day 19 defendant serves a 12(e) motion for a more definite statement; on Day 40 the 12(e) motion is granted; on Day 45 plaintiff serves the more definite statement, revealing for the first time possible grounds for a 12(b)(6) motion; on Day 50 defendant serves a 12(b)(6) motion; and on Day 75 the 12(b)(6) motion is denied. How much time does defendant have to serve an answer?

(21) When learning the mechanics of the Rules, you should give thought to the policies behind them. A general policy underlying many of the Rules is the elimination of traps for the unwary or, equivalently, the protection of clients from the effects of their lawyers' mistakes. Yet Rule 12 bristles with notions of waiver. What countervailing policies account for this?

———

BLACK, SIVALLS & BRYSON, INC. v. SHONDELL
United States Courts of Appeals, Eighth Circuit, 1949.
174 F.2d 587.

[This action was brought in a Missouri state court for damages for breach of express and implied warranties in the sale of five oil storage tanks manufactured by the defendant. The case was removed to the federal court on the ground of diversity of citizenship.

[Plaintiff[i] alleged that he ordered the tanks from a retailer who thereafter ordered them from defendant; that defendant had been told of the proposed use of the tanks and defendant had expressly and impliedly warranted their fitness for the disclosed purpose; and that the tanks were then manufactured, delivered, and paid for but they collapsed when put to the intended use.

[Defendant's answer in essence denied that any special purpose was communicated to it and denied that it warranted the tanks to be fit for such purpose.

[Defendant did not move against the complaint for failure to state a claim. Upon a jury trial, it neither moved for a directed verdict nor excepted to the jury instructions stating in effect that plaintiff could recover upon proof of his allegations. Verdict and judgment were given for the plaintiff. Defendant's subsequent motion in the trial court for judgment notwithstanding the verdict was denied.]

Before GARDNER, CHIEF JUDGE, and WOODROUGH and THOMAS, CIRCUIT JUDGES.

WOODROUGH, CIRCUIT JUDGE.

. . . .

It is contended on this appeal that the plaintiff's petition did not state a cause of action and that when the facts alleged in it are considered in the light of the evidence it affirmatively appears that no right of recovery against the defendant existed. The contention is grounded upon the assertion that under the law of Missouri the right to maintain an action ex contractu for breach of warranty depends upon privity of contract and that a sub-purchaser who is not in privity with the seller cannot maintain an action for the seller's breach of warranty. It is contended that as plaintiff assumed no obligation to the defendant manufacturer but bought the tanks from and agreed to and did pay the independent dealer Midwest therefor, and Midwest ordered them from and agreed to and did pay defendant for them, there was no privity of contract between plaintiff and defendant and that Missouri law denies plaintiff any right to recover from defendant manufacturer for breach of any warranty it may have made in respect to the tanks. [Citations omitted.] The plaintiffs concede that

[i] Shondell was the plaintiff.

In the district court, the caption of the case is, of course, in the form of Plaintiff v. Defendant; if there are several parties on either side, only the first is named in citing the case. Cf. Rule 10(a). In the courts of appeals, it was long the usual practice to reformulate the caption as Appellant v. Appellee; but since 1968, when the Federal Rules of Appellate Procedure were adopted, the title given to the action in the district court is retained on appeal. See App. Rule 12(a). In the Supreme Court, the practice is still to caption the case as: party who seeks review versus adverse party.

So in this case from a court of appeals in 1949, because defendant was appealing Shondell's victory in the district court, the caption of the case is Appellant (i.e., defendant) v. Appellee (i.e., plaintiff).

their action is ex contractu for breach of warranty but insist that the Missouri courts would hold that in the exceptional case where the manufacturer of an article itself enters into the negotiations for the sale thereof to an intending purchaser as defendant did through its agent Traylor in this instance, and, to get the business and induce the sale, makes a warranty respecting the article and its fitness for a certain purpose as alleged and shown here, then and in that case the action for breach of the warranty may be maintained by such purchaser against the manufacturer. [Citations omitted.]

It is clear that Missouri law is controlling in this case because the warranty and transactions involved, including the delivery of the tanks, occurred in Missouri,[j] but it does not appear that said question now sought to be raised has been properly brought here for review. Under Rule 12, Rules of Civil Procedure, 28 U.S.C.A., a defendant waives all defenses and objections which he does not present either by motion or in his answer except that the defense of failure to state a claim upon which relief may be granted may also be made by a later pleading if one is permitted or by motion for judgment on the pleadings or at the trial on the merits.[k] The record shows no such defense presented by defendant in a motion or answer and it must be deemed to have waived the defense that the petition did not state a claim upon which relief may be granted. The motion which defendant made for judgment notwithstanding the verdict was on the grounds that "the plaintiff's petition and the evidence discloses that there was no privity of contract between the plaintiff and the defendant" and that "it is uncontroverted in the evidence that the five tanks delivered by defendant complied with the terms specified in the [written] order" given by Midwest to defendant. It was made after the trial and not on the trial and did not preserve the defense of failure of the petition to state a claim. The defendant is therefore in the position of having waived that defense and may not urge it here.

[The remainder of the opinion dealing with other alleged errors is omitted.]

No error has been found in any of the matters properly preserved for review. The judgment is affirmed.

(c) Replying to Defenses

[Rules 7(a), 8(d)]

If the defendant's answer is confined to denials, there is no occasion for a response by the plaintiff, because the matters in dispute appear on the face of the complaint and the answer.

[j] The reason why state law controls here relates to 28 U.S.C. § 1652, which is considered later.

[k] Is this an entirely accurate summary of the effect of the present Rule?

Suppose, however, that the answer sets up an affirmative defense. May the plaintiff respond to it? Must he respond to it or have it taken as admitted? Rule 7(a)—differing sharply from the practice at common law and under many state codes of procedure—indicates that the plaintiff is not only not required to plead, but not permitted to do so unless the court orders a reply. The court ordinarily will not order a reply unless it is the defendant who moves for such an order, and there are relatively few cases in which it will order a reply even on the defendant's motion.

Questions: (22) What is the purpose of the general prohibition on replies to defenses?

(23) In what circumstances should an order compelling or allowing a reply be granted?

Rule 8(d) is the necessary complement of Rule 7(a). It provides: "Averments in a pleading to which no responsive pleading is required or permitted shall be taken as *denied or avoided.*" (Emphasis added.)

If, then, plaintiff makes allegations 1, 2, 3, and 4, and defendant in his answer denies 1 and asserts 5, 6, and 7 by way of affirmative defense, and there is no order compelling or allowing plaintiff to reply, what are the matters in dispute? Allegation 1 is in dispute because the plaintiff asserts the affirmative and the defendant the negative of it. Allegations 2, 3, and 4 stand admitted under Rule 8(d). Allegations 5, 6, and 7 are in dispute, likewise by reason of Rule 8(d). Defendant asserts the affirmative on 5, 6, and 7. Plaintiff's position with respect to these allegations is not fully disclosed by the pleadings. At the trial, or otherwise, he may (a) assert the negative (denial), (b) assert that, granting for the sake of argument the truth of the allegations, there are further matters that vitiate their effect (avoidance), or (c) take both such positions. For instance, if defendant alleges the affirmative defense that plaintiff for consideration released his claim against defendant, plaintiff without filing a reply is free at trial to deny that he received consideration for the release; or he can assert that it was procured by fraud; or both.

It should be added that by a motion to strike under Rule 12(f) plaintiff may raise the point that a defense in an answer is "insufficient"—a point that Rule 12(h)(2) preserves through the stage of trial. This is the analogue of a Rule 12(b)(6) motion addressed to a complaint.

Also under Rule 12(f) plaintiff may move to strike matter from an answer as being redundant or the like, much as a defendant can object to a complaint.

(d) Counterclaims

[Rule 13]

Defendant, whether or not he asserts defenses or objections to plaintiff's statement of claim, may desire to assert one or more claims against plaintiff. Must he resort to a separate action against plaintiff, or may or must he assert such claims in his answer to plaintiff's complaint? Rule 13 deals with this problem of "counterclaims." Rule 13(a) covers "compulsory counterclaims" and Rule 13(b) "permissive counterclaims." It is important to examine the differences between the two.

Compulsory counterclaims.—*A* sues *B* for slander. *B* wishes to contend (1) that he has a good defense to *A*'s claim, because he did not use the slanderous words alleged, and (2) that at the time and place of the alleged slander *A* struck him, so that he has a claim against *A* for battery. The events involved in the two claims are closely interwoven. If it were necessary for *B* to bring a separate action, the same witnesses might well have to be brought to court again, and much of the same testimony would have to be repeated. The wisdom of permitting enlargement of plaintiff's action to take in defendant's claim against plaintiff when the latter arises out of the same "transaction or occurrence that is the subject matter of" plaintiff's claim is generally recognized. The Federal Rules, however, go further, making enlargement in those circumstances compulsory and not merely permissive. The plaintiff can thus choose the forum for the defendant's claim.

The language of Rule 13(a) is mandatory (*"Compulsory counterclaims.* A pleading *shall* state as a counterclaim . . . .") (emphasis added). Of course, this does not mean that defendant is jailed or fined for failing to assert a compulsory counterclaim. It does suggest that if he fails to assert the claim in his answer, he is thereafter precluded from asserting it against the plaintiff either (1) in the plaintiff's pending action or (2) in an independent action. As to the first preclusion, however, Rule 13(f) provides: "When a pleader fails to set up a counterclaim through oversight, inadvertence, or excusable neglect, or when justice requires, he may by leave of court set up the counterclaim by amendment." The federal courts have commonly been generous in applying this provision, particularly where the omitted counterclaim was a compulsory one. The second preclusion involves an application of the principle of finality in litigation. If a person who has failed to assert a compulsory counterclaim later sues on that claim, res judicata or possibly estoppel or waiver can then be pleaded as a defense.

Question: (24) *P* sues *D*, who moves under Rule 12(b)(6) for failure to state a claim upon which relief can be granted. The motion is granted and the case dismissed, *D* never having filed an answer. There is no appeal. Then *D* sues *P* on a claim arising out of the same transaction or occurrence as *P*'s earlier attempted claim. *P* defends solely on the ground that *D*'s claim is precluded by *D*'s failure to interpose it as a counterclaim in the first action. What judgment? Does the word "pleading" as used in the first sentence of Rule 13(a) include a motion? Consider Rule 7. See Lawhorn v. Atlantic Ref. Co., 299 F.2d 353 (5th Cir.1962) (judgment for *D*).

Permissive counterclaims.—Suppose that when *A* sues *B* for breach of contract, *B* has a claim against *A* for battery arising out of a transaction or occurrence wholly unrelated to the subject matter of *A*'s claim. Rule 13(b) permits but does not compel *B* to assert such an unrelated claim by way of counterclaim in his answer in *A*'s action. If *B* chooses not to assert the counterclaim, he is free to bring an independent action on the claim.

It should be mentioned here that, in furtherance of convenience or to avoid prejudice, the court may order a separate trial of any claim, counterclaim, or issue in an action. See Rule 42(b). There will naturally be more frequent occasion to apply Rule 42(b) to permissive than to compulsory counterclaims.

Separate Trial

"Transaction or occurrence."—Having been warned that words like "claim" and "cause of action" are legal chameleons that may change their meaning as the context changes, you may wonder whether the key phrase of Rule 13(a) and (b), "transaction or occurrence," is also a chameleon. It is certainly wise, in seeking to find the meaning of a phrase in the context of a particular Rule, to bear steadily in mind what the purposes of the Rule may be.

There are relatively few decided cases in which Rule 13(a) has been invoked in an attempt to bar a later suit, and hence there is a dearth of judicial decisions defining "transaction or occurrence" for purposes of Rule 13 in those circumstances.

Question: (25) What probably accounts for the dearth of cases on this point?

In some state codes of procedure there is no such thing as a compulsory counterclaim; the defendant is permitted, not required, to interpose certain kinds of counterclaims. One of these kinds is often defined thus: "a cause of action arising out of the contract or transaction set forth in the complaint as the foundation of the plaintiff's claim, or connected with the subject of the action."

Questions: (26) Consider whether the defendant should be permitted to interpose his counterclaim in the following cases under the code language above given. Then consider whether the counterclaim would be compulsory under Federal Rule 13(a).

(a) Lyric Piano Co. v. Purvis, 194 Ky. 826, 241 S.W. 69 (1922): *P* sues *D* for the balance due on an installment contract for the sale of a piano. *D* seeks to counterclaim for a battery by *P*'s representative while engaged in collecting the sum due.

(b) Mulcahy v. Duggan, 67 Mont. 9, 214 P. 1106 (1923): *P* sues *D* for a battery occurring on May 17. *D* seeks to counterclaim for a libel published by *P* about *D* on May 8, with *D* alleging that the subsequent altercation was the result of the publication of the libel.

(27) Is there an undesirable inconsistency between Rule 18(a), which states that a plaintiff *may* join his claims, and Rule 13(a), which states that a defendant *must* assert his claims arising from the same transaction or occurrence as the plaintiff's claim?

Also bear in mind that the meaning of "transaction or occurrence," even only for the purposes of a particular Rule such as Rule 13, may vary with the type of circumstances of the case and the consequent effects on the parties and the public.

WILLIAMS v. ROBINSON

United States District Court, District of Columbia, 1940.
1 F.R.D. 211.

LETTS, JUSTICE. By way of background it may be stated that the following matters transpired in sequence as related; the defendant's wife filed a suit for maintenance; the defendant filed his answer with a cross-complaint[1] seeking an absolute divorce upon the ground of adultery, naming this plaintiff as co-respondent; in his answer to such cross-complaint this plaintiff contented himself with denying the acts of adultery with which he was charged; such maintenance cause is identified as Civil Action No. 5224, and is pending in this court.

Plaintiff brings this suit entitling his complaint as one for libel and slander. He alleges that he was libeled and slandered by the matters set up by the defendant in the cross-complaint wherein the defendant falsely and maliciously charged that this plaintiff had been guilty of adultery with the defendant's wife.

The defendant has filed no answer but moves to dismiss the complaint upon the ground that plaintiff has failed to assert his claim, if any he has, in his answer to the cross-complaint in the maintenance suit. Defendant invokes Rule 13(a) of the Federal Rules of Civil Procedure, 28 U.S.C.A. following section 723c, and insists that plaintiff was obliged thereunder to then assert the claim which he now brings as an independent action. It is the defendant's position that since plaintiff failed so to do by way of counterclaim he is now precluded from asserting it here.

Rule 13(a) relates to compulsory counterclaims and clearly required this plaintiff in the maintenance suit to state as a counterclaim any claim which at the time of filing his answer in the maintenance case he had against this defendant if such claim arose out of the transaction or occurrence that was the subject matter of the defendant's cross-complaint in the maintenance suit.

[1] In the terminology of the Federal Rules, this cross-complaint would properly be called a counterclaim.

But one question arises for consideration: was the slander and libel of which plaintiff complains part and parcel of the transaction or occurrence that was the subject matter of the defendant's cross-complaint in the maintenance suit? The question may be otherwise stated; the defendant in his cross-complaint charged this plaintiff with specific acts of adultery; these charges were in response to the wife's complaint for maintenance; can it be said that the acts of adultery alleged and relied upon by defendant and his subsequent accusations respecting such adultery may be grouped together as one and the same transaction or the same occurrence within the meaning of the rule?

The word "transaction" has abundant use in many statutes as; requiring or permitting joinder of causes of action growing out of the same transaction; making it necessary or optional for a defendant to plead as a counterclaim a cause of action arising out of the transaction which is the subject matter of the plaintiff's suit; relating to the admissibility of evidence pertaining to personal transactions with persons since deceased; statutes of limitation and many others which the courts have had occasion to construe. As a result of judicial determination the word "transaction" as so used has acquired a well defined meaning which, if applied to Rule 13(a), will give to it the intended sense and meaning.

The decided cases indicate that the word "transaction" denotes something done; a completed action; an affair as a whole; in Craft Refrigerating Mach. Co. v. Quinnipiac Brewing Co., 63 Conn. 551, 29 A. 76, 25 L.R.A. 856, the word "transaction" is defined to mean something which has been acted out to the end. In Cheatham v. Bobbitt, 118 N.C. 343, 24 S.E. 13, it is said the word "transaction" as found in the North Carolina Code in reference to the joinder of actions is used in the sense of the conduct of finishing up an affair, which constitutes as a whole the subject of an action. A right of action for slander and one for false imprisonment of plaintiff at the time the words were uttered cannot be united in one action, under the New York Code of Civil Procedure, as being causes arising out of the same transaction; DeWolfe v. Abraham, 151 N.Y. 186, 45 N.E. 455.

The use of the word "occurrence" in the rule in connection with the word "transaction" can serve no other purpose than to make clear the meaning of the word "transaction". An "occurrence" is defined to be a happening; an incident; or event. The word "transaction" is somewhat broader in its scope than the word "occurrence". The word "transaction" commonly indicates an act of transacting or conducting business but in the rule under consideration it is not restricted to such sense. It is broad enough to include an occurrence. It seems apt to say that the words "transaction" and "occurrence" as used in Rule 13(a) include the facts and circumstances out of which a cause of action may arise; Scarborough v. Smith, 18 Kan. 399. The words "transaction" and "occurrence" probably mean, whatever may

[margin note: cause of action test]

be done by one person which affects another's rights and out of which a cause of action may arise. Whether the subject matter of opposing claims is the same requires an examination into the basic facts underlying each of them. A familiar test may be applied by *[margin note: How to know it same if or]* inquiring whether the same evidence will support or refute the opposing claims. *[margin note: Same evidence test]*

It is clear that the use of the defamatory language of which plaintiff complains constituted no portion of the facts or circumstances alleged and relied on by this defendant in his cross-complaint filed in his wife's maintenance suit. There is no common point between the causes of action. The rule is in accordance with modern trend and the general prevailing policy to have the whole subject matter of any controversy settled in one action. It does not apply to causes growing out of separate transactions.

To sustain defendant's motion to dismiss would be in effect to require plaintiff to admit that there was a transaction or occurrence within the meaning of the rule, and as alleged by defendant in his cross-complaint in the maintenance suit. He makes no such admission but specifically denies the acts of adultery with which he is charged. *[margin note: Not a valid argument for every claim would have this argument]*

It follows that defendant's motion to dismiss the complaint must be overruled.

Question: (28) It has been suggested that the test of compulsoriness should be whether there is a "logical relationship" between claim and counterclaim. What do you think of this possible criterion?

Responding to a counterclaim.—A counterclaim, whether compulsory or permissive, is treated very much like a complaint for pleading purposes, with the counterclaiming defendant assuming to that extent the role of a plaintiff and the original plaintiff the role of a defendant. See Rules 7(a) and 12(a). Note that the plaintiff is required to reply to the counterclaim in much the same way as a defendant is required to answer a complaint. And, reading the remainder of Rule 12, you will see that the plaintiff may make motions in respect to the counterclaim in roughly the same way that a defendant may move in respect to a complaint.

Questions: (29) What would be the consequence if the plaintiff failed to reply or to move with respect to the counterclaim? See Rules 8(d) and 55(d).

(30) *P* sues *D* on a contract. *D* sets up in his answer a counterclaim on an unrelated contract. *P* replies, denying that he committed any breach of the second contract. The action, including the counterclaim, is tried and disposed of. Thereafter *P* sues *D* for a breach of the second contract occurring before he interposed his reply to *D*'s counterclaim in the first suit. *D* sets up a defense based upon *P*'s failure to counterclaim in the first suit. Is *P*'s second suit precluded? See 5 Wright & Miller § 1188, at 25–26. Why were we careful to say that the breach of the second contract occurred before the interposition of the reply?

Recoveries on claim and counterclaim.—In an action that involves a counterclaim, the plaintiff may prevail on his claim and the defendant on his counterclaim. If the defendant's recovery is for a smaller sum than the plaintiff's, the result is a judgment for the plaintiff for the difference. If the defendant's recovery is for a larger amount than the plaintiff's, there will be an affirmative judgment for the defendant for the difference. See Rule 13(c). An affirmative judgment for the defendant will also follow where the plaintiff fails on his claim and the defendant succeeds on his counterclaim.

(e) Amending the Pleadings

[Rule 15]

Rule 15 reflects the idea that a party ought not to be irretrievably bound to stand by his first formulation of a pleading, by way of either claim or defense—that the contours of the controversy should not be frozen beyond change. A party may commit an innocent mistake in framing his pleading; or he may see the need for altering it in the light of his opponent's subsequent pleading; or the investigation of the facts, carried on privately or by means of the discovery methods shortly to be described, may show that the matters in dispute are not as first supposed. One who finds himself in such a situation will naturally want to amend his pleading.

The question of the degree of freedom of amendment that should be permitted turns on the answer to the general question already posed: what are the purposes of the pleading process? In this light consider why Rule 15 attaches importance to the stage of the lawsuit at which the amendment is sought to be made.

Amendments before trial.—Rule 15(a) permits a party to amend his pleading "once as a matter of course at any time before a responsive pleading is served."[m] For the meaning of "responsive pleading," consider Rule 7. An answer is plainly a responsive pleading; a motion is not. Therefore, if defendant presents by motion under Rule 12(b)(6), before answer, the defense that the complaint fails to state a claim, plaintiff can reexamine his complaint and amend it without applying to the court for leave.

After the period of grace above mentioned, the allowance of an amendment rests in the discretion of the court, but the Rule prescribes that "leave shall be freely given when justice so requires."[n] Leave to amend is sought by a motion in accordance with Rule 7(b). The proposed amendment should be presented with the motion. As a general rule the court on such a motion will not pass on the legal sufficiency of the proposed amended pleading, and clearly

---

[m] Observe what the Rule has to say about the amendment of a pleading to which no responsive pleading is permitted.

[n] Alternatively, a party may amend if he has obtained the written consent of the adverse party.

the granting of the motion is not an adjudication on this point. If, however, it is obvious that the proposed amended pleading is insufficient, the court is likely in the exercise of its discretion to disallow the amendment.

Questions: (31) What factors should influence the court in granting or refusing amendment?

(32) Should a court be more ready to allow amendment of an answer than of a complaint?

(33) Note the time that Rule 15(a) gives a party to plead in response to an amended pleading. May the party instead move in response?

Amendments at or after trial.—Rule 15(a) imposes no absolute time limit on seeking amendment. Rule 15(b) shows that a motion to amend made during the course of the trial is not necessarily too late, and indeed that there are circumstances in which an amendment may be sought and allowed even after the trial is concluded and judgment is entered.

Question: (34) Why should an amendment of the pleadings ever be sought after judgment?

Rule 15(b) specially handles two situations within the general scope of Rule 15(a). The first two sentences of Rule 15(b) provide for treating the pleadings as amended if the disadvantaged party failed to object fully to trial evidence unambiguously going beyond the pleadings and thus tried those new issues by consent. The last two sentences of Rule 15(b) make provision for a different situation: where a party seeks to amend after his opponent has successfully objected to trial evidence as going beyond the pleadings.

Questions: (35) How does the objecting party show, under the next to the last sentence of Rule 15(b), that he will be prejudiced by the admission of evidence not within the issues made by the pleadings?

(36) What is a "continuance," referred to in the last sentence of Rule 15(b)? Is this device feasible in jury trials?

Relation back of amendments.—What is the purpose of Rule 15(c)?

BLAIR v. DURHAM

United States Circuit Court of Appeals, Sixth Circuit, 1943.
134 F.2d 729.

Before HICKS, SIMONS, and HAMILTON, CIRCUIT JUDGES.

HAMILTON, CIRCUIT JUDGE. Appellant, Algernon Blair, doing business as the Algernon Blair Construction Company, was general contractor for the repair of and improvements on, the United States Post Office, Customs House and United States Court Building in the city of Nashville, Tennessee, and appellant, C.W. Roberts, was the Superintendent and Manager for his co-appellant. The work was being done while the building was occupied and in use by officers and employees of the United States.

On or about August 17, 1938, appellee, Nelle B. Durham, a stenographic clerk in the Social Security Division in the office of the Collector of Internal Revenue, while at work in one of the rooms where the rebuilding under appellant's contract was going on, was struck in the head and injured by a heavy piece of timber falling from a scaffold.

Appellee originally filed this action on January 14, 1939, and alleged in her complaint that "by reason of the negligence and carelessness of defendants, their agents and servants in handling certain heavy timbers on and about the scaffolding that was erected in the office in which the plaintiff was working, a large and heavy piece of board approximately 2 × 4 inches in width and thickness and about 3 feet long was permitted to fall from said scaffolding, which was about 10 feet above the floor, and onto plaintiff's head with great force and violence injuring her."

Issue was joined on this complaint and the cause came on for trial before a jury. In the course of the trial on August 15, 1940, appellee with the consent of the court filed an amended complaint alleging the same facts with the following revision: "The defendants had erected said scaffolding and provided it for the use of persons engaged in the installation of air-conditioning equipment in said building and said scaffold was erected in such a manner that it did not protect persons, including the plaintiff, who were required to work thereunder, but was erected in such a manner that the defendants might have reasonably anticipated that heavy objects would be likely to fall therefrom."

At the time the amendment was filed, the empanelling of the jury was set aside and the cause continued. Thereupon appellants moved to dismiss the amended complaint on the ground it stated a new cause of action and was barred by the Tennessee Statute of Limitations of one year. (Code of Tennessee, Sec. 8595.) Said motion was overruled by the court.

On retrial, the jury returned a verdict on behalf of plaintiff for $6,500. Appellants assign the following points:

1. Appellee's amended complaint was barred by the one-year statutory period of limitation.

[Two other assignments of error are omitted.]

Rule 15(a) of the Rules of Civil Procedure, 28 U.S.C.A. following section 723c, provides that a party may amend his pleadings by leave of court, which leave shall be freely given when justice so requires at any time during the proceedings, and subsection (c) of the rule provides that whenever the amended pleading arose out of the conduct, transaction or occurrence set forth or attempted to be set forth in the original pleadings, the amendment relates back to the date of the original pleading. The issue here as to whether the statute of limitations was tolled by the original complaint depends upon whether the amendment stated a new cause of action.

A cause of action is the unlawful violation of a right or failure to discharge a duty which the facts show. The variety of facts alleged does not establish more than one cause of action so long as their result, whether they be considered severally or in combination, is the violation of but one right by a single legal wrong. A multiplicity of grounds of negligence alleged as causing the same injury does not result in pyramiding as many causes of action as separate allegations of actual negligence.

An amendment does not set up a new cause of action so long as the cause of action alleged grows out of the same transaction and is basically the same or is identical in the essential elements upon which the right to sue is based and upon which defendant's duty to perform is alleged to have arisen. As long as a plaintiff adheres to a legal duty breached or an injury originally declared on, an alteration of the modes in which defendant has breached the legal duty or caused the injury is not an introduction of a new cause of action. The true test is whether the proposed amendment is a different matter or the same matter more fully or differently laid.

[handwritten margin note: when there's a new cause of action]

A comparison between the appellee's original complaint and the amendment leaves no room for doubt that in both she relies on the same unlawful violation of a duty which appellants owed her at the place and in the position where she worked.

The original complaint which alleged that appellee's injuries were due to the negligence of appellant's employees in the use of the scaffold states no different cause of action as respects limitation than the amended complaint which stated that her injuries were due to the negligent manner in which the scaffold was constructed, because the two acts alleged were but different invasions of appellee's primary right and different breaches of the same duty. There was but one injury and it is immaterial whether it resulted from the negligence of the users of the scaffold or from its construction, since in either case it was a violation of the same obligation. [Citations omitted.]

[The remainder of the opinion, dealing with the other assignments of error, is omitted. However, in the course of its discussion the court did mention this: the evidence at trial had shown that at the time of the accident, the scaffold was being used solely by employees of a subcontractor.]

. . . Judgment affirmed.

Questions: (37) Some state codes in terms prohibit amendments that would have the effect of changing or substantially changing the "cause of action" or "defense." Do you find a comparable limitation in Rule 15? Do you agree with the court's statement in Blair v. Durham that "[t]he issue

here . . . depends upon whether the amendment stated a new cause of
action"?

(38) It does not appear that the defendants objected to the making of the
amendment itself. Why did they not do so?

"Cause of action" and "claim."—Of "cause of action" the Supreme Court has said: "One of the most theory-ridden of legal concepts is a 'cause of action.' This Court has recognized its 'shifting
meanings' and the danger of determining rights based upon definitions of 'a cause of action' unrelated to the function which the concept serves in a particular situation." United States v. Dickinson, 331
U.S. 745, 748, 67 S.Ct. 1382, 1385 (1947). The Federal Rules avoid
use of "cause of action," but do use the word "claim" in a number of
places. We shall have to observe how far the avoidance of the former phrase actually obviates the difficulties to which the Court referred.

(f) Discovery

[Rules 26, 30–37, 45]

Purposes of discovery.—The pleadings and motions attacking the
pleadings serve among other things to acquaint the parties with the
scope and character of the controversy. But the pleadings often contain little detail; for example, Form 9 does no more than identify the
accident and charge the defendant with negligence; the accident is
not described with precision, nor does the plaintiff state in what way
the defendant was negligent. Moreover, even when the pleadings do
go into detail, they do not often disclose the witnesses or documents
or other things by which the parties propose to make their proof.

If, apart from the pleadings, the parties knew all about the relevant facts and how the proof would be made by both sides at the
trial, the pretrial exchange of information might nevertheless stop
with the pleadings. But this is rarely the situation in practice. Even
after the pleading process is completed, the parties are often quite in
the dark about the facts and about each other's positions and sources
of proof; indeed, they may not know precisely what detailed positions
they will ultimately take or how they will prove their own claims or
defenses.

Private investigation is possible. But no one is bound to talk or
display papers to an investigator, and an adverse party or a person
friendly to an adverse party is unlikely to cooperate voluntarily.

When the time for trial comes, any person, including an adverse
party, may be compelled by subpoena to attend court and testify; and
he may also be commanded by subpoena duces tecum to bring with
him and produce designated documents and the like. See Rule 45. [Subpoena]
Knowledge acquired through testimony or other evidence given during the course of the trial itself, however, may well not come in time
for effective use. It may, for instance, point to a new line of inquiry,

revealed too late to undertake. Moreover, if a party is surprised at trial by unexpected adverse testimony, he may suffer seriously from lack of opportunity for further investigation to rebut it. And counsel's decision whether to call a given witness may quite properly turn on his advance knowledge of what the witness will say—the practical hazard in calling a witness whose testimony may boomerang is obvious.

The Federal Rules on "discovery" establish a machinery, much of which is a striking departure from tradition, for a further sifting of facts and exploration of positions and evidence before trial. See Rule 26(a) and (d). By the use of the discovery devices a party may uncover facts or sources of proof not hitherto known to him that will aid him in establishing his own contentions, or he may obtain leads that will help him to search out and uncover such facts or sources of proof for himself. He may also learn to a considerable extent what his adversary will seek to prove in support of a claim or defense and how his adversary expects to prove it. He may simply discover what a particular witness will say in court. By the skillful use of these devices he may eliminate from the trial issues on which there is no real dispute.

A major motive behind these Rules is to prevent the trial from being a drama of surprises with the happy ending for the side with the more extensive facilities for private investigation or the more agile court performer. Accordingly, the discovery provisions not only shape the preparation for trial but also profoundly affect the strategy and tactics of the trial itself. They affect other aspects of procedure as well. For example, as the Sierocinski case suggests, the availability of discovery devices will often influence decision on how much detail shall be required in the pleadings; the whole problem of pleading under the Federal Rules is indeed bound up with the discovery provisions and ultimately cannot be fruitfully considered apart from them. This suggests that another major motive behind the discovery Rules is to facilitate the efficient presentation and resolution of controversies.

General provisions governing discovery [Rule 26]. What may be inquired into? The scope of discovery is wide. Basic is Rule 26(b)(1): as a general proposition,[o] the "[p]arties may obtain discovery regarding any matter, not privileged,[p] which is relevant to the subject matter involved in the pending action,"[q] whether relating to the discovering party's claim or defense or to that of any other party, and including the identity and location of documents or other things and

---

[o] The introductory clause of Rule 26(b)(1) is: "Unless otherwise limited by order of the court in accordance with these rules." See, e.g., Rule 26(c) (protective orders).

[p] The reference is to such limitations as the attorney-client privilege. The subject of privilege is considered in connection with the trial, infra p. 117.

[q] See Rule 27 (discovery in anticipation of the commencement of an action and discovery after judgment to perpetuate testimony).

the identity and whereabouts of persons having knowledge of any discoverable matter. "It is not ground for objection that the information sought will be inadmissible at the trial if the information sought appears reasonably calculated to lead to the discovery of admissible evidence." (The rules of evidence are considered infra pp. 110–32.)

Questions: (39) In an action based on alleged negligence of the defendant in maintaining a skylight through which the plaintiff fell, may the plaintiff discover from the defendant what repairs to the skylight were made following the accident? See Caulk v. Baltimore & O.R.R., 306 F.Supp. 1171 (D.Md.1969) (discovery allowed). Consider also Federal Rule of Evidence 407, which is in the Rules pamphlet.

(40) In an action for alleged violation of the antitrust laws, plaintiff during discovery refuses to answer (a) questions concerning the circumstances surrounding the bringing of the suit, including possibly unethical financial arrangements between plaintiff and his counsel for bearing the costs of this litigation, and (b) questions concerning plaintiff's net worth, including his ability to satisfy a judgment for costs if defendant were to prevail in the action. Defendant moves to compel answers. What should be the decision? See Bogosian v. Gulf Oil Corp., 337 F.Supp. 1228 (E.D.Pa.1971); 4 Moore ¶ 26.56[2].

This general formula of Rule 26(b)(1) is followed by specific provisions regarding discovery of the existence and contents of insurance policies (see Rule 26(b)(2)), discovery of certain materials prepared by or for a party or his representative in anticipation of litigation or for trial (see Rule 26(b)(3)),[r] and discovery of expert information (see Rule 26(b)(4)).

Questions: (41) Do these specific provisions broaden or restrict the general formula of Rule 26(b)(1)?

(42) Was Rule 26(b)(2) with respect to discovery of insurance policies necessary? Would not the general formula of Rule 26(b)(1) have sufficed to permit that discovery?

Discovery is expected to work almost wholly by action of the parties without intervention by the court. Physical or mental examination under Rule 35, already considered in Sibbach v. Wilson & Co., is the only discovery device that must be initiated by motion addressed to the court. The five other devices—depositions upon oral examination, depositions upon written questions, interrogatories to parties, production of documents and things, and requests for admission—start and generally move along by party initiative with application to the court only in special situations, as where discovery is sought before commencement of an action or after judgment, or when something goes awry, as when a request for discovery is refused or a misuse of discovery is threatened.

Question: (43) Why should a request for a physical or mental examination require an order made only on motion for good cause shown?

[r] Rule 26(b)(3) raises some of the most far-reaching problems of modern procedure. It is reserved to a later stage of the course. But students may be interested in reading now the case of Hickman v. Taylor, infra p. 472.

Note that for each discovery request or response, Rule 26(g) imposes a certification requirement analogous to the provision for pleadings and motions in Rule 11. Note also the sanctions set forth for violations of Rule 26(g).

Depositions upon oral examination [Rule 30].—This method of discovery comprises oral examination of anyone, party or nonparty, thought to have information within the scope of discovery as set out in Rule 26. It may be well to begin by asking why a party might want to take a deposition. Here are some possible reasons, which in a sense particularize the purposes of discovery discussed above:

1. The discovering party may know or suspect that his adversary or some other person has information that would aid him in his own investigation and preparation for trial. For example, under Rule 26(b)(1) the person deposed may be required to reveal the names and addresses of other witnesses to the events in suit.

2. The discovering party may be left genuinely in the dark by his adversary's pleadings, and so may want to take the adversary's deposition to uncover the nature of the claim or defense that he must be prepared to meet at trial.

3. He may have a witness with whose story he is fully familiar, so there is no occasion to "discover" it. But the witness may be old and likely to die before trial, or he may be young and about to join the armed forces, or he simply may live far from the place of trial, or there may be some other danger that he will be unavailable to testify at trial. A deposition serves to record testimony and, as we shall see, may be used at trial upon a proper showing that the witness is unavailable.

4. He may know the story his adversary or some other witness will tell well enough for purposes of his own preparation. But he nevertheless may want a deposition to pin the witness down by sworn testimony in advance of trial. If, as sometimes happens, the story told at trial is different, the deposition may be used to discredit the witness.

5. He may hope that he can by a deposition expose a fatal weakness in his adversary's claim or defense, and thus be able to avoid a trial altogether by a motion for summary judgment pursuant to Rule 56, which is examined infra p. 85.

To follow the main features of the oral-deposition process, read these provisions in order: Rules 30(a) and (b)(1) and (2), 45(d), 28(a), 30(c), (e), and (f), and 29. See also Rules 37(a), 30(d), and 26(c).

In the usual case, leave of court is not needed to initiate the deposition procedure.[8] The discovering party gives reasonable notice in writing to the other parties to the action, specifying the time and

---

[8] Reread Rule 30(a), describing the situations in which leave of court is required. Consider why these provisions were thought necessary. Consider also Rule 27.

place of the deposition and naming the person to be examined ("deponent"). A nonparty deponent is officially summoned to appear at the deposition by the service upon him of a subpoena.[t] If the deponent is a party, a subpoena need not be used; the notice of examination itself suffices as a command.[u]

Question: (44) With regard to the place specified by the discovering party for taking the deposition, what is the significance of Rule 45(d)(2)?

The taking of the deposition resembles the taking of testimony at a trial.[v] The deponent is sworn, interrogated by counsel for the discovering party, cross-examined by counsel for the other party or parties, and so on, the questions and answers being taken down stenographically.[w]

There is no judge present, however, as at a trial. The person presiding at the deposition does not have judicial powers. The difference becomes important when there is an objection to a question. At a trial, the judge would rule on the objection and the question would be answered or not, depending on the ruling. At a deposition, there is no one on hand to make the ruling. How, then, is the objection disposed of?

Consider the possible reasons for objection: (1) A question put at deposition may be within the scope of discovery described in Rule 26, but would be objectionable at trial under the rules of evidence. (2) A question may be objectionable as not falling within the scope of discovery; in such case, it would in all likelihood also be objectionable at the trial proper.

In situation (1), the Rules contemplate that the deponent will answer the question and that the objection will simply be recorded. See Rule 30(c). Then, if the deposition is offered in evidence at the trial, the objection will in effect be renewed and the trial judge will pass on it as if the deponent were testifying orally. In fact, when a deposition is offered at the trial, objection under the rules of evidence may ordinarily be made to questions even though they were not objected to while the deposition was being taken. See Rule 32(b) and (d)(3)(A) and (B). But when the ground for objection is one that might have been obviated or removed if presented at the taking of the deposition, the objection cannot be raised for the first time at the trial. It is patently unfair to be able to have deposition testimony excluded at

[t] A nonparty deponent may also be commanded by a subpoena duces tecum to bring with him and produce documents and other things. See Rule 45(b) and (d).

[u] See also Rule 30(b)(5), which provides that the notice to a party deponent may be accompanied by a request under Rule 34 to produce documents and other things at the taking of the deposition.

[v] But see Rule 30(b)(7), which permits a stipulation or order that a deposition be taken by telephone.

[w] But see Rule 30(b)(4), which permits a stipulation or order for recordation by other than stenographic means, such as by tape recorder or videotape. Compare Colonial Times, Inc. v. Gasch, 509 F.2d 517 (D.C.Cir.1975), with UAW v. National Caucus of Labor Comms., 525 F.2d 323 (2d Cir.1975).

the trial where the examining party could have remedied the error if alerted to the danger by an objection during the deposition. For example, a leading question on direct examination is objectionable in form, but a rephrasing of the question provides a ready corrective. If that objection could be made for the first time at trial, the error might be fatal because the deponent might not be then available to answer the rephrased question. Other problems are more difficult. Suppose a doctor at deposition is asked a question calling for an expert opinion on a medical question, and an objection is first made at trial on the ground that his expert qualifications were not sufficiently shown. Is the objection untimely because the ground for it was obviable? Uncertainty in the few precedents in this area often leads lawyers either to attempt to protect themselves by excessive objections at the deposition or to stipulate at the time of the deposition that all objections except as to form may be first made at the trial.

Even in situation (2)—where the examining party puts a question at deposition that is not within the scope of discovery—the deponent and the other parties may be willing to have it answered if the answer would not prove damaging or offensive. But suppose the question is thought to enter the field of privilege. Here there may be strong reason to decline to give an answer unless the court actually orders one, for the answer may be harmful in itself, and the harm would perhaps not be cured by the question being ruled improper at the subsequent trial.

Question: (45) What may an examining party do in the face of a deponent who has been advised by an opposing party not to answer or who himself refuses to answer? See Rule 37(a).

Note that the examining party may request payment of expenses for proceedings occasioned by unreasonable failure to answer a proper question, and the deponent or opposing party may make a corresponding request in case of unreasonable insistence on an answer to an improper question. Counsel advising unreasonable action may be obliged to pay these expenses personally. See Rule 37(a)(4).

UMPHRES v. SHELL OIL CO.

United States District Court, Southern District of Texas, 1971.
15 Fed.R.Serv.2d (Callaghan) 1116.

Cox, District Judge. A motion to compel the plaintiff to answer certain questions asked of him during the taking of his oral deposition by the defendant is before the court.

. . . .

Apparently, defendant commenced plaintiff's deposition as scheduled, on August 30, 1971. As pointed out by the defendant in its memorandum in support of its motion to compel answers, counsel for the defendant commenced interrogating the plaintiff with regard to an alleged conspiracy pleaded by him. Plaintiff's counsel advised his client not to answer any questions about conspiracy, to which the attorney for the defendant observed, in effect, that conspiracy is a question of fact and the proper subject for interrogation, and the defendant should be entitled "to inquire of him what he thinks the conspiracy was." Plaintiff's counsel, Mr. Conde Anderson, replied, "Well, you know full well, Mr. Kingdon, that I prepared the complaint and that Mr. Umphres didn't. And I attempted to prepare it, keeping in mind what I understood the law to be, and I don't think this is a proper line of inquiry and I'm going to instruct him not to answer."

Mr. Kingdon then continued with his next question, being, "Mr. Umphres, do you have any information regarding the allegation in the complaint that Shell exercised control of numerous retail dealers with whom it contracted in areas elsewhere in the state of Texas other than Harris County, Texas, and in many other states, do you have any information to support that claim that there was a conspiracy in areas other than Harris County, Texas?" The plaintiff did not answer this question under instructions from his counsel.

The court is of the opinion that the oral interrogatory may very well ask for plaintiff's conclusion as to the legal meaning of conspiracy, and, if so, since plaintiff is not an experienced man in the field and the subject matter which is involved in such question, he should not be required to answer the question as asked. However, it seems to the court that defendant is certainly entitled to interrogate plaintiff about the facts upon which the claim of conspiracy was based. But, up to now, defendant's counsel has not asked Mr. Anderson for the details upon which he relied to plead conspiracy.

This court considers any motion relating to discovery to be premature until the party making such request has first explored all reasonable avenues of agreement as to discovery problems by conference with counsel for the other side. Therefore, counsel for the plaintiff and counsel for the defendant are here directed to sit down, face to face, and in good faith discuss the question of conspiracy as alleged by the plaintiff, and the attorney for the plaintiff is to detail for the benefit of the defendant those facts which he took into account in making his allegations of conspiracy. Upon the furnishing of such factual information to the defendant, then the deposition of plaintiff should resume and the defendant's counsel is at liberty to interrogate the plaintiff with regard to the particular facts which his counsel has divulged, or which may be developed during the interrogation.

. . . .

BRANDENBERG v. EL AL ISRAEL AIRLINES, 79 F.R.D. 543 (S.D.N.Y.1978). Plaintiff sued two airlines for $900,000, alleging negligent and reckless treatment that had caused physical stress and mental injuries.

Defendants deposed the 72-year-old plaintiff. Mrs. Brandenberg's position was "that in view of her age and physical condition (she suffered from diabetes), the airlines were obligated to treat her with particular care, and that they failed in that obligation, on the contrary, 'abandoning' her in times of need." Counsel for British Airways questioned her concerning the events of its leg of the flight that had carried her abroad to visit her daughter. "It is fair to say that the plaintiff . . . had some difficulty in remembering the sequence of events." The court further noted: "It is also fair to say that, having studied her account of the events involving British Airways, the precise complaint or complaints which the plaintiff makes concerning her treatment at the hands of that defendant are not clear." Contrariwise, her criticism of the other airline had been "entirely clear."

"In these circumstances, counsel for British Airways posed, or attempted to pose, the following questions to plaintiff at the end of the deposition:

'Q. Do you know of any factual basis to support the allegations in your complaints against British—'

'Q. Do you know of anything that British Airways did that was not proper treatment of you at Heathrow Airport in March of 1976?'

'Q. Mrs. Brandenberg, can you tell me in your own words what the basis of your claim against British Airways—'

'Q. Do you know of anything that British Airways did to you that was not in accordance with the way you thought you should be treated by them?'

'Q. What facts do you contend show that British Airways did not properly treat you?'

"On direction of her attorney, the plaintiff declined to answer any of these questions. British Airways now moves for an order under Rule 37(a) compelling answers. Plaintiff resists on the ground that the questions call for legal conclusions of a lay witness."

The court concluded that such contentions could be sought:

"British Airways is understandably left in the dark, on the present deposition record, as to the factual basis perceived by plaintiff for the charge of negligence against it. British Airways is entitled to inquire on that score, and plaintiff is directed to respond to such questions, at a continuation of her deposition at a place and time to be mutually agreed or, failing such agreement, as directed by the Court."

———

The Rules give a party (or the deponent himself) certain opportunities to take the initiative against the examining party, halt the examination, and obtain a court order to limit the deposition if it is going too far afield or being abusively conducted or to furnish other kinds of protection. See Rules 30(d) and 26(c). Again an offending person may be ordered to pay expenses.

Question: (46) In what circumstances may a party (or the deponent himself) seek court protection against the deposition before the stated date for the appearance of the deponent?

Moreover, Rule 26(b)(1) encourages district courts on their own to curb discovery overuse.

When the examination of the deponent has been completed, the testimony is transcribed if requested by any party. The transcript is then submitted to the deponent for review; any changes requested by the deponent are entered with the reasons given by the deponent; and the deponent signs the transcript (often the parties will have stipulated to waive the signing). Finally, the person who presided at deposition certifies the transcript, seals it, and delivers it to the court in which the action is pending.

Question: (47) Suppose there is no stipulation to waive the signing of the transcript and the deponent refuses to sign it. What effect does this have?

Depositions upon written questions [Rule 31].—The typical notice to take a deposition upon oral examination does not specify the particular matters to be inquired into, but rather might at most refer generally to the matters involved in the action. The notice for taking a deposition upon written questions, on the other hand, is accompanied by the questions to be put to the deponent, who may be a party or nonparty. Within 30 days after being served with the notice and questions, any party may serve questions for cross-examination, which may be followed by questions for redirect and recross. All questions are delivered to the person designated to preside at the deposition. He swears the deponent (summoned to appear in the same way as for a Rule 30 deposition), and he reads the questions one by one. The deponent responds, and the testimony is recorded. The deposition may be transcribed, and it is then reviewed, signed, certified, sealed, and delivered.

Again consult Rule 37(a) to see when and how an examining party may secure an order directing a deponent to answer a written question, and see Rule 26(c) as to when and how a party or deponent may secure a protective order in respect to a deposition upon written questions.

Questions: (48) Why is there no equivalent of Rule 30(d) in Rule 31?

(49) Is it proper for counsel, who has received the Rule 31 questions from his opponent in advance, to rehearse his client or a friendly nonparty deponent by reading the questions to him? Compare 4A Moore ¶ 31.02, with 8 Wright & Miller § 2133.

Rule 31 depositions upon written questions are typically cheaper than Rule 30 depositions upon oral examination. The saving under Rule 31 arises from the fact that counsel can with reasonable safety absent themselves from the examination. But counsel labor under the handicap of having to frame questions without knowing what answers will have been given to the previous questions. Hence questions must be framed on predictions or on alternative assumptions about the content of prior answers. This procedure is uncertain and cumbersome. And if the deponent is unfriendly to the examining side, it may be harder to pin him down by written questions than by oral examination.

Question: (50) What may a party do in an effort to save the expense of attending an oral deposition called by another party? See Rule 30(c). What difficulties can be foreseen?

Interrogatories to parties [Rule 33].—This method of discovery is relatively simple and inexpensive. The discovering party serves written interrogatories, similar to the written questions in a Rule 31 deposition, upon any other party to the action. The responding party and his lawyer sit down on their own to prepare responses. "Each interrogatory shall be answered[x] separately and fully in writing under oath, unless it is objected to, in which event the reasons for objection shall be stated in lieu of an answer." Rule 33(a). Answers are signed by the person making them; objections are signed by the attorney.

Questions: (51) Give some typical reasons why an interrogatory might fairly be objected to.

(52) What may the interrogating party do to compel an answer when he considers an objection insufficient? When he considers an answer, unaccompanied by an objection, insufficient?

(53) May a party to whom interrogatories are directed seek any protection against them otherwise than by written objections in lieu of answers?

(54) May a party to whom interrogatories are directed serve cross-interrogatories, i.e., interrogatories directed to himself? Compare the following questions: May a party who is being deposed upon oral examination be cross-examined by his own counsel? Might any useful purpose be so achieved? Indeed, may a party initiate a deposition upon oral examination in which he himself is the deponent? Might any useful purpose be achieved by such a deposition? In a deposition upon written questions, may a deposed party direct cross-questions to himself? May a party depose himself upon written questions?

---

[x] Under Rule 33(c), in certain cases involving business records, the interrogated party instead of actually answering the interrogatories may invite the discovering party to inspect the records from which answers can be derived. This subdivision was added as part of the very extensive 1970 amendments and refined in 1980. See in the Rules pamphlet the Advisory Committee's notes thereon.

O'BRIEN v. INTERNATIONAL BROTHERHOOD
OF ELECTRICAL WORKERS

United States District Court, Northern District of Georgia, 1977.
443 F.Supp. 1182.

EDENFIELD, DISTRICT JUDGE.

This action was brought pursuant to the Labor Management Reporting and Disclosure Act, 29 U.S.C. §§ 401, et seq., against a local union and its parent international union. . . .

Plaintiff was charged by a fellow union member with violating certain sections of the IBEW constitution when he distributed certain information which was allegedly detrimental to the union. Local 613's executive board heard the charges on January 27, 1976 and found plaintiff guilty, fining him $2,725.00 and temporarily suspending him from local union activities. The decision of Local 613 was rescinded when it was discovered that defendant IBEW, not Local 613, had jurisdiction over the charges pursuant to the IBEW constitution. On March 15, 1976 plaintiff was notified of a new hearing to be held before the International Executive Council of IBEW on May 6, 1976. At this hearing, plaintiff was found guilty and fined $100. Thereafter, plaintiff filed this action.

Plaintiff has alleged that the charges, trials and disciplinary measures violated plaintiff's rights of free speech and assembly as guaranteed by the LMRDA in 29 U.S.C. § 411(a)(2).* . . .

[The court first disposed of a number of other motions.]

Lastly, the court must concern itself with plaintiff's motion to compel answers to interrogatories from Local 613. Plaintiff's interrogatories, filed May 18, 1977, seek to have defendants explain why they found plaintiff guilty of the union charges. Local 613 has registered a general objection to plaintiff's interrogatories which may be readily disposed of. Local 613 claims that since its decision to fine and suspend defendant was rescinded, its reasons for trying plaintiff and finding him guilty are now irrelevant. However, plaintiff is charging that both defendants in their respective actions taken against plaintiff violated plaintiff's free speech rights under the LMRDA. Plaintiff seeks, among other relief, the expenses incurred

---

* Section 411(a)(2) of Title 29, U.S.C., provides:

"Every member of any labor organization shall have the right to meet and assemble freely with other members; and to express any views, arguments, or opinions; and to express at meetings of the labor organization his views, upon candidates in an election of the labor organization or upon any business properly before the meeting, subject to the organization's established and reasonable rules pertaining to the conduct of meetings: *Provided,* That nothing herein shall be construed to impair the right of a labor organization to adopt and enforce reasonable rules as to the responsibility of every member toward the organization as an institution and to his refraining from conduct that would interfere with its performance of its legal or contractual obligations." [Footnote by court.— Ed.]

in defending and appealing Local 613's decision. While the decision may have been rescinded, the expenses were not.

A second objection listed by Local 613 is that plaintiff has not sought to compel discovery as against IBEW. While that is a matter for plaintiff to decide, it must be noted that plaintiff cannot expect the local union to answer interrogatories that are within the distinct knowledge of the international union, specifically interrogatories numbered 1(c) and (d), 2(2), and 5.

Interrogatory numbers 1(a) and (b) ask for the specific statements allegedly made by plaintiff for which he was tried. The court sees no reason why defendant should not be required to set out these statements, despite the fact that plaintiff might be able to cull this information from the hearing transcript. The same may be said with respect to interrogatory number 2, wherein plaintiff asks that defendant Local 613 state which provisions of the IBEW constitution were violated by which statements.

Interrogatory number 3 seeks an explanation as to why these statements violated these constitutional provisions. While defendant Local 613 argues that this question seeks a legal theory which is not discoverable, when the constitutional provisions presumably involved are examined, the interrogatory appears to be one that Local 613 should answer. All but one of the provisions proscribe false statements. Plaintiff is entitled to know the facts which render his utterances untrue. One constitutional provision deals with conduct which causes dissension and dissatisfaction among union members. Plaintiff is entitled to know the facts which, in Local 613's view, constituted dissension caused by plaintiff's statements.

Interrogatory number 4 provides as follows:

> In respect to each act and/or utterance listed in response to Interrogatory 1. above, explain the manner in which each said act and/or utterance (a) violated plaintiff's responsibility toward Local 613, IBEW and IBEW as institutions, and (b) interfered with Local 613, IBEW's, and IBEW's performance of their respective legal or contractual obligations. (If any of said acts/utterances violated neither standard, please indicate which did not.)

Clearly this question seeks to discover defendant's legal theory based on the facts elicited from the other interrogatories. Interrogatory number 4 is based on the exceptions in the free speech section of the LMRDA [the court here quoted again the proviso of 29 U.S.C. § 411(a)(2)]. Anticipating that defendant will rely on this language as a defense to this action, plaintiff asks defendant to explain its application to the communications made by the plaintiff.

Rule 33(b), Fed.R.Civ.P., makes clear that such discovery is in fact permissible [the court here quoted the last paragraph of Rule 33(b)]. This rule cuts against many older cases which imposed a strict rule against opinions, contentions and conclusions. The Advisory Committee Note only excludes those interrogatories which "extend to issues of 'pure law,' i.e., legal issues unrelated to the facts of the case." Note to 1970 Amendment of Rule 33(b), 48 F.R.D. 485, 524 (1970), see Wright & Miller, Federal Practice and Procedure, § 2167 at 513. Interrogatory number 4 seeks an application of law to the central facts of the case, and accordingly is permissible under Rule 33(b). Since the discovery period is nearly complete, there is no danger of tying defendant to a legal theory before he has had an opportunity to fully explore the case, see Wright & Miller, supra, at 514.

Interrogatory number 6 reads as follows:

> In respect to each and every constitutional provision listed in response to Interrogatory 2., state and explain the reasons why each provision is *not* deprived of force and effect by operation of 29 U.S.C. § 411(b) [y] in respect to plaintiff and the acts and utterances listed in response to Interrogatory 1.

In contrast to the interrogatory previously discussed, this question seeks pure legal conclusions which are related not to the facts, but to the law of the case. While the line demarcating permissible discovery under Rule 33(b) may be obscure, the court concludes that this interrogatory exceeds the bounds of permissible discovery under the rule.

For these reasons, plaintiff's motion to compel discovery is DENIED as to interrogatories numbered 1(c) and (d), 2(2), 5 and 6, but is GRANTED as to the balance of the interrogatories in dispute. The court further concludes that each party should bear the cost incurred in bringing and opposing these discovery motions.

. . . . .

———

Questions: (55) In the Sierocinski case, would it be proper under present Rule 33 for the defendant to put to the plaintiff the interrogatory: "What specific acts or omissions by the defendant do you contend constituted negligence?" How about the interrogatory: "Do you intend to rely on the doctrine of res ipsa loquitur?"

(56) If Sierocinski were to answer any such interrogatory, how binding on Sierocinski should his answer be?

(57) Would it be proper for the defendant instead to put those same questions when deposing the plaintiff? when deposing the plaintiff's lawyer?

A most significant point is that, unlike depositions, interrogatories may not be used to question nonparties. But what is the difference between depositions upon written questions, when addressed to parties, and interrogatories to parties? In the former case, the party as deponent is at least formally on his own when he testifies and gives answers to the written questions read out to him. In the latter case,

[y] That statute provides: "(b) Any provision of the constitution and bylaws of any labor organization which is inconsistent with the provisions of [29 U.S.C. § 411(a)] shall be of no force or effect."

the party answering can and commonly does sit down with his attorney, examine the questions at leisure, and make use of his attorney's advice in framing the answers. Despite the studied and artful answers that may be returned to Rule 33 interrogatories, this discovery method is a good and relatively cheap means of obliging one's adversary to specify his position on the issues arising in the case; in addition, of course, it can be used simply to obtain evidence or leads to evidence.

Requests for admission [Rule 36].—A party may serve upon any other party a written request to admit the truth of matters set forth in the request or to admit the genuineness of described documents. See Form 25. Observe how a request is made, what action or inaction by the requested party may result in an admission, what may be done about improper objections or inadequate answers, and what the effect of an admission is. A denial defeats the attempt to obtain an admission, but consider the sanctions contained in Rule 37(c) which are designed to discourage capricious denials.

Questions: (58) How do Rule 36 requests for admission differ from Rule 33 interrogatories, and wherein do the functions of these devices differ?

(59) Prior to 1970, Rule 36 admissions could be sought only as to genuineness of described documents and as to matters of "fact." Compare present Rule 36(a). Was not the earlier version preferable?

(60) What is the practical likelihood of securing a Rule 37(c) order? What is the meaning of "proves" as used in Rule 37(c)?

(61) A lawyer lecturing at a meeting of the Federal Bar Association said that he thought "the best time to file a request for admissions is at the same time the complaint or answer is filed because the opponent has not had time to figure out his litigation strategy." 51 U.S.L.W. 2170, 2172 (Sept. 21, 1982). What do you think of that suggestion?

Production of documents and things for inspection and other purposes [Rule 34].—Witnesses, including parties, may be compelled to produce documents and other things during trial, but this may be too late for effective use. Rule 34 enables a party to anticipate trial and cause any other party to produce any designated documents or tangible things within his control, so that the discovering party may inspect, copy, and (in the case of things) test or sample them.[z] (All this must of course be within the scope of Rule 26.) The process begins by service of a request in writing. See Form 24. The requested party serves a written response either acquiescing in the request or objecting with reasons. The discovering party has a remedy under Rule 37(a) for a failure to respond or an improper refusal.

The description of "documents" was expanded by the 1970 amendments to reflect changing technology. It includes electronic data compilations, which the responding party may be required to translate into reasonably usable form. Often he will supply a print-out of

---

[z] Rule 34 also provides for securing entry on any other party's land or other property for the purposes of inspection and measuring or the like.

computer data, but the court has flexible powers sufficient to assure the discovering party adequate information and at the same time to protect the responding party against undue burden or expense. See the Advisory Committee's note on the 1970 amendment of Rule 34(a).

Questions: (62) Rule 34(a)(1) refers to "designated documents." What should a party do if he is not sufficiently informed to identify the documents he wants?

(63) Requests under Rule 34 can be addressed only to parties. Suppose a document or thing is under the control of a nonparty. How can its production for discovery be compelled?

Physical and mental examination [Rule 35].—Physical or mental condition is frequently in question in lawsuits, and almost invariably in actions for personal injuries. In an injury case, the defendant will generally want his physician to conduct an examination of the plaintiff. Otherwise he will be at a disadvantage in meeting an exaggerated or fraudulent claim by the plaintiff, and also in evaluating the claim for purposes of settlement. The plaintiff will often agree to examination by the defendant's physician because he also is interested in settlement, and he is aware that the trier might be impressed unfavorably by a disclosure at trial that he had declined to allow himself to be examined. Rule 35, however, is useful where for any reason a party refuses to be examined.[a]

Only a party (or a person in the custody or legal control of a party) can be reached under Rule 35.

Question: (64) How, then, does a litigant prepare himself on the condition of a nonparty, e.g., the eyesight of a witness to the accident in suit?

The discovering party initiates the procedure by a motion—he must show "good cause," and the physical or mental condition must be "in controversy" in the action. In the Schlagenhauf case below, the Supreme Court said this about the requirements of "good cause" and "in controversy":

"They are not met by mere conclusory allegations of the pleadings—nor by mere relevance to the case—but require an affirmative showing by the movant that each condition as to which the examination is sought is really and genuinely in controversy and that good cause exists for ordering each particular examination. Obviously, what may be good cause for one type of examination may not be so for another. The ability of the movant to obtain the desired information by other means is also relevant.

"Rule 35, therefore, requires discriminating application by the trial judge . . . .

"Of course, there are situations where the pleadings alone are sufficient to meet these requirements. A plaintiff in a negligence action who asserts mental or physical injury, cf. Sibbach v. Wilson & Co.,

---

[a] Note that certain provisions of Rule 35 apply even when examinations are   made by agreement of the parties. See Rule 35(b)(3).

supra, places that mental or physical injury clearly in controversy and provides the defendant with good cause for an examination to determine the existence and extent of such asserted injury."

Question: (65) In what circumstances would it be necessary in a personal-injury case to establish "good cause" and "in controversy" otherwise than by the pleadings?

The party against whom an order is made is entitled upon request to receive from the discovering party a detailed written report of the examination made under the Rule and also like reports of earlier examinations of the same condition to which the latter may have access.

Question: (66) If the discovering party delivers these reports, what does he become entitled to? See Rule 35(b)(1) and (2).

SCHLAGENHAUF v. HOLDER, 379 U.S. 104, 85 S.Ct. 234 (1964). In a diversity action involving a collision between a bus and the rear of a tractor-trailer, the plaintiff bus passengers named as defendants the bus owner, bus driver, tractor owner, tractor driver, and trailer owner. Bus owner cross-claimed against tractor owner, tractor driver, and trailer owner for damage to the bus; bus owner claimed that the tractor-trailer was driven at a dangerously low speed, had not remained in lane, and was not equipped with proper rear lights. Tractor owner and driver, answering the cross-claim, denied their own negligence; alleged contributory negligence on the part of the bus driver, one Schlagenhauf; and further alleged that Schlagenhauf was "not mentally or physically capable" of driving a bus at the time of the accident.

Tractor owner, tractor driver, and trailer owner together applied for an order directing Schlagenhauf to submit to mental and physical examinations by one specialist each in the fields of internal medicine, ophthalmology, neurology, and psychiatry. The application was accompanied by an affidavit of counsel stating that Schlagenhauf admitted on deposition that he had seen the red lights of the trailer 10 to 15 seconds prior to the collision and yet had driven on without change of speed or course; that the only eyewitness testified that he also had been approaching the trailer from the rear and had seen the lights from three-quarters to one-half mile away; and that Schlagenhauf also admitted in his deposition that he had been involved in a prior rear-end collision of a similar type.

While the application was pending, trailer owner answered the cross-claim and, in addition, made a claim against bus owner and Schlagenhauf for damage to the trailer caused by his negligence when both knew he had defective vision.

The district court granted the requested examinations, and the court of appeals refused to vacate this order upon a petition for mandamus.[b] The denial of mandamus reached the Supreme Court upon its granting Schlagenhauf's petition for certiorari.

After considering the threshold problem whether mandamus was a proper avenue for review and deciding that it was, the Supreme Court dealt with Schlagenhauf's contentions that application of Rule 35 to defendants (which no federal court had previously done) was a violation of the Rules Enabling Act and an unconstitutional invasion of privacy. How might it be argued that these issues remained open after Sibbach v. Wilson & Co.? The Court also considered Schlagenhauf's contentions that he was not an opposing party vis-à-vis the discovering parties, that his physical and mental condition was not "in controversy," and that "good cause" had not been shown.

How should the case be decided?

———

Questions: (67) One of the Justices thought that the problem should be referred to the Civil Rules Committee of the Judicial Conference so that, if the Rule was to be applied to defendants, the standards and conditions might be made discriminating and precise. He referred to the need in that setting to safeguard "against the awful risks of blackmail." What do you think he meant by "blackmail" ? What standards and conditions would you prescribe to safeguard against those "risks" ?

(68) Should the examined party be entitled to have his attorney present during the medical examination? See Brandenberg v. El Al Israel Airlines, 79 F.R.D. 543 (S.D.N.Y.1978) (no, with respect to a court-ordered psychiatric examination of Mrs. Brandenberg).

Supplementation of responses (Rule 26(e)).—If discovery answers that were actually or presumably correct and complete when given come to be revealed as inaccurate or incomplete by reason of later events or newly acquired knowledge, the discovering party may be seriously misled by relying upon them. But an obligation to supplement may be extremely onerous because it will force the responding party's lawyer to keep checking for new bits of information and matching them against the prior answers.

Prior to the 1970 amendments, the law was in an uncertain state as to the duty of keeping answers up-to-date. What could, say, an interrogating party do to protect himself? He could put later interrogatories, but this was a burden on both parties. Some courts by local rule or judicial decision imposed a general duty of supplementation. Some litigants in particular cases tried to do the equivalent by including in their initial set of interrogatories a request to that effect or by seeking a court order or party agreement to similar effect.

Rule 26(e) now deals with the problem in a way designed to minimize the burden on the responding party and at the same time to protect the discovering party from being seriously misled. It pro-

[b] Petitioning for the extraordinary remedy of mandamus sometimes functions as a kind of irregular means of se- curing review of district-court action by the court of appeals. See 28 U.S.C. § 1651 and Topic D of Part Eight.

vides that there is no duty to supplement responses except in three main situations: (1) when the responding party has new information about the identity or location of persons with knowledge of discoverable matters; ᶜ (2) when the responding party obtains information from which he actually knows that his response was incorrect when made; and (3) when the responding party obtains information from which he actually knows that his response is no longer true and the circumstances are such that a failure to amend it would be "in substance a knowing concealment." See also Rule 26(e)(3).

It is to be noted that although problems about supplementation have arisen chiefly with respect to interrogatories, the new Rule applies in terms to all requests for discovery.

Questions: (69) Apart from any provision by Rule, is an attorney ethically justified in standing silently by and letting an opponent be deceived by answers he knows are no longer true? Cf. N.Y. County Lawyers' Ass'n Comm. on Professional Ethics, Op. 309 (1933), which is reprinted infra p. 266.

(70) What might a federal trial judge appropriately do if a party called at trial a witness whose identity had not been disclosed by the party in either original or supplemental answers to interrogatories directed to the point?

(71) Suppose you are counsel in a personal-injury case in which, during the discovery phase, you have fully complied with a request to identify all known witnesses with knowledge of the facts in litigation. When the trial is nearly over, a witness previously unknown to you appears and tells you that he read of the case in the newspaper and that he was an eyewitness to the accident. His story is favorable to your client's case. What should you do? Suppose instead his story is very unfavorable to your client's case. What, if anything, should you do?

Use of products of discovery in court proceedings [Rule 32].— The mere presence of, say, a deposition in the court files does not mean that the court will consider it in deciding the action. Usually a deposition will be ignored unless a party elects to offer it in evidence. Indeed, the use by the court of a deposition that has not been introduced into evidence is generally improper and may amount to reversible error.

Rule 32 deals with the use by parties of depositions. The big barrier to introducing a deposition at a hearing or at the trial is the hearsay rule, which as we shall soon see is a rule of evidence that in general renders out-of-court statements inadmissible and thus would tend to exclude all depositions. Rule 32(a) lists a series of circumstances—such as sometimes when the deponent is presently unavailable to testify—and provides that in those circumstances the hearsay rule should not apply to exclude a deposition simply because it embodies out-of-court statements. In sum, in those circumstances a deposition may be used "so far as admissible under the rules of evi-

---

ᶜ There is also a provision for supplementing information concerning persons to be called as expert witnesses at trial.

dence applied as though the witness were then present and testifying."

Questions: (72) Rule 32(a)(3)(E) overrides the hearsay rule if the court finds "exceptional circumstances," but in making its finding the court is to give "due regard to the importance of presenting the testimony of witnesses orally in open court." See also Rule 43(a). Why the preference for live testimony?

(73) What explains the special treatment in Rule 32(a)(2) of the deposition of a party?

Rule 32 regulates only the use of depositions in court proceedings. What about the use in court proceedings of the products of other discovery methods—answers to interrogatories, documents, etc.? In general, it is correct to say simply that these may be used so far as admissible under all the rules of evidence. For example, the plaintiff in the Freed case below could introduce at trial the defendant's answer to an interrogatory under the rule that relevant out-of-court statements by the party-opponent are generally admissible in evidence, as soon to be explained.

FREED v. ERIE LACKAWANNA RAILWAY

United States Court of Appeals, Sixth Circuit, 1971.
445 F.2d 619, cert. denied, 404 U.S. 1017, 92 S.Ct. 678 (1972).

Before PECK, BROOKS and KENT, CIRCUIT JUDGES.

BROOKS, CIRCUIT JUDGE. Plaintiff-appellant, Floyd W. Freed, III, brought this action under the Federal Employers' Liability Act against defendant-appellee, Erie Lackawanna Railway Company, for personal injuries sustained when he was struck by a train. This appeal follows a jury verdict for the defendant [in 1969].

At the time plaintiff was injured, he was the head brakeman on a freight train running from Cleveland to Youngstown, Ohio. The accident occurred in the North Randall switching area where there were numerous sets of tracks and switching operations were frequent. The plaintiff and the fireman, a fellow crewman, had just dropped off their train and had started walking down a right-of-way adjacent to a side track on their way to lunch when plaintiff was struck by a caboose, which was the lead car of a switching train that was slowly backing in performance of its switching assignment. Seconds before getting in the path of the train, plaintiff's attention was diverted when the fireman turned and called to the engineer of the freight train to throw him his cigarettes which he had forgotten and left in the cab of the locomotive.

The principal issue raised by plaintiff on appeal is whether an answer made by the defendant to an interrogatory is binding on it although contradicted by other evidence adduced by the defendant. In response to one of plaintiff's interrogatories, defendant stated that the location of the switch train at the time of the accident was not within the yard limits. A train that is not within yard limits was subject to road rule Number 103 which requires cars being pushed by engines in an area outside the yard limits to have a lookout posted on the lead car. There was no such lookout on the car of the switch train that injured the plaintiff. At trial the defendant produced testimony that the switch train was actually operating within the yard limits and, therefore, no lookout on the lead car was required, thus contradicting the answer given in the interrogatory as to the location of the train at the time of the accident.

While the jury was deliberating, the jury foreman submitted a question to the court asking if the switch train was within the yard limits at the time of the accident. The court declined to answer the question on the grounds that it involved a question of fact which it was the duty of the jury to resolve. Plaintiff argues that the answer to the interrogatory, when introduced in evidence, was . . . binding on the defendant, and therefore the court should have answered the jury's question in accordance with the answer given in the interrogatory. . . . As stated in Victory Carriers, Inc. v. Stockton Stevedoring Company, [388 F.2d 955 (9th Cir.1968)]:

> "An answer to an interrogatory is comparable to answers, which may be mistaken, given in deposition testimony or during the course of the trial itself. Answers to interrogatories must often be supplied before investigation is completed and can rest only upon knowledge which is available at the time. When there is conflict between answers supplied in response to interrogatories and answers obtained through other questioning, either in deposition or trial, the finder of fact must weigh all of the answers and resolve the conflict."

The court properly declined to answer the question dealing with the location of the switch train at the time of the accident.

. . . .

Affirmed.

[The concurring opinion of Judge Peck is omitted.]

Questions: (74) Would the decision in the Freed case have been different if the plaintiff had utilized Rule 36 rather than Rule 33?

(75) Would the decision have been different under present Rule 26(e)?

Sanctions for failure to make discovery [Rule 37].—We have referred at a number of points to the discovering party's motion under Rule 37(a) for a directive order—an order compelling discovery. Note the court to which such a motion is addressed; the use of the motion to enforce various duties under Rules 30, 31, 33, and 34; and the possibilities of securing reimbursement of expenses incurred in making or defending against the motion. Rule 37(b) states the sanctions for refusals to obey such directive orders.

In general, when the discovering party is faced with recalcitrance, he must assume the burden, first, of going to court to get a directive order and, second, in case of continued recalcitrance, of going to court to obtain a sanction. And although it may be open to another party or a deponent to seek a protective order under Rule 26(c) or relief under Rule 30(d) in anticipation of an application for a directive order, this is optional and is not a condition of avoiding a directive order. But some qualifications are needed here.

First, Rule 37(d) provides that in certain cases of gross failure of a party to comply with the process for giving discovery, the discovering party need not first apply for a directive order but instead may apply for a sanction forthwith; and the party from whom discovery is sought is not permitted to excuse his failure on the ground that the discovery sought was objectionable unless he has applied previously for a protective order. The gross failures referred to are failure to appear for deposition, to serve any answers or objections to interrogatories, or to serve any written response to a request for inspection. See also Rule 45(f).

Second, because Rule 35 requires a preliminary court order, Rule 37(a) and (d) has no application. The discovering party may proceed immediately to seek sanctions for disobedience under Rule 37(b).

Third, orders and sanctions for failure to make discovery under Rule 36 are specially treated in Rules 36(a) and 37(c).

General problems.—Discovery on the broad scale envisaged by the Federal Rules gradually came to be generally accepted by the bar, but not without some lingering doubts and second thoughts. Thus it has been suggested that compliant or unscrupulous witnesses, having gone through the informing experience of testifying on deposition themselves, or having learned about the results of other discovery, can contrive to manipulate their stories to meet all exigencies when they finally testify at trial. The critics of discovery view "surprise" at trial—at least up to a point—as a promoter of truth rather than the opposite.

Apart from this basic dispute over the value of discovery, there is the risk of discovery abuse and recalcitrance. Thus, for example, all would agree that if carried on without decent restraint, discovery could give wealthy litigants excellent opportunities to browbeat their weaker adversaries. For discovery can be made very expensive. And, of course, the oppressive sword of discovery cuts both ways. It may be used in nuisance suits to extort unjust settlements from wealthy litigants, who realize it is sometimes cheaper to buy off opponents than to defend. A survey conducted by the Columbia Project for Effective Justice in aid of the 1970 revision of the discovery Rules tended to indicate that discovery has generally been kept within reasonable bounds of expense;[d] but the possibility that a party will attempt through discovery to price a lawsuit out of the market for his adversary—and might succeed despite the protections offered by such provisions as Rule 26(c)—must be real in many cases.

Added to these truth and fairness costs are simple laments over the time and expense consumed even by proper discovery, especially in those *occasional* cases where that consumption reaches almost unimaginable heights. Ultimately, an argument that can be made is that together all these different kinds of costs outweigh any benefits of discovery—at the least, a conclusion that cannot be denied is that the system must make an effort to lower those costs.

During the 1970's these complaints about the burdens of discovery grew more intense. Various proposals to limit and control discovery circulated.[e] In response, the Supreme Court in 1980 and 1983 adopted a series of relatively modest amendments to the discovery Rules. See the sections of the Rules pamphlet containing those amendments and the Advisory Committee's notes thereon.

Perhaps the singly most significant of these changes is the new Rule 26(f), which aims at controlling abuse of discovery in a big or unusual case by establishing a plan for discovery. If the parties and attorneys are unable to frame a plan by agreement, the court can step in through the mechanism of a "discovery conference," which culminates in a court order governing discovery. For enforcement, see Rule 37(g) and (b)(2). This innovation should to some degree facilitate a more active but selective case-by-case supervision of discovery by the court—such supervision probably being the most effective remedy for discovery abuse and recalcitrance, and explicit amendments to the Rules arguably being required to overcome judicial reluctance to use existing powers of control.

(g) Pretrial Conferences

[Rule 16]

Playing in with pleadings and with discovery—serving some of the same functions and also having distinct missions—are the pretrial conferences provided for by Rule 16. Note the objectives and range of this procedure as given in Rule 16(a) and (c).

Until 1983, Rule 16 was a brief and relatively uncomplicated Rule. Practice thereunder, although highly variable in response to obvious

[d] See Advisory Committee's Explanatory Statement Concerning Amendments of the Discovery Rules, which begins the section of the Rules pamphlet containing the 1970 amendments. See generally W. Glaser, Pretrial Discovery and the Adversary System (1968).

[e] See, e.g., Section of Litigation, ABA, Report of the Special Committee for the Study of Discovery Abuse (1977), reprinted in 92 F.R.D. 149 (1982). See generally D. Segal, Survey of the Literature on Discovery from 1970 to the Present: Expressed Dissatisfactions and Proposed Reforms (1978).

tensions, was generally rather noncoercive, informal, simple, and flexible. See McCargo v. Hedrick, 545 F.2d 393 (4th Cir.1976). The court could call the attorneys together and would do so typically once late in the litigation to consider with them what the points in controversy were and how the trial of the action might be facilitated.

In 1983, Rule 16 was rewritten in expansive form, certainly changing the tone thereof if not the practice thereunder. Case management by the judge from the institution of suit was the new emphasis, motivated by the "widespread feeling" that modern litigation demanded a move in that direction. See the lengthy Advisory Committee's note on the amended Rule in the section of the Rules pamphlet dealing with the 1983 amendments. The empirical and theoretical bases for this change were, respectively, quite scanty and disputed. Moreover, it was not clear that detailed rulemaking was the most desirable route to reform. But only the future can rule on the wisdom of the amendment.

The initial step in the new procedure is the scheduling order of Rule 16(b). In most cases, within 120 days of commencement, the court *must* after consultation fix time limits for settling pleadings, hearing motions, and completing discovery.

Then there *may* be one or more pretrial conferences. Indeed, a scheduling conference may have preceded the scheduling order under Rule 16(b). One or more pretrial conferences may be held relatively early in the litigation to address some of the pretrial concerns listed in Rule 16(c). A final pretrial conference, which can be especially useful when the parties have obtained substantial discovery, may be held shortly before trial to formulate a plan for trial, as prescribed in Rule 16(d).

Although Rule 16 does not in terms provide for it, most courts require the attorneys for both sides to confer prior to a pretrial conference and to agree if possible upon a joint pretrial statement, or to file separate pretrial statements indicating their respective positions. Many districts have local rules on this subject, some of which at least literally require fairly extensive preparation by counsel.

The actual conduct of a pretrial conference is not specified by the Rule and is the subject of considerable disagreement. For example, judges differ in their views about the propriety and wisdom of introducing the subject of settlement or urging it on the parties. (Why so?) Perhaps settlement talk should arise, if at all, only as a natural by-product of a businesslike pretrial conference aimed at shaping the litigation. Or perhaps judges should take an active role in pushing for settlement. There has in fact been a wide range of practice, but recently there has been a noticeable shift toward activism. Since 1983, Rule 16(c)(7) expressly mentions settlement and the note thereon even suggests the possibility of a settlement conference. The Rule's new emphasis can only accelerate that shift toward activism.

More generally, use of the pretrial conference is optional with the court. The actual practice varies from district to district: in some districts there is a conference in each case, in others its use is confined to selected cases, and in still others it has been resorted to perfunctorily if at all. The degree to which particular judges take an active part in molding the case varies considerably, depending not only upon the temperaments of the judges but also upon their views of what their role is or should be in the litigation process.

Question: (76) Can a question of propriety ever arise as to whether the pretrial judge should be permitted to preside at the trial?

The role of the pretrial conference likewise may vary from case to case. The expense and effort entailed in a conference may not be warranted for a small, simple case. In an average case there might be a single, "final" pretrial conference. And in large or complex litigation, such as antitrust cases and class actions, extensive use of conferences is found nearly indispensable; the semi-official Manual for Complex Litigation gives elaborate advice about how to employ conferences at intervals (usually in a series of at least four conferences) to elucidate the issues, organize and control discovery, and otherwise prepare the "big case" for trial.

IDENTISEAL CORP. v. POSITIVE IDENTIFICATION SYSTEMS, INC.

United States Court of Appeals, Seventh Circuit, 1977.
560 F.2d 298.

Before SWYGERT and BAUER, CIRCUIT JUDGES, and JAMESON, SENIOR DISTRICT JUDGE.[1]

SWYGERT, CIRCUIT JUDGE. The outcome of this appeal turns on whether the district court, in presiding over the pretrial phase of the case, had the power to compel plaintiff to conduct discovery instead of permitting it to litigate the entire suit at trial. We conclude that the district court lacked the authority to compel involuntary discovery and we reverse the court's order dismissing the complaint.

. . . . .

On April 26, 1973, plaintiff Identiseal Corporation of Wisconsin filed a complaint against defendant Positive Identification Systems, Inc. in the district court for the Eastern District of Wisconsin. The complaint charged that defendant induced plaintiff to enter into a franchising agreement for the sale of a product known as "Identiseal"; that defendant represented to plaintiff that defendant was successful in the promotion of its products, causing plaintiff to invest $15,000 in defendant's products; and that in fact defendant was not

[1] The Honorable William J. Jameson, Senior District Judge for the District of Montana, is sitting by designation.

successful in the promotion of its products. Plaintiff sought relief under a common law theory of misrepresentation and under Wisconsin statutes relating to franchising. Jurisdiction was based on diversity of citizenship.

After a delay caused by the death of plaintiff's attorney, the litigation proceeded and a final pretrial conference was held on February 26, 1976. On March 8, 1976, the district court issued an order in which it concluded "that the pretrial work necessary to efficiently try this action had not been done." It ordered that the action be dismissed for want of prosecution, but stayed the order until June 4, 1976 and stated that the order would be vacated if plaintiff's counsel had conducted specified discovery . . . by that date.[2]

. . . Plaintiff's counsel [argued to no avail] that he had "made a considered judgment that discovery would in no way be beneficial to the plaintiff's interest and would at most be of some significant support or assistance to the defendant." He also asserted that the court had exceeded its authority under the Federal Rules of Civil Procedure in ordering plaintiff to conduct discovery or suffer dismissal of the complaint.

[The district court ultimately dismissed the action without prejudice pursuant to the March 8 order, and the plaintiff appealed.]

Discovery in lawsuits in the federal courts is governed by Rules 26 to 37 of the Federal Rules of Civil Procedure. Although these rules provide for judicial intervention to settle disputes about the scope of discovery and to enforce a legitimate request by one party for information or documents from the other party, they do not give district judges the authority to compel a litigant to engage in discovery in the first place.

Therefore, the district court's March 8 order can only be upheld if the court had the power, under its general authority over the pretrial phase of a lawsuit, to compel plaintiff to conduct discovery. Pretrial procedure in the district courts is governed by Fed.R.Civ.P. 16, which states in relevant part that "the court may in its discretion direct the attorneys for the parties to appear before it for a conference to consider . . . [t]he possibility of obtaining admissions of fact and of documents which will avoid unnecessary proof." Under the rule,

---

[2] The court held that its order of dismissal would be vacated if plaintiff's counsel satisfied the following conditions:

1. Counsel shall, by means of discovery such as written interrogatories, requests for production of documents, or requests for admissions, ascertain the identity of those persons who have knowledge of the facts relevant or material to the issues of this action and those documents containing information relevant or material to the issues of this action.

2. Counsel shall then, by means of further discovery such as oral depositions or deposition on written questions, determine the actual knowledge of such persons disclosed as having knowledge of the facts. Counsel shall also, by means of requests for production of documents or requests for admissions, obtain copies of relevant documents not already within their possession.

. . . . .

"the court has wide discretion and power to advance the cause and simplify the procedure before the cause is presented to the jury." O'Malley v. Chrysler Corp., 160 F.2d 35, 36 (7th Cir.1947).

This discretion, however, is not unlimited. The language of the rule does not, by its terms, confer upon the court the power to *compel* the litigants to obtain admissions of fact and of documents even if it is clear that such admissions would simplify the trial of the case. Instead, the rule requires the parties to appear and *consider the possibility* of admissions which would lessen their task at trial.

We have recently decided a case in which we made clear that there are limitations on the district court's power at the pretrial conference. In J.F. Edwards Construction Co. v. Anderson Safeway Guard Rail Corp., 542 F.2d 1318 (7th Cir.1976) (per curiam), we held that a district court lacks the authority under Rule 16 to dismiss an action because one of the parties would not agree to a stipulation of facts. We noted that Rule 16 was noncoercive in nature, and we concluded that a dismissal based on a party's refusal to follow the trial judge's wishes expressed at the pretrial conference could only be upheld if that refusal could be characterized as a "failure to prosecute." Because the party that would not agree to the stipulation of facts was clearly not attempting to avoid trial, the district court's order could not stand.

In our judgment this appeal is controlled by J.F. Edwards. Like the appellant in J.F. Edwards, plaintiff in the case at bar did not engage in conduct that could be characterized as a failure to prosecute. Plaintiff was ready to go to trial, and simply disagreed with the district court about the desirability of eliminating the need to develop all of the facts at trial. Although we recognize that its order was based on a commendable desire to simplify the lawsuit, the court had no more authority under Rule 16 to command discovery than the district court in J.F. Edwards had to require a stipulation of facts. The limit of the court's power was to compel plaintiff to consider the possibility of conducting discovery,[7] and there is no evidence in the record that plaintiff's attorney rejected the district court's preferred method of litigating the action without giving it serious consideration.

Our decision is predicated on more than the absence of express authority in Rule 16 authorizing compulsory discovery. It is also based on the traditional principle that the parties, rather than the court, should determine litigation strategy. See Chayes, The Role of the Judge in Public Law Litigation, 89 Harv.L.Rev. 1281, 1283 (1976); Developments in the Law—Class Actions, 89 Harv.L.Rev. 1318, 1414 (1976). It was the judgment of plaintiff's attorney that his client's chances of prevailing would be maximized if he did not conduct discovery but instead developed his entire case at trial. We cannot say whether this decision was correct. We can say, however, that the

[7] We note that our resolution of this issue is in conflict with the Third Circuit's decision in Buffington v. Wood, 351 F.2d 292 (3d Cir.1965). . . .

decision was for plaintiff's attorney, and not the district court, to make.

The judgment of the district court is reversed and the cause is remanded for further proceedings consistent with this opinion.

Question: (77) Is Identiseal still good law under amended Rule 16? Is J.F. Edwards?

A pretrial conference culminates in an order that, according to Rule 16(e), "shall control the subsequent course of the action unless modified." The order may articulate in a convenient and helpful way the remaining controverted issues. Even though the pleadings are not in terms amended by the order (as they may be), in practice the order has the effect of superseding the pleadings. And as the order is binding on the parties, evidence need not be offered at the trial to prove a proposition established in the order, nor will contrary evidence be admitted.

Question: (78) Should a party be permitted to offer evidence on a proposition established in his favor in the pretrial order? Why might he want to do so?

SHUBER v. S.S. KRESGE CO., 458 F.2d 1058 (3d Cir.1972), aff'g 55 F.R.D. 52 (W.D.Pa.1970). Wife-plaintiff brought a diversity action against Kresge in federal court for personal injuries, in which her husband joined with a claim for her medical expenses and the loss of her services. The theory of recovery was that defendant had been negligent in installing or having installed a light fixture that fell upon wife-plaintiff while she was working in defendant's store in 1965. As required by the local rule for pretrial procedure, plaintiffs set forth this theory in a narrative pretrial statement and also listed therein "plaintiff" (not "plaintiffs") as a witness on the issue of liability. There was no indication that husband-plaintiff, an electrician by trade, was to testify concerning the fixture. At trial plaintiffs' evidence, including wife-plaintiff's testimony, pointed to the contention that the fixture had been negligently installed by an electrical subcontractor to the construction company employed by Kresge's landlord; but the evidence failed to connect Kresge with the negligence. Kresge moved for a directed verdict at the close of plaintiffs' case. After argument on the motion, plaintiffs moved for leave to reopen to call a witness not listed in the pretrial statement. Counsel announced that he intended to call husband-plaintiff to testify that Kresge itself installed the ceiling tiles and, in doing so, disconnected the light fixtures and reinstalled them negligently; husband-plaintiff was further to testify that the defective installation would be apparent on reasonable inspection. Defendant objected to the complete change of the theory of liability. Wife-plaintiff had testified on deposition that her husband had no knowledge of the facts of the accident, and he had been present throughout the trial without any suggestion that he had such evidence to offer.

The trial judge refused to allow plaintiffs' case to be reopened and granted defendant's motion for a directed verdict, saying:

"[T]he Court has an interest to support the integrity of its pretrial procedures. The Pretrial Order in the case binds and limits the parties to what they have presented and revealed in their Pretrial Narratives and at the Pretrial Conference. Neither at the Pretrial Conference, nor in the trial was this new line of evidence suggested. We must either require adherence to our Pretrial Rules or abandon them utterly in this case. We think that the interests of the efficient administration of justice require their enforcement."

The court of appeals affirmed, expressing itself as thoroughly in accord with the trial judge's statement. The court of appeals commented that counsel's inadequate prosecution of his clients' cause "would appear to be in violation of the Code of Professional Responsibility of the American Bar Association requiring a lawyer to represent his client competently and zealously within the bounds of the law."

The trial judge in Shuber referred to the statement of Judge (now Chief Justice) Burger in Washington Hospital Center v. Cheeks, 394 F.2d 964, 965 (D.C.Cir.1968), that liberal modification of pretrial orders encourages careless preparation but that an unbending attitude may work grave injustice. In that case, a medical malpractice action, the testimony of plaintiff's attending physician surprised plaintiff's counsel, who sought leave the next day to offer an expert medical witness not on the pretrial list. The court modified the pretrial order and let the expert testify the following day, first giving defendant a chance to depose him; defendant did not request a longer continuance or mistrial, but took the deposition and sought only to exclude the new testimony. The expert's testimony supported plaintiff's claim, and verdict and judgment were for plaintiff. The court of appeals held that there was no abuse of discretion.

Question: (79) A complaint alleged that *P* and *D* had entered into an oral partnership to sell certain oil-well drilling equipment on commission, that any commission was to be equally divided, and that a commission of over $39,000 had been paid to *D*, who had paid *P* only $3000. The answer denied any partnership, and stated that *P* had demanded a portion of the commission for services performed in the sale and that *D* had paid *P* $3000 in full satisfaction of *P*'s claim. The pretrial order included agreement as to the amount of the commission and the amount paid to *P*, and it recited that the only matter of controversy to be determined by the jury was whether a partnership existed. At trial the jury was charged on the question of partnership without any objection, but at the end of the charge the judge refused to instruct on the issue of compromise settlement on the ground that it was not within the pretrial order. Should *D*'s appeal from this refusal be sustained? See Case v. Abrams, 352 F.2d 193 (10th Cir.1965) (no). Should it matter that *D*'s proof in support of the compromise settlement had been admitted without objection? Of what relevance is Rule 15(b)?

Finally, Rule 16(f) expressly provides for sanctions that might be imposed for certain violations of the Rule.

(h) Devices for Terminating Litigation Without Trial

[Rules 12(c), 56]

We have already seen a number of ways in which a case may be terminated short of trial. For example, if defendant presents by motion under Rule 12(b)(6) the defense that the complaint fails to state a claim upon which relief can be granted, and the motion is granted, and the complaint is not thereafter amended, then the case is ripe for a judgment for defendant.

Question: (80) In what other ways may a case be terminated short of trial?

Motion for judgment on the pleadings.—We call attention now to another device that may also conclude the case without trial. Rule 12(c) provides for a motion for judgment on the pleadings. This motion is made after the pleadings are closed, and it asserts that upon the pleadings the moving party is entitled to judgment in his favor on a particular claim. It can be used only to resolve questions of law, not disputes as to facts.

Suppose the complaint adequately alleges a claim, and the answer admits the allegations of the complaint but sets up two purported affirmative defenses. If one but not both of the defenses is insufficient as a matter of law, a timely motion lies under Rule 12(f) to strike that defense; when that motion is granted, the insufficient defense is eliminated, but the case will stand for trial on the other defense. If, however, both defenses are insufficient, plaintiff may move for judgment on the pleadings.

The moving party admits his adversary's allegations for purposes of the Rule 12(c) motion, but his own allegations are taken as true only if they have been admitted by his opponent's pleading. Thus, in the example last given, if defendant, besides setting up the two insufficient defenses, had denied in his answer material allegations of the complaint, plaintiff's motion for judgment on the pleadings would have been denied, although a motion under Rule 12(f) to strike the affirmative defenses would have been granted.

A motion by defendant for judgment on the pleadings ordinarily challenges the legal sufficiency of the complaint only, just as does a motion under Rule 12(b)(6). It takes on no added strength by reason of one or more affirmative defenses in the answer. For, as we have seen, the allegations of such defenses are taken as denied or avoided under Rule 8(d).

Questions: (81) *P* files a complaint attempting to allege defamation. *D* answers, admitting *P*'s factual allegations and attempting to assert the defense of privilege. *D* moves for judgment on the pleadings. What are the facts for purposes of the motion? What legal issues are raised by the motion? *P* moves for judgment on the pleadings at the same point. What are the facts for purposes of this motion? What legal issues are raised?

(82) Suppose that, instead of admitting *P*'s factual allegations, *D* denies them and also attempts to assert the defense of privilege. What relief can *P* get if the privilege defense is insufficient as a matter of law? In what manner may *P* pursue that relief? Does it matter how much time has elapsed since service of *D*'s answer?

Motion for summary judgment.—The motion for judgment on the pleadings is available where a pleading is legally insufficient. But must there necessarily be a trial whenever the pleadings show a disputed issue of fact, either by an actual denial of an adversary's allegation or through the operation of Rule 8(d)? If so, the "just, speedy, and inexpensive determination of every action" set forth as the ideal in Rule 1 could not be achieved. In certain district courts, the trial list for civil cases is in such a congested condition that the median lapse of time between the filing of an answer and a trial on the merits is over two years. A defendant against whom a just claim has been asserted is likely to want to put off the day of reckoning as long as possible. There is a temptation, despite Rule 11, to file an answer with denials or affirmative defenses for purposes of delay, even though the pleader knows that he is doomed to defeat at the trial. Similarly, a plaintiff may assert a baseless claim in order to harass.

Rule 56, "Summary Judgment," provides a means of going behind the pleadings to see whether there really is any genuine issue as to any material fact. If there is not, there is no occasion for a trial, and the case is ripe for a motion for summary judgment. Such a motion may be filed by either a plaintiff or a defendant in any type of case. The motion may be made even before the pleadings are closed. See Rule 56(a) and (b).

On such a motion, the movant maintains that there is no genuine issue of material fact and that, upon resolution of any disputed questions of law, he is entitled to judgment as a matter of law. Ordinarily the motion will be accompanied by affidavits (of the moving party or of others) in support of the contention of the moving party that there is no genuine issue of fact. The affidavits may incorporate exhibits; the affidavits must be on the personal knowledge of the affiants; and the contents of the affidavits must be such as would be admissible in evidence. The opposing party may file like counter-affidavits. See Rule 56(e). On the motion the court will also consider the pleadings—and may consider depositions, answers to interrogatories, admissions, and similar material on file, to the extent they represent admissible evidence.

A motion for summary judgment is not intended as a means of trying questions of fact upon conflicting affidavits. The function of the court on this motion is to determine whether there is a genuine factual dispute, not to resolve a genuine factual dispute found to exist. Hence, if on the motion such a dispute is found, the motion must be denied even though the judge has strong ground for the belief that one set of affidavits is true and the other false.

Questions: (83) May summary judgment ever be granted by a judge where the case is of a type in which trial by jury is constitutionally guaranteed and proper demand for a jury has been made?

(84) Rule 32(a) speaks of the use of a deposition not only at trial, but also "upon the hearing of a motion or an interlocutory proceeding." Can Rule 32 be applied according to its terms when depositions are used upon a motion for summary judgment under Rule 56(c)? (This question should be renewed after reading the American Airlines case below.)

A summary judgment may be granted on the entire case or only on a part of it. For example, a summary judgment may be granted on the issue of liability alone, although there is a genuine issue on the amount of damages. See Rule 56(c). You will note further from Rule 56(d) that upon motion for summary judgment an order may be made "specifying the facts that appear without substantial controversy," thus narrowing the issues for trial in somewhat the same way as the pretrial procedure under Rule 16.

AMERICAN AIRLINES v. ULEN

United States Court of Appeals, District of Columbia Circuit, 1949.
186 F.2d 529.

Before CLARK, WILBUR K. MILLER, and PRETTYMAN, JUDGES.

CLARK, JUDGE. Appellant, American Airlines, Inc., a certified carrier engaged in the business of transporting passengers for hire, separately appeals from two final judgments of the District Court. The appeal in No. 9921 attacks the judgment based upon a jury verdict for $25,000 in favor of appellee, Violet Ulen, for personal injuries and property damage. The appeal in No. 9922 was taken from a judgment based on a jury verdict for $2,500 in favor of appellee, Francis Graeme Ulen, husband of Violet Ulen, for medical and other expenses resulting from his wife's injuries and for loss of her services. These two appeals were consolidated for the purpose of filing briefs and for hearing and decision by order of this court dated July 24, 1948. Accordingly, this opinion shall dispose of both appeals.

At about midnight on February 22–23, 1945, Violet Ulen boarded appellant's plane at Washington National Airport with a ticket entitling her to transportation to Mexico City, Mexico. The plane took off from Washington at 12:15 A.M. on February 23, 1945. At approximately 2:25 A.M. that morning, appellant's plane, with Violet Ulen aboard, crashed close to the summit of Glade Mountain near the town of Rural Retreat in Southwest Virginia. The crash, in which both the pilot and the co-pilot of the plane lost their lives, resulted, admittedly, in very serious and aggravated injury to Violet Ulen and in her permanent partial disability.

On January 11, 1946, the Ulens both filed complaints in the District Court alleging that their injuries and losses directly resulted from the negligence of agents of the appellant in carelessly planning and approving the flight and in unskillfully operating the plane. The complaint filed by Violet Ulen sought recovery in the amount of $257,500. Mr. Ulen's complaint asked for $50,000 in damages. Appellant carrier answered both complaints by admitting the facts alleged but denying that the injuries were caused by its negligence and disclaiming any knowledge of the extent of Violet Ulen's injuries. Thereupon the Ulens served a set of 55 interrogatories on appellant and these were answered in detail by appellant. The Ulens then filed motions for summary judgment in their favor and to impanel a jury for the purpose of determining damages. As grounds for these motions the Ulens asserted that the pleadings together with the carrier's answers to the interrogatories demonstrated that there was no genuine issue as to any material fact except as to damages. After these motions for summary judgment came on for oral argument in the court below, appellant carrier filed a motion for leave to amend its answers to the complaints by including additional defenses. At the same time appellant filed its opposition to the motions for summary judgment. On July 14, 1947, Judge Morris entered a memorandum opinion in which he indicated his intention of granting the motions for summary judgment in favor of the Ulens, but in which he also indicated that decision on the motions would be continued in order to allow the filing by the carrier of an amended answer. A court order to that effect was entered below and appellant filed its amended answer which added the additional defense that Violet Ulen was a passenger in international transportation within the purview of the Warsaw Convention,[1] and hence that total recovery, if any, is limited thereby to the sum of $8,291.87.[2]

On November 12, 1947, the motions for summary judgment were granted and the cases were assigned for inquisition by a jury as to the amount of damages. The court expressly reserved the defense based upon the Warsaw Convention for disposition by the court at the time of such inquisition. In April, 1948, the two cases were tried together before a jury. Defendant-appellant moved for directed verdicts both at the close of plaintiffs' case and at the close of all the evidence, but said motions were overruled. The jury then returned verdicts for Violet Ulen in the amount of $25,000 and for her husband in the amount of $2,500 and judgments thereon were entered. Fol-

[1] 49 Stat. (Part 2) 3000 (1929).

[2] Under Article 22 of the Warsaw Convention the liability of the carrier for each passenger was limited to the sum of 125,000 francs. It is agreed by the parties to this appeal that the figure above is the equivalent, in United States currency, of $8,291.87.

lowing the denial of various other motions of the carrier, separate appeals were taken from those judgments.

Appellant raises two major issues on these appeals which shall be dealt with separately herein. First, appellant asserts that plaintiff-appellees were not entitled to summary judgment. Second, it is vigorously urged that, if there is any liability at all, it is definitely limited in amount by the applicable provisions of the Warsaw Convention.

Appellant's first point is that summary judgment was erroneously granted and to its great prejudice, because the *pleadings* (that is, the complaint alleging negligence and the answer as amended denying any negligence) raised genuine issues as to material facts which could only have been properly determined by a trial on the merits. Thus far, we have no difficulty in agreeing with appellant and, in fact, appellees concede that this contention, so far as it goes, is correct. However, it is vitally significant that *before* summary judgment was granted the trial judge had before him not only the complaint and the answer as amended but also the 55 interrogatories of plaintiffs and all of defendant's detailed, sworn answers thereto as well as a lengthy "Defendant's Brief in Opposition to Motion for Summary Judgment." . . .

The answers to the interrogatories which Judge Morris had before him in this case show undeniably that appellant was negligent. The answers show that appellant's authorized and experienced agents planned, agreed upon, and were in the process of executing, a flight plan which called for the plane to fly at an altitude of 4000 feet on the leg of the flight on which the accident occurred (Pulaski to Tri-City). From the flight log kept by the pilot during this particular flight it is clear that he was following this flight plan up to the time of his last entry. The last radio contact with the plane while in flight was received at 2:05 A.M. (about 20 minutes before the crash) when the pilot reported his altitude as 4000 feet. At the time this flight was planned and flown there was in effect a Civil Air Regulation [No. 61.7401] promulgated by the Civil Aeronautics Board which read as follows:

"No scheduled air carrier aircraft shall be flown at an altitude of less than 1000 feet above the highest obstacle located within a horizontal distance of 5 miles from the center of the course intended to be flown, ..."

The answers to the interrogatories show further that appellant's plane crashed at an elevation of 3910 feet near the summit of Glade Mountain which was located near the center of Green Airway No. 5, a strip ten miles wide over which the plane was scheduled to, and did, fly. The answers admit that a certain chart apparently in appellant's possession indicates that "the terrain [Glade Mountain] is more than 3500 ft. high but less than 4000 ft. above sea level."

We have no difficulty in finding, as did the lower court, that negligence and proximate cause were sufficiently established so as to justify entry of summary judgment in favor of appellees subject only to a determination of the amount of damages and the applicability of the Warsaw Convention.

Appellant's second major contention is that, because of the applicability of the Warsaw Convention, appellant's liability is limited to the sum of $8,291.87. This Convention, to which the United States was not a signatory but to which, pursuant to Presidential Proclamation, this country adheres, applies to "all international transportation of persons, baggage, or goods performed by aircraft for hire." In the view which we take of this case it is unnecessary for this court to decide whether or not the Convention applies since the result would be the same either way. Assuming, without deciding, that the Convention does apply here, we are of the opinion that one of the Articles of the Convention itself precludes appellant's claim of limited liability in this case. Article 25(1) of the Convention as it appears in the official translation from the original French reads as follows:

"The carrier shall not be entitled to avail himself of the provisions of this convention which exclude or limit his liability, *if the damage is caused by his wilful misconduct or by such default on his part as, in accordance with the law of the court to which the case is submitted, is considered to be equivalent to wilful misconduct.*" (Emphasis supplied.)

The words "wilful misconduct" as they twice appear in the language quoted above were represented in the original French of the Convention by the word "dol." Appellant vigorously urges that the word "dol" was improperly translated and that properly translated it means "fraud" or "deceit." As we understand appellant's argument, the carrier must be guilty of well-nigh criminal intent before Article 25(1) has application. Stated somewhat differently, it is appellant's claim that its liability, if any, is limited unless it can be successfully shown that the pilot, or other agents of appellant, with malicious or felonious intent, planned to fly the plane into the mountain to the injury of its passengers. We cannot agree that the language of Article 25 quoted above goes, or was intended to go, this far.

Appellant has gone to the trouble of having translated (by a translator of its own selection) a portion of the official minutes of the Conference which later formulated the Convention. We see nothing in these minutes which would justify a holding that the official translation of "dol" into "wilful misconduct" is incorrect. Those minutes show little more than that the delegates were at the time in disagreement as to what terms would express their intent when translated into various languages. In fact, one statement by an English delegate to the Conference lends force to appellees' claim that the term is properly translated. That delegate said: "We have in English the expression 'wilful misconduct'. I think that it covers all that you want to say; it covers not only the acts accomplished deliberately, but also of insouciance, without concern for the consequences."

We, therefore, see no basis for questioning the correctness of the official translation as quoted above. The problem thus becomes one of deciding whether the trial judge properly applied the "law of the court to which the case is submitted" when, in his charge to the jury he said as follows:

"Now, wilful misconduct is not, as I have said, merely misconduct, but wilful misconduct. So if the carrier, or its employees or agents, wilfully performed any act with the knowledge that the performance of that act was likely to result in injury to a passenger, or performed that act with reckless and wanton disregard of its probable consequences, then that would constitute wilful misconduct; and if the result of that wilful misconduct was injury to Mrs. Ulen, then her recovery would not be limited by this sum of some eight thousand dollars.

. . . .

"Now, the mere violation of those [safety rules and regulations], . . . even if intentional, would not necessarily constitute wilful misconduct, but if the violation was intentional with knowledge that the violation was likely to cause injury to a passenger, then that would be wilful misconduct, and likewise, if it was done with a wanton and reckless disregard of the consequences."

We are of the opinion that this charge to the jury was substantially correct and that there was ample evidence upon which the jury could base its verdict, finding appellant guilty of wilful misconduct. One recent federal court decision defines the term as follows: " 'Wilful misconduct' means a deliberate purpose not to discharge some duty necessary to safety." [15] This definition squarely fits the facts in the instant case. The obvious and sole purpose of Civil Air Regulation 61.7401, supra, is safety. It imposed a duty upon all scheduled carriers which appellant deliberately, knowingly and intentionally violated. Appellant attempts to excuse itself by stating that the "center of the course intended to be flown" is not the same as the center of the airway and by arguing that it was possible for the airplane, by zigzagging first to the right of the airlane and then to the left, to fly at 4000 feet and still more than five miles distant from and 1000 feet above the highest obstacle and thereby comply, appellant says, with Regulation 61.7401. We need not pass upon the technical distinction between "center of the course" and "center of the airway," because, even adopting appellant's theory, the evidence clearly establishes a deliberate violation of the safety regulation.

The flight plan, drawn up, approved, and partially executed by appellant's admittedly experienced and otherwise qualified personnel, indicates that the "course intended to be flown" by this plane from Pulaski to Tri-City (the leg of the flight on which the accident oc-

[15] Circuit Judge Minton in Rowe v. Gatke Corporation, 7 Cir., 1942, 126 F.2d 61, 66.

curred) was 246 degrees magnetic. The aeronautical chart introduced in evidence at the trial shows Glade Mountain to be 4080 feet in
elevation and lying very close to the center of the *airway* over which
this plane was to fly. That chart also shows clearly that a plane proceeding at an altitude of 4000 feet from Pulaski toward Tri-City on a
magnetic bearing of 246 degrees—*the course intended to be flown*—
would pass *within 1½ miles, or at most 2 miles, from Glade Mountain, a mountain 4080 feet high!* Under these circumstances, it requires no stretch of the imagination whatever to visualize what *could*
happen and what *did* happen in this case. Appellant's case is only
weakened by its proof that the same pilot had flown this same route
in the same manner several times before. This is only evidence of
deliberateness and full knowledge which renders appellant's actions
the more reprehensible. One further fact of record cannot escape
note. In appellant's answers to the interrogatories it made the aston-
ishing admission that "we do not know the official elevation of Glade
Mountain." From the foregoing it is evident that wilful misconduct
in planning and executing this flight has been completely and conclusively shown in this case. Finally, there is nothing in either the flight
plan or the flight log of this plane to show that the zigzag course,
which appellant now argues would safely carry the plane through the
mountains in compliance with Regulation 61.7401, was ever contemplated or attempted in the case of this flight. The fact that there
might have been a safe way to fly this flight over this route cannot
help this appellant where all the evidence of record shows indisputably that an obviously unsafe method was employed and planned.

It follows that the Warsaw Convention, by its own terms, is inapplicable and does not operate to limit appellant's liability in these
cases. Both judgments appealed from in these cases must be, and
are hereby

Affirmed.[f]

---

[f] On or after September 28, 1955, a
good number of countries including the
United States signed the Hague Protocol.
This was a new treaty incorporating important amendments to the Warsaw Convention. The Protocol doubled the Convention's limitation on liability for
personal injury or death to passengers.
However, the Protocol eliminated the
Convention's reference to "dol" or "wilful misconduct," and instead provided
that the limitation on liability was not to
apply "if it is proved that the damage resulted from an act or omission of the carrier, his servants or agents, done with intent to cause damage or recklessly and
with knowledge that damage would probably result." Although in force elsewhere, the Protocol has never been ratified by the United States.

On November 15, 1965, the United
States gave notice of "denunciation" of
the Warsaw Convention (meaning withdrawal in accordance with the terms of
the Convention), emphasizing that such
action was solely because of the Convention's low limitation on liability. The notice was to become effective six months
later. Within that period, the International Air Transport Association made efforts to effect an arrangement among domestic and foreign air carriers that
would raise the limitation and provide a
basis upon which the United States could
withdraw its notice of denunciation. The
result was the so-called Montreal Agreement among numerous carriers by which
they bound themselves to include in their
tariffs a special contract providing for liability regardless of fault up to $75,000

Questions: (85) Would you expect summary judgment to be granted often in favor of plaintiffs in actions based on charges of negligence?

(86) How would the plaintiffs in the American Airlines case go about proving to the jury the defendant's "wilful misconduct"? Could they rely simply on the answers to interrogatories?

(87) What did the district court in the American Airlines case accomplish by granting summary judgment as to liability?

Interchangeability of motion for summary judgment and motion for judgment on the pleadings.—Rule 56(c) refers to "the pleadings," among other things; and it is clear that if on the pleadings, unassisted by affidavits or other material, the moving party is entitled to judgment, summary judgment should be granted in his favor. Correspondingly, Rule 12(c) states that if on a motion for judgment on the pleadings the court chooses to receive matters outside the pleadings, the motion shall be treated as one for summary judgment (which means giving the parties an opportunity to present any further material they may have pertinent to a summary judgment motion). There is no point in insistence on mere form—here the names of the motions.

Questions: (88) What can be said of the interchangeability of a motion for summary judgment and a motion under Rule 12(b)(6) for failure to state a claim upon which relief can be granted or a motion under Rule 12(f) to strike an insufficient defense?

(89) Why would a party ever use Rule 12(c) in preference to Rule 56?

SECTION 2. PROVISIONAL REMEDIES

[Rules 64, 65]

It is worth pausing to make the point that although we are canvassing the "phases" of a lawsuit, a word that might suggest a set order of proceedings, modern lawsuits do not exhibit a fixed or invariant pattern—they are fluid affairs. It is true that under the Rules certain moves necessarily precede other moves, and in this sense any lawsuit has a certain sequential order. The complaint precedes the answer, and a motion for a more definite statement necessarily fol-

per passenger. There was no change in the wilful misconduct exception to limited liability. This contract was to be applicable to international transportation that included a place in the United States as a point of origin, point of destination, or agreed stopping place. Thereupon, the United States officially withdrew its notice of denunciation of the Convention.

Since then, on March 8, 1971, in Guatemala City and on September 25, 1975, in Montreal, controversial new treaties have been signed by the United States and others in an attempt to amend further the Warsaw Convention. These treaties provide for no-fault liability of the airline up to approximately $120,000 per passenger, with the possibility of supplemental mandatory insurance coverage. However, there is to be no exception, on wilful misconduct or other grounds, to this limited liability. Neither the Guatemala City Protocol nor the Montreal Protocols are yet in force. See 1 L. Kreindler, Aviation Accident Law ch. 12B (rev.ed.1981).

lows the pleading to which it is addressed, and so on. But a lawsuit is not a cotillion in which the litigants invariably take the same steps according to a definite routine. Only some of the large variety of moves that are theoretically available to the litigants under the Rules will be made in a particular litigation; the moves will not be made in an absolutely fixed order; a given move may be responded to in one or more of a variety of ways; and a number of moves may be carried out more or less simultaneously. It is the mark of the first-class litigating lawyer to be able to hold the entire litigation in view while considering particular steps.

One of the things a litigant must bear in mind is that his adversary will sometimes not remain in a condition of repose while the lawsuit is taking its course. Suppose plaintiff begins an action for a money judgment. If he wins, he can then take steps to have defendant's property in the court's jurisdiction seized and sold to satisfy the judgment. But what is to prevent defendant from concealing his property or removing it from the jurisdiction so that it cannot be reached? Or, for that matter, what is to prevent him from dissipating his property? In either case, plaintiff's victory might be a hollow one, leaving him with an uncollectible judgment.

State legislatures have provided various devices designed to secure a plaintiff against these hazards, and Rule 64 makes available in the district court whatever remedies of this sort are available under the law of the state in which the district court sits.[a] There are considerable differences in the remedies available from state to state, in the circumstances in which they can be used, and in the types of property that can be reached thereby. Because the district courts follow the local state practice, the result is a divergence in practice among the district courts. Speaking generally, the most important of the remedies are attachment and garnishment. Attachment is the seizure of defendant's property in advance of judgment, commonly at a very early stage in the proceedings, to give plaintiff security that the judgment he hopes to obtain will be collectible. Garnishment is a process whereby a debt owed by a third person to defendant, or more generally property in the hands of a third person but belonging to defendant, is similarly made subject to plaintiff's claim. A typical example of a garnishable debt is defendant's bank deposit. By the service of proper process upon the bank, the bank is warned not to pay defendant the amount deposited, but to hold it for application to plaintiff's judgment if he gets one. The garnishment excuses the bank from paying defendant; indeed, if the bank nevertheless does pay defendant, it can be made to pay again to the successful plaintiff. Similarly, state statutes have long provided for garnishment of wages by service of proper process upon the employer.[b]

[a] This adoption of state law by reference is subject to the qualification that any statute of the United States governs in federal court as far as applicable.

[b] However, of late the power to garnish wages has been made subject to varying but increasing statutory restrictions. Most importantly, in 1970 by Title III of

These remedies are drastic ones, particularly if the seizure takes effect upon plaintiff's say-so, thus depriving defendant of control of his property before there has been any sort of impartial adjudication that plaintiff's claim is sound or even prima facie sound. Accordingly, the fundamental fairness of these remedies, and therefore their constitutional validity, has been repeatedly challenged in recent years, often with success. Of course, much turns on the details of the attachment or garnishment procedure provided by the particular state, the kinds of claims and the classes of creditors and debtors covered by the procedure, the type of property involved, and the like. We shall examine this question later, in Topic C of Part Five. In any event, the district courts follow the local statutes unless those statutes are determined to be unconstitutional.

Attachment and garnishment are possible provisional remedies when plaintiff is seeking a money judgment. But the ultimate relief sought may be a judgment directing defendant to do or to refrain from doing particular acts. In appropriate circumstances, the court will issue such a judgment, denominated an "injunction," after a decision for plaintiff on the merits of the dispute. Disobedience of such an order will result in severe action by the court. Yet here again the effectiveness of the final relief may be frustrated by intervening events. Suppose defendant is about to conduct blasting operations in dangerous proximity to plaintiff's property, and plaintiff seeks an injunction directing defendant to desist. The harm feared by plaintiff may be done before the court can hear and decide the case.

Rule 65 shows that plaintiff is not helpless in this situation. On a sufficient showing of urgency the court may issue a "temporary restraining order" without a hearing and, in particularly exigent cases, even without notice to the adverse party. But such an order should be followed promptly by an application for a "preliminary injunction," requiring notice and hearing.

Question: (1) Note the strict limitations imposed by Rule 65(a)(1), (b), (c), and (d) on the issuance of both temporary restraining orders and preliminary injunctions. Why were they deemed necessary?

---

the Consumer Credit Protection Act, Congress greatly restricted this device not only in the federal courts, but in the state courts as well. Title III overrode state law except to the extent that state law imposes more stringent restrictions on wage garnishment.

Title III generally provides that the maximum amount that may be garnished is the lesser of (1) 25% of the defendant's weekly disposable earnings or (2) the amount by which those earnings exceed 30 times the federal minimum hourly wage. Title III also makes it a criminal offense to discharge an employee because of a single garnishment of his wages. See 15 U.S.C. §§ 1671–1677.

HAMILTON WATCH CO. v. BENRUS WATCH CO.
United States Court of Appeals, Second Circuit, 1953.
206 F.2d 738.

Before SWAN, CHIEF JUDGE, and CLARK and FRANK, CIRCUIT JUDGES.

The complaint of Hamilton Watch Company alleges that, in violation of Section 7 of the Clayton Act, 15 U.S.C.A., Section 18,[1] the defendant, Benrus Watch Company, Inc., has bought a large block of shares of the common (voting) stock of Hamilton, a competitor, for the purpose of obtaining control of Hamilton, and that, should Benrus succeed in achieving such control, it would control so considerably larger a percentage than it had previously of the interstate industry in which both companies are competitively engaged as to substantially lessen competition in a "line of commerce". The complaint prayed, inter alia, that Benrus be required to divest itself of all its Hamilton shares and be restrained from acquiring additional Hamilton shares; and that, pending final disposition of the suit, a preliminary injunction issue enjoining Benrus from voting its Hamilton shares. Plaintiff moved for a preliminary injunction. It filed affidavits, and defendant filed counteraffidavits. Plaintiff, then, at a hearing on the motion before the district judge, introduced oral testimony through two of its officers who appeared as witnesses; defendant called no witnesses. The trial judge, having filed findings of fact and legal conclusions, entered an order enjoining defendant, pending a trial and a final order, from voting such Hamilton stock, provided defendant gave bond in the sum of $10,000. Defendant has appealed from this order.

FRANK, CIRCUIT JUDGE. The trial judge's opinion, findings of fact and conclusions of law are reported in D.C., 114 F.Supp. 307. As the facts are there fully set forth, we do not repeat them in detail.

1. Defendant argues that it appears unmistakably that defendant did not violate Section 7 of the Clayton Act. Were that true, we would now know that plaintiff could have no final relief, and that therefore the granting of the preliminary injunction was an obvious error; indeed, we might direct dismissal of the complaint. But we think that the present record sufficiently discloses that the court, after a trial, may be required to conclude that Benrus was not innocent of a Section 7 violation. To justify a temporary injunction it is not

---

[1] This section reads in part as follows:

"No corporation engaged in commerce shall acquire, directly or indirectly, the whole or any part of the stock or other share capital and no corporation subject to the jurisdiction of the Federal Trade Commission shall acquire the whole or any part of the assets of another corporation engaged also in commerce, where in any line of commerce in any section of the country, the effect of such acquisition may be substantially to lessen competition, or to tend to create a monopoly.

. . .

"This section shall not apply to corporations purchasing such stock solely for investment and not using the same by voting or otherwise to bring about, or in attempting to bring about, the substantial lessening of competition."

necessary that the plaintiff's right to a final decision, after a trial, be absolutely certain, wholly without doubt; if the other elements are present (i.e., the balance of hardships tips decidedly toward plaintiff), it will ordinarily be enough that the plaintiff has raised questions going to the merits so serious, substantial, difficult and doubtful, as to make them a fair ground for litigation and thus for more deliberate investigation.

As here the trial judge's findings derived from evidence presented at a preliminary hearing, they may perhaps be altered after a full-dress one. Yet, although we recognize them as necessarily tentative, they have such support in the oral testimony that we cannot possibly declare them "clearly erroneous"; we must therefore accept them on this appeal. Nor, on the basis of those findings, can we hold that the judge erred in temporarily holding, in effect, as follows: (a) The acquisition of control of Hamilton by Benrus very probably would substantially lessen competition in "a line of commerce" within the meaning of Section 7. (b) The purchases by Benrus of Hamilton shares were not made "solely for investment" but for the primary purpose of obtaining such control; had this purpose not been frustrated by action of Hamilton's management, Benrus would successfully have carried it out. (c) The purchases therefore violated Section 7. (d) Purchases thus unlawfully made do not cease to be unlawful—so as to preclude an order of divestment—because the purpose is balked.

. . . .

The judge's legal conclusions, like his fact-findings, are subject to change after a full hearing and the opportunity for more mature deliberation. For a preliminary injunction—as indicated by the numerous more or less synonymous adjectives used to label it—is, by its very nature, interlocutory, tentative, provisional, ad interim, impermanent, mutable, not fixed or final or conclusive, characterized by its for-the-time-beingness. It serves as an equitable policing measure to prevent the parties from harming one another during the litigation; to keep the parties, while the suit goes on, as far as possible in the respective positions they occupied when the suit began.

For the foregoing reasons, we cannot hold that the judge should have dismissed the complaint on the merits.

2. There remains the question whether the judge—assuming, as he did, for the time being, that the complaint was not without merit—went outside the bounds of his discretion in ordering a preliminary injunction. We read Section 16 of the Clayton Act, 15 U.S.C.A. § 26,[6]

---

[6] So far as pertinent, 15 U.S.C.A. § 26 reads as follows:

"Injunctive relief for private parties; exception

"Any person, firm, corporation, or association shall be entitled to sue for and have injunctive relief, in any court of the United States having jurisdiction over the parties, against threatened loss or damage by a violation of the antitrust laws, including sections 13, 14, 18 and 19 of this title, when and under the same conditions and principles as injunctive relief against threatened conduct that will cause loss or damage is granted by courts of equity, under the rules govas declaratory of the usual rule relative to the exercise of such discretion: The judge must consider whether irreparable harm is likely to result to plaintiff if pendente lite (i.e., "immediately") the injunction is denied, and against this harm he must balance the harm to defendant likely to result if the relief is granted. The "hardship plaintiff will suffer . . . may make interlocutory relief imperative where the same showing at a final hearing would not outweigh the hardship the defendant would suffer from a permanent injunction. Thus in view of the character and extent of the emergency presented, of the provisional and temporary character of the relief sought, of the probable period of its duration, and of the court's tentative opinion on the substantive issues involved, the factor of relative hardship is measured, on an application for interlocutory injunction, with a different yardstick from that used at final hearing." [8]   Here no substantial harm from the injunction to defendant is perceptible; but the hardship to plaintiff, were there no injunction, would be very considerable. We agree with the trial judge that the private harm to plaintiff required as a condition of granting injunctive relief under Section 16 need not be at all the same as the public harm condemned by Section 7. In the light of the evidence before the judge and his findings not unreasonably derived therefrom, we hold that he surely did not "abuse" his discretion.

Affirmed.

SWAN, C.J., concurs in the result.

———

CHECKER MOTORS CORP. v. CHRYSLER CORP., 405 F.2d 319 (2d Cir.), cert. denied, 394 U.S. 999, 89 S.Ct. 1595 (1969). Plaintiff, a manufacturer of taxicabs, brought suit under the antitrust laws, seeking treble damages and injunctive relief, against Chrysler, its competitor in the taxicab market. The district court denied the plaintiff's motion for a preliminary injunction that would enjoin the defendant from continuing an allegedly illegal rebate plan during the pendency of the litigation, finding "that there was serious doubt as to whether Checker will ultimately prevail in this action [and] that a review of the involved hardships and equities did not disclose a balance favoring injunctive relief." The Second Circuit affirmed, observing that a preliminary injunction "is an extraordinary remedy, and will not be granted except upon a clear showing of probable success *and* possible irreparable injury."

———

erning such proceedings, and upon the execution of proper bond against damages for an injunction improvidently granted and a showing that the danger of irreparable loss or damage is immedi- ate, a preliminary injunction may issue: . . .."

[8] Restatement of Torts, Section 94, comment f.

SECTION 3. TRIAL

If the case has survived the pretrial maneuvers and has not been settled by the parties or otherwise accelerated to termination, a trial is in order. Each district court is directed to provide by local rule for the placing of cases upon the calendar for trial. See Rule 40. These local rules vary. In some districts, one of the parties must take the initiative in order to secure a trial; in others, the matter is handled exclusively by the court. One way or another, the case is set for trial—although bear in mind that about only one in ten federal lawsuits makes it to trial.

(a) The Jury

[Rules 38, 39, 47, 48]

Right to jury trial.—Shall the trial be to a judge alone or to a jury under the supervision of a judge? Read the seventh amendment to the Constitution of the United States. Until fairly recently, it could have been said with a fair amount of accuracy that the measure of the jury right preserved by the Constitution was whether the case was of a type that was triable by jury in one of the superior courts of common law in England in 1791 when the seventh amendment was adopted.[a] Although that historical test is still of central importance, it no longer tells the whole story. Complications arise primarily from the fact that under the Federal Rules the federal courts hear cases in a procedural context unknown to the English courts; particularly significant here is the merger of law and equity effectuated by the Rules. The question is a difficult one. We reach it at Topic E of Part Four.

The fact that a case falls into a category making it triable by jury as a matter of constitutional right does not necessarily mean that a jury will ultimately render a verdict upon it. The jury right is waived unless timely demand for it is made as prescribed by Rule 38(b) and (c). And even if a jury is impanelled, it may never be given anything to decide, for the jury's sole function is to pass upon contested questions of fact. If, for instance, the judge has reserved until trial, as he may do under Rule 12(d), the question whether the plaintiff has stated a claim upon which relief can be granted, his determination of this question of law adversely to the plaintiff may dispose of the case without the intervention of the jury. Similarly, a ruling of law that

---

[a] The superior courts of common law were the Court of Common Pleas (also called Common Bench), the Court of King's Bench, and the Court of Exchequer. These courts generally utilized trial by jury. Actions at law typically were those that sought relief in the form of money damages.

In the Court of Chancery, which had jurisdiction of suits in equity, the jury method of trial was not used, except that the chancellor sometimes referred a case to a jury for advisory purposes. Suits in equity typically sought relief in the form of an order commanding the defendant to do or not to do some act.

the proof is insufficient to warrant a jury in finding that a claim or defense has been established may result in withdrawal of the case from the jury.

Incidents of jury trial.—A common-law jury numbered twelve, and its verdict had to be unanimous. Are these incidents of a civil jury trial preserved by the seventh amendment?

Consider first the number of jurors. It was long the common assumption that a party in federal court was entitled to a twelve-person jury under the seventh amendment, although under Rule 48 a lesser number could be agreed to. Some states, on the other hand, had provided in certain civil cases for juries of fewer than twelve persons, as the seventh amendment itself does not restrict the states.[b] A few states had gone further, prescribing juries of fewer than twelve in certain criminal cases; here the sixth amendment is applicable through the fourteenth amendment; however, in Williams v. Florida, 399 U.S. 78, 90 S.Ct. 1893 (1970), the Supreme Court rejected precedent to hold that a six-person jury, acting unanimously, in a state criminal trial does not constitute a violation of the Federal Constitution. Encouraged by these developments on the criminal side, most federal district courts came to provide by local rule for six-person civil juries.[c]

COLGROVE v. BATTIN

Supreme Court of the United States, 1973.
413 U.S. 149, 93 S.Ct. 2448.

MR. JUSTICE BRENNAN delivered the opinion of the Court.

Local Rule 13(d)(1) of the Revised Rules of Procedure of the United States District Court for the District of Montana provides that a jury for the trial of civil cases shall consist of six persons.[1] When respondent District Court Judge set this diversity case for trial before a jury of six in compliance with the Rule, petitioner sought mandamus from the Court of Appeals for the Ninth Circuit to direct re-

[b] By interpretation of the fourteenth amendment, most of the rights in the Bill of Rights have been held fundamental enough to be guaranteed against invasion by the states; but the seventh amendment right to a civil jury is not one of those. That is to say, the seventh amendment applies to actions in the federal courts, but not to state-court actions. State constitutions, however, often contain provisions similar to the seventh amendment.

On the other hand, the sixth amendment right to a criminal jury does apply to the states through the fourteenth amendment. Why this distinction?

[c] Federal district courts were precluded from experimenting with the criminal jury, because the Federal Rules of Criminal Procedure, independently of the Constitution, did and still do normally require in federal criminal cases a twelve-person jury that acts unanimously.

[1] Rule 13(d)(1) provides:

"A jury for the trial of civil cases shall consist of six persons plus such alternate jurors as may be impaneled."

Similar local rules have been adopted by 54 other federal district courts, at least as to some civil cases. . . .

spondent to impanel a 12-member jury. Petitioner contended that the
local Rule (1) violated the Seventh Amendment; (2) violated the statutory provision, 28 U.S.C. § 2072, that rules "shall preserve the right
of trial by jury as at common law and as declared by the Seventh
Amendment . . ."; and (3) was rendered invalid by Fed.Rule Civ.
Proc. 83 because "inconsistent with" Fed.Rule Civ.Proc. 48 that provides for juries of less than 12 when stipulated by the parties. The
Court of Appeals found no merit in these contentions, sustained the
validity of local Rule 13(d)(1), and denied the writ, 456 F.2d 1379
(1972). We granted certiorari, 409 U.S. 841, 93 S.Ct. 44 (1972). We
affirm.

I

In Williams v. Florida, 399 U.S. 78, 90 S.Ct. 1893 (1970), the Court
sustained the constitutionality of a Florida statute providing for six-
member juries in certain criminal cases. The constitutional challenge
rejected in that case relied on the guarantees of jury trial secured the
accused by Art. III, § 2, cl. 3, of the Constitution and by the Sixth
Amendment. We expressly reserved, however, the question whether
"additional references to the 'common law' that occur in the Seventh
Amendment might support a different interpretation" with respect to
jury trial in civil cases. Id., at 92 n. 30, 90 S.Ct., at 1901 n. 30. We
conclude that they do not.

The pertinent words of the Seventh Amendment are: "In Suits at
common law . . . . . the right of trial by jury shall be preserved
. . . ." On its face, this language is not directed to jury characteristics, such as size, but rather defines the kind of cases for which
jury trial is preserved, namely, "suits at common law." And while it
is true that "[w]e have almost no direct evidence concerning the intention of the framers of the seventh amendment itself," [7] the historical setting in which the Seventh Amendment was adopted highlighted
a controversy that was generated, not by concern for preservation of
jury characteristics at common law, but by fear that the civil jury
itself would be abolished unless protected in express words. Almost
a century and a half ago, this Court recognized that "[o]ne of the
strongest objections originally taken against the constitution of the
United States, was the want of an express provision securing the
right of trial by jury in civil cases." Parsons v. Bedford, 3 Pet. 433,
445 (1830). But the omission of a protective clause from the Constitution was not because an effort was not made to include one. On
the contrary, a proposal was made to include a provision in the Constitution to guarantee the right of trial by jury in civil cases but the
proposal failed because the States varied widely as to the cases in
which civil jury trial was provided, and the proponents of a civil jury

---

[7] Henderson, The Background of the
Seventh Amendment, 80 Harv.L.Rev.
289, 291 (1966).

guarantee found too difficult the task of fashioning words appropriate to cover the different state practices. The strong pressures for a civil jury provision in the Bill of Rights encountered the same difficulty. Thus, it was agreed that, with no federal practice to draw on and since state practices varied so widely, any compromising language would necessarily have to be general. As a result, although the Seventh Amendment achieved the primary goal of jury trial adherents to incorporate an explicit constitutional protection of the right of trial by jury in civil cases, the right was limited in general words to "suits at common law." We can only conclude, therefore, that by referring to the "common law," the Framers of the Seventh Amendment were concerned with preserving the *right* of trial by jury in civil cases where it existed at common law, rather than the various incidents of trial by jury. In short, what was said in Williams with respect to the criminal jury is equally applicable here: constitutional history reveals no intention on the part of the Framers "to equate the constitutional and common-law characteristics of the jury." 399 U.S., at 99, 90 S.Ct., at 1905.

Consistently with the historical objective of the Seventh Amendment, our decisions have defined the jury right preserved in cases covered by the Amendment, as "the substance of the common-law right of trial by jury, as distinguished from mere matters of form or procedure . . . ." Baltimore & Carolina Line, Inc. v. Redman, 295 U.S. 654, 657, 55 S.Ct. 890, 891 (1935). The Amendment, therefore, does not "bind the federal courts to the exact procedural incidents or details of jury trial according to the common law in 1791," Galloway v. United States, 319 U.S. 372, 390, 63 S.Ct. 1077, 1087 (1943); see also Ex parte Peterson, 253 U.S. 300, 309, 40 S.Ct. 543, 546 (1920); Walker v. New Mexico & S.P.R. Co., 165 U.S. 593, 596, 17 S.Ct. 421, 422 (1897), and "[n]ew devices may be used to adapt the ancient institution to present needs and to make of it an efficient instrument in the administration of justice. . . ." Ex parte Peterson, supra, 253 U.S. at 309–310, 40 S.Ct. at 546; Funk v. United States, 290 U.S. 371, 382, 54 S.Ct. 212, 215 (1933).

Our inquiry turns, then, to whether a jury of 12 is of the substance of the common-law right of trial by jury. Keeping in mind the purpose of the jury trial in criminal cases to prevent government oppression, Williams, 399 U.S., at 100, 90 S.Ct., at 1905, and, in criminal and civil cases, to assure a fair and equitable resolution of factual issues, Gasoline Products Co. v. Champlin Co., 283 U.S. 494, 498, 51 S.Ct. 513, 514 (1931), the question comes down to whether jury performance is a function of jury size. In Williams, we rejected the notion that "the reliability of the jury as a factfinder . . . [is] a function of its size," 399 U.S., at 100–101, 90 S.Ct., at 1906, and nothing has been suggested to lead us to alter that conclusion. Accordingly, we think it cannot be said that 12 members is a substantive aspect of the right of trial by jury.

It is true, of course, that several earlier decisions of this Court have made the statement that "trial by jury" means "a trial by a jury of 12 . . . ." Capital Traction Co. v. Hof, 174 U.S. 1, 13, 19 S.Ct. 580, 585 (1899); see also American Publishing Co. v. Fisher, 166 U.S. 464, 17 S.Ct. 618 (1897); Maxwell v. Dow, 176 U.S. 581, 586, 20 S.Ct. 448, 450 (1900). But in each case, the reference to "a jury of twelve" was clearly dictum and not a decision upon a question presented or litigated. . . . Insofar as the Hof statement implied that the Seventh Amendment required a jury of 12, it was at best an assumption. And even if that assumption had support in common-law doctrine, our canvass of the relevant constitutional history, like the history canvassed in Williams concerning the criminal jury, "casts considerable doubt on the easy assumption in our past decisions that if a given feature existed in a jury at common law . . . then it was necessarily preserved in the Constitution." 399 U.S., at 92–93, 90 S.Ct., at 1902. We cannot, therefore, accord the unsupported dicta of these earlier decisions the authority of decided precedents.

There remains, however, the question whether a jury of six satisfies the Seventh Amendment guarantee of "trial by jury." We had no difficulty reaching the conclusion in Williams that a jury of six would guarantee an accused the trial by jury secured by Art. III and the Sixth Amendment. Significantly, our determination that there was "no discernible difference between the results reached by the two different-sized juries," 399 U.S., at 101, 90 S.Ct., at 1906, drew largely upon the results of studies of the operations of juries of six in civil cases. Since then, much has been written about the six-member jury, but nothing that persuades us to depart from the conclusion reached in Williams.[15] Thus, while we express no view as to whether any number less than six would suffice,[16] we conclude that a jury of six satisfies the Seventh Amendment's guarantee of trial by jury in civil cases.

[Parts II and III of the Court's opinion dealt with those of the petitioner's arguments based on § 2072 and on Rules 48 and 83, and are omitted.]

Affirmed.

. . . .

[15] Arguments, pro and con, on the effectiveness of a jury of six compared to a jury of 12 will be found in Devitt, [The Six Man Jury in the Federal Court, 53 F.R.D. 273 (1971)]; . . . Zeisel, . . . And Then There Were None: The Diminution of the Federal Jury, 38 U.Chi. L.Rev. 710 (1971) . . . .. [On the dangers of the use by courts of social science research, see Lermack, No Right Number? Social Science Research and the Jury-Size Cases, 54 N.Y.U.L.Rev. 951 (1979).—Ed.]

[16] What is required for a "jury" is a number large enough to facilitate group deliberation combined with a likelihood of obtaining a representative cross section of the community. Williams v. Florida, 399 U.S., at 100, 90 S.Ct., at 1905. It is undoubtedly true that at some point the number becomes too small to accomplish these goals, but, on the basis of presently available data, that cannot be concluded as to the number six. [Citations omitted.]

MR. JUSTICE MARSHALL, with whom MR. JUSTICE STEWART joins, dissenting.

Some 30 years ago, Mr. Justice Black warned his Brethren against the "gradual process of judicial erosion which . . . has slowly worn away a major portion of the essential guarantee of the Seventh Amendment." Galloway v. United States, 319 U.S. 372, 397, 63 S.Ct. 1077, 1090 (1943) (dissenting opinion). Today, the erosion process reaches bedrock. . . .

. . . No one need be fooled by reference to the six-man trier of fact utilized in the District Court for the District of Montana as a "jury." . . . We deal here not with some minor tinkering with the role of the civil jury, but with its wholesale abolition and replacement with a different institution which functions differently, produces different results, and was wholly unknown to the Framers of the Seventh Amendment.

.   .   .   .

When a historical approach is applied to the issue at hand, it cannot be doubted that the Framers envisioned a jury of 12 when they referred to trial by jury. . . .

.   .   .   .

The Court today elects to abandon the certainty of this historical test, as well as the many cases which support it, in favor of a vaguely defined functional analysis which asks not what the Framers meant by "trial by jury" but rather whether some substitute for the common-law jury performs the same functions as a jury and serves as an adequate substitute for one. . . .

. . . But the composition of the jury itself is a matter of arbitrary, a priori definition. As Mr. Justice Harlan argued "[t]he right to a trial by jury . . . has no enduring meaning apart from historical form." Williams v. Florida, 399 U.S., at 125, 90 S.Ct., at 1919 (separate opinion).

It is senseless, then, to say that a panel of six constitutes a "jury" without first defining what one means by a jury, and that initial definition must, in the nature of things, be arbitrary. One could, of course, define the term "jury" as being a body of six or more laymen. But the line between five and six would then be just as arbitrary as the line between 11 and 12. There is no way by reference to abstract principle or "function" that one can determine that six is "enough," five is "too small," and 30 "too large." [8] These evaluations can only

[8] The Court asserts that "[w]hat is required for a 'jury' is a number large enough to facilitate group deliberation combined with a likelihood of obtaining a representative cross section of the community." See ante, at . . . n. 16. We can bypass for the moment the intriguing question of where the majority finds this requirement in the words of the Seventh Amendment. For our purposes, it is sufficient to note that, upon examination, this "test" turns out to be no test at all. It may be that the ideal jury would provide "enough" group deliberation and community representation. But the question in this case is how much

be made by reference to a hypothetical ideal jury of some arbitrarily chosen size. All one can say is that a jury of six functions less like a jury of 12 than would a jury of, say eight, but more like a jury of 12 than would a jury of three.[9] Although I think it clear that my Brethren would reject, for example, a jury of one, the Court does not begin to tell us how it would go about drawing a line in a nonarbitrary fashion, and it is obvious that in matters of degree of this kind, nonarbitrary line drawing is a logical impossibility.

Of course, there is nothing intrinsically wrong with drawing arbitrary lines and, indeed, . . . in order to resolve certain problems they are essential. Thus, this Court has not hesitated in the past to rely on arbitrary demarcations in cases where constitutional rights depend on matters of degree. See, e.g., Burns v. Fortson, 410 U.S. 686, 93 S.Ct. 1209 (1973). But in cases where arbitrary lines are necessary, I would have thought it more consonant with our limited role in a constitutional democracy to draw them with reference to the fixed bounds of the Constitution rather than on a wholly ad hoc basis.

I think history will bear out the proposition that when constitutional rights are grounded in nothing more solid than the intuitive, unexplained sense of five Justices that a certain line is "right" or "just," those rights are certain to erode and, eventually, disappear altogether. Today, a majority of this Court may find six-man juries to represent a proper balance between competing demands of expedition and group representation. But as dockets become more crowded and pressures on jury trials grow, who is to say that some future Court will not find three, or two, or one a number large enough to satisfy its unexplicated sense of justice? It should be clear that constitutional rights which are so vulnerable to pressures of the moment are not really protected by the Constitution at all. . . .

. . . It may well be that the number 12 is no more than a "historical accident" and is "wholly without significance 'except to mystics.' " Williams v. Florida, supra, 399 U.S., at 102, 90 S.Ct., at 1907. But surely there is nothing more significant about the number six, or three, or one. The line must be drawn somewhere, and the difference between drawing it in the light of history and drawing it on an ad hoc basis is, ultimately, the difference between interpreting a constitution and making it up as one goes along.

. . . .

is "enough." Obviously, the larger the jury the more group representation it will provide. . . . Merely observing that a certain level of group representation is constitutionally required fails to tell us what that level is. And, more significantly, it fails to tell us how to go about deciding what that level is.

[9] It thus will not do to argue, as has my Brother White, that one "can get off the 'slippery slope' before he reaches the bottom. . . ." Williams v. Florida, 399 U.S. 78, 91 n. 28, 90 S.Ct. 1893, 1901 n. 28 (1970). This begs the question how one knows at what point to get off—a question for which the Court apparently has no answer.

[Justices Douglas and Powell dissented on other grounds, allowing them to avoid reaching the constitutional issue. Their opinions are omitted.]

Questions: (1) What arguments can you make each way on the petitioner's contentions concerning (a) § 2072 and (b) Rules 48 and 83?

(2) Can parties in the District of Montana stipulate to a jury of eleven?

In Ballew v. Georgia, 435 U.S. 223, 98 S.Ct. 1029 (1978), the Court held that in a state criminal trial a five-person jury, even though acting unanimously, constitutes a violation of the Federal Constitution. All the Justices supported this holding, although the case produced five opinions. Justice Blackmun, through a lengthy review of the numerous post-Williams empirical studies on the jury, explained that reducing the jury below six members would adversely affect group deliberation and cross-sectional representation. Among other points, he observed that the smaller the jury, the less likely is the group to remember accurately, to overcome the biases of its members, and to exhibit self-criticism; also, "the data now raise doubts about the accuracy of the results achieved by smaller and smaller panels." Furthermore, smaller juries erect barriers to "the representation of minority groups in the community." Meanwhile, he argued, reducing the jury below six members would offer only minimal savings in court time and financial costs. Accordingly, the line was drawn.

In the meantime, a similar scenario is working itself out on the unanimity front. It has long been generally assumed that a party in federal court is entitled to a unanimous verdict under the seventh amendment. Indeed, here it is more than assumption, the Supreme Court having in fact so held in Springville v. Thomas, 166 U.S. 707, 17 S.Ct. 717 (1897), and apparently also in American Publishing Co. v. Fisher, 166 U.S. 464, 17 S.Ct. 618 (1897). Again, under Rule 48 the parties may stipulate to a verdict or finding by a stated majority. Some states, on the other hand, abolished the unanimity requirement for certain civil and criminal cases. When the issue finally arose, in Apodaca v. Oregon, 406 U.S. 404, 92 S.Ct. 1628 (1972), and Johnson v. Louisiana, 406 U.S. 356, 92 S.Ct. 1620 (1972), a sharply divided Supreme Court held that a nonunanimous verdict, by a twelve-person jury, in a state criminal trial passes federal constitutional muster; there was some indication by the Court, however, that a "substantial majority of the jury" is needed and that a 9–3 verdict is at or very near the constitutional floor for twelve-person state criminal juries.

Questions: (3) Springville and American Publishing are obviously being buffeted by the winds of change. Do you see any way that their requirement of unanimity for federal civil juries can survive the trend of the modern cases? Is there an argument to be built on the fact that Apodaca and Johnson are criminal cases, as contrasted to civil cases governed by the seventh amendment? Is there an argument based on the fact that Apodaca and Johnson are state cases, thus leaving open the question whether unanimity is

still a requirement for federal juries? Is there an argument tied to the undeniable fact that unanimity is a much more important concern than is the
number of jurors, thus allowing Colgrove to be distinguished? Is there an
argument to be found in the fact that the Court here faces actual holdings
directly in point, unlike the situation confronting the Court in Colgrove?

(4) Assuming that nonunanimous verdicts by federal civil juries are to be
authorized, what combinations of reduced numbers of jurors and majority
verdicts will be deemed constitutionally permissible? Eight-out-of-nine?

In Burch v. Louisiana, 441 U.S. 130, 99 S.Ct. 1623 (1979), the Court
held that in a state criminal trial a nonunanimous verdict, by a six-
person jury, violates the Federal Constitution. All the Justices were
in agreement that a 5–1 verdict is invalid. Writing for the Court,
Justice Rehnquist addressed this " 'close' " question "at the intersection of our decisions concerning jury size and unanimity" by first noting that "having already departed from the strictly historical requirements of jury trial, it is inevitable that lines must be drawn
somewhere if the substance of the jury trial right is to be preserved."
He then quickly concluded that "much the same reasons that led us
in Ballew to decide that use of a five-member jury threatened the
fairness of the proceeding and the proper role of the jury, lead us to
conclude now that conviction for a nonpetty offense by only five
members of a six-person jury presents a similar threat to preservation of the substance of the jury trial guarantee and justifies our requiring verdicts rendered by six-person juries to be unanimous."

Jury selection.—The selection of the jury is largely a matter of
local rule and practice, but some general description is possible. A
panel of jurors, summoned by the statutory officials from the general
body of citizens,[d] is brought to the courtroom. The jurors for the
particular trial are tentatively drawn by lot from this larger group.

These jurors are then subjected to the questioning process referred to in Rule 47(a), which is called the voir dire examination and
which is usually conducted by the judge in federal court, to determine
whether there is good reason why any of them should not serve in
the case. If, for example, a juror is related to a party, or if he has a
financial interest in the outcome of the case, or if he is prejudiced
against a party, he may be challenged "for cause." He will be excluded if the court finds that the cause exists. In addition, at some
point in the process, each side is allowed a limited number of "peremptory challenges."[e] These may be exercised at the party's appar-

[d] The Jury Selection and Service Act of
1968, 28 U.S.C. §§ 1861–1869, is designed
to ensure selection of federal jurors at
random from a fair cross section of the
community without discrimination on account of race, color, religion, sex, national origin, or economic status. Generally,
each district court must adopt a selection
plan tied to voter lists.

[e] 28 U.S.C. § 1870 provides that in civil
cases each party is entitled to three peremptory challenges; where there are
multiple plaintiffs or defendants, the trial
judge in his discretion may treat each
side as a single party or may allow additional peremptory challenges. See also
Rule 47(b).

ently uncontrolled pleasure. (Why should this type of challenge, which will be used only when cause is not found, be permitted?)

Jurors who have been excluded by either type of challenge are replaced by others similarly drawn by lot from the panel and similarly subject to questioning and challenge. When the process of selection is completed, the jury is sworn and the trial proceeds.

(b) Order and Method of Proof [f]

[Rules 41(b), 50(a)]

Burden of proof.—Who must prove what? What happens if no evidence is presented on a disputed issue, or not enough evidence to persuade the jury? [g]

Speaking broadly, the burden of persuading the jury on particular disputed issues is allotted between the parties in the same way that the rules of pleading assign the burden of allegation.[h] Thus, plaintiff will lose if the jury is not persuaded of the truth of the allegations of the complaint that have been denied in the answer. So also, defendant's affirmative defenses controverted by plaintiff will fail if the jury is not persuaded of their truth. The party who thus suffers the consequences of non-persuasion on an issue is said to have the "burden of proof" with respect to it.

Plaintiff's case.—Ordinarily, plaintiff has the initial obligation to bring forward the evidence in support of the disputed elements of his claim.

Question: (5) Why is this ordinarily so? Suggest cases where it is not so.

Before calling his witnesses, plaintiff's attorney customarily makes an opening statement in which he tells the jury what the issues in the action are and what he proposes to prove. The purpose of the opening is to explain the case in such a way that the jury will be better able to follow the testimony. Commonly, defendant's attorney follows immediately with a comparable opening statement, although he sometimes can choose to postpone this until the beginning of defendant's case.

[f] The conduct of a trial is largely confided to the trial judge's discretion. We resort in much of this Section to an account of the usual course of trial.

The main elements of the trial are much the same whether the trial is by judge and jury or by the judge alone. For the purpose of the present account, we assume that the trial is with a jury.

[g] We pass over at this point the question of the degree of persuasion to which the minds of the jurors must be brought before they are warranted in deciding that a proposition has been established. Suffice it now to say that the required degree of persuasion in a civil case is normally a "preponderance of the evidence," which requires a showing of more-probable-than-not.

[h] This is not invariably so. For example, contributory negligence is to be pleaded as an affirmative defense under Rule 8(c), but we shall see that the burden of proving the absence of contributory negligence is sometimes cast upon the plaintiff.

Then plaintiff's first witness is called to the stand, sworn to tell the truth, and questioned first by plaintiff's attorney (direct examination) and next by defendant's attorney (cross-examination), following which there may be redirect examination, recross-examination, and so on. Other witnesses for plaintiff are called and subjected to the same process of direct and cross-examination until plaintiff's attorney is satisfied that he has done all that he can to establish the elements of the claim. In theory he is not supposed at this stage of the case to anticipate defenses and rebut them, but matters of claim and defense are frequently so interwoven that it is not practicable to try to separate them; the trial judge usually allows considerable leeway. Upon the completion of the testimony in support of his "case in chief," plaintiff's attorney announces that he rests his case.

Motion at the close of plaintiff's case.—When plaintiff rests, he may have failed to present any evidence on an issue upon which he has the burden of proof, or his evidence on it may be plainly insufficient to persuade reasonable triers of fact. In such a situation, defendant may move for a directed verdict pursuant to Rule 50(a). If such a motion is granted, the judge directs the jury to bring in a given verdict and the jury does so in a mechanical way. Indeed, under the last sentence of Rule 50(a), the formal act by the jury can be dispensed with. Thus, granting this motion here would mean that the case is withdrawn from the jury and that judgment will be entered for defendant.

Questions: (6) The corresponding motion by the defendant where the action is being tried without a jury is a motion for an involuntary dismissal; however, here the standard that the defendant must meet is the much less stringent one "that upon the facts and the law the plaintiff has shown no right to relief." Rule 41(b). Do you see why such very different standards should prevail under Rules 50(a) and 41(b)?

(7) Rule 41(b) says that the dismissal "operates as an adjudication upon the merits" unless "the court in its order for dismissal otherwise specifies." [i] When should the court "otherwise specify"?

(8) Judgment entered upon a directed verdict is taken to be an adjudication on the merits, although Rule 50(a) does not say so. In circumstances such that the court would "otherwise specify" in a dismissal under Rule 41(b), may it make some similar provision upon directing a verdict under Rule 50(a)?

Defendant does not risk his all by making a motion at the close of plaintiff's case. If the motion is not granted, defendant may proceed with his case just as if he had not made the motion.

Defendant's case.—If plaintiff has presented evidence sufficient to permit reasonable triers to find in his favor, defendant's motion would be futile because such a case will not then be withdrawn from the jury. Yet defendant may still cut short the scenario—by resting

---

[i] Or unless the dismissal is for lack of jurisdiction, for improper venue, for failure to join a party under Rule 19, or (by judicial construction of Rule 41(b)) for some similar reason not linked to the merits of plaintiff's claim.

without offering proof. Why would he do so? After plaintiff rests, the condition of the evidence may be such that reasonable triers might differ as to whether he has sustained his burden of proof. For example, plaintiff's burden has been sustained only if a given piece of evidence is believed, and a reasonable jury might either believe or disbelieve it. By resting, defendant stakes his chances upon argument to the jury that plaintiff's story should not be accepted as true. Defendant would do so where he has little evidence to offer or a lot of confidence.

Ordinarily, however, defendant will proceed to offer his own evidence. This evidence may be designed to disprove one or more of the disputed matters on which plaintiff has the burden of proof. Or it may break new ground, being designed to prove matters of affirmative defense upon which defendant has the burden of proof. The process of direct examination by defendant's attorney and cross-examination by plaintiff's attorney is the same as that already described. Upon completion of his presentation of evidence, defendant's attorney rests.

Motion at the close of defendant's case.—When defendant rests, plaintiff may move for a directed verdict pursuant to Rule 50(a), without waiving his right to put in rebuttal evidence if his motion is denied.

Questions: (9) May plaintiff make a corresponding motion at this point if the case is being tried without a jury? See Rule 41(b).

(10) May defendant, at this point, make a motion for a directed verdict or a motion for an involuntary dismissal? See Rules 50(a) and 41(b).

Rebuttal and rejoinder.—Assuming that plaintiff has not moved for a directed verdict, or that his motion has not been granted, he now has the chance to offer rebuttal evidence. Properly speaking, the rebuttal should be limited to evidence that meets new facts put in evidence by defendant. It is not, however, limited to evidence designed to meet an affirmative defense. For instance, defendant may have presented an alleged eyewitness to an automobile accident whose testimony contradicted that of plaintiff's witnesses. It would be proper rebuttal on the part of plaintiff to put on a witness to testify that defendant's witness was elsewhere at the time of the accident. On the other hand, mere reiteration of plaintiff's own evidence for the purpose of giving it added emphasis so as to overcome the effect of contradictory testimony is improper rebuttal. It is also improper to reserve for rebuttal material that was properly a part of the case in chief, as defendant may reasonably have supposed that the case in chief was the entire case he had to meet. However, the trial judge has a wide discretion in these matters; he is likely, for example, to permit in rebuttal testimony that was inadvertently omitted earlier.[j]

---

[j] Even after both parties have rested, the court has discretion in the interests of justice to permit the introduction of evidence to repair the damage of an inadvertent omission in a party's proof.

Again, examination of rebuttal witnesses is the same as that already described. After presenting all his evidence in rebuttal, plaintiff rests. And again, defendant may move for a directed verdict.

After the rebuttal, the defendant may present evidence in rejoinder, as to which the same general principles apply. And there may be still further stages until finally both parties rest.ᵏ

(c) The Rules of Evidence

The process of proof that we have described in general terms is governed throughout by the rules of evidence. These rules had their origin in the decisions of common-law judges and were changed over the years by the traditional common-law method of case-by-case adjudication. Progress was inevitably sporadic, uncertain, and unsystematic; the administration of justice was hampered by the accidents of history. The rules developed differently from jurisdiction to jurisdiction, just as did the rules of substantive law.

When the Federal Rules of Civil Procedure were adopted they contained only minimal provisions ˡ about the rules of evidence instead of detailed rules covering actions in federal courts.

On November 20, 1972, the Supreme Court prescribed Federal Rules of Evidence, effective on July 1, 1973, to govern civil and criminal cases in the federal courts; this was the culmination of years of study by an advisory committee, the publication of two drafts, revision in the light of comments from the bench and bar, and approval by the standing committee and the Judicial Conference of the United States. However, taking into account serious objections that had arisen concerning some of those rules, Congress enacted a statute, signed by the President on March 30, 1973, as Pub.L. No. 93–12, 87 Stat. 9, providing that those rules should have no force or effect except as they might be expressly approved by act of Congress. A two-year redrafting project produced a substantially revised, less revolutionary House bill (see H.R.Rep. No. 93–650), Senate amendments that moved back toward the Court-proposed rules (see S.Rep. No. 93–1277), and a compromise conference bill (see H.R.Conf.Rep. No. 93–1597) that finally was passed and signed into law on January 2, 1975, as Pub.L. No. 93–595, 88 Stat. 1926. That law (1) adopted the Federal Rules of Evidence, as redrafted; (2) amended the Rules Enabling Act by adding 28 U.S.C. § 2076; and (3) made minor conforming changes to the Federal Rules of Civil Procedure and the

---

ᵏ In Subsection (d) we shall pick up with the motions that may be made at the stage when both parties have rested.

ˡ Rule 43(a) provided for admissibility of evidence if it fell in any one of three categories: (1) evidence admissible under federal statutes, of which there were few; (2) evidence admissible under the rules "heretofore" applied in federal courts in suits in equity; or (3) evidence admissible under the rules applied in the courts of the state in which the federal court was held. This was a rule of admissibility, not a rule of exclusion; thus, the statute or rule favoring reception of the evidence governed.

Federal Rules of Criminal Procedure. The effective date for the new Federal Rules of Evidence [m] and the conforming changes was set at July 1, 1975.

The following pages constitute a brief survey of the law of evidence.[n] Focus will be centered on the Evidence Rules, not only because they are controlling in the federal courts but also because to an extent they reflect current thinking as to what modern rules of evidence should be—they have already spurred many states to adopt similar rules, and other states are likely to follow, just as was the case with the Federal Rules of Civil Procedure. Nevertheless, for the purpose of contrast, we shall make frequent reference to the practice at common law and to the practice prevailing in the several states.

Kinds of evidence.—Testimony does not always consist of the simple narration by a witness of what he observed. Sometimes a witness is permitted to give *opinion evidence.*

When the evaluation of evidence calls for specialized knowledge not possessed by the ordinary juror, a qualified expert may be called in to assist the jury. On a given point, the needed expert may be a doctor, a chemist, a fingerprint specialist, a musician, a carpenter, or anyone with a specialty. The expert is allowed to express opinions in his field of expertness. See Evidence Rules 702, 703, and 705. Determination of an expert's qualifications is in the first instance for the judge. See Evidence Rule 104(a) and (c). Counsel examine and cross-examine experts much as they examine and cross-examine lay witnesses. The testimony of experts is of course often in sharp conflict. The credibility of experts and the weight to be given their testimony are for the jury. See Evidence Rule 104(e).

How about opinion evidence from a lay witness? Clearly he cannot give an opinion upon a matter as to which he is not qualified, but there are many matters upon which an ordinary adult is capable of giving a valid opinion.[o] Nevertheless, the jury is presumably equally capable of forming its own opinion if it has before it the data on which the witness's opinion is based. Is not the forming of such opin-

[m] Hereinafter cited as Evidence Rules. These rules are in the Rules pamphlet.

[n] Certainly, the brevity will raise some questions without answering them. Answers are often readily available, however. Many can be had by reading the Evidence Rules themselves; where the text or footnotes refer to particular Evidence Rules, it is meant that you should read them. In further study of a particular Evidence Rule, the original Advisory Committee's notes, together with the above-cited legislative reports, are often invaluable; a multi-volume work, keyed to the Evidence Rules and containing the notes and the legislative history, is J. Weinstein & M. Berger, Weinstein's Evidence (rev. ed. 1976–1982); a single-volume study is M. Graham, Handbook of Federal Evidence (1981). If further information of a more general nature is desired, an excellent one-volume treatise is McCormick's Handbook of the Law of Evidence (2d ed. E. Cleary 1972 & Supp. 1978).

[o] It has perhaps already become obvious that what we have called "the simple narration by a witness of what he observed" necessarily embodies a certain quantum of inference and hence in a sense is opinion evidence. "I saw *B*" is an opinion or product of inference.

ions precisely what the jury's job is? If the witness is allowed to express his opinion, is he not usurping the jury's function? Shall we then confine the non-expert to matters of "fact"? See Evidence Rules 701, 704, and 602.

Question: (11) Consider the admissibility under the Evidence Rules of the following statements by an ordinary witness, who was a bystander to the automobile accident at issue in a personal-injury suit: (a) "The defendant's automobile was going 30 miles per hour" (or "about 30 miles per hour"). (b) "The defendant's automobile was going very fast" (or "too fast"). (c) "The road was very slippery." (d) "The plaintiff was drunk." (e) "The defendant was driving his automobile in a very negligent manner."

We have so far spoken of testimony given in court by witnesses. There is also, as it is sometimes rather uninformatively called, *real evidence*: a person or thing shown to the jury for use of the jurors' own powers of direct observation. A jury might be shown a scarred face, a bloodstained garment, a sample of seized narcotics, or a document. If an object cannot be produced in court, the jury may at the court's discretion be taken elsewhere to view it; for example, the jury might be taken to the scene of an automobile accident to observe how the roads intersect. Before the jury views real evidence, that evidence must be authenticated. See Evidence Rule 901(a). Authentication in the first instance is a question for the judge, not the jury. However, the jury again has the ultimate say, because it has the option of giving no weight to the evidence offered.

Experiments performed in the presence of the jury fall into the same general category as real evidence. So do charts, models, and diagrams. These items, which have not played a part in the events in suit but which are offered to illustrate or explain testimony, are sometimes called *demonstrative evidence*.

Finally, *judicial notice* may be thought of as another medium of presenting evidence at a trial. It is a means of dispensing with proof. When the judge can safely assume that a matter to be proved is indisputably true as a matter of public knowledge (not his own private knowledge), he may "notice" it, that is, instruct the jury that it is true. The judge may have to inform himself of the fact before "noticing" it. For example, he may consult a calendar to ascertain that August 26, 1984, fell on a Sunday, or an almanac to ascertain that the sun set at 4:43 p.m. on December 31, 1977. The object of judicial notice is to save the time and expense of proving matters not subject to reasonable dispute. See Evidence Rule 201.

Relevance.—With regard to admissibility, we take it as our starting point that evidence will be received only if it is relevant, that is, only if it has some rational tendency to make more or less probable any proposition of fact that is of consequence to the action. See Evidence Rules 401 and 402.

To determine what propositions are of consequence, we look to the issues shown by the pleadings as narrowed or sharpened by the pretrial techniques already considered. When proof of a proposition of fact could have no effect on the outcome of the case, either because as a matter of substantive law it makes no difference whether it is true or false or because the parties have not chosen to put it in issue, evidence bearing on that proposition is inadmissible.

Relevant evidence may be probative of propositions of consequence with varying degrees of directness or persuasiveness. For illustration, imagine that *A* sues *B* on a promissory note and that the genuineness of *B*'s signature on the note is in dispute. On the one hand, *W–1*'s testimony, "I saw *B* sign the note," bears directly on the disputed issue, and if the jury believes *W–1*'s testimony the issue may be determined. On the other hand, *W–2*'s testimony, "I saw *B* in bed in a Boston hospital on the morning of July 1, 1984" (the day the note was allegedly signed in Los Angeles), bears more remotely on the disputed issue. (Lawyers often term such evidence "circumstantial.") In each case the witness is testifying to what he observed, but in the latter case what he observed is significant only if the jury takes account of certain general propositions and infers that *B* did not sign the note in Los Angeles. The general propositions are that a flight to Los Angeles takes a certain number of hours, that a man in a hospital bed is probably sick and unable or unwilling to fly, and so on. In order for evidence thus inferentially connected to be admissible, the inference need not be a necessary one. *W–2*'s testimony is admissible although the possibility has not been excluded that *B* left his hospital bed and went by plane to Los Angeles in time to sign the note. It is open to *A* to attempt to overcome *W–2*'s testimony by proving these facts.

Question: (12) There may of course be several links in the chain of inference between the evidence and the proposition to be proved. Suppose the proposition to be proved is that *Y* killed *X*, and a love letter from *Y* to *X*'s wife is offered in evidence.[p] Spell out the series of inferences that the jury is being asked to make.

Thus, not all relevant evidence is entitled to the same amount of weight. The weight of a piece of evidence depends upon the number of successive inferences that must be made to connect it with the proposition to be proved and upon the probability of each inference.[q] Sometimes a single piece of evidence will be enough to induce the jury to infer the proposition. Often many pieces of evidence will have to be presented before their cumulative effect is such as to induce the jury so to conclude.

Rules excluding relevant evidence.—So, to be admissible, evidence must be relevant. It is not true, however, that all relevant evi-

[p] The illustration is from Morgan, Introduction to Evidence, in A. Scott & S. Simpson, Cases and Other Materials on Civil Procedure 941, 943 (1950).

[q] Of course, the testimony may be subject to an initial discount if there is a question whether the witness correctly and truthfully reported his observation. The man in the hospital bed may not have been *B* but *Z*; the witness may be mistaken or lying.

dence is admitted. The rules of evidence sometimes have the effect of excluding relevant evidence. Some persons who could give relevant testimony are not allowed to testify at all; some witnesses are not permitted to give certain kinds of testimony although relevant; and some kinds of relevant evidence are inadmissible no matter who the witness is. To return to the case of the promissory note, testimony tending to show that B signed the note is relevant. Yet a lunatic, prepared to swear that he saw B sign, may not be permitted to testify (a question of competency). Nor can B's attorney testify that B told him the signature was genuine (a question of privilege). Nor can W testify that one X told him that he, X, saw B sign (a question of hearsay).

As we examine these and other rules that prevent relevant evidence from being presented to the jury, you should ask yourself whether the claimed justification for them is valid.

Competency of witnesses.—We have said that some persons are not permitted to testify at all—they are "incompetent." For example, some states have the rule that a person may be so lacking in mental capacity that he is unfit to be a witness. The judge would therefore not allow a two-year-old child or a raving lunatic to testify. But how about a four-year-old, six-year-old, or eight-year-old child? How about an inmate of an insane asylum who although "of unsound mind" has sufficient mental capacity to observe an event, remember it, and narrate what he saw?

Question: (13) Of what effect is lack of understanding of the nature and meaning of an oath? What about an atheist who says that the oath means nothing to him? See Evidence Rule 603 and Federal Rule 43(d); cf. Evidence Rule 610.

How does the judge go about determining whether a person is competent to be a witness? In some instances, such as extreme infancy or insanity, mere observation may be enough. In others, preliminary questioning of the prospective witness may satisfy the judge. But it may become necessary to supplement these methods by calling witnesses to testify about the mental capacity of the witness in question. Suppose the incapacity is disclosed for the first time in the course of the direct examination or cross-examination of the witness. The judge may then strike out the testimony already given and tell the jury to disregard it. (But is it realistic to assume that the jurors can or will eliminate from their minds testimony that they have heard, merely because the judge instructs them to do so?)

It is well to remember that although the judge has the first word as to the competency of a witness, the jury will (if the judge allows him to testify) have the last as to his worth. The judge may decide that a six-year-old child has sufficient mental capacity so that he may testify, but the jury may give no credence or weight to what he says. Does this suggest that in a doubtful case the judge should allow the testimony to come in and leave it to the jury to appraise it?

A very few states still hold to an old common-law rule rendering a person incompetent as a witness if he has been convicted of a serious crime.

Questions: (14) What justification could be offered for this rule? Is the rule a sound one?

(15) Assuming that a state has no such rule rendering incompetent a person convicted of a crime, to what extent if any should it be permissible to inform the jury of the witness's conviction? Cf. Evidence Rule 609.

Another type of incompetency demands a word, although today only a vestige of it remains among the states. Until the middle of the nineteenth century the common-law courts took the cynical view that a party to the litigation was rendered so unreliable by his interest in the outcome that he should not be allowed to testify at all. This frequently produced the bizarre result that those who knew most about the controversy were silenced. Nowadays this disqualification in its broad form is entirely abolished. Instead, jurors are warned by the judge to take into account the interest of the party when they come to appraise the credibility of his testimony.

A vestige, however, remains. Many states have a so-called Dead Man's Act which, in suits prosecuted or defended by an executor or administrator on behalf of the decedent, renders the surviving opponent-party incompetent as a witness concerning some or all matters in issue. The various states' statutes vary widely in scope, and their interpretation has given rise to much litigation. Note that under these statutes the incompetency question arises only with respect to a survivor in actions with an executor or administrator; there is no general principle silencing a party where the only person who could have contradicted him has died before trial.

Question: (16) Do these statutes reflect the same purpose as the old disqualification of parties for interest? Do you think the statutes are wise?

The common-law rule was that husband and wife were incompetent to testify either for or against each other in any case, civil or criminal. Today this rule has largely disappeared, eroding down to a privilege in criminal cases whereby the accused may elect to keep his or her spouse off the stand except when the charge is the commission of a crime against the spouse and whereby the accused's spouse may refuse to testify adversely, and most often eroding still further.[r]

Against the background of this patchwork of competency rules applied by the states, Evidence Rule 601 as originally proposed by the Supreme Court represented a major advance. It simply provided that "[e]very person is competent to be a witness except as otherwise provided in these rules," thus virtually abolishing the concept of competency in federal courts because the Evidence Rules "otherwise provid-

---

[r] The dying rule of spousal incompetency and the eroding criminal privilege to exclude adverse spousal testimony are to be distinguished from the privilege against disclosure of confidential communications between husband and wife, which is mentioned below.

ed" in only very special circumstances. See Evidence Rules 605 and
606; cf. Evidence Rules 602 and 603. Included among the grounds of
incompetency to be abolished were mental incapacity, conviction of
crime, party status, and spousal status; also, state Dead Man's Acts
were to be rendered ineffective in federal courts. The rationale was
that it is generally better to let a witness testify and then—in order
to counter the effects of mental incapacity, moral turpitude, and interest—to rely on cross-examination, extrinsic evidence, and warnings
by the judge to the jury. The common law's total exclusion of testimony from a doubtful witness was thought to be a rather inept and
primitive manner of handling the problem. Instead, the reformers
said, the judge should let in the testimony of almost all witnesses,
and the jury should be permitted to appraise its weight and credibility.

The congressional redrafting of Evidence Rule 601 cut back the
extent of this advance. This was done by adding a second sentence
providing that in civil cases "with respect to an element of a claim or
defense as to which State law supplies the rule of decision, the competency of a witness shall be determined in accordance with State
law." This change will not be fully understood until you have studied Section 9 of this Topic. However, in very gross terms, the new
rule, its significance, and its rationale can be described as follows.

As we have already seen in several cases, state substantive law is
sometimes applied in federal court; that is to say, state law sometimes supplies the rule of decision. For example, if a New Yorker is
run down in New York City by a New Jersey driver and if the New
Yorker sues in the United States District Court for the Southern District of New York, that court will apply New York State's negligence
law, not some uniform federal law of negligence. Evidence Rule 601
now says that as to testimony tending to support or defeat a finding
of negligence in such a suit, New York State's rules as to competency
will control. The federal court will apply not only state substantive
law, but also state evidence law dealing with competence.

What this means in practical terms is that the Evidence Rules do
not provide for uniform practice in federal district courts on the subject of competency. In federal court the competency of some witnesses will be treated under the uniform federal rule embodied in the
first sentence of Evidence Rule 601, while the competency of others
will be judged under diverse state rules incorporated by the second
sentence thereof. So, in the area of competency, the federal practitioner must be the master of both federal and state evidence law.

The legislators' rationale for introducing this note of confusion into the Evidence Rules was, in part, that the federal interest in a uniform law of evidence for federal courts is not strong enough to override the state policies embodied in the states' competency rules. The
states had no strong policies wrapped up in rules of, say, judicial no-

tice, but it was thought that competency rules (especially the Dead Man's Acts) might involve more important state policies.

Privilege.—There are various rules protecting certain persons from disclosure of particular matters. To take a familiar example: if *L*, a lawyer, is called as a witness and asked about what *B*, his client, confidentially told him in the course of seeking legal advice, *B* may prevent *L* from responding. Assuming, as we shall see may be the case, that if *B* told the same things to a layman, the layman could testify to what *B* said, why are statements to a lawyer dealt with differently? Confidential communications between husband and wife, patient and physician, and penitent and clergyman are also commonly recognized as privileged. What are the reasons for and against each of these privileges?

What would you say about confidential communications to an accountant by his client? How about confidential communications between parent and child? How about a communication made to any person on a pledge of secrecy? The communications just listed are commonly not privileged. Should they be?[s]

In addition to privileged communications, there are topics privileged from disclosure. For example, the public interest may require that state secrets be privileged—an increasingly important question as much governmental activity is "classified." Within limits, too, trade secrets important to the existence of a particular business may be privileged. Here also falls the familiar privilege against self-incrimination. (This privilege can be claimed in all kinds of proceedings: criminal and civil actions, administrative hearings, and legislative investigations. Note that although a witness is privileged not to reveal facts tending to incriminate himself, he has no such privilege as to facts incriminating someone else.)[t]

We do not here attempt to draw a logically satisfying distinction between incompetency and privilege, although the key to it would lie in the differing purposes of the two doctrines. Competency rules are centrally concerned with the reliability of evidence, whereas the rules of privilege are based on social policies extrinsic to the courtroom.

[s] Would you compel a newspaper reporter to disclose the source of information given to him in confidence? See the absorbing case of Branzburg v. Hayes, 408 U.S. 665, 92 S.Ct. 2646 (1972), regarding newspaper reporters' obligation to testify before grand juries. That case held that the first amendment does not give rise to a general newsman's privilege but left plenty of room for distinguishing the holding. And, of course, the absence of a privilege of constitutional origin does not preclude a judge-made or statutory privilege. Thus, most of the federal circuits have molded some degree of qualified privilege for newsmen, and more than half the states have enacted legislation according reporters some form of privilege as to their confidential sources. See also Herbert v. Lando, 441 U.S. 153, 99 S.Ct. 1635 (1979). See generally 23 Wright & Graham § 5426.

[t] Restrictions on the use in criminal cases of confessions and evidence illegally obtained may be mentioned here.

Under "privilege" is also classed the question whether the President, a state governor, or a foreign ambassador can claim immunity from compulsory process to testify as a witness.

Privilege is not aimed at the ascertainment of truth, but rather at some other goal often pursued at the price of shutting out the truth.

Each particular privilege, being tied to some extrinsic social policy, must be considered individually as to how broad it is in scope, as to who may claim it, and as to how it may be waived. It is worth thinking about how these three questions should be answered for each of the privileges mentioned above.

Questions: (17) If a judge erroneously upholds a witness's privilege and excludes testimony, should the party damaged by the ruling be able to attack it on appeal?

(18) What if the judge erroneously denies the privilege and admits the testimony? See McCormick's Handbook of the Law of Evidence 152–53 (2d ed. E. Cleary 1972).

Again, against this background of the accepted rules regarding privilege, the Evidence Rules as originally proposed by the Supreme Court represented a major change. Evidence Rules 501 to 513 codified the rules of privilege for federal courts in accordance with modern thinking on the subject; their effect was, in general, to restrict the realm of privilege, eliminating some common-law privileges and modifying others. However, these privilege provisions generated more controversy in Congress than did any other aspect of the Evidence Rules, and the result was the enactment of a redrafted version of Evidence Rule 501 and the passage of 28 U.S.C. § 2076.

Evidence Rule 501, as enacted, is similar in effect to Evidence Rule 601. It provides for the application of federal privilege rules in certain circumstances and state privilege rules in others. Thus, just as for competence, the federal practitioner must be the master of both federal and state privilege law. But there is an important difference between Evidence Rules 501 and 601. The first sentence of Evidence Rule 601 represents a codification of federal competence law. The first sentence of Evidence Rule 501, on the other hand, leaves federal privilege rules to continuing case-by-case development; the codification attempted in proposed Evidence Rules 502 to 513 was deleted. This is a reflection of the furor that the proposed privilege provisions generated in Congress.

A further reflection of that controversy is found in 28 U.S.C. § 2076. This new provision specifically restricts the Supreme Court's rulemaking power in the area of privilege.

Question: (19) Would the codification of privilege rules as proposed by the Supreme Court have been within the terms of 28 U.S.C. § 2072?

Hearsay.—We have already given one example of hearsay: in the suit on the promissory note, W testifies that X told him that he, X, saw B sign the note. This testimony is objectionable as hearsay. See Evidence Rule 802. Why is it objectionable? Because W may be mistaken in his memory as to what X said? Suppose then that W produces in court a written statement, identifying it as having been prepared by X. The testimony is still objectionable. Is this because

X was not under oath? Suppose then that W is a notary public and has taken X's oath that the statement is true. Even this does not cure the hearsay difficulty. Why all this squeamishness about hearsay? Responsible persons daily make important decisions in their own lives in reliance upon patent hearsay; indeed, normal life could hardly go on if this were not so. Why should courts reject a type of evidence so commonly relied upon outside the courtroom?

The heart of the objection to hearsay is the absence of an opportunity for cross-examination of the declarant (the person who made the out-of-court statement offered in evidence by the testimony of another). Cross-examination may bring out important matters omitted from the original statement; it may lay falsehood bare; it may expose errors in observation, memory, or narration; or it may at least raise doubts as to the credence and weight the jury should give to the testimony. Often, of course, cross-examination fails of its purposes and, particularly if it is unskillful, may serve only to reinforce the original story. But the chance for cross-examination is regarded as such an essential check on the reliability of testimony that where cross-examination is not possible the testimony is ordinarily not admissible.[u]

The concern generated by lack of an opportunity for cross-examination largely explains the hearsay rule, but not entirely. The rule may be invoked even where the declarant is sitting in court, readily available for cross-examination. Indeed, testimony in a previous trial or hearing where the declarant was in fact subject to cross-examination may in certain circumstances run afoul of the hearsay rule. In such situations the hearsay rule is better explained by the simple proposition that calling the declarant to the stand to testify as to what he said is, as a method of proof, clearly superior to letting some witness testify as to what the declarant previously said. If the declarant is called, his demeanor on the stand can be considered along with his statements.

How sound is the hearsay rule? Granting that there is a risk of falsehood or error that cross-examination and demeanor might expose, does this risk so overcome the probative value of the testimony that the fact-finder should not be given the chance to hear and appraise it, making what the fact-finder may think to be due allowance for its infirmity? Basic to the rule excluding hearsay and to some other exclusionary rules is a distrust of the capacity of the jury to appraise the evidence properly. You will find that such rules are frequently not applied when the trier of fact is an expert administrative tribunal.

[u] For example, if the witness dies after his direct examination, thus defeating the opportunity for cross-examination, the testimony already given under oath in open court may be stricken. See 5 J. Wigmore, Evidence § 1390 (J. Chadbourn rev. 1974).

Question: (20) Should the hearsay rule apply when the trier of fact is a judge sitting in a nonjury case? See McCormick's Handbook of the Law of Evidence 137–38 (2d ed. E. Cleary 1972).

Do not fall into the error of assuming that repetition in court of an out-of-court statement of another person invariably raises a hearsay problem. Assume that *A* is suing *B* for slander, alleging that *B* called him a thief, and *B* by answer has denied that he made such a statement. *W* testifies that at the time and place in question he heard *B* say that *A* was a thief. In this case, although *W* is testifying to what he heard *B* say, *W*'s testimony is admissible. No question of hearsay is involved. What is the difference between this case and the one where *W* testified as to what *X* said about seeing *B* sign the note? There the purpose of the testimony was to prove that *B* signed the note, and the credibility and weight of *X*'s out-of-court statement were therefore important. In the present case, the purpose of offering *W*'s testimony is simply to prove that *B* made the slanderous statement that *W* says he made, and for that purpose the credibility and weight of *B*'s statement are unimportant. The credibility and weight of *W*'s testimony are important, but *W* is on the stand and subject to cross-examination. We can generalize and say that it is only when the statement of the declarant is offered to prove the truth of the statement—when, in effect, testimony by the declarant is being offered through the mouth of another—that a question of hearsay arises. See Evidence Rule 801(c).

Question: (21) *P* sued Dr. *D* for negligence in leaving a sponge in the incision after an operation on *P*'s spine. Several doctors had operated on *P*'s spine at various times prior to the discovery of the sponge. To establish liability it was necessary to prove (a) that a sponge was left in the incision by Dr. *D* and (b) that it was left there as the result of Dr. *D*'s failure to exercise proper skill and care. *P* offered testimony by a witness, *W*, that someone in the operating room told Dr. *D* that the sponge count had not come out right. This testimony was excluded on the ground that it was hearsay. There was a verdict and a judgment for Dr. *D*, and *P* appealed. The question on appeal was the propriety of excluding the proffered testimony. What argument would you make for *P*, and what do you think the decision should be? See Smedra v. Stanek, 187 F.2d 892 (10th Cir.1951).

Exceptions to the hearsay rule.—The rule excluding hearsay is riddled with exceptions. We shall not catalogue them all or probe the refinements of any of them. Were we to do so, you would quickly see that the pattern is haphazard rather than logical. Not only does the law differ greatly from state to state, but the law of any one state is likely to be shifting, uncertain, and abounding in inconsistencies; on the federal level, the twenty-nine exceptions listed in Evidence Rules 803 and 804 suggest a similar complexity. Rather we shall consider in a general way the reasons why the rejection of hearsay has not been complete and the conditions that must exist before an exception to the rule is made.

In the first place, it is apparent that not all forms of hearsay are inherently unreliable; a rational system would attempt to segregate and admit hearsay evidence that falls high on the reliability scale. In the second place, although an out-of-court utterance is a less desirable method of proof than in-court testimony, it is recognized that a rigorous exclusion of all hearsay, or of all but the most reliable hearsay, would sometimes block effective proof of an essential issue. Because of these considerations, some types of hearsay have always been admitted.

Accordingly, exceptions to the hearsay rule have arisen where there is something about the out-of-court utterance that can be pointed to as a justification for relying on that evidence in the absence of accompanying demeanor evidence and cross-examination. In other words, the circumstances in which the declarant's statement was made must be such as to make it seem trustworthy. See Evidence Rule 803. Absolute trustworthiness is not, of course, required—even the testimony of a witness on the stand and subjected to cross-examination does not approach that ideal.

For certain hearsay exceptions, circumstances surrounding the declarant's statement that suggest some degree of reliability do not constitute a sufficient condition for admission. There is imposed the additional requirement that the declarant be unavailable to testify (for example, because he is dead or absent from the jurisdiction). In other words, there is an explicit notion of necessity linked to the hearsay exception. See Evidence Rule 804. However, careful examination of most hearsay exceptions, even those that apply whether or not the declarant is unavailable, will reveal implicit notions of necessity or at least of practicality.

With these generalities in mind, consider the following examples of major exceptions to the hearsay rule.

1. Our first illustration comes originally from the criminal law. *A* is charged with the murder of *B*. Testimony of *W* is offered to the effect that *B*, knowing that death was imminent, said, "*A* shot me," or, for that matter, "*C* shot me." *W*'s testimony is clearly hearsay, but the likelihood that *B* told the truth under the circumstances set forth is supposed to be strong enough to justify admitting *W*'s account. Of course, *B* may have been mistaken or may have lied to get revenge upon *A* or *C*, to protect someone, or for some other reason; but these considerations will go only to the weight and credence to be given to the evidence. You may well ask how much scientific support there is for the supposition upon which this "dying declaration" exception rests.[v] Indeed, distrust of its scientific support perhaps ex-

[v] "The existing rule, with its strict limitations, has been introduced into India where it appears to have worked badly, according to Mr. Justice Stephen, who says: 'I have heard that in the Punjab the effect of it is that a person mortally wounded frequently makes a statement bringing all his hereditary enemies on to the scene at the time of his receiving his wound, thus using his last opportunity ex-

plains the fact that the common law and many states have construed this exception narrowly. Traditionally, for it to apply, (a) the case has to be a criminal prosecution for homicide, (b) the declarant has to have died, a victim of that homicide, (c) the utterance had to be made by the declarant while believing that his death was imminent, and (d) the utterance had to concern the circumstances of that impending death. You may find it odd that in many states, then, *W*'s testimony of *B*'s dying declaration, admissible in a murder trial, is not admissible in a civil action for *B*'s wrongful death.

Evidence Rule 804(b)(2) significantly expands the exception by modifying requirements (a) and (b), although that expansion was based not on a belief in the reliability of dying declarations, but rather on a feeling that the traditional requirements were illogical and arbitrary. It should be specially noted that the dying declaration exception to the hearsay rule is now available in civil cases in federal court.

2. *A*, injured by a hit-and-run driver, sues *B* for the injuries he sustained. The identity of the driver is in dispute. *B* offers the testimony of *W* that *C*, now dead, said to *W*, "I ran over *A* and was lucky enough to get away." Should it be admitted? How is the requirement of reliability satisfied? The theory is that a person is unlikely to make a statement against his own interest unless it is true. This "declaration against interest" exception to the hearsay rule is well recognized. It is, however, narrowly limited. Traditionally, the statement has to have been against a *proprietary* or a *pecuniary* interest. Some courts say that a statement that would inferentially subject the declarant to tort liability is not sufficiently against his pecuniary interest to be admissible, and such courts would therefore exclude the statement of the hit-and-run driver given above. (Is there any rational basis for this limitation?) Furthermore, the declarant must be unavailable. (Does this second requirement make sense?)

Evidence Rule 804(b)(3) extends the exception to cover a statement of a declarant unavailable as a witness that "so far tended to subject him to civil or criminal liability, or to render invalid a claim by him against another, that a reasonable man . . . would not have made the statement unless he believed it to be true."

3. "Admissions" form another traditional exception. These are out-of-court statements by a party or his representative offered by an opponent as evidence of their content.ʷ They were usually against

do them an injury. A remark made on the policy of the rule by a native of Madras shows how differently such matters are viewed in different parts of the world. "Such evidence," he said, "ought never to be admitted in any case. What motive for telling the truth can any man possibly have when he is at the point of death."'

(1 Stephen's Hist. Crim. Law of England, 448, 449.)" People v. Becker, 215 N.Y. 126, 147, 109 N.E. 127, 133 (1915).

ʷ Contrast these "evidential" admissions with binding "judicial" admissions such as those made under Federal Rule

interest when made, but they need not have been so. *A* is suing *B* for negligently inflicted injuries; *A* can introduce testimony of *W* that *B* said, "I had only one drink before the accident, but I didn't see *A* until after I hit him," or, "It was all my fault." Dean McCormick cited this example: someone has stated that a note is forged, but then buys the note and sues on it; the statement can come in against him as an admission. McCormick's Handbook of the Law of Evidence 630 (2d ed. E. Cleary 1972).

Admissions and declarations against interest are frequently confused. But note: (a) admissions are utterances attributable to parties, while a declaration against interest can be uttered by anyone; (b) admissions need not be against interest when made, while a declaration against interest obviously must be; and (c) for admissions availability of the declarant is immaterial, while for a declaration against interest the declarant must be unavailable.

Question: (22) What is the justification for the exception regarding admissions?

Admissions receive similar treatment under the Evidence Rules; that is, they are admissible. However, the analytic approach differs. As just explained, admissions have traditionally been treated as an exception to the hearsay rule, but the Evidence Rules treat admissions as simply not hearsay in the first place. See Evidence Rule 801(d)(2). The Advisory Committee's note thereto says: "Admissions by a party-opponent are excluded from the category of hearsay on the theory that their admissibility in evidence is the result of the adversary system rather than satisfaction of the conditions of the hearsay rule."

4. Courts have also created a hearsay exception for statements relating to a startling event made while the declarant was under the stress of excitement caused by the event. This is one of several hearsay exceptions often lumped together under the label "res gestae" without serious analysis.[x]

Questions: (23) What is the voucher of trustworthiness for this "excited utterance" exception?

(24) Should it make any difference whether the declarant is available?

---

36. See Freed v. Erie L. Ry., supra p. 74.

[x] "The marvelous capacity of a Latin phrase to serve as a substitute for reasoning, and the confusion of thought inevitably accompanying the use of inaccurate terminology, are nowhere better illustrated than in the decisions dealing with the admissibility of evidence as 'res gestae.' It is probable that this troublesome expression owes its existence and persistence in our law of evidence to an inclination of judges and lawyers to avoid the toilsome exertion of exact analysis and precise thinking." Morgan, A Suggested Classification of Utterances Admissible as Res Gestae, 31 Yale L.J. 229, 229 (1922).

HANDEL v. NEW YORK RAPID TRANSIT CORP.

Supreme Court of New York, Appellate Division, Second Department, 1937.
252 A.D. 142, 297 N.Y.S. 216, aff'd mem., 277 N.Y. 548, 13 N.E.2d 468 (1938).

TAYLOR, J. In an action to recover damages for the death of plaintiff-appellant's intestate alleged to have resulted from the negligence of the defendant-respondent, judgment dismissing the complaint, entered upon a nonsuit, affirmed, with costs. The plaintiff's proofs failed to establish, prima facie, a cause of action. The claimed declaration of the intestate after the happening of the accident, to wit, "Save me. Help me—why did that conductor close the door on me," was incompetent as evidence and properly excluded by the trial court. The declaration was not admissible as part of the res gestae. [Citations omitted.] It was narrative of a past event and within the hearsay rule.

DAVIS, ADEL and TAYLOR, JJ., concur; CLOSE, J., with whom HAGARTY, J., concurs, dissents and votes for reversal of the judgment and for a new trial, with opinion.

CLOSE, J. (dissenting). In my opinion the evidence, offered in behalf of the plaintiff, of a statement made by the decedent after the accident was admissible as a part of the res gestae, and the trial court erred in excluding it. A recital of the circumstances under which the statement was made will serve to define the point of law.

The decedent was a police officer attached to Precinct 60, located at West Eighth street, Brooklyn. At some time between three-forty and four o'clock in the morning of April 22, 1934, Timothy Downing, another policeman, saw him coming from a nearby lunch wagon. Handel was off duty, having finished at midnight, and was not due back at the station house until the following afternoon. After a brief conversation, the two policemen crossed the street to the West Eighth Street station of the defendant's elevated railroad, located almost opposite the precinct station house. Handel passed through the door, and Downing last saw him as he was going up the stairs toward the elevated platform. As Downing walked back across the street he heard the rumble of an approaching train. It was then about four o'clock.

Mrs. Ida Pfeifer lived on the top floor of an apartment house on West Third street, with her bedroom window directly facing the elevated structure. She slept with the window open. She testified that at about four o'clock in the morning she was awakened by the sound of someone screaming. Looking out the window, she saw a train come to a stop and something that looked like "a big bundle" fall from the side door of the last car down to Park place. The screaming continued. Mrs. Pfeifer put on a bathrobe and slippers, ran down three flights of stairs to the front entrance of her house, and proceeded from there to Park place, a distance of about seventy feet. There she found the body of Handel. He was moaning, and made a statement to the witness which was excluded from evidence on the defendant's objection. The record shows that the witness would have testified, if permitted, that Handel said, "Save me. Help me—why did that conductor close the door on me."

John Leyton also lived in the vicinity of West Third street and Park place. A little before four o'clock in the morning he had taken his dog out for a walk. When he returned it was "Pretty near four o'clock." As he approached the house he heard the noise of an elevated train, and looking up he saw a train stop near West Third street. Leyton put the dog in the house and stepped out again. As he did so he heard someone moaning under the elevated structure. He estimated that it took him about half a minute to get to where Handel lay, and that about two and one-half minutes elapsed between the time when he heard the train and his arrival at the place where the deceased lay. Mrs. Pfeifer was already there. Leyton would also have testified to Handel's statement if permitted to do so. One of Handel's shoes was missing, and his pants were torn off from the hips down.

Officer Downing testified that he received word of the accident about three-quarters of an hour after he had left Handel at the station entrance. In company with a detective named Fitzsimmons, he went up to the station platform, walked to the end of the platform, and then proceeded along a "catwalk" beside the tracks. The "catwalk" ended about fifty feet from West Third street. The two men then walked on the ties between the rails to a point just over the curb of West Third street, about 1,000 feet distant from the station entrance. There they found a shoe, with the laces broken out of it, wedged between the rail and a wooden beam. The toe of the shoe pointed back toward West Eighth street.

Downing returned and examined the station platform. He found two dark marks running parallel with the edge of the platform for a distance of about 125 to 150 feet, increasing in width as they approached the end of the platform. The inference is that the marks were made by the rubber heels of Handel's shoes as he was dragged along by a moving train. Beyond the end of the platform no marks were visible.

When the decedent was examined by a doctor it was found that, in addition to numerous lacerations and contusions, he had suffered a concussion of the brain, a broken right hand, a fracture of the right femur, a broken pelvis, and a ruptured bladder. He was also in profound shock. Of course, this must have been his condition at the time when he made his statement to Mrs. Pfeifer and Leyton. Apparently, he died later in the day.

The foregoing is substantially all the evidence offered by the plaintiff. At the close of the plaintiff's case, the trial court dismissed the complaint. We are all agreed that the dismissal was proper if the declaration of the decedent was properly excluded; because without that declaration the record is wholly lacking in proof of negligence on the part of the defendant. From the drag marks on the platform, the broken shoe wedged between the rails, and the fact that the deceased was seen to fall from the car door at just about the point where the shoe was found, it might reasonably be inferred that the deceased had, in some manner, been caught in the door at the station platform; that he had been dragged along with his body hanging outside the train as far as West Third street; that his foot had then become caught between the ties or the rails; and that his shoe had been torn off and his body jerked from the train at the same time. But the circumstances throw no light on how the deceased came to be trapped in the door, and the proof is therefore insufficient to warrant an inference of negligence.

However, the declaration of the deceased, if admissible, would constitute some evidence of negligence. . . . The question to be determined is whether this evidence was competent as a part of the res gestae. The trial court concluded . . . that the evidence was not admissible under that exception to the hearsay rule. A majority of this court are of the same opinion. With that conclusion I disagree.

. . . .

. . . We must answer two questions: (1) Was the declaration "spontaneously expressive of the injured person's observation" of the occurrence? (2) Was the utterance made "within such limit of time as presumably to preclude fabrication?"

Handel's statement was of a spontaneous character. It was not made in response to any question . . .. The spontaneous nature of the utterance is shown by the words "Save me. Help me," which preceded the reference to the action of the conductor. . . . The statement about the conductor took the form of a question, "why did that conductor close the door on me," which in itself is an indication of spontaneity. A construction which holds this declaration merely a narrative of a past event ignores the language used and its plain implications.

The other element is that of time. We are asked to consider the fact that the deceased had traveled from West Eighth street to West Third street before he fell. I would disregard that entirely. On a journey so perilous, one has little leisure for plotting fiction. The only material period of time is that which elapsed after the deceased fell to the street. The best estimate of the interval is that given by the witness Leyton, who said that about two and one-half minutes elapsed between the time when he heard the train and his arrival at the place where Handel was found. . . . But it is not a question of precisely how many seconds or minutes elapsed. The question is whether "the utterance is made within such limit of time as presumably to preclude fabrication."

My conclusion is that Handel's utterance came within the confines of the rule. It seems to me incredible that a man so broken in body and so profoundly shocked in mind could have spent the slight interval before aid arrived in manufacturing a false explanation of the extremity in which he was found.

If there is a "spontaneous exclamation exception to the hearsay rule," here is a case for its application. In my opinion the evidence was wrongly excluded, and the error requires a reversal of the judgment and a new trial.

———

Questions: (25) Assuming the Handel case arose today in federal court, would the evidence be admissible under Evidence Rule 803(2)? under Evidence Rule 803(1)?

(26) Adopting the same assumption, would Handel's statement be admissible as a dying declaration under Evidence Rule 804(b)(2)? See Shepard v. United States, 290 U.S. 96, 54 S.Ct. 22 (1933) (Cardozo, J.) ("There must be a 'settled hopeless expectation' [citation omitted] that death is near at hand, and what is said must have been spoken in the hush of its impending presence.").

5. Entries contemporaneously made in books and records in the ordinary course of business generally may be admitted in evidence without producing the persons who actually made the entries. This "business records" exception serves to point up the important fact that writings may present hearsay problems, e.g., where a document is offered in evidence to prove the facts it relates.[y] In order to get such evidence in, the document must be authenticated and an applicable hearsay exception (such as business records) must be found.

For the contours of the federal exception, see Evidence Rule 803(6), as well as the subsequent subdivisions of that Evidence Rule.

6. We close with some other illustrative exceptions to the hearsay rule. (a) *Testimony given at another hearing of the same or a different proceeding by a witness now unavailable.* This is an easy exception to justify when the parties to the former hearing were the same and the issues substantially identical. But suppose the testimony is now offered against a person not a party before. Should the opportunity for cross-examination by someone else with similar motive and interest suffice as a voucher of reliability? See Evidence Rule 804(b)(1).[z] (b) *Declarations concerning family history.* See Evidence Rule 804(b)(4). If it were not for this exception, proof of

---

[y] See Evidence Rule 801(a)(1). Another example would be where a witness testifies that he read, "Died 1928," on a tombstone. Cf. Evidence Rule 803(13).

Similarly, it should be noted that nonverbal conduct may also present hearsay problems. A witness testifying that someone nodded his head provides an example. See Evidence Rule 801(a)(2).

Was there a hearsay problem with Mrs. Pfeifer testifying that she had heard someone scream?

[z] Cf. Federal Rule 32(a)(3). Apparently, Federal Rule 32(a)(1) to (4) provides alternative exceptions to the hearsay rule. A deposition satisfying either Federal Rule 32(a) or the Evidence Rules is admissible. See Evidence Rule 802.

matters of pedigree might be extremely difficult. What is the basis for holding such declarations reliable? (c) *Statements in ancient writings.* The usual requirement of authentication of a document may be satisfied with respect to an ancient document by a showing that its condition is such as to create no suspicion concerning its authenticity and that it was in a place where, if authentic, it would be likely to be. See Evidence Rule 901(b)(8). There is a separate requirement of admissibility as against a hearsay objection, if the document is offered for the truth of statements made in it. See Evidence Rule 803(16). (d) *Other exceptions.* Consider the potential of Evidence Rules 803(24) and 804(b)(5). Do you think that these residual exceptions portend the demise of the hearsay rule?

Multiple hearsay.—Finally, there is the problem of, as Evidence Rule 805 puts it, "hearsay within hearsay." The rule here is that when testimony includes multiple levels of hearsay, each level must come within a hearsay exception in order for the testimony to be admissible.

Question: (27) In a civil wrongful-death action brought in federal court by *X*'s wife against *K*, *W* is called by plaintiff to testify that *W* saw *X* and his wife walking together, that *X* fell, that *W* ran over, that *X* was then dead, and that *W* heard *X*'s wife cry, "*X* just groaned that *K* had told him that *K* had poisoned him." Can the quoted testimony come in, over objection?

The "best evidence" rule.—Suppose a defendant wishes to prove payment by means of proving the content of a written receipt given by the plaintiff.[a] The "best evidence" of the content consists of the original paper, which will be admitted upon sufficient authentication. May the party prove the content not by means of the original paper but by means of a copy of the paper or by means of oral testimony regarding the content by a witness who read it? Evidence Rules 1001 and 1002 tell us that this usually may not be done. But exceptions exist. See Evidence Rules 1003, 1004, and 1007.

Remote, confusing, and prejudicial evidence.—The fact that a piece of relevant evidence does not run afoul of any of the foregoing rules does not necessarily mean that it will be admitted. The judge has discretion to exclude evidence of comparatively slight probative value when he believes that it is not worth the time it will take to hear it.[b] A similar discretion exists when the probative value of the evidence is outweighed by the confusion or the prejudice that its admission would produce. See Evidence Rule 403.

---

[a] The student should be clear that payment can be proved otherwise than through the content of the receipt, even if a receipt was in fact given.

[b] To prevent the piling up of merely cumulative testimony, the judge has discretion to limit the number of witnesses on a particular issue, a discretion frequently exercised with respect to the number of expert witnesses. Such a limitation is often prescribed in a pretrial order under Federal Rule 16.

For example, will the plaintiff suing for injuries from an allegedly defective condition on the defendant's premises be permitted to prove other accidents occurring there for the purpose of showing that the situation was dangerous? Generally yes. Will the defendant be allowed to show an absence of other accidents as evidence of nonexistence of danger? Generally not. Why this distinction? Should the plaintiff be permitted to prove that the defendant is protected by liability insurance (as the basis for an inference that he had nothing to lose by his carelessness and hence was less likely to be careful)? See Evidence Rule 411.

In a suit for injuries allegedly due to a defective condition on the defendant's premises, should evidence that the defendant made repairs after the accident be admissible as some proof of his negligence? See Evidence Rule 407. Should the defendant's offer to make a compromise settlement be received as evidence for the plaintiff? See Evidence Rule 408. Are your conclusions with respect to these last two questions tied exclusively to notions of remoteness, confusion, and prejudice?

Objections to evidence.—When evidence is being offered that the opponent believes to be inadmissible, he should object specifically and immediately, as soon as the ground for objection appears. The objection has a two-fold purpose: (1) to keep the evidence out, or to have it stricken; and (2) to lay the foundation for a later appeal if the evidence is admitted.[c] Any evidence admitted without objection may be given such weight as the jury thinks it deserves, and any error in its admission is usually unavailable upon appeal. See Evidence Rule 103(a)(1) and (d). For instance, if testimony regarding the content of a document is admitted without the objection that it is not the "best evidence," the jury may properly base a finding upon it. Similarly, a finding may properly be based upon hearsay testimony to which no objection is made. In either case, of course, the jury may nevertheless discount or disregard the testimony because of the inherent weakness that gives rise to the exclusionary rule in question.

It will often happen that evidence is offered that is properly admissible for one purpose but inadmissible for another. The fact that the jury might improperly apply it to an inadmissible purpose does not ordinarily require its exclusion. But the party against whom it is offered may acquire some protection by asking the judge to instruct the jury as to the limited purpose for which it is being admitted. See Evidence Rule 105. If no such request is made, the jury may properly give the evidence its natural probative force for any purpose.

---

[c] Examine Federal Rule 46, and you will find that formal "exceptions" are not necessary, although the Rule indicates that "heretofore" they were. This is a reference to the old requirement of such ritualistic words as, "I except," or, "Please note my exception," in order for a party to have the right to appeal an adverse ruling. By virtue of this Rule, it is now necessary in the federal courts only to state an objection. However, the old requirement still prevails in some states.

Question: (28) In the case in question (21) involving the statement that the sponge count did not come out right, if the proffered testimony were admitted over objection, what should the objecting party then do?

A piece of evidence is often offered that will become relevant only after or in connection with other evidence not yet presented. Practical necessities prevent it from being excluded. A party must start somewhere, and the connecting evidence would very likely be subject to the same infirmity if presented first. The dilemma is resolved by admitting it conditionally on the reasonable assurance of counsel that it will be "connected up" later. If it turns out not to be, it will be stricken on motion and the jury instructed to disregard it. See Evidence Rule 104(b).

If evidence is erroneously admitted over objection, the record is clear for purposes of appeal. If, however, the objection is sustained and the evidence is excluded, the party against whom the ruling is made should make known to the judge by "offer of proof" the substance of the proffered evidence (for example, the answer the party expects from the witness), unless the substance is apparent from the context. If he does not do so, he cannot predicate error on the exclusion, for it is only in this way that the appellate court can appraise the seriousness of the error. See Evidence Rule 103(a)(2) and (b). For obvious reasons the offer of proof should be made out of the hearing of the jury. See Evidence Rule 103(c).

Question: (29) Suppose the opponent does not agree that the witness would answer the objectionable question as the party making the offer of proof expects him to do. How can this difficulty be resolved?

It should be pointed out that what is in appearance a ruling on evidence is often actually a ruling on substantive law. Suppose in an action for breach of contract to deliver 1000 tons of coal at a stated price, the plaintiff offers evidence that he was emotionally upset and suffered a nervous breakdown because of his loss of faith in the contract-breaking defendant, who had been his close friend. The defendant objects on the ground of irrelevance. If the court excludes the evidence, this is in effect a ruling of substantive law that in such a case emotional disturbance is not a proper element of damages.

Ways of combating admissible evidence.—Let us assume that a party has called a witness whose direct testimony, if believed, will be damaging to the opponent. What may the opponent do to combat it?

He may try in various ways to impeach (that is, discredit) the witness.[d] His first chance is on cross-examination, when he may ask questions designed to bring out bias; weakness of perception, of memory, or of narration; prior inconsistent statements; bad character; or the like. See, e.g., Evidence Rules 608 and 609. Or he may wait until he puts on his own case, and then impeach the witness by

[d] We shall pass over the counterstep of rehabilitating an impeached witness. See, e.g., Evidence Rule 608(a)(2).

the testimony of other witnesses or documentary evidence bringing out similar defects; however, to prevent unreasonable excursions such impeachment by extrinsic evidence is limited to the more significant defects; on lesser matters, the opponent must "take the witness's answer" on cross-examination. See, e.g., Evidence Rule 608(b).

In addition to impeaching the witness in these ways, the story of the witness may be contradicted (that is, disproved) by other evidence. In line with the constant objective of keeping a trial within bounds, there are also limitations on the extent to which contradiction of "collateral" matters in a witness's testimony will be permitted.

Traditionally, a prior statement inconsistent with the testimony of a witness on the stand has been admissible for the purpose of discrediting his court testimony, but normally not for the purpose of proving the truth of what he is alleged to have previously said. For the former purpose it is not hearsay. (Why not?) For the latter purpose it has been considered hearsay by the great majority of courts, including the Supreme Court of the United States. Bridges v. Wixon, 326 U.S. 135, 65 S.Ct. 1443 (1945). Evidence Rule 801(d)(1)(A) alters the definition of hearsay somewhat so that when a declarant testifies and is subject to cross-examination concerning a prior inconsistent statement made under certain formal circumstances, that statement is not hearsay and can therefore be used for its truth. The argument for this change is that the trier of fact, being able to observe demeanor and the nature of the testimony, is in as good a position to determine the truth or falsity of such a prior statement as it is to determine the truth or falsity of the inconsistent testimony given in court.

Now let us assume that a witness has unexpectedly given testimony damaging to the party who called him. That party may of course contradict him through other evidence, but the traditional rule has been that a party is not allowed to "impeach his own witness," that is, discredit a witness he himself has called. This rule has long been subject to criticism. It was rejected in a few states, and inroads upon it by way of limitations and exceptions were made in others. Evidence Rule 607 abandons it entirely. The Advisory Committee's note thereto says that the traditional rule was "based on false premises. A party does not hold out his witnesses as worthy of belief, since he rarely has a free choice in selecting them."

The combination of Evidence Rules 607 and 801(d)(1)(A) is especially helpful in dealing with the turncoat witness who changes his story and deprives the party calling him of essential testimony.

Scope and manner of cross-examination.—Beyond impeaching a witness, how far may the cross-examining party go in the course of the cross-examination in seeking to support his own case out of the mouth of the witness? Not far, according to the rule in most states and in the federal courts. See Evidence Rule 611(b). Accordingly, a witness may be cross-examined only as to facts and circumstances connected with the matters covered in direct examination, in addition to matters affecting credibility.[e] Departures from this rule are, however, permitted in the discretion of the trial judge.

Question: (30) What reasons can you advance for and against so limiting the scope of cross-examination?

A conventional technique of cross-examination is to put "leading questions," that is, questions that suggest the desired answer. One such type is, "Isn't it a fact that . . . ?" Leading questions are usually improper on direct examination, although they generally pass without objection on routine matters of a preliminary nature and they may be permitted in specified situations including interrogation of a hostile witness. See Evidence Rule 611(c); cf. Evidence Rule 611(a).

Question: (31) Why are leading questions ordinarily objectionable on direct but permissible on cross-examination?

Where the scope of cross-examination is limited as under Evidence Rule 611(b), it may be necessary for a party who has cross-examined to recall the witness at a later stage of the trial to get additional testimony. In doing so the party is held to "make the witness his own," thus subjecting the questioning on recall to the rules governing direct rather than cross-examination.

(d) Motions at the Close of All the Evidence

We continue our consideration of the course of a jury trial. When all the evidence is in, either party may move for a directed verdict. See Rule 50(a) and (b). Note that the motion "shall state the specific grounds therefor." The granting of this motion results in the withdrawal of the case from the jury. When may this drastic step be taken without impinging upon the constitutional right to trial by jury? This brings us to examine in greater detail the difficult question of the standard to be applied in the direction of a verdict.

Suppose that plaintiff has the burden of proof on propositions A, B, and C, all essential to his case, and defendant has the burden on propositions D and E. When the evidence is closed, no evidence bearing on A has been offered by either party. Defendant's motion for a directed verdict should be granted. It is immaterial that there may be a conflict in the evidence as to B, C, D, and E, because the jury's resolution of these conflicts could make no difference in the result. There is no more infringement of the right to trial by jury here than there would be if the plaintiff failed to allege A and his complaint was dismissed for failure to state a claim upon which relief could be granted.

---

[e] On the other hand, in some states the cross-examination may cover all aspects of the case, including matters on which the cross-examining party has the burden of proof. Evidence Rule 611(b) as originally proposed by the Court adopted this minority position. However, Congress redrafted the Rule to return to the traditional federal practice.

Next let us assume that there is some evidence bearing on *A* but so little that the judge is satisfied that, looking only to the evidence favorable to the plaintiff, a reasonable jury would not be justified in finding *A*. Granting that it is the function of the jury and not of the judge to resolve disputed issues of fact, is it not wholly proper to say that there is here no basis for a genuine dispute as to *A*? The almost universal answer to this question, and the answer given by the federal courts, is that a directed verdict is proper in these circumstances.

Suppose, however, that there is testimony that, standing alone, would warrant a finding of *A*, but there is overwhelming evidence to the contrary. If the judge is satisfied that no reasonable jury properly considering the evidence could find *A*, must he nevertheless submit the case to the jury? This is a debated question. It is argued on the one hand that to direct a verdict here would be an invasion of the jury's right to determine the credibility of witnesses and on the other hand that a jury ought not to be permitted to act unreasonably.

Now let us assume that the plaintiff has offered highly persuasive testimony as to *A*, *B*, and *C* and that the defendant has rested without impeaching the testimony and without putting in any evidence of his own.[f] We know that in a courtroom, as well as outside, people sometimes lie and honest people are sometimes mistaken. It could be argued, then, that the credibility of the testimony is necessarily at issue and, because this is a matter for the jury to decide, the defendant is entitled to the chance to argue to the jury that it should disbelieve the unimpeached and uncontradicted evidence of the plaintiff's witnesses. So, can the party with the burden of proof ever obtain a directed verdict when highly persuasive testimony in support of all of his essential allegations is unimpeached and uncontradicted? The usual answer to this question, and the answer given by the federal courts, is that a directed verdict is theoretically available in such circumstances.

Finally, suppose that defendant has offered only some slight impeachment or contradiction of highly persuasive testimony tending to establish *A*, *B*, and *C* and that the testimony in support of plaintiff's essential allegations is indeed overwhelming. If the judge is satisfied that no reasonable jury properly considering the evidence could find for defendant, must the judge nevertheless submit the case to the jury? This is also a much debated question.

How can one generalize? There is some formula to be applied that is tied to a notion of whether reasonable minds could not differ. But this formula is applied only to a certain portion of the evidence, including all evidence that is favorable to the opponent of the motion and also apparently including unquestionable evidence, such as unimpeached and uncontradicted testimony from disinterested wit-

---

[f] The same problems are raised if the defendant offers highly persuasive evidence as to *D* and *E*, constituting a complete defense if believed, and the plaintiff offers nothing to counteract it.

nesses, that is favorable to the movant. How does the standard for directing a verdict compare with the standard for granting summary judgment? May a verdict ever properly be directed when summary judgment for the same movant has properly been denied?

Question: (32) Is there, when an action is tried without a jury, any motion analogous to a motion for a directed verdict at the close of all the evidence? Is there a need for one?

(e) Submission to Jury and Return of Verdict

[Rules 49, 51, 52]

If a motion for a directed verdict is not made, or is made but not granted, the disputed issues of fact will be decided (at least in the first place) by the jury, which announces its decision in the form of a verdict. But before the case is submitted to the jury, counsel for the plaintiff and the defendant will make closing arguments to the jury that the proof is with their respective side; the party who could make the initial opening statement will now have the right to make the final closing argument. Then, the judge will instruct, or charge, the jury as to the law.[g] See Rule 51.

Because the nature of the judge's instructions is affected by the kind of verdict that the jury is asked to return, it is appropriate to deal first with the kinds of verdict authorized by the Rules. This subject is treated in Rule 49. The verdict may be a general one, for example, "The jury find for the plaintiff and assess damages in the sum of $_____," or, "The jury find for the defendant."[h] Or the verdict may be a general one accompanied by "written interrogatories upon one or more issues of fact the decision of which is necessary to a verdict." Rule 49(b). Or the verdict may be special, "in the form of a special written finding upon each issue of fact." Rule 49(a).

Questions: (33) Who determines which kind of verdict will be used?

(34) On what basis should the determination be made?

The judge in his instructions to the jury will customarily state the issues that are in dispute and the contentions of the parties with respect to them; state who has the burden of proof on which issues, and to what degree of persuasion the jury must be brought before it decides that a party has successfully sustained a burden of proof; and analyze or at least summarize the evidence. A federal judge may also, if he chooses, express his views on the facts, provided he

---

[g] In a few states, instructions to the jury precede closing arguments. What are the advantages and disadvantages of the federal position?

[h] Alternative forms of verdict are given to the jury when it retires to deliberate. When a decision has been reached, the foreman of the jury signs the appropriate form.

makes clear to the jury that matters of fact are submitted for its determination and that his views are not binding.[i]

Whenever a general verdict is to be returned, whether or not accompanied by written interrogatories, the judge must instruct the jury on the rules of substantive law that govern the case. For the jurors cannot rationally find a verdict "for the plaintiff" or "for the defendant" without applying the rules of substantive law to the facts as they find them, and they do not and should not know these rules except as they are told them by the judge. The rules of substantive law that the judge imparts to the jury may be rather vague or general, leaving a considerable range of judgment to the jury (instructions on the standard of "due care" in most negligence cases are perforce general), or they may be fairly specific. In all events, the judge's instructions on the law will usually be a good deal more particularized than the legal rubrics that were invoked or suggested in the pleadings. For example, in an action for battery the defendant may have pleaded self-defense in a general way, but the judge may have to explain to the jury in detail the factors that should go into a determination of whether a defendant is justified in striking a plaintiff in response to what appears to be a threatened attack.

If only a special verdict is to be returned by the jury, the judge's instructions on the applicable rules of substantive law may be reduced in scope, because the judge will himself apply those rules to the jury's special findings on the issues of fact.

What is the lawyer's role in connection with the judge's instructions? In the first place Rule 51 gives the parties the right to file written requests for specific instructions. But the lawyer has other opportunities to urge on the judge his views of what the instructions should include.

Question: (35) *P* sues *D* for damage to *P*'s truck allegedly caused by *D*'s negligence. Because of industry-wide shortages the requisite repair parts cannot be obtained for some time, nor can *P* obtain a substitute truck. As a result, he loses the anticipated profit from a trucking contract. *P*'s attorney wants the jury to award as an element of damages the loss of this profit. Suppose: (a) *P*'s attorney requests an instruction that the jury may properly consider the loss of profit as an element of damages, and the judge refuses so to instruct; (b) *P*'s attorney makes no such request, and the judge's charge expressly excludes from the jury's consideration every element of damages except the diminution in value of the truck caused by the accident; (c) *P*'s attorney makes no such request, and the judge's charge makes no reference to the matter. In case (a), what must *P*'s attorney next do if he thinks the judge is in error on the law and if he wants to preserve the point for appeal? Has he lost appeal rights in case (b) or (c) by not requesting an instruction?

[i] Despite their acknowledged power to "comment on the evidence," including the power to indicate who in their judgment should prevail on the facts, many federal judges refrain from expressing their views. In the majority of state courts, the judges do not have the power. What arguments can be made for and against the federal position of allowing comment?

After receiving the instructions, the jury retires to deliberate. It is usually kept isolated from the time it retires until it is finally discharged. If the jurors are unable to reach a verdict, the judge will discharge the jury and the case may have to be retried. If a verdict is reached, it will be returned in open court with the jury present; the verdict will then be recorded; and the jury will be discharged.

Questions: (36) In an action tried without a jury, should the parties have a right to make closing argument to the judge?

(37) Our discussion of instructions and verdict is obviously inapplicable when the case is being tried without a jury. In a nonjury case "the court shall find the facts specially and state separately its conclusions of law thereon." Rule 52(a); see Rule 41(b). Why should the judge be required to find the facts specially when the jury is not required to do so (at least when it returns a general verdict)?

(f) Motions After Verdict

[Rules 50, 59]

Suppose the jury has come in with a verdict for one of the parties. Will the result of the litigation in the district court necessarily conform to the verdict? No. It will be made clear shortly that judgment is normally entered (at least in the first place) in accordance with the verdict. But even after that judgment has been entered, the party against whom the judgment went still has two "ten-day motions" available to him that may change the result.[j]

Motion for judgment notwithstanding the verdict.—Rule 50(b)— passing over the first sentence, which has a curious meaning and history to be later examined— permits a party whose motion for a directed verdict at the close of all the evidence has been denied or not granted to move to have the verdict and any judgment entered on the verdict set aside and to have judgment entered in his favor despite the adverse verdict.[k] This motion for judgment notwithstanding the verdict (often called judgment n.o.v., from the Latin *non obstante veredicto*) must be made not later than the tenth day after entry of judgment on the verdict. As the text of Rule 50(b) suggests, the standard for granting a motion for judgment notwithstanding the verdict is in theory the same as the standard for granting a motion for a directed verdict at the close of all the evidence. What hope is there, then, that the judge will grant a motion for judgment n.o.v. when he has previously denied the same party's motion for a directed

---

[j] Besides the motions for judgment notwithstanding the verdict (Rule 50(b)) and for a new trial (Rule 59(a)(1)), which will be discussed in the text, see Rule 59(e) (motion to amend judgment) and Rule 60 (motion for relief from judgment).

[k] Note carefully that it is a condition of a party's making an effective motion for judgment notwithstanding the verdict that he shall have previously moved at the close of all the evidence for a directed verdict. In light of this rule, reconsider Black, Sivalls & Bryson, Inc. v. Shondell, supra p. 43.

verdict at the close of all the evidence? Will not the jury's verdict fortify the judge in the view that he supposedly expressed in denying the directed verdict?

In seeking an answer to these questions, consider a situation where defendant moves for a directed verdict in his favor at the close of all the evidence, and the judge inclines to the belief that the motion should be granted but he is not certain and wants time to reflect. Will he perhaps deny the motion, or refrain from granting it, and pass the case to the jury believing that the jury will probably find for defendant, thus rendering it unnecessary to deal further with the question posed by the motion for a directed verdict? And if the jury does find for defendant, has not the judge avoided the appearance of intruding into the sphere of the jury? But if the jury returns a verdict for plaintiff, may he not grant defendant's motion for judgment n.o.v. in accordance with his original inclination?

The value of this practice will be more apparent if we anticipate the course of later proceedings on appeal.

Questions: (38) Suppose the judge directs a verdict for defendant at the close of all the evidence, and the appellate court later decides that he was wrong and that the case should have gone to the jury. What happens after that?

(39) Suppose the judge instead denies defendant's motion for a directed verdict, submits the case to the jury, and, after a verdict for plaintiff and on defendant's motion, enters judgment notwithstanding the verdict. The appellate court later finds him in error in entering judgment n.o.v. What then happens?

(40) So there are excellent reasons for a judge to deny a directed verdict motion even though he would feel bound to grant the same party's motion for judgment n.o.v., if necessary. Then why would judges ever direct a verdict at the close of all the evidence, as they sometimes do?

Motion for a new trial.—A party dissatisfied with a verdict has yet another motion—the motion for a new trial under Rule 59(a)(1)—that must be made not later than ten days after entry of judgment on the verdict. See Rule 59(b). A new trial motion asks that the verdict and any judgment entered on the verdict be set aside and that the case be retried. Such a motion may be granted on any of numerous grounds.

1. One possible ground is that the verdict is "against the weight of the evidence." The jury by its verdict will have decided one or more disputed factual issues. If the judge, looking at all the evidence, is clearly convinced that the jury was wrong in deciding as it did, that it grossly misjudged the credibility of the testimony or misconceived where the weight of the evidence lay, he should order a new trial. Here we touch upon a difficult problem. On the one hand, the judge is not justified in ordering a new trial merely because he disagrees with the jury's resolution of the issues. On the other hand, there are cases where the verdict is so far against the general cur-

rent of the evidence that to let it stand would be to countenance injustice; and here the judge may properly set the verdict aside and order a new trial.

Questions: (41) What is the difference in practical result between (a) directing a verdict or entering judgment n.o.v. for the defendant and (b) setting aside a verdict for the plaintiff and ordering a new trial?

(42) How does the standard for ordering a new trial on the ground that the verdict is against the weight of the evidence compare with the standard under Rule 50(a) and (b)? May a party's new trial motion on such ground ever properly be granted when the same party's motions for a directed verdict and judgment n.o.v. have properly been denied?

(43) Suppose a verdict is returned, but the verdict is set aside as against the weight of the evidence and a new trial is ordered. On the second trial before a new jury and possibly before a new judge, the same verdict is returned. May a new trial be ordered? Should there be a limit to the number of times a new trial may be ordered?

2. Sometimes the judge will order a new trial because it is clear that the jury has failed to follow his instructions.

Question: (44) Can you imagine a situation where it would be manifest from a general verdict that such error has occurred?

Another reason for granting a new trial is that the judge believes that he himself committed an error, for example, in instructing the jury or ruling on the admissibility of evidence. The motion for a new trial in a sense gives the judge a chance to reconsider his own actions; if he believes they were wrong in any material respect, he may order a new trial. Indeed, Rule 59(d) provides that "the court of its own initiative may order a new trial for any reason for which it might have granted a new trial on motion of a party."

The list of irregularities that may occur during the course of a trial, on the basis of which the court would be justified in granting a new trial after verdict and judgment to prevent injustice, is a lengthy one. But see Rule 61.

3. A new trial may also be granted on the ground of newly discovered evidence.

Joinder of motions.—A motion for a new trial may be and usually is made together with a motion for judgment notwithstanding the verdict. [See Rule 50(b).] If alternative motions for judgment n.o.v. and for a new trial are both denied, judgment on the verdict will stand. If the motion for judgment n.o.v. is denied but the motion for a new trial is granted, the verdict and any judgment entered thereon will be set aside, and the case will again stand for trial. If the motion for judgment n.o.v. is granted, the verdict and any judgment entered thereon will be set aside, and a contrary judgment will be entered; in such case, the new trial motion will also be ruled on, being either *conditionally* granted or *conditionally* denied pursuant to Rule 50(c)(1).[1]

Question: (45) Is there, when an action is tried without a jury, any motion analogous to a motion for judgment n.o.v.? Cf. Rule 52(b). Is there any motion analogous to a motion for a new trial? Cf. Rule 59(a)(2).

SECTION 4. JUDGMENT

(a) Entry of Judgment

[Rule 58]

The upshot of litigation in the district court is a judgment setting out any relief to which the parties have been held entitled. This may come about short of, or after, trial.

Where the judgment is a simple one—a jury has returned a general verdict, or in a nonjury case the court has decided that a party shall recover a sum of money or has denied all relief—the clerk prepares, signs, and enters the judgment immediately. In the more complicated cases, the court promptly approves the form of judgment and the clerk enters it. See Rule 58; Forms 31 and 32.

(b) Kinds of Relief Afforded by Judgment

[Rules 54, 57]

It is worth pausing on the kinds of relief that may be afforded by a judgment. We should perhaps have dealt with this subject at the outset of our discussion of the phases of a lawsuit, for the questions, "What kinds of relief are available in this type of case?" and, "How shall I make my election if I have a choice?" are often of first importance to an intending plaintiff, and he will consider them before he frames his complaint. Observe, however, that under Rule 54(c), "every final judgment shall grant the relief to which the party in whose favor it is rendered is entitled, even if the party has not demanded such relief in his pleadings"—except that "[a] judgment by default shall not be different in kind from or exceed in amount that prayed for in the demand for judgment."

Question: (1) What are the reasons for these provisions of Rule 54(c)?

A common type of judgment for a successful plaintiff is one for money damages designed to compensate him for the defendant's wrong. Thus, an ordinary measure of damages for breach of contract is the difference between what the plaintiff was promised and what he got. In an action for personal injuries, the measure of dam-

---

[1] The interplay of these motions is explored in Section 5 of Topic D of Part Four.

ages is the sum that will supposedly restore the plaintiff as nearly as possible to the position he would have been in if the wrong had not been committed; the difficulties in putting a dollar figure on such things as pain and suffering or facial disfigurement are obvious. Interest, accruing after and in some cases before judgment, may be awarded.

In some kinds of cases punitive damages—designed to punish or make an example of the defendant—may be given. And sometimes an award of nominal damages, which is a trifling sum given in recognition of a legal right, or a restitutionary measure of damages, which prevents the defendant's unjust enrichment, may be appropriate.

Another type of judgment may award the restoration of property wrongfully withheld by the defendant from the plaintiff, as where the defendant has wrongfully appropriated the plaintiff's watch and retains it, or where the defendant has wrongfully entered upon the plaintiff's land and occupies it.

The foregoing types of judgment are historically associated with the courts of common law. There is another type of judgment, historically associated only with the courts of equity, that orders the losing party to do or to refrain from doing some act.[a] For instance, in proper cases a party in default under a contract may be directed by the judgment to carry out the contract according to its terms. In some situations the judgment will not go so far as to order the party to carry out his promise, but it will order him to refrain from acting inconsistently with his promise. So, if the defendant, a famous opera singer, has promised to sing exclusively for the plaintiff over a certain period of time and wrongfully refuses to perform, the judgment may order the defendant not to sing for the plaintiff's competitors during the time in question.

Questions: (2) Why should the court not order the singer to sing for the plaintiff?

(3) What can be said for prohibiting her from singing for any competitor of the plaintiff during the contract period?

An equitable judgment may order the defendant to refrain from committing some other kind of wrong. If defendant is wrongfully selling chewing gum packaged so as to imitate plaintiff Wrigley's, the judgment may order him to desist from this unfair competition. Or a defendant who has wrongfully constructed a dam that floods the plaintiff's land may be ordered to tear it down.

A judgment may combine one kind of relief with another. Thus, a judgment for plaintiff ordering defendant to perform a promise may also award damages to plaintiff for past breaches by defendant.

---

[a] Judgments in suits in equity were called decrees. In Rule 54(a) "judgment" is defined as including a decree.

RITTER v. RITTER, 381 Ill. 549, 46 N.E.2d 41 (1943). Joseph Ritter agreed with defendant Louis Ritter, a relative, that they would buy two pieces of real estate upon foreclosure sale, taking title in their names as joint tenants; and that if there was no redemption, Joseph would take the "Nixon property" and defendant the "brick building." After the purchase Joseph became critically ill; he asked defendant whether, in case of his death, his wife and daughter would have any trouble securing the Nixon property; and defendant assured him they would not. Nevertheless, when Joseph had died and the redemption period had passed, defendant procured a master's deed to both properties to be issued in his own name. Thus, Joseph's widow and daughter were obliged to start a chancery suit against defendant to impose a constructive trust upon the Nixon property in their favor. They succeeded in the suit.

The widow and daughter then sued Louis to recover the expenses of the chancery suit that had not been assessed therein as costs. After trial without jury, judgment was entered in plaintiffs' favor for $2007, representing primarily counsel fees paid in prosecuting the prior suit.

On appeal, the intermediate appellate court affirmed. But the Supreme Court of Illinois reversed, holding that the subsequent action would not lie. Among the reasons given were the following: (1) Under Illinois law recovery of litigation expenses depends on statute, and here there was none in point. (2) As defendant had the "right" to resist plaintiffs' claim, it cannot be contended that he is liable on general principles for the consequences of his conduct in refusing to convey the property. (3) It is true there are cases where A has been held liable to B for wrongful conduct that involved B in litigation with third parties, and there the measure of damages has included B's expenses of litigation with the third parties, but those cases are not relevant to an attempt by a successful litigant to recover his expenses against his immediate adversary. (4) The rule urged by plaintiffs would involve endless litigation; if plaintiffs recover here, they could institute another action for expenses of the present action, and so on in an infinite series. (5) True, in some jurisdictions litigation expenses may be considered in situations where punitive damages are allowed, but that is different from recovery in a separate action. (6) Illinois has permitted an action for "malicious prosecution of a civil suit without probable cause" only if accompanied by arrest, seizure of property, or other special injury (in refusing to extend this tort, the court has stressed the need to leave the courts "open to every citizen"); the converse must be true, namely, that a plaintiff cannot bring an action against a defendant who made a "groundless and causeless defense."

COSTS

"Costs" are normally awarded to the prevailing party, either plaintiff or defendant, as a part of any judgment. After decision in the case, the clerk "taxes" costs, subject to the judge's review and ultimately to his discretion. See Rule 54(d).

Taxable costs may include certain direct expenses incurred in conducting the litigation, such as fees of clerk and marshal, statutory fees and disbursements for witnesses, docket fees, some deposition expenses, and like items. Defining the bounds on such costs is a complicated and variable matter, but suffice it to say that certainly not even all out-of-pocket expenses are reimbursed. Of crucial importance is the precept that costs in American courts (other than in Alaska) ordinarily cannot include counsel fees, so that each party ordinarily pays his own lawyer. Thus, although sometimes rather significant in absolute terms, costs represent only a small percentage of the total expenses of litigation.

In most of the rest of the Western world, including England, the losing party also pays the attorneys' fees of the prevailing party. Indeed, the so-called American rule against fee-shifting might be better termed the "American exception." But using comparative law to leap to conclusions of heresy must be resisted. It is true that the historical reasons for our early departure from the English rule are murky and largely obsolete. Nevertheless, the reasons behind the persistence of the difference in practice may well lie in profound societal differences, especially differing views on the nature of law, the role of courts, and the desirability of litigation.

Here and today, the American rule appears firmly entrenched. See Alyeska Pipeline Service Co. v. Wilderness Society, 421 U.S. 240, 95 S.Ct. 1612 (1975). Yet academic criticism of that rule is mounting, and exceptions to it are multiplying on both federal and state levels. Therefore, the complexities of adopting the English rule in America deserve consideration.

Considering the effects of a change to fee-shifting on the litigants' economic incentives, there has been no effective empirical work. There has been some theoretical work, but it is surprisingly inconclusive. For purposes of illustration, picture the Ritter plaintiffs' initial chancery suit under a regime that would require the loser to pay, in addition to his own counsel fees, the winner's counsel fees as costs; so victory will be more complete, but the risk of loss is greater. First—on the decision to pursue the claim—probably the English rule relatively encourages small meritorious suits, while somewhat discouraging larger dubious suits and nuisance suits; however, risk aversion discourages the middle class from resorting to litigation under the English rule. Second—on the subsequent decision whether to settle—although the effects of implementing the English rule on the likelihood and timing of settlement are unclear, it can be said that strong claims would tend to be settled for more and weak claims for less than under the American rule. Third—on the conduct of litigation—although the English rule might relatively encourage the litigants to escalate expenditures, its influence on the overall economic costs of the litigation system is unknown and arguably unknowable. In any event, predicting the direction of an effect tells us nothing of the size of the effect, the interplay of countervailing effects, or the importance of side effects. The lesson seems to be this: beware of simplistic analysis of the English-American dispute.

There are many considerations other than these economic concerns, of course. In a perspicacious article, Professor Rowe lists five other common rationales for fee-shifting:

"The first is a sense of simple fairness: the idea that it is only just for the loser to have to pay, at least in considerable part, the winner's legal costs appears to be a major underpinning of the English indemnity rule. The second, the theme of making a litigant financially whole for a legal wrong suffered, is probably most familiar as the idea of compensation in the substantive law of remedies. A punitive emphasis on fee shifting to deter and punish misconduct, either in litigation or in the underlying transaction, is a third rationale. Fourth, the 'private attorney general' theory justifies a fee award on the basis of the public usefulness of advancing a particular type of claim. A fifth justification is a desire to affect the relative strengths of the parties, a theme that appears in discussion of schemes for fee shifting against government, particularly when the private party involved is an individual or a small concern."

Rowe, The Legal Theory of Attorney Fee Shifting: A Critical Overview, 1982 Duke L.J. 651, 653. But as he demonstrates, the validity or at least the reach of each of these arguments is also open to serious question or qualification. And counterarguments remain, including an effective claim that the weak rationales for the English rule fail generally to justify the undeniably substantial transaction costs of fee-shifting. Moreover, all these conflicting policies must be considered in a broader context, which would take into account at least the presence or absence of contingent fees, legal aid, legal insurance, small-claims courts, alternative dispute-resolution mechanisms, class actions, and other representative litigation and also the effects of any security-for-costs or offer-of-judgment provisions. See, e.g., Rule 68. The lesson here seems to be this: beware of thinking too narrowly.

One should recognize that neither the English rule nor the American rule exists in pure form anywhere. There are exceptions on whether to shift fees; and given shifting, there are variations on how much of the fees should shift in the particular case. One should also recognize that the English and American rules do not exhaust the possible fee-shifting regimes. An obvious alternative is one-way fee-shifting, most probably shifting only in favor of a prevailing plaintiff. Indeed, Professor Rowe apparently supports a one-way pro-prevailing-plaintiff scheme, although he would allow a shift in favor of any prevailing defendant who had been subjected to a truly baseless action. Id. at 679. Very importantly, because of the interplay of policies, the chosen rules for fee-shifting should probably differ according to the type or size of the case or the characteristics or behavior of the litigants. See Mause, Winner Takes All: A Re-examination of the Indemnity System, 55 Iowa L.Rev. 26 (1969). The lesson here seems to be this: beware of thinking too generally.

In summary, the English-American dispute raises very complex issues. In all likelihood, we shall retain the American rule; but the courts and especially the legislatures will continue to move cautiously by a sort of common-law incremental method away from that polar position, adopting numerous targeted exceptions such as the federal ones that currently allow discretionary shifting of reasonable fees when the opponent has litigated in bad faith or, under 42 U.S.C. § 1988, when in a civil rights action a plaintiff has prevailed or a prevailing defendant has been subjected to a truly baseless suit or, under 28 U.S.C. § 2412, when certain private parties have prevailed against the federal government. Perhaps by now this approach does not appear so inappropriate as it might at first have seemed to you.

DECLARATORY RELIEF

The judgments so far considered are plainly coercive. The power of government is behind them, as we shall see shortly. A judgment for the defendant is less plainly coercive, because the result of the litigation is a denial rather than a grant of the relief sought. The force of government may, however, be invoked to secure by execution against the defeated plaintiff the recovery of the costs awarded to the prevailing defendant. More importantly, such a judgment is a determination of rights and other legal relations, which the principle of res judicata may make conclusive.

Finally, Rule 57 speaks of "Declaratory Judgments" and refers to 28 U.S.C. § 2201. See also § 2202. The action for a declaratory judgment differs from the usual action in that the party instituting it need not in the first instance seek the imposition of any sanction apart from a declaration of rights and other legal relations. He may, for example, seek a declaration as to whether a particular act that he proposes to commit will be tortious, the defendant, a person who would be affected, having asserted that he will so regard it.

Questions: (4) Rule 57 says: "The existence of another adequate remedy does not preclude a judgment for declaratory relief in cases where it is appropriate." What does Rule 57 mean thereby? Why does Rule 57 so provide?

(5) What is the "further relief" that is mentioned in § 2201, and what is the "further relief" mentioned in § 2202?

(6) What are the meaning and the purpose of the opening clause of § 2201? (Part of the answer can be found in article III, section 2 of the Constitution.)

AMERICAN MACHINE & METALS, INC. v. DE BOTHEZAT IMPELLER CO.

United States Circuit Court of Appeals, Second Circuit, 1948.
166 F.2d 535.

Before SWAN, CHASE and FRANK, CIRCUIT JUDGES.

SWAN, CIRCUIT JUDGE. This appeal presents a question under the Declaratory Judgment Act, 28 U.S.C.A. § 400,[b] which authorizes the courts of the United States "in cases of actual controversy" to declare "rights and other legal relations of any interested party petitioning for such declaration," without regard to whether further relief is or could be sought. Before answering the complaint, the defendant moved, pursuant to Rule 12(b) of the Federal Rules of Civil Procedure, 28 U.S.C.A. following section 723, for dismissal of the action on the ground that (a) the complaint fails to state a claim upon which relief can be granted, and (b) the court lacks jurisdiction because there is no matter in controversy between the parties. This motion was granted for the reason, as we read the district court's opinion, that the facts alleged in the complaint did not show the existence of an "actual controversy." From the judgment of dismissal the plaintiff has appealed.

In summary the allegations of the complaint are the following:

In 1934 the parties entered into a contract under which the defendant conveyed to the plaintiff certain patents and certain physical equipment for the making of fans and other products and the plaintiff agreed to pay the defendant license fees (not less than $5,000 annually) based on the "net sales" of its products. So long as the contract continued the fees were to be paid on "net sales" regardless of whether the plaintiff's products were covered by the patents or whether the patents had expired. The contract contained no expiration date but could be terminated at any time by the plaintiff on six months' notice. In the event of such termination the plaintiff was to transfer the patents back to the defendant and to cease using the name "De Bothezat," which it agreed to use in its literature and sales promotion while the contract continued. Since February 19, 1946, the plaintiff has neither manufactured nor sold any product for which possession of the patents is essential. The plaintiff "desires and intends" to exercise its right of termination under the contract and "desires and intends" to continue in the business of selling fans and

[b] With changes this section, originally enacted in 1934, now appears as 28 U.S.C. § 2201.

ventilating equipment. The defendant at various times has made claims and assertions to the plaintiff and other persons to the effect that upon termination of the contract the plaintiff will no longer have the right to continue the manufacture of fans and ventilating equipment, and "has led plaintiff to believe" that upon termination of the contract defendant will sue plaintiff if it does not cease the manufacture and sale of fans and ventilating equipment. Said claims and assertions by defendant "are without basis and an actual controversy exists between the parties," and plaintiff seeks a declaration of the rights of the parties in order to avoid the possible accrual of avoidable damages. The prayer requests a declaration "particularly with respect to the proper interpretation and effect of the agreement" and that the court declare the right of plaintiff to continue to manufacture and sell fans and other noninfringing products after termination of the agreement and without the payment of further sums to defendant.

In concluding that no controversy exists the district judge noted that the plaintiff has not yet given notice of termination of the contract and may never do so; the opinion states [75 F.Supp. 421, 424]:

"In this case, if the court should decide that plaintiff might terminate and continue its manufacture and sale of products other than those covered by patents, plaintiff might and probably would terminate. If the court should decide otherwise, plaintiff would probably continue under the agreement until its termination and no controversy such as now claimed to exist might ever be present. In other words, plaintiff has not elected what it wishes to do and its action might and could render academic the very declaration which it seeks.

"The complaint is, therefore, dismissed because no justiciable controversy exists which would justify the maintenance of an action under the Declaratory Judgment Statute. The relief prayed for should not be granted at this time either as a matter of discretion or otherwise."

We think the judge construed the statute too narrowly. As the Supreme Court said in Maryland Casualty Co. v. Pacific Coal & Oil Co., 312 U.S. 270, 273, 61 S.Ct. 510, 85 L.Ed. 826, the difference between an abstract question and a "controversy" is one of degree. If notice of termination had been given, the defendant apparently concedes that there might be an actual controversy, although even after termination it would still be optional with the plaintiff whether to continue the business and an adverse decision would probably induce him not to continue. Before termination, the controversy is one step further removed from actuality but not so far removed as to present only an abstract question, in our opinion. Once the notice of termination is given, it is beyond recall; the dispute between the parties concerns the right of the plaintiff to continue business if that contingency happens. Where there is an actual controversy over contingent rights, a declaratory judgment may nevertheless be granted. Pennsylvania Casualty Co. v. Upchurch, 5 Cir., 139 F.2d 892, 894; Franklin Life Ins. Co. v. Johnson, 10 Cir., 157 F.2d 653, 658; Sigal v. Wise, 114 Conn. 297, 158 A. 891, 892, 893; Borchard, Declaratory Judgments, pp. 422–3. In Sigal v. Wise, supra, the tenant of premises destroyed by fire sought a declaration of his right to use the premises if the landlord should rebuild. Although the right claimed was contingent, the court thought that "its present determination may well serve a very real practical need of the parties for guidance in their future conduct." There, it is true, the contingency was within the control of the defendant, not of the plaintiff as here, but that does not seem to be a material distinction. After bringing the contingency to pass it will be too late to avoid an action for damages if the plaintiff acts as he intends by continuing the business. The very purpose of the declaratory judgment procedure is to prevent the accrual of such avoidable damages. This procedure has long been recognized in the law of Scotland and we may well be guided by Lord Justice Dunedin's opinion in Russian C. & I. Bank v. British Bank (1921), 2 A.C. 438, 448. There the British bank had obtained a loan from the Russian bank and pledged securities to protect the lender. In order to decide whether to exercise its privilege of redeeming the pledged securities, the British bank wanted to know whether the loan was repayable in rubles or sterling—a question on which the parties were in dispute. Lord Dunedin was of opinion that the case was an appropriate one for a declaratory judgment even though it was probable that if sterling was declared to be the required currency the British bank would not exercise its privilege of redemption. This seems indistinguishable from the case at bar. Also pertinent are Altvater v. Freeman, 319 U.S. 359, 63 S.Ct. 1115, and Sola Electric Co. v. Jefferson Electric Co., 317 U.S. 173, 63 S.Ct. 172. In the latter case the Supreme Court permitted a patent licensee to seek a declaratory judgment as to the validity of certain patents without previously relinquishing its rights under the license.

Johnson v. Interstate Transit Lines, 10 Cir., 163 F.2d 125, and Perlberg v. Northwestern Mut. Life Ins. Co., E.D.Pa., 62 F.Supp. 76, relied upon by the appellee, did not involve such an irrevocable choice as the termination of the contract presents to the plaintiff in the case at bar. Failure to declare his seniority rights did not seriously affect the employee in the Johnson case, since he was not threatened with immediate loss of employment or status; and the insured in the Perlberg case, seeking a declaration as to the consequences of a default, would have been able even in the event of a default to reinstate his policy without penalty, or failing that to receive paid-up insurance or the cash surrender value. By the decision below the appellant here must "act on his own view of his rights" and risk an otherwise profitable business in order to present a justiciable "controversy." The Declaratory Judgments Act was designed to obviate just this sort of peril, and we believe its benefits should be available to one in the appellant's situation. S.Rep. No. 1005, 73d Cong., 2 Sess., pp. 2–3; Borchard, Declaratory Judgments, pp. 58, 930.

Judgment reversed and cause remanded for trial on the merits.[c]

INTERNATIONAL LONGSHOREMEN'S LOCAL 37 v. BOYD

Supreme Court of the United States, 1954.
347 U.S. 222, 74 S.Ct. 447.

MR. JUSTICE FRANKFURTER delivered the opinion of the Court.

This is an action by Local 37 of the International Longshoremen's and Warehousemen's Union and several of its alien members to enjoin the District Director of Immigration and Naturalization at Seattle from so construing § 212(d)(7) of the Immigration and Nationality Act of 1952[*] as to treat aliens domiciled in the continental United States returning from temporary work in Alaska as if they were aliens entering the United States for the first time. Declaratory relief to the same effect is also sought. Since petitioners asserted in the alternative that such a construction of the challenged statute would be unconstitutional, a three-judge district court was convened.[d] The case came before it on stipulated facts and issues of law, from which it appeared that the union has over three thousand members who work every summer in the herring and salmon canneries of Alaska, that some of these are aliens, and that if alien workers going to Alaska for the 1953 canning season were excluded on their return, their "contract and property rights [would] be jeopardized and forfeited." The District Court entertained the suit but dismissed it on the merits. 111 F.Supp. 802. In our order of October 12, 1953, we

[c] After the decision set out in the text, defendant moved under Rule 12(b)(6) to dismiss the complaint and for other relief, this time presenting affidavits to show that there was no controversy. The motion was denied, 8 F.R.D. 324 (S.D.N.Y.1948). Later reported steps in the case will be found at 8 F.R.D. 306; 8 F.R.D. 459; 82 F.Supp. 556; and 173 F.2d 890. Finally, plaintiff obtained a declaration that it could terminate the contract and continue to sell "any and all fans, ventilating equipment and other products, not infringing upon valid patents owned by defendant after such termination." This judgment was affirmed, 180 F.2d 342 (2d Cir.), cert. denied, 339 U.S. 979, 70 S.Ct. 1025 (1950).

[*] This section states that the exclusionary provisions of § 212(a) shall, with exceptions not here relevant, "be applicable to any alien who shall leave Hawaii, Alaska, Guam, Puerto Rico, or the Virgin Is-

lands of the United States, and who seeks to enter the continental United States . . . ." 8 U.S.C. § 1182(d)(7). [Footnote by Court.—Ed.]

[d] For the three-judge district court referred to, see 28 U.S.C. § 2284.

Prior to 1976, three-judge district courts were required not infrequently. Most importantly, federal actions seeking injunctive relief against the enforcement of a federal or state statute, on the ground that the statute in question was contrary to the Federal Constitution, had to be heard by a district court composed of three judges.

Now, the three-judge requirement is much more limited in scope, applying primarily to reapportionment suits and to certain cases under the 1964 Civil Rights and 1965 Voting Rights Acts. See generally C. Wright, The Law of Federal Courts § 50 (4th ed. 1983).

postponed the question of jurisdiction to a hearing on the merits. 346 U.S. 804, 74 S.Ct. 43.

On this appeal, appellee contends [inter alia] that the District Court should not have reached the statutory and constitutional questions—that it should have dismissed the suit for want of a "case or controversy" . . . .

Appellants in effect asked the District Court to rule that a statute the sanctions of which had not been set in motion against individuals on whose behalf relief was sought, because an occasion for doing so had not arisen, would not be applied to them if in the future such a contingency should arise. That is not a lawsuit to enforce a right; it is an endeavor to obtain a court's assurance that a statute does not govern hypothetical situations that may or may not make the challenged statute applicable. Determination of the scope and constitutionality of legislation in advance of its immediate adverse effect in the context of a concrete case involves too remote and abstract an inquiry for the proper exercise of the judicial function. United Public Workers v. Mitchell, 330 U.S. 75, 67 S.Ct. 556; see Muskrat v. United States, 219 U.S. 346, 31 S.Ct. 250, and Alabama State Federation of Labor v. McAdory, 325 U.S. 450, 65 S.Ct. 1384. Since we do not have on the record before us a controversy appropriate for adjudication, the judgment of the District Court must be vacated, with directions to dismiss the complaint.

It is so ordered.

MR. JUSTICE BLACK, with whom MR. JUSTICE DOUGLAS concurs, dissenting.

This looks to me like the very kind of "case or controversy" courts should decide. With the abstract principles of law relied on by the majority for dismissing the case, I am not in disagreement. Of course federal courts do not pass on the meaning or constitutionality of statutes as they might be thought to govern mere "hypothetical situations . . . . ." Nor should courts entertain such statutory challenges on behalf of persons upon whom adverse statutory effects are "too remote and abstract an inquiry for the proper exercise of the judicial function." But as I read the record it shows that judicial action is absolutely essential to save a large group of wage earners on whose behalf this action is brought from irreparable harm due to alleged lawless enforcement of a federal statute. My view makes it necessary for me to set out the facts with a little more detail than they appear in the Court's opinion.

Every summer members of the appellant union go from the west coast of continental United States to Alaska to work in salmon and herring canneries under collective-bargaining agreements. As the 1953 canning season approached the union and its members looked forward to this Alaska employment. A troublesome question arose, however, on account of the Immigration and Nationality Act of 1952,

66 Stat. 163. Section 212(d)(7) of this new Act has language that given one construction provides that all aliens seeking admission to continental United States from Alaska, even those previously accepted as permanent United States residents, shall be examined as if entering from a foreign country with a view to excluding them on any of the many grounds applicable to aliens generally. This new law created an acute problem for the union and its numerous members who were lawful alien residents, since aliens generally can be excluded from this country for many reasons which would not justify deporting aliens lawfully residing here. The union and its members insisted on another construction. They denied that Congress intended to require alien workers to forfeit their right to live in this country for no reason at all except that they went to Alaska, territory of the United States, to engage in lawful work under a lawfully authorized collective-bargaining contract. The defendant immigration officer announced that the union's interpretation was wrong and that workers going to Alaska would be subject to examination and exclusion. This is the controversy.

It was to test the right of the immigration officer to apply § 212(d)(7) to make these workers subject to exclusion that this suit was filed by the union and two of its officers on behalf of themselves and all union members who are aliens and permanent residents. True, the action was begun before the union members went to Alaska for the 1953 canning season. But it is not only admitted that the Immigration official intended to enforce § 212(d)(7) as the union and these workers feared. It is admitted here that he has since done precisely that. All 1953 alien cannery workers have actually been subjected to the wearisome routine of immigration procedure as though they had never lived here. And some of the union members are evidently about to be denied the right ever to return to their homes on grounds that could not have been legally applied to them had they stayed in California or Washington instead of going to Alaska to work for an important American industry.

Thus the threatened injury which the Court dismisses as "remote" and "hypothetical" has come about. For going to Alaska to engage in honest employment many of these workers may lose the home this country once afforded them. This is a strange penalty to put on productive work. Maybe this is what Congress meant by passing § 212(d)(7). And maybe in these times such a law would be held constitutional. But even so, can it be that a challenge to this law on behalf of those whom it hits the hardest is so frivolous that it should be dismissed for want of a controversy that courts should decide? Workers threatened with irreparable damages, like others, should have their cases tried.

Question: (7) Four years after the International Longshoremen's case, there was an appeal to the Supreme Court from dismissal of an action on the

ground that there was no "actual controversy." The plaintiff's complaint
sought a declaration that a Tennessee statute requiring segregated seating
arrangements on transportation facilities on account of race, was unconstitutional, and, also sought an injunction against enforcement of this statute.
The three-judge district court found that the plaintiff boarded a bus in Memphis, Tennessee, seated himself in the front, and was told by the driver that
he must move to the rear, the driver stating that the law required it because
of his color; that the plaintiff refused, and two police officers shortly thereafter boarded the bus and ordered the plaintiff to go to the back of the bus,
get off, or be arrested; and that thereupon the plaintiff left the bus. The
record further showed that the defendants, who were officials and officers
of the City of Memphis and of the company operating the bus, intended to
enforce the Tennessee statute until final adjudication of unconstitutionality.
The Supreme Court decided the appeal in a per curiam opinion without hearing argument. What would you expect the decision to be? Is the case distinguishable from the International Longshoremen's case? Should it matter
that the plaintiff boarded the bus for the purpose of instituting this litigation? See Evers v. Dwyer, 358 U.S. 202, 79 S.Ct. 178 (1958).

(c) Enforcement of Judgment

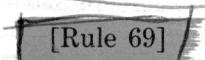

Do not be deceived into thinking that an unappealed judgment
concludes the scenario. The maneuvering may have just begun. An
unenforced judgment often does one little good, and the losing party
is not always a good sport about compliance. In short, there are frequently extensive post-judgment proceedings.

An equitable judgment is in the form and nature of a court order
to the defendant. If he disobeys, the defendant could be imprisoned
until he complies (or fined conditionally) and thus be coerced into
compliance. This would be done under the court's civil contempt
powers. Criminal contempt is not, strictly speaking, a means of enforcement, but the possibility of criminal contempt incidentally benefits the plaintiff by encouraging compliance with the judgment.

Legal relief, on the other hand, is typically not expressed as an
order to the defendant to pay or to restore, but rather as a statement
that the plaintiff shall recover a sum of money or certain property
from the defendant. This signifies more than a matter of form or a
historical oddity. A legal judgment is not an order to the defendant;
it is up to the plaintiff to enforce the judgment.

Take as an example a judgment for money damages, and assume
that the defendant does not voluntarily pay it. The first step for the
plaintiff is to identify and locate the defendant's assets. This sometimes requires extensive investigation. The discovery devices of the
Federal Rules can be utilized for this purpose; state law may provide
other means of discovery, which can be used in connection with the
enforcement of a federal judgment. See Rule 69(a).

The plaintiff is then in a position to invoke the force of government in order to secure for himself the relief to which he has been found entitled. In federal court the procedure for this generally conforms to the local state law, as provided in Rule 69(a). The precise interplay of federal and state law here is similar to that prevailing under Rule 64 for provisional remedies.

Question: (8) What are the advantages and disadvantages of such incorporation by the Rules of state procedure?

Typically, the plaintiff will obtain from the court a writ of execution addressed to a federal marshal. Pursuant to this writ, the marshal will seize, or levy on, so much of the defendant's nonexempt property within the state (state laws provide many and varied exemptions) as is necessary to pay the judgment. If the defendant still does not pay, the marshal will sell that property, use the proceeds to cover his own fees and expenses and to satisfy the plaintiff's judgment, and then give any remainder to the defendant.

If execution is less than fully successful, there are other remedies available to the plaintiff by permission of the federal judge, namely, state-law devices called supplementary proceedings. For example, state statutes commonly provide a means for compelling the judgment debtor to appear for sworn examination before the court as to his assets and his ability to pay the judgment. If the court finds that he has property not exempt from execution, he may be ordered to produce it so that it may be taken on execution. Now the defendant is the subject of a court order, and failure to obey an order of the court in supplementary proceedings is punishable as contempt. Under the law of some states, the court may order the debtor to make installment payments on the judgment debt, from time to time out of future income, the payment schedule to be fixed after taking into account the reasonable requirements of the debtor and his dependents. Imprisonment for contempt under such a procedure has been upheld against constitutional attack. Reeves v. Crownshield, 274 N.Y. 74, 8 N.E.2d 283 (1937) ("To compel the judgment debtor to obey the order of the court is not imprisonment for debt, but only imprisonment for disobedience of an order with which he is able to comply."). Apparently, such imprisonment would be impermissible if the order were not reasonably within the defendant's means.

GABOVITCH v. LUNDY, 584 F.2d 559 (1st Cir.1978). A federal judgment creditor of appellee Lundy obtained a writ of execution from the clerk for the District of Massachusetts. "The writ was returned on May 5, 1976, certifying a levy on appellee Taunton Co-Operative Bank in the amount of $3000, representing Lundy's deposits in the bank. The bank ignored appellant's numerous demands that it pay over the $3000. On February 24, 1978, appellant petitioned the district court" to enforce the writ. The district court denied relief, holding the writ ineffective because of the creditor's failure to comply with state procedure. The creditor appealed.

The court of appeals affirmed. The appellant had argued that Rule 69(a) makes state law applicable to procedures in aid of execution but not to the mere issuance of process. "Unfortunately for appellant, the legislative history and judicial application of Rule 69(a) make clear that the first sentence of the Rule expresses a limitation on the means of enforcement of money judgments and does not create a general power to issue writs of execution in disregard of the state law incorporated by the rest of the Rule."

Rule 69(a) was meant only (1) to adopt a prior practice of following state law on both the procedure for obtaining process and the effect of such writs and (2) to extend this practice to purely monetary equitable judgments.

"Finally, the courts have consistently read Rule 69(a) as limiting all federal process on money judgments to the type of process available under state law. This court held in First National Bank of Boston v. Antonio Santisteban & Co., Inc., 285 F.2d 855 (1st Cir.1961), that a federal writ of execution did not reach unearned wages of a Puerto Rican judgment debtor because Puerto Rican law gave no effect to such a writ. See Traveler's Insurance Co. v. Lawrence, 509 F.2d 83, 86–88 (9th Cir.1974) (Rule 69 makes availability and effect of federal process subject to state law); United States ex rel. Marcus v. Lord Elec. Co., 43 F.Supp. 12 (W.D.Pa.1942) (bank deposits affected by writ of execution because state law so provides). Thus, we have no difficulty concluding that the writ of execution issued by the clerk had no effect. Under Massachusetts law, attachment of bank accounts takes place by trustee process. Mass.Gen.Laws Ann. ch. 246. Attachment on trustee process requires court approval. Mass.Rules Civ.Proc. 4.2(c). Because a writ issued solely on the authority of a court clerk has no effect on a bank account under Massachusetts law, it has no effect under Rule 69(a).[3]"

---

[3] Although the forms of the process would, of course, be federal, the essential elements of state procedure for obtaining the writ must be followed. Mass.Gen. Laws Ann. ch. 246 § 5 and Mass.Rules Civ.Proc. 4.2(a) provide for trustee process to attach the 'credits' of a defendant. Receipt of a trustee summons notifies a bank of attachment of a depositor's credits. Mass.Gen.Laws Ann. ch. 246 § 20; Mass.Rules Civ.Proc. 4.2(b). But a trustee summons cannot issue without a prior court approval of the attachment. Mass.Rules Civ.Proc. 4.2(c). Under the same rule, the attachment usually will not be approved without a prior adversary hearing. Once the trustee process issues, the trustee must answer specifying the property subjected to the attachment. Mass.Gen.Laws Ann. ch. 246 § 10. If the court then adjudges the bank to be a trustee, it must pay over to the creditor or be subject to a trustee writ of execution. Mass.Gen.Laws Ann. ch. 246 § 45. Because appellant failed to obtain court approval of his process, it could not be effective to attach the property held by the bank.

Question: (9) In a state where a plaintiff's lawyer can prepare the documents for execution, as under NYCPLR § 5230(b), must the holder of a federal-court judgment go to the court clerk for a writ of execution?

Here, as is the case with provisional remedies, some of the more pro-plaintiff enforcement mechanisms may be quite drastic in effect. Consequently, some have of late been attacked, and a few struck down, on the ground of fundamental unfairness. As a matter of constitutional law, then, the state remedial procedure must be carefully drawn to provide equal protection of the laws, and to accord with the dictates of procedural due process later explored in Topic C of Part Five.

SECTION 5.   APPELLATE REVIEW

(a) Appeal to the Court of Appeals

[Rule 62]

Avenues of appeal.—According to 28 U.S.C. § 1291, a party, dissatisfied with a final decision [a] of a district court and claiming that it is erroneous, has a right to appeal to the United States Court of Appeals for the appropriate circuit [b] for correction of the error, that is, for reversal or modification of the decision. What is a final decision within the meaning of § 1291 may become a serious question, but the basic design was to accord an appeal of right when the case had been fully treated and had reached a full stop in the court below.

RUSSELL v. BARNES FOUNDATION
United States Circuit Court of Appeals, Third Circuit, 1943.
136 F.2d 654.

Before MARIS, JONES, and GOODRICH, CIRCUIT JUDGES.

PER CURIAM. In this case the district court entered a summary judgment in favor of the plaintiff and against the defendant under Civil Procedure Rule 56, 28 U.S.C.A. following section 723c, and ordered that the case proceed to trial for the determination of the

---

[a] We shift here from the word "judgment" because the appeals statutes usually do not use that more inclusive term. Note again the wording of Rule 54(a).

[b] There are special situations in which decisions of the district courts, final or interlocutory, are subject to direct review by the Supreme Court. The statutes are cited and summarized in C. Wright, The Law of Federal Courts § 105 (4th ed. 1983). See, e.g., 28 U.S.C. § 1252, which, in any civil action to which the United States is a party, gives any party a right of direct appeal to the Supreme Court from an interlocutory or final judgment, decree, or order of a district court holding a federal statute unconstitutional; and 28 U.S.C. § 1253, which gives any party a right of direct appeal from an order granting or denying an interlocutory or permanent injunction in an action required to be heard by a three-judge district court.

amount of damages to which the plaintiff is entitled. From the order thus entered the defendant took the present appeal.

The plaintiff has moved to dismiss the appeal upon the ground that the order appealed from is not a final decision subject to appellate review by this court under Section 128 of the Judicial Code, 28 U.S.C.A. § 225.[c] The motion must be granted since the order appealed from, although it determines the liability of the defendant to the plaintiff, will not become a final adjudication of the controversy between them until the damages to which the plaintiff is entitled have been assessed. See Guarantee Co. v. Mechanics' S.B. & Trust Co., 173 U.S. 582, 19 S.Ct. 551, 43 L.Ed. 818.

The appeal is dismissed.

Question: (1) What are the arguments for and against generally limiting the right of appeal to final decisions?

When the Federal Rules came in to permit the inclusion in a single action of a number of claims to be litigated among a number of parties—a condition that could exist in the prior practice but was now to become more common—it was thought desirable to permit appeal from the disposition of a clearly divisible part of a complicated case. See Rule 54(b), noting that the district court must make an "express determination that there is no just reason for delay" before it directs the entry of a "final judgment" as to one or more of several claims or parties, which in effect releases a part of the case for appeal under § 1291.

There is also a right of appeal from certain interlocutory, that is, nonfinal, decisions of the district court. The most important class is described in 28 U.S.C. § 1292(a)(1)—interlocutory orders that grant, refuse, modify, or otherwise affect injunctions. (By interpretation, temporary restraining orders are generally not within § 1292(a)(1), but preliminary injunctions are within it.) Recall Hamilton Watch Co. v. Benrus Watch Co., supra p. 95.

Question: (2) Why are these particular interlocutory orders singled out for appeal of right?

Section 1292(b) permits appeal of an interlocutory order other than one covered by § 1292(a) when, first, the district judge states that it involves a "controlling question of law" as to which there is "substantial ground for difference of opinion" and that immediate appeal "may materially advance the ultimate termination of the litigation" and, second, the court of appeals in its discretion agrees to hear the appeal. Because of these multiple requirements, appeals under § 1292(b) are not common.

An appeal is taken from and attacks the "final decision" or "interlocutory order," but what is really claimed in many appeals is that

[c] With changes this section now appears as 28 U.S.C. § 1291.

some action of the district court taken prior to the entry or making of the final decision or interlocutory order, and objected to at the time, was erroneous and that this error has infected the final decision or interlocutory order with material error. The district court during the course of the litigation may have ruled on a variety of questions— motions attacking the pleadings, objections to the admission and exclusion of evidence, motions for directed verdicts, and so on. On appeal the losing party may be urging that one or more of these rulings were wrong and, hence, that the final decision or interlocutory order appealed from is wrong. For example, a losing plaintiff may be urging on appeal that the judgment for the defendant is wrong and must be reversed and a new trial ordered because the district court erroneously excluded evidence offered by the plaintiff that, had it been received and considered, might have caused the jury to bring in a different verdict. It is of the utmost importance to our understanding of any case in an appellate court to single out the precise act or acts of the lower court that are complained of as having been erroneous.

This is a convenient point to ask whether it makes sense to have any system of appeals and, if so, what limits should be placed on appellate review. In all events, why the particular arrangements set out in the current statutes with their emphasis on the distinction between final decisions and interlocutory orders and their peculiar mix of appeals of right and discretionary appeals?

Appellate procedure.—The procedure for taking appeals is outlined in the Federal Rules of Appellate Procedure. This procedure will not be recounted here, but students should familiarize themselves with it in a general way, especially App. Rules 3 and 4 (appeal of right), 5 (appeal under § 1292(b)), 7 (bond for costs), 10 and 11 (record on appeal), 12 (docketing appeal; filing record), 28 and 31 (briefs), 30 (appendix to briefs; appeal on original record), and 34 (oral argument). In addition to the uniform provisions of the Federal Rules of Appellate Procedure, the courts of appeals may severally adopt their own rules of procedure not inconsistent with them. See 28 U.S.C. § 2071; App. Rule 47.

Despite local variations, the chief business of the courts of appeals is conducted in much the same way throughout the country, and it is largely the way traditional to our appellate courts. The appeal is heard on the record and on the briefs of counsel; usually there is also oral argument. The appellate court applies to the particular alleged errors the appropriate standard of review, which might be a fresh determination by the appellate judges or might involve some degree of deference to the trial judge's view. By majority vote of the usual three-judge panel, the appellate court affirms, reverses, or modifies the decision appealed from. If it follows from the view of the case adopted by the appellate court that further testimony should be taken, this will not be done by the appellate court, but rather by the lower court on remand. See 28 U.S.C. § 2106.

Stay of proceedings to enforce a judgment.—What happens to an appealable decision before the appeal can be disposed of? Does it remain effective or is it held in abeyance until the court of appeals decides? The arrangements are rather complex.

Where the judgment is the usual one for money, there is an automatic stay of enforcement for ten days after entry of judgment, see Rule 62(a), a period dovetailing with the time limit for making the various post-judgment motions. If such a motion is made, the district court may stay enforcement until the disposition of that motion, this being done as a matter of discretion and "on such conditions for the security of the adverse party as are proper." Rule 62(b). If an appeal is taken, the appellant is entitled to a stay upon giving a supersedeas bond that meets the approval of the district court; normally such a bond is in an amount sufficient to cover the judgment, costs on appeal, interest, and damages for delay consequent to the stay. See Rule 62(d) and (e); see also Rule 62(f) and (h).

Question: (3) The plaintiff you represent has won a money judgment of a type to which neither Rule 62(f) nor Rule 62(h) applies. The defendant made no post-judgment motions, but he did file a notice of appeal on the thirtieth day after entry of the judgment, in accordance with App. Rule 4(a). On that same day, the defendant gave a supersedeas bond and the district court approved it. The appeal is still pending. When could you have executed? What could the defendant have done to foreclose such possibility?

Consider now an interlocutory or final judgment in an action for an injunction. There is no provision for an automatic stay. However, the district court in its discretion may order a stay (or modify, restore, or grant an injunction) in the period prior to appeal, see Rule 62(a) and (b), or after an appeal is taken, see Rule 62(c), always "upon such terms as to bond or otherwise as it considers proper for the security of the rights of the adverse party."

Matters regarding stays of enforcement are, in the first instance, within the purview of the district court. But if a stay could not be there obtained, and if an appeal has been taken, relief can be sought in the court of appeals. See Rule 62(g); App. Rule 8(a); 28 U.S.C. § 1651(a). Again, such relief "may be conditioned upon the filing of a bond or other appropriate security in the district court." App. Rule 8(b). In exceptional situations where a hearing by a panel of the court of appeals would be impracticable because of the requirements of time, the application for a stay may be made to a single judge of that court. See App. Rule 8(a).

LONG v. ROBINSON, 432 F.2d 977 (4th Cir. 1970). In a class action a federal district court declared unconstitutional a Maryland statute and the corresponding local ordinance exempting Baltimore City from the uniform state definition of juvenile age as under 18 years and providing that a person in Baltimore City ceases to be a juvenile at the age of 16. (The age for determining who is a juvenile is important because juveniles charged with crime are treated differently from adults.) The order required persons between 16 and 18 years of age currently in jail in Baltimore City awaiting trial to be turned over to the juvenile authorities as expeditiously as possible. It was on August 6, 1970, that this judgment was handed down, 316 F.Supp. 22 (D.Md.1970).

The district judge refused a stay. The defendants applied to a single judge of the court of appeals, Circuit Judge Winter, for a stay pending appeal. They asserted that the district judge's legal conclusions were incorrect and that the administrative and economic burdens in complying with the order would be very heavy. It was estimated that the order would double the yearly caseload of juvenile cases in the city and would require expansion of detention facilities, training schools, courts and court personnel, social workers, and other personnel. It was said that until these facilities and personnel could be provided, the treatment program for juveniles under 16 would be adversely affected. Finally, it was argued that the unavailability of sufficient funds to meet the costs of the additional juvenile cases might make it necessary to convene a special session of the General Assembly of Maryland to make the needed appropriations.

Judge Winter stated the legal principles by which such an application is to be judged: "a party seeking a stay must show (1) that he will likely prevail on the merits of the appeal, (2) that he will suffer irreparable injury if the stay is denied, (3) that other parties will not be substantially harmed by the stay, and (4) that the public interest will be served by granting the stay." He found: (1) that the defendants' probability of success on appeal was not substantial; (2) that the principal irreparable injury that the defendants claimed they would suffer was of their own making (state legislation to abolish the lower age for juveniles in Baltimore City had been enacted in 1966, to be effective in 1969, but nothing had been done to effectuate the change; the effective date had been twice postponed for a year, but still no steps beyond some preliminary planning had been taken; and it "would seem elementary that a party may not claim equity in his own defaults"); (3) that a stay's deleterious consequences to the 16- and 17-year-old members of the plaintiff class by reason of their incarceration with older persons were clear; and (4) that the public interest lay in the immediate implementation of the order.

Judge Winter denied the stay but ordered hearing of the appeal expedited. The stay was denied on August 11, 1970. The expedited appeal was argued on September 17, 1970. On January 18, 1971, the district court decision was affirmed on the merits, 436 F.2d 1116 (4th Cir.1971).

If the court of appeals denies a stay of enforcement of the district-court judgment, immediate relief can be sought in the Supreme Court. See 28 U.S.C. § 1651(a). Application is made to the single

Justice assigned to the particular circuit from which the case comes. If the stay is granted, it may be conditioned upon the giving of adequate security. If the stay is denied, the applicant may (with scant hope of success) renew his request to any other Justice, and so on. Any Justice may refer a request for a stay to the entire Court for action.

If a stay is obtained somewhere along this line, the aggrieved party may seek to modify or vacate the stay, on good grounds shown, by pursuing relief up the line in similar manner.

If no stay is obtained, the party who prevailed in the district court may proceed to enforce his money judgment or take the benefit of an injunction in his favor.

Question: (4) What then is the situation if the court of appeals ultimately reverses?

(b) Review by the Supreme Court

The litigant disappointed by an adverse decision of the court of appeals has still another chance. See 28 U.S.C. § 1254, which provides for review by the Supreme Court of cases in the courts of appeals by certiorari, appeal, or certified questions. Appeal as of right under § 1254(2) is strictly limited, and certification of questions by courts of appeals is extremely unusual. The usual avenue to the Supreme Court is the petition for certiorari.

Review on certiorari is not a matter of right, but of discretion, and "will be granted only when there are special and important reasons therefor." S.Ct. Rule 17.1, further quoted supra p. 17. A showing of a conflict in decisions of the courts of appeals on a point involved in the case is likely to weigh strongly with the Court as a factor favoring review, but the fact that it is strongly arguable that the decision below was wrong is not in itself a "special and important" reason for review. So a denial of certiorari, theoretically, says nothing as to the merits of the case.

Question: (5) Is certiorari available to review a decision of the court of appeals that is nonfinal? Is it actually necessary to await a decision by the court of appeals before applying for certiorari? At what point, precisely, can certiorari be sought, and by whom?

The procedure for review by the Supreme Court is prescribed in the Rules of the Supreme Court of the United States. Return your focus to review on certiorari. The petition for a writ of certiorari must contain the questions presented for review, a concise statement of the case, and the reasons relied on for allowance of the writ. Certiorari is granted or denied by the Supreme Court upon consideration of the petition, the brief in opposition, and any reply brief; there is no oral argument at this stage. If the petition is granted, which requires the vote of only four Justices, the Court has thereby agreed to consider the merits. The case is normally then briefed on the merits and heard on oral argument. Finally, the Supreme Court—by majority vote, with six Justices constituting a quorum—affirms, reverses, or modifies the decision being reviewed, possibly remanding to a court below for further proceedings.

A stay with respect to a decision of the court of appeals is available from that court or a judge thereof, or from a single Justice of the Supreme Court, under circumstances and in a manner analogous to the stay procedure described above for district-court judgments.

Final decision in the Supreme Court brings the federal court case to the end of the line, and to the end of this survey of the conduct of a lawsuit. As Justice Jackson observed in Brown v. Allen, 344 U.S. 443, 540, 73 S.Ct. 397, 427 (1953) (concurring opinion), "We are not final because we are infallible, but we are infallible only because we are final."

SECTION 6. SELECTING A PROPER COURT: GENERAL DIVISION OF BUSINESS BETWEEN STATE AND FEDERAL COURT SYSTEMS

Having described the conduct of lawsuits in the district courts and their review in the courts of appeals and the Supreme Court, we shall now return to a question put at the beginning of the survey: in which courts may particular actions be instituted? Our concern then shifts to jurisdiction or, as it is called more specifically, jurisdiction over the subject matter. We start with a consideration of the division of business between the state court systems, on the one hand, and the federal court system, on the other hand.

(a) The Judicial Power of the States

The tenth amendment to the Constitution of the United States, which is largely declaratory of the relationships created by the Constitution proper, declares: "The powers not delegated to the United States by the Constitution, nor prohibited by it to the States, are reserved to the States respectively, or to the people." The Constitution nowhere expressly prohibits any judicial power to the states.

As we shall see, article III declares that the federal judicial power shall extend to various enumerated "cases" and "controversies," but these constitute only a fraction of all the disputes that require adjudication. The rest of those disputes can constitutionally be handled only in the state courts.

Moreover, even the article III "cases" and "controversies" may be handled by the states except as Congress decides that they shall not be. In other words, although a limited judicial power is delegated to the federal government by article III, it does not follow that that power may not be exercised by the states; they are free to exercise it unless Congress steps in and says no. Much of the jurisdiction of the federal courts is thus *concurrent* with that of the state courts; that is, a plaintiff often has a choice of instituting a particular action in a federal or a state court.

Finally, there are indeed some acts of Congress that declare certain classes of article III "cases" and "controversies" shall be handled exclusively by the federal courts, but such statutes are relatively few. Examples of this *exclusive* federal jurisdiction are bankruptcy proceedings and actions under the federal antitrust laws.

The net result is that the states are free to handle a very large amount of business. A state may choose not to exert its full judicial power: subject to some vague but slight constitutional limitations not of immediate concern, a state may by provisions in its constitution or statutes restrict the kinds of disputes that its courts will handle. Nevertheless, a very large percentage of this nation's judicial business is handled by state courts. Of course, a state may set up such a hierarchy of courts as it wishes and allocate business among its courts as it sees fit, and there is no uniformity of pattern among the states in these respects. *Dis. Ct. can be less than (Constit. allowed)*

(b) The Judicial Power of the United States

The outer bound on the judicial power of the United States is fixed by article III of the Constitution. After reading the entire article, consider: section 2, paragraph 1;[a] section 1, first sentence; and section 2, paragraph 2. Try to get a sense of what is meant by the statement that the federal courts are courts of *limited* jurisdiction, as opposed to *general* jurisdiction.

Questions: (1) To what extent can the "cases" and "controversies" enumerated in article III, section 2, paragraph 1 be classified as dependent on

---

[a] This is to be read in conjunction with the eleventh amendment. The Supreme Court in Chisholm v. Georgia, 2 U.S. (2 Dall.) 419 (1793), allowed an action in a federal court by a citizen of South Carolina against the State of Georgia. Dissatisfaction with that decision led to the adoption of the eleventh amendment, providing that the federal judicial power should not be construed to extend to any action brought against one of the states by citizens of another state or by citizens or subjects of any foreign state.

The language of the eleventh amendment indicates that involvement of a federal question makes no difference. But the scope of the amendment cannot be determined solely by reference to its wording. On the theory that the amendment was intended simply to overturn the Chisholm holding and to return to the original understanding of article III, and

that the original understanding was that a nonconsenting state could not be sued in federal court by anyone other than a sister state or the United States, the Supreme Court has far departed from the wording of the amendment. On the one hand, the states' immunity has been broadly read. For example, in Hans v. Louisiana, 134 U.S. 1, 10 S.Ct. 504 (1890), it was held that a federal court could not entertain a suit by a citizen against his *own* state although it involved a federal question. On the other hand, the amendment has not been read to bar an otherwise proper federal suit by an out-of-state citizen against a state if the state consents to such suit. E.g., Petty v. Tennessee-Missouri Bridge Comm'n, 359 U.S. 275, 79 S.Ct. 785 (1959).

Note exactly what language of article III, section 2, paragraph 1 is thus affected by the eleventh amendment.

the nature of the claim asserted? as dependent on the types of parties involved?

(2) What importance attaches to the use of the words "cases" and "controversies"? See C. Wright, The Law of Federal Courts § 12 (4th ed. 1983).

(3) Is there any constitutional requirement that there be a Supreme Court? that there be inferior federal courts? [b]

(4) Is it constitutionally required that all or any of the enumerated "cases" or "controversies" shall be handled by federal courts?

Again apart from fairly slight but vague constitutional limitations not of immediate concern, although potentially of great political import, Congress appears to have a free hand in allocating to the inferior federal courts that it establishes, and in withholding from them, *original* jurisdiction over the enumerated "cases" and "controversies" constituting the federal judicial power. Thus, when the problem is whether such a federal court is authorized to hear a particular "case" or "controversy," resort must be had to federal statutes. Similarly, the *appellate* jurisdiction of the federal courts appears largely confided to congressional control. So, when considering an issue of federal jurisdiction, reference should be made first to congressional enactment and then to article III. Generally, for such jurisdiction to exist, the particular action must fall within the bounds of both.

(c) How Congress Has Vested Original Jurisdiction in the District Courts

Examine, as examples of how Congress has vested original jurisdiction in the district courts, 28 U.S.C. §§ 1331 (federal question), 1332 (diversity of citizenship), 1337 (commerce), 1338 (patents and the like), and 1343 (civil rights).

Questions: (5) With respect to each of the foregoing provisions: (a) Can you relate it to one of the classes of "cases" or "controversies" enumerated in article III, section 2, paragraph 1? (b) Does it comprehend the entire class or only a portion of the class? (c) Is the jurisdiction conferred exclusive or concurrent? (d) Is the jurisdiction dependent upon the amount in controversy?

(6) What is the relation between § 1331 and § 1337? between § 1331 and § 1338? between § 1331 and § 1343?

(d) The "Federal Question" Provision

Congress could constitutionally have given the district courts jurisdiction over all civil actions arising under the Constitution, laws, or

---

[b] The most important "inferior Courts" established by Congress are the district courts and the courts of appeals. Congress has also established certain other article III courts of specialized jurisdiction, currently including most significantly the United States Court of International Trade, which handles certain civil actions relating to import transactions.

treaties of the United States and made such jurisdiction exclusive. It has not done so. ✗ ONLY ?'s arising on P's complaint

LOUISVILLE & NASHVILLE RAILROAD v. MOTTLEY
Supreme Court of the United States, 1908.
211 U.S. 149, 29 S.Ct. 42.

The appellees (husband and wife), being residents and citizens of Kentucky, brought this suit in equity in the Circuit Court of the United States for the Western District of Kentucky [c] against the appellant, a railroad company and a citizen of the same State. The object of the suit was to compel the specific performance of the following contract:

"Louisville, Ky., Oct. 2nd, 1871.

"The Louisville & Nashville Railroad Company in consideration that E.L. Mottley and wife, Annie E. Mottley, have this day released Company from all damages or claims for damages for injuries received by them on the 7th of September, 1871, in consequence of a collision of trains on the railroad of said Company at Randolph's Station, Jefferson County, Ky., hereby agrees to issue free passes on said Railroad and branches now existing or to exist, to said E.L. & Annie E. Mottley for the remainder of the present year, and thereafter, to renew said passes annually during the lives of said Mottley and wife or either of them."

The bill alleged that in September, 1871, plaintiffs, while passengers upon the defendant railroad, were injured by the defendant's negligence, and released their respective claims for damages in consideration of the agreement for transportation during their lives, expressed in the contract. It is alleged that the contract was performed by the defendant up to January 1, 1907, when the defendant declined to renew the passes. The bill then alleges that the refusal to comply with the contract was based solely upon that part of the act of Congress of June 29, 1906, 34 Stat. 584, which forbids the giving of free passes or free transportation. The bill further alleges: First, that the act of Congress referred to does not prohibit the giving of passes under the circumstances of this case; and, second, that if the law is to be construed as prohibiting such passes, it is in conflict with the Fifth Amendment of the Constitution, because it deprives the plaintiffs of their property without due process of law. The defendant demurred to the bill. The judge of the Circuit Court overruled the demurrer, entered a decree for the relief prayed for, and the defendant appealed directly to this court.

---

[c] These circuit courts have since been abolished. They are not to be confused with the present United States Courts of Appeals, formerly called United States Circuit Courts of Appeals.

MR. JUSTICE MOODY, after making the foregoing statement, delivered the opinion of the court.

Two questions of law were raised by the demurrer to the bill, were brought here by appeal, and have been argued before us. They are, first, whether that part of the act of Congress of June 29, 1906 (34 Stat. 584), which forbids the giving of free passes or the collection of any different compensation for transportation of passengers than that specified in the tariff filed, makes it unlawful to perform a contract for transportation of persons who in good faith, before the passage of the act, had accepted such contract in satisfaction of a valid cause of action against the railroad; and, second, whether the statute, if it should be construed to render such a contract unlawful, is in violation of the Fifth Amendment of the Constitution of the United States. We do not deem it necessary, however, to consider either of these questions, because, in our opinion, the court below was without jurisdiction of the cause. Neither party has questioned that jurisdiction, but it is the duty of this court to see to it that the jurisdiction of the Circuit Court, which is defined and limited by statute, is not exceeded. This duty we have frequently performed of our own motion. [Citations omitted.]

There was no diversity of citizenship and it is not and cannot be suggested that there was any ground of jurisdiction, except that the case was a "suit . . . arising under the Constitution and laws of the United States." Act of August 13, 1888, c. 866, 25 Stat. 433, 434.[d] It is the settled interpretation of these words, as used in this statute, conferring jurisdiction, that a suit arises under the Constitution and laws of the United States only when the plaintiff's statement of his own cause of action shows that it is based upon those laws or that Constitution. It is not enough that the plaintiff alleges some anticipated defense to his cause of action and asserts that the defense is invalidated by some provision of the Constitution of the United States. Although such allegations show that very likely, in the course of the litigation, a question under the Constitution would arise, they do not show that the suit, that is, the plaintiff's original cause of action, arises under the Constitution. In Tennessee v. Union & Planters' Bank, 152 U.S. 454, 14 S.Ct. 654, the plaintiff, the State of Tennessee, brought suit in the Circuit Court of the United States to recover from the defendant certain taxes alleged to be due under the laws of the State. The plaintiff alleged that the defendant claimed an immunity from the taxation by virtue of its charter, and that therefore the tax was void, because in violation of the provision of the Constitution of the United States, which forbids any State from passing a law impairing the obligation of contracts. The cause was held to be beyond the jurisdiction of the Circuit Court, the court saying, by Mr. Justice Gray (p. 464), "a suggestion of one party, that the other will or may set up a claim under the Constitution or laws of

---

[d] Now 28 U.S.C. § 1331.

the United States, does not make the suit one arising under that Constitution or those laws." Again, in Boston & Montana Consolidated Copper & Silver Mining Company v. Montana Ore Purchasing Company, 188 U.S. 632, 23 S.Ct. 434, the plaintiff brought suit in the Circuit Court of the United States for the conversion of copper ore and for an injunction against its continuance. The plaintiff then alleged, for the purpose of showing jurisdiction, in substance, that the defendant would set up in defense certain laws of the United States. The cause was held to be beyond the jurisdiction of the Circuit Court, the court saying, by Mr. Justice Peckham (pp. 638, 639):

"It would be wholly unnecessary and improper in order to prove complainant's cause of action to go into any matters of defence which the defendants might possibly set up and then attempt to reply to such defence, and thus, if possible, to show that a Federal question might or probably would arise in the course of the trial of the case. To allege such defence and then make an answer to it before the defendant has the opportunity to itself plead or prove its own defence is inconsistent with any known rule of pleading so far as we are aware, and is improper.

"The rule is a reasonable and just one that the complainant in the first instance shall be confined to a statement of its cause of action, leaving to the defendant to set up in his answer what his defence is and, if anything more than a denial of complainant's cause of action, imposing upon the defendant the burden of proving such defence.

"Conforming itself to that rule the complainant would not, in the assertion or proof of its cause of action, bring up a single Federal question. The presentation of its cause of action would not show that it was one arising under the Constitution or laws of the United States.

"The only way in which it might be claimed that a Federal question was presented would be in the complainant's statement of what the defence of defendants would be and complainant's answer to such defence. Under these circumstances the case is brought within the rule laid down in Tennessee v. Union & Planters' Bank, 152 U.S. 454, 14 S.Ct. 654. That case has been cited and approved many times since."

. . . . The application of this rule to the case at bar is decisive against the jurisdiction of the Circuit Court.

It is ordered that the

Judgment be reversed and the case remitted to the Circuit Court with instructions to dismiss the suit for want of jurisdiction.

Question: (7) Suppose the action were instead structured as one for a declaratory judgment under a statute analogous to present 28 U.S.C. § 2201, with the railroad as plaintiff seeking a declaration of its obligation in light of the statute prohibiting free passes. Would federal question jurisdiction then exist?

(e) The "Diversity of Citizenship" Provision

The cases comprehended in 28 U.S.C. § 1332, as in § 1331, are not prohibited to the states, and so the state courts are free to entertain them in the first instance.

Question: (8) Does the required diversity under § 1332 exist in each of the following cases? The matter in controversy exceeds $10,000 in each case.

(a) *A*, a citizen of Canada, sues *B*, a citizen of Massachusetts.

(b) *A*, a citizen of Canada, sues *B*, a citizen of England.

Now suppose that *A*, a citizen of New York, sues *B*, a citizen of Massachusetts, in a United States District Court. While the suit is pending, *A* becomes a citizen of Massachusetts. Diversity is not destroyed. It is citizenship at the time when the action is commenced that controls, and any change thereafter is immaterial.

In the ordinary case there is little difficulty in determining the citizenship of a litigant. At times, however, the facts regarding citizenship are seriously disputed and must be resolved.

BAKER v. KECK

United States District Court, Eastern District of Illinois, 1936.
13 F.Supp. 486.

LINDLEY, DISTRICT JUDGE. Plaintiff has filed herein his suit against various individuals and the Progressive Miners of America charging a conspiracy, out of which grew certain events and in the course of which, it is averred, he was attacked by certain of the defendants and his arm shot off. This, it is said, resulted from a controversy between the United Mine Workers and the Progressive Miners of America.

Plaintiff avers that he is a citizen of the state of Oklahoma. Defendants filed a motion to dismiss, one ground of which is that plaintiff is not a citizen of the state of Oklahoma, but has a domicile in the state of Illinois, and that therefore there is no diversity of citizenship. To this motion plaintiff filed a response, with certain affidavits in support thereof.

Upon presentation of the motion, the court set the issue of fact arising upon the averments of the complaint, the motion to dismiss, and the response thereto for hearing. A jury was waived. Affidavits were received and parol evidence offered.

It appears that plaintiff formerly resided in Saline county, Ill., that he was not a member of United Mine Workers, but was in sympathy with their organization. The averment of the declaration is

FACTS

that he was attacked by members of, or sympathizers with, the Progressive Mine Workers of America. He was a farmer, owning about 100 acres of land. After his injury, he removed to the state of Oklahoma, taking with him his family and all of his household goods, except two beds and some other small items. His household furniture was carried to Oklahoma by truck, and the truckman was paid $100 for transportation. Near Ulan, Okl., he rented 20 acres and a house for $150 per year, and began occupancy thereof October, 1934. He testified that he had arrangements with another party and his own son, living with him, to cultivate the ground, but that farming conditions were not satisfactory, and that it was impossible, therefore, to produce a crop in 1935. He produced potatoes, sweet corn, and other garden products used in the living of the family. He had no horses or other livestock in Oklahoma. He was unable to do any extensive work himself because of the loss of his arm. In the summer of 1935 he leased for the year 1936 the same 20 acres and an additional 20 acres at a rental of $150.

At the first opportunity to register as a qualified voter in Oklahoma after he went there, he complied with the statute in that respect and was duly registered. This was not until after he had been in the state for over a year, as, under the state statute, a qualified voter must have resided within the state for twelve months prior to registration. He has not voted, but he testified that the only election at which he could have voted after he registered was on a day when he had to be in Illinois to give attention to his lawsuit. He has returned to Illinois for short visits three or four times.

He testified that he moved to Oklahoma for the purpose of residing there, with the intention of making it his home and that he still intends to reside there. He testified that the family started out to see if they could find a new location in 1934. Upon cross-examination it appeared that the funds for traveling and removal had been paid by the United Mine Workers or their representative; that he left his livestock on the Illinois farm, but no chickens; that he had about 60 chickens on his farm in Oklahoma; that, when he removed to Oklahoma, he rented his Illinois farm for a period of five years; that the tenant has recently defaulted upon the same.

In the affidavits it appears that plaintiff's house in Illinois was completely destroyed by fire shortly after he left. It was not insured and was a total loss. Witnesses for the defense testified that he had told them that he intended to move back to Illinois after he got his case settled; that he had told one witness in 1935 that he was going to Oklahoma but did not know for how long. Plaintiff denies that he told these witnesses that he expected to return to Illinois as soon as his litigation was completed.

I think it is a fair conclusion from all the evidence that at the time plaintiff removed to Oklahoma one of his motives was to create diversity of citizenship so that he might maintain a suit in the United

ISSUE

States courts. But that conclusion is not of itself decisive of the question presented. There remains the further question of whether there was at the time this suit was begun an intention upon his part to become a citizen of Oklahoma. One may change his citizenship for the purpose of enabling himself to maintain a suit in the federal court, but the change must be an actual legal change made with the intention of bringing about actual citizenship in the state to which the removal is made.

Citizenship and domicile are substantially synonymous. Residency and inhabitance are too often confused with the terms and have not the same significance. Citizenship implies more than residence.[e] It carries with it the idea of identification with the state and a participation in its functions. As a citizen, one sustains social, political, and moral obligation to the state and possesses social and political rights under the Constitution and laws thereof. . . . Change of domicile arises when there is a change of abode with the absence of any present intention not to reside permanently or indefinitely in the new abode. This is the holding of the Supreme Court in Gilbert v. David, 235 U.S. 561, 35 S.Ct. 164, 167, 59 L.Ed. 360, where the court said: "As Judge Story puts it in his work on 'Conflict of Laws' (7th Ed.) § 46, page 41, 'If a person has actually removed to another place, with an intention of remaining there for an indefinite time, and as a place of fixed present domicil, it is to be deemed his place of domicil, notwithstanding he may entertain a floating intention to return at some future period.' The requisite animus is the present intention of permanent or indefinite residence in a given place or country, or, negatively expressed, the absence of any present intention of not residing there permanently or indefinitely.'"

∗ It will be observed that, if there is an intention to remain, even though it be for an indefinite time, but still with the intention of making the location a place of present domicile, this latter intention will control, even though the person entertains a floating intention to return at some indefinite future period. In this respect the court in Gilbert v. David, supra, further said: "Plaintiff may have had, and probably did have, some floating intention of returning to Michigan after the determination of certain litigation. . . . But, as we have seen, a floating intention of that kind was not enough to prevent the new place, under the circumstances shown, from becoming his domicil. It was his place of abode, which he had no present intention of changing; that is the essence of domicil."

. . . .

The statement of the Restatement of the Law, Conflict of Laws, § 15, Domicil of Choice, is as follows:

[e] The fourteenth amendment defines citizenship in terms of residence. However, that definition is not controlling for diversity-jurisdiction purposes.

"(1) A domicil of choice is a domicil acquired, through the exercise of his own will, by a person who is legally capable of changing his domicil.

"(2) To acquire a domicil of choice, a person must establish a dwelling-place with the intention of making it his home.

"(3) The fact of physical presence at a dwelling-place and the intention to make it a home must concur; if they do so, even for a moment, the change of domicil takes place." f

In Holt v. Hendee, 248 Ill. 288, 93 N.E. 749, 752, 21 Ann.Cas. 202, the court said: "The intention is not necessarily determined from the statements or declarations of the party but may be inferred from the surrounding circumstances, which may entirely disprove such statements or declarations. On the question of domicile less weight will be given to the party's declaration than to his acts."

Though it must be confessed that the question is far from free of doubt, I conclude that, under the facts as they appear in the record, despite the fact that one of the plaintiff's motives was the establishment of citizenship so as to create jurisdiction in the federal court, there was at the time of his removal a fixed intention to become a citizen of the state of Oklahoma. He testified that he worked on a community project in that state without compensation. It appears that he registered as a voter; he thus became a participant in the political activities of the state. Such action is inconsistent with any conclusion other than that of citizenship, and in view of his sworn testimony that it was his intention to reside in Oklahoma and to continue to do so, it follows that the elements constituting the status of citizenship existed.

True, there is some evidence that he had said he might return to Illinois as soon as his case was settled. The language of the cases above indicates that such a floating intention is insufficient to bar citizenship, where active participation in the obligations and enjoyment of the rights of citizenship exist.

Defendants contend that the fact that the costs of plaintiff's transportation and maintenance were paid by the United Mine Workers is of decisive weight upon this issue. I cannot agree. It seems to me immaterial what motives may have inspired the United Mine Workers to help him, and the court is not now concerned with their alleged charitable and philanthropic practices.

I conclude, therefore, that plaintiff was at the time of the commencement of the suit, and is now, a citizen of the state of Oklahoma. The findings herein embraced will be adopted as findings of fact of

f Among the changes in § 15 made by Restatement (Second) of Conflict of Laws § 15 (1969) is the omission of the phrase "through the exercise of his own will," this being omitted to avoid any implication that the significant intention is one to acquire a domicile rather than one to make a home. Section 18, "Requisite Intention," now provides: "To acquire a domicil of choice in a place, a person must intend to make that place his home for the time at least."

the court and entered as such. It is ordered that the motion to dismiss because of lack of diversity of citizenship be, and the same is hereby, denied. An exception is allowed to defendants.

. . . .

Question: (9) Does the required diversity under § 1332 exist in each of the following cases? The matter in controversy exceeds $10,000 in each case.

(a) The soprano Felice Lyne, born in Missouri, abandoned her home there and took up residence in London, England, declaring it to be her home and that it was her intention to remain there indefinitely. She has taken no steps toward naturalization in England. While on a temporary visit to Missouri she is sued in the United States District Court for the Western District of Missouri by Oscar Hammerstein, a citizen of New York. The court finds that she is domiciled in England. See Hammerstein v. Lyne, 200 F. 165 (W.D.Mo.1912) (no).

(b) *A*, a citizen of New York, sues *B*, a Cuban refugee domiciled in Florida with the status of stateless alien.

(c) *A*, a citizen of New York, sues *B*, a Cuban citizen domiciled in Florida.

DOMICILE OF STUDENTS

An unemancipated minor has the same domicile as the parent with whom he or she lives, but the student who is emancipated or who is not a minor may acquire a domicile of choice. Cf. Restatement (Second) of Conflict of Laws § 22 (1969).

Question: (10) Should students be free to select either their parents' home or their college residence as their domicile? If not, what should be the standards for determining domicile? Should it matter whether a student lives in a dormitory or rented apartment or buys a house? whether the student returns to his or her parents' home during vacations? Should the student's present intention regarding post-educational residence matter? What if he or she intends to return to the parents' home? intends to remain in the college community? intends to move elsewhere? does not know? Cf. Restatement (Second) of Conflict of Laws § 18 comment f, illustrations 13–14 (1969).

Although the issue of interest here is jurisdiction, the determination of a student's domicile may carry with it other consequences. For instance, voting rights, state income tax liability, automobile registration, automobile excise tax, and automobile insurance premiums may all be affected by domicile. For these different purposes, a student may have different domiciles. Restatement (Second) of Conflict of Laws § 11(2) (1969) recognized this possibility by providing: "Every person has a domicil at all times and, at least for the same purpose, no person has more than one domicil at a time." The conventional learning, reflected in Restatement of Conflict of Laws § 11

(1934), had been simply that every person has one and only one domicile at a time.

DOMICILE OF WIVES

At common law, a wife was not able to acquire a domicile of choice, but was instead assigned the domicile of her husband by operation of law. This rule is close to expiration. Today a wife, particularly when she lives apart from her husband, may acquire a separate domicile of choice. Cf. Restatement (Second) of Conflict of Laws § 21 (1969).

"CITIZENSHIP" OF CORPORATIONS

What about diversity of citizenship with respect to corporations? The Constitution does not mention corporations, and for various constitutional purposes a corporation is not a citizen. For instance, a corporation cannot claim the benefits of article IV, section 2 of the Constitution, which provides: "The Citizens of each State shall be entitled to all Privileges and Immunities of Citizens in the several States."

Does this mean that corporations are excluded from diversity jurisdiction? The Supreme Court of the United States avoided this result by deciding that the citizenship of the stockholders effectively determined the citizenship of a corporation, and the Court then blandly laid down the conclusive presumption that for diversity purposes all the stockholders were citizens of the state of incorporation. Marshall v. Baltimore & Ohio Railroad, 57 U.S. (16 How.) 314 (1853). Thus the General Motors Corporation would be treated as though it and all its stockholders were citizens of Delaware, the state of incorporation. Here is one of the many instances in the law where results thought desirable were achieved through the use of transparent fictions.

By statute since 1958, a corporation is for diversity purposes "deemed a citizen of any State by which it has been incorporated and of the State where it has its principal place of business." 28 U.S.C. § 1332(c). The preferred interpretation of this language is that an American corporation is deemed a citizen of each and every state (a corporation may be incorporated by more than one state) by which it has been incorporated, and also of any state (there can be at most one) in which it has its principal place of business. Naturally, the more states of which a corporation is a citizen, the less likely diversity jurisdiction is to exist.

The proviso in § 1332(c), added in 1964, was aimed at preventing the exercise of diversity jurisdiction where it would be dependent on the mere fact that under local law the plaintiff can sue the liability insurer directly without joining the insured.

Some of the problems of interpreting § 1332(c) should be becoming apparent. As for a foreign corporation, it is seemingly still deemed a citizen only of the country of incorporation, but this is a matter of considerable dispute.

———

KELLY v. UNITED STATES STEEL CORP., 284 F.2d 850 (3d Cir. 1960). The question for determination was whether United States Steel, then incorporated in New Jersey, had its principal place of business in New York or Pennsylvania.

The plaintiffs, Pennsylvania citizens, sought to invoke diversity jurisdiction. They urged that the test should be where the "nerve center" of the corporation's business was, that the nerve center was in New York, and hence that diversity of citizenship existed. The court did not find the "pleasant and alluring figure of speech" helpful and turned therefore "to a consideration of the facts of the Steel Corporation's life." These included the following activities in New York: the Board of Directors regularly meets there (although it can choose its own place of meeting and has met in Pittsburgh); the Chairman of the Board is there, spending one day a week in Pittsburgh; the Executive Committee and the Finance Committee meet regularly there; the Secretary, the Treasurer, the Comptroller, and the General Counsel have their offices there; the dividends are declared, the income tax returns filed, and the annual report mailed there; the Public Relations Department is centered there; and the major banking and financing activities are there. To the court this adds up to the conclusion that if the test of principal place of business is where the final decisions are made on corporate policy, including its financing, the principal place is New York.

The activities in Pennsylvania included the following: the Operation Policy Committee, to which the Board of Directors has delegated the duty of conducting the manufacturing, mining, transportation, and general operation of the corporation, sits and conducts its affairs there (this Committee is composed of the Chairman of the Board, the President, the Chairman of the Finance Committee, the General Counsel, and the seven Executive Vice Presidents, and it makes policy decisions subject to the Board of Directors); the Executive Vice Presidents, one heading each of the seven great branches of the corporation, have headquarters and staffs there; and 34 per cent of the management personnel are located there, fourteen times as many as in New York. All this points, the court says, to "the conclusion that business by way of activities is centered in Pennsylvania."

The court then adds some other facts "of lesser importance" but having "some significance": Pennsylvania has 32.13 per cent of employee personnel (twenty-five times as many as New York); more than one-third of the tangible property is there (with less than one per cent in New York); and about 35 per cent of the total productive capacity is there (New York has none). "These facts," the court concludes, "added to what we have found to be the headquarters of day-to-day corporate activity and management, add up to the irresistible conclusion that the principal place of business of this giant corporation is in Pennsylvania."

Holding

———

Questions: (11) American Airlines, a Delaware corporation, had its overall business policy prescribed in and directed from New York, where its activities were substantial but represented only a modest fraction of the company's total. In states with a greater volume of activity, however, its local officers were concerned mostly with local activities. The company repaired and serviced most of its aircraft in Oklahoma; it flew more miles in Texas and carried more passengers in California than it did in New York. Was New York its principal place of business? See Egan v. American Airlines, 211 F.Supp. 292 (E.D.N.Y.1962) (yes), aff'd, 324 F.2d 565 (2d Cir.1963).

(12) Central Foundry Company, a Maine corporation, manufactures soil pipe and fittings, which it sells throughout the United States and abroad. All of its production is in Holt, Alabama. Its executive offices are in New York, and all its officers are there except one in Alabama who has the title of vice president and plant manager; but he works under the director of Holt operations, who is located in New York and who spends only fifteen per cent of his time in Alabama. The sales staff is in New York, where all sales policy is made and sales activity directed. All invoices are directed to be paid in New York. The company's books and records are kept in New York, and its financial affairs are conducted there. New York has 55 employees; Alabama has 1890. Annual payroll in New York is $500,000; that in Alabama is $9,200,000. Physical assets in New York have a book value of $60,000; those in Alabama have a book value of $5,695,000. Is New York its principal place of business? See Anniston Soil Pipe Co. v. Central Foundry Co., 216 F.Supp. 473 (N.D.Ala.1963) (no), aff'd on opinion below, 329 F.2d 313 (5th Cir. 1964).

———

"CITIZENSHIP" OF UNINCORPORATED ASSOCIATIONS

Treated as real persons not as corps

For diversity purposes unincorporated associations, such as partnerships, fraternal benefit societies, trade associations, and labor unions, are covered by neither the judicial fiction nor the legislative treatment extended to corporations. Hence, such an association is deemed a citizen of each and every state and country of which one of its members is actually a citizen. This rule was reconsidered by the Supreme Court in United Steelworkers v. R.H. Bouligny, Inc., 382 U.S. 145, 86 S.Ct. 272 (1965), but it was there decided that change was a task for Congress and not for the courts.

———

DESIRABILITY OF DIVERSITY JURISDICTION

It is not too early to ask whether Congress has been wise in its allocation of diversity of citizenship cases to the federal courts. Compare § 1332 with 28 U.S.C. § 1335. In forming a judgment on this question you should consider what the purposes of the Founders were in extending the federal judicial power to diversity cases. Have any changes come about since 1789 that have any bearing on the general problem? These questions were among the many considered by the American Law Institute before it proposed rather drastic restrictions on the scope of diversity jurisdiction. See ALI Study of the Division of Jurisdiction Between State and Federal Courts 99–110 (1968). More recently, in an effort to lessen the growing congestion in federal court, numerous commentators, judges, and legislators have called for virtually complete abolition by Congress of federal jurisdiction based solely on diversity of citizenship. But see Marsh, Diversity Jurisdiction: Scapegoat of Overcrowded Federal Courts, 48 Brooklyn L.Rev. 197 (1982).

As you read the next Subsection, ask yourself what difference there is between original and removal jurisdiction so far as the right of access to a federal court in a diversity case is concerned. Is the difference a logical one?

(f) "Removal" Jurisdiction of the District Courts

Suppose an action that could have been commenced in a district court as falling within the original but nonexclusive jurisdiction of those courts is commenced in a state court instead. Are there circumstances in which either party may remove the case from the state system into the federal system of courts? What reasons of policy suggest that such a course should at least in some situations be open? The basic removal statute is 28 U.S.C. § 1441.

Questions: In the following questions, assume that the matter in controversy exceeds $10,000.$ 50000

(13) *A*, a citizen of New York, sues *B*, a citizen of Pennsylvania, in a New York state court. The only possible basis of federal jurisdiction is diversity of citizenship. Can *B* properly remove to the United States District Court?

(14) *A*, a citizen of New York, sues *B*, a citizen of Pennsylvania, in a Pennsylvania state court. The only possible basis of federal jurisdiction is diversity of citizenship. Can *B* properly remove?

(15) A corporation incorporated in Delaware and having its principal place of business in New York commences a trademark action based on federal statute in a Massachusetts state court against a New York corporation having its principal place of business in Massachusetts. Can defendant properly remove?

(16) Suppose the Louisville & Nashville R.R. v. Mottley litigation were instead brought originally in Kentucky state court by the Mottleys. Could defendant railroad properly remove the action to federal court under a statute analogous to present 28 U.S.C. § 1441?

There are exceptions to the general rule of § 1441, as is indeed suggested by the opening clause of the section. For example, 28 U.S.C. § 1445(a) provides that a civil action arising under the Federal Employers' Liability Act (45 U.S.C. §§ 51–60) and commenced in a state court may not be removed to a federal district court. The FELA is a statute designed to make it easier for an injured railroad worker engaged in interstate commerce to recover damages from his employer. Substantively, it abrogates the common-law rule that prevented an employee from recovering from his employer for injuries sustained through the negligence of a fellow servant; and it provides that the plaintiff's contributory negligence is not a complete defense, but is to be considered only in reduction of damages on a comparative-negligence basis. Procedurally, it gives the injured worker a choice between a state court and a federal district court that cannot be frustrated by the defendant employer.

It may be noted parenthetically that the Jones Act (46 U.S.C. § 688) gives to seamen the same substantive benefits in actions against their employers for injuries suffered in the course of their employment that the FELA gives to railroad workers. It also gives seamen the same procedural benefits by allowing them the choice between a state and a federal court and forbidding removal by the employer. Indeed, the Jones Act incorporates by reference "all statutes of the United States modifying or extending the common-law right or remedy in cases of personal injury to railway employees."

Removal must be sought promptly, normally within thirty days of the receipt of the complaint. The mechanics of removal are covered by 28 U.S.C. §§ 1446–1450. Briefly, the defendant files in the United States District Court sitting in the same locality a petition for removal in which he sets forth the facts entitling him to removal, and also a bond sufficient to cover costs in case of improper removal. The defendant then gives the plaintiff and the state court notice of the filing. By this activity solely on the part of the defendant, removal is complete. The state court can proceed no further with the action unless and until the United States District Court remands it to the state court upon a finding that it was improperly removed. See also Rule 81(c).

(g) Possible Review by the Supreme Court of State-Court Actions

If an action is properly commenced in or removed to a district court, it will remain in the federal court system to the end. There is no such thing as removal from a federal court to a state court.[g]

But can an action commenced in a state court appear in the federal court system at any later stage if (1) it was not removable to a federal court or (2) it was removable but was not in fact removed? The matter is governed by 28 U.S.C. § 1257, which should be read in contrast to 28 U.S.C. § 1254, discussed supra p. 159.

Consider the subsequent history of Louisville & Nashville Railroad v. Mottley. After that federal suit was dismissed for want of jurisdiction, the Mottleys brought a new action in a state circuit court in Kentucky seeking the same relief. The railroad company based its defense upon the federal statute prohibiting free passes. The state circuit court, granting the relief asked, by its judgment required the railroad company to issue annual passes over its lines to the plaintiffs during their respective lives. On appeal, the Kentucky Court of Appeals, the highest court of the state, affirmed the judgment. Then the railroad company took the case to the Supreme Court of the United States again for the determination of the same federal issue that had been unsuccessfully relied upon to give the federal court original jurisdiction in the first suit. In Louisville & Nashville Railroad v. Mottley, 219 U.S. 467, 31 S.Ct. 265 (1911), the Court held that by reason of the federal statute the railroad company rightly refused further to comply with its agreement to issue passes to the plaintiffs and that the judgment of the Kentucky court requiring performance of the agreement was erroneous.

Questions: (17) What are the purposes, in a state-federal arrangement of courts, of § 1257?

(18) Why does § 1257 confine review by the Supreme Court of state-court decisions to "[f]inal judgments or decrees rendered by the *highest* court of a State in which a decision could be had" (emphasis added)?

(19) Why is review by the Supreme Court under § 1257 in some cases to be had by "appeal" and in others by "writ of certiorari"?

(20) Under present § 1257, would Supreme Court review in the second Mottley suit be by appeal or by certiorari? See also 28 U.S.C. § 2103. Is such review here constitutionally within the Court's jurisdiction?

(21) Where a plaintiff has a choice between commencing his action in a state or a federal court, what are the considerations that would be likely to affect his choice?

---

[g] To be distinguished is the remand to the state court of a case improperly removed to the federal court.

SECTION 7. SELECTING A PROPER COURT: LIMITATIONS RESULTING FROM PROVISIONS AS TO VENUE AND SERVICE OF PROCESS

Suppose a person has a case that fits within article III as well as within one of the sections of the United States Code vesting original jurisdiction in the United States District Courts, so that he may (if the jurisdiction is concurrent) or must (if it is exclusive) commence his action in one of these courts. Is he free to select any district court in any state? Manifestly he should not be altogether free to do so.

Question: (1) What are the factors that should enter rationally into a solution of the general problem here posed? (When you complete your study of this Section, try to make a tentative determination of how well the federal scheme takes these factors into account.)

In fact there are two types of regulation that control the plaintiff's choice of a district court in which to commence his lawsuit.[a]

(a) Venue Requirements as a Limitation

Rules of venue specify where the sovereign will exercise its authority to adjudicate, i.e., in what place it will exercise its jurisdiction. The general precepts regarding venue in the federal system appear in 28 U.S.C. § 1391.

Question: (2) Why the difference between cases where jurisdiction is founded only on diversity of citizenship and cases where jurisdiction is otherwise founded?

Note the use of the word "reside" in § 1391(a) and (b). Strangely, under the case law this term is generally equated with "citizenship" as used in the diversity statute. The restrictive consequences with respect to venue are mitigated by the 1966 amendment making the place where the claim arose a proper venue.

Questions: (3) Is there any policy that should prevent a person from having more than one residence for venue purposes?

(4) In a suit seeking to recover for anticipatory repudiation of a contract, did the claim arise for venue purposes in the district where the repudiation was made or in the district where the contract was to be performed or elsewhere?

Read carefully § 1391(c), added in 1948, with its definition of the residence of a corporation for venue purposes as lying in each district in which it is incorporated or is licensed to do business or is doing business. The statute appears on its face to apply to a corporation either as plaintiff or defendant, but it has been authoritatively held that the statute was intended to cover a corporate defendant only.[b]

[personal jurisdiction]

---

[a] For now we put to one side whether, despite these regulations, the case may go forward if the defendant consents or if he raises no appropriate objection. But do recall Rule 12.

[b] See Manchester Modes, Inc. v. Schuman, 426 F.2d 629 (2d Cir.1970). Judge Friendly's opinion in this case well illustrates the resort to legislative history in construing a statute.

This evidently leaves unaltered the earlier doctrine that, when suing as a plaintiff, a corporation resides for venue purposes only in its home-office district in the state (or states) by which it was incorporated. Compare § 1391(c) with 28 U.S.C. § 1332(c).

For venue purposes unincorporated associations are analogized to corporations. Hence, such an association as defendant is deemed to reside in each district in which it is doing business, and as plaintiff is deemed to reside only in the district in which it has its principal office. See Denver & Rio Grande Western Railroad v. Brotherhood of Railroad Trainmen, 387 U.S. 556, 87 S.Ct. 1746 (1967). Compare this rule with the treatment of unincorporated associations for diversity purposes.

As for an alien defendant, either individual or corporate, § 1391(d) means that venue lies in any district, so that here the venue requirements place no limitation on the plaintiff's choice of a district court. As for an alien plaintiff, he "resides" in no district, thus restricting the available places to sue.

Question: (5) In which United States District Courts would venue be proper in each of the following cases? The matter in controversy exceeds $10,000 in each case.

(a) *A*, a resident of the Southern District of New York, wishes to sue *B*, a resident of Vermont, the only possible basis of jurisdiction being diversity of citizenship. The claim arose in Buffalo in the Western District of New York.

(b) Same as the preceding case except that this case presents a federal question that would support jurisdiction.

(c) *A*, a resident of the Southern District of New York, wishes to sue *B* Company, a Delaware corporation with its principal place of business in Michigan. *B* Company does business in each of the fifty states. The only possible basis of jurisdiction is diversity of citizenship. The claim arose in Buffalo.

There are various statutes and some judge-made doctrines that lay down special venue rules for particular classes of cases. Most of these special rules have been interpreted to supplement § 1391, broadening the choice of venue. E.g., 28 U.S.C. § 1401. Others have been read to override § 1391(a) and (b), thus controlling venue for the particular class of cases. E.g., 28 U.S.C. § 1397. One such exclusive provision is unique and deserves special mention: when a case is removed from a state court to a federal district court, it always passes "to the district court of the United States for the district and division [c] embracing the place where such action is pending." 28 U.S.C. § 1441(a)

Question: (6) Assume that a case in state court is properly removed to the district court sitting in the same locality. Is that district court necessari-

---

[c] Many districts are subdivided into divisions. A plaintiff suing in federal district court has to select a proper division in a manner somewhat analogous to selecting among the districts themselves, but the statutory divisional scheme is poorly drafted and therefore quite confusing. See generally 15 Wright, Miller & Cooper § 3809.

ly a court in which, under venue requirements for actions originally brought in the district courts, the plaintiff might initially have commenced the action?

(b) Service of Process Requirements as a Limitation

[Rules 3, 4; Form 1]

The second type of regulation limiting the plaintiff's choice of a district court in which to commence his action comprises the rules regarding service of process. These rules concern the means (1) of officially informing the defendant that an action has been brought against him and that he must defend himself or suffer the entry of judgment by default and (2) of formally subjecting the defendant to the adjudicatory authority of the sovereign.

Rule 3 of the Federal Rules tells us that "[a] civil action is commenced by filing a complaint with the court." Rule 4(a) says that, upon the filing of the complaint, the clerk shall issue a summons. Rule 4(b) states the requirements as to the form of the summons; note how Form 1, the form of summons, carries out the requirements of Rule 4(b). Rule 4(c) specifies who can serve the summons, and ordinarily this is any nonparty at least eighteen years old. Rule 4(d) says that "[t]he summons and complaint shall be served together."

Question: (7) Consider the likely reaction of an inexperienced layman when confronted with these formidable documents. Would it be desirable to couch them in simpler language?

Rule 4(d) also describes the manner of service. Take a typical lawsuit for a money recovery against an individual who is found in the state in which the district court sits or is an inhabitant of that state, and who is neither an infant nor an incompetent. Rule 4(d)(1) says that the service shall be made by delivering a copy of the summons and of the complaint to the defendant personally, or by leaving these papers at his dwelling house or usual place of abode with some person of suitable age and discretion residing there, or by delivering them to an agent authorized to receive them. According to Rule 4(c)(2)(C), it is also sufficient if the papers are served in the manner prescribed by the law of the state in which the district court is held, or by a fairly complicated procedure for serving by mail. Thus, Rule 4(d) incorporates Rule 4(c)(2)(C).

Question: (8) How is service to be carried out on a domestic corporation?

What about service outside the state? By Rule 4(e) this is to be carried out in the manner prescribed by any applicable federal statute or state law.[d] Service under 28 U.S.C. § 2361 is an example of a fed-

---

[d] Although a literal reading of Rule 4(d) and (e) might suggest that service is to be made under Rule 4(d) unless it is made upon a party not found within the state *and* not an inhabitant thereof, this is not the way the relation between the two subdivisions of the Rule has in fact been worked out. In general, Rule 4(e) is to be used whenever service is made outside the state; Rule 4(d) is to be used only for service within the state boundaries. See Kaplan, Amendments of the Federal

eral statute within Rule 4(e). An example of a state law within Rule
4(e) is one of the familiar "nonresident motorist" statutes: where *A*
is injured on a State *X* highway through the alleged negligence of a
nonresident motorist *B*, a State *X* statute says that *A* may start his
action in State *X* and serve process upon *B* through a prescribed system, which may involve the medium of registered or certified mail to
B in his home state.[e]

Rule 4(f) regulates the "Territorial Limits of Effective Service."
In the first place, service in the manner prescribed by Rule 4(d) may
be made anywhere within the state in which the district court is held
(not merely within the district). In the second place, service outside
the state is authorized only where the federal statute or state law
referred to in Rule 4(e) provides for such service.[f] (See the special
provisions of Rule 4(i) for cases where the service is to be made in a
foreign country.)[g]

Rule 4 is somewhat intricate because, by the nature of its historical growth, it combines specific federal regulations with adopted features of state law. But to go back to the heading of this Section, it is
clear that the place-restrictions on making service themselves impose
limits on the plaintiff's choice of a district court in which to commence his action. Thus, for simple illustration, in a diversity action
for breach of contract, a plaintiff may well be disabled from suing in
a district court in his own state—where venue requirements are satisfied—and obliged to sue in a district court in the defendant's state (at
least if the defendant takes care to remain outside the plaintiff's
state). We are not at the moment intimating any opinion that this
result is bad or regrettable; we are noting the fact that it comes
about through the rules regarding service of process. We shall have
to come finally to the question whether the territorial limitations of
Rule 4 do make sense; and here we should remark that they do not
seem to be compelled by any constitutional requirement.[h]

Rules of Civil Procedure, 1961–63 (I), 77
Harv.L.Rev. 601, 621 n.90 (1964).

[e] Another example of a state law within Rule 4(e) is a State *X* statute permitting *A*, claiming as creditor of a nonresident debtor *B*, to commence an action
against *B* in State *X* by attaching property of *B* located in State *X* and providing
some form of reasonable notice to *B* as
prescribed in the statute. Such an attempt to base a suit on the attachment of
property is classified as a nonpersonal action. The study of such actions, and the
question of their constitutional validity,
we put off until Part Five.

[f] The first sentence of Rule 4(f) refers
expressly to the federal statutes. It invokes the state laws through the phrase
"by these rules," which points to Rule
4(e).

[g] In addition to all the foregoing authority, when a pending action is enlarged to bring in certain kinds of additional parties that will be studied in the
next Section ("third-party defendants"
under Rule 14 or "persons needed for
just adjudication" under Rule 19), service
upon those parties may be made at any
place within the sweep of a radius of 100
miles from the courthouse if that place is
outside the state but within the United
States. See Rule 4(f). This provision
may be useful in a metropolitan area
spanning more than one state.

[h] One purpose of service of process is
to provide notice. As fair notification to
the defendant is a constitutional requirement for the exercise by any American
court of the authority to adjudicate (a requirement deriving from the due process

(c) Transfer of Cases from One District Court to Another

Operation of the ordinary rules will not infrequently result in a case being commenced in or removed to a district court that is not the most convenient for the conduct of the action. Congress has sought to meet this problem principally by 28 U.S.C. § 1404(a).

Question: (9) What problems of interpretation are raised by the language of § 1404(a)?

(d) Addendum on Allocation of Court Business Among the States

A word is in order about the allocation of court business among the states. With fifty states, each having a court system, some allocation among the states would seem to be needed. The matter is controlled, most importantly, by the Constitution of the United States, particularly the due process clause of the fourteenth amendment as it has been interpreted by the courts. The control is largely negative: a defendant who has no adequate connection with a particular state may be held to be beyond the state's adjudicatory authority.

1. A highway accident occurs in Nebraska, both parties are domiciled there, the defendant has not gone outside the state and has no property outside the state, and all the witnesses reside in the state. It would seem that Nebraska is a proper state in which to conduct any lawsuit. If Wyoming or some other state purports to handle the case at the plaintiff's request and to give judgment after the defendant's default, perhaps its judgment should be open to attack or denied recognition.

2. But suppose the defendant wanders into Wyoming and is there handed summons and complaint in an action commenced in a Wyoming court based on the Nebraska accident. Does Wyoming now have constitutional authority to adjudicate?

clauses of the fifth and fourteenth amendments), the power to regulate the service of process is not unlimited. Nevertheless, this consideration creates no constitutional barrier to obliterating *territorial limitations* on service of process.

Service of process also works to subject the defendant to the adjudicatory authority of the sovereign. Here the due process clauses require an adequate connection between sovereign and defendant, and so they do limit the power to extend the effective service of process. However, again there is no constitutional barrier to obliterating, for service of process in *federal actions*, the territorial limitations in Rule 4 that are tied to *state boundaries*.

This is not to say that a particular federal action against a particular defendant could be tried consistently with the fifth amendment anywhere in the United States. Due process may demand that the place of federal trial be reasonably fair for the defendant. But this requirement is not so much a restriction on service of process as one on venue, and in all likelihood the current federal statutory scheme regarding venue satisfies in virtually all cases this possible constitutional requirement.

All this goes to support the proposition that Congress has the power to provide generally for nationwide service of process issuing from federal courts, as indeed it has done in instances such as 28 U.S.C. § 2361.

The broad question is this: what must be the relation between a given state and the defendant, in light of the nature of the particular matter in dispute, so that the state will have the constitutional authority to render a judgment? Again it should be noted that a state may by statute or otherwise decline to exert its utmost constitutional powers of adjudication. For example, even if service of process on the defendant in the state would be sufficient, constitutionally, to support a valid judgment against the defendant although he fails to appear in the action, Wyoming might say that there are reasons of convenience and efficiency for declining to entertain the action and that the action will accordingly not be allowed.

Each state naturally makes its own internal arrangements for allocating business on a territorial basis among the various courts in its court system. For instance, in personal-injury cases between residents, a state may provide by statute that the action shall be brought in the county of residence of the plaintiff or of the defendant.

SECTION 8. MORE COMPLICATED LITIGATION: MULTIPLE PARTIES AND MULTIPLE CLAIMS

Thus far we have spoken of lawsuits mostly in terms of two parties—one plaintiff and one defendant. Even within this two-party framework, litigation may become ramified by the assertion of a considerable number of claims. Rule 18 permits a plaintiff to join in a single proceeding as many claims as he may have against the defendant, however unrelated they may be. The defendant similarly may by counterclaim under Rule 13 expand the lawsuit so as to include whatever claims he may have against the plaintiff. And of course each such claim may be met by a number of defenses.

A lawsuit may be further complicated by the presence in it of more than two parties and also by the parties' assertion of various claims among themselves. The number of these multi-party actions in the courts has increased markedly in recent years. This has been due not only to the adoption of rules and statutes liberalizing the joinder of parties and claims, but also to the increased complexity of financial and other transactions in our society.

The subject of multiple parties and multiple claims is a large and difficult one, as even a casual reading of Rule 14 and Rules 19 through 24 (and a rereading of Rules 13 and 18) will indicate. We shall survey the field in a very general and necessarily superficial way.

JURISDICTION AND VENUE

There is a certain fitness in dealing with this subject of complicated litigation after the Sections on subject-matter jurisdiction, venue, and service, for among the major difficulties (felt especially keenly in the federal system with its limited jurisdiction) is that of finding a proper court for the multi-party, multi-claim lawsuit. We shall illustrate this point by touching upon some of the problems of jurisdiction and venue in actions involving more than one plaintiff or defendant.

The diversity of citizenship required to satisfy 28 U.S.C. § 1332 is complete diversity; that is, no two opposing parties can be citizens of the same state.[a] Here is an illustration: a plaintiff who is a citizen of New York cannot join as defendants a citizen of Michigan and another citizen of New York, because the presence of a New Yorker on each side of the controversy destroys the required diversity.

Question: (1) Does the required diversity under § 1332 exist in each of the following cases? The matter in controversy exceeds $10,000 in each case.

(a) *A*, a citizen of New York, and *B*, a citizen of Ohio, sue *C*, a citizen of Michigan.

(b) *A*, a citizen of New York, and *B*, a citizen of Ohio, sue *C*, a citizen of France.

(c) *A*, a citizen of New York, and *B*, a citizen of France, sue *C*, a citizen of Ohio.

(d) *A*, a citizen of New York, and *B*, a citizen of France, sue *C*, a citizen of Ohio, and *D*, a citizen of France.

(e) *A*, a citizen of New York, and *B*, a citizen of France, sue *C*, a citizen of France.

The alignment of the parties as plaintiffs and defendants in the pleadings is not conclusive in determining diversity jurisdiction. The court will realign the parties according to their ultimate interests.[b] Realignment thus may either defeat or create jurisdiction.

It is provided in the basic removal statute, 28 U.S.C. § 1441, that "the defendant or the defendants" have the right, under the conditions there prescribed, to remove an action to the federal court.

Questions: In the following questions, assume that the matter in controversy exceeds $10,000.

---

[a] This statement is being made about the general diversity statute. The diversity clause of article III has not been so narrowly interpreted. Thus Congress has the constitutional power to bestow jurisdiction based on minimal diversity (any two opposing parties being of diverse citizenship); and, indeed, Congress has done so for interpleader actions under 28 U.S.C. § 1335, as interpreted by the Supreme Court in State Farm Fire & Cas. Co. v. Tashire, infra p. 1203.

[b] See City of Indianapolis v. Chase Nat'l Bank, 314 U.S. 63, 62 S.Ct. 15 (1941), for a frequently cited statement of the principles. In that case realignment defeated jurisdiction.

(2) *A*, a citizen of New York, sues *B* and *C*, citizens of California, in a New York state court. *B* is content with the state court. Can *C* alone properly remove to the local United States District Court?

(3) *A*, a citizen of New York, sues *B*, a citizen of New York, and *C* Company, a Connecticut corporation having its principal place of business in California, in a New York state court. Can *C* Company alone properly remove? Can *C* Company and *B* together properly remove?

(4) *A*, a citizen of California, sues *B*, a citizen of California, in a California state court for personal injuries. *C* Ins. Co., *B*'s liability insurer, refuses to defend, contending that its policy does not cover the kind of accident in question. Thereupon *B* brings an action in the same state court for a declaratory judgment of coverage, naming *C* Ins. Co., a Connecticut corporation with its principal place of business in Connecticut, and *A* as defendants. Can *C* Ins. Co. properly remove? See Bonell v. General Accident Fire & Life Assur. Corp., 167 F.Supp. 384 (N.D.Cal.1958) (yes).

Multi-party actions also create problems with reference to venue. Note that the general venue statute, 28 U.S.C. § 1391 refers to "all plaintiffs" and "all defendants." See also 28 U.S.C. § 1392(a).

Question: (5) In which United States District Courts would venue be proper in each of the following cases? The matter in controversy exceeds $10,000 in each case.

(a) *A*, a resident of Maine, wishes to sue *B*, a resident of Vermont, and *C*, a resident of New Hampshire, the only possible basis of jurisdiction being diversity of citizenship. The claim arose in Maine.

(b) *A*, a resident of Maine, wishes to sue *B*, a resident of Buffalo in the Western District of New York, and *C*, a resident of Manhattan in the Southern District of New York, the only possible basis of jurisdiction being diversity of citizenship. The claim arose in Maine.

(c) *A*, a resident of Manhattan, and *B*, a resident of Buffalo, wish to sue *C*, a resident of Vermont, and *D*, a resident of New Hampshire, the only possible basis of jurisdiction being diversity of citizenship. The claim arose in Maine.

(d) Same as the preceding case except that this claim arose in Quebec.

We have couched the foregoing cases in terms of the plaintiff or plaintiffs "wishing" to sue. Insofar as the venue requirements merely impose obstacles to a *permissive* joinder of parties, the consequence is only that the plaintiff must content himself with suing fewer defendants than he would like, or that several intending co-plaintiffs will have to sue separately. But we shall see shortly that there is a graver problem. Sometimes party joinder is *compulsory;* that is, the action cannot go forward in the absence of certain parties plaintiff or defendant. When this situation exists, the requirements of venue taken together with limitations on effective service of process may result in closing the door of the federal courts to a meritorious claim cognizable there in point of subject-matter jurisdiction. It may also turn out to be impossible to find a suitable state court for the action because no state may be in a position to issue process that will be effective to bring in all the defendants that must be joined.

With this introduction behind us, we turn to a consideration of the Federal Rules dealing with multiple parties and multiple claims. However, for the most part we shall postpone until Part Five further study of the interplay between these Rules and the law of subject-matter jurisdiction, venue, and service; such problems rapidly become much thornier and require extensive treatment. For the moment, then, your task is primarily to understand how these particular Rules are structured.

(a) Permissive Joinder of Parties

[Rule 20]

There are numerous situations where a group of plaintiffs, each of whom would be free to sue separately, may consider it desirable to pool their resources and join in a single action. Rule 20 permits them to do this, subject only to the requirements that their rights grow out of the same transaction, occurrence, or series of transactions or occurrences and that some question of law or fact common to all of them will arise in the action. Thus, for instance, ten passengers in a bus may join in suing the bus company for personal injuries sustained by them in a collision. Such joinder may not only be advantageous to the parties, but also serve the public interest by preventing relitigation of the same facts in a succession of actions—and with a possibility of inconsistent results.

Correspondingly liberal provisions allow a plaintiff (or several plaintiffs) to join a number of defendants in one action.[c] Here are some examples of situations in which a plaintiff may join all persons claimed to be liable to him: plaintiff A is injured by a collision of three cars owned and negligently driven by B, C, and D respectively; or plaintiff T is injured through the negligence of employee S for which employer M is also responsible on the ground of respondeat superior. In situations of these types the plaintiff may select his targets—he may sue all or any of those liable. Form 10 is illustrative of a claim for relief against defendants "in the alternative," which Rule 20 also expressly permits.

Questions: (6) A sues B and C for libel, alleging that B falsely wrote of him on May 1 that he was a thief and that C did the same on July 1. Is the joinder proper under Rule 20?

(7) What is the Federal Rules' remedy for an attempted joinder that is improper under Rule 20?

[c] The territorial limitations on effective service of process impose practical restrictions on joinder of defendants. Joinder otherwise proper may also be prevented by requirements of subject-matter jurisdiction or venue.

(b) Compulsory Joinder of Persons Needed for Just Adjudication

[Rule 19]

The party-structure of a lawsuit is determined in the first instance by the plaintiff (or plaintiffs) instituting the action. But he is not entirely free to do as he pleases. As we have just seen, there are outer limits on who *may* be joined as "proper" parties. And inner limits exist to tell the plaintiff who *must* be joined, limits enforceable by the defendant or the court: there are occasions when he must enlist other persons who should have joined him as plaintiffs, and there are also occasions when he must bring in certain additional persons to defend the lawsuit.[d]

Rule 19(a) declares that persons sustaining certain relationships to the action shall be joined as parties if their joinder is feasible, that is, if they can be reached by effective service of process and if their joinder will not deprive the court of subject-matter jurisdiction.[e] The relationships are expressed, first, in terms of whether "complete relief" can be given to those already parties if the particular person is not joined and remains outside the action and, second, in terms of whether the disposition of the action in the absence of the particular person either may as a practical matter impair his ability to protect an interest that he claims in the subject of the action[f] or may leave those already parties exposed to a substantial risk of incurring double liability as the result of a later suit by that person. It will be seen that the relationships, as described, are rather broadly inclusive.[g]

Suppose the person in question is within the net of subdivision (a) of Rule 19 and thus termed "necessary," but his joinder is not feasible. The court then faces the alternatives of dismissing the action or of continuing it without the full cast of characters that we would prefer to have as parties. Subdivision (b) sets out a series of factors to

---

[d] Suppose a defendant to an action desires to assert a counterclaim that involves persons not already joined. See Rule 13(h).

[e] Ultimately, venue will also have to be satisfied unless the point is waived. See the last sentence of Rule 19(a).

[f] Ordinarily the judgment in an action between *A* and *B* cannot affect *C in a legal sense:* due process ordinarily dictates that no judgment shall go against *C* or alter his legal position unless he has been summoned as a party and has had an opportunity to present his side of the case. *C*, however, may be affected *in a practical sense* by an action between *A* and *B*.

Here is a simple example: *B* is holding a certain amount of money for *A* and *C*

in disputed shares, and *A* recovers the whole sum from *B* in an action in which *C* has not been joined. *C* is not precluded from suit—he is unaffected legally—but as a practical matter he may be left without an adequate remedy against either *B* or *A.*

[g] Rule 19(a) is not so broad, however, as to take in the concurrent-negligence and employee-employer cases hypothesized above in connection with Rule 20. Joinder of defendants in those cases is not required under Rule 19(a) even if feasible; it is entirely optional with the plaintiff under Rule 20. The explanation is found in the character of the substantive rights and duties of the persons involved.

be considered in deciding between these alternatives. Examine the statement of factors. Try to imagine situations in which the second and fourth factors would tend to the conclusion that the action should go forward notwithstanding the absence of a person embraced by the definition of subdivision (a). A person whose joinder is not feasible is denominated "indispensable" if upon consideration of the terms of Rule 19, including the factors of subdivision (b), the court finds that he is so urgently needed for just adjudication that the case should be dismissed; the word "indispensable" is simply a convenient way of stating this conclusion, but does not itself assist in the analysis leading to it.

The present text of Rule 19 went into effect in 1966, superseding a text that had been written at a high level of abstraction and that did not lay as much stress on tracing out the practical consequences of nonjoinder and making the critical elections in that light. The older text derived from the leading case of Shields v. Barrow, 58 U.S. (17 How.) 130 (1855), digested below and quoted infra p. 1094.

Robert R. Barrow, a citizen of Louisiana, in 1836 sold his plantations in Louisiana to Thomas R. Shields, a citizen of Louisiana, for $227,000 payable in installments, the obligations being evidenced by notes. The notes were each indorsed by six persons, of whom four were citizens of Louisiana and two were citizens of Mississippi. Payment up to $107,000 was made; the rest was defaulted. In 1842 Barrow, Shields, and the six indorsers agreed to a compromise under which the original transaction was to be undone, the plantations were to be returned to Barrow, Barrow was to retain the $107,000 paid, and the six indorsers were to execute notes in varying amounts aggregating $32,000. (A tough proposition for the debtors: the panic of 1837 had intervened.) This compromise was carried out to the point where Barrow went into possession of the plantations and discontinued litigation previously begun, and the indorsers executed the new notes.

Barrow now claimed that he had been induced to enter the compromise by fraud. He commenced the present suit in the United States Circuit Court for the Eastern District of Louisiana against only the two Mississippi parties, seeking rescission of the compromise and recovery on the defendants' original obligations as indorsers.

The question in the Supreme Court was whether the suit could be maintained in the absence of the other interested persons, whose joinder would destroy diversity. The Court, reversing the circuit court, ordered the case dismissed for nonjoinder of Shields and the Louisiana indorsers, whose presence was deemed indispensable.

Questions: (8) Should the result be the same under the present Rule 19? See Kaplan, Continuing Work of the Civil Committee: 1966 Amendments of the Federal Rules of Civil Procedure (I), 81 Harv.L.Rev. 356, 360–62 (1967).

(9) Under the Federal Rules, how and when does the defendant raise the defense of a failure to join persons as required by Rule 19?

(c) Interpleader

[Rule 22]

As stated above, Rule 20 and Form 10 make provision for a plaintiff who is doubtful which of two or more defendants is liable to him. But what of the prospective defendant who is in doubt as to which of two or more claimants is entitled to payment of a debt admittedly owed to one of them?

Assume, for example, that the *A* Life Insurance Co. insured *B*'s life. *B* has died, and *C* and *D* each claim to be the sole beneficiary under the policy. There is the uncomfortable possibility that *C* might sue *A* Co. and recover, and that *D* might thereafter sue *A* Co. and likewise recover. The imposition of such a double recovery is unjust to *A* Co., but it can easily happen if each claimant sues separately. Different evidence might be presented in the two cases, or different fact-finders might take different views of substantially identical evidence. Nor can *A* Co. defend in *D*'s action by saying, "We do not have to pay you because we have already been held liable to *C* on this policy." (Why is this not a defense?)

Rule 22 provides an escape from this dilemma. *A* Co. may commence a suit against *C* and *D* and require them to make their respective claims in the same action, thus avoiding the hazard of double liability. Moreover, suppose *A* Co. contends that it is not liable to either *C* or *D* because *B* had procured the policy by false representations. The interpleader machinery of Rule 22 is still available; an admission of liability to one of the claimants is not a prerequisite to its use. See Form 18.

If *A* Co. is sued by one of the claimants, it may still interplead. The Rule provides that a defendant in such a position may interplead the other claimant and say in effect to the two of them, "Fight it out and we'll pay the winner," or, "We'll pay the winner unless it is held that we don't have to pay either." [h]

[h] If interpleader is based on a federal question, Rule 22(1) must be utilized, and the usual rules of subject-matter jurisdiction, venue, and service apply. But most interpleader cases in federal court are based on diversity of citizenship. For these the stakeholder may have a choice between two devices: "rule interpleader" under Rule 22(1) or "statutory interpleader" referred to in Rule 22(2).

Where the interpleader action rests on diversity and proceeds under Rule 22(1), the general diversity statute (28 U.S.C. § 1332) is applicable; the stake must exceed $10,000, and the diversity of citizenship called for is complete diversity between the adverse claimants on the one side and the stakeholder on the other.

Venue for such an interpleader action initiated by the stakeholder is governed generally by 28 U.S.C. § 1391(a). And process runs within the usual territorial limits of Rule 4.

Rule 22(2) refers to the federal statute providing for interpleader (see 28 U.S.C. §§ 1335, 1397, and 2361). Here the jurisdictional amount is "$500 or more"; and the required diversity is defined specially—we look to diversity of citizenship among the claimants, and the Supreme Court has held that minimal as distinguished from complete diversity suffices. Venue for such an interpleader action initiated by the stakeholder lies in any district in which any claimant resides. Also, process runs nationwide.

(d) Third-Party Practice

[Rule 14]

A defendant may wish to extend the lawsuit in another way. He may want to reach a third person, not joined in the action, who he believes is or may be liable to him for all or part of the claim that the plaintiff is making against him.[i]

To illustrate: *A* sues *B*, a restaurant proprietor, claiming damage as a result of eating contaminated food. *B*'s contention is that if he is held liable to *A*, the loss ought to be made good by *C*, his supplier, who furnished the food. If *B* waits until *A* has recovered a judgment against him and he has paid it, and then brings a separate action against *C*, *B* may find himself in a position not dissimilar to that of the insurance company in the interpleader situation described above. *C* is not bound by what occurred in the *A* versus *B* litigation in his absence; and the two fact-finders may arrive at inconsistent conclusions on the facts. Even if this does not happen, there will remain the wasteful business of repeating the ground already covered in the first action.

Rule 14 permits such a defendant to bring the third person into the case as a party if he can be reached by effective service of process. (Note when leave of court is required, and see Forms 22–A and 22–B.) This device, called impleader, is optional with the defendant; he is free to wait and bring a separate action if he chooses. If Rule 14 is availed of, the result is a kind of lawsuit within a lawsuit. The defendant becomes a "third-party plaintiff" and the impleaded newcomer becomes a "third-party defendant" with respect to the claim between them. The premise of the claim between them is not that the third-party defendant might be liable to the original plaintiff, but rather that the third-party defendant should cover part or all of the third-party plaintiff's liability to the original plaintiff. The theory of the claim might be indemnity, contribution, subrogation, or warranty. So the focus of this lawsuit within a lawsuit will be on whether, under the substantive law and the facts, such secondary liability exists.

What then is the strategic structure of the *A–B–C* litigation above described, after *B* has impleaded *C*? *A* wants to establish his case against *B*. *B* wants to defeat *A*'s claim against him, especially if he lacks confidence in his claim against *C* or in *C*'s ability to satisfy a judgment; *B* also wants to establish *C*'s liability to him if *A*'s claim succeeds. *C* wants to see *A*'s claim against *B* defeated; *C* also wants to prove that in no event does *B* have a right of reimbursement from him, *C*.

Question: (10) Referring to Rule 14(a), how should *C* plead?

---

[i] Suppose a plaintiff against whom a counterclaim has been asserted wishes to reach a third person who is or may be liable to him for the counterclaim. See Rule 14(b).

The original plaintiff may have a related claim of his own against the impleaded newcomer, but originally elected not to press it. Injection of the third-party defendant into the case cannot of itself force the plaintiff to sue an unwanted adversary. Nevertheless, a plaintiff who finds a potential adversary injected into the case may well change his mind. Likewise, the third-party defendant may wish to assert a related claim against the original plaintiff. Once a two-party lawsuit has become a three-cornered affair through a Rule 14 impleader, the whole matter of claims and counterclaims among the parties requires careful examination. See generally 6 Wright & Miller §§ 1455–1459.

Questions: (11) *S*, driving *M*'s car on *M*'s business, collides with an automobile owned and operated by *T*. Both cars are damaged, and both *T* and *S* are injured. It is a matter of doubt whether *T* or *S* or both were negligent. Under the applicable substantive law: (a) *If S was negligent and T was not, T* can recover from *S* and can recover also from *M*, although *T* of course cannot actually collect from *M* and *S* more than the total amount of his damages; if *M* is forced to pay because of *S*'s negligence, *M* is entitled to be repaid by *S*; *M* is also entitled to recover against *S* for the damage to *M*'s car. (b) *If S was not negligent and T was, S* can recover against *T* for *S*'s personal injuries, and *M* can recover against *T* for the damage to *M*'s car. (c) *If both S and T were negligent, M* can recover against *S* for the damage to *M*'s car but cannot recover against *T* for that damage. Furthermore, under that applicable law: there is no doctrine of comparative negligence and no right to contribution among concurrent tortfeasors. Assume that *T*, who might sue *M* or *S* or both, elects to sue *M* only. *M* brings in *S* as a third-party defendant. If the three parties wish to assert all the claims that they may assert under Rule 14, how should they plead? And how should they respond to the claims made against them? What claims are foreclosed from presentation in a later lawsuit if they are not asserted here?

(12) Suppose *M*, more than ten days after serving his answer to *T*'s complaint, had sought leave to implead *S;* *T* had opposed the impleader on the ground that *S* is impecunious and without personal-liability insurance and would be unable to reimburse *M* to any substantial extent; and *T* had also argued that the jurors would be likely to render a smaller verdict if they were required to find that *S* is ultimately responsible for its payment. What action should the court have taken? Would your answer be different if *M* had impleaded *S* at the time he served his answer and *T* had moved to strike the third-party claim?

(e) Cross-claims

[Rule 13(g)]

Once it is recognized that there may be several plaintiffs, several defendants, and several third-party defendants in an action, the possibility of conflict among the co-parties (so called to distinguish them from opposing parties) becomes apparent. The effect of Rule 13(g) is to permit, but not to compel, co-parties to assert against one another claims that bear certain prescribed relations to the rest of the controversy—such claims are called cross-claims. This provision is but an-

other reflection of the general aim of the Rules to allow related quarrels to be disposed of under the umbrella of a single action.

To illustrate with a simple example: *A* sues *B* and *C*. *B* has a claim against *C* arising out of the same transaction. *B* may proceed by cross-claim against *C*, but he may instead elect to bring a separate action against *C*.

Questions: (13) Why should a counterclaim arising out of the same transaction be compulsory while a cross-claim against a co-party is merely permissive?

(14) Why must a cross-claim bear a certain prescribed relation to the rest of the controversy while a permissive counterclaim may be entirely unrelated?

Now suppose *A* and *B* sue *C* for breach of contract. *C* pleads a permissive counterclaim against *A* and *B* for negligence. According to the second sentence of Rule 13(g), *A* may plead a cross-claim against *B* to establish that *B* is liable to *A* in respect to *C*'s counterclaim. If *A* pleads this cross-claim against *B* and if *B* has a claim against *A* arising out of the transaction or occurrence that is the subject matter of that cross-claim, *B* must assert his claim as a compulsory counterclaim under Rule 13(a), because to that extent *A* is an opposing party within the Rule.

Rule 13(g) specifies no time limit for asserting cross-claims, leaving this to judicial discretion.

(f) Class Actions

[Rules 23, 23.1, 23.2]

We have thus far considered who may and who must be included in an action as parties plaintiff, parties defendant, and third-party defendants, and what claims may be tried out among the parties. Rule 23 opens up a different concept, the class action, by which persons may sue or defend not merely on their own behalf but on behalf of others not before the court as parties.

The law knows a variety of people who as parties in litigation are "stand-ins" for, or represent, others not joined as parties, just as they may represent those others in ordinary transactions. Thus a trustee sues or defends on behalf of his beneficiaries in respect to the trust property; a guardian stands in for his ward; an executor represents the estate or those interested in it. And similarly an adjudication in an action by or against a person owning an interest in land may inure to the benefit of or limit the rights of successors to that interest in the land by purchase or devolution—the predecessor may be thought of as representing those who follow him in ownership.

Class actions also involve a version of representation, but of a somewhat different order. Suppose a large number of persons have similar claims (or similar liabilities) arising from the same matrix of facts. If each person had to commence his own individual action (or

defend an action brought against him alone), we would have repetitious proceedings with a large expenditure of time and effort. We would also run into the possible embarrassment of inconsistent results, and this would be especially painful where the party opposing the numerous claimants (or defenders) would find himself unable or very hard put to carry out the conflicting commands comprised in the inconsistent judgments. The operation of Rules 19 and 20 might result in a joinder of the claimants (or defenders) in a single action, which would be helpful as far as it went; but joinder under either Rule encounters obstacles of subject-matter jurisdiction, venue, and service, and Rule 20 joinder is strictly permissive; furthermore, as the group reaches a certain size, presence of all the members makes the action simply unmanageable. The inability to hear from all interested persons, or indeed the practical inability to maintain small individual actions, might have deleterious effects on the full realization of substantive policies. To meet these problems the class action envisaged by Rule 23 uses a justificatory principle of adequate representation: under stated conditions and subject to certain safeguards, one or a few members may sue (or defend) on behalf of the class. Plainly such a device must be carefully delimited and controlled lest it run roughshod over the "represented" absentee members of the class or abuse the parties or overwhelm the court. Examine Rule 23, which was substantially revised in 1966.

Subdivision (a) of Rule 23 sets out prerequisites for maintaining any class action: the class must be so numerous as to make joinder of all members impracticable; there must be questions of law or fact common to the class; the claims or defenses of the representative parties must be typical of the class; and there must be assurance that the representatives will be vigorous and competent champions of the class interests. These are necessary conditions for maintaining a class action, but they are not sufficient. The provisions of subdivision (b) must also be satisfied; that is, the case must be shown to fit into one of the categories of that subdivision.

Subdivision (b)(1)(A) and (B) was framed with an eye to the evident inconveniences or absurdities or unfairnesses involved in individual adjudications; illustrative of (1)(A) is a taxpayer suit against a municipality to declare a bond issue invalid; and (1)(B) is exemplified by an action involving numerous persons claiming against a fund insufficient to satisfy all the claims. Subdivision (b)(2) takes in cases where a defendant has made the characteristics of the class a basis for his own conduct, and final class-wide injunctive or corresponding declaratory relief is thus rendered appropriate; the prime example is a desegregation case.

Coming to subdivision (b)(3), we find situations that are not as readily amenable to class treatment as those in (b)(1) and (b)(2), but in which that procedure may yet have definite advantages. For example, hypothesize false statements in a stock prospectus, or a conspira-

cy to fix the prices of commodities in violation of the antitrust laws. In the former case, any element of reliance may vary among the purchasers making up the class, and the amount of damages certainly will vary; there may, in addition, be quite legitimate reasons why the individual defrauded purchasers might want to institute and control their own lawsuits. Like considerations apply to the price-fixing example. Note that a class action is permitted by (b)(3) only upon findings, first, that the questions common to the class "predominate" over those affecting individual members and, second, that a class action is "superior" to other methods of handling the controversy. Examine the factors listed in (b)(3) as pertinent to the findings. But even when the court is prepared to make the findings favorable to maintaining a class action, the individual member is allowed to "opt out" of the class and proceed on his own. Under subdivision (c)(2), the court is required to give the best practicable notice to the members of a (b)(3) class of the right of any member to withdraw from the class by simply informing the court.[j]

Question: (15) Why did the draftsmen of Rule 23 not prescribe this notice and opting-out procedure for (b)(1) and (b)(2) cases?

As soon as practicable after commencement of the proposed class action, the court must determine the propriety of allowing it to be maintained as a class action. See subdivision (c)(1). You will see that class treatment may be possible or advisable only as to certain issues in a case; the other issues may have to be treated individually. See subdivision (c)(4). Similarly, class treatment may be deemed proper only for certain subclasses of a proposed class.

Apart from the (c)(2) notice, Rule 23 has ample provision for discretionary notices as part of the process of the court's running any class action. See the variety of "management" provisions in subdivision (d).

A class action, when carried out to the end (note subdivision (e) on dismissal or compromise), results in a judgment extending by its terms to the class, but excluding in (b)(3) cases the opters-out. The judgment so extends whether or not it is favorable to the class.[k]

---

[j] The best notice practicable under (c)(2) might consist of notice by mail to reasonably identifiable individuals together with published notice in newspapers or trade magazines or the like addressed to the class as a whole. The plaintiff must initially bear the cost of notice. See Eisen v. Carlisle & Jacquelin, infra p. 1144.

If the member does not inform the court of his desire to be excluded from the class, he remains tied into the class. He then has the option of entering an appearance in the action through counsel, which would ensure his being kept currently informed about the case. Beyond that, he may be in a position to intervene under Rule 24, as discussed in the next Subsection.

[k] See subdivision (c)(3). The design is that the judgment will be respected according to its terms as res judicata in subsequent litigation, but that cannot be assured until the subsequent litigation occurs and a plea of res judicata is made and decided. If, for instance, a (b)(3) plaintiff class action is sloppily handled and no reasonable effort is made to notify class members, might a member who got no notice of the class action pursue his separate action and attack the prior class-action judgment that nominally included him? See Topic B of Part Seven.

When jurisdiction turns on an amount in controversy, the individual claim involving each class member must satisfy the jurisdictional amount requirement, if that claim is separate and distinct from the other class claims.[l] As to satisfying any diversity of citizenship requirement, however, it is settled that only the citizenship of the representative parties is considered, not the citizenship of all the members of the class—if the citizenship of all members were counted, the federal court would of course more often be ousted of jurisdiction. Similarly, for purposes of venue and service only the representative parties are considered.

Actions relating to unincorporated associations.—The preceding paragraph leads to a mention of Rule 23.2 governing actions involving unincorporated associations. These organizations are not viewed as entities with unitary citizenship for diversity of citizenship purposes, so class actions naming a few members as representatives have been used as a device for satisfying any diversity requirement. Because of the special reasons for utilizing the class device here, the specifically tailored Rule 23.2 was added in 1966, with references where appropriate therein to Rule 23.

Derivative actions by shareholders.—A shareholder of a corporation,[m] believing that the corporation should be asserting a right of action against a third party (who may be a wrongdoing director or officer of the corporation), makes demand on the directors, and if necessary on the shareholders, to sue; the demand is refused. A right to sue upon the corporation's claim may then accrue to the shareholder; if he succeeds in the suit, the recovery goes into the treasury of the corporation and is shared (in a manner of speaking) by all the shareholders. These derivative actions have their place even when there are few shareholders. When the number of shareholders is large, the derivative action has the character of a class action, with one or several shareholders suing on behalf of all. See Rule 23.1, also added in 1966 but having antecedents in the original Rule 23.

Only the corporation's claim need satisfy any jurisdictional amount requirement. Although the corporation must be joined as a defendant, it is sometimes realigned for diversity purposes with the plaintiff-shareholder. Note also the special supplementary provisions for venue and service in these actions: 28 U.S.C. §§ 1401 and 1695.

(g) Intervention

[Rule 24]

Rule 19(a)(2)(i) requires that persons claiming certain described interests in the subject of an action shall be joined as parties if feasible; if joinder is not feasible, Rule 19(b) indeed puts the question whether

---

[l] See Snyder v. Harris, infra p. 751; Zahn v. International Paper Co., infra p. 754.

[m] What is said here applies also to a member of an unincorporated association suing derivatively.

the action should not be dismissed. Rule 24(a) takes the plausible position that when such a person, instead of waiting to be forced into the action, timely applies to the court to intervene, he must be granted the right to do so—assuming that his interest is not already adequately represented by one of the parties. This is "intervention of right."

There is also "permissive intervention," that is, intervention in the discretion of the court under the terms of Rule 24(b), which echoes Rule 20 in part.

The procedure for intervention is prescribed by Rule 24(c). See also Form 23. Intervention normally means that the intervenor becomes a full party on the appropriate side of the action, but the court may impose some conditions or restrictions on an intervenor's participation.

Intervention is common in class actions. The intervening class member is typically claiming that for one reason or another the representative parties do not adequately represent his particular interest. You will notice that Rule 23(d)(2) reminds the court that it may on occasion decide to give notice to class members of their opportunity to intervene. See also Rule 23(d)(3).

(h) General Observations

Even taking into account the practical restrictions imposed by territorial limitations on effective service, by venue requirements, and by limitations on the kinds of cases that the federal courts may entertain, it is clear that an action under the Federal Rules may become greatly proliferated.

The issues of fact and law may of course be highly complex even when few parties and few claims are involved; a single plaintiff's antitrust case against a single defendant, for instance, may produce issues of vast difficulty. But multi-party actions raise peculiar problems of both management for the court and planning for the parties. How far, for example, may a court justifiably limit examination and cross-examination of a particular witness by the several parties to a lawsuit? May the court require that parties aligned in interest speak through one lawyer only? Often problems of this order are solved by informal arrangements. The strategic problems of counsel may also be aggravated in multi-party actions. The tactic of divide and conquer, for example, is not unknown in the courtroom; plaintiff may join two defendants for the very purpose of driving between them. Likewise, perplexing problems of management and planning are sometimes posed by multi-claim actions.

Criticism of the Rules has been made on this account: it is said that they allow litigation to get "too big" in terms of parties and claims. The Rules themselves recognize the dangers of delay, expense, confusion, and prejudice that spring from attempting to handle too many claims and parties as a bundle. Accordingly, the court is given certain discretionary powers to reshape the litigation. That is, even for a case properly pleaded between the limits of compulsory and permissive joinder, the court can reduce the bundle in the interests of fairness and efficiency. See Rules 42(b) (separate trials in general), 21 (severance in general), 13(i) (separate trials of counter-claims and cross-claims), 14(a) (discretion in allowing third-party claims; severance and separate trials of third-party claims), 20(b) (protective orders and separate trials in relation to permissive joinder of parties), 23(c) (effective discretion in allowing class actions), and 24(b) (discretion in allowing permissive intervention).[n]

SECTION 9.   WHAT LAW GOVERNS A PARTICULAR ACTION

(a) State Law in Federal Court

The Erie problem.—We complete this preliminary survey of the phases of a lawsuit in the federal courts by considering what law applies in particular actions. We know that the Federal Rules are the principal body of law governing matters of "practice and procedure" but that the Rules may not "abridge, enlarge or modify any substantive right." 28 U.S.C. § 2072. We have seen, too, that to draw the line between "procedure" and "substance," for this or any other purpose, is sometimes a difficult task. But assuming that a matter can be clearly classified as one of substance, what then?

It is no mystery to the student by this time that not all courts arrive at the same answer to a given question of substantive law. The substantive law, both statutory and common, differs from state to state. But further: suppose that because diversity of citizenship exists and the jurisdictional amount is present, a plaintiff has a choice between bringing his action in the United States District Court for the Southern District of New York and instituting it in a state court of New York. Can he gain an advantage by examining the federal and state precedents and selecting the forum where the decisions on the relevant points of substantive law are more favorable to his case? For nearly a century after the decision in Swift v. Tyson, 41 U.S. (16 Pet.) 1 (1842) (Story, J.), the answer to this question was yes.

In that case Norton and Keith were drawers of a bill of exchange of which Tyson was the drawee-acceptor, Norton the payee, and Swift the indorsee. Tyson had accepted the bill in part payment for land sold to him by Norton and Keith, but Tyson now claimed that the sale had been induced by fraudulent representations on the part of Norton and Keith. Swift had taken the bill in satisfaction of a

[n] The court also has discretion to make the bundle larger when this will avoid de- lay or reduce costs. See Rule 42(a) (joint trials and consolidation).

promissory note due to him from Norton and Keith. ~~Swift~~, the indorsee, sued Tyson, the drawee-acceptor, in a federal court in New York
upon the bill of exchange. Jurisdiction was based on diversity of citizenship. The drawee-acceptor's defense was that he had accepted
the bill as the result of the drawers' fraud.

The indorsee, acting in good faith without notice of the fraud, had
taken the bill in satisfaction of a pre-existing debt. Did this make the
indorsee a "bona fide holder without notice for a valid consideration,"
so that the drawee-acceptor's defense of fraud would be cut off as
against the indorsee? The issue thus became whether the indorsee
had given an invalid consideration. It was assumed that under the
common (i.e., non-statutory) law of New York (the place of the acceptance), satisfaction of a pre-existing debt would not serve as a valid
consideration. Nevertheless, the Supreme Court of the United States
ultimately held that it would so serve. Thus the indorsee was entitled to prevail.

The Court said that the question was one of general commercial
law as to which the state-court decisions were not controlling. Concededly, if the New York rule had been laid down by statute rather
than developed through judicial decisions, or if the rule were a long-
established local custom having the force of law, the Rules of Decision Act of 1789, now 28 U.S.C. § 1652, would have required the opposite result. The essential holding of Swift, then, was that the word
"laws" in § 1652 included only state statutes and local usages, not
the state's general common law; and that in the absence of a congressional directive, the federal courts had the power to come to an
independent conclusion as to the "true" general common law.

"Swift Rule"

What arguments could be marshaled in favor of the Swift rule?
What happened in the ensuing century to undercut those arguments?
Some answers to these questions can be derived from a careful reading of the following case, which will allow you to reconstruct Swift's
reasoning, policies, and jurisprudence.

ERIE RAILROAD v. TOMPKINS
Supreme Court of the United States, April 25, 1938.
304 U.S. 64, 58 S.Ct. 817.

Mr. Theodore Kiendl, with whom Messrs. William C. Cannon and
Harold W. Bissell were on the brief, for petitioner.

. . . .

We do not question the finality of the holding of this Court in
Swift v. Tyson . . . ..

. . . .

The Pennsylvania decisions denying permissive rights on longitudinal pathways, as distinguished from crossings, declare a Pennsylvania rule sufficiently local in nature to be controlling . . . .

. . . .

MR. JUSTICE BRANDEIS delivered the opinion of the Court.

The question for decision is whether the oft-challenged doctrine of Swift v. Tyson shall now be disapproved.

Tompkins, a citizen of Pennsylvania, was injured on a dark night by a passing freight train of the Erie Railroad Company while walking along its right of way at Hughestown in that state. He claimed that the accident occurred through negligence in the operation, or maintenance, of the train; that he was rightfully on the premises as licensee because on a commonly used beaten footpath which ran for a short distance alongside the tracks; and that he was struck by something which looked like a door projecting from one of the moving cars. To enforce that claim he brought an action in the federal court for Southern New York, which had jurisdiction because the company is a corporation of that state. It denied liability; and the case was tried by a jury.

The Erie insisted that its duty to Tompkins was no greater than that owed to a trespasser. It contended, among other things, that its duty to Tompkins, and hence its liability, should be determined in accordance with the Pennsylvania law; that under the law of Pennsylvania, as declared by its highest court, persons who use pathways along the railroad right of way—that is, a longitudinal pathway as distinguished from a crossing—are to be deemed trespassers; and that the railroad is not liable for injuries to undiscovered trespassers resulting from its negligence, unless it be wanton or willful. Tompkins denied that any such rule had been established by the decisions of the Pennsylvania courts; and contended that, since there was no statute of the state on the subject, the railroad's duty and liability is to be determined in federal courts as a matter of general law.

The trial judge refused to rule that the applicable law precluded recovery. The jury brought in a verdict of $30,000; and the judgment entered thereon was affirmed by the Circuit Court of Appeals, which held (2 Cir., 90 F.2d 603, 604), that it was unnecessary to consider whether the law of Pennsylvania was as contended, because the question was one not of local, but of general, law, and that "upon questions of general law the federal courts are free, in absence of a local statute, to exercise their independent judgment as to what the law is; and it is well settled that the question of the responsibility of a railroad for injuries caused by its servants is one of general law. . . . Where the public has made open and notorious use of a railroad right of way for a long period of time and without objection, the company owes to persons on such permissive pathway a duty of care in the operation of its trains. . . . It is likewise generally recognized law that a jury may find that negligence exists toward a pedestrian using a permissive path on the railroad right of way if he is hit by some object projecting from the side of the train."

The Erie had contended that application of the Pennsylvania rule was required, among other things, by § 34 of the Federal Judiciary Act of September 24, 1789, c. 20, U.S.C. § 725, which provides: "The laws of the several States, except where the Constitution, treaties, or statutes of the United States otherwise require or provide, shall be regarded as rules of decision in trials at common law, in the courts of the United States, in cases where they apply." [a]

Because of the importance of the question whether the federal court was free to disregard the alleged rule of the Pennsylvania common law, we granted certiorari. 302 U.S. 671, 58 S.Ct. 50.

First. Swift v. Tyson, 16 Pet. 1, 18, held that federal courts exercising jurisdiction on the ground of diversity of citizenship need not, in matters of general jurisprudence, apply the unwritten law of the state as declared by its highest court; that they are free to exercise an independent judgment as to what the common law of the state is—or should be; and that, as there stated by Mr. Justice Story, "the true interpretation of the 34th section limited its application to state laws strictly local, that is to say, to the positive statutes of the state, and the construction thereof adopted by the local tribunals, and to rights and titles to things having a permanent locality, such as the rights and titles to real estate, and other matters immovable and intraterritorial in their nature and character. It never has been supposed by us, that the section did apply, or was designed to apply, to questions of a more general nature, not at all dependent upon local statutes or local usages of a fixed and permanent operation, as, for example, to the construction of ordinary contracts or other written instruments, and especially to questions of general commercial law, where the state tribunals are called upon to perform the like functions as ourselves, that is, to ascertain, upon general reasoning and legal analogies, what is the true exposition of the contract or instrument, or what is the just rule furnished by the principles of commercial law to govern the case."

The Court in applying the rule of § 34 to equity cases, in Mason v. United States, 260 U.S. 545, 559, 43 S.Ct. 200, 204, said: "The statute, however, is merely declarative of the rule which would exist in the absence of the statute." The federal courts assumed, in the broad field of "general law," the power to declare rules of decision which Congress was confessedly without power to enact as statutes. Doubt was repeatedly expressed as to the correctness of the construction given § 34, and as to the soundness of the rule which it introduced. But it was the more recent research of a competent

---

[a] With minor changes this section now appears as 28 U.S.C. § 1652. The words "in civil actions" were substituted for "in trials at common law" in the 1948 revision of title 28, but this change was intended only to conform the statute to the existing judicial interpretation.

scholar, who examined the original document, which established that the construction given to it by the Court was erroneous; and that the purpose of the section was merely to make certain that, in all matters except those in which some federal law is controlling, the federal courts exercising jurisdiction in diversity of citizenship cases would apply as their rules of decision the law of the state, unwritten as well as written.[5]

Criticism of the doctrine became widespread after the decision of Black & White Taxicab Co. v. Brown & Yellow Taxicab Co., 276 U.S. 518, 48 S.Ct. 404 [(1928)]. There, Brown & Yellow, a Kentucky corporation owned by Kentuckians, and the Louisville & Nashville Railroad, also a Kentucky corporation, wished that the former should have the exclusive privilege of soliciting passenger and baggage transportation at the Bowling Green, Ky., railroad station; and that the Black & White, a competing Kentucky corporation, should be prevented from interfering with that privilege. Knowing that such a contract would be void under the common law of Kentucky, it was arranged that the Brown & Yellow reincorporate under the law of Tennessee, and that the contract with the railroad should be executed there. The suit was then brought by the Tennessee corporation in the federal court for Western Kentucky to enjoin competition by the Black & White; an injunction issued by the District Court was sustained by the Court of Appeals; and this Court, citing many decisions in which the doctrine of Swift v. Tyson had been applied, affirmed the decree.

[Second.] Experience in applying the doctrine of Swift v. Tyson, had revealed its defects, political and social; and the benefits expected to flow from the rule did not accrue. Persistence of state courts in their own opinions on questions of common law prevented uniformity;[7] and the impossibility of discovering a satisfactory line of demarcation between the province of general law and that of local law developed a new well of uncertainties.

On the other hand, the mischievous results of the doctrine had become apparent. Diversity of citizenship jurisdiction was conferred in order to prevent apprehended discrimination in state courts against those not citizens of the state. Swift v. Tyson introduced grave discrimination by noncitizens against citizens. It made rights enjoyed under the unwritten "general law" vary according to whether enforcement was sought in the state or in the federal court; and the privilege of selecting the court in which the right should be determined was conferred upon the noncitizen. Thus, the doctrine rendered impossible equal protection of the law. In attempting to pro-

[5] Charles Warren, New Light on the History of the Federal Judiciary Act of 1789 (1923) 37 Harv.L.Rev. 49, 51–52, 81–88, 108. [See C. Wright, The Law of Federal Courts § 54, at 350 (4th ed. 1983).—Ed.]

[7] [The Court's footnote cited, among other writings, Frankfurter, Distribution of Judicial Power Between United States and State Courts, 13 Cornell L.Q. 499, 524–30 (1928).]

mote uniformity of law throughout the United States, the doctrine had prevented uniformity in the administration of the law of the state.

The discrimination resulting became in practice far-reaching. This resulted in part from the broad province accorded to the so-called "general law" as to which federal courts exercised an independent judgment. In addition to questions of purely commercial law, "general law" was held to include the obligations under contracts entered into and to be performed within the state, the extent to which a carrier operating within a state may stipulate for exemption from liability for his own negligence or that of his employee, the liability for torts committed within the state upon persons resident or property located there, even where the question of liability depended upon the scope of a property right conferred by the state, and the right to exemplary or punitive damages. Furthermore, state decisions construing local deeds, mineral conveyances, and even devises of real estate were disregarded.

In part the discrimination resulted from the wide range of persons held entitled to avail themselves of the federal rule by resort to the diversity of citizenship jurisdiction. Through this jurisdiction individual citizens willing to remove from their own state and become citizens of another might avail themselves of the federal rule. And, without even change of residence, a corporate citizen of the state could avail itself of the federal rule by reincorporating under the laws of another state, as was done in the Taxicab Case.

The injustice and confusion incident to the doctrine of Swift v. Tyson have been repeatedly urged as reasons for abolishing or limiting diversity of citizenship jurisdiction. Other legislative relief has been proposed. If only a question of statutory construction were involved, we should not be prepared to abandon a doctrine so widely applied throughout nearly a century. But the unconstitutionality of the course pursued has now been made clear, and compels us to do so.

Third. Except in matters governed by the Federal Constitution or by acts of Congress, the law to be applied in any case is the law of the state. And whether the law of the state shall be declared by its Legislature in a statute or by its highest court in a decision is not a matter of federal concern. There is no federal general common law. Congress has no power to declare substantive rules of common law applicable in a state whether they be local in their nature or "general," be they commercial law or a part of the law of torts. And no clause in the Constitution purports to confer such a power upon the federal courts. As stated by Mr. Justice Field when protesting in Baltimore & Ohio R. Co. v. Baugh, 149 U.S. 368, 401, 13 S.Ct. 914, 927 [(dissenting opinion)], against ignoring the Ohio common law of fellow-servant liability: "I am aware that what has been termed the general law of the country—which is often little less than what the judge advancing the doctrine thinks at the time should be the general law on a particular subject—has been often advanced in judicial opinions of this court to control a conflicting law of a state. I admit that learned judges have fallen into the habit of repeating this doctrine as a convenient mode of brushing aside the law of a state in conflict with their views. And I confess that, moved and governed by the authority of the great names of those judges, I have, myself, in many instances, unhesitatingly and confidently, but I think now erroneously, repeated the same doctrine. But, notwithstanding the frequency with which the doctrine has been reiterated, there stands, as a perpetual protest against its repetition, the constitution of the United States, which recognizes and preserves the autonomy and independence of the states—independence in their legislative and independence in their judicial departments. Supervision over either the legislative or the judicial action of the states is in no case permissible except as to matters by the constitution specifically authorized or delegated to the United States. Any interference with either, except as thus permitted, is an invasion of the authority of the state and, to that extent, a denial of its independence."

The fallacy underlying the rule declared in Swift v. Tyson is made clear by Mr. Justice Holmes.[23] The doctrine rests upon the assumption that there is "a transcendental body of law outside of any particular State but obligatory within it unless and until changed by statute," that federal courts have the power to use their judgment as to what the rules of common law are; and that in the federal courts "the parties are entitled to an independent judgment on matters of general law":

"But law in the sense in which courts speak of it today does not exist without some definite authority behind it. The common law so far as it is enforced in a State, whether called common law or not, is not the common law generally but the law of that State existing by the authority of that State without regard to what it may have been in England or anywhere else. . . .

"The authority and only authority is the State, and if that be so, the voice adopted by the State as its own [whether it be of its Legislature or of its Supreme Court] should utter the last word."

Thus the doctrine of Swift v. Tyson is, as Mr. Justice Holmes said, "an unconstitutional assumption of powers by the courts of the United States which no lapse of time or respectable array of opinion should make us hesitate to correct." In disapproving that doctrine we do not hold unconstitutional § 34 of the Federal Judiciary Act of 1789 or any other act of Congress. We merely declare that in applying the doctrine this Court and the lower courts have invaded rights which in our opinion are reserved by the Constitution to the several states.

[23] Kuhn v. Fairmont Coal Co., 215 U.S. 349, 370–72, 30 S.Ct. 140, 147–48; Black & White Taxicab Co. v. Brown & Yellow Taxicab Co., 276 U.S. 518, 532–36, 48 S.Ct. 404, 408–10. [The citations are both to dissenting opinions.—Ed.]

Fourth. The defendant contended that by the common law of Pennsylvania as declared by its highest court in Falchetti v. Pennsylvania R. Co., 307 Pa. 203, 160 A. 859, the only duty owed to the plaintiff was to refrain from willful or wanton injury. The plaintiff denied that such is the Pennsylvania law. In support of their respective contentions the parties discussed and cited many decisions of the Supreme Court of the state. The Circuit Court of Appeals ruled that the question of liability is one of general law; and on that ground declined to decide the issue of state law. As we hold this was error, the judgment is reversed and the case remanded to it for further proceedings in conformity with our opinion.

Reversed.

MR. JUSTICE CARDOZO took no part in the consideration or decision of this case.

[Justice Butler filed a separate opinion concurred in by Justice McReynolds. In the course of arguing that Swift v. Tyson should not be overruled, Justice Butler gave attention to the Court's manner of proceeding:]

This Court has often emphasized its reluctance to consider constitutional questions and that legislation will not be held invalid as repugnant to the fundamental law if the case may be decided upon any other ground. In view of grave consequences liable to result from erroneous exertion of its power to set aside legislation, the Court should move cautiously, seek assistance of counsel, act only after ample deliberation, show that the question is before the Court, that its decision cannot be avoided by construction of the statute assailed or otherwise, indicate precisely the principle or provision of the Constitution held to have been transgressed, and fully disclose the reasons and authorities found to warrant the conclusion of invalidity. . . .

. . . Against the protest of those joining in this opinion, the Court declines to assign the case for reargument. It may not justly be assumed that the labor and argument of counsel for the parties would not disclose the right conclusion and aid the Court in the statement of reasons to support it. . . .

The course pursued by the Court in this case is repugnant to the Act of Congress of August 24, 1937, 50 Stat. 751.[b] . . .

. . . [N]ear the end of the last page the Court states that it does not hold § 34 unconstitutional, but merely that, in applying the doctrine of Swift v. Tyson construing it, this Court and the lower courts have invaded rights which are reserved by the Constitution to the several states. But, plainly through the form of words employed,

[b] This Act (with changes now 28 U.S.C. § 2403(a)) required, "whenever the constitutionality of any Act of Congress affecting the public interest is drawn in question in any court of the United States," that the court give notice to the Attorney General and allow intervention by the United States. This Act was not followed in this case, the majority apparently feeling that the Act did not apply. Why did it not apply?

the substance of the decision appears; it strikes down as unconstitutional § 34 as construed by our decisions; it divests the Congress of power to prescribe rules to be followed by federal courts when deciding questions of general law. In that broad field it compels this and the lower federal courts to follow decisions of the courts of a particular state.

I am of opinion that the constitutional validity of the rule need not be considered, because under the law, as found by the courts of Pennsylvania and generally throughout the country, it is plain that the evidence required a finding that plaintiff was guilty of negligence that contributed to cause his injuries and that the judgment below should be reversed upon that ground.

MR. JUSTICE REED. I concur in the conclusion reached in this case, in the disapproval of the doctrine of Swift v. Tyson, and in the reasoning of the majority opinion except in so far as it relies upon the unconstitutionality of the "course pursued" by the federal courts.

The "doctrine of Swift v. Tyson," as I understand it, is that the words "the laws," as used in § 34, line one, of the Federal Judiciary Act of September 24, 1789, did not include in their meaning "the decisions of the local tribunals." Mr. Justice Story, in deciding that point, said, 16 Pet. 1, 19: "Undoubtedly, the decisions of the local tribunals upon such subjects are entitled to, and will receive, the most deliberate attention and respect of this Court; but they cannot furnish positive rules, or conclusive authority, by which our judgments are to be bound up and governed."

To decide the case now before us and to "disapprove" the doctrine of Swift v. Tyson requires only that we say that the words "the laws" include in their meaning the decisions of the local tribunals. As the majority opinion shows, by its reference to Mr. Warren's researches and the first quotation from Mr. Justice Holmes, that this Court is now of the view that "laws" includes "decisions," it is unnecessary to go further and declare that the "course pursued" was "unconstitutional," instead of merely erroneous.

The "unconstitutional" course referred to in the majority opinion is apparently the ruling in Swift v. Tyson that the supposed omission of Congress to legislate as to the effect of decisions leaves federal courts free to interpret general law for themselves. I am not at all sure whether, in the absence of federal statutory direction, federal courts would be compelled to follow state decisions. There was sufficient doubt about the matter in 1789 to induce the first Congress to legislate. No former opinions of this Court have passed upon it. Mr. Justice Holmes evidently saw nothing "unconstitutional" which required the overruling of Swift v. Tyson, for he said in the very opinion quoted by the majority, "I should leave Swift v. Tyson undisturbed, as I indicated in Kuhn v. Fairmont Coal Co., but I would not allow it to spread the assumed dominion into new fields." Black & White Taxicab Co. v. Brown & Yellow Taxicab Co., 276 U.S. 518, 535,

48 S.Ct. 404, 409. If the opinion commits this Court to the position that the Congress is without power to declare what rules of substantive law shall govern the federal courts, that conclusion also seems questionable. The line between procedural and substantive law is hazy but no one doubts federal power over procedure. Wayman v. Southard, 10 Wheat. 1. The Judiciary Article and the "necessary and proper" clause of Article One may fully authorize legislation, such as this section of the Judiciary Act.

In this Court, stare decisis, in statutory construction, is a useful rule, not an inexorable command. Burnet v. Coronado Oil & Gas Co., 285 U.S. 393, dissent, page 406, note 1, 52 S.Ct. 443, 447 n. 1. Compare Read v. Bishop of Lincoln, [1892] A.C. 644, 655; London Street Tramways Co. v. London County Council, [1898] A.C. 375, 379. It seems preferable to overturn an established construction of an act of Congress, rather than, in the circumstances of this case, to interpret the Constitution. Cf. United States v. Delaware & Hudson Co., 213 U.S. 366, 29 S.Ct. 527.

There is no occasion to discuss further the range or soundness of these few phrases of the opinion. It is sufficient now to call attention to them and express my own non-acquiescence.

Questions: (1) What exactly did the Erie Court hold unconstitutional? Is that holding a restriction on the federal legislative power, or only on the federal judicial power?

(2) Why did the Court instruct a lower federal court sitting in New York to apply the law of Pennsylvania?

(3) According to Justice Brandeis, how should the federal court determine what the law of Pennsylvania is?

(4) According to Justice Brandeis, in diversity cases what matters will be decided under state law and what matters will be governed by federal law? Where would Justice Reed apparently draw that line?

BURDEN OF PROOF IN DIVERSITY ACTIONS

In Cities Service Oil Co. v. Dunlap, 308 U.S. 208, 60 S.Ct. 201 (1939), the plaintiff sued to remove a cloud on its title to certain Texas land that was covered by its deed. The defendants alleged in a counterclaim that the land had been included in the deed by mistake. The plaintiff replied that it had purchased the land in good faith, without notice of mistake, and for value. No evidence was offered by either side on the question raised by the plaintiff's reply. The district court and the circuit court of appeals found for the defendants, taking the view that the burden of proving bona fide purchase without notice for value was on the plaintiff; the circuit court explained that the recognized Texas rule to the contrary could be ignored because burden of proof in a diversity case like this was "a

matter of practice or procedure and not a matter of substantive law."
The Supreme Court reversed, briefly explaining: "We cannot accept
the view that the question presented was only one of practice in
courts of equity. Rather we think it relates to a substantial right
upon which the holder of recorded legal title to Texas land may confidently rely."

In Palmer v. Hoffman, 318 U.S. 109, 63 S.Ct. 477 (1943), the Court
peremptorily disposed of the contention that an instruction to the jury, to the effect that the burden of proving contributory negligence in
federal court is on the defendant, was proper because of Rule 8(c).
The Court said: "Rule 8(c) covers only the manner of pleading. The
question of the burden of establishing contributory negligence is a
question of local law which federal courts in diversity of citizenship
cases . . . must apply." Cities Service Oil Co. v. Dunlap was cited in support of this conclusion.

KLAXON CO. v. STENTOR ELECTRIC MANUFACTURING
CO., 313 U.S. 487, 61 S.Ct. 1020 (1941). Plaintiff brought a diversity
action for breach of contract in the United States District Court for
the District of Delaware and obtained a verdict for $100,000. The
court, applying the law of New York (the place of performance of the
contract), added pre-judgment interest to that sum. The Third Circuit affirmed this addition of interest, saying: (1) that the right to
pre-judgment interest is a matter of substance, not procedure, and so
is governed by state law; (2) that such right "should be settled by
reference to the law of the appropriate state according to the type of
case being tried"; and (3) that in this contract case, under general
principles of conflict-of-laws doctrine, the "appropriate" state is the
place of performance. On certiorari, the Supreme Court reversed.
Justice Reed, for a unanimous Court, said in part:

"The principal question in this case is whether in diversity cases
the federal courts must follow conflict of laws rules prevailing in the
states in which they sit. We left this open in Ruhlin v. New York
Life Insurance Company, 304 U.S. 202, 208, note 2, 58 S.Ct. 860, 862
n. 2. The frequent recurrence of the problem, as well as the conflict
of approach to the problem between the Third Circuit's opinion here
and that of the First Circuit in Sampson v. Channell, 110 F.2d 754,
759–762, led us to grant certiorari.

"We are of opinion that the prohibition declared in Erie R. Co. v.
Tompkins, 304 U.S. 64, 58 S.Ct. 817, against such independent determinations by the federal courts extends to the field of conflict of
laws. The conflict of laws rules to be applied by the federal court in
Delaware must conform to those prevailing in Delaware's state
courts. Otherwise, the accident of diversity of citizenship would constantly disturb equal administration of justice in coordinate state and

federal courts sitting side by side. See Erie R. Co. v. Tompkins, supra, 304 U.S. at 74–77, 58 S.Ct. at 820–822. Any other ruling would do violence to the principle of uniformity within a state upon which the Tompkins decision is based. Whatever lack of uniformity this may produce between federal courts in different states is attributable to our federal system, which leaves to a state, within the limits permitted by the Constitution, the right to pursue local policies diverging from those of its neighbors. It is not for the federal courts to thwart such local policies by enforcing an independent 'general law' of conflict of laws. Subject only to review by this Court on any federal question that may arise, Delaware is free to determine whether a given matter is to be governed by the law of the forum or some other law. Cf. Milwaukee County v. White Co., 296 U.S. 268, 272, 56 S.Ct. 229, 231. This Court's views are not the decisive factor in determining the applicable conflicts rule. Cf. Funkhouser v. J.B. Preston Co., 290 U.S. 163, 54 S.Ct. 134. And the proper function of the Delaware federal court is to ascertain what the state law is, not what it ought to be." *Vary from state to state but not w/in a state*

The case was remanded for determination of which state's law would be applied by Delaware state courts on the question of prejudgment interest. On remand, the circuit court of appeals found that Delaware would apply New York law, 125 F.2d 820 (3d Cir.), cert. denied, 316 U.S. 685, 62 S.Ct. 1284 (1942).

Question: (5) Reexamine Justice Roberts' statement of the plaintiff's dilemma in Sibbach v. Wilson & Co., supra p. 7. How did he handle the conflict-of-laws problem there? How is the plaintiff's "dilemma" affected by the Court's later decision in Klaxon? (This question—how Sibbach's "dilemma" is properly to be posed under prevailing doctrine—should be renewed periodically as you progress through this study of Erie's progeny.)

GUARANTY TRUST CO. v. YORK

Supreme Court of the United States, 1945.
326 U.S. 99, 65 S.Ct. 1464.

[In a class action brought in the United States District Court for the Southern District of New York, jurisdiction being based on diversity of citizenship, noteholders of Van Sweringen Corporation sued Guaranty Trust Company, the noteholders' trustee, for its alleged breach of trust. The defendant's motion for summary judgment was granted. The Second Circuit reversed (2–1), holding inter alia that the state statute of limitations did not apply in this federal-court case in the face of a federal tolling doctrine. On certiorari, the Supreme Court reversed the decision of the circuit court of appeals. Justice Frankfurter, speaking for the majority, said in part:]

S.Ct. says follow state statute of lim. idea

Our only concern is with the holding that the federal courts in a suit like this are not bound by local law.

. . . .

Our starting point must be the policy of federal jurisdiction which Erie R. Co. v. Tompkins, 304 U.S. 64, 58 S.Ct. 817, embodies. In overruling Swift v. Tyson, 16 Pet. 1, Erie R. Co. v. Tompkins did not merely overrule a venerable case. It overruled a particular way of looking at law which dominated the judicial process long after its inadequacies had been laid bare. [Citations omitted.] Law was conceived as a "brooding omnipresence" of Reason, of which decisions were merely evidence and not themselves the controlling formulations. Accordingly, federal courts deemed themselves free to ascertain what Reason, and therefore Law, required wholly independent of authoritatively declared State Law, even in cases where a legal right as the basis for relief was created by State authority and could not be created by federal authority and the case got into a federal court merely because it was "between Citizens of different States" under Art. III, § 2 of the Constitution of the United States.

. . . .

In relation to the problem now here, the real significance of Swift v. Tyson lies in the fact that it did not enunciate novel doctrine. Nor was it restricted to its particular situation. It summed up prior attitudes and expressions in cases that had come before this Court and lower federal courts for at least thirty years, at law as well as in equity. The short of it is that the doctrine was congenial to the jurisprudential climate of the time. Once established, judicial momentum kept it going. Since it was conceived that there was "a transcendental body of law outside of any particular State but obligatory within it unless and until changed by statute," [Black & White Taxicab & Transfer Co. v. Brown & Yellow Taxicab & Transfer Co.,] 276 U.S. 518, 532, 533, 48 S.Ct. 404, 408, 409, State court decisions were not "the law" but merely someone's opinion—to be sure an opinion to be respected—concerning the content of this all-pervading law. Not unnaturally, the federal courts assumed power to find for themselves the content of such a body of law. The notion was stimulated by the attractive vision of a uniform body of federal law. . . .

. . . .

Matters of "substance" and matters of "procedure" are much talked about in the books as though they defined a great divide cutting across the whole domain of law. But, of course, "substance" and "procedure" are the same key-words to very different problems. Neither "substance" nor "procedure" represents the same invariants. Each implies different variables depending upon the particular problem for which it is used. See Home Ins. Co. v. Dick, 281 U.S. 397, 409, 50 S.Ct. 338, 341. And the different problems are only distantly related at best, for the terms are in common use in connection with situations turning on such different considerations as those that are relevant to questions pertaining to ex post facto legislation, the impairment of the obligations of contract, the enforcement of federal rights in the State courts and the multitudinous phases of the conflict of laws. [Citations omitted.]

Here we are dealing with a right to recover derived not from the United States but from one of the States. When, because the plaintiff happens to be a non-resident, such a right is enforceable in a federal as well as in a State court, the forms and mode of enforcing the right may at times, naturally enough, vary because the two judicial systems are not identic. But since a federal court adjudicating a State-created right solely because of the diversity of citizenship of the parties is for that purpose, in effect, only another court of the State, it cannot afford recovery if the right to recover is made unavailable by the State nor can it substantially affect the enforcement of the right as given by the State.

And so the question is not whether a statute of limitations is deemed a matter of "procedure" in some sense. The question is whether such a statute concerns merely the manner and the means by which a right to recover, as recognized by the State, is enforced, or whether such statutory limitation is a matter of substance in the aspect that alone is relevant to our problem, namely, does it significantly affect the result of a litigation for a federal court to disregard a law of a State that would be controlling in an action upon the same claim by the same parties in a State court?

It is therefore immaterial whether statutes of limitation are characterized either as "substantive" or "procedural" in State court opinions in any use of those terms unrelated to the specific issue before us. Erie R. Co. v. Tompkins was not an endeavor to formulate scientific legal terminology. It expressed a policy that touches vitally the proper distribution of judicial power between State and federal courts. In essence, the intent of that decision was to insure that, in all cases where a federal court is exercising jurisdiction solely because of the diversity of citizenship of the parties, the outcome of the litigation in the federal court should be substantially the same, so far as legal rules determine the outcome of a litigation, as it would be if tried in a State court. The nub of the policy that underlies Erie R. Co. v. Tompkins is that for the same transaction the accident of a suit by a non-resident litigant in a federal court instead of in a State court a block away should not lead to a substantially different result. And so, putting to one side abstractions regarding "substance" and "procedure," we have held that in diversity cases the federal courts must follow the law of the State as to burden of proof, Cities Service Oil Co. v. Dunlap, 308 U.S. 208, 60 S.Ct. 201, as to conflict of laws, Klaxon Co. v. Stentor Co., 313 U.S. 487, 61 S.Ct. 1020, as to contributory negligence, Palmer v. Hoffman, 318 U.S. 109, 117, 63 S.Ct. 477, 482. And see Sampson v. Channell, 110 F.2d 754. Erie R. Co. v. Tompkins has been applied with an eye alert to essentials in avoiding disregard of State law in diversity cases in the federal courts. A policy so important to our federalism must be kept free from entanglements with analytical or terminological niceties.

Plainly enough, a statute that would completely bar recovery in a suit if brought in a State court bears on a State-created right vitally and not merely formally or negligibly. As to consequences that so intimately affect recovery or non-recovery a federal court in a diversity case should follow State law.

. . . .

Diversity jurisdiction is founded on assurance to non-resident litigants of courts free from susceptibility to potential local bias. The Framers of the Constitution, according to Marshall, entertained "apprehensions" lest distant suitors be subjected to local bias in State courts, or, at least, viewed with "indulgence the possible fears and apprehensions" of such suitors. Bank of the United States v. Deveaux, 5 Cranch 61, 87. And so Congress afforded out-of-State litigants another tribunal, not another body of law. The operation of a double system of conflicting laws in the same State is plainly hostile to the reign of law. Certainly, the fortuitous circumstance of residence out of a State of one of the parties to a litigation ought not to give rise to a discrimination against others equally concerned but locally resident. The source of substantive rights enforced by a federal court under diversity jurisdiction, it cannot be said too often, is the law of the States. Whenever that law is authoritatively declared by a State, whether its voice be the legislature or its highest court, such law ought to govern in litigation founded on that law, whether the forum of application is a State or a federal court and whether the remedies be sought at law or may be had in equity.

[Justices Roberts and Douglas did not participate. Justice Rutledge, joined by Justice Murphy, dissented, and in passing observed:]

Applicable statutes of limitations in state tribunals are not always the ones which would apply if suit were instituted in the courts of the state which creates the substantive rights for which enforcement is sought. The state of the forum is free to apply its own period of limitations, regardless of whether the state originating the right has barred suit upon it. Whether or not *the action* will be held to be barred depends therefore not upon the law of the state which creates the substantive right, but upon the law of the state where suit may be brought.

———

Consider the following cases (all decided by the Supreme Court on the same day, June 20, 1949) in the light of the Erie Railroad v. Tompkins doctrine as further spelled out in the Guaranty Trust case. The basis of jurisdiction in each case is diversity of citizenship.

RAGAN v. MERCHANTS TRANSFER & WAREHOUSE CO., 337 U.S. 530, 69 S.Ct. 1233 (1949). *P* sues *D* in the District Court for the

District of Kansas for personal injuries arising out of a highway accident on October 1, 1943. The applicable state statute of limitations is two years. The complaint is filed with the court on September 4, 1945, and the summons and complaint are served on December 28, 1945. Rule 3 provides that "[a] civil action is commenced by filing a complaint with the court." A Kansas statute says that for statute-of-limitations purposes an action shall be deemed commenced at the date of the service of the summons. *D* pleads the statute of limitations and moves for summary judgment. Is the action barred? (8–1 decision.) (YES) - stat. of lim - changes outcome of case → follow state law

WOODS v. INTERSTATE REALTY CO., 337 U.S. 535, 69 S.Ct. 1235 (1949). *P*, a Tennessee corporation, sues *D*, a citizen of Mississippi, in the District Court for the Northern District of Mississippi for a broker's commission. A Mississippi statute requires a foreign corporation doing business in the state to file a written power of attorney designating an agent for service of process and provides that any foreign corporation not complying with this requirement "shall not be permitted to bring or maintain any action or suit in any of the courts of this state." The effect of the statute, as construed by the highest court of the state, is not to make the contracts of such a corporation void but only to make them unenforceable in the Mississippi state courts. Prior to the Erie case, in David Lupton's Sons v. Automobile Club of America, 225 U.S. 489, 32 S.Ct. 711 (1912), the Supreme Court had held that such a state statute was not a bar to a diversity suit by such a corporation, saying: "The State could not prescribe the qualifications of suitors in the courts of the United States, and could not deprive of their privileges those who were entitled under the Constitution and laws of the United States to resort to the Federal courts for the enforcement of a valid contract." Note, although the Woods Court did not advert to it, Rule 17(b). *P* has not complied with the state statute. *D* moves for summary judgment on that ground. Should the motion be granted? (6–3 decision.) (YES) - Sim. to stat. of lim → follow state law

COHEN v. BENEFICIAL INDUSTRIAL LOAN CORP., 337 U.S. 541, 69 S.Ct. 1221 (1949). A small stockholder, *P*, brings a shareholders' derivative action in the District Court for the District of New Jersey, the defendants being the corporation and certain of its managers and directors who are alleged to have wasted or diverted corporate assets through mismanagement and fraud. A New Jersey statute provides that when stockholders whose holdings amount to less than 5% of the total stock outstanding and not more than $50,000 in market value bring an action of this type, the corporation shall be entitled to require the plaintiffs to give security for the reasonable expenses, including counsel fees, that may be incurred in defending the action, and against that security the corporation shall have recourse in such amount as the court may determine upon termination of the action. Compare Rule 23.1. The corporation moves to require *P* to give security as provided by the state statute, in the amount of $125,000. Is the statute applicable in the federal court? The Su-

∴ outcome would be diff.

YES - follow state law b/c small stockholder can't file if bond must be posted!

preme Court divided on this question. One of the opinions said: "We see no reason why the policy stated in Guaranty Trust . . . should not apply." Another said: "The measure of the cause of action is the claim which the corporation has against the alleged wrong-doers. This New Jersey statute does not add one iota to nor subtract one iota from that cause of action. . . . [It] regulates only the procedure for instituting a particular cause of action and hence need not be applied in this diversity suit in the federal court." Which do you think was the majority opinion and which a dissent? (6–3 decision.) 1st diss. 2nd maj.

FEDERAL DETERMINATION OF STATE LAW

Questions as to scope of state law applicability are not the only problem that Erie has raised for the federal courts. What is to be done when the state law clearly governs but there is no clear state law on the point in issue? What if the only state-court decision is a very old one by the state's highest court but wholly out of line with the modern trend of authority elsewhere? What if the highest court of the state has not passed upon the point but there is a decision of an intermediate state court of appeals? The Supreme Court said in an early case that such a decision "is not to be disregarded by a federal court unless it is convinced by other persuasive data that the highest court of the state would decide otherwise." West v. AT & T, 311 U.S. 223, 237, 61 S.Ct. 179, 183 (1940). Where would a federal judge look for such "persuasive data"? What if there is a recent decision of an intermediate state court that is inconsistent with an old decision of the state's highest court? What if there are only state-court dicta? What if there is no state law of any kind on the particular point in issue?

BERNHARDT v. POLYGRAPHIC CO. OF AMERICA, 350 U.S. 198, 76 S.Ct. 273 (1956). An employment contract made in New York between the plaintiff, an individual residing in New York, and the defendant, a New York corporation, called in case of dispute for arbitration under the law of New York by the American Arbitration Association. The plaintiff subsequently moved to Vermont where he was to carry out the contract. In this action for wrongful discharge, removed on the basis of diversity of citizenship from the state court to the United States District Court for the District of Vermont, the defendant applied for a stay pending resort to arbitration. The district court denied the application on the ground that Vermont law controlled and under that law there would be no stay because agreements to arbitrate were not enforceable, giving as its authority Mead's Admx. v. Owen, 83 Vt. 132, 74 A. 1058 (1910). On appeal, the court of appeals reversed, holding that state law did not govern this matter because it was not "substantive" in the Erie sense and that a stay was called for by section 3 of the United States Arbitration Act, 9 U.S.C. § 3, which was construed to apply in any federal action with respect to any agreement to arbitrate.

On certiorari, the Court by Justice Douglas said that section 3 should be narrowly read and limited to arbitration agreements in maritime transactions and in interstate or foreign commerce transactions; otherwise "a constitutional question might be presented" in light of the Erie decision. (The student should attempt to formulate that question. See Prima Paint Corp. v. Flood & Conklin Mfg. Co., 388 U.S. 395, 87 S.Ct. 1801 (1967).)

With the Arbitration Act thus considered inapplicable to this particular contract, the Court next decided that state law applied to the issue of enforceability. "If the federal court allows arbitration where the state court would disallow it, the outcome of litigation might depend on the courthouse where suit is brought. For the remedy by arbitration, whatever its merits or shortcomings, substantially affects the cause of action created by the State. The nature of the tribunal where suits are tried is an important part of the parcel of rights behind a cause of action. The change from a court of law to an arbitration panel may make a radical difference in ultimate result."

As to what Vermont law was, Justice Douglas said:

"That case [Mead's Admx. v. Owen] was decided in 1910. But it was agreed on oral argument that there is no later authority from the Vermont courts, that no fracture in the rules announced in those cases has appeared in subsequent rulings or dicta, and that no legislative movement is under way in Vermont to change the result of those cases. Since the federal [district] judge making those findings is from the Vermont bar, we give special weight to his statement of what the Vermont law is. . . . Were the question in doubt or deserving further canvass, we would of course remand the case to the Court of Appeals to pass on this question of Vermont law. But, as we have indicated, there appears to be no confusion in the Vermont decisions, no developing line of authorities that casts a shadow over the established ones, no dicta, doubts or ambiguities in the opinions of Vermont judges on the question, no legislative development that promises to undermine the judicial rule. We see no reason, therefore, to remand the case to the Court of Appeals to pass on this question of local law."

The Court, citing Klaxon, instead remanded the case to the district court with authority to consider whether, as a matter of conflict of laws, the Vermont Supreme Court would apply New York rather than Vermont law to the enforcement of this agreement to arbitrate. (It was not clear that the district court had considered that question in rendering its decision.)

Justices Frankfurter and Harlan, concurring separately, agreed that state law controlled, but they would have remanded to the court of appeals to consider whether the Vermont Supreme Court would not now change its attitude toward the enforcement of agreements to arbitrate. Justice Frankfurter said:

"As long as there is diversity jurisdiction, 'estimates' are necessarily often all that federal courts can make in ascertaining what the state court would rule to be its law. . . . The Supreme Court of Vermont last spoke on this matter in 1910. The doctrine that it referred to was not a peculiar indigenous Vermont rule. The attitude reflected by that decision nearly half a century ago was the current traditional judicial hostility against ousting courts, as the phrase ran, of their jurisdiction.. . . To be sure, a vigorous legislative movement got under way in the 1920's expressive of a broadened outlook of view on this subject. But courts do not always wait for legislation to find a judicial doctrine outmoded. . . .

"Surely in the light of all that has happened since 1910 in the general field of the law of arbitration, it is not for us to assume that the Court of Appeals, if it had that question for consideration, could not have found that the law of Vermont today does not require disregard of a provision of a contract made in New York, with a purposeful desire to have the law of New York govern, to accomplish a result that today may be deemed to be a general doctrine of the law. Of course, if the Court of Appeals, versed in the general jurisprudence of Vermont and having among its members a Vermont lawyer, should find that the Vermont court would, despite the New York incidents of the contract, apply Vermont law and that it is the habit of the Vermont court to adhere to its precedents and to leave changes to the legislature, it would not be for the federal court to gainsay that policy."

Justice Burton dissented, viewing arbitration as merely a "form of trial" as to which the federal courts were not bound to follow state law under Erie or Guaranty Trust.

These incidental problems of federal determination of state law persist to the present. Consider this installment of the curious case of Factors Etc., Inc. v. Pro Arts, Inc., 701 F.2d 11 (2d Cir.1983), in which the majority opinion was as follows:

"On June 29, 1981, this panel of the Court, by a divided vote, issued an opinion reversing the District Court's grant of summary judgment in favor of the plaintiffs-appellees and the issuance of a permanent injunction barring the defendants-appellants from marketing a poster depicting Elvis Presley. Factors, Etc., Inc. v. Pro Arts, Inc., 652 F.2d 278 (2d Cir. 1981) [, cert. denied, 456 U.S. 927, 102 S.Ct. 1973 (1982)]. The basis for that ruling . . . was that in the absence of authoritative guidance from the courts of Tennessee, we would deem controlling in this diversity case the decision of the Sixth Circuit in Memphis Development Foundation v. Factors, Etc., Inc.,

616 F.2d 956 (6th Cir.), cert. denied, 449 U.S. 953, 101 S.Ct. 358, 66 L.Ed.2d 217 (1980). Memphis Development, also a diversity case requiring application of Tennessee law, had held that Tennessee does not recognize a descendible right of publicity. Upon the return of the instant case to the District Court for the Southern District of New York, plaintiffs called to Judge Tenney's attention a decision of the Tennessee Chancery Court, issued October 2, 1981, which held that Tennessee law does recognize a descendible right of publicity. Commerce Union Bank v. Coors of the Cumberland, Inc., 7 Media L.Rptr. 2204 (Chan.Ct.Davidson Cty.Tenn.1981). That decision, not officially reported, was issued prior to the issuance of our mandate in the instant case.

"Judge Tenney thereupon stayed entry of judgment for the defendants pending an application by the plaintiffs to petition this Court to recall its mandate and consider an untimely petition for rehearing in light of the alleged intervening change in state law. [Citation omitted.] Plaintiffs diligently sought such relief, and we granted leave to file their petition for rehearing to assess the significance of the Chancery Court's decision in Commerce Union Bank. Supplemental briefs have been received.

"Fortunately, a recent development in the Tennessee Chancery Court has made it unnecessary for us to determine whether Commerce Union Bank is of sufficient authoritativeness to warrant our disregard of the Sixth Circuit's decision in Memphis Development. On November 24, 1982, the Chancery Court, acting through a different judge from the one who rendered the decision in Commerce Union Bank, ruled that Tennessee does not recognize a descendible right of publicity. Lancaster v. Factors, Etc., Inc., [9 Media L.Rptr. 1109] (Chan.Ct.Shelby Cty.Tenn.1982). The Lancaster decision is surely entitled to no less weight than the decision in Commerce Union Bank and may even have a special pertinence since it involves a claim by the same parties who are plaintiffs in the instant litigation with respect to a descendible right of publicity concerning Elvis Presley. Whatever the weight to be given an unreported decision of the Tennessee Chancery Court by a diversity court at any stage of litigation, much less at the point where a mandate is sought to be recalled on the basis of an alleged intervening change of state law, we have no doubt that the appearance of two conflicting decisions of the Chancery Court on the precise point at issue affords us no basis for considering the law of Tennessee to have authoritatively been changed since our June 29, 1981, decision. The motion to recall the mandate and the petition for rehearing are denied."

Judge Mansfield dissented, saying that "the internal Tennessee state court conflict provides an additional reason for our following the usual practice, where we disagree with the reasoning of another circuit on an issue, of deciding a case according to what we believe to be the more rational basis."

STATE DETERMINATION OF STATE LAW

Erie imposes on the federal courts the duty of, "in effect, sitting as a state court" when deciding certain issues of law. Commissioner v. Estate of Bosch, 387 U.S. 456, 465, 87 S.Ct. 1776, 1783 (1967). The various burdens attendant upon such duty should now be obvious. Is there any way for the federal court to shift those burdens?

A possibility is abstention, a complex doctrine under which a federal court, in deference to a state's interests, declines to exercise the federal jurisdiction. There are a number of circumstances where a federal court might abstain; the Supreme Court has indicated that "[a]bstention is also appropriate where there have been presented difficult questions of state law bearing on policy problems of substantial public import whose importance transcends the result in the case then at bar. Louisiana Power & Light Co. v. City of Thibodaux, 360 U.S. 25, 79 S.Ct. 1070 (1959), for example, involved such a question. In particular, the concern there was with the scope of the eminent domain power of municipalities under state law." Colorado River Water Conservation District v. United States, 424 U.S. 800, 814, 96 S.Ct. 1236, 1244–45 (1976) (dictum). Accordingly, a district court faced under the Erie doctrine with an unsettled but publicly significant state-law issue might dismiss or stay the federal diversity case, leaving the parties to pursue a coercive or declaratory remedy in the state-court system.

There is a less drastic course that in this context is more broadly applicable, viz., a process of certification of the unsettled question of state law by the federal court directly to the highest court of the state. By this device the federal court retains jurisdiction, eventually handling the case in accordance with the state court's answer. The first state provision for answering certified questions was in a Florida statute, which had never been used until the Supreme Court gave its blessing to the procedure in Clay v. Sun Insurance Office Ltd., 363 U.S. 207, 80 S.Ct. 1222 (1960). Many states have since by statute or rule authorized their highest court to answer certified questions. The National Conference of Commissioners on Uniform State Laws in 1967 approved, and recommended for adoption by the states, a Uniform Certification of Questions of Law Act. The American Law Institute, over the objections of its Reporters, proposed a federal statute specifically authorizing federal courts to certify to states having a certification procedure; see ALI Study of the Division of Jurisdiction Between State and Federal Courts § 1371(e) commentary at 292–96 (1968). The Supreme Court emphatically restated its approval of certification in Lehman Brothers v. Schein, 416 U.S. 386, 94 S.Ct. 1741 (1974) (instructing the Second Circuit, in a diversity case, to reconsider the possibility of certifying a question to the Florida Supreme Court).

Certification does offer a neat means of avoiding the anomaly of different answers to the same question of law from a state and a federal court. (Is this anomaly more of a reproach to the judicial process than the anomaly of different juries coming to opposite conclusions on the same evidence?) But this neat solution comes at a stiff price.

First, certification inevitably causes delay and increased expense for the parties. At the least, this requires the federal court to balance the interests involved, taking into account the type of question and the circumstances of the particular case. Lehman Brothers v. Schein involved a question of corporate fiduciary obligation arising in a shareholders' derivative suit. Contrast this with an unsettled question of state tort law arising in a case brought by an injured infant, as in Hatfield v. Bishop Clarkson Memorial Hospital, 701 F.2d 1266 (8th Cir.1983).

Second, certification imposes a burden on the state court. The unavoidably abstract nature of the question may make it difficult to answer; indeed, certification may run aground if the state has a constitutional prohibition against giving advisory opinions. These problems are lessened by allowing certification, as Florida does, only from a federal appellate court; but most state provisions, the Uniform Act, and the ALI proposal all allow a federal district court to certify as well.

Third, certification poses a possible threat to the judicial function of the federal courts in diversity cases, diminishing their authority and their sense of responsibility.

————

BYRD v. BLUE RIDGE RURAL ELECTRIC COOPERATIVE

Supreme Court of the United States, 1958.
356 U.S. 525, 78 S.Ct. 893.

[This was a diversity action in a federal district court in South Carolina for injuries allegedly caused by the defendant's negligence. The plaintiff was employed as a lineman by a contractor, which held a construction contract with the defendant. The plaintiff was injured while performing work under that contract. One of the defenses was that the South Carolina Workmen's Compensation Act imposed upon the plaintiff—because the work contracted to be done by his employer was work of the kind also done by the defendant's own construction and maintenance crews—the status of a statutory employee of the defendant; the defendant would therefore be immune from an action at law, and the plaintiff would be obliged to accept workers' compensation benefits as his exclusive remedy. The Supreme Court on certiorari considered, among other things, whether the factual issue raised by this defense should be decided by the trial judge, as held in a South Carolina decision, Adams v. Davison-Paxon Co., 230

S.C. 532, 96 S.E.2d 566 (1957), or by a jury, in line with federal practice.] Justice Brennan, for the majority, explained:]

First. It was decided in Erie R. Co. v. Tompkins that the federal courts in diversity cases must respect the definition of state-created rights and obligations by the state courts. We must, therefore, first examine the rule in Adams v. Davison-Paxon Co. to determine whether it is bound up with these rights and obligations in such a way that its application in the federal court is required. Cities Service Oil Co. v. Dunlap, 308 U.S. 208, 60 S.Ct. 201.

The Workmen's Compensation Act is administered in South Carolina by its Industrial Commission. The South Carolina courts hold that, on judicial review of actions of the Commission . . . ., the question whether the claim of an injured workman is within the Commission's jurisdiction is a matter of law for decision by the court, which makes its own findings of fact relating to that jurisdiction. The South Carolina Supreme Court states no reasons in Adams v. Davison-Paxon Co. why, although the jury decides all other factual issues raised by the cause of action and defenses, the jury is displaced as to the factual issue raised by the affirmative defense . . . .. The conclusion is inescapable that the Adams holding is grounded in the practical consideration that the question had theretofore come before the South Carolina courts from the Industrial Commission and the courts had become accustomed to deciding the factual issue of immunity without the aid of juries. We find nothing to suggest that this rule was announced as an integral part of the special relationship created by the statute. Thus the requirement appears to be merely a form and mode of enforcing the immunity, Guaranty Trust Co. v. York, 326 U.S. 99, 108, 65 S.Ct. 1464, 1469, and not a rule intended to be bound up with the definition of the rights and obligations of the parties. The situation is therefore not analogous to that in Dice v. Akron, C. & Y.R. Co., 342 U.S. 359, 72 S.Ct. 312 . . . .

Second. But cases following Erie have evinced a broader policy to the effect that the federal courts should conform as near as may be—in the absence of other considerations—to state rules even of form and mode where the state rules may bear substantially on the question whether the litigation would come out one way in the federal court and another way in the state court if the federal court failed to apply a particular local rule. E.g., Guaranty Trust Co. v. York, supra; Bernhardt v. Polygraphic Co., 350 U.S. 198, 76 S.Ct. 273. Concededly the nature of the tribunal which tries issues may be important in the enforcement of the parcel of rights making up a cause of action or defense, and bear significantly upon achievement of uniform enforcement of the right. It may well be that in the instant personal-injury case the outcome would be substantially affected by whether the issue of immunity is decided by a judge or a jury. Therefore, were "outcome" the only consideration, a strong case might appear for saying that the federal court should follow the state practice.

But there are affirmative countervailing considerations at work here. The federal system is an independent system for administering justice to litigants who properly invoke its jurisdiction. An essential characteristic of that system is the manner in which, in civil common-law actions, it distributes trial functions between judge and jury and, under the influence—if not the command [10]—of the Seventh Amendment, assigns the decisions of disputed questions of fact to the jury. Jacob v. City of New York, 315 U.S. 752, 62 S.Ct. 854.[11] The policy of uniform enforcement of state-created rights and obligations, see, e.g., Guaranty Trust Co. v. York, supra, cannot in every case exact compliance with a state rule [12]—not bound up with rights and obligations—which disrupts the federal system of allocating functions between judge and jury. Herron v. Southern Pacific Co., 283 U.S. 91, 51 S.Ct. 383. Thus the inquiry here is whether the federal policy favoring jury decisions of disputed fact questions should yield to the state rule in the interest of furthering the objective that the litigation should not come out one way in the federal court and another way in the state court.

We think that in the circumstances of this case the federal court should not follow the state rule. It cannot be gainsaid that there is a strong federal policy against allowing state rules to disrupt the judge-jury relationship in the federal courts. In Herron v. Southern Pacific Co., supra, the trial judge in a personal-injury negligence action brought in the District Court for Arizona on diversity grounds directed a verdict for the defendant when it appeared as a matter of law that the plaintiff was guilty of contributory negligence. The federal judge refused to be bound by a provision of the Arizona Constitution which made the jury the sole arbiter of the question of contributory negligence. This Court sustained the action of the trial judge, holding that "state laws cannot alter the essential character or function of a federal court" because that function "is not in any sense a local matter, and state statutes which would interfere with the appropriate performance of that function are not binding upon the federal court under either the Conformity Act or the 'Rules of Decision' Act." Id., 283 U.S. at page 94, 51 S.Ct. at page 384. Perhaps even more clearly in light of the influence of the Seventh Amendment, the function assigned to the jury "is an essential factor in the process for which the Federal Constitution provides." Id., 283 U.S. at page 95,

---

[10] Our conclusion makes unnecessary the consideration of—and we intimate no view upon—the constitutional question whether the right of jury trial protected in federal courts by the Seventh Amendment embraces the factual issue of statutory immunity when asserted, as here, as an affirmative defense in a common-law negligence action.

[11] The Courts of Appeals have expressed varying views about the effect of Erie R. Co. v. Tompkins on judge-jury problems in diversity cases. [Citations omitted.]

[12] This Court held in Sibbach v. Wilson & Co., 312 U.S. 1, 61 S.Ct. 422, that Federal Rules of Civil Procedure 35 should prevail over a contrary state rule.

51 S.Ct. at page 384. Concededly the Herron case was decided before Erie R. Co. v. Tompkins, but even when Swift v. Tyson, 16 Pet. 1, was governing law and allowed federal courts sitting in diversity cases to disregard state decisional law, it was never thought that state statutes or constitutions were similarly to be disregarded. Green v. Neal's Lessee, 6 Pet. 291. Yet Herron held that state statutes and constitutional provisions could not disrupt or alter the essential character or function of a federal court.[14]

Third. We have discussed the problem upon the assumption that the outcome of the litigation may be substantially affected by whether the issue of immunity is decided by a judge or a jury. But clearly there is not present here the certainty that a different result would follow, cf. Guaranty Trust Co. v. York, supra, or even the strong possibility that this would be the case, cf. Bernhardt v. Polygraphic Co., supra. There are factors present here which might reduce that possibility. The trial judge in the federal system has powers denied the judges of many States to comment on the weight of evidence and credibility of witnesses, and discretion to grant a new trial if the verdict appears to him to be against the weight of the evidence. We do not think the likelihood of a different result is so strong as to require the federal practice of jury determination of disputed factual issues to yield to the state rule in the interest of uniformity of outcome.

[Justice Whittaker dissented from the ruling that the plaintiff was entitled to a jury determination of his status, arguing that Guaranty Trust required the application of state law. Justices Frankfurter and Harlan also dissented, but they did not reach the jury-trial point.]

Question: (6) Reexamine Woods v. Interstate Realty Co. Do you think its decision to apply state law is still sound after Byrd?

HANNA v. PLUMER

Supreme Court of the United States, 1965.
380 U.S. 460, 85 S.Ct. 1136.

Mr. Chief Justice Warren delivered the opinion of the Court.

The question to be decided is whether, in a civil action where the jurisdiction of the United States district court is based upon diversity of citizenship between the parties, service of process shall be made in the manner prescribed by state law or that set forth in Rule 4(d)(1) of the Federal Rules of Civil Procedure.

---

[14] Diederich v. American News Co., 10 Cir., 128 F.2d 144, decided after Erie R. Co. v. Tompkins, held that an almost identical provision of the Oklahoma Constitution was not binding on a federal judge in a diversity case.

On February 6, 1963, petitioner, a citizen of Ohio, filed her complaint in the District Court for the District of Massachusetts, claiming damages in excess of $10,000 for personal injuries resulting from an automobile accident in South Carolina, allegedly caused by the negligence of one Louise Plumer Osgood, a Massachusetts citizen deceased at the time of the filing of the complaint. Respondent, Mrs. Osgood's executor and also a Massachusetts citizen, was named as defendant. On February 8, service was made by leaving copies of the summons and the complaint with respondent's wife at his residence, concededly in compliance with Rule 4(d)(1) [the Court here quoted the Rule]. Respondent filed his answer on February 26, alleging, inter alia, that the action could not be maintained because it had been brought "contrary to and in violation of the provisions of Massachusetts General Laws (Ter.Ed.) Chapter 197, Section 9." That section provides:

> "Except as provided in this chapter, an executor or administrator shall not be held to answer to an action by a creditor of the deceased which is not commenced within one year from the time of his giving bond for the performance of his trust, or to such an action which is commenced within said year unless before the expiration thereof the writ in such action has been served by delivery in hand upon such executor or administrator or service thereof accepted by him or a notice stating the name of the estate, the name and address of the creditor, the amount of the claim and the court in which the action has been brought has been filed in the proper registry of probate. . . ." Mass.Gen.Laws Ann., c. 197, § 9 (1958).

On October 17, 1963, the District Court granted respondent's motion for summary judgment, citing Ragan v. Merchants Transfer Co., 337 U.S. 530, 69 S.Ct. 1233, and Guaranty Trust Co. v. York, 326 U.S. 99, 65 S.Ct. 1464, in support of its conclusion that the adequacy of the service was to be measured by § 9, with which, the court held, petitioner had not complied. On appeal, petitioner admitted noncompliance with § 9, but argued that Rule 4(d)(1) defines the method by which service of process is to be effected in diversity actions. The Court of Appeals for the First Circuit, finding that "[r]elatively recent amendments [to § 9] evince a clear legislative purpose to require personal notification within the year,"[1] concluded that the conflict of

---

[1] Section 9 is in part a statute of limitations, providing that an executor need not "answer to an action . . . which is not commenced within one year from the time of his giving bond . . . .." This part of the statute, the purpose of which is to speed the settlement of estates, Spaulding v. McConnell, 307 Mass. 144, 146, 29 N.E.2d 713, 715 (1940); Doyle v. Moylan, 141 F.Supp. 95 (D.C.D. Mass.1956), is not involved in this case, since the action clearly was timely com-

menced. (Respondent filed bond on March 1, 1962; the complaint was filed February 6, 1963; and the service—the propriety of which is in dispute—was made on February 8, 1963.) 331 F.2d, at 159. Cf. Guaranty Trust Co. v. York, supra; Ragan v. Merchants Transfer Co., supra.

Section 9 also provides for the manner of service. Generally, service of process must be made by "delivery in hand," al-state and federal rules was over "a substantive rather than a procedural matter," and unanimously affirmed. 331 F.2d 157. Because of the threat to the goal of uniformity of federal procedure posed by the decision below, we granted certiorari, 379 U.S. 813, 85 S.Ct. 52.

[margin note: S.Ct. reversed - Not Sub. is not against REA.]

We conclude that the adoption of Rule 4(d)(1), designed to control service of process in diversity actions, neither exceeded the congressional mandate embodied in the Rules Enabling Act nor transgressed constitutional bounds, and that the Rule is therefore the standard against which the District Court should have measured the adequacy of the service. Accordingly, we reverse the decision of the Court of Appeals.

. . . . Under the cases construing the scope of the Enabling Act, Rule 4(d)(1) clearly passes muster. Prescribing the manner in which a defendant is to be notified that a suit has been instituted against him, it relates to the "practice and procedure of the district courts." Cf. Insurance Co. v. Bangs, 103 U.S. 435, 439.

> "The test must be whether a rule really regulates procedure,—the judicial process for enforcing rights and duties recognized by substantive law and for justly administering remedy and redress for disregard or infraction of them." Sibbach v. Wilson & Co., 312 U.S. 1, 14, 61 S.Ct. 422, 426.[4]

In Mississippi Pub. Corp. v. Murphree, 326 U.S. 438, 66 S.Ct. 242, this Court upheld Rule 4(f), which permits service of a summons anywhere within the State (and not merely the district) in which a district court sits:

> "We think that Rule 4(f) is in harmony with the Enabling Act . . . . Undoubtedly most alterations of the rules of practice and procedure may and often do affect the rights of litigants. Congress' prohibition of any alteration of substantive rights of litigants was obviously not addressed to such incidental effects as necessarily attend the adoption of the prescribed new rules of procedure upon the rights of litigants who, agreeably to rules of practice and procedure, have been brought before a court authorized to determine their rights. Sibbach v. Wilson & Co., 312 U.S. I, 11–14, 61 S.Ct. 422, 425–427. The fact that the application of Rule 4(f) will operate to subject petitioner's rights to adjudication by the district court for northern Mississippi will undoubtedly af-

[margin note: Doesn't prohibit when rights affected are only incidentally affected]

---

though there are two alternatives: acceptance of service by the executor, or filing of a notice of claim, the components of which are set out in the statute, in the appropriate probate court. The purpose of this part of the statute, which *is* involved here, is, as the court below noted, to insure that executors will receive actual notice of claims. Parker v. Rich, 297 Mass. 111, 113–114, 8 N.E.2d 345, 347 (1937). Actual notice is of course also the goal of Rule 4(d)(1); however, the Federal Rule reflects a determi-

nation that this goal can be achieved by a method less cumbersome than that prescribed in § 9. In this case the goal seems to have been achieved; although the affidavit filed by respondent in the District Court asserts that he had not been served in hand nor had he accepted service, it does not allege lack of actual notice.

[4] See also Schlagenhauf v. Holder, 379 U.S. 104, 112–114, 85 S.Ct. 234, 239–240.

[margin note: Why it's not a valid law! (Court says)]

fect those rights. But it does not operate to abridge, enlarge or modify the rules of decision by which that court will adjudicate its rights." Id., at 445–446, 66 S.Ct. at 246.

Thus were there no conflicting state procedure, Rule 4(d)(1) would clearly control. National Rental v. Szukhent, 375 U.S. 311, 316, 84 S.Ct. 411, 414. However, respondent, focusing on the contrary Massachusetts rule, calls to the Court's attention another line of cases, a line which—like the Federal Rules—had its birth in 1938. Erie R. Co. v. Tompkins, 304 U.S. 64, 58 S.Ct. 817, overruling Swift v. Tyson, 16 Pet. 1, held that federal courts sitting in diversity cases, when deciding questions of "substantive" law, are bound by state court decisions as well as state statutes. The broad command of Erie was therefore identical to that of the Enabling Act: federal courts are to apply state substantive law and federal procedural law. However, as subsequent cases sharpened the distinction between substance and procedure, the line of cases following Erie diverged markedly from the line construing the Enabling Act. Guaranty Trust Co. v. York, 326 U.S. 99, 65 S.Ct. 1464, made it clear that Erie-type problems were not to be solved by reference to any traditional or common-sense substance-procedure distinction:

> "And so the question is not whether a statute of limitations is deemed a matter of 'procedure' in some sense. The question is . . . does it significantly affect the result of a litigation for a federal court to disregard a law of a State that would be controlling in an action upon the same claim by the same parties in a State court?" 326 U.S. at 109, 65 S.Ct. at 1470.[5]

Respondent, by placing primary reliance on York and Ragan, suggests that the Erie doctrine acts as a check on the Federal Rules of Civil Procedure, that despite the clear command of Rule 4(d)(1), Erie and its progeny demand the application of the Massachusetts rule. Reduced to essentials, the argument is: (1) Erie, as defined in York, demands that federal courts apply state law whenever application of federal law in its stead will alter the outcome of the case. (2) In this case, a determination that the Massachusetts service requirements obtain will result in immediate victory for respondent. If, on the other hand, it should be held that Rule 4(d)(1) is applicable, the litigation will continue, with possible victory for petitioner. (3) Therefore, Erie demands application of the Massachusetts rule. The syllogism possesses an appealing simplicity, but is for several reasons invalid.

In the first place, it is doubtful that, even if there were no Federal Rule making it clear that in-hand service is not required in diversity actions, the Erie rule would have obligated the District Court to follow the Massachusetts procedure. "Outcome-determination" analy-

[*marginalia: Respondents argument for State law*]

[*marginalia: S.Ct. says arg. invalid*]

---

[5] See also Ragan v. Merchants Transfer Co., supra; Woods v. Interstate Realty Co., 337 U.S. 535, 69 S.Ct. 1235; Bernhardt v. Polygraphic Co., 350 U.S. 198, 203–204, 207–208, 76 S.Ct. 273, 276, 278–279; cf. Byrd v. Blue Ridge Cooperative, 356 U.S. 525, 78 S.Ct. 893.

sis was never intended to serve as a talisman. Byrd v. Blue Ridge Cooperative, 356 U.S. 525, 537, 78 S.Ct. 893, 900. Indeed, the message of York itself is that choices between state and federal law are to be made not by application of any automatic, "litmus paper" criterion, but rather by reference to the policies underlying the Erie rule. Guaranty Trust Co. v. York, supra, 326 U.S. at 108–112, 65 S.Ct. at 1469–1471.

[margin note: Policy ① of Erie]

The Erie rule is rooted in part in a realization that it would be unfair for the character or result of a litigation materially to differ because the suit had been brought in a federal court.

"Diversity of citizenship jurisdiction was conferred in order to prevent apprehended discrimination in state courts against those not citizens of the state. Swift v. Tyson introduced grave discrimination by noncitizens against citizens. It made rights enjoyed under the unwritten 'general law' vary according to whether enforcement was sought in the state or in the federal court; and the privilege of selecting the court in which the right should be determined was conferred upon the noncitizen. Thus, the doctrine rendered impossible equal protection of the law." Erie R. Co. v. Tompkins, supra, 304 U.S. at 74–75, 58 S.Ct. at 820–821.[7]

[margin note: Policy ② of Erie]

The decision was also in part a reaction to the practice of "forum-shopping" which had grown up in response to the rule of Swift v. Tyson. 304 U.S. at 73–74, 58 S.Ct. at 819–820.[8] That the York test was an attempt to effectuate these policies is demonstrated by the fact that the opinion framed the inquiry in terms of "substantial" variations between state and federal litigation. 326 U.S. at 109, 65 S.Ct. at 1469. Not only are nonsubstantial, or trivial, variations not likely to raise the sort of equal protection problems which troubled the Court in Erie; they are also unlikely to influence the choice of a forum.

[margin note: York trys to further these policies]

The "outcome-determination" test therefore cannot be read without reference to the twin aims of the Erie rule: discouragement of forum-shopping and avoidance of inequitable administration of the laws.[9]

[7] See also Klaxon Co. v. Stentor Co., 313 U.S. 487, 496, 61 S.Ct. 1020, 1021; Woods v. Interstate Realty Co., supra, note 5, 337 U.S. at 538, 69 S.Ct. at 1237.

[8] Cf. Black & White Taxicab Co. v. Brown & Yellow Taxicab Co., 276 U.S. 518, 48 S.Ct. 404.

[9] The Court of Appeals seemed to frame the inquiry in terms of how "important" § 9 is to the State. In support of its suggestion that § 9 serves some interest the State regards as vital to its citizens, the court noted that something like § 9 has been on the books in Massachusetts a long time, that § 9 has been amended a number of times, and that § 9 is designed to make sure that executors receive actual notice. See note 1, supra.

The apparent lack of relation among these three observations is not surprising, because it is not clear to what sort of question the Court of Appeals was addressing itself. One cannot meaningfully ask how important something is without first asking "important for what purpose?" Erie and its progeny make clear that when a federal court sitting in a diversity case is faced with a question of whether or not to apply state law, the importance of a state rule is indeed relevant, but only in the context of asking whether application of the rule would make so important a difference to the character or result of the litigation that failure to enforce it would unfairly dis-

The difference between the conclusion that the Massachusetts rule is applicable, and the conclusion that it is not, is of course at this point "outcome-determinative" in the sense that if we hold the state rule to apply, respondent prevails, whereas if we hold that Rule 4(d)(1) governs, the litigation will continue. But in this sense *every procedural variation is "outcome-determinative."* For example, having brought suit in a federal court a plaintiff cannot then insist on the right to file subsequent pleadings in accord with the time limits applicable in the state courts, even though enforcement of the federal timetable will, if he continues to insist that he must meet only the state time limit, result in determination of the controversy against him. So it is here. Though choice of the federal or state rule will at this point have a marked effect upon the outcome of the litigation, the difference between the two rules would be of scant, if any, relevance to the choice of a forum. Petitioner, in choosing her forum, was not presented with a situation where application of the state rule would wholly bar recovery;[10] rather, adherence to the state rule would have resulted only in altering the way in which process was served.[11] Moreover, it is difficult to argue that permitting service of defendant's wife to take the place of in-hand service of defendant himself alters the mode of enforcement of state-created rights in a fashion sufficiently "substantial" to raise the sort of equal protection problems to which the Erie opinion alluded.

There is, however, a more fundamental flaw in respondent's syllogism: the incorrect assumption that the rule of Erie R. Co. v. Tompkins constitutes the appropriate test of the validity and therefore the applicability of a Federal Rule of Civil Procedure. The Erie rule has never been invoked to void a Federal Rule. It is true that there have been cases where this Court has held applicable a state rule in the face of an argument that the situation was governed by one of the Federal Rules. But the holding of each such case was not that Erie commanded displacement of a Federal Rule by an inconsistent state rule, but rather that the scope of the Federal Rule was not as broad as the losing party urged, and therefore, there being no Fed-

---

criminate against citizens of the forum State, or whether application of the rule would have so important an effect upon the fortunes of one or both of the litigants that failure to enforce it would be likely to cause a plaintiff to choose the federal court.

[10] See Guaranty Trust Co. v. York, supra, 326 U.S. at 108–109, 65 S.Ct. at 1469; Ragan v. Merchants Transfer Co., supra, 337 U.S. at 532, 69 S.Ct. at 1234; Woods v. Interstate Realty Co., supra, note 5, 337 U.S. at 538, 69 S.Ct. at 1237.

Similarly, a federal court's refusal to enforce the New Jersey rule involved in Cohen v. Beneficial Loan Corp., 337 U.S. 541, 69 S.Ct. 1221, requiring the posting

of security by plaintiffs in stockholders' derivative actions, might well impel a stockholder to choose to bring suit in the federal, rather than the state, court.

[11] Cf. Monarch Insurance Co. of Ohio v. Spach, 281 F.2d 401, 412 (C.A.5th Cir. 1960). We cannot seriously entertain the thought that one suing an estate would be led to choose the federal court because of a belief that adherence to Rule 4(d)(1) is less likely to give the executor actual notice than § 9, and therefore more likely to produce a default judgment. Rule 4(d)(1) is well designed to give actual notice, as it did in this case. See note 1, supra.

eral Rule which covered the point in dispute, Erie commanded the enforcement of state law.

"Respondent contends, in the first place, that the charge was correct because of the fact that Rule 8(c) of the Rules of Civil Procedure makes contributory negligence an affirmative defense. We do not agree. Rule 8(c) covers only the manner of pleading. The question of the burden of establishing contributory negligence is a question of local law which federal courts in diversity of citizenship cases (Erie R. Co. v. Tompkins, 304 U.S. 64, 58 S.Ct. 817) must apply." Palmer v. Hoffman, 318 U.S. 109, 117, 63 S.Ct. 477, 482.[12]

(Here, of course, the clash is unavoidable; Rule 4(d)(1) says—implicitly, but with unmistakable clarity—that in-hand service is not required in federal courts.) At the same time, in cases adjudicating the validity of Federal Rules, we have not applied the York rule or other refinements of Erie, but have to this day continued to decide questions concerning the scope of the Enabling Act and the constitutionality of specific Federal Rules in light of the distinction set forth in Sibbach. E.g., Schlagenhauf v. Holder, 379 U.S. 104, 85 S.Ct. 234.

Nor has the development of two separate lines of cases been inadvertent. The line between "substance" and "procedure" shifts as the legal context changes. "Each implies different variables depending upon the particular problem for which it is used." Guaranty Trust Co. v. York, supra, 326 U.S. at 108, 65 S.Ct. at 1469; Cook, The Logical and Legal Bases of the Conflict of Laws, pp. 154–183 (1942). It is true that both the Enabling Act and the Erie rule say, roughly, that federal courts are to apply state "substantive" law and federal "procedural" law, but from that it need not follow that the tests are identical. For they were designed to control very different sorts of decisions. When a situation is covered by one of the Federal Rules, the question facing the court is a far cry from the typical, relatively unguided Erie choice: the court has been instructed to apply the Federal Rule, and can refuse to do so only if the Advisory Committee, this Court, and Congress erred in their prima facie judgment that the Rule in question transgresses neither the terms of the Enabling Act nor constitutional restrictions.

We are reminded by the Erie opinion[14] that neither Congress nor the federal courts can, under the guise of formulating rules of decision for federal courts, fashion rules which are not supported by a

[12] To the same effect, see Ragan v. Merchants Transfer Co., supra; Cohen v. Beneficial Loan Corp., supra, note 10, 337 U.S. at 556, 69 S.Ct. at 1230; id., at 557, 69 S.Ct. at 1230 (Douglas, J., dissenting); cf. Bernhardt v. Polygraphic Co., supra, note 5, 350 U.S. at 201–202, 76 S.Ct. at 275; see generally Iovino v. Waterson, [274 F.2d 41, 47–48 (2d Cir. 1959), cert. denied, 362 U.S. 949, 80 S.Ct. 860 (1960)].

[14] Erie R. Co. v. Tompkins, supra, 304 U.S. at 77–79, 58 S.Ct. at 822–823; cf. Bernhardt v. Polygraphic Co., supra, note 5, 350 U.S. at 202, 76 S.Ct. at 275; Sibbach v. Wilson & Co., supra, 312 U.S. at 10, 61 S.Ct. at 424; Guaranty Trust Co. v. York, supra, 326 U.S. at 105, 65 S.Ct. at 1467.

grant of federal authority contained in Article I or some other section of the Constitution; in such areas state law must govern because there can be no other law. But the opinion in Erie, which involved no Federal Rule and dealt with a question which was "substantive" in every traditional sense (whether the railroad owed a duty of care to Tompkins as a trespasser or a licensee), surely neither said nor implied that measures like Rule 4(d)(1) are unconstitutional. For the constitutional provision for a federal court system (augmented by the Necessary and Proper Clause) carries with it congressional power to make rules governing the practice and pleading in those courts, which in turn includes a power to regulate matters which, though falling within the uncertain area between substance and procedure, are rationally capable of classification as either. Cf. M'Culloch v. Maryland, 4 Wheat. 316, 421. Neither York nor the cases following it ever suggested that the rule there laid down for coping with situations where no Federal Rule applies is coextensive with the limitation on Congress to which Erie had adverted. Although this Court has never before been confronted with a case where the applicable Federal Rule is in direct collision with the law of the relevant State,[15] courts of appeals faced with such clashes have rightly discerned the implications of our decisions.

> "One of the shaping purposes of the Federal Rules is to bring about uniformity in the federal courts by getting away from local rules. This is especially true of matters which relate to the administration of legal proceedings, an area in which federal courts have traditionally exerted strong inherent power, completely aside from the powers Congress expressly conferred in the Rules. The purpose of the Erie doctrine, even as extended in York and Ragan, was never to bottle up federal courts with 'outcome-determinative' and 'integral-relations' stoppers—when there are 'affirmative countervailing [federal] considerations' and when there is a Congressional mandate (the Rules) supported by constitutional authority." Lumbermen's Mutual Casualty Co. v. Wright, 322 F.2d 759, 764 (C.A.5th Cir. 1963).

Erie and its offspring cast no doubt on the long-recognized power of Congress to prescribe housekeeping rules for federal courts even though some of those rules will inevitably differ from comparable state rules. Cf. Herron v. Southern Pacific Co., 283 U.S. 91, 51 S.Ct. 383. "When, because the plaintiff happens to be a non-resident, such a right is enforceable in a federal as well as in a State court, the forms and mode of enforcing the right may at times, naturally

---

[15] In Sibbach v. Wilson & Co., supra, the law of the forum State (Illinois) forbade the sort of order authorized by Rule 35. However, Sibbach was decided before Klaxon Co. v. Stentor Co., supra, note 7, and the Sibbach opinion makes clear that the Court was proceeding on the assumption that if the law of any State was relevant, it was the law of the State where the tort occurred (Indiana), which, like Rule 35, made provision for such orders. 312 U.S. at 6–7, 10–11, 61 S.Ct. at 423, 424–425.

enough, vary because the two judicial systems are not identic."
Guaranty Trust Co. v. York, supra, 326 U.S. at 108, 65 S.Ct. at 1469;
Cohen v. Beneficial Loan Corp., 337 U.S. 541, 555, 69 S.Ct. 1221, 1229.
Thus, though a court, in measuring a Federal Rule against the standards contained in the Enabling Act and the Constitution, need not
wholly blind itself to the degree to which the Rule makes the character and result of the federal litigation stray from the course it would
follow in state courts, Sibbach v. Wilson & Co., supra, 312 U.S. at 13–
14, 61 S.Ct. at 426–427, it cannot be forgotten that the Erie rule, and
the guidelines suggested in York, were created to serve another purpose altogether. To hold that a Federal Rule of Civil Procedure must
cease to function whenever it alters the mode of enforcing state-created rights would be to disembowel either the Constitution's grant of
power over federal procedure or Congress' attempt to exercise that
power in the Enabling Act. Rule 4(d)(1) is valid and controls the instant case.

Reversed.

MR. JUSTICE BLACK concurs in the result.

MR. JUSTICE HARLAN, concurring.

It is unquestionably true that up to now Erie and the cases following it have not succeeded in articulating a workable doctrine governing choice of law in diversity actions. I respect the Court's effort
to clarify the situation in today's opinion. However, in doing so I
think it has misconceived the constitutional premises of Erie and has
failed to deal adequately with those past decisions upon which the
courts below relied.

Erie was something more than an opinion which worried about
"forum-shopping and avoidance of inequitable administration of the
laws," ante, . . .   although to be sure these were important elements of the decision. I have always regarded that decision as one of
the modern cornerstones of our federalism, expressing policies that
profoundly touch the allocation of judicial power between the state
and federal systems. Erie recognized that there should not be two
conflicting systems of law controlling the primary activity of citizens,
for such alternative governing authority must necessarily give rise to
a debilitating uncertainty in the planning of everyday affairs.[1] And
it recognized that the scheme of our Constitution envisions an allocation of law-making functions between state and federal legislative
processes which is undercut if the federal judiciary can make substantive law affecting state affairs beyond the bounds of congressional legislative powers in this regard. Thus, in diversity cases Erie
commands that it be the state law governing primary private activity
which prevails.

[1] Since the rules involved in the present
case are parallel rather than conflicting,
this first rationale does not come into
play here.

The shorthand formulations which have appeared in some past decisions are prone to carry untoward results that frequently arise from oversimplification. The Court is quite right in stating that the "outcome-determinative" test of Guaranty Trust Co. v. York, 326 U.S. 99, 65 S.Ct. 1464, if taken literally, proves too much, for any rule, no matter how clearly "procedural," can affect the outcome of litigation if it is not obeyed. In turning from the "outcome" test of York back to the unadorned forum-shopping rationale of Erie, however, the Court falls prey to like oversimplification, for a simple forum-shopping rule also proves too much; litigants often choose a federal forum merely to obtain what they consider the advantages of the Federal Rules of Civil Procedure or to try their cases before a supposedly more favorable judge. To my mind the proper line of approach in determining whether to apply a state or a federal rule, whether "substantive" or "procedural," is to stay close to basic principles by inquiring if the choice of rule would substantially affect those primary decisions respecting human conduct which our constitutional system leaves to state regulation.[2] If so, Erie and the Constitution require that the state rule prevail, even in the face of a conflicting federal rule.

primary decisions of human conduct

The Court weakens, if indeed it does not submerge, this basic principle by finding, in effect, a grant of substantive legislative power in the constitutional provision for a federal court system (compare Swift v. Tyson, 16 Pet. 1), and through it, setting up the Federal Rules as a body of law inviolate.

> "[T]he constitutional provision for a federal court system . . . carries with it congressional power . . . to regulate matters which, though falling within the uncertain area between substance and procedure, are *rationally capable of classification as either.*" Ante, ... (Emphasis supplied.)

So long as a reasonable man could characterize any duly adopted federal rule as "procedural," the Court, unless I misapprehend what is said, would have it apply no matter how seriously it frustrated a State's substantive regulation of the primary conduct and affairs of its citizens. Since the members of the Advisory Committee, the Judicial Conference, and this Court who formulated the Federal Rules are presumably reasonable men, it follows that the integrity of the Federal Rules is absolute. Whereas the unadulterated outcome and forum-shopping tests may err too far toward honoring state rules, I submit that the Court's "arguably procedural, ergo constitutional" test moves too fast and far in the other direction.

---

[2] See Hart and Wechsler, The Federal Courts and the Federal System 678.

Byrd v. Blue Ridge Coop., Inc., 356 U.S. 525, 536–540, 78 S.Ct. 893, 900–902, indicated that State procedures would apply if the State had manifested a particularly strong interest in their employment. Compare Dice v. Akron, C. & Y.R. Co., 342 U.S. 359, 72 S.Ct. 312. However, this approach may not be of constitutional proportions.

The courts below relied upon this Court's decisions in Ragan v. Merchants Transfer Co., 337 U.S. 530, 69 S.Ct. 1233, and Cohen v. Beneficial Loan Corp., 337 U.S. 541, 69 S.Ct. 1221. Those cases deserve more attention than this Court has given them, particularly Ragan which, if still good law, would in my opinion call for affirmance of the result reached by the Court of Appeals. Further, a discussion of these two cases will serve to illuminate the "diversity" thesis I am advocating.

In Ragan a Kansas statute of limitations provided that an action was deemed commenced when service was made on the defendant. Despite Federal Rule 3 which provides that an action commences with the filing of the complaint, the Court held that for purposes of the Kansas statute of limitations a diversity tort action commenced only when service was made upon the defendant. The effect of this holding was that although the plaintiff had filed his federal complaint within the state period of limitations, his action was barred because the federal marshal did not serve a summons on the defendant until after the limitations period had run. I think that the decision was wrong. At most, application of the Federal Rule would have meant that potential Kansas tort defendants would have to defer for a few days the satisfaction of knowing that they had not been sued within the limitations period. The choice of the Federal Rule would have had no effect on the primary stages of private activity from which torts arise, and only the most minimal effect on behavior following the commission of the tort. In such circumstances the interest of the federal system in proceeding under its own rules should have prevailed.

Cohen v. Beneficial Loan Corp. held that a federal diversity court must apply a state statute requiring a small stockholder in a stockholder derivative suit to post a bond securing payment of defense costs as a condition to prosecuting an action. Such a statute is not "outcome determinative"; the plaintiff can win with or without it. The Court now rationalizes the case on the ground that the statute might affect the plaintiff's choice of forum (ante, . . . n. 10), but as has been pointed out, a simple forum-shopping test proves too much. The proper view of Cohen is, in my opinion, that the statute was meant to inhibit small stockholders from instituting "strike suits," and thus it was designed and could be expected to have a substantial impact on private primary activity. Anyone who was at the trial bar during the period when Cohen arose can appreciate the strong state policy reflected in the statute. I think it wholly legitimate to view Federal Rule [23.1] as not purporting to deal with the problem. But even had the Federal Rules purported to do so, and in so doing provided a substantially less effective deterrent to strike suits, I think the state rule should still have prevailed. That is where I believe the Court's view differs from mine; for the Court attributes such overriding force to the Federal Rules that it is hard to think of a case where a conflicting state rule would be allowed to operate, even though the state rule reflected policy considerations which, under Erie, would lie within the realm of state legislative authority.

It remains to apply what has been said to the present case. The Massachusetts rule provides that an executor need not answer suits unless in-hand service was made upon him or notice of the action was filed in the proper registry of probate within one year of his giving bond. The evident intent of this statute is to permit an executor to distribute the estate which he is administering without fear that further liabilities may be outstanding for which he could be held personally liable. If the Federal District Court in Massachusetts applies Rule 4(d)(1) of the Federal Rules of Civil Procedure instead of the Massachusetts service rule, what effect would that have on the speed and assurance with which estates are distributed? As I see it, the effect would not be substantial. It would mean simply that an executor would have to check at his own house or the federal courthouse as well as the registry of probate before he could distribute the estate with impunity. As this does not seem enough to give rise to any real impingement on the vitality of the state policy which the Massachusetts rule is intended to serve, I concur in the judgment of the Court.

Question: (7) Consider once again Woods v. Interstate Realty Co. Would you expect its result to be affected by Hanna? What of Rule 17(b)? See 6 Wright & Miller § 1569. Assuming that Rule 17(b) does not extend to the situation in Woods (as the Supreme Court apparently assumed, knowingly or unknowingly, when it decided Woods itself, and also when it referred to Woods in Hanna), then reference must be made not to the portion of Hanna that deals with the applicability of the Federal Rules but rather to the discussion in Hanna of the more general Erie problem. So, under Hanna's refined "outcome-determinative" test, was Woods rightly decided?

SZANTAY v. BEECH AIRCRAFT CORP., 349 F.2d 60 (4th Cir. 1965). Szantay bought a Beech aircraft in Nebraska and flew it to Florida and thence to South Carolina, where it was serviced by Dixie Aviation Co. during a brief stopover. Szantay and his passengers then left for Illinois, where they lived, but the plane crashed in Tennessee, killing all its occupants. The Illinois personal representatives of the decedents each brought a diversity action in a federal district court in South Carolina against Beech and Dixie, alleging negligent design and manufacture on the part of Beech and negligent servicing by Dixie. The requirements for diversity jurisdiction were satisfied, as Beech was a Delaware corporation with its principal place of business in Kansas, Dixie was a South Carolina corporation doing business only in that state, and the amount in controversy exceeded $10,000. By virtue of Beech's doing business in South Carolina, venue requirements were met and in-state service of process was properly effected.

Beech moved to dismiss the actions on the ground that a South Carolina "door-closing" statute provided that a foreign corporation could be sued in a South Carolina court only by (1) any South Carolina resident for any cause of action or (2) a nonresident plaintiff when the cause of action arose in South Carolina. It was conceded that a South Carolina state court could not entertain a suit brought by a nonresident against a foreign corporation on a foreign cause of action. Beech maintained that this statute should likewise bar suit in federal court. The motion to dismiss was denied, and Beech was granted an interlocutory appeal pursuant to 28 U.S.C. § 1292(b).

Judge Sobeloff, in a unanimous opinion for the court of appeals, began by discussing prior decisions, including the Erie, Guaranty Trust, Woods, Byrd, and Hanna cases. He generalized:

"The spirit of these decisions makes it appropriate for a court attempting to resolve a federal-state conflict in a diversity case to undertake the following analysis:

1. If the state provision, whether legislatively adopted or judicially declared, is the substantive right or obligation at issue, it is constitutionally controlling.

2. If the state provision is a procedure intimately bound up with the state right or obligation, it is likewise constitutionally controlling.[5]

3. If the state procedural provision is not intimately bound up with the right being enforced but its application would substantially affect the outcome of the litigation, the federal diversity court must still apply it unless there are affirmative countervailing federal considerations. This is not deemed a constitutional requirement but one dictated by comity."

Deciding that the case before it fell into the third category, the court proceeded with the necessary further analysis.

The court first considered the outcome-determinative factor. Rejection of the South Carolina statute in the federal court would apparently have a forum-shopping effect. However, rejection of state law would not result in discrimination against South Carolina residents; indeed, such rejection would do no more than give to nonresidents what residents enjoyed anyway, viz., a South Carolina forum for a case such as this one.

The court next explored the state policies underlying the door-closing statute. Faced with a total absence of legislative history and prior judicial discussion, the court concluded that the state interests were uncertain and that the conceivable ones appeared weak. Among other possibilities, the statute could be viewed as a formulation of the doctrine of forum non coveniens or as a measure to relieve

[5] [In a footnote here the court gave Cohen, Ragan, and Guaranty Trust as examples.]

state docket congestion, but such interests would be irrelevant for Erie purposes "since federal cognizance of the case would in no way frustrate state policy."

The court then found "[t]he countervailing federal considerations [to be] explicit, and they are numerous." The list included: (1) avoidance of discrimination against nonresidents, the very purpose of the diversity clause itself; (2) maximum enforcement in each state of the rights and duties created by sister states, the consideration underlying the full faith and credit clause; (3) the policy that a federal court sitting in diversity should hear and adjudicate the issues before it, citing Meredith v. Winter Haven, 320 U.S. 228, 64 S.Ct. 7 (1943); (4) encouragement of efficient joinder in multi-party actions, which interest was threatened because Dixie could be served only in South Carolina; and (5) the interest in providing a convenient forum for federal litigants.

After a final word distinguishing Woods, the court of appeals affirmed the decision below.

————

Question: (8) Reexamine Blair v. Durham, supra p. 53. Assume that a Tennessee state court would not allow the amendment of the complaint to relate back for the purposes of the Tennessee statute of limitations. What decision would you expect in the federal court after Guaranty Trust but before Byrd? after Byrd but before Hanna? after Hanna? See Welch v. Louisiana Power & Light Co., 466 F.2d 1344, 1345–46 (5th Cir.1972) (federal law controls).

————

MARSHALL v. MULRENIN, 508 F.2d 39 (1st Cir.1974). Mrs. Marshall was injured in a fall occurring on certain business premises located in Massachusetts. Mr. and Mrs. Marshall consequently brought this diversity action in the District of Massachusetts against Mr. and Mrs. Kirk, whose names appeared, as the people conducting the business, on a certificate filed in accordance with law. However, several years before the accident the Kirks had conveyed the premises to Mr. and Mrs. Mulrenin, who continued the business operation; but neither the Kirks nor the Mulrenins had changed the certificate.

After the Massachusetts statute of limitations had run, the plaintiffs learned the true facts as to ownership and then sought to amend by substituting the Mulrenins for the Kirks as defendants. Because of lack of timely notice to the Mulrenins, Federal Rule 15(c) apparently would not allow relation back and would thus bar suit. A more permissive Massachusetts statute, which required no such notice to new defendants, would relate the amendment back and would thus permit the suit to proceed. The district court, following Hanna, applied Rule 15(c) and held the amendment ineffective.

The court of appeals unanimously reversed, ruling that Hanna did not require application of the Federal Rule and that instead the Massachusetts statute should apply to permit the amendment to relate back. Judge Aldrich, for the court of appeals, wrote that Hanna stated only "a principle for resolving a direct conflict between two strictly procedural rules" and that Hanna did not dictate "that the Federal Rules be woodenly applied irrespective of a discoverable substantive, as distinguished from a merely procedural, state purpose." Looking at the federal interests behind the Federal Rule in question (what are those interests and how strong are they in the context of this case?), the "state purpose" behind its statute (what are those state interests and how strong are they?), and the outcome-determinative effect (how strong is this factor here?), he concluded that the latter two variables overcame any federal interests at stake. Therefore, this state law should apply in this federal case.

DAY & ZIMMERMANN, INC. v. CHALLONER, 423 U.S. 3, 96 S.Ct. 167 (1975). In May of 1970, in the midst of combat in Cambodia between American and North Vietnamese forces, a 105 mm. howitzer round prematurely exploded in the gun's barrel. The blast killed one of the gun's operators, a soldier named Daniel Nelms from Tennessee. Another soldier, Hawley Challoner of Wisconsin, was seriously wounded. The round had been manufactured in Texas by Day & Zimmermann, incorporated in Maryland with its principal place of business in Pennsylvania. A diversity action was brought by Nelms's parents and Challoner against the manufacturer in the United States District Court for the Eastern District of Texas.

The district judge submitted the case to the jury under the strict liability principles of Texas law, and sizable verdicts were returned for the plaintiffs. On appeal, the defendant contended that Klaxon compelled the district court to apply the Texas conflict-of-laws rule and that, because Texas had a law-of-the-place-of-the-injury rule and because Cambodian law required proof of fault, the judgment based on a strict liability standard had to be reversed. The court of appeals nevertheless affirmed, 512 F.2d 77 (5th Cir.1975).

The court of appeals began by acknowledging that Klaxon "held, as a general rule," that the conflict-of-laws rules of the forum state apply in diversity cases. The court next conceded that a Texas state court would certainly look to Cambodian tort law in the wrongful-death action, and perhaps in the personal-injury action as well. Yet the Fifth Circuit went on to hold that a federal court in this situation could make an independent choice of law, thus permitting the district court here to look to the tort law of Texas rather than that of Cambodia.

The reasoning of the court of appeals in support of its assumed power to apply a federal conflict-of-laws rule was somewhat obscure. Yet its approach was unmistakably ad hoc, with the court weighing the federal interests at stake in this particular case against the forum state's interests in having its conflict-of-laws rule applied in this federal case. The federal interests predominated, and hence federal law was applied.

In a per curiam opinion, the Supreme Court ruled:

"The Court of Appeals .   .   .   supported its decision on the grounds that the rationale for applying the traditional conflicts rule applied by Texas 'is not operative under the present facts'; and that it was 'a Court of the United States, an instrumentality created to effectuate the laws and policies of the United States.'

"We believe that the Court of Appeals either misinterpreted our longstanding decision in Klaxon Co. v. Stentor Electric Mfg. Co., 313 U.S. 487, 61 S.Ct. 1020 (1941), or else determined for itself that it was no longer of controlling force in a case such as this. We are of the opinion that Klaxon is by its terms applicable here and should have been adhered to by the Court of Appeals. In Klaxon, supra, at 496, 61 S.Ct., at 1021, this Court said:

'The conflict of laws rules to be applied by the federal court in Delaware must conform to those prevailing in Delaware's state courts. Otherwise, the accident of diversity of citizenship would constantly disturb equal administration of justice in coordinate state and federal courts sitting side by side. See Erie R. Co. v. Tompkins . . . .'

"By parity of reasoning, the conflict-of-laws rules to be applied by a federal court in Texas must conform to those prevailing in the Texas state courts. A federal court in a diversity case is not free to engraft onto those state rules exceptions or modifications which may commend themselves to the federal court, but which have not commended themselves to the State in which the federal court sits. The Court of Appeals in this case should identify and follow the Texas conflicts rule. What substantive law will govern when Texas' rule is applied is a matter to be determined by the Court of Appeals.

"The petition for certiorari is granted, the judgment of the Court of Appeals is vacated, and the case is remanded for further proceedings in conformity with this opinion."

Questions: (9) Does the Court's approach in Day & Zimmermann call into question the result in Marshall v. Mulrenin? See Britt v. Arvanitis, 590 F.2d 57, 60–61 (3d Cir.1978) (federal law controls).

(10) On the question of whether a supplemental pleading under Rule 15(d) relates back, does federal law or a more restrictive state provision govern? See Davis v. Piper Aircraft Corp., 615 F.2d 606, 611–12 (4th Cir.) (federal law controls), cert. dismissed, 448 U.S. 911, 101 S.Ct. 25 (1980). Which branch of Hanna is relevant: the branch interpreting Erie or the branch interpreting Sibbach?

WALKER v. ARMCO STEEL CORP., 446 U.S. 740, 100 S.Ct. 1978 (1980). This case from the United States District Court for the Western District of Oklahoma presented anew, on similar facts, the legal issue of Ragan v. Merchants Transfer & Warehouse Co. The district court and the Tenth Circuit barred suit by following Ragan, but the Supreme Court granted certiorari to resolve a conflict among the circuits. Justice Marshall, writing for a unanimous Supreme Court, ruled:

"The present case is indistinguishable from Ragan. The statutes in both cases require service of process to toll the statute of limitations, and in fact the predecessor to the Oklahoma statute in this case was derived from the predecessor to the Kansas statute in Ragan. See Dr. Koch Vegetable Tea Co. v. Davis, 48 Okl. 14, 22, 145 P. 337, 340 (1914). Here as in Ragan the complaint was filed in federal court under diversity jurisdiction within the two-year statute of limitations, but service of process did not occur until after the two-year period . . . had run. In both cases the suit would concededly have been barred in the applicable state court, and in both instances the state service statute was held to be an integral part of the statute of limitations by the lower court more familiar than we with state law. Accordingly, as the Court of Appeals held below, the instant action is barred by the statute of limitations unless Ragan is no longer good law.

"Petitioner argues that the analysis and holding of Ragan did not survive our decision in Hanna [v. Plumer, 380 U.S. 460, 85 S.Ct. 1136 (1965)]. Petitioner's position is that Okla.Stat., Tit. 12, § 97 (1971) is in direct conflict with the federal rule. Under Hanna, petitioner contends, the appropriate question is whether Rule 3 is within the scope of the Rules Enabling Act and, if so, within the constitutional power of Congress. In petitioner's view, the federal rule is to be applied unless it violates one of those two restrictions. This argument ignores both the force of stare decisis and the specific limitations that we carefully placed on the Hanna analysis.

"We note at the outset that the doctrine of stare decisis weighs heavily against petitioner in this case. Petitioner seeks to have us overrule our decision in Ragan. Stare decisis does not mandate that earlier decisions be enshrined forever, of course, but it does counsel that we use caution in rejecting established law. In this case, the reasons petitioner asserts for overruling Ragan are the same factors which we concluded in Hanna did not undermine the validity of Ragan. A litigant who in effect asks us to reconsider not one but two prior decisions bears a heavy burden of supporting such a change in our jurisprudence. Petitioner here has not met that burden.

"This Court in Hanna distinguished Ragan rather than overruled it, and for good reason. Application of the Hanna analysis is premised on a 'direct collision' between the federal rule and the state law. 380 U.S., at 472, 85 S.Ct., at 1143. In Hanna itself the 'clash' between Rule 4(d)(1) and the state in-hand service requirement was 'unavoidable.' Id., at 470, 85 S.Ct., at 1143. The first question must therefore be whether the scope of the federal rule in fact is suffi-ciently broad to control the issue before the Court. It is only if that question is answered affirmatively that the Hanna analysis applies.[9]

" . . . [W]e recognized in Hanna that the present case is an instance where 'the scope of the Federal Rule [is] not as broad as the losing party urge[s], and therefore, there being no Federal Rule which cover[s] the point in dispute, Erie command[s] the enforcement of state law.' Ibid. Rule 3 simply states that '[a] civil action is com-menced by filing a complaint with the court.' There is no indication that the Rule was intended to toll a state statute of limitations,[10] much less that it purported to displace state tolling rules for purposes of state statutes of limitations. In our view, in diversity actions [11] Rule 3 governs the date from which various timing requirements of the federal rules begin to run, but does not affect state statutes of limitations. Cf. 4 C. Wright & A. Miller, Federal Practice and Proce-dure, § 1057, at 190–191 (1969); id., § 1051, at 165–166.

"In contrast to Rule 3, the Oklahoma statute is a statement of a substantive decision by that State that actual service on, and accord-ingly actual notice by, the defendant is an integral part of the several policies served by the statute of limitations. See C & C Tile Co. v.

[9] This is not to suggest that the Feder-al Rules of Civil Procedure are to be nar-rowly construed in order to avoid a 'di-rect collision' with state law. The Federal Rules should be given their plain meaning. If a direct collision with state law arises from that plain meaning, then the analysis developed in Hanna v. Plumer applies.

[10] 'Rule 3 simply provides that an ac-tion is commenced by filing the complaint and has as its primary purpose the mea-suring of time periods that begin running from the date of commencement; the rule does not state that filing tolls the statute of limitations.' 4 C. Wright & A. Miller, Federal Practice and Procedure, § 1057, at 191 (1969) (footnote omitted).

The Note of the Advisory Committee on the Rules states that

'[w]hen a Federal or State statute of limi-tations is pleaded as a defense, a ques-tion may arise under this rule whether the mere filing of the complaint stops the running of the statute, or whether any further step is required, such as, service of the summons and complaint or their delivery to the marshal for service. The answer to this question may depend on whether it is competent for the Supreme Court, exercising the power to make rules of procedure without affecting sub-stantive rights, to vary the operation of statutes of limitations. The requirement

of Rule 4(a) that the clerk shall forthwith issue the summons and deliver it to the marshal for service will reduce the chances of such a question arising.' 28 U.S.C.App., pp. 394–395.

This Note establishes that the Adviso-ry Committee predicted the problem which arose in Ragan and arises again in the instant case. It does not indicate, however, that Rule 3 was *intended* to serve as a tolling provision for statute of limitations purposes; it only suggests that the Advisory Committee thought the Rule *might* have that effect.

[11] The Court suggested in Ragan that in suits to enforce rights under a federal statute Rule 3 means that filing of the complaint tolls the applicable statute of limitations. 337 U.S., at 533, 69 S.Ct., at 1234, distinguishing Bomar v. Keyes, 162 F.2d 136, 140–141 (CA2), cert. denied, 332 U.S. 825, 68 S.Ct. 166 (1947). See Ely, The Irrepressible Myth of Erie, 87 Harv. L.Rev. 693, 729 (1974). See also Walko Corp. v. Burger Chef Systems, Inc., 180 U.S.App.D.C. 306, 308, n. 19, 554 F.2d 1165, 1167, n. 19 (1977); 4 C. Wright & A. Miller, supra, § 1056, and authorities col-lected therein. We do not here address the role of Rule 3 as a tolling provision for a statute of limitations, whether set by federal law or borrowed from state law, if the cause of action is based on federal law.

[margin note: Policy aspects of state law]

Independent School District No. 7 of Tulsa County, 503 P.2d 554, 559 (Okl.1972). The statute of limitations establishes a deadline after which the defendant may legitimately have peace of mind; it also recognizes that after a certain period of time it is unfair to require the defendant to attempt to piece together his defense to an old claim. A requirement of actual service promotes both of those functions of the statute. See generally ibid.; Seitz v. Jones, 370 P.2d 300, 302 (Okl.1961). See also Ely, The Irrepressible Myth of Erie, 87 Harv.L. Rev. 693, 730–731 (1974). It is these policy aspects which make the service requirement an 'integral' part of the statute of limitations both in this case and in Ragan. As such, the service rule must be considered part and parcel of the statute of limitations.[13] Rule 3 does not replace such policy determinations found in state law. Rule 3 and Okla.Stat., Tit. 12, § 97 (1971) can exist side-by-side, therefore, each controlling its own intended sphere of coverage without conflict.

[margin note: Policy makes rule subst.]

[margin note: R3 & state does so be not of "direct collision"]

[margin note: .. Hanna doesn't apply]

"Since there is no direct conflict between the federal rule and the state law, the Hanna analysis does not apply. Instead, the policies behind Erie and Ragan control the issue whether, in the absence of a federal rule directly on point, state service requirements which are an integral part of the state statute of limitations should control in an action based on state law which is filed in federal court under diversity jurisdiction. The reasons for the application of such a state service requirement in a diversity action in the absence of a conflicting federal rule are well explained in Erie and Ragan . . . and need not be repeated here. It is sufficient to note that although in this case failure to apply the state service law might not create any problem of forum shopping,[15] the result would be an 'inequitable administration' of the law. Hanna v. Plumer, supra, 380 U.S., at 468, 85 S.Ct., at 1142. There is simply no reason why, in the absence of a controlling federal rule, an action based on state law which concededly would be barred in the state courts by the state statute of limitations should proceed through litigation to judgment in federal court solely because of the fortuity that there is diversity of citizenship between the litigants. The policies underlying diversity jurisdiction do not support such a distinction between state and federal plaintiffs, and Erie and its progeny do not permit it.

[margin note: State law applies b/c inequit. appl. of law]

[margin note: inequit. law]

[13] The substantive link of § 97 to the statute of limitations is made clear as well by another provision of Oklahoma law. Under Okla.Stat., Tit. 12, § 151 (1971), '[a] civil action is deemed commenced by filing in the office of the court clerk of the proper court a petition and by the clerk's issuance of summons thereon.' This is the state law corollary to Rule 3. However, § 97, not § 151, controls the commencement of the lawsuit for statute of limitations purposes. See Tyler v. Taylor, 578 P.2d 1214 (Okl. App.1977). Just as § 97 and § 151 can both apply in state court for their separate purposes, so too § 97 and Rule 3 may both apply in federal court in a diversity action.

[15] There is no indication that when petitioner filed his suit in federal court he had any reason to believe that he would be unable to comply with the service requirements of Oklahoma law or that he chose to sue in federal court in an attempt to avoid those service requirements.

"The judgment of the Court of Appeals is affirmed."

MASINO v. OUTBOARD MARINE CORP.

United States Court of Appeals, Third Circuit, 1981.
652 F.2d 330, cert. denied, 454 U.S. 1055, 102 S.Ct. 601 (1981).

Before ALDISERT, WEIS and SLOVITER, CIRCUIT JUDGES.

ALDISERT, CIRCUIT JUDGE.

The question presented by this appeal from a unanimous jury verdict for the defendant in a diversity of citizenship case is whether the district court sitting in the Eastern District of Pennsylvania erred in refusing to apply a Pennsylvania statute providing that a civil jury vote of five-sixths suffices for entry of judgment. The district court reasoned, inter alia, that the long-standing federal policy favoring unanimous civil jury verdicts compelled application of the unanimity rule in this case. Masino v. Outboard Marine Corp., 88 F.R.D. 251 (E.D.Pa.1980). We agree and accordingly affirm.

Gerald and Sheila Masino, appellants, initiated this diversity action alleging that appellee had manufactured and sold a defective lawnmower that had injured Mrs. Masino. The case was tried to a jury of eight persons pursuant to the local rules of the Eastern District of Pennsylvania, and counsel for appellants requested a charge based on Pa.Cons.Stat.Ann. tit. 42, § 5104(b) (Purdon Supp.1980): "In any civil case a verdict rendered by at least five-sixths of the jury shall be the verdict of the jury and shall have the same effect as a unanimous verdict of the jury." The trial judge refused the instruction, and the jury returned a unanimous verdict for appellee.

Although federal courts sitting in diversity actions must usually apply the substantive law of the forum state, the same principle does not apply with equal force to procedural rules. The line of demarcation between "substantive" rules and "procedural" rules, however, is often blurred, and the Supreme Court has cautioned that the line "shifts as the legal context changes." Hanna v. Plumer, 380 U.S. 460, 471, 85 S.Ct. 1136, 1143, 14 L.Ed.2d 8 (1965). One test for determining whether a federal or state rule should be applied is the "outcome determinative" test, but the Supreme Court has warned against its mechanical application. Byrd v. Blue Ridge Electric Cooperative, Inc., 356 U.S. 525, 537–38, 78 S.Ct. 893, 900–01, 2 L.Ed.2d 953 (1958); see also Hanna, 380 U.S. at 467, 85 S.Ct. at 1141. Recognizing the complexity of the inquiry, this court has eschewed reliance on "litmus paper" tests, and has instead examined the choice of law question in light of the policies underlying the doctrine developed from Erie R.R. v. Tompkins, 304 U.S. 64, 58 S.Ct. 817, 82 L.Ed. 1188 (1938). See, e.g., Edelson v. Soricelli, 610 F.2d 131, 141 (3d Cir.1979); Witherow v. Firestone Tire & Rubber Co., 530 F.2d 160, 163 (3d Cir.1976).

In Edelson v. Soricelli and Stoner v. Presbyterian University Hospital, 609 F.2d 109 (3d Cir.1979), we held that Pennsylvania's requirement that medical malpractice claims be arbitrated before judicial resolution binds federal courts in diversity actions. We characterized the arbitration requirement as "a condition precedent to entry into the state judicial system," Edelson, 610 F.2d at 134, and we recognized the advantage that would have resulted to federal plaintiffs if federal courts did not enforce the precondition, id. at 141. We noted that the arbitration requirement did not affect the trial of the federal action once the case ripened for trial, but merely regulated the time at which trial could occur. See generally Edelson, 610 F.2d at 134–35, 141.

In contrast, the five-sixths majority verdict statute does affect the way the trial is conducted, and in this fundamental respect this case differs from Edelson and Stoner. We therefore believe the proper analysis of this question may be derived from Byrd v. Blue Ridge Electric Cooperative, Inc. In Byrd, the Court held that the determination of employee status for purposes of South Carolina's Workmen's Compensation Act must be submitted to the jury in a federal diversity action even though South Carolina courts would leave that issue to the trial judge. Edelson isolated three premises underlying the Byrd decision: the lack of a strong and explicit state policy justifying the removal of this discrete factual determination from the jury; the federal interest in insuring access by litigants in federal courts to a jury; and the continuing viability of the outcome determinative analysis of Guaranty Trust Co. v. York, 326 U.S. 99, 65 S.Ct. 1464, 89 L.Ed. 2079 (1945). See Edelson, 610 F.2d at 138–40. Although Edelson concluded that these three premises would be served better by applying the state requirement of arbitration of medical malpractice claims as a precondition to suit in federal court, we conclude that the federal requirement of jury unanimity is the appropriate rule in the present case.[2]

The single apparent state interest in application of a five-sixths majority rule is greater efficiency of judicial administration by reducing the number of deadlocked juries. Pennsylvania has no concern, however, with the administration of the federal judicial system. Indeed, we noted in Edelson that Byrd "implicates no more than trial management in federal courts . . . ." 610 F.2d at 141. Because trial management in the federal courts is a weighty concern of the federal judiciary and of no concern to the state judiciary, the absence of a state interest in application of the five-sixths majority rule fulfills the first premise of Byrd.

---

[2] The federal unanimity requirement is implicit in Fed.R.Civ.P. 48: "The parties may stipulate that the jury shall consist of any number less than twelve or that a verdict or a finding of a stated majority of the jurors shall be taken as the verdict or finding of the jury."

The federal interest in unanimity, although not rising to constitutional dimensions, is cloaked in a strong tradition, see Johnson v. Louisiana, 406 U.S. 356, 370, 92 S.Ct. 1620, 1637, 32 L.Ed.2d 152 (1972) (Powell, J., concurring) ("unanimity . . . is mandated by history"), and this interest meets the second premise of Byrd. Assuming, and this would be a most generous assumption, that the tradition favoring unanimous verdicts could be reversed by a contrary local rule, just as the tradition favoring twelve jurors may be altered, see Colgrove v. Battin, 413 U.S. 149, 160, 163, 93 S.Ct. 2448, 2454, 2456, 37 L.Ed.2d 522 (1973), no local rule to that effect exists in the Eastern District of Pennsylvania. The federal interest need not be of constitutional magnitude to outweigh an insubstantial state interest, however, if all other aspects of Byrd are met. See Byrd, 356 U.S. at 357 & n.10, 78 S.Ct. at 900 & n.10; Edelson, 610 F.2d at 139.

Finally, we are not convinced that application of the federal unanimity rule instead of the state five-sixths majority rule will alter a substantial number of outcomes and thereby frustrate the policy of discouraging forum shopping underlying Erie and its progeny. See Witherow, 530 F.2d at 164. The concern with forum shopping in this case is minimal because the appellants brought suit in federal court even though they had notice that the federal verdict requirement would very likely differ from the one they advocated. This action therefore demonstrates that the rule chosen is not so determinative as to dictate choice of forum. The concern with preventing discrimination against residents, another policy underlying Erie, is also minimal; it is improbable that a party who has lost a verdict unanimously would have prevailed had he been required to persuade only seven, rather than eight, jurors to vote the other way. The predominant effect of a majority verdict rule in comparison to a unanimous verdict rule is to reduce the likelihood of deadlocked juries. See Wieser v. Chrysler Motors Corp., 69 F.R.D. 97, 100–01 (E.D.N.Y.1975) (examining New York's experience with majority verdicts). As a result, the concern with state-federal relationships in this case is minimal because the state simply has no interest in managing trials conducted in federal courts. Thus, the final premise of Byrd is not offended by our decision.

. . . .

The role of Congress.—The Supreme Court in Article V of the Evidence Rules proposed to create uniform rules of privilege for the federal courts. Congress eventually provided instead for the application of state privilege rules in certain circumstances. Evidence Rule 501. The House Committee on the Judiciary, in H.R.Rep. No. 93–650, explained:

"The rationale underlying the proviso is that federal law should not supersede that of the States in substantive areas such as privilege absent a compelling reason. The Committee believes that in civil cases in the federal courts where an element of a claim or defense is not grounded upon a federal question, there is no federal interest strong enough to justify departure from State policy. In addition, the Committee considered that the Court's proposed Article V would have promoted forum shopping in some civil actions, depending upon differences in the privilege law applied as among the State and federal courts. The Committee's proviso, on the other hand, under which the federal courts are bound to apply the State's privilege law in actions founded upon a State-created right or defense, removes the incentive to 'shop'."

Question: (11) A diversity action is brought in a federal court in State *A*, based on an automobile accident in State *B*. During a deposition being taken in State *C* and bearing on the issue of negligence, the physician-patient privilege is asserted with respect to a consultation that took place in State *D*. A motion for an order compelling an answer is made in the federal court for State *C*. Which state's privilege law applies?

By way of contrast, Congress apparently chose federal law to govern admissibility of subsequent remedial measures and then formulated an appropriate rule. So, in federal court, Evidence Rule 407 should apply despite contrary state law. See Oberst v. International Harvester Co., 640 F.2d 863, 867 n.2 (7th Cir.1980) (separate opinion).

Federal common law.—Justice Brandeis in Erie wrote: "There is no federal general common law." But have we not already seen post-Erie examples of federal common law being created and applied?

———

CLEARFIELD TRUST CO. v. UNITED STATES, 318 U.S. 363, 63 S.Ct. 573 (1943). Justice Douglas for a unanimous Court stated the facts as follows:

"On April 28, 1936, a check was drawn on the Treasurer of the United States through the Federal Reserve Bank of Philadelphia to the order of Clair A. Barner in the amount of $24.20. It was dated at Harrisburg, Pennsylvania and was drawn for services rendered by Barner to the Works Progress Administration. The check was placed in the mail addressed to Barner at his address in Mackeyville, Pa. Barner never received the check. Some unknown person obtained it in a mysterious manner and presented it to the J.C. Penney Co. store in Clearfield, Pa., representing that he was the payee and identifying himself to the satisfaction of the employees of J.C. Penney Co. He endorsed the check in the name of Barner and transferred it to J.C. Penney Co. in exchange for cash and merchandise. Barner never authorized the endorsement nor participated in the proceeds of the check. J.C. Penney Co. endorsed the check over to the Clearfield Trust Co. which accepted it as agent for the purpose of collection and endorsed it as follows: 'Pay to the order of Federal Reserve Bank of

Philadelphia, Prior Endorsements Guaranteed.'[1] Clearfield Trust Co. collected the check from the United States through the Federal Reserve Bank of Philadelphia and paid the full amount thereof to J.C. Penney Co. Neither the Clearfield Trust Co. nor J.C. Penney Co. had any knowledge or suspicion of the forgery. Each acted in good faith. On or before May 10, 1936, Barner advised the timekeeper and the foreman of the W.P.A. project on which he was employed that he had not received the check in question. This information was duly communicated to other agents of the United States and on November 30, 1936, Barner executed an affidavit alleging that the endorsement of his name on the check was a forgery. No notice was given the Clearfield Trust Co. or J.C. Penney Co. of the forgery until January 12, 1937, at which time the Clearfield Trust Co. was notified. The first notice received by Clearfield Trust Co. that the United States was asking reimbursement was on August 31, 1937.

"This suit was instituted in 1939 by the United States against the Clearfield Trust Co., the jurisdiction of the federal District Court being invoked pursuant to the provisions of § 24(1) of the Judicial Code, 28 U.S.C. § 41(1).[c] The cause of action was based on the express guaranty of prior endorsements made by the Clearfield Trust Co. J.C. Penney Co. intervened as a defendant. The case was heard on complaint, answer and stipulation of facts. The District Court held that the rights of the parties were to be determined by the law of Pennsylvania and that since the United States unreasonably delayed in giving notice of the forgery to the Clearfield Trust Co., it was barred from recovery under the rule of Market St. Title & Trust Co. v. Chelten Tr. Co., 296 Pa. 230, 145 A. 848. It accordingly dismissed the complaint. On appeal the Circuit Court of Appeals reversed. 3 Cir., 130 F.2d 93."

Justice Douglas then said: "We agree with the Circuit Court of Appeals that the rule of Erie R. Co. v. Tompkins . . . does not apply to this action. The rights and duties of the United States on commercial paper which it issues are governed by federal rather than local law." Accordingly, the Court affirmed the application of old federal case law, under which mere delay in giving notice did not bar suit.

Questions: (12) Why did the Erie rule not apply to this action?

(13) In a diversity action, between two private parties, based on an alleged conversion of United States bonds, two issues arise: (a) who has the burden of proof on whether the defendant took the bonds in good faith; and (b) were the bonds, which had been called but were not yet mature, "over-

---

[1] Guarantee of all prior indorsements on presentment for payment of such a check to Federal Reserve banks or member bank depositories is required by Treasury Regulations. 31 Code of Federal Regulations § 202.32, § 202.33.

[c] Jurisdiction was based on that part of § 24(1) vesting original jurisdiction in the district courts over civil actions in which the United States is plaintiff, now 28 U.S.C. § 1345.

due" at that time. Should these issues be governed by state law or federal common law? See Bank of America Nat'l Trust & Sav. Ass'n v. Parnell, 352 U.S. 29, 77 S.Ct. 119 (1956).

(14) In a federal action under 28 U.S.C. § 1345, the United States sought to collect from Mrs. Yazell of Texas on a federal disaster loan. An issue arose as to the capacity of the defendant to bind herself personally by the loan contract. Under the peculiar Texas law of coverture that then existed, a wife could not so bind herself in the circumstances of this case. In the absence of a congressional directive, did that Texas law apply? See United States v. Yazell, 382 U.S. 341, 86 S.Ct. 500 (1966) (yes).

(15) Many federal statutes creating causes of action fail to provide a limitations period. In such cases, federal courts ordinarily apply the forum state's statute of limitations for the most closely analogous state cause of action. See, e.g., Johnson v. Railway Express Agency, 421 U.S. 454, 95 S.Ct. 1716 (1975) (civil rights action). How does this rule mesh with the Erie-Clearfield doctrine? See generally Special Project, Time Bars in Specialized Federal Common Law: Federal Rights of Action and State Statutes of Limitations, 65 Cornell L.Rev. 1011 (1980).

UNITED STATES v. KIMBELL FOODS, INC., 440 U.S. 715, 99 S.Ct. 1448 (1979). The two cases decided under this caption, both of which came from the Fifth Circuit, required a choice between federal and state law on "whether contractual liens arising from certain federal loan programs take precedence over private liens, in the absence of a federal statute setting priorities."

The first case, coming from Texas, involved a loan guaranteed by the Small Business Administration (SBA) and a debt to a private party, both obligations being secured by competing liens on the same collateral. The second case from a Georgia federal court arose in Georgia and involved loans from the Farmers Home Administration (FHA) to a farmer, secured in part by a lien on his tractor; when the farmer later brought the tractor to a private repairman but could not pay for the repairs, the repairman retained the tractor and thus asserted a lien thereon; when still later the farmer defaulted on the federal loans, the United States sued the repairman to obtain the tractor, with jurisdiction invoked under 28 U.S.C. § 1345. State law concerning the relative priority of competing liens would have favored the private lienholders on the facts of these two cases, so the government argued for a more favorable federal common law.

On the choice-of-law problem, Justice Marshall for a unanimous Supreme Court wrote:

"This Court has consistently held that federal law governs questions involving the rights of the United States arising under nationwide federal programs. As the Court explained in Clearfield Trust Co. v. United States, [318 U.S. 363, 366–67, 63 S.Ct. 573, 575 (1943)]:

'When the United States disburses its funds or pays its debts, it is exercising a constitutional function or power. . . . The authority [to do so] had its origin in the Constitution and the statutes of the United States and was in no way dependent on the laws [of any State]. The duties imposed upon the United States and the rights acquired by it . . . find their roots in the same federal sources. In absence of an applicable Act of Congress it is for the federal courts to fashion the governing rule of law according to their own standards.' (Citations and footnote omitted.)

"Guided by these principles, we think it clear that the priority of liens stemming from federal lending programs must be determined with reference to federal law. The SBA and FHA unquestionably perform federal functions within the meaning of Clearfield. Since the agencies derive their authority to effectuate loan transactions from specific acts of Congress passed in the exercise of a 'constitutional function or power,' Clearfield Trust Co. v. United States, supra, at 366, 63 S.Ct., at 575, their rights, as well, should derive from a federal source. When Government activities 'aris[e] from and bea[r] heavily upon a federal . . . program,' the Constitution and Acts of Congress ' "require" otherwise than that state law govern of its own force.' United States v. Little Lake Misere Land Co., 412 U.S. 580, 592, 593, 93 S.Ct. 2389, 2396, 2397 (1973). In such contexts, federal interests are sufficiently implicated to warrant the protection of federal law.[19]

"That the statutes authorizing these federal lending programs do not specify the appropriate rule of decision in no way limits the reach of federal law. It is precisely when Congress has not spoken ' "in an area comprising issues substantially related to an established program of government operation," ' id., at 593, 93 S.Ct., at 2397, quoting Mishkin, supra, n. 19, at 800, that Clearfield directs federal courts to fill the interstices of federal legislation 'according to their own standards.' Clearfield Trust Co. v. United States, supra, at 367, 63 S.Ct., at 575.

"Federal law therefore controls the Government's priority rights. The more difficult task, to which we turn, is giving content to this federal rule.

. . . .

"Controversies directly affecting the operations of federal programs, although governed by federal law, do not inevitably require resort to uniform federal rules. See Clearfield Trust Co. v. United States, supra, at 367, 63 S.Ct., at 575; United States v. Little Lake Misere Land Co., supra, at 594–595, 93 S.Ct., at 2397–2398. Whether to adopt state law or to fashion a nationwide federal rule is a matter

[19] See [citation omitted]; Mishkin, The Variousness of 'Federal Law': Competence and Discretion in the Choice of National and State Rules for Decision, 105 U.Pa.L.Rev. 797, 800, and n. 15 (1957) (hereinafter Mishkin); Comment, Adopting State Law as the Federal Rule of Decision: A Proposed Test, 43 U.Chi.L.Rev. 823, 825 (1976); see also Bank of America National Trust & Savings Assn. v. Parnell, 352 U.S. 29, 33–34, 77 S.Ct. 119, 121–122 (1956); Miree v. DeKalb County, 433 U.S. 25, 29, 31–32, 97 S.Ct. 2490, 2493, 2494–2495 (1977).

of judicial policy 'dependent upon a variety of considerations always relevant to the nature of the specific governmental interests and to the effects upon them of applying state law.' United States v. Standard Oil Co., 332 U.S. 301, 310, 67 S.Ct. 1604, 1609 (1947).[21]

"Undoubtedly, federal programs that 'by their nature are and must be uniform in character throughout the Nation' necessitate formulation of controlling federal rules. United States v. Yazell, 382 U.S. 341, 354, 86 S.Ct. 500, 507 (1966); see Clearfield Trust Co. v. United States, supra, at 367, 63 S.Ct., at 575; United States v. Standard Oil Co., supra, at 311, 67 S.Ct., at 1609; Illinois v. City of Milwaukee, 406 U.S. 91, 105 n. 6, 92 S.Ct. 1385, 1393 n. 6 (1972). Conversely, when there is little need for a nationally uniform body of law, state law may be incorporated as the federal rule of decision. Apart from considerations of uniformity, we must also determine whether application of state law would frustrate specific objectives of the federal programs. If so, we must fashion special rules solicitous of those federal interests. Finally, our choice of law inquiry must consider the extent to which application of a federal rule would disrupt commercial relationships predicated on state law."

The Court decided "to reject generalized pleas for uniformity as substitutes for concrete evidence":

"We are unpersuaded that in the circumstances presented here, nationwide standards favoring claims of the United States are necessary to ease program administration or to safeguard the federal treasury from defaulting debtors. Because the state commercial codes 'furnish convenient solutions in no way inconsistent with adequate protection of the federal interest[s],' United States v. Standard Oil Co., supra, at 309, 67 S.Ct., at 1609, we decline to override intricate state laws of general applicability on which private creditors base their daily commercial transactions.

. . . .

"Because the ultimate consequences of altering settled commercial practices are so difficult to foresee, we hesitate to create new uncertainties, in the absence of careful legislative deliberation. Of course, formulating special rules to govern the priority of the federal consensual liens in issue here would be justified if necessary to vindicate important national interests. But neither the Government nor the Court of Appeals advanced any concrete reasons for rejecting well-established commercial rules which have proven workable over time. Thus, the prudent course is to adopt the readymade body of

---

[21] As explained by one commentator:

'Whether state law is to be incorporated as a matter of federal common law . . . involves the . . . problem of the relationship of a particular issue to a going federal program. The question of judicial incorporation can only arise in an area which is sufficiently close to a national operation to establish competence in the federal courts to choose the governing law, and yet not so close as clearly to require the application of a single nationwide rule of substance.' Mishkin, supra, n. 19, at 805.

state law as the federal rule of decision until Congress strikes a different accommodation.

. . . . .

"Accordingly, we hold that absent a congressional directive, the relative priority of private liens and consensual liens arising from these Government lending programs is to be determined under non-discriminatory state laws [here Texas and Georgia law, respectively]."

The government had also argued that a federal rule was "needed to prevent States from 'undercutting' the agencies' liens by creating 'arbitrary' rules." The Court met this by noting: "Adopting state law as an appropriate federal rule does not preclude federal courts from excepting [particular] local laws that prejudice federal interests."

———

ILLINOIS v. CITY OF MILWAUKEE, 406 U.S. 91, 92 S.Ct. 1385 (1972). The State of Illinois brought a federal action against four cities and two local sewerage commissions in Wisconsin, seeking to abate the public nuisance allegedly caused by the defendants' pollution of the interstate waters of Lake Michigan. The Court held that here the federal court should, in the absence of applicable federal statutes, apply a uniform federal common law of nuisance; and that such an action founded on federal common law would arise under the "laws" of the United States within the meaning of 28 U.S.C. § 1331.[d]

After the lower courts gave relief under the federal common law, the parties once again came before the Supreme Court. City of Milwaukee v. Illinois, 451 U.S. 304, 101 S.Ct. 1784 (1981). In the meantime, however, Congress had enacted the Federal Water Pollution Control Act Amendments of 1972, "a comprehensive regulatory program supervised by an expert administrative agency." The Supreme Court concluded that here no remedy under the federal common law was still available, the common law having been implicitly displaced by the enactment. The Court explained that "when Congress addresses a question previously governed by a decision rested on federal common law the need for such an unusual exercise of law-making by federal courts disappears."

———

(b) Federal Law in State Court

HINDERLIDER v. LA PLATA RIVER & CHERRY CREEK DITCH CO., 304 U.S. 92, 58 S.Ct. 803 (1938). A Colorado corporation

[d] The Fourth Circuit refused to extend the reach of the federal common law to a federal question suit by private citizens to enjoin intrastate stream pollution. Committee for Jones Falls Sewage System v. Train, 539 F.2d 1006 (4th Cir. 1976) (in banc).

brought suit in a Colorado state court against the State Engineer of Colorado to enjoin him from depriving the plaintiff of the use of the water of the La Plata River, which runs from Colorado into New Mexico. An issue arose as to the relative rights of the two states to its water. On the very day that Erie was decided, a unanimous Court, again speaking through Justice Brandeis, held: "[W]hether the water of an interstate stream must be apportioned between the two States is a question of 'federal common law' upon which neither the statutes nor the decisions of either State can be conclusive." This federal common law was applicable and binding in the state court, apparently by virtue of the supremacy clause of article VI of the Constitution.

DICE v. AKRON, CANTON & YOUNGSTOWN RAILROAD, 342 U.S. 359, 72 S.Ct. 312 (1952). Plaintiff brought an FELA action in an Ohio state court. The railroad's defenses included a release of all claims signed by plaintiff. Plaintiff contended that the purported release was void because he had relied on defendant's deliberately false statement that the document was merely a receipt for back wages. The Ohio Supreme Court, reversing the intermediate appellate court, sustained the trial court's entry of judgment for the defendant notwithstanding the verdict, holding that (1) Ohio, not federal, law governed the validity of the release; (2) under that Ohio law, the plaintiff, a man of ordinary intelligence who could read, was bound by the release even though he had been induced to sign it by a deliberately false statement; and (3) under controlling Ohio law, factual issues as to fraud in the execution of the release were properly decided by the judge rather than by the jury. Certiorari was granted.

The Supreme Court, in an opinion by Justice Black, held that federal common law controlled the validity of the release, that the correct federal rule was that a release of rights under the Act was void when induced by a deliberately false statement as to the contents of the release, and that the factual issues as to fraud had to be determined by the jury. On the last point, the Court said:

"*Third.* Ohio provides and has here accorded petitioner the usual jury trial of factual issues relating to negligence. But Ohio treats factual questions of fraudulent releases differently. It permits the judge trying a negligence case to resolve all factual questions of fraud 'other than fraud in the factum.' The factual issue of fraud is thus split into fragments, some to be determined by the judge, others by the jury.

"It is contended that since a state may consistently with the Federal Constitution provide for trial of cases under the Act by a nonunanimous verdict, Minneapolis & St. Louis R. Co. v. Bombolis,

241 U.S. 211, 36 S.Ct. 595,[e] Ohio may lawfully eliminate trial by jury as to one phase of fraud while allowing jury trial as to all other issues raised. The Bombolis case might be more in point had Ohio abolished trial by jury in all negligence cases including those arising under the federal Act. But Ohio has not done this. It has provided jury trials for cases arising under the federal Act but seeks to single out one phase of the question of fraudulent releases for determination by a judge rather than by a jury. Compare Testa v. Katt, 330 U.S. 386, 67 S.Ct. 810.

"We have previously held that 'The right to trial by jury is "a basic and fundamental feature of our system of federal jurisprudence"' and that it is 'part and parcel of the remedy afforded railroad workers under the Employers Liability Act.' Bailey v. Central Vermont R. Co., 319 U.S. 350, 354, 63 S.Ct. 1062, 1064. We also recognized in that case that to deprive railroad workers of the benefit of a jury trial where there is evidence to support negligence 'is to take away a goodly portion of the relief which Congress has afforded them.' It follows that the right to trial by jury is too substantial a part of the rights accorded by the Act to permit it to be classified as a mere 'local rule of procedure' for denial in the manner that Ohio has here used. Brown v. Western R. Co., 338 U.S. 294, 70 S.Ct. 105."

Justice Frankfurter, with whom Justices Reed, Jackson, and Burton joined, dissented from that portion of the opinion requiring a jury determination of the fraud issues. He said:

"To require Ohio to try a particular issue before a different fact-finder in negligence actions brought under the Employers' Liability Act from the fact-finder on the identical issue in every other negligence case disregards the settled distribution of judicial power between Federal and State courts where Congress authorizes concurrent enforcement of federally-created rights.

. . . .

". . . The fact that Congress authorized actions under the Federal Employers' Liability Act to be brought in State as well as in Federal courts seems a strange basis for the inference that Congress overrode State procedural arrangements controlling all other negligence suits in a State, by imposing upon State courts to which plaintiffs choose to go the rules prevailing in the Federal courts regarding juries. Such an inference is admissible, so it seems to me, only on the theory that Congress included as part of the right created by the Employers' Liability Act an assumed likelihood that trying all issues to juries is more favorable to plaintiffs. At least, if a plaintiff's right to

[e] In this FELA case decided in 1916, the jury in state court was allowed, over the defendant's objection, to return a five-sixths verdict after twelve hours of deliberation, as permitted by the constitution and statutes of Minnesota. It was then unquestioned that the seventh amendment required a unanimous verdict, but it was unsuccessfully urged that this was controlling in a state-court action to enforce a right created by Congress.

have all issues decided by a jury rather than the court is 'part and
parcel of the remedy afforded railroad workers under the Employers
Liability Act,' the Bombolis case should be overruled explicitly instead of left as a derelict bound to occasion collisions on the waters of
the law."

BROWN v. WESTERN RAILWAY, 338 U.S. 294, 70 S.Ct. 105
(1949). Plaintiff brought an FELA action in a Georgia state court.
The railroad filed a general demurrer on the ground that the complaint failed to "set forth a cause of action and is otherwise insufficient in law." The trial court sustained the demurrer and dismissed
the action, applying a Georgia rule to construe pleading allegations
"most strongly against the pleader." The intermediate appellate
court affirmed, and the Georgia Supreme Court denied review. Under Georgia law, this was a final adjudication barring recovery in any
future state proceedings. Certiorari was granted.

The Supreme Court reversed in an opinion by Justice Black. He
said:

"Strict local rules of pleading cannot be used to impose unnecessary burdens upon rights of recovery authorized by federal laws.
'Whatever springes the State may set for those who are endeavoring
to assert rights that the State confers, the assertion of federal rights,
when plainly and reasonably made, is not to be defeated under the
name of local practice.' Davis v. Wechsler, 263 U.S. 22, 24, 44 S.Ct.
13, 14. Cf. Maty v. Grasselli Chemical Co., 303 U.S. 197, 58 S.Ct. 507.
Should this Court fail to protect federally created rights from dismissal because of over-exacting local requirements for meticulous pleadings, desirable uniformity in adjudication of federally created rights
could not be achieved. See Brady v. Southern R. Co., 320 U.S. 476,
479, 64 S.Ct. 232, 234.

"Upon trial of this case the evidence offered may or may not support inferences of negligence. We simply hold that under the facts
alleged it was error to dismiss the complaint and that petitioner
should be allowed to try his case."

Justice Frankfurter, with whom Justice Jackson joined, dissented.
He said:

"States have varying systems of pleading and practice. One State
may cherish formalities more than another, one State may be more
responsive than another to procedural reforms. If a litigant chooses
to enforce a Federal right in a State court, he cannot be heard to
object if he is treated exactly as are plaintiffs who press like claims
arising under State law with regard to the form in which the claim
must be stated—the particularity, for instance, with which a cause of
action must be described. . . .

. . . . .

TOPIC C.   CHARACTERISTICS OF A PROCEDURAL SYSTEM

SECTION 1.   THE ADVERSARY SYSTEM

L. FULLER, THE PROBLEMS OF JURISPRUDENCE
706–07 (1949).

Adjudication involves a complex of factors that may appear in various combinations and that may be present in varying degrees. We may, however, say that the moral force of a judgment or decision will be at a maximum when the following conditions are satisfied: 1) The judge does not act on his own initiative, but on the application of one or both of the disputants. 2) The judge has no direct or indirect interest (even emotional) in the outcome of the case. 3) The judge confines his decision to the controversy before him and attempts no regulation of the parties' relations going beyond that controversy. 4) The case presented to the judge involves an existing controversy, and not merely the prospect of some future disagreement. 5) The judge decides the case solely on the basis of the evidence and arguments presented to him by the parties. 6) Each disputant is given ample opportunity to present his case.

It is seldom that all of these conditions can be realized in practice, and it is not here asserted that it is always wise to observe all of them. What is asserted is merely that adjudication as a principle of order achieves its maximum force when all of these conditions are satisfied. Some of this moral or persuasive force may wisely be sacrificed when other considerations dictate a departure from the conditions enumerated above, and where the tribunal, as an agent of legitimated power, has the capacity to compel respect for its decision.

The connection between the conditions enumerated above and the moral force of the judgment rendered is not something irrational and fortuitous. The key to it is found in the fact that men instinctively seek to surround the process of adjudication with those conditions that will tend to insure that the decision rendered is the closest possible approximation of the common need. This obviously explains the conditions of disinterestedness on the part of the judge and the opportunity for a full hearing of both sides, that is, conditions 2 and 6 in the enumeration above. Underlying the other four conditions is a single insight, namely, that men's interests and desires form a complex network, and that to discover the most effective and least disruptive pattern of order within this network requires an intimate acquaintance with the network itself and the interests and desires of which it is composed. In other words, these conditions are designed to obviate an evil that may be broadly called "absentee management." The

253

judge must stick to the case before him (condition 3), because if he ventures beyond it he may attempt to regulate affairs on which he is inadequately informed. The judge must work within the framework of the parties' arguments and proof (condition 5), because if he goes beyond these he will lack the guidance given him by the parties and may not understand the interests that are affected by a decision rendered outside that framework. The case must involve a present controversy (condition 4), because neither the parties nor the judge can be sure that they fully understand the implications of a possible, future controversy or the precise interests that may be affected by it when it arises. The first condition (that the judge should act on the application of the parties) is perhaps the most difficult to justify. It arises from the fact that the judge who calls the parties in and himself sets the framework of the hearing lays himself open to the suspicion of planning a general regulation in which the controversy on which he hears evidence and arguments appears as a mere detail. Thus a violation of condition 1 tends to carry with it a strong suspicion that condition 3 is being violated.

If this discussion seems abstract, it may perhaps be given a more concrete meaning by recurring to an example . . ., that of the father who decides a dispute between two of his children. If, implored by the disputants to hear their arguments, such a father, at the conclusion of the evidence and arguments and without rendering any decision on the case before him, were to declare, "Well, now that I see what's going on around here, I announce that the following rule must be observed . . ." it is fairly obvious that he would be sacrificing his moral position as judge for that of legislator. If he were then to decide the case before him, his ruling would not seem like a decision but an order. If he wishes to preserve his moral position as judge, he would be well advised to proceed by first deciding the controversy submitted to him, and to postpone for a day or so any legislation based on the information gained through his adjudicative activities.[a]

JOINT CONFERENCE ON PROFESSIONAL RESPONSIBILITY, REPORT
44 A.B.A.J. 1159, 1160–61 (1958).

The lawyer appearing as an advocate before a tribunal presents, as persuasively as he can, the facts and the law of the case as seen from the standpoint of his client's interest. It is essential that both the lawyer and the public understand clearly the nature of the role thus discharged. Such an understanding is required not only to ap-

---

[a] See also Fuller, The Forms and Limits of Adjudication, 92 Harv.L.Rev. 353 (1978) (elaborating his views on adjudication). See generally R. Summers, Lon L. Fuller 74–109 (1984). Professor Fuller was also an author of the Report next set out in the text.

preciate the need for an adversary presentation of issues, but also in order to perceive truly the limits partisan advocacy must impose on itself if it is to remain wholesome and useful.

In a very real sense it may be said that the integrity of the adjudicative process itself depends upon the participation of the advocate. This becomes apparent when we contemplate the nature of the task assumed by any arbiter who attempts to decide a dispute without the aid of partisan advocacy.

Such an arbiter must undertake, not only the role of judge, but that of representative for both of the litigants. Each of these roles must be played to the full without being muted by qualifications derived from the others. When he is developing for each side the most effective statement of its case, the arbiter must put aside his neutrality and permit himself to be moved by a sympathetic identification sufficiently intense to draw from his mind all that it is capable of giving,—in analysis, patience and creative power. When he resumes his neutral position, he must be able to view with distrust the fruits of this identification and be ready to reject the products of his own best mental efforts. The difficulties of this undertaking are obvious. If it is true that a man in his time must play many parts, it is scarcely given to him to play them all at once.

It is small wonder, then, that failure generally attends the attempt to dispense with the distinct roles traditionally implied in adjudication. What generally occurs in practice is that at some early point a familiar pattern will seem to emerge from the evidence; an accustomed label is waiting for the case and, without awaiting further proofs, this label is promptly assigned to it. It is a mistake to suppose that this premature cataloguing must necessarily result from impatience, prejudice or mental sloth. Often it proceeds from a very understandable desire to bring the hearing into some order and coherence, for without some tentative theory of the case there is no standard of relevance by which testimony may be measured. But what starts as a preliminary diagnosis designed to direct the inquiry tends, quickly and imperceptibly, to become a fixed conclusion, as all that confirms the diagnosis makes a strong imprint on the mind, while all that runs counter to it is received with diverted attention.

An adversary presentation seems the only effective means for combatting this natural human tendency to judge too swiftly in terms of the familiar that which is not yet fully known. The arguments of counsel hold the case, as it were, in suspension between two opposing interpretations of it. While the proper classification of the case is thus kept unresolved, there is time to explore all of its peculiarities and nuances.

These are the contributions made by partisan advocacy during the public hearing of the cause. When we take into account the preparations that must precede the hearing, the essential quality of the advocate's contribution becomes even more apparent. Preceding the hearing, inquiries must be instituted to determine what facts can be proved or seem sufficiently established to warrant a formal test of their truth during the hearing. There must also be a preliminary analysis of the issues, so that the hearing may have form and direction. These preparatory measures are indispensable whether or not the parties involved in the controversy are represented by advocates.

Where that representation is present there is an obvious advantage in the fact that the area of dispute may be greatly reduced by an exchange of written pleadings or by stipulations of counsel. Without the participation of someone who can act responsibly for each of the parties, this essential narrowing of the issues becomes impossible. But here again the true significance of partisan advocacy lies deeper, touching once more the integrity of the adjudicative process itself. It is only through the advocate's participation that the hearing may remain in fact what it purports to be in theory: a public trial of the facts and issues. Each advocate comes to the hearing prepared to present his proofs and arguments, knowing at the same time that his arguments may fail to persuade and that his proofs may be rejected as inadequate. It is a part of his role to absorb these possible disappointments. The deciding tribunal, on the other hand, comes to the hearing uncommitted. It has not represented to the public that any fact can be proved, that any argument is sound, or that any particular way of stating a litigant's case is the most effective expression of its merits.

The matter assumes a very different aspect when the deciding tribunal is compelled to take into its own hands the preparations that must precede the public hearing. In such a case the tribunal cannot truly be said to come to the hearing uncommitted, for it has itself appointed the channels along which the public inquiry is to run. If an unexpected turn in the testimony reveals a miscalculation in the design of these channels, there is no advocate to absorb the blame. The deciding tribunal is under a strong temptation to keep the hearing moving within the boundaries originally set for it. The result may be that the hearing loses its character as an open trial of the facts and issues, and becomes instead a ritual designed to provide public confirmation for what the tribunal considers it has already established in private. When this occurs adjudication acquires the taint affecting all institutions that become subject to manipulation, presenting one aspect to the public, another to knowing participants.

These, then, are the reasons for believing that partisan advocacy plays a vital and essential role in one of the most fundamental procedures of a democratic society. But if we were to put all of these detailed considerations to one side, we should still be confronted by the fact that, in whatever form adjudication may appear, the experienced judge or arbitrator desires and actively seeks to obtain an adversary presentation of the issues. Only when he has had the benefit of intelligent and vigorous advocacy on both sides can he feel fully confident of his decision.

Viewed in this light, the role of the lawyer as a partisan advocate appears not as a regrettable necessity, but as an indispensable part of a larger ordering of affairs. The institution of advocacy is not a concession to the frailties of human nature, but an expression of human insight in the design of a social framework within which man's capacity for impartial judgment can attain its fullest realization.

When advocacy is thus viewed, it becomes clear by what principle limits must be set to partisanship. The advocate plays his role well when zeal for his client's cause promotes a wise and informed decision of the case. He plays his role badly, and trespasses against the obligations of professional responsibility, when his desire to win leads him to muddy the headwaters of decision, when, instead of lending a needed perspective to the controversy, he distorts and obscures its true nature.[b]

At the outset, one must ask what is the aim of our system of justice. But, to say the very least, justice is not a concept that lends itself readily to definition.

So assume for the moment that some aim can be intuited. The next question is how effective is the adversarial method in accomplishing that aim. The answer to this question is of critical importance: here public opinion becomes concerned, and it is to the public that the system of justice must ultimately look for support. There is no public debate on the aim of the system—that is unthinkingly taken for granted. But on the implementation everyone has an opinion.

"Unlike abstract principle, a system of justice calls for rules to make it work, rules that take a principle off the shelf and dirty it up with people. The rules need explaining to those who don't know them, and they have got to be explained in terms more earthy than truth and beauty and empyrean harmonies. It takes a bit of explaining, for example, to have it understood why under our system of justice a lawyer is not a scoundrel when he pleads the statute of limitations to defeat an honest debt. It is not self-evident even to a dishonest man. It is insufficient and misleading to lace fingers and gravely assure everyone that 'We are searching for truth as much as you do if not more so.' "[c]

---

[b] See also Finman & Schneyer, The Role of Bar Association Ethics Opinions in Regulating Lawyer Conduct: A Critique of the Work of the ABA Committee on Ethics and Professional Responsibility, 29 UCLA L.Rev. 67, 156–67 (1981) (arguing that Committee's procedures should be made more adversarial).

[c] D. Mellinkoff, The Conscience of a Lawyer 10 (1973).

POUND, THE CAUSES OF POPULAR DISSATISFACTION
WITH THE ADMINISTRATION OF JUSTICE
29 A.B.A.Rep. 395, 404–06 (1906).

A no less potent source of irritation lies in our American exaggerations of the common law contentious procedure. The sporting theory of justice, the "instinct of giving the game fair play,"[2] as Professor Wigmore has put it, is so rooted in the profession in America that most of us take it for a fundamental legal tenet. But it is probably only a survival of the days when a lawsuit was a fight between two clans in which change of venue had been taken to the forum. So far from being a fundamental fact of jurisprudence, it is peculiar to Anglo-American law; and it has been strongly curbed in modern English practice. With us, it is not merely in full acceptance, it has been developed and its collateral possibilities have been cultivated to the furthest extent. Hence in America we take it as a matter of course that a judge should be a mere umpire, to pass upon objections and hold counsel to the rules of the game, and that the parties should fight out their own game in their own way without judicial interference. We resent such interference as unfair, even when in the interests of justice. The idea that procedure must of necessity be wholly contentious disfigures our judicial administration at every point. It leads the most conscientious judge to feel that he is merely to decide the contest, as counsel present it, according to the rules of the game, not to search independently for truth and justice. It leads counsel to forget that they are officers of the court and to deal with the rules of law and procedure exactly as the professional football coach with the rules of the sport. It leads to exertion to "get error into the record" rather than to dispose of the controversy finally and upon its merits. It turns witnesses, and especially expert witnesses, into partisans pure and simple. It leads to sensational cross-examinations "to affect credit," which have made the witness stand "the slaughter house of reputations."[1] It prevents the trial court from restraining the bullying of witnesses and creates a general dislike, if not fear, of the witness function which impairs the administration of justice. . . .

The effect of our exaggerated contentious procedure is not only to irritate parties, witnesses and jurors in particular cases, but to give to the whole community a false notion of the purpose and end of law. Hence comes, in large measure, the modern American race to beat the law. If the law is a mere game, neither the players who take part in it nor the public who witness it can be expected to yield to its spirit when their interests are served by evading it. And this is doubly true in a time which requires all institutions to be economically efficient and socially useful. We need not wonder that one part of the community strain their oaths in the jury box and find verdicts

[2] 1 Wigmore, Evidence, 127.   [1] 2 Wigmore, Evidence, 1112.

against unpopular litigants in the teeth of law and evidence, while another part retain lawyers by the year to advise how to evade what to them are unintelligent and unreasonable restrictions upon necessary modes of doing business. Thus the courts, instituted to administer justice according to law, are made agents or abettors of lawlessness.

————

At the National Conference on the Causes of Popular Dissatisfaction with the Administration of Justice, held to commemorate the seventieth anniversary of Roscoe Pound's address to the American Bar Association, Chief Justice Burger delivered the keynote address. Burger, Agenda for 2000 A.D.—A Need for Systematic Anticipation, 70 F.R.D. 83, 91 (1976), reprinted in The Pound Conference: Perspectives on Justice in the Future 23, 30–31 (1979). He said:

"Nor should we be surprised at the loss of public confidence caused by lawyers' using the courts for their own ends rather than with a consideration of the public interest. If Pound was correct in his analysis that excessive contentiousness was an impediment to fair administration of justice in 1906, I doubt that anyone could prove it is less so today. Correct or not, there is also a widespread feeling that the legal profession and judges are overly tolerant of lawyers who exploit the inherently contentious aspects of the adversary system to their own private advantage at public expense."

————

J. FRANK, COURTS ON TRIAL
80–81 (1949).

When we say that present-day trial methods are "rational," presumably we mean this: The men who compose our trial courts, judges and juries, in each law-suit conduct an intelligent inquiry into all the practically available evidence, in order to ascertain, as near as may be, the truth about the facts of that suit. That might be called the "investigatory" or "truth" method of trying cases. Such a method can yield no more than a guess, nevertheless an educated guess.

. . . .

. . . Our mode of trials is commonly known as "contentious" or "adversary." It is based on what I would call the "fight" theory, a theory which derives from the origin of trials as substitutes for private out-of-court brawls.

Many lawyers maintain that the "fight" theory and the "truth" theory coincide. They think that the best way for a court to discover the facts in a suit is to have each side strive as hard as it can, in a keenly partisan spirit, to bring to the court's attention the evidence

favorable to that side. Macaulay said that we obtain the fairest decision "when two men argue, as unfairly as possible, on opposite
sides," for then "it is certain that no important consideration will altogether escape notice."

Unquestionably that view contains a core of good sense. The
zealously partisan lawyers sometimes do bring into court evidence
which, in a dispassionate inquiry, might be overlooked. Apart from
the fact element of the case, the opposed lawyers also illuminate for
the court niceties of the legal rules which the judge might otherwise
not perceive. The "fight" theory, therefore, has invaluable qualities
with which we cannot afford to dispense.

But frequently the partisanship of the opposing lawyers blocks
the uncovering of vital evidence or leads to a presentation of vital
testimony in a way that distorts it.

By now it should be apparent that one cannot responsibly attack
or defend the adversary system without first facing the question of
what the aim of our system of justice is. As reexamination will suggest, Fuller, Pound, and Frank all faced this question, although arriving perhaps at different answers. The question is further explored in
the following excerpts.

SCHAEFER, IS THE ADVERSARY SYSTEM WORKING IN OP-
TIMAL FASHION?, 70 F.R.D. 159, 159–60 (1976). "The assigned
question, whether the adversary system is operating in optimal fashion, immediately prompts another: What is the purpose of the adversary system. The fundamental purpose of that system, as I see it, is
the ascertainment of the truth with respect, most frequently, to an
event which took place in the past. All aspects of the adversary system must be measured, in my opinion, against that objective. There
are peripheral considerations, but the ultimate question is whether
the adversary system as we know it today is doing the best that it
can to determine the truth with respect to litigated controversies."

SIMPSON, "THE PROBLEM OF TRIAL," in David Dudley Field
Centenary Essays 141, 141–42 (A. Reppy ed. 1949). "Of course, even
in the most primitive societies, it has been important that some heed
be paid to such moral sentiments and ideas of justice as may have
received common acceptance. This was essential to the maintenance
of group morale even in the early despotisms which so often emerged
from expanding groups of kindred. But the fact remains that originally the essential factor in the judicial settlement of disputes has
been that those disputes be settled definitely and finally, rather than
that they be settled on the basis of an accurate determination of the
facts.

"In considerable measure this is still true. Finality in adjudication
is as essential now as it was in more primitive times. But the pur-

pose of the legal order has changed. It is no longer merely to keep the peace. The law is now a principal means whereby mankind seeks consciously to control its collective social destiny. The accent has therefore shifted from the mere settlement of disputes to their just settlement—and by just settlement I mean the decision of controversies not only finally, and not only in a way which does not give major offense to the beliefs and moral standards of the mass of the community, but in a manner which takes account of the reality of the controversies presented and seeks to adjudicate them according to standards which the law consciously lays down. Indeed in most of the civilized world it is not too much to say that continued failure to adjudicate controversies on the basis of their real nature and in accordance with established legal standards would of itself, if that failure became a matter of public notoriety, produce a revulsion of popular feeling against the established legal and political order."

SCOTT, TWO MODELS OF THE CIVIL PROCESS, 27 Stan.L. Rev. 937, 937–39 (1975). "One possible view of the civil process is a Conflict Resolution Model that sees civil process primarily as a method of achieving peaceful settlement of private disputes. . . . So in the interests of preserving the peace, society offers through the courts a mechanism for the impartial judgment of personal grievances, as an alternative to retaliation or forcible self-help. . . .

"This model has only weak implications for the precise content of the legal rules whereby judgment is rendered. To facilitate acceptance of the outcome and resort to the process, the rules should be seen as 'fair' in terms of prevailing community values, but notions of what is fair may vary a great deal from one era or society to another. Such variations are of only secondary importance; it is more important for society that the dispute be settled peaceably than that it be settled in any particular way. . . .

. . . .

"A Behavior Modification Model, on the other hand, sees the courts and civil process as a way of altering behavior by imposing costs on a person. Not the resolution of the immediate dispute but its effect on the future conduct of others is the heart of the matter. Consistency and predictability of outcome, therefore, assume an importance that they do not possess in the Conflict Resolution Model.

"The implications of the Behavior Modification Model are at their most powerful if coupled with a view of the substantive rules of civil liability as designed to contribute to economic efficiency. If a person negligently injures another, the law of torts requires him to pay for the damages he has caused; if he breaches his agreement, contract law requires him to make whole the person who has relied on it. As a result he is led to take appropriate precautions to avoid injury and to make appropriate judgments about honoring agreements; and consequently, the social loss from such conduct is minimized.[2] The imposition of legal liability is, in economists' jargon, a way of making a person 'internalize' or take into account the costs of his actions, thereby inducing appropriate levels of care and performance toward others.[3] . . . Whatever their actual merits may be, if legal rules are seen as attempts to alter public behavior in ways that have been deemed desirable, the civil sanction contributes toward that end by depriving one who violates them of his gains or by imposing on him the costs occasioned by his violation."

GOLDING, "ON THE ADVERSARY SYSTEM AND JUSTICE," in Philosophical Law 98, 107 (R. Bronaugh ed. 1978). "The truth-finding conception of the trial process rests on the connection it perceives between legal justice and truth. It argues that the disposition of a case according to the applicable law of a system presupposes that correct answers are given to the disputed questions of fact. If a case is decided on wrong answers, the case is (legally speaking) wrongly decided, with the result that one of the parties is not given his legal due. A finding of correct answers to the disputed questions of fact is therefore a necessary condition for doing legal justice. A similar connection holds between truth and justice in the moral sense. Thus, if the applicable law in a case is also a just law according to some moral standard, then a decision made on wrong answers to the disputed questions of fact is also morally unjust, and one of the parties is not being given what moral justice requires."

BARRETT, THE ADVERSARY SYSTEM AND THE ETHICS OF ADVOCACY, 37 Notre Dame Law. 479, 479 (1962). " 'The purpose of a lawsuit is,' indeed, 'to arrive at the truth of the controversy, in order that justice may be done.'[2] Undoubtedly the courts of the Spanish Inquisition and the Supreme Court of the United States would alike assent to this. It is at least another of those 'decencies of civilization that no one would dispute.'[3] However, given the ideal and given also the inescapably human features of a lawsuit, how can

---

[2] This assumes that social costs and the private damages to the plaintiff are the same, which is not always the case.

[3] For a more adequate exposition, see R. Posner, Economic Analysis of Law (1973). [See also Posner, An Economic Approach to Legal Procedure and Judicial Administration, 2 J. Legal Stud. 399, 400–01 (1973) ("An important purpose of substantive legal rules (such as the rules of tort and criminal law) is to increase economic efficiency [in the sense of value-maximizing]. It follows . . . that mistaken imposition of legal liability, or mistaken failure to impose liability, will reduce efficiency. Judicial error is therefore a source of social costs and the reduction of error is a goal of the procedural system. . . . Even when the legal

process works flawlessly, it involves costs—the time of lawyers, litigants, witnesses, jurors, judges, and other people, plus paper and ink, law office and court house maintenance, telephone service, etc. These costs are just as real as the costs resulting from error: in general we would not want to increase the direct costs of the legal process by one dollar in order to reduce error costs by 50 (or 99) cents. The economic goal is thus to minimize the sum of error and direct costs.").—Ed.]

[2] McCarty, Psychology & the Law 223 (1960).

[3] Holmes, J., in Michigan Trust v. Ferry, 228 U.S. 346, 353 (1913).

the truth of the matter in dispute between the parties be most practically arrived at in order that justice (not justice in the abstract but justice according to law) may be done? We have no archangel on the bench. The jury is not drawn from a venire of Cherubim or Seraphim. The litigants, their lawyers and their witnesses are not saints. The trial of a lawsuit is a very human thing."

MORGAN, FOREWORD to Model Code of Evidence 3–4 (1942). "Thoughtful lawyers realize that a lawsuit is not, and cannot be made, a scientific investigation for the discovery of truth. The matter to be investigated is determined by the parties. They may eliminate many elements which a scientist would insist upon considering. The court has no machinery for discovering sources of information unknown to the parties or undisclosed by them. It must rely in the main upon data furnished by interested persons. The material event or condition may have been observed by only a few. The capacities and stimuli of each of these few for accurately observing and remembering will vary. The ability and desire to narrate truly may be slight or great. The trier of fact can get no more than the adversaries are able and willing to present. The rules governing the acceptable content of the data and the methods and forms of presenting them must be almost instantly applied in the heat and hurry of the trial. Prompt decision on the merits is imperative, for justice delayed is often justice denied. Sometimes a wrong decision quickly made is better than a right decision after undue procrastination. 'Some concession must be made to the shortness of human life'. The trier must assume that the data presented are complete, and the litigants must be satisfied with a determination of the preponderance of probability. If the data leave the mind of the trier in equilibrium, the decision must be against the party having the burden of persuasion. No scientist would think of basing a conclusion upon such data so presented. The court is not a scientific body. It is composed of one or more persons skilled in the law, skilled in the general art of investigation, but not necessarily skilled in the field which the dispute concerns, acting either alone or with a body of men not necessarily trained in investigation of any kind. Its final determination is binding only between the parties and their privies. It does not pronounce upon the facts for any purpose other than the adjustment of the controversy before it. Consequently there must be a recognition at the outset that nicely accurate results cannot be expected; that society and the litigants must be content with a rather rough approximation of what a scientist might demand. And it must never be forgotten that in the settlement of disputes in a court room, as in all other experiences of individuals in our society, the emotions of the persons involved—litigants, counsel, witnesses, judge and jurors—will play a part. A trial cannot be a purely intellectual performance."

CURTIS, THE ETHICS OF ADVOCACY, 4 Stan.L.Rev. 3, 12 (1951). " 'I must be cruel only to be kind,' said Hamlet, on his way to his mother. And so likewise a lawyer has to tell himself strange things on his way to court. But they are strange only to those who do not distinguish between truth and justice. Justice is something larger and more intimate than truth. Truth is only one of the ingredients of justice. . . . The administration of justice is no more designed to elicit the truth than the scientific approach is designed to extract justice from the atom."

SMITH, COMPONENTS OF PROOF IN LEGAL PROCEEDINGS, 51 Yale L.J. 537, 575 (1942). "In trial by battle we see the primitive concept of letting the best man win by 'might and main,' using all the strength and means at his command short of actual foul play. This combat aspect of litigation has psychological connotations running deeper than self vindication of one's cause by valor or might. It expresses the animosity factor in litigation, the desire to be at one's assailant and 'have it out.' Later we see the more primitive arrangement giving way to combat by proxy in the form of bilateral litigation. Each party still fends for himself under rules of diligence but aided by a lawyer as his paid champion. The law suit here still retains a dual character, on the one hand being a means of settling disputes with approximate justice, and on the other a sublimation mechanism for combat feelings and expression of grudges."

C. CURTIS, IT'S YOUR LAW 3–4 (1954). "There are some subjects of litigation in which the adversary proceeding is an admirable way of administering justice. One wise judge implied as much when Charles E. Wyzanski said, 'A political libel suit is the modern substitute for ordeal by battle. It is the means which society has chosen to induce bitter partisans to wager money instead of exchanging bloody noses.'[5] But litigation by an adversary proceeding is the way we cut the knot of many disputes in which it is disastrously inappropriate. Divorces, the custody of children, will contests, almost any kind of dispute which springs from family or equally intimate dissension—there a broken bone is more easily mendable. And it is intolerably too often true that a criminal trial turns into an adversary proceeding. . . .

"What, then, is the justification for this approach to justice, other than the fact we are several centuries used to it and aside from the fact that spectators in small communities and newspaper readers in cities enjoy the spectacle? It seems to me that the justification of the adversary proceeding is the satisfaction of the parties, and not our satisfaction, except as we too are prospective litigants. This is a rational justification of the adversary approach to justice. Along this line, what the law is trying to do is give the algebraic maximum of satisfaction to both parties. This is a crude, but indeed it is not a bad, definition of the justice which the adversary proceeding provides. The law is trying to do justice between the parties for the

[5] [Wyzanski, A Trial Judge's Freedom and Responsibility, 65 Harv.L.Rev. 1281, 1283 (1952)].

parties rather than for us, trying to give them their own justice so far as possible and so far as compatible with what may be distinguished as our justice.

"It is necessary, to be sure, to apply the general terms of what we regard as justice to their particular case. For we too must be satisfied. We are prospective customers. But the difference is not great. They are some of us, and they are much influenced by what we regard as just. The law pays more attention to the satisfaction of the needs of the parties in the particular case than it does to our ideas about justice in general. The law takes the position that we ought to be satisfied if the parties are; and it believes that the best way to get that done is to encourage them to fight it out, and dissolve their differences in dissension. We are still a combative people, not yet so civilized and sophisticated as to forget that combat is one way to justice."[d]

R. SUMMERS, LAW: ITS NATURE, FUNCTIONS, AND LIMITS 75–76 (2d ed. 1972). After quoting Sir Frederick Pollock to the effect that "[p]erhaps the greatest of all fallacies entertained by lay people about the law is . . . that the business of a court of justice is to discover the truth," Professor Summers continues:

"Surely, the reader will ask, 'How can there be any inconsistency between justice and truth? Indeed, justice can only be done on the basis of the facts. Justice cannot be done in the dark.' So? A distinction between substantive justice and procedural justice may help here. Pollock may be referring to procedural justice. And giving each side an equal chance to present his case *may*, in a particular case, lead to substantive injustice. One side, the weaker side factually, may nonetheless be able to *demonstrate* a better case factually than can the other side. Yet recognition of this risk has not induced us to deny each side an equal opportunity to be heard.

"Pollock's remark can be generalized. Actually, the pursuit of truth may, in an adjudicative process, be subordinated to still other social aims. One of these is that of offering the parties a 'day in court,' a 'forum in which to have it out.' In the end, the truth may get lost sight of, but the parties will have had their say 'against each other,' and this will have served as a substitute for disorderly forms of self-help. Furthermore, 'evidentiary privileges' may frustrate the pursuit of truth. Thus the adjudicator may be forced to apply rules of evidence that limit or close off relevant lines of factual inquiry altogether. A rule that, say, privileges a witness not to testify because his testimony would violate a confidential relation may operate to keep an adjudicator in the dark in the particular case. When this

[d] Compare J. Thibaut & L. Walker, Procedural Justice: A Psychological Analysis (1975) (experiments tending to prove that adversary system maximizes satisfaction), with Sarat, Studying American Legal Culture: An Assessment of Survey Evidence, 11 Law & Soc'y Rev. 427, 438–41 (1977) (surveys tending to show that experience with courts disillusions parties).

happens, substantive justice (insofar as it is necessarily premised on truth) is sacrificed to the social policy of inducing and protecting confidential relations. One way to sum all this up is to say that the private-remedial mode, with its elaborate procedures for resolving disputes over the factual premises of particular remedies, is a multipurpose institutional scheme, only one of the purposes of which is the pursuit of truth, with other purposes thereof either cooperatively or antagonistically involving themselves in this pursuit of truth."

Question: (1) To what extent does the Constitution dictate an adversary system?

SECTION 2.   ALTERATIONS AND ALTERNATIVES

Even if one can identify the aims of our system of justice, there remains the question of how well the adversary system accomplishes those aims and at what cost. Such a question cannot be answered in a vacuum. The effectiveness of the current adversary system can only be gauged relative to other methods of striving to accomplish those aims. In other words, the remaining question is not simply how effective is the adversarial method in accomplishing those aims, but rather what is the best way available to find truth, satisfy the parties, ensure fairness, and so on.

In considering other methods, it is necessary to distinguish the need for tinkering from the need for a totally new direction. There are many problems (e.g., access of the poor to our system of justice) and abuses (e.g., excesses of cross-examination) that might be solved or eliminated without endangering or abandoning the adversary system itself. But some remedies—including some that might appear quite minor—would have unavoidably broad and profound repercussions.

(a) Changing the Advocate's Role

NEW YORK COUNTY LAWYERS' ASSOCIATION COMMITTEE ON PROFESSIONAL ETHICS, OPINIONS
Op. 309 (1933).

Question. In an action on behalf of an infant three years of age, for injuries sustained by falling off a porch owned by the defendant, due to the alleged negligence of the defendant, where there is no eyewitness known to the plaintiff's attorney, and thereafter when the case came to trial, the infant's case was dismissed on motion of the defendant's attorney on the ground that the infant plaintiff was unable to make out a sufficient case of circumstantial evidence. During the presentation of the plaintiff's case, said attorney for the defendant had an eyewitness to said accident actually present in court, and did not mention said fact, either to the plaintiff's attorney or to the Court and kept the Court in ignorance of the fact that a person did exist who actually saw said accident, and was present in court. Was the failure of the defendant's attorney to disclose said information to the Court improper professional conduct?

Answer. In the opinion of the Committee the conduct of the defendant's attorney is not professionally improper. The fact of infancy does not call for a different reply.[e]

———

At the time of the foregoing opinion, the relevant provisions of the ABA's Canons of Professional Ethics (1908) were: (1) "The lawyer owes 'entire devotion to the interest of the client, warm zeal in the maintenance and defense of his rights and the exertion of his utmost learning and ability,' to the end that nothing be taken or be withheld from him, save by the rules of law, legally applied," Canon 15; and (2) "The conduct of the lawyer before the Court and with other lawyers should be characterized by candor and fairness," Canon 22. The newer Code of Professional Responsibility (1969) was no more informative, with DR 7–102(A)(3) providing that in his representation of a client a lawyer shall not "[c]onceal or knowingly fail to disclose that which he is required by law to reveal." Today the Model Rules of Professional Conduct (1983) provide in Model Rule 3.3(a)(2) that a lawyer shall not knowingly "fail to disclose a material fact to a tribunal when disclosure is necessary to avoid assisting a criminal or fraudulent act by the client," and the preamble to the Model Rules defines "fraudulent" as denoting "conduct having a purpose to deceive and not merely negligent misrepresentation or failure to apprise another of relevant information."

In his autobiography, Life and Law 271 (1941), Professor Williston tells of an incident in his brief practice where, in preparing the defense in a financial matter, he went carefully over his client's file of correspondence between the parties. The opposing lawyer did not demand production of this correspondence, and Williston did not feel bound to disclose it. At the end of the trial the judge gave judgment orally, citing as one reason for his decision a supposed fact that Williston knew to be unfounded. Williston says: "I had in front of me a letter that showed his error. Though I have no doubt of the propriety of my behavior in keeping silent, I was somewhat uncomfortable at the time."

Question: (2) Should the ethical duty to disclose adverse facts be any different in a jurisdiction with extensive discovery procedures like the Federal Rules from what it is in one permitting only limited discovery? Compare Brazil, The Adversary Character of Civil Discovery: A Critique and Propos-

———

[e] The soundness of the New York opinion is "queried" (without further comment) in H. Drinker, Legal Ethics 77 n.42 (1953) (the author was for many years Chairman of the ABA Committee on Professional Ethics and Grievances). It is approved in L. Patterson & E. Cheatham, The Profession of Law 101 (1971).

als for Change, 31 Vand.L.Rev. 1295 (1978), with Shapiro, Some Problems of Discovery in an Adversary System, 63 Minn.L.Rev. 1055 (1979).

Thus, a lawyer need not disclose adverse facts in many circumstances. Indeed, a lawyer normally has a duty not to "reveal information relating to representation of a client unless the client consents" expressly or impliedly. Model Rules of Professional Conduct Rule 1.6(a) (1983). So, for the advocate, just what does that so-called duty of candor entail? Here are some suggestive provisions:

1. Model Rule 3.3(d) provides: "In an ex parte proceeding, a lawyer shall inform the tribunal of all material facts known to the lawyer which will enable the tribunal to make an informed decision, whether or not the facts are adverse." Does this exception tell us something about the reasons for the rule against disclosing adverse facts?

2. Model Rule 3.8(d) provides that a prosecutor shall "make timely disclosure to the defense of all evidence or information known to the prosecutor that tends to negate the guilt of the accused or mitigates the offense . . . ." Does this exception suggest more generally when the rule against disclosing adverse facts should not apply?

3. Model Rules 3.3(a)(1), 4.1(a), and 3.3(a)(4) provide that a lawyer shall not knowingly "make a false statement of material fact or law" to a tribunal or to a third person or "offer evidence that the lawyer knows to be false" or leave such evidence unremedied. So regardless of any duty of disclosure, there is a duty of truthfulness. Moreover, a comment accompanying the Model Rules says without elaboration: "There are circumstances where failure to make a disclosure is the equivalent of an affirmative misrepresentation."

4. Model Rule 3.3(a)(3) provides that a lawyer shall not knowingly "fail to disclose to the tribunal legal authority in the controlling jurisdiction known to the lawyer to be directly adverse to the position of the client and not disclosed by opposing counsel." The Code of Professional Responsibility had essentially the same provision, but the Canons of Professional Ethics had not specifically addressed this matter.

Question: (3) Must an attorney disclose to a federal district court an adverse legal ruling of a federal court for another district or circuit? See Ass'n of the Bar of the City of N.Y. Comm. on Professional Ethics, Op. 80–4 (1980) (usually no).

ABA Comm. on Professional Ethics and Grievances, Formal Op. 280 (1949), had gone further with reference to disclosure of adverse authority than the language of the Model Rules seems to require, saying:

"We would not confine the Opinion[f] to 'controlling authorities'— i.e., those decisive of the pending case—but, in accordance with the

---

[f] The reference was to ABA Comm. on Professional Ethics and Grievances, For-   mal Op. 146 (1935), which had ruled that a lawyer should disclose a decision ad-

tests hereafter suggested, would apply it to a decision directly adverse to any proposition of law on which the lawyer expressly relies, which would reasonably be considered important by the judge sitting on the case.

"Of course, if the court should ask if there are any adverse decisions, the lawyer should make such frank disclosure as the question seems to warrant. Close cases can obviously be suggested, particularly in the case of decisions from other states where there is no local case in point.[1] A case of doubt should obviously be resolved in favor of disclosure, or by a statement disclaiming the discussion of all conflicting decisions.

"Canon 22 should be interpreted sensibly, to preclude the obvious impropriety at which the Canon is aimed. In a case involving a right angle collision or a vested or contingent remainder, there would seem to be no necessity whatever of citing even all the relevant decisions in the jurisdiction, much less those from other states or by inferior courts. Where the question is a new or novel one, such as the constitutionality or construction of a statute, on which there is a dearth of authority, the lawyer's duty may be broader. The test in every case should be, is the decision which opposing counsel has overlooked one which the court should clearly consider in deciding the case? Would a reasonable judge properly feel that a lawyer who advances, as the law, a proposition adverse to the undisclosed decision, was lacking in candor and fairness to him? Might the judge consider himself misled by an implied representation that the lawyer knew of no adverse authority?"

Questions: (4) Is the position that a lawyer is under a duty to disclose adverse legal authority consistent with the position that a lawyer need not disclose adverse facts? Which is the court more likely to discover for itself?

(5) You are attorney for the defendant, and a contract action has just been decided by the judge against your client (although you believe wrongfully). In computing the damages, both the plaintiff's counsel and the judge err, so that the computed damages are nearly $5000 less than they should be under the judge's decision. Should you inform the court or opposing counsel of this error? See Ass'n of the Bar of the City of N.Y. Comm. on Professional Ethics, Op. 477 (1939) (yes).

---

verse to his client's contentions but unknown to his adversary. This opinion had been criticized in Tunstall, Ethics in Citation: A Plea for Re-Interpretation of a Canon, 35 A.B.A.J. 5, 6 (1949) (The lawyer "is not called upon to volunteer detractions from the force of his own authorities. His march to a conclusion need not be interrupted by self-sought skirmishes, nor continued to the accompaniment of dubitandos. He is an advocate, not an umpire. He is participating in an argument, not a speculative inquiry; a trial, not a confessional."). See generally Commentary—The Advocate's Duty, 16 Ga.L.Rev. 821 (1982).

[1] See Glebe Company v. Trustees, 37 T.L.R. 436 (1921 A.C. 66) where the dicta of Lord Birkenhead are very broad [duty to disclose "any authority which might throw light upon the matters under debate"—Ed.]. Also 15 Law Quarterly Rev. 259, 273–275; 69 Albany L.J. 300, 303; "The Seven Lamps of Advocacy" by Edward A. Parry (1923) pages 19–20, "The Advocate" (Cecil Walsh) (2d Ed.) page 100.

FRANKEL, THE SEARCH FOR TRUTH: AN UMPIREAL VIEW
123 U.Pa.L.Rev. 1031, 1055–58 (1975).

We should consider whether the paramount commitment of counsel concerning matters of fact should be to the discovery of truth rather than to the advancement of the client's interest. . . .

We should face the fact that the quality of "hired gun" is close to the heart and substance of the litigating lawyer's role. As is true always of the mercenary warrior, the litigator has not won the highest esteem for his scars and his service. Apart from our image, we have had to reckon for ourselves in the dark hours with the knowledge that "selling" our stories rather than striving for the truth cannot always seem, because it is not, such noble work as befits the practitioner of a learned profession. The struggle to win, with its powerful pressures to subordinate the love of truth, is often only incidentally, or coincidentally, if at all, a service to the public interest.

We have been bemused through the ages by the hardy (and somewhat appealing) notion that we are to serve rather than judge the client. Among the implications of this theme is the idea that lawyers are not to place themselves above others and that the client must be equipped to decide for himself whether or not he will follow the path of truth and justice. . . .

It is impossible to guess closely how prevalent this view may be as a practical matter. Nor am I clear to what degree, if any, received canons of legal ethics give it sanction. My submission is in any case that it is a crass and pernicious idea, unworthy of a public profession. It is true that legal training is a source of power, for evil as well as good, and that a wicked lawyer is capable of specially skilled wrongdoing. It is likewise true that a physician or pharmacist knows homicidal devices hidden from the rest of us. Our goals must include means for limiting the numbers of crooked and malevolent people trained in the vital professions. We may be certain, notwithstanding our best efforts, that some lawyers and judges will abuse their trust. But this is no reason to encourage or facilitate wrongdoing by everyone.

Professional standards that placed truth above the client's interests would raise more perplexing questions. The privilege for client's confidences might come in for reexamination and possible modification. We have all been trained to know without question that the privilege is indispensable for effective representation. The client must know his confidences are safe so that he can tell all and thus have fully knowledgeable advice. We may want to ask, nevertheless, whether it would be an excessive price for the client to be stuck with the truth rather than having counsel allied with him for concealment and distortion. . . .

If the lawyer is to be more truth-seeker than combatant, trouble-some questions of economics and professional organization may demand early confrontation. How and why should the client pay for loyalties divided between himself and the truth? Will we not stultify the energies and resources of the advocate by demanding that he judge the honesty of his cause along the way? Can we preserve the heroic lawyer shielding his client against all the world—and not least against the State—while demanding that he honor a paramount commitment to the elusive and ambiguous truth? It is strongly arguable, in short, that a simplistic preference for the truth may not comport with more fundamental ideals—including notably the ideal that generally values individual freedom and dignity above order and efficiency in government. Having stated such issues too broadly, I leave them in the hope that their refinement and study may seem worthy endeavors for the future.

. . . .

The rules of professional responsibility should compel disclosures of material facts and forbid material omissions rather than merely proscribe positive frauds. This final suggestion is meant to implement the broad and general proposition that precedes it. In an effort to be still more specific, I submit a draft of a new disciplinary rule . . . .. The draft says:

(1) In his representation of a client, unless prevented from doing so by a privilege reasonably believed to apply, a lawyer shall:

(a) Report to the court and opposing counsel the existence of relevant evidence or witnesses where the lawyer does not intend to offer such evidence or witnesses.

(b) Prevent, or when prevention has proved unsuccessful, report to the court and opposing counsel the making of any untrue statement by client or witness or any omission to state a material fact necessary in order to make statements made, in the light of the circumstances under which they were made, not misleading.

(c) Question witnesses with a purpose and design to elicit the whole truth, including particularly supplementary and qualifying matters that render evidence already given more accurate, intelligible, or fair than it otherwise would be.

(2) In the construction and application of the rules in subdivision (1), a lawyer will be held to possess knowledge he actually has or, in the exercise of reasonable diligence, should have.[k]

---

[k] Mr. Frankel apparently would now abandon the privilege exception in his draft rule. See Frankel, The Search for Truth Continued: More Disclosure, Less Privilege, 54 U.Colo.L.Rev. 51 (1982). For a defense of giving the advocate an extremely adversarial role, see M. Freedman, Lawyers' Ethics in an Adversary System (1975).

(b) Changing the Adjudicator's Role

G. JOUGHIN & E. MORGAN, THE LEGACY OF
SACCO AND VANZETTI
184–85, 189–91 (1948).

Ours is an adversary system of litigation. In civil litigation the parties must overcome the inertia of the courts. The parties must frame the issues to be tried; they must make the necessary investigations, discover the pertinent data, locate the necessary witnesses, and see that steps are taken to procure their attendance. The court has no duty to make an independent investigation and no facilities for doing so. At the trial the parties present the testimony and other evidence. Neither has any obligation to bring forward material which will aid his adversary or will weaken his own case. The theory of the system is that each party will discover and present everything that will favor his own cause and disclose the weaknesses of his adversary. Thus the truth will emerge to the view of the impartial tribunal. This, it will be noted, assumes that each side will be equally intelligent, equally diligent, and equally fortunate in investigation and discovery of pertinent data, that there will be no fortuitous circumstances to deprive one party of an available witness or to make any of his relevant and important evidence inaccessible or inadmissible without a corresponding disadvantage to the other, and that both parties will be equally skillful in presenting the material and equally able and persuasive in expounding its bearing upon the issues. No argument is necessary to convince the most unobserving that these assumptions are without any basis in fact. Rarely, if ever, in a contested case do they even approximate the truth. With our system of pleading and evidence, a layman is incapable of handling his own litigation. From a bar, whose membership includes men of every degree of learning, skill, and experience, to say nothing of awareness of moral responsibility, it is difficult for the average person to select competent conscientious counsel; for the ignorant and inexperienced, it is well-nigh impossible. Thorough investigation is often costly. Proper preparation for trial on the law and the facts involves expenditures of time and money. Persuasive presentation requires skill beyond the capacity of many practicing lawyers. Indeed, many lawsuits are what popular opinion believes all lawsuits to be, a battle of wits between the advocates of the parties.

. . . .

Some of the most distressing effects of our adversary system appear in its application to the rules governing evidence and witnesses. They are more than ordinarily harmful where matters in issue require special skill in observation or in drawing deductions from observed data. Judicial experience has made it abundantly clear that in numerous cases, both civil and criminal, the testimony of experts is not merely desirable; it is essential. As early as the fourteenth century courts called experts to their aid. These men, learned in arts and in science, were originally called not as witnesses for a party but as assistants to the court. As the form of trial by jury changed and the jury came to rely principally upon matter offered in court rather than upon matter within their own knowledge or learned by private inquiry, these helpers of the court took on the functions of witnesses to the jury. As witnesses they were and are selected by the parties. It is true that as to ordinary data a party can offer from among the persons having relevant information those whose observation and recollection are favorable to his cause. But they will speak about things familiar to jurors. Their testimony can be valued in the light of common experience. Their perception, memory and sincerity can be adequately tested by cross-examination in terms understandable by the ordinary man. Such inferences or conclusions as they may express will carry no undue weight because of their superior capacities for making relevant observations and drawing sound deductions. The subject of expert testimony, however, is generally beyond the ken of the layman. It calls for special skill, knowledge, experience, or training in the perception of data or in the process of drawing accurate inferences, or in both. Where experts who are equally skillful in exposition disagree, the jury is practically helpless.

Consequently it is of the highest importance that the expert witnesses should be properly qualified, honest, and impartial. So long as they were helpers of the court, these qualities could be assured in most cases. When they became witnesses in an adversary system, the temptation to make them partisans became great; and it has not been resisted. Indeed in the majority of instances they have deserted their role as witnesses and have become expert advocates. Even this would be sufferable, if they were competent and honest. The ugly truth is, however, that in many fields the most incompetent is the most glib and persuasive in presenting his views and the most positive in his statements. He can also adjust his opinions to suit the necessities of the party who retains him. He acquires skill in the use of obscure and misleading phrasing. Expert testimony as to mental responsibility in criminal cases, as to diagnosis and prognosis in personal-injury litigation, has become a scandal. . . .

. . . The conduct of the experts in this case [Sacco-Vanzetti] should cause no surprise: [h] so long as experts are chosen by the par-

---

[h] The conduct to which the authors were alluding included that of Captain Proctor, ballistics expert called by the prosecution, part of whose direct examination was as follows:

"Q. Have you an opinion as to whether bullet 3 was fired from the Colt Automatic [Sacco's pistol] which is in evidence?

"A. I have.

"Q. And what is your opinion?

"A. My opinion is that it is consistent with being fired by that pistol." 1 The Sacco-Vanzetti Case: Transcript of the Record of the Trial of Nicola Sacco and Bartolomeo Vanzetti in the Courts of Massachusetts and Subsequent Proceedings 1920–7, at 896 (1928).

No clarification was sought on cross-examination. In connection with post-tri-

ties and are willing to lend their services as advocates, so long will
the jury be at their mercy and the decision or verdict will rest on
nothing much better than conjecture. Even the honest expert, if he
conceives himself an advocate, will follow the recognized attitude of
the lawyer; he will emphasize the data which favor his client and
minimize those which favor the opponent. He will have the hypothetical questions so framed as to enable him to give an apparently
favorable opinion and convince himself that it is for the adverse expert to do a corresponding job for his client. The vices of the adversary system carried to this extent, especially in criminal cases, are
outrageous and intolerable. In this situation also the trial judge
should hold the key. He should be given power to select impartial,
competent experts wherever expert assistance will be helpful. The
jury should be informed that these experts have been chosen by the
court. It is probably impossible to prevent the parties from calling
other experts, but their testimony will be subject to discount on account of their partisanship.[i]

Read Evidence Rules 614 and 706, which allow the court to interrogate witnesses and even to call its own witnesses. The Advisory
Committee's notes thereto make it clear that these judicial powers are
well established. But these are powers and not duties. Extremely
few cases can be found holding it to be reversible error for the judge
to fail to question or call a witness.

In Johnson v. United States, 333 U.S. 46, 68 S.Ct. 391 (1948), Johnson, a seaman on a tanker owned and operated by the United States,
brought action under the Jones Act for injuries sustained when a
block being held by Dudder, a shipmate, fell and hit Johnson on the
head. Plaintiff's version of the episode was the only evidence as to
how the injury occurred. He testified that the block, which Dudder
had the duty to hold, was permitted to fall on him as he was bending
over to coil the line that ran through the block. Although available,
Dudder was not called as a witness by either party. The issue before
the Court was whether the rule of res ipsa loquitur applied. The majority, in an opinion by Justice Douglas reversing the court below,
held that there was no reason why res ipsa loquitur was not applica-

al proceedings Captain Proctor explained
what he actually meant, and what the
prosecution knew he meant, in the following affidavit:

"At no time was I able to find any evidence whatever which tended to convince
me that the particular model [mortal?]
bullet found in Berardelli's body, which
came from a Colt automatic pistol,
. . . came from Sacco's pistol and I so
informed the District Attorney and his
assistant before the trial. . . . Had I
been asked the direct question: whether
I had found any affirmative evidence

whatever that this so-called mortal bullet
had passed through this particular Sacco's pistol, I should have answered then,
as I do now without hesitation, in the
negative." 4 id. at 3642–43.

[i] Charging that the nonexpert courts
with their adversary system cannot effectively handle high-technology cases, Yel-
lin, High Technology and the Courts:
Nuclear Power and the Need for Institutional Reform, 94 Harv.L.Rev. 489 (1981),
argues for a much broader use of masters by the courts.

ble to acts of a fellow servant and that the falling of the block alone was sufficient basis for an inference of Dudder's negligence. Justice Frankfurter, dissenting in part, did not believe that res ipsa loquitur was applicable, because it is a rule of necessity to be invoked only when necessary evidence is absent and not readily available. He took the position that when neither party saw fit to call Dudder, the person who actually knew what happened, it was the trial judge's duty to call him as the court's witness. "Federal judges are not referees at prize-fights but functionaries of justice," he said. "As such they have a duty of initiative to see that the issues are determined within the scope of the pleadings, not left to counsel's chosen argument." He further explained:

"While a court room is not a laboratory for the scientific pursuit of truth, a trial judge is surely not confined to an account, obviously fragmentary, of the circumstances of a happening, here the meagre testimony of Johnson, when he has at his command the means of exploring them fully, or at least more fully, before passing legal judgment. A trial is not a game of blind man's buff; and the trial judge—particularly in a case where he himself is the trier of the facts upon which he is to pronounce the law—need not blindfold himself by failing to call an available vital witness simply because the parties, for reasons of trial tactics, choose to withhold his testimony."[j]

Questions: (6) Why do you suppose the plaintiff did not call Dudder? Why did not the defendant do so? See Note, Trial Judge's Duty to Call Witnesses in Res Ipsa Loquitur Cases, 58 Yale L.J. 183 (1948).

(7) If the judge's failure to call a witness were reversible error, how would the trial tactics of the parties be affected?

RESERVE MINING CO. v. LORD, 529 F.2d 181 (8th Cir.1976). In a major environmental action against a mining company that was allegedly polluting Lake Superior, District Judge Lord in November 1975 ruled against the defendant on a certain motion. On petition for a writ of mandamus, the Eighth Circuit undid that defeat, citing various irregularities that occurred when the trial judge, in his own words, "dispensed with the usual adversary proceeding." Furthermore, the court of appeals sua sponte ordered the recusal of the district judge, observing:

"It is urged that the district court's actions were nothing more than a judge acting upon his deep convictions formed after nine and one-half months of trial. No one can doubt that Judge Lord does

[j] In Canada, it has been held reversible error in an uncontested divorce case for the trial judge to call the defendants (wife and co-respondent) as witnesses. The judge had been skeptical of the evidence as to the alleged adultery; he called both defendants to the stand, they denied adultery, and he dismissed the action. A new trial was ordered because he had thus "assumed the functions of counsel rather than of judge." Fowler v. Fowler, [1949] Ont.W.N. 244. See generally Saltzburg, The Unnecessarily Expanding Role of the American Trial Judge, 64 Va.L.Rev. 1, 52–80 (1978).

have deep convictions in this matter or that such convictions largely
influenced his actions. However, the record reveals more than a trial
judge merely acting in accord with his prior judgment. In the November proceeding Judge Lord called and examined the witnesses
and interspersed testimony of his own; the trial judge announced on
the record that witnesses called by Reserve could not be believed,
'that in every instance Reserve Mining Company hid the evidence,
misrepresented, delayed and frustrated the ultimate conclusions;'
and that he did not have 'any faith' in witnesses to be called by Reserve. Transcript of November 14, 1975 hearing at 2–5, 56, 109. He
further announced that the court would have to take depositions since
the lawyers opposing Reserve 'did not know anything about it.'
Transcript of November 19, 1975 hearing at 25.

"Judge Lord seems to have shed the robe of the judge and to have
assumed the mantle of the advocate. The court thus becomes lawyer, witness and judge in the same proceeding, and abandons the
greatest virtue of a fair and conscientious judge—impartiality.

"A judge best serves the administration of justice by remaining
detached from the conflict between the parties. As Justice McKenna
stated long ago, '[T]ribunals of the country shall not only be impartial
in the controversies submitted to them but shall give assurance that
they are impartial . . . .' Berger v. United States, 255 U.S. 22,
35–36, 41 S.Ct. 230, 235, 65 L.Ed. 481 (1921). When the judge joins
sides, the public as well as the litigants become overawed, frightened
and confused."

———

The student should consider how far Rule 16, dealing with pretrial
conferences, authorizes or obligates the judge to join actively in
readying the case for trial or in pushing for settlement. See Topic E
of Part Three.

Generally on the role of the trial judge, compare Frankel, The
Search for Truth: An Umpireal View, 123 U.Pa.L.Rev. 1031 (1975),
with Wyzanski, A Trial Judge's Freedom and Responsibility, 65 Harv.
L.Rev. 1281 (1952).

Question: (8) Justice Jackson, concurring in Youngstown Sheet & Tube
Co. v. Sawyer, 343 U.S. 579, 635, 72 S.Ct. 863, 870 (1952), said: "And court
decisions are indecisive because of the judicial practice of dealing with the
largest questions in the most narrow way." Should this judicial practice be
changed? If so, how?

———

WEBSTER EISENLOHR, INC. v. KALODNER
United States Circuit Court of Appeals, Third Circuit, 1944.
145 F.2d 316, cert. denied, 325 U.S. 867, 65 S.Ct. 1404 (1945).

Before BIGGS, MARIS, JONES, GOODRICH, and McLAUGHLIN, CIR-
CUIT JUDGES.

GOODRICH, CIRCUIT JUDGE. The proceedings at bar are upon a petition to this court for writs of mandamus and prohibition to be directed to the Honorable Harry E. Kalodner, one of the Judges of the District Court of the United States for the Eastern District of Pennsylvania, and David Bortin, Esq., a Special Master appointed pursuant to his order.

[The underlying case was a class action brought by Andrew Speese on behalf of the preferred stockholders against their company, with the plaintiffs claiming exclusive voting power as a consequence of dividend defaults. The certificate of incorporation provided that the preferred stock was not entitled to vote unless two quarterly dividends were in arrears, whereupon "full voting power" would be vested in the preferred stock until the arrearages were paid. The dispute was whether "full voting power" meant exclusive voting power or only the power in the preferred stock to vote along with the common stock.]

Between hearings upon the matter before the District Court the company sent to its stockholders copies of its annual report for the year 1942. Following the sending of the report the company also wrote its preferred stockholders, offering to purchase their interests. Copies of these documents were supplied to the District Judge upon his request although not introduced in evidence in the litigation. At one of the hearings Judge Kalodner indicated his belief that the financial statement sent by the corporation to stockholders was misleading and he criticized the letter sent to preferred stockholders for failure to state facts which he deemed material. Then, at a hearing on April 24, 1943, counsel for Speese stated to the court that he had no client since the shares of Speese and other stockholders which he had represented had been purchased. Judge Kalodner again expressed his dissatisfaction with the actions of the company and stated: "I will advise you gentlemen that I am going to appoint an examiner to look into this matter." Subsequently the court did appoint Mr. Bortin as Special Master under Rule 53 of the Rules of Civil Procedure, 28 U.S.C.A. following section 723c. The Special Master was directed "to investigate: the acts, conduct, property, liabilities, financial condition, books, records and assets . . . [of Webster Eisenlohr, Inc.]; all the circumstances relating to an Offer made March 26, 1943 to the Holders of 7% Cumulative Preferred Stock . . .; the arrangement made by and between . . . [Webster Eisenlohr, Inc.] with White, Weld & Co. of New York and Bertram K. Wolfe, Esq. with reference to the Offer made to the Preferred Stockholders; the conduct of the Board of Directors . . . with reference to the making of said Offer to the Preferred Stockholders; the propriety, reasonableness and adequacy of the said Offer to the Preferred Stockholders; the question as to whether or not there was any violation of Rule X–10B–5 'Employment of Manipulative and Deceptive Devices' of the Securities and Exchange Commission, and any other matters which may be referred to the Special Master by the Court as relevant to these proceedings."

Counsel for Webster Eisenlohr, Inc., sought vacation of the order in the District Court and, failing that, asks a writ of mandamus directing the District Court to vacate this appointment and a writ of prohibition directed to the Special Master to prevent him from carrying out his commission. A majority of the court believe the company's position to be well taken.

The fundamental proposition which probably no one would dispute is that a court's power is judicial only, not administrative nor investigative. A judgment may only be properly given for something raised in the course of a litigation between the parties. Now, what was the litigation in this case? The complaint presents the question of the legal effect of the provision that preferred stockholders, under given circumstances, shall have full voting power. . . .

If the plaintiff's contentions on voting rights are upheld as a matter of law, the preferred stockholders are entitled to determine who shall manage the corporation, and other questions which may be determined by stockholders. They are entitled to court help to get those rights if they need it. On the other hand, if the plaintiff's contentions as to the meaning of the phrase are incorrect, they have alleged no legal grounds for complaint. . . .

The directions given the Master went far beyond anything involved in the issues presented in the litigation, as will be seen from the reading of the order appointing him.

. . . .

. . . If the court is limited in its judicial duties, to deciding the issues presented in the litigation before it, the master's function can go no further than to aid in the court's discharge of its duties.

In this case the report made by the company to its stockholders and the circumstances under which some of the preferred stockholders disposed of their interests were not before the court in the then pending lawsuit. The District Judge felt that there were indications that the company had not been entirely aboveboard in the matter. The company, through its counsel, earnestly contended that it had been entirely fair. This court refused to hear counsel on that point, for we thought the matter not relevant. None of these stockholders was under guardianship; all had the full legal power to sell their shares under such circumstances as it pleased them to sell. If any one felt that he had been deceived, he could take the steps necessary to protect his rights. There was no indication that any party to the transaction was complaining. We think that neither the report to the stockholders nor the sale of their stock was involved in the litigation. It was therefore outside the scope of investigation both by the Special Master and the court itself.

We do not think this view imposes unduly restrictive limitations upon courts. The judicial power is limited to deciding controversies. That has been its function historically; that is its function under the Constitution of the United States. No doubt a great deal goes on in the world which ought not to go on. If courts had general investigatory powers, they might discover some of these things and possibly right them. Whether they would do as well in this respect as officers or bodies expressly set up for that purpose may be doubted, but until the concept of judicial power is widened to something quite different from what it now is courts will better serve their public function in limiting themselves to the controversies presented by parties in litigation.

[The court here observed that the class action remained pending, presenting an opportunity for any remaining preferred stockholders to intervene, so that Rule 23(e) was not involved.]

In view of the above discussion we think it unlikely that the formal issuing of the writs prayed for will be necessary. The applicant may later apply to this court if the need presents itself. No order for costs will be made.

[The strong dissenting opinion of Judge Biggs, with whom Judge McLaughlin joined, is omitted.]

Question: (9) Professor James distinguished between "party-presentation" and "party-prosecution." The former represents the principle that the parties are to decide what is submitted for decision, and the latter the principle that the parties are to move the case along. Assumption of responsibility by judges, he thought, is more readily justifiable with respect to the latter than with respect to the former. F. James, Civil Procedure 3–8 (1965). Does this suggest a way of reconciling the foregoing materials on the role of the judge?

CHAYES, THE ROLE OF THE JUDGE IN PUBLIC LAW LITIGATION, 89 Harv.L.Rev. 1281, 1284 (1976). After arguing that the traditional view of a lawsuit as a vehicle for settling disputes between private parties about private rights is invalid as a description of much current civil litigation in the federal district courts, Professor Chayes sketches an emerging conception of "public law litigation":

"The characteristic features of the public law model are very different from those of the traditional model. The party structure is sprawling and amorphous, subject to change over the course of the litigation. The traditional adversary relationship is suffused and intermixed with negotiating and mediating processes at every point. The judge is the dominant figure in organizing and guiding the case, and he draws for support not only on the parties and their counsel, but on a wide range of outsiders—masters, experts, and oversight personnel. Most important, the trial judge has increasingly become the creator and manager of complex forms of ongoing relief, which have widespread effects on persons not before the court and require the judge's continuing involvement in administration and implementation. School desegregation, employment discrimination, and prisoners' or inmates' rights cases come readily to mind as avatars of this new form of litigation. But it would be mistaken to suppose that it is confined to these areas. Antitrust, securities fraud and other aspects of the conduct of corporate business, bankruptcy and reorganizations, union governance, consumer fraud, housing discrimination, electoral reapportionment, environmental management—cases in all these fields display in varying degrees the features of public law litigation."[k]

(c) Changing the System

Questions: (10) Judge Frank proposed a different idea. Rather than change the roles of lawyer and judge, he would have enlarged the role of the government. After observing that a court's judgment is a solemn governmental act with potentially grave consequences and that courts are alone among governmental bodies in not accepting any responsibility for establishing the facts upon which they act, he suggested for many civil cases "that we should consider whether it is not feasible to provide impartial government officials—who are not court employees, and who act on their own initiative—to dig up, and present to the courts, significant evidence which one or the other of the parties may overlook or be unable to procure. No court would be bound to accept that evidence as true. Nor would any of the parties be precluded from trying to show the unreliability of such evidence (by cross-examination or otherwise) or from introducing additional evidence. Trials would still remain adversary." J. Frank, Courts on Trial 98 (1949). Are you impressed by this suggestion?

(11) Mr. Frankel suggested a "lawyerless tribunal" for many civil cases. The aggrieved person would complain directly to a judge. "The putative claimant may be persuaded at this stage that the claim is not worth pursuing. If that does not happen, the opposed party is summoned. Efforts to settle may follow. If there is no early compromise, the judge will assign staff to investigate, to examine and cross-examine witnesses, to collect other evidence—to do, in short, whatever is necessary to reconstruct as accurately as possible the events giving rise to the dispute. Similarly, the law will be researched, perhaps by subordinates assigned to develop the best adversary stance for each of the disputants. The end of the researches, with both parties having had a chance to contest witnesses or other evidence against them, will be a decision more or less of the familiar kind our courts render." M. Frankel, Partisan Justice 116 (1980). Are you impressed by this suggestion?

---

[k] For development of the implications of public law litigation, see Topics B and C of Part Seven.

R. SUMMERS, LAW: ITS NATURE, FUNCTIONS, AND LIM-ITS 110–11 (2d ed. 1972). "It may be . . . that if a social thinker really wanted to justify abandonment of *adversarial* adjudication he ought to urge abandonment of adjudication. Adjudication—referral of two-sided disputes to impartial third parties for decision—begets *adversarial* adjudication, does it not? But how could the need for adjudication itself be eliminated and aggrieved citizens still be left with something resembling a grievance-remedial mode? Actually this is not impossible, at least for *some* types of remedial claims.

"In the Swimming Pool episode [a negligence case against the operator of a swimming pool for injuries sustained from diving into the pool], the relevant principle of law might have provided that 'any person suffering personal injuries caused by another in the course of leisure activity shall be entitled to compensation therefor from *public funds* upon application to the appropriate public official. Satisfactory proof of such injuries and that they were caused by another must be submitted.'

"Observe that an arrangement of this kind would not, in the first instance, call for adjudication at all. It would not even call for the loss causer to be present at the official determination of loss and causation, let alone pay out of his own pocket (or that of his insurer). In short, here we do not have a *two*-sided dispute for reference to a third party. Of course, a dispute could arise between the aggrieved and the relevant public official over facts of loss and causation, and *this* dispute would be of a two-sided kind which might then be referred to a third party adjudicative body for resolution. But absent this, no need for adjudication would arise. Moreover, there is no need to give the loss causer himself an elaborate day in court (the chief value of our present system?), for he does not himself bear the loss. He is not being branded a 'wrongdoer.' He is involved only quite indirectly.

"Would you recommend a system of the foregoing kind to handle personal injury claims arising from auto accidents?"

———

SANDER, VARIETIES OF DISPUTE PROCESSING
70 F.R.D. 111, 111–17, 130–31 (1976).

Thus one concern to which we ought to address ourselves here is how we might escape from the specter [of exploding caseloads]. This might be accomplished in various ways. First, we can try to prevent disputes [4] from arising in the first place through appropriate changes in the substantive law, such as the adoption of a no-fault principle for automobile injuries or the removal of a criminal sanction for certain

---

[4] For present purposes I use the word "dispute" to describe a matured controversy, as distinguished, for example, from a "grievance" which may be inchoate and unexpressed.

conduct. A less obvious substantive law issue that may have a bearing on the extent of litigation that arises is whether we opt for a discretionary rule or for one that aims to fix more or less firmly the consequences that will follow upon certain facts. For example, if a statute says that marital property on divorce will be divided in the court's discretion there is likely to be far more litigation than if the rule is, as in the community property states, that such property will normally be divided 50–50. I wonder whether legislatures and law revision commissions are sufficiently aware of this aspect of their work.

Another method of minimizing disputes is through greater emphasis on preventive law. Of course lawyers have traditionally devoted a large part of their time to anticipating various eventualities and seeking, through skillful drafting and planning, to provide for them in advance. But so far this approach has been resorted to primarily by the well-to-do. I suspect that with the advent of prepaid legal services this type of practice will be utilized more widely, resulting in a probable diminution of litigation.

A second way of reducing the judicial caseload is to explore alternative ways of resolving disputes outside the courts, and it is to this topic that I wish to devote my primary attention. By and large we lawyers and law teachers have been far too single-minded when it comes to dispute resolution. Of course, as pointed out earlier, good lawyers have always tried to prevent disputes from coming about, but when that was not possible, we have tended to assume that the courts are the natural and obvious dispute resolvers. In point of fact there is a rich variety of different processes, which, I would submit, singly or in combination, may provide far more "effective" conflict resolution.[7]

Let me turn now to the two questions with which I wish to concern myself:

1) What are the significant characteristics of various alternative dispute resolution mechanisms (such as adjudication by courts, arbitration, mediation, negotiation, and various blends of these and other devices)?

2) How can these characteristics be utilized so that, given the variety of disputes that presently arise, we can begin to develop some rational criteria for allocating various types of disputes to different dispute resolution processes?

. . .

. . . .

[7] I would suggest the following criteria for determining the effectiveness of a dispute resolution mechanism: cost, speed, accuracy, credibility (to the public and the parties), and workability. In some cases, but not in all, predictability may also be important.

The chart reproduced below attempts to depict a spectrum of some of the available processes arranged on a scale of decreasing external involvement.[12]

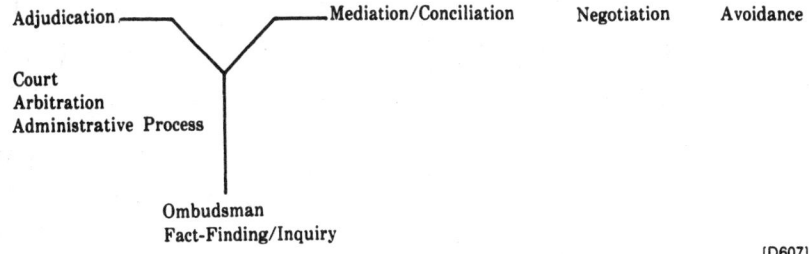

[D607]

At the extreme left is adjudication, the one process that so instinctively comes to the legal mind that I suspect if we asked a random group of law students how a particular dispute might be resolved, they would invariably say "file a complaint in the appropriate court." Professor Lon Fuller, one of the few scholars who has devoted attention to an analysis of the adjudicatory process, has defined adjudication as "a social process of decision which assures to the affected party a particular form of participation, that of presenting proofs and arguments for a decision in his favor."[13] Although he places primary emphasis on process, I would like for present purposes to stress a number of other aspects—the use of a third party with coercive power, the usually "win or lose" nature of the decision, and the tendency of the decision to focus narrowly on the immediate matter in issue as distinguished from a concern with the underlying relationship between the parties. Although mediation or conciliation[14] also involves the use of a third party facilitator (and is distinguished in that regard from pure negotiation), a mediator or conciliator usually has no coercive power and the process in which he engages also differs from adjudication in the other two respects just mentioned. Professor Fuller puts this point well when he refers to "the central quality of mediation, namely, its capacity to reorient the parties toward each other, not by imposing rules on them, but by helping them to achieve

[12] I have selected this factor as one that seems to me rather critical, but there are obviously other aspects in which the various processes differ and which must be considered (e.g., method and cost of selection of third party, qualifications and tenure of third party, formality of proceedings, role of advocates, number of disputants, etc.). Some of these are referred to interstitially in the ensuing discussion. Another factor that is often said to play a differing part in the various processes is the relevance of norms. But see M. Eisenberg, Private Ordering Through Negotiation: Dispute Settlement and Rulemaking, 89 Harv.L. Rev. 637 (1976), suggesting that dispute settlement negotiation closely resembles adjudication in its frequent recourse to norms. See also A. Sarat & J. Grossman, Courts and Conflict Resolution: Problems in the Mobilization of Adjudication, 69 Am.Pol.Sci.Rev. 1200 (1975).

[13] L. Fuller, Collective Bargaining and the Arbitrator, 1963 Wis.L.Rev. 1, 19.

[14] For present purposes the terms mediation and conciliation will be used interchangeably, although in some settings conciliation refers to the more unstructured process of facilitating communication between the parties, while mediation is reserved for a more formal process of meeting first with both parties and then with each of them separately, etc.

a new and shared perception of their relationship, a perception that will redirect their attitudes and dispositions toward one another." [15]

Of course quite a variety of procedures fit under the label of adjudication. Aside from the familiar judicial model, there is arbitration, and the administrative process. Even within any one of these, there are significant variations. Obviously there are substantial differences between the Small Claims Court and the Supreme Court. Within arbitration, too, although the version used in labor relations is generally very similar to a judicial proceeding in that there is a written opinion and an attempt to rationalize the result by reference to general principles, in some forms of commercial arbitration the judgment resembles a Solomonic pronouncement and written opinions are often not utilized. Another significant variant is whether the parties have any choice in selecting the adjudicator, as they typically do in arbitration. Usually a decision rendered by a person in whose selection the parties have played some part will, all things being equal, be less subject to later criticism by the parties.

There are important distinctions, too, concerning the way in which the case came to arbitration. There may be a statute (as in New York and Pennsylvania) requiring certain types of cases to be initially submitted to arbitration (so-called compulsory arbitration). More commonly arbitration is stipulated as the exclusive dispute resolution mechanism in a contract entered into by the parties (as is true of the typical collective bargaining agreement and some modern medical care agreements). In this situation the substantive legal rules are usually also set forth in the parties' agreement, thus giving the parties control not only over the process and the adjudicator but also over the governing principles.

As is noted on the chart, if we focus on the indicated distinctions between adjudication and mediation, there are a number of familiar hybrid processes. An inquiry, for example, in many respects resembles the typical adjudication, but the inquiring officer (or fact finder as he is sometimes called) normally has no coercive power; indeed, according to Professor Fuller's definition, many inquiries would not be adjudication at all since the parties have no right to any agreed-upon form of presentation and participation.

But a fact finding proceeding may be a potent tool for inducing settlement. Particularly if the fact finder commands the respect of the parties, his independent appraisal of their respective positions will often be difficult to reject. This is especially true of the Ombudsman who normally derives his power solely from the force of his position. These considerations have particular applicability where there is a disparity of bargaining power between the disputants (e.g., citizen and government, consumer and manufacturer, student and universi-

---

[15] L. Fuller, Mediation—Its Forms and Functions, 44 So.Cal.L.Rev. 305, 325 (1971).

ty). Although there may often be a reluctance in these situations to give a third person power to render a binding decision, the weaker party may often accomplish the same result through the use of a skilled fact finder.

There are of course a number of other dispute resolution mechanisms which one might consider. Most of these (e.g., voting, coin tossing, self-help) are not of central concern here because of their limited utility or acceptability. But one other mechanism deserves brief mention. Professor William Felstiner [, Influences of Social Organization on Dispute Processing, 9 Law & Soc'y Rev. 63 (1974),] pointed out that in a "technologically complex rich society" avoidance becomes an increasingly common form of handling controversy. He describes avoidance as "withdrawal from or contraction of the dispute-producing relationship" (e.g., a child leaving home, a tenant moving to another apartment, or a businessman terminating a commercial relationship). . . .

[Professor Sander explores criteria that may help determine how particular disputes might best be resolved, including nature of dispute, relationship between disputants, and cost and speed of available processes. He goes on to advocate] a flexible and diverse panoply of dispute resolution processes, with particular types of cases being assigned to differing processes (or combinations of processes), according to some of the criteria previously mentioned. Conceivably such allocation might be accomplished for a particular class of cases at the outset by the legislature; that in effect is what was done by the Massachusetts legislature for malpractice cases. Alternatively one might envision by the year 2000 not simply a court house but a Dispute Resolution Center, where the grievant would first be channelled through a screening clerk who would then direct him to the process (or sequence of processes) most appropriate to his type of case. The room directory in the lobby of such a Center might look as follows:

Screening Clerk	Room 1
Mediation	Room 2
Arbitration	Room 3
Fact Finding	Room 4
Malpractice Screening Panel	Room 5
Superior Court	Room 6
Ombudsman	Room 7

Of one thing we can be certain: once such an eclectic method of dispute resolution is accepted there will be ample opportunity for everyone to play a part. Thus a court might decide of its own to refer a certain type of problem to a more suitable tribunal. Or a legislature might, in framing certain substantive rights, build in an appropriate dispute resolution process. Institutions such as prisons, schools, or mental hospitals also could get into the act by establishing indigenous dispute resolution processes.

LANDSMAN, THE DECLINE OF THE ADVERSARY SYSTEM: HOW THE RHETORIC OF SWIFT AND CERTAIN JUSTICE HAS AFFECTED ADJUDICATION IN AMERICAN COURTS, 29 Buffalo L.Rev. 487, 488, 528–30 (1980). "Pound's remarks have served as a manifesto for those championing judicial efficiency and celerity. Their goal has been to secure the adoption of what they deem to be the speediest methods of resolving disputes. In pursuit of this goal the architects of change have ignored the aims and values of those aspects of the adversary process they seek to alter. They have substituted the rhetoric of swift and certain justice for a reasoned assessment of the impact of change on the court system and society.

. . . .

"The adversary method is not of equal utility in resolving all types of disputes. . . . [S]everal situations can be identified in which the adversary process would seem particularly useful. The most outstanding of these is litigation involving a dispute between a citizen and the government. In such a dispute, whether it be a civil rights case, a criminal matter, or a contract action, the adversary [system's] judge and jury serve as a vital counterbalance to the power of the state.

"On the other hand, there are a number of settings in which adversary procedure does not seem appropriate. When the parties must continue to work or live together in intimate contact or in a cooperative relationship, the adversary method may not be the best means of resolving their dispute. Adversary procedure may exacerbate rather than resolve tensions and may not foster the kind of compromise essential to the restoration of harmony. For this reason, disputes like those between labor and management, or between family members in an intact family unit should usually be resolved in nonadversarial proceedings.

"It is also sensible to utilize nonadversarial methods when *all the parties* strongly desire speed, simplicity, and economy in adjudication. In such settings adversary process will tend to intrude undesired deliberation and expense. The labor grievance process provides an example of the type of case in which certain adversary procedures are avoided for reasons of economy and celerity. Finally, where there is no dispute, adversary machinery is not needed. In situations like the uncontested divorce, adoption, or name change, there is little call for the panoply of procedures built into the adversary process.

"While it is possible to list types of cases that seem more or less suited to adversarial adjudication, any a priori designation threatens to unfairly exclude some litigants from access to procedures they view essential to the proper consideration of their cases. An arbitrary ban on adversarial consideration of 'repetitious' cases, or cases involving small sums of money, or cases involving some 'institutional relationship' raises serious problems of social and political judgment as well as accusations of unequal treatment. A better approach than categorical exclusion may be a system that allows the parties to choose the type of process best suited to their needs. Where all the parties make an *uncoerced* choice to avoid adversarial process it seems eminently sensible to honor their decision. Use of an election mechanism may ease the burden on the adversarial courts, while protecting the rights of those who believe they cannot obtain redress outside the adversarial framework.

"Only when the nature of the adversary process and the values it vindicates are clearly understood and considered is it possible to determine the extent nonadversary processes should be utilized by American courts to resolve disputes. If these issues are ignored, intelligent change is impossible. Arguments like that concerning swift and certain justice, which tend to obscure the fundamental issues, must be rejected as a basis upon which to premise change."

CURRENT DEVELOPMENTS IN JUDICIAL ADMINISTRATION:
PAPERS PRESENTED AT THE PLENARY SESSION OF
THE AMERICAN ASSOCIATION OF LAW
SCHOOLS, DECEMBER, 1977
80 F.R.D. 147, 167–68, 173–74, 179–84 (1979).

Remarks of Earl Johnson, Jr. as Presentor

. . . .

Though there are some differences in analysis and emphasis in these various articles and speeches, they share a common theme: we have become too dependent upon an over-legalized, over-formalized method of resolving disputes in the U.S. . . .

There is less consensus about the cures. Nonetheless, one does often hear about the four de's: de-legalize, de-lawyer, de-formalize and de-judicialize. In other words, let's reduce the number of laws. Let's make them simple enough so that it isn't necessary for a citizen to hire a lawyer before he takes any major step or every time he attempts to resolve any dispute. Let's take some of the time-consuming, confounding formalities out of the judicial process itself. And finally, let's take as many disputes as possible completely out of the judicial framework and resolve them through other means.

. . . .

But why consider using any of these alternative forums. What is wrong with our tried and tested centuries old Anglo-American judicial model? That is an important threshold question that is related intimately to the issue of which criteria one might employ in allocating different categories of disputes to different kinds of forums.

Nor is there a single answer to this question. I suspect that different reformers would provide this audience with different answers. It is, however, possible to detect at least three independent rationales for diverting civil cases away from the traditional judicial forum. For some, the primary goal is to relieve the court workload. For a second, the primary purpose is to improve access for disputes and disputants that cannot economically reach the judicial forum. A third group of reformers feels that the judicial mode is at best an inferior way of resolving at least some kinds of disputes and furthermore that it is a socially and psychologically disruptive approach to such controversies. For convenience, I will label the first motive for channelling disputes to alternative forums as the "judicial overload" rationale, the second as the "access to justice" rationale, and the third as the "superior process" rationale.

This is not to say that a given forum must be supported by only one of these rationales. Some alternative forums are seen as contributing to two or more of these purposes. Nonetheless they are very distinct rationales. Deciding which one is the predominant motive will largely determine which kinds of disputes should be allocated to the non-judicial forum and the criteria which should be applied in judging the performance of that alternative forum.

. . . .

Whichever rationale is under consideration, it is apparent we do not yet have all the answers as to what forums work or which disputes should be channeled to which tribunals. In fact we are just beginning to ask the right questions.

The next decade is apt to see an enormous amount of activity in this field. New forums will be devised, experiments will be undertaken, evaluations will be conducted, debates will rage. In one way or another, through careful planning or confused groping I submit American society will move toward a new justice system: one in which the courts as we know them will still occupy an important position but alongside a variety of alternative forums offering disputants other methods of resolving disputes, other types of dispute resolvers and even other aspirations. It is also a justice system where non-lawyers will have a prominent role.

The entire enterprise offers both challenge and opportunity to the law schools. The chances for creative scholarship and particularly for empirical research are exciting. Meanwhile, there will be need to be flexible in our educational programs to adjust them to the needs of a rapidly evolving and probably dramatically restructured justice system. Who is to train the lay arbitrators, the mediators and other dispute resolvers, both professional and amateur? And how do we equip law students to function effectively in a multi-faceted justice system where they may be called upon to be neutral mediators as often as they are expected to be partisan advocates?

I'm sure there are many in this audience who are skeptical that anything nearly so dramatic as I have suggested will happen ever, to say nothing of within the next decade. But I submit that the three rationales I discussed today are each supported by different but very powerful constituencies. These constituencies range from right to left across the political spectrum, and are found within and without legal profession. Pushing from different directions and for different reasons I suggest they will thrust what might be viewed as revolutionary change upon the judiciary and the legal profession. It may be the historic role of the law schools not only to respond to that change but to help shape it.

Remarks of Paul D. Carrington as Commentator

.   .   .   .

.   .   . I have some doubts about a complex system of alternative procedures for dispute resolution. My doubts are of two kinds. First, I find the task of measuring the supposed benefits and the apparent risks of the proposal to be very troubling. And, secondly, I am not clear to whom the benefits would flow.

[Dean Carrington first observes that the necessary cost-benefit analysis is extremely complex and elusive. Given current understanding, "[w]e are in a very poor position to give guidance to the officer who would match disputes with procedures according to the degree of adversariness appropriate." In particular, there is the risk of encouraging "overuse of legal institutions" and giving "too little reinforcement to the virtue of forbearance."]

Let me now proceed to a brief discussion of my second level of concern. My question here is not whether there is a cost or benefit to be measured, but who receives it. This question is more political and less economic. But it appears that Professor Johnson and I share a common premise that judicial reform should serve the interests of those who are generally least advantaged by the legal system.

There is a lesson to be learned from our relatively recent experience in creating small claims courts to serve as forums for the poor. That reform is about 50 years old. What happened to the small claims courts is that they were quickly captured by institutional litigants. Institutions have employees who quickly gain the experience needed to make effective lay presentations; [these] lay persons can usually be expected to roll over the beleaguered poor who appear to contest their claims as tenants or consumers. It is a rare tenant or consumer who leaves the small claims court with the warm feeling that he has secured justice at a low price. The lesson to be learned from this experience is this: Do not underestimate the ability of those who seem to exploit the present system to exploit its substitute or alternative even more effectively.

.   .   .   .

Similarly, we might ask: who benefits from the complexity of a system of alternatives? Rarely, I suspect, will it be those citizens who are disadvantaged by the flaws in the present system of justice. The one group that is generally advantaged by complexity is the professional class who learn to manipulate the complexity and turn it to their own profit. Again, we have experience to draw on. Perhaps the most notable contribution of Roscoe Pound was his leadership in the unification movement. For decades, efforts proceeded under his guidance to simplify the judicial hierarchy and to consolidate courts and jurisdictions. This movement was intended to serve those who might be disadvantaged by the complexity of the law, who would be burdened by the costs of jurisdictional squabbling. Let us not draw more costly jurisdictional lines without a good purpose clearly in mind. As we populate our courthouses with various levels of para-judges, including such figures as magistrates, referees, court-appointed arbitrators, and other retainers, we are likely to be increasing the value of the professional lawyer's skill. We may well be making justice more of a game to be won by the side who has the best champion. And so it is by no means clear that the beneficiaries of alternative dispute-resolving processes will be those who are intended to benefit.

SINGER, NONJUDICIAL DISPUTE RESOLUTION MECHANISMS: THE EFFECTS ON JUSTICE FOR THE POOR, 13 Clearinghouse Rev. 569, 571–72 (1979). "The supporters of nonjudicial forums . . . have different, sometimes unstated, objectives. Judicial endorsement of informal dispute resolution, for example, frequently proceeds from the desire to make the courts more efficient by reducing caseloads, costs and delays. Government sponsorship of community dispute centers generally is based on the hypothesis that the centers are faster and less expensive to operate than courts and that the courts themselves can be made to operate more efficiently if congestion is reduced by diverting minor disputes to other forums. A different, and possibly conflicting, objective is to augment the access of citizens to a variety of tribunals which can resolve their complaints. Achievement of this objective would bring a large number of disputes into some forum, whether judicial or nonjudicial, and thus, presumably, increase the total resources devoted to dispute resolution.

"A third objective of alternative forums is to reduce conflict by settling individual disputes that, if unresolved, might fester, recur or escalate into violent confrontations. In this regard, supporters of mediation frequently cite its superiority to formal adjudication in addressing the 'root causes,' as opposed to the most recent symptoms, of ongoing conflicts.

"On the other hand, the achievement of a fourth objective—the use of the legal system to further social, economic and political conceptions of equal justice—sometimes may result in the escalation of conflict. For the past generation legal efforts to achieve equal justice have frequently been concentrated on class action litigation. Recently, some scholars and practitioners have begun to question such

heavy reliance on the courts to enforce rights and deter unfair practices. They advocate a variety of forums and procedures to redress
the grievances of members of underrepresented constituencies, rang-
ing from prisoners to consumers. Such advocates are sometimes vocal supporters of nonjudicial forums.

"Many advocates of nonjudicial dispute resolution are motivated
by still other objectives such as increased fairness of both legal
processes and their results, increased satisfaction with the legal system on the part of participants, and increased ability of various seg-
ments of society to govern their own affairs without having to resort
regularly to judicial intervention. The last objective has been expressed quite differently in different contexts. In institutional contexts, the objective is expressed as one of self-governance or avoidance of the imposition of rules by outsiders. In neighborhoods or,
occasionally, in tightly knit ethnic communities, it may be expressed
as community empowerment or neighborhood justice. Finally, on an
individual level, the objective is one of increased self-sufficiency or
the capacity to manage one's own affairs without heavy reliance on
representatives of the legal system." [1]

SECTION 3.   A COMPARATIVE LOOK

KAPLAN, CIVIL PROCEDURE—REFLECTIONS ON THE COMPARISON OF SYSTEMS
9 Buffalo L.Rev. 409, 409–14 (1960).

To begin, the rules governing civil procedure in Germany today
are laid down by legislative enactment stemming from the famous
code of 1877; judicial rule-making plays virtually no part. There is
no jury. The courts, at least those concerned in the regular proceedings for cases of consequence, are collegial in structure, acting
through benches of three or—in the court of final review—five judges. To some extent, however, the plural bench may use a single
judge as a representative or helper.

One of the leitmotifs of the German process is sounded by the
Siegfried horn of the summons in the action. This invites appearance
at a *Termin zur mündlichen Verhandlung*, a court-session for oral-
argument, or rather for conference, since the ideal style of proceeding is less that of a contentious confrontation than a cooperative discussion. The conference is set perhaps three to four weeks after initial service of the papers—which by the way is usually accomplished
by mail—and it is commonly attended by the parties as well as counsel. Now the point to be made is that the whole procedure up to
judgment may be viewed as being essentially a series of such confer-

---

[1] For an anthropological approach to
dispute resolution, see The Disputing
Process—Law in Ten Societies (L. Nader
& H. Todd eds. 1978).

ences, the rest of the process having a sort of dependent status. Prooftaking occurs to the extent necessary in the spaces, as it were, between conferences. Intermediate decisions are made along the way. But the conferences are the heart of the matter. Very promptly, then, the litigants are brought under the eye of the court and the case begins to be shaped; and this treatment is applied to the action at intervals until it is fully opened and finally broken. "Conference" betokens informality and this characterizes the entire German procedure. "Conference" also suggests what is the fact, that possibilities of settlement are openly, vigorously, and continually exploited.

I must relate German pleadings to the conference method—I shall use the word "pleadings" although these writings are quite different from the American variety. The action starts with a complaint served together with the summons, but beyond this there is no prescribed number or sequence of pleadings. Pleadings are to be put in in such numbers and at such times as to prepare for, strengthen, and expedite the conferences and thereby the general movement of the case. They have no position independent of the conferences. Indeed the framers of the code of 1877 looked to a free, oral restatement of the pleadings at conference. Such oral recapitulation no longer occurs: the court reads the pleadings in advance and the lawyers are assumed to adopt the pleadings except as they speak up to the contrary. Still no question arises as to the sufficiency of the pleadings as such, nor is there any motion practice directed to the pleadings themselves. In short, pleadings merge into, are an ingredient of the conferences. What is wanted from the pleadings as adopted and perhaps revised at conference is a narrative of the facts as the parties see them at the time, with offers of proof—mainly designated witnesses and documents—and demands for relief. There is no insistence on niceties of form, and legal argumentation, though strictly out of place, is common in today's pleadings. Amendments, even drastic amendments, of the statements can be made until the end of the case, normally without any penalty for late change. This malleability of the pleadings flows from the realization and expectation that a case may change its content and color as it is repeatedly discussed and as proof is from time to time adduced.

Returning to the conduct of the conferences, we find the presiding judge highly vocal and dominant, the parties themselves often voluble, the lawyers relatively subdued. To understand the judicial attitude and contribution at conference, we must take account of two related concepts. First, there is the principle jura novit curia, the court knows and applies the law without relying on the parties to bring it forward. Second, article 139 of the code, as strengthened in recent years, imposes a duty on all courts to clarify the cause and lead the parties toward full development of their respective positions. Thus with awareness of the law implicit in the case, the court is obliged to discuss it freely with the litigants, and in that light to indicate what will be material to decision. By discussion with counsel and the parties the court completes the picture of the controversy as presented by the litigants, throwing light upon obscurities, correcting misunderstandings, marking out areas of agreement and disagreement. It spurs and guides the parties to any necessary further exploration of facts and theories, and may suggest appropriate allegations, proof offers, and demands. The court, however, is not bound to take over and commandeer the litigation, nor does it have the power to do so in an ultimate sense. To some degree—the power is greater in "family" matters than in ordinary cases—the court may call up evidence and background information. The calling of experts is basically a matter for the court. But, in general, allegations, proof offers, and demands can be made only by the parties and so in the last analysis major control of the cause-materials remains with them. Nevertheless, as the parties are likely to follow the court's suggestions, we have here a significant potential in the court which imparts a special quality to the procedure; and this is so despite the fact that clarification and leading are hardly noticeable in simpler cases where the lawyers seem to be providing competent representation. The role of the court not only at conference but throughout the proceedings is envisioned as being both directive and protective. The court as vigorous chairman is to move the case along at a good pace, stirring the parties to action on their own behalf, exercising its limited sua sponte powers where necessary, conscious of a duty to strive for the right solution of the controversy regardless of faults of advocacy.

Conferences propel the lawsuit. Most dates are set by the court in open session. It acts in discretion with due regard to the convenience of the parties: few "iron" time provisions are laid down in the code, and the parties cannot control the pace by stipulation. When discussions disclose ripe questions of law, a time will be set for decision. If they show up disputed issues of fact, there will be an order and a time set for prooftaking.

To understand German prooftaking, we have first to ask what investigation of the facts a German lawyer customarily makes. He consults his client and his client's papers. But he has substantially no coercive means of "discovering" material for the purpose of preparing his proof offers or readying himself for prooftaking. Moreover he is by no means at liberty to go out and talk informally with prospective witnesses. He is hobbled by the principle that he is to avoid all suspicion of influencing those who may be later called to give evidence in court. I shall not attempt to mark the exact boundaries of this inhibition or to dredge up the possible evasive contrivances. I shall simply say that German lawyers are not prime movers with respect to the facts. The régime just described does make for unrehearsed witnesses. It begins to explain why a party in German litigation is not charged with any "proprietorship" over the witnesses whom he has nominated and neither "vouches" for them nor is "bound" by their testimony.

The court draws up the order for prooftaking, the *Beweisbeschluss*, from the nominations set out in the pleadings as they may have been revised at conference. Prooftaking need not be concentrated at a single session, and is in fact not often so concentrated. Accordingly the court may pick and choose what it wants to hear at particular sessions. It can take proof in any order—evidence on a defense ahead of evidence on the main case, even evidence on the negative of an issue ahead of the affirmative.

Witnesses are sequestered, kept out of the courtroom until called. The court asks the witness to state what he knows about the proof theme on which he has been summoned. When the witness has done that in narrative without undue interruption, the court interrogates him, and this is the principal interrogation. Counsel put supplemental questions. Lawyers' participation is likely to be meager. If a lawyer puts too many questions he is implying that the court does not know its business, and that is a dubious tactic. A full stenographic transcript is not kept. Instead the court dictates a summary of the witness' testimony for the minutes which is then read back and perhaps corrected.

German law has few rules excluding relevant evidence. In general relevant evidence is admissible and when admitted is freely evaluated: thus there is no bar to the admission of hearsay. But a few qualifications must be made. German law recognizes a series of privileges. It is somewhat irresolute in compelling production in court of various kinds of documentary proof. Testimony will be received from the parties themselves only in particular circumstances defined by law, and in no event may a party be compelled to testify. Party-testimony is viewed as a kind of last resort. This raises a quiddity, for parties are regularly heard in conference, nominally for purposes of clarification, not proof. I say "nominally" because German law tends to blur the line between evidence stricto sensu and other happenings in the courtroom.

Prooftaking is succeeded by conference, conference by prooftaking, and so on to the end of the regular proceedings in the first-instance court; and now we naturally ask, are there any shortcuts, any special devices for closing a case out promptly when it appears that there is overwhelming strength on one side and corresponding weakness on the other? The answer is no. The German system relies on the succession of conferences and prooftakings to show up strength or weakness with reasonable dispatch. Nor is there much in the way of stage-preclusion, that is, rules intended to discourage delaying afterthoughts by requiring that particular offers or objections be made at fixed points in the proceeding on pain of being otherwise lost to the party. The German action is not segmented into clear-cut stages—recall how pleadings may be thrown in late in the day—and it has in general a quality of "wholeness" or unity. But we do need to say here that the German system makes interestingly brisk provision for handling defaults; and we should also call attention to certain special speed-up devices: "dunning" proceedings, *Mahnverfahren*, available for "collection" cases and carried on regardless of amount in the inferior one-judge court; and "documentary-process," *Urkundenprozess*, used chiefly in suits on commercial paper, with proof initially limited to documents and party-testimony.

We come now to appellate review. The most notable fact about it is that on appeal to the court of second instance from final judgment, or from the important type of intermediate judgment which determines liability but leaves damages to be ascertained, the parties are entitled to a redoing of the case. The record made below, so far as it is thought to be free of error, stands as part of the proceedings, but the parties may add new proofs and invoke new legal theories, and the conduct of the cause is quite similar to that in the court below. Remember that article 139 on clarification and leading, with related duties and powers, continues to apply. The final court of review hears "revisions" on questions of law. As to matters of substance as distinguished from procedure, the court is not confined to the grounds urged by counsel. It seems a mark of the reality of the principle jura novit curia that this national court, dealing with a very large number of revisions coming up from the lower courts administered by the states, the *Länder*, is served by a bar limited by law to less than a score of lawyers.

The German court system is manned by a quite sizeable number of judges. They are career men, appointed on the basis of government examinations, modestly paid, of good but not exalted social prestige, looking primarily to ministerial departments of justice for advancement. In normal times men customarily enter into judicial service at an early age, generally without substantial experience in practice. Judges have traditionally been chided for *Lebensfremdheit*, undue detachment from the rough-and-tumble of life. We have caught a hint of their paternalistic role in the court procedure. This is not far distant from, indeed it comprises, an element of the bureaucratic. Working, many of them, in collegial courts whose judgments, stiffly authoritative in style, disclose neither individual authorship nor individual dissent, German judges live rather anonymous lives. And they are desk-bound through a large part of their working time, for files must be read in preparation for court sessions, and most decisions in actions large and small must be compendiously written up.

As to the German lawyers, I must avoid leaving the impression that their contribution to litigation is unimportant, or that their attitude is flaccid. Despite the court's capacity for active interposition, the frame of the case is made by the lawyers and there is room for contentious striving. Still the procedural system we have outlined does not make for notably vigorous performance by counsel. Moreover the education of lawyers tends against their full identification with clients as combatants: a significant part of their post-University required training is as apprentice-judges. Most important, we must notice some economic facts. Lawyers' fees for litigation, generally corresponding with statutory scales fixed in relation to the amount in controversy, are low.

Court costs are also fixed by statute in relation to the amount in suit, so that a litigant is on the one hand prompted to moderate his demand for judgment, and can on the other hand make a reasonably accurate advance estimate of the expense of litigation. Taking all elements of expense into consideration, German litigation is cheap by comparison with the American brand. But on the threshold a German litigant must conjure with the fact that if as plaintiff or defendant he turns out loser in the lawsuit, he will have to reimburse his opponent's expenses—counsel fees and court costs at the statutory rates together with ordinary disbursements. Let us note here that contingent-fee arrangements—agreements for quota litis—are proscribed in German practice. A comprehensive system of state-provided legal aid aims to enable not only downright paupers but any citizens of insufficient means to prosecute or defend civil cases upon a plausible showing of a prospect of success.

Lastly I must respond to the nervous question which any American lawyer would surely want to ask: Does the German system get over its court business without undue delay? German court statistics—at least those publicly available and not held in subterranean tunnels by the ministries—are curiously sparse; but these figures combine with the opinion of German lawyers familiar with the scene to indicate that the courts, although handling a very considerable volume of cases, are disposing of their calendars with fair speed. However, the court of final review—the *Bundesgerichtshof* sitting in Karlsruhe, successor to the famous *Reichsgericht* which used to reside in Leipzig—has had a hard time in recent years overcoming a serious backlog.[m]

Exercise: Set out below is a series of notes and catch phrases intended to remind you of the characteristics of American civil procedure. With respect

[m] For a more complete account of the German procedure, see Kaplan, von Mehren & Schaefer, Phases of German Civil Procedure (pts. 1–2), 71 Harv.L.Rev. 1193, 1443 (1958). Obviously, since the time of these accounts, there have been changes in that procedure. Most significantly, there has been a movement, based on efficiency concerns, toward greater concentration of the proceedings in a single hearing. See Fisch, Recent Reforms in German Civil Procedure: The Constitutional Dimension, 1 Civ.Just.Q. 33 (1982). See generally Gottwald, Simplified Civil Procedure in West Germany, 31 Am.J.Comp.L. 687 (1983).

For a look at a system closer to ours, a comparison with its own distinctive lessons, see Kaplan, An American Lawyer in the Queen's Courts: Impressions of English Civil Procedure, 69 Mich.L.Rev. 821 (1971). For a more up-to-date account, see Kaplan & Clermont, Ordinary Proceedings in First Instance: England and the United States, 16 Int'l Ency. Comp.L. ch. 6 (1984).

For a look at systems more distant from ours, one might begin by contrasting the socialist civil procedure described in M. Glendon, M. Gordon & C. Osakwe, Comparative Legal Traditions in a Nutshell 336–43 (1982).

to each item, try to describe the analogous or contrasting feature of German civil procedure.

    I. *Lack of nationwide uniformity*

       51 systems

       Abundance of detailed procedural regulation in older state systems

       Spread of rulemaking and increasing adoption of Federal Rules pattern

       Query how far there is or should be functional adaptation of procedure to the type of case

   II. *Inherent problems in allocation of cases to courts*

       Federal-state cleavage

       State-state divisions

       Persistence of artificial determinants of case-allocation, e.g., continued importance of place of service of process

       Cf. search for proper law to be applied

  III. *Emphasis on full exploration of facts by parties before trial*

       Importance of facts in the system of justice

       Single-episode trial as compelling exploration of facts beforehand

       Three sorties into facts: unsanctioned, discovery, trial

       Free recourse to prospective witnesses

       Influence of strong adversary spirit of litigation

       No ex officio investigation

  IV. *Pretrial effort to frame issues by pleadings and pleading-motions*

       Single-episode trial as compelling formal definition of issues beforehand

       Use of pleadings and pleading-motions to secure summary disposition

       Generalized style of pleadings: no legal argumentation, no recital of evidence or nomination of sources of proof (relation to discovery)

   V. *Mechanisms for disposition of cases before trial*

       Motion for summary judgment (relation to discovery)

       Failure to prosecute; default; voluntary dismissal; settlement

  VI. *Growing use of pretrial conferences as corrective*

       Use of conferences to rationalize materials developed by discovery

       To sharpen issues

       To produce early disposition

       To facilitate trial proper

       Emergent tendency to center regulation of all pretrial activities in conferences

       Tendency toward assumption by judge of greater management power and protective responsibility

Extent to which conferences (and discovery) soften adversary climate of litigation

  VII. *Characteristics of trial*

Single-episode; relatively dramatic; oral and "immediate"

Fixed order of proceeding

Parties as combatants

Judge as umpire administering exclusionary rules of evidence

Question-and-answer and the verbatim transcript

Jury as centerpiece

Interaction of judge and jury

Effects on system of infusion of lay triers of fact

  VIII. *Characteristics of appeal*

Three-level system, with only appellate courts collegial

"Final decision" standard

Confinement of review substantially to rulings of law by trial court challenged by party when made

Simplicity of appellate procedure

  IX. *Access to courts as related to expenses of litigation*

Court costs controlled, low, reimbursed to winner

Other expenses uncontrolled, high, not reimbursed

Role of the contingent fee

Actions in forma pauperis; legal aid; legal insurance plans

  X. *Condition of calendars as related to number of judges and character of cases*

  XI. *Image of the judge*

  XII. *Image of the lawyer*

In doing this exercise, consider the following from the above-excerpted article (9 Buffalo L.Rev. at 422):

"Possibilities of lifting pieces from a foreign system and incorporating them in the domestic must be approached with a sense of the interdependencies, the syndromes, so to speak, within the system a quo and the system ad quem. This is not to say that it is no use trying to import mechanisms for domestic use unless the foreign system is brought over entire. For some procedural devices can stand up pretty well in isolation from the rest of the system. I put as possible examples the special 'dunning' and documentary processes successfully employed in many cases in Germany. Another example which may make the point is service by mail, a traditional usage in Germany and elsewhere, much admired by Bentham. This has in fact been progressively adopted in our country, although its original parentage may not always have been recognized. . . . Consider the feasibility of introducing here the German practice of having witnesses give their testimony in narrative, followed by interrogation by the court; this to be followed in turn by interrogation in our conventional way by counsel for both sides. This may seem a simple change that could be commended on various imaginable grounds, but I would ask you to reflect on whether it could be effectively or safely engrafted on our present system without other profound changes."

Part Two

THE UNITARY CIVIL ACTION

TOPIC A. INTRODUCTION—FEDERAL RULE 2

WILLIAMSON v. COLUMBIA GAS & ELECTRIC CORP., 110 F.2d 15 (3d Cir.1939), cert. denied, 310 U.S. 639, 60 S.Ct. 1087 (1940). On September 16, 1938, one Williamson, as trustee in bankruptcy of Inland Gas Corporation, commenced an action in the United States District Court for the District of Delaware against Columbia Gas & Electric Corporation. He charged in his complaint that Columbia had injured Inland by committing various acts in violation of § 7 of the Clayton Act, 15 U.S.C. § 18, which then provided in part: "No corporation engaged in commerce shall acquire . . . the whole or any part of the stock . . . of another corporation engaged also in commerce, where the effect of such acquisition may be to substantially lessen competition between the corporation whose stock is so acquired and the corporation making the acquisition." He demanded treble damages in accordance with § 4 of the Clayton Act, 15 U.S.C. § 15.

Columbia presented by motion under Rule 12(b)(6) the defense that the complaint failed to state a claim upon which relief could be granted, contending that plaintiff's claim was barred by the applicable statute of limitations. The parties entered into a stipulation, which accompanied the motion, to the effect that "the right of action accrued not later than January 1, 1931."

As there was no act of Congress fixing a period of limitations for commencing actions under the Clayton Act, the district court resorted to the laws of Delaware to find the applicable period. A Delaware statute provided in part: "No action of trespass, no action of replevin, no action of detinue, no action of debt not found upon a record or specialty, no action of account, no action of assumpsit, and no action upon the case shall be brought after the expiration of three years from the accruing of the cause of such action." [a] Plaintiff contended that his action was in the nature of an action of "debt on a specialty," [b] which was not covered by the quoted Delaware statute and as to which the Delaware courts had said that the only limitation was the presumption of satisfaction after twenty years. Defendant con-

---

[a] The problem of this case could not arise today in Delaware for two reasons. First, with the adoption in 1948 of the Delaware Rules of Civil Procedure, including a rule corresponding to Federal Rule 2, the Delaware statute of limitations was amended to eliminate references to the forms of action. See Del. Code Ann. tit. 10, § 8106. Second, in 1955 Congress added a four-year period of limitations for actions arising under the antitrust laws. See 15 U.S.C. § 15b.

[b] See infra p. 338.

299

tended that the action was one on the "case," [c] which was therefore barred.

The district court granted the motion, and the circuit court of appeals affirmed. The opinion of the circuit court of appeals went at some length into the differences among the ancient forms of action mentioned in the Delaware statute, citing not only Delaware cases but English cases and treatises, and concluded that the action was one on the "case."

Plaintiff had contended that "since the 'civil action' provided for by the Federal Rules of Civil Procedure . . . has abolished all distinctions in the forms of actions the state statutes of limitations based upon differences in forms of action no longer apply." Answering this contention, the appellate court said:

"Exactly the same contention was made in England, after the abolition of forms of action by the Judicature Act of 1873. In Gibbs v. Guild, 1882, 9 Q.B.D. 59, page 67, Brett, L.J., said: 'It was said that inasmuch as the names of actions are altered, and there is no longer an action on the case, or an action of trespass, the Statute of Limitations did no longer apply; but I am of opinion that the Judicature Act, 1873, did not alter or touch the Statute of Limitations at all, and that the statute still applies to the circumstances which constituted the actions named in it, that is to say, that if the circumstances would have constituted an action on the case or an action of trespass, although the action which involves the remedy sought would not now be called an action on the case or an action of trespass, yet, notwithstanding the Statute of Limitations applies to it, if the facts are such as would have supported an action on the case or an action of trespass.' *Even tho not now called "case" or "trespass" → stat. of lim. still applies if facts support action on case, tress.*

"We fully agree with the views expressed by the Circuit Court of Appeals of the Fifth Circuit, in City of El Paso v. West et al., 104 F.2d 96, 97, in which that court disposed of a similar argument with the statement 'Even under the new rules, when limitation depends on the State law and that law refers to a form of action as determinative, it will be necessary to ascertain what sort of case the pleader is presenting.' We find no evidence in the Federal Rules of Civil Procedure or in the notes thereto of an intent to cover the field of limitations of actions. . . .

To apply State Stat. of lim ct. must determine what form of action would have been at C.L. "In order to apply a statute of limitations, such as that of Delaware, which reads in terms of common law actions, to a civil action brought in a district court, it is necessary for the court through a consideration of the nature of the cause of action disclosed in the complaint to determine the form of action which would have been brought upon it at common law. It is evident that the complaint in the case before us discloses a cause of action which, under the com-

[c] See infra p. 318.

mon law of Delaware, would be enforceable in an action on the case and not in an action of debt on a specialty. The district court, therefore, properly held that the action was barred by the Delaware statute of limitations."

What, then, is the meaning of Federal Rule 2, which provides: *"One Form of Action.* There shall be one form of action to be known as 'civil action' "?

A large number of states have statutes or rules of court substantially to the same effect. Section 103(a) of New York Civil Practice Law and Rules is somewhat more explicit than Rule 2. It provides: *"One form of civil action.* There is only one form of civil action. The distinctions between actions at law and suits in equity, and the forms of those actions and suits, have been abolished." This language, stemming from the famous New York Code of Procedure of 1848 associated with the name of David Dudley Field, suggests that there was once a distinction between "actions at law" and "suits in equity" and further that there were various "forms" at least of those actions; that the distinction and the forms have been abolished; and that consequently there is only one form of civil action.

In the following passages from the English legal historian F.W. Maitland, we find a statement of what the one form of civil action entails. He contrasts the position in England during the time of Blackstone with the position after the English legislation of 1873, effective in 1875, finally adopting the concept of the unitary civil action. (Maitland is addressing himself chiefly to the forms of action at law and their abolition. He does not here consider at any length the erasure of the dividing line between actions at law and suits in equity.[d])

F. MAITLAND, THE FORMS OF ACTION AT COMMON LAW
2–5, 8–9 (1936).[e]

The forms of action we have buried, but they still rule us from their graves. Let us then for awhile place ourselves in Blackstone's day, or, for this matters not, some seventy years later in 1830, and let us look for a moment at English civil procedure.

Let it be granted that one man has been wronged by another; the first thing that he or his advisers have to consider is what form of action he shall bring. It is not enough that in some way or another he should compel his adversary to appear in court and should then

[d] In this country there is a constitutional barrier to the complete procedural merger of law and equity. What is that barrier?

[e] This book consists of a course of seven lectures given by Maitland at Cambridge around the turn of the last century.

state in the words that naturally occur to him the facts on which he relies and the remedy to which he thinks himself entitled. No, English law knows a certain number of forms of action, each with its own uncouth name, a writ of right, an assize of novel disseisin or of *mort d'ancestor*, . . . an action of covenant, debt, detinue, replevin, trespass, assumpsit, ejectment, case. This choice is not merely a choice between a number of queer technical terms, it is a choice between methods of procedure adapted to cases of different kinds. Let us notice some of the many points that are implied in it.

Certain cts. take certain actions

(i) There is the competence of the court. For very many of the ordinary civil cases each of the three courts which have grown out of the king's court of early days, the King's Bench, Common Pleas and Exchequer is equally competent, though it is only by means of elaborate and curious fictions that the King's Bench and the Exchequer can entertain these matters, and the Common Pleas still retains a monopoly of those actions which are known as real.

Diff ways to Get def. to appear

(ii) A court chosen, one must make one's adversary appear; but what is the first step towards this end? In some actions one ought to begin by having him summoned, in others one can at once have him attached, he can be compelled to find gage and pledge for his appearance. In the assize of novel disseisin it is enough to attach his bailiff.

(iii) Suppose him contumacious, what can one do? Can one have his body seized? If he can not be found, can one have him outlawed? This stringent procedure has been extending itself from one form of action to another. Again, can one have the thing in dispute seized? This is possible in some actions, impossible in others.

(iv) Can one obtain a judgment by default, obtain what one wants though the adversary continues in his contumacy? Yes in some forms, no in others.

(v) It comes to pleading, and here each form of action has some rules of its own. For instance the person attacked—the tenant he is called in some cases, the defendant in others—wishes to oppose the attacker—the demandant he is called in some actions, the plaintiff in others—by a mere general denial, casting upon him the burden of proving his own case, what is he to say? In other words, what is the general issue appropriate to this action? In one form it is *Nihil debet*, in another *Non assumpsit*, in another 'Not guilty,' in others, *Nul tort, nul disseisin*.

Lots of Diff types of juries

(vi) There is to be a trial; but what mode of trial? Very generally of course a trial by jury. But it may be trial by a grand or petty assize, which is not quite the same thing as trial by jury; or in Blackstone's day it may still conceivably be a trial by battle. Again in some forms of action the defendant may betake himself to the world-old process of compurgation or wager of law. Again there are a few issues which are tried without a jury by the judges who hear witnesses.

(vii) Judgment goes against the defendant, what is the appropriate form of execution? Can one be put into possession of the thing that has been in dispute? Can one imprison the defendant? Can one have him made an outlaw? or can he merely be distrained?

(viii) Judgment goes against the defendant. It is not enough that he should satisfy the plaintiff's just demand; he must also be punished for his breach of the law—such at all events is the theory. What form shall this punishment take? Will an amercement suffice, or shall there be fine or imprisonment? Here also there have been differences.

(ix) Some actions are much more dilatory than others; the dilatory ones have gone out of use, but still they exist. In these oldest forms—forms invented when as yet the parties had to appear in person and could only appoint attorneys by the king's special leave—the action may drag on for years, for the parties enjoy a power of sending essoins, that is, excuses for non-appearance. The medieval law of essoins is vast in bulk; time is allowed for almost every kind of excuse for non-appearance—a short essoin *de malo veniendi*, a long essoin *de malo lecti*. Now-a-days all is regulated by general rules with a wide discretion left in the Court. In the Middle Ages discretion is entirely excluded; all is to be fixed by iron rules. This question of essoins has been very important—in some forms, the oldest and solemnest, a party may betake himself to his bed and remain there for year and day and meanwhile the action is suspended.

These remarks may be enough to show that the differences between the several forms of action have been of very great practical importance—'a form of action' has implied a particular original process, a particular mesne process, a particular final process, a particular mode of pleading, of trial, of judgment. But further to a very considerable degree the substantive law administered in a given form of action has grown up independently of the law administered in other forms. Each procedural pigeon-hole contains its own rules of substantive law, and it is with great caution that we may argue from what is found in one to what will probably be found in another; each has its own precedents. It is quite possible that a litigant will find that his case will fit some two or three of these pigeon-holes. If that be so he will have a choice, which will often be a choice between the old, cumbrous, costly, on the one hand, the modern, rapid, cheap, on the other. Or again he may make a bad choice, fail in his action, and take such comfort as he can from the hints of the judges that another form of action might have been more successful.[f] The plaintiff's

[f] A judgment for the defendant solely on the ground that the plaintiff had selected the wrong form of action terminated that lawsuit and made the losing plaintiff liable for costs. Because it was not an adjudication on the merits, the principle of res judicata did not come into play. The plaintiff could therefore commence a new action under the proper form unless the period of limitations had run meanwhile. Compare R. Casad, Res Judicata in a Nutshell 19–20 (1976), with C. Clark, Handbook of the Law of Code Pleading 473–74 (2d ed. 1947).

choice is irrevocable; he must play the rules of the game that he has chosen. Lastly, he may find that, plausible as his case may seem, it just will not fit any one of the receptacles provided by the courts and he may take to himself the lesson that where there is no remedy there is no wrong.

The key-note of the form of action is struck by the original writ, the writ whereby the action is begun. From of old the rule has been that no one can bring an action in the king's court of common law without the king's writ; we find this rule in Bracton—*Non potest quis sine brevi agere.*[g]   . . .

. . . .

The final blow was struck by the Judicature Act of 1873 and the rules made thereunder, which came into force in 1875. This did much more than finally abolish the forms of actions known to the common law for it provided that equity and law should be administered concurrently. Since that time we have had what might fairly be called a Code of Civil Procedure. Of course we can not here speak of the details of that Code; but you will not misunderstand me if I say that the procedure which it enjoins is comparatively formless. Of course there are rules, many rules.

We can not say that whatever be the nature of the plaintiff's claim the action will always take the same course and pass through the same stages. For instance, when the plaintiff's claim falls within one of certain classes he can adopt a procedure whereby when he has sworn positively to the truth of his claim the defendant can be shut out from defending the action at all unless he first makes oath to some good defence. So again there are cases in which either party can insist that the questions of fact, if any, shall be tried by jury; there are other cases in which there will be no trial by jury. Again, I must not allow you to think that a lawyer can not do his client a great deal of harm by advising a bad or inappropriate course of procedure, though it is true that he can not bring about a total shipwreck of a good cause so easily as he might have done some years ago. The great change gradually brought about and consummated by the Judicature Acts is that the whole course of procedure in an action is not determined for good and all by the first step, by the original writ. It can no longer be said, as it might have been said in 1830 that we have about 72 forms of action, or as it might have been said in 1874 that we have about 12 forms of action. This is a different thing from saying that our English law no longer attempts to classify *causes* of action, on the contrary a rational, modern classification of causes of action is what we are gradually obtaining—but the forms of action belong to the past.

[g] Bracton's formula must be taken with certain qualifications. See Richardson & Sayles, Introduction to 60 Selden Society, Select Cases of Procedure Without Writ Under Henry III (1941).

Since the Judicature Acts there are, of course, differences of procedure arising out of the character of the various actions, whether for divorce, probate of a will, specific performance of a contract: such differences there must be, but they can now be regarded as mere variations of one general theme—procedure in an action in the High Court of Justice.

Among the questions of civil procedure most in need of basic research are: "[S]hould the drive toward a unitary procedure be abated, should special procedures be set up that are better accommodated to the intrinsic qualities of the problems presented? I suggest that we need to think less about 'procedure' eo nomine and more about the particular social matrix; we should go from the problem in its setting to the appropriate procedure; whether or how the courts or any other dispute-resolving mechanisms are to be invoked will be conditioned by the other material solutions." Kaplan, An American Lawyer in the Queen's Courts: Impressions of English Civil Procedure, 69 Mich.L. Rev. 821, 845 (1971). This article goes on to note: "With regard to variations on a standard procedure, recall that the English are not as much attached to unitary procedure as we have been; a number of variant procedures are today in use in the High Court, but whether the particular variations are justified functionally may be doubted."

For example, it has been argued that the Federal Rules' notions of notice pleading, liberal joinder, and wide discovery have "produced a nightmare" when applied to smaller cases. "We need a less-expansive process. Otherwise, ordinary disputes will continue to blossom into Federal cases." Subrin, The Law and the Rules, N.Y. Times, Nov. 10, 1979, at 23, col. 4. Think of this argument as we trace the history of procedure.

TOPIC B.   EVOLUTION OF THE COMMON LAW

SECTION 1.   EMERGENCE OF THE FORMS OF ACTION AT LAW

F. MAITLAND, THE CONSTITUTIONAL HISTORY OF ENGLAND
105–09, 111–15 (1908).[a]

We will now take a brief review of the whole system of law courts as it stands in Edward the First's day. [Reigned 1272–1307.—Ed.]

There are we may say courts of four great kinds. (1) There are the very ancient courts of the shire and the hundred; these we may call popular courts, or still better, communal courts—they are courts which in time past have been constituted by the free men of the district; they are courts which are now constituted by the freeholders of the district; but a good many of the hundred courts have fallen into private hands. (2) There are the feudal courts, courts which have their origin in tenure, in the relation between man and lord; there is the manorial court baron for the freehold tenants of the manor, in which they sit as judges; there is the hall-moot or customary court of the manor for the tenants in villeinage, in which (at least according to the theory of later times) the lord's steward is the only judge. (3) There are the king's own central courts. (4) There are the courts held by the king's itinerant justices—visitorial courts, we may for the moment call them. We leave out of sight the ecclesiastical courts, or courts Christian, though these were important courts for the laity as well as for the clergy.

Now the preliminary notions with which we ought to start are, I think, these:—(a) The communal courts of the shire and the hundred are, to start with, fully competent courts for all causes criminal as well as civil. The kings of the pre-Conquest period had apparently no desire to draw away justice from these courts. Over and over again they ordain that no one is to bring his suit before the king before justice has failed him in the hundred and the shire. We must not think of the witenagemot even as a court of appeal—to introduce the notion of an appeal from court to court is to introduce a far too modern conception. The suitor who comes before the king comes there not to get a mistake corrected but to lodge a complaint against his judges; they have wilfully denied him justice.

[a] This book consists of a course of lectures given by Maitland at Cambridge in 1887–88.

(b) By the side of the ancient courts there have grown up the feudal courts. This process had in all probability been going on for a century before the Conquest. After the Conquest the principle seems admitted that any lord who has tenants may, if he can, hold a court for them. In this disputes between tenants are adjudged; in particular if land is in dispute and both parties admit that the land is holden of this lord, then his court is the proper tribunal. A great deal of jurisdiction has thus been taken away from the communal courts, but jurisdiction of a civil kind. Mere tenure cannot give a criminal jurisdiction; if the lord has this, he has it by virtue of some grant from the king.

(c) After the Norman Conquest the king's court has, we may say, three main functions: (i) as of old it is a court of last resort in case of default of justice, (ii) on feudal principle it is a court for the tenants in chief, (iii) it is admitted that there are certain causes in which the king has a special interest and which must come either before his own court or before a court held by some officer of his:—these are the pleas of the crown.

We have now to watch the growth of this royal jurisdiction and will begin by speaking of the pleas of the crown.

Already before the Conquest we find that there are certain criminal cases in which the king is conceived to have a special interest. Thus in the Laws of Canute [1017–35] it is said 'These are the rights which the king has over all men in Wessex—*mund-bryce, ham-socne, forstal, flymena-fyrmde* and *fyrd-wite.*' Apparently in case of any of these crimes no lord may presume to exercise jurisdiction—unless it has been expressly granted to him; such cases must come before the king, or his officer the sheriff, and the consequent forfeitures are specially the king's. A word as to the nature of these crimes:— *mund-bryce* is breach of the king's special peace or protection, this as we shall soon see becomes a matter of the utmost moment; *ham-socne* is housebreaking, the seeking of a man in his house; *forstal* seems to mean ambush; *flymena-fyrmde* the receipt of outlaws; *fyrd-wite* the fine for neglecting the summons to the army. In these cases, it is conceived there is something more than ordinary crime, e.g. homicide or theft, there is some injury to the king, some attack upon his own peculiar rights.

The next list of pleas of the crown that we get is found in the *Leges Henrici Primi* [1100–35]. It is much longer and so instructive that I will translate it: 'Breach of the king's peace given by his hand or writ; danegeld; contempt of his writs or precepts; death or injury done to his servants; treason and breach of fealty; every contempt or evil word against him; [castle building—*castellatio trium scannorum;*] outlawry; theft punishable with death; murder; counterfeiting his money; arson; *hamsoken; forestal; fyrdwite; flymena-fyrmde;* premeditated assault; robbery; streetbreach; taking the king's land or money; treasure trove; shipwreck; waif of the sea;

rape; forests; reliefs of barons; fighting in the king's house or household; breach of peace in the army; neglecting to repair castles or bridges; neglecting a summons to the army; receiving an excommunicate or outlaw; breach of surety; flight in battle; unjust judgment; default of justice; perverting the king's law.' It is a most disorderly list. The writer has apparently strung together all cases in which either in ancient or modern times the king has asserted a special interest. Observe how criminal cases are mixed up with the king's fiscal rights—by fiscal rights I mean such rights as that to treasure trove, to shipwreck and goods thrown up by the sea. This is very instructive; one of the chief motives that the king has for amplifying his rights is the want of money; the criminal is regarded as a source of income. It will strike you that by a little ingenuity on the part of royal judges almost all criminal cases and very many civil cases also can be brought within the terms of this comprehensive list. But you will further observe that no such generalization has yet been made, it is not yet said that all crime, or all serious crime, or all acts of violence are causes for royal cognizance.

There is one term, however, which occurs in both these lists which can be so extended as to cover a very large space—that is the *mundbryce* of Canute's laws, which in the *Leges Henrici* appears as *infortio pacis regiae per manum vel breve datum.* Let us go back a little. The idea of law is from the first very closely connected with the idea of peace—he who breaks the peace, puts himself outside the law, he is outlaw. But besides the general peace which exists at all times and in all places, and which according to ancient ideas is the peace of the nation rather than of the king, every man has his own special peace and if you break that you injure him. Thus if you slay *A* in *B*'s house, not only must you pay *A*'s price or wergild to his kinsfolk, but you have broken *B*'s peace and you will owe *B* a sum of money, the amount of which will vary with *B*'s rank—you have broken *B*'s peace or *mund*; the *mund* of an archbishop is worth so much, that of an ealdorman so much, and so forth. Like other men the king has his peace. In course of time, we may say, the king's peace devours all other peaces—but that has not been effected until near the end of the twelfth century. In the *Leges Edwardi Confessoris* [1042–66] which represent the law of the first half of the century, the king's peace covers but certain times, places, and persons. *Pax Regis multiplex est*—the king's peace is manifold. First there is that which he gives with his own hand. Then there is the peace of his coronation day, and this extends eight days. Then the peace of the three great festivals, Christmas, Easter, Pentecost: each endures for eight days. Then there is the peace of the four great highways— the four ancient Roman roads which run through England. To commit a crime in one of these peaces is to offend directly against the king.

Before the end of the century there has been a great change, a great simplification; apparently it has been effected thus:—Under the Norman kings, the mode of bringing a criminal to justice was called an appeal (*appellum*); this word is not used in our modern way to imply the going from one court to a superior court—but means an accusation of crime brought by the person who has been wronged—the person, e.g., whose goods have been stolen or who has been wounded. Well, the king's justices seem to have allowed any appellor to make use of the words 'in the king's peace' whenever he pleased, and did not allow the appellee to take exception to these words—did not allow him to urge that though he might have committed theft or homicide still he had not broken the king's peace, since the deed was not done against a person, or at a time or place which was covered by the king's peace. Fictions of this kind are very common in our legal history, they are the means whereby the courts amplify their jurisdiction. Any deed of violence then, any use of criminal force, can be converted into a breach of the king's peace and be brought within the cognizance of the king's own court.

. . . .

I think we may say that from the beginning of the thirteenth century onwards, all causes that are regarded as criminal are pleas of the crown, *placita coronae*, save some petty offences which are still punished in the local courts, but even over these the sheriff is now regarded as exercising a royal jurisdiction. . . . [W]e have meanwhile to watch the growth of royal jurisdiction in civil causes.

This is by no means a simple matter; the process is very slow, and indeed even in the present century our civil procedure bore witness of a time when the king's court had not yet taken upon itself to act as a court of first instance in the ordinary disputes of ordinary people. We may, however, indicate six principles which serve to bring justice to the king's court.

(1) From the outset it is a court to which one may go, for default of justice in lower courts. Under the Norman kings we find that frequently a litigant, who in the ordinary course is going to sue in the court of a feudal lord, will go to the king in the first instance, and procure a writ, a mandate directing the lord, ordering him to do justice in his court to the applicant and adding a threat, *quod nisi feceris vicecomes meus faciet* —if you won't do it my sheriff will—the action will be removed out of your court into the county court, and thence it can be removed into the king's own court. This is a writ *de recto tenendo*, a writ of right.

(2) Henry II [1154–89] must, it would seem, have ordained that no action for freehold land shall be begun in a manorial court without such a writ. I say he must have ordained it: we have no direct evidence of this: but Glanvill lays down the principle in the broadest terms, no one need answer for his freehold without the king's writ, a writ directing the lord to do right—and we can say pretty positively that this was not law before Henry's day. You will notice that it is a serious invasion on feudal principles; when freehold is at stake, the

lord cannot hold his court or do justice until the king sets him in motion—the jurisdiction may spring out of tenure, but it is not beyond royal control. The excuse for such an interference may lie in that royal protection of possession of which we are soon to speak.

(3) In an action for land in a manorial court begun by writ of right, Henry II by some ordinance, the words of which have not come down to us but which was known as the grand assize, enabled the holder of the land to refuse trial by battle and to put himself upon the oath of a body of twelve neighbours sworn to declare which of the two parties had the greater right to the land. This was called putting oneself on the grand assize; and the body of sworn neighbours was known as the grand assize.

(4) Henry II . . . took seisin, possession as distinct from ownership, under his special protection—men who consider that land is unjustly withheld from them are not to help themselves; there is to be no disseisin without a judgment. He who is thus disseised shall be put back into possession without any question as to his title. This protection of possession is, I think, closely connected with that extension of the king's peace which we have been watching. He who takes upon himself to eject another from his freehold, breaks the peace, and the peace is the king's. This possessory procedure the king keeps in his own hands—it is a royal matter, the feudal courts have nothing to do with it. Thus there grows up a large class of actions (the possessory assizes) relating to land, which are beyond the cognizance of any but the king's justices, and these justices take good care that the limits of these actions shall not be narrow; perhaps indeed they are not always very careful to draw the line between disputes about possession which belong to them, and disputes about ownership which should go to the manorial courts.

(5) If we turn back to the list of royal rights contained in the *Leges Henrici,* we find among them—*placitum brevium vel praeceptorum ejus contemptorum* —pleas touching the contempt of his writs or precepts. Now here is an idea of which great use can be made: *B* detains from *A* lands or goods or owes *A* a debt; this may not be a case for the royal jurisdiction—but suppose that the king issues a writ or precept ordering *B* to give up the land or goods or to pay the debt, and *B* disobeys this order, then at once the royal jurisdiction is attracted to the case. The king's chancellor begins to issue such writs with a liberal hand. A writ is sent to the sheriff in such words as these: Command *B* (*Praecipe B*) that justly and without delay he give up to *A* the land or the chattel or the money which, as *A* says, he unjustly detains from him, and if he will not do so command him to be before our court on such a day to answer why he hath not done it. Thus the dispute between *A* and *B* is brought within the sphere of the king's justice; if *B* is in the wrong he has been guilty of contemning the king's writ. Such writs in Henry II's time are freely sold to litigants: but this is somewhat too high-handed a

proceeding to be stood, for in the case of land being thus demanded, the manorial courts are deprived of their legitimate jurisdiction. So we find that one of the concessions extorted from John [1199–1216] by Magna Carta is this: The writ called *Praecipe* shall not be issued for the future, so as to deprive a free man of his court, i.e., so as to deprive the lord of the manor of cases which ought to come to his court, his court being one of his sources of income. To a certain extent in cases of land this puts a check on the acquisitiveness of the royal court. But even as regards land, it is evaded in many different ways, in particular, by an extension of the possessory actions which make them serve the purpose of proprietary actions. As regards chattels and debts the king has a freer hand.

(6) The notion of the king's peace is by no means exhausted when it has comprehended the whole field of criminal law: mere civil wrongs, "torts" as we call them, can be brought within it—a mere wrongful step upon your land, a mere wrongful touch to your goods or to your person can be regarded as a breach of the peace; any wrongful application of force, however slight, can be said to be made *vi et armis et contra pacem domini Regis*: in such cases there may be no felony and no intention to do what is wrong—I may believe the goods to be mine when they are yours, and carry them off in that belief; still this may be called a breach of the peace. Hence in the thirteenth century a large class of writs grows up known as writs of trespass; for a long time the procedure is regarded as half-civil, half-criminal: the vanquished defendant has not only to pay damages to the plaintiff, he has to pay a fine to the king for the breach of the peace. Gradually (but this is not until the end of the Middle Ages) the fine becomes an unreality: actions of trespass are regarded as purely civil actions—and in course of time this form of action and forms derived out of it are made to do duty instead of all, or almost all, the other forms.

Armed with these elastic principles it was easy for the king's courts to amplify their province. By the beginning of Edward's reign we may, I think, say that all serious obstacles to the royal jurisdiction had been removed. The royal courts had in one way and another become courts of first instance for almost all litigation. But the extremely active legislation of his reign and the growth of parliament set a limit to the invention of new actions. It was now recognized that there were a certain number of actions to which no addition could be made except by statute. There were a certain number of writs in the royal Chancery; these were at the disposal of every subject; they were to be had on payment of the customary fees; they could not be denied; by these writs actions were begun, were originated; they were *brevia originalia*, original writs. A certain power of varying the stereotyped forms was allowed by the Statute of Westminster II (1285), and of this in course of time some good use was made; but from Edward's day down to the middle of the present century the development of common law was fettered by this system of original writs—writs which had been devised for the purpose of bringing before the king's court litigation which in more ancient times would have gone to other tribunals.

But the king's court could not have succeeded in thus extending the sphere of its activity if it had not been able to offer to suitors advantages which they could not get elsewhere. Royal justice was a good article—that is to say, a masterful thing not to be resisted. There were many processes which the king could give which were not to be had in lower courts. To describe some of these would take us too deeply into the technicalities of legislation. But there is one royal boon, *regale beneficium*, as Glanvill calls it, which has had a most important influence on the whole of our national history—trial by jury. In order to understand its history we must say a little about these modes of trial and of proof which in course of time gave way before it.

F. MAITLAND, THE FORMS OF ACTION AT COMMON LAW

15–19 (1936).

In modern German books dealing with ancient procedure we find the startling proposition that judgment preceded proof; it was a judgment that one party or the other to the litigation was to prove his case. Now when in our own day we speak of proof we think of an attempt made by each litigant to convince the judge, or the jurors, of the truth of the facts that he has alleged; he who is successful in this competition has proved his case. But in old times proof was not an attempt to convince the judges; it was an appeal to the supernatural, and very commonly a unilateral act. The common modes of proof are oaths and ordeals. It is adjudged, for example, in an action for debt that the defendant do prove his assertion that he owes nothing by his own oath and the oaths of a certain number of compurgators, or oath-helpers. The defendant must then solemnly swear that he owes nothing, and his oath-helpers must swear that his oath is clean and unperjured. If they safely get through this ceremony, punctually repeating the right formula, there is an end of the case; the plaintiff, if he is hardy enough to go on, can only do so by bringing a new charge, a criminal charge of perjury against them. They have not come there to convince the court, they have not come there to be examined and cross-examined like modern witnesses, they have come there to bring upon themselves the wrath of God if what they say be not true. This process is known in England as 'making one's law.' A litigant who is adjudged to prove his case in this way is said to 'wage his law' (*vadiare legem*), when he finds security that on a future day he will bring compurgators and perform this solemnity; then when on the appointed day he comes and performs that ceremony with success, he is said to 'make his law' (*facere legem*). An ordeal is still more obviously an appeal to the supernatural; the judgment of God is given; the burning iron spares the innocent, the water rejects the guilty. Or again the court adjudges that there must be trial by battle; the appellor charges the appellee with a crime, the appellee gives him the lie; the demandant's champion swears that he saw the demandant seised of the land, and is ready to prove this by his body; the wit of man is at fault in presence of a flat contradiction; God will show the truth. It is hard for us to say how this ancient procedure worked in practice, hard to tell how easy it was to get oath-helpers who would swear falsely, hard to tell how much risk there was in an ordeal. The rational element of law must, it would seem, have asserted itself in the judgment which decided how and by whom the proof should be given; the jurisprudence of the old courts must have been largely composed of the answers to this question; and some parts of it are being recovered, for example we can see that even before the Norman Conquest the man who has been often accused has to go to the ordeal instead of being allowed to purge himself with oath-helpers. But the point now to be seized is that the history of the forms of action presupposes this background of ancient courts with their unprofessional judges, their formal, supernatural modes of proof.

In its constitution and in its procedure the king's court is ahead of the other courts. Theoretically, from the Conquest onwards, it may be a feudal court, one in which all the king's tenants in chief, or such at least of them as are deemed barons, are entitled and bound to sit under the presidency of the king, his high steward or his chief justiciar. To this day the king's highest court of all is the assembly of the lords spiritual and temporal. But practically a small knot of trained administrators, prelates and barons, becomes the king's court for ordinary judicial purposes. The reforms of Henry II, the new actions invented in his reign, brought an ever-increasing mass of litigation before the royal court. It became more and more a group of men professionally learned in the law. Gradually, as is well known, this group breaks up into three courts, there are the three courts of common law, the King's Bench, Common Bench, and Exchequer. This process is not complete until Edward I's reign; but we may say that for a century before this the king's court for ordinary judicial purposes has been no feudal court of tenants in chief, but a court of professional justices; the justices of Henry III's time [1216–72] are often men who have had a long education in the subordinate offices of the court and the chancery.

As to procedure, all the old formal modes of proof have been known in the king's court. It made use of the ordeal until that ancient process was abolished by the Lateran Council of 1215.[b] Trial by

---

[b] There has been much recent, original work in legal history that casts doubt on some of Maitland's specific positions. For example, it now appears that by 1215

battle, as we all know, was not abolished until 1819, and wager of law was not abolished until 1833. For a very long time before this any practical talk of these barbarisms had been very rare, and for a still longer time pent within ever narrowing limits; still, if we are to understand the history of the forms of action, we must be mindful of these things; a long chapter in that history might be entitled 'Dodges to evade Wager of Battle,' a still longer chapter, 'Dodges to evade Wager of Law.' We must not suppose that the unreasonableness of these archaic institutions was suddenly perceived; the cruelties of the *peine forte et dure* had their origin in the sentiment that trial by jury is not a fair mode of trial save for those who have voluntarily consented to it; the remembrance of the ordeal was dear to the people; they would 'swim a witch' long centuries after the Lateran Council; so late as 1376 we find that wager of law is still popular with the commons of England, they pray that there may be wager of law in the Exchequer as in the other courts. But to a very great extent the early history of the forms of action is the history of a new procedure gradually introduced, the procedure which in course of time becomes trial by jury. It would be needless to repeat here what has been sufficiently said elsewhere about the first germs of the jury. The Frankish kings, perhaps assuming to themselves the rights of the Roman fiscus, had placed themselves outside the ancient formal procedure of the popular courts, had sought to preserve and enforce their royal rights by compelling the inhabitants of the district, or a representative body of such inhabitants, to swear that they would tell the truth as to the nature and extent of these rights. Further, they gave or sold this privilege to specially favoured persons, especially to the churches which were under their patronage. The favoured person, if possessions were attacked, need not defend them by battle or ordeal, or any of the ancient modes of proof, but might have an inquest of neighbours sworn to tell the truth about the matter in hand. Immediately after the Norman Conquest we find that this procedure has been introduced into England, and it is employed on a magnificent scale. Domesday Book is the record of the verdicts of bodies of neighbours sworn to tell the truth, and its main object is the ascertainment and preservation of the king's rights. Very soon after this we find the inquest or jury employed in the course of litigation; for instance, in a suit touching the rights of the Church of Ely the Conqueror commands that those who best know how the lands lay in the days of the Confessor shall be sworn to tell the truth about them; so a number of the good folk of Sandwich are sworn to tell the truth about a certain ship, and they testifying in favour of the Abbot of St. Augustine's, the Abbot is 'reseised' of the ship. The right to a jury makes its appearance as a royal prerogative, a prerogative, the bene-

the ordeal had long been discredited in ordinary practice. Hyams, "Trial by Ordeal: The Key to Proof in the Early Common Law," in On the Laws and Customs of England 90 (1981). Nevertheless, the pioneering work of Maitland exposes the grand themes of the emergence of the common law.

fit of which the king can give or sell to those who obtain his grace. We see traces of this origin even at a very late time; it is an established maxim that one can not wage one's law against the king. In an action for debt upon simple contract, were the plaintiff a subject, the defendant would be allowed to purge himself with oath-helpers in the ancient way, but when the king is plaintiff he must submit to trial by jury.

In the competition of courts, therefore, the king's court has a marked advantage; to say nothing of its power to enforce its judgments it has, for those who can purchase or otherwise obtain such a favour, a comparatively rational procedure. As yet, indeed, trial by jury is far from being what it became in later times; the jurors are not 'judges of fact,' they are witnesses; but they are not like the witnesses and the compurgators of the old procedure; they are not brought in by the party to swear up to a set form of words in support of his case, they are summoned as impartial persons by a royal officer, and they swear to tell the truth, whatever the truth may be. This is the procedure, far more rational than battle, or ordeal, or wager of law, which the king's court has at its command when it begins to bid against the communal and feudal courts.

F. MAITLAND, THE CONSTITUTIONAL HISTORY OF ENGLAND
137, 141 (1908).

(d) It remains to speak of the visitatorial courts:—

From an early time a great deal of the work of royal justice is done not by the central tribunal but by itinerant justices, sent out by royal commission to hear cases in the various counties. We hear of such judges in the reign of Henry I; their visitations become normal and systematic under the rule of Henry II. The king commissions justices to transact this and that judicial business in the various counties of England. . . .

. . . . .

The general result of this system of commissions was that a great deal of royal justice was done not by the permanent central courts, but in the counties, by commissioners sent out just for that occasion. They could completely dispose of the criminal business of the county, and could preside over the trial by jury of civil actions depending in the central courts. In course of time more and more of this circuit work was done by the judges of the king's permanent courts.

H. STEPHEN, A TREATISE ON THE PRINCIPLES OF PLEADING IN CIVIL ACTIONS
3–7 (S. Williston ed. 1895).[c]

Actions are divided into *real, personal,* and *mixed. Real* actions are those brought for specific recovery of lands, tenements, or hereditaments; *personal,* are those brought for specific recovery of goods and chattels,—or for damages, or other redress, for breach of contract, or other injuries, of whatever description, the specific recovery of lands, tenements, and hereditaments, only excepted. *Mixed* actions are such as appertain, in some degree, to both the former classes, and, therefore, are properly reducible to neither of them; being brought both for specific recovery of lands, tenements, or hereditaments, and for damages for injury sustained in respect of such property. But the learning which relates to this ancient division of legal remedies, has now lost much of its importance, in consequence of the recent statute, 3 & 4 Will. IV c. 27, s. 36 [1833], by which provision is made for the abolition, within a short prospective period, of all real and mixed actions, except four.

There are three Superior courts of the common law, in each of which actions may be brought. These are the Queen's Bench, the Common Pleas, and the Exchequer,—each consisting, at present, of five judges. The original distribution of business among them, upon their first establishment, was as follows: the cognisance of crime, and of such matters of litigation in general, as directly concerned the crown (those relating to the revenue excepted), was exclusively appropriate to the first of the Courts above mentioned; civil suits between subject and subject, (called communia placita,) to the second; and matters relating to the royal revenue, to the last. In course of time, considerable violations of this arrangement took place, usurpation on the province of the Common Pleas being made by each of the other courts. Of these changes the general result is as follows. The Queen's Bench has now jurisdiction not only in those matters which belonged to it by its original constitution, but in *all personal actions whatever.* The case is the same with the Exchequer; but both these courts are still excluded from the cognisance of actions *real* and *mixed.* The Common Pleas retains its original province, and therefore entertains all actions whatever between subject and subject, whether of the real, mixed, or personal class.

Anciently it was essential to the due institution of all actions in the Superior Courts, that they should commence by *original writ;* in the case of real and mixed actions this is still necessary. But in personal actions the use of original writs is abolished by the recent statute 2 Will. IV c. 39 [1832].

[c] The Williston edition is based on the fifth English edition of 1843.

The *original writ* (breve originale) is a mandatory letter issuing out of the Court of Chancery, under the great seal, and, in the King's name, directed to the sheriff of the county where the injury is alleged to have been committed, containing a summary statement of the cause of complaint, and requiring him to command the defendant to satisfy the claim; and, on his failure to comply, then to summon him to appear in one of the superior courts of common law, there to account for his non-compliance. In some cases, however, it omits the former alternative, and requires the sheriff simply to enforce the appearance.

.   .   .   .

An original writ (as already stated) was formerly essential in every case, to the due institution of the suit. These instruments have consequently had the effect of limiting and defining the right of action itself; and no cases are even now considered as within the scope of judicial remedy, in the English law, but those to which some known original writ (when these instruments were in universal use) would have applied, or for which some new original writ, framed on the analogy of those already existing, might, under the provisions of the statute of Westminster 2, have been lawfully devised. The enumeration of writs, and that of actions, have become, in this manner, identical.

SECTION 2. EVOLUTION THROUGH LOGIC–CHOPPING (HEREIN CHIEFLY OF TRESPASS AND CASE)

(a) Trespass

WRIT OF TRESPASS
[From A. Fitz-Herbert, Natura Brevium 86 I (9th ed. London 1794)]

The King to the Sheriff, &c. If A. shall make you secure, &c. then put by gages and safe pledges B. that he be before us on the morrow of All Souls, wheresoever we shall then be in England, to show wherefore with force and arms he made an assault upon him the said A. at N. and beat, wounded and ill treated him, so that his life was despaired of, and other enormous things to him did, to the great damage of him the said A. and against our peace: and have there the names of the pledges and this writ. Witness, &c.

Question: (1) Does the language of the writ provide any apparent confirmation of Maitland's account of the growth of royal civil jurisdiction?

There were variant forms of the writ of trespass,[d] including forms for injury to personal property, carrying away of personal property (trespass de bonis asportatis), entry upon real property (trespass quare clausum fregit), and false imprisonment. A medieval affray might have involved all these wrongs, and more besides, but a single writ could be used to cover the whole affray.

ANONYMOUS
Court of Common Pleas, 1304.
Y.B.Trin. 32 & 33 Edw. (Rolls Series) 258–59.

One R. brought his writ against J. and others &c., and said that they tortiously came with force and arms, and his wood cut and carried away &c. The defendants said that they were not guilty.—THE INQUEST came and said that they did cut his trees, but not with force and arms. Therefore it was adjudged by BEREFORD that he should recover his damages &c.; and that the defendants should be taken notwithstanding they did not come with force or arms.

"By the close of the thirteenth century the process of differentiation [of trespass] was complete and the adoption of set terms had clipped the exuberance of earlier litigants and their pleaders. But when phrase becomes formula, fact declines into fiction." C. Fifoot, History and Sources of the Common Law 55–56 (1949).

(b) The Rise of Case

C. FIFOOT, HISTORY AND SOURCES OF THE COMMON LAW
66 (1949).

The writs established at the accession of Edward I offered a respectable measure of redress for injury to property and, less amply, for personal injury. But their limitations were patent. Even trespass, potentially the most fruitful, would lie only for a direct and unauthorised interference with land, goods or person. A plaintiff could not use it who had voluntarily submitted himself or his property to the defendant's ministrations, as where he complained of the carelessness of a doctor or a farrier or a veterinary surgeon. A bail-

---

[d] Scholars have differed in their explanations of how trespass originated. Holmes, Ames, and Maitland look to the appeal of felony as the source of trespass. Woodbine traces its origin to the writ of novel disseisin. Plucknett thinks it is an adaptation of proceedings of local courts. Finally, there is evidence that trespass developed out of certain "innominate" actions—actions commenced without writ, but rather by petition to the central courts or the king's itinerant justices. In all events, trespass appears as an established, "formed" writ by the time of the accession of Edward I.

or could not use it if the bailee damaged or destroyed the goods.[e] It would not avail where the injury was not the direct but merely consequential result of the defendant's misfeasance. So, if the defendant by operations on his own land succeeded in flooding other land of which the plaintiff was a lessee for years, the latter had no remedy. Finally, the plaintiff could not sue where he was injured not by an act, but by an omission: 'not doing is no trespass.' It is common knowledge that these gaps were in time filled by the development of actions on the case . . . .

———

The earliest reported modification of trespass to fill the lacunae left by the early writ system dates from the second half of the fourteenth century. Gradually a category of "special trespass" or "trespass on the case" may be identified. By the sixteenth century "case" had become a distinct form of action.[f] Fifoot says: "Its one essential feature was that the plaintiff should set out at large in his writ the facts upon which he sought redress. . . . Litigants were thus offered a wide choice in the framing of writs to meet the substance of their complaints, and, within the limits of professional decency, judges had equal liberty to accord or to withhold their sanction as expediency or temperament might dictate. The opportunity offered was eagerly grasped. Not only did the judges sustain what, in substance if not in name, were writs of Nuisance on the Case and Detinue on the Case, but they were prepared to envisage actions where no basic

[e] This statement may require qualification, at least if we look to cases of later vintage. There was some authority to the effect that the owner might maintain trespass against a bailee, whether for a term or at will, who destroyed the bailed chattel. And there was some authority for trespass by the owner against a bailee at will who injured the bailed chattel.

Moreover, Fifoot notes that in certain circumstances the plaintiff in some of his textual illustrations might have other remedies, such as detinue or the assize of nuisance.

[f] There was a learned dispute as to the origin of actions on the case, centering about the meaning and effect of the Statute of Westminster II, 1285, 13 Edw., ch. 24. The Statute deals with three cases where certain existing writs (assize of nuisance, quod permittat, and assize utrum) have failed to cover situations requiring remedy, and it declares that henceforth the writs shall be varied to cover these cases. Then comes a more general clause (translation by Fifoot): "And whensoever from henceforth it shall happen in the Chancery that in one case a writ is found and in a similar case [*in consimili casu*] falling under the same law and needing a similar remedy there is no writ found, the clerks of the Chancery shall agree in making a writ, or they shall adjourn the complainants to the next Parliament and they shall write down the cases in which they cannot agree and refer them to the next Parliament, and a writ shall be made by those learned in the law; so that from henceforth it shall not befall that the court shall fail those who seek justice." C. Fifoot, History and Sources of the Common Law 79 (1949). The view that case derived from trespass through the *in consimili casu* clause of the Statute had long been prevalent and was guardedly accepted by F. Maitland, The Forms of Action at Common Law 51 (1936). It was, says Professor Milsom, "destroyed" by Plucknett, Case and the Statute of Westminster II, 31 Colum.L.Rev. 778 (1931). S. Milsom, Historical Foundations of the Common Law 284 n.2 (2d ed. 1981). Fifoot concludes: "The action on the case derived, not from the statutory powers of Chancery clerks, but from the fiat of the judges." C. Fifoot, supra, at 74.

analogy existed at all. The way was open for the development of such modern torts as Defamation and Negligence." Id. at 77–78.[g]

WRIT OF TRESPASS ON THE CASE OR CASE
[From A. Fitz-Herbert, Natura Brevium 92 F (9th ed. London 1794)]

The King to the Sheriff, &c. [Continue as in Trespass], to show wherefore he fixed piles across the water of Plim, along which, between the Humber and Gaunt, there is a common passage for ships and boats, whereby a certain ship, with thirty quarters of malt of him the said W. was sunk under water, and twenty perished; and other wrongs, &c. [continue as in Trespass].

(c) Drawing the Line Between Trespass and Case

REYNOLDS v. CLARKE, 93 Eng.Rep. 747 (K.B.1726). "Trespass for entering the plaintiff's yard, and fixing a spout there, *per quod* the water came into the yard and rotted the walls of the plaintiff's house. The defendant justifies, that before the trespass John Fountain was seised in fee of the plaintiff's house and yard, and two other houses adjoining, and demised the plaintiff's house and yard to one Tyler, except the free use of the yard and privy for the tenants of the other two houses jointly with the tenant of the plaintiff's house: then he shews how the house of the defendant, which was one of the two

---

[g] Professor Milsom, in Trespass from Henry III to Edward III (pts. 1–3), 74 L.Q.Rev. 195, 407, 561 (1958), challenges the received view that "what came into being in the thirteenth century was a single entity, a definite tort with the essential ingredient of direct forcible injury, and that out of or around this entity there developed, by a process beginning in the late fourteenth century, the mass of actions on the case." Professor Milsom "does not believe that there was in the thirteenth or fourteenth century an entity equivalent to the modern trespass, or that the word trespass at that time even meant anything narrower than just wrong. The concept was unlimited. Limitation came from without rather than within: the question was not whether a wrong qualified as a trespass, but whether it was the kind of trespass which the royal court could or would handle." Id. at 195. The proportion of trespasses, i.e., wrongs, admitted to the royal court gradually increased. The commonest reason for taking the actions there was breach of the king's peace, but that

was not the only reason—a "royal interest" would do, and we can even say that the king's courts were not debarred from hearing cases with no royal interest, but that "normally they would not." The development around 1370 conventionally taken to be the origin of case was simply that "the requirement of a royal interest was abandoned; and private trespasses came to the royal court in their own right." One of the reasons why this could have happened almost imperceptibly was that "[e]ven genuine breaches of the peace had come to be seen primarily as private wrongs, with the king's interest important mainly for the process it gave; and sometimes breach of the peace was alleged untruthfully." Id. at 588–89. So he concludes: "This then is how actions on the case began. . . . A jurisdictional adjustment had allowed some wrongs which had long come to the king's courts to come there without fictitious allegations, and other wrongs to come there for the first time." S. Milsom, Historical Foundations of the Common Law 304 (2d ed. 1981).

houses, came to him, and that he entered the yard and fixed the spout for his necessary use, to carry off the rain, *prout ei bene licuit.*" Plaintiff demurred. Held, judgment for defendant.

Lord Raymond, C.J., said: "We must keep up the boundaries of actions, otherwise we shall introduce the utmost confusion: if the act in the first instance be unlawful, trespass will lie; but if the act is *prima facie* lawful (as it was in this case) and the prejudice to another is not immediate, but consequential, it must be an action upon the case; and this is the distinction."

Fortescue, J., said: "[I]f a man throws a log into the highway, and in that act hits me, I may maintain trespass, because it is an immediate wrong; but if as it lies there I tumble over it, and receive an injury, I must bring an action upon the case; because it is only prejudicial in consequence, for which originally I could have no action at all."

SCOTT, an Infant, by his next Friend v. SHEPHERD,
an Infant, by Guardian

Court of Common Pleas, 1773.
96 Eng.Rep. 525.

Trespass and assault for throwing, casting, and tossing a lighted squib at and against the plaintiff, and striking him therewith on the face, and so burning one of his eyes, that he lost the sight of it, whereby, &c. On not guilty pleaded, the cause came on to be tried before Nares, J., last Summer Assizes, at Bridgwater, when the jury found a verdict for the plaintiff with 100*l.* damages, subject to the opinion of the Court on this case:—On the evening of the fairday at Milborne Port, 29th October, 1770, the defendant threw a *lighted squib*, made of gun-powder, &c. from the street into the market-house, which is a covered building, supported by arches, and enclosed at one end, but open at the other and both the sides, where a large concourse of people were assembled; which lighted squib, so thrown by the defendant, fell upon the standing of one Yates, who sold gingerbread, &c. That one Willis instantly, and to prevent injury to himself and the said wares of the said Yates, took up the said lighted squib from off the said standing, and then threw it *across* the said market-house, when it fell upon another standing there of one Ryal, who sold the same sort of wares, who instantly, and to save his own goods from being injured, took up the said lighted squib from off the said standing, and then threw it to another part of the said market-house, and, in so throwing it, struck the plaintiff then in the said market-house in the face therewith, and the combustible matter then bursting, put out one of the plaintiff's eyes. *Qu.* If this action be maintainable?

This case was argued last term by *Glyn*, for the plaintiff, and *Burland*, for the defendant: and this term, the Court, being divided in their judgment, delivered their opinions *seriatim*.

NARES, J., was of opinion, that trespass would well lie in the present case. That the natural and probable consequence of the act done by the defendant was injury to somebody, and therefore the act was illegal at common law. And the throwing of squibs has by Statute W. 3 [1697], been since made a nuisance. Being therefore unlawful, the defendant was liable to answer for the consequences, be the injury *mediate* or *immediate*. . . . The principle I go upon is what is laid down in Reynolds and Clarke, Stra. 634, that if the act in the first instance be unlawful, trespass will lie for the consequences of it. . . . I do not think it necessary, to maintain trespass, that the defendant should personally touch the plaintiff; if he does it by a mean it is sufficient.—*Qui facit per aliud facit per se.* He is the person, who, in the present case, gave the mischievous faculty to the squib. That mischievous faculty remained in it till the explosion. No new power of doing mischief was communicated to it by Willis or Ryal. It is like the case of a mad ox turned loose in a crowd. The person who turns him loose is answerable in trespass for whatever mischief he may do. The intermediate acts of Willis and Ryal will not purge the original tort in the defendant. But he who does the first wrong is answerable for all the consequential damages. [Citations omitted.] And it was declared by this Court, in Slater and Baker, M. 8 Geo. 3, 2 Wils. 359, that they would not look with eagle's eyes to see whether the evidence applies exactly or not to the case: but if the plaintiff has obtained a verdict for such damages as he deserves, they will establish it if possible.

BLACKSTONE, J., was of opinion, that an action of *trespass* did not lie for Scott against Shepherd upon this case. He took the settled distinction to be, that where the injury is *immediate*, an action of *trespass* will lie; where it is only *consequential*, it must be an action on the *case*: Reynolds and Clarke, Lord Raym. 1401. Stra. 634; [other citations omitted]. The *lawfulness* or *unlawfulness* of the original act is not the criterion; though something of that sort is put into Lord Raymond's mouth in Stra. 635, where it can only mean, that if the act then in question, of erecting a spout, had been in itself unlawful, trespass might have lain; but as it was a lawful act (upon the defendant's own ground), and the injury to the plaintiff only consequential, it must be an action on the case. But this cannot be the general rule; for it is held by the Court in the same case, that if I throw a log of timber into the highway (which is an unlawful act), and another man tumbles over it, and is hurt, an action on the case only lies, it being a *consequential* damage; but if in throwing it I hit another man, he may bring trespass, because it is an *immediate* wrong. Trespass may sometimes lie for the consequences of a lawful act. If in lopping my own trees a bough accidentally falls on my neighbour's ground, and I go thereon to fetch it, trespass lies. This is the case cited from 6 Edw. 4, 7. But then the entry is of itself an immediate wrong. And case will sometimes lie for the consequence of an unlawful act. If by false imprisonment I have a special damage, as if I forfeit my recognizance thereby, I shall have an action on the case; *per* Powell, J., 11 Mod. 180. Yet here the original act was unlawful, and in the nature of trespass. So that *lawful* or *unlawful* is quite out of the case; the solid distinction is between *direct* or *immediate* injuries on the one hand, and *mediate* or *consequential* on the other. And trespass never lay for the latter. If this be so, the only question will be, whether the injury which the plaintiff suffered was *immediate*, or *consequential* only; and I hold it to be the latter. The original act was, as against Yates, a trespass; not as against Ryal, or Scott. The tortious act was complete when the squib lay at rest upon Yate's stall. He, or any bystander, had, I allow, a right to protect themselves by removing the squib, but should have taken care to do it in such a manner as not to endamage others. But Shepherd, I think, is not answerable in an action of trespass and assault for the mischief done by the squib in the new motion impressed upon it, and the new direction given it, by either Willis or Ryal; who both were free agents, and acted upon their own judgment. This differs it from the cases put of turning loose a wild beast or a madman. They are only instruments in the hand of the first agent. Nor is it like diverting the course of an enraged ox, or of a stone thrown, or an arrow glancing against a tree; because there the original motion, the *vis impressa*, is continued, though diverted. Here the instrument of mischief was at rest, till a new *impetus* and a new direction are given it, not once only, but by two successive rational agents. But it is said that the act is not complete, nor the squib at rest, till after it is spent or exploded. It certainly has a power of doing fresh mischief, and so has a stone that has been thrown against my windows, and now lies still. Yet if any person gives that stone a new motion, and does farther mischief with it, trespass will not lie for that against the original thrower. No doubt but Yates may maintain trespass against Shepherd. And, according to the doctrine contended for, so may Ryal and Scott. Three actions for one single act! nay, it may be extended *in infinitum*. If a man tosses a football into the street, and after being kicked about by one hundred people, it at last breaks a tradesman's windows; shall he have *trespass* against the man who first produced it? Surely only against the man who gave it that mischievous direction. But it is said, if Scott has no action against Shepherd, against whom must he seek his remedy? I give no opinion whether *case* would lie against Shepherd for the *consequential* damage; though, as at present advised, I think, upon the circumstances, it would. But I think, in strictness of law, trespass would lie against Ryal, the immediate actor in this unhappy business. Both he and Willis have exceeded the bounds of self-defence, and not used sufficient circumspection in removing the danger from themselves. The throwing it *across* the market-house, instead of brushing it down, or throwing [it]

out of the open sides into the street (if it was not meant to continue
the sport, as it is called), was at least an unnecessary and incautious
act. Not even menaces from others are sufficient to justify a trespass against a third person; much less a fear of danger to either his
goods or his person;—nothing but inevitable necessity; Weaver and
Ward, Hob. 134; Dickenson and Watson, T. Jones, 205; Gilbert and
Stone, Al. 35, Styl. 72. So in the case put by Brian, J., and assented
to by Littleton and Cheke, C.J., and relied on in Raym. 467,—"If a
man assaults me, so that I cannot avoid him, and I lift up my staff to
defend myself, and, in lifting it up, undesignedly hit another who is
behind me, an action lies by that person against me; and yet I did a
lawful act in endeavouring to defend myself." But none of these
great lawyers ever thought that trespass would lie, by the person
struck, against him who first assaulted the striker. . . . Slater
and Barker was first a motion for a new trial after verdict. In our
case the verdict is suspended till the determination of the Court.
And though after verdict the Court will not look with eagle's eyes to
spy out a variance, yet, when a question is put by the jury upon such
a variance, and it is made the very point of the cause, the Court will
not wink against the light, and say that evidence, which at most is
only applicable to an action on the case, will maintain an action of
trespass. 2. It was an action on the case that was brought, and the
Court held the special case laid to be fully proved. So that the present question could not arise upon that action. 3. The same evidence
that will maintain *trespass*, may also frequently maintain *case*, but
not *e converso*. Every action of trespass with a *"per quod"* includes
an action on the case. I may bring trespass for the immediate injury,
and subjoin a *"per quod"* for the consequential damages;—or may
bring case for the consequential damages, and pass over the immediate injury, as in the case from 11 Mod. 180, before cited. But if I
bring trespass for an immediate injury, and prove at most only a consequential damage, judgment must be for the defendant; Gates and
Bailey, Tr. 6 Geo. 3, 2 Wils. 313. It is said by Lord Raymond, and
very justly, in Reynolds and Clarke, "we must keep up the boundaries of actions, otherwise we shall introduce the utmost confusion."
As I therefore think no immediate injury passed from the defendant
to the plaintiff (and without such immediate injury no action of trespass can be maintained), I am of opinion, that in this action judgment
ought to be for the defendant.

GOULD, J., was of the same opinion with Nares, J., that this action
was well maintainable. . . .

DE GREY, C.J.—This case is one of those wherein the line drawn
by the law between actions on the case and actions of trespass is very
nice and delicate. Trespass is an injury accompanied with force, for
which an action of trespass *vi et armis* lies against the person from
whom it is received. The question here is, whether the injury received by the plaintiff arises from the force of the original act of the
defendant, or from a new force by a third person. I agree with my

brother Blackstone as to the principles he has laid down, but not in his application of those principles to the present case. The real question certainly does not turn upon the lawfulness or unlawfulness of the original act . . . . But the true question is, whether the injury is the direct and immediate act of the defendant; and I am of opinion, that in this case it is. The throwing the squib was an act unlawful and tending to affright the bystanders. So far, mischief was originally intended; not any particular mischief, but mischief indiscriminate and wanton. Whatever mischief therefore follows, he is the author of it;—*Egreditur personam*, as the phrase is in criminal cases. And though criminal cases are no rule for civil ones, yet in trespass I think there is an analogy. Every one who does an unlawful act is considered as the doer of all that follows; if done with a deliberate intent, the consequence may amount to murder; if incautiously, to manslaughter; Fost. 261. So too, in 1 Ventr. 295, a person breaking a horse in Lincoln's Inn Fields hurt a man; held, that trespass lay: and, 2 Lev. 172, that it need not be laid *scienter*. I look upon all that was done subsequent to the original throwing as a continuation of the first force and first act, which will continue till the squib was spent by bursting. And I think that any innocent person removing the danger from himself to another is justifiable; the blame lights upon the first thrower. The new direction and new force flow out of the first force, and are not a new trespass. The writ in the Register, 95a. for trespass in maliciously cutting down a head of water, which thereupon flowed down to and overwhelmed another's pond, shews that the immediate act need not be instantaneous, but that a chain of effects connected together will be sufficient. It has been urged, that the intervention of a free agent will make a difference: but I do not consider Willis and Ryal as free agents in the present case, but acting under a compulsive necessity for their own safety and self-preservation. On these reasons I concur with Brothers Gould and Nares, that the present action is maintainable.

Postea to the plaintiff.

———

DAY v. EDWARDS, 101 Eng.Rep. 361 (K.B.1794). Action on the case for a collision on the highway. The declaration alleged that "the said defendant then and there so furiously, negligently and improperly drove the said cart and horse of him the said defendant, that . . . the said cart was then and there, to wit, &c. driven and struck with great force and violence upon and against the said carriage of the plaintiff, and thereby then and there overturned and damaged the same, to the loss of the plaintiff, &c." Defendant entered a special demurrer assigning for cause, among other things, that the action should have been trespass. Held, judgment for defendant.

Lord Kenyon, C.J., quoting the example of the log in the Reynolds case, said: "The distinction between the actions of trespass *vi et armis* and on the case is perfectly clear. If the injury is committed by the immediate act complained of, the action must be trespass; if the injury be merely consequential upon that act, an action upon the case is the proper remedy."

———

OGLE v. BARNES, 101 Eng.Rep. 1338 (K.B.1799). Action on the case, the declaration describing a collision between the ships "Anne" and "Acteon," possessed by plaintiffs and defendants respectively. In the first count it was alleged that the defendants, having the care, direction, and management of their ship, "so incautiously, carelessly, negligently, and inexpertly" managed and steered it, and took such bad care of the management and steering of it, that it struck and damaged the plaintiffs' ship. The second count differed from the first in stating that the defendants' ship was under the care and direction of Barnes, one of the defendants, and of certain servants of the defendants. Plaintiffs obtained a verdict. On rule nisi to arrest the judgment on the ground that trespass should have been brought, and not an action on the case, held, rule discharged.

Lord Kenyon, C.J., said: "[I]t cannot be said, that in this case the defendants *vi et armis* did an injury to the plaintiffs, when it appears that they did not do any act at all. The charge imputed to these defendants is, that they so carelessly and negligently steered their vessel, that by reason of such negligence, their vessel sailed against and ran afoul of the plaintiff's; and for that negligence they are liable in an action upon the case."

Lawrence, J., said: "Such an injury as the present may be occasioned, either by the wilful act or by the negligence of the defendants: it is a question of evidence. If the former, trespass is the proper action; if the latter, an action on the case."

———

LEAME v. BRAY, 102 Eng.Rep. 724 (K.B.1803). Trespass. Defendant, driving his carriage on a dark night on the wrong side of the road, ran down plaintiff's curricle, which was being driven by plaintiff's servant. The servant was thrown to the ground, and the horses ran away with the curricle; plaintiff jumped to save his life and fractured his collarbone. Plea, not guilty. On the trial defendant objected that the injury having happened from negligence, and not wilfully, the proper remedy was case, not trespass. Plaintiff was nonsuited. On rule nisi to set aside the nonsuit, held, rule absolute.

Lord Ellenborough, C.J., reverted to the Blackstone criterion of directness in Scott v. Shepherd. "It is immaterial whether the injury be wilful or not." Day v. Edwards supported this proposition, for "the allegation of the act having been done furiously was understood to imply an act of force immediately proceeding from the defendant." Ogle v. Barnes gave trouble, presumably because the injury seemed direct, but "it [was] not even alleged that [the defendants] were on board the ship at the time."

Lawrence, J., was of the same opinion. "It is more convenient that the action should be trespass than case; because if it be laid in trespass, no nice points can arise upon the evidence by which the plaintiff can be turned round upon the form of the action, as there may in many instances if case be brought; for there if any of the witnesses should say that in his belief the defendant did the injury wilfully, the plaintiff will run the risk of being nonsuited. . . . As to Ogle v. Barnes, I certainly did not mean to say that the distinction turned on the wilfulness of the act; I only made use of the word wilful to distinguish that from other cases which had been mentioned where the injurious acts were averred to be wilfully done, and where as the acts complained of were charged as intentional, and the injuries done immediately referred to them, trespass was determined to be the proper remedy."

WILLIAMS v. HOLLAND

Court of Common Pleas, 1833.
131 Eng.Rep. 848.

The declaration stated that Plaintiff, on, &c., was lawfully possessed of a certain cart, and of a certain horse drawing the same; in which said cart certain persons, to wit, John Williams, being the son and servant, and Mary Ann Williams, being the infant daughter of the Plaintiff, were then riding in and along a certain public and common highway: and the Defendant was then and there possessed of a certain gig, and of a certain other horse drawing the same, which said gig and horse were then and there under the care, government, and direction of the Defendant, in and along the said highway, to wit, at, &c. Nevertheless the Defendant so carelessly, unskilfully, and improperly drove, governed, and directed his said gig and horse, that, by and through the carelessness, negligence, unskilfulness, and improper conduct of the Defendant, the said gig and horse of the Defendant then and there ran and struck with great violence upon and against the cart and horse of the Plaintiff, and thereby then and there crushed, broke to pieces, and damaged the same; and the said cart of the Plaintiff thereby then and there became and was rendered of little or no value to the Plaintiff: and thereby the said John Williams and Mary Ann Williams were then and there cast and thrown with great force and violence from and out of the said cart to and upon the ground there, and by means of the several premises aforesaid, the Plaintiff was deprived of the service of his son, and put to expense for doctor's bills, &c. Plea, not guilty.

At the trial before Tindal, C.J., it appeared that the Plaintiff's cart was standing at the side of a road twenty-four feet wide, with the near wheel on the footway, when the [defendant] in a gig, and, in the act of racing with another gig, drove against the cart, upset and broke it to pieces, and severely injured the Plaintiff's children.

The defence was, that the Defendant's horse had run away with him. And the Chief Justice left it to the jury to say whether the collision was the result of accident, or of negligence and carelessness in the Defendant. The jury found the latter, and gave a verdict with damages for the Plaintiff. It was also contended, on the part of the Defendant, that the action was misconceived, and ought to have been trespass instead of case. The Chief Justice having reserved that point for the consideration of the Court,

Bompas Serjt. obtained, thereupon, a rule nisi to set aside the verdict and enter a nonsuit.

. . . .

TINDAL, C.J.

. . . .

But upon examining the cases cited in argument, both in support of, and in answer to, the objection, we cannot find one in which it is distinctly held, that the present form of action is not maintainable under the circumstances of this case.

For as to Leame v. Bray, on which the principal reliance is placed by the Defendant, in which the form of action was trespass, and the circumstances very nearly the same as those in the case now under consideration, the only rule established is, that an action of trespass might be maintained, not that an action on the case could not. The case of Savignac v. Roome, [101 Eng.Rep. 470 (K.B.1794),] in which the Court held that case would not lie where the defendant's servant wilfully drove against the plaintiff's carriage, was founded on the principle, that no action would lie against the master for the wilful act of his servant; and in that of Day v. Edwards, in which it was ruled that trespass was the proper remedy, and not case, it should be observed that the question arose upon a special demurrer to the declaration; and that the declaration stated that the defendant "so furiously, negligently, and improperly drove his cart and horse, that through the furious, negligent, and improper conduct of the defendant, the cart and horse were driven and struck with great force and violence upon and against the carriage of the plaintiff;" the question therefore arising upon a special demurrer, where the Court could look to nothing but the legal construction of the declaration, is very differently circumstanced from this, where the jury have found that negligence was the ground of the injury. On the other hand, the cases of Rogers v. Imbleton, [127 Eng.Rep. 568 (C.P.1806),] and Ogle v. Barnes and Others, are simply in favour of the proposition, that the present form of action, is, under the circumstances, maintainable.

We hold it, however, to be unnecessary, to examine very minutely the grounds of the various decisions; for the late case of Moreton v. Hardern and Others [, 107 Eng.Rep. 1042 (K.B.1825),] appears to us to go the full length of deciding, that where the injury is occasioned by the carelessness and negligence of the Defendant, although it be occasioned by his immediate act, the Plaintiff may, if he thinks proper, make the negligence of the Defendant the ground of his action, and declare in case. It has been urged, indeed, in answer to that case, that is was decided on the ground, that the action was brought against one of the proprietors who was driving, and against his co-proprietors who were absent, but whose servant was on the box at the time; and that as trespass would not have been maintainable against the co-proprietors who were absent, so case was held maintainable in order that all the proprietors might be included. But it is manifest that the Court did not rest their opinion upon so narrow a ground; nor indeed would it have been a solid foundation for the judgment, that the master, who was present, should be made liable to a different form of action than he otherwise would have been if the servant of the other proprietors had not been there.

We think the case last above referred to has laid down a plain and intelligible rule, that where the injury is occasioned by the carelessness and negligence of the Defendant, the Plaintiff is at liberty to bring an action on the case, notwithstanding the act is immediate, so long as it is not a wilful act; and, upon the authority of that case, we think the present form of action maintainable to recover damages for the injury.

Rule discharged.[h]

———

SHARROD v. LONDON & NORTH WESTERN RAILWAY, 154 Eng.Rep. 1345 (Ex.1849). Trespass. Defendant company's railway engine, negligently driven by defendant's servant, ran down and killed plaintiff's sheep. Defendant objected at the trial that the proper form of action was case. A verdict was entered for the plaintiff by consent, leave being reserved to the defendant to move to enter a nonsuit. On rule nisi, held, rule absolute.

Baron Parke said, on analogy to an ordinary carriage drawn by horses, "the law is well established, on the one hand, that, whenever the injury done to the plaintiff results from the immediate force of the defendant himself, whether intentionally or not, the plaintiff may bring an action of trespass; on the other hand, that if the act be that of the servant, and be negligent, not wilful, case is the only remedy against the master." Trespass will not lie against the master for his servant's trespass unless the act was done by the master's command, that is, "unless the particular act which constitutes the trespass is ordered to be done by the principal, or some act which comprises it; or some act which leads by a physical necessity to the act complained of."

———

[h] See Prichard, Trespass, Case and the Rule in Williams v. Holland, 1964 Cambridge L.J. 234, for an account of the evolution of the Williams rule.

Question: (2) As a barrister representing the plaintiff in a highway collision case in England in 1850, which form of action would you employ and
why?[i]

American cases.—Problems quite similar to those dealt with by
the English courts in the preceding cases—and in the cases considered later in this Topic—arose in American jurisdictions prior to the
various state provisions abolishing the forms of action, and they may
still perhaps arise in jurisdictions that have not wholly abandoned the
forms. Justice Morton was to echo Lord Raymond in saying: "We
cannot break down the well known distinctions between different
modes of declaring, without endangering the principles of justice upon which they are founded." Miner v. Bradley, 39 Mass. (22 Pick.)
457, 457–58 (1839). But the common-law development could not be
contained.

ADAMS v. HEMMENWAY, 1 Mass. 145 (1804). Trespass improper to recover for the freight and passage money lost to plaintiff
through defendant's firing upon plaintiff's vessel and wounding the
captain, thus compelling a discontinuance of the voyage.

At the same term of court, the captain recovered in trespass for
the injury done to him. Adams v. Hemmenway, 1 Mass. 146 (1804).

KELLY v. LETT, 35 N.C. 50 (1851). Case improper where defendant wilfully and designedly raised a head of water behind his own
dam and discharged it, injuring plaintiff's dam.

BROWN v. KENDALL, 60 Mass. (6 Cush.) 292 (1850). Trespass
proper where defendant, while trying to separate fighting dogs, negligently struck plaintiff with a stick. The court relied heavily on
Leame v. Bray, supra. But the court further indicated that plaintiff
could not recover even in trespass unless he could prove unlawfulness, intention, or negligence.

DALTON v. FAVOUR, 3 N.H. 465 (1826). Case proper where defendant, "having in his hands a firelock, highly charged with powder,
and a great quantity of wadding, so exceedingly carelessly managed
his said firelock, that he discharged its contents into the foot of the
plaintiff." The language of the court somewhat anticipated Williams
v. Holland, supra.

---

[i] In Winfield & Goodhart, Trespass and
Negligence, 49 L.Q.Rev. 359, 365–66
(1933), there is some discussion of practical considerations—such as costs and advantages in pleading—that might determine the choice between theoretically
available forms.

The distinction between trespass and
case was reexamined in Fowler v. Lanning, [1959] 1 Q.B. 426, noted in 1959
Cambridge L.J. 33; 75 L.Q.Rev. 161
(1959); 22 Mod.L.Rev. 538 (1959), where
the question was whether a statement of
claim was sufficient if it alleged merely
that "the defendant shot the plaintiff"
without any reference to intention or
negligence; the statement was held insufficient, the court deciding that even
trespass would "not lie if the injury to
the plaintiff, although the direct consequence of the act of the defendant, was
caused unintentionally and without negligence on the defendant's part." See also
Letang v. Cooper, [1965] 1 Q.B. 232
(C.A.1964), noted in 1964 Cambridge L.J.
200; 28 Mod.L.Rev. 92 (1965).

In a later New Hampshire case, Merrill v. Perkins, 59 N.H. 343 (1879), plaintiff was allowed to amend his declaration, after verdict and judgment, to add a count in trespass to a count in case in order to obviate the objection that trespass, rather than case, was the proper remedy. This would have been unthinkable at strict common law: an amendment changing the form of action from case to trespass, or vice versa, was not permitted.[j]

In contrast to the liberal approach in New Hampshire without benefit of statute, consider the treatment given by the Maine court to a legislative attempt at reform. In Lawry v. Lawry, 88 Me. 482, 34 A. 273 (1896), the court held that trespass would not lie for consequential injury and that the action had to be in case. The plaintiff was nonsuited, and an amendment was disallowed. There was in force at the time a Maine statute that provided: "The distinction between trespass and case is abolished. A declaration in either form is good." (The statute in this form had been on the books since 1857, and its substance, although in a much wordier version, dates back to 1835.) In reference to the statute, the court said: "But this relates to the distinction in form only. In cases where the distinction is really of substance, rather than of form, the statute is inapplicable."

BROKAW v. NEW JERSEY RAILROAD & TRANSPORTATION CO., 32 N.J.L. 328 (1867). Trespass proper against the railroad company for its servant's forcibly ejecting plaintiff from a car in which he was riding. "[I]f the act of the agent was authorized by the rules and regulations of the company, or was necessary to accomplish the purposes of his employment, the company is answerable [in trespass], even for the unnecessary violence of the agent."

(d) The "Possession" Necessary to Maintain Trespass

Trespass was conceived of as a form of action protecting "possession." This became material in actions for entry upon or injury to land or for injury to or asportation of personal property.

1. Suppose *A*, owning Blackacre, had leased it for a term of ten years to *B*, who had gone into possession. *C*, during the term, wrongfully entered upon the land and destroyed a dwelling house. Might *A* maintain trespass against *C*? The answer was no, for *A* did not have possession (or, indeed, the right to possession) at the time of the wrongful act. *B*, on the other hand, could bring trespass against *C*, recovering the whole amount of the damage but being responsible over to *A* for so much of the recovery as represented the injury to *A*'s reversionary interest in the land. Unless *B* had already recovered in this fashion, *A* could maintain an action on the case against *C* for the injury to his reversionary interest.

---

[j] The opinion in the Merrill case was by Chief Justice Doe. For accounts of this exceptional man, see J. Reid, Chief Justice: The Judicial World of Charles Doe (1967); Note, Doe of New Hampshire: Reflections on a Nineteenth Century Judge, 63 Harv.L.Rev. 513 (1950).

2.   What of the situation where direct injury was done to land by a stranger while it was in the possession of a tenant at will? The tenant at will could maintain trespass. But there was some dispute whether the owner could. Although he had a continuing right to immediate possession of the land as against the tenant at will, he did not have possession at the time of the injury. Here was a nice point. Ames thought the owner could maintain trespass against the stranger in this situation, but generally the availability of trespass turned on plaintiff's *possession* rather than *right to possession* at the time of the wrong.

3.   Reasoning similar to that set out in the foregoing paragraphs was employed in defining the rights of the bailor and bailee (for a term or at will) against third parties who directly injured the bailed chattel while in the hands of the bailee or who wrongfully took it from him.

4.   It was thought that a bailee for a term who damaged the chattel while it was in his possession under the bailment, or who wrongfully gave it away or sold it to a stranger, was not suable in trespass by the owner.[k]

Question: (3) Argue for and against this position.

5.   *A* owned a chattel. *B* wrongfully took it from *A*. *C* wrongfully took it from *B*. *A* could maintain trespass against *B*. *B*, although himself a wrongdoer, could maintain trespass against *C*. According to early authority (with some contrary authority in later times), *A* could not maintain trespass against *C*.

6.   For many purposes a servant having physical control of his master's goods was said to have "custody" rather than "possession."

Questions: (4) While driving *M*'s horse and carriage, *S* is held up by a stranger, *X*, who steals the horse and carriage. May *M* bring trespass against *X*?

(5) Suppose *S* had himself made off with the horse and carriage. Could *M* maintain trespass against *S*?[l]

The student need hardly be warned that the account here given is superficial. "Possession" and "right to possession" are far from being simple concepts and, as we already have ample reason to suspect, their meanings may change according to the context.[m]

---

[k] Compare supra p. 319 note e.

[l] The social consequences of the answer to the latter question will appear when it is noted that larceny—a felony that used to entail capital punishment—required a trespassory taking, while the lesser offense of embezzlement did not.

[m] In trespass, as in case, the successful plaintiff recovered only damages. Suppose *B* wrongfully took a chattel from *A*.

Was there any way in which *A* could recover the chattel in specie? By the form of action known as replevin—originally a remedy only for wrongful "distress," later extended to other wrongful takings—the plaintiff could compel such restitution; indeed, seizure of the chattel by the sheriff and its restitution to the plaintiff were interlocutory steps in the action. Speaking very generally, in order to qualify as a plaintiff in replevin at common

SECTION 3.   EVOLUTION THROUGH FICTION [n]
(HEREIN CHIEFLY OF TROVER)

WRIT OF DEBT OR DETINUE

[From A. Fitz-Herbert, Natura Brevium 119 L, I (9th ed. London 1794)]

The King to the Sheriff of Surrey, greeting: Command A. that justly and without delay he render to B. one hundred shillings, which he owes to him, and unjustly detains, as it is said (or, render to B. a certain book, or a certain cup, or a certain horse, or two lambs of the price of, &c. which he unjustly detains from him, &c.); and unless he will do it, and the aforesaid B. shall make you secure to prosecute his claim, then summon by good summons the aforesaid A. that he be before our justices at Westminster [on such a day] to show wherefore he hath not done it. And have there the summoners and this writ.

Question: (6) Does the language of the writ provide any apparent confirmation of Maitland's account of the growth of royal civil jurisdiction?

As the wording of the writ suggests, detinue was at first quite indistinguishable from debt, but in the thirteenth century became differentiated from it and lay for specific chattels. It could be used by the bailor against a bailee who wrongfully withheld (detained) the bailed chattel. Through alterations in the set language of the declaration sanctioned by the courts, detinue was extended to cover a number of situations, outside the bailment field, where a chattel was withheld against a person entitled to its possession. Thus detinue would lie by the owner against a finder who refused on demand to return the found article.

Question: (7) Give an example where detinue and trespass d.b.a. were available as alternative remedies.

In detinue, as in "simple debt," the ancient method of trial by wager of law rather than trial by jury was often available to the defendant. From the plaintiff's point of view this was a serious objection to the use of that form. Moreover, the defeated defendant could satisfy a judgment in detinue, at his option, either by returning the chattel to the plaintiff or by keeping it and paying damages; and it seems that where the defendant had injured the chattel, he could satisfy the judgment by returning it in its injured condition.

law, it was necessary to show the same "possession" at the time of the taking as was required for trespass; however, in the United States, it came to be held generally that replevin could be brought for a mere wrongful detention.

[n] The nature and role of fictions in the law are analyzed in L. Fuller, Legal Fictions (1967).

Ejectment, a form of action deriving from trespass, showed perhaps the greatest proliferation of fiction. See the description infra pp. 386–87. Ejectment was ultimately generalized as a means of recovering the possession of real property, superseding the ancient real actions.

For these and other reasons, pleaders began to cast about for a better remedy. The courts commenced to entertain actions on the case on analogy to detinue, and by the middle of the sixteenth century "trover" appears as a differentiated form of action. Trial was by jury, and the successful plaintiff recovered damages. The set language of the writ, which was tracked in the declaration, ran as follows.

WRIT OF TRESPASS ON THE CASE IN TROVER
[From H. Stephen, Pleading 18 (London 1824)]

The King to the Sheriff, &c. [Continue as in Trespass], to show for that whereas the said A.B. heretofore, to wit, on the _____ day of _____ in the year of our Lord _____ at _____ in the county of _____ was lawfully possessed, as of his own property, of certain goods and chattels, to wit, twenty tables and twenty chairs of great value, to wit, of the value of _____ pounds, of lawful money of Great Britain; and being so possessed thereof, he, the said A.B., afterwards, to wit, on the day and year aforesaid, at _____ aforesaid, in the county aforesaid, casually lost the said goods and chattels out of his possession; and the same afterwards, to wit, on the day and year aforesaid, at _____ aforesaid, in the county aforesaid, came to the possession of the said C.D. by finding; Yet the said C.D., well knowing the said goods and chattels to be the property of the said A.B., and of right to belong and appertain to him, but contriving and fraudulently intending, craftily and subtilly, to deceive and defraud the said A.B. in this behalf, hath not as yet delivered the said goods and chattels, or any part thereof, to the said A.B. (although often requested so to do); but so to do hath hitherto wholly refused, and still refuses; and afterwards, to wit on the _____ day of _____ in the year _____ at _____ aforesaid, in the county aforesaid, converted and disposed of the said goods and chattels to his, the said C.D.'s own use, to the damage of the said A.B. of _____ pounds, as it is said; and have you there the names of the pledges, and this writ. Witness, &c.

The use of this writ was extended to a great many situations other than cases of finding. The method was not to change the set form of the writ and declaration, but rather to dispense with the need of proving what was alleged. In time virtually none of these required allegations had to be proved. Lord Mansfield frankly said of trover: "In form it is a fiction: in substance a remedy to recover the value of personal chattels wrongfully converted by another to his own use." Cooper v. Chitty, 97 Eng.Rep. 166, 172 (K.B.1756). Plaintiff need not have lost the goods, nor need defendant have found them; "a trover and conversion well lies, although [the defendant] came to them by a lawful delivery, and not by trover." Ratcliff v. Davies, 79 Eng.Rep. 210, 210 (K.B.1611). The allegations "lawfully possessed" and "as of his own property" were taken in a highly qualified sense. Request and refusal to deliver did not need to be shown, at least in many instances. Not only did the plaintiff not have to establish the truth of these atrophied allegations, the defendant was not allowed to prove their falsity.

Again speaking very generally, trover could be maintained by the person entitled to possession of the goods for any "conversion" thereof by the defendant: the chief problem became one of defining what was meant by "conversion." Professors Scott and Kent say that acts of conversion included "a wrongful taking of possession of the chattel, a wrongful user of a chattel in the defendant's possession, a wrongful sale by the defendant of a chattel in his possession, or a wrongful detention." A. Scott & R. Kent, Cases and Other Materials on Civil Procedure 40 (1967).

Questions: (8) Did trover cover all the ground covered by trespass d.b.a.?

(9) Did it cover all the ground of trespass for injury to personal property?

In Ward v. Macauley, 100 Eng.Rep. 1135 (K.B.1791), plaintiff had leased a house with furniture for a term to *T*. Defendants, who had been plaintiffs in a separate action against *T*, levied execution on the furniture during the term in the mistaken belief that the furniture belonged to *T*. Plaintiff during the term brought trespass against the levying defendants. Lord Kenyon held that plaintiff could not maintain trespass, but intimated that he could maintain trover. In Gordon v. Harper, 101 Eng.Rep. 828 (K.B.1796), it was held that trover would not lie on such facts. Lord Kenyon said: "I forbear to deliver any opinion as to what remedy the landlord has in this case, not being at present called upon so to do: but it is clear that he cannot maintain trover."

Questions: (10) Why was trespass not maintainable?

(11) Why was trover not maintainable?

(12) What form of action was available to plaintiff?

(13) If plaintiff had commenced his action after the end of the term, what form or forms of action might be available to him?

B stole goods from *A* and sold them for a fair price to *C*, who knew nothing of the theft.

Questions: (14) Could *A* bring trespass against *B*?

(15) Could *A* bring trover against *B*?

(16) Could *A* bring trespass against *C*?

(17) Could *A* bring trover against *C*?

Read the following case closely and see how far the decision and reasoning conform to the models we have been building up.

———

SWIFT v. MOSELEY

Supreme Court of Vermont, 1838.

10 Vt. 208.

Trover, for two oxen, three cows and nine sheep.

Plea—Not guilty.

On the trial of the cause in the county court, it appeared in evidence, that, in the spring of 1835, the plaintiff [Eliphalet Swift] leased a farm, lying in Bridport, (of which he was possessed in right of his wife,) together with the above mentioned cattle and sheep, to one Jirah Swift, for the term of one year. By the terms of said lease, the plaintiff and said Jirah Swift, were, at the end of the year, to divide the profits of the farm and the increase of the stock, equally between them, which stock was to remain upon the farm during the year, unless sold or taken off by the consent of the plaintiff and said Jirah Swift;—that some time in the month of August, 1835, the said Jirah Swift sold said cattle and sheep to the defendants, without the consent of the plaintiff, and absconded, and that the defendants, immediately after making the purchase, drove the cattle and sheep away from the farm. The plaintiff introduced testimony tending to prove, that the defendants knew that Jirah Swift had no right to dispose of the cattle and sheep, and that they purchased them much under their value. Upon this evidence, the county court decided, that this action could not be sustained, as the plaintiff brought the suit previous to the termination of said lease, by the terms of which he had parted with his right of possession of the property in question, during its continuance, and rendered a judgment for the defendants, to which decision the plaintiff excepted.

REDFIELD, J. It seems to be well settled, that the plaintiff, in trespass de bonis asportatis, or trover, in order to maintain the action, must have had, at the time of the injury complained of, either the actual custody of the thing injured or taken, or a property in it, either general or special, with the right to immediate possession. If he had the actual custody of the thing, even wrongfully, he may maintain the action against every one, whose right is not superior to his. Perhaps a mere servant could not be said to have any such custody. His possession is that of the master. The general owner of a chattel may always maintain the action, unless he have parted with the possession, for a "definite term." Ward v. Macauley, 4 T.R. 489. Lord Kenyon in that case intimates an opinion, that trover will lie, but in Gordon v. Harper, 7 T.R. 12, it is expressly held, that case is the only remedy for an injury done to the thing bailed, during the continuance of the bailment.

In the present case it is contended, that the act of the lessee or bailee, in selling to the defendants, did, ipso facto, determine his right, and revive the right of the plaintiff to immediate possession.

If so, the plaintiff may maintain this action. It may be well to inquire what acts will determine a bailment of this character.

It is certain the act of a mere stranger will not operate to revive the plaintiff's right to immediate possession. Any misuse or abuse of the thing bailed, in the particular use for which the bailment was made, will not enable the general owner to maintain trespass or trover against the bailee. His only remedy is case. But if the thing be put to a *different* use from that for which it was bailed, by the consent of the bailee, we think the bailor may maintain trespass or trover.

It has been long settled that if the bailee kill or destroy the thing bailed, trespass or trover will lie. Coke's In. a. 53. It was early held, too, that the interest of the tenant in standing trees was so far determined by their being severed from the freehold, that the landlord might maintain trespass.

In the case of Farrant v. Thompson, 5 Barn. & Ald. 826, found in the 7th Com.Law R. it was held that machinery, leased and by the lessee severed from the freehold, became *instanter* re-vested in the lessor, and he might maintain trover even during the continuance of the term. The case is expressly put by the court upon the ground, that the lessee, by his wrongful act, forfeits his right, and thus "puts an end to his qualified possession." If so in that case, much more in this, where the bailee sells the property. The same doctrine here decided is held in the case of Sanborn v. Colman, 6 N.H. 14.

The judgment of the County Court is reversed, and a new trial granted.

SECTION 4.   DEVELOPMENT OF REMEDIES FOR BREACH OF PROMISE

(a) Debt and Covenant and Their Deficiencies

B struck *A* and injured him ten pounds' worth. Debt would not lie for the £10 although in a sense *B* "owed" *A* the money. The early conception of debt appears to have been quite different. "The conception [as in the writ of right for land] was that the debtor was holding back something which he had granted, and which therefore actually belonged, to the creditor, not that he was merely under an obligation to pay money." E. Morgan, Introduction to the Study of Law 92–93 (2d ed.1948). Examine again the wording of the writ of debt in the preceding Section.

A and *B* orally agreed, *A* to deliver the horse Dobbin, *B* then to pay £10. *A* delivered Dobbin; *B* did not pay. Debt would lie by *A* against *B* to recover the promised price.[o] This was an instance of "simple debt." One could rationalize the result by saying that by the agreement and upon the delivery of Dobbin, *B* had granted and *A* had acquired ownership of the £10. An action could be brought not on *B*'s promise to perform, but on the half-completed transaction that created *A*'s property right. The horse having been given, debt lay to recover the definite, fixed sum that remained owing. But the thing that was given need not have been an article of personal property. It might be money lent, work performed, or the like. So long as a fixed sum [p] was owed for the thing by agreement, express or implied, simple debt lay to recover the sum.

A variant form of debt, "debt on a specialty," lay for breach of a promise, made in a sealed instrument, to pay a fixed sum of money.[q]

The ancient form of action named "covenant" could be brought for breach of a promise under seal other than a promise to pay a fixed sum of money.[r] Such promises to do something in the future should be contrasted with a grant, which transfers an immediate right or interest to the grantee. Covenant could be used only to compel performance, and not to compensate for misperformance.

There were at least two grave sorts of deficiencies from which this array of forms suffered. In the first place, as has already been noted, wager of law was often open to the defendant as the method of trial in simple debt. In the second place, some important kinds of defaults in elementary commercial transactions were at this stage beyond the range of debt and covenant, being thus left to the local courts.

Question: (18) Give examples justifying the last statement.

By adroit manipulation of specialty instruments, commercial transactions could be and were so rigged as to provide easy access to the established forms of action in case of a breach of promise.[s] There was, however, a lengthy development by which new forms of action were devised to supply the omissions of debt and covenant.

---

[o] Detinue would also lie against *B* to recover Dobbin or the value of Dobbin. But here the value came to be equated to the promised price. Hence, this remedy had no usefulness to *A* beyond that of simple debt. Similarly, the later development of trover did not expand *A*'s remedial arsenal.

[p] The requirement in debt that the sum be fixed was watered down somewhat in later cases.

[q] Other variants of debt were "debt on a record" (i.e., a judgment) and "debt on a statute" (e.g., a statute prescribing a penalty recoverable by private suit; cf. Williamson v. Columbia Gas & Elec. Corp., supra p. 299).

[r] Covenant later came to cover the case of a promise under seal to pay a fixed sum of money, so that debt and covenant overlapped.

[s] "Statutes merchant and statutes staple" provided other correctives for the deficiencies of the old forms. See Thorne, Tudor Social Transformation and Legal Change, 26 N.Y.U.L.Rev. 10, 19–21 (1951).

(b) Rise of Special Assumpsit to Fill Lacunae
Left by Debt and Covenant

A germinal situation in this development was one where defendant negligently injured a chattel entrusted to his care. An action on the case would lie.

Question: (19) What of trespass? detinue?

The pleader in the action on the case would take care to allege in his declaration that defendant undertook (*assumpsit*) to care for the goods properly. Why the allegation of *assumpsit*? It has been surmised that this was intended to negative the implication that the plaintiff shared somehow in the blame by entrusting the chattel to *this* defendant. And similarly *assumpsit* appears in actions on the case for negligence of barbers, surgeons, and others.

The *assumpsit* then began to live a life of its own, so that in time the defendant in an action on the case on assumpsit might be held liable for breaking a promise (1) even where he had not been negligent and (2) even where his violation of the promise consisted of his not doing anything at all. There was at work also a nontechnical notion of deceit, especially so where defendant had received value and then misperformed his promise or failed to perform it.

The following report shows the action on the case on assumpsit in midpassage. The judges are concerned over the failure of the plaintiff to allege what in later days would be termed "consideration" for the defendant's promise sued on, and also over the failure to allege a misfeasance as distinguished from a nonfeasance. (For "trespass" in this report, read "trespass on the case." "Covenant" is used in some places in the report as the equivalent of agreement or promise, in others as signifying the action of covenant.)

WATKINS' CASE
Court of Common Pleas, 1425.
Y.B.Hil. 3 Hen. 6, f. 36, pl. 33.[t]

A writ of Trespass was brought by one W.B. against Watkins of London, mill-maker. And he counted by *Strangeways sur ce cas*, that is to say, that on such a day and year in London in such a ward he took upon himself (*emprist sur luy*) to make a mill for the said plaintiff; and he showed that the mill was to be all ready and built by the following Christmas, but that by this time the mill was not built, *a tort* and to the damage of the plaintiff ten marks.

[t] The translation is by C. Fifoot, History and Sources of the Common Law 341–43 (1949). Siegel v. Spear & Co., 234 N.Y. 479, 138 N.E. 414 (1923), is a modern analogue of Watkins' Case.

Rolfe: Judgment of the writ: for by the writ it is supposed that the defendant should make a mill, and he has not declared for certain how much he should have for the making.

Strangeways: Since you have said nothing, we ask judgment and pray our damages.[u]

BABINGTON, C.J. If I bring a writ of Deceit against one, for that the defendant was my attorney and that by his negligence I have lost my land, etc., in this case I must declare how he was retained by me, or else the writ shall be abated. So here.

MARTIN, J. I do not know that I have seen in the Law that a writ *sur tiel mattere* lies, where no tort is alleged in the writ, but only that the defendant has promised to do something and he has not done it: for in such case a good writ of Covenant lies, supposing that he has a specialty. But if he had made a mill which was not good but altogether badly made, then a good writ of Trespass would lie. Suppose we put the case that a farrier makes a covenant with me to shoe my horse, and by his negligence he lames my horse, on this matter shewn a good writ of Trespass lies, for notwithstanding that in the rehearsal of the matter a covenant is supposed, I say that, inasmuch as he has done badly what he had covenanted to do, the covenant is thereby changed and made into a tort, for which a good writ of Trespass lies. But in the case at bar there is no such thing; for no tort is alleged in the writ by any feasance, but only a nonfeasance, which sounds only in covenant.

BABINGTON, C.J. I think the contrary. Put the case that one makes a covenant with me to roof my hall or a certain house by a certain time, and within this time he does not roof it, so that by default of the roofing the furniture of the house is all damaged by the rain; in this case I say that I shall have a good writ of Trespass *sur le mattere monstre* against him who made the covenant with me. So too I shall recover damages because I have suffered loss by the not making the mill.

COKAYNE, J. To the same intent. As to the first argument, that he should have declared that he made the covenant with him for a sum certain, it seems to me, Sir, that he has thus declared in effect. For it is not to be supposed that he should make the mill for nothing, and so it is all one as if he had expressly said so in his pleading, and on the matter shown the writ is well enough. And put the case that one makes a covenant to repair certain ditches on my land, and he does not do so, so that by his default the water which should run into

[u] "A young barrister had been talking for about four hours to a jury who, when he had finished, felt somewhat exhausted. His opponent then arose and, looking sweetly at the judge, said: My lord, I will follow the example of my friend who has just finished and submit the case without argument." R. Fountain, The Wit of the Wig 110 (1968).

the ditches floods my land and destroys my corn; I say that I shall have a good writ of Trespass for this nonfeasance. So here.

. . . .

MARTIN, J. . . . But truly, as it seems to me, if this action be maintainable *sur cette mattere*, for every broken covenant in the world a man shall have an action of Trespass.

BABINGTON, C.J. All our talk is vain; for as yet they have not demurred in law.

Wherefore he said to *Strangeways* and *Rolfe*, Plead and say what you will, or demur; and then there can be debate and dispute enough.

Wherefore *Rolfe* pleaded over, and said that, long after the time when it was supposed that he made the covenant, that is to say, on such a day, etc., the defendant came to the plaintiff in such a ward and said to him that the mill was quite ready and built, and asked him when he would have the mill, and discharged himself completely of the mill. And so we demand judgment if the action lies.

Strangeways: He did not discharge himself.

Issue joined.

Quaere de l'opinion de MARTIN.[v]

———

By 1589 the action named "special assumpsit" had become a differentiated form of action. It was said broadly in Strangborough v. Warner, 74 Eng.Rep. 686 (Q.B.1589), that "a promise against a promise will maintain an action upon the case, as in consideration that you do give me £ 10 on such a day, I promise to give you £10 such a day after."

Question: (20) Whom does the reporter in the Strangborough case envisage as plaintiff, *you* (lender) or *I* (borrower)? What would be the measure of damages?

———

DECLARATION IN SPECIAL ASSUMPSIT
[From 2 J. Chitty, Pleading 99–100 (London 1809)]

In the Common Pleas.

Hilary Term, 47 Geo. 3, Middlesex, (to wit) C.D. was attached to answer A.B. of a plea of trespass on the case, &c. and thereupon the said A.B. by E.F. his attorney, complains, For that whereas heretofore, to wit, on, &c. at, &c. the said A.B. at the special instance and request of the said C.D. bargained with the said C.D. to buy of him the said C.D. and the said C.D. then and there sold to the said A.B. a large quantity, to wit, ten loads of wheat at the rate or price of

———

[v] This last observation is a note by the reporter.

£ _____ for each and every load thereof, to be delivered by the said C.D. to the said A.B. in a week then next following, at _____, and to be paid for by the said A.B. to the said C.D. on the delivery thereof as aforesaid; and in consideration thereof, and that the said A.B. at the like special, &c. had then and there undertaken and faithfully promised the said C.D. to accept and receive the said wheat, and to pay him for the same at the rate or price aforesaid; he the said C.D. undertook, &c. to deliver the said wheat to him the said A.B., as aforesaid; and although the said time for the delivery of the said wheat, as aforesaid, hath long since elapsed, and the said A.B. hath always been ready and willing to accept and receive the said wheat, and to pay for the same at the rate or price aforesaid, to wit, at, &c. aforesaid; yet the said C.D. not regarding, &c. but contriving, &c. to deceive and defraud the said A.B. in this behalf, did not nor would within the time aforesaid, or at any time afterwards, deliver the said wheat, or any part thereof for the said A.B. at, &c. aforesaid, or elsewhere, but wholly neglected and refused so to do, whereby the said A.B. hath lost and been deprived of divers great gains and profits, which might and otherwise would have arisen and accrued to him from the delivery of the said wheat to him the said A.B., as aforesaid, to wit, at, &c. aforesaid. Wherefore the said A.B. saith that he is injured, and hath sustained damages to the value of £ _____, and therefore he brings his suit, &c.

To return to the case of the horse Dobbin: special assumpsit now lay by *B* to recover damages in the event of *A*'s nondelivery of the horse. But if *B* failed to pay after *A* had delivered, *A* could not maintain special assumpsit to recover the agreed price. Here the remedy remained simple debt, with its attendant wager of law. The notion seems to have been that *B*'s promise to pay was "merged" in the debt, so that it afforded no ground for special assumpsit.

(c) Assumpsit Engulfs Simple Debt

Now began a movement by which assumpsit became a remedy alternative to simple debt.

The first step. Suppose *B*, being indebted for Dobbin, made a *fresh* promise to pay (*indebitatus, assumpsit*). It was held that assumpsit would lie on the fresh promise. The pleading did not have to contain specifics on how the original debt accrued, because the plaintiff was suing on the fresh promise.

The second step. Then in Slade's Case, 76 Eng.Rep. 1072 (K.B.1602),[w] it was held after much deliberation that even if *B* had

---

[w] See J. Baker, An Introduction to English Legal History 282–90 (2d ed. 1979); S. Milsom, Historical Foundations of the Common Law 339–56 (2d ed. 1981); A. Simpson, A History of the Common Law of Contract 281–313 (1975); Lücke, Slade's Case and the Origin of the Com-

not actually made a subsequent promise to pay, assumpsit would nevertheless lie if the plaintiff pleaded specifics concerning the original debt.

The third step. In the years immediately following Slade's Case, a new variant of assumpsit, named "general assumpsit," came to be accepted as an alternative to simple debt. The averment of a fresh promise to pay had to appear in the declaration, but it was now recognized as fictitious and was non-traversable. Some information about the original debt had to be pleaded, but complete specifics were now deemed unnecessary: a general rather than a special pleading sufficed. As a consequence of the plaintiff's being freed from the need of specifically pleading the original debt and of proving a subsequent promise, the path to expansion of the form of action was open wide.

(d) Extension of General Assumpsit Beyond the Range of Simple Debt

In the sweep of time, general assumpsit was extended far beyond the province of simple debt. It was no objection to the maintenance of general assumpsit that the amount involved was not fixed. A common situation for general assumpsit was one where plaintiff had delivered goods or performed work for defendant without agreement as to the amount of compensation; if plaintiff was successful, he recovered a judgment for the reasonable value, as determined in the action.

A series of simple, stylized forms of declaration evolved within general assumpsit. These "common counts" may be classed as follows: (1) the indebitatus or debt counts, including the money counts (money lent; money paid; money had and received; and so on) and other counts (goods sold and delivered; work, labor, and materials; and so on); and (2) the value counts (quantum meruit, for the reasonable value of work done; and quantum valebant, for the reasonable value of goods supplied). Here follows a form of declaration in general assumpsit for goods sold and delivered.

DECLARATION IN GENERAL ASSUMPSIT
[From H. Stephen, Pleading 47–48 (London 1824)]

In the King's Bench.

_____ Term, in the _____ year of the reign of King George the Fourth.

_____ to wit, C.D. was attached to answer A.B. of a plea of trespass on the case; and thereupon the said A.B., by _____ his attorney, complains: For that, whereas the said C.D. heretofore, to wit, on

mon Counts (pts. 1–3), 81 L.Q.Rev. 422, 539 (1965), 82 L.Q.Rev. 81 (1966).

the _____ day of _____ in the year of our Lord _____ at _____
in the county of _____ was indebted to the said A.B. in the sum of
_____ pounds, of lawful money of Great Britain, for divers goods,
wares and merchandizes, by the said A.B. before that time sold and
delivered to the said C.D. at his special instance and request; and
being so indebted he the said C.D., in consideration thereof, afterwards to wit, on the day and year aforesaid, at _____ aforesaid, in
the county aforesaid, undertook and faithfully promised the said A.B.
to pay him the said sum of money when he the said C.D. should be
thereto afterwards requested. Yet the said C.D. not regarding his
said promise and undertaking, but contriving and fraudulently intending craftily and subtilly to deceive and defraud the said A.B. in
this behalf, hath not yet paid the said sum of money, or any part
thereof, to the said A.B. (although oftentimes afterwards requested).
But the said C.D., to pay the same, or any part thereof, hath hitherto
wholly refused, and still refuses, to the damage of the said A.B. of
_____ pounds; and therefore he brings his suit, &c.

Consider now the case of Lamine v. Dorrell, 92 Eng.Rep. 303 (Q.B.
1705). A man died intestate owning certain Irish debentures. Defendant wrongfully procured his own appointment as administrator and
wrongfully sold the debentures, apparently asserting them to be his
own. Administration was then granted to plaintiff, who sued to recover the price received by defendant, using general assumpsit "for
money received by the defendant to the use of the plaintiff as administrator." It was held that the action could be maintained.

Questions: (21) Could any argument be made that simple debt would lie,
and hence general assumpsit?

(22) To what extent must the language of the declaration in general assumpsit be fictionalized in order to bring a situation like Lamine v. Dorrell
within the scope of the declaration?

If the Lamine case could be maintained in general assumpsit, it
was plain that the way was open for the use of that form of action as
a remedy for a wide variety of cases of unjust enrichment.

Note that trover could have been brought for the conversion of
the debentures. Powell, J., said in the Lamine case: "But the plaintiff may dispense with the wrong, and suppose the sale made by his
consent, and bring an action for the money they were sold for, as
money received to his use." Here is the germ of a powerful idea.
You will now begin to understand what is meant by the lawyer's
phrase, "waiving the tort and suing in (general) assumpsit" for the
proceeds of the tort.[x]

[x] May the concept of waiving the tort
and suing in (general) assumpsit be extended to the case where the converter
has not sold the goods but retains them?
See Manhattan Egg Co. v. Seaboard Terminal & Refrigeration Co., infra p. 403.

The classic justification for these new uses of general assumpsit was by Lord Mansfield in Moses v. Macferlan, 97 Eng.Rep. 676, 678 (K.B.1760):

"The 1st objection is, 'that an action of debt would not lie here; and no *assumpsit* will lie, where an action of debt may not be brought:' some sayings at *nisi prius,* reported by note takers who did not understand the force of what was said, are quoted in support of that proposition.   But there is no foundation for it.

"It is much more plausible to say, 'that where debt lies, an action upon the case ought not to be brought.'   And that was the point relied upon in Slade's case: but the rule then settled and followed ever since is, 'that an action of *assumpsit* will lie in many cases where debt lies, and in many where it does not lie.'

"A main inducement, originally, for encouraging actions of *assumpsit* was, 'to take away the wager of law:' and that might give rise to loose expressions, as if the action was confined to cases only where that reason held.

"2d objection.—'That no assumpsit lies, except upon an express or implied contract: but here it is impossible to presume any contract to refund money . . . .'

"Answer.   If the defendant be under an obligation, from the ties of natural justice, to refund;   the law implies a debt, and gives this action, founded in the equity of the plaintiff's case, as it were upon a contract ('quasi ex contractu,' as the Roman law expresses it)."

The bounds on this idea of unjust enrichment were difficult to fix. From a formal point of view, one might be tempted to agree with Scrutton, L.J., that ever since Lord Mansfield, "the whole history of this particular form of action has been what I may call a history of well-meaning sloppiness of thought."   Holt v. Markham, [1923] 1 K.B. 504, 513 (C.A.1922).

(e) Relation Between Special and General Assumpsit

General assumpsit thus would lie as an alternative to simple debt, as a means for recovery of reasonable value under contracts implied in fact, and as a remedy for unjust enrichment.   Speaking perhaps too simply, special assumpsit came to be recognized as a remedy for breach of any express promise not under seal.   It is evident that this scheme involved considerable overlap.

To round out our account, we return again to the case of the horse Dobbin.   We have seen that debt would lie by *A* for the promised price after delivery of the horse.   When the common-law development was over, special and general assumpsit would also lie for the price.

Some of the relations among the forms of action for breach of promise, at the close of the entire development that has just been reviewed, will be brought out by considering the following problem cases.

Questions: (23) *X* and *Y* contract orally, or in an instrument not under seal, *X* to perform work over a period of time, *Y* to pay a stated sum upon completion of the work. When *X* has performed in part, *Y* wrongfully discharges him from the job. What forms of action were available to *X* against *Y*, and how would the recoveries be figured in each instance?

(24) *B* promises to pay *A* an agreed price, *A* then to deliver Dobbin. *B* pays, but *A* fails to deliver. What forms of action were available to *B* against *A*? Will *B*'s choice of a form of action depend on what he thinks he can prove to be the reasonable value of the horse?

(25) *A* is to deliver Dobbin, and *B* is then to pay an agreed price. If *B* receives the horse and fails to pay the price, may *A* use general assumpsit to recover not the agreed price, but the reasonable value of the horse, where that value exceeds the price? See Restatement (Second) of Contracts § 373(2) (1979) (no).

(26) Defendant put up at auction a certain cow and 400 pounds of hay, which was then in a bay with other hay. Plaintiff bid off the cow and the hay for one gross sum of $17, which he paid at the time. He then received the cow and afterwards made demand for the hay, which was refused by defendant, who had used it. What forms of action were available to plaintiff, and what would be his recovery under each? See Miner v. Bradley, 39 Mass. (22 Pick.) 457 (1839).

SECTION 5. THE COMMON–LAW SYSTEM OF PLEADING

Because the reform movement that swept away the forms of action at law was also directed, almost as a corollary, at the amelioration of the common-law system of pleading, it is convenient to examine that system briefly at this point.[y]

1. Reaching a single issue.—The fundamental notion behind common-law pleading was that the parties usually should, by as extensive an interchange of written statements of position as was necessary, wind up with a single issue of law or of fact upon the resolution of which the controversy would depend. We shall review briefly the moves and countermoves by which this result was achieved.

2. Declaration.—After determining the proper form of action and obtaining the appropriate writ, the plaintiff's first step toward the production of an issue was to prepare a *declaration*. The declaration had to conform to the writ, and it had to contain a statement sufficient in law to sustain the action. Declarations under most of the forms of action took on set and rigid forms. Some of them, notably the declaration in trover, were loaded with fictitious allegations frequently giving the defendant no hint of what the plaintiff would

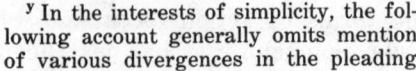

[y] In the interests of simplicity, the following account generally omits mention of various divergences in the pleading techniques among the several forms of action.

later seek to prove. They also varied greatly in the specificity of allegation that was required. The declaration on the common counts in general assumpsit, for example, was generalized, while the declaration in special assumpsit was pretty detailed although containing a number of fictitious allegations.

3. Responses to declaration.—The defendant, in order to prevent the entry of judgment against him, had to make a choice among three types of countermoves:

a. The defendant might *demur.* Demurrers were of two kinds, *general* and *special.* The former attacked defects of substance, the latter defects in form. For the moment we shall confine our attention to the general demurrer. A general demurrer was appropriate when, supposing the assertions in the declaration to be true, the defendant believed that the plaintiff was not entitled to the redress he sought. Thus the parties were at issue immediately, the plaintiff affirming and the defendant denying the sufficiency in law of the declaration. This question of law was resolved by the court on argument. In England the hearing on such an issue of law was before the full bench of the court sitting at Westminster. There was no occasion for a trial of the facts because for purposes of the demurrer the allegations of the declaration stood as admitted. Originally, a judgment on demurrer ended the case, but in due time leave to plead over came to be given as a matter of course.

b. The defendant might interpose a *dilatory plea.* Such a plea did not dispute the justice of the plaintiff's claim on the merits; its aim was simply to show that the particular suit could not be maintained in that court at that time. If successful, it defeated the particular action but did not preclude the plaintiff from starting afresh if he could cure the defect. One such plea was a *plea to the jurisdiction,* by which the defendant challenged the jurisdiction of the court to entertain the action. Another, and more common, class of dilatory plea was a *plea in abatement,* by which several kinds of defect could be attacked, including lack of capacity of the plaintiff to sue or of the defendant to be sued, misjoinder (too many) or nonjoinder (too few) of plaintiffs or defendants, and pendency of another action between the same parties for the same cause. Successive pleas in abatement could be made in the same action, but there was a set order that had to be followed. Any matter in abatement was treated as waived if it was preceded by or combined with another matter in abatement that, according to the prescribed order, was supposed to come after it.[z] Courts looked with disfavor on pleas in abatement and required them to be framed with great exactness. It was necessary for the defendant to point out the defect with particularity so that the plaintiff could correct it in a new action. For example, if the basis of the plea

---

[z] A plea in abatement was similarly waived if it was preceded by or combined with a plea in bar.

was the nonjoinder of a necessary party defendant, the missing defendant had to be named.

c.   The defendant might interpose a *plea in bar.* If the declaration was sufficient in law and there was no basis for a dilatory plea, the defendant had to meet the plaintiff's case on the merits by a plea in bar. Such a plea might be (i) by way of *traverse* or (ii) by way of *confession and avoidance.*

A traverse was the denial of a material allegation of the plaintiff's declaration. Originally the insistence upon the singleness of issue was so strong that only one such allegation could be denied even though several were untrue. We shall refer below to the relaxation of this restriction. A denial produced an issue of fact, the plaintiff affirming and the defendant denying the truth of the allegation. This closed the pleadings, and the action was ripe for trial. In England the trial of an issue of fact ordinarily took place not at Westminster, but at nisi prius, i.e., before a judge on circuit sitting with a local jury.

When the declaration was true in fact, the defendant might be able to resort to a plea in confession and avoidance. As the name implies, such a plea confessed the truth of the declaration but asserted further matter thought to be sufficient to avoid a judgment. These further facts might show some justification or excuse for the matters alleged in the declaration, as where in an action for trespass to the person the defendant admitted striking the plaintiff but asserted that he acted in self-defense. Or the avoidance might show the release or discharge of an obligation that had once existed, as by payment, release, accord and satisfaction, or the running of the statute of limitations. The confession was an essential part of the plea: the defendant had to confess before he was allowed to set up new matter in avoidance.

4.   **Replication and later pleadings.**—If the defendant's plea was in confession and avoidance, no issue was produced and the pleading process was continued. The next move was up to the plaintiff. If he believed that the matter asserted in avoidance was insufficient in law, he could demur to the plea. Otherwise he filed a *replication.* Like the defendant's plea in bar, the replication might either (a) deny a material allegation in the plea or (b) admit the truth of the plea but set forth new matter by way of confession and avoidance. For an example of the latter, if the defendant pleaded his infancy as a defense to an action of assumpsit for goods sold and delivered, the plaintiff might in his replication admit the defendant's infancy but assert that the goods were necessaries. (As a matter of substantive law, infants were chargeable in assumpsit for necessaries.)

If the replication was in the nature of denial, an issue of fact was created and a trial of that issue followed. If, however, the replication contained new matter by way of avoidance, no issue was reached and it was again the defendant's turn to plead. He might demur to the replication, or he might file a *rejoinder* either denying the new matter in the replication or confessing it and pleading further matter in avoidance. If he took the latter course, still another round of pleading was required from the plaintiff. This process continued until either a demurrer created an issue of law or a denial created an issue of fact. The succeeding pleadings were called respectively the *surrejoinder*, the *rebutter*, and the *surrebutter*. Subsequent rounds after the surrebutter were theoretically possible, but they were of such rarity that no names were assigned to them. As a matter of fact, it was an unusual case that would not wind up at issue well before the named pleadings were exhausted.

5. **Departures.**—In his later rounds of pleading, a party could not desert his ground of complaint or defense and rely upon another. The replication had to support the declaration; the rejoinder had to support the plea; and so on through the later stages of pleading on both sides. Otherwise the pleader was guilty of a *departure*, and his pleading was demurrable. To illustrate, if the plaintiff alleged one cause of action in his declaration and in his replication introduced a new cause of action, this would be a departure. Similarly, a defendant asserting infancy as a defense in his plea would be guilty of a departure if he responded to a replication of necessaries with a rejoinder alleging payment. It should be noted that a departure, although demurrable, was "cured" by verdict; that is, the objection had to be raised at an early stage and was not available to the party after a verdict had been rendered.

6. **Motions in arrest and n.o.v.**—The demurrer was not the only device for challenging the legal sufficiency of pleadings. If an issue of fact was made on the pleadings, a trial held, and a verdict rendered for the plaintiff, the defendant could file a *motion in arrest of judgment*. This was in essence a delayed demurrer, raising the same question of law that would have been open on demurrer. A similar delayed attack could be made by the plaintiff after a verdict for the defendant by a *motion for judgment notwithstanding the verdict* (non obstante veredicto). If successful, it resulted in a judgment for the plaintiff despite the verdict for the defendant, for the verdict would have been rendered on an insufficient defense.

7. **Demurrer searches the record.**—When a line of pleadings ended with a demurrer, the demurrer not only challenged the validity of the immediately prior pleading, but was said to "open the record." Thus, if the declaration was found to be deficient in substance, judgment on the demurrer went against the plaintiff even though there had been no demurrer to the declaration. This was equally true whether the demurrer was interposed by the defendant (for example, to the plaintiff's replication) or by the plaintiff (for example, to the defendant's rejoinder). Similarly, if the declaration was sufficient and the defendant's plea insufficient, judgment on the demurrer went against the defendant. A concomitant of this rule was the proposi-

tion that certain deficiencies in a pleading might be cured by a later pleading. For example, let us assume a declaration from which an essential allegation was omitted. At this point a demurrer by the defendant would have been sustained. Instead of demurring, however, the defendant answered to the merits and in his plea supplied the missing allegation. Upon a demurrer to the plea or to any later pleading, the defect in the declaration was disregarded. In other words, judgment on a demurrer went against the party who made the first uncorrected pleading error.

8. Subsidiary rules of pleading.—There were various subsidiary rules of pleading, most of them calculated to further the objective of producing a single, clear-cut, and definite issue. Many were highly technical, and some to the modern eye appear to be flatly absurd. Some of the rules, on the other hand, enunciated principles of pleading that remain sound today (even though the consequences of error are mitigated in modern practice). We shall mention a few of the guiding ideas.

Duplicity was a cardinal sin of common-law pleading. A declaration, for instance, could not ask for the same relief on two distinct grounds. Nor could a plea or any later pleading contain more than one distinct answer to the pleading that preceded it. The reason for the rule was to preserve the singleness of issue. Illustrative of the same principle was the proposition that a party could not simultaneously demur and plead to the same matter. That is, he could not in effect say, "Your pleading is untrue, but even if it were true it is insufficient in law."

There were also numerous rules designed to produce precision and particularity in the issue. Thus a pleading might be fatally defective for *uncertainty* if facts were not pleaded distinctly and explicitly in detail.

Hypothetical and *alternative* pleadings were also forbidden by the common-law rules. Both the "if" and "either-or" forms of allegation were bad for uncertainty and also as violating the requirement of singleness of issue.

There were, in addition, rules designed to prevent confusion or obscurity. Naturally, if a pleading was unintelligible (or, in the language of the common law, *insensible*), the defect was fatal. Further, if a pleading was inconsistent within itself, it was demurrable as *repugnant*. Another pleading fault was *ambiguity*, and pursuant to the general principle that pleadings were construed most strongly against the pleader, the construction of an ambiguous pleading was adopted that was the most unfavorable to the pleader. An illustration of ambiguity was the *negative pregnant*, a form of negative statement implying within itself an affirmative. If the plaintiff alleged that the defendant "struck and kicked" the plaintiff and if the defendant denied that he "struck and kicked" him, the denial that the defendant did both of these things would be taken impliedly to admit that he did one or the other. Because either one would be sufficient to establish the defendant's liability, such a plea raised no defense, and on a demurrer to the plea the plaintiff would be entitled to judgment.

Nor could pleadings be *argumentative*. The rule against argumentativeness required that a denial be negative in form as well as substance. For instance, if the plaintiff alleged that X was dead and if the defendant pleaded that X was alive, this was argumentative. The proper form of pleading would be to allege that X was not dead.

9. Joinder of causes of action.—The plaintiff could combine under a single writ as many separate causes of action as he might have against the defendant so long as they fell within the same form of action. Each cause would then in effect be separately pleaded in the same action.[a] It was no objection to joinder that such causes were entirely unrelated to each other. Thus the plaintiff could combine in an action on the case claims (a) that the defendant negligently ran him down in May and (b) that the defendant obstructed his right of way over Blackacre in October. But if the same street affray included both blows and slanderous words, the aggrieved plaintiff could not join (a) the cause of action for slander with (b) the cause for trespass to the person. This was a fatal misjoinder.

There was some possibility of relief from the effects of the restrictions on joinder of causes. Matter not joinable when made the subject of an independent claim, because it would require a different form of action, might sometimes be shown in *aggravation* of the damages. In an action for trespass q.c.f., the damages might be increased by proof of the taking of goods, a personal assault, seduction of the plaintiff's wife or daughter, and even slander. Such matters in aggravation, called consequential damages, had to be set forth specifically in the declaration introduced by a per quod ("whereby"). But if the plaintiff failed to establish his main claim of trespass q.c.f., it did him no good to prove matters in aggravation, as there was nothing to aggravate. If, however, causes of action were properly joined, the failure to establish any one of them would have no effect upon the others.

Reforms up to the 1830's.—The stringency of these pleading requirements produced sporadic pressures over the years for reform. We shall here tell something of this story up to the 1830's.

Originally, many purely formal defects were open to challenge at any stage in the case, even after verdict, with the result that the fruits of victory were frequently snatched away from a litigant for

---

[a] Without going into the antique learning, it may be said that for this purpose a form included its variants. Thus counts under all the varieties of debt could be joined in a declaration, and so could counts in special and general assumpsit. Debt and detinue were joinable, as were case and trover.

pleading flaws. The first step in the reform was a statute in the time of Queen Elizabeth I.[b] The aim of this statute was to require defects in form to be challenged by a special demurrer specifying the particular fault. Any merely formal defect not so challenged was waived, and the judges were to give judgment, in the words of the statute, "according as the very right of the cause and matter in law shall appear unto them." Thus a defect in the form of the pleading could still be fatal to the pleader's case, but only if it was timely challenged with particularity. The distinction between defects in form and defects of substance was not found easy to draw, but the former category included such things as duplicity and argumentativeness.

The onerous requirement of singleness of issue was doomed eventually to break down. From early times the plaintiff could avoid its rigors by declaring in separate *counts*. A plaintiff with several separate causes of action falling within the same form of action could declare in separate counts for each of them. Why should not the same device be available to a plaintiff who had only a single cause but was uncertain as to what in law he had to prove or what in fact he would be able to prove? Although he was required to make the elaborate pretense that separate causes were involved, a plaintiff indeed could state the same cause of action in various ways in separate counts. He thus gained by indirection the benefit of pleading in the alternative. This device was frequently used in order to lessen the possibility of a *variance.* A variance occurred when the matters proved did not correspond to the allegations of the pleading; only a few kinds of allegations were excepted from this requirement of conforming proof. Even a minor variance was fatal until the nineteenth century, when by statute [c] the judge was empowered to allow an amendment at the trial to correct a variance immaterial to the merits of the case.

While the plaintiff could avoid the singleness requirement by using separate counts, the defendant had no such opportunity. For any particular count, he might have several possible defenses and be forced to select one of them and abandon the others. If he chanced to lose on the defense he selected, the fact that he might have succeeded on another defense would do him no good. By statute in 1705,[d] a defendant was permitted to interpose several pleas in bar to the same count. There was no requirement that these several pleas be consistent with each other: an admission of an allegation in one plea did not prevent its denial in another plea. This reform did not extend to the replication or later pleadings, however, so there still could be only as many issues as there were pleas.

Another step toward breaking down the requirement of singleness was to allow the defendant to enter a plea in bar called the *general issue*—"nil debet" in debt, "not guilty" in trespass and case, and so

---

[b] 27 Eliz., ch. 5, § 1 (1585). This statute was supplemented by the statute of 4 Anne, ch. 16, § 1 (1705).

[c] 3 & 4 Will. 4, ch. 42, § 23 (1833).

[d] 4 Anne, ch. 16, § 4 (1705).

on. This not only constituted a blanket denial of the plaintiff's allegations, but also allowed proof of some matters in avoidance, the matters varying from one form to another. A plea of the general issue thus permitted a certain freedom in interposing defenses, but at the same time it left the plaintiff in the dark as to the exact grounds of defense that the defendant would urge.[e] The demand to eliminate such uncertainty of pleading culminated in 1834 in a reform embodied in rules of court known as the Hilary Rules. These Rules sharply restricted the scope of the general issue. To illustrate, before the Hilary Rules, a defendant under the general issue in trover ("not guilty") could show not only that he had not converted the goods, but almost any matter in justification, excuse, or discharge (but not release or the statute of limitations, which had to be specially pleaded); after the Hilary Rules, the plea amounted only to a denial of the conversion. It is generally conceded that the Hilary Rules were unsuccessful, as they had the effect of placing even more emphasis on niceties of pleading.

In appraising the merits and demerits of the common-law system, it is worth bearing in mind that there was no device available at law comparable to the modern discovery devices (although in some situations discovery was obtainable by a bill in equity in aid of the action at law), nor was any device available at law comparable to the modern motion for summary judgment. Examination of the difficulties in procedures at law will be renewed in Topic D of this Part.

[e] A similar type of blanket denial known as the *replication de injuria* was available to the plaintiff in certain situations.

TOPIC C. THE COMPLEMENTARY SYSTEM OF EQUITY

SECTION 1. DEVELOPMENT OF EQUITY

The law courts showed considerable ingenuity in accommodating the forms of action to changing needs. Nevertheless the formulary system was essentially a rigid one, and it is a question, and an intrinsically unanswerable question, whether it would not have collapsed under the pressures of a vastly ramified and complexified society if it had stood alone and been obliged to meet alone the hammer blows of time. That the formulary system continued well into the nineteenth century seems attributable in part to the coexistence and side-by-side growth of a complementary system of justice known as equity, developed and administered principally by a separate Court of Chancery. This system was not pinned to any "forms" of action and had its own distinctive procedures.

Consider the following well-known passage from Sir Henry Maine: "A general proposition of some value may be advanced with respect to the agencies by which Law is brought into harmony with society. These instrumentalities seem to me to be three in number, Legal Fictions, Equity, and Legislation. Their historical order is that in which I have placed them. Sometimes two of them will be seen operating together, and there are legal systems which have escaped the influence of one or other of them. But I know of no instance in which the order of their appearance has been changed or inverted." H. Maine, Ancient Law 24–25 (London 1861).

ADAMS, THE ORIGIN OF ENGLISH EQUITY
16 Colum.L.Rev. 87, 94–97 (1916).

When we go into the thirteenth century, we pass into a time when the older system of law and courts was rapidly falling into insignificance before the advance of the newer system, and when this latter, the Common Law system, was coming to be looked upon as the normal and prevailing law of the community. It is a time also when differentiation was slowly but steadily taking place in the judicial system. A new central court, the later Common Pleas court, had early been found to be a necessary adjunct of the itinerant justice system and it took from the middle of the reign of Henry II a distinct and fairly well defined position. The reservation of difficult cases from this court, or from the Itinerant Justice courts, to the Council, or small curia regis, forced by degrees upon that body, as the Common Law became more and more technical in character, an increasing

354

amount of technical, or professional, judicial work. This body of work was further increased by the tendency to regard some portion of what was original conciliar judicial work from the technical or professional point of view. By slow degrees, scarcely perceptible in the thirteenth century, this tendency created a distinct court, the *coram rege*, or King's Bench court. Meantime the Exchequer, as another phase of the Council, or small curia, gradually becoming distinct both from Council and from *coram rege*, had continued its judicial function, its power to try cases as a court of original jurisdiction, and as in the thirteenth century the advantages of the Common Law procedure had become so evident as to make it now the prevailing system, the Exchequer showed a tendency to assume a Common Law jurisdiction or, to put it in terms which are appropriate to the thirteenth century, to adopt a Common Law procedure. The natural effect of these developments was to bring forward as never before, probably not into very clear consciousness but as a practical matter, the question of jurisdiction, of boundary lines and fields of action.

As parallel to this tendency there must also be noticed another affecting the history of the writ. It is the increasing attitude of suspicion from before the middle of the century which the community at large adopted towards the growing number of writs and the power of Chancery to make new writs at will. Growing out of this are various attempts at the middle of the century and later to regulate and limit the issue of writs. If we recall the principle which had been early established in the Common Law that the action as developed before the court must not be different from that foreshadowed in the writ, and the consequent fact that the multiplication of writs which characterized the first century of the Common Law was a process of the multiplying and classifying of actions, it will be clear that a limitation upon the making of new writs was a marking out of the field of Common Law to a certain extent and a setting of boundaries to it.

The effect of both these tendencies to mark out for the courts the boundaries of their jurisdiction and also the boundaries of the law which they applied, was the same. The Common Law was becoming a hard and fast system with certain clearly defined things which it could not do. I do not intend to assert that this point in the development was reached at the end of the thirteenth century. It is very evident that it was not, though considerable approach had been made towards it. When the fourteenth century opened, boundary lines still seem now and then vague, fields overlap, content is still variable, the same body will do things that are later regarded as quite distinct, two different bodies will do the same thing, but as compared with the beginning of the thirteenth century great progress had been made towards definition and exclusion. It is possible to say I think that this progress had gone much further in the case of judicial institutions than it had in those which afterwards formed, or were then forming, the legislative, administrative, and conciliar systems, the Council and Parliament.

It is in this situation, as carried on into the fourteenth century, that we must find the origin of Equity as a separate system and by which we must account for its late origin as compared with the Common Law. So long as the Common Law remained a flexible system, its field undefined, its power of inclusion unlimited, its organs undifferentiated, there was no reason for distinguishing between it and Equity, and all that was later done by Equity could still be done in the field of the Common Law. Such a distinction between them was indeed impossible. All acts of the king in opening his prerogative procedure to the community were alike in the teeth of the existing system, furnishing unusual remedies, and founded upon his duty to secure justice to all. There was no ground upon which they could be divided into two great classes by the later tests which distinguished Equity and the Common Law. It is only as the Common Law became a hard and fast system, as men began to ask themselves about boundaries of action and limitations upon the new, that a new field must be found for the action of the royal prerogative in securing general justice not specially provided for in the ordinary way, for this duty and this function still remained to the king.

The seat of this action was found in a place where it had always existed, in an organ which had come to be more and more recognized, as definition and differentiation increased, as being the special organ of the king's prerogative, in the Council.[a]

T. PLUCKNETT, A CONCISE HISTORY OF THE COMMON LAW

180–81 (5th ed. 1956).

A variety of theories have been proposed to account for the origins of Chancery jurisdiction, but the general trend has been to estab-

[a] Writing of the rise of courts of equity in the Tudor age, Professor Plucknett speaks of "the need for newer institutions." Common-law procedure, he says, was "generally patient and long-suffering," for the common law originally centered upon the law of land, the litigants were predominantly landowners, and "land at least could not be removed." As the common law ramified beyond the law of real property and as litigants "could not be identified with certain acres," common-law procedure became strikingly ineffective. Also, "there were matters which could best be settled by securing the prompt personal attendance of parties, and by giving them direct personal commands to act or to desist." Yet the "common law rarely achieved anything so logically direct as this action in per- sonam." So also, "the common law was slow to admit the evidence of parties and witnesses." The need for such evidence was not strongly felt while the chief concern of the law was land; attention was rather focused on records and documents, and on notorious facts such as seisin "which were better proved by a jury than by the interested statements of parties or their friends." With the evolution of other branches of law, evidence of parties and witnesses became necessary. And by the fifteenth century the jury had fallen into disrepute for a variety of reasons. "Distrust of juries is an important factor in the early popularity of the equity courts." T. Plucknett, A Concise History of the Common Law 177–78 (5th ed. 1956). See also id. at 157–59.

lish an old theory first put forward by Palgrave. According to this view the Chancellor's jurisdiction was not by virtue of his office; still less had it anything to do with his supposed position of keeper of the King's conscience. At a later date, it is true, Chancery became a court of conscience, with a jurisprudence deliberately based upon that idea, but this was a later development and will not account for the earliest period of Chancery history. It now seems clear that the Chancellor's position was originally that of a delegate of the Council. Overburdened with work of every description, the Council delegated particular matters to the Chancellor, who of all the officials was the one who was most constantly in attendance. Moreover, the Chancellor already had a well-organized office staff which had long been familiar with the judicial work arising on the common law side of Chancery,[b] and for a long time had exercised the power of issuing writs both judicial and administrative to all the King's officials, central and local. The Chancellor, therefore, commanded the machinery which sooner or later would have to be set in motion in order to give redress to the petitioners, and so nothing could be simpler than for the Council to transmit the petitions addressed to it to the Chancellor, sometimes (but not always) endorsing them with a brief instruction what to do. Both on the common law and on the equity sides the Chancellors frequently called upon the judges of the common law courts to sit in Chancery, and it may well be the case that a good deal of genuine collaboration took place in the great task of creating the system of equity.

Early petitions, says Maitland, were "often couched in piteous terms." F. Maitland, Equity 5 (1909). The petitioner complained that by reason of his poverty or illness, or the wealth and power of his adversary, he was unable to get a remedy in the ordinary course of law. Petitioners were not complaining, or not so much complaining, about the substantive rules of the common law, as about the defects in its procedures. At first, as noted by Plucknett, the petitions would be referred by the Council to the chancellor; during the fourteenth century, they came to be addressed to the chancellor directly. On examining the petition or *bill*, the chancellor might issue a writ of subpoena ordering the adversary to appear and answer. The *answer* would be made on oath and would respond to each of the particular charges of the bill.

The chancellor was as yet for the most part dealing with matters cognizable by the law courts. This was objected to by the law courts and Parliament, especially as it was related to the exercise by the Council of an extraordinary criminal jurisdiction (a jurisdiction that later fell in part to the Court of Star Chamber). "And so," says

[b] Chancery had an important common-law jurisdiction, consisting largely of cases based on the king's feudal rights and powers.

Maitland, "the Chancellor is warned off the field of common law
. . . . But then just at this time it is becoming plain that the Chancellor is doing some convenient and useful works that could not be
done, or could not easily be done by the courts of common law. He
has taken to enforcing uses or trusts."   Id. at 6.

USES

What was a "use"? Let us take the date 1500. *A* owned land in
fee simple. When *A* died and the land passed to his heir—we speak
now of a time when the power to transfer land by will was very limited—certain feudal dues or taxes became payable to *A*'s overlord.
However, the old feudal justifications for these taxes had disappeared, or were at least not felt as creating a strong moral obligation.

To avoid or minimize these exactions, *A* during his lifetime might
convey the land in fee simple to *B*, *C*, and *D*, jointly, "to the use of"
A during his lifetime and thereafter to the use of *A*'s designate, *X*
(say, *A*'s eldest son). This meant that *B*, *C*, and *D* were thenceforth
the technical owners of the land (the holders of the title "at law"), but
they were bound in conscience and confidence to recognize that the
substantial benefits of ownership belonged to the use-holders, *A* and
X; for instance, they would be expected to pay over any income of
the property to the use-holders. *B*, *C*, and *D* were the "feoffees to
uses" (trustees); *A* and *X* the "cestuis que usent" (beneficiaries).

The law courts acted largely as if they were oblivious of the purpose of this maneuver. They considered *B*, *C*, and *D* as the owners
of the land and largely disregarded the existence of the use. No feudal taxes were due when *A* died, for he was not the legal owner. Nor
were the taxes due when *B* died, leaving *C* and *D* surviving, for as *B*,
C, and *D* were *joint* legal owners they were dealt with as a kind of
unit. It was only when the last survivor of *B*, *C*, and *D* died that the
taxes would become due. But the last survivor might again in his
lifetime convey to *E*, *F*, and *G* to the same uses.

There was a difficulty with this arrangement. What would happen if the trustees should at any point become faithless, deny the use,
and violate the confidence reposed in them? Suppose they began to
collect the income for themselves and refused to pay over to the beneficiaries? The common-law courts could not be looked to for relief.
It was the Court of Chancery that came to the aid of the beneficiaries
by ordering the trustees to carry out their trust. In this way a large
class of cases passed into the domain of the chancellor.

This example of the use will have prepared your mind for the
ideas (1) that equity acts in personam and (2) that equity does not act
in opposition to law—ideas that must be appreciated even if they

were not entirely or in all cases accurately descriptive of how equity acted.

Observe that when the Court of Chancery gave relief in the use case, it did not do so according to the style or manner of an ordinary law judgment. You will recall that the law judgment for money was that plaintiff do recover so much from defendant; even in ejectment the judgment was that plaintiff do recover possession of the land. The sheriff was prepared to execute on defendant's property and sell it to satisfy the judgment for money, and he was prepared to eject defendant to satisfy the judgment in ejectment. Yet neither judgment was in the form of a command to defendant. Chancery's decree was typically just such a command. In the use case Chancery ordered the trustees to behave according to the use, on pain of going to jail if they did not.[c]

Especially because of the form of the decree, it could be plausibly, if not altogether convincingly, argued that equity had not acted in derogation of law. For nothing had been done to disturb the legal title. That was still in the trustees, and the law courts still continued to regard them as essentially the sole owners.

This oversimplified story of the use introduces you to the potent concept of the separation of the "legal" from the "beneficial" (we are now prepared to say "equitable") ownership.[d] We do not pause to give you in full depth the reasons for the emergence of the use device; nor shall we describe its tortuous development or the attempts over the years to combat it, of which the most notable effort was the Statute of Uses, 1536. These matters are dealt with in the courses in Property and Trusts. The familiar family and commercial trusts of today are lineal descendants of the old use.

------

[c] Ames was especially insistent on this point. He said: "[T]ime has strengthened the conviction of the present writer that the principle 'Equity acts upon the person' is, and always has been, the key to the mastery of equity. The difference between the judgment at law and the decree in equity goes to the root of the matter. The law regards chiefly the right of the plaintiff, and gives judgment that he recover the land, debt, or damages because they are his. Equity lays stress upon the duty of the defendant, and decrees that he do or refrain from doing a certain thing because he ought to act or forbear. It is because of this emphasis upon the defendant's duty that equity is so much more ethical than law." J. Ames, "The Origin of Uses," in Lectures on Legal History 233, 233–34 (1913).

[d] Ideas developed in equity were capable of being fictionalized. Suppose a person acquired property by unjust means and was thereby unjustly enriched. Was it not possible to say that he held the legal title impressed with a trust in favor of the person justly entitled (a "constructive" trust)? Cf. Moses v. Macferlan, supra p. 345. Take even the case of mistake. "Owing to a mutual mistake of fact, say as to the existence of a debt, Doe delivers to Roe in payment of the supposed debt a horse. What are Doe's rights? They may possibly be at least: (1) A right to rescind as in the case of personal property obtained by fraud, and so to sue in trover or statutory replevin [where a trespassory taking might not be required] after a demand for return or perhaps without demand; (2) assumpsit for goods sold and delivered; (3) bill in equity for specific restitution." Cook, The Place of Equity in Our Legal System, 37 A.B.A.Rep. 997, 1007 (1912).

EMERGING SCOPE OF EQUITY JURISDICTION ᵉ

Holdsworth classified under five main heads the matters dealt with by the Court of Chancery up to the middle of the seventeenth century. 1 W. Holdsworth, A History of English Law 454–59 (7th ed. 1956). They were:

"Firstly, the recognition, protection and development of uses and trusts."

"Secondly, the court of Chancery interfered to enforce contracts on principles very different from any known to the common lawyers." While the law courts were painfully evolving remedies for breach of promise, the chancellors are said to have "enforced agreements, just as they enforced trusts, whenever they thought that in the interests of good faith and honest dealing they ought to be enforced." As the law courts perfected their remedies, Chancery tended to withdraw from the field. Yet all the law courts would usually give by way of relief was damages. Chancery could give specific performance—order the defendant to perform his promise. "But in this period it was not settled what cases did, and what did not entitle a plaintiff to specific relief."

"Thirdly, the Chancellor interfered in a class of cases where, owing to the rigidity of the law, the enforcement of the strict legal right was clearly contrary to equity. Fraud, forgery and duress were some of the chief grounds of his interference." "Mistake" and "accident" were further grounds.

"Fourthly, the procedure of the court enabled the Chancellor to give remedies in cases where the common law either could not act at all, or could not act with effect." The injunction is an instance in point. Chancery could examine the parties, and it could compel discovery (that is, production and examination) of documents even in aid of proceedings in the law courts.

"Fifthly, the organization of the court of Chancery made it a tribunal much more efficient than the courts of common law for the investigation of matters of account." The administration of estates became for this reason an important part of equity jurisdiction.

———

But in the second decade of the seventeenth century equity was challenged by law. The dual systems of law and equity had many potentialities of conflict, and at this time the question of primacy came to a head.

———

ᵉ "Jurisdiction" is here used in the sense of the "aggregate of those cases, controversies, and occasions which form proper subjects for the exercise of the powers of a chancery court." Black's Law Dictionary 485 (5th ed. 1979).

COURTNEY v. GLANVIL
Court of King's Bench, 1615.
79 Eng.Rep. 294.

Glanvil was committed to the Fleet the last day of Michaelmas term, 11 Jac. 1, for not performing a decree in Chancery; and upon a *habeas corpus* returned, the case was informed to be thus:

Glanvil sold to Courtney, being a young gentleman, a jewel, which he pretended to be of the value of three hundred and sixty pounds, whereas in truth it was worth but twenty pounds, and three other jewels to the value of one hundred pounds; and for his security he took a bond of six hundred pounds in the name of one Hampton, and procured an action to be brought in the said Hampton's name, and the action to be confessed, and Glanvil paid all the charges of both parties, and the confession was out of Court in the vacation.

Courtney finding this deceit, that the jewel was not worth above twenty pounds, which was delivered to him at the rate of three hundred and sixty pounds, exhibited his bill in chancery for relief, and afterward brought a writ of error to reverse this judgment; but the judgment was affirmed.

Afterwards, upon a hearing in Chancery, it was decreed, that Glanvil should take again his jewel and one hundred pounds, and that he should procure Hampton to release and acknowledge satisfaction: and for not performing this decree he was imprisoned.

COKE, CHIEF JUSTICE, said, that this decree and imprisonment, being after a judgment at the common law, was unlawful, and that this Court ought to relieve him; and for proof he cited a judgment in Easter term, 5 Edw. 4. Roll 35. Cobb v. Moor, where Cobb procured an action of debt to be brought against Moor, and the action to be confessed by attorney, and a writ of error to be brought thereupon, and the judgment to be affirmed; and all this was done in the absence of Moor, who, being beyond sea, upon his return exhibited his bill in Chancery, to be relieved concerning this practice, there being no debt due: and it was resolved, that after a judgment at the common law he could not be relieved there, but was inforced to exhibit his bill in Parliament. And there was a special Act made for his relief. . . . Wherefore Coke and all the Court held here, that the party ought to be bailed; and they let him to bail until the next term, and he was then discharged. . . . . .

————

ELLESMERE ON THE NATURE OF EQUITY

Lord Ellesmere's contention that equity did not act in opposition to law was put in these words: "[I]n this Case there is no Opposition to the Judgment; neither will the Truth or Justice of the Judgment be examined in this Court, nor any Circumstance depending thereupon; but the same is justified and approv'd; and therefore a Judgment is no Let to examine it in Equity, so as all the Truth of the Judgment, &c., be (not) examin'd. . . . [W]hen a Judgment is obtained by Oppression, Wrong and a hard Conscience, the Chancellor will frustrate and set it aside, not for any error or Defect in the Judgment, but for the hard Conscience of the Party . . .." Earl of Oxford's Case, 21 Eng.Rep. 485, 486–87 (Ch.1615).

JUDGMENT OF JAMES I

The celebrated judgment of James I on the Coke-Ellesmere controversy, rendered in 1616, is as follows:

"Forasmuch as Mercy and Justice be the true Supporters of our Royal Throne, and that it properly belongeth unto us in our Princely Office to take Care and provide, that our Subjects have equal and indifferent Justice ministred unto them: And that where their Case deserveth to be relieved in Course of Equity by Suit in our Court of Chancery, they should not be abandoned and exposed to perish under the Rigor and Extremity of our Laws, We in our Princely Judgment . . . do will and command that our Chancellor, or Keeper of the Great Seal for the Time being, shall not hereafter desist to give unto our Subjects, upon their several Complaints now or hereafter to be made, such Relief in Equity (notwithstanding any Proceedings at the Common Law against them) as shall stand with the Merit and Justice of their Cause, and with the former, ancient and continued Practice and Presidency of our Chancery have done: And for that it appertaineth to our Princely Office only to judge over all Judges, and to discern and determine such Differences, as at any time may and shall arise between our several Courts touching their Jurisdictions, and the same to settle and determine, as we in our Princely Wisdom shall find to stand most with our Honour, and the Example of our Royal Progenitors in the best Times, and the general Weals and Good of our People, for which we are to answer unto God who hath placed us over them: Our Will and Pleasure is, that our whole Proceedings therein, by the Decrees formerly set down, be inrolled in Chancery, there to remain of Record, for the better Extinguishing of the like Differences and Questions that may arise in future Times." [f]

---

[f] Taken from a tract entitled "Arguments Proving from Antiquity the Dignity, Power, and Jurisdiction of the Court of Chancery," which is printed in 21 Eng. Rep. 576, 588.

The full story of the controversy is much richer than these materials indicate, with lengthy arguments from and sophisticated maneuvering by both sides. With some understatement, Holdsworth says of the judgment of James I: "It may be that the decision was slightly tinged by political considerations. The common law judges, especially Coke, were already tending to manifest an independence opposed to James's absolutist claims. The Chancellor, as a minister of state, was more favourable to these claims. But, considering the rigidity of the practice of the courts of common law

Question: (1) Professor Goebel said that the Coke-Ellesmere dispute was a battle for the principle of res judicata. Appraise this statement.[K]

As may be gathered from the foregoing materials, a defendant in a law action might be obliged to "go across the hall" for an injunction staying the action. He would do so where he had some matter that ought to defeat the action and that would be recognized by equity but not by law. Against whom would such an injunction run? Do you see any administrative or other advantage in such a bifurcated procedure?

KATZ, "THE POLITICS OF LAW IN COLONIAL AMERICA"

Law in American History 257, 260–61 (1971).

By the late sixteenth century, and especially with the accession of the Stuarts, the court of chancery was closely associated with the royal prerogative and became the target of opposition. Equity was therefore disadvantageously contrasted with common law in an era when the "ancient law" took on revolutionary constitutional overtones. The struggle between the two systems of law became explicit in Glanville's case, the 1616 litigation, jurisdiction over which was sought by Chancellor Ellsmere, who enjoined suitors from proceeding at law, and by Chief Justice Coke, who prohibited the same litigants from proceeding in equity, and in which James I finally intervened on the side of the chancery. The common lawyers of the early Stuart period strongly objected to the prerogative character of equity law, but they also attacked particular abuses: the use of chancery jobs as royal patronage, the delay and expense of chancery proceedings, and the increasing formalism of equity litigation. At bottom, of course, they anticipated Selden, who sneered that "Equity is a roguish thing. For the law we have a measure . . . [but] equity is according to the conscience of him that is Chancellor, and as that is larger or narrower, so is equity. 'Tis all one as if they should make the standard for measure a Chancellor's foot."[5]

The High Court of Chancery was one of the leading targets of Puritan legal reformers during the Interregnum, and an attempt to abolish the court was made during the Barebones Parliament. The other prerogative courts had been destroyed in 1641, but the attack on chancery failed because the court was simply too useful to be lost, and because the courts of common law were not sufficiently adapta-

[Handwritten margin notes: "Equity attacked", "Eg. Stays b/c too useful"]

at that period, it cannot be said that the views for which the Chancellor contended were unreasonable." 1 W. Holdsworth, A History of English Law 463 (7th ed. 1956).

[K] J. Goebel, Cases and Materials on the Development of Legal Institutions 267 (1930). A measured answer to this question is given by Dawson, Coke and Ellesmere Disinterred: The Attack on Chancery in 1616, 36 Ill.L.Rev. 127 (1941), which also provides a fine picture of the setting in which the whole controversy took place.

[5] John Selden, Table Talk (London, 1821), p. 52.

ble to incorporate the equitable jurisdiction. Perhaps even more important, most of the critics of chancery objected to the administration of the court rather than to the character of equity law. The court of chancery therefore operated under a commission in the absence of a chancellor, but resumed its traditional operation with the Restoration. The chancery of the late-seventeenth century was unsystematic and inefficient, however, until the administration of Chancellor Nottingham, 1673–1682, whose emphasis on the importance of precedent introduced a new element of rationality into its proceedings—although not without raising the question of whether the principle of stare decisis did not contradict the precepts of natural equity.

Thus the early history of equity in England involves a gradual emergence of a legal system in response to primitive deficiencies of the common law in the later Middle Ages, and an attempt to provide judicial processes adequate to the increasing complexity of English society. Even by the seventeenth century, however, equity displayed signs of rigidities peculiar to itself, and the eighteenth century was a period in which for the first time the probable results of suits in chancery could be predicted with some accuracy. The end result was an important legal system which was very imperfectly synchronized with the dominant common law, and which fostered delay, inefficiency, and even injustice—until the nineteenth century legislative intervention was necessary to effect a rational fusion of law and equity.

One problem which disappeared from view in England after the Restoration, was the objection to chancery as a prerogative court. In effect, the High Court of Chancery reappeared in the 1660's with undiminished powers and prestige, but seemingly without acquiring a rationalization of its existence to replace the traditional concept of the chancery as the personal expression of the sovereign's power to do justice. This may not be surprising, but the result was a theoretical void which did not go unquestioned in the colonies of North America.

SECTION 2. EQUITY MATURED

(a) Scope of Equity Jurisdiction

In opening a series of lectures on equity, Maitland said: "[W]e are driven to say that Equity now is that body of rules administered by our English courts of justice which, were it not for the operation of the Judicature Acts [the legislation effective in 1875], would be administered only by those courts which would be known as Courts of Equity." He added: "This, you may well say, is but a poor thing to call a definition. . . . Still I fear that nothing better than this is possible." By way of generalization, however, he finally offered this: "In my view equity has added to our legal system, together with a number of detached doctrines, one novel and fertile institution, namely the trust; and three novel and fertile remedies, namely the decree for specific performance, the injunction, and the judicial administration of estates. Round these, as it seems to me, most of the equitable rules group themselves." F. Maitland, Equity 1, 22 (1909).

Judge Phelps in 1894 attempted, on the basis of a previous attempt by Professor Venable, to write a catalogue of the heads of equity jurisdiction. This appears in C. Phelps, Juridical Equity Abridged 222–24 (1894):

"*Principal heads of equity jurisdiction.* The *heads* of equity jurisdiction have been long established, and cover all possible cases which may properly be brought within the cognizance of courts of equity. Those of most frequent occurrence in practice are as follows: ACCIDENT, MISTAKE, FRAUD, TRUST, specific performance, account, administration, mortgages and liens, partnerships, creditors' bills, partition, injunctions, receivers, interpleader, bills of peace, *quia timet*, divorce, alimony, infants, persons of unsound mind, married women.

"More particularly, equity has jurisdiction: to relieve against a class of unforeseen and injurious occurrences, not attributable to mistake, neglect or misconduct—(ACCIDENT, and herein of *re-execution*); to relieve against acts, or contracts, done, or made, from ignorance of fact, forgetfulness or inadvertence—(MISTAKE, and herein of *reformation* and *rescission*); to set aside, correct, annul, or prevent advantage being taken of, instruments and acts induced by FRAUD, (and herein of *cancellation*); to enforce a beneficial interest in property against the holder of the legal title—(TRUST, and herein of trusts, *active* and *passive*, *express* and *implied*, the latter including *constructive* and *resulting* trusts); to compel *specific performance* of contracts; to adjust accounts between co-owners, partners, principal and agent, principal and surety, debtor and creditor, &c.— (*account*, and herein of *set-off*, *contribution*, *exoneration*, *subrogation* and *marshalling* of assets and securities); to superintend, in certain cases, the settlement of decedent's estates—(*administration*, and herein of *election*, *conversion*, *satisfaction* and *performance*); to establish the true *construction of wills*; to enforce *mortgages* by foreclosure, or to extinguish them by redemption; to enforce *liens* generally; to provide for the dissolution and settlement of *partnerships*; to entertain applications to charge the real property of deceased owners, or the real and personal property of living owners, beyond the reach of ordinary legal process, with their debts—(*creditors' bills*); among co-owners to make *partition*; to prevent persons from enforcing judgments, prosecuting suits, or setting up defences, in a court of law, where the claim or defence is inequitable, and to prevent the performance of acts which, if performed, would inflict an injury on a person, for which he would have no adequate remedy— (*injunction*); to secure property in dispute pending litigation—(*receiver*); to prevent vexatious litigation by protecting a party liable to the suit of two or more conflicting claimants (*interpleader*), or of a numerous class insisting upon the same adverse right, or of the same party repeating an unsuccessful claim (*bills of peace*); to preserve the means by which existing rights may be secured from impending violations (*quia timet*); to dissolve, either partially or absolutely, the marriage relation, with incidental provision for *pendente lite,* or permanent, support (*divorce alimony*); to guard and administer the estates of *infants*, persons of *unsound mind*, and *married women*; and to compel a party to a suit at law to disclose facts and produce documents within his knowledge and control—(*discovery*)."

There has been a great expansion of the field of equity in America during the past century. Perhaps one should speak of a filling-in of an already existing outline. Thus the simple "receiver" of the Phelps list foreshadows the complex corporate receiverships of the Twenties and Thirties. But perhaps new paths are being blazed. The reference to "injunction" only dimly suggests the interpolation of the courts as the ultimate enforcer of elaborate schemes of governmental controls and as the last line of defense of citizens seeking protection against governmental abuses. The involvement of the courts in effectuating social change in such areas as legislative reapportionment, civil rights, and environmental protection has carried equity to a point far beyond what Judge Phelps could have envisaged. Indeed, the "weight of important business of the courts today (the bias of contemporary legal education notwithstanding) seems to have shifted toward the equity side." Weinberg, The New Meaning of Equity, 28 J. Legal Educ. 532, 532 (1977).

In the following pages we examine briefly some characteristic equitable doctrines and attitudes.

(b) Equitable Relief Against Penalties; Mortgages

The form of the old "penal bond" was that the obligor promised to pay a sum to the obligee on a stated day, but this promise was to be void and of no effect if the obligor had done thus-and-so on a previous day. There was often a great disproportion between the penal sum of the bond and the value of the condition: in loan transactions the penal sum might be twice the amount of the actual loan, payment of which appeared as the condition of the bond. The law courts enforced these bonds according to their terms, a result not surprising if you consider the importance that was attached to the seal and the fact that even fraud in the inducement was not a defense to an action on a sealed instrument. Equity, however, seems first to have given relief where through accident the obligor had not performed the condition on the due date. Later it intervened to prevent collection of penalties without even the pretext of accident; for example, in the loan cases it would stay the action at law or enjoin collection of the law judgment and confine the recovery to the amount borrowed with interest. In the study of Contracts you will see the spread of the

idea of "penalty," study the distinction between "penalty" and "liquidated damages," and examine to what extent the equitable ideas
were absorbed by law.

A similar development took place in mortgage cases where the intervention of equity was necessary to protect the mortgagor who defaulted on the mortgage loan. The initial excuse of accident as a basis for the chancellor's action gave way to routine, with the end result
being complex foreclosure proceedings involving sale of the property,
payment of the loan out of the proceeds, and establishment of any
deficiency against the mortgagor or payment of any surplus to him.
This falls within the boundaries of Property courses.

(c) Specific Performance of Contracts

Inadequacy of legal relief.—In the eighteenth century equity's
enforcement of contracts polarized around the idea that it would give
specific performance only if the law remedy was "inadequate." An
enormous gloss was written over this idea of inadequacy.

Suppose V and P contract in writing for the sale by V and the
purchase by P of a parcel of real property, the payment and conveyance to take place at a future day. On that day V defaults. Of
course, P may go to law and recover the difference between the price
and the value of the land. But does P have the option to go to equity
and get a decree ordering V to convey the land (conditioned on P's
paying the price [h])? This in theory turns on whether law damages
are thought to be an adequate remedy. It is easy to say that damages are inadequate if the land has a dwelling house on it and P
wants the place as a residence. But is the case the same if the land
is vacant and there is a similar adjacent parcel that is available for
purchase by P with the proceeds of his law judgment plus the original agreed price? Even in such a case it was held that P was entitled
to specific performance, seemingly on the ground that land is intrinsically unique.

What of the case where P defaults in making payment: may V
get specific performance as against P? The answer is yes. But how
is V's law remedy inadequate? There have been some rather ingenious explanations. It does seem, however, that where contracts for
the sale of interests in land are concerned, the inadequacy formula
became somewhat detached from the facts.

It may be said generally that outside the land cases some real
showing of the inadequacy of law damages must be made in order to
obtain specific performance of a contract.

Question: (2) May specific performance be had of a promise to deliver a
quantity of bales of cotton, where there is a free and fair market for the

[h] Note that an equity decree may be,
and often is, cast in conditional form.
This was not true of judgments at law.

commodity? What of a promise to deliver a hundred shares of General Motors stock? or shares of a close corporation not previously traded in? or an heirloom? What of a promise to supply at a fixed price all the output of a mine until it is exhausted an indefinite number of years hence?

V, having contracted to sell to *P* property of such a type that *P* would have a right to specific performance against him, in breach of his promise conveys or delivers the property to *X*. What are *P*'s rights against *X*? Equity considers that *P* has a kind of beneficial ownership in the property from the date of the contract, because he has a right to specific performance against *V*; *V* is in a sense "trustee" for *P*. *X* did indeed obtain the legal title from *V*; but what of *P*'s equitable interest? If *X* knew of the contract between *V* and *P* (and in the case of land, if the *V–P* contract had been publicly recorded, *X* might not be heard to say that he did not have knowledge), *X*'s legal title is subject to *P*'s equity, which means that *P* can compel *X* to convey to him (*P* paying the agreed price to *X*). The same result follows if *X* did not know of the contract between *V* and *P* but received the property from *V* by way of gift. But if *X* paid a fair price to *V* without knowledge of the *V–P* contract (that is, if *X* is a "bona fide purchaser for value without notice"), *P*'s equitable interest is extinguished; he cannot secure specific performance (or, indeed, any other kind of relief) against *X*, and he is left only with rights against *V*. What would be *P*'s measure of damages against *V*?

Question: (3) Suppose *P* contracted to buy Blackacre from *V* for $10,000, and *V* then sold to *X*, a bona fide purchaser without notice, for $15,000. If *P* does not believe that he can establish the fair market value to be as much as $15,000 (the fact that *X* paid $15,000 would not be decisive on the question of value), what recourse should *P* have against *V*, and on what theories?

Difficulty of administering equitable relief.—Thus far we have spoken of contracts respecting the sale of property. What other types of contract are specifically enforceable? The test of inadequacy of law damages is still to the fore, but additional factors may enter.

X Construction Company undertakes to build a house for *Y* but fails to perform its promise. May *Y* get specific performance? Ordinarily the law remedy is adequate: *Y* may build the house himself and recover from *X* the difference between the cost and the contract price. But suppose *Y* has bought from *X* one of the lots in a real estate development, and *X* has agreed to put in roads and sewers on *X*'s own land. Here the remedy at law is inadequate: *Y* cannot have the work done himself. But there is the further argument, successfully made in many situations, that specific performance should not be decreed because of the difficulties of enforcing and supervising the execution of the decree. The modern tendency is to weigh the difficulties of administration against the importance to the plaintiff of the equitable relief sought. Here is an instance of the balancing of interests by an equity court to determine whether to grant or withhold relief. See Zygmunt v. Avenue Realty Co., 108 N.J.Eq. 462, 155 A. 544 (1931).

How about a contract for personal services? A shoe clerk refuses to perform his contract to work in a department store, or Birgit Nilsson refuses to sing for the Metropolitan Opera. Plainly the Metropolitan has a better case for specific performance than the department store, but is it good enough? We have indicated that equity will not command Nilsson to sing, but in some situations a negative decree may be granted; that is, Nilsson may be forbidden to sing for others for some time.[i] Are the objections to an affirmative decree really obviated by this device? Should it matter whether the promise to sing for no one else was an express term of the contract, or was rather an implied term? whether Nilsson now seeks to sing for a company in New York or one in San Francisco? See Lumley v. Wagner, 42 Eng.Rep. 687 (Ch.1852). Compare Fuller, The Forms and Limits of Adjudication, 92 Harv.L.Rev. 353, 404–05 (1978), with Restatement (Second) of Contracts § 367 (1979).

Discretionary character of equitable relief.—Courts of equity have traditionally taken the view that even if the damages at law are inadequate, specific performance will be decreed only in the sound judicial discretion of the court. Thus equitable relief may be denied because the plaintiff drove an unconscionable bargain; because the contract was induced by misrepresentation, concealment, nondisclosure, or mistake; or because specific enforcement would cause undue hardship to the defendant or third persons or be detrimental to the public interest.

Questions: (4) In 1854, *P* leased a Washington hotel from *D* for a ten-year term with an option to buy for $22,500. After (a) the Civil War had made property values in Washington much higher and (b) Congress had enacted legislation making greenbacks legal tender (previously only gold had been legal tender) and they had depreciated to slightly more than half their gold equivalent, *P* tendered $22,500 in greenbacks and demanded a conveyance pursuant to the option. *D* refused. Should *P* have been able to get specific performance? See Willard v. Tayloe, 75 U.S. (8 Wall.) 557 (1870).

(5) *A* is the owner of land *X*. *B* is a manufacturer who intends to locate a factory in the town where land *X* lies. *B* does not disclose his intentions to *A*. In consideration of $100 in cash, *A* contracts to sell his land to *B* at the latter's option for $10,000 if paid within three months. This is a fair purchase price at existing market prices. Later *B*'s intentions become generally known, prices of land rise immediately, and *A* repudiates his contract. *B* sues for specific performance within the three months and pays $10,000 into court. What should be the result? See Restatement (Second) of Contracts § 364 comment a, illustration 2 (1979).

Sometimes the reason that prevents the plaintiff from getting specific performance would equally defeat him at law. In other cases this is not so, so that the plaintiff will be denied equitable relief but will be remitted to his legal remedy.

[i] See supra p. 140.

Question: (6) Do you approve this double standard? Should a contract that is too unfair to be specifically enforced nevertheless furnish the basis for an action for damages?

———

CARMEN v. FOX FILM CORP.

United States Circuit Court of Appeals, Second Circuit, 1920.
269 F. 928, cert. denied, 255 U.S. 569, 41 S.Ct. 323 (1921).

[Jewel Carmen, a twenty-year-old moving-picture actress, made a contract with Fox, which if Fox chose to exercise its options would run for several years, with a salary starting at $125 a week and gradually increasing to $250. A few months later, while still a minor, she made a contract for her exclusive services with Keeney Corporation at a starting salary of $400 a week, which would increase to $1000. Keeney was ignorant of the Fox contract. Shortly afterward she came of age and repudiated her Fox contract because it was made during her infancy. Fox threatened Keeney with suit if Keeney employed her, and thereafter Keeney refused to do so.

[Miss Carmen sued for an injunction restraining Fox from interfering with her contractual relations with Keeney and for damages. The district court entered a decree in her favor, and Fox appealed.]

Before WARD, ROGERS, and HOUGH, CIRCUIT JUDGES.

ROGERS, CIRCUIT JUDGE.

. . . .

. . . . [T]he conduct of the plaintiff has been such as entitles her to no relief in this court. According to her own allegations in her complaint, she was a minor when she entered into the contract with Keeney, and she misled him into making the contract by representing that she was free to make it, when in fact she was morally not free to make the contract, and there was doubt whether she was legally free to make it. If the contracts with defendants were valid, she was under a legal and moral obligation not to make the contract with the Keeney corporation. And if the contracts were voidable because of her infancy, then, while she was under no legal obligation to recognize them, she was under a moral obligation to abide by them, and good faith required her to continue to render the services she had agreed to give. In either case her action in repudiating her pledged word was misconduct of which no person of honor and conscience would have been guilty. That no action could be brought against her at law because of what she did does not alter the moral character of her act. And when she comes into a court of conscience and asks its affirmative aid to assist her in carrying into effect the inequitable arrangement into which she unfaithfully entered, the appeal falls on deaf ears. One who comes into equity must come with clean hands, and her hands are not clean. The testimony discloses that reliance cannot be placed upon her agreements which the law does not oblige her to keep, and that for a money gain to herself she unscrupulously disregarded her express contracts.

. . . .

The maxim that one who comes into equity must come with clean hands expresses rather a principle of inaction than one of action.[j] It means that equity will refuse its aid in any manner to one seeking its active interposition if he has been guilty either of unlawful or inequitable conduct respecting the subject-matter of the litigation.

[margin handwriting: Equity will not help D who has been unlawful or inequitable conduct]

An illustration of the maxim is found in the attitude of courts of equity in the matter of specific performance. A court of equity always refuses specific performance of a contract which has been obtained by the plaintiff by sharp and unscrupulous practices, by overreaching, by concealment of important facts, even though not actually fraudulent. The contract may be a legal one, against which no defense could be set up at law, and one which a court of equity would not cancel. But if it has been procured by unconscientious means a court of equity refuses specific performance. Pomeroy's Equity Jurisprudence (3d Ed.) vol. 1, § 400.

The right which one seeks to enforce in a court of equity must be one which in and of itself appeals to the conscience of a chancellor. Mr. Justice Brewer, speaking for the court in Deweese v. Reinhard, 165 U.S. 386, 390, 17 Sup.Ct. 340, 341 (41 L.Ed. 757), said:

"A court of equity acts only when and as conscience commands, and if the conduct of the plaintiff be offensive to the dictates of natural justice, then, whatever may be the rights he possesses and whatever use he may make of them in a court of law, he will be held remediless in a court of equity."

. . . .

The fact that a contract has been dishonestly or dishonorably obtained is a bar to relief in equity.

Decree reversed.

———

Professor Chafee says of this case: "Of course, the ancient doctrine of 'infantile paralysis,' designed to protect children from improvident bargains, becomes absurd when applied to annul a contract entitling the minor to over $6,500 a year. The remedy is to change the doctrine by statute, as California has since done, and not to call the minor immoral. Furthermore, if her contract right was not worth protecting in equity, it should not have been worth protecting at law

[j] "I propose to show that the clean hands doctrine does not definitely govern anything, that it is a rather recent growth, that it ought not to be called a maxim of equity because it is by no means confined to equity, that its supposed unity is very tenuous and it is really a bundle of rules relating to quite diverse subjects, that insofar as it is a principle it is not very helpful but is at times capable of causing considerable harm." Z. Chafee, Some Problems of Equity 2 (1950).

against this sort of interference. Yet the jury in a New York state court made Fox pay Jewel over $60,000. What did she care that Judge Rogers called her unethical, so long as she brought home the bacon?" Z. Chafee, Some Problems of Equity 98 (1950).

Mutuality of remedy.—A word is in order about the much-discussed rule of "mutuality of remedy." This rule took two forms: one, affirmative ("you have a right to specific performance, so I also should have one"); the other, negative ("you must give up your right to specific performance, because I have none"). The former, sometimes used as a justification for granting the seller of land a right to specific performance for the price, is relatively harmless. Usually in the situations where it is applied there is some other sound basis for equitable relief. If not, no great injustice is done by compelling the defendant to perform his contract, instead of breaking it and becoming liable for damages. The negative aspect of the rule, on the other hand, often resulted in obvious injustice. It has now been either flatly repudiated [k] or largely nullified by exceptions.

There is, however, one doctrine, akin to but distinguishable from "negative mutuality," that is generally adhered to by courts of equity. It can be illustrated by the following situation. *V* agrees to convey Blackacre to *P* on May 1, 1984, *P* agreeing to pay the purchase price in five annual installments thereafter. Should *P* be able to get specific performance if *V* refuses to convey? In this case, unlike those where the conveyance and the payment are to be concurrent, a court of equity cannot be certain that *P* will perform when the time comes. To be sure, this risk of nonperformance was inherent in *V*'s bargain, but equity is reluctant specifically to impose it upon him. Ames put it thus: "Equity will not compel specific performance by a defendant, if after performance the common law remedy of damages would be his sole security for the performance of the plaintiff's side of the contract." Ames, Mutuality in Specific Performance, 3 Colum. L.Rev. 1, 12 (1903).

Question: (7) Do you see any way in which equity might grant relief in this case without violating the rule laid down by Ames? See Van Scoten v. Albright, 5 N.J.Eq. 467 (1846); Durfee, Mutuality in Specific Performance, 20 Mich.L.Rev. 289, 298–305 (1922).

Closing thought.—As all the foregoing suggests, in our law specific performance of contracts has for some time been regarded as being available only in the exceptional case. There are signs that courts are now becoming more liberal in granting this kind of relief.

Question: (8) What reasons can you suggest for this change of attitude?

[k] "[T]he fact that specific performance or an injunction is not available to one party is not a sufficient reason for refus-ing it to the other party." Restatement (Second) of Contracts § 363 comment c (1979).

(d) Equitable Intervention for Misconduct and Mistake

Fraud.—We take fraud as an example of the many kinds of misconduct against which equity undertook to give relief. Particularly through the action on the case for deceit, the action of general assumpsit (as broadly conceived), and the allowance of fraud as a defense in an action on simple contract, the law courts in the nineteenth century were able to deal effectively with a large number of fraud cases. Equity, which had largely pioneered the field, seems to have retained a concurrent jurisdiction with law over some of these cases. And there were many situations where it was only in equity that a fully satisfactory remedy could be had. Equity's distinctive powers and procedures were especially needed where the fraudulent transaction had been executed and must be undone (rescinded) or changed (reformed). This of course extended to the cancellation or reformation of documents delivered in consummation of the transaction.[1]

Suppose *V* has been induced by fraud to enter into a contract with *P* to sell Blackacre to *P* for $5000, and the transaction has actually been carried out, *V* signing and delivering a deed with intent to pass title. At law *V* can recover damages for the fraud, but surely he ought to be able to recover Blackacre in specie from *P*. In equity he can get this relief under a conditional decree of rescission, by which *P* will be ordered to reconvey to *V* if *V* repays the price he received.

Question: (9) What remedies are available to *V* when *P*, the fraudulent buyer, has resold the property to *X*?

What is the meaning of "fraud" in equity? Is innocent misrepresentation to be dealt with on the same footing as fraud, or in some other way? See H. McClintock, Handbook of the Principles of Equity §§ 79–80 (2d ed. 1948). These and many other questions we must pass over.

Mistake.—By a mutual mistake of fact *V* conveys to *P* a larger amount of land than was actually bargained for. The conveyance was thought by both parties to describe just the property the parties had in mind, but in truth it extended to additional property owned by *V*. The effect at law of the transaction is to vest *P* with legal title in accordance with the conveyance. A judgment at law for damages

[1] The bill quia timet ("because he fears") may be mentioned at this point. Suppose *A* had signed a negotiable instrument in *B*'s favor. The giving of the instrument had been induced by *B*'s fraud, or for some other reason the instrument was voidable while in *B*'s hands. Yet if *B* should negotiate it to *C*, a bona fide purchaser for value without notice, and if *C* should sue *A*, *A* would have no defense. To forestall this possibility, *A* could bring a bill quia timet against *B* and get the instrument canceled. This principle was extended to certain other cases where a person feared future injury and could not be relieved of the fear by bringing an action at law. The bill to remove a cloud on title to property proceeded on a similar principle. In these situations, and in many others, equity granted preventive relief; law did not do so. In a sense, the bill quia timet may be regarded as a forerunner of the modern declaratory judgment.

would hardly do full justice. But the chancellor may direct *P* to re-convey the surplus property, or he may direct *P* to give up the deed and *V* to deliver a fresh deed in proper form.

In the case imagined there is an anterior agreement of the parties to which the transaction may be made to conform. Imagine a case where both parties were mistaken but the relief fairly called for is to restore the parties to their condition as before they entered into their deal and so to undo the transaction completely, rather than to rectify it. Rescission, rather than reformation, would be the appropriate remedy.

Is mistake of "law" to be treated differently from mistake of "fact," and can "law" and "fact" be satisfactorily distinguished in the context of mistake? Should the chancellor treat unilateral mistake differently from mutual mistake? Should it make any difference whether the plaintiff delays in seeking equitable relief after discovery of the mistake (or misconduct)?

(e) Equitable Relief Against Torts

Recaption or protection of personal property.—The form of action called replevin might fail of its object because the defendant could put the chattel beyond the reach of the sheriff or could destroy it before the sheriff was able to reach it. If the chattel was "unique," there was reason for equity to use its compulsive procedures against the tortfeasor to compel him to deliver it, and equity did so in proper cases. In a variety of cases, also, equity used its injunctive process to prevent threatened injury to tangible personal property.

Waste.—*L* is life tenant of a dwelling house and land. *R* owns the remainder interest. It is intended that *R* shall have the enjoyment of the house when *L* dies. If *L* meanwhile commences to destroy the house, we have a case of "waste" for which a law judgment for damages is not satisfactory.[m] In this and many cognate cases where ownership of real estate was divided and one part-owner threatened injury, relief by injunction (with incidental recovery of damages for past injury) could be obtained by another part-owner.[n]

Trespass.—Suppose *B*, without right and claiming no right, commits continuing or repeated acts of trespass on land owned and possessed by *A*, and he threatens to continue his tortious behavior. After early hesitation to deal with trespass, equity began to grant injunctions in such cases, for *A* would otherwise be required to bring

---

[m] What form of action is available to *R* at law?

[n] In suits to enjoin waste, the chancellor did not follow the common law in determining the parties' rights. Thus, relief could be secured in equity against some kinds of injury for which no relief would be available at law. These cases often appear under the caption of "equitable waste."

a series of actions at law for the damage.[o] Where *B*'s acts resulted in permanent damage, the case for an injunction would appear to be even clearer.

If wilful trespass is established and the remedy at law is inadequate to prevent its continuance or repetition, should a court of equity consider the degree of hardship to the defendant in relation to the value of the plaintiff's right and perhaps exercise its discretion against granting relief?

Questions: (10) *A* owned valuable mining property and also owned water rights, without use of which the mine could not be operated. Between the mine and the water, however, was a strip of barren, rocky, unusable land owned by *B*. *A*'s negotiations for a right of way across the strip failed. *A* then dug a trench across the strip, laid a pipeline, replaced the soil, and employed a force of armed men to patrol the pipeline and prevent *B*'s interference with it. The mine employed several hundred men and yielded a large and highly profitable output. "The laying of the pipeline across this barren, valueless land caused no appreciable injury" to *B*. *B* seeks an injunction against the maintenance of the pipeline. What arguments would you make for *B*? for *A*? What do you think the result should be? See Crescent Mining Co. v. Silver King Mining Co., 17 Utah 444, 54 P. 244 (1898).

(11) The court in the above-cited case, in addition to the above-quoted sentence, said: "No peculiar, present, speculative, or other value is attached to the land crossed by the line." Do you agree with this statement?

(12) If an injunction is denied to *B* and he is remitted to his right to damages at law, what should the measure of *B*'s legal relief be? See Restatement (Second) of Torts §§ 929–930 (1977); McCormick, Damages for Anticipated Injury to Land, 37 Harv.L.Rev. 574 (1924).

(13) If an injunction is denied to *B* and he employs a larger force of armed men who eject *A*'s men, should *A* be able to get injunctive relief to prevent *B* from digging up the pipeline?

Where the title to land was genuinely in dispute, equity approached the question of enjoining acts of trespass in a gingerly way, for trial of title to real estate was the historic preserve of the law courts. At first it seems that equity would not touch the case at all, at least if the title turned on a question of fact. Later equity might go so far as to grant a temporary injunction, remitting the plaintiff to

---

[o] The notion that equity may be resorted to in order to prevent a multiplicity of actions was at the heart of the so-called bill of peace. When a large number of persons with similar but separate grievances sued or threatened to sue one or more defendants, the latter could resort to a bill of peace, the effect of which was to prevent the maintenance of separate actions and to allow all the grievances to be heard as a single suit. Similarly, an intending plaintiff might avoid multiplicity of actions by bringing a bill of peace against a large number of defendants when he had separate grievances against them that involved one or more common questions. Often in these cases the basic dispute was one appropriate for a law court, but the joinder of parties and claims was so restricted at common law that separate individual actions would be required. The only reason for coming into equity was to avoid litigating the same question over and over again. We do not attempt to catalogue the situations in which the bill of peace could be maintained. See Chafee, Bills of Peace with Multiple Parties, 45 Harv.L.Rev. 1297 (1932), reprinted with slight revisions in Z. Chafee, Some Problems of Equity 149–98 (1950).

an action at law to try the title, after which the injunction was made
permanent or dissolved. See Durfee, Trial of Legal Issues in Injunction Against Tort, 57 Mich.L.Rev. 539 (1959).

Suppose A, out of possession but claiming title and the right to
possession of land, wants to prevent B, in possession and also claiming title and right to possession, from cutting the timber and ex-
tracting the minerals. A's remedy at law would be an action of ejectment. This would, in due time, restore the land to him if he
succeeded in establishing his claim, but it would not give him damages for what B had done up to the termination of the action. A
would have to bring a second action at law in "trespass for mesne
profits" to collect for this damage. Here again, because title was in
dispute, there was trouble in getting equity to intervene, but in later
years some courts would grant a temporary injunction against those
acts of B going beyond normal use of the land until the title could be
tried at law.[p]

Nuisance.—A landowner allows smoke to escape from his factory,
causing injury to an adjacent property owner. The noxious odors
from a piggery cause annoyance to nearby residents. A tannery pol-
lutes the water of a stream, damaging the crops of a lower riparian
owner. These are examples of "nuisances," the continuance of which
a court of equity may in appropriate circumstances enjoin.[q] Is a nuisance case a proper one for the consideration of such discretionary
factors as relative hardship to the parties, the public interest, and the
like? Should it make any difference whether it is possible for the
defendant to install protective devices that will eliminate the nuisance
and still enable him to conduct his business? Are the considerations
any different from those in the case of wilful trespass, which we have
just discussed?

Question: (14) A factory supplying the city of Pittsburgh with light and
power emitted smoke and soot that damaged an adjoining nursery. The installation of the latest devices reduced but could not eliminate the nuisance.
The nursery sought an injunction. What arguments might be made in support of and against equitable relief? What, if any, additional facts would it
be useful for each of the parties to show? See Elliott Nursery Co. v. Duquesne Light Co., 281 Pa. 166, 126 A. 345 (1924).

Unfair competition.—Equity intervened not only to protect tangible property, real and personal, from tortious conduct, but also to
protect intangible property interests. Injunctions against infringe-
ments of patents and copyrights are familiar. Trademarks, trade-
names, and trade secrets have been similarly protected. A large array of miscellaneous wrongs to business interests, usually collected

[p] Students should read this paragraph
of text carefully to prepare for Avery v.
Spicer, infra p. 399.

Conceivably, equity could install a receiver to manage and exploit the property during the interval, holding the avails

for the party ultimately held to be entitled.

[q] The relations between law and equity
in the field of nuisance are considered infra pp. 676–77.

under the head of "unfair competition," have been enjoined in equity courts.

Labor injunctions.—Injunctions in labor disputes forbidding various kinds of conduct by striking employees have gone on the ground of protecting tangible property or intangible property interests of the employers. The question of what conduct may be enjoined has been a difficult one. One of the claimed abuses in the past was the issuance of broad temporary injunctions ex parte, that is, without notice to the defendant unions or employees affected. In federal courts the availability of injunctions in labor disputes is dealt with by special legislation. See Rule 65(e). There are similar state statutes.

Other types of injunctions.—The extent to which equity will make use of its injunctive power to protect or vindicate citizens' claims of right is far from static. Our examination of typical equitable remedies has so far involved protection of property interests. But what of interests of "personality" more or less unconnected with property interests? Is there, for instance, a right of privacy—a right to be let alone—that equity will protect by injunction? May a libel ever be enjoined?

The attempt of the United States to enjoin publication of a classified study entitled "History of U.S. Decision-Making Process on Viet Nam Policy," popularly called the Pentagon Papers, illustrates the proposition that " '[a]ny system of prior restraints of expression comes to this Court bearing a heavy presumption against its constitutional validity.' " The majority of the Court held that the government had not met the " '. . . heavy burden of showing justification for the imposition of such a restraint.' " New York Times Co. v. United States, 403 U.S. 713, 91 S.Ct. 2140 (1971). The three dissenters, Chief Justice Burger and Justices Harlan and Blackmun, recognized the constitutional limitations on prior restraint of expression. All of them objected to the "frenetic haste" in which the case had been conducted and the dealing with rights of great magnitude without an adequate record and without time for adequate consideration.[r] Justices Harlan and Blackmun, "forced" to reach the merits, dissented thereon. The Chief Justice did not address the merits but would have remanded for development of the issues—the district court, meanwhile, continuing the restraint on publication.

The emerging model of American public law litigation[s]—exemplified by legislative reapportionment and desegregation cases—entails heavy reliance on the injunctive remedy. "One of the most striking

[r] The district-court hearing in the New York Times case was on June 18, and the decision came on June 19. The court of appeals heard the appeal on June 22 and decided it on June 23. The petition for certiorari and motion for accelerated consideration thereof were filed in the Supreme Court on June 24. Certiorari was granted and the record was filed on June 25. The briefs were received less than two hours before argument on June 26. The case was decided on June 30. Each Justice wrote a separate opinion.

[s] See infra pp. 1172–73.

procedural developments of this century is the increasing importance of equitable relief." Chayes, The Role of the Judge in Public Law Litigation, 89 Harv.L.Rev. 1281, 1292 (1976). But this model looks to no ordinary injunction. "The traditional prohibitory injunction contained large discretionary elements: deciding whether to grant equitable relief, balancing the equities of the case and the interests of the often numerous parties, and shaping the exact contours of the decree. But in contemporary affirmative orders, especially structural injunctions—decrees establishing an ongoing regime governing the institution that is the real target of the lawsuit—the discretionary component is dramatically enhanced. To be sure, the purpose of the decree is to rectify a course of conduct that has been found to abridge rights asserted by the plaintiffs. But the trial judge has broad discretion to elaborate remedial arrangements in response to the particular characteristics of the situation and parties before him. This discretion makes it impossible to identify a unique remedial regime that follows ineluctably from and is measured by the determination of substantive liability." Chayes, The Supreme Court, 1981 Term—Foreword: Public Law Litigation and the Burger Court, 96 Harv.L.Rev. 4, 46 (1982). See also O. Fiss, The Civil Rights Injunction (1978).

(f) Accounting; Debtor and Creditor Relationships

Beneficiaries may call upon their trustees to account for their management of the trust; and similarly where it is conceived that there is a "fiduciary" relationship, although not strictly a trust, as in the case of partners and of principal and factor, an accounting might be compelled in equity. Even where the relationship was not considered "fiduciary," but was that of creditor-debtor, resort might sometimes be had to equity to compel an accounting if the job was likely to be too complicated for the law court, with its adjunct, the jury. Accountings, particularly in the case of trusts, might involve elements of continuous administration.

A creditor who obtained a judgment at law might require aid in equity to obtain satisfaction of the judgment, for example, to force disclosure of concealed assets or to set aside fraudulent conveyances made by the debtor. See Rule 18(b). He might also have to go to equity to reach assets of the debtor not subject to execution at law, for example, property interests of an equitable as distinguished from a legal type.

We have already mentioned the receiver, appointed to preserve or care for property during the pendency of an equity suit. American courts, especially the federal courts, developed the receivership idea as a means of superintending the operations of corporations in financial trouble and preventing their being disemboweled at the suit of particular creditors until some final arrangement could be made, often a reorganization of financial structure. Here equity took on very large tasks of administration. See also Morgan v. McDonough, 540

F.2d 527 (1st Cir.1976) (affirming appointment of receiver for Boston high school as part of desegregation effort), cert. denied, 429 U.S. 1042, 97 S.Ct. 743 (1977), on remand, 456 F.Supp. 1113 (D.Mass.1978).

(g) Complicated Litigation

An action at law was basically conceived to be a contest between two and only two adversary sides (although there might be more than one party on each side), in which one side would eventually get a single judgment against the other. Even at a relatively late date, law narrowly restricted the types of setoffs and counterclaims that it would allow in an action. Equity could and did deal with litigation of a much more complex character. It was not only more liberal in allowing setoffs and counterclaims, but it also allowed multi-sided controversies (interpleader, for example, is an equity contrivance) and considerable complication of the party-structure of the suit. Where a number of parties were before it, equity would grant whatever relief inter se appeared necessary; for example, one plaintiff might emerge with a decree against a co-plaintiff. Many of the modern statutes and rules regulating complex litigation are traceable to equity practice.

(h) Discovery

In an action at law a party had no effective way to prove facts within the exclusive knowledge of his adversary. Parties were not permitted to testify, and there was no process for compelling the production of documents in an opponent's possession. In a suit in equity the position was quite different, as we shall see shortly. To remedy the defective procedures at law, equity assumed an auxiliary jurisdiction and permitted bills of discovery in aid of law actions. By such a bill a party could ascertain the facts necessary for success in the legal action. The remedy was, however, hedged in by such restrictive requirements that its use was much less general than one might expect. But the bill of discovery was the precursor of modern discovery devices, illustrated by Rules 26 to 37.

(i) Flexibility of Equity Decrees

The flexibility of equity decrees is in striking contrast to the rigidity of a judgment for damages at law. Not only will equity order a defendant to do or refrain from doing specified things, but it will also cast its decree in a conditional mold when justice so requires. A typical instance already mentioned is the decree that V shall convey Blackacre on condition that P pay the agreed price. On occasion, too, equity will condition its relief upon the doing by the plaintiff of an act he was not legally bound to do. ("He who seeks equity must do equity." ᵗ) For instance, a plaintiff seeking specific performance may in the interests of fairness be compelled to accept some modification of his contract as a condition of obtaining equitable relief. If he does not consent, he will be left to his legal remedy on the contract as made.

A decree, moreover, is subject to modification on the initiative of any party in the light of changing conditions. Indeed, a decree may be frankly of an experimental, "let's-see-how-it-works" type. We find in nuisance cases some particularly good examples of such decrees. See, e.g., Georgia v. Tennessee Copper Co., 237 U.S. 474, 35 S.Ct. 631, decree entered, 237 U.S. 678, 35 S.Ct. 752 (1915).

The prime example of flexibility in an equity decree is Brown v. Board of Education, 349 U.S. 294, 75 S.Ct. 753 (1955), where the Supreme Court, having declared in 1954 the fundamental principle that racial discrimination in public education is unconstitutional and that all provisions of federal, state, or local law requiring or permitting such discrimination must yield to this principle, decided to leave the matter of relief to the district courts. The Court directed the district courts to be guided by equitable principles. Equity was traditionally characterized "by a practical flexibility in shaping its remedies and by a facility for adjusting and reconciling public and private needs." The district courts were to proceed "with all deliberate speed."

Question: (15) Was this delegation of responsibility for achieving compliance with the constitutional mandate wise? Is a court well equipped to approve or disapprove plans for compliance proposed by school authorities? to devise plans of its own?

(j) The "Clean-Up" Doctrine

When separate law and equity courts were operating side by side, there were frequent occasions when equity took jurisdiction of a claim for an equitable remedy and then retained it—at least if the plaintiff so wished—to clean up the entire controversy by granting "legal" relief in addition to or in lieu of "equitable" relief. This saved the plaintiff the inconvenience, expense, and delay of beginning a new action in a court of law. In some instances, moreover, a new action could not be brought because meanwhile the statute of limitations had run. The precise extent to which an English equity court would thus act was not wholly clear, nor were the pre-merger precedents in the American courts.

A typical example of *additional* relief of a legal type in equitable proceedings was when equity took jurisdiction to grant specific performance of a contract and also gave damages for delay in performance or past breach. The equitable clean-up doctrine has also been

ᵗ This and other so-called maxims of equity may perhaps give some sense of how the conscience of the chancellor works, but on the whole they probably confuse more than they clarify. See H. McClintock, Handbook of the Principles of Equity §§ 24–25 (2d ed. 1948).

frequently applied in suits to enjoin a tort, where the plaintiff seeks compensation for the injury already suffered as well as an injunction. For instance, *P* successfully shows that *D* has damaged him by means of unfair competition; equity courts have enjoined the defendant from continuing the conduct complained of and also assessed damages for the past wrongs.

As an example of legal relief *in lieu of* equitable relief consider the situation where *P* sued *V* to compel the conveyance of Blackacre pursuant to a contract of sale and in the course of the trial it was discovered that, while the suit was pending, *V* had conveyed the land to *X*, a bona fide purchaser for value without notice. This wrongful act of the defendant made specific performance impossible, but equity would retain the case and award damages to *P*. The same result ordinarily followed when the defendant's act was prior to the commencement of suit but *P* did not know of it.

If the plaintiff knew the facts precluding equitable relief above when he brought suit in an equity court, should the equity court retain the case and give legal relief? Should it make any difference if, knowing the facts, the plaintiff mistakenly but in good faith believed that he was entitled to equitable relief?

Now suppose that the case is one where specific performance is denied as a discretionary matter because of difficulties in supervising enforcement of a decree or because specific relief would be contrary to the public interest. Should a court denying equitable relief that the plaintiff might reasonably have expected to be granted retain the case for assessment of damages? Or suppose that the plaintiff is denied specific enforcement because of conduct on her part so unconscionable that it offends the conscience of the chancellor, although the contract would be enforceable in a law court. Should the equity court give legal damages?

Bear in mind that the defendant's right to jury trial turned on all this. The extent to which the clean-up doctrine has survived the merger of law and equity into the unitary action will be examined later in its bearing on the present-day American right to trial by jury. See Topic E of Part Four.

(k) Enforcement of Equity Decrees

The classical method of enforcing an equitable decree was through imprisonment for contempt.[u] The object of the imprisonment was to coerce the defendant into doing what the court had ordered him to do. When he tired of imprisonment and complied with the decree, he was released. Thus he was said to "carry the keys to

[u] Fines conditional on continued noncompliance could also be imposed through contempt proceedings in order to coerce obedience. And contempt proceedings might be supplemented by the coercive measure of seizure of property under a writ of sequestration.

his prison in his own pocket." A defendant might, and sometimes did, remain recalcitrant and frustrate the plaintiff's relief by simply staying in prison. This state of affairs, in theory at least, might continue indefinitely.

In addition to imprisonment for contempt to coerce obedience, which was civil in nature, there was also criminal contempt, the purpose of which was to vindicate the dignity of the court by punishing disobedience of its orders. A fixed prison term or an unconditional fine was the form of punishment. The same conduct might lead to proceedings for either civil or criminal contempt, or both, and attempts to distinguish between the two have frequently caused difficulties. See R. Goldfarb, The Contempt Power 49–67 (1963).

Under later practice, equity secured satisfaction of simple decrees for the payment of money by the same method of execution that law courts used.[v] See Rule 69(a). Also, under modern statutes, a decree for the conveyance of real estate may be made self-executing; that is, the decree itself is given by statute the effect of a deed. An alternative statutory approach is to authorize an officer of the court to execute a deed on behalf of the defendant, the statute giving such deed full effect. See Rule 70. Where applicable, these devices furnish relief to the plaintiff by means other than coercing the defendant.

(*l*) Equity in the Infant United States

In the early colonial period in this country, conditions of life were simple as compared to those in England. There was no real need for a sophisticated legal system, and there were very few lawyers to make such a system work if there had been one. The colonial courts administered a sort of homespun justice, presumably neither knowing nor caring whether they were doing the work of a chancellor or of a common-law court in the mother country. In addition, the lingering identification of equity courts with the Crown impeded their development. As equity slowly came to develop, it did so in greatly varying ways in the several colonies and continued to do so after the colonies became states.[w] In 1789, while some states had separate courts of equity, there were several states where equity jurisdiction was either in a very primitive form or nonexistent.[x]

One result of these disparities was that federal equity, not hampered by any conformity act, was uniform from the start. The first

[v] Constitutional or statutory provisions against imprisonment for debt now may, in some circumstances, prevent enforcement of a simple money decree by imprisonment for contempt.

[w] See Katz, "The Politics of Law in Colonial America," in Law in American History 257 (1971); Walsh, "The Growing Function of Equity in the Development of the Law," in 3 Law: A Century of Progress 139, 145–55 (1937).

[x] For an extreme example, Massachusetts did not have full equity jurisdiction until 1877.

Congress in a stop-gap fashion [y] and the second Congress in a permanent formulation, which lasted until the merger of the federal courts' law and equity sides in 1938, provided for forms and modes of equity proceedings "according to the principles, rules and usages which belong to courts of equity" but with the vital additional provision that these rules could be altered "as the supreme court of the United States shall think proper from time to time by rule to prescribe." [z] This rulemaking authority, later confirmed in more specific and sweeping language, was first exercised in 1822, when equity rules were prescribed for the lower federal courts.

[y] Act of September 29, 1789, ch. 21, § 2, 1 Stat. 93.

[z] Act of May 8, 1792, ch. 36, § 2, 1 Stat. 275.

TOPIC D. ABOLITION OF THE FORMS OF ACTION;
MERGER OF LAW AND EQUITY

SECTION 1. THE CONDITION OF CIVIL PROCEDURE
AROUND 1840

BOWEN, "PROGRESS IN THE ADMINISTRATION OF JUSTICE
DURING THE VICTORIAN PERIOD"

1 Select Essays in Anglo-American Legal History 516, 517–28 (1907).

The ancient barrier which separated the several Courts of the
Common Law from the Court of Chancery still subsisted in the year
1837. Two systems of judicature, in many respects at variance with
each other, flourished side by side under the famous roof of Westminster Hall. The principle of a division of labour by which distinct machinery can be accommodated to special subject-matter is based upon
reason and convenience. A large portion of the law business of the
country is made up of litigation in the result of which no one is directly interested but the rival combatants. But there are many matters
of which the law takes cognisance that necessitate a special and a
more complicated mechanism for their adjustment. The property of
infants, for example, requires to be protected—trusts to be managed
day by day during a long period of years—the estates of deceased
persons to be dealt with for the benefit of creditors, the assets to be
collected and distributed, accounts to be taken, directions to be given,
questions to be settled once for all that affect the interests of many.
It is desirable that special tribunals should be armed with the particular organization requisite for purposes such as these. The distinction
between law and equity went, however, far beyond what was needed
to carry out this natural division of labour. The two jurisdictions had
no common historical origin, and the principles on which they administered justice were unlike. The remedies they afforded to the suitor
were different; their procedure was irreconcilable; they applied diverse rules of right and wrong to the same matters. The common
law treated as untenable claims and defences which equity allowed,
and one side of Westminster Hall gave judgments which the other
restrained a successful party from enforcing. The law had always
cherished as its central principle the idea that all questions of fact
could best be decided by a jury. Except in cases relating to the possession of land, the relief it gave took, as a rule, the shape of money
compensation, in the nature either of debt or of damages. The procedure of the Court of Chancery, on the other hand, was little adapted
for the determination of controverted issues of fact, and it was constantly compelled to have recourse for that purpose to the assistance
of a court of law. The common law had no jurisdiction to prevent a

threatened injury; could issue no injunctions to hinder it; was incompetent to preserve property intact until the litigation which involved the right to it was decided; had no power of compelling litigants to disclose what documents in their possession threw a light upon the dispute, or to answer interrogatories before the trial. In all such cases the suitor was driven into equity to assist him in the prosecution even of a legal claim. The Court of Chancery, in its turn, sent parties to the Law Courts whenever a legal right was to be established, when a decision on the construction of an Act of Parliament was to be obtained, a mercantile contract construed, a point of commercial law discussed. Suits in Chancery were lost if it turned out at the hearing that the plaintiff, instead of filing his bill in equity, might have had redress in a law court; just as plaintiffs were nonsuited at law because they should have rather sued in equity, or because some partnership or trust appeared unexpectedly on the evidence when all was ripe for judgment. Thus the bewildered litigant was driven backwards and forwards from law to equity, from equity to law. The conflict between the two systems, and their respective modes of redress, was one which, if it had not been popularly supposed to derive a sanction from the wisdom of our forefathers, might well have been deemed by an impartial observer to be expressly devised for the purpose of producing delay, uncertainty, and untold expense.

The common law tribunals of Westminster Hall consisted of three great courts, each with a different history and originally different functions. In the growth of time, and by dint of repeated legislation, all, so far as the bulk of the litigation of the country was concerned, had acquired equal jurisdiction, and no practical necessity was left for the maintenance side by side of three independent channels of justice, in each of which the streams ran in a similar fashion and performed the same kind of work. First came the Queen's Bench, composed of a chief justice and four puisne judges. Its authority was supreme over all tribunals of inferior jurisdiction. It took sovereign cognisance of civil and criminal causes alike—kept the Ecclesiastical Courts and the Admiralty within bounds, controlled magistrates and justices, supervised the proceedings of civil corporations, repressed and corrected all usurpations, all encroachments upon common right. It wielded two great weapons of justice over public bodies; mandamus, whereby, when no other remedy appeared available, it compelled them to fulfil the law; prohibition, by means of which it confined all inferior authorities strictly to their respective provinces and powers. The Court of Common Pleas, historically the most ancient of the three, which had retained, with no particular benefit to society, supervision over the few ancient forms of real actions that still survived, exercised also a general authority over personal actions. It was directed by a chief justice and four puisne justices. It laboured, however, under the disadvantage that, as far as the general bar of England was concerned, it was a 'champ clos.' Serjeants-at-law had exclusive audience in it during term time, and it was not till 1847 that this vexatious and injurious monopoly was finally abolished. The Court of Exchequer had been from early years the special tribunal for dealing with matters in which the king's revenue was interested. It still retained in revenue cases and some other matters a particular jurisdiction, though clothed by this time (like the Queen's Bench and the Common Pleas) with power over all actions that were personal. Besides these functions, it was also a Court of Equity, and took part from time to time in the Chancery business of the realm. A chief baron was at the head, assisted by four puisne barons . . ..

The procedure at the common law, as compared with the wants of the country, had become antiquated, technical, and obscure. In old days the courts at Westminster were easily able to despatch, during four short terms of three weeks each, together with the assizes and sittings at Guildhall, the mass of the business brought before them. But, from the beginning of the century, the population, the wealth, the commerce of the country had been advancing by great strides, and the ancient bottles were but imperfectly adapted to hold the new wine. At a moment when the pecuniary enterprises of the kingdom were covering the world, when railways at home and steam upon the seas were creating everywhere new centres of industrial and commercial life, the Common Law courts of the realm seemed constantly occupied in the discussion of the merest legal conundrums, which bore no relation to the merits of any controversies except those of pedants, and in the direction of a machinery that belonged already to the past. Frivolous and vexatious defences upon paper delayed the trial of a litigant's cause. Merchants were hindered for months and years from recovering their just dues upon their bills of exchange. Causes of action had become classified, as if they were so many Aristotelian categories—a system which secured learning and precision, but at the risk of encouraging technicality; and two causes of complaint could not be prosecuted in one and the same action unless they belonged to the same metaphysical 'form.' An action on a bond could not be joined with a claim upon a bill of exchange. A man who had been assaulted and accused of theft in the market-place of his town was obliged, if he wished redress for the double wrong, to issue two writs and to begin two litigations, which wound their course through distinct pleadings to two separate trials. If surprise occurred at Nisi Prius or the assizes, the court was unable to adjourn the proceedings beyond a single day. Old fictions still survived, invented in bygone ages to assist justice—with no particular harm left in them, it is true, but which were well fitted to encourage the popular delusion that English law was a mass of ancient absurdity. In order to recover possession of any piece of land, the claimant began his action by delivering to the defendant a written statement narrating the fictitious adventures of two wholly imaginary characters called John Doe and Richard Roe, personages who had in reality no more existence than Gog and Magog. The true owner of the land, it was averred, had given John Doe a lease of the property in question, but John Doe had been forcibly and wrongly ejected by Richard Roe, and had in consequence begun an action of trespass and ejectment against him. Richard Roe, meanwhile, being a 'casual ejector' only, advised the real defendant to appear in court and procure himself to be made defendant in the place of the indifferent and unconcerned Richard Roe, otherwise the defendant would infallibly find himself turned out of possession. Till within the last twenty-six years, this tissue of invention of unreal persons and of non-existent leases preceded every investigation of the claim to possession of land. Nor was the trial itself of a common law cause productive of certain justice. Right was liable to be defeated by mistakes in pleading, by variances between the case as previously stated upon paper and the case as it stood ultimately upon the evidence, or by the fact that the right party to the suit had not been nominally joined, or that some wrong party had been accidentally joined with him. Perhaps the most serious blemish of all consisted in the established law of evidence, which excluded from giving testimony all witnesses who had even the minutest interest in the result, and, as a crowning paradox, even the parties to the suit themselves. 'The evidence of interested witnesses,' it was said, 'can never induce any rational belief.' The merchant whose name was forged to a bill of exchange had to sit by, silent and unheard, while his acquaintances were called to offer conjectures and beliefs as to the authenticity of the disputed signature from what they knew of his other writings. If a farmer in his gig ran over a foot-passenger in the road, the two persons whom the law singled out to prohibit from becoming witnesses were the farmer and the foot-passenger. In spite of the vigorous efforts of Lord Denman and others, to which the country owes so much, this final absurdity, which closed in court the mouths of those who knew most about the matter, was not removed till the year 1851.

In a strictly limited number of cases the decisions of the three courts could be reviewed in the Exchequer Chamber—a shifting body composed of alternate combinations of the judges, and so arranged that selected members from two of the courts always sat to consider such causes as came to them by writ of error from the third. The House of Lords, in its turn, was the appointed Court of Error from the Exchequer Chamber. The modern system of appeal, rendered necessary in our day by the weakening of the Courts in Banc and the development of what has been called the single-judge system, had not yet come into existence. Nor, in truth, on the common law side of Westminster Hall was there any great necessity for it. The Queen's Bench, the Common Pleas, and the Exchequer—whatever the imperfection of the procedure—were great and powerful tribunals. In each of them sat a chief of mark, with three puisnes to assist him, and the weight of authority of four judges, amongst whom there could not well fail to be present one or more men of the first rank of intellect and experience, was sufficient as a rule to secure sound law and to satisfy the public. The prestige, again, of the Exchequer

Chamber in such cases as were allowed to reach it upon error was of the highest order. But the principle upon which appeals were allowed by the law in some matters, and refused in others, was full of anomalies. Only matters of 'error' which were apparent on the record could be the subject of a hearing in the Exchequer Chamber. No appeal lay on subjects so important as a motion for a new trial or to enter a verdict or a nonsuit—motions which proceeded on the assumption of miscarriages in law by the judge or the jury who tried the cause. If the aggrieved party had not succeeded in complying at the trial with the difficult formalities of the rule as to bills of exceptions—an old-fashioned and often impracticable method of challenging the direction of a judge—no review of it was possible. Error lay from a special verdict, where the parties had arranged, or the judge directed at the trial, a special statement of the facts. No error lay upon a special case framed without a trial by consent. That is to say, no appeal was permitted unless the expensive preliminary of a useless trial had first been thrown away.

The technicalities which encumbered the procedure of the courts furnished one reason, no doubt, for the arrears which loaded the lists at the accession of her Majesty. . . .

The Court of Chancery was both a judicial tribunal and an executive department of justice for the protection and administration of property, but the machinery that it employed for the two purposes was, unfortunately, not kept distinct. Its procedure in contentious business served as the basis of its administrative operations, and persons between whom there was no dispute of fact at all found themselves involved in the delays and the embarrassments of a needless lawsuit. In its judicial capacity the Court of Chancery gave effect to rights beyond the reach of the common law, corrected the evils that flowed from the imperfect jurisdiction and remedies of the Common Law Courts, and dealt with whole classes of transactions over which it had acquired a special cognisance. The code of ethics which it administered was searching and precise—academical, perhaps, rather than worldly, the growth of the brains of great masters of learning and of subtlety, whose maxims and refinements had crystallised into a system. But its practice was as dilatory and vexatious as its standard of right and wrong was noble and accurate. For deciding matters of conflicting testimony it was but little fitted. It tossed about as hopelessly in such cases as a ship in the trough of the sea, for want of oral testimony—a simple and elementary method of arriving at the truth, which no acuteness can replace. It had no effective machinery at all for the examination or the cross-examination of witnesses, and (as we have seen) fell back upon the Common Law Courts whenever questions of pure law were raised, or as soon as depositions and affidavits became hopelessly irreconcilable. Oral evidence had always been at common law the basis of the entire system, although the common law perversely excluded from the witness-box the parties to the cause who naturally knew most about the truth.

The Court of Chancery, on the other hand, allowed a plaintiff to search the conscience of the defendants, and the defendants, by a cross bill, to perform a similar operation upon their antagonist, but only permitted the inquiry to be on paper. A bill in a Chancery suit was a marvellous document, which stated the plaintiff's case at full length and three times over. There was first the part in which the story was circumstantially set forth. Then came the part which 'charged' its truth against the defendant—or, in other words, which set it forth all over again in an aggrieved tone. Lastly came the interrogating part, which converted the original allegations into a chain of subtly framed inquiries addressed to the defendant, minutely dovetailed and circuitously arranged so as to surround a slippery conscience and to stop up every earth. No layman, however intelligent, could compose the 'answer' without professional aid. It was inevitably so elaborate and so long, that the responsibility for the accuracy of the story shifted, during its telling, from the conscience of the defendant to that of his solicitor and counsel, and truth found no difficulty in disappearing during the operation. Unless the defendant lived within twenty miles of London, a special commission was next directed to solicitors to attest the oath upon which the lengthy answer was sworn, and the answer was then forwarded by sworn messenger to London. Its form often rendered necessary a restatement of the plaintiff's whole position, in which case an amended bill was drawn requiring another answer, until at last the voluminous pleadings were completed and the cause was at issue. By a system which to lawyers in 1887 appears to savour of the Middle Ages, the evidence for the hearing was thereupon taken by interrogatories written down beforehand upon paper and administered to the witnesses in private before an examiner or commissioner. At this meeting none of the parties were allowed to be present, either by themselves or their agents, and the examiner himself was sworn to secrecy. If cross-examined at all (for cross-examination under such conditions was of necessity somewhat of a farce), the witnesses could only be cross-examined upon written inquiries prepared equally in advance by a counsel who had never had the opportunity of knowing what had been said during the examination-in-chief. If the examination was in the country, it took place at some inn before the commissioner and his clerk, the process seldom costing less than £60 or £70. It often lasted for days or weeks, at the end of which its mysterious product was sealed up and forwarded to London. On the day of the publication of the depositions copies were furnished to the parties at their own expense; but, from that moment, no further evidence was admissible, nor could any slip in the proofs be repaired, except by special permission of the court, when, if such leave was granted, a fresh commission was executed with the same formalities and in the same secret manner as before. The expense of the pleadings, of the preparation for the hearing, and of the other stages of the litigation may be imagined, when we recollect that it was a necessary maxim of the

Court of Chancery that all parties interested in the result must be parties to the suit. If, for example, relief was sought against a breach of trust, all who were interested in the trust estate had to be joined, as well as all who had been privy to the breach of trust itself. During the winding journey of the cause towards its termination, whenever any death occurred, bills of review or supplemental suits became necessary to reconstitute the charmed circle of litigants which had been broken. On every such catastrophe the plaintiff had again to begin wearily to weave his web, liable on any new death to find it unravelled and undone. It was satirically observed that a suit to which fifty defendants were necessary parties (a perfectly possible contingency) could never hope to end at all, since the yearly average of deaths in England was one in fifty, and a death, as a rule, threw over the plaintiff's bill for at least a year. The hearing in many cases could not terminate the cause. Often inquiries or accounts were necessary, and had still to be taken under the supervision of a master. Possibly some issue upon the disputed facts required to be sent for trial at the assizes, or a point of law submitted to a common law court. In such cases, the verdict of the jury, or the opinions of the court so taken, in no way concluded the conscience of the Court of Chancery. It resumed charge of the cause again, when the intermediate expedition to the common law was over, and had the power, if it saw fit, to send the same issue to a new trial, or to disregard altogether what had been the result. In a case which was heard in February 1830, there had been seven trials, three before judges and four before the Chancellor, at the close of which the suit found its way upwards to the House of Lords. When a cause had reached its final stage—when all inquiries had been made, all parties represented, all accounts taken, all issues tried—justice was done with vigour and exactitude. Few frauds ever in the end successfully ran the gauntlet of the Court of Chancery. But the honest suitor emerged from the ordeal victorious rather than triumphant, for too often he had been ruined by the way. Courts where ultimate justice is achieved, but where delay and expense reign supreme, become at last a happy hunting-ground for the fraudulent. The hour for reform has struck when the law can be made an instrument of abuse. . . . With all its distinction and excellence, the Court of Equity was thus practically closed to the poor. The middle classes were alarmed at its very name, for it swallowed up smaller fortunes with its delays, its fees, its interminable paper processes. The application of such a procedure to the large class of transactions, where no fact was in dispute, and only the careful administration of an estate required, was a cruel burden upon property. . . .

The judges of the court were the Lord High Chancellor (who then, as now, was a political officer and changed with every change of Ministry); the Master of the Rolls stood next in dignity; last came the Vice-Chancellor of England—a judge who in 1813 had been created to relieve the pressure. Some equity work was also done by the Chief

Baron, or, in his stead, a puisne baron sitting on the equity side of the Exchequer; but this could only be during a limited portion of the year. The appellate system was defective in the extreme. The Chancellor sat singly on appeals from the Vice-Chancellor of England and from the Master of the Rolls (whose inferior in the science of equity he easily might be), and presided in the House of Lords over the hearing of appeals from himself—a position the less satisfactory inasmuch as, owing to the imperfect constitution of that august tribunal, the Chancellor was very often its ruling spirit. These appellate functions left him not too much time to bestow on his own duties as a Chancery judge of first instance. To a court so loaded with procedure and so undermanned in its judicial strength, the Chancery business of this kingdom, contentious or non-contentious, metropolitan or provincial, all flowed. A formidable list of arrears naturally blocked the entrance of the Temple of Equity.

The situation in the United States.—The situation in the United States can be appreciated from the following summary by Hepburn of the vices in civil procedure stressed by American reformers. Hepburn speaks of "an inveterate incongruity between our law of procedure and our substantive law. The former had early lost the power of developing along with the substantive law. It had petrified while our modern substantive law was still in its budding growth. But the chief grounds of complaint which were urged against common law pleading were more specific. They related to the wall of separation between legal and equitable relief; to the labyrinth of arbitrary forms of action at law; to the artificial restrictions of the common law as to joining parties and as to joining causes of action; to the concealment of the real facts of a case through the verbiage or the vagueness of common law pleading." C. Hepburn, The Historical Development of Code Pleading 18–19 (1897). A statement in greater detail by David Dudley Field, who was chiefly responsible for the New York Code of Procedure of 1848, can be found in his 1847 essay, "What Shall Be Done with the Practice of the Courts?," in 1 Speeches, Arguments, and Miscellaneous Papers of David Dudley Field 226 (A. Sprague ed. 1884).

SECTION 2. THE REFORM MOVEMENT

Filled with revulsion at Blackstone's parochial and self-satisfied laudation of the common law, Jeremy Bentham (1748–1832), a law-trained philosopher, launched and sustained for many years a brilliant and bitter attack on English law both substantive and procedural.[a] His ideas attracted a group of able and influential supporters, including in this country the powerful figure of David Dudley Field, a leading lawyer of his time. The entire movement was associated with a reaction against case-made law and in favor of legislative codification. Although the movement got its initial impetus from Englishmen, perhaps the greatest early success in procedural reform was achieved in New York with its Code of Procedure of 1848. This success may in turn have encouraged the effort in England.

The English movement counted among its adherents some practicing lawyers and judges, but Professor Sunderland in 1926 concluded thus: "England has just completed a century of struggle for procedural reform, and it is to the energy and determination of the public, and not to the leadership of the bar, that the credit for the present English practice is due." Sunderland, The English Struggle for Procedural Reform, 39 Harv.L.Rev. 725, 727 (1926). And Field similarly observed that credit for the American reforms must be given principally to non-lawyers. This rather sad record of the legal profession in cleaning its own house is relieved by the story of the more recent procedural reform movement that culminated in the Federal Rules and has not yet spent its force. Here the American legal profession may claim to have made a very solid contribution.

English advances.—In England reform on a substantial scale began in the 1830's.

Most of the "real" and "mixed" forms of action at law were abolished by legislation of 1833 and 1860, leaving in their place a few statutory actions. In 1832, process in the main "personal" forms of action was made substantially uniform by statute. Advances toward abolishing the personal forms of action appeared in an act of 1852, but the final dissolution of the forms came with the Judicature Act of 1873.

Certain changes in pleading at law came in the Hilary Rules of 1834, written by the judges under legislative authority. As we have noted, these rules proved largely abortive. More effective reforms in pleading both at law and in equity can be traced in legislation from the 1850's onward.

Parties were made competent to testify at law by legislation dating from 1851. The reform of Chancery practice was accomplished in large part by legislation, although practice orders issued by several chancellors played a part. Among many reforms, radically transforming the outlandish procedures lampooned by Dickens in Bleak House, was the allowance in 1852 of oral testimony in open court in lieu of the cumbersome depositions.

[a] Maine said: "I do not know a single law-reform effected since Bentham's day which cannot be traced to his influence . . . ." H. Maine, Early History of Institutions 397 (1888).

The steps by which law and equity were fused or merged in England will not be recounted here. Complete fusion came through the Judicature Act of 1873—law and equity were now to be "administered concurrently," to use Maitland's phrase, and although there remained "differences of procedure arising out of the character of the various actions, . . . they can now be regarded as mere variations of one general theme—procedure in an action in the High Court of Justice."

These reforms called for a reconstitution of the courts, which was effected by the Judicature Act and later legislation. At present there is in England a Supreme Court of Judicature into which have been merged the three superior courts of law, the Court of Chancery, the Court of Exchequer Chamber, and certain other courts. The Supreme Court has a general branch, the High Court of Justice (in turn divided administratively into three divisions: Queen's Bench Division, Chancery Division, and Family Division); a special criminal branch, the Crown Court; and an appellate branch, the Court of Appeal. The court of highest appeal is the House of Lords.

A significant feature of the Judicature Act remains to be mentioned. The judges were given wide rulemaking powers over procedure. Either House of Parliament might secure an annulment of a rule by resolution, and Parliament of course might enact any procedural legislation on its own initiative.

The Field Code.—In the United States the bellwether of reform, as we have suggested, was the Field Code. Its major provisions, basic to all others, were these: [b]

§ 69. The distinction between actions at law and suits in equity, and the forms of all such actions and suits, heretofore existing, are abolished; and, there shall be in this state, hereafter, but one form of action, for the enforcement or protection of private rights and the redress of private wrongs, which shall be denominated a civil action.[c]

§ 142. The complaint shall contain:

1. The title of the cause, specifying the name of the court in which the action is brought, the name of the county in which the plaintiff desires the trial to be had, and the names of the parties to the action, plaintiff and defendant;

[b] Quotations in the text are from the Code of Procedure as it stood in 1851, the Act of 1848 (1848 N.Y.Laws ch. 379) having been amended in 1849 and again in 1851 (1849 id. ch. 438; 1851 id. ch. 479).

[c] Section 1 divided remedies in courts into "actions" and "special proceedings." Section 2 defined an "action" as "an ordinary proceeding in a court of justice, by which a party prosecutes another party for the enforcement or protection of a right, the redress or prevention of a wrong, or the punishment of a public offence." "Every other remedy is a special proceeding" (§ 3). Actions were then classified as either civil or criminal (§§ 4–6).

2. A plain and concise statement of the facts constituting a cause of action without unnecessary repetition; [d]

3. A demand of the relief, to which the plaintiff supposes himself entitled. If the recovery of money be demanded, the amount thereof shall be stated.

The precept of § 142(2) was carried forward through other sections of the Code. For instance, the provision dealing with the answer declared:

§ 149. The answer of the defendant must contain:

1. A specific denial of each material allegation of the complaint controverted by the defendant, according to his knowledge, information or belief, or of any knowledge or information thereof sufficient to form a belief.

2. A plain and concise statement of any new matter constituting a defence or set-off without unnecessary repetition.

Question: (1) What significant differences do you observe between § 142 and Federal Rule 8(a)?

The New York Code embodied a number of other changes and reforms. It required verification of most pleadings; cut down the number of permissible pleadings by the parties to complaint, answer, reply, and demurrers; limited the use of demurrers; revised the old rules on joinder of causes of action; altered and made more pliant the rules as to joinder of, and relief against, parties in an action; reformed the rules governing permissible counterclaims (this came into the Code by an amendment in 1852); liberalized the granting of amendments and softened the consequences of variances between pleadings and proof; set out a flexible system of provisional remedies; provided for general and special verdicts of juries; facilitated the waiver of jury trial; modernized the procedures on execution and simplified proceedings supplementary to execution; made the parties

[d] In the 1848 Act, § 120(2) read as follows: "A statement of the facts constituting the cause of action, in ordinary and concise language, without repetition, and in such manner as to enable a person of common understanding to know what is intended."

The New York lawyer-diarist George Templeton Strong made this sardonic entry on September 28, 1847: "Report of the Commissioners on Practice and Pleading indicating the course of their intended reformation, which is to be root and branch work, all existing law and usage to be swept away and a new system created *in vacuo* by these enlightened and modest jurists. Rather like their plan. I shall know as much law as Daniel Lord the moment it's adopted, or rather I shall know more, for I won't have so much to forget. And with such a bench as we're likely soon to have, this reduction of legal practice to a Hottentot standard of simplicity and despatch is indispensable. Being ignorant, our elected judges will be thereby preserved from blunders; being inclined to be mischievous, they'll not be protected in partisan decisions and wilful injustice by mysteries and formalities unintelligible to the public at large. *Vive la République* and *à bas* the Common money counts! To the Lantern with John Doe and Richard Roe, and let there be a *noyade* and a *fusillade* and a general extermination done upon all extant reporters and writers of treatises." 1 The Diary of George Templeton Strong 301 (A. Nevins & M. Thomas eds. 1952).

to some extent competent as witnesses; and enlarged discovery procedures before trial.[e] The New York Constitution had previously been amended to provide that "the testimony in equity cases shall be taken in like manner as in cases at law."

The New York code system was promptly copied in many states including California, and the California version became itself the basis of codes in several western states. The Federal Rules owe a great deal to the Field Code model,[f] as naturally do the rules of the great many states now patterned upon the Federal Rules. There remains only a handful of states—and the number is steadily dwindling—that can be said still to show noticeable allegiance to the common-law practice, and these bear little resemblance to the pristine form of the classic common law. In the very few states where law and equity have not been merged in a unitary action, the consequences have been softened by provisions for easy transfer from one side of the court to the other.

More recent reform has been achieved in the majority of states through legislation confiding rulemaking power in some form to the courts, most often by statutes similar to the Federal Rules Enabling Act. Some states, however, still choose to proceed directly by the enactment of a code by the legislature.

Federal reform.—Recall that article III, section 2 of the Constitution of the United States says that the judicial power shall extend to "all Cases, in Law and Equity" falling into described categories; and the seventh amendment provides that in "suits at common law," where the value in controversy is more than twenty dollars, the right of trial by jury shall be preserved. Do these provisions prevent a merger of law and equity? Reading "in Law and Equity" as merely an emphatic repetition of "all," they do not prevent a merger; but of course the guarantee of jury trial may not be abridged. The federal constitutional situation is not materially different in this respect from the situation of those states with similar guarantees of jury trial written into their several constitutions.

Until 1938, however, law and equity were kept separate in the lower federal courts. In these courts the same judges administered the two systems of jurisprudence not "concurrently," but in separate law and equity sides and according to separate procedures.

Under the Conformity Act, the procedure in actions at law in the district courts was a reflection of procedure for like actions in the

---

[e] Field's Code, which was notably simple and brief, received unsympathetic treatment by the New York courts, and the legislature persisted in amending and enlarging it until it became a structure with incredible over-detail. The same thing happened to a number of state codes modeled on the Field Code. All this necessitated renewed reform.

[f] Judge Clark said that the Federal Rules "represent a present-day interpretation and execution of what are at bottom the Field principles." Clark, "Code Pleading and Practice Today," in David Dudley Field Centenary Essays 55, 64 (A. Reppy ed. 1949).

forum state, subject always to particular federal statutes regulating procedure and to various intractable elements deriving from the very nature of the federal judicial power. Thus there was no uniformity of procedure in the district courts at law.

On the equity side, Congress had authorized the Supreme Court to regulate procedure by rules, and under this rulemaking power the Supreme Court laid down a uniform equity procedure for the district courts.[g]

Separation of law from equity was of course not so complete as in England during the classical period of Lord Eldon. For example, the following sections were enacted in 1915 (they appear here as formerly codified in title 28, but they have since been repealed):

§ 397. *Amendments to pleadings.* In case any United States court shall find that a suit at law should have been brought in equity or a suit in equity should have been brought at law, the court shall order any amendments to the pleadings which may be necessary to conform them to the proper practice. Any party to the suit shall have the right, at any stage of the cause, to amend his pleadings so as to obviate the objection that his suit was not brought on the right side of the court. The cause shall proceed and be determined upon such amended pleadings. All testimony taken before such amendment, if preserved, shall stand as testimony in the cause with like effect as if the pleadings had been originally in the amended form.

§ 398. *Equitable defenses and equitable relief in actions at law.* In all actions at law equitable defenses may be interposed by answer, plea, or replication without the necessity of filing a bill on the equity side of the court. The defendant shall have the same rights in such case as if he had filed a bill embodying the defense or seeking the relief prayed for in such answer or plea. Equitable relief respecting the subject matter of the suit may thus be obtained by answer or plea. In case affirmative relief is prayed in such answer or plea, the plaintiff shall file a replication. Review of the judgment or decree entered in such case shall be regulated by rule of court. Whether such review be sought by writ of error or by appeal the appellate court shall have full power to render such judgment upon the records as law and justice shall require.[h]

[g] It was not until the adoption of the Equity Rules of 1912 that the method of taking testimony in federal equity cases was finally assimilated to the method at law. Up to that time, depositions were used in much the way described supra p. 389.

[h] Statutes that allow so-called equitable defenses to be interposed in actions at law (presupposing that law and equity are otherwise to be kept distinct) have given rise to some intricate questions. It was perhaps easiest to deal with a case where the equitable matter would under the classical practice have entitled the defendant to an unconditional decree enjoining the plaintiff from prosecuting the action. But suppose the equitable matter would have resulted in a conditional decree or a decree of reformation? This type of relief was quite foreign to law,

A lawyer practicing in the state courts and the United States District Courts of a particular locality must thus have mastered three systems of procedure: the state procedure (which might be unmerged and therefore comprise two procedures); the federal law-procedure (which was the state procedure in law actions but with a federal overlay); and the federal equity-procedure. A lawyer practicing in federal courts throughout the country (as a government lawyer, for example, might well do) had to beware of the state procedure at law (as modified by the federal overlay) for each state in which he appeared.

The movement for reform of the procedures of lower federal courts has a history dating back to the nineteenth century. It culminated in 1934 in the Rules Enabling Act and in 1938 in the Federal Rules of Civil Procedure. The story of these developments, and the continuing series of amendments and the Federal Rules of Evidence, has already been told.[i]

Currently, the advisory function with respect to the Supreme Court's rulemaking power is entrusted to the Judicial Conference of the United States, a body of federal judges headed by the Chief Justice, which has long been charged with improving the administration of federal courts. Under legislation of 1958 amending 28 U.S.C. § 331, the Judicial Conference is directed to carry on a continuous study of the rules of practice prescribed by the Supreme Court for the inferior federal courts and to make recommendations to the Court. The Judicial Conference works through a standing committee, appointed by the Chief Justice, and advisory committees, also appointed by the Chief Justice, which report to the standing committee. There are now four advisory committees respectively for Civil, Criminal, Bankruptcy, and Appellate Rules, each assisted by a reporter who is usually a law professor. The advisory committees draft new or amended rules with explanatory notes, circulate them under the aegis of the standing committee to the bench and bar for comment, rework the rules in the light of the comments, and transmit them to the standing committee with an additional explanatory report. The standing committee in turn makes recommendations to the Judicial Conference, which finally advises the Court. At this point the procedure of the Rules Enabling Act, 28 U.S.C. § 2072, takes over with respect to the rules to which the Act refers. See also 28 U.S.C. § 2076.

This rulemaking machinery is currently very much under attack and reconsideration. Its contribution has been great, but some argue for radical change. Concerns center on process (e.g., lack of openness), institutional structure (e.g., involvement of the Supreme Court), and content (e.g., dealing with subjects too important for

and notwithstanding the statutes some law courts declined to entertain equitable matter that envisioned such relief. Would the situation be clarified by broadening the statutes to cover so-called equitable counterclaims? In many jurisdictions the statutes were thus broadened.

[i] See especially supra pp. 19–20.

rulemaking).   See generally W. Brown, Federal Rulemaking: Problems and Possibilities (1981).

TOPIC E.   PROBLEMS IN ADMINISTERING THE UNITARY CIVIL ACTION

SECTION 1.   USE AND MISUSE OF OLD LEARNING

AVERY v. SPICER

Supreme Court of Errors of Connecticut, 1916.
90 Conn. 576, 98 A. 135.

Action, under § 1097 of the General Statutes, to recover damages for unlawfully cutting trees, timber and poles upon land alleged to belong to the plaintiff, brought to the Superior Court in New London County and tried to the jury before Bennett, J.; verdict and judgment for the defendants, and appeal by the plaintiff.   No error.

PRENTICE, C.J.   The plaintiff, claiming to be the owner and possessor of a certain tract of land, brings this action to recover damages, as provided by § 1097 of the General Statutes, for the alleged unlawful cutting and carrying away by the defendants of trees, timber and poles growing upon said tract, and particularly described in the complaint.   The complaint alleges that the plaintiff owned and possessed the land, and that the defendant Ingalls, acting under the authority and direction of the defendant Spicer, unlawfully entered upon it and cut and carried away the trees, timber and poles.   The defendant Ingalls justifies his acts of cutting and removal under the rights and authority of the defendant Spicer, and in their joint answer they aver that the latter owned in fee simple the land upon which the cutting was done, and then was and ever since had been in possession thereof.   These allegations of title and possession in Spicer the plaintiff denies in his reply.   The parties were thus at issue to the jury in respect to both the title to and the possession of the land.

It appeared by the undisputed evidence that the plaintiff and Spicer were the owners in fee simple of adjoining farms, and both were able to trace their respective titles as such owners back for a long period of years.   The dispute between them as to the ownership of the locus grows out of a disagreement as to the location of the boundary line between their properties at the point in controversy.   The plaintiff claims that he owns, as evidenced by his title deeds, up to a line beyond which, upon his side of it, the cutting complained of was done.   The defendant's contention, on the other hand, is that Spicer's paper title extends his ownership to a line over and beyond which there was no cutting, that he and his predecessors in title had long occupied up to that line, and that he was so occupying at the time of the cutting.

399

No question presented by the appeal calls for the observance of a distinction between the defendant Ingalls, who did the actual cutting, and the defendant, Spicer, whose ownership, possession and authority are pleaded in justification of it. For the sake of convenience, therefore, the former's connection with the alleged wrong may be ignored, and his acts treated as though done by the latter.

The evidence having shown this situation, the plaintiff requested the court to instruct the jury that the first question for their consideration was whether or not the plaintiff was the owner of the land in dispute, and that if they should find that he was such owner and that the defendant Ingalls had entered upon it without his license and cut, the plaintiff was entitled to a verdict. The court did not comply with this request. On the contrary, its instructions were, in effect, that the plaintiff, to entitle himself to a verdict, must prove that he was in actual or constructive possession of the land. In further elaboration of this subject it stated that it was not necessary that the plaintiff show actual possession, but that sufficient proof of possession would be produced by proof of title and the absence of actual and exclusive possession in another.

The action of the court in thus charging and in refusing to charge as requested, furnishes the chief ground of complaint on the appeal. That complaint is not that the instructions were erroneous in their statement of how possession sufficient to maintain the action might be shown. On the contrary, they were full and clear upon that subject, and all that could have been desired. The complaint is the narrower, but fundamental one, that, whereas the court was asked to tell the jury that the plaintiff could recover upon proof of title without proof of possession, it told them that the plaintiff must show possession, actual or constructive, as a prerequisite of recovery.

This complaint might be summarily disposed of by reference to the fact that the plaintiff himself alleges possession, and that upon the pleadings the parties were at direct issue upon that matter. The plaintiff, having put up his case and helped to frame the issues on the basis that possession was a material and issuable fact, is not in a position to charge the court with error in accepting the allegations made by him and the issues framed as material, and instructing the jury accordingly and in such a way that those issues could be intelligently decided by them. Knapp v. Tidewater Coal Co., 85 Conn. 147, 157, 81 A. 1063; Jacobs v. Williams, 85 Conn. 215, 218, 82 A. 202.

But the court's action finds justification upon more substantial grounds. The complaint sounds in trespass. It alleges the plaintiff's possession of the land, an unlawful entry by the defendants and acts done thereon by them to its direct injury by force. Here are all the essentials of an action quare clausum fregit, if we revert to the distinctions and employ the terminology of the common-law system of pleading. That, however, is not of importance save as it shows that the complaint is one seeking recovery for a tort which lies within the broad field of trespass. It is brought to recover damages resulting from a direct injury done by force to property in actual or constructive possession, and that spells trespass according to the common-law classification of personal actions. Actions of trespass for injuries to property were actions for the recovery of damages for wrongs done to the possessory right. They were founded on possession only. The gist of the action was the injury to the plaintiff's possession, and it was requisite that his possession, actual or constructive, be shown to authorize recovery. This was the rule of universal application. Toby v. Reed, 9 Conn. 216, 223; Church v. Meeker, 34 Conn. 421, 422.

The plaintiff's action being unmistakably one in the nature of trespass, the court did not err in giving a charge appropriate to it. But that is not all. Its instructions, when examined in the light of the facts before the court and regardless of the pleadings and the issues raised by them, were correct.

Passing by trespass with its requirement of possession as a prerequisite of recovery, there was in the common-law system a form of action providing for the redress of an injury suffered by one having an interest in property but not having the possession. By an action of trespass on the case, one whose reversionary interest had been invaded by a wrongdoer might have redress. But the action could not be resorted to by one whose interest, instead of being reversionary, was such as the right of possession attached to it. A fee owner, for example, might not avail himself of it to redress a wrong done to his property by direct force, express or implied. His interest is possessory and not reversionary, as is that of a landlord, remainderman, and the like.

These two forms of action, to wit, trespass and trespass on the case, supplemented one another, and together covered the entire field of personal actions for damages for injury to property, whether that property was or was not in the plaintiff's possession when the wrong was committed, so that by resort to one or the other every one so injured in his rights might find redress.

Two pertinent facts of present interest and importance thus appear. The first is that a person whose interest was not reversionary was not permitted to recover for injury to property unless he could show possession, actual or constructive. The second is but its corollary, to wit, that a title owner disseized could not sue his disseizor for the latter's acts of wrongdoing to the property as long as the disseizin continued. The disseizee in such case must either first regain possession by legal action or otherwise, and then bring his action of trespass for the injury to the property, or recover for those injuries as an incident of his action to regain possession. He could not sue the disseizor for the tort independently until he had come into possession. [Citations omitted.] [a]

---

[a] See supra p. 376.

The substitution of our Practice Act [b] for the common-law system of pleading has not changed the situation save as it has abolished certain formal distinctions and employed a new nomenclature. The same facts will entitle one to the same redress as before, and to no other redress. It still remains true, save as some statute may provide otherwise, that possession is a necessary condition precedent to recovery by one whose interest is not reversionary in its character for a direct injury done to tangible property by force, actual or implied, and that a disseizor cannot be sued by the disseizee for such injury while the disseizin continues.

The plaintiff faced the obstacles interposed by these principles. The defendant claimed and offered evidence to prove that he was in possession of the locus long before the cutting was done, and has so remained ever since. If so, the plaintiff was not only not in possession, but also, assuming that he had established his claimed title, was in the position of a disseizee at the hands of the defendant. It is apparent, therefore, that the court's instructions, which required of the plaintiff proof of his possession, actual or constructive, as a prerequisite to his recovery, were in their application to the situation disclosed by the case correct, unless some statute has provided a redress unknown to the common law. This is all the more apparent in view of the fact, called to the attention of the jury in the court's charge, that the plaintiff has offered no evidence of his actual and exclusive possession of the locus at the time the cutting was done, and so was compelled to rely upon proof of title and the absence of actual exclusive possession in another.

This brings us to an examination of § 1097 of the General Statutes, which is the only statute having any bearing upon the situation. The plaintiff contends that it gives to the title owner of land as such a new and independent right of action under circumstances like those disclosed by this case, and one which dispenses with the necessity of proof of the plaintiff's possession to entitle him to recover.

[Section 1097 provided: "Every person who shall cut, destroy, or carry away any trees, timber, or underwood, standing or lying on the land of another, . . . without license of the owner, and all who shall aid therein, shall pay to the party injured one dollar for every tree or pole under one foot diameter; and for all trees of a diameter of one foot or more three times their value . . . ."]

. . . . .

The authorities, as far as we have observed them, hold, with substantial unanimity, that statutes similar to ours do not give a new and independent right of action and that their sole office is to prescribe the measure of damages in cases where compensatory damages would, in the absence of the statute, be recoverable. . . .

[b] This contained the usual provision about "one form of civil action."

To hold that the statute creates a new and independent right of action and gives to an owner of land as such a right of recovery for a wrong done to it, would be to permit the title to the property, upon which the alleged wrong was committed, to be put in issue in every action wherein the special statutory damages were sought and to put the plaintiff in every such case to proof of his title. Thus the personal action brought for the recovery of damages would become one necessarily calling for an adjudication of title. In this connection it is to be noted that the statute does not provide that the owner of the land may recover the statutory damages. Its language is that the wrong-doer shall pay those damages to "the party injured." By "the party injured" is, of course, meant the party legally injured, and that necessarily means some one to whom the law affords redress. "An injury is a wrong; and for the redress of every wrong there is a remedy: a wrong is a violation of one's right; and for the vindication of every right there is a remedy. Want of right and want of remedy are justly said to be reciprocal. Where therefore there has been a violation of a right, the person injured is entitled to an action." Parker v. Griswold, 17 Conn. 288, 303.

. . . .

There is no error.

In this opinion the other judges concurred.

Question: (1) How would this case be decided if Connecticut had adopted rules similar to the Federal Rules? Would Rule 18(b) be pertinent?

MANHATTAN EGG CO. v. SEABOARD TERMINAL & REFRIGERATION CO.

City Court of New York, 1929.
137 Misc. 14, 242 N.Y.S. 189.

SHIENTAG, J. The motion is by the plaintiff to strike out the counterclaim contained in the defendant's answer upon the ground that it is not one which may be interposed in the action. Plaintiff sues for money had and received. Defendant counterclaims, alleging that 220 cases of eggs which were in the defendant's possession were stolen from it and sold to the plaintiff; that defendant, before the commencement of the present action, demanded their return from plaintiff or payment therefor, which the plaintiff refused; that by reason thereof plaintiff became indebted to defendant for their value, which it agreed to pay to defendant. Concededly the counterclaim, if in tort for conversion, sets forth a good cause of action, but if so it cannot be interposed in this case, for it does not arise out of the transaction set forth in the complaint.[c] Two questions are presented: (1) Does the counterclaim set up a good cause of action in quasi-contract, i.e., an obligation imposed by law? [d] (2) May an action in quasi-contract be set up as a counterclaim in an action on an independent contract under subdivision 2 of section 266 of the Civil Practice Act?

1. If *A* stole goods belonging to *B* the latter could sue him at common law in trover for conversion. With the development of indebitatus assumpsit it was held that if the thief converted the stolen property into money the owner could waive the tort; that is, his remedy for tort, and resort to the new and more convenient remedy, the law implying an obligation on the part of the converter of the goods to pay over the proceeds to the rightful owner. To bring the case within the new writ the fiction of a contract was created. There developed a conflict in the authorities as to whether or not the remedy in assumpsit would apply against one who converted goods but did not turn them into cash. At an early date it was held in this State, in accordance with the prevailing view, that such remedy would apply. If *A* stole goods belonging to *B* and sold them to *C*, a purchaser without notice, what rights would he have against *C*? Clearly he could not be deprived of his ownership by *A*'s wrongful act, and after demand on *C* for the goods and his refusal to turn them over could sue *C* in trover for conversion. *C*'s wrong consisted in withholding the goods from the owner after the latter's demand for them. Under the older cases the remedy in assumpsit would not lie as against *C*, because, being a purchaser in good faith and for value, it was held that he was not unjustly enriched at the expense of the true owner. A historical review of the development of the various forms of action and the writs issued thereunder would be necessary to show the reasons for this distinction. Suffice it to say they have no application under our modern code system. I hold, therefore, in all cases of conversion, whether involving the original wrongdoer or one acquiring from him by purchase, the true owner may waive his remedy in tort and proceed in assumpsit on the theory of an obligation imposed by law or a quasi-contract. [Citations omitted.]

[c] At the time of decision of the Manhattan Egg case, New York's main provision on counterclaims was NYCPA § 266:

"*Counterclaim defined.* A counterclaim . . . must tend to diminish or defeat the plaintiff's recovery, and must be one of the following causes of action against the plaintiff, or, in a proper case, against the person whom he represents, and in favor of the defendant, or of one or more defendants, between whom and the plaintiff or the plaintiff and another person or persons alleged to be liable a separate judgment may be had in the action:

1. A cause of action arising out of the contract or transaction set forth in the complaint as the foundation of the plaintiff's claim or connected with the subject of the action;

2. In an action on contract, any other cause of action on contract existing at the commencement of the action."

The present New York law, NYCPLR § 3019(a), reads as follows:

"*Subject of Counterclaims.* A counterclaim may be any cause of action in favor of one or more defendants or a person whom a defendant represents against one or more plaintiffs, a person whom a plaintiff represents or a plaintiff and other persons alleged to be liable."

[d] See supra pp. 344–45.

2. Under subdivision 2 of section 266 of the Civil Practice Act, "in an action on contract, any other cause of action on contract existing at the commencement of the action" may be set up as a counterclaim. Is an action on quasi-contract based upon a conversion, "an action on contract" within the meaning of this provision? The subject is discussed in another connection and the question left open in Kittredge v. Grannis (244 N.Y. 182, 188–91, 155 N.E. 93). It would seem that without attempting to reconcile the authorities in this and other jurisdictions the adoption of the following principles would bring about the most practical and equitable solution: (a) Give the owner of converted goods his choice of remedies, tort or assumpsit. (b) Having chosen his remedy, make the nature of the action selected rather than the underlying nature of the obligation "the determinative factor," so far as matters of practice are concerned at any rate. The common law invented the fiction of a contract in these cases. That fiction to a considerable extent has outlived its usefulness. It should either be wiped out entirely and the necessary readjustments made, or it should be treated at its face value. For the courts, the latter solution would seem the more feasible. Provisions dealing with counterclaims particularly should receive a liberal construction in order to avoid multiplicity of actions. I hold, therefore, that the counterclaim is properly interposed. (Job & Co. v. Sanders, 121 Misc. 760, 202 N.Y.S. 752.) Motion denied. Order signed.

RAAB v. BOWERY SAVINGS BANK

Civil Court of the City of New York, 1974.
77 Misc.2d 1054, 355 N.Y.S.2d 748.

IRVING YOUNGER, JUDGE.   In 1965, plaintiff and her husband bought a house. Defendant is their mortgagee.

The mortgage says that the mortgagors shall make certain monthly payments "to be held in trust by the mortgagee." Plaintiff has made the payments. Defendant enters them in an "escrow account" out of which it pays taxes and other assessments on the house. The amount received has exceeded the amount expended for at least the last six years. In 1968, the average monthly balance in plaintiff's favor was $346.76; in 1969, $351.09; in 1970, $485.00; in 1971, $456.56; in 1972, $604.05; and in 1973, $731.87.

In January, 1974, plaintiff commenced this Small Claims action "for interest on tax escrow money given to defendant from January, 1968. Breach of fiduciary relationship." Defendant has not objected to the failure to join plaintiff's husband as a party, CPLR 1001, and the facts are stipulated.

In Tierney v. Whitestone Savings & Loan Ass'n, Civ.Ct., Queens Co., 77 Misc.2d 284, 353 N.Y.S.2d 104, a case indistinguishable from this case, Judge Margulies found for the plaintiff. With all diffidence, I decline to follow him.

Plaintiff must establish some basis for holding defendant liable. Since the mortgage contains no promise by the bank to pay interest on the escrow balances, there has been no breach of an express contract. Since plaintiff has offered no evidence of an unstated agreement to pay interest, there has been no breach of an implied contract. Since the legislature had not spoken, there has been no breach of a statutory obligation. (But see chapter 119 of the Laws of 1974, providing henceforth for payment of interest on escrow accounts.)

Not seriously disputing any of these conclusions, plaintiff argues that "the rule of just compensation," derived from dicta in Bevier v. Covell, 87 N.Y. 50 (1881); [other citations omitted], requires a decision in her favor. Although it would be rash to quarrel with the idea that people should be compensated where it is just that they be compensated, I can hardly accept it as a basis for liability. Alas, litigants must do something more than demand justice: they must demonstrate a cause of action.

So plaintiff urges that her claim is for money had and received, a theory which usually avails when a plaintiff has given money to a defendant who should, for whatever reason, be made to return it. Here, plaintiff does not sue for the return of anything she gave defendant. Her contention is a more subtle one.

Defendant took plaintiff's escrow payments and commingled them with its general funds. It invested its general funds in the money market—commercial paper, certificates of deposit, treasury bills, etc.—earning whatever interest the money market was then paying. Plaintiff argues that these earnings rightly belong to her, and hence that she has a cause of action for money had and received.

When plaintiff says that the bank's earnings on her escrow payments rightly belong to her, she speaks words of equity. We are taught, however, that this does not convert an action for money had and received into an equity action. Chapman v. Forbes, 123 N.Y. 532, 537, 26 N.E. 3, 5 (1890):

"That an action is of an equitable nature does not make it an action in equity.

"When, in an action for money had and received, all the facts show that the plaintiff is ex aequo et bono entitled to recover, his right to recover is a legal one, and maintainable in a court of law."

We must go further. In Chapman, the allegation was that defendant refused to pay to plaintiff money which defendant had been given by a third person who had received it as the agent of plaintiff's testatrix. There was no fiduciary relationship between plaintiff's testatrix and defendant, a circumstance which limits the Court of Appeals' holding. "And in the particular case before the court there is no such relation of trust between the parties as would render the

cause of action cognizable in equity. Equitable relief is not demanded, nor is a case made by the complaint for granting any relief of an
equitable nature." Id. Here, by contrast, there was a relation of
trust between the parties: defendant agreed in the mortgage to hold
plaintiff's escrow payments "in trust" for the purposes specified.
The complaint alleges "breach of fiduciary relationship," which, allowing for the succinctness customary in Small Claims cases, sounds
in equity. And the transactions at issue, looked at closely, show an
equitable cause of action. Defendant was to hold plaintiff's escrow
payments in trust. Defendant was thus obliged not to commingle
them and not to use them for its own gain. Defendant did both. It
follows that, although none of the escrow payments have been dissi-
pated, defendant may be made to disgorge to plaintiff the fruits of its
breach of fiduciary obligation.

Plaintiff's remedy, in short, is an accounting of defendant's gain,
that is, the interest defendant earned by investing plaintiff's escrow
payments in the money market. This may be more or less than the
sum obtained by computing interest on the escrow balances, but
whatever the amount, the cause of action is equitable. I am therefore obliged to dismiss the complaint for lack of subject-matter jurisdiction, NYCCCA §§ 202, 1801,[e] and I do.

CLASSIFICATION

Reconsider the Williamson case with which this Part began. Notwithstanding Federal Rule 2, with its invocation of one form of action, it is apparent that the court cannot fly in the face of any applicable statute that attempts to make some regulation, whether of
substance or procedure, through the medium of classifying actions
and attaching different consequences to the different classes. In the
Williamson case the subject of regulation was limitations of time for
the commencement of actions, and actions were for this purpose classified by the Delaware statute in terms of the old forms of action. In
the Manhattan Egg case the subject was permissible counterclaims,
and the New York statute used the characterization "cause of action
on contract." The courts could not in these instances escape the task
of exegesis, and they felt compelled to go back to old law.

In regulating various aspects of litigation, classification and differentiation of cases are often desirable, for not all civil litigation
should be carried out in exactly the same way. But classification is
intelligent only if it keeps in view the purposes for which it is being
made. Unfortunately, draftsmen have sometimes harked back to the
old forms of action or to broader categories such as "on contract" or

[e] The reference here was to the jurisdictional statutes of the Small Claims
Part of the Civil Court, which provide in
pertinent part for jurisdiction over "any
cause of action for money only" not in
excess of the jurisdictional amount, then
$500.

"in tort" when the typing of cases in those terms bore no wise relation to the underlying purposes of the regulation that was being attempted.

In all events, we point to the truth that Rule 2 cannot and does not avoid all problems of classification.

With respect to the right to jury trial, the constitutional provision itself points to the category "suits at common law." Are we then obliged to resort to ancient history? Is this the only resort? Are the results defensible functionally? The problem is dealt with in Topic E of Part Four.

SECTION 2. "THEORY OF THE PLEADINGS"

In some states there developed under the early codes a theory of the pleadings doctrine, the creation of judges seemingly reluctant to pull away too far from the comforting rigidities of the forms of action. The code provision requiring the pleader merely to make "a plain and concise statement of the facts constituting a cause of action" seemed to these judges to countenance, indeed to encourage, an undisciplined approach to pleading wholly at odds with the system that they had known all their professional lives, which they believed to be not only right but eternally so. In 1858, a decade after the Field Code, Justice Grier of the Supreme Court of the United States put it this way: "The distinction between the different forms of action for different wrongs, requiring different remedies, lies in the nature of things; it is absolutely inseparable from the correct administration of justice in common-law courts." McFaul v. Ramsey, 61 U.S. (20 How.) 523, 525 (1858).

A leading case espousing the theory of the pleadings requirement was Supervisors of Kewaunee County v. Decker, 30 Wis. 624, 629–30, 632–33 (1872). Chief Justice Dixon said:

"It thus appears that the authorities relied upon do not sanction the position, that a complaint in the first instance and where challenged by demurrer, may be uncertain and ambulatory, purposely so made, now presenting one face to the court and now another, at the mere will of the pleader, so that it may be regarded as one in tort, or one on contract, or in equity as he is pleased to name it and the necessities of argument require, and if discovered to be good in any of the turns or phases which it may thus be made to assume, that it must be upheld in that aspect, as a proper and sufficient pleading by the court. As already observed, the opinion of the court is quite to the contrary. We have often held that the inherent and essential differences and peculiar properties of actions have not been destroyed, and from their very nature cannot be. Howland v. Needham, 10 Wis. 495, 498. These distinctions continuing, they must be regarded by the courts now as formerly, and now no more than then . . . can any one complaint or count be made to subserve the purposes of two or more distinct and dissimilar causes of action at the option of the party presenting it. It cannot be 'fish, flesh or fowl' according to the appetite of the attorney preparing the dish set before the court. If counsel disagree as to the nature of the action or purpose of the pleading, it is the province of the court to settle the dispute. It is a question when properly raised which cannot be left in doubt, and the court must determine with precision and certainty upon inspection of the pleading to what class of actions it belongs or was intended, whether of tort, upon contract, or in equity, and, if necessary or material, even the exact kind of it within the class must also be determined. [Citations omitted.]

. . . .

". . . And this we take to be the true rule, that the court must in the first instance decide with certainty what the specific cause of action counted and relied upon is, and, having decided that, it must next determine whether the complaint contains a sufficient statement of such cause, and if it does not, the demurrer must be sustained."

The question posed by this doctrine is not whether the plaintiff must have a theory. He would always be well advised not to institute an action if his analysis discloses none. The real and recurring problem arises when he wants to shift his position and embrace a new theory.

The application of the theory of the pleadings requirement may be illustrated by the following case. *P*'s complaint alleges that *D* owned a gray mare, represented by him to be worth $100, which he offered to exchange for *P*'s horse, worth $100; that *P* relying on *D*'s representations left his horse at an agreed place, where *D* picked it up; that *D* failed to leave his gray mare there as agreed, but instead left a bay mare of no value, which later died; that *P* promptly notified *D* of his dissatisfaction with the bay mare; that *D* did not have the gray mare in his possession and did not intend to deliver it as agreed, but falsely and fraudulently represented to *P* that he would do so and thereby induced *P* to part with his horse; and that *D* made his statements knowing them to be false with intent to defraud *P*. The complaint asks for $100 damages. The answer is a denial of the material allegations of the complaint. The court finds the facts as alleged by *P*, except that *D* did not make knowingly false statements to induce *P* to part with his horse. The court also finds the value of the gray mare promised by *D* to be $30. *D* argues, in true theory of the pleadings fashion, that *P*'s theory was fraud (what form of action at common law?) and that, not having proved fraud, *P* must fail. *P* argues that, without proof of fraud, he has nevertheless alleged and proved all the elements of breach of contract. What result?

The court in the case from which the illustration is drawn, Knapp v. Walker, 73 Conn. 459, 47 A. 655 (1900), accepted *P*'s argument and allowed recovery. The Wisconsin court of Chief Justice Dixon's day,

and later, would not. Indeed, that court would not even allow an
amendment changing the theory before trial. See Supervisors of
Kewaunee County v. Decker, 34 Wis. 378 (1874) (a second appeal);
Klipstein v. Raschein, 117 Wis. 248, 94 N.W. 63 (1903). Wisconsin did
a complete turnabout, however, and by 1911 the theory of the pleadings doctrine was dead in that state. The change may be observed in
Bieri v. Fonger, 139 Wis. 150, 120 N.W. 862 (1909); Bruheim v. Stratton, 145 Wis. 271, 129 N.W. 1092 (1911); and Frechette v. Ravn, 145
Wis. 589, 130 N.W. 453 (1911). (The last-named case poses a peculiarly difficult problem, as to which Klingbeil v. Saucerman, 165 Wis. 60,
160 N.W. 1051 (1917), is instructive.)

In some code states, theory of the pleadings philosophy seems
never to have exerted much influence. Other states, like Wisconsin,
were at one time attracted to it but have since abandoned it. In very
few jurisdictions must it still be reckoned with as a factor at the trial
level.

Question: (2) As a plaintiff's lawyer operating under the theory of the
pleadings doctrine, how could you seek to avoid its pitfalls? Would such
stratagem undermine any justifiable rationale of the doctrine?

It was undoubtedly the intent of the framers of the Federal Rules
to do away with the theory of the pleadings doctrine, and the decided
cases show that a great measure of success has been achieved.

Question: (3) Apart from Rule 2 itself, which provisions of the Rules can
be said to have outlawed the theory of the pleadings doctrine in federal practice? Which can be said to preserve some of its spirit? See 5 Wright &
Miller § 1219.

In 1931, the following proposal[f] was advanced in New York:

"A party shall no longer be permitted to plead several causes of
action or counterclaims arising out of a single transaction or connected set of facts, but shall be required to make a single statement of
the transaction or facts, followed by a statement of the various legal
theories upon which he claims to be entitled to recover under those
facts. He may demand one or more kinds of relief warranted by the
facts and legal theories pleaded, whether legal or equitable or both.
He shall not be required to elect as between the various theories, but
a verdict shall be rendered upon each separate claim, unless the court
shall dismiss the action or direct a verdict as to such claim. If there
are different measures of damage for the various legal theories
pleaded, he shall be entitled to recover the highest measure of damages on any of the theories proven."

As pointed out by Professor Millar,[g] this proposal precisely corre-
sponds to a method of pleading that has long been followed in Scotland, where each party "is required to append to his unitary state-

[f] Committee on Law Reform of the As-
sociation of the Bar of the City of New
York, Tentative Proposals for Changes in
Civil Procedure and Practice 14 (1931).

[g] R. Millar, Civil Procedure of the Trial
Court in Historical Perspective 196
(1952).

ment of facts a 'concise note of the legal propositions' upon which he rests his claim or defense."

Questions: (4) Was the New York proposal a meritorious one?

(5) If it were adopted, to what extent should a party be bound by his statement of legal theory?

SECTION 3. CHANGE OF THEORY ON APPEAL

APEX SMELTING CO. v. BURNS

United States Court of Appeals, Seventh Circuit, 1949.
175 F.2d 978, cert. denied, 338 U.S. 911, 70 S.Ct. 350 (1950).

Before MAJOR, CHIEF JUDGE, KERNER and DUFFY, CIRCUIT JUDGES.

MAJOR, CHIEF JUDGE. This is an appeal from a judgment in defendants' favor, entered September 14, 1948, following a directed verdict, allowed on defendants' motion, at the conclusion of plaintiff's case.

Plaintiff filed its complaint against the defendants, alleging that it was the owner and in possession of certain described premises located in the city of Chicago, Illinois, and was in the exercise of due care and caution for the preservation of such premises from injury and harm, and was active in the conduct and operation of a large and commodious manufacturing plant. That its plant might have care and protection from sabotage and other interruption of efficient operation, plaintiff and defendants on February 2, 1943, entered into a certain written agreement, which is set forth verbatim in the complaint, the salient portions of which are as follows: The defendants agreed to furnish a uniformed armed guard service consisting of five armed guards or more as might be agreed upon from time to time between the parties for the protection of the property. Such guards were to be guided by a set of general rules and written instructions issued by the plaintiff through its designated representatives. Defendants agreed to pay the expense of equipping the guards, as well as social security, unemployment taxes and employers' liability insurance. Supervision of the guards was made the responsibility of defendants, who in turn were to be responsible to and receive instructions from the plaintiff. The guards were charged with the function of guarding plaintiff's plant in the manner best suited, depending upon the circumstances. It was agreed that the wishes of the plaintiff would be honored at all times consistent with good judgment in replacing guards who in its opinion did not fill the requirements of the service as outlined. The agreement set forth the compensation to be paid defendants by the plaintiff for the services thus rendered and provided that the supervisor in charge of the guard force was to be responsible at all times for the proper functioning of the operation.

The service provided was to begin on Monday, February 15, 1943, at 6 a.m., and was to remain in force until the expiration of thirty days' written notice by either or both of the parties to the agreement.

The complaint alleged that the defendants entered upon the performance of the agreement at the time and in the manner provided and that among the armed guards furnished by the defendants was one Harry Frontczak, who on or about the 8th of September, 1946, "while active in his duties, as the servant of the defendants, in, upon and about the premises of the plaintiff, and coincident therewith, from infirmity of temper, and under the influence of passion aroused by real or fancied grievance, did, wilfully and with intent to wreak vengeance upon the plaintiff, cause combustion to take place within the premises of the plaintiff and a conflagration to ensue thereon, to the harm and injury of said premises and to the contents therein." The complaint concluded by alleging that as a result of the combustion caused by the servant of the defendants, plaintiff's premises and contents were damaged by the fire and that it expended large sums of money in the restoration and repair of the same and was damaged by the interruption of operation and delayed production in the amount of $20,000.00 for which judgment against the defendants was sought.

Defendants filed a motion to strike the complaint as insufficient in law and to dismiss the action, specifying the following grounds as reason therefor: (1) the complaint did not charge any act of negligence against the defendants nor that any damage was suffered by the plaintiff through the negligence of or as a direct and proximate result of any negligence on the part of the defendants; (2) the complaint did not charge any breach of contract on the part of the defendants, and (3) the complaint did not charge that the alleged damage was caused as a direct and proximate result of any negligence or breach of contract by any of the defendants' agents, servants or employees, acting within the scope of their authority or employment.

The court took the motion to dismiss under advisement and briefs were filed by the respective parties upon the issues raised by defendants' motion to dismiss. Subsequently the court denied such motion, "without prejudice to the right of the defendants to renew said motion on the same grounds at the end of the plaintiff's case." Thereupon, the defendants by their answer admitted the execution of the agreement with the plaintiff and that they entered upon the performance of the same, as alleged in the complaint. Also, defendants admitted that Harry Frontczak was one of the guards employed by the defendants and assigned to plaintiff's plant, but denied that the acts complained of and committed by him were within the scope of his employment or that such acts were committed while performing any act incident to his employment, and that plaintiff's damage was not sustained as a result of any of defendants' agents or servants acting within the scope of their employment. Defendants' answer, as its motion to dismiss, specifically averred that the complaint did not charge any acts of negligence against the defendants or that any damage was suffered as a result of such negligence, and that the complaint did not charge a breach of contract on the part of the defendants.

In the view which we take of the situation before us, there appears no occasion to narrate plaintiff's testimony in detail. . . .

. . . .

We agree with the lower court that there was no basis for recovery upon the theory of negligence. Plaintiff's evidence showed that Frontczak had been employed by the government in various capacities, in handling its mail, finances, records and personnel during the time of war. Under such circumstances, we think there was no negligence in his employment by defendants. More than that, plaintiff had an equal opportunity to observe his conduct, as well as that of all other guards, and it did not complain or request his removal. We also agree that in setting the fires he was not acting within the scope of his employment or in furtherance of the master's business. [Citations omitted.]

We need not pursue this negligence theory further, however, because it is no longer relied upon. Here, for the first time, plaintiff advances the theory that defendants were liable for breach of contract. As already noted, no such breach was alleged in the complaint and the record is plain that such a theory was not relied upon below. Neither is the liberalized rule which permits the amendment of a pleading to conform to the proof of any benefit to plaintiff. No such amendment was proposed, but even if it had been we doubt if it could have been properly permitted in view of plaintiff's proof. . . .

. . . .

Finally, if we were impressed with the theory of liability argued before this court, which we are not, we would not be justified in reversing the judgment because the case was neither tried nor decided below on such theory. As was said in Helvering v. Rubinstein, 8 Cir., 124 F.2d 969, 972:

"The rule that an appellate court will not ordinarily consider questions not tried below is an important rule of appellate procedure and one which is usually not unjust to litigants. It requires them to deal fairly and frankly with each other and with the trial tribunal with respect to their controversies. It prevents the trial of cases piecemeal or in installments. It tends to put an end to litigation."

And as said by this court in Maloney v. Brandt, 7 Cir., 123 F.2d 779, 782:

"It has long been a rule of practice that a reviewing Court will not consider assignments of error not called to the attention of the trial court where such matters do not concern the jurisdiction of the court. It would manifestly be unfair to hold that the trial court had erred in a matter it had not considered. Litigants are not entitled to hide a point in an obscure pleading and present it for the first time on review, but should fully and fairly acquaint the trial court with all matters relied upon."

This rule announced in the Maloney case was cited with approval by this court in Chatz v. Midco Oil Corp., 7 Cir., 152 F.2d 153, 154. In fact, the cases are legion where the same or a similar rule has been announced and followed. [Citations omitted.]

True, there are cases which, while recognizing the general rule, have held that where an injustice will result owing to the particular circumstances of the case, a reviewing court may consider questions which have not been pressed below. See Hormel v. Helvering, 312 U.S. 552, 556–557, 61 S.Ct. 719, 85 L.Ed. 1037. In Lambur v. Yates, 8 Cir., 148 F.2d 137, 138, the reviewing court in noticing an error not raised on the record stated, "This power is and should be sparingly exercised only for the purpose of preventing a miscarriage of justice and in cases in which the public interest is directly and substantially involved." And the exception to the general rule was followed in Schaff v. Claxton, Inc., 79 U.S.App.D.C. 207, 144 F.2d 532, 533, because a decision rendered subsequent to the trial below had changed the law as it was thought to be at the time of trial.

Plaintiff tried its case below on the negligence theory of liability and lost, and we discern nothing in the situation which would justify this court in reversing that decision so that plaintiff may again try its case on a different theory of liability. If the instant plaintiff be permitted to do that, it would seem that the losing party could do it in any case, and the general rule against such procedure would soon become an empty gesture.

The judgment appealed from is affirmed.

KERNER, CIRCUIT JUDGE, dissenting.

———

SEARS, ROEBUCK & CO. v. MARHENKE, 121 F.2d 598 (9th Cir. 1941). Infant *P* was scalded by hot water leaking from a hot water bag purchased from *D*. *P* sued for the resulting injuries. The case was tried before the court without a jury, and *P* obtained a judgment based upon a finding that *D* was negligent. On appeal, the circuit court of appeals held the evidence insufficient to sustain a finding of negligence. *P*'s brief on appeal had relied solely upon the theory of negligence. *D* had briefed and argued the question of implied warranty, contending it was not involved, and *P* had agreed that the real question was one of negligence and not warranty. The court then had directed the parties' attention to the state statute on implied warranty, and additional briefs had been filed on the question. *P* at this point had contended "that the allegations of the complaint were sufficient to sustain the judgment upon the ground of a breach of the warranty implied by statute."

The court then said that to recover under the statute *P* must plead and prove (1) that the buyer informed the seller of the particular purpose for which the goods were required and (2) that the buyer relied upon the seller's skill and judgment. "But," said the court, "the complaint failed to allege [the first] of these essential facts and the trial court made no finding as to the other." It found the pleadings and findings "altogether inconsistent with the theory of liability for breach of an implied warranty advanced in the supplementary brief." Nor was this a case, according to the court, where issues not raised by the pleadings were tried by express or implied consent, so Rule 15(b) had no application. The judgment was reversed "without prejudice to the right of plaintiff" to amend.

Judge Healy dissented. He thought that breach of warranty was sufficiently alleged, that *D* was apprised of the essential facts relied upon, that these facts were fully established by the evidence, and that *D* was not prejudiced by *P*'s "insistence on the theory of negligence." He pointed out that *D* made no claim of surprise and could not well do so because a substantial portion of its opening brief on appeal was devoted to a discussion of the warranty theory. He would have affirmed.[h]

———

WALL v. BRIM, 138 F.2d 478 (5th Cir.1943), after remand, 145 F.2d 492 (5th Cir.1944), cert. denied, 324 U.S. 857, 65 S.Ct. 858 (1945). *P* sued Dr. *D* for malpractice, claiming negligence in removal of a cyst from *P*'s neck and proving serious facial injury. *D*'s motion for a directed verdict was denied, as was his motion for judgment n.o.v. after a verdict for *P*. On appeal from the ensuing judgment, the circuit court of appeals held that there was no evidence of negligence, because *P* had failed to present any expert evidence. It noted, however, the undisputed evidence from both sides that *D* discovered after making his incision that the operation would not be the simple one he had secured *P*'s consent to perform ("simply pull it out like hulling a pea out of a pod") and that instead it would be a serious and difficult one, and that *D* nevertheless went ahead without disclosing these difficulties to the plaintiff, who was still conscious, and without obtaining a new consent. This, the court said, would amount to a battery or trespass for which *D* would be liable. Hence judgment for *D* was not ordered. Nor was the court willing to affirm the judgment for *P*, because the issue as to battery or trespass had not been developed and tried out below as it should have been. The cause was re-

[h] A similar last-ditch argument was made by the plaintiff in the Sierocinski case, supra p. 34. The case had been pleaded and tried on the ground of negligence, and on appeal *P* attempted to sustain his judgment on the basis of breach of warranty. The court rejected the argument and reversed, ordering final judgment for the defendant. The reversal was not, as in Marhenke, without prejudice to *P*'s right to amend, very likely because the court thought there was no merit in the breach of warranty theory.

manded for a new trial "with full right to the parties to amend their pleadings."

On remand, the case was tried again on amended pleadings asserting a claim for trespass. This time D testified that he told P of the unexpected conditions he found and that she consented to his going ahead. P testified that there was no such warning or consent. On this conflicting evidence the jury returned a verdict for P, and D again appealed the ensuing judgment. The most strongly argued point on appeal was D's contention that a new cause of action was introduced by the amendment more than two years after it arose and that the two-year statute of limitations was therefore a bar. The court rejected this contention, saying: "As was pointed out in the reversing opinion on the former appeal, the evidence on that trial definitely presented this ground for recovery and, under Federal Rules of Civil Procedure, rule 15(b), 28 U.S.C.A. following section 723c, it could then have been submitted to the jury if requested, though no formal amendment had been made. Under these circumstances, it would be a sticking in the bark of pure technicality to say that when the pleadings were later formally amended to conform to the evidence, the claim was then first presented. If, therefore, we could agree that the claim on which the verdict and judgment appealed from were based did present a new cause of action, it is quite clear that the introduction of that claim into the case long antedated the filing of the amended pleading." The court added that it could not agree that the claim on which recovery was based constituted a new cause of action, so that Rule 15(c) provided an additional reason to reject D's statute of limitations argument. The judgment was affirmed.

DIEMER v. DIEMER, 8 N.Y.2d 206, 168 N.E.2d 654, 203 N.Y.S.2d 829 (1960). This was a separation action. The complaint alleged that H, a Protestant, and W, a Catholic, were married, W agreeing to take up H's faith. After a child was born, religious conflict revolved around the child. Finally W told H that they were not married in the eyes of her church, and that there would be no more sexual relations unless there was a second ceremony in the Catholic Church. H refused such a ceremony, and W refused further sexual relations. On these facts, H sought a separation, characterizing W's conduct as "cruel and inhuman treatment." W counterclaimed for a separation, but neither in her answer nor at the trial did she deny the essentials of H's story. After making findings of fact, the trial court denied a separation to either spouse, saying that cruel and inhuman treatment was not established. The appellate division affirmed. The New York Court of Appeals reversed (5–2), awarding H a separation and holding that the facts alleged and proved established H's right to separation on the ground of abandonment.

Judge Fuld, for the majority, rejected the argument that *H* must fail because he did not denominate *W*'s conduct as "abandonment." He said: "Surely, we have advanced far beyond that hypertechnical period when form was all-important and a pleader had to attach the correct label to his complaint, at the risk of having it dismissed. It is enough now that a pleader states the facts making out a cause of action, and it matters not whether he gives a name to the cause of action at all or even that he gives it a wrong name."

Chief Judge Desmond, dissenting, quoted earlier opinions: "Pleadings and a distinct issue are essential to every system of jurisprudence . . . . It is fundamental that in civil actions the plaintiff must recover on the facts stated in his complaint, or not at all. In case a complaint proceeds on a definite, clear and certain theory, it will not support or permit another theory because it contains isolated or subsidiary statements consistent therewith." He added: "For no reason at all we are making a precipitous retreat from the good old rule that the parties to a private lawsuit fix the theory of suit and that no appellate court can present the losing side with a new theory."

UNIVERSE TANKSHIPS, INC. v. UNITED STATES, 528 F.2d 73 (3d Cir.1975). On appeal from a judgment for defendant in a negligence action tried without a jury, plaintiff attempted to invoke res ipsa loquitur. The court of appeals rebuffed the attempt and affirmed the judgment, explaining:

"[A] different theory of recovery may not be urged on appeal where prejudice would result to the other party. The test for prejudice in this context is whether the other party 'had a fair opportunity to defend and whether it could offer any additional evidence on the different theory.' Jurinko v. Edwin L. Wiegand Co., 477 F.2d 1038, 1045 (3d Cir.), vacated on other grounds, 414 U.S. 970, 94 S.Ct. 293, 38 L.Ed.2d 214 (1973); [other citations omitted].[3]

"We feel that consideration of plaintiff's argument in the nature of res ipsa loquitur would be prejudicial to the government. At the very least, if the government had been aware of this theory at trial it might have been more contentious about the facts of the accident. The government stipulated to several facts . . . and . . . relied primarily on the plaintiff's burden of proving the government negligent rather than offering its own version of the accident. Accordingly, we decline the invitation to reverse the district court on the

[3] We recognize that, in Jurinko, we considered the different theory on appeal. There, however, we found no prejudice to the defendant. Moreover, the theory was advanced to affirm the judgment of the district court, rather than to reverse it. . . . [To affirm the plaintiff's judgment after nonjury trial in that employment discrimination case, the court of appeals shifted the theory from discrimination against married women to discrimination against women, saying that the facts disclosed by the proof supported this theory.—Ed.]

theory in the nature of res ipsa loquitur, which was not raised in the district court."

ALTMAN v. ALTMAN, 653 F.2d 755 (3d Cir.1981). Sydney sued his brother Ashley to dissolve their partnerships. Defendant alleged that the partnerships had been dissolved years earlier by plaintiff's retirement, which would change the financial picture considerably. The court by a nonjury trial gave judgment for plaintiff, finding no retirement. On appeal, defendant contended that plaintiff was estopped from denying retirement by his sworn contrary statements in his Florida divorce proceedings. The court of appeals rejected that contention and affirmed the judgment, explaining:

"Our review of the record reveals that Ashley did not raise this issue in the district court. He did not plead judicial estoppel or argue to the court that Sydney should be estopped from denying he had retired by his statements in the Florida proceedings.[1] We have emphasized that 'absent exceptional circumstances, an issue not raised in the district court will not be heard on appeal.' Franki Foundation Co. v. Alger-Rau & Associates, Inc., 513 F.2d 581, 586 (3d Cir.1975). Exceptional circumstances have been recognized when the public interest requires that the issue be heard or when manifest injustice would result from the failure to consider the new issue. Id.; see Princeton Community Phone Book, Inc. v. Bate, 582 F.2d 706, 708 n.1 (3d Cir.), cert. denied, 439 U.S. 966, 99 S.Ct. 454, 58 L.Ed.2d 424 (1978) (first amendment issue not raised in district court considered on appeal because of great public interest); Richerson v. Jones, 572 F.2d 89, 97 (3d Cir.1978) (public interest served by hearing on appeal issue concerning exhaustion of administrative remedies under title VII). In addition, we have considered the merits of an issue raised for the first time on appeal when the new theory was advanced to affirm the district court and prejudice would not result to the other party.[2] See Jurinko v. Edwin L. Wiegand Co., 477 F.2d 1038 (3d Cir.), vacated on other grounds, 414 U.S. 970, 94 S.Ct. 293, 38 L.Ed.2d 214 (1973); cf.

---

[1] Ashley notes that he confronted Sydney with his Florida statements at trial and argued to the court that in light of those statements Sydney's testimony that he had not retired should not be 'believed.' As a result, Ashley maintains that the 'facts' supporting judicial estoppel were presented to the district court, and that any failure to use the term estoppel was merely a technical omission. However, under the estoppel theory now espoused by Ashley, Sydney's statements in the Florida proceedings would be deemed to have conclusively established the fact of his retirement in this litigation. Thus, Ashley's failure to use the term estoppel in the district court cannot be said to be a mere technical omission. Cf. Fed.R.Civ.P. 8(c) (estoppel must be pled as affirmative defense).

[2] We do not read Universe Tankships, Inc. v. United States, 528 F.2d 73 (3d Cir. 1975), as creating a rule that an issue may be raised for the first time on appeal solely because prejudice to the other party would not occur.

Walker v. Sinclair Refining Co., 320 F.2d 302, 305 (3d Cir.1963) (district court should not be reversed on grounds not argued before it).

"We find no exceptional circumstances in this case that would allow Ashley to raise judicial estoppel on appeal. No great public interest would be advanced by consideration of this issue. Moreover, Ashley offers no explanation for his failure to raise judicial estoppel in the district court, and we are not aware of any obstacles that prevented him from doing so. Cf. Princeton Community Phone Book, 582 F.2d at 708 n.1 (first amendment issue heard for first time on appeal because controlling Supreme Court case decided after district court's decision). Therefore, no manifest injustice to Ashley would result if we do not consider this issue. In addition, the new issue raised on appeal is presented as a ground for reversing the district court. As a result, we find that the rule barring a party from raising new issues on appeal precludes our consideration of Ashley's judicial estoppel argument."

Part Three

PLEADINGS, DISCOVERY, AND PRETRIAL CONFERENCES

TOPIC A. GENERAL OBSERVATIONS

SECTION 1. THE OBJECTIVES OF MODERN PLEADING

The aim of the Federal Rules, as stated in Rule 1, is "to secure the just, speedy, and inexpensive determination of every action." Any procedural system must aspire to this goal. In our adversary system of litigation, however, the initiative for taking procedural steps rests primarily on parties whose interest in attaining justice in the particular case is ordinarily less than their interest in victory. The person against whom a remedy is sought is generally not interested in a speedy determination of the action, and indeed he is likely to embrace any opportunity for delay that is open to him. Making litigation as expensive as possible for one's opponent is a tactic as old as the adversary system itself. Although we may deplore it, we must recognize the fact that counsel cannot be counted upon to cooperate fully in achieving the objectives of the procedural rules when it appears to be to their clients' advantage to thwart them. Hence the efficacy of a procedural system must be measured in part by the court's power to enforce the rules in the face of resistance by parties and counsel.

In appraising the role of pleading in the judicial process, we must consider not only its legitimate part in advancing a lawsuit to the point where it can be properly tried, but also its susceptibility to misuse and the effectiveness of judicial sanctions against misuse. Procedural reform in England and the United States was actuated by resentment against a system under which justice was defeated or delayed by overemphasis on the niceties of special pleading. The substitution of the "fact pleading" of the codes for the elaborate "issue pleading" of the common law did not, however, obviate the preliminary skirmishes, so often sham battles, over pleading points. The framers of the Federal Rules believed that the trouble lay in seeking to accomplish too much through the pleading process. Their solution was to subordinate the role of pleading still further and to place increased emphasis upon discovery, pretrial conferences, and the like as preliminary steps toward trial.

A central problem of this Part will be to try to put pleading in its proper perspective as one, but not the sole, method of pretrial interchange among the parties. In coming to a judgment as to what should be expected of pleading, it is only good sense to consider the extent to which other devices can better carry the burdens traditionally assigned to pleading.

What, then, should be accomplished prior to trial, either by pleading or by some other means? Professor Cleary has put it thus, in The Uses of Pleading, 40 Ky.L.J. 46, 46 (1951):

"Regardless of the means employed to achieve them, these factors seem to inhere inescapably in the concept of an orderly judicial process:

1. Notice to the opponent which is adequate to enable him to prepare and present his side of the case effectively;

2. Determination of the elements which are relevant to the ultimate decision and allocating between the parties the responsibility for bringing them into the litigation;

3. Isolation of the area of actual controversy;

4. Ascertaining the governing substantive principles.

"Without them, litigation has no apparent origin or discernible destination." [a]

It may be taken as a fair working hypothesis that each party to a lawsuit wants to find out as much as possible about his adversary's case and to disclose as little as possible about his own; the tactical advantage of being able to present testimony at the trial that an opponent is unprepared to meet is obvious. Equally obvious is the advantage of using such weapons as the rules provide to limit the opponent's area of offense or defense and, where possible, so to expose the barrenness of the opponent's claim or defense as to avoid a trial entirely. A party's pleading moves will often spring from these strategic considerations.

Whatever their purpose, attacks on pleadings entail delay and expense for the defender, and it will sometimes seem apparent that this was the attacker's goal.[b] Integral to the problem is the modern free-

---

[a] Judge Clark made this further observation as to the minimum that can be expected of pleadings: "They must sufficiently differentiate the situation of fact which is being litigated from all other situations to allow of the application of the doctrine of res judicata, whereby final adjudication of this particular case will end the controversy forever. As a natural corollary, they will also show the type of case brought, so that it may be assigned to the proper form of trial, whether by the jury in negligence or contract, or to a court, referee, or master, as in foreclosure, divorce, accounting, and so on." Clark, Simplified Pleading, 2 F.R.D. 456, 456–57 (1943).

[b] Judge Clark pointed to figures from Connecticut state courts collected for a period shortly predating the Federal Rules to demonstrate how rarely final judgment results from a hearing on demurrer or no motion to correct. He wrote: "As some available statistics show, even in the limited number of cases actually heard on demurrer or motion—perhaps roughly 2 per cent of all for each form of objection—judgment rarely follows (after perhaps 7 per cent of the cases where demurrer is filed, and 2 per cent where motion is filed). Clark and Shulman, A Study of Law Administration in Connecticut (1937) 218, 219; A Study of the Business of the Federal Courts (1934) Pt. II, cc. V, VI. Since amendment is free, even these are necessarily cases where the parties were content with this means of trial." Id. at 457 n.3.

dom of amendment, with the result that a challenge to a pleading, whether successful or not, is ordinarily not dispositive of the case in the trial court. And under some procedural systems a ruling on the sufficiency of a pleading may be immediately reviewed on appeal, thus causing further delay and expense and often still not finally ending the case. Shall we conclude that interlocutory appeal on pleading matters ought to be wholly prohibited? On the one hand, speedy and inexpensive justice is not achieved by forcing a defendant to go through what may be a long and costly trial on a claim that the appellate court eventually says is legally insufficient. On the other hand, the plaintiff whose trial is delayed by what turns out to be a fruitless appeal is equally denied speedy and inexpensive justice. Yet we cannot be certain who is aggrieved until the appellate court speaks.

Question: (1) To what extent should the judicial handling of pleading problems in the trial court be affected by the availability or nonavailability of interlocutory appeals?

SECTION 2. THE RELATION OF PLEADING TO PROOF

Professor James Bradley Thayer lists as the first of the "four great, fundamental rules which are said to govern the production of testimony" that "evidence must be relevant to what is alleged in pleading." J. Thayer, A Preliminary Treatise on Evidence at the Common Law 484–85 (1898). If the pleadings determine the elements upon which the ultimate decision depends, it readily follows that evidence not relevant to the allegations in the pleadings serves no proper purpose. Successful objections to evidence on this ground are a commonplace in the trial of cases.

1. Suppose proffered evidence is objected to at the trial as "not within the pleadings." The first question for the judge is whether the evidence bears on some proposition that is in issue under the pleadings. Is this always apparent from an inspection of the language of the pleadings, or are other problems involved? Will it make any difference in decision whether the pleadings are particularized or general?

2. Assume that proffered evidence is found not to be within the pleadings. Shall the evidence be excluded? Shall it be admitted then and there, the pleadings being amended to correspond to the proof? When will it be the proper course to allow an amendment at trial and let the evidence come in under it, but only after a continuance? When evidence not within the pleadings is offered, should a voluntary dismissal ever be allowed or a mistrial declared, with leave to amend the pleadings and retry the case?

3. If evidence is excluded on objection as not being within the pleadings and the appellate court holds that it was error to exclude it, the result may well be a new trial where the evidence might have

changed the outcome of the trial had it been received. But suppose evidence is erroneously received over the objection that it is outside the pleadings: what should be the consequences on appeal?

It will be seen that it is not enough to consider whether the proof conforms to the pleading. The further question is what consequences should attach to such a discrepancy—commonly called a variance. And again it is worth asking whether a court's attitude toward variance should be affected by the devices available in the jurisdiction for discovery and pretrial conference, and the extent to which those devices were employed in the particular case.

Related problems arise when evidence not within the pleadings is admitted without objection. To what extent should a party be entitled later to go back to the pleadings and complain of the absent allegations?

MANNING v. LOEW

Supreme Judicial Court of Massachusetts, 1943.
313 Mass. 252, 46 N.E.2d 1022.

Lummus, J. In this action of contract the plaintiff was the only witness on the question of liability. Her testimony tended to prove the following facts. The defendant lives in Boston, but the parties met in January, 1941, in a restaurant in Miami, Florida, where the plaintiff was employed as a waitress. The defendant owned a chain of moving picture theatres in New England, and also had such a theatre in Miami, where he gave the plaintiff employment. Later, at the invitation of the defendant, the plaintiff came to Boston, where the defendant met her. She later went to New York, but returned to Boston on request of the defendant.

When the plaintiff got back to Boston, the defendant met her, and told her, to use her words, that "if I would stay here in Boston, and not go back to New York, and be like a daughter to him, accompany him to his home and on trips and see him any time that he wanted to see me, and be a companion and daughter to him, that he would then put me in the movies; he would get me a screen test. He would see that I got this screen test; if I couldn't that he would produce a picture himself, he would star me in it." It could be found that the plaintiff accepted this offer and agreed to perform its terms.

Subsequently the plaintiff accompanied the defendant to his house, to eating places, to New York and other cities, and on a yachting trip. The defendant was living apart from his wife. In December, 1941, the defendant told the plaintiff that he was through with her and that he was not serious about the alleged agreement. The plaintiff then consulted a lawyer, and this action was begun. At the trial a verdict was directed for the defendant, subject to the plaintiff's exception.

The declaration set forth as the consideration for the defendant's promise that the plaintiff agreed "that she would devote herself at all times required by him [the defendant] to the companionship and service of the defendant and to accompany him to such places as he should designate." Nothing was said in the declaration about being a daughter, or like a daughter, to him, though that was an essential part of the contract according to the plaintiff's testimony, by which she is bound. There was therefore a variance between the declaration and the proof. The action of the judge in directing a verdict for the defendant was not error, even though there was no express statement that the ruling was made with the pleadings in mind. Ferris v. Boston & Maine Railroad, 291 Mass. 529, 533, 197 N.E. 506.

But if we consider the merits without regard to the pleadings, the direction of a verdict for the defendant was not error. Not only did the plaintiff admit that she had sexual intercourse at various times with the defendant (French v. Boston Safe Deposit & Trust Co., 282 Mass. 600, 607, 185 N.E. 493), but she also admitted that she had been in bed with another man, and had gone to resorts with that man after the defendant had left her at her hotel for the night, as he thought. Her admitted conduct was not consistent with her promise to act as a daughter to the defendant.

Exceptions overruled.

Questions: (2) Might the plaintiff have avoided the hazard of variance by pleading differently? Suppose she had merely alleged that the defendant's promise was made for "a valuable consideration"? Would this be held sufficient under a typical code? Compare California Packing Corp. v. Kelly Storage & Distrib. Co., 228 N.Y. 49, 126 N.E. 269 (1920), with Foley v. Cowan, 80 Cal.App.2d 70, 181 P.2d 410 (1947). Should it be held sufficient under the Federal Rules?

(3) If such a generalized statement is acceptable and if Miss Manning has so pleaded, what can Mr. Loew's lawyer do, under a procedural system like the Federal Rules, to expedite a decision of the case if in fact the consideration for the promise, although "valuable," was also illegal? Cf. Richardson v. Gregory, 219 A.D. 211, 219 N.Y.S. 397 (1927).

VARIANCE

Variance was heavily penalized at common law, and the same was true in some states long after ameliorative provisions had been introduced by statute in England.[c] A plaintiff who offered evidence of all

---

[c] 3 & 4 Will. 4, ch. 42, § 23 (1833). This statute gave the nisi prius judge power to amend at trial to cure a variance between pleading and proof that was "not material to the merits of the case," upon reasonable terms as to costs and postponement. Previously, no amendment could be allowed except by the full bench of the court sitting at Westminster. In much earlier times, Parliament had provided remedies for purely formal defects in pleadings. For a chronological list of these "Statutes of Jeofails and Amendments," commencing

the necessary elements to prove a cause of action might nevertheless be deprived of the chance for a jury verdict if in some particular his proof failed to conform to the allegations in his declaration. Illustrative of the extremes to which this doctrine went are two Illinois cases. In Spangler v. Pugh, 21 Ill. 85 (1859), the plaintiff declared upon a promissory note for $2579.57. The note offered in evidence, and received over the defendant's objection, was for $2579.57½. The appellate court reversed the lower court's judgment for the plaintiff on account of this variance and remanded the cause with leave to amend, saying: "However much courts may regret that a slip in pleading should delay the party in the administration of justice, the rules of law must be observed. If the rule were relaxed in this case, it would be to sanction a looseness in practice that might eventually be productive of more injury than benefit." In Wabash Western Ry. v. Friedman, 146 Ill. 583, 30 N.E. 353 (1892), the defendant railroad ran from Point A through Points B and C to Point D. The plaintiff, suing for personal injuries, alleged that he became a passenger at Point B and was being carried to Point C when the accident occurred. The evidence showed that the plaintiff became a passenger at Point A and was going to Point D when injured between Points B and C. The defendant's objection on the ground of variance was overruled in the trial court, but the appellate court reversed and remanded, saying that although there was no need to have alleged the termini, it was necessary, having alleged them, to prove them as laid.

B. Shipman, Handbook of Common-Law Pleading 515–16 (3d ed. 1923), says:

"The harsh rule by which the courts punish a party who pleads immaterial facts by compelling him to prove them literally as alleged, although they need never have been set out to state the cause of action, is shockingly illustrated in negligence cases. New trials have frequently been granted for want of proof of wholly unnecessary allegations. The pleader has to steer his course between Scylla and Charybdis, and is driven to state his case in a confusing variety of counts, which multiply and complicate the issues. He has to learn just how general he may make his allegations, avoiding all unnecessary detail, on the one hand, and the danger of stating mere conclusions of law or fact, on the other. By unnecessary particularity in a descriptive statement, he binds himself to prove this surplusage in addition to the essential facts of the case." [d]

So there were various ways in which a variance might occur, but to generalize, they all revolved around the more general rule that a

in 1340, see Clark & Yerion, Amendment and Aider of Pleadings, 12 Minn.L.Rev. 97, 125 (1928).

[d] If the unnecessary matter pleaded was wholly foreign and irrelevant, it would be ignored or on motion stricken out, but it would not vitiate the pleading or require conforming proof. The rule Shipman discusses dealt instead with pleaded matter that was "descriptive" of what was essential to the case.

claim or defense could be sustained only if it was both pleaded in full *and* proved in conformity therewith.

Even at common law, as Shipman suggests, the harshness of the rule against variance was mitigated by the possibility of stating the same cause of action in various ways in different counts. If, for example, in a negligence action the plaintiff was uncertain what the proof would show, he could plead several specifications of negligence. There was no penalty for such over-pleading; if the proof supported any one of the specifications, a verdict for the plaintiff could be sustained.[e] Today there are in most states statutes or rules that provide less cumbersome and more general antidotes.

CALIFORNIA CODE OF CIVIL PROCEDURE

§ 469. No variance between the allegation in a pleading and the proof is to be deemed material, unless it has actually misled the adverse party to his prejudice in maintaining his action or defense upon the merits. Whenever it appears that a party has been so misled, the Court may order the pleading to be amended, upon such terms as may be just.

§ 470. *Immaterial variance, how provided for.* Where the variance is not material, as provided in the last section, the Court may direct the fact to be found according to the evidence, or may order an immediate amendment, without costs.

§ 471. *What not to be deemed a variance.* Where, however, the allegation of the claim or defense to which the proof is directed, is unproved, not in some particular or particulars only, but in its general scope and meaning, it is not to be deemed a case of variance, within the last two sections, but a failure of proof.

WASIK v. BORG

United States Court of Appeals, Second Circuit, 1970.
423 F.2d 44.

Before LUMBARD, CHIEF JUDGE, and FRIENDLY and FEINBERG, CIRCUIT JUDGES.

FEINBERG, CIRCUIT JUDGE. While driving his station wagon in Rutland, Vermont, Robert W. Borg rammed into the rear of a vehicle operated by appellee Albert J. Wasik, injuring both Wasik and his automobile. Wasik sued Borg, a resident of Maryland, in the United States District Court for the District of Vermont, basing jurisdiction on diversity of citizenship. Borg served a third-party complaint on appellant Ford Motor Company, alleging that the accident was due to

[e] See supra p. 352.

a dangerous defect in the design or manufacture of the automobile, which had caused it to accelerate suddenly. Ford answered, denying Borg's claims and alleging his contributory negligence. Ford also filed an answer to Wasik's original complaint, denying knowledge of the facts of the accident. Trial was held in the summer of 1969 before the late Ernest W. Gibson, J., and a jury, which found that Ford—but not Borg—was liable to Wasik. Damages were assessed at $8,700, and judgment was entered in that amount. On Ford's appeal, we affirm.

The jury indicated by its verdict that it believed that Borg was free from negligence, and that the accident was caused exclusively by a defect in the design or manufacture of his vehicle. Ford contends that it was improper to hold it directly liable to Wasik because Ford was a mere third-party defendant whose liability was contingent on the liability of Borg, for whom the jury found. In another age this argument might have been persuasive, but appellant has ignored two vital factors which we consider dispositive—the course of the proceedings below and the Federal Rules of Civil Procedure. While it would doubtless have been better if appellee Wasik had amended his complaint to include a claim against Ford once it became obvious that a major theory of recovery was to be Ford's liability as manufacturer of a defective product, Wasik's failure to do so does not require reversal.

Rule 14(a) specifically contemplates that

The plaintiff may assert any claim against the third-party defendant arising out of the transaction or occurrence that is the subject matter of the plaintiff's claim against the third-party plaintiff

. . . .

and Rule 15(b) provides:

When issues not raised by the pleadings are tried by express or implied consent of the parties, they shall be treated in all respects as if they had been raised in the pleadings. Such amendment of the pleadings as may be necessary to cause them to conform to the evidence and to raise these issues may be made upon motion of any party at any time, even after judgment; but failure so to amend does not affect the result of the trial of these issues.

. . .

Borg's complaint put Ford on notice that it would be called to account for alleged defects in its product leading to the accident. Throughout the trial, Ford was apparently treated by counsel and the trial judge as a defendant subject to direct liability. The trial record makes it clear that Ford had the opportunity to, and did, litigate all the factual issues essential to the jury verdict, particularly Borg's claim that the throttle cable on his Ford vehicle was in a "runaway condition." All the issues were raised, either by Wasik's pleadings or by Borg's. And it is also evident that counsel for Wasik early sought the benefit of Borg's theory of the accident. Borg was cross-examined as part of

Wasik's main case; Wasik's counsel encouraged Borg to describe his non-negligent operation of the vehicle both before and after its sudden "take off." Appellant cross-examined both Wasik and Borg during this early stage of the trial. Had the parties not understood that Ford could be held directly liable to appellee, this tactic of Wasik would hardly be explicable; if the jury were to find, as it ultimately did, that Borg had not been negligent and that the vehicle had been defective, appellee could recover only from Ford, if at all. We see no reason to treat issues which were fully litigated as if they had not been litigated, where no prejudice to appellant has been suggested or is apparent from the record.[1] Under these circumstances, we do not think it was error for the trial judge to treat appellant as a defendant potentially subject to primary liability. See Falls Industries, Inc. v. Consolidated Chemical Industries, Inc., 258 F.2d 277, 283–287 (5th Cir.1958); 3 J. Moore, Federal Practice ¶ 15.13.

[Discussion of other alleged errors is omitted.]

Judgment affirmed.

ROBBINS v. JORDAN

United States Court of Appeals, District of Columbia Circuit, 1950.
181 F.2d 793.

Before EDGERTON, CLARK and FAHY, CIRCUIT JUDGES.

CLARK, CIRCUIT JUDGE. The court below directed a verdict in favor of the defendant at the close of the plaintiffs' case. The plaintiffs have prosecuted this appeal to test the validity of that judgment.

The action sounds in tort for malpractice. The plaintiffs claim negligence on the part of Dr. Jordan in that he failed to take pelvic measurements of Mrs. Robbins at the proper time and as a result a normal birth was attempted when timely measurements would have indicated to a practitioner of average skill and knowledge in this locality that a Caesarean operation was necessary. The husband asks damages for loss of services and consortium while Mrs. Robbins asks compensation for certain resulting injuries including pain and suffering.

The principal error assigned by the appellants to the proceedings below involves the failure of the trial judge to allow them to amend their pleadings in order to introduce evidence to the effect that the defendant held himself out to them as a specialist in obstetrics.

The complaint alleged that the defendant was a "duly licensed physician practicing medicine in the District of Columbia and holding

---

[1] It is undisputed that Wasik never formally sought to amend his complaint prior to or during trial to assert a claim directly against Ford. Such a formal motion was made in this court, and if it were necessary to rule upon it, we would grant it.

himself out to the general public, including the plaintiffs, as a practicing physician, and a doctor of medicine, and one well qualified in the treatment of disorders and diseases of women." But the court ruled that these allegations were not broad enough to permit proof that the defendant had represented himself to the plaintiffs as an obstetrician. After this ruling the appellants sought permission to amend their complaint so as to enable them to introduce the evidence, but the court again ruled against them and disallowed the amendment.

There can be no question that the plaintiffs were prejudiced by these rulings. Instead of being able to proceed on the theory that the defendant was a specialist and was therefore held to a standard of care and skill normally exercised by such specialists, they were compelled to try their case on the theory that the duty owed them by the defendant was to be measured by that standard of skill and knowledge required of a general practitioner. That the standard of care and skill required of the specialist in obstetrics is stricter than that required of the general practitioner is demonstrable from the record. Take for example the testimony of the roentgenologist who examined Mrs. Robbins with reference to the anticipated delivery of her second child.[1] He stated on cross-examination that in his experience, since 1930, no general practitioner had resorted to the use of pelvimetry.[2] And yet since he testified that he had made a great many thousand of such measurements, it is reasonable to suppose that they were made at the behest of specialists.

Having found that the court's refusal to grant the plaintiffs leave to amend their complaint worked to their prejudice, the only other problem for us to decide,[3] therefore, is whether or not the learned trial judge exceeded the limits of his discretion in so refusing. Rule 15(b) of the Federal Rules of Civil Procedure, 28 U.S.C.A., provides in part: ". . . If evidence is objected to at the trial on the ground that it is not within the issues made by the pleadings, the court may allow the pleadings to be amended and shall do so freely when the presentation of the merits of the action will be subserved thereby and the objecting party fails to satisfy the court that the admission of such evidence would prejudice him in maintaining his action or defense on the merits. The court may grant a continuance to enable the objecting party to meet such evidence."

As was said in International Ladies' Garment Workers' Union v. Donnelly Garment Co., 8 Cir., 1941, 121 F.2d 561, 563: "The Supreme Court of the United States has fixed the limits of permissible amendments with increasing liberality and has ruled that a change of the

---

[1] The second child was delivered by Caesarean section.

[2] The measurement of the female pelvis by X-ray.

[3] Although we do not necessarily mean to imply that we agree with the trial judge that the allegations of the complaint are not broad enough to permit in proof that the defendant held himself out as a specialist in obstetrics, we prefer to decide this case on other grounds.

legal theory of the action is no longer accepted as a test of the propriety of a proposed amendment. . . . Rule 15 of the Rules of Civil Procedure . . . expresses the same liberality with respect to the amendment of pleadings."

. . . .

In the instant case the amendment proposed by the plaintiffs did not state a new cause of action. It simply altered the theory of their case. The only reason for denying the proposed amendment was stated by the lower court in the following discussion which was had at the beginning of the trial.

"The Court: Well, I think that would come too late, because that prejudices the defendant in his defense.

"Mr. Quimby: The case has not started.

"The Court: I know, but I am assuming that, being the type of lawyer that I know Mr. Daily is, he has prepared his defense. If the plaintiff is going to change his theory of the case, then he is in a position where he ought to be protected from going forward on a change of theory."

There can be no question that a defendant should be protected from surprise resulting from a change of theory; but it is our opinion that the court erred in the method it chose to protect him. The proper procedure would have been to grant the defendant a continuance in order to meet the new evidence. But it was beyond the limits of its judicial discretion to refuse to allow the amendment.

. . . .

Reversed and remanded.

Questions: (4) The court in Robbins v. Jordan said the proper procedure would have been to grant the defendant a continuance. How might a continuance have been helpful to him?

(5) Suppose testimony that the defendant had represented himself to the plaintiffs as an obstetrician had been admitted without objection. What would you expect the subsequent course of the proceedings to have been?

(6) Suppose the specified testimony had been admitted over objection by the defendant, and there had been a verdict for the plaintiffs. Should the plaintiffs be able to hold their verdict on appeal if the appellate court believes that the objection ought to have been sustained? Should it make any difference whether the defendant, after the overruling of his objection, had requested a continuance? Should it make any difference if the defendant, after the overruling of his objection, had either tried to discredit the testimony by cross-examination or presented evidence of his own to discredit it?

COX v. FREMONT COUNTY PUBLIC BUILDING AUTHORITY, 415 F.2d 882 (10th Cir.1969). This was an action against a building contractor and his surety for breach of contract for construction of a courthouse. Leaking and breaking of glass in a skylight in the court-house roof were the center of the controversy. The trial judge re-fused to charge on the defense that the skylight problem resulted from defective design, stating that the assertion of this theory was outside the pleadings and was untimely. In affirming a judgment for the plaintiff, the appellate court said:

"Appellants say that since proof on the defective design theory was admitted without objection, any contention that the issue was not pleaded was waived. Objection was made when the principal testimo-ny on the theory was offered. The trial court stated that the proof was admitted because of its relevance to the separate issue of wheth-er a lack of maintenance caused the skylight problem. We conclude that the defective design issue was not tried by consent. It was not raised in the answers filed or in the pretrial order fixing the issues. Refusal of the instruction was not error. Miller v. Brazel, 300 F.2d 283 (10th Cir.1962). Complaint is also made of denial of a motion to amend during the trial to include the defense of a defective design. The circumstances show no abuse of the trial court's discretion by denying the motion. Heilig v. Studebaker Corporation, 347 F.2d 686 (10th Cir.1965)."

Question: (7) How do the Federal Rules solve the Shipman problem of a lack of conforming proof with respect to wholly unnecessary allegations?

ALLEGATIONS OF TIME AND PLACE

Common-law pleading required certainty in pleadings, including certainty of time and place. Somewhat paradoxically, although alle-gations of time and place had to be specifically made, else the plead-ing would be defective, they generally were considered exceptions to the rule forbidding variance and did not have to be proved as alleged. For instance, the allegation of one time and the proof of another would not be a fatal variance, the allegation of time being regarded as immaterial. As another consequence of immateriality, a declara-tion seeming to show on its face that the action was barred by the statute of limitations was not demurrable. This rule, formalistic in its origin, was later rationalized on the ground that if the defense of limitations could be raised by demurrer, the plaintiff would be de-prived of his chance to assert in his replication to the limitations de-fense that special circumstances, such as conduct of the defendant constituting estoppel or waiver, avoided the statute.

Some of the codes specifically provide for a demurrer, or its equiv-alent, when the complaint shows that the action is barred by the stat-ute of limitations. In the absence of such codified guidance, there has been diversity of opinion as to when a demurrer will put the timeliness of suit in issue. See Atkinson, Pleading the Statute of Limitations, 36 Yale L.J. 914 (1927).

In making allegations of time and place material for the purpose of testing the sufficiency of a pleading, Federal Rule 9(f) departs from the earlier practice. It is silent as to the necessity of such allegations, but simply states their materiality when they are made.

Questions: (8) In the light of Rule 9(f), should a federal action be dismissed on a motion under Rule 12(b)(6) if the complaint on its face shows that it is time-barred? Does Rule 8(c), listing the statute of limitations as an affirmative defense, have any bearing on your answer? See 5 Wright & Miller § 1277.

(9) If a federal complaint makes no allegation as to time or place, what remedy should be open to the defendant? See id. § 1309.

BURLINGTON TRANSP. CO. v. JOSEPHSON
United States Circuit Court of Appeals, Eighth Circuit, 1946.
153 F.2d 372.

[Plaintiff sued for false arrest and imprisonment at Rapid City, South Dakota, and obtained judgment on a jury verdict in the amount of $19,500, with costs in the sum of $44.50. Defendants appealed. Several errors were assigned, but only those relating to damages are discussed herein.

[The allegations in the complaint as to damages were as follows:

"III. Plaintiff was thereby damaged and injured in his character, good name and reputation; he has suffered intense embarrassment, humiliation and mental anguish; he was compelled to incur and pay attorneys fees and costs in a large amount to obtain his release from said arrest and confinement; he was thereby necessarily compelled to be away from his business and suffered a large consequent loss, all to his damage in the sum of $100,000.00."]

Before SANBORN, THOMAS, and RIDDICK, CIRCUIT JUDGES.

THOMAS, CIRCUIT JUDGE.

. . . .

Josephson testified in his own behalf saying that he resides in New York City; that his business or profession is that of a physician engaged in the specialized practice relating to the eye, ear, nose and throat . . . .

. . . .

On the question of damages he testified that he was worried and anxious and quite a bit embarrassed by the arrest; and that his attorney's fees and costs for his release were approximately $500.

Over the objection of counsel for the defendants he testified that due to his delay in returning to New York occasioned by his remain-

ing in Rapid City for his trial he sustained large losses in connection
with the remodeling of a building which he had recently purchased;
that because of the delay he missed a conference with a contractor
with whom he was negotiating for the remodeling, and the delay resulted in a loss of rentals and increased cost of material and labor.

. . . .

The gist of defendants' complaint . . . is that damages, if sustained by reason of remodeling a building in New York, are special
and not general damages, and that recovery for such damages could
not be had because they were not pleaded and because they are speculative.

[The court here quoted Rule 9(g).]

In the case of Simmons v. Leighton, 60 S.D. 524, 244 N.W. 883,
884, the Supreme Court of South Dakota said: "The distinction between general and special damages and the necessity of a special allegation to permit proof and recovery of damages is well settled. Special, as distinguished from general, damages are those which are the
natural but not the necessary consequence of the act complained of.
17 C.J. 715. The plaintiff under a general allegation of damages may
recover all such damages as are the natural and necessary result of
such injuries as are alleged for the law implies their sequence. 2
Sutherland on Damages (4th Ed.) § 418. Not every loss which may
result from an injury is a natural and necessary result of the injury.
To permit recovery of other or special damages, there must be allegation of the specific facts showing such damages to apprise the defendant of the nature of the claim against him."

This distinction between general and special damages prevails
generally. C.J.S., Damages, § 2; 15 Am.Jur., Damages, § 10. General compensatory damages only were claimed in this case. In other
words, only such damages were alleged in the complaint as are the
natural consequence of the false arrest and false imprisonment, such
as humiliation, embarrassment and the costs incident to obtaining a
release from detention. In the federal courts an indispensable allegation in a demand for special damages is a statement "of the special
circumstances giving rise to the special damages." Huyler's v. Ritz-
Carlton Restaurant & Hotel Co., D.C., 6 F.2d 404, 406, 407.

But the plaintiff claims that the pleading was sufficient to entitle
him to special damages. Such claim is unwarranted. . . . His
proof showed that he is a professional, not a business, man. The allegation that "he was thereby necessarily compelled to be away from
his business" specifies only loss of time in the practice of his profession. The rule is well settled that "In the case of a professional man
the proper measure for damages for loss of time is the amount he
would have earned by the practice of his profession." 15 Am.Jur.,
Damages, § 97. No loss of professional earnings whatever was
shown.

The damages, if any, arising out of the remodeling of the apartment building in New York were special damages, and the court erred . . . in admitting the objectionable evidence, and in permitting recovery under the instructions. We need not pass upon the denial of defendants' motion for a new trial on the ground of these erroneous rulings, since a new trial must be granted anyway.

. . . .

For the errors pointed out the judgment appealed from is reversed and the case remanded with instructions to grant a new trial.

_____

PLEADING SPECIAL DAMAGES

The requirement of Rule 9(g) that special damages be specifically stated reflects the traditional doctrine. The line between general and special damages is not, however, clearly drawn, nor is the degree of specificity called for by Rule 9(g) settled by the cases.

When special damages are sought in addition to general damages, the specific pleading requirement is aimed to protect the defendant from surprise at trial. This gives a handle on what kind of damages should be deemed special. Moreover, this sheds light on the required specificity: great detail is not necessary to give notice. The defendant alerted to a claim for special damages may resort to a motion for a more definite statement if he cannot frame a responsive pleading, and he may pursue discovery in order to prepare for trial.

In certain types of cases special damages are an essential element of the plaintiff's claim for relief. If special damages are not pleaded, the complaint is subject to dismissal for failure to state a claim. This requirement exists primarily in "disfavored causes of action," such as defamation where the words are not actionable per se, disparagement of property, and trade libel. Here considerable particularity of allegation may be required. See generally Note, The Definition and Pleading of Special Damage Under the Federal Rules of Civil Procedure, 55 Va.L.Rev. 542 (1969).

Questions: (10) In a diversity of citizenship case, to what extent is state law controlling with respect to special damages and to what extent federal law?

(11) What, if any, relationship is there between the pleading requirement as to special damages and the reasoning of Hadley v. Baxendale, 156 Eng. Rep. 145 (Ex.1854), to the effect that damages not within the contemplation of the defendant at the time of contracting are not recoverable?

_____

NIEDLAND v. UNITED STATES, 338 F.2d 254 (3d Cir.1964). Plaintiff, operator of an Arthur Murray School of Dancing, sued the United States under the Federal Tort Claims Act, 28 U.S.C. § 1346(b), for personal injuries sustained in a collision between his car and a

Post Office vehicle. Plaintiff offered testimony at trial to prove that by reason of his injuries, it had been necessary for him to employ a full-time assistant at a certain salary. There was no objection to this testimony, and the government did not request a continuance to meet this evidence; and government counsel cross-examined plaintiff and plaintiff's medical witness on the need for an assistant, and also questioned the defense medical witnesses on this point. At the close of the testimony, government counsel stated that he objected to any argument respecting the cost of hiring an assistant because this matter had not been specially pleaded. The court overruled this objection. On appeal from a judgment for plaintiff, the government asserted error with respect to the damage award. The appellate court said: "It is clear that even under the more generalized notice pleadings of the Federal Civil Rules, special damages must be specifically pleaded. . . . It is equally clear that expenditures for the hiring of a substitute are special damages, under both federal and state law."

Question: (12) Having reached this conclusion, should the court sustain the government's claim of error?

TOPIC B. THE COMPLAINT

SECTION 1. STATING THE CLAIM

The essential elements of a cause of action or a claim for relief are drawn from the substantive law. The form of statement required of a complaint is a matter of procedure. No attempt will be made here to explore the substantive requirements, but the following generalizations, from F. James & G. Hazard, Civil Procedure 98, 112 (2d ed. 1977), on the elements of negligence and breach of contract claims may be helpful examples for use in studying the upcoming pages:

"The elements of a cause of action or claim for negligence are these: (1) A duty to use care must be owed by defendant to plaintiff; (2) there must be a breach of that duty, (3) which is a proximate cause of (4) injury to plaintiff. In general, the plaintiff must cover each of these elements in his complaint. A few states also require plaintiff in a negligence case to allege his own freedom from contributory negligence.

"The elements of a cause of action or claim for breach of contract are these: (1) a contract or agreement involving a quid pro quo (or the presence of some other factor which under substantive law makes an agreement binding); (2) performance by plaintiff of all conditions precedent to be performed by him; and (3) breach of the contract by defendant. Actual damage caused by breach of contract is not an essential element of a claim in the way it is for negligence . . . . Plaintiff is, of course, also entitled to actual damages if he satisfies the rules of pleading and proof . . . ."

DEGREE OF SPECIFICITY REQUIRED

A major problem is the degree of detail or specificity required. The broad outline of the federal approach has already been considered.[a] We have also adverted to the contrast between Federal Rule 8(a) and § 142 of the Field Code, typical of the provisions still prevailing in many code jurisdictions.[b] Garcia v. Hilton Hotels International, Inc., 97 F.Supp. 5 (D.P.R.1951), further illustrates the difference between a permissible federal complaint and the customary code requirements. A former employee alleged that he "was violently discharged by the defendant, being falsely and slanderously accused[c] of

[a] See supra pp. 33 – 36.

[b] See supra pp. 393 – 94.

[c] The introduction of an allegation by the participial phrase "being . . . accused" would have made it subject to special demurrer at common law. This is

436

being engaged in bringing women from outside the Hotel and introducing them into the rooms thereof for the purpose of developing prostitution in the Hotel." This would be demurrable under the typical code provision calling for a statement of the facts constituting a cause of action, just as it would have been at common law.[d] Publication of a defamation was and is a necessary substantive element of the cause of action, failure of proof of which is fatal. In Garcia, the court agrees that the complaint fails to state "in so many words" a publication, but nevertheless upholds the complaint as stating a claim upon which relief can be granted. The court explains its result thus: "While in a technical sense, this language states a conclusion, it is clear that plaintiff used it intending to charge publication of the slanderous utterance and it would be unrealistic for defendant to claim that it does not so understand the allegations. See, Edelman v. Locker, D.C., 6 F.R.D. 272, 274. Clearly, under such allegations it reasonably may be conceived that plaintiff, upon trial, could adduce evidence tending to prove a publication. If the provisions of rule 8(a) are not to be negatived by recourse to rule 12(b), the statement in . . . the complaint must be deemed sufficient."

If the pleader's failure lies in the statement of claim as distinguished from the existence in fact of a valid claim, as is very often the case, the expensive paper battle as to formal sufficiency causes delay, takes up valuable judicial time, and may end merely in giving

an illustration of "recital pleading." Its vice is that it assumes facts instead of alleging facts. Other types of recital pleading were allegations commencing with "whereas" or "notwithstanding the fact that." Some decisions in code states have even held such pleading insufficient against a general demurrer. E.g., Malott v. Sample, 164 Ind. 645, 74 N.E. 245 (1905); Thompson v. Read, 63 Misc. 235, 118 N.Y.S. 452 (1909) ("The foregoing words being spoken in the presence of . . . " held to be an insufficient allegation of publication in a slander action). How would you answer the contention that recital pleading is prohibited by Rule 8(e)(1)? Whether forbidden or not, recital pleading is not artistic pleading under the Federal Rules or in code-pleading states.

[d] Slander was one of those disfavored actions as to which the common-law pleading requirements were extremely strict. After setting forth the essentials of a declaration in slander, Shipman characterizes them as "an elaborate and absurd jargon of recitals and explanations which obscure the real issues to be tried almost as effectually as if the pleadings were still drawn in Latin." He then quotes Odgers in his work on libel and slander as follows: "Again, in Ball v. Roane (1593) Cro.Eliz. 308, the words were: 'There was never a robbery committed within forty miles of Wellingborough but thou hadst thy part in it.' After a verdict for the plaintiff, the court arrested judgment, 'because it was not averred there was any robbery committed within forty miles, etc., for otherwise it is no slander.' So in Foster v. Browning (1625) Cro.Jac. 688, where the words were, 'Thou art as arrant a thief as any is in England,' the court arrested judgment 'because the plaintiff had not averred that there was any thief in England.' But the climax was reached in a case cited in Dacy v. Clinch (1661) 1 Sid. 53, where the defendant had said to the plaintiff, 'As sure as God governs the world, or King James this kingdom, you are a thief.' After verdict for the plaintiff, the defendant moved in arrest of judgment, on the ground that there was no averment on the record that God did govern the world, or King James this kingdom. But here the court drew the line, and held that 'these things were so apparent' that neither of them need be averred." B. Shipman, Handbook of Common-Law Pleading 219–20 (3d ed. 1923).

plaintiff's counsel a lesson in pleading. It will not, however, finally dispose of the action because of the freedom in obtaining leave to amend. A lack of clarity in the complaint would seemingly be better handled via Rule 12(e) or, better yet, discovery or a pretrial conference. In the relatively rare case where the real problem is inability to state a good claim because there is not one in fact, devices other than pleading challenges make it possible to expose the situation without a trial. For example, if publication were genuinely a problem in Garcia, the defendant could raise the point by a motion for summary judgment under Rule 56, showing by affidavit or otherwise that there was no publication.

How far does this tolerance for lack of detail in a complaint extend in federal practice? The Supreme Court said in Conley v. Gibson, supra p. 35, echoing similar pronouncements in lower-court cases, that "a complaint should not be dismissed for failure to state a claim unless it appears beyond doubt that the plaintiff can prove no set of facts in support of his claim which would entitle him to relief."

Questions: (1) *P*'s complaint simply alleges that *D* is legally liable to *P* for damages in a named amount. *D* moves to dismiss under Rule 12(b)(6). What result?

(2) *P* alleges a contract claim with no reference to consideration. Assuming that a gratuitous promise is as a matter of substantive law not enforceable on the given facts, should a motion to dismiss be granted? If not, what might *D* do?

(3) *P*, asserting that he was a guest passenger in *D*'s automobile, states a personal-injury claim in language drawn from Form 9 to the effect that *D* drove his motor vehicle negligently. Assuming that as a matter of substantive law gross negligence is an essential element of a guest passenger's case (as is the law in many states), should a motion to dismiss be granted? If so, what might *P* do?

PLEADING FACTS NECESSARY TO CONSTITUTE CAUSE OF ACTION: PROS AND CONS

The arguments of the adherents of the code requirement of pleading the facts necessary to constitute a cause of action include the following:

1. The code pleader must think through his case, evolving a tenable theory and ascertaining what facts are necessary to support that theory. This process may satisfy him that his client has no valid claim, whereas the sloppy pleading permitted under the Federal Rules does not necessitate this disciplined thinking and hence leads to unfounded lawsuits.

2. The imprecision of pleading tolerated under the Federal Rules creates a needless uncertainty as to the issues and a resultant risk of surprise at trial. To guard against this hazard the litigant has to

undertake extensive discovery, costing him time and money that could be saved by maintaining the code-pleading requirements.

3. The clarification of issues required under code pleading facilitates summary judgment motions.

4. The trial is likely to take longer under the Federal Rules. The trial judge will let in doubtful evidence because it will not be clear to him, especially in the early stages of the case, what the bounds of relevance are going to be. It is the course of safety not to risk reversal by excluding testimony the significance of which may become apparent as the case develops.

5. The clarification of issues required under code pleading facilitates the application of the doctrine of res judicata.

Although the number of states with a rule patterned on Federal Rule 8(a)(2) has steadily increased, the adherents of the code form have successfully held the line in many states. In modernizing the procedure of New Jersey by comprehensive rules of court in 1948, the New Jersey Supreme Court followed the Federal Rules to a substantial extent but did not accept Rule 8(a)(2). The parallel New Jersey Court Rule 4:5–2 reads as follows: "A pleading which sets forth a claim for relief, whether an original claim, counterclaim, cross-claim or third-party claim, shall contain a statement of the facts on which the claim is based showing that the pleader is entitled to relief . . . ."

There have also been guerrilla attacks on the Federal Rule itself. The Judicial Conference of the Ninth Circuit that was held on September 11, 1952, adopted a resolution recommending the amendment of Rule 8(a)(2) to read substantially as follows: "a short and plain statement of the claim showing that the pleader is entitled to relief, which statement shall contain the facts constituting a cause of action." The reports and the discussion preceding the adoption of this resolution appear at 13 F.R.D. 253 (1953).

The Advisory Committee, in its 1955 report proposing numerous amendments to the Federal Rules, resisted the pressure to change Rule 8(a)(2), with the following explanation:

"*Note.* Rule 8(a)(2) is retained in its present form. This Note is appended to it in answer to various criticisms and suggestions for amendment which have been presented to the Committee.

"The criticisms appear to be based on the view that the rule does not require the averment of any information as to what has actually happened. That Rule 8(a) envisages the statement of circumstances, occurrences, and events in support of the claim presented is clearly indicated not only by the forms appended to the rules showing what should be considered as sufficient compliance with the rule, but also by other intermeshing rules; see, inter alia, Rules 8(c) and (e), 9(b)–(g), 10(b), 12(b)(6), 12(h), 15(c), 20, and 54(b). Rule 12(e), providing for a motion for a more definite statement, also shows that the complaint must disclose information with sufficient definiteness. The intent and effect of the rules is to permit the claim to be stated in general terms; the rules are designed to discourage battles over mere form of statement and to sweep away the needless controversies which the codes permitted that served either to delay trial on the merits or to prevent a party from having a trial because of mistakes in statement. The decision in Dioguardi v. Durning, 139 F.2d 774 (2d Cir.1944), to which proponents of an amendment to Rule 8(a) have especially referred, was not based on any holding that a pleader is not required to supply information disclosing a ground for relief. The complaint in that case stated a plethora of facts and the court so construed them as to sustain the validity of the pleading.

"While there has been some minority criticism, the consensus favors the rule and the reported cases indicate that it has worked satisfactorily and has advanced the administration of justice in the district courts. The rule has been adopted verbatim by a number of states in framing their own rules of court procedure. This circumstance appears to the Committee to confirm its view that no change in the rule is required or justified.

"It is accordingly the opinion of the Advisory Committee that, as it stands, the rule adequately sets forth the characteristics of good pleading; does away with the confusion resulting from the use of 'facts' and 'cause of action'; and requires the pleader to disclose adequate information as the basis of his claim for relief as distinguished from a bare averment that he wants relief and is entitled to it."

PLEADING EVIDENCE, ULTIMATE FACTS, AND CONCLUSIONS

There was a beguiling appearance of simplicity in the requirement adopted by the framers of the codes that a pleader should give a "plain and concise statement of the facts constituting a cause of action." The pleader was not to "plead his evidence," for that was being too specific; nor was he to "plead conclusions of law," for that was being too general; he was to plead the "ultimate facts." [e] The codifiers would probably be amazed to see the vast accumulation of cases that somewhat more than a century of interpreting this simple-sounding mandate has produced.[f]

[e] Compare the English requirement in Rules of the Supreme Court, O. 18, r. 7(1), which provides: "[E]very pleading must contain, and contain only, a statement in a summary form of the material facts on which the party pleading relies for his claim or defence, as the case may be, but not the evidence by which those facts are to be proved, and the statement must be as brief as the nature of the case admits." See Bruce v. Odhams Press, [1936] 1 K.B. 697.

[f] Scanning the West digest system under Pleading nos. 8, 11 will disclose the volume of litigation but will not reveal clear guidelines for decision.

Where did they go astray? The difficulty was the apparent failure to realize that every statement of fact is generalized to some degree, and that the appropriate degree depends upon the objective. Any statement of fact about a given situation necessarily involves a process of selection and rejection, the choice again depending upon the objective. One can scarcely imagine a lawyer asking his client for a "plain and concise statement of the facts" and finding a transcript of that statement to be a suitable pleading. The lawyer's training and experience supposedly enable him to cull from a client's story the facts relevant to his purpose and to couch them in terms neither too specific nor too general.

Suppose the lawyer knows the substantive rule into which he hopes to fit his client's cause. From what source does he learn how to steer between "evidence" and "conclusion"? [k] Surely not from the sterile statement of the code itself. Under a typical code the object should perhaps be, as Judge Clark suggested, "fair notice of each material fact of the pleader's cause," [h] but the pleader may find that this is merely a restatement of the problem rather than a solution.

Does he plead a contract by reciting that "*A* said this, *B* said that, and so on" or by reciting that "*A* and *B* mutually agreed such and such"? Is "*A* converted to his own use" a proper statement of ultimate fact or bad as a conclusion? (See Federal Form 11.) How about "*A* negligently drove a motor vehicle against plaintiff"? (See Federal Form 9.) Are "*A* is the owner of Blackacre" and "*A* is the wife of *B*" proper statements of fact? Either may involve one or more intricate matters of law. Should the required particularity of statement be made to depend on whether the allegation is likely to be in serious dispute in the litigation?

About all that the pleader has to go on is precedent and analogy. Most of the common pleading problems have by now been dealt with by the courts of the code states (although frequently with varying results from state to state and inconsistencies within a single state), so the careful lawyer is likely to find a precedent with judicial blessing. Many states have provided officially approved forms for common types of action, and unofficial practice books with forms are numerous.

In New York, NYCPLR § 3013 tries to avoid the morass of the evidence/ultimate fact/conclusion distinctions. It reads: "Statements in a pleading shall be sufficiently particular to give the court and parties notice of the transactions, occurrences, or series of transactions or occurrences, intended to be proved and the material elements of each cause of action or defense." See Foley v. D'Agostino,

[k] For more extensive development of the problem raised in the text, see Cook, 'Facts' and 'Statements of Fact,' 4 U.Chi. L.Rev. 233 (1937); Morris, Law and Fact, 55 Harv.L.Rev. 1303 (1942).

[h] C. Clark, Handbook of the Law of Code Pleading 232 (2d ed. 1947).

21 A.D.2d 60, 248 N.Y.S.2d 121 (1964), in which the court gave this section a liberal construction that substantially equates "cause of action" to the federal "claim for relief." In discouraging time-consuming attacks on pleadings, the court also relied upon NYCPLR § 3026, which provides: "Pleadings shall be liberally construed. Defects shall be ignored if a substantial right of a party is not prejudiced."

A leading commentator made this wry comment on Federal Rule 8(a)(2): "You will notice the words 'cause of action' do not appear; neither does the word 'fact'. The reason for that is, nobody knows what 'facts' are; courts have been trying for five hundred years to find 'facts' and nobody has ever been able to draw a line between what were and what were not 'facts.' Since the word 'facts' has given a great deal of trouble the suggestion was, Why not eliminate it? Since the phrase 'cause of action' has given trouble, eliminate that also. Whether this will do any good is very doubtful, for both terms are embedded in the literature of the law and in the vocabulary of the profession." Sunderland, The New Federal Rules, 45 W.Va.L.Q. 5, 12 (1938).

Question: (4) The Colorado Rules, patterned on the Federal Rules, add this sentence to rule 8(e)(1): "Pleadings otherwise meeting the requirements of these rules shall not be considered objectionable for failure to state ultimate facts as distinguished from conclusions of law." Is this provision necessary? Is it wise? See 5 Wright & Miller § 1218.

THE COMMON COUNTS

The common counts in general assumpsit [i] were brief and summary statements giving the defendant notice of no more than that the plaintiff was seeking to recover on a money claim of one of several generalized types. They were used in lieu of simple debt, and they also were used where there was no express contract to pay a stated price but where the circumstances were such as to give rise to a mutual understanding of the parties that payment of the reasonable value of the goods, services, or the like was to be made.[j] The common counts came to be used as well in "waiver-of-the-tort" situations and, more broadly, in cases where "the ties of natural justice" imposed an implied legal obligation to make payment although there was in fact no intention to pay; this class of cases embraced a wide variety of claims now termed "quasi contracts."

The question naturally arose whether the summary form of statement used in the common counts was permissible under the "facts" requirement of code pleading. Some early commentators thought

------

[i] See supra pp. 343–44.

[j] A common count was also frequently pleaded as an additional count in an action of special assumpsit for fear that the proof would fail to show a binding express contract but would nevertheless reveal the necessary elements of an implied undertaking to pay the reasonable value of a benefit conferred upon the defendant.

not, because the common counts tended to conceal rather than to disclose the facts. But the common counts were so convenient and so favorably regarded by the bar that their use was sanctioned in most states, at least in the consensual types of cases first mentioned above.

Where the common counts are now used, the old requirement of stating a fictitious promise to pay has usually been abandoned. See, e.g., New York Official Form 11, which runs as follows:

> Defendant owes plaintiff twenty thousand dollars for money had and received from one G.H. on June 1, 1965, to be paid by defendant to plaintiff.

> Wherefore plaintiff demands judgment against defendant for the sum of twenty thousand dollars, interest from June 1, 1965, and costs and disbursements.

Questions: (5) Should a complaint like a common count be sufficient under a typical code in a "waiver-of-the-tort" case? in a case where the obligation to pay is imposed only by "the ties of natural justice"?

(6) To what extent are pleadings like the common counts permissible under the Federal Rules? See Federal Forms 4 to 8 and the note to Form 5.

(7) A plaintiff suing in a federal court on a complaint similar to Form 8 offers evidence that G.H. paid money to the defendant under a contract obtained by fraud. It is objected to as not within the pleadings. Should the objection be sustained? Does Rule 9(b) have any bearing? See 5 Wright & Miller § 1222.

JUDICIAL NOTICE OF FACT AND LAW

We have discussed judicial notice as a means of dispensing with ordinary testimony.[k] The doctrine also has its place in pleading. A proposition of which the court takes judicial notice need not be alleged in a pleading, however material to the pleader's case it may be. An allegation in a pleading that contradicts a proposition judicially noticed will be disregarded; thus a demurrer or motion to dismiss does not admit any allegation in the attacked pleading running counter to the court's judicial knowledge. The court reads the attacked pleading as if such untenable allegations were omitted and any material propositions judicially noticed were added. The classic illustrative case at common law was Cole v. Maunder, 2 Rolle's Abr. 548 (K.B.1635), where an allegation that stones were thrown "*molliter et molli manu*" ("gently and with a gentle hand") was held not to be admitted by demurrer, "for the judges say that one cannot throw stones *molliter*." In Southern Ry. v. Covenia, 100 Ga. 46, 29 S.E. 219 (1896), the court took judicial notice that a child under two years of age was unable to have any earning capacity and held on

[k] See supra p. 112.

demurrer that an allegation that such a child performed valuable services did not stand as admitted.

The courts of a state take judicial notice of local law, common and statutory, and of the United States Constitution and other federal law. This is done without pleading or proof; but counsel will naturally call attention to the appropriate sources so that the judge's actual knowledge will match what he judicially "knows"; however, neither the trial nor the appellate courts are limited to the sources to which their attention is called. The law of sister states and of foreign countries was traditionally a matter of "fact" to be pleaded and proved, although failure to do so was sometimes relieved by a presumption that such foreign law was the same as the forum's. The "fact" characterization was sometimes carried to the extreme of leaving the determination to the jury if there was a dispute, and it considerably complicated the process of appellate review of the findings on foreign-law issues. This whole tradition of law as "fact" is now approaching extinction as a result of the Uniform Judicial Notice of Foreign Law Act—approved by the National Conference of Commissioners on Uniform State Laws in 1936 and since adopted by a majority of the states—and of similar reform statutes providing for the extension of judicial notice to the law of other states.[1] The Act further provides that to enable a party to ask that judicial notice be taken of another state's law, reasonable notice shall be given either in the pleadings or otherwise. There has been a conflict of decisions as to whether the Act dispenses with pre-existing pleading requirements. In Litsinger Sign Co. v. American Sign Co., 11 Ohio St.2d 1, 227 N.E.2d 609 (1967), the court held that the law of a sister state could be judicially noticed so long as the reasonable-notice provision of the Act was satisfied, even though it was not pleaded. In Scott v. Scott, 153 Neb. 906, 46 N.W.2d 627 (1951), the court held that the Act related to proof only and, the sister state's law not having been pleaded, refused to take judicial notice of it but instead resorted to the presumption that the sister state's law was the same as that of Nebraska. Some state statutes or court rules specifically negate the need of pleading foreign law.

Lower federal courts, and the Supreme Court on review of their decisions, take judicial notice of federal law and of the law of all the states. Moreover, a federal court sitting in Nebraska in a diversity case has taken judicial notice of the law of another state despite the fact that it was not pleaded, thus refusing to follow the state law referred to above. Simmons v. Continental Casualty Co., 410 F.2d 881 (8th Cir.1969). But on review of a case from a state court, the Supreme Court judicially notices only such law as the state court would notice. See Hanley v. Donoghue, 116 U.S. 1, 6 S.Ct. 242 (1885).

[1] The law of foreign countries is not covered by the Uniform Judicial Notice of Foreign Law Act, other than in a section providing that an issue of such law is for the court rather than for the jury; but some of the similar statutes do not distinguish between the law of foreign countries and that of sister states.

Traditionally, the law of foreign countries was treated in the lower federal courts as a matter of "fact." Rule 44.1, adopted by amendment in 1966, changed that practice. Also, there had been uncertainty in the federal courts as to whether the law of a foreign country had to be pleaded under Rule 8. Rule 44.1 was stated by the Advisory Committee, and has since been held, to eliminate that uncertainty by providing that reasonable written notice of the intention to raise an issue concerning foreign law be given in the pleadings or otherwise. (Note, however, that similar language in the Uniform Judicial Notice of Foreign Law Act has not been universally held to dispense with pleading requirements.) When the relevance of the law of a foreign country is apparent from the outset, the easy and sensible way of complying with the notice requirement of Rule 44.1 is to give in the pleading notice of the intention to raise the foreign-law issue.

Rule 44.1 represents a new approach to the problems of handling the law of foreign countries. The Uniform Interstate and International Procedure Act—which was intended to supersede the Uniform Judicial Notice of Foreign Law Act, was approved by the National Conference of Commissioners on Uniform State Laws in 1962, and since has been adopted by a number of states—takes the same approach as Rule 44.1 but applies to the law of sister states as well as of foreign countries. Neither the Rule nor the new Uniform Act uses the term "judicial notice." These and similar provisions render obsolete much of the old learning about judicial notice and should simplify litigation in which foreign law is involved. See Miller, Federal Rule 44.1 and the "Fact" Approach to Determining Foreign Law: Death Knell for a Die-Hard Doctrine, 65 Mich.L.Rev. 613 (1967), which deals thoroughly with the entire problem. As to the procedure for determining whether a foreign law is applicable, see D. Cavers, The Choice-of-Law Process 272–79 (1965).

LEGGETT v. MONTGOMERY WARD & CO.

United States Court of Appeals, Tenth Circuit, 1949.
178 F.2d 436.

[Plaintiff, seeking damages for malicious prosecution, alleged in his amended complaint that defendant, through an authorized agent, maliciously and without probable cause filed with a justice of the peace in Wyoming a criminal complaint charging plaintiff with the crime of embezzlement; that plaintiff was arrested and required to furnish bail; that on advice of counsel he waived preliminary hearing (for tactical reasons that the complaint went on to explain); that plaintiff was tried on such charge and acquitted; and that he was damaged. Defendant filed a motion to dismiss the action on the ground that it appeared from the face of the amended complaint that plaintiff waived preliminary hearing upon the charge; that by reason of such waiver there was prima facie evidence of probable cause to believe that plaintiff was guilty of the offense charged in the criminal complaint; and that therefore the allegation of want of probable cause contained in the amended complaint was insufficient to state a claim against defendant upon which relief could be granted. The court dismissed the action, and plaintiff appealed.]

Before BRATTON and HUXMAN, CIRCUIT JUDGES, and RICE, DISTRICT JUDGE.

BRATTON, CIRCUIT JUDGE.

. . . .

The motion to dismiss the action for failure of the amended complaint to state a cause of action for which relief could be granted admitted all facts well pleaded in the amended complaint. But whether the facts thus pleaded and admitted constituted a cause of action for which relief could be granted in the form of damages for malicious prosecution was a question to be determined by the law of Wyoming. Van Sant v. American Express Co., 3 Cir., 158 F.2d 924.

[The court held the Wyoming law, as enunciated in Penton v. Canning, 57 Wyo. 390, 118 P.2d 1002 (1941), to be that waiver of preliminary hearing and binding over for trial were equivalent in law to a hearing and a finding of probable cause and that, in the absence of allegation and proof that the binding over was procured by perjury, false testimony, or other improper means on the part of defendant, an action like this for malicious prosecution could not be maintained.]

Apparently in an effort to avoid the impact of Penton v. Canning, supra, plaintiff argues in effect that the question whether the amended complaint stated a cause of action for which relief could be granted must be determined by the rules of pleading applicable to the United States District Courts, and that under such rules the amended complaint was not fatally defective. . . . It is the general rule of pleading that where a complaint alleges facts constituting a cause of action and also alleges facts which constitute a valid defense, unless it alleges further facts avoiding such defense, it may be attacked by demurrer or motion to dismiss. St. Louis, Kennett and Southeastern Railroad Company v. United States, 267 U.S. 346, 45 S.Ct. 245, 69 L.Ed. 649; [other citations from Indiana and Georgia omitted]. Alleging that the criminal complaint was filed, that plaintiff waived preliminary examination, and that he was bound over to the district court; and failing to allege that the action of the justice of the peace in binding plaintiff over to the district court was procured by perjury, false testimony, or other improper means on the part of defendant, the pleading did not state a claim for which relief could be granted under the law of Wyoming. Sheffield v. Cantwell, 7 Cir., 101 F.2d 351.

[The court also held that it did not appear that the trial court abused its discretion in the denial of the application further to amend.]

The judgment is affirmed.

RICE, DISTRICT JUDGE (dissenting). . . . Apparently the test of the sufficiency of a complaint in federal court, under the majority opinion, now is—would the complaint if filed as a petition in the state court be sustained when attacked by a general demurrer? . . .

Questions: (8) Would you expect this case to be decided differently after Hanna v. Plumer, supra p. 220?

(9) How should the point be decided in a federal question case? See Kozlowski v. Ferrara, 117 F.Supp. 650 (S.D.N.Y.1954).

DEFENSIVE MATTER IN THE COMPLAINT

Suppose the plaintiff alleges a good cause of action and goes on to allege further facts constituting a good defense. At common law one can find statements that a matter of defense set forth in a declaration is surplusage and should be disregarded on demurrer. But these statements usually appear in cases where the plaintiff after anticipating a defense proceeded to avoid it. The common-law approach was to disregard both the defense and the avoidance, and thus to hold the declaration good against a demurrer.

There is some code support for this view. For instance, in Trotter v. Mutual Reserve Fund Life Ass'n, 9 S.D. 596, 70 N.W. 843 (1897), the plaintiff sued on a life insurance policy. In his complaint he anticipated the defense of a release but alleged that it was procured by fraud. The defendant's demurrer was overruled on the theory that both the defense and the avoidance were surplusage. However, the more usual code approach is to hold that a demurrer will be sustained if the complaint discloses a defense and does not avoid it, but that a good avoidance of the defense saves the complaint.

The difference is important at the next step in pleading. What should the defendant do on the facts of the Trotter case? Because he cannot demur, he must answer. Suppose he pleads the release, ignoring the fraud, and the plaintiff demurs to the answer or moves for judgment on the pleadings. It was held in Canfield v. Tobias, 21 Cal. 349 (1863), following the strict common-law view, that on these facts the plaintiff's motion for judgment on the pleadings would not lie. The court reasoned that only material allegations were admitted if not denied and that the plaintiff's allegations of release and fraud, being pure surplusage, were properly to be disregarded. On the more usual code approach, the plaintiff's complaint would fall if he alleged a defense without avoiding it. Accordingly the allegation of fraud, being necessary to save the complaint, is material. Being material, it must be denied in the answer or be taken as admitted.

Hence the plaintiff's motion would lie. This latter analysis is generally regarded as more in harmony with the code objectives.

Question: (10) How would this problem of what the defendant should plead be treated under the Federal Rules? Does Rule 8(d) shed any light on the point?

O'DONNELL v. ELGIN, JOLIET & EASTERN RAILWAY, 338 U.S. 384, 70 S.Ct. 200 (1949). The plaintiff, seeking recovery for a death resulting from the breaking of a coupler, had joined in a single count (1) a claim under the Safety Appliance Act, 45 U.S.C. § 2, for which the Supreme Court held negligence need not be shown, with (2) an FELA claim for negligence. The trial court had indiscriminately submitted the whole to the jury as a negligence case. Judgment for the defendant, affirmed by the Seventh Circuit, was reversed by the Supreme Court because the trial court had failed to give a peremptory instruction that equipping a car with a coupler that broke in a switching operation was a violation of the Safety Appliance Act, thus rendering the defendant liable without a showing of negligence. Justice Jackson observed in passing:

"We no longer insist upon technical rules of pleading, but it will ever be difficult in a jury trial to segregate issues which counsel do not separate in their pleading, preparation or thinking. We think the unfortunately prolonged course of this litigation is in no small part due to the failure to heed the admonition well stated by the Court of Appeals of the Seventh Circuit in a similar case: 'Of course, it is not proper to plead different theories in the same paragraph, but it is not necessarily fatal especially when the adversary makes no objection.' Vigor v. Chesapeake & Ohio R. Co., 101 F.2d 865, 869 (1939). Pleadings will serve the purpose of sharpening and limiting the issues only if claims based on negligence are set forth separately from those based on violation of the appliance acts.[6]"

Questions: (11) Was the plaintiff's pleading actually inconsistent with Rule 10(b)? with Rule 8(e)(2)? with any other provision of the Rules? By what procedure might the defendant have sought to enforce any violated pleading Rules?

(12) In what other ways might "the unfortunately prolonged course of this litigation" have been shortened?

[6] This, after all, is the command of Rule 10(b), Federal Rules of Civil Procedure, which provides: 'All averments of claim or defense shall be made in numbered paragraphs, the contents of each of which shall be limited as far as practicable to a statement of a single set of circumstances . . . .'

Professor Moore, in discussing this Rule with reference to claims based upon both common law and statutory grounds, states: 'Separate statement by way of counts is not required; separate paragraphing in setting out the grounds in the above actions is desirable and required.' 2 Moore's Federal Practice, 2006–2007 (2d ed. 1948).

(13) *P* set forth in the same paragraph of a single count alternative allegations of wilfulness and negligence in an automobile collision. The court dismissed the action for failure to state separately these allegations, although leave to amend was granted. Sherman v. Renth, 22 F.R.D. 59 (E.D.Ill.1957) (separate paragraphs required and separate counts desirable). Was the decision correct?

(14) How would you rewrite Rule 10(b)?

SECTION 2. CHALLENGING THE STATEMENT OF THE CLAIM

MOTION FOR MORE DEFINITE STATEMENT

Clarification of the complaint may be sought under the codes by a motion for a more definite statement or a motion for a bill of particulars. In some jurisdictions the two have become substantially interchangeable, but in others a distinction is made. A motion for a more definite statement is appropriate when further details are required in order to enable the moving party to frame a responsive pleading. A bill of particulars can be required in order to enable the moving party to prepare for trial and especially to protect against surprise and to limit the issues at trial. Originally used in connection with declarations in general assumpsit under the common counts, the bill of particulars has come to be available, at the discretion of the court, in any kind of action; this enlarged use of the bill is common under the codes, but some codes restrict its use to contract actions. When there is no provision for discovery comparable to that obtainable under Federal Rules 26 to 37, the value of bills of particulars is obvious.

Originally, Rule 12(e) allowed both types of motion. It was found, however, after a few years of actual operation, that Rule 12(e) had been subject to more judicial rulings than any other part of the Rules. In a large percentage of the cases the rulings were adverse to the moving party, but motions under the Rule were nevertheless productive of considerable delay and confusion. The original Rule accordingly was much criticized by commentators, judges, and lawyers, who pointed out that as an aid in preparation for trial it was superfluous in the light of the more effective provisions for discovery.

In 1948, Rule 12(e) was amended by eliminating the bill of particulars entirely and permitting a motion for a more definite statement only when the moving party shows that the pleading is so vague or ambiguous that he cannot reasonably be required to frame a responsive pleading. Cases where the motion should be granted are rare. Indeed, the motion has been characterized as "superfluous and unnecessary." Comment, Federal Rule 12(e): Motion for More Definite

Statement—History, Operation and Efficacy, 61 Mich.L.Rev. 1126, 1138 (1963).

MOTION TO STRIKE

The motion to strike may be used to eliminate "any redundant, immaterial, impertinent, or scandalous matter." Rule 12(f). We have seen the adjurations against "pleading evidence." But suppose the pleader does so plead. Obviously, saying too much is less of a sin than saying too little, and the needless pleading of evidence ordinarily does the adversary no harm. There is not much point in seeking to prune harmless evidentiary matter from pleadings, and the court will most often deny a motion to strike if it is made. See, e.g., Mitchell v. Hart, 41 F.R.D. 138 (S.D.N.Y.1966). But a statement of the claim that is neither short nor plain because of flagrant violation of the mandate of Rule 8(e)(1) that the averments of a pleading be "simple, concise, and direct" may be stricken on motion even in the absence of other prejudice. See, e.g., Johns-Manville Sales Corp. v. Chicago Title & Trust Co., 261 F.Supp. 905 (N.D.Ill.1966) (single count runs to 69 paragraphs covering 39 pages, including numerous exhibits containing evidentiary material, some of it extraneous to any issue). There are more cases where the court strikes matter that it finds to be prejudicial in other ways. See, e.g., Bernstein v. N.V. Nederlandsche-Amerikaansche Stoomvaart-Maatschappij, 7 F.R.D. 63 (S.D.N.Y.1946) (allegations concerning general attitude of Nazis toward Jews and defendant's knowledge that plaintiff was Jewish and at mercy of Nazis stricken from complaint for money had and received), appeal dismissed, 161 F.2d 733 (2d Cir.), cert. denied, 332 U.S. 771, 68 S.Ct. 84 (1947); Hughes v. Kaiser Jeep Corp., 40 F.R.D. 89 (D.S.C.1966) (allegations characterizing automobile manufactured by defendant as "death trap" stricken from complaint in death action).

Whether there is in fact prejudice usually turns on whether the pleadings are read or shown to the jury. There is a great variation in the rules of practice or custom on this point, in both state and federal courts. Some jurisdictions espouse the very strict rule that it is reversible error if the court or counsel reads or comments upon any pleading, except where a particular pleading is admissible in evidence and has in fact been introduced. See Louisville & N.R.R. v. Hull, 113 Ky. 561, 68 S.W. 433 (1902). A substantial number of jurisdictions allow counsel to read the pleadings upon which the parties go to trial, whether or not such pleadings have been or could be introduced in evidence. In Woodworth v. Fuller, 235 Mass. 443, 446, 126 N.E. 781, 782 (1920), the court stated: "In this Commonwealth from time immemorial, in opening, the pleadings have been read to the jury. Howe's Practice (1834) 252; Colby's Practice (1848) 238. At the close of trial, the writ and declaration and answers in their final form customarily go to the jury. [Citation omitted.] It is not necessary to consider whether this practice is founded on right rather than upon discretionary authority."

Apparently, the increasingly common practice today is routinely to keep the jury from hearing or seeing pleadings not introduced in evidence or at least to do so in any case where they contain prejudicial matter. See H.E. Miller Oil Co. v. Socony-Vacuum Oil Co., 37 F.Supp. 831 (E.D.Mo.1941) (pleadings not evidence and may not be read to jury over objection).

DREWETT v. AETNA CASUALTY & SURETY CO.

United States District Court, Western District of Louisiana, 1975.
405 F.Supp. 877.

[Plaintiffs sued insurers to recover on flood insurance policies issued under the National Flood Insurance Act of 1968, 42 U.S.C. §§ 4001–4127, and also demanded penalties and attorneys' fees under the state insurance law.]

NAUMAN, S. SCOTT, DISTRICT JUDGE. Defendants . . . have moved the Court to strike plaintiffs' demands for penalties and attorneys fees.

Federal Rules of Civil Procedure, Rule 12(f) provides that the motion to strike is directed toward any insufficient defense [m] or redundant, immaterial, impertinent or scandalous matter. Defendants' motion to strike herein is directed toward a specific allegation in the complaint; that is, plaintiffs' demand for penalties and attorneys fees theoretically provided for by Louisiana Revised Statutes 22:658. It is clear that this specific allegation of the complaint constitutes neither an insufficient defense nor a redundant, immaterial, impertinent or scandalous allegation such as covered by the motion to strike. Therefore, that particular procedural device is inappropriate in this case. Wright & Miller, Federal Practice and Procedure, Section 1380.

On the other hand, the subject matter of this motion may be properly presented to the Court by means of a motion directed to the failure to state a claim upon which relief can be granted. F.R. C.P.12(b)(6). Authorities indicate that this motion may be used to challenge the sufficiency of part of a pleading such as a single count or

[m] The motion to strike an insufficient defense was added to Rule 12(f) by a rather clumsy amendment in 1948. It is used when the plaintiff wishes to challenge the legal sufficiency of a defense. Such a motion to strike, if granted, will dispose of a question of law in advance of trial and may significantly simplify the trial.

Courts show reluctance to strike a defense as insufficient. If the defense presents a question of law that can better be determined in the context of facts proved at trial, it plainly should not be stricken. There are many cases, however, where a purely legal question is involved and the court nevertheless says that its function on a motion to strike is not to determine disputed questions of law.

claim for relief. Wright & Miller, Federal Practice and Procedure, Section 1358. . . .

. . . .

. . . We think it clear that Congress intended only Federal law to apply to claims arising under the National Flood Insurance Act.

In light of the above considerations, defendants' motion to dismiss the demand for penalties and attorneys fees for failure to state a claim upon which relief can be granted is hereby granted.

CONSEQUENCES OF THE MOTION TO DISMISS FOR FAILURE TO STATE A CLAIM

Consider a motion under Federal Rule 12(b)(6) that is aimed at the whole complaint. Under the Rules the plaintiff may amend once as of right even after a motion to dismiss is interposed, for under Rule 7(a) a motion is not a "responsive pleading" within the meaning of Rule 15(a). See United States v. Newbury Mfg. Co., 123 F.2d 453 (1st Cir.1941). Thus the plaintiff may render the motion moot by filing an amended complaint.

Now let us assume that the motion to dismiss is *granted*. The right to amend as a matter of course "at any time before a responsive pleading is served" is subject to the qualification that this right ceases with dismissal for failure to state a claim." The order for dismissal will often expressly provide for leave to amend, and counsel will be well advised to request such a provision if he contemplates the possibility of amendment. In view of the admonition of Rule 15(a) that leave to amend "shall be freely given when justice so requires," the refusal to allow leave is likely to be reversed as an abuse of discretion. See Britton v. Atlantic Coast Line Railroad, 303 F.2d 274 (5th Cir.1962). But denial of leave to amend may be a proper exercise of discretion, especially if the plaintiff has made several unsuccessful efforts to state a claim and it seems unlikely that he will be able to do so. See Shall v. Henry, 211 F.2d 226 (7th Cir.1954) (after four amended complaints, no abuse of discretion to deny further opportunity to amend). If judgment of dismissal is entered without leave to amend, amendment should be allowed only if motion for relief is made under Rule 59(e) within the ten-day time limit there provided, or perhaps under Rule 60(b) if the plaintiff can satisfy its requirements. See Keene Lumber Co. v. Leventhal, 165 F.2d 815 (1st Cir.1948).

" A few courts have refused to recognize this qualification and have indicated that amendment may be made as of right even after dismissal. E.g., Fuhrer v. Fuhrer, 292 F.2d 140 (7th Cir.1961). Professor Moore says: "These holdings seem incorrect." 3 Moore ¶ 15.07[2]. At the least, it would seem that any such amendment must be made within a reasonable time after dismissal. See 6 Wright & Miller § 1483.

If the plaintiff amends, the question may arise whether he thereby waives any subsequent chance to argue that the dismissal was erroneous. In some states it appears that there is such a waiver, and there are federal cases to the same effect. E.g., Loux v. Rhay, 375 F.2d 55 (9th Cir.1967). A more reasonable approach would seem to be to reverse an adverse judgment on the amended complaint if the plaintiff can show that his defeat is directly traceable to the alteration of his case made necessary by the erroneous dismissal of his original complaint. See Blazer v. Black, 196 F.2d 139 (10th Cir.1952). So if the plaintiff pleads over, he naturally cannot thereafter argue any claimed error in the dismissal of his original complaint for technical defects. He should still be able to argue, however, the substantive validity of his original claim for relief and that the dismissal "struck a vital blow to a substantial part of plaintiff's cause of action." Williamson v. Liverpool & London & Globe Ins. Co., 141 F. 54, 57 (8th Cir.1905).

On the other hand, if the plaintiff stands on his pleading and appeals from the judgment of dismissal,[e] a reversal by the appellate court will reinstate the complaint and naturally the defendant may then answer. But what if the appellate court agrees that the complaint was insufficient and affirms the judgment? The appellate court may in the interest of justice include in its mandate express leave to amend or to apply to the district court for such relief. See 28 U.S.C. § 2106. If the mandate does not grant leave, it seems that the district court, at least in ordinary circumstances, lacks power to allow an amendment. See Tkaczyk v. Gallagher, 265 F.Supp. 791 (D.Conn.1967).

Now let us assume instead that the motion to dismiss is *denied.* After denial the defendant may answer; this is now universally recognized. Suppose the defendant then answers, and he loses at trial. May he on appeal from judgment for the plaintiff urge again the legal insufficiency of the plaintiff's claim, or has he foregone that opportunity by answering?

Question: (15) How is this question different from the question of plaintiff's waiver by amending the complaint after a motion to dismiss has been granted?

If the defendant answers, it may be that the appellate court will not reexamine as such the action of the trial court in denying the motion to dismiss, but the same question may reappear in a different guise. When the case is tried, the defendant will presumably move for a directed verdict and judgment n.o.v., contending that on the proof the plaintiff has not made out a claim for relief. The trial court's denial of those motions will be reviewable on appeal from the judgment. Thus the appellate court may in effect be passing on the

---

[e] Once the appeal has been taken, the district court no longer has jurisdiction to allow an amendment without leave of the appellate court. See Thompson v. Harry C. Erb, Inc., 240 F.2d 452 (3d Cir.1957).

same question of law that confronted the trial judge on the motion to dismiss the complaint, inasmuch as the question will be the same when the proof has established the allegations of the complaint and nothing more.

On the other hand, if the defendant declines to answer, judgment will be entered for the plaintiff. Should the judgment be reversed on appeal because of the complaint's insufficiency, plaintiff ought to have leave to replead. But if the judgment is affirmed, we have the question whether the judgment for plaintiff should stand without more, or whether leave to answer should ever be given by the appellate or lower court. Consider again the applicability of 28 U.S.C. § 2106.

The foregoing discussion with respect to the consequences both of a grant and of a denial of a motion to dismiss has been set in the context of federal practice with limited rights of interlocutory appeal. In the jurisdictions where interlocutory appeals are freely allowed from rulings on such motions, the considerations are obviously different.

Question: (16) Is it fair to say that allowance of a right to replead after a party has stood on his pleading, appealed, and lost is tantamount to allowing an interlocutory appeal in derogation of the final decision rule? What bearing, if any, does 28 U.S.C. § 1292(b) have on the problem?

SECTION 3. COMPLETING THE COMPLAINT

Rule 8(a)(1) requires the federal plaintiff to set forth the grounds upon which subject-matter jurisdiction depends. See Form 2. This requirement stems from the limited jurisdiction of the federal courts, and so it generally does not exist in state practice. See also 28 U.S.C. § 1653.

Question: (17) In federal court plaintiff alleges that he is not a citizen of Texas and defendant is a citizen of Texas, and that the matter in controversy exceeds, exclusive of interest and costs, $10,000. Defendant moves under Rule 12(b)(1). What decision? Cf. Bryant v. Harrelson, 187 F.Supp. 738 (S.D.Tex.1960) (suggesting dismissal).

Rule 8(a)(3) requires a demand for judgment. See also Rule 54(c). This requirement is common in state practice, but there are a few states in which no demand for a specific sum is required, as under Fla.R.Civ.P. 1.110(b), or in which such a specific demand is expressly forbidden, N.J.Ct.R. 4:5–2. A majority of the states, although requiring or permitting such a specific demand, do permit recovery of damages in excess of those demanded, except in default cases, either because of a provision adopted from the Field Code or because of a rule modeled on Rule 54(c). A minority of states do not allow recovery in excess of the amount demanded, but in such states an amendment of the ad damnum clause is likely to be permitted, even after verdict.

Questions: (18) Under 28 U.S.C. § 1441 the right of removal is generally confined to actions over which the federal court has original jurisdiction. The defendant in a state-court action in which no specific sum need be demanded, or one in which judgment in excess of the amount demanded may be recovered, wishes to remove to the federal court. What problems does he have in establishing that the matter in controversy exceeds $10,000? See ALI Study of the Division of Jurisdiction Between State and Federal Courts § 1381(c)(2) commentary at 344–48 (1968).

(19) Even in Massachusetts, where the pleadings can routinely be read and shown to the jury, some judges except a specific ad damnum clause from this practice. Assume, however, you are a plaintiff before a judge who allows such an ad damnum to be read to the jury. Would doing so be tactically wise? See McNaught & Aronson, Trial Without Error—Plaintiff's Presentation, 57 Mass.L.Q. 171, 172–73 (1972).

(20) Plaintiff, suing in a federal court for her husband's wrongful death, prays in her complaint for damages "in the sum of $500,000.00." Defendant moves to strike from the complaint this portion of the prayer, contending that it is prejudicial for the jury to be informed as to the amount plaintiff is seeking. Plaintiff points to Rule 8(a)(3). What action should the court take on the motion? See 5 Wright & Miller § 1259.

TOPIC C. THE RESPONSIVE PLEADING

SECTION 1. FORM AND SCOPE OF DEFENSES

VERIFICATION OF PLEADINGS

Rule 11 requires a pleading to be verified or supported by affidavit only when it is specifically required by federal rule or statute. Such provisions are found in Rules 23.1, 27(a), and 65(b) and, inferentially, in Rule 66 (because "the practice heretofore followed in the courts of the United States" required verification of a complaint seeking appointment of a receiver). A few federal statutes also require verification. See 2A Moore ¶ 11.03.

Question: (1) 28 U.S.C. § 1446(a) requires that the petition for removal of an action to federal court be verified. Does this serve any useful purpose? See ALI Study of the Division of Jurisdiction Between State and Federal Courts § 1381(a) commentary at 338–39 (1968).

There are extensive statutory provisions for verification in some states.

NEW YORK CIVIL PRACTICE LAW AND RULES

§ 3020. *Verification*

(a) **Generally.** A verification is a statement under oath that the pleading is true to the knowledge of the deponent, except as to matters alleged on information and belief, and that as to those matters he believes it to be true. Unless otherwise specified by law, where a pleading is verified, each subsequent pleading shall also be verified, except the answer of an infant and except as to matter in the pleading concerning which the party would be privileged from testifying as a witness. Where the complaint is not verified, a counterclaim, crossclaim or third-party claim in the answer may be separately verified in the same manner and with the same effect as if it were a separate pleading.

. . . .

Question: (2) A verified complaint is filed in a diversity action in the Southern District of New York. Must the answer be verified? Cf. Follenfant v. Rogers, 359 F.2d 30 (5th Cir.1966) (indicating no).

456

SUROWITZ v. HILTON HOTELS CORP.

Supreme Court of the United States, 1966.
383 U.S. 363, 86 S.Ct. 845.

[Plaintiff, a Polish immigrant with a very limited English vocabulary and practically no formal education, saved several thousand dollars from her work as a seamstress and invested it in stocks on the advice of her son-in-law, Irving Brilliant, a professional investment adviser who was a graduate of the Harvard Law School and possessed a master's degree in economics from Columbia University— "and in addition to his degrees and his financial acumen, he wore a Phi Beta Kappa key." Among these investments was stock in Hilton Hotels Corporation, for which she paid over $2000 in 1957. The plaintiff sought her son-in-law's advice in 1962 about a mailed notice from Hilton announcing its plan to purchase a large amount of its own stock, and in 1963 about Hilton's failure to pay its dividend. He and a lawyer friend named Rockler investigated and concluded that Hilton's management had wrongfully damaged the corporation by a fraudulent scheme. Brilliant advised her to bring suit, and she agreed. Rockler prepared the complaint for a shareholders' derivative action. The plaintiff verified it as required by Rule 23(b), now Rule 23.1, stating that some of the allegations were true and "on information and belief" she thought that all the other allegations were true. She did this not on the basis of her own knowledge, but on faith in her son-in-law's advice and his explanation of the complaint to her.

[The district court, over her counsel's objection, allowed the defendants before answer to take the oral deposition of the plaintiff. In the deposition the plaintiff showed that she did not understand the complaint at all and that in signing it she had relied upon her son-in-law. Thereupon defendants moved to dismiss the complaint, alleging that the pleading was a sham. Rockler filed two affidavits about the extensive investigation preceding the commencement of the action. The court, holding that the plaintiff's verification was "false" and hence a "sham," dismissed the case "with prejudice." The court of appeals affirmed. The Supreme Court granted certiorari.]

MR. JUSTICE BLACK delivered the opinion of the Court.

.   .   .   .   .

We assume it may be possible that there can be circumstances under which a district court could stop all proceedings in a derivative cause of action, relieve the defendants from filing an answer to charges of fraud, and conduct a pre-trial investigation to determine whether the plaintiff had falsely sworn that the facts alleged in the complaint were either true or that he had information which led him to believe they were true. And conceivably such a pre-trial investigation might possibly reveal facts surrounding the verification of the complaint which could justify dismissal of the complaint with prejudice. However, here we need not consider the question of whether, if ever, Federal Rule 23(b) might call for such summary action. Certainly it cannot justify the court's summary dismissal in this case. Rule 23(b) was not written in order to bar derivative suits. Unquestionably it was originally adopted and has served since in part as a means to discourage "strike suits" by people who might be interested in getting quick dollars by making charges without regard to their truth so as to coerce corporate managers to settle worthless claims in order to get rid of them. On the other hand, however, derivative suits have played a rather important role in protecting shareholders of corporations from the designing schemes and wiles of insiders who are willing to betray their company's interest in order to enrich themselves. And it is not easy to conceive of anyone more in need of protection against such schemes than little investors like Mrs. Surowitz.

When the record of this case is reviewed in the light of the purpose of Rule 23(b)'s verification requirement, there emerges the plain, inescapable fact that this is not a strike suit or anything akin to it. Mrs. Surowitz was not interested in anything but her own investment made with her own money. Moreover, there is not one iota of evidence that Mr. Brilliant, her son-in-law and counselor, sought to do the corporation any injury in this litigation. In fact his purchases for the benefit of his family of more than $50,000 of securities in the corporation, including a $10,000 debenture, all made years before this suit was brought, manifest confidence in the corporation, not a desire to harm it in any way. The Court of Appeals in affirming the District Court's dismissal, however, indicated that whether Mrs. Surowitz and her counselors acted in good faith and whether the charges they made were truthful were irrelevant once Mrs. Surowitz demonstrated in her oral testimony that she knew nothing about the content of the suit. . . . In fact the opinion of the Court of Appeals indicates in several places that a woman like Mrs. Surowitz, who is uneducated generally and illiterate in economic matters, could never under any circumstances be a plaintiff in a derivative suit brought in the federal courts to protect her stock interests.

We cannot construe Rule 23 or any other one of the Federal Rules as compelling courts to summarily dismiss, without any answer or argument at all, cases like this where grave charges of fraud are shown by the record to be based on reasonable beliefs growing out of careful investigation. The basic purpose of the Federal Rules is to administer justice through fair trials, not through summary dismissals as necessary as they may be on occasion. These rules were designed in large part to get away from some of the old procedural booby traps which common-law pleaders could set to prevent unsophisticated litigants from ever having their day in court. If rules of procedure work as they should in an honest and fair judicial system, they not only permit, but should as nearly as possible guarantee that bona fide complaints be carried to an adjudication on the merits.

Rule 23(b), like the other civil rules, was written to further, not defeat the ends of justice. The serious fraud charged here, which of course has not been proven, is clearly in that class of deceitful conduct which the federal securities laws were largely passed to prohibit and protect against. There is, moreover, not one word or one line of actual evidence in this record indicating that there has been any collusive conduct or trickery by those who filed this suit except through intimations and insinuations without any support from anything any witness has said. The dismissal of this case was error. It has now been practically three years since the complaint was filed and as yet not one of the defendants has even been compelled to admit or deny the wrongdoings charged. They should be. The cause is reversed and remanded to the District Court for trial on the merits.

Reversed and remanded.

[Chief Justice Warren and Justice Fortas did not participate.]

MR. JUSTICE HARLAN, concurring.

Rule 23(b) directs that in a derivative suit "the complaint shall be verified by oath" but nothing dictates that the verification be that of the plaintiff shareholder. See Bosc v. 39 Broadway, Inc., D.C., 80 F.Supp. 825. In the present circumstances, it seems to me the affidavit of Walter J. Rockler, counsel for Mrs. Surowitz, amounts to an adequate verification by counsel, which I think is permitted by a reasonable interpretation of the Rule at least in cases such as this. On this premise, I agree with the decision of the Court.

DENIALS

The common-law plea of the general issue, [a] a means of making a blanket denial of the plaintiff's allegations, has its analogue under the codes called the general denial. There was dispute as to whether use of the general denial conformed to the spirit of code pleading. It was forbidden in a few states, but its convenience was appealing and it has generally been allowed. Note, however, that where, as is done in many codes, the use of the general denial is in terms allowed only when the defendant "intends in good faith to controvert all the allegations," it is in theory unavailable in most cases.

The traditions of the bar are such that routine general denials are habitually filed in many states when they should not be. Neither published criticisms [b] nor ethical pronouncements [c] nor attempted regulation in the form of statutory imposition of costs for unfair use of

---

[a] See supra pp. 352–53.

[b] E.g., Bolster, The Municipal Court, 134 Boston B.Bull. 3, 7–8 (1938), reprinted in the first edition of this book at p. 418.

[c] E.g., N.Y.S.B.A. Comm. on Professional Ethics, Op. 469 (1977).

the general denial [d] has been significantly effective. See C. Clark, Handbook of the Law of Code Pleading 582 (2d ed. 1947). In explanation, if not justification, of the indiscriminate use of the general denial, it may be said that typically it involves neither deception nor the intent to deceive. Counsel recognize that later developments will clarify what is actually in controversy. This form of pleading is looked upon as merely an easy way to satisfy a formal requirement.

Question: (3) Does this practice, and the attitude of the bar toward it, suggest the wisdom of abolishing the requirement of a responsive pleading, at least in some constantly recurring types of cases?

Federal Rule 8(b) preserves the general denial. However, it is available in theory even less frequently than under the codes. (Why so?)

Question: (4) What sanctions are available under the Federal Rules for abuse of the general denial? See United States v. Long, 10 F.R.D. 443 (D.Neb.1950); cf. American Auto. Ass'n v. Rothman, 104 F.Supp. 655 (E.D. N.Y.1952).

Rule 8(b) also authorizes the "qualified general denial" which denies everything not expressly admitted, the "specific denial" which denies designated portions of the complaint, and the denial based on lack of "knowledge or information." In addition to these forms of denial set forth in Rule 8(b), the federal courts allow a party without firsthand knowledge but with sufficient information to form a belief as to the truth of an allegation to deny it "upon information and belief"; this has been the general practice under state codes, and the provision of Rule 11 that the signature to a pleading certifies "knowledge, information, and belief" lends further support for the use of this form of denial.

Questions: (5) In the light of these rules, consider how in each of the following situations the defendant's attorney should plead in response to the plaintiff's assertion in his federal complaint of a fact upon which the plaintiff has the burden of proof:

(a) The defendant tells his attorney that he knows the fact to be true but does not think the plaintiff can prove it.

(b) Neither the defendant nor his attorney knows whether the fact is true, but it involves a matter of public record easily verifiable.

(c) The only person with firsthand knowledge of the fact is *W*, an apparently disinterested witness. The defendant's attorney interviews *W*, who tells him the fact is true. The attorney is impressed by his seeming candor and believes that he is telling the truth.

(d) What if the attorney is unimpressed by *W* and believes that he may well be lying or mistaken?

(6) *P*'s complaint includes allegations that, if true, would establish that *D* was guilty of a crime. *D* in his answer refuses to respond to these allegations upon the ground that a response might tend to incriminate him. *P*

[d] E.g., Conn.Gen.Stat. § 52–99.

moves for judgment on the pleadings. What decision? See National Acceptance Co. of America v. Bathalter, 705 F.2d 924 (7th Cir.1983) (deny motion).

AFFIRMATIVE DEFENSES

Federal Rule 8(c) enumerates nineteen affirmative defenses, but the list is not exhaustive, as "any other matter constituting an avoidance or affirmative defense" must be pleaded affirmatively.[e] The pleader may have difficulty in determining whether a particular matter is an affirmative defense or one that can be shown under a denial. There is no sure test, but precedent and form books will often provide the answer. If not, one must look to considerations of apparent logic and of convenience, fairness, and good policy similar to those that govern allocation of the burden of proof.[f]

Customarily, the allocation of the burden of pleading parallels the allocation of the burden of proof, but this is not invariably so. Indeed, the Supreme Court of the United States has indicated that Rule 8(c) governs pleading in federal court even though burden of proof must under Erie follow state law. Palmer v. Hoffman, supra p. 206.

Questions: (7) *P* sues *D* for damage to his growing crops by reason of *D*'s negligent failure to keep open a drainage ditch. *D*'s answer is a general denial. Should evidence be admissible that the flooding of *P*'s property was caused by such an unprecedented rain as to be regarded as an act of God and not by any fault of *D*? See Chesapeake & O.Ry. v. Carmichael, 298 Ky. 769, 184 S.W.2d 91 (1944) (yes).

(8) *P* sues *D* for breach of contract. *D*'s answer is a general denial. Should evidence that the alleged offer and acceptance were made in jest be admissible under these pleadings? See Good v. Chiles, 57 S.W.2d 1100 (Tex. Comm'n App.1933) (no).

NYCPLR § 3018(b) provides: "*Affirmative defenses.* A party shall plead all matters which if not pleaded would be likely to take the adverse party by surprise or would raise issues of fact not appearing on the face of a prior pleading such as [here are listed twelve affirmative defenses generally corresponding to those in Federal Rule 8(c)]. The application of this subdivision shall not be confined to the instances enumerated."

Question: (9) Does this New York provision make easier or harder the task of an attorney trying to decide whether to treat a matter as an affirmative defense?

---

[e] For example, in Schmidtke v. Conesa, 141 F.2d 634 (1st Cir.1944), the plaintiff sued for overtime pay under the Fair Labor Standards Act, 29 U.S.C. § 216(b). After nonjury trial the district court dismissed his complaint on the ground that his employment had been in a professional capacity and hence was exempt under § 213(a)(1) of the Act. This matter had not been specifically pleaded or tried. The court of appeals reversed, holding that exemption was a matter of defense that had to be raised under Rule 8(c), although not specifically enumerated there.

[f] See infra pp. 541–42.

An example of an affirmative defense not listed in Federal Rule
8(c) is the defense of truth in libel or slander. The plaintiff must
allege falsity in the complaint, but the defendant cannot offer evidence of truth under a general denial. Similarly, the plaintiff suing
on an obligation to pay money must allege nonpayment, but payment
is nevertheless an affirmative defense which the defendant must
plead.

Question: (10) Under the Federal Rules should a specific denial of the
plaintiff's allegation of nonpayment be sufficient to raise the defense of payment? See FDIC v. Siraco, 174 F.2d 360 (2d Cir.1949) (no).

PLEADING CONTRIBUTORY NEGLIGENCE

There are various views with respect to the pleading and proof of
contributory negligence, including the following:

1. The plaintiff must plead and prove his own due care.

2. The plaintiff must prove his due care, but need not in terms
allege it, the allegation that the defendant's negligence caused the
injury being sufficient.

3. The defendant must plead and prove contributory negligence.
(This is now the most common view.)

4. The defendant must prove contributory negligence, but may
do so under a denial that the defendant's negligence caused the injury.

A problem may arise in a federal court sitting in a state that takes
position (1), as Illinois did until 1981 when it converted to comparative
negligence. It was held in Francis v. Humphrey, 25 F.Supp. 1 (E.D.
Ill.1938), decided after Erie and the adoption of the Federal Rules,
that an allegation of due care was necessary in order to state a claim.
(Should this be so? See Merit Insurance Co. v. Colao, 603 F.2d 654,
659 (7th Cir.1979) (no), cert. denied, 445 U.S. 929, 100 S.Ct. 1318
(1980).) Assuming that the plaintiff does allege his own due care,
must the defendant still plead contributory negligence pursuant to
Rule 8(c) in order to have the issue in the case or does a specific denial of the plaintiff's allegation of due care suffice? It does not seem
that the defendant should have to plead contributory negligence, but
the cautious defendant would be wise to heed the literal language of
Rule 8(c). He should be careful, however, to avoid the possible impact of certain state cases holding that when a party needlessly assumes the burden of pleading a matter, he thereby also assumes the
burden of proving it. E.g., Boyd v. Geary, 126 Conn. 396, 12 A.2d
644 (1940). This doctrine has little to recommend it and is, moreover,
pretty clearly a procedural matter that a federal court would not be
bound to follow under Erie. The cautious defendant should make it
plain, nevertheless, that he is not assuming the burden of proof.

Questions: (11) In a jurisdiction taking position (3), the plaintiff unnecessarily alleges his own due care. The answer specifically denies this allegation. Is the issue of contributory negligence in the case?

(12) Suppose instead that the answer is a general denial. Is the issue of contributory negligence in the case?

GUNDER v. NEW YORK TIMES CO.
United States District Court, Southern District of New York, 1941.
37 F.Supp. 911.

CONGER, DISTRICT JUDGE. Plaintiff has moved for an order striking out all of the affirmative defenses in the answer as legally insufficient, and striking out specific paragraphs as irrelevant, etc.

Although opposing the motion on the merits, defendant has challenged the sufficiency of the complaint, and asks that it be dismissed. Both under the state and federal practice, the principle is well settled that a bad answer is good enough for a bad complaint. In Baxter v. McDonnell, 154 N.Y. 432, at page 436, 48 N.E. 816, at page 817, it is stated: "The rule is that, on demurrer to an answer for insufficiency, the defendant may attack the complaint on the ground that it does not state facts sufficient to constitute a cause of action. . . . A demurrer searches the record for the first fault in pleading, and reaches back to condemn the first pleading that is defective in substance, because he who does not so plead as to invite an issue cannot compel his adversary to so plead as to accept it. . . ." See also Gise v. Brooklyn Society for the Prevention of Cruelty to Children, 262 N.Y. 114, 186 N.E. 412. In Cheatham v. Wheeling & L.E. Ry. Co., D.C., 37 F.2d 593, 598, the court stated: "It is a settled, though oft-forgotten, rule that a plaintiff's demurrer to a defense tests his own pleading. . . . A motion to strike out pleadings or parts thereof as insufficient in law is the modern equivalent of a demurrer. Carmody, Pleading and Practice in New York, § 246. When addressed to a defense in the answer of a defendant or to a replication by a plaintiff, it opens up the whole record as a demurrer did of old.

"The rationale of this principle is that such an attack, whether by motion or demurrer, has to be based on, and necessarily presupposes, a sound pleading in behalf of the party making it. Otherwise, it would be futile to grant the relief, however great the infirmity of the pleading attacked might be." See also Gay v. E.H. Moore, Inc., D.C., 26 F.Supp. 749; Ashman v. Coleman, D.C., 25 F.Supp. 388.

The sound reasons underlying this rule are just as cogent since the advent of the new Federal Rules as they were before. A bad complaint tenders no issue and requires no answer. Thus it is necessary to examine into the sufficiency of the complaint at bar.

I am satisfied that no cause of action is stated in this complaint.

[A discussion of the substantive law of libel is omitted.]

Feeling as I do that the matter set forth in the complaint is clearly not libelous, I am constrained to dismiss the complaint. The motion, therefore, is denied, and plaintiff's complaint dismissed. Settle order on notice.

WATERTOWN MILK PRODUCERS' CO–OPERATIVE ASS'N v. VAN CAMP PACKING CO., 199 Wis. 379, 226 N.W. 378 (1929). After pointing out that an essential allegation was lacking in the complaint, the court said:

"A demurrer to the complaint would have been sustained. But there was no demurrer to the complaint. The defendants answered, and by their answers they supplied the substance of this essential allegation. A demurrer to the answer searches the record. It goes back to the complaint. If the complaint is bad the demurrer will be overruled, as a bad answer is considered good enough for a bad complaint. However, where the entire record reveals facts constituting a good cause of action, a demurrer to the answer will not be overruled on the ground that the complaint does not state facts sufficient to constitute a cause of action. Colwell Lead Co. v. Home Title Ins. Co., 154 App. Div. 83, 138 N.Y.S. 738; Sill v. Sill, 31 Kan. 248, 1 P. 556. While there are decisions holding that upon a demurrer to the answer the averments in the answer will not be permitted to supply a deficiency in the complaint, we find very little considerate discussion of the subject. . . .

". . . Upon mature consideration, it would seem that the cause of simplified procedure is illy served by a rule which ignores the allegations of the answer where the complaint is under scrutiny by virtue of a demurrer to the answer. Where in such case it appears that essential facts omitted in the complaint are supplied by the answer of the one who challenges the complaint, why should the litigants be required to retrace their steps and frame new pleadings all along the line?"

SECTION 2.   COUNTERCLAIMS

Recoupment.—At common law there were narrowly confined situations where a defendant, by asserting a claim of his own in the action, could reduce the recovery to which the plaintiff would otherwise be entitled. A building contractor sues the owner for work done and materials furnished; in that action the owner might seek a recoupment on the ground that the work was not well done, and if the recoupment succeeded, the contractor's recovery would be reduced accordingly. Sedgwick says that "recoupment, in its original sense, was a mere right of deduction from the amount of the plaintiff's recovery, on the ground that his damages were not really as high as he alleged," but in time the sharpness of this definition was lost. 3 T. Sedgwick, Damages 2162 (9th ed. 1912). For instance, where the plaintiff sued on a promissory note given for the sale of his business, the defendant was allowed to recoup for the plaintiff's breach of an agreement not to compete with the business. Stacy v. Kemp, 97 Mass. 166 (1867).

A recoupment must have arisen out of the same transaction as the plaintiff's claim. It could reduce the plaintiff's claim but could not result in an affirmative judgment in the action in the defendant's favor. However, to maintain a recoupment it was not necessary that the plaintiff's or the defendant's claim be liquidated or certain in amount.

Question: (13) Would recoupment be available to a defendant in a highway accident case where both plaintiff and defendant were injured and each asserts that the other was solely to blame?

As the matter asserted by way of recoupment must have arisen out of the same transaction as plaintiff's claim, it would naturally follow in most cases that if plaintiff's action was not barred by the statute of limitations, the recoupment matter would not be barred if an independent action had been brought on it on the date of commencement of plaintiff's action. In a small number of cases this would not be true. Moreover, defendant's recoupment might be barred as an independent action at the time defendant pleaded, even if timely when plaintiff's action was commenced. It was laid down as a general rule, however, that if plaintiff's action was timely, defendant's recoupment was also timely.

Setoff.—Where the defendant's claim arose out of a different transaction, recoupment was unavailable. So, at early common law the defendant could secure adjudication of his claim only by bringing an independent action. Equity, however, borrowed the Roman and civil-law doctrine of compensatio and allowed the setoff of mutual debts. See 3 J. Story, Commentaries on Equity Jurisprudence § 1881 (14th ed. 1918). In the course of time this principle of equity was taken over by the law courts. The first step was the statute of 4 Anne, ch. 17, § 11 (1705), by which setoff was made available at law in cases where the parties were mutually indebted and the plaintiff was insolvent. Then the statute of 2 Geo. 2, ch. 22, § 13 (1729), as amended by 8 Geo. 2, ch. 24, § 5 (1735), eliminated the requirement of insolvency and made setoff generally available wherever there were mutual debts.

This statutory setoff, like recoupment, could not be used as a basis for affirmative relief; its only effect was to reduce or defeat the plaintiff's claim. The plea of setoff was allowed only where the claims on both sides involved liquidated debts or debts that could be readily and without difficulty ascertained. See Stooke v. Taylor, 5 Q.B.D. 569 (1880). (There were some inroads on these rules in the United States.)

Unlike recoupment, the defendant's claim in setoff was not immune from the bar of the statute of limitations. But the crucial date was the day when the plaintiff instituted his suit. The setoff was timely even though the statutory period for bringing an independent action upon it had expired between the commencement of the plaintiff's suit and the bringing of the claim in setoff. See Walker v. Clements, 117 Eng.Rep. 755 (Q.B.1850).

Counterclaim.—In New York provision was made by amendment to the Field Code in 1852 for counterclaims, which were materially broader than common-law recoupment or statutory setoff. Many code states soon followed New York's lead. The most striking change was to permit the defendant to recover an affirmative judgment. Thus the defendant whose claim was adjudged to exceed that of the plaintiff could wind up with a money judgment in his favor, as could the defendant whose counterclaim succeeded when the plaintiff's claim failed. Nor did contract claims arising from different transactions have to be certain in amount, as their setoff ancestor required. The New York provision allowed as a counterclaim: (1) "A cause of action arising out of the contract or transaction set forth in the complaint, as the foundation of the plaintiff's claim, or connected with the subject of the action"; or (2) "In an action arising on contract, any other cause of action arising also on contract, and existing at the commencement of the action." [g] Code provisions in other states were usually to the same effect.

Words like "transaction" give the usual troubles. [h] The other restrictions also give rise to problems. [i] A number of the codes provide expressly or have been construed to mean that the counterclaim must tend to diminish or defeat the plaintiff's recovery. This requirement may have a curiously restrictive effect. It has been held, for instance, that in a suit in equity for cancellation of a deed to real property, a counterclaim for a money judgment for expenditures made in the operation of the property is improper. Bandy v. Westover, 200 Cal. 222, 252 P. 593 (1927).

In recent years a good many states, including New York, [j] have extended the scope of the permissive counterclaim in the same fashion as Federal Rule 13(b). A good many other states have gone further to provide as well for compulsory counterclaims along the lines of Federal Rule 13(a).

STATUTE OF LIMITATIONS

Courts have had difficulty in dealing with the statute of limitations as applied to counterclaims. They have generally heeded the

[g] 1852 N.Y.Laws ch. 392, amending Code of Procedure § 150.

[h] See supra pp. 48–51.

[i] See supra pp. 403–05.

[j] NYCPLR § 3019(a).

common-law precedents developed in recoupment and setoff cases. Accordingly, in the absence of a statute dictating a different result, the usual view is that a counterclaim of the old-fashioned recoupment type may be used "defensively," that is, in reduction of the plaintiff's claim, no matter when the events giving rise to the counterclaim occurred; but that a counterclaim arising from a different transaction cannot be maintained if an independent action upon it was barred when the plaintiff's suit was instituted. However, some jurisdictions take different approaches, falling along a spectrum we shall now sketch. Note for each situation whether the counterclaim merely relates back to the time of the complaint or is timely if the plaintiff's action was timely, whether or not there is a requirement of transactional relation, and whether or not only "defensive" relief is allowed.

In several states, statutes deal specifically with the problem of time limitations on counterclaims. Occasionally these statutes seem more restrictive than the common-law approach. For example, a former Wisconsin statute provided: "A cause of action upon which an action cannot be maintained, as prescribed in this chapter [on limitations of actions], cannot be effectually interposed as a defense, counterclaim or set-off." Wis.Stat. § 893.27 (1977) (repealed 1979).

Questions: (14) Under a statute like that of Wisconsin, a doctor sues a patient for his professional services within the period of limitations for a contract action, but the patient is quite unhappy with those services. (a) After institution of suit but before answer, the shorter statute on malpractice actions runs. Can the patient set up "defensively" that the services were negligently performed, a matter that was a basis for recoupment at common law? (b) Can the patient do so if the doctor's suit was brought after the malpractice statute had run? See Peterson v. Feyereisen, 203 Wis. 294, 234 N.W. 496 (1931) (indicating yes).

(15) On June 1, 1984, *A* sues *B* on a note for $1000. On June 15, 1984, *B* counterclaims on another note for $3000, upon which the limitations period expired on June 5, 1984. The counterclaim statute is like Rule 13(b), and the statute of limitations contains no specific reference to counterclaims. *A* moves against the counterclaim. What result? An English court in dealing with this problem followed Walker v. Clements, supra p. 466, to the extent of allowing the "defensive" use of the counterclaim but denied affirmative recovery, pointing out that affirmative relief was unknown when Walker v. Clements was decided. Lowe v. Bentley, 44 T.L.R. 388 (K.B.1928). Would you follow Lowe v. Bentley, dismiss the counterclaim, or allow the defendant an affirmative recovery? Would your answer be different if both claims were contract claims for uncertain amounts? or unrelated torts?

AZADA v. CARSON

United States District Court, District of Hawaii, 1966.
252 F.Supp. 988.

TAVARES, DISTRICT JUDGE. On October 12, 1963, plaintiff Mariano Azada was driving a car which collided with a car driven by defendant Roger Carson. Plaintiff and his wife filed suit for personal injuries three days before the running of the two-year statute of limitations.

Defendant was not served with process until nearly three months after the complaint was filed; thus the counterclaim later filed by the defendant was filed more than two years following the date of the collision. Plaintiffs move to dismiss the counterclaim on the ground that it was filed after the statute of limitations had become a bar.

Jurisdiction here is based upon diversity of citizenship, and therefore this Court must apply Hawaii law. However, no Hawaii statute nor reported decision had been found that disposes of the question here.

Authorities outside of Hawaii are divided on the question. C.J.S. Limitations of Actions § 285, pp. 342–343, reports:

> "There is a conflict of opinion as to when a claim interposed as a set-off or counterclaim becomes barred by the statute of limitations. The weight of authority supports the rule, said to be the better rule, that, where defendant's claim, asserted in a set-off or counterclaim, was an existing debt not barred by the statute of limitations at the time plaintiff's action was begun, it will be a valid set-off or counterclaim, although the statutory period may have elapsed before the filing of the answer setting it up, provided, under some of the statutes, the counterclaim arose out of the same transaction as gave rise to the main action."

Plaintiff argues that most of the cases allowing a counterclaim, if it was not barred at the time the action was begun, involved contracts and not torts. But there seems to be no logical reason for making such a distinction. The same considerations of fair play and justice apply, whether the action is based upon contract or tort.

Statutes of limitation are statutes of repose—they are designed to bar stale claims. Where, as in this case, the counterclaim arises from the same incident as the complaint, the counterclaim is no more stale than the complaint.

Simple justice dictates that if the plaintiffs are given an opportunity to present a claim for relief based upon a particular automobile collision, the defendant should not be prevented from doing so by a mere technicality.

Without meaning to suggest in any way that the instant suit involves frivolous claims, the rule adopted by this Court will also have the beneficial effect of tending to discourage the filing of frivolous claims just before the running of the statute of limitations.

Therefore plaintiffs' motion to dismiss the counterclaim is hereby denied.

NEW YORK CIVIL PRACTICE LAW AND RULES

§ 203. *Method of computing periods of limitation generally*

. . . .

(c) **Defense or counterclaim.** A defense or counterclaim is interposed when a pleading containing it is served. A defense or counterclaim is not barred if it was not barred at the time the claims asserted in the complaint were interposed, except that if the defense or counterclaim arose from the transactions, occurrences, or series of transactions or occurrences, upon which a claim asserted in the complaint depends, it is not barred to the extent of the demand in the complaint notwithstanding that it was barred at the time the claims asserted in the complaint were interposed. [k]

. . . .

Question: (16) The Federal Tort Claims Act provides in 28 U.S.C. § 2401(b) that a tort claim against the United States must be asserted within two years after such claim accrues. The United States sues for damage to a government-owned motor vehicle more than two years after the date of the accident but well within the applicable statute of limitations for motor vehicle torts. The defendant counterclaims for his own damage, seeking affirmative relief. Should the counterclaim be dismissed on the government's motion? Compare United States v. Capital Transit Co., 108 F.Supp. 348 (D.D.C.1952) (no), with United States v. Yellow Cab Co., 188 F.Supp. 660 (E.D.Pa.1960) (yes).

UNITED STATES CODE, TITLE 28

§ 2415. *Time for commencing action brought by the United States*

. . . .

(f) The provisions of this section shall not prevent the assertion, in an action against the United States or an officer or agency thereof, of any claim of the United States or an officer or agency thereof against an opposing party, a co-party, or a third party that arises out of the transaction or occurrence that is the subject matter of the opposing party's claim. A claim of the United States or an officer or agency thereof that does not arise out of the transaction or occurrence that is the subject matter of the opposing party's claim may, if time-

---

[k] Massachusetts, which now has a counterclaim rule modeled on Federal Rule 13, has a limitations statute to the same effect as this New York provision. Mass.Gen.Laws Ann. ch. 260, § 36. For the background of the Massachusetts statute, see Bose Corp. v. Consumers Union of United States, 367 Mass. 424, 326 N.E.2d 8 (1975) (Kaplan, J.).

barred, be asserted only by way of offset and may be allowed in an amount not to exceed the amount of the opposing party's recovery.

. . . .

Questions: (17) To close out the spectrum, imagine that *P* sues *D* for breach of contract within the applicable period of limitations but after the statute has run on *D*'s unrelated tort claim. Can any argument be made to allow *D* affirmative relief by way of counterclaim?

(18) Assume that a claim upon which the statute of limitations has run would, if pleaded as a counterclaim in the answer interposed by the defendant in a federal-court action, be saved by one or another of the above-suggested approaches under the applicable law. However, it is omitted from the answer and only later added by amendment under Rule 13(f). The plaintiff moves against the counterclaim. What result? See Diematic Mfg. Corp. v. Packaging Indus., 412 F.Supp. 1367 (S.D.N.Y.1976) (applying Rule 15(c)).

SECTION 3. THE REPLY

In the absence of a counterclaim, to which a responsive pleading is required, pleading under the Federal Rules stops with the answer save in the rare case where the court orders a reply. The majority of codes, however, carry the pleading process somewhat further, although none of them adheres to the common-law scheme of continuing the pleadings until they terminate in an issue of fact or law. Typically, further pleadings after the reply (the common-law replication) are forbidden.

The codes vary in their provisions with respect to the reply. Frequently a reply to new matter in the answer is required, else the new matter stands as admitted. Under the New Jersey Court Rules such a reply is required only if the plaintiff wishes to raise new matter in avoidance of the defense; a reply simply to deny new matter in the answer is neither necessary nor proper. N.J.Ct.R. 4:5–1. Whatever the arrangement may be, there comes a point where no further pleading is allowed and new matter in the last permitted pleading is "taken as denied or avoided," as it is under Federal Rule 8(d). This means that the pleadings may leave the parties in ignorance of the exact issues to be tried, with clarification coming, if at all, from any discovery and pretrial conference devices that may exist or from informal discussion between counsel.

The requirement of a reply to new matter creates pitfalls for the pleader that do not exist when pleadings are cut off with the answer. We have, for instance, already seen something of the difficulties in deciding whether a particular matter of defense can be shown under a general denial. If the defendant's answer unnecessarily includes matter that would be open to him under a general denial, it is not "new matter" that is taken as admitted if not denied in a reply. But the consequences of a wrong guess may be serious. Suppose the defendant in a case involving the facts of question (7) pleads that the plaintiff's loss was due to an act of God. The plaintiff's attorney does not reply, believing that this is provable under a general denial (as the Kentucky court in the cited Carmichael case held) and hence that no reply is necessary. The defendant moves for judgment on the pleadings. If the court takes a view opposed to the Carmichael case (as some courts have), then the plaintiff has unwittingly admitted the existence of a good defense to his claim.

A reply may also involve the hazards of departure. Just as at common law, a code plaintiff may not in his reply abandon the claim stated in his complaint and rely upon another. With the present-day freedom of amendment a plaintiff can ordinarily avoid a departure by simply amending his complaint when the need to do so becomes manifest. It has been suggested that for this reason a rigid enforcement of the rule against departure would be inconsistent with the spirit of the Federal Rules. Commentary, Departure in the Reply, 4 Fed.R. Serv. (Callaghan) 889 (1941). On the other hand, in Grobart v. Society for Establishing Useful Manufactures, 2 N.J. 136, 65 A.2d 833 (1949), the court inveighs against permitting a pleader to shift his ground from pleading to pleading, as distinguished from allowing in the same pleading alternative or hypothetical or inconsistent positions.

TOPIC D.   DISCOVERY

SECTION 1.   SCOPE OF DISCOVERY

HICKMAN v. TAYLOR

Supreme Court of the United States, 1947.
329 U.S. 495, 67 S.Ct. 385.

MR. JUSTICE MURPHY delivered the opinion of the Court.

This case presents an important problem under the Federal Rules of Civil Procedure as to the extent to which a party may inquire into oral and written statements of witnesses, or other information, secured by an adverse party's counsel in the course of preparation for possible litigation after a claim has arisen. Examination into a person's files and records, including those resulting from the professional activities of an attorney, must be judged with care. It is not without reason that various safeguards have been established to preclude unwarranted excursions into the privacy of a man's work. At the same time, public policy supports reasonable and necessary inquiries. Properly to balance these competing interests is a delicate and difficult task.

On February 7, 1943, the tug "J.M. Taylor" sank while engaged in helping to tow a car float of the Baltimore & Ohio Railroad across the Delaware River at Philadelphia. The accident was apparently unusual in nature, the cause of it still being unknown. Five of the nine crew members were drowned. Three days later the tug owners and the underwriters employed a law firm, of which respondent Fortenbaugh is a member, to defend them against potential suits by representatives of the deceased crew members and to sue the railroad for damages to the tug.

A public hearing was held on March 4, 1943, before the United States Steamboat Inspectors, at which the four survivors were examined. This testimony was recorded and made available to all interested parties. Shortly thereafter, Fortenbaugh privately interviewed the survivors and took statements from them with an eye toward the anticipated litigation; the survivors signed these statements on March 29. Fortenbaugh also interviewed other persons believed to have some information relating to the accident and in some cases he made memoranda of what they told him. At the time when Fortenbaugh secured the statements of the survivors, representatives of two of the deceased crew members had been in communication with him. Ultimately claims were presented by representatives of all five of the deceased; four of the claims, however, were settled without litigation. The fifth claimant, petitioner herein, brought suit

472

in a federal court under the Jones Act on November 26, 1943, naming as defendants the two tug owners, individually and as partners, and the railroad.

One year later, petitioner filed 39 interrogatories directed to the tug owners. The 38th interrogatory read: "State whether any statements of the members of the crews of the Tugs 'J.M. Taylor' and 'Philadelphia' or of any other vessel were taken in connection with the towing of the car float and the sinking of the Tug 'John M. Taylor.' Attach hereto exact copies of all such statements if in writing, and if oral, set forth in detail the exact provisions of any such oral statements or reports."

Supplemental interrogatories asked whether any oral or written statements, records, reports or other memoranda had been made concerning any matter relative to the towing operation, the sinking of the tug, the salvaging and repair of the tug, and the death of the deceased. If the answer was in the affirmative, the tug owners were then requested to set forth the nature of all such records, reports, statements or other memoranda.

The tug owners, through Fortenbaugh, answered all of the interrogatories except No. 38 and the supplemental ones just described. While admitting that statements of the survivors had been taken, they declined to summarize or set forth the contents. They did so on the ground that such requests called "for privileged matter obtained in preparation for litigation" and constituted "an attempt to obtain indirectly counsel's private files." It was claimed that answering these requests "would involve practically turning over not only the complete files, but also the telephone records and, almost, the thoughts of counsel."

In connection with the hearing on these objections, Fortenbaugh made a written statement and gave an informal oral deposition explaining the circumstances under which he had taken the statements. But he was not expressly asked in the deposition to produce the statements. The District Court for the Eastern District of Pennsylvania, sitting en banc, held that the requested matters were not privileged. 4 F.R.D. 479. The court then decreed that the tug owners and Fortenbaugh, as counsel and agent for the tug owners, forthwith "answer Plaintiff's 38th interrogatory and supplementary interrogatories; produce all written statements of witnesses obtained by Mr. Fortenbaugh, as counsel and agent for Defendants; state in substance any fact concerning this case which Defendants learned through oral statements made by witnesses to Mr. Fortenbaugh whether or not included in his private memoranda and produce Mr. Fortenbaugh's memoranda containing statements of fact by witnesses or to submit these memoranda to the Court for determination of those portions which should be revealed to Plaintiff." Upon their refusal, the court adjudged them in contempt and ordered them imprisoned until they complied.

The Third Circuit Court of Appeals, also sitting en banc, reversed the judgment of the District Court. 153 F.2d 212. It held that the information here sought was part of the "work product of the lawyer" and hence privileged from discovery under the Federal Rules of Civil Procedure. The importance of the problem, which has engendered a great divergence of views among district courts, led us to grant certiorari. 328 U.S. 876, 66 S.Ct. 1337.

The pre-trial deposition-discovery mechanism established by Rules 26 to 37 is one of the most significant innovations of the Federal Rules of Civil Procedure. Under the prior federal practice, the pre-trial functions of notice-giving, issue-formulation and fact-revelation were performed primarily and inadequately by the pleadings. Inquiry into the issues and the facts before trial was narrowly confined and was often cumbersome in method. The new rules, however, restrict the pleadings to the task of general notice-giving and invest the deposition-discovery process with a vital role in the preparation for trial. The various instruments of discovery now serve (1) as a device, along with the pre-trial hearing under Rule 16, to narrow and clarify the basic issues between the parties, and (2) as a device for ascertaining the facts, or information as to the existence or whereabouts of facts, relative to those issues. Thus civil trials in the federal courts no longer need be carried on in the dark. The way is now clear, consistent with recognized privileges, for the parties to obtain the fullest possible knowledge of the issues and facts before trial.

Should have used R34 Production of documents [The Court here said that in using interrogatories to obtain documents the petitioner misconceived his remedy, but the Court decided to overlook this procedural irregularity and reach the underlying problem of scope of discovery.]

Arguments for no Priv. In urging that he has a right to inquire into the materials secured and prepared by Fortenbaugh, petitioner emphasizes that the deposition-discovery portions of the Federal Rules of Civil Procedure are designed to enable the parties to discover the true facts and to compel their disclosure wherever they may be found. It is said that inquiry may be made under these rules, epitomized by Rule 26, as to any relevant matter which is not privileged; and since the discovery provisions are to be applied as broadly and liberally as possible, the privilege limitation must be restricted to its narrowest bounds. On the premise that the attorney-client privilege is the one involved in this case, petitioner argues that it must be strictly confined to confidential communications made by a client to his attorney. And since the materials here in issue were secured by Fortenbaugh from third persons rather than from his clients, the tug owners, the conclusion is reached that these materials are proper subjects for discovery under Rule 26.

As additional support for this result, petitioner claims that to prohibit discovery under these circumstances would give a corporate defendant a tremendous advantage in a suit by an individual plaintiff.

Thus in a suit by an injured employee against a railroad or in a suit by an insured person against an insurance company the corporate defendant could pull a dark veil of secrecy over all the pertinent facts it can collect after the claim arises merely on the assertion that such facts were gathered by its large staff of attorneys and claim agents. At the same time, the individual plaintiff, who often has direct knowledge of the matter in issue and has no counsel until some time after his claim arises could be compelled to disclose all the intimate details of his case. By endowing with immunity from disclosure all that a lawyer discovers in the course of his duties, it is said, the rights of individual litigants in such cases are drained of vitality and the lawsuit becomes more of a battle of deception than a search for truth.

But framing the problem in terms of assisting individual plaintiffs in their suits against corporate defendants is unsatisfactory. Discovery concededly may work to the disadvantage as well as to the advantage of individual plaintiffs. Discovery, in other words, is not a one-way proposition. It is available in all types of cases at the behest of any party, individual or corporate, plaintiff or defendant. The problem thus far transcends the situation confronting this petitioner. And we must view that problem in light of the limitless situations where the particular kind of discovery sought by petitioner might be used.

We agree, of course, that the deposition-discovery rules are to be accorded a broad and liberal treatment. No longer can the time-honored cry of "fishing expedition" serve to preclude a party from inquiring into the facts underlying his opponent's case. Mutual knowledge of all the relevant facts gathered by both parties is essential to proper litigation. To that end, either party may compel the other to disgorge whatever facts he has in his possession. The deposition-discovery procedure simply advances the stage at which the disclosure can be compelled from the time of trial to the period preceding it, thus reducing the possibility of surprise. But discovery, like all matters of procedure, has ultimate and necessary boundaries. As indicated by Rules 30(b) and (d) and 31(d), [a] limitations inevitably arise when it can be shown that the examination is being conducted in bad faith or in such a manner as to annoy, embarrass or oppress the person subject to the inquiry. And as Rule 26(b) provides, further limitations come into existence when the inquiry touches upon the irrelevant or encroaches upon the recognized domains of privilege.

We also agree that the memoranda, statements and mental impressions in issue in this case fall outside the scope of the attorney-client privilege and hence are not protected from discovery on that basis. It is unnecessary here to delineate the content and scope of that privilege as recognized in the federal courts. For present purposes, it suffices to note that the protective cloak of this privilege

[margin note: Not ATTY-Client Priv]

---

[a] Old Rules 30(b) and 31(d) now appear as Rule 26(c).

does not extend to information which an attorney secures from a witness while acting for his client in anticipation of litigation. Nor does this privilege concern the memoranda, briefs, communications and other writings prepared by counsel for his own use in prosecuting his client's case; and it is equally unrelated to writings which reflect an attorney's mental impressions, conclusions, opinions or legal theories.

But the impropriety of invoking that privilege does not provide an answer to the problem before us. Petitioner has made more than an ordinary request for relevant, non-privileged facts in the possession of his adversaries or their counsel. He has sought discovery as of right of oral and written statements of witnesses whose identity is well known and whose availability to petitioner appears unimpaired. He has sought production of these matters after making the most searching inquiries of his opponents as to the circumstances surrounding the fatal accident, which inquiries were sworn to have been answered to the best of their information and belief. Interrogatories were directed toward all the events prior to, during and subsequent to the sinking of the tug. Full and honest answers to such broad inquiries would necessarily have included all pertinent information gleaned by Fortenbaugh through his interviews with the witnesses. Petitioner makes no suggestion, and we cannot assume, that the tug owners or Fortenbaugh were incomplete or dishonest in the framing of their answers. In addition, petitioner was free to examine the public testimony of the witnesses taken before the United States Steamboat Inspectors. We are thus dealing with an attempt to secure the production of written statements and mental impressions contained in the files and the mind of the attorney Fortenbaugh without any showing of necessity or any indication or claim that denial of such production would unduly prejudice the preparation of petitioner's case or cause him any hardship or injustice. For aught that appears, the essence of what petitioner seeks either has been revealed to him already through the interrogatories or is readily available to him direct from the witnesses for the asking.

The District Court, after hearing objections to petitioner's request, commanded Fortenbaugh to produce all written statements of witnesses and to state in substance any facts learned through oral statements of witnesses to him. Fortenbaugh was to submit any memoranda he had made of the oral statements so that the court might determine what portions should be revealed to petitioner. All of this was ordered without any showing by petitioner, or any requirement that he make a proper showing, of the necessity for the production of any of this material or any demonstration that denial of production would cause hardship or injustice. The court simply ordered production on the theory that the facts sought were material and were not privileged as constituting attorney-client communications.

In our opinion, neither Rule 26 nor any other rule dealing with discovery contemplates production under such circumstances. That is not because the subject matter is privileged or irrelevant, as those concepts are used in these rules. Here is simply an attempt, without purported necessity or justification, to secure written statements, private memoranda and personal recollections prepared or formed by an adverse party's counsel in the course of his legal duties. As such, it falls outside the arena of discovery and contravenes the public policy underlying the orderly prosecution and defense of legal claims. Not even the most liberal of discovery theories can justify unwarranted inquiries into the files and the mental impressions of an attorney.

Historically, a lawyer is an officer of the court and is bound to work for the advancement of justice while faithfully protecting the rightful interests of his clients. In performing his various duties, however, it is essential that a lawyer work with a certain degree of privacy, free from unnecessary intrusion by opposing parties and their counsel. Proper preparation of a client's case demands that he assemble information, sift what he considers to be the relevant from the irrelevant facts, prepare his legal theories and plan his strategy without undue and needless interference. That is the historical and the necessary way in which lawyers act within the framework of our system of jurisprudence to promote justice and to protect their clients' interest. This work is reflected, of course, in interviews, statements, memoranda, correspondence, briefs, mental impressions, personal beliefs, and countless other tangible and intangible ways—aptly though roughly termed by the Circuit Court of Appeals in this case as the "work product of the lawyer." Were such materials open to opposing counsel on mere demand, much of what is now put down in writing would remain unwritten. An attorney's thoughts, heretofore inviolate, would not be his own. Inefficiency, unfairness and sharp practices would inevitably develop in the giving of legal advice and in the preparation of cases for trial. The effect on the legal profession would be demoralizing. And the interests of the clients and the cause of justice would be poorly served.

We do not mean to say that all written materials obtained or prepared by an adversary's counsel with an eye toward litigation are necessarily free from discovery in all cases. Where relevant and non-privileged facts remain hidden in an attorney's file and where production of those facts is essential to the preparation of one's case, discovery may properly be had. Such written statements and documents might, under certain circumstances, be admissible in evidence or give clues as to the existence or location of relevant facts. Or they might be useful for purposes of impeachment or corroboration. [b] And production might be justified where the witnesses are no longer available or can be reached only with difficulty. Were production of writ-

---

[b] What differences do you perceive with respect to use at trial for impeachment purposes between (i) the signed statement of a witness and (ii) memoranda made by the attorney as to oral statements of the witness, whether made contemporaneously with the interview or later pursuant to a discovery order such as that of the district court in this case?

ten statements and documents to be precluded under such circumstances, the liberal ideals of the deposition-discovery portions of the Federal Rules of Civil Procedure would be stripped of much of their meaning. But the general policy against invading the privacy of an attorney's course of preparation is so well recognized and so essential to an orderly working of our system of legal procedure that a burden rests on the one who would invade that privacy to establish adequate reasons to justify production through a subpoena or court order. That burden, we believe, is necessarily implicit in the rules as now constituted.

Policy against giving atty's papers so strong that burden on other to prove good reason for showing info

Rule 30(b), as presently written, gives the trial judge the requisite discretion to make a judgment as to whether discovery should be allowed as to written statements secured from witnesses. But in the instant case there was no room for that discretion to operate in favor of the petitioner. No attempt was made to establish any reason why Fortenbaugh should be forced to produce the written statements. There was only a naked, general demand for these materials as of right and a finding by the District Court that no recognizable privilege was involved. That was insufficient to justify discovery under these circumstances and the court should have sustained the refusal of the tug owners and Fortenbaugh to produce.

But as to oral statements made by witnesses to Fortenbaugh, whether presently in the form of his mental impressions or memoranda, we do not believe that any showing of necessity can be made under the circumstances of this case so as to justify production. Under ordinary conditions, forcing an attorney to repeat or write out all that witnesses have told him and to deliver the account to his adversary gives rise to grave dangers of inaccuracy and untrustworthiness. No legitimate purpose is served by such production. The practice forces the attorney to testify as to what he remembers or what he saw fit to write down regarding witnesses' remarks. Such testimony could not qualify as evidence; and to use it for impeachment or corroborative purposes would make the attorney much less an officer of the court and much more an ordinary witness. The standards of the profession would thereby suffer.

Can't get oral stmts bk inaccurate & atty then not officer of ct.

Denial of production of this nature does not mean that any material, non-privileged facts can be hidden from the petitioner in this case. He need not be unduly hindered in the preparation of his case, in the dicovery of facts or in his anticipation of his opponents' position. Searching interrogatories directed to Fortenbaugh and the tug owners, production of written documents and statements upon a proper showing and direct interviews with the witnesses themselves all serve to reveal the facts in Fortenbaugh's possession to the fullest possible extent consistent with public policy. Petitioner's counsel frankly admits that he wants the oral statements only to help prepare himself to examine witnesses and to make sure that he has overlooked nothing. That is insufficient under the circumstances to permit him an exception to the policy underlying the privacy of Fortenbaugh's professional activities. If there should be a rare situation justifying production of these matters, petitioner's case is not of that type.

We fully appreciate the wide-spread controversy among the members of the legal profession over the problem raised by this case. It is a problem that rests on what has been one of the most hazy frontiers of the discovery process. But until some rule or statute definitely prescribes otherwise, we are not justified in permitting discovery in a situation of this nature as a matter of unqualified right. When Rule 26 and the other discovery rules were adopted, this Court and the members of the bar in general certainly did not believe or contemplate that all the files and mental processes of lawyers were thereby opened to the free scrutiny of their adversaries. And we refuse to interpret the rules at this time so as to reach so harsh and unwarranted a result.

We therefore affirm the judgment of the Circuit Court of Appeals.

Affirmed.

MR. JUSTICE JACKSON, concurring.

. . . . .

The primary effect of the practice advocated here would be on the legal profession itself. But it too often is overlooked that the lawyer and the law office are indispensable parts of our administration of justice. Law-abiding people can go nowhere else to learn the ever changing and constantly multiplying rules by which they must behave and to obtain redress for their wrongs. The welfare and tone of the legal profession is therefore of prime consequence to society, which would feel the consequences of such a practice as petitioner urges secondarily but certainly.

. . . . .

To consider first the most extreme aspect of the requirement in litigation here, we find it calls upon counsel, if he has had any conversations with any of the crews of the vessels in question or of any other, to "set forth in detail the exact provision of any such oral statements or reports." Thus the demand is not for the production of a transcript in existence but calls for the creation of a written statement not in being. But the statement by counsel of what a witness told him is not evidence when written. Plaintiff could not introduce it to prove his case. What, then, is the purpose sought to be served by demanding this of adverse counsel?

Counsel for the petitioner candidly said on argument that he wanted this information to help prepare himself to examine witnesses, to make sure he overlooked nothing. He bases his claim to it in his brief on the view that the Rules were to do away with the old situation where a lawsuit developed into "a battle of wits between counsel." But a common law trial is and always should be an adversary proceeding. Discovery was hardly intended to enable a learned profession to perform its functions either without wits or on wits borrowed from the adversary.

why no oral stmts retold by atty

The real purpose and the probable effect of the practice ordered by the district court would be to put trials on a level even lower than a "battle of wits." I can conceive of no practice more demoralizing to the Bar than to require a lawyer to write out and deliver to his adversary an account of what witnesses have told him. Even if his recollection were perfect, the statement would be his language, permeated with his inferences. Everyone who has tried it knows that it is almost impossible so fairly to record the expressions and emphasis of a witness that when he testifies in the environment of the court and under the influence of the leading question there will not be departures in some respects. Whenever the testimony of the witness would differ from the "exact" statement the lawyer had delivered, the lawyer's statement would be whipped out to impeach the witness. Counsel producing his adversary's "inexact" statement could lose nothing by saying, "Here is a contradiction, gentlemen of the jury. I do not know whether it is my adversary or his witness who is not telling the truth, but one is not." Of course, if this practice were adopted, that scene would be repeated over and over again. The lawyer who delivers such statements often would find himself branded a deceiver afraid to take the stand to support his own version of the witness's conversation with him, or else he will have to go on the stand to defend his own credibility—perhaps against that of his chief witness, or possibly even his client.

Every lawyer dislikes to take the witness stand and will do so only for grave reasons. This is partly because it is not his role; he is almost invariably a poor witness. But he steps out of professional character to do it. He regrets it; the profession discourages it. But the practice advocated here is one which would force him to be a witness, not as to what he has seen or done but as to other witnesses' stories, and not because he wants to do so but in self-defense.

And what is the lawyer to do who has interviewed one whom he believes to be a biased, lying or hostile witness to get his unfavorable statements and know what to meet? He must record and deliver such statements even though he would not vouch for the credibility of the witness by calling him. Perhaps the other side would not want to call him either, but the attorney is open to the charge of suppressing evidence at the trial if he fails to call such a hostile witness even though he never regarded him as reliable or truthful.

Having been supplied the names of the witnesses, petitioner's lawyer gives no reason why he cannot interview them himself. If an employee-witness refuses to tell his story, he, too, may be examined under the Rules. He may be compelled on discovery, as fully as on the trial, to disclose his version of the facts. But that is his own disclosure—it can be used to impeach him if he contradicts it and such a deposition is not useful to promote an unseemly disagreement between the witness and the counsel in the case.

. . . .

The question remains as to signed statements or those written by witnesses. Such statements are not evidence for the defendant. Palmer v. Hoffman, 318 U.S. 109, 63 S.Ct. 477. Nor should I think they ordinarily could be evidence for the plaintiff. But such a statement might be useful for impeachment of the witness who signed it, if he is called and if he departs from the statement. There might be circumstances, too, where impossibility or difficulty of access to the witness or his refusal to respond to requests for information or other facts would show that the interests of justice require that such statements be made available. [No sufficient showing was made in this case.]

Still have to show good reason why need written stmts.

I agree to the affirmance of the judgment of the Circuit Court of Appeals which reversed the district court.

MR. JUSTICE FRANKFURTER joins in this opinion.

————

TRIAL PREPARATION MATERIALS: BEFORE AND AFTER HICKMAN

Prior to the decision in Hickman v. Taylor, the law in state courts had been unclear with respect to discovery of materials obtained or prepared in anticipation of litigation or in preparation for trial. There was authority that statements of third persons prepared for the lawyer's use were within the scope of professional privilege, just as were statements of the client's agents to the lawyer. There was some reliance on English precedents, themselves not entirely clear, giving a broad protection to materials gathered by or for the solicitor in connection with litigation.

Before the Federal Rules, decisions by the federal courts had been rare in this area. Under the Federal Rules before the Hickman decision, some courts had denied discovery of witness statements on the ground of privilege, others simply on the broad ground that discovery "would penalize the diligent and place a premium on laziness." McCarthy v. Palmer, 29 F.Supp. 585, 586 (E.D.N.Y.1939). Still others, a minority, had rejected these objections and permitted discovery. See, e.g., Hoffman v. Palmer, 129 F.2d 976 (2d Cir.1942), aff'd on other grounds, 318 U.S. 109, 63 S.Ct. 477 (1943).

It was generally held that federal discovery could be freely used to learn the identity and location of persons having knowledge of discoverable matter. This information was not privileged and was often an essential starting point in the adversary's own investigation. A party could be interrogated under Rule 33 about such persons, and he could not refuse to answer on the ground that the information sought was solely within the knowledge of his attorney. A distinction was made, however, between disclosing the witnesses to the events and disclosing the witnesses whom the party planned to call at trial. The latter was usually not permitted at the discovery stage, although there were a few decisions to the contrary. It was plain, nevertheless, that such disclosure could be required at pretrial conference.

Questions: (1) Why should there be any distinction between witnesses to the events and witnesses to be called at trial?

(2) Is there any reason to deny disclosure of trial witnesses through discovery when it is required at pretrial conference?

After the grant of certiorari in Hickman v. Taylor, the Advisory Committee submitted to the Supreme Court a large number of proposed amendments, including the following provision on trial preparation materials which appears at 5 F.R.D. 433, 456–57 (1946):

Proposed Amendment

"The court shall not order the production or inspection of any writing obtained or prepared by the adverse party, his attorney, surety, indemnitor, or agent in anticipation of litigation or in preparation for trial unless satisfied that denial of production or inspection will unfairly prejudice the party seeking the production or inspection in preparing his claim or defense or will cause him undue hardship or injustice. The court shall not order the production or inspection of any part of the writing that reflects an attorney's mental impressions, conclusions, opinions, or legal theories, or, except as provided in Rule 35, the conclusions of an expert."

When the Court adopted most of the proposed amendments, at a time after Hickman v. Taylor had been argued, it did not adopt this proposal. It seems plain that the Court believed it preferable to leave the protection of work product [c] to the processes of adjudication on a case-by-case basis. [d]

Questions: (3) What is the rationale of the Hickman decision? What matters did it definitively settle?

(4) To what extent were the policy determinations underlying the Hickman opinion in accord with those underlying the rejected 1946 proposal?

(5) Was it wise for the Supreme Court in 1947 to deal with the problem by judicial decision rather than by rule?

Whether it was right or wrong at the time to refrain from adopting a rule, the result was a welter of conflicting decisions. There was disagreement as to whether work-product protection should be limited to the preparatory work of lawyers only or should extend to such work by lay investigators like claim agents. Compare Alltmont v. United States, 177 F.2d 971 (3d Cir.1949) (protecting statements

---

[c] The label "work product" was used in the argument in the court of appeals and by that court in its opinion. Hickman v. Taylor, 153 F.2d 212, 223 (3d Cir.1945). Despite that court's expressed misgivings about adopting it, the phrase has stuck.

[d] New Jersey adopted the Advisory Committee's proposal with minor changes in phrasing, and a good number of states followed its lead.

obtained by FBI agents for use of government counsel in a civil action), cert. denied, 339 U.S. 967, 70 S.Ct. 999 (1950), with Southern Railway v. Campbell, 309 F.2d 569 (5th Cir.1962) (denying protection to statements taken by claim agents). The question was whether, as the Alltmont court put it, the rationale of Hickman "applies to all statements of prospective witnesses which a party has obtained for his trial counsel's use." There was apparently no dissent, however, from the proposition that materials assembled in the ordinary course of business or for purposes unrelated to litigation were not entitled to work-product protection. See, e.g., Goosman v. A. Duie Pyle, Inc., 320 F.2d 45 (4th Cir.1963) (statements made pursuant to ICC regulations).

Probably the most perplexing area of controversy centered on the showing necessary to overcome the qualified protection given to ordinary work product. Because Rule 34 then required "good cause" for the production of any document, there was difficulty in determining the relationship between the general "good cause" requirement of that Rule and the showing required under Hickman v. Taylor to obtain disclosure of work product, which the courts often characterized as "good cause." (The Court in Hickman did not use the term "good cause," but referred to "adequate reasons," "necessity or justification," and failure to demonstrate "that denial of production would cause hardship or injustice.") It was confusing to have "good cause" mean one thing for obtaining routine documents and another for piercing work-product protection. Yet it was also confusing, as the Advisory Committee pointed out in 1970, to have "two verbally distinct requirements of justification that the courts have been unable to distinguish clearly."

"Good cause" under Rule 34 was commonly equated to relevance and the absence of privilege in cases not involving trial preparation materials, and no more than a perfunctory showing of need was required. But when trial preparation materials were involved, even if they were held not to be entitled to work-product protection because they did not entail the work of a lawyer, courts demanded a much more rigorous showing. In a much-cited case, Guilford National Bank v. Southern Railway, 297 F.2d 921 (4th Cir.1962), the court avoided passing upon the trial judge's ruling that statements taken by claim agents were not entitled to the protection of the Hickman doctrine by finding on the facts that good cause under Rule 34 had not been shown. The same result would clearly have been reached if the work-product test had been applied. In Southern Railway v. Lanham, 403 F.2d 119 (5th Cir.1968), the court upheld an order for production of statements taken by a claim agent, saying that "good cause" under Rule 34 "requires something more than relevance and something less than the demonstration required to overcome the work product immunity." On the facts of that case it seems likely that there was a sufficient showing to compel production even if the statements had been taken by a lawyer. Indeed, when trial preparation materials were involved, there was far less disparity in results reached under the two formulations than there was in the verbalizations of the ways in which they were reached.

TRIAL PREPARATION MATERIALS:
THE 1970 AMENDMENTS

The 1970 amendments to the discovery Rules did much to dispel the confusion engendered by the accumulation of lower-court decisions after Hickman v. Taylor. Firstly, the elimination of the "good cause" requirement in Rule 34 made documents unconnected with trial preparation routinely discoverable. Secondly, Rule 26(b)(3) was introduced to deal with the scope of discovery of trial preparation materials. A careful examination of Rule 26(b)(3) is essential to a clear understanding of the attempted resolution of the uncertainties that had plagued the courts.

It is to be noted that this new subdivision pertains to documents and tangible things otherwise discoverable under subdivision (b)(1). Relevance to the subject matter is naturally still required, and privileged matter continues to be protected. The rules of privilege here referred to are the evidentiary rules applicable at trial. See Evidence Rules 1101(c) and 501.

Questions: (6) What is the effect of giving work-product protection to documents and tangible things prepared "by or for another party or by or for that other party's representative (including his attorney, consultant, surety, indemnitor, insurer, or agent)"?

(7) What of a statement dictated by a witness to the attorney's secretary at his request but in his absence?

(8) What of a written statement of a witness obtained by a party himself on his own initiative and turned over to his attorney?

(9) What of an unsolicited letter written to the attorney giving the writer's version of the events he observed?

Consider the special showing required by the Rule in order to obtain discovery of ordinary work product. The party seeking discovery must show that he has substantial need of the materials and that he is unable without undue hardship to obtain their substantial equivalent by other means. The Advisory Committee noted that this provision conforms to the holdings of the prior cases when viewed in the light of their facts, as distinguished from the courts' explanations of the results reached under the "good cause" formulations.

It has been said that a witness statement taken immediately after an accident is "a catalyst of unique value in the development of the truth through the judicial process." De Bruce v. Pennsylvania R., 6 F.R.D. 403, 406 (E.D.Pa.1947). Of what significance are the words "substantial equivalent" in relation to disclosure of a contemporaneous statement? It is arguable that disclosure of a contemporaneous statement should be freely ordered whenever there has been a substantial lapse of time between its taking and the interview of the witness by the party seeking discovery, and there is case authority for this approach. E.g., Clower v. Walters, 51 F.R.D. 288 (S.D.Ala. 1970). But see, e.g., Almaguer v. Chicago, Rock Island & Pacific Railroad, 55 F.R.D. 147 (D.Neb.1972). Should the diligence or lack of diligence of the party seeking discovery be material?

The Advisory Committee's note cited as factors lapse of memory of the witness or his reluctance or hostility. Should the party be required to take a deposition first in order to demonstrate the need for discovery of a statement? Is great inequality of investigative resources a suitable consideration? The Rule does not provide categorical answers to these questions, and it is not feasible to devise rules that would answer them all. Rather this subdivision establishes guidelines within the framework of which decisions may be made on a discretionary case-by-case basis.

RACKERS v. SIEGFRIED, 54 F.R.D. 24 (W.D.Mo.1971). Plaintiff sued for his child's injuries from being hit by defendant's automobile. Plaintiff requested production of documents, including "any notes, measurements and diagrams made by Max Miller [an insurance adjuster] or anyone else on behalf of defendant within seven days after the accident which show the length of skidmarks left by defendant's automobile at the scene of said accident." Defendant objected, invoking Rule 26(b)(3). Plaintiff moved under Rule 37(a). The court ruled:

"The critical materiality of the measurement of the skid marks in the case at bar is apparent from the direct bearing the measurement may have on the issues of both negligence and injuries (causation). If one party were to have knowledge of the precise measurements and the other party were to be without such knowledge, a distinct trial advantage would accrue to the former party. Therefore, plaintiff has shown a substantial need for the discovery of the documents within the meaning of the applicable rule. Defendant, however, suggests two possible alternative sources: (1) the personal observation of plaintiff after the accident, and (2) the accident report of the highway patrol. With respect to the former, however, it is observable that plaintiff's observations after an accident in which his infant child was involved could in no way approximate the precision of the measurements made by an insurance adjuster 'on the spot' soon after the accident. It is not shown that plaintiff made any exact measurements and, under the circumstances appearing from the file, it is not presumable that he did. With respect to the accident report, plaintiff states that it is erroneous and this statement is not contradicted by defendant. But, assuming that there is presently a disagreement over the accuracy of the highway patrol report, plaintiff should, for that reason, have access to the notes, measurements and diagrams made by defendant's agent after the accident. In these circumstances the alternative source cannot be deemed sufficient."

Question: (10) Could plaintiff have discovered by interrogatory and without any special showing the length of the skid marks measured by defendant's representatives, instead of seeking the documents embodying that fact? *Yes*

DUPLAN CORP. v. MOULINAGE ET RETORDERIE DE CHAVANOZ

United States Court of Appeals, Fourth Circuit, 1974.
509 F.2d 730, cert. denied, 420 U.S. 997, 95 S.Ct. 1438 (1975).

Before ADAMS,* FIELD and WIDENER, CIRCUIT JUDGES.

what about work prod. from prior lit.!?

WIDENER, CIRCUIT JUDGE. This case presents the question whether an attorney's opinion work product material developed in prior terminated litigation may properly become the subject of discovery in connection with subsequent litigation. The issue involves the work product doctrine of Hickman v. Taylor, 329 U.S. 495, 67 S.Ct. 385, 91 L.Ed. 451 (1947), and the scope of the protection afforded a lawyer's "mental impressions, conclusions, opinions, or legal theories" by Rule 26(b)(3) of the Federal Rules of Civil Procedure.

HOLDING: Immune, even tho other lit. final.

We hold that such opinion work product material, as distinguished from material not containing mental impressions, conclusions, opinions, or legal theories, is immune from discovery although the litigation in which it was developed has been terminated. Thus, for reasons which follow, we vacate the judgment of the district court and remand.

Facts:

This patent-antitrust litigation presently consists of 37 cases which have been consolidated in the district court. Duplan Corporation (the throwsters) brought this suit charging Moulinage et Retorderie de Chavanoz (Chavanoz) and others with violating Sections 1 and 2 of the Sherman Act by denying the throwsters a free and open market for the purchase of unlicensed royalty-free false twist machines.[e] Claiming patent misuse and inequitable conduct on the part of Chavanoz in dealing with the United States Patent Office, the throwsters also seek a declaratory judgment that 21 patents owned by Chavanoz are invalid, unenforceable, and not infringed.

In this context, the throwsters seek discovery of work product material developed by Chavanoz's attorneys and others relating to 1964 settlement agreements with Leesona Corporation,[2] and also relating

---

* United States Court of Appeals for the Third Circuit; sitting by designation.

[e] These machines are used to produce texturized yarn.

[2] In the early 1960's, Leesona Corporation claimed in a series of lawsuits that United States patents which it owned were infringed by the sale and operation of machines manufactured by a licensee

to knowledge by Chavanoz of the state of the prior art involved in its patented process.[3]

In an earlier appeal, Duplan Corp. v. Moulinage et Retorderie de Chavanoz, 487 F.2d 480 (4th Cir.1973), we held, "upon the narrow question whether upon the termination of litigation the work product documents prepared incident thereto lose the qualified immunity extended to them under Rule 26(b)(3), Federal Rules of Civil Procedure," they do not automatically "become freely discoverable in subsequent and unrelated litigation." Because we were not then confronted with any claim relating to opinion work product, we dealt solely with the first sentence of Rule 26(b)(3) as applied to factual materials contained in an attorney's files.

[margin note: Not re: opinion w.p.]

Upon remand, the district court separately reviewed the documents in question, and in an order dated December 21, 1973 directed Chavanoz to produce 105 of them. Fifty-eight of these 105 documents have been produced; the remaining 47 were the subject of a motion for reconsideration by Chavanoz. As to these, Chavanoz claimed they were protected from discovery under Rule 26(b)(3) since they contained mental impressions, conclusions, opinions, and legal theories of attorneys and other representatives of Chavanoz prepared in anticipation of litigation or for trial. Nevertheless, on February 5, 1974, the district court ordered production of 22 of the 47 documents, finding that as to each of these the throwsters had demonstrated "substantial need" and "undue hardship." And although it acknowledged that Rule 26(b)(3) accords an absolute privilege during pending litigation to opinion work product materials prepared incident thereto, the court held that immunity ceases and the protection becomes only "qualified" once the litigation for which they were prepared terminates.

[margin note: What dis. ct. ruled]

. . . .

of Chavanoz. These lawsuits were settled in 1964 by agreement between Leesona and Chavanoz.

[3] "In particular, the throwsters request that documents should be produced dealing with the following matters:

(a) *Patent Procurement.* What knowledge did Chavanoz possess about prior 'false twist' art at the time that it filed and prosecuted each patent application in the U.S. Patent Office? Did the French patent agent, Leo Soep, disclose to the U.S. Patent Office the pertinent facts he knew about the prior art? Did the American patent attorneys Armitage and Mueller disclose to Chavanoz or to the U.S. Patent Office the pertinent facts they knew about the prior art? Were representations to the appropriate Patent Office officials accurate and candid?

. . .

(b) *Patent Enforcement.* When the patent owner and/or the exclusive U.S. uselicensee filed infringement suits against the defaulting sublicensee throwsters, did they know or have reason to know that they were attempting to enforce invalid or inapplicable patents? . . . .

(c) *Termination of Patent Litigation.* . . . what facts were known by the Chavanoz/Deering Milliken Research Corporation Group about the alleged invalidity and inapplicability of Chavanoz' patents when entering the 1964 agreements with the Leesona/Permatwist Group? [What evidence is there] . . . about the alleged invalidity and inapplicability of Leesona patents . . . [involved in the same] settlement agreements . . . ."[?] Opinion of district court, pp. 4–5.

. . . . The first sentence [of Rule 26(b)(3)] grants a qualified immunity to "documents and tangible things . . . prepared in anticipation of litigation." The second sentence, however, provides "[i]n ordering discovery of *such materials* . . . the court *shall* protect against disclosure of the mental impressions. . . ." [Emphasis added] By their terms, the two sentences are complementary. Thus, it is apparent that the clear command of the second sentence to "protect against disclosure" applies to all the materials referred to in the first sentence. In our view, no showing of relevance, substantial need or undue hardship should justify compelled disclosure of an attorney's mental impressions, conclusions, opinions or legal theories. This is made clear by the Rule's use of the term "shall" as opposed to "may."

[handwritten margin note: Nothing can justify disclosing mental imps, etc.]

The district court, however, reasoned that what was a mental impression, opinion, conclusion, or legal theory, although absolutely protected during the pendency of a lawsuit, may change to an "operative fact" in a subsequent case once the earlier lawsuit is terminated. And should this happen, upon a proper showing of substantial need and undue hardship, the district court held that it might in its discretion order the production of opinions and conclusions where the denial of such production would frustrate the demands of justice and result in suffocation of the truth.

The district court then devised an operative fact exception to the otherwise absolute immunity accorded opinion work product by Rule 26(b)(3).[7] In our view, this construction fails to comport with the policies underlying Hickman v. Taylor and Rule 26(b)(3).

It seems clear from the whole tenor of the Hickman opinion that the court was concerned with protecting the thought processes of lawyers and thus the very adversary system. . . . Should an advocate's thoughts, theories, opinions, and impressions, collected and developed during pending litigation, become discoverable in connection with later litigation because they are thought to be relevant, our adversary system would clearly suffer. Its foundation would be undermined. . . .

. . . . .

We are mindful that certain documents may contain both discoverable material and non-discoverable material. On remand, the district

---

[7] Because it was contended here that the 1964 settlement agreements between Leesona Corporation and the patent owner, Chavanoz, were in fact an antitrust conspiracy, the district court ordered production of certain opinion work product materials since "the mental impressions, opinions, conclusions, and legal theories of the attorney in the prior litigation are now operative facts as to the motive and intent of the parties at the time of the settlement." District court opinion at p.

16. As to the contentions that fraud was practiced on the U.S. Patent Office, the court ordered production of similar materials since "the mental impressions, opinions, conclusions, and legal theories of the attorneys prosecuting the patent applications for Chavanoz are now operative facts as to the motive and intent of the patent owner in its dealing with the Patent Office." District court opinion at p. 16.

court may, providing the other prerequisites for discovery have been met, excise from such documents the mental impressions, conclusions, opinions, or legal theories of an attorney or other representative, and order the balance of the documents to be produced. See Note of the Advisory Committee, etc., 48 F.R.D. 457, 502; 8 Federal Practice and Procedure, Civil, Wright and Miller (1970), pp. 231–2. The district court also may require Chavanoz to abstract such documents for turning over to the throwsters, or may itself abstract the documents, in either case taking care to protect against disclosure of mental impressions, conclusions, opinion, or legal theories as directed by the last sentence of F.R.C.P. 26(b)(3).

Reversed and remanded.

Question: (11) Instead of seeking the documents, could the throwsters have discovered by interrogatories or depositions the mental impressions, etc.? *yes*

PETERSON v. UNITED STATES, 52 F.R.D. 317 (S.D.Ill.1971). Plaintiffs sued for alleged overpayments of federal income taxes. *Trying to* Plaintiffs by interrogatories requested a detailed description of the *discover* contents of certain audit reports prepared by IRS agents concerning *description* plaintiffs. The government objected, arguing that the reports were *of doc's* work product and also that they consisted entirely of mental impres- *is same* sions, conclusions, opinions, or legal theories. The court observed: *as trying* "The only things protected by rule 26(b)(3) are 'documents and tangi- *to disc* ble things.' It is clear to this court that discovery of a detailed *doc's* description of the contents of documents through interrogatories is *themselves* equivalent to the discovery of the documents themselves. The discovery sought by plaintiff through the interrogatories is therefore covered by rule 26(b)(3)." However, the court ultimately decided that the government had to respond to the interrogatories because the reports were not prepared in anticipation of litigation or for trial but were instead prepared in the assessment and review process of the IRS.

Questions: (12) Rule 26(b)(3) "is an accurate codification of the doctrine announced in the Hickman case and developed in later cases in the lower courts. . . . Rule 26(b)(3) provides protection only for 'documents and tangible things.' There is a distinction . . . between documents that a party has assembled and the facts he has learned from those documents. The courts have consistently held that the work product concept furnishes no shield against discovery, by interrogatories or by deposition, of the facts that the adverse party's lawyer has learned . . . , even though the documents themselves may not be subject to discovery." 8 Wright & Miller § 2023, at 193–94; cf. id. § 2026. Was the court in Peterson correct, then, in expanding the Rule as suggested in the passage quoted from its opinion?

(13) "It is to be noted that the 'work product' doctrine, as announced in Hickman, was not limited to documents, but applies with special force to discovery of the mental impressions of the attorney, as illustrated by the recollections of oral interviews with witnesses sought by the plaintiff in that case. Since Rule 26(b)(3) is limited in terms to the discovery of documents and other tangible things, it leaves the 'work product' doctrine unchanged in this regard." 4 Moore ¶ 26.64[1], at 26–414. "Thus, when discovery of 'work product' is sought through interrogatories or through questions propounded at the taking of depositions, the Rule has no application and one must revert to the principles enunciated in Hickman." Id. ¶ 26.64[4], at 26–451. Was the court in Peterson correct, then, in concluding that even mental impressions, etc., are protected only if formed in anticipation of litigation or for trial?

FORD v. PHILIPS ELECTRONICS INSTRUMENTS CO., 82 F.R.D. 359 (E.D.Pa.1979). "Defendant's counsel subpoenaed Frederic J. Prior, who is not a party to this action, to appear for oral deposition. Because of objections raised by plaintiff's counsel during the course of the deposition, the deposition was suspended, and plaintiff has moved for an order limiting the scope of examination. Plaintiff, relying on Federal Rule of Civil Procedure 26(b)(3) and Hickman v. Taylor, 329 U.S. 495, 67 S.Ct. 385, 91 L.Ed. 451 (1947), contends that defendant's questioning impermissibly impinged upon protected work product of plaintiff's attorney.

"The dispute arose when defendant's counsel questioned Mr. Prior concerning a discussion between the witness and Mr. Feldman, plaintiff's counsel, that had occurred the morning of the deposition. Plaintiff interpreted this exchange as an attempt to reveal his counsel's mental impressions and legal theories concerning the present case."

The court observed that this dispute was not directly governed by Rule 26(b)(3), which pertains only to documents and tangible things. However, that Rule in no way implies that mental impressions not embodied in documents are discoverable, which would fly in the face of Hickman's "general policy against invading the privacy of an attorney's course of preparation."

Hence, the court ruled: "Insofar as defendant's question attempted to elicit from the witness the specific questions that plaintiff's counsel posed to him, or even the area of the case to which he directed the majority of his questions, it exceeds the permissible bounds of discovery and begins to infringe on plaintiff's counsel's evaluation of the case. However, insofar as it was directed to the substance of the witness' knowledge of relevant facts, it is clearly an acceptable line of inquiry."

The court closed by observing that to the extent defendant was seeking to uncover the basis of plaintiff's claim, Rules 33(b) and 36(a) might provide more appropriate vehicles.

Question: (14) To what degree does Hickman protect against an interrogatory asking for the substance of a witness statement?

UNITED STATES v. NOBLES, 422 U.S. 225, 95 S.Ct. 2160 (1975). In the course of ruling that in a criminal trial admission of impeachment testimony by a defense investigator based on his interviews with prosecution witnesses could be conditioned on production by the defense of the relevant parts of the investigator's report, the Court stated:

"The work product doctrine, recognized by this Court in Hickman v. Taylor, 329 U.S. 495, 67 S.Ct. 385 (1947), reflects the strong 'public policy underlying the orderly prosecution and defense of legal claims.' . . .

"Although the work product doctrine most frequently is asserted as a bar to discovery in civil litigation, its role in assuring the proper functioning of the criminal justice system is even more vital. The interests of society and the accused in obtaining a fair and accurate resolution of the question of guilt or innocence demand that adequate safeguards assure the thorough preparation and presentation of each side of the case.

"At its core, the work product doctrine shelters the mental processes of the attorney, providing a privileged area within which he can analyze and prepare his client's case. But the doctrine is an intensely practical one, grounded in the realities of litigation in our adversary system. One of those realities is that attorneys often must rely on the assistance of investigators and other agents in the compilation of materials in preparation for trial. It is therefore necessary that the doctrine protect material prepared by agents for the attorney as well as those prepared by the attorney himself. Moreover, the concerns reflected in the work product doctrine do not disappear once trial has begun. Disclosure of an attorney's efforts at trial, as surely as disclosure during pretrial discovery, could disrupt the orderly development and presentation of his case. We need not, however, undertake here to delineate the scope of the doctrine at trial, for in this instance it is clear that the defense waived such right as may have existed to invoke its protections.

"The privilege derived from the work product doctrine is not absolute. Like other qualified privileges, it may be waived. Here respondent sought to adduce the testimony of the investigator and contrast his recollection of the contested statements with that of the prosecution's witnesses. Respondent, by electing to present the investigator as a witness, waived the privilege with respect to matters covered in his testimony.[14] "

_____

[14] What constitutes a waiver with respect to work product materials depends, of course, upon the circumstances. . . . [The throwsters in Duplan subse-

Question: (15) As for a former party's trial preparation materials not reduced to tangible form, to what degree are they protected in subsequent litigation to which he is not a party? What of his tangible trial preparation materials? See Special Project, The Work Product Doctrine, 68 Cornell L.Rev. 760, 861–64 (1983).

PERSON'S OWN STATEMENT

A party may obtain, without the showing of need generally required for discovery of statements of witnesses, his own previously made statement about the subject matter of the action. Rule 26(b)(3). Note the definition therein of "statement previously made."
(concerning the action or it's subject matter)

The typical situation is in a personal-injury case where an attorney, insurance company investigator, or other claim agent interviews a prospective plaintiff before he has obtained counsel [f] and takes a signed statement from him, and later his attorney wants to obtain the statement. There had been conflicting cases in the federal courts and also in the state courts as to the discoverability of such statements. Compare Smith v. Central Linen Service Co., 39 F.R.D. 15 (D.Md.1966) (discovery allowed), with Safeway Stores v. Reynolds, 176 F.2d 476 (D.C.Cir.1949) (discovery denied). In the Smith case, Chief Judge Thomsen (long a member of the Advisory Committee) said: "There is justification for a different treatment of the request of a party to obtain his own statement, and his request to obtain the statement of a witness."

Questions: (16) What is that justification?

(17) What arguments are there against allowing routine discovery of a party's own statement?

Chief Judge Thomsen coupled his order for discovery with a ruling that the defendant would be entitled, if he wished, to take the plaintiff's deposition before making his statement available to him. The 1970 Advisory Committee's note on Rule 26(b)(3) stated that in appropriate cases a similar order may be made.

Question: (18) What is the purpose of ordering a party to be deposed before his statement is produced?

quently claimed that production of some work product in the course of discovery had waived protection for other work product dealing with the same subject matter. This contention was rejected. Duplan Corp. v. Deering Milliken, Inc., 540 F.2d 1215 (4th Cir.1976) (throwsters also argued for exception to strict protection of opinion work product if prepared in furtherance of crime or fraud, but court ruled that if such exception existed it did not here apply). The defendants ultimately lost on the merits. Duplan Corp. v. Deering Milliken Inc., 594 F.2d 979 (4th Cir.1979), cert. denied, 444 U.S. 1015, 100 S.Ct. 666 (1980), after remand sub nom. Burlington Indus. v. Milliken & Co., 690 F.2d 380 (4th Cir.1982), cert. denied, 103 S.Ct. 1893 (1983).—Ed.]

[f] It is impermissible under the rules of ethics to communicate directly with a party known to be represented by a lawyer without that lawyer's prior consent. See Model Rules of Professional Conduct Rule 4.2 (1983).

It has been asserted by a perceptive commentator that on the whole it would be better to deny special protection to all witness statements, making them discoverable as a matter of course but affording, as in the Smith case, an opportunity to depose the witness before producing his statement. Cooper, Work Product of the Rules-makers, 53 Minn.L.Rev. 1269, 1322–28 (1969).

Question: (19) Is this proposal a sound one?

Interestingly, Rule 26(b)(3) goes partway toward routine discoverability of all witness statements by providing that a nonparty witness may obtain his own statement upon request without making the showing of need required of a party for ordinary work product. It is a fair assumption that in most cases such a request will be instigated by a party to whom the witness is favorably disposed and that the statement will then be made available to that party. A party may thus by indirection achieve a result that he could not get directly. See Friedenthal, The Rulemaking Power of the Supreme Court: A Contemporary Crisis, 27 Stan.L.Rev. 673, 681–82 (1975).

Question: (20) Could a party, by means of a subpoena duces tecum, compel even an unfriendly witness to obtain his statement under Rule 26(b)(3) and then to produce it at his deposition?

———

EXPERT INFORMATION

Rule 26(b)(4) sought to resolve the prior disagreement in the cases concerning the discovery of facts known and opinions held by experts. There had been many decisions denying discovery of expert information acquired or developed in anticipation of litigation or for trial because that information was held to be privileged, or protected as work product, or simply because it was deemed unfair for a party to learn from discovery what his adversary had paid to acquire. Other cases, especially the later ones, had allowed discovery; they rejected the arguments of privilege and work product and met the claim of unfairness by requiring the discovering party in appropriate cases to share the payment of the expert's fees and expenses. In general, scholarly commentary supported discovery.[g]

The new Rule 26(b)(4)(A) is favorable to disclosure of facts known and opinions held by experts expected to be called at trial, although it is more restrictive than some of the prior decisions. The Rule provides for disclosure, as a matter of course and through the use of interrogatories, of the identity of experts expected to be trial witnesses, the subject matter of their testimony, and the substance of the facts and opinions to which each expert is expected to testify, includ-

[handwritten margin notes: 26 b 4 A / Can find out who, what, why testify what they're testifying]

---

[g] Friedenthal, Discovery and Use of an Adverse Party's Expert Information, 14 Stan.L.Rev. 455 (1962), was the best-known article in the field. It was cited in the 1970 Advisory Committee's note on Rule 26(b)(4) and in numerous judicial opinions.

ing a summary of the grounds for each opinion. This enables the party seeking discovery to check the qualifications of the opponent's experts and to prepare for cross-examination and rebuttal. Further discovery, such as taking an expert's deposition, is allowed only upon motion, and it may be restricted by the court as to scope and conditioned upon payment of fees and expenses by the discovering party.

Have to motion to do further discovery (depos, etc.)

Questions: (21) The Advisory Committee's note said that it was establishing substantially the procedure adopted by Chief Judge Thomsen in Knighton v. Villian & Fassio, 39 F.R.D. 11 (D.Md.1965). However, that case had allowed discovery of expert information "by any appropriate method." What was the purpose of the Rule in allowing discovery beyond interrogatories only upon motion?

(22) What restriction as to the scope of a deposition do you think the rulemakers had in mind? The Advisory Committee's original proposal in 1967 had limited discovery of the expert's opinions (and the grounds therefor) to those previously given by the expert or those to be given by him on direct examination at trial. See 43 F.R.D. 211, 225–26 (1968). Would such a limitation be suitable? See Bailey v. Meister Brau, Inc., 57 F.R.D. 11 (N.D. Ill.1972) (suggesting yes).

(23) May an opposing party under any circumstances obtain the report itself, as distinguished from the facts and opinions embodied therein, of an expert expected to be called at trial? See Graham, Discovery of Experts Under Rule 26(b)(4) of the Federal Rules of Civil Procedure: Part One, an Analytical Study, 1976 U.Ill.L.F. 895, 921–31.

Experts not witnesses → need "exceptional" circumstances to discover facts or opinions

The new Rule 26(b)(4)(B) deals separately with experts who are not expected to be called as witnesses and requires a showing of "exceptional circumstances" for discovery of facts known or opinions held by them.

Question: (24) What was the rationale behind this separate treatment?

Outside the coverage of Rule 26(b)(4), and apparently subject to ordinary discovery, are expert information not acquired or developed in anticipation of litigation or for trial, see Spaulding v. Denton, 68 F.R.D. 342 (D.Del.1975), and information obtained by an expert as an actor or viewer with respect to the events in suit, see Duke Gardens Foundation v. Universal Restoration, Inc., 52 F.R.D. 365 (S.D.N.Y. 1971). It also has been held that the identity of an expert who falls within Rule 26(b)(4)(A) or (B) is freely discoverable under Rule 26(b)(1), because the matter of identity falls outside the introductory language of Rule 26(b)(4). Baki v. B.F. Diamond Construction Co., 71 F.R.D. 179 (D.Md.1976); Sea Colony, Inc. v. Continental Insurance Co., 63 F.R.D. 113 (D.Del.1974). Contra Perry v. W.S. Darley & Co., 54 F.R.D. 278 (E.D.Wis.1971). See generally Note, Discovery of Retained Nontestifying Experts' Identities Under the Federal Rules of Civil Procedure, 80 Mich.L.Rev. 513 (1982).

ID of experts freely discov. b/c outside of R 26(b)(4)

Still more difficult questions arise in connection with expert information that seemingly falls within the introductory language of Rule 26(b)(4) but that is possessed by an expert treated arguably in neither subdivision (A) nor subdivision (B).

Questions: (25) May a party discover the identity of, facts known by, and opinions held by an expert who has acquired or developed his information in anticipation of litigation or for trial, who is not expected to be called at trial, and who is a regular employee of the opposing party? See Seiffer v. Topsy's Int'l, Inc., 69 F.R.D. 69 (D.Kan.1975) (subdivision (B) applies). Compare Virginia Elec. & Power Co. v. Sun Shipbldg. & Dry Dock Co., 68 F.R.D. 397 (E.D.Va.1975) (outside Rule 26(b)(4), hence normal discovery), with Breedlove v. Beech Aircraft Corp., 57 F.R.D. 202 (N.D.Miss.1972) (semble) (within Rule 26(b)(4) but outside subdivisions (A) and (B), hence no discovery).

(26) What of an expert not "retained or specially employed" by the opposing party but only "informally consulted" (the Advisory Committee's note~~*yes*~~ used the latter phrase, although the Rule itself does not)? What is the test for distinguishing between the two roles? Compare Ager v. Jane C. Stormont Hosp. & Training School for Nurses, 622 F.2d 496, 501–02 (10th Cir.1980), with Nemetz v. Aye, 63 F.R.D. 66, 68 (W.D.Pa.1974). What happens if the informally consulted expert destroys in tests the only existing sample?

(27) What should the attorney do when he has obtained a mildly unfavorable opinion from an expert whom he may or may not call, depending upon later developments in preparation for trial or at trial?

Professor Michael Graham has conducted a survey to ascertain the actual practice of discovery of expert information. His results suggest that for experts expected to be called at trial, "full discovery is the rule, and practitioners use all available means of disclosure including both the discovery of expert's reports and depositions." His results suggest that the restrictions of subdivision (B) also are ignored by practitioners to some extent. He proposes amending Rule 26(b)(4) to make it better reflect actual practice. Graham, Discovery of Experts Under Rule 26(b)(4) of the Federal Rules of Civil Procedure: Part Two, an Empirical Study and a Proposal, 1977 U.Ill.L.F. 169, 172, 192–94, 200.

Question: (28) "As we read Rule 26(b)(4)(B), factual information, even when acquired [by an expert] in expectation of litigation, is shielded only if discovery is attempted from the expert, and not at all if the effort is to obtain it from a party or another sharing it." Marine Petroleum Co. v. Champlin Petroleum Co., 641 F.2d 984, 994 (D.C.Cir.1979). Do you agree?

———————

BERKEY PHOTO, INC. v. EASTMAN KODAK CO., 74 F.R.D. 613 (S.D.N.Y.1977). An issue in this antitrust case was the discoverability of four notebooks, which had been prepared by Kodak's attorney to synthesize the facts in preparation for trial and which had been shown to Kodak's experts to help in preparing their deposition testimony. Kodak argued that the notebooks comprised ordinary and opinion work product. Judge Frankel in his discretion denied discovery here, but he warned that in future cases a party's delivery of materials to an expert to prepare testimony might waive work-product immunity in accordance with the broadly read Evidence Rule 612(2).

[handwritten: — If witness uses writing to testify or b/y tst. → adverse party gets to see it too (writing used to refresh memory...)]

[handwritten: p. 516]

IMPEACHMENT EVIDENCE

There is no doubt about using discovery to obtain information that will impeach an opposing witness. When, on the other hand, a party wants to discover what information the adversary has acquired to impeach the discovering party's witness, the considerations are different.

MARGESON v. BOSTON & MAINE RAILROAD, 16 F.R.D. 200 (D.Mass.1954). The plaintiff in a personal-injury action made a voluminous demand for statements and records, including his own statement. In denying the motion, Judge Aldrich said:

"The adoption of the Civil Procedure Rules was not a denial of the concept that the court is the forum and the trial the procedure best calculated to uncover the truth. The enthusiasm which greeted the discovery provisions of the Rules when carried, as it has been, to the extent here advocated, that 'the truth should be known before the trial, and nobody be surprised', seems calculated, however, to weaken the efficacy of ordinary trial procedure. There is a vast difference between surprise and unfair surprise. The one is as beneficial as the other is harmful. Not merely may too many rehearsals, in the form of too much discovery, take the bloom off the opening night, but this absence of freshness may make the performance sterile. A certain amount of surprise is often the catalyst which precipitates the truth. Alternatively it may serve as a medium by which the court or jury may gauge the accuracy of the account.

[handwritten margin note: Need some surprise in adversary system]

"If every witness consistently told the truth, and none cut his cloth to the wind, little possible harm and much good might come from maximum pretrial disclosure. Experience indicates, however, that there are facile witnesses whose interest in 'knowing the truth before trial' is prompted primarily by a desire to find the most plausible way to defeat the truth. For this, and other reasons, I believe the requirement of good cause for compulsory pretrial production should mean more than mere relevancy and competency, or ordinary desirability from the standpoint of the movant, and should be something in the nature of special circumstances." [h]

[handwritten margin note: "Good cause" should mean more than relevancy & competency should be special circumstance]

---

[h] Judge Dawson expressed somewhat comparable views in this single sentence: "While it may be true that, in the language of the vernacular, a party involved in a lawsuit under the present Federal Rules may be required, when entering Court, to 'put all his cards upon the table', this is no basis for assuming that he must also put all his clothes upon the table." Service Liquor Distribs., Inc. v. Calvert Distillers Corp., 16 F.R.D. 344, 347 (S.D.N.Y.1954).

Although the Rules as amended in 1970 do date some of Judge Aldrich's statements (how so?), his words have been much cited. They raise the question whether material that has value only for impeachment of a party or a witness should be treated for discovery purposes differently from substantive evidence tending to establish a claim or defense. A party or witness with advance knowledge of impeaching material may on that account refrain from giving false or distorted testimony, but the adversary will then be deprived of the opportunity dramatically to unmask him before the fact-finder and thus discredit not only the impeached testimony but his general credibility as well. It may be persuasively urged that this type of surprise is a legitimate aid to ascertainment of the truth.

One problem is evidence that is not only impeaching but also relevant to the merits of the case. For example, evidence that a party in a negligence action was intoxicated is of major importance in establishing negligence or contributory negligence, as well as for impeachment. It would seem that such evidence should be as readily discoverable as any other substantive evidence.

There is another problem with nondisclosure. Even for purely impeaching evidence, the impeaching witness may himself be subject to impeachment if the party has an opportunity to investigate him before trial. The same is true of nontestimonial impeaching material. Moreover, full knowledge of all admissible evidence would help the parties to reach a fair settlement, as well as to prepare for trial.

Finally, we have moved toward much fuller discovery in general, changing the context of the policy argument. And the remaining pockets of immunity from discovery do raise line-drawing difficulties.

Surveillance of a plaintiff in a personal-injury action and his prior medical history constitute forms of impeachment the disclosure of which is required by some courts and not by others. Suppose, for instance, that witnesses have observed the plaintiff performing labor inconsistent with his claim of disability, or that an investigator has taken films showing the same thing. Some federal judges have refused to allow discovery of such impeachment evidence, including the identity of the witnesses or the existence of such evidence. E.g., Bogatay v. Montour Railroad, 177 F.Supp. 269 (W.D.Pa.1959); Stone v. Marine Transport Lines, 23 F.R.D. 222 (D.Md.1959). In the latter case Chief Judge Thomsen said: "Ordinarily a party need not divulge facts necessarily known to his opponent where the only purpose of the interrogatory is to prevent effective cross-examination." The Supreme Court of Minnesota has forcefully put the case for requiring disclosure, making the point that the impeaching evidence itself may be fraudulent and that the plaintiff should have a chance to investigate it. Boldt v. Sanders, 261 Minn. 160, 111 N.W.2d 225 (1961). Stressing the substantive import of this kind of evidence, the Supreme Court of Arizona reached the same result, Zimmerman v. Su-

perior Court, 98 Ariz. 85, 402 P.2d 212 (1965), over the strongly
worded dissent of Vice Chief Justice Struckmeyer who said:

"The category of surveillance evidence, which is the only issue before the Court, has two obvious attributes: First, it pertains to facts
which come into existence after an accident occurs. As such, it has
nothing to do with the merits of the plaintiff's right of action. Second, it almost invariably concerns facts which are better known to the
plaintiff than to the defendant, facts which in all fairness should be
known equally to both parties but which, because of their nature, oft-
en are impossible for the defendant to discover with certainty. It is,
therefore, a fertile field for fraud and magnification, and a field in
which the parties are not on even terms. Because of the strong public policy against perjury and because the parties are often not on
even terms in the presentation of evidence of the exact extent of a
plaintiff's injuries, a defendant should not be required to disclose the
results of his surveillance.

"This does not mean that there is embraced a 'sporting theory' of
litigation for nothing is hidden from the plaintiff which he does not
already know. Rather, I call it 'sporting' to take from a defendant
the ability to surprise a dishonest witness thereby leaving the cause
vulnerable to perjury. As has been aptly said, 'An honest witness
cannot be discredited and a dishonest one ought to be.' "

Questions: (29) What about not requiring disclosure in the discovery process, but requiring submission of the impeachment evidence to the court in
camera at pretrial conference for a discretionary ruling as to whether it
should then be disclosed? Cf. Frank, Pretrial Conferences and Discovery—
Disclosure or Surprise?, 1965 Ins.L.J. 661, 664–67.

(30) What about requiring disclosure at a time shortly before trial, after
the party with the impeachment evidence has been given an opportunity to
commit the other side by depositions to a final version of its position? See
Cooper, Work Product of the Rulesmakers, 53 Minn.L.Rev. 1269, 1314–18
(1969).

(31) If a federal judge were inclined to establish some such special procedure for discovery of certain impeachment evidence, or if for that matter he
were inclined to prohibit such discovery, where could he find authority in the
current Federal Rules to do so?

Since the 1970 amendments to the Rules, the trend in the federal
courts is to allow discovery of impeachment evidence, while affording
in appropriate cases an opportunity to depose the adverse party or his
witness before disclosure. See, e.g., Snead v. American Export-Isbrandtsen Lines, 59 F.R.D. 148 (E.D.Pa.1973).

RICHARDS OF ROCKFORD, INC. v. PACIFIC GAS & ELEC-
TRIC CO. 71 F.R.D. 388 (N.D.Cal.1976). Plaintiff sued defendant
utility seeking to recover payment for certain spray cooling modules.
Defendant asserted that the modules did not adequately perform. A
research assistant for a university professor had confidentially inter-

viewed employees of defendant as part of a study of the manner in
which utilities make environmental decisions, and the decision to install those modules had been one subject of inquiry. Plaintiff sought
to depose the research assistant concerning those interviews. Upon
meeting refusal to answer, plaintiff moved for an order compelling
answers. The court said that the discovery Rules required it to "balance the interests of the private litigant in obtaining the information
sought against the costs of providing it." Here, the profound interest of society in the research of its scholars, the necessity of maintaining confidential relationships if their research is to be accomplished, and the rather tenuous relation of this research to the subject
matter of this claim all argued against compelling disclosure. And
the court so ruled.

[handwritten margin note: Balance interests of party wanting dis. against costs of providing it]

FOIA

There are, of course, means other than discovery for obtaining information to prepare one's case. For example, since 1966 the Freedom of Information Act, 5 U.S.C. § 552, has provided a means of access to all federal agency records subject to certain exemptions—a
means separate from discovery in a lawsuit. See generally Toran,
Information Disclosure in Civil Actions: The Freedom of Information
Act and the Federal Discovery Rules, 49 Geo.Wash.L.Rev. 843 (1981).

SECTION 2. SUPERVISION OF DISCOVERY

The discovery Rules reflect the desirability of having discovery
carried on so far as practicable without the intervention of the court.
Needless trips to court are costly and wasteful of time. It is necessary, however, to provide the opportunity for supervision of discovery
by the court and to prescribe sanctions against misuse of and noncompliance with the discovery procedure.

Rule 26(c) sets up the ground rules for protective orders to prevent harassing and oppressive use of oral depositions and the other
discovery devices by resort to the court before discovery has begun.
Because the typical notice for taking an oral deposition does not even
reveal the subject matter of the examination, often the need for protection cannot be demonstrated before commencement of the examination. Resort may then be made to Rule 30(d) for an order to check
abuses developing during the taking of the examination. The deposition must be suspended on demand of either the objecting party or
the witness for the time necessary to go to court to seek an order.
Of course, the witness may instead simply refuse to answer, doing
this on his own or at the direction of a party. Rule 37(a) provides for
court orders to compel answers from a balky deponent. Commonly,

however, if a witness refuses to answer a question, the examiner continues with other lines of inquiry instead of rushing immediately into court. Unanswered questions may thus pile up until a convenient time for resort to court, and frequently later questioning leads the examiner to conclude that it is not worthwhile to pursue the resisted matters further.

Question: (32) Supervision may be invoked by the objecting party or the witness, under Rule 26(c) or 30(d), *or* by the discovering party, under Rule 37(a). Should the burden of proof depend on this difference?

Excessive resort to the court can plainly make a shambles out of a deposition, and the Rules attempt to forestall this by costs sanctions against parties, deponents, or counsel. It may be questioned, however, whether the theoretical protection of these Rules is likely to be a sufficient actual protection against insistent abuse or stubborn recalcitrance. Even if they are administered with sternness and vigor, delay and the consumption of the court's time inevitably result. The court will often find it difficult to determine the propriety of the questioning when presented out of context. An extended inquiry is likely to be necessary, which constitutes an added burden on a busy court and an added expense to the litigants.

One current approach to limiting the burden on judges is the greatly increasing reliance on United States magistrates to play the judicial role in supervision of the discovery procedure. Judges may designate these salaried court officials so to act under 28 U.S.C. § 636(b) and may review their decisions subject to a "clearly erroneous or contrary to law" standard. See generally Streepy, The Developing Role of the Magistrate in the Federal Courts, 29 Clev.St.L.Rev. 81 (1980).

Another approach is to appoint special masters under Rule 53 to supervise discovery closely in cases of considerable need, especially big cases. See, e.g., Eggleston v. Chicago Journeymen Plumbers' Local Union No. 130, 657 F.2d 890, 904 (7th Cir.1981), cert. denied, 455 U.S. 1017, 102 S.Ct. 1710 (1982); see also W. Brazil, G. Hazard & P. Rice, Managing Complex Litigation: A Practical Guide to the Use of Special Masters (1983). The special master differs from a magistrate in being normally an outsider, whose compensation is fixed by the court and paid by the parties upon court-directed terms. To cut down on delay, some courts have even resorted to the use of a special master to preside at depositions with authority to rule on disputes on the spot, but that is expensive. See, e.g., Fisher v. Harris, Upham & Co., 61 F.R.D. 447 (S.D.N.Y.1973), appeal dismissed, 516 F.2d 896 (2d Cir. 1975); cf. Park Tower Development Group v. Goldfeld, 87 F.R.D. 96 (S.D.N.Y.1980) (suggesting special master be available by telephone for ruling during depositions). In Hirsch v. Glidden Co., 79 F.Supp. 729 (S.D.N.Y.1948), such an appointment of a special master was authorized, but at the cost of the party requesting the appointment. Shapiro v. Freeman, 38 F.R.D. 308 (S.D.N.Y.1965), followed this lead under unusual circumstances. The infant plaintiff's claim for personal injuries included permanent psychiatric shock resulting from the crash into her home of the defendant's private airplane. After her school teachers on instructions from the plaintiff's attorneys had declined to talk informally, the defendant took depositions of the teachers to obtain information about her pre-injury adjustment to everyday life. At the depositions the plaintiff's lawyer objected to almost every question and successfully instructed the deponents not to answer, making the depositions a complete waste of time. On a motion to compel answers, the court, finding that the plaintiff's attorneys had acted "in the utmost bad faith," appointed a special master to take the depositions and rule on all objections and motions relating to discovery. The fees and expenses of the master were ordered to be paid by the plaintiff's attorneys without reimbursement from their client, as were the defendant's expenses in bringing the motion.

The possibilities of harassment and oppression through the setting up of oral depositions [i] at inconvenient places so as to involve costly travel and counsel fees provide an obvious illustration of the necessity and operation of discovery supervision. A subpoena need not be served on a party in order to take his deposition; even if the party is far beyond the reach of a subpoena, a simple notice served upon his attorney pursuant to Rule 5(b) is sufficient.[j] Resort to a seasonal motion under Rule 26(c) is required if a party wants protection from an inconvenient deposition. Ordinarily a plaintiff must appear for a deposition in the district he selected for institution of his action, but more solicitude is likely to be shown to a defendant notified to appear in a district where he has been sued but that is distant from his home. Some district courts have bolstered Rule 26(c) by local rules providing that the court, as a condition of refusing to vacate a notice for taking a deposition, may order the discovering party to pay prior to the examination expenses of the adverse party. Other courts have ordered prepayment of expenses under the general authority of Rule 26(c) to protect a party from "undue burden or expense" or its special authority to order that "discovery may be had only on specified terms and conditions."

The cases summarized below further illustrate how flexibly discretion has been exercised in an effort to achieve fairness in the use of the deposition machinery.

V.O. MACHINOIMPORT v. CLARK EQUIPMENT CO., 11 F.R.D. 55 (S.D.N.Y.1951). Plaintiff, a Soviet corporation not engaging in

---

[i] Burdensome and costly requests may also be made under the other discovery Rules. See, e.g., Niagara Duplicator Co. v. Shackleford, 160 F.2d 25 (D.C.Cir.1947) (Rule 34 order for production of books and records for inspection and copying should require production in San Francisco, where the defendant company's records were kept, rather than in Washington, D.C., where the action was brought).

[j] A nonparty witness can be compelled to appear for a deposition only by a subpoena and only within the geographical limits set by Rule 45(d)(2).

business in the United States, brought suit in the Southern District of New York against defendant, a Michigan corporation, seeking to recover about $2,500,000 for breach of contract. Defendant asserted a counterclaim. Plaintiff took rather extensive depositions of defendant's officers and employees, lasting over a period of four days. Then defendant served notice to take the deposition of plaintiff in New York, designating nine individuals, all residents of the U.S.S.R., as the persons to be examined. Plaintiff moved (1) that no oral examination be taken because only two of the named individuals were officers, directors, or managing agents of plaintiff and those two had not participated in any of the transactions at issue, (2) that the depositions be confined to matters not previously covered by plaintiff's answers to Rule 33 interrogatories, (3) that the depositions be taken in Russia, not New York, and (4) that defendant be ordered to pay plaintiff's expenses and attorneys' fees incurred by reason of any order entered.

(1) The court ruled that because of the technical and complex problems involved, the denial of oral examination would result in serious prejudice to defendant and so would be improper. (2) The motion to limit the depositions to matters not covered by answers to Rule 33 interrogatories was denied. (3) The court further ruled that the place of examination should be New York, saying: "The plaintiff experienced little difficulty in sending its representatives here when it sought to obtain the benefits of a contract and the know-how of American industry; it should have no trouble in sending the persons to be examined and the documents which may be required when it is seeking a very substantial recovery from the defendant." (4) Plaintiff's request for expenses and counsel fees was denied.

Examination of two of the named individuals was ordered, but decision as to the rest was held in abeyance until their status as officers, directors, or managing agents of plaintiff was clarified. Only persons of such status can be designated by the examining party in a notice of deposition of a corporate party.

Plaintiff did not comply with the order. The court then granted a motion by defendant under Rule 37(b)(2) for the dismissal of plaintiff's complaint with prejudice and the direction of a default judgment in defendant's favor on its counterclaim, the amount of damages to be determined by an inquest, 12 F.R.D. 191 (1951).[k]

CONNELL v. BILTMORE SECURITY LIFE INSURANCE CO., 41 F.R.D. 136 (D.S.C.1966). A South Carolina plaintiff sued defendant, an Arizona corporation, in federal court in South Carolina and sought to depose defendant's president in that state. Defendant

---

[k] For an opinion without the 1951 cold war overtones of this case, see Grotrian, Helfferich, Schulz, Th. Steinweg Nachf. v. Steinway & Sons, 54 F.R.D. 280 (S.D. N.Y.1971). In that case plaintiff sought to take the oral deposition in Germany of one of its executive officers. Defendant's motion for a protective order that the deposition be taken in New York was granted. A claim of hardship because of the age (72) and the state of health of the witness was found not to be established.

moved that the deposition be upon written questions or that the oral deposition be taken in St. Paul, where the corporation's principal place of business was located and where the president maintained his office and residence. The court ordered that there be an oral deposition in South Carolina, that the parties share equally the deponent's travel expense, that plaintiff pay the deponent's living expenses on the days of his testimony, and that all expenses be taxed as costs to be paid by the losing party in the litigation.

SULLIVAN v. SOUTHERN PAC. CO., 7 F.R.D. 206 (S.D.N.Y. 1947). Plaintiff, a resident of Minneapolis, brought an FELA action in the Southern District of New York for injuries sustained in Arizona. Defendant served a notice to take his deposition in New York. Plaintiff sought an order that the examination be held in Minneapolis. Plaintiff had lost both legs in the accident, had no artificial legs, and could travel only if accompanied by an attendant. He was also without funds. The court granted the motion, and it refused to impose a condition that the expenses of defendant's counsel be paid.

OLIVER v. KALAMAZOO BOARD OF EDUCATION, 346 F.Supp. 766 (W.D.Mich.1972). Plaintiffs brought a class action under the civil rights laws to declare unconstitutional an order of the board of education rescinding a school integration plan and to force implementation of that plan. The plan had been adopted a month before a school board election in which two new members were elected on a platform pledging the rescission of the integration plan. Defendant board served notice to take the depositions of the two defeated members of the board that had adopted the plan. Plaintiffs moved for a protective order on the ground that defense counsel, who had acted for the board for over twenty years, had been in such a relation of trust and confidence to the deponents as board members that defendant was unlikely to discover any relevant facts by taking their deposition and that the deponents would be subjected to needless annoyance, harassment, and friction. The court ruled that the depositions could be taken, but it ordered that they should be taken by attorneys other than members of the firm that had represented the board.

D'IPPOLITO v. AMERICAN OIL CO., 272 F.Supp. 310 (S.D.N.Y. 1967). Plaintiffs brought a civil antitrust action against corporate defendants, following which the government brought a related criminal action against the same defendants. Shortly after discovery from the defendants was begun, the defendants moved to stay discovery until the conclusion of the criminal action. Plaintiffs, standing to benefit from a criminal conviction, had turned over to the prosecutor testimony so far obtained from defendants. On the other hand, the criminal case would probably not go to trial for some time, and some of the prospective deponents were of advanced years and plaintiffs had need to preserve their testimony. The court ordered that the depositions be taken with no one present except the deponent, the parties, and counsel, and it also ordered that the depositions be immediately sealed, not to be opened until conclusion of the criminal trial or further order of the court.

KOSTER v. CHASE MANHATTAN BANK

United States District Court, Southern District of New York, 1982.
93 F.R.D. 471.

GOETTEL, DISTRICT JUDGE:

Carolee Koster commenced this action against the Chase Manhattan Bank (the Bank) and Allan Ross, a former vice-president of the Bank, alleging, inter alia, violations of Title VII of the Civil Rights Act of 1964, 42 U.S.C. § 2000e et seq. The gist of her claim is that, while she and Ross were employed by the Bank, Ross forced her to engage in a sexual relationship with him and abused her and interfered with her career when she terminated the relationship. She seeks injunctive relief, a declaratory judgment, and damages.

To say the least, this lawsuit has attracted more than the usual amount of media attention. . . . According to the defendants, this widespread and, at times, somewhat sensationalized coverage has resulted in injury to the reputations of Ross, the Bank, and its employees. To avoid further embarrassment, therefore, the defendants have moved for a protective order pursuant to Rule 26(c) of the Federal Rules of Civil Procedure and this Court's general equitable powers—a course of action vigorously opposed by the plaintiff and several representatives of the news media who have submitted briefs as amicus curiae. The order proposed by the defendants would require that all documents filed in this action be sealed and would prohibit disclosure of information obtained through discovery to anyone other than a party to this action and that party's authorized representatives and attorneys. Disclosure to third parties of information not obtained through the Court's processes or of information in a party's possession prior to the inception of this lawsuit, however, would be permitted. . . .

I. Rule 26(c) and the First Amendment

. . . .

Rule 26(c) "emphasizes the complete control that the court has over the discovery process." 8 C. Wright & A. Miller . . . § 2036, at 267. Recently, however, there has been recognition of a potential conflict between this power to supervise discovery and the First Amendment. In In re Halkin, 598 F.2d 176 (D.C.Cir.1979), and In re San Juan Star Co., 662 F.2d 108 (1st Cir.1981), the D.C. Circuit and the First Circuit held that an order precluding dissemination of information obtained as a result of discovery implicates First Amendment interests and that the good cause standard embodied in Rule 26(c) does not protect those interests sufficiently. . . .

The present motion raises questions in this now controversial and relatively uncharted area of the law.[10] . . .

A. The First Amendment Interest In Disseminating Information Obtained Through Discovery

It appears fair to conclude that litigants and their lawyers have a First Amendment interest in disseminating information procured through discovery. [Citations omitted.] All persons have an interest in communicating ideas and information to others, In re San Juan Star Co., supra, at 115, regardless of the manner in which the information was acquired. [Citations omitted.] Moreover, one cannot state categorically that the fruits of discovery fall within one of the traditional classifications of speech unprotected by the First Amendment. . . . Finally, the First Amendment rights of litigants and lawyers are not checked at the door of the courthouse upon the commencement of litigation, [citations omitted], and in particular, these rights are not waived when the parties embark upon the discovery process. . . .

Another point that is seemingly undisputed is that the nature of this First Amendment interest is somewhat limited, and thus, a Rule 26(c) order restricting expression should not be evaluated by the stringent standards governing classic prior restraints. . . .

Although Rule 26(c) orders that restrict expression are similar in form to other orders that have been characterized as prior restraints, [citations omitted], the special nature of discovery as a source of information justifies a reduced level of scrutiny. [Citations omitted.] First, a stringent standard that precludes issuance of virtually all Rule 26(c) orders restricting expression could have a pernicious effect on the smooth functioning of the discovery system. In re San Juan Star Co., supra, at 115. One of the purposes of discovery is to expedite the conduct of litigation. Id., at 115. Moreover, the entire system is premised on cooperation between the parties, that is, voluntary compliance with discovery requests without the constant supervision of a judge or magistrate. Dore, Confidentiality Orders—The Proper Role of the Courts in Providing Confidential Treatment for Information Disclosed Through the Pre-Trial Discovery Process, 14 N.Eng.L. Rev. 1, 6 (1978). If it is extremely difficult to obtain an order restricting dissemination of discovery materials, however, a litigant may be discouraged from complying with discovery requests voluntarily when he perceives that his interests will be harmed by public disclosure of the requested information. This would force the other

---

[10] This motion also raises the question whether the public and the media have a First Amendment right of access to pretrial discovery materials. Amici imply that such a right exists, and in support of this proposition, they appear to rely primarily on Richmond Newspapers, Inc. v. Virginia, 448 U.S. 555, 100 S.Ct. 2814, 65 L.Ed.2d 973 (1980) [(first amendment right to attend criminal trials)]. Although our disposition of this motion makes resolution of this question unnecessary, we observe that Richmond Newspapers does not seem to support such a proposition.

 . . . . .

party to seek sanctions or a court order compelling disclosure. See Fed.R.Civ.P. 37. A series of such occurrences would delay the discovery process considerably and amount to an undue burden on the resources of the judiciary and the litigants. Similarly, if it is difficult to protect litigants from injury as a result of disclosure, judges may be apt to deny access to discovery materials altogether. In re San Juan Star Co., supra, at 115. This could subvert the goal of allowing "parties to obtain the fullest possible knowledge of the issues and facts before trial." Hickman v. Taylor, . . . 329 U.S. at 501, 67 S.Ct. at 389 (footnote omitted).

Second, the nature of discovery makes it unfair to allow the recipient of discovery materials the virtually unlimited right to disseminate those materials. As noted above, the discovery rules are very liberal and accord litigants a broad right of access to information. See Fed. R.Civ.P. 26(b). Consequently, production of much irrelevant and inadmissible information could be compelled by the processes of the court. As the First Circuit noted,

> [s]uch undigested matter, forced from the mouth of an unwilling deponent, is hardly material encompassed within a broad public "right to know". Its disclosure would not advance the informed civic and political discussion that the First Amendment is intended to protect. We do not see present in the case of civil discovery those interests that make publicity in a criminal trial an important "safeguard against any attempt to employ our courts as instruments of persecution." Nor can the discovery processes lay claim to the long tradition of openness enjoyed by criminal or civil trials. We conclude, therefore, that although there is a First Amendment interest in information produced at trial that warrants full protection, a judicially-powered process compelling information that has not yet passed through the adversary-judicial filter for testing admissibility does not create communications that deserve full protection.

In re San Juan Star Co., supra, at 115 (citations omitted). It seems only fitting that a court should be allowed to exercise reasonable control over information that it has compelled a litigant to disclose. See In re Halkin, supra, 598 F.2d at 206–08 (Wilkey, J., dissenting) (Because access results from a system that reserves to the court the power to restrict the use of discovered information, the litigant obtains only a limited interest in information received through the discovery system, that is, he accepts it subject to the possibility that the court may restrict its use.).

B. The Standards for Protecting the First Amendment Interest

The major area of disagreement concerns what showing must be made to justify an infringement on this somewhat limited First Amendment interest. Three standards have been utilized: the good cause standard of Rule 26(c), the Halkin standard, and the San Juan Star standard.

The ostensibly strictest test was enunciated by the D.C. Circuit in In re Halkin, supra.[12] Because of its view that a restriction on dissemination of discovery materials "constitutes direct governmental action limiting speech," id. at 183, the court concluded that such an order can be entered only after "close scrutiny of its impact on protected First Amendment expression." Id. at 186. Specifically, it adopted a two-tiered approach. The initial inquiry is to determine the nature of the restraint. "An order restraining publication of official court records open to the public, or an order restraining political speech, implicates different interests than an order restraining commercial information." Id. at 191 (footnotes omitted). The next step is for the court to determine if three criteria have been satisfied. First, the nature of the harm threatened by dissemination must be substantial and serious. Id. at 191, 192–93. There must be a "specific showing that dissemination of the discovery materials would pose a concrete threat to an important countervailing interest." Id. at 193 (footnote omitted). Second, the order must be narrowly drawn and precise. Id. at 191, 193–95. Third, there must be no alternative means of avoiding the harm that will be less restrictive of expression. Id. at 191, 195.

In attempting to strike a balance between the First Amendment interests of litigants and society's interest in the effective operation of the discovery system, the First Circuit, in In re San Juan Star Co., supra, adopted a standard that is described as midway between the Halkin standard and one of good cause. At 116.[15] Before issuing a

---

[12] Halkin was a non-jury case in which the plaintiffs sued the Federal Government for alleged violations of their constitutional and statutory rights arising from a program of government surveillance. Pursuant to a discovery request, the Government provided the plaintiffs with documents relating to the surveillance operation. No protective order was sought, and there was no agreement between the parties concerning the use of the documents. (The Government, however, had deleted "sensitive" information before delivering the documents.) Shortly after receiving the documents, the plaintiffs informed the defendants that they intended to make the documents available to the public. In response, the defendants moved for a Rule 26(c) order "restraining the parties and their counsel from publicly disclosing information obtained through discovery." In re Halkin, supra, 598 F.2d at 182. They argued that public disclosure would compromise their right to a fair adjudication of the issues. Although this motion was unsupported by affidavits or other evidence, the district court issued the protective order. The Court of Appeals reversed be-

cause issuance of the order was based upon a mere finding of good cause. See id. at 179–82.

[15] In San Juan Star, relatives of two suspected Puerto Rican terrorists who had been killed in a shootout with police brought a federal civil rights action in the District of Puerto Rico, alleging that government officials had conspired to arrange the killings. Because the shooting was one of the most controversial events "in recent Puerto Rico history," the lawsuit received intense media coverage and generated much public interest. For example, the depositions of the defendants were reported, and both sides then attempted to explain the testimony to the press. Consequently, the district court entered several orders, one of which forbade "attorneys from disclosing any evidence obtained through subsequent depositions to the press . . . or to any third party." In re San Juan Star Co., supra, at 111. The San Juan Star Co., a newspaper, intervened in the lawsuit and challenged the order. The Court of Appeals affirmed. See id., at 118.

protective order that restricts the dissemination of information obtained through discovery, three factors must be considered. First, the trial court must look to the magnitude and imminence of the threatened harm. Id., at 116. In considering this factor, however, the trial court should maintain a good degree of flexibility by viewing the magnitude and imminence of harm "on a sliding scale: as the potential harm grows more grave, the imminence necessary is reduced." Id., at 116. The court characterized this standard as one of " 'good cause' that incorporates a 'heightened sensitivity' to the First Amendment concerns at stake." Id., at 116. Second, the court must be reasonably certain that the protective order will prevent the threatened harm. Id., at 116. Third, the restraint must be the least restrictive means of avoiding the harm. Id., at 116.

The third standard that can be used when considering the propriety of a protective order that will limit expression is, of course, the good cause standard embodied in Rule 26(c). See In re Halkin, supra (Wilkey, J., dissenting). Good cause is a rather amorphous concept, not amenable to precise definition. Nevertheless, a few general observations can be made.

Good cause is a highly discretionary standard. [Citations omitted.] Its application can perhaps best be conceptualized as a two step process. Initially, the moving party must show that a "clearly defined and very serious injury" will result if a protective order is not issued. United States v. International Business Machines Corp., 67 F.R.D. 40, 46 (S.D.N.Y.1975) (emphasis deleted); [other citations omitted]. The showing necessary to establish such potential harm depends upon the type of harm being threatened and the type of order being sought. [Citations omitted.] At the least, the moving party must provide the court with "information from which it can reasonably conclude that the nature and magnitude of the moving party's interest are such that protective intervention by the court is justified." In re Halkin, supra, 598 F.2d at 211 (Wilkey, J., dissenting).

Once such a showing has been made,the court should consider other factors that may militate [for or] against issuing a protective order. United States v. Hooker Chemicals & Plastics Corp., 90 F.R.D. 421, 425 (W.D.N.Y.1981). For example, it should consider whether the order will prevent the threatened harm, whether there are less restrictive means of preventing the threatened harm, the interests of the party opposing the motion, and the interests of the public. In the context of a motion to prevent dissemination of information obtained through discovery, it is appropriate to consider the other party's First Amendment interests, the nature of the information, and whether the public has an interest in learning of that information.

It is interesting to note that, when using the good cause standard, a court may consider factors similar, if not identical, to those mandated by Halkin and San Juan Star. A significant difference among the three, however, lies in the discretionary nature of the good cause standard. In determining whether there is good cause to enter a Rule 26(c) order, a court may, but does not have to, weigh these factors. Moreover, because a determination that good cause has been shown is reviewed under an abuse of discretion standard, it is less likely that the appellate court would substitute its judgment for that of the trial court even if, for example, it believed that more deference should have been given to the other party's First Amendment interests. Under either of the "heightened" standards, on the other hand, the court must find that definite criteria have been satisfied before issuing a protective order, and failure to do so will result in a reversal. To the extent that the discretion of the trial court is limited by these "heightened" standards, therefore, they do provide more protection for a litigant's First Amendment rights. See Brink v. DaLesio, 82 F.R.D. 664, 678 (D.Md.1979).

The controversy about what standard should be used is not easily resolved and, indeed, could expand. . . . At the present time, however, we need not resolve the questions whether the good cause standard is constitutionally deficient and, if so, what standard should be used, for we conclude that there is not good cause to issue the protective order proposed by the defendants. [Citation omitted.]

II. Good Cause Applied

. . . As a result of the plaintiff's decision to publicize her allegations against the defendants last August, the Bank claims that it and its employees suffered embarrassment and injury to reputation. Ross claims that the dissemination of this information had injurious effects on his business and personal life, and he cites specific examples. . . .

Even if it is assumed that these injuries will reoccur and that they are sufficiently "defined and serious," other factors militate against issuing the protective order proposed by the defendants. Our first concern is the breadth of the proposed order, which would prohibit dissemination of discovery materials that are as yet nonexistent. [This inclined the court to wait; for example, if the defendants wanted to restrict dissemination of specific deposition testimony, they could move before, during, or after the particular deposition—and if unforeseen information was revealed at a deposition and if the defendants informed the plaintiff that they planned to move, "we trust that the plaintiff and her attorneys will follow the spirit of this opinion and not publicize the information" in the meantime. The court's other concerns were (2) that the proposed order might not eliminate the harm because it would not prohibit dissemination of information in a party's possession prior to the lawsuit and (3) that information concerning the sexual relationship was central to the lawsuit, had already been revealed to some extent, and would be revealed at any trial.]

These are but some of the reasons that, when taken together, lead
this Court to the conclusion that issuance of this proposed order at
this particular juncture of the lawsuit is not warranted. By no
means do we foreclose the possibility that some information revealed
through discovery will be the proper subject of a narrowly drawn protective order.[22] Whether such information will be revealed, however,
cannot be foretold. Rather, we must await the commencement of the
discovery process.

One final point merits discussion. Throughout this opinion, we
have dealt primarily with that portion of the proposed order that concerns the dissemination of discovery materials. The proposed order,
however, also contains a provision requiring that all papers filed in
this action be sealed.

Although the Court's inherent equitable powers unquestionably
allow it to take this course of action, International Products Corp. v.
Koons, 325 F.2d 403, 407–08 (2d Cir.1963), sealing is not appropriate
at this time. No purpose would be served by sealing depositions and
other discovery materials that must be filed with the Court in view of
our refusal to preclude dissemination of the information contained in
these papers. Nor is the sealing of the pleadings, legal memoranda,
and affidavits in support of this motion warranted. The information
contained in these papers either has been substantially disclosed already or is not of the type that, if disclosed, will result in serious
harm to the defendants' interests. Of course, if, in the future, any
party believes that a particular document should be sealed, the appropriate motion can be made.

So ordered.

Question: (33) "We agree that plaintiffs do not have a First Amendment
right of access to information not generally available to members of the public." In re Halkin, 598 F.2d 176, 190 (D.C.Cir.1979) (thus "discovery may be
denied completely without implicating the First Amendment"). How can the
first amendment seemingly permit a judge to deny discovery altogether,
even because of fear of dissemination, but possibly prohibit a nondissemina-
tion order?

SEQUENCE OF DEPOSITIONS

Although there was nothing in the Rules prior to the 1970 amendments to require it, courts tended to adopt a rule of thumb giving
priority to the party first serving notice of the taking of a deposition.

------

[22] There is also the possibility that media coverage will become so intense that
the defendants' right to have the issues
adjudicated fairly will be threatened.
This, however, seems unlikely. It should
also be noted that the penchant of the
plaintiff to try her case in the media may
become a consideration in determining
the scope of discovery to be afforded her.

This meant that a party was ordinarily allowed to complete the taking of all depositions for which he had first served notice before an adversary could start taking his own. Field studies showed that a race for priority did not occur very often, but it was unseemly when it did. See Caldwell-Clements, Inc. v. McGraw-Hill Pub. Co., 11 F.R.D. 156 (S.D.N.Y.1951). Moreover, the plaintiff entered the race with a built-in handicap. He was allowed to serve notice within 20 days after commencement of the action only by obtaining leave of court, but the defendant might do so at any time without leave. The reason for this disparity was to protect the defendant who might be without counsel until he was served with process, but the result was to give the vigilant defendant priority. (Illogically, the 20-day period ran from the date of commencement of the action to the date of notice rather than from the date of service of process to the date of taking the deposition.) It was true that the courts always recognized their power to change the sequence, but they usually did so only for obviously compelling reasons.

Question: (34) What tactical advantages do you see in having priority of examination?

Rule 26(d) of the 1970 amendments did away with the notion that a party's commencement of discovery should ordinarily await the other party's completion. The parties may proceed concurrently, unless the court finds special considerations for providing otherwise. In practice the parties usually work out their own arrangements without seeking intervention of the court.

Rule 30(a) now measures the period within which leave of court must be obtained, lengthened to 30 days, from the date of service of process upon any defendant to the date of taking the deposition, thus correcting the anomaly in the prior Rule.

Question: (35) *A*'s action against *B* and *C* is commenced on July 1. *B* is served with process on July 3. On July 15, *A* serves notice on *B* of the taking of *W*'s oral deposition on August 2. *C* is not served with process until August 1, when he is simultaneously served with notice of the taking of *W*'s deposition. Can *W*'s deposition be taken on August 2 and, if so, with what effect?

ENFORCEMENT OF DISCOVERY ORDERS

The discovery procedure would not be effective unless adequate machinery were provided for its enforcement. Rule 37(b) sets forth the wide-ranging choice of sanctions open to the court for failure to comply with a discovery order. And the discovery Rules enable the court to impose expenses on those who unjustifiably attempt either to prevent or to obtain discovery.

Although the Rules did not in terms so prescribe, the practice of the courts had long been to impose the lightest remedial sanction thought to be consistent with effective administration of the discovery procedure. See Waterman, An Appellate Judge's Approach When Reviewing District Court Sanctions Imposed for the Purpose of Insuring Compliance with Pretrial Orders, 29 F.R.D. 420 (1962). Indeed, the original Advisory Committee's note on Rule 37 recognized that there were due process limitations upon the power of the court to order dismissal or default without giving the party an opportunity for hearing on the merits, and the Supreme Court said that "substantial constitutional questions" would be raised if a pleading were stricken for noncompliance with a discovery order with which the party had made a good faith effort to comply. Société Internationale pour Participations Industrielles et Commerciales, S.A. v. Rogers, 357 U.S. 197, 210, 78 S.Ct. 1087, 1095 (1958) (dismissal with prejudice, for failure to comply with order under Rule 34 to produce Swiss banking records, not warranted where disclosure would subject party to criminal sanctions in Switzerland).

More recently, however, the drastic sanction of entry of a default judgment has been upheld for willful and deliberate disregard of discovery orders. TWA v. Hughes, 449 F.2d 51 (2d Cir.1971) (default entered upon Howard Hughes's failure to comply with order to appear for deposition, and judgment entered for over $145 million), rev'd on other grounds sub nom. Hughes Tool Co. v. TWA, 409 U.S. 363, 93 S.Ct. 647 (1973). And in language that will undoubtedly encourage some degree of increased severity, the Supreme Court itself has approved dismissal of an action for bad faith failure to comply with discovery orders. National Hockey League v. Metropolitan Hockey Club, 427 U.S. 639, 96 S.Ct. 2778 (1976).

Moreover, the 1970 amendments revised Rule 37 in order to tighten the sanctions for failure to make discovery (one revision was to change "refusal" in the caption and at several places in the body of the Rule, thus negating the idea of a requirement of willfulness). The new Advisory Committee's note reflected dissatisfaction with the reluctance of the courts to use their powers more vigorously. For instance, Rule 37(a)(4) now requires an award of expenses *unless* the non-prevailing person's position "was substantially justified." The former Rule provided for such an order *if* his position was "without substantial justification." It may be doubted whether this shifting of the burden will of itself often change the result, but the Advisory Committee pointed out that the change in language was intended to encourage judges to be more alert to abuses in the discovery process.

Then, in 1983 the Advisory Committee used even tougher talk. Referring to the "widespread recognition that there is a need for more aggressive judicial control and supervision," the Committee provided mandatory sanctions for violations of the new Rule 26(g), stressing the aim of deterrence.

It may indeed be doubted whether this shift in emphasis from the remedial to the deterrent will have a dramatic impact on the actual practice of the courts. See R. Rodes, K. Ripple & C. Mooney, Sanctions Imposable for Violations of the Federal Rules of Civil Procedure 5–31 (1981). In any event, an empirical study indicates that parties in fact do not use the compelling process of Rule 37(a) or the sanction process of Rule 37(b) very often and that, when the Rule is invoked, the court usually grants the motion. P. Connolly, E. Holleman & M. Kuhlman, Judicial Controls and the Civil Litigative Process: Discovery 18–26 (1978). So if the goal is case management, perhaps the district court cannot rely on party-initiative but must act on its own— a prospect considered in the next Topic.

RUBENSTEIN v. KLEVEN

United States District Court, District of Massachusetts, 1957.
150 F.Supp. 47.

ALDRICH, DISTRICT JUDGE. This is an action by an unmarried woman for breach of an alleged agreement to render companionship and other services to a married man. The defendant has answered that the agreement was against public policy. While this is not an express assertion of illegal consideration, viz., an illicit relationship, I would regard evidence of such admissible under this general allegation. The plaintiff has taken defendant's deposition, and has asked certain questions to which affirmative answers might indicate adultery. The defendant has refused to answer on the ground of incrimination. Plaintiff moves for an order compelling him to answer.

. . . .

Since it would be to plaintiff's disadvantage for defendant to testify to an illicit relationship, I inquired of her counsel why he was pressing for an answer. He replied that he was of opinion that the answers would, in fact, be in the negative, and that defendant, being unable to testify truthfully to anything of a criminal nature, was seeking to create the impression of such, to plaintiff's disfavor, by the inference which would attach to his refusal. The suggestion that the defendant is a sheep in wolf's clothing presents a novel reverse-English to the Fifth Amendment. I do not, however, find it necessary to pursue it. Defendant can not work both sides of the street. Illegality is an affirmative defence. If he is going to assert it predicated upon criminal acts involving himself, to be established through the testimony of any witness, or even simply by inference, he cannot remain aloof, asking the jury to find that such acts occurred, and at the same time claim a privilege against incrimination on cross-examination. Since he refuses on his deposition to incriminate himself, I will assume, as the rule of the case, that equally he does not intend to prove criminality, through his own testimony or otherwise, at the trial. Unless within twenty days he notifies plaintiff that he proposes to answer the questions, plaintiff's motion will be denied and the issue of criminality foreclosed.[l]

APPELLATE REVIEW OF DISCOVERY RULINGS

Even though compliance with a discovery order or submission to a discovery sanction may be very burdensome or harmful, there are serious obstacles to prompt review.

A discovery order ordinarily is merely interlocutory and hence not appealable under the final decision rule of 28 U.S.C. § 1291. See Borden Co. v. Sylk, 410 F.2d 843 (3d Cir.1969). However, there is the possibility that an occasional discovery order will be held appealable as a "collateral order," a final determination of an important question separable from the main litigation that needs review before final adjudication of the whole action. And rarely a discovery order may come within some other judge-made exception to the normal final decision rule. E.g., United States v. Nixon, 418 U.S. 683, 94 S.Ct. 3090 (1974).[m]

In O'Malley v. Chrysler Corp., 160 F.2d 35 (7th Cir.1947), Chrysler appealed from a discovery order compelling it to prepare extensive computations, which would require much additional time and expense over and above the 90 days and $10,000 spent in compliance with a prior order. The appeal was on the theory that the order was an interlocutory mandatory injunction under 28 U.S.C. § 1292(a). The court of appeals dismissed the appeal for want of jurisdiction.

The chance of an interlocutory appeal under 28 U.S.C. § 1292(b) is rather remote, although use of this procedure has occasionally been successful. E.g., Garner v. Wolfinbarger, 430 F.2d 1093 (5th Cir. 1970) (review of denial of attorney-client privilege claimed by a corporation against its stockholders, where ruling would affect scope of evidence in complex case), cert. denied, 401 U.S. 974, 91 S.Ct. 1191 (1971); Groover, Christie & Merritt v. LoBianco, 336 F.2d 969 (D.C. Cir.1964) (question of propriety of order in malpractice action requiring defendant partnership of doctors to produce for inspection and copying a letter to its liability insurer reporting about the events in suit; the appeal was permitted over the vigorous dissent of Judge Wright, who called it "a garden variety discovery motion" and "a

---

[l] In the plaintiff's deposition she testified that the defendant paid her $1000 a month for over six years pursuant to the alleged agreement. The defendant, contending no payments were ever made, filed a motion under Rule 34 for production of her bank records and her state and federal income tax returns for the period in question. The court ordered that the bank records be produced, and that the tax returns also be produced unless the plaintiff would admit that there was nothing in them directly or indirectly relating to the alleged payments, 21 F.R.D. 183 (1957). The defendant eventually obtained summary judgment on his plea of the New York Statute of Frauds, 163 F.Supp. 237 (1958).

[m] See Topic B of Part Eight.

graphic illustration of the mischief that results when the Interlocutory Appeals Act is misused").[n]

The likelihood of successful resort to the extraordinary writ of mandamus is also remote, but some discovery orders have been reviewed by this means. E.g., Schlagenhauf v. Holder, infra p. 1244; Pfizer Inc. v. Lord, 456 F.2d 545 (8th Cir.1972) (mandamus to review ruling in complex case that attorney-client privilege was not available because relationship employed to perpetrate crime or fraud).[o]

A discovery order is of course reviewable on appeal from a final judgment, but there is certain to be great difficulty in demonstrating that a grant of too extensive discovery was prejudicially erroneous. Not only is the trial court's discretion so broad that a finding of abuse would be made only rarely, but once disclosure has been made there is no effective way to correct an erroneous order. If the discovery order is too niggardly, prejudicial error may be somewhat more readily shown. E.g., Mellon v. Cooper-Jarrett, Inc., 424 F.2d 499 (6th Cir.1970) (plaintiff in automobile accident erroneously protected from answering whether he had ever been convicted of a lesser criminal offense than a felony or of driving under the influence of alcohol or drugs); Edgar v. Finley, 312 F.2d 533 (8th Cir.1963) (erroneous refusal to order disclosure of identity of witness given to plaintiff's attorney by another attorney "in confidence").

Assuming that a party is unable to get immediate review of a discovery order, there remains the question of what happens if he violates the order. The cases indicate that even a decision adjudging a party to be in civil contempt is not final for purposes of review. See Fox v. Capital Co., 299 U.S. 105, 57 S.Ct. 57 (1936). On the other hand, if a party is held to be guilty of criminal contempt for failure to comply with a discovery order, the contempt judgment is deemed final and hence immediately appealable; on appeal the court will review the propriety of the discovery order. See Hanley v. James McHugh Construction Co., 419 F.2d 955 (7th Cir.1969). If an adjudication for contempt has both a civil and a criminal character, "the criminal feature of the order is dominant and fixes its character for purposes of review." Union Tool Co. v. Wilson, 259 U.S. 107, 110, 42 S.Ct. 427, 428 (1922).

If a person not a party to the action disobeys a discovery order and is held to be in civil or criminal contempt, he is entitled to appeal from the contempt judgment. He could not appeal from the ultimate final judgment in the case, so the contempt judgment is as to him considered final. See Fenton v. Walling, 139 F.2d 608 (9th Cir.1943), cert. denied, 321 U.S. 798, 64 S.Ct. 938 (1944). This proposition derives from Cobbledick v. United States, 309 U.S. 323, 60 S.Ct. 540 (1940), where Cobbledick moved to quash a subpoena duces tecum to appear and produce documents before a federal grand jury and then

[n] See Topic C of Part Eight.   [o] See Topic D of Part Eight.

appealed from denial of his motion. The decision was held to be non-final, and the appeal was therefore dismissed. The Court said that one to whom a subpoena is directed may refuse to obey, contest its validity if he is cited for contempt, and then appeal if his contentions are rejected. The contempt, the Court pointed out, is "so severed from the main proceeding as to permit an appeal." The continuing validity of Cobbledick was affirmed in 1971 in United States v. Ryan, infra p. 770.

The appellate review in Sibbach v. Wilson & Co., supra p. 5, is hard to account for under these principles. The plaintiff was ordered jailed until she submitted to the physical examination. This was plainly a civil contempt designed to coerce her into being examined rather than a criminal contempt designed as a punishment. The Supreme Court nevertheless decided the case without mention of any problem of appealability. Similarly, in Hickman v. Taylor, supra p. 472, no question of appealability was raised. The Third Circuit characterized the contempt as criminal. The Supreme Court did not label it as either civil or criminal, but its recital that "the court adjudged them in contempt and ordered them imprisoned until they complied" made it sound like a civil contempt proceeding "in which the defendant had the key to the jail house door." Southern Railway v. Lanham, 408 F.2d 348, 350 n.2 (5th Cir.1969) (Brown, C.J., dissenting). What of the presence of Fortenbaugh as an appellant?

TOPIC E. PRETRIAL CONFERENCES

JAQUETTE v. BLACK HAWK COUNTY, IOWA, 710 F.2d 455 (8th Cir.1983). A terminated employee brought a civil rights action for violation of her first and fourteenth amendment rights. Eventually she settled for $1500. She then requested almost $93,000 in attorneys' fees, for 1034.45 hours' work, under 42 U.S.C. § 1988. The district court awarded about $20,000, finding the time expended to be excessive. She appealed.

The court of appeals remanded for an evidentiary hearing on the reasons behind expending excessive hours and for consideration of sanctions. The court added:

"This case, although not unusual on its facts, exemplifies not only society's concern, but the profession's acknowledgment that there exists excessive cost and delay in litigation. The direct effect is the denial of reasonable access to justice in our courts. The entire administration of justice is involved. The searching question is why. Assuming counsel for each side acted in good faith, and we have no reason at this stage to suggest otherwise, nonetheless the time, expense and delay involved in the litigation of a relatively simple claim demands full judicial attention. . . .

"In almost all cases the key to avoiding excessive costs and delay is early and stringent judicial management of the case. Sending counsel off into extended 'paper chases' in compliance with pretrial orders has now been demonstrated not to be the answer. See Peckham, The Federal Judge as a Case Manager: The New Role in Guiding a Case from Filing to Disposition, 69 Calif.L.Rev. 770 (1981); Pollack, Pretrial Procedures More Effectively Handled, 65 F.R.D. 475 (1975); Solomon, Techniques for Shortening Trials, 65 F.R.D. 485 (1975); Will, Judicial Responsibility for the Disposition of Litigation, 75 F.R.D. 117 (1978). The recognition of early judicial management, not by the clerk, not by the magistrate, but by the trial judge before whom the case will be tried is essential. Management conferences at the pleading stage, which simplify the extent of discovery as well as the issues involved, have proven successful. The newly adopted Federal Rule of Civil Procedure 16(b) contemplates such a practice.[19] We request each district judge to re-evaluate local rules with the view toward early case management. With such management procedure, we are confident that litigation such as this, extending almost three years in the district court, would be avoided. Excessive costs of liti-

[19] [The court, deciding on June 27, 1983, here quoted the new Rule 16(b), promulgated by the Supreme Court on April 28 and due to become effective August 1. The court also cited Rule 26(f).]

517

gation is as much the court's concern as it is of counsel and litigants. We fully recognize district judges are busy people; it has been argued that they do not have time for pretrial skirmishes because they are too busy in the 'adjudication' of cases (that is, the trial itself). However, it is time to recognize that the adjudication process begins at the time of the filing of the complaint and carries through to the last appeal. Lack of proper judicial supervision in the pretrial stage leads to excessive discovery, the development of complex and multiple issues, extended motion practice, and long and expensive trials. Conversely, time expended wisely by counsel and the district judge at the early stages will save many hours of unnecessary labor later in the process. We suggest that under the newly amended rules of civil procedure requiring early judicial supervision and management, the present litigation could have been resolved within six to nine months. The litigation should have terminated long before the plaintiff's counsel could have expended 1,000 hours. Early and ongoing judicial management is essential if the judicial process is to survive. It is now obvious that adversarial lawyers are unable to achieve proper management alone. This new procedure may necessitate changes in the practice of many judges and attorneys, but unless we are willing to innovate and break away from our present conduct, excess costs and delays will geometrically multiply, and the result will be the denial of justice in our courts."

S. FLANDERS, CASE MANAGEMENT AND COURT MANAGEMENT IN UNITED STATES DISTRICT COURTS

ix–xi, 18–19, 35–37 (1977).

This volume reports the overall results of the District Court Studies Project, a long-range effort by the Federal Judicial Center to assist the work of the United States district courts. . . . Specifically, the project has been designed to determine what procedures are associated with the greatest possible speed and productivity, consistent with the highest standards of justice. A secondary goal is to determine precisely what some of the statistical measures in use actually measure. This report is based on visits to ten courts. It presents extensive data from the civil dockets of six of those courts. The visits included detailed discussions with judges and most supporting personnel, and observation of the widest possible variety of proceedings.

. . . .

The following factors primarily distinguish the fast and/or highly productive courts from the others:

An automatic procedure assures, for every civil case, that pleadings are strictly monitored, discovery begins quickly and is completed within a reasonable time, and a prompt trial follows if needed. These procedures are automatic in that they are invoked at the start of every case, subject only to a small number of necessary exceptions. Although all the courts visited have procedures designed to achieve early and effective control, most do not attain that goal. In slow courts, much of the time during which a typical case is pending is either unused or violates the time limits in the Federal Rules of Civil Procedure.

Procedures minimize or eliminate judges' investment of time through the early stages of a case, until discovery is complete. Docket control, attorney contacts, and most conferences are delegated, generally to the courtroom deputy clerk or a magistrate. A case comes to the judge's attention only when he is indispensable to resolve preliminary matters, handle dispositive motions, or plan the preparation of an exceptionally complex case.

The role of the court in settlement is minimized; judges are highly selective in initiating settlement negotiations, and normally do so only when a case is ready, or nearly ready, for trial. Some judges also arrange to raise the issue early in each case, or have a magistrate do so.

Relatively few written opinions are prepared for publication.

All proceedings that do not specifically require a confidential atmosphere are held in open court.

We recommend that widespread adoption of these approaches be considered. . . .

. . . .

The District Court Studies Project research revealed problems with some widely accepted opinions about speed and productivity, such as:

—*"It all comes down to strong case management."* Most courts visited are characterized by "strong case management" in one form or another. The differences lie in the relative effectiveness of alternative forms of case management.

. . . .

—*"A comprehensive pretrial order is essential."* None of the courts enforced this requirement fully in routine cases. The ones that enforced it most vigorously were not necessarily the speediest or most efficient.

—*"Get the lawyers in early and often."* Our observations suggest that frequent conferences are a poor use of time.

. . . .

. . . Each court was visited in late 1975 or in 1976 to obtain data on approximately 500 randomly selected civil cases. A group of highly skilled researchers (most of them present or past law clerks to district judges) filled out a detailed form for each case, under the direction of Paul Connolly of the Federal Judicial Center staff. Cases were selected from a list of all cases terminated in the district in fiscal 1975, listed in order of their docket numbers (therefore also the order in which they were filed). From a random starting point, every third, or fifth, or *n*th case was selected; the interval was chosen to yield approximately 500 cases from each court.

. . . .

TABLE 5

Overall Disposition Times

Fiscal 1975

	All cases sampled	
	Median (days)	Number (cases)
FL/S	121	595
CA/C	166	541
MD	223	502
LA/E	313	494
PA/E	352	497
MA	500	468
Average	279	516

Table 5 shows overall disposition times in the six courts, according to the collected data. As in all tables through table 23, the courts are listed in order of their disposition time for all cases, from the court with the fastest overall disposition time to the court with the slowest. This permits easy scanning of each table, allowing the reader to determine to what extent a particular column falls in the same order as the overall disposition time of the courts. . . .

. . . .

Some courts could save several months by asserting earlier control of civil cases. The controls asserted are fairly effective, once imposed.

TABLE 21

Scheduling Pretrials

	Initiation time *		Control time **		Overall time: answer until first pretrial	
	Median (days)	Number (cases)	Median (days)	Number (settings)	Median (days)	Number (cases)
FL/S	18	250	49	401	94	77
CA/C	21	196	63	342	186	96
MD	82	145	33	266	71	169
LA/E	104	305	43	603	158	253
PA/E	175	122	42	203	192	193
MA	595	58	28	91	763	84
Average........	165.8	179.3	43	317.7	244	145.3

* Time interval between the answer to the original complaint and the first date on which a pretrial date is set.
** Time interval between the date on which a pretrial date is set and the date pretrial is set for.

. . . Table 21 shows the courts' pretrial conference scheduling practices. (. . . Maryland and Eastern Pennsylvania figures are affected by several judges' practice of holding pretrial conferences, no record of which appears in the file or on the docket sheet.)

The key variable seems to be the time interval between the answer to the original complaint and the date on which the first pretrial was scheduled. The range of differences here is extraordinarily large, from 18 and 21 days, respectively, in Southern Florida and Central California, up to 595 days (in a very small number of cases) in Massachusetts. This appears to be a crucial variable. Eastern Pennsylvania, for example, could possibly save four or five months of "dead time" in many cases by earlier scheduling of the first pretrial conference.

There is a smaller range of differences among the intervals between the date on which the pretrial date was set and the date the pretrial was set for—from 28 days in Massachusetts to 63 days . . . in the Central District of California. Very large differences appear again among the time intervals between the answer to the original complaint and the time a first pretrial is actually held. Maryland and Southern Florida are fastest in this respect, with 71 and 94 days, respectively. Eastern Louisiana, Central California, and Eastern Pennsylvania are clustered between 158 and 192 days, and Massachusetts is much slower, with 763 days.[7]

[7] It should be noted that these figures . . . are not additive. One cannot add the median initiation time to the median control time. Medians in general are not additive. Beyond that, different groups of cases are involved in the variables displayed in this table, and a time interval measured for one group is not necessarily applicable to another. The clearest instance is the three medians shown for Maryland. The median overall time is actually shorter than the median initiation time. It is much shorter than the sum of initiation plus control time.

[Other data on the courts' setting of a discovery cutoff date generally showed a similar effectiveness of early control.]

The data on pretrials and discovery cutoffs, in summary, show great differences among the courts in the nature and extent of case management control—differences that appear to have a powerful impact on disposition time.

LUSKIN, BUILDING A THEORY OF CASE PROCESSING TIME
62 Judicature 115, 117, 120–23 (1978).

Writing on court delay is voluminous, but much of it might simply be termed inspirational. Judges, administrators and prosecutors who feel that they have been successful in reducing delay in their own courts describe their actions and report "significant" reductions in delay or backlog. The authors assume the actions have caused the reduction in delay but make no attempt to actually separate the effect of the innovation from that of other potential causes nor to measure the size of the effect that can be attributed to the action taken by the court relative to other variables. In the absence of a theory of case processing time, these reports may be helpful to court administrators, judges and prosecutors looking for suggestions about how they might approach problems of court delay, but they contribute little or nothing to the development of a theory of case processing time.

More analytic works on court delay specify variables thought to affect case processing time and backlog and describe the relationships among them. The articles discussed below vary in the degree to which they do this, in appropriateness of the statistical models used to represent their theory, and, thus, in their contribution to a theory of case processing time. I have organized this work under four general headings: (1) inventories of causes, (2) experiments, (3) surveys, and (4) process models.

. . . .

Surveys are by far the most common research designs for studying court delay. In surveys, unlike experiments, the researcher does not manipulate the independent variables; both the independent and dependent variables vary naturally. The researcher observes variation in the dependent variable, hypothesizes causes for it, and seeks to sort out and estimate the effects produced by these causes.

This characteristic lack of control over the independent variables means that the causal ordering of the variables is more problematic in surveys than in experiments. . . . Lack of control over the independent variables also means that statistical techniques must be used to disentangle the effects of multiple causes of the dependent variable.

. . . .

Often, however, the theoretical and policy utility of court delay studies using survey designs has been limited by the inadequacy of the statistical models used to test the researcher's hypotheses. Most researchers hold, at least implicitly, theories of case processing time that are multivariate and asymmetric, that is, theories that say that variation in case processing time is produced by at least two independent variables and that influence flows *to* the dependent variable *from* these variables . . . . The analysis models many of these same researchers use, however, are bivariate (they examine the association between two variables only) and symmetric (the statistic estimates the degree to which the independent and dependent variable vary together, but not the change in the dependent variable produced by the change in the independent variable). If the theory is multivariate and asymmetric but the analysis model is bivariate and associational, the model is mis-specified.

. . . From a seriously mis-specified model (e.g., one that omits an important causal variable), one can develop neither satisfactory theory nor satisfactory policy recommendations.

Some examples will illustrate the shortcomings of a bivariate, symmetric model for analyzing case processing time. . . .

. . . Sovern and Rosenberg looked at the relationships between case characteristics and case processing time in civil cases.[13] They reported that the size of the claim has the single largest correlation with case processing time. Because they measure bivariate associations without having introduced controls for variables that affected the size of those associations, they did not rule out the alternative hypothesis that the association is spurious—that is, that some other variable produced the observed association between claim size and case processing time. Furthermore, if the relationship is real, do we want to know only that size of claim and case processing time vary together? Or do we want an estimate of the magnitude of the effect of size of claim given the presence of the other causes? If we believe that differences in the size of the claim cause differences in case processing time, a symmetric statistical model is inappropriate to our theory and does not yield the information we want.

. . . .

The District Court Studies Project . . . seeks to relate differences in speed and productivity to differences in the practices of courts. The project has two goals: to identify differences below "slow" courts and "fast" courts and to identify the ways in which current measures of speed and delay may be misleading. To accomplish these goals, [certain] metropolitan federal courts representing the extremes in speed and delay in the federal system were studied. Once again, the design looks at a small group of fast and slow courts

[13] Michael I. Sovern and Maurice Rosenberg, Delay and the Dynamics of Personal Injury Litigation, 59 Colum.L.Rev. 1115 (1959).

that vary on many dimensions. Because of the small number of courts studied and the cross-sectional nature of the data, most of the analysis relies on informal observations of associations between various activities—opinion writing, for example—and measures of speed or productivity.

. . . .

In the reports on this project, the informal analysis model used, for the most part, is bivariate even though the implicit theoretical model is multivariate. As a result, the authors cannot assess the relative importance of differences among courts in the speed of processing nor can they rule out the possibility that the relationships they observe are spurious. The District Court Studies Project can point to some variables that may be related to delay and may be susceptible to manipulation, but it cannot assess the size of the effects to be expected.

J. BARTLETT, THE LAW BUSINESS: A TIRED MONOPOLY 93–94 (1982). "In the course of implementing reforms, one must come to grips with the argument that the causes of delay in the court system are mysterious and complex, the efficacy of currently recommended solutions has not in many cases been supported by empirical data and further research is necessary. To give this view its due, it is certainly the fact that some of the current suggestions for slaying the dragon of delay have been off the mark—indeed some, like the pretrial conference, may even foster the opportunities for delay in certain instances. On the other hand, the lack of a study is not . . . a necessary or sufficient reason for delaying change that experience and common sense recommends. The business of studying delay in the courts has become an industry in itself. And, the product of those studies has been, in many instances, disappointing; the 'findings' too often reflect what is or should be obvious to any one with experience in the field.

. . . .

". . . The vice of interminable studies is that studies condition people who are already cautious by nature (as lawyers undoubtedly are) and who are protected by lifetime tenure (as judges generally are) to think in terms of 'more studies, more data' before acting. Moreover, studies usually don't uncover quirks in the system—actual practice does; systems can only be debugged in use."

BRAZIL, IMPROVING JUDICIAL CONTROLS OVER THE PRETRIAL DEVELOPMENT OF CIVIL ACTIONS: MODEL RULES FOR CASE MANAGEMENT AND SANCTIONS

1981 Am.B.Found.Research J. 873, 916–20.

[Based on extensive interviews with lawyers and judicial officers, Professor Brazil develops his own comprehensive model rule for judicial pretrial management. Nevertheless, he approves the basic purposes and concepts of the 1983 revision of Rule 16. He goes on to suggest further changes in that revision:]

Subdivision (a) of the revised rule would confer upon courts the power to convene pretrial conferences and would describe in general terms some of the major purposes such conferences could serve. For reasons outlined above, I believe this subdivision should explicitly recognize the courts' discretionary power to direct the parties, even when represented by counsel, to attend pretrial conferences. While the committee's notes could suggest that this discretion be exercised only after balancing the potential benefits against the burdens of compelling party attendance, there are sufficient potential advantages of requiring parties (as well as their lawyers) to participate to warrant an explicit reminder to the judiciary that the power exists.

Subdivision (a) also should acknowledge that responsibility to be alert to the need for or potential utility of an early pretrial conference is not confined to the court. One way to incorporate such an acknowledgment in the rule itself (as opposed to merely discussing it in accompanying notes) is to indicate that the litigants or their lawyers may file a motion requesting the court to convene a conference. It is not clear, however, that the court should be *obligated* to schedule a conference merely because a potential participant requests one. A rule that would give the parties or their attorneys an essentially unqualified right to compel the convening of these kinds of conferences might be abused to delay the movement of an action toward trial or to burden (e.g., economically) an opponent. This possibility, coupled with the notion that pretrial conferences should remain primarily *judges'* tools for case control, suggest that at least in the absence of the kinds of requirements Rule 26(f) imposes on a party moving for a discovery conference, Rule 16(a) should leave the court with the discretion to deny a motion for any pretrial conference not required by the language of the federal rule itself or by a local rule adopted by a district court.

Subdivision (b) of the new rule would require the courts, except in categories of cases exempted by local rule, to consult at least informally (e.g., by telephone or correspondence) with counsel and unrepresented parties about the time requirements for joinder, amended pleadings, motions, and discovery, and then within [120] days of the filing of the complaint, to issue an order fixing the dates for completion of these matters. Some matters 16(b) leaves optional for the court to include in a scheduling order should be moved to the mandatory list: at least the dates for the final pretrial conference and for the trial itself. As discussed above, the data produced by our interviews and by other studies indicate that fixing early and firm dates *for the completion of trial preparation and for the trial itself* is probably the single most effective device thus far developed for encouraging prompt and well-focused case development. There does not appear to be any consequential practical obstacle to setting these dates very shortly after an action is commenced. Several judges we interviewed reported that they routinely follow such a procedure and that it has had very beneficial effects. Other studies and commentaries have described the successful use of this approach in several federal courts.

As the description of my model rule for pretrial management should make clear, I believe there is a need for a more fundamental change in proposed 16(b). That subdivision (or some other part of Rule 16) should set forth criteria for identifying "potentially complex or protracted cases" or should require each district court to adopt a local rule that does so. Thereafter, the rule should separately set forth additional requirements for managing actions that satisfy the criteria. For potentially complex or protracted cases, these additional requirements should convert the scheduling conference into a broader and more formal management session by expanding the list of mandatory subjects for consultation and incorporation in an order to include: (1) exploring, at least briefly, the possibility of settlement and various means to achieve it, (2) formulating and attempting to narrow the issues genuinely in dispute, (3) devising means to secure stipulations to as many matters as possible, (4) discussing possibilities for voluntary, informal exchanges of information, (5) deciding whether to hold a Rule 26(f) discovery conference and, if not, estimating the amount and kinds of discovery the case will require and setting guidelines for the first round of discovery, (6) deciding whether to refer any pretrial matters to a magistrate or special master and, if so, specifying the scope of his authority as well as procedures for appealing his decisions and the standards to be applied on such appeals, and (7) fixing an early date and an agenda for the next pretrial or status conference.

It is particularly important that the federal rules assure that the courts take affirmative steps at the outset of each action to identify potentially complex cases. Clause 10 of 16(c) of the proposed rule identifies four "illustrative" characteristics, any one of which, according to the note, makes "a case a strong candidate for special treatment." Because the discovery stage consumes such a significant percentage of the overall litigation time of complex actions and because of the great need for control during that stage, I recommend adding a fifth characteristic to the list in clause 10: "extensive discovery." This addition should encourage judges to focus on the potential for inefficiency and delay during discovery when they are deciding whether to adopt "special procedures for managing potentially difficult or protracted actions."

It also is important that the rules compel prompt and meaningful judicial involvement in assessing discovery needs and shaping and pacing discovery proceedings. Rule 26(f) does not accomplish this purpose. There is reason to question the potential effectiveness of any rule that, like 26(f), relies primarily on initiatives by counsel to involve the judiciary in case management. Even though most of the big case litigators we interviewed said they would favor, at least as an abstract proposition, "greater judicial involvement in the discovery stage of litigation," some of our respondents suggested that attorneys might feel considerable reluctance, in specific cases, to take steps that would foreseeably reduce the scope of their freedom to maneuver by vesting significant control over pretrial developments in a judicial officer. Widely shared beliefs that many judges and magistrates are not interested in discovery matters and, under current procedures, tend to be superficial or arbitrary in ruling on discovery disputes could intensify that reluctance. Considerations like these, plus the demanding prerequisites of Rule 26(f), may help account for reports that litigators are filing motions for discovery conferences only in a small percentage of cases. In any event, one thing seems clear: prompt, close, and continuous judicial or parajudicial monitoring of the discovery process is too important in big cases to be left to chance. Either Rule 16 or Rule 26 should establish compulsory procedural machinery to secure that kind of monitoring in all potentially complex actions.

Rule 16(b) and (c) should also describe counsel's obligations with respect to both scheduling and pretrial conferences more clearly . . . . Responsibilities of participants in scheduling or pretrial conferences are mentioned in two places in the proposed rule. The first of these is the last sentence of 16(c), which appears to relate only to pretrial conferences. It requires counsel to "have authority to enter into stipulations and to make admissions regarding all matters that the participants may reasonably anticipate may be discussed." The only other reference to the duties of parties and counsel is in 16(f), which is devoted to "Sanctions." That paragraph authorizes courts to impose sanctions if

> a party or party's attorney fails to obey a scheduling or pretrial order, or if no appearance is made on behalf of a party at a scheduling or pretrial conference, or if a party or party's attorney is substantially unprepared to participate in the conference, or if a party or party's attorney fails to participate in good faith.

Together, these passages in essence require counsel to "substantially" prepare for scheduling or pretrial conferences, to acquire authority to enter stipulations and make admissions during pretrial conferences (but not during scheduling conferences), and to appear (when ordered) and to participate in good faith in both kinds of conferences.

There are several ways in which these duty provisions could be improved. The rule would communicate much more clearly what counsels' obligations are if it described them in a separately lettered subdivision to precede the subdivision authorizing sanctions. The subdivision devoted to articulating the obligations the rule imposes should explicitly require the court to give counsel (and unrepresented parties) timely advance notice of any subjects the court expects to cover or tasks the court intends to accomplish that are not described with particularity in a standing order or local rule applying to the type of conference involved. The "duties" subdivision also should compel counsel, in advance of the scheduling conference or within 60 days after commencement of the action, to draft estimates of the amount of time required for joinder, amending pleadings, presenting Rule 12 motions, completing discovery, and preparing for the final pretrial conference. Such estimates are necessary to enable the judge to make the decisions required by 16(b). By failing to make the duty to prepare such estimates clear, the rule invites either irrational judicial decision making or delays while counsel scramble belatedly to respond to the court's initial effort at "consultation."

The duties section of Rule 16 also should have a separate subdivision setting forth additional obligations that counsel or parties involved in potentially complex cases must fulfill. That subdivision should require counsel, in advance of the first judicially hosted conference, (1) to draft and exchange statements of the major issues and narrative descriptions of the events or acts on which the lawsuit is based, (2) to explore the possibility of arranging for voluntary, informal exchanges of information, (3) to estimate the amount and kinds of discovery they will conduct, and (4) to discuss the advisability of referring matters to a magistrate or special master and, if appropriate, to exchange lists of names of acceptable masters.

[Professor Brazil would also tighten up the sanctions subdivision and recognize a right to compensation for violations.]

———

RESNIK, MANAGERIAL JUDGES

96 Harv.L.Rev. 374, 376–80, 388–90, 400–02, 422, 431–32, 444–45 (1982), reprinted in Rand R–3002–ICJ (1982).

Until recently, the American legal establishment embraced a classical view of the judicial role. Under this view, judges are not supposed to have an involvement or interest in the controversies they adjudicate. Disengagement and dispassion supposedly enable judges to decide cases fairly and impartially. . . .

Many federal judges have departed from their earlier attitudes; they have dropped the relatively disinterested pose to adopt a more active, "managerial" stance.[4]   In growing numbers, judges are not only adjudicating the merits of issues presented to them by litigants, but also are meeting with parties in chambers to encourage settlement of disputes and to supervise case preparation.   Both before and after the trial, judges are playing a critical role in shaping litigation and influencing results.

.   .   .   .

.   .   .   Judges have described their new tasks as "case management"—hence my term "managerial judges."   As managers, judges learn more about cases much earlier than they did in the past.   They negotiate with parties about the course, timing, and scope of both pretrial and posttrial litigation.   These managerial responsibilities give judges greater power.   Yet the restraints that formerly circumscribed judicial authority are conspicuously absent.   Managerial judges frequently work beyond the public view, off the record, with no obligation to provide written, reasoned opinions, and out of reach of appellate review.

This new managerial role has emerged for several reasons.   One is the creation of pretrial discovery rights.   The 1938 Federal Rules of Civil Procedure embodied contradictory mandates: a discovery system ("give your opponent all information relevant to the litigation") was grafted onto American adversarial norms ("protect your client zealously" and therefore "withhold what you can").   In some cases, parties argued about their obligations under the discovery rules; such disputes generated a need for someone to decide pretrial conflicts.   Trial judges accepted the assignment and have become mediators, negotiators, and planners—as well as adjudicators.   Moreover, once involved in pretrial discovery, many judges became convinced that their presence at other points in a lawsuit's development would be beneficial; supervision of discovery became a conduit for judicial control over all phases of litigation and thus infused lawsuits with the continual presence of the judge-overseer.

Partly because of their new oversight role and partly because of increasing case loads, many judges have become concerned with the volume of their work.   To reduce the pressure, judges have turned to efficiency experts who promise "calendar control."   Under the experts' guidance, judges have begun to experiment with schemes for speeding the resolution of cases and for persuading litigants to settle rather than try cases whenever possible.   During the past decade, enthusiasm for the "managerial movement" has become widespread; what began as an experiment is likely soon to become obligatory. Unless the Supreme Court and Congress reject proposed amendments to [rule 16], pretrial judicial management will be required in virtually all cases.

[4] I focus on changes in the federal courts, but similar changes are underway in many state courts.   See P. Ebener, Court Efforts to Reduce Pretrial Delay (1981); L. Freedman, State Legislation on Dispute Resolution (1982).

In the rush to conquer the mountain of work, no one—neither judges, court administrators, nor legal commentators—has assessed whether relying on trial judges for informal dispute resolution and for case management, either before or after trial, is good, bad, or neutral. Little empirical evidence supports the claim that judicial management "works" either to settle cases or to provide cheaper, quicker, or fairer dispositions.[21] Proponents of judicial management have also failed to consider the systemic effects of the shift in judicial role. Management is a new form of "judicial activism," a behavior that usually attracts substantial criticism. Moreover, judicial management may be teaching judges to value their statistics, such as the number of case dispositions, more than they value the quality of their dispositions. Finally, because managerial judging is less visible and usually unreviewable, it gives trial courts more authority and at the same time provides litigants with fewer procedural safeguards to protect them from abuse of that authority. In short, managerial judging may be redefining sub silentio our standards of what constitutes rational, fair, and impartial adjudication.

[Professor Resnik constructs some hypothetical but realistic cases to demonstrate the ways in which the new managerial role influences litigation. For example:]

2. Paulson v. Danforth, Ltd.—On July 1, 1980, Sarah Paulson bought a "Zip," a car manufactured by the small British company Danforth, Ltd., from a dealer in Manhattan. She drove the car home to the state of Essex in the fall of 1980. On March 4, 1981, while driving at about fifty miles per hour on an interstate highway in Essex, Ms. Paulson lost control of the car and skidded into a side railing. The gas tank exploded immediately, and Ms. Paulson was badly burned. On January 4, 1982, Ms. Paulson's attorney, Robert Adams, filed Paulson v. Danforth, Ltd. in the United States District Court for

---

[21] [Here Professor Resnik cross-refers to a later section where she points out the limits of currently available information and includes these observations:]

Commentators and rulemakers rely heavily on Flanders' work for the proposition that pretrial management techniques actually promote efficiency. Perhaps the most prominent example of this reliance is found in the Advisory Committee's notes to draft rule 16:

Empirical studies reveal that when a trial judge intervenes personally at an early stage to assume judicial control over a case and to schedule dates for completion by the parties of the principal pretrial steps, the case is disposed of by settlement or trial more efficiently and with less cost and delay than when the parties are left to their own devices.

. . . Flanders, however, measured neither parties' costs nor court management costs.

Some commentators also rely on Flanders' data to assert that case management does not "necessarily" diminish quality. [Omitted citations include Professor Brazil's above-excerpted article.] But Flanders provides no measurement of quality; instead he assumes a "close positive relationship between speed and quality." . . . He concedes that "no staff member on this project could be considered qualified to attempt a comprehensive evaluation of the quality of justice rendered in the several courts we observed. That evaluation is a task well left to others . . . ."

the District of Essex. The complaint alleged that defective design had caused the gas tank to explode upon impact, and sought $750,000 in damages. The case was randomly assigned to Judge Edward Kinser.

Danforth's counsel in New York City received a copy of the complaint on January 15 and promptly telecopied it to Danforth's headquarters in London. Danforth retained Deborah Alford, an Essex City lawyer, on January 18. On February 4, Danforth filed a motion to dismiss the suit for lack of personal jurisdiction. Danforth claimed that, because its only business offices in the United States were in New York and California, it could not be sued in Essex. Ms. Paulson countered that Danforth was a commercial enterprise that voluntarily and deliberately did business with people coming from and going to Essex.

On June 10, Judge Kinser denied Danforth's motion to dismiss. On June 18, Danforth filed its answer denying liability. Thereafter, pursuant to rules 33 and 34 of the Federal Rules of Civil Procedure, Mr. Adams served a set of interrogatories and a notice to produce documents. Among the fifty interrogatories were the following:

13. From 1977 until 1982, did Danforth test the gas tank on the "Zip" to learn about the tank's durability and ability to withstand impact?

14. If the tests described in question 13 above were performed, list below the names of all personnel who had any responsibility for the tests.

Plaintiff also made several document requests, including this one:

8. Provide all data on the results of any tests performed on the "Zip" from January 1, 1977, through June 1, 1982.

Plaintiff served these discovery requests on Danforth's attorney on July 10, 1982. After the thirty days that the Federal Rules permit for response had passed, Mr. Adams reminded Ms. Alford of the discovery requests. She expressed reservations about the propriety of several questions. Aware of the local district court rule requiring counsel to negotiate discovery disputes "in good faith" before filing discovery motions, the lawyers discussed the questions for several minutes but could not resolve their differences.

Twenty days later, defendant moved for a protective order. Danforth asked Judge Kinser to rule that: (1) twenty-nine of the fifty interrogatories were vague, irrelevant, or overly burdensome, or requested privileged information, and therefore need not be answered; (2) Danforth need not produce crash test data for 1977–1979 and for 1981–1982, because such statistics were irrelevant; and (3) only plaintiff's attorney could see the information produced, because of its "commercial" nature. In opposition to the motion, Mr. Adams asserted the relevance of the information and the absence of any special reason to protect the disclosure. Claiming that Danforth had no legal basis for a protective motion, Mr. Adams requested that his client be awarded the costs and attorney's fees incurred in opposing the motion.

After Judge Kinser read the papers on the pending discovery motion, he decided that he did not know enough about plaintiff's theories to decide the questions presented. He called the attorneys to his chambers and asked them to explain more about the case. After listening for several minutes to the lawyers' posturing, Judge Kinser asked whether all these legal battles were really necessary: was not settlement the least expensive, quickest, and fairest resolution of most disputes? When the attorneys insisted upon pursuing their arguments, the judge asked whether the lawyers were acting in their clients' best interests. Had they thought about how costly the litigation would be? Did the clients know how risky trials were? That the loser would have to pay the victor's court costs? That discovery could take years and that he, the judge, had control over the schedule?

Judge Kinser then asked Mr. Adams to leave the room so that the judge could confer privately with defendant's lawyer. Judge Kinser explained to Ms. Alford that he had learned a bit about plaintiff's case and that it looked "sound" to him. Did Danforth understand that a jury would surely be sympathetic to an injured plaintiff? What harm would there be in giving this injured victim some money? Had the parties talked numbers? Perhaps she could tell her client that $250,000 seemed "about right" to the judge. And perhaps she could mention that his court looked with disfavor upon uncompromising litigants.

Judge Kinser then called in plaintiff's counsel for a private meeting. Did Mr. Adams know how hard it was to prove a products liability claim? Had he thought about how long it might take to get to trial? What numbers would his client "go for"? The judge thought that $250,000 "sounded right" and that the case looked like one that "should settle."

Summoning both attorneys before him once more, Judge Kinser concluded the conference by announcing that he would defer ruling on the discovery motion until the parties had had time to negotiate further. He set a date to hold another conference in six weeks.

. . . .

Under [rule 16's] new regime of judicial management, discovery disputes and efforts to promote settlement would not be the only occasions upon which Judge Kinser would become acquainted with the parties' attorneys and the details of lawsuits. Rather, by virtue of rule 16, he would be obliged to issue pretrial orders within 120 days of filing of a complaint. To do so with any intelligence, he would need to learn a good deal about the lawsuits to which he was assigned.

"Replaying" Paulson v. Danforth, Ltd. as if proposed rule 16 were in effect illustrates that the grant of pretrial power to federal judges would be expansive. In the hypothetical, Ms. Paulson's attorney, Mr. Adams, filed the complaint on January 4, 1982. But suppose that, instead of promptly replying, defendant asked for an additional twenty days to respond. Plaintiff's counsel readily agreed, and the parties filed a stipulation to that effect. However, Judge Kinser refused to permit any extension beyond the time permitted by the Federal Rules—twenty days after receipt of service.

On May 14, Judge Kinser held a rule 16 pretrial conference. Although he had not yet decided Danforth's pending motion to dismiss for lack of personal jurisdiction, rule 16 required him to issue a pretrial order "in no event more than 120 days after filing of the complaint." Ms. Alford argued that it would be a substantial waste of time and money for her to present discovery plans, because (she believed) the case should be dismissed on the jurisdictional ground. Mr. Adams was reluctant to discuss the case at all; he explained to the judge that, because no answer had been filed, he did not know what defenses would be raised, and he certainly did not want to suggest any.

Judge Kinser agreed that the conference was premature. He decided to postpone issuing a pretrial order (although he was not sure that rule 16 permitted the postponement). But he told the lawyers that the case should be resolved "quickly." "Looking down the road," the judge would neither tolerate further requests for delay nor let discovery "get out of hand." This case, like most, should be settled. He instructed the parties to return to his chambers on June 30 prepared to "talk settlement" with "real numbers."

On June 10, Judge Kinser denied Danforth's motion to dismiss. On June 18, Danforth filed its answer denying liability. A week later the parties once again met with the judge in chambers. After the attorneys reported that they had no settlement proposals to offer, the judge responded by announcing his schedule for the lawsuit. He ordered each side to inform him, by August 16, of the names of their prospective deponents. He directed the parties to exchange their first interrogatories by July 15, to begin taking depositions by August 25, and to finish discovery by November 30. Both sides objected, but the judge issued a pretrial order with this timetable.

Subsequently, the parties requested and obtained changes in the original scheduling order. Experts for both sides were unavailable for most of the summer of 1982, and a shipment of documents disappeared in the mail and required several months to replace. At each of the three pretrial conferences that Judge Kinser has conducted to date, he has raised the issue of settlement, but with little success. As a result of his efforts, however, the parties have begun to discuss the same "ball park" settlement figures.

Although this description of Paulson was presented as though proposed rule 16 were in effect, the scenario is not futuristic: under current rule 16, many federal judges manage their cases much as Judge Kinser did in the revised hypothetical. As they gain more experience with such new procedures, judges are acting more forcefully. Indeed, not all judges are as circumspect as Judge Kinser. Some warn the parties that the judge would take a dim, and possibly hostile, view of either side's insistence on going to trial.

. . . .

In the preceding discussion, I have argued for reflection before we plunge headlong into judicial management. I do not mean to suggest, however, that adjudication must be frozen into earlier forms or that more efficient decisionmaking is an unworthy aim. Rather, as we reorient the judicial system to accommodate contemporary demands, I believe that we should preserve the core of adjudication. To help judges remain impartial, we should limit the flow of untested information. To ensure that judges have the time and patience for deliberation, we should refrain from giving them too many distracting new responsibilities. To hold judges accountable for the quality—not merely the quantity—of their actions, we should require judges to act in public and to state reasons for their decisions.

With these goals in mind, I outline below some alterations of and alternatives to judicial management. . . .

. . . .

Ideas about statutory timetables for litigation, diverse procedural rules for different categories of cases, alternative dispute resolution centers, curtailed discovery rights, state-controlled case preparation, limitations on court access, and penalties for those who do not settle lawsuits should give us pause, for these reforms would drastically alter the civil litigation world. But equally far-reaching changes, instituted by the judiciary itself and carried out in the name of increased efficiency, are already under way. Unfortunately, these changes are being carried out piecemeal and with little reflection on their cumulative implications for the adversarial system.

If, as many of their critics assert, the courts cannot meet the demands they face, revamping adjudication may well be appropriate. But if the time to reappraise the process of adjudication has arrived, the work should not be left to the judiciary, its support staff, a handful of academics, or a few American Bar Association committees. Rather, the hard questions about pace (how quickly should lawsuits proceed?), allocation of authority (should the pace be decided by judges, the parties, or Congress?), and the continued existence of the adversary process (who should be responsible for case investigation, preparation, and presentation?) should be subjected to a more searching and free-ranging public debate.

. . . .

In the debate over appropriate responses to the increasingly heavy work load of the federal courts, I am concerned about preserving the uniqueness of the judicial function. Seduced by controlled calendars, disposition statistics, and other trappings of the efficiency era and the high-tech age, managerial judges are changing the nature of their work. The old judiciary was doing something different from the modern managerial ideal, something quite out of step with the world of time and motion studies. Among all of our official decisionmakers, judges—and judges alone—are required to provide reasoned explanations for their decisions. Judges alone are supposed to rule without concern for the interests of particular constituencies. Judges alone are required to act with deliberation—a steady, slow, unhurried task.

I want to take away trial judges' roving commission and to bring back the blindfold. I want judges to balance the scales, not abandon them altogether in the press to dispose of cases quickly. No one has convincingly discredited the virtues of disinterest and disengagement, virtues that form the bases of the judiciary's authority. Our society has not yet openly and deliberately decided to discard the traditional adversarial model in favor of some version of the continental or inquisitorial model. Until we do so, federal judges should remain true to their ancestry and emulate the goddess Justicia. I fear that, as it moves closer to administration, adjudication may be in danger of ceasing to be.

EBERSOLE, "DISCOVERY AND PRETRIAL PROCEDURES," in The Improvement of the Administration of Justice 137, 138, 143–44 (F. Klein 6th ed. 1981). In the 1970's, with the full flowering of the discovery and pretrial rules, judges clearly assumed new roles in addition to "the traditional role of umpire."

"*Case Manager.* This role is based on the premise that the flow of the court calendar should be controlled by the court, not by the attorneys. It recognizes the court has a responsibility for assuring just resolutions of disputes expeditiously and inexpensively. Effective case management requires a personal concern that a just, speedy and inexpensive determination be reached in every action and the belief that managing the flow of litigation in the pretrial phases is an essential and important part of the art of judging. Thus, attitude is all important as a necessary (although not sufficient) condition.

. . . .

"*Mediator.* This role is based on the premises that (1) in most cases the absolute result of a trial is not as high a quality of justice as is a freely negotiated settlement, (2) it is appropriate for a judge to function as a mediator, and (3) a judge who is familiar with a case can often be the most effective mediator for that case. It is normally not advisable for a judge to 'force' settlement discussions. Formal settlement conferences held on a routine basis tend not to be effective. However, where judges make it known they are available for settlement discussions and ask counsel when the opportunity occurs whether they wish to discuss settlement possibilities fruitful mediation often occurs.

"It should be recognized that judicial settlement of lawsuits is . . . an art and some judges may find it more comfortable to serve as mediators than others. Further, mediation of a nonjury case by the judge who will try the case if it is not settled is considered inadvisable by many judges and attorneys. Therefore, each court should have procedures under which a judge who will not try the case can serve the role of mediator."

Questions: (1) As the mediator role begins to look more like negotiation or arbitration, or as the pretrial judge begins actively to adjudicate by formulation of the issues through eliminating frivolous claims or defenses and by disposition of pending motions, does this judicial role of case mover come into conflict with that of case manager? If so, does recognition of this conflict inform the specific decision on whether pretrial conferences should be held in the courtroom or in chambers? with or without a court reporter?

(2) Does either the role of case manager or that of case mover conflict with the traditional role of umpire?

BEARY v. CITY OF RYE, 601 F.2d 62 (2d Cir.1979). This diversity action alleged malicious prosecution for sex crimes.

"Appellant brought the instant suit in federal court on January 26, 1977. A pretrial order provided that

[t]he parties shall, in order to prevent delay or interruption of the trial, have sufficient witnesses present at all times during the trial and shall perpetuate before trial the testimony of any essential witnesses, on direct and cross examination, . . . likely to be unavailable when required upon the trial.

The pretrial order also provided that failure to comply with any of its provisions 'may result in this court's imposing appropriate sanctions, including termination of the action.'

"Trial of the federal action commenced on Monday, November 27, 1978. Appellant's counsel had, on November 24, subpoenaed six witnesses to appear on Wednesday, November 29, one at 9:00 a.m. and five at 9:30 a.m. At the luncheon recess on the first day of the trial appellant's first witness, appellant himself, was still testifying; opposing counsel subjected him to a vigorous cross-examination which continued after the luncheon recess. After redirect examination of appellant, appellant then called two other witnesses . . . . At this point in the trial, which was 3:30 p.m., the following occurred:

Mr. Greenspan [counsel for plaintiff]: I have no further questions.

. . . .

Mr. Zawacki [counsel for defendant]: I have no questions.

The Court: You are excused.

(Witness excused.)

The Court: Next witness.

Mr. Greenspan: I have no further witnesses today, your Honor. I request a continuance until tomorrow morning.

The Court: You rest.

Mr. Greenspan: No, sir, I do not rest.

The Court: Put in your defense.

Mr. Zawacki: The defendant moves to dismiss the complaint.

The Court: Granted. The jury may be excused.

(Jury leaves courtroom.)

The court did not give appellant time to explain, as he contends on appeal, that he had a number of depositions of witnesses taken for use at the trial or any opportunity to read those depositions into the record.

"Immediately after the jury left the courtroom the following occurred:

Mr. Greenspan: Your Honor, at this time—

The Court: Just a moment. Let the record reflect . . . .

Mr. Greenspan: If your Honor please, at this point I would move for a new trial.

The Court: Denied.

In the court's remarks above elided, the court referred to the pretrial order above quoted, stated that counsel came in 'without sufficient witnesses to complete the day' and went on to hold that the plaintiff had failed to make out a prima facie case. . . . The court went on to say that 'we cannot tolerate waste of time, interruption of trials and delays which have a ripple effect on our whole docket . . . .' "

The plaintiff appealed. The court of appeals reversed the judgment dismissing the complaint, explaining:

"This appeal is an example of a trial court's permitting its zeal for clearing its calendar to overcome the right of a party to a full and fair trial on the merits. . . .

"In striking the balance between alleviating court calendar congestion and protecting a party's right to due process and a fair chance to be heard, we have repeatedly given a great deal of latitude

to the individual district judges laboring conscientiously in a day of ever-rising filings closely to control their dockets. [Citations omitted.] At the same time this court has always recognized that 'a court must not let its zeal for a tidy calendar overcome its duty to do justice.' Peterson v. Term Taxi, Inc., 429 F.2d 888, 891 (2d Cir.1970).
. . .

. . . .

"In our view justice has been impaired by such a 'close inflexible attention to the docket.' [Id.] Here we have no flagrant or intentional disregard of the pretrial order but rather an understandable mistake of judgment in thinking that the examination of appellant, who had a criminal record and other habits and problems which would prompt a rather extensive cross-examination for impeachment as well as to show a diminished reputation, combined with the examination of two other witnesses, would probably consume the entire first day of trial. At least counsel could reasonably have thought that if they did not do so depositions would enable counsel to make valuable use of the court's and the jury's time. Counsel's belief was particularly reasonable because appellant was still on the stand at the luncheon recess. There was clearly no failure on appellant's part to prosecute his action. Here the plaintiff had obtained the necessary subpoenas for his witnesses, selected a jury, made his opening statement, and presented the testimony of three witnesses. We believe that the ordering of the plaintiff's rest, especially without giving him an opportunity to use the time alternatively, was an abuse of discretion under the circumstances.

"We direct a retrial to take place before a different judge."

Part Four

TRIAL

TOPIC A. PRELIMINARY QUESTIONS ABOUT FORENSIC PROOF

SECTION 1. BURDEN OF PROOF

Professor John Maguire says in Evidence: Common Sense and Common Law 175–77 (1947):

"Under our law the term burden of proof has been used to express two rather different ideas, and as might be expected this usage has led to a jumble. Incisive thinkers have framed a more particularized vocabulary, duly segregating the ideas, but have not managed to get their vocabulary into universal use. Let us try to phrase the two ideas:

"During a trial the evidence concerning an issue of fact may become decisively one-sided. If no controlling counter-evidence is presented before the end of the trial, the judge must remove that issue from the jury's deliberations and cause it to be resolved in favor of the party whose contentions have thus overwhelmed opposition. When at the end of the trial an issue is more nearly in balance, so that it should be submitted to the jury for a deliberative verdict, the judge must decide which party has to make his contentions of fact prevail or suffer an adverse determination. If the issue is commonplace, there will be precedents for this decision; if it is unusual, the judge may find precedents or may have to decide the question as an original problem. Having decided, the judge transmits the effect of the decision to the jury to prevent their verdict from being merely the chance result of unregulated discussion. He may do the transmitting in either of two ways. More commonly, perhaps, he simply states his decision for the jury's guidance. Alternatively he puts to the jury one or more questions, carefully but colloquially worded, the answers to which will show whether the party with the laboring oar has successfully wielded that implement.

"Both these situations are sometimes lumped under the term burden of proof. Careful verbalists therefore feel that we should have a brace of subordinate terms to keep the distinction clear. Speaking of the deliberative verdict, they say that the litigant in whose hands we have put the laboring oar has 'the burden of persuasion of the fact.' Verbalists who are *very* careful, noting that any litigant may derive useful evidence from the probative mischances of his opponent as well as from his own efforts, abandon the metaphors of oarsmanship and burden bearing in favor of 'risk of non-persuasion of the fact.'

This last refinement has not gained much practical support. Careful phraseology about the other situation is that while opposition is overwhelmed, the opponent has 'the burden of producing evidence of the fact' in order to escape an adverse directed verdict rather than an adverse deliberative verdict.

"As to the self-same issue of fact, burden of persuasion may be on one party in case of ultimate submission to the jury, and burden of producing evidence, in the course of the case, now on him and now on his opponent as evidence or counter-evidence is called for to avoid a directed verdict."

Let us illustrate Professor Maguire's remarks with a simple case in which there is but one disputed issue of fact. The plaintiff asserts *A*, the defendant denies it, and the persuasion-burden is on the plaintiff. Ordinarily, if the plaintiff offered no proof of *A*, the judge would direct a verdict against him. Hence it may be said, in Professor Maguire's terms, that the plaintiff is "overwhelmed" at the moment when the trial commences and that the production-burden is upon him. He is, therefore, bound to go forward with his evidence until he satisfies the judge that the jury would be warranted in finding *A*. When the plaintiff has thus carried his production-burden, he is in the hands of the jury in the sense that if both parties rest at this point, the case will be submitted to the jury for decision.

But the plaintiff realizes that the minimum amount of evidence needed to prevent the direction of an adverse verdict may not be enough to bring the minds of the jurors to the required degree of persuasion regarding *A*; that is, he may fail to sustain the persuasion-burden. Hence he may well be advised to go on with his evidence in order to strengthen his case with the jury.

Sometimes the plaintiff's evidence may be overwhelming, so that the judge will hold that no reasonable juror could fail to find *A*. If on this posture of the evidence both parties rested, the judge would direct a verdict for plaintiff. (We reserve for the present such questions as the propriety of the judge's passing on the credibility of witnesses in ruling on a motion for a directed verdict.) At this stage the production-burden has shifted to the defendant. To avoid a directed verdict for the plaintiff, the defendant is bound in his turn to go forward with such evidence that it will become reasonable for the jury to decline to find *A*.

The defendant's evidence may do more than push the issue back into the area of doubt where the jury is the arbiter. It may be overwhelming, in which case the production-burden shifts to the plaintiff. As a theoretical matter, the production-burden may thus shift several times with the pull and haul of the evidence. As a practical matter, however, such multiple shifting on a single issue of fact is very unlikely. The reason is that conflicting evidence on a single issue would in most realistic settings leave the matter in the realm where decision is properly for the jury: a reasonable jury could find *A* or decline to find *A*, and so the judge should not direct a verdict. Thus the pull and haul of the evidence will result only in oscillation within the jury's realm.

A diagram adapted from 9 J. Wigmore, Evidence § 2487 (J. Chadbourn rev. 1981), should help to visualize this process:

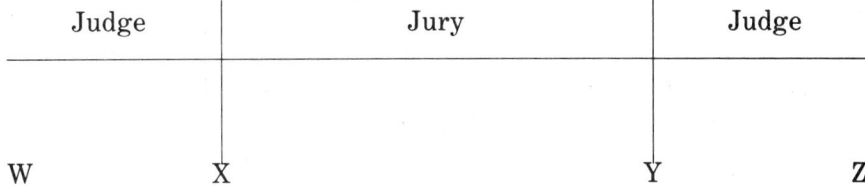

Judge	Jury	Judge
W X	Y	Z

The plaintiff in our illustrative case starts at point W. He must get beyond point X to make a jury question of *A*, our assumed single issue of fact. If he gets beyond point Y, he is entitled to a directed verdict in his favor unless the defendant comes forward with enough evidence to push the case back beyond point Y into the X–Y area. If the defendant succeeds in this, it is again a case for the jury. He may, however, be so successful that his evidence carries the case beyond point X into the W–X area. If so, the defendant becomes entitled to a directed verdict unless the plaintiff in his turn comes forward with more evidence. But whenever, at the close of all the evidence, the case lies between points X and Y, it goes to the jury and the plaintiff has the persuasion-burden. He will lose if the jury is not persuaded of *A*.[a]

Where the case involves more than one disputed issue of fact, we can conveniently use a separate diagram for each such issue. In the typical case, the persuasion-burden will rest upon the plaintiff on some issues and upon the defendant on others.

Question: (1) How must the foregoing description of burden of proof be altered to describe accurately the situation in trials by judge without jury? Cf. Rule 41(b).

ALLOCATION OF THE PERSUASION–BURDEN

Whether one or the other of the parties has sustained or failed to sustain the production-burden is a matter for the judge to decide, and there is no occasion for the jury to hear anything about it. But as it is for the jury to decide, when a case is submitted to it, whether the party carrying the persuasion-burden on a particular issue of fact has sustained it, the judge must explain to the jury in his charge (1) upon whom this burden rests with regard to each issue that is left to the

[a] For a criticism of the Wigmore diagram and approach and for some more sophisticated diagrams, see McNaughton, Burden of Production of Evidence: A Function of a Burden of Persuasion, 68 Harv.L.Rev. 1382 (1955).

jury and (2) the degree of persuasion to which the minds of the jurors must be brought before they are warranted in finding that the burden has been carried with respect to the particular issue.

Problem (2) is reserved for Section 2 of this Topic. With respect to problem (1), Professor Morgan says in Some Observations Concerning Presumptions, 44 Harv.L.Rev. 906, 910–11 (1931):

"Inasmuch as under our adversary system of litigation the court conducts no independent investigation of its own, it must distribute between the litigants the burden of making the facts appear. In assigning to the plaintiff the burden of persuasion of the existence of X, it in substance notifies him that unless he makes X appear, the court will assume for the purposes of the litigation that X does not exist. In reaching its determination to put this burden upon plaintiff or defendant, it is influenced by substantially the same considerations as those which obtain in the determination of any question of substantive law. As in many branches of substantive law, precedents have developed rules of thumb, so here at least four a priori tests for placing this burden have emerged. These respectively make it fall upon (1) the party having the affirmative of the issue, (2) the party to whose case the fact in question is essential, (3) the party having peculiar means of knowing the fact, and (4) the party who has the burden of pleading it. Needless to say, these formulae are not self-executing; frequently to apply one is to repudiate another. Ordinarily the one selected is used only as a facile form of statement of the result. The real decision is made upon the judicial judgment based upon experience as to what is convenient, fair, and good policy; and some opinions frankly so declare."

Not only would it be erroneous to assume that the burden of persuasion is inevitably allocated between the parties in the same way as the burden of allegation, although this is typically the case,[b] but also it would be erroneous to assume that the burden of persuasion and the initial burden of production necessarily are allocated to the same party. A familiar illustration to the contrary from the criminal law is the matter of the defendant's insanity: normally the defendant must plead and initially present some evidence of insanity, but the prosecution must ultimately persuade the jury that the defendant was sane.

Question: (2) What considerations of convenience, fairness, and good policy dictate a difference in the allocation of the burdens as to insanity?

---

[b] See supra pp. 32, 107, 461.

TEXAS DEPARTMENT OF COMMUNITY AFFAIRS v. BURDINE

Supreme Court of the United States, 1981.
450 U.S. 248, 101 S.Ct. 1089.

JUSTICE POWELL delivered the opinion of the Court.

This case requires us to address again the nature of the evidentiary burden placed upon the defendant in an employment discrimination suit brought under Title VII of the Civil Rights Act of 1964, 42 U.S.C. § 2000e et seq. The narrow question presented is whether, after the plaintiff has proved a prima facie case of discriminatory treatment, the burden shifts to the defendant to persuade the court by a preponderance of the evidence that legitimate, nondiscriminatory reasons for the challenged employment action existed.

I

Petitioner, the Texas Department of Community Affairs (TDCA), hired respondent, a female, in January 1972, for the position of accounting clerk in the Public Service Careers Division (PSC). PSC provided training and employment opportunities in the public sector for unskilled workers. When hired, respondent possessed several years' experience in employment training. She was promoted to Field Services Coordinator in July 1972. Her supervisor resigned in November of that year, and respondent was assigned additional duties. Although she applied for the supervisor's position of Project Director, the position remained vacant for six months.

PSC was funded completely by the United States Department of Labor. The Department was seriously concerned about inefficiencies at PSC. In February 1973, the Department notified the Executive Director of TDCA, B.R. Fuller, that it would terminate PSC the following month. TDCA officials, assisted by respondent, persuaded the Department to continue funding the program, conditioned upon PSC's reforming its operations. Among the agreed conditions were the appointment of a permanent Project Director and a complete reorganization of the PSC staff.

After consulting with personnel within TDCA, Fuller hired a male from another division of the agency as Project Director. In reducing the PSC staff, he fired respondent along with two other employees, and retained another male, Walz, as the only professional employee in the division. It is undisputed that respondent had maintained her application for the position of Project Director and had requested to remain with TDCA. Respondent soon was rehired by TDCA and assigned to another division of the agency. She received the exact salary paid to the Project Director at PSC, and the subsequent promotions she has received have kept her salary and responsibility commensurate with what she would have received had she been appointed Project Director.

Respondent filed this suit in the United States District Court for the Western District of Texas. She alleged that the failure to promote and the subsequent decision to terminate her had been predicated on gender discrimination in violation of Title VII. After a bench trial, the District Court held that neither decision was based on gender discrimination. The court relied on the testimony of Fuller that the employment decisions necessitated by the commands of the Department of Labor were based on consultation among trusted advisers and a nondiscriminatory evaluation of the relative qualifications of the individuals involved. He testified that the three individuals terminated did not work well together, and that TDCA thought that eliminating this problem would improve PSC's efficiency. The court accepted this explanation as rational and, in effect, found no evidence that the decisions not to promote and to terminate respondent were prompted by gender discrimination.

The Court of Appeals for the Fifth Circuit reversed in part. 608 F.2d 563 (1979). . . . [T]he court affirmed the District Court's finding that respondent was not discriminated against when she was not promoted. The Court of Appeals, however, reversed the District Court's finding that Fuller's testimony sufficiently had rebutted respondent's prima facie case of gender discrimination in the decision to terminate her employment at PSC. The court reaffirmed its previously announced views that the defendant in a Title VII case bears the burden of proving by a preponderance of the evidence the existence of legitimate nondiscriminatory reasons for the employment action . . . . It, therefore, reversed the judgment of the District Court and remanded the case for computation of backpay. Because the decision of the Court of Appeals as to the burden of proof borne by the defendant conflicts with interpretations of our precedents adopted by other Courts of Appeals, we granted certiorari. 447 U.S. 920, 100 S.Ct. 3009 (1980). We now vacate the Fifth Circuit's decision and remand for application of the correct standard.

II

In McDonnell Douglas Corp. v. Green, 411 U.S. 792, 93 S.Ct. 1817 (1973), we set forth the basic allocation of burdens and order of presentation of proof in a Title VII case alleging discriminatory treatment. First, the plaintiff has the burden of proving by the preponderance of the evidence a prima facie case of discrimination. Second, if the plaintiff succeeds in proving the prima facie case, the burden shifts to the defendant "to articulate some legitimate, nondiscriminatory reason for the employee's rejection." Id., at 802, 93 S.Ct., at 1824. Third, should the defendant carry this burden, the plaintiff must then have an opportunity to prove by a preponderance of the evidence that the legitimate reasons offered by the defendant were not its true reasons, but were a pretext for discrimination. Id., at 804, 93 S.Ct., at 1825.

The nature of the burden that shifts to the defendant should be understood in light of the plaintiff's ultimate and intermediate burdens. The ultimate burden of persuading the trier of fact that the defendant intentionally discriminated against the plaintiff remains at all times with the plaintiff. See Board of Trustees of Keene State College v. Sweeney, 439 U.S. 24, 25, n. 2, 99 S.Ct. 295, 296, n. 2 (1978); id., at 29, 99 S.Ct., at 297 (Stevens, J., dissenting). See generally 9 J. Wigmore, Evidence § 2489 (3d ed. 1940) (the burden of persuasion "never shifts"). The McDonnell Douglas division of intermediate evidentiary burdens serves to bring the litigants and the court expeditiously and fairly to this ultimate question.

The burden of establishing a prima facie case of disparate treatment is not onerous. The plaintiff must prove by a preponderance of the evidence that she applied for an available position for which she was qualified, but was rejected under circumstances which give rise to an inference of unlawful discrimination.[6] The prima facie case serves an important function in the litigation: it eliminates the most common nondiscriminatory reasons for the plaintiff's rejection. See Teamsters v. United States, 431 U.S. 324, 358, and n. 44, 97 S.Ct. 1843, 1866, and n. 44 (1977). As the Court explained in Furnco Construction Corp. v. Waters, 438 U.S. 567, 577, 98 S.Ct. 2943, 2949 (1978), the prima facie case "raises an inference of discrimination only because we presume these acts, if otherwise unexplained, are more likely than not based on the consideration of impermissible factors." Establishment of the prima facie case in effect creates a presumption that the employer unlawfully discriminated against the employee. If the trier of fact believes the plaintiff's evidence, and if the employer is silent in the face of the presumption, the court must enter judgment for the plaintiff because no issue of fact remains in the case.[7]

[6] In McDonnell Douglas, supra, we described an appropriate model for a prima facie case of racial discrimination. The plaintiff must show:

"(i) that he belongs to a racial minority; (ii) that he applied and was qualified for a job for which the employer was seeking applicants; (iii) that, despite his qualifications, he was rejected; and (iv) that, after his rejection, the position remained open and the employer continued to seek applicants from persons of complainant's qualifications." 411 U.S., at 802, 93 S.Ct., at 1824.

We added, however, that this standard is not inflexible, as "[t]he facts necessarily will vary in Title VII cases, and the specification above of the prima facie proof required from respondent is not necessarily applicable in every respect in differing factual situations." Id., at 802, n. 13, 93 S.Ct., at 1824, n. 13.

In the instant case, it is not seriously contested that respondent has proved a prima facie case. She showed that she was a qualified woman who sought an available position, but the position was left open for several months before she finally was rejected in favor of a male, Walz, who had been under her supervision.

[7] The phrase "prima facie case" not only may denote the establishment of a legally mandatory, rebuttable presumption, but also may be used by courts to describe the plaintiff's burden of producing enough evidence to permit the trier of fact to infer the fact at issue. 9 J. Wigmore, Evidence § 2494 (3d ed. 1940). McDonnell Douglas should have made it apparent that in the Title VII context we use "prima facie case" in the former sense.

The burden that shifts to the defendant, therefore, is to rebut the presumption of discrimination by producing evidence that the plaintiff was rejected, or someone else was preferred, for a legitimate, nondiscriminatory reason. The defendant need not persuade the court that it was actually motivated by the proffered reasons. See Sweeney, supra, at 25, 99 S.Ct., at 296. It is sufficient if the defendant's evidence raises a genuine issue of fact as to whether it discriminated against the plaintiff.[8] To accomplish this, the defendant must clearly set forth, through the introduction of admissible evidence, the reasons for the plaintiff's rejection.[9] The explanation provided must be legally sufficient to justify a judgment for the defendant. If the defendant carries this burden of production, the presumption raised by the prima facie case is rebutted,[10] and the factual inquiry proceeds to a new level of specificity. Placing this burden of production on the defendant thus serves simultaneously to meet the plaintiff's prima facie case by presenting a legitimate reason for the action and to frame the factual issue with sufficient clarity so that the plaintiff will have a full and fair opportunity to demonstrate pretext. The sufficiency of the defendant's evidence should be evaluated by the extent to which it fulfills these functions.

The plaintiff retains the burden of persuasion. She now must have the opportunity to demonstrate that the proffered reason was not the true reason for the employment decision. This burden now merges with the ultimate burden of persuading the court that she has been the victim of intentional discrimination. She may succeed in this either directly by persuading the court that a discriminatory reason more likely motivated the employer or indirectly by showing that the

[8] This evidentiary relationship between the presumption created by a prima facie case and the consequential burden of production placed on the defendant, is a traditional feature of the common law. "The word 'presumption' properly used refers only to a device for allocating the production burden." F. James & G. Hazard, Civil Procedure § 7.9, p. 255 (2d ed. 1977) (footnote omitted). See Fed.Rule Evid. 301. See generally 9 J. Wigmore, Evidence § 2491 (3d ed. 1940). Cf. J. Maguire, Evidence, Common Sense and Common Law 185–186 (1947). Usually, assessing the burden of production helps the judge determine whether the litigants have created an issue of fact to be decided by the jury. In a Title VII case, the allocation of burdens and the creation of a presumption by the establishment of a prima facie case is intended progressively to sharpen the inquiry into the elusive factual question of intentional discrimination.

[9] An articulation not admitted into evidence will not suffice. Thus, the defendant cannot meet its burden merely through an answer to the complaint or by argument of counsel.

[10] See generally J. Thayer, Preliminary Treatise on Evidence 346 (1898). In saying that the presumption drops from the case, we do not imply that the trier of fact no longer may consider evidence previously introduced by the plaintiff to establish a prima facie case. A satisfactory explanation by the defendant destroys the legally mandatory inference of discrimination arising from the plaintiff's initial evidence. Nonetheless, this evidence and inferences properly drawn therefrom may be considered by the trier of fact on the issue of whether the defendant's explanation is pretextual. Indeed, there may be some cases where the plaintiff's initial evidence, combined with effective cross-examination of the defendant, will suffice to discredit the defendant's explanation.

employer's proffered explanation is unworthy of credence. See Mc-Donnell Douglas, 411 U.S., at 804–805, 93 S.Ct., at 1825–1826.

III

. . . .

The Court of Appeals has misconstrued the nature of the burden that McDonnell Douglas and its progeny place on the defendant. . . . It is plain that the Court of Appeals required much more: it placed on the defendant the burden of persuading the court that it had convincing, objective reasons for preferring the chosen applicant above the plaintiff.[11]

The Court of Appeals distinguished Sweeney on the ground that the case held only that the defendant did not have the burden of proving the absence of discriminatory intent. But this distinction slights the rationale of Sweeney and of our other cases. We have stated consistently that the employee's prima facie case of discrimination will be rebutted if the employer articulates lawful reasons for the action; that is, to satisfy this intermediate burden, the employer need only produce admissible evidence which would allow the trier of fact rationally to conclude that the employment decision had not been motivated by discriminatory animus. The Court of Appeals would require the defendant to introduce evidence which, in the absence of any evidence of pretext, would *persuade* the trier of fact that the employment action was lawful. This exceeds what properly can be demanded to satisfy a burden of production.

The court placed the burden of persuasion on the defendant apparently because it feared that "[i]f an employer need only *articulate*—not prove—a legitimate, nondiscriminatory reason for his action, he may compose fictitious, but legitimate, reasons for his actions." Turner v. Texas Instruments, Inc., [555 F.2d 1251, 1255 (5th Cir.1977)] (emphasis in original). We do not believe, however, that limiting the defendant's evidentiary obligation to a burden of production will unduly hinder the plaintiff. First, as noted above, the defendant's explanation of its legitimate reasons must be clear and reasonably specific. [Citations omitted.] This obligation arises both from the

---

[11] The court reviewed the defendant's evidence and explained its deficiency:

"Defendant failed to introduce comparative factual data concerning Burdine and Walz. Fuller merely testified that he discharged and retained personnel in the spring shakeup at TDCA primarily on the recommendations of subordinates and that he considered Walz qualified for the position he was retained to do. Fuller failed to specify any objective criteria on which he based the decision to discharge Burdine and retain Walz. He stated only that the action was in the best interest of the program and that there had been some friction within the department that might be alleviated by Burdine's discharge. Nothing in the record indicates whether he examined Walz' ability to work well with others. This court in [a previous case] found such unsubstantiated assertions of 'qualification' and 'prior work record' insufficient absent data that will allow a true *comparison* of the individuals hired and rejected." 608 F.2d, at 568.

necessity of rebutting the inference of discrimination arising from the prima facie case and from the requirement that the plaintiff be afforded "a full and fair opportunity" to demonstrate pretext. Second, although the defendant does not bear a formal burden of persuasion, the defendant nevertheless retains an incentive to persuade the trier of fact that the employment decision was lawful. Thus, the defendant normally will attempt to prove the factual basis for its explanation. Third, the liberal discovery rules applicable to any civil suit in federal court are supplemented in a Title VII suit by the plaintiff's access to the Equal Employment Opportunity Commission's investigatory files concerning her complaint. See EEOC v. Associated Dry Goods Corp., 449 U.S. 590, 101 S.Ct. 817 (1981). Given these factors, we are unpersuaded that the plaintiff will find it particularly difficult to prove that a proffered explanation lacking a factual basis is a pretext. We remain confident that the McDonnell Douglas framework permits the plaintiff meriting relief to demonstrate intentional discrimination.

.   .   .   .

PRESUMPTIONS

A full-dress treatment of burden of proof would involve us deeply in "presumptions," all the intricacies of which cannot be explored here. The word has, as Professor Maguire says, suffered badly from rough and careless handling. J. Maguire, Evidence: Common Sense and Common Law 183 (1947).

1. To the layman its most common use is doubtless the "presumption of innocence" in criminal cases. This is not really a presumption at all, but rather another way of saying that the prosecution must prove its case beyond a reasonable doubt, that there is to be no inference against the defendant because of his arrest, indictment, and presence in the dock, and so on. In instructions to the jury the phrase does, however, have a satisfying ring to defense counsel, and the judge's refusal to use it may be reversible error, no matter how accurately and meticulously he tells the jury in other words what it means. See Taylor v. Kentucky, 436 U.S. 478, 98 S.Ct. 1930 (1978).

2. Another use of the word is in the phrase "conclusive presumption." This is not a presumption in any useful sense, but a rule of law that so equates one fact (the basic fact) to another (the presumed fact) that no one will be heard to say the latter does not exist if the former is proved. For instance, the statement in a workers' compensation act that the children under sixteen living in a worker's household at the time of his or her death are conclusively presumed to be dependent upon him or her really means that the law is not concerned with dependency in fact so long as the prescribed circumstances exist.

3. The word is also loosely used, by lawyers as well as laymen, as a synonym for inference ("Dr. Livingstone, I presume"), a matter of logic and experience and not of law. All circumstantial evidence is a matter of inference, and the use of presumption terminology in this context can only be confusing. Nevertheless, "permissive presumption" is sometimes used to describe certain inferences that by law the jury is authorized but not required to draw.[c] These inferences are usually based on reasonable probabilities, but are occasionally arbitrary in the sense that the rule authorizing the particular inference may be based instead on policy concerns. If the jury is authorized to find the existence of the presumed fact from proof of the basic fact when the raw probabilities alone would not justify the finding, the judge may so instruct the jury without violation of the common ban in state practice against comment on the evidence. It is argued that this is as much a rule of law as that about to be discussed.

4. We finally come to the more general view, held by Thayer, Wigmore, Morgan, Maguire, and other commentators and illustrated recurringly in common and statutory law, that the word "presumption" should be used only to denote the convention that when a designated basic facts exists, a certain presumed fact *must* be taken to exist in the absence of adequate *rebuttal*.[d] It is in this sense that we shall use it hereafter. For convenience in the discussion which follows, the basic fact will be designated as B and the presumed fact as P.

Assume that the single disputed issue of fact in a civil case is P, the plaintiff asserts the affirmative and initially has the production-burden and the persuasion-burden thereon, and there is a common-law or statutory presumption that when B exists P is presumed to exist. Assume further that the presumption is grounded upon reasonable probabilities; that is, proof of B would have sufficient evidentiary value to warrant the jury in finding P if there were no presumption. (We shall refer in a moment to the less common presumptions that are arbitrary; that is, apart from such a presumption, proof of the basic fact would not be sufficient to warrant the jury's finding the presumed fact.) Assume still further that the plaintiff offers overwhelming evidence of B, and there is no other evidence bearing on B or P. The judge will direct a verdict for the plaintiff. But suppose that the defendant introduces evidence of non-B to the point where the jury could reasonably find either way as to B's existence, and there is still no other evidence bearing on P. The presumption compels the judge to instruct the jury: "If, but only if, you find B,

[c] According to most courts, this is the situation in res ipsa loquitur cases. See W. Prosser, Handbook of the Law of Torts 228–31 (4th ed. 1971).

[d] "This careful, particularized use of the word presumption, by the way, is getting more and more consistent accept-ance in the courts; nobody has ever succeeded in making consistent the legislative use of this or any other important word." J. Maguire, Evidence: Common Sense and Common Law 183–84 (1947).

you are bound to find *P*." There is no advantage in mentioning the presumption to the jury in the charge.

Questions: (3) How does the action of the judge in these two situations differ from what it would be in the absence of the presumption?

(4) When there are other disputed issues in addition to *P*, how does the judge instruct the jury if the evidence as to *B* is overwhelming and there is no other evidence bearing on *P*? if the evidence as to *B* is conflicting and there is no other evidence bearing on *P*?

So long as the only evidence relates to *B*, the basic fact, the courts are in universal agreement that when *B* is established, *P*, the presumed fact, must be taken as true. But when evidence of non-*P* is introduced, that unanimity disappears and the decisions are in what Wigmore termed a state of "variegated inconsistency." [e] There is little point in running down these inconsistencies, which were reflected in the deliberations of the American Law Institute in drawing up its Model Code of Evidence, promulgated in 1942.[f] The Institute, over the opposition of its Reporter, Professor Morgan, finally wound up adopting what is often called the Thayer approach, because of the distinguished early pioneering in the field by Professor Thayer. The Institute generalized as follows: when the basic fact has been established, the presumed fact must be assumed until other evidence has been introduced that would warrant a finding of its nonexistence; when such evidence has been introduced, the existence or nonexistence of the presumed fact is to be determined exactly as if no presumption had ever been applicable.[g] In other words, the presumption affects the production-burden only; when other evidence warranting a finding of the nonexistence of the presumed fact appears, the presumption has spent itself like a "bursting bubble." If the presumption was grounded upon the reasonable probability that *P* exists when *B* is shown, that probability remains for the jury to consider against the evidence to the contrary, but without any artificial weight by reason of the presumption. There is no occasion for the judge to mention the presumption in charging the jury. This Thayer approach had attracted considerable judicial support prior to the Model Code and still does.[h]

The original Uniform Rules of Evidence, approved by the National Conference of Commissioners on Uniform State Laws in 1953, took a very different tack.[i] Adopting the view of Professor Morgan, the

[e] Professor Morgan lists eight different views exhibited in judicial opinions. E. Morgan, Basic Problems of Evidence 34–37 (1962).

[f] 18 A.L.I. Proc. 197–226 (1941).

[g] Model Code of Evidence Rule 704 (1942).

[h] Probably a majority of states follow the Thayer-Model Code approach. See Annot., 5 A.L.R.3d 19 (1966). It is doubtful whether the Model Code itself was of significant influence in this development. The Code was not very well received by the bench and bar. Its proposed relaxation of the rules as to admission of hearsay evidence, for example, was widely thought to be dangerously radical.

[i] Unif.R.Evid. 14 (1953 version).

Uniform Rules provided that if the basic fact has any probative value as evidence of the existence of the presumed fact, the presumption continues and the burden of proof (that is, the burden of persuasion) of the nonexistence of the presumed fact is upon the party against whom the presumption operates. The traditional dogma of Wigmore that the burden of persuasion never shifts is thus violated. A plaintiff who starts out with the burden of proving P has the benefit, once he proves B, of placing the burden of proving non-P on the defendant.

However, the 1953 Uniform Rules gave less procedural effect to presumptions where the basic fact proved has no probative value with respect to the fact presumed. When such probative value is lacking, the Uniform Rules provided that only the burden of production is affected. Thus, the presumption disappears when other evidence is offered that would warrant a finding that the presumed fact does not exist. (The draftsmen of the Uniform Rules were frightened off by Western & Atlantic Railroad v. Henderson, 279 U.S. 639, 49 S.Ct. 445 (1929). There a Georgia statute provided that a railroad company would be liable for damage from its locomotive unless the company made it appear that it had exercised due care, the presumption in all cases being against the company. The Court held the statute unconstitutional because it shifted the burden of persuasion when the basic fact, damage, had no probative value in establishing the presumed fact, negligence. The Supreme Court distinguished Mobile, Jackson & Kansas City Railroad v. Turnipseed, 219 U.S. 35, 31 S.Ct. 136 (1910), in which a somewhat similar Mississippi statute had been construed to affect only the burden of production and had been upheld.) The effect of the Uniform Rules, then, was to treat arbitrary presumptions in precisely the same way that the Thayer-Model Code approach treated all presumptions.

The Federal Rules of Evidence, as originally proposed by the Supreme Court in 1972 but not as eventually enacted, treated all presumptions in exactly the same way that the 1953 Uniform Rules treated presumptions grounded upon reasonable probabilities. That is, the proposed Federal Rules provided that a presumption imposes on the party against whom it is directed the burden of persuasion of the nonexistence of the presumed fact, as well as the usual burden of production. Once the plaintiff proves B, the defendant must produce evidence and must ultimately persuade the jury of non-P. Again, there is no occasion for the judge to mention the presumption in charging the jury. The rationale for this approach is that the reasons giving rise to presumptions are too important to permit them to disappear entirely like bursting bubbles. Shifting the burden of persuasion gives presumptions lasting effect without hopelessly confusing the jury. (Under the proposed Federal Rules, no distinction was drawn between reasonable and arbitrary presumptions. It was thought that the social policies behind arbitrary presumptions might be no less important than the evidentiary value underlying reasonable presumptions and, indeed, might be more in need of special procedural treatment. The draftsmen found no constitutional infirmity in this view, believing that the Henderson case would not be followed today.) The new Uniform Rules of Evidence, approved by the National Conference of Commissioners on Uniform State Laws in 1974 to supersede the 1953 Uniform Rules, followed the approach of the proposed Federal Rules.[j]

Question: (5) The distinction between reasonable and arbitrary presumptions is complicated by the fact that different jurisdictions may take different views as to whether a particular presumption falls within one category or the other. For instance, State X may regard proof of employment as warranting a finding that the employee was acting within the scope of his employment on a given occasion; State Y may not. In other words, in an action in State X, proof of employment will take the issue of scope of employment to the jury; in State Y, proof of employment alone will not suffice to prevent a directed verdict. Now superimpose a presumption of scope from the fact of employment on the law of each state. In a case where the plaintiff has the burden of proving scope and where the only evidence bearing on scope is overwhelming evidence of employment, what would be the effect of the presumption in State X and State Y respectively under (a) the Thayer-Model Code approach, (b) the 1953 Uniform Rules, and (c) the 1974 Uniform Rules? If the defendant were to introduce other evidence warranting a finding that the employee was not acting within the scope of his employment, what would then be the effect of the presumption in those two states respectively under these three approaches?

The Federal Rules of Evidence, as ultimately enacted into law in 1975, appear to have reverted in Evidence Rule 301 to the Thayer-Model Code approach. Evidence Rule 302 provides that state law is controlling as to the effect of a presumption respecting a fact which is an element of a claim or defense itself governed by state law. This naturally cuts down the impact of Evidence Rule 301, but it is in accord with the decisions holding that burden of proof is within the realm of state law under the Erie doctrine.

Finally, it should be noted that some states give varying procedural effect to different presumptions, depending upon the nature and force of the reasons giving rise to each. See Gausewitz, Presumptions in a One-Rule World, 5 Vand.L.Rev. 324 (1952). The Federal Rules of Evidence, preferring the greater ease of administration, treat all presumptions alike in civil cases. However, the proposed Federal Rules had included a special provision covering presumptions in criminal cases. This provision was omitted by Congress with the intention of treating the matter in subsequent legislation. Evidence Rules 301 and 302 are thus left extending only to the civil side.[k]

---

[j] Unif.R.Evid. 301(a) (1974 version).

[k] The Model Code generally treated all presumptions alike, there being only a minor exception. Model Code of Evidence Rule 703 (1942). Putting aside the distinction based on probative value, the same can be said for the 1953 Uniform Rules. Unif.R.Evid. 16 (1953 version). The 1974 Uniform Rules followed the approach of the proposed Federal Rules, distinguishing between civil and criminal cases. Unif.R.Evid. 303 (1974 version).

Questions: (6) How are the constitutional questions as to presumptions different in a criminal case? See 21 Wright & Graham § 5148.

(7) How must the foregoing description of presumptions be altered to describe accurately the situation in trials by judge without jury?

SUMMERS v. TICE, 33 Cal.2d 80, 199 P.2d 1 (1948). The plaintiff and two defendants were hunting quail. In the course of hunting, plaintiff went ahead. One of the defendants flushed a quail, and both defendants fired simultaneously in the direction of the plaintiff. One shot struck the plaintiff in the eye. Both defendants were using 12-gauge shotguns with shells containing $7\frac{1}{2}$-size shot, making it substantially impossible to determine from which gun the shot causing the damage came. The trial judge sitting without a jury found that the plaintiff's injury was the "direct result of the shooting by the defendants," that both defendants were negligent in so shooting, and that the plaintiff was not contributorily negligent. Judgment was entered against both defendants. On appeal, judgment was affirmed. The court said:

"When we consider the relative position of the parties and the results that would flow if plaintiff was required to pin the injury on one of the defendants only, a requirement that the burden of proof on that subject be shifted to defendants becomes manifest. They are both wrongdoers—both negligent toward plaintiff. They brought about a situation where the negligence of one of them injured the plaintiff, hence it should rest with them each to absolve himself if he can. The injured party has been placed by defendants in the unfair position of pointing to which defendant caused the harm. If one can escape the other may also and plaintiff is remediless."

SECTION 2. STANDARD OF PROOF

Preponderance of evidence

In Livanovitch v. Livanovitch, 99 Vt. 327, 131 A. 799 (1926), the following charge was given: "If . . . you are more inclined to believe from the evidence that he did so deliver the bonds to the defendant, even though your belief is only *the slightest degree* greater than that he did not, your verdict should be for the plaintiff." The appellate court said: "The instruction was not erroneous. It was but another way of saying that the slightest preponderance of the evidence in his favor entitled the plaintiff to a verdict. . . . All that is required in a civil case of one who has the burden of proof is that he establish his claim by a preponderance of the evidence. . . . When the equilibrium of proof is destroyed, and the beam inclines toward him who has the burden, however slightly, he has satisfied the requirement of the law, and is entitled to the verdict. 'A bare preponderance is sufficient, though the scales drop but a feather's weight.' This rule accords with the practice in this State as remembered by the Justices of this Court, and is well supported by the authorities."

In Lampe v. Franklin American Trust Co., 339 Mo. 361, 96 S.W.2d 710 (1936), one of the defendant's contentions was that the note in suit had been altered after it had been signed by the defendant's decedent. The trial court refused the defendant's request for an instruction that the jury should find that the instrument was not the decedent's note "if you find and believe that it is *more probable* that such changes or alterations have been made in the instrument after it was signed by the deceased and without his knowledge and consent, than it is that such alterations and changes were made at or about the time that the deceased signed the instrument and under his direction and with his knowledge and consent." On appeal the refusal was held to have been proper. The court said: "The trouble with this statement is that a verdict must be based upon what the jury finds to be facts rather than what they find to be 'more probable.'"

These cases are but random samplings of the contrariety of views on a subject that has long plagued trial judges and appellate courts. The problem is present in every charge to a jury. If the trial judge meets it by resorting to the conventional language of "preponderance of the evidence," does he convey any meaningful concept to the ordinary juror? In replies of 843 former jurors in Ohio to a questionnaire submitted by Judge Wanamaker, 232 thought that this phrase was the most difficult to understand. ("Proximate cause" was runner-up with 203 votes.) Trial by Jury, 11 U.Cin.L.Rev. 119, 192 (1937). And in replies of 173 former jurors in the District of Columbia to a questionnaire asking them to pick the most accurate definition of preponderance of the evidence from (1) one party's evidence is stronger than the other's, (2) a slow and careful pondering of the evidence, and (3) looking at the exhibits in the jury room, 76 chose one of the latter two. O'Reilly, Why some Juries Fail, D.C.B.J., Jan.-June 1974, at 69.

The use of pattern jury instructions has developed in recent years. In some jurisdictions their use where applicable is mandatory. See, e.g., Ill.Sup.Ct.R. 239(a). More often they are available for the trial judge to use in his discretion. For example, the New York pattern instruction on burden of proof, prepared by a panel of New York judges, is as follows: "The burden of proof rests on the plaintiff. That means that it must be established by a fair preponderance of the credible evidence that the claim plaintiff makes is true. The credible evidence means the testimony or exhibits that you find to be worthy to be believed. A preponderance means the greater part of such evidence. That does not mean the greater number of witnesses or the greater length of time taken by either side. The phrase refers to the quality of the evidence, that is, its convincing quality, the weight and the effect that it has on your minds. The law requires that, in order for the plaintiff to prevail, the evidence that supports his claim must appeal to you as more nearly representing what took place than that opposed to his claim. If it does not, or if it weighs so evenly that you are unable to say that there is a preponderance on either side, then you must resolve the question in favor of the defendant. It is only if the evidence favoring the plaintiff's claim outweighs the evidence opposed to it that you can find in favor of plaintiff." New York Pattern Jury Instructions 1:23 (2d ed. 1974).

In attacking a similar pattern instruction as "gobbledygook," Professor Mellinkoff argues that the "judge would have done his job much better telling the jury: Jones brought this case to court and it is his job to satisfy you that Smith hit him." D. Mellinkoff, The Language of the Law 433–34 (1963).

Is there a feasible means of avoiding this confusion? Professor Morgan has this suggestion: "If the trial judge tells the jury that the burden is upon a party to prove a specified fact by a preponderance of the evidence, he should explain that this means only that they must find that the fact does not exist unless the evidence convinces them that its existence is more probable than its non-existence. Indeed, there is no need for him to talk of burden of proof or of preponderance of evidence. He may well confine his instruction on this matter to a specification of the disputed propositions of fact and a direction as to which party must fail on each proposition unless the jury is convinced by the evidence that the truth of that proposition is more probable than its falsity." Morgan, Instructing the Jury upon Presumptions and Burden of Proof, 47 Harv.L.Rev. 59, 66–67 (1933). See generally A. Elwork, B. Sales & J. Alfini, Making Jury Instructions Understandable (1982).

On certain issues in civil cases some courts have imposed stricter standards than preponderance of the evidence. These standards are usually expressed in such phrases as "clear and convincing" or "clear, precise, and indubitable." See, e.g., Johnson v. Johnson, 172 N.C. 530, 90 S.E. 516 (1916) (fraud and undue influence). In certain kinds of civil cases these stricter standards apply generally to the issues involved. See, e.g., Santosky v. Kramer, 455 U.S. 745, 102 S.Ct. 1388 (1982) (termination of parental rights). For other issues and cases as to which stricter standards may be applied, see 9 J. Wigmore, Evidence § 2498 (J. Chadbourn rev. 1981).

In criminal cases the degree of persuasion must be beyond a reasonable doubt, a concept that has also been a source of confusion. One of the best-known formulations of reasonable doubt is that of Chief Justice Shaw: "It is not mere possible doubt; because everything relating to human affairs, and depending on moral evidence, is open to some possible or imaginary doubt. It is that state of the case, which, after the entire comparison and consideration of all the evidence, leaves the minds of jurors in that condition that they cannot say they feel an abiding conviction, to a moral certainty, of the truth of the charge." Commonwealth v. Webster, 59 Mass. (5 Cush.) 295, 320 (1850). There are holdings that whenever in a civil case a criminal act is charged, proof of the act must be beyond a reasonable doubt. An example would be proof of forgery in a proceeding to set aside an allegedly forged deed. This view has not been widely adopted. See McCormick's Handbook of the Law of Evidence 802 (2d ed. E. Cleary 1972).

Professor Morgan, following the quotation with respect to preponderance of the evidence above set forth, goes on to deal with the stricter standards as follows: "In like manner, if he charges that the burden is upon a party to prove a proposition by clear and convincing evidence, or by clear, satisfactory and convincing evidence, he should interpret this by saying that it requires the jury to be convinced not only that the truth of this proposition is more probable than its falsity, but also that its truth is much more probable than its falsity, though it is not necessary that the preponderance of probability of its truth shall be so great as to dissipate all reasonable doubt. Here too it is entirely unnecessary to use the orthodox phraseology, though it can do no harm if elucidated. As to issues which must be proved beyond reasonable doubt, there is no necessity for abandoning the familiar formula though there could be no rational objection to charging, instead, that the preponderance of probability must be so great as to banish all reasonable doubts." 47 Harv.L.Rev. at 67.

Question: (8) In a diversity case, would the required degree of persuasion be governed by federal or state law?

REID v. SAN PEDRO, LOS ANGELES & SALT LAKE RAILROAD

Supreme Court of Utah, 1911.
39 Utah 617, 118 P. 1009.

[The plaintiff's first cause of action was for the death of a three-year-old heifer, which strayed onto the defendant's right of way and was killed by a train. There was no evidence of negligence on the part of the train crew. On the one hand, a Utah statute absolved the railroad from liability in such a case if the cow got onto the track through an open gate at a private crossing. On the other hand, if the cow entered through the fence inclosing the railroad's right of way at a point where the fence was out of repair, the railroad might be held liable. There was evidence that part of the fence between the land where the cow was pastured and the right of way was down and out of repair. There was also evidence that a gate opening into the pasture had been left open almost continuously prior to the accident. Verdict and judgment were for the plaintiff. The defendant appealed.]

McCARTY, J.

. . . .

There is no direct evidence as to where the cow got onto the right of way. It is conceded, however, that she was killed in the immediate vicinity of the gate mentioned, and, as shown by the evidence, about one mile from the point where the fence inclosing the right of way was down and out of repair. The inference, therefore, is just as strong, if not stronger, that she entered upon the right of way through the open gate as it is that she entered through the fence at the point where it was out of repair. The plaintiff held the affirmative, and the burden was on her to establish the liability of the defendant by a preponderance of the evidence. It is a familiar rule that where the undisputed evidence of the plaintiff, from which the existence of an essential fact is sought to be inferred, points with equal force to two things, one of which renders the defendant liable and the other not, the plaintiff must fail. So in this case, in order to entitle respondent to recover, it was essential for her to show by a preponderance of the evidence that the cow entered upon the right of way through the broken down fence. This the respondent failed to do.

We are of the opinion that the verdict rendered on the first cause of action is not supported by the evidence, and that the trial court should have directed a verdict for appellant on that cause of action in accordance with appellant's request. [Citations omitted.]

. . . .

Questions: (9) Should the verdict have been upheld if the cow had been killed at a point in the immediate vicinity of the break in the fence?

(10) If the cow had been killed at the equidistant point between the break in the fence and the gate, should the case have been submitted to the jury upon a showing that the break in the fence was twice as wide as the open gate? ten times as wide? What if it were also shown that the barn was closer to the gate than to the break?

(11) Is there any sensible difference between saying that because all the evidence points with equal force to opposite inferences a reasonable jury could not decide either way and saying that because evidence of equal force supports each of opposite inferences a reasonable jury could decide either way? See Wratchford v. S.J. Groves & Sons Co., 405 F.2d 1061 (4th Cir. 1969).

SARGENT v. MASSACHUSETTS ACCIDENT CO., 307 Mass. 246, 29 N.E.2d 825 (1940). This was an action to recover on an accident insurance policy. The insured, a young man of twenty-one, had attempted to go down the perilous Nottaway River to James Bay in a kayak. He was never heard from again, nor was his body recovered, but his paddle and a part of the kayak were found downstream. Perhaps he died by accidental injury or drowning. But perhaps he did not die or he died by disease or starvation, which would not be covered by the policy.

The question was whether there was evidence on which the jury might find death by accident within the terms of the policy or whether the court should say that it was a case where the plaintiff must fail because "the evidence tended equally to support two inconsistent propositions as to what happened" and consequently neither could be found to be true. The trial judge directed a verdict for the defendant insurance company. In reversing, Justice Lummus said in a much-quoted paragraph:

"The burden of proof that is on the plaintiff in this case does not require him to establish beyond all doubt, or beyond a reasonable doubt, that the insured died from [accident]. He must prove that by a preponderance of the evidence. It has been held not enough that mathematically the chances somewhat favor a proposition to be proved; for example, the fact that colored automobiles made in the current year outnumber black ones would not warrant a finding that an undescribed automobile of the current year is colored and not black, nor would the fact that only a minority of men die of cancer warrant a finding that a particular man did not die of cancer. [Citations omitted.] Compare Commonwealth v. Clark, 292 Mass. 409, 415, 198 N.E. 641. The weight or ponderance of evidence is its power to convince the tribunal which has the determination of the fact, of the actual truth of the proposition to be proved. After the evidence has been weighed, that proposition is proved by a preponderance of the evidence if it is made to appear more likely or probable in the sense that actual belief in its truth, derived from the evidence, exists in the mind or minds of the tribunal notwithstanding any doubts that may still linger there."

The reference by Justice Lummus to mathematical chances in the Sargent case was in no way necessary to the decision. No effort had been made to resort to mathematical proof. The question was simply whether the inference of accidental death could reasonably be drawn from the evidence. The use of mathematics as a tool of decisionmaking has, however, been much discussed in recent years, and the Lummus passage has been frequently quoted. The large volume of writing in the field reflects, on the one hand, the desire to enhance the objectivity and precision of judicial proof and, on the other hand, the costs of misusing and indeed of merely using mathematical tools. Professor Tribe's article, Trial by Mathematics: Precision and Ritual in the Legal Process, 84 Harv.L.Rev. 1329 (1971), is recommended as a starting point for a student seriously interested in the problems and should aid in answering the questions posed below.[1]

[1] See also Hart & McNaughton, Evidence and Inference in the Law, 87 Daedalus 41 (1958); Ball, The Moment of Truth: Probability Theory and Standards of Proof, 14 Vand.L.Rev. 807 (1961); Finkelstein & Fairley, A Bayesian Approach to Identification Evidence, 83 Harv.L.Rev. 489 (1970); Broun & Kelly, Playing the Percentages and the Law of Evidence, 1970 U.Ill.L.F. 23; Gerjuoy, The Relevance of Probability Theory to Problems of Relevance, 18 Jurimetrics J.

The hazards of improper use of mathematics are illustrated in People v. Collins, 68 Cal.2d 319, 438 P.2d 33, 66 Cal.Rptr. 497 (1968). There the alleged perpetrators of a robbery in Los Angeles were described as a white woman with her blond hair in a ponytail and a black man with moustache and beard, who were said to flee in a partly yellow automobile. The defendants, who seemed to match these descriptions, were arrested later. At trial the identification evidence was weak, and the prosecutor tried to bolster it through the testimony of a mathematics instructor designed to show that there was but one chance in twelve million that a couple chosen at random would possess the described characteristics. The prosecutor argued to the jury in effect that there was therefore only one chance in twelve million that the defendants were innocent. The California Supreme Court reversed the conviction, holding that the mathematical testimony was inadmissible and the prosecutor's argument improper.

The hazards become more apparent upon a closer inspection of Collins. The mathematician testified to the "product rule," which states that the probability of the joint occurrence of a number of mutually independent events is the product of the probabilities of each event. Then the prosecutor suggested probabilities for the various characteristics at issue: partly yellow automobile, $1/10$; man with moustache, $1/4$; woman with ponytail, $1/10$; woman with blond hair, $1/3$; black man with beard, $1/10$; and interracial couple in car, $1/1000$. The product rule yielded the one-in-twelve-million figure. The most obvious error in all this was that the prosecutor picked out of the air specific probability factors for each of the specified characteristics and asked the witness to assume their accuracy without any supporting evidence. The court went on, however, to point out three additional flaws in the mathematical evidence that would be fatal even if each of the assumed probabilities could be shown to be correct: there was no proof of statistical independence of the six factors; the mathematical approach hid the fact that the characteristics of the true perpetrators might not have been accurately established; and, all other errors aside, a one-in-twelve-million chance that a random couple would have the specified characteristics can be proven, by complicated mathematics, to mean that there was a better than forty per cent chance of the existence of a couple in the Los Angeles area other than the Collinses who also had those same characteristics. The court concluded that "under the circumstances the 'trial by mathematics' so distorted the role of the jury and so disadvantaged counsel for the defense, as to constitute in itself a miscarriage of justice." [m]

1 (1977); Kaye, The Limits of the Preponderance of the Evidence Standard: Justifiably Naked Statistical Evidence and Multiple Causation, 1982 Am.B.Found. Research J. 487. For a further interchange between Messrs. Finkelstein and Fairley and Professor Tribe, see The Continuing Debate over Mathematics in the Law of Evidence, 84 Harv.L.Rev. 1801 (1971).

[m] See Professor Tribe's discussion of the Collins case, 84 Harv.L.Rev. at 1334–37, 1342 n.40. Cf. id. at 1340 & nn.35 & 36.

Questions: (12) A jet plane bearing U.S. Air Force markings flies low over a field that *P* is plowing with his mule Emma. Emma, frightened by the buzzing plane, bolts; and *P* is injured. *P* sues the United States under the Federal Tort Claims Act. It is shown that there is a base twenty miles away, the Air Force planes at which are piloted by both Air Force and National Guard pilots. As a matter of substantive law, the United States is liable for negligence of the former but not of the latter. If there was no direct evidence of the pilot's identity, would proof that 60 per cent of the pilots flying out of the base were Air Force personnel be enough to warrant a finding of operation by a servant of the United States? 80 per cent? 99 per cent? Cf. Guenther v. Armstrong Rubber Co., 406 F.2d 1315, 1318 (3d Cir. 1969) (plaintiff injured by exploding tire; dictum that 75 to 80 per cent likelihood it came from defendant manufacturer not enough for case to go to jury); Sawyer v. United States, 148 F.Supp. 877 (M.D.Ga.1956).

(13) A criminal defendant seeking a change of venue offers testimony of a pollster that, using standard scientific techniques, he has taken a sampling of public opinion in the district where the case is pending and the sampling shows a widespread prejudice against the defendant. Should the pollster's evidence be admitted? Should it, if believed, be enough to support a grant of the motion for change of venue? What, if any, difference is there between this case and that of the Air Force plane?

(14) Should the cooperation or lack of cooperation of the United States in seeking to identify the pilot have any bearing upon your answer to the question regarding the Air Force plane?

(15) Should it matter whether *P* could reasonably have produced more evidence of the pilot's identity?

(16) Should the sufficiency of *P*'s evidence be measured differently if his claim was for $100 than if it was for $100,000?

(17) Assume a case, plainly an extremely rare one, where there is literally no possibility of discovering any evidence except a showing of mathematical probabilities. What if the mathematical chances of the single disputed fact being true are 60 per cent? 80 per cent? 99 per cent? Should the jury ever be allowed to decide the case on its view of these odds or should there always be a directed verdict for one party or the other?

(18) If there were some direct evidence identifying the pilot as an Air Force pilot, should evidence of the proportion of Air Force pilots flying out of the base be admissible in support of such identification?

(19) The issue in a workers' compensation case is whether the employee's death from cancer was causally related to an injury sustained in the course of his employment when he fell off a truck. The only medical evidence supporting causation is from a specialist in internal medicine who had not treated the employee and whose testimony is based upon the medical records. He expresses the opinion that the force of the fall directly affected the pre-existent cancerous tissue of the pancreas and thereby hastened the metastatic spread of the cancer to other parts of the employee's body, thus hastening his death. On cross-examination, the doctor concedes that there is no direct clinical evidence of pre-existing cancer or of disturbance of cancerous tissue by the accident. It would, he admits, be conceivable that the cancer of the pancreas originated after the accident, but he says: "This would be unusual in view of the widespread metastasis; the size and the spread indicate it has probably been present for years." He adds: "I answer in terms of likeli-

hood." Does this testimony support a finding of causal relation? Does the quoted statement of Justice Lummus in Sargent v. Massachusetts Accident Co. have any bearing on your answer? Compare King's Case, 352 Mass. 488, 225 N.E.2d 900 (1967), with McCormick's Handbook of the Law of Evidence 494 n.49 (2d ed. E. Cleary 1972) (judicial preference for nonnumerical estimates).

STIMPSON v. HUNTER, 234 Mass. 61, 125 N.E. 155 (1919). *P* sued *D* for dental services rendered to *D*'s minor son. *D* rested at the close of the plaintiff's case. The trial judge put to the jury the special question: "Was the work done by the plaintiff authorized or ratified by the defendant?" The jury answered in the affirmative and thereupon, by order of the judge, found for *P*. *D*'s exceptions were sustained, the Supreme Judicial Court holding that the evidence did not warrant submission of the question to the jury and saying: "The failure of the defendant and of his son to testify although present in court was not equivalent to affirmative proof of facts necessary to maintain the action. The defendant was not bound to offer any evidence unless and until evidence was offered by the plaintiff warranting the submission of the case to the jury."

[handwritten margin note: Failure to testify NOT equal to affirm. proof of facts...]

Question: (20) If there had been a case for the jury and the defendant had not testified, would it have been proper argument on behalf of the plaintiff that the defendant's failure to testify justified an inference against him? See Mitchell v. Silverstein, 323 Mass. 239, 81 N.E.2d 364 (1948) (yes). What if the defendant's failure to testify had been premised on the privilege against self-incrimination? Cf. Baxter v. Palmigiano, 425 U.S. 308, 96 S.Ct. 1551 (1976) (suggesting same result).

CRUZAN v. NEW YORK CENTRAL &
HUDSON RIVER RAILROAD

Supreme Judicial Court of Massachusetts, 1917.
227 Mass. 594, 116 N.E. 879.

[The deceased, brakeman on a freight train that was backing into a siding, was coming down a ladder on the side of one of the cars to set a switch when he was struck by the locomotive of a passenger express train going about sixty miles per hour on the other main track. The plaintiff sued under the FELA to recover for the death of her intestate. The judge refused to rule that there was no evidence of negligence. The jury returned a verdict for the plaintiff, and the defendant alleged exceptions.]

[handwritten margin note: Facts]

RUGG, C.J.

. . . .

The only negligence alleged in the case at bar is that of the fireman and engineer of the passenger express train. We are of the

opinion that there is no evidence of negligence on the part of either.
There is nothing to indicate that it was their duty to be observant of
the movements of brakemen upon other trains in the position in
which Cruzan was. The only rule pertinent in this connection was
this: "Firemen and Helpers. . . . They must keep a constant
lookout ahead (except as to firemen when engaged in firing), and give
instant notice to the engineman or motorman of any danger signals
or obstructions on the track." It is manifest that this rule relates
only to the safety of the train on which they are at work. It imposes
no duty to be on the watch for other employees on other tracks and
trains. The duty of exercising care for their own safety was placed
by explicit rule upon such other employees. There can be no negligence in the ordinary case when no duty has been violated. It is
manifest that the danger of Cruzan was momentary. So long as he
kept close to the car even coming down the ladder on its side, he was
in a safe place. It was only for the instant when he swung out from
the body of the car as he was on the point of jumping to the ground
that he came within the sweep of the rapidly moving express train.
It may be assumed that, if the fireman or engineer of the passenger
express train had seen him, there would have been evidence of their
negligence. But there was no evidence that either the engineer or
fireman saw Cruzan in time to give him any warning. Both testified
that they did not see him earlier than an instant before he was
struck. Mere disbelief of denials of facts which must be proved is
not the equivalent of affirmative evidence in support of those facts."
Wakefield v. American Surety Co., 209 Mass. 173, 177, 95 N.E. 350;
Southern Ry. v. Gray, 241 U.S. 333, 337, 36 S.Ct. 558.

. . . .

It becomes unnecessary to consider the other questions raised.
The request that a verdict be ordered for the defendant should have
been granted. In accordance with St.1909, c. 236, judgment may be
entered for the defendant.

So ordered."

GUINAN v. FAMOUS PLAYERS–LASKY CORP., 267 Mass. 501,
167 N.E. 235 (1929). The plaintiff was injured by the igniting of

"This decision is representative of
many cases. These include Moore v.
Chesapeake & O. Ry., 340 U.S. 573, 71
S.Ct. 428 (1951) (FELA case where engineer, the sole eyewitness, testified that
he saw decedent brakeman fall from car
and then he made emergency stop; plaintiff's theory was that engineer's sudden
stop threw decedent off). The Court
there said: "True, it is the jury's function
to credit or discredit all or part of the testimony. But disbelief of the engineer's
testimony would not supply a want of
proof." In Clairmont v. Cilley, 85 N.H.
1, 7, 153 A. 465, 468 (1931), the court
made the point thus: "Falsity of testimony is no proof of what is true, and disbelief does not supply the need of proof.
[Citation omitted.] Otherwise any fact
might be proved by discrediting testimony to the contrary. While the falsehood
of testimony may add to the weight to be
given evidence to the contrary, the testimony by itself does not go far enough to
establish the fact it denies."

scrap film given to one Shirley by Doherty, the defendant's agent. Shirley had carried it away in a burlap bag in which it had been stuffed in the presence of Doherty. The bag caught fire when Shirley set it against a heater in a subway car. The issue was whether Doherty had been acting in the scope of his employment. Doherty testified that he had authority to dispose of scrap film only by delivering it to the Film Transfer Company, which was paid to carry it away, and that he had forgotten that limitation when he gave the film to Shirley. It was held that this testimony created an issue of fact for the jury on scope of employment. The court said: "Although mere disbelief of testimony is not proof of facts of an opposite nature or tendency, [citations omitted], the jury might have believed that part of Doherty's testimony that related to his authority to dispose of the scrap film, and disbelieved the alleged limitation of his authority to dispose of it only to the Film Transfer Company."

Question: (21) Does the Guinan decision suggest a possible basis for a different result in the Cruzan case?

DYER v. MacDOUGALL, 201 F.2d 265 (2d Cir.1952). The plaintiff brought an action for slander, based on alleged defamatory statements by the defendants to one Almirall and a Mrs. Hope. The defendants moved for summary judgment, supporting their motion by affidavits of the defendants and Almirall and by a deposition of Mrs. Hope previously taken by the plaintiff; the defendants unequivocally denied utterance of the slanders attributed to them, and Almirall and Mrs. Hope denied that they had heard the slanders uttered. When the motion came on for hearing, the court offered the plaintiff an opportunity to take the depositions of the defendants and Almirall and a further deposition of Mrs. Hope. After a continuance for this purpose, the plaintiff told the court that he did not wish to take the depositions. Thereafter the court granted summary judgment on the ground that the plaintiff would have no evidence to offer in support of the slanders except the testimony of witnesses all of whom would deny their utterance. On appeal, the court of appeals affirmed. Judge Learned Hand for the court said:

"The question is whether, in view of the defendants' affidavits and Mrs. Hope's deposition, there was any 'genuine issue' under Rule 56(c) as to the utterance of the slanders. The defendants had the burden of proving that there was no such issue; on the other hand, at a trial the plaintiff would have the burden of proving the utterances; and therefore, if the defendants on the motion succeeded in proving that the plaintiff would not have enough evidence to go to the jury on the issue, the judgment was right. As the plaintiff has refused to avail himself of the privilege under Rule 56(f) of examining by deposition the witnesses whom the defendants proposed to call at the trial, we must assume that what they said in their affidavits they would have repeated in their depositions; and that what they would have said in their depositions, they would say at a trial, with one possible exception, the consideration of which we will postpone for the time being."

Judge Hand observed that the only witnesses by whom the plaintiff could prove the slanders would deny that they had been uttered, and on this showing the plaintiff could not escape a directed verdict. He conceded that the demeanor of a witness was part of the evidence and might satisfy the tribunal not only that the witness's testimony was not true, but that the truth was the opposite of his story. The opinion continued as follows:

"Nevertheless, although it is therefore true that in strict theory a party having the affirmative might succeed in convincing a jury of the truth of his allegations in spite of the fact that all the witnesses denied them, we think it plain that a verdict would nevertheless have to be directed against him. This is owing to the fact that otherwise in such cases there could not be an effective appeal from the judge's disposition of a motion for a directed verdict. . . . It may be argued that such a ruling may deprive a party of a possibly rational verdict and indeed that is theoretically true, although the occasions must be to the last degree rare in which the chance so denied is more than fanciful. Nevertheless we do not hesitate to set against the chance so lost, the protection of a review of the judge's decision.

"There remains the second point which we reserved for separate discussion: i.e. whether by an examination in open court the plaintiff might extract from the four witnesses admissions which he would not have got on the depositions that he refused. Although this is also at best a tenuous possibility, we need not say that there could never be situations in which it might justify denying summary judgment. It might appear for example that upon a deposition a witness had been recalcitrant, or crafty, or defiant, or evasive, so that the immediate presence of a judge in a court-room was likely to make him tell more. That would be another matter; and it might be enough. But the plaintiff is in no position to invoke such a possibility for he has refused to try out these witnesses upon deposition, where he might discover whether there was any basis for supposing that awe of a judge was necessary to make them more amenable. A priori we will not assume that that is true. The course of procedural reform has all indeed been towards bringing witnesses before the tribunal when it is possible; but that is not so much because more testimony can be got out of them as because only so can the 'demeanor' evidence be brought before the tribunal."

RELATION OF SUMMARY JUDGMENT TO DIRECTED VERDICT

A party moving for summary judgment has the burden of establishing that there is no genuine issue of material fact and that he is entitled to judgment as a matter of law. But where the plaintiff will have the burden of proof on an essential issue at trial, the defendant may successfully move for summary judgment when it is clear that he would be entitled to a directed verdict at trial if the plaintiff presented nothing more than was before the court at the hearing on the motion. Plaintiff has the opportunity to adduce evidence—by deposition, affidavit, and the like—that would justify submission of his claim to a jury. He cannot choose to hold back his evidence until the time of trial and nevertheless escape summary judgment by the mere assertion that he may or will then produce evidence. Here is no battle of affidavits, which would of course be improper on a summary judgment motion. The plaintiff fails simply for lack of proof. See Engl v. Aetna Life Ins. Co., 139 F.2d 469 (2d Cir.1943).

Denial of summary judgment does not necessarily rule out the possibility of a directed verdict at trial, even though the standards are theoretically the same. The motion for a directed verdict comes at a later stage in the litigation and is decided upon a more complete and effective airing of the evidence. The result is a practical difference in standards, with the test for directed verdict being slightly easier to meet. See 9 Wright & Miller § 2532; 10 Wright, Miller & Kane § 2713.1.

Moreover, some courts are especially cautious about granting a motion for summary judgment in certain kinds of cases. For example, they may be reluctant so to act in cases requiring determination of a state of mind; there they prefer to give an opportunity to see and hear the witnesses during direct and cross-examination, even though it may then appear that there was no genuine issue as to a material fact. See, e.g., Croley v. Matson Navigation Co., 434 F.2d 73 (5th Cir.1970). Similarly, there have been cases to the effect that when the facts are within the personal knowledge of the movant, the opponent is entitled to a trial at which the movant may be examined, his demeanor observed, and his credibility evaluated. See, e.g., Subin v. Goldsmith, 224 F.2d 753 (2d Cir.1955).

A plaintiff is in a difficult position if, as in Dyer v. MacDougall, he must prove his case through the adverse party or hostile witnesses. It would be unfair to render summary judgment against him on the basis of their affidavits negating his claim without an opportunity to test their stories by deposition. If, given the opportunity to take the deposition of an affiant, he elects not to do so, he normally cannot maintain that summary judgment should be denied because he hopes to break the affiant down on examination at trial. If he pursues full discovery but fails to unearth evidence sufficient to suggest a genuine issue of material fact, most courts will likewise grant summary judgment. See, e.g., Jones v. Borden Co., 430 F.2d 568 (5th Cir.1970).

It is not, however, a wholly satisfactory answer to say that the plaintiff's opportunity to examine on deposition is the equivalent of an opportunity to do so at trial. And the examination on deposition necessary to prevent summary judgment may well give a crafty witness a lesson in how to handle himself that will make examination at trial less likely to be effective. This may account for the reluctance or refusal of some courts to grant summary judgment in cases where questions of state of mind or personal knowledge are involved. See, e.g., Friedman v. Meyers, 482 F.2d 435 (2d Cir.1973); Arnstein v. Porter, 154 F.2d 464 (2d Cir.1946). In the latter case, which involved a claim of plagiarism against Cole Porter, defendant moved for summary judgment. In his deposition defendant had denied copying, and plaintiff had little evidence to support his contention to the contrary. The court of appeals, speaking through Judge Frank, an obdurate opponent of summary judgment, especially in state-of-mind and personal-knowledge cases, reversed a grant of the motion on the ground that plaintiff should have the opportunity to discredit defendant's denial by cross-examination in a jury trial. Judge Clark strongly dissented, saying that the majority opinion was "a novel method of amending rules of procedure" and that it gave impetus to strike suits. In fact, the jury returned a verdict for the defendant after a long trial. The Second Circuit, by a panel including Judge Frank but not Judge Clark, affirmed per curiam, but stated that there was undoubtedly enough evidence to make a jury issue, 158 F.2d 795 (2d Cir.1946), cert. denied, 330 U.S. 851, 67 S.Ct. 1096 (1947).

TOPIC B.   DIRECTED VERDICT

SECTION 1.   GENERAL OBSERVATIONS

Attrition of the right of voluntary dismissal.—The plaintiff had the right at common law voluntarily to abandon his action at any time before the verdict. He could and frequently did take this course in order to forestall either the direction of a verdict against him or an expected adverse verdict from the jury. The result was a nonsuit, which ended the case and made the plaintiff liable for costs but did not preclude a new action on the same cause.

There have been substantial inroads upon this common-law doctrine, some by statute or rule of court and others by judicial decision. The inroads vary widely as to when the plaintiff loses the right to abandon his case without precluding a new action. The critical point may be, for example, the commencement of the trial, the opening of the defendant's case, the beginning of argument to the jury, the close of argument, the submission to the jury, or the time when the jury is ready to give in the verdict.

The federal rulemakers in Rule 41(a)(1) limited the unqualified right to voluntary dismissal without prejudice to the period prior to service of the answer or a motion for summary judgment (not a motion to dismiss for failure to state a claim). When this right exists, the filing of a notice of dismissal ends the case. The court has no occasion to pass upon it and is without power to impose "terms and conditions" on the dismissal.

The right to voluntary dismissal by notice of dismissal under Rule 41(a)(1) is subject to the "two-dismissal" rule. Cf. 5 Moore ¶ 41.04 (arguing that both dismissals must be by notice of dismissal for rule to apply).

Questions: (1) Plaintiff voluntarily dismisses a state-court action, then sues on the same claim in federal court and dismisses that action also. Is a third action in a federal court barred by reason of Rule 41(a)(1)? in a state court that has no comparable rule?

(2) Plaintiff voluntarily dismisses a federal-court action, then sues on the same claim in state court and dismisses that action also. Is a third action in a federal court barred by reason of Rule 41(a)(1)?

Once the grace period is over, unilateral voluntary dismissal requires a motion and court order, which may be "upon such terms and conditions as the court deems proper." Rule 41(a)(2). After some early authority that the right to voluntary dismissal without prejudice remained absolute as at common law, with the court's discretion relating only to the terms and conditions of dismissal, it has been settled that the whole matter rests in the court's discretion, which is

reviewable only for abuse.   See Grivas v. Parmelee Transp. Co., 207
F.2d 334 (7th Cir.1953), overruling Bolten v. General Motors Corp.,
180 F.2d 379 (7th Cir.1950).   Courts in exercising this discretion adhere to the principle of allowing dismissal unless the defendant will
suffer disadvantage other than the prospect of having to defend another action.   The terms and conditions ordinarily include a requirement that the plaintiff pay court costs, and sometimes that he pay
attorneys' fees.

Question: (3) Suppose the plaintiff wants a voluntary dismissal with
prejudice, which will bar further action.   Should the court have discretion to
refuse dismissal at the behest of a defendant who wants the vindication of a
trial?   See Smoot v. Fox, 340 F.2d 301 (6th Cir.1964) (plaintiff, a television
and radio broadcaster, sues the League of Women Voters for libel, the action
stirring a great deal of public interest; the judge refuses to dismiss with
prejudice; plaintiff obtains mandamus to force dismissal).

Rule 41(d), dealing with costs of previously dismissed actions, has
its counterpart in many state statutes.   This type of provision gives
inadequate protection to a defendant harassed by repeated actions in
which the plaintiff takes voluntary nonsuits at a stage in proceedings
early enough under the applicable rules not to foreclose a new action
on the same cause.   Does the defendant have any effective remedy
against such tactics?   In Steinberg v. McKay, 295 Mass. 139, 3
N.E.2d 23 (1936), the plaintiff successfully sought equitable relief in
the nature of a bill of peace [a] to enjoin the defendant from instituting
repeated groundless actions for false arrest.   In Renfro v. Johnson,
142 Tex. 251, 177 S.W.2d 600 (1944), the plaintiff sued twice on the
same promissory notes, taking a nonsuit each time after the statute
of limitations was pleaded.   His counsel announced in open court, at
the time of the first nonsuit, his intention to file a new suit against
the defendants at every term of court in the future.   The defendants
filed a cross-action in the second suit for an injunction to prevent the
filing of any more suits on these notes.   The requested relief was
granted.   See Restatement (Second) of Torts § 679 (1976); see also
id. § 681 (damages).

Preventing unreasonable verdicts.—The demurrer to the evidence (to be sharply distinguished from a demurrer to pleadings) was
the earliest means of withdrawing a case from the jury in the course
of trial, before verdict.   A defendant would demur to the evidence
where at the close of plaintiff's case it appeared that plaintiff's evidence was insufficient to warrant a verdict for plaintiff even if the
evidence was taken as true and construed as strongly as possible in
plaintiff's favor.   The device was a cumbersome one, for the demurrer had to contain a statement of the evidence demurred to and (in
later years) a distinct admission of every fact that plaintiff's evidence
tended to prove.[b]   It was hazardous as well as cumbersome, because
defendant's admission was final, not provisional.   If the demurrer

---

[a] See supra p. 375 note *o*.   [b] Gibson v. Hunter, 126 Eng.Rep. 499
                                                  (H.L.1793), spelling out the latter re-

was sustained, judgment went for defendant, terminating the action and barring a later action on the same cause. But if the demurrer was overruled, judgment went for plaintiff; defendant could not offer evidence of his own, nor could the case be submitted to the jury with argument that plaintiff's evidence should not be believed. Only in instances where plaintiff's evidence was very plainly insufficient would a defendant take this risk. See generally Comment, Trial Practice—Demurrer upon Evidence as a Device for Taking a Case from the Jury, 44 Mich.L.Rev. 468 (1945).

The compulsory nonsuit on motion of the defendant was another means of preventing a case from reaching the jury. It is said that the compulsory nonsuit was unknown at common law, but in many American jurisdictions the practice developed of nonsuiting the plaintiff against his will for failure of proof. See Henderson, The Background of the Seventh Amendment, 80 Harv.L.Rev. 289, 301 (1966). The defendant would move for a nonsuit when the plaintiff rested. If the motion was granted, judgment would go for the defendant, but this was not a bar to a new action on the same cause. See Restatement (Second) of Judgments § 20 comment g (1980). If the motion was denied, the defendant could proceed with his own evidence as though no motion had been made. In doing so the defendant might supply the deficiency in the plaintiff's proof, and his exception to the denial of his motion would then be unavailing. See Gagnon v. Dana, 69 N.H. 264, 39 A. 982 (1898). Furthermore, even if the deficiency in the plaintiff's proof was not supplied in the defendant's evidence, it had been held that the exception to denial of the nonsuit at the close of the plaintiff's case was still unavailing and that the defendant had to make an appropriate motion at the close of all the evidence in order to have the court scrutinize the record to determine the sufficiency of the evidence. See Spencer v. State, 187 N.Y. 484, 80 N.E. 375 (1907).

Finally, there is the motion for a directed verdict.[c] If such a motion is granted, the judgment entered thereon has the same preclusive effect as a judgment entered on a verdict of the jury; that is, a judgment on a directed verdict is a bar to a new action on the same cause. Some states follow the original rule that a directed verdict can be sought by a party at the close of his opponent's case only by immediately resting his own case; that is, the price of making the motion is that the moving party forgoes his chance to offer any evidence thereafter. Thus, in jurisdictions that still recognize the compulsory nonsuit and also exact the price just described for a motion

quirement, meant the end of the demurrer to the evidence in England. The device was little used in the United States, except where the requirement of Gibson v. Hunter was not adopted.

[c] A word of warning about terminology: in some states what is in practical effect a motion for a directed verdict, as here described, is called a demurrer to the evidence, but it has no kinship with the old common-law device of that name. In Virginia, where a statute forbids the trial court to direct a verdict, the same result can be achieved by a "demurrer to the evidence" or "motion to strike out the evidence." See Va.Code § 8.01–378; Davis v. Rodgers, 139 Va. 618, 124 S.E. 408 (1924).

for a directed verdict, a defendant may be put to a choice at the close of the plaintiff's case: (1) He can move for a nonsuit with no serious consequences if the motion is denied; but if the motion is granted, he is exposed to the possibility of a second action on the same cause. (2) If he wants protection against a second action, he must move for a directed verdict; but then he must rest his own case and lose the opportunity to put in his own proof. Even if the motion is denied, however, he may still have a chance for a favorable verdict from the jury on the basis of the plaintiff's evidence, including any material developed in cross-examination of the plaintiff's witnesses. (3) When the defendant has evidence that he thinks will be persuasive with the jury, he may well prefer not to rest at the close of the plaintiff's case and move at that point for a directed verdict; instead, he will go ahead with his own evidence and move for a directed verdict at the close of all the evidence. Then if his motion is denied, he may still have a chance for a jury verdict based on all the evidence, including his own.

The Federal Rules provide a means for the defendant to test the sufficiency of the plaintiff's evidence before he decides whether to offer evidence of his own. In an action tried to a jury, the defendant may move under Rule 50(a) for a directed verdict at the close of the plaintiff's case. In an action tried without a jury, he may move for an involuntary dismissal under Rule 41(b) after the plaintiff rests (this Rule permits the judge, who will be the eventual fact-finder anyway, to evaluate the evidence objectively and order a dismissal at this point if, in his view, the plaintiff has failed to carry the burden of persuasion—even though enough evidence has been adduced to have prevented direction of a verdict in a jury case). If a motion under either Rule is denied, the defendant may proceed with his own evidence, as he could have done under the prior practice after denial of a motion for a compulsory nonsuit.[d]

Question: (4) In what way were the consequences of the grant of a compulsory nonsuit different from those of the grant of a Rule 50(a) directed verdict or a Rule 41(b) involuntary dismissal?

The defendant in federal court cannot on appeal rely upon any error in the denial of his motion for a directed verdict at the close of the plaintiff's case if he goes forward with his own evidence. As Judge Magruder said in Home Ins. Co. v. Davila, 212 F.2d 731, 733 (1st Cir.

[d] The second sentence of Rule 50(a) is designed to do away with the rule, which apparently originated in New York and has been abandoned there but which still prevails in some states, that when both parties at the close of all the evidence present motions for a directed verdict, the effect is a mutual waiver of the right to a jury and thus a submission of all questions, both of fact and law, to the court. Even under the mutual-waiver doctrine it was held that a party might, by an express reservation at the time he joined in the motion for a directed verdict, preserve his right to go to the jury in case neither party was entitled to a directed verdict. See Sampliner v. Motion Picture Patents Co., 254 U.S. 233, 41 S.Ct. 79 (1920). Thus the doctrine was merely a trap for the uninformed lawyer.

1954): "It is well-settled that if a motion under Rule 50(a) . . . asking for a directed verdict at the close of the plaintiff's case is denied, and the defendant thereupon presents his own evidence, this constitutes a waiver of the motion; unless a renewed motion for a directed verdict is made at the close of all the evidence, the defendant is precluded from questioning on appeal the sufficiency of the evidence to take the case to the jury." Likewise, if the defendant presents evidence after his Rule 41(b) motion on the ground of insufficiency of the evidence is denied, he waives that motion and cannot on appeal rely upon any error in its denial.

Revising improper verdicts.—Perhaps the most venerable device for controlling the jury was the attaint. Where it was claimed that the verdict was "false," a jury of twenty-four was summoned to reexamine the issue; if the verdict was then found to be false, it would be reversed and the first jury might be severely punished. The attaint may have been tolerable when the jury was a body of witnesses drawn from the vicinage who decided issues on their own knowledge. It could not survive when the trial of issues came to be upon evidence offered in open court. In Bushell's Case, 124 Eng.Rep. 1006 (C.P.1670), jurors who had failed to find William Penn guilty of unlawful assembly and who had been fined and imprisoned for their verdict were released on habeas corpus. Although it was a ground of this decision that the jurors had not been proceeded against by the ancient method of attaint, it was understood that that method was already obsolete. The decision "therefore amounted to a declaration of the irresponsibility of the jury." T. Plucknett, A Concise History of the Common Law 134 (5th ed. 1956).

Meanwhile, the practice of granting new trials for misconduct of jurors and for improper verdicts was being elaborated. Eventually, the motion for judgment n.o.v. also developed into a tool for revising unreasonable verdicts. We shall deal with these matters in Topic D of this Part.

SECTION 2. DIRECTION AGAINST PARTY WITH BURDEN OF PROOF

What is the proper standard to be applied by the court upon a motion for a directed verdict against the party with the burden of proof? This is a question to which courts give different answers. Professor McBaine stated that there were two possible tests: (1) if the judge looking at all the evidence, both favorable and unfavorable to the proponent (by "proponent" is meant the party having the burden of proof), determines that he would be duty bound to set aside a verdict for the proponent because it would be against the weight of the evidence, he may direct a verdict; and (2) if the judge considering only the evidence favorable to the proponent, and completely disregarding all unfavorable evidence, determines that a reasonable jury, viewing the evidence in the light most favorable to the proponent, could find every essential fact in the proponent's favor, he may not direct a verdict. (The two tests are often termed for convenience the "set aside" and the "most favorable evidence" tests.) Professor McBaine added: "In each test the judge must determine what a reasonable jury can conclude. The first test involves passing upon credibility of witness; the second does not." McBaine, Trial Practice: Directed Verdicts; Federal Rule, 31 Calif.L.Rev. 454, 460–61 (1943).

PEDRICK v. PEORIA & EASTERN RAILROAD, 37 Ill.2d 494, 229 N.E.2d 504 (1967). In this case the court reviewed the standards for a directed verdict prevailing in other states as indicated in their recent decisions, reexamined its own standards, and concluded: "In our judgment verdicts ought to be directed and judgments n.o.v. entered only in those cases in which all of the evidence, when viewed in its aspect most favorable to the opponent, so overwhelmingly favors movant that no contrary verdict based on that evidence could ever stand."

The only allegation of the railroad's negligence submitted to the jury was that the electrically operated red-flasher warning signals that protected the crossing where the train-automobile collision occurred were not working. The testimony of the two plaintiffs and their passenger that the flashers were not operating was weak, highly equivocal, and of "dubious probative value," the court said, when considered in the light of unequivocal testimony by two disinterested witnesses that they saw the flashers working, the corroborative testimony of four of the train crew, and the testimony of the signal maintenance man that the flashers were working a few days before and two-and-a-half hours after the accident. The court held that a verdict should have been directed for the defendant.

There are more disparities in the language of the formulation than in the results of the cases. Professors James and Hazard refer to these expressions of doctrinal differences as largely battles of words and suggest that, despite some shadings in application, there is now a pretty uniform test of the sufficiency of the evidence to withstand a directed verdict motion. Whatever the nomenclature, they say, there is "a fairly uniform reluctance to go very far in taking matters of credibility from the jury." As for equating the directed verdict test to that for setting aside a verdict and granting a new trial, they concede that the equation is more nearly valid in some jurisdictions than in others but argue that the differences are rather because of variations in the new trial test than because of any variation in the directed verdict test.   F. James & G. Hazard, Civil Procedure 285–87 (2d ed. 1977).

A few matters not involving possible differences in standards for directing a verdict may be disposed of without difficulty.   First, if there is literally no evidence on an element of his case, a verdict will naturally be directed against the plaintiff.[e]   Second, the same is true if, looking only at the evidence favorable to him, the court is satisfied that no properly functioning jury could find for him (except perhaps in Alabama, which still professes to follow the almost universally discredited "scintilla" rule).   Such a situation in which a jury could not reasonably find for the plaintiff may result either from uncertainty as to what the facts were, leaving the case within the realm of conjecture or speculation, or from the failure of facts fully known to measure up to the requirements set by the court to establish, for example, negligence on the part of the defendant.   Third, we come to the trickier course of rejecting otherwise adequate evidence on the ground that it is simply unbelievable.   Whatever may be the attitude of courts with respect to evidence asserted to be contrary to the physical facts or in other ways incredible, an area in which we shall see there is some room for manipulation, any court will consider incredible as a matter of law testimony flatly contrary to the laws of nature. E.g., Seiwell v. Hines, 273 Pa. 259, 116 A. 919 (1922) (no issue for jury on plaintiff's testimony that his stationary automobile on an upward grade with the brakes on was drawn by suction into the rear wheels of the locomotive of a passing train).   The concept of incredibility as a matter of law may be extended by some courts beyond the area of what is judicially recognized to be in defiance of natural laws, but it is a fair generalization to say that testimony that is not incredible nor even improbable when viewed by itself does not become incredible as a matter of law merely because many witnesses have told a diametrically different story.   See Shannon v. Dow, 133 Me. 235, 175 A. 766 (1934).

This brings us to the more difficult questions that arise where there is evidence that, standing alone, would warrant a finding for the plaintiff but where there is overwhelming evidence to the contrary.

---

[e] In the interest of clarity we speak of the party with the burden of proof as the "plaintiff," instead of as the "proponent."   In the typical case it is the defendant who moves for a directed verdict on the ground that the plaintiff has not sustained his burden of proof.   At times, however, as when the sole issue is one on which the defendant has the burden of proof, the plaintiff will move for a directed verdict.

By "burden of proof" here we mean burden of persuasion, except that where little or no evidence on the relevant issue has been introduced we mean the initial burden of production.

PENNSYLVANIA RAILROAD v. CHAMBERLAIN

Supreme Court of the United States 1933.
288 U.S. 333, 53 S.Ct. 391.

MR. JUSTICE SUTHERLAND delivered the opinion of the Court.

This is an action brought by respondent against petitioner to recover for the death of a brakeman, alleged to have been caused by petitioner's negligence. The complaint alleges that the deceased, at the time of the accident resulting in his death, was assisting in the yard work of breaking up and making up trains and in the classifying and assorting of cars operating in interstate commerce; that in pursuance of such work, while riding a cut of cars, other cars ridden by fellow employees were negligently caused to be brought into violent contact with those upon which deceased was riding, with the result that he was thrown therefrom to the railroad track and run over by a car or cars, inflicting injuries from which he died.

[margin: Prior Hist]

At the conclusion of the evidence, the trial court directed the jury to find a verdict in favor of petitioner. Judgment upon a verdict so found was reversed by the court of appeals, Judge Swan dissenting. 59 F.2d 986.

[margin: Facts]

That part of the yard in which the accident occurred contained a lead track and a large number of switching tracks branching therefrom. The lead track crossed a "hump," and the work of car distribution consisted of pushing a train of cars by means of a locomotive to the top of the "hump," and then allowing the cars, in separate strings, to descend by gravity, under the control of hand brakes, to their respective destinations in the various branch tracks. Deceased had charge of a string of two gondola cars, which he was piloting to track 14. Immediately ahead of him was a string of seven cars, and behind him a string of nine cars, both also destined for track 14. Soon after the cars ridden by deceased had passed to track 14, his body was found on that track some distance beyond the switch. He had evidently fallen onto the track and been run over by a car or cars.

[margin: All people able to see say no collision]

The case for respondent rests wholly upon the claim that the fall of deceased was caused by a violent collision of the string of nine cars with the string ridden by deceased. Three employees, riding the nine-car string, testified positively that no such collision occurred. They were corroborated by every other employee in a position to see, all testifying that there was no contact between the nine-car string and that of the deceased. The testimony of these witnesses, if believed, establishes beyond doubt that there was no collision between these two strings of cars, and that the nine-car string contributed in no way to the accident. The only witness who testified for the respondent was one Bainbridge; and it is upon his testimony alone that respondent's right to recover is sought to be upheld. His testimony is concisely stated, in its most favorable light for respondent, in the prevailing opinion below by Judge Learned Hand, as follows:

"The plaintiff's only witness to the event, one Bainbridge, then employed by the road, stood close to the yardmaster's office, near the 'hump.' He professed to have paid little attention to what went on, but he did see the deceased riding at the rear of his cars, whose speed when they passed him he took to be about eight or ten miles. Shortly thereafter a second string passed which was shunted into another track and this was followed by the nine, which, according to the plaintiff's theory, collided with the deceased's. After the nine cars had passed at a somewhat greater speed than the deceased's, Bainbridge paid no more attention to either string for awhile, but looked again when the deceased, who was still standing in his place, had passed the switch and onto the assorting track where he was bound. At that time his speed had been checked to about three miles, but the speed of the following nine cars had increased. They were just passing the switch, about four or five cars behind the deceased. Bainbridge looked away again and soon heard what he described as a 'loud crash,' not however an unusual event in a switching yard. Apparently this did not cause him at once to turn, but he did so shortly thereafter, and saw the two strings together, still moving, and the deceased no longer in sight. Later still his attention was attracted by shouts and he went to the spot and saw the deceased between the rails. Until he left to go to the accident, he had stood fifty feet to the north of the track where the accident happened, and about nine hundred feet from where the body was found."

The court, although regarding Bainbridge's testimony as not only "somewhat suspicious in itself, but its contradiction . . . so manifold as to leave little doubt," held, nevertheless, that the question was one of fact depending upon the credibility of the witnesses, and that it was for the jury to determine, as between the one witness and the many, where the truth lay. The dissenting opinion of Judge Swan proceeds upon the theory that Bainbridge did not testify that in fact a collision had taken place, but inferred it because he heard a crash, and because thereafter the two strings of cars appeared to him to be moving together. It is correctly pointed out in that opinion, however, that the crash might have come from elsewhere in the busy yard and that Bainbridge was in no position to see whether the two strings of cars were actually together; that Bainbridge repeatedly said he was paying no particular attention; and that his position was such, being 900 feet from the place where the body was found and less than 50 feet from the side of the track in question, that he necessarily saw the strings of cars at such an acute angle that it would be physically impossible even for an attentive observer to tell whether the forward end of the nine-car cut was actually in contact with the rear end of the two-car cut. The dissenting opinion further points out that all the witnesses who were in a position to see testified that there was no collision; that respondent's evidence was wholly circumstantial, and the inferences which might otherwise be drawn from it were shown to be utterly erroneous unless all of petitioner's witnesses were willful perjurers. "This is not a case," the opinion proceeds, "where direct testimony to an essential fact is contradicted by direct testimony of other witnesses, though even there it is conceded a directed verdict might be proper in some circumstances. Here, when all the testimony was in, the circumstantial evidence in support of negligence was thought by the trial judge to be so insubstantial and insufficient that it did not justify submission to the jury."

We thus summarize and quote from the prevailing and dissenting opinions, because they present the divergent views to be considered in reaching a correct determination of the question involved. It, of course, is true, generally, that where there is a direct conflict of testimony upon a matter of fact, the question must be left to the jury to determine, without regard to the number of witnesses upon either side. But here there really is no conflict in the testimony as to the facts. The witnesses for petitioner flatly testified that there was no collision between the nine-car and the two-car strings. Bainbridge did not say there was such a collision. What he said was that he heard a "loud crash," which did not cause him at once to turn, but that shortly thereafter he did turn and saw the two strings of cars moving together with the deceased no longer in sight; that there was nothing unusual about the crash of cars—it happened every day; that there was nothing about this crash to attract his attention except that it was extra loud; that he paid no attention to it; that it was not sufficient to attract his attention. The record shows that there was a continuous movement of cars over and down the "hump," which were distributed among a large number of branch tracks within the yard, and that any two strings of these cars moving upon the same track might have come together and caused the crash which Bainbridge heard. There is no direct evidence that *in fact* the crash was occasioned by a collision of the two strings in question; and it is perfectly clear that no such fact was brought to Bainbridge's attention as a perception of the physical sense of sight or of hearing. At most there was an inference to that effect drawn from observed facts which gave equal support to the opposite inference that the crash was occasioned by the coming together of other strings of cars entirely away from the scene of the accident, or of the two-car string ridden by deceased and the seven-car string immediately ahead of it.

We, therefore, have a case belonging to that class of cases where proven facts give equal support to each of two inconsistent inferences; in which event, neither of them being established, judgment, as a matter of law, must go against the party upon whom rests the necessity of sustaining one of these inferences as against the other, before he is entitled to recover. United States F. & G. Co. v. Des Moines Nat. Bank, 145 F. 273, 279–280, and cases cited; [other citations omitted].

. . . .

That Bainbridge concluded from what he himself observed that the crash was due to a collision between the two strings of cars in question is sufficiently indicated by his statements. But this, of course, proves nothing, since it is not allowable for a witness to resolve the doubt as to which of two equally justifiable inferences shall be adopted by drawing a conclusion, which, if accepted, will result in a purely gratuitous award in favor of the party who has failed to sustain the burden of proof cast upon him by the law.

And the desired inference is precluded for the further reason that respondent's right of recovery depends upon the existence of a particular fact which must be inferred from proven facts, and this is not permissible in the face of the positive and otherwise uncontradicted testimony of unimpeached witnesses consistent with the facts actually proved, from which testimony it affirmatively appears that the fact sought to be inferred did not exist. This conclusion results from a consideration of many decisions, of which the following are examples: Wabash R. Co. v. De Tar, 141 F. 932, 935; [other citations omitted]. A rebuttable inference of fact, as said by the court in the Wabash Railroad case, "must necessarily yield to credible evidence of the actual occurrence." And, as stated by the court in George v. Missouri Pac. R. Co., [213 Mo.App. 668, 674, 251 S.W. 729, 732 (1923)], "It is well settled that where plaintiff's case is based upon an inference or inferences, that the case must fail upon proof of undisputed facts inconsistent with such inferences." Compare Fresh v. Gilson, 16 Pet. 327, 330–331. In Southern Ry. Co. v. Walters, [284 U.S. 190, 52 S.Ct. 58 (1931)], the negligence charged was failure to stop a train and flag a crossing before proceeding over it. The court concluded that the only support for the charge was an inference sought to be drawn from certain facts proved. In rejecting the inference, this court said:

"It is argued that it may be inferred from the speed of the train when some of the witnesses observed it crossing other streets as well as Bond Avenue, and from such a guess of the engineer as to the time required to get up such speed after a full stop, that none could have been made at Bond Avenue. But the argument amounts to mere speculation in view of the limited scope of the witnesses' observation, the down grade of the railway tracks at the point, and the time element involved. (Compare Chicago, M. & St. P.R. Co. v. Coogan, 271 U.S. 472, 46 S.Ct. 564.) Five witnesses for defendant [employees] testified that a full stop was made and the crossing flagged, and that no one was hit by the rear of the tender, which was the front of the train.

"An examination of the record requires the conclusion that the evidence on the issue whether the train was stopped before crossing Bond Avenue was so insubstantial and insufficient that it did not justify a submission of that issue to the jury."

Not only is Bainbridge's testimony considered as a whole suspicious, insubstantial and insufficient, but his statement that when he turned shortly after hearing the crash the two strings were moving together is simply incredible, if he meant thereby to be understood as saying that he saw the two in contact; and if he meant by the words "moving together" simply that they were moving at the same time in the same direction but not in contact, the statement becomes immaterial. As we have already seen he was paying slight and only occasional attention to what was going on. The cars were eight or nine hundred feet from where he stood and moving almost directly away from him, his angle of vision being only 3° 33′ from a straight line. At that sharp angle and from that distance, near dusk of a misty evening (as the proof shows), the practical impossibility of the witness being able to see whether the front of the nine-car string was in contact with the back of the two-car string is apparent. And, certainly, in the light of these conditions, no verdict based upon a statement so unbelievable reasonably could be sustained as against the positive testimony to the contrary of unimpeached witnesses, all in a position to see, as this witness was not, the precise relations of the cars to one another. The fact that these witnesses were employees of the petitioner, under the circumstances here disclosed, does not impair this conclusion. Chesapeake & Ohio Ry. v. Martin, 283 U.S. 209, 216–220, 51 S.Ct. 453.

We think, therefore, that the trial court was right in withdrawing the case from the jury. It repeatedly has been held by this court that before evidence may be left to the jury, "there is a preliminary question for the judge, not whether there is literally no evidence, but whether there is any upon which a jury can properly proceed to find a verdict for the party producing it, upon whom the onus of proof is imposed." Pleasants v. Fant, 22 Wall. 116, 120–121. And where the evidence is "so overwhelmingly on one side as to leave no room to doubt what the fact is, the court should give a peremptory instruction to the jury." Gunning v. Cooley, 281 U.S. 90, 94, 50 S.Ct. 231, 233; Patton v. Texas & Pacific Ry. Co., 179 U.S. 658, 660, 21 S.Ct. 275. The rule is settled for the federal courts, and for many of the state courts, that whenever in the trial of a civil case the evidence is clearly such that if a verdict were rendered for one of the parties the other would be entitled to a new trial, it is the duty of the judge to direct the jury to find according to the views of the court. Such a practice, this court has said, not only saves time and expense, but "gives scientific certainty to the law in its application to the facts and promotes the ends of justice." Bowditch v. Boston, 101 U.S. 16, 18; Barrett v. Virginian Ry. Co., 250 U.S. 473, 476, 39 S.Ct. 540, and cases cited; Herbert v. Butler, 97 U.S. 319, 320. The scintilla rule has been definitely and repeatedly rejected so far as the federal courts are concerned. [Citations omitted.]

Leaving out of consideration, then, the inference relied upon, the case for respondent is left without any substantial support in the evidence, and a verdict in her favor would have rested upon mere speculation and conjecture. This, of course, is inadmissible. [Citations omitted.]

The judgment of the Circuit Court of Appeals is reversed and that of the District Court is affirmed.

MR. JUSTICE STONE and MR. JUSTICE CARDOZO concur in the result.

Question: (5) Would the direction of the verdict for the defendant have been upheld (a) if Bainbridge had been the only witness on the issue of negligence or (b) if Bainbridge, standing 900 feet away and at an angle making accurate observation difficult but not "physically impossible," had testified that he "saw the two strings collide" and if the testimony of all the other witnesses had been as summarized in the opinion?

LAVENDER v. KURN, 327 U.S. 645, 66 S.Ct. 740 (1946). In this FELA case, Haney, the decedent, was found unconscious on the ground near the railroad track with a skull fracture from which he died. There were no eyewitnesses. Plaintiff's theory was that Haney was struck by the curled end of a mail hook that extended from a mail car; defendant contended that plaintiff's theory was practically a physical impossibility and that in fact Haney was probably murdered by one of the hoboes shown to frequent the area at night. The examining doctor testified that the fatal blow might have come from an object attached to a moving train, but also admitted that it might have resulted from a pipe or club wielded by an individual. The Missouri Supreme Court overturned a verdict for the plaintiff and said the case should not have gone to the jury. On certiorari, the Supreme Court of the United States reversed, saying: "It is no answer to say that the jury's verdict involved speculation and conjecture. Whenever facts are in dispute or the evidence is such that fair-minded men may draw different inferences, a measure of speculation and conjecture is required on the part of those whose duty it is to settle the dispute by choosing what seems to them to be the most reasonable inference. Only when there is a complete absence of probative facts to support the conclusion reached does a reversible error appear."

WILKERSON v. McCARTHY, 336 U.S. 53, 69 S.Ct. 413 (1949). In this FELA case, the plaintiff was injured when he fell from a narrow board stretching across a deep work pit in the railroad yard. The central issue in determining the defendant's negligence was whether its employees habitually used the plank as a walkway. On this there

was conflicting evidence, with the plaintiff and another employee testifying that such practice was an established one but with strong testimony to the contrary from other employees. The Utah Supreme
Court affirmed a directed verdict for the defendant. On certiorari,
the Supreme Court of the United States reversed. In the course of
his opinion for the Court, Justice Black said: "It is the established
rule that in passing upon whether there is sufficient evidence to submit an issue to the jury we need look only to the evidence and reasonable inferences which tend to support the case of a litigant against
whom a peremptory instruction has been given." Justice Frankfurter, concurring, put the standard this way: "When a plaintiff claims
that an injury which he has suffered is attributable to a defendant's
negligence—want of care in the discharge of a duty which the defendant owed to him—it is the trial judge's function to determine whether the evidence in its entirety would rationally support a verdict for
the plaintiff, assuming that the jury took, as it would be entitled to
take, a view of the evidence most favorable to the plaintiff." Justices Black and Frankfurter agreed that there was enough evidence
here to go to the jury. Chief Justice Vinson and Justice Jackson dissented.

Questions: (6) What, if any, significant difference is there between these
two formulations in Wilkerson?

(7) Should the result in Pennsylvania R.R. v. Chamberlain be different
under Justice Black's formulation? under Justice Frankfurter's formulation?

(8) In Reid v. Nelson, 154 F.2d 724 (5th Cir.1946), plaintiff sued husband
and wife for injuries allegedly caused by their dog. Plaintiff's only evidence
tending to show the essential fact of ownership in the wife was that she had
referred to "our dog." If the wife rested at the close of the plaintiff's case
and moved for a directed verdict, should the motion be granted? In fact, the
defendants went on to offer uncontradicted and unimpeached direct evidence
of the husband's sole ownership. Should the wife's motion for a directed
verdict now be granted?

STANDARD IN FELA ACTIONS

The pro-plaintiff tilt of the FELA itself may have led to what
seems to be an especially lenient standard for avoiding a directed verdict in cases brought under that Act. The test of a jury case thereunder has been expressed as "whether the proofs justify with reason
the conclusion that employer negligence played any part, even the
slightest, in producing the injury or death for which damages are
sought." Rogers v. Missouri Pacific Railroad, 352 U.S. 500, 506, 77
S.Ct. 443, 448 (1957). This test has been held to require submission
to the jury of cases that some lower courts have regarded as based
on conjecture, speculation, or surmise. Indeed, the states' Confer-

ence of Chief Justices in 1966, reflecting its dissatisfaction with the numerous reversals by the Supreme Court of state-court decisions in FELA cases, adopted a resolution that these actions should by amendment to the statute be placed exclusively within federal jurisdiction.

Perhaps the seemingly lenient FELA standard merely reflects the tilt in the substantive law, or perhaps there is a difference in kind between the standard in FELA cases and the standard in other actions. This is the subject of much dispute. Compare Boeing Co. v. Shipman, 411 F.2d 365 (5th Cir.1969) (likening the FELA test to the long-rejected scintilla test, the court held it to be not controlling in other federal cases), with Wratchford v. S.J. Groves & Sons Co., 405 F.2d 1061 (4th Cir.1969) (FELA decisions control in other federal cases).

There is nothing in Justice Black's opinion in Wilkerson v. McCarthy, nor in Justice Frankfurter's concurrence, to indicate a difference between FELA cases and other actions with respect to the standard for avoiding direction of a verdict. And it may be that the dampening oscillation of the common-law method is bringing the courts in FELA cases to the same point at which they are arriving in other types of actions.

O'CONNOR v. PENNSYLVANIA RAILROAD

United States Court of Appeals, Second Circuit, 1962.
308 F.2d 911.

[Plaintiff slipped on the terrace of Pennsylvania Station in New York City during a snowstorm on February 16, 1958. Suit was brought in New York state court, but the case was removed on the basis of diversity of citizenship. (It was not an FELA case.) Defendant was liable only if the ice on which plaintiff had allegedly slipped had persisted from earlier snowfalls. The issue on appeal, arising from the grant of defendant's motion for judgment n.o.v., was whether there was sufficient evidence for plaintiff to reach the jury.]

Before LUMBARD, CHIEF JUDGE, and FRIENDLY and KAUFMAN, CIRCUIT JUDGES.

KAUFMAN, CIRCUIT JUDGE.

. . . .

. . . The plaintiff . . . fell . . . on what he described as a "rugged" patch of ice "roughly two by four feet". The usual conflict of testimony as to the condition of the premises was present here as in most negligence suits. There was testimony on behalf of the plaintiff that the center of the terrace floor was almost complete-

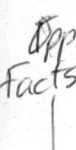

ly clear of snow while there was an accumulation of snow along the edges. The plaintiff testified that the ice on which he slipped was dirty gray and that all the irregular bits and patches of ice on the stone terrace floor were dirty. He further said that he did not remember whether the falling snow was being blown and whipped. The defendant submitted testimony to the effect that there was an accumulation of approximately two inches of wet snow on the terrace floor and that a gale was blowing the snow onto the terrace, which showed no traces of ice.

[United States Weather Bureau records indicated that in the preceding week only unmeasurably small amounts ("traces") of snow fell or remained on the ground, and that in the snowstorm of February 15 and 16 nine inches of snow fell, with drifts of two feet and with strong winds gusting to 54 miles per hour.]

[All of these factors, supported by unquestioned documentary evidence, tend strongly to contradict the evidence offered on behalf of the plaintiff.] Even if it could reasonably be assumed that some traces of snow from the earlier February snowfalls might possibly have persisted on the terrace floor through some negligence of the defendant, the evidence overwhelmingly supports the inference that the snow or ice upon which O'Connor fell at 7:20 a.m. on February 16 was a product of the snowfall raging at the time. To warrant submitting this case to the jury, it was incumbent upon the plaintiff to offer other evidence which could more convincingly overcome the proven physical facts offered on behalf of the defendant.]

[The court avoided the Erie question by observing that the federal and state standards for reaching the jury were "substantially similar."]

"The propriety of granting or denying a motion for a directed verdict [or for judgment non obstante veredicto] is tested both in the trial court and on appeal by the same rule. The trial court must view the evidence and all inferences most favorably to the party against whom the motion is made. The reviewing court must do the same with respect to a judgment entered on a directed verdict or the denial of a motion for a directed verdict or a judgment entered notwithstanding the verdict." 2B Barron & Holtzoff, Federal Practice and Procedure, § 1075 at 378 (1961). In granting such a motion for a judgment notwithstanding the verdict, and in affirming it on appeal, the function of the jury is not usurped. The jury is simply not being permitted to make unreasonable findings of fact. The case is withdrawn from them "as a matter of law" because no jury could reasonably bring in a verdict for the opponent of the moving party. To decide upon the propriety of granting this motion, the court looks to the substantial evidence tending to bolster the case of the non-moving party and draws all reasonable inferences therefrom. But the evidence cannot properly be deemed substantial nor the inferences rea-

sonable if they are contrary to proven physical facts. The inferences
which may be drawn must be within the range of reasonable
probability, Ford Motor Co. v. McDavid, 259 F.2d 261 (4th Cir.), cert.
denied, 358 U.S. 908, 79 S.Ct. 234, 3 L.Ed.2d 229 (1958) and must not
be at war with undisputed facts.

This is not a case where two competing versions of the facts, depending upon the credibility of oral testimony, are to be resolved but
instead one where the uncontested documentary evidence of weather
conditions at the time in question overwhelms the plaintiff's testimony so as to render the inference sought to be drawn unreasonable.
Here, the documentary evidence reveals that the snowfall of February 15 and 16 was so severe that it would be grossly unreasonable to
find that the plaintiff's icy nemesis was the result of the traces of
snow falling several days earlier and of ground precipitation too
small to measure, rather than of the snowfall in progress. Since the
weather records so overwhelmingly outweigh the oral testimony offered in behalf of the plaintiff, [citations omitted], it would have been
improper to permit the jury's verdict to stand.

Affirmed.

SECTION 3.   DIRECTION FOR PARTY WITH BURDEN OF PROOF

The refusal to direct a verdict against the party with the burden
of proof although a verdict in his favor would be contrary to the
weight of the evidence is explainable by the unwillingness to invade
the jury's province of assessing the credibility of witnesses. The direction of a verdict in favor of the party with the burden of proof
involves passing on credibility in almost every case. Does it follow
then that a verdict can never be directed for such a party on the basis
of oral testimony because the jury might not accept it as true? Only
a few states reach this conclusion.[f]

---

[f] In Giles v. Giles, 204 Mass. 383, 90
N.E. 595 (1910), the direction of a verdict
in favor of the party with the burden of
proof was held to have been erroneous,
the court saying: "We know of no case
in this Commonwealth in which it has
been determined that a jury can be directed to return a verdict, upon the oral
testimony of witnesses, in favor of a party who has the burden of proving the
facts to which they have testified."

No such Massachusetts case has yet
been found. A direction in favor of the
party having the burden is possible in
Massachusetts where his case does not
depend on the credibility of witnesses,
e.g., where his case is documentary and
there is no question about the genuineness of the documents. See Goldstein v.
D'Arcy, 201 Mass. 312, 87 N.E. 584
(1909).

CHESAPEAKE & OHIO RAILWAY v. MARTIN

Supreme Court of the United States, 1931.
283 U.S. 209, 51 S.Ct. 453.

[The respondents sued in a Virginia state court for misdelivery of a carload of potatoes transported from Michigan to Richmond, Virginia, on a through bill of lading. The bill of lading required claim for loss or injury to be made within six months after a reasonable time for delivery had elapsed. This claim was made six months and twenty days after shipment from Michigan. The railroad's freight agent at Richmond, qualified to speak by twenty years' experience, testified that a reasonable time after shipment for delivery to the consignee in Richmond would be about eight days and that if any longer time were taken it would be considered a delayed movement. There was no evidence to the contrary. The railroad demurred to the evidence [k] on the ground that the claim was barred by the provision of the bill of lading. The demurrer was overruled, and judgment was entered upon a verdict against the railroad. The judgment was affirmed on appeal, and the railroad's petition for certiorari was granted to review the federal question of compliance with the provisions of a bill of lading authorized by the Interstate Commerce Act.]

MR. JUSTICE SUTHERLAND delivered the opinion of the Court.

. . . .

Not only is the estimate of the agent reasonable upon its face and in accordance with probability; and not only is it wholly unchallenged by other evidence or circumstances; but it is so completely corroborated by the undisputed facts in respect of this very shipment as to put it beyond the reach of a fair doubt. The movement of the car from the point of origin to the yards of petitioner in Richmond actually was made in six days; and, if there be added full forty-eight hours thereafter for completing delivery to the Bowman warehouse, the testimony of the agent as to time stands verified by indubitable test. [The evidence was that the shipment was mistakenly delivered by the railroad not to the Bowman warehouse, as directed by the respondents, but to the Harwood warehouse, where it was eventually located by the respondents in a spoiled condition.] In the face of this record, the conclusion of the court that it was still open for the jury to say that not eight days merely, but twenty days, fell short of being a reasonable time for delivery, is so clearly erroneous as to cause the ruling of the court, in effect, to rest upon nothing more substantial than the power of a jury arbitrarily to disregard established facts.

We recognize the general rule, of course, as stated by both courts below, that the question of the credibility of witnesses is one for the

---

[k] This is the equivalent under Virginia practice of a motion for a directed verdict. See supra p. 569 note c.

jury alone; but this does not mean that the jury is at liberty, under the guise of passing upon the credibility of a witness, to disregard his testimony, when from no reasonable point of view is it open to doubt. The complete testimony of the agent in this case appears in the record. A reading of it discloses no lack of candor on his part. It was not shaken by cross-examination; indeed, upon this point, there was no cross-examination. Its accuracy was not controverted by proof or circumstance, directly or inferentially; and it is difficult to see why, if inaccurate, it readily could not have been shown to be so. The witness was not impeached; and there is nothing in the record which reflects unfavorably upon his credibility. [The only possible ground for submitting the question to the jury as one of fact was that the witness was an employee of the petitioner. In the circumstances above detailed, we are of opinion that this was not enough to take the question to the jury, and that the court should have so held.]

It is true that numerous expressions are to be found in the decisions to the effect that the credibility of an interested witness always must be submitted to the jury, and that that body is at liberty to reject his testimony upon the sole ground of his interest. But these broad generalizations cannot be accepted without qualification. Such a variety of differing facts, however, is disclosed by the cases that no useful purpose would be served by an attempt to review them. In many, if not most, of them, there were circumstances tending to cast suspicion upon the testimony or upon the witness, apart from the fact that he was interested. We have been unable to find any decision enforcing such a rule where the facts and circumstances were comparable to those here disclosed. . . .

. . . .

Judgment reversed.

———

POWERS v. CONTINENTAL CASUALTY CO.

United States Court of Appeals, Eighth Circuit, 1962.
301 F.2d 386.

[Plaintiff sued in an Arkansas state court on two $50,000 insurance policies issued by defendants on June 15, 1959, for a period of 60 days against the risk of accidental bodily injury; the case was removed on the basis of diversity of citizenship. Thirteen days after issuance of the policies, plaintiff while on a fishing trip with three companions had been shot in the back of the left arm by a shotgun borrowed and brought on the trip by one of his companions. The injury had necessitated amputation of plaintiff's arm above the elbow. The only issue at trial was whether the injury was accidental, on which plaintiff had the burden of proof. At the close of all the evidence, plaintiff's motion for a directed verdict was denied. The jury returned a verdict for the defendants. Plaintiff's motion for judgment n.o.v. was denied. The plaintiff appealed, claiming error in denial of these motions.]

Before JOHNSEN, CHIEF JUDGE, and VAN OOSTERHOUT and MAT-THES, CIRCUIT JUDGES.

PER CURIAM.

. . . .

It is an exceptional case wherein the party on whom rests the burden of proof is entitled to a directed verdict in his behalf. 88 C.J.S. Trial § 257(g).

[handwritten margin: When can have Dir. Ver. for party w/ bofp 1. fact admitted 2. fact established by undisputed test. of ≥1 dis-interested witnesses]

"A verdict upon an issue of fact should not be directed in favor of the party who has the burden of proof with respect thereto, unless such fact is admitted, or is established by the undisputed testimony of one or more disinterested witnesses and different minds cannot reasonably draw different conclusions from such testimony. . . ." Woodmen of the World Life Ins. Soc. v. Reese, 206 Ark. 530, 176 S.W.2d 708, 712.

. . . .

Defendants here have denied plaintiff's allegation that the injury was accidental. While plaintiff has offered testimony to establish the accidental nature of his injuries, we cannot say from the record as a whole that plaintiff has established as a matter of law that he is entitled to a directed verdict. Plaintiff and his fishing companion Tucker are the only witnesses who purported to testify as to the facts surrounding the discharge of the gun. Their companions heard the discharge of the gun but were not in a position to see and did not attempt to testify as to the facts relating to the shooting. The testimony of plaintiff and Tucker if believed would support a finding that the shooting was accidental. However, it is obvious from the verdict that the jury did not accept this testimony. Arguments to the jury were completed at 10:30 a.m. The jury returned its verdict for defendants at 11:40 that same morning. . . .

[handwritten margin: Only witnesses here = ℗ & friend (interested parties)]

[handwritten margin: Jury didn't believe their testimony]

The factfinder is not compelled to believe the testimony of a witness even if it is uncontradicted. Northwest Airlines, Inc. v. Rowe, 8 Cir., 226 F.2d 365, 371; Noland v. Buffalo Ins. Co., 8 Cir., 181 F.2d 735, 738.

[handwritten margin: dicta]

This rule has particular application in the case of an interested witness such as the plaintiff. It would also seem that Tucker may have a personal interest in supporting the accident theory as it was defendants' contention that Tucker fired the gun. The evidence discloses that Tucker was at a place where he could reach and discharge the gun and that he was the only person in such position.

Where there were no other eyewitnesses who could contradict directly the testimony of plaintiff and Tucker as to the shooting, we believe that the jury could well have found that the explanation of the shooting was [unsatisfactory]. There is much evidence to squarely contradict much of the plaintiff's testimony relating to the rather unusual procurement by him of three large accident policies and the reasons assigned by him for obtaining them.

Plaintiff is 44 years old. He was in military service for about nine months and draws a disability pension of $262.50 per month. He owns no property and has no other income and has been unemployed since January, 1953.

[The court here stated the facts about procurement of the policies in suit, for which plaintiff had paid $64.80 and $75.35 respectively, and of a third policy in the amount of $100,000 (no longer involved in the action), which he had obtained from another company a month earlier for $157. It appeared that plaintiff had given conflicting explanations of why he wanted the policies, all of which might be found unconvincing. In filing proof of loss with the three companies, plaintiff had used three separate attorneys and had made false statements in the forms.]

The jury saw and heard the witnesses. It is the historic function of the jury to determine the credibility of witnesses and the weight to be given their testimony. There is evidence before the jury which, if believed, would warrant the jury in determining that the testimony of the plaintiff and Mr. Tucker was untrue in some respects. The jury had a right to consider such evidence in determining the credibility of such witnesses.

The record in our present case is such that reasonable minds could differ as to the fact issue of the accidental nature of plaintiff's injury. This is particularly true in light of the law placing the burden upon the plaintiff to prove that the injury was accidental. We can not say that the plaintiff has conclusively met this burden. The court did not err in denying plaintiff's motion for a directed verdict, made at the close of the evidence. For the same reasons, no error was committed in overruling plaintiff's post-trial motion for judgment in accordance with his motion for directed verdict.

. . . .

The judgment appealed from is affirmed.

———

Questions: (9) In an action on a fidelity bond designed to protect an employer from loss through defalcation by his employees, the plaintiff employer offers in evidence against the defendant surety company the testimony of *W*, an employee, that he stole the money and used it for his own purposes. There is no other evidence bearing upon the issue of loss. Should the plaintiff's motion for a directed verdict be granted? See Nanty-Glo Boro. v. American Sur. Co., 309 Pa. 236, 163 A. 523 (1932) (no).

(10) In an action on a note, defendant pleads a material alteration of the note after delivery (an affirmative defense on which defendant has the burden of proof). Defendant's testimony as to the alteration is such that if it were not true, plaintiff could deny it of his own knowledge. Plaintiff does

not testify, and no explanation is offered for his failure to do so. Should defendant's motion for a directed verdict be granted? See Scribner v. Cyr, 148 Me. 329, 93 A.2d 126 (1952) (yes). (The actual motion in Scribner was for a new trial after a verdict for plaintiff, but in Maine, contrary to the prevailing view, the standards for granting this motion and for direction of a verdict are identical. See 1 R. Field, V. McKusick & L. Wroth, Maine Civil Practice 664 (2d ed. 1970).)

SIMBLEST v. MAYNARD

United States Court of Appeals, Second Circuit, 1970.
427 F.2d 1.

[A car driven by plaintiff collided with a fire engine, a 500-gallon pumper driven by defendant, at the intersection of Main Street and South Willard Street, Burlington, Vermont, during the electric power blackout that left most of New England in darkness on the night of November 9, 1965. Both parties were experienced drivers thoroughly familiar with the intersection. Plaintiff was driving west on Main Street and defendant, responding to a fire alarm, was driving south on South Willard Street as they approached the intersection, at which there was an overhead traffic light. The neighborhood was partly business, partly residential. It was dark, the traffic was light, and the weather was clear. Defendant struck plaintiff's car on the front right side. Plaintiff was knocked unconscious for about a minute.

[Plaintiff testified that the traffic light was green in his favor as he entered the intersection, but that when he was partway through it the power failure extinguished all lights, including the traffic light. All other witnesses for both sides testified that the power failure occurred at least 10 to 15 minutes earlier. Plaintiff testified that he was going 12 to 15 miles per hour as he approached the intersection, that he did not look to the right before he entered, that he looked to his right for the first time when he was one-half to three-quarters of the way through the intersection and then saw the fire engine within 12 feet of him, and that he did not hear the fire engine's siren or see the flashing lights or any other lights on the engine. Plaintiff further testified that his vision was obstructed to the right as he entered the intersection by traffic signs, trees, and an information booth. All of the evidence, including photographs, demonstrated that he could have seen the engine if he had looked between the obstructions or after he passed the information booth; one of plaintiff's witnesses testified that he might have seen the fire truck "maybe five to ten seconds" before he was struck.

[Defendant testified that he approached the intersection at 20 to 25 miles per hour (the highest estimate of speed was 30 to 35 miles per hour from another witness) and that the following warning devices were in operation on the fire engine: the penetrator making a wailing sound, the usual fire siren, a flashing red light attached to the dome of the fire engine, two red lights on either side of the cab, and the usual headlights. He saw plaintiff's car before it passed the information booth and next as it entered the intersection. He testified that he applied his brakes and turned to his right in an attempt to avoid the collision. He estimated his speed at 15 to 20 miles per hour at the time of impact.

[Other witnesses virtually bracketed the intersection from various vantage points. The two called by plaintiff saw the flashing lights of the engine, and one of those two also heard the siren. The two called by defendant both heard the warning signals and saw the flashing lights.]

[Defendant's motion for a directed verdict at the close of all the evidence was denied, the jury returned a verdict for plaintiff, and the trial judge granted defendant's motion for judgment n.o.v. The plaintiff appealed.]

Before KAUFMAN and FEINBERG, CIRCUIT JUDGES, and TIMBERS, DISTRICT JUDGE.

TIMBERS, DISTRICT JUDGE.

. . . . .

In determining whether the motion for judgment n.o.v. should have been granted, a threshold question is presented as to the correct standard to be applied. This standard has been expressed in various ways. Simply stated, it is whether the evidence is such that, without weighing the credibility of the witnesses or otherwise considering the weight of the evidence, there can be but one conclusion as to the verdict that reasonable men could have reached. See, e.g., Brady v. Southern Railway Company, 320 U.S. 476, 479–80 (1943); O'Connor v. Pennsylvania Railroad Company, 308 F.2d 911, 914–15 (2 Cir. 1962). See also 5 Moore's Federal Practice ¶ 50.02[1], at 2320–23 (2d ed. 1968); Wright, Law of Federal Courts § 95, at 425 (2d ed. 1970). On a motion for judgment n.o.v., the evidence must be viewed in the light most favorable to the party against whom the motion is made and he must be given the benefit of all reasonable inferences which may be drawn in his favor from that evidence. O'Connor v. Pennsylvania Railroad Company, supra, at 914–15; 5 Moore, supra, at 2325; Wright, supra, at 425.

We acknowledge that it has not been settled in a diversity action whether, in considering the evidence in the light most favorable to the party against whom the motion is made, the court may consider all the evidence or only the evidence favorable to such party and the uncontradicted, unimpeached evidence unfavorable to him. Under Vermont law, all the evidence may be considered. Kremer v. Fortin, 119 Vt. 1, 117 A.2d 245 (1955) (intersection collision between fire engine and passenger car). Plaintiff here urges that under the federal standard only evidence favorable to him should have been considered, citing Wilkerson v. McCarthy, 336 U.S. 53, 57 (1949). As plaintiff reads that case, the court below should not have considered anything else, not even the uncontradicted, unimpeached evidence unfavorable to him. However, we are committed to a contrary view in a diversity case. O'Connor v. Pennsylvania Railroad Company, supra.

The Supreme Court at least twice has declined to decide whether the state or federal standard as to the sufficiency of the evidence is controlling on such motions in diversity cases. Mercer v. Theriot, 377 U.S. 152, 156 (1964) (per curiam); Dick v. New York Life Insurance Company, 359 U.S. 437, 444–45 (1959). Our Court likewise has declined to decide this issue in recent cases. [Citations omitted.] [3]

Under either standard (P) contrib. neg. [Our careful review of the record in the instant case leaves us with the firm conviction that, under either the Vermont standard or the more restrictive federal standard, plaintiff was contributorily negligent as a matter of law; and that Chief Judge Leddy correctly set aside the verdict and entered judgment for defendant n.o.v.[Citations omitted.]

Under Vt.-all evid. → clearly contrib. neg. Under the Vermont standard which permits all the evidence to be considered, Kremer v. Fortin, supra, plaintiff was so clearly guilty of contributory negligence that no further dilation is required.

Under the more restrictive federal standard—i.e., considering only the evidence favorable to plaintiff and the uncontradicted, unimpeached evidence unfavorable to him—while a closer question is presented than under the Vermont standard, we nevertheless hold that plaintiff was guilty of contributory negligence as a matter of law. [4]

Critical issue: If fire truck sirens & lights going) In our view, applying the federal standard, the critical issue in the case is whether the fire engine was sounding a siren or displaying a red light as it approached the intersection immediately before the col-

[3] Assuming that the federal standard were controlling, plaintiff's contention that under that standard evidence introduced by the moving party may not be considered is open to question. Plaintiff relies on Wilkerson v. McCarthy, 336 U.S. 53, 57 (1949). But most Courts of Appeals have held that evidence introduced by the moving party may be considered, distinguishing Wilkerson on the ground that FELA cases are sui generis. 5 Moore, supra, at 2329.

See especially the comprehensive opinion of the Fifth Circuit in Boeing Company v. Shipman, 411 F.2d 365 (5 Cir. 1969) (en banc), holding (1) that in diversity cases a federal rather than state standard should be applied in testing the sufficiency of the evidence in connection with motions for a directed verdict and for judgment n.o.v.; (2) that the FELA standard for testing the sufficiency of the evidence on such motions is not applicable in diversity cases; and (3) that the federal standard to be applied in diversity cases requires the court to consider "all of the evidence—not just that evidence which supports the nonmover's case—but in the light and with all reasonable inferences most favorable to the party opposed to the motion." 411 F.2d at 374.

[4] We emphasize that, solely for the purpose of testing the validity of plaintiff's claim under the federal standard, we assume without deciding that the federal standard is as stated. But compare, e.g., Boeing Company v. Shipman, supra note 3, at 373–75.

lision. Upon this critical issue, Chief Judge Leddy accurately and succinctly summarized the evidence as follows:

> "All witnesses to the accident, except the plaintiff, testified that the fire truck was sounding a siren or displaying a flashing red light. All of the witnesses except Miss Burgess and the plaintiff testified that the fire truck was sounding its siren and displaying a flashing red light."

[margin note: All witnesses say yes to lights & siren]

The reason such evidence is critical is that under Vermont law, 23 V.S.A. § 1033, upon the approach of a fire department vehicle which is sounding a siren or displaying a red light, or both, all other vehicles are required to pull over to the right lane of traffic and come to a complete stop until the emergency vehicle has passed.[5] Since the emergency provision of this statute supersedes the general right of way statute regarding intersections controlled by traffic lights, 23 V.S.A. § 1054, the lone testimony of plaintiff that the traffic light was green in his favor as he approached and entered the intersection is of no moment. And since the emergency provision of 23 V.S.A. § 1033 becomes operative if *either* the siren is sounding *or* a red light is displayed on an approaching fire engine, we focus upon plaintiff's own testimony that he did not see the fire engine's flashing light, all other witnesses having testified that the red light was flashing.

[margin note: Vt. law re: emergency vehicles]

As stated above, plaintiff testified that he first saw the fire engine when he was one-half to three-quarters of the way through the intersection and when the fire engine was within 12 feet of his car. At the speed at which the fire engine was traveling, plaintiff had approximately one-third of a second in which to observe the fire engine prior to the collision. Accepting plaintiff's testimony that his eyesight was excellent, and assuming that the fire engine's flashing red light was revolving as rapidly as 60 revolutions per minute, plaintiff's one-third of a second observation does not support an inference that the light was not operating, much less does it constitute competent direct evidence to that effect. Opportunity to observe is a necessary ingredient of the competency of eyewitness evidence. Plaintiff's opportunity to observe, accepting his own testimony, simply was too short for his testimony on the operation of the light to be of any probative value whatsoever.

[margin note: P's testimony re: light not OK]

Plaintiff's testimony that he did not see the fire engine's flashing red light, in the teeth of the proven physical facts, we hold is tantamount to no proof at all on that issue. O'Connor v. Pennsylvania Railroad Company, supra, at 915. As one commentator has put it, ". . . the question of the total absence of proof quickly merges into the question whether the proof adduced is so insignificant as to

---

[5] . . . Violation of this statute under Vermont law constitutes prima facie evidence of negligence. Dashnow v. Myers, 121 Vt. 273, 155 A.2d 859 (1959).

be treated as the equivalent of the absence of proof." 5 Moore, supra, at 2320. . . . .

. . . .

Affirmed.

Questions: (11) What if plaintiff and defendant had both rested after the plaintiff alone had testified on the issue of liability?

(12) How should Simblest v. Maynard be decided under the Wilkerson v. McCarthy formulations?

STANDARD IN DIVERSITY ACTIONS

Generally, diversity of citizenship actions are controlled by state law as to the substantive elements of the case, and we have seen that under the command of Erie burden of proof in such actions is also governed by state law. But the Supreme Court has never decided whether or not the quantum of evidence necessary to take a diversity case to the jury is state controlled. The assertion by Chief Judge Parker in Davis Frozen Foods, Inc. v. Norfolk Southern Ry., 204 F.2d 839, 842 (4th Cir.1953), that the applicability of federal law "is too well settled to admit of argument," appears to have been an overstatement. However, there is by now a trend toward applying federal law, as was done in Boeing Co. v. Shipman, 411 F.2d 365 (5th Cir. 1969). Accord Wratchford v. S.J. Groves & Sons Co., 405 F.2d 1061 (4th Cir.1969); cf. Donovan v. Penn Shipping Co., 429 U.S. 648, 97 S.Ct. 835 (1977). But see Lykos v. American Home Insurance Co., 609 F.2d 314 (7th Cir.1979), cert. denied, 444 U.S. 1079, 100 S.Ct. 1030 (1980); cf. Cooper, Directions for Directed Verdicts: A Compass for Federal Courts, 55 Minn.L.Rev. 903, 972–89 (1971).

Questions: (13) Should it matter whether the state law is more or less lenient than the federal law in allowing the case to go to the jury?

(14) Should state law control on permissive-inference doctrines, such as res ipsa loquitur?

SERVICE AUTO SUPPLY CO. v. HARTE & CO., 533 F.2d 23 (1st Cir.1976). Plaintiff wholesaler from Puerto Rico sued defendant manufacturer from New York for breach of contract, alleging delivery of defective car mats. Three witnesses "sympathetic" to plaintiff testified. For defendant only its president testified, but he failed to contradict and in part corroborated the testimony of plaintiff's witnesses as to the condition of the delivered goods. At the close of all the evidence, the district court granted plaintiff's motion for a directed verdict as to liability. A verdict and judgment for almost $90,000 followed. On defendant's appeal, the court of appeals said:

"The most troublesome issue lies in the direction of the verdict for plaintiff on liability. While such a direction in favor of the party having the burden of proof is rare, it is permitted where that party 'has established his case by testimony that the jury is not at liberty to disbelieve.' [2] But the standard of proof to be met is a strict one. The Supreme Court in Brady v. Southern Ry. Co., 320 U.S. 476, 479, 64 S.Ct. 232, 234, 88 L.Ed. 239, 243 (1943), has defined the evidence meriting such a sudden death result as 'such that without weighing the credibility of the witnesses there can be but one reasonable conclusion as to the verdict.' . . .

Standard for dir. ver. for (P)

"In ordinary cases, such as this one, where the issues are factual, oral testimony is dominant, and the testimony from each side is likely to be given by witnesses who are committed in their views to one party or the other, whether or not legally 'interested', the making of a motion for directed verdict by a party having the burden is a long shot gamble. In the generality of cases, it saves perhaps a few hours of jury time but nothing else. Affirmance requires the most detailed combing of the record and exposition by the appellate court. Reversal means an entire new trial and possibly another appeal. Perhaps its only merit is that if made and refused, the motion preserves, for a plaintiff, the issue of sufficiency of defendant's evidence in the event of a verdict for defendant. While counsel may feel obligated to make the motion, we advise caution on the part of the court.

. . . . .

". . . We conclude, though not without travail and antipathy for this kind of analysis, that a jury could not have found for the defendant on the issue of liability. The directed verdict on this issue may stand."

[2] 9 Wright and Miller, Federal Practice and Procedure, 591. See authorities gathered in § 2535.

TOPIC C.   VERDICT

SECTION 1. DIVISION OF FUNCTIONS BETWEEN JUDGE AND JURY

The statement that questions of fact are for the jury and questions of law are for the judge has been reiterated over the centuries, but "this conventional brocard cannot be taken as a trustworthy guide to the solution of any particular controversy on the subject." 9 J. Wigmore, Evidence § 2549 (J. Chadbourn rev. 1981).

Judges have always decided questions of fact. For example, threshold matters such as jurisdictional challenges often involve questions of fact, but these matters are normally decided by the judge. The admissibility of evidence likewise may turn on preliminary questions of fact, which are routinely decided by the judge.[a] And Judge Madden said in Wunderlich v. United States, 117 Ct.Cl. 92, 212 (1950), rev'd on other grounds, 342 U.S. 98, 72 S.Ct. 154 (1951): "We are, of course, aware that questions of the interpretation of written documents are not, speaking with analytical accuracy, in most cases questions of law in the sense that a lawyer or a judge has the special skill needed to answer them. They may be questions of agriculture, or engineering, or finance, or medicine, or law. In the division of judicial functions between the judge and the lay jury which only by accident would have the requisite skill in a particular case, the judge reserved this function to himself, presumably as being more competent than the jury. And judges and lawyers began to call the questions 'questions of law,' as a short way of saying that they should be decided by the judge. This method of expression, though analytically inaccurate was, so far as we know, quite universal."

Among the "issues of fact" assigned to the jury, there may be two types of questions: (1) determining what happened, that is, what the parties did and what the circumstances were; and (2) evaluating those facts in terms of their legal consequences, for instance, whether the conduct of the defendant in the circumstances was not that of a reasonable person. But the court always sets the outside limits within which the jury may perform its function. For example, with respect to the latter type of question the Court, in Railroad Co. v. Stout, 84 U.S. (17 Wall.) 657, 663 (1874), said: "So if a coach-driver intentionally drives within a few inches of a precipice, and an accident happens, negligence may be ruled as a question of law. On the other hand, if he had placed a suitable distance between his coach and the precipice, but by the breaking of a rein or an axle, which could not

---

[a] By way of illustration, the competency of a witness (see supra p. 114) and the admissibility in evidence of a copy of a writing when the absence of the original is satisfactorily explained (see supra p. 128) may be cited. See also Federal Evidence Rule 104(a) and (c).

594

have been anticipated, an injury occurred, it might be ruled as a question of law that there was no negligence and no liability." [b]

Although the line between what is fact for the jury and what is law for the court is not always bright and clear, reversals are not uncommon for leaving to the jury questions that the judge should have decided for himself or for committing the converse error. In Savannah, F. & W. Ry. v. Daniels, 90 Ga. 608, 17 S.E. 647 (1892), a statute prescribed a speed limit for a train crossing "any drawbridge over a stream." In a negligence action the trial judge left it to the jury whether the term included the trestles and approaches or only the bridge proper, of which the "draw" or movable section forms a part. This was held to be error. But suppose the action were one on a written contract to paint a certain "drawbridge." Does it necessarily follow that in an action for breach of contract the meaning of the term is for the court? It may be that extrinsic evidence is necessary to determine what the parties meant or to resolve an ambiguity. Or it may be contended that the parties contracted in the light of a trade usage giving words other than their natural meaning.[c] It is for the jury to resolve conflicts in the evidence on such matters, these situations being recognized as exceptions to the general rule that interpretation of writings is for the judge. See Western Petroleum Co. v. Tidal Gasoline Co., 284 F. 82 (7th Cir.1922) ("tank wagon price").

SECTION 2. INSTRUCTIONS

At common law the trial judge was under a duty to instruct the jury on the law, whether or not the parties made any requests to charge. He would commonly sum up the evidence, indicating how the rules of law should be applied to the findings of fact the jury might make. He could also comment on the credibility of the witnesses and the weight of the evidence, giving his own opinion on these matters, provided he made clear to the jurors that the ultimate decision was theirs.[d] The instructions came following the arguments of counsel and before the jury retired to deliberate.

[b] See F. James & G. Hazard, Civil Procedure 266–67 (2d ed. 1977). Professors James and Hazard point out that the rules of law can thus be formulated in such a detailed fashion as to reduce greatly the role of the jury, with considerations of policy dictating whether this will be done. The prevailing approach today in negligence cases is increasingly to commit to the jury the application of the objective community standard of what the reasonably prudent person would do in the circumstances, but the judge tends to play a much bigger role in actions for malicious prosecution. What are the considerations of policy that explain this difference? Does the seventh amendment have a role to play here?

[c] We are here assuming that the proffered evidence does not run afoul of the parol evidence rule. Cf. Hennepin Paper Co. v. Fort Wayne Corrugated Paper Co., infra p. 969.

[d] At common law and now where comment is permitted, it must be fair: the judge must not assume the advocate's role. Reversals for prejudicial comments do occur. Compare Virginian Ry. v. Armentrout, 166 F.2d 400 (4th Cir.1948) (re-

The federal courts and some state courts still adhere to the common-law tradition, but many states have departed from it in various ways, primarily as part of an old popular movement to diminish the role of the judge and increase that of the jury. There are provisions in the majority of states, some of them in state constitutions, forbidding comment on the evidence. A good many states do not even allow the judge to sum up the evidence. Some do not require instructions on the law governing the case generally but only upon points covered by specific requests. In a few states the charge precedes the arguments of counsel. All these rules are considered procedural matters as to which state law is not controlling in federal court.

In Commonwealth v. Barry, 91 Mass. (9 Allen) 276 (1864), the defendant's counsel in his argument to the jury made adverse comments as to the testimony of policemen. The judge told the jury that the same rules were applicable to policemen as to other witnesses in determining their credibility, adding that policemen had testified in many cases tried during that term of court and he thought the jury would agree with him that in these cases they had manifested great intelligence and testified with apparent candor and impartiality. The Supreme Judicial Court reversed for comment on the evidence, which Massachusetts does not permit. It should be noted that a judge could achieve much the same effect by a generalized statement that the jury is entitled to consider as to all witnesses their interest or lack of it in the outcome, their training and experience in observation, and the like. Furthermore, a judge may, if he is so disposed, convey his views to the jury by a tone of voice or gesture that a stenographic transcript does not reveal. See Note, Judges' Nonverbal Behavior in Jury Trials: A Threat to Judicial Impartiality, 61 Va.L.Rev. 1266 (1975).

Question: (1) What do you think of requiring a videotape of the charge to be made part of the record on appeal?

Many judges in jurisdictions where the power to comment on the evidence exists exercise it only infrequently. The existence of the power to comment then serves as a shield against reversal when the trial judge, perhaps inadvertently, says something that may be construed as a comment on credibility or weight.

Following are a few guiding ideas widely, but not universally, applied in framing instructions to the jury:[e]

versed for "an argumentative presentation of the case which must necessarily have prejudiced defendant's cause"), with Trezza v. Dame, 370 F.2d 1006 (5th Cir. 1967) (comments leaving no doubt of judge's conclusion that defendant was negligent "came dangerously close to usurping the function of the jury" and "would have been better left unsaid," but were not prejudicial in light of the strong evidence and the instruction that jury was free to disagree with judge).

[e] The differences from state to state are so great that generalizations are difficult. See generally F. James & G. Hazard, Civil Procedure 289–95 (2d ed. 1977). The generalizations given do accord with the federal approach. See generally 1 E. Devitt & C. Blackmar, Federal Jury Practice and Instructions 198–255 (3d ed. 1977).

1. The trial judge must tell the jury what questions of fact it has to decide. The trial judge typically instructs the jury, even in the absence of requests, on the rules of law applicable generally to the case and necessary to the jury's task.

2. It is error to give an instruction that assumes as true a disputed proposition of fact. To illustrate, in Barnett v. H.L. Green Co., 233 Ala. 453, 171 So. 911 (1936), the charge in an assault case was: "I charge you, gentlemen of the jury, if you believe from the evidence that the defendant . . . used no more force than was necessary to repel the attack, your verdict cannot be for the plaintiff." There had been a sharp conflict in the evidence as to whether the plaintiff did attack the defendant. The charge was held to be error.

Questions: (2) How should the instruction on this point have been framed?

(3) A Nebraska statute provides that "the fact that the plaintiff may have been guilty of contributory negligence shall not bar a recovery when the contributory negligence of the plaintiff was slight and the negligence . . . of the defendant was gross in comparison." The trial judge instructed the jury as follows: "If you find negligence on the part of the plaintiff but that such negligence of the plaintiff was slight in comparison with the gross negligence of the defendant, then you will find for the plaintiff." In what way was the instruction erroneous? How should it have been framed? See Pratt v. Western Bridge & Constr. Co., 116 Neb. 553, 218 N.W. 397 (1928).

3. The correctness of a particular statement is not to be determined from the isolated language. The charge is to be taken as a whole in the light of the evidence.

4. The trial judge is not required to charge the jury in the precise language of any request even though it is a proper and correct statement of the law. A party has no vested right to his own carefully couched form of words. If the substance of the request is given, there is no basis for complaint.

5. A party is entitled to specific instructions on his theory of the case if there is evidence to support it and timely request is made. The fact that the request is not strictly accurate in form or content should not be fatal. If the meaning is reasonably apparent and sufficiently calls the court's attention to the point, the court should instruct the jury with reference to it.

6. The trial judge is not required, however, to single out a part of all the evidence and give an instruction upon that part. The combinations of facts that may be found by the jury are likely to be so numerous that instructions cannot reasonably be compelled as to the legal effect of every fragment of the evidence upon which the jury might rest a finding. There is also the danger that singling out a particular fact and instructing upon it will lead the jury to believe it to be of greater weight than other unmentioned facts. Such undue emphasis may constitute reversible error. The obvious difficulties in applica-

tion of this principle, in conjunction with that of point (5), are discussed in Barnes v. Berkshire Street Railway, 281 Mass. 47, 183 N.E. 416 (1932).

7. The charge is delivered orally in open court. The trial judge may in his discretion also submit a copy of his instructions to the jury, but most judges do not do it. Commonly the charge is not formally and completely written out in advance, and to await a stenographic transcript would cause delay. Moreover, there is danger that jurors might pick passages out of context and give them a distorted effect. If during deliberations the jury is in doubt about the instructions that have been given, it may request the judge to repeat a portion of the charge or give a supplemental charge.

Questions: (4) How can this scheme for giving instructions be improved? What do you think of giving the retiring jury a tape recording of the charge? See United States v. Watson, 669 F.2d 1374, 1385–87 (11th Cir.1982) (not reversible error).

(5) What of letting the jurors take notes during the trial? See Flango, Would Jurors Do a Better Job If They Could Take Notes?, 63 Judicature 436 (1980); Note, Taking Note of Note-taking, 10 Colum.J.L. & Soc.Probs. 565 (1974).

(6) What of giving specific instructions at the outset and periodically throughout the trial? See Comment, Memory, Magic, and Myth: The Timing of Jury Instructions, 59 Or.L.Rev. 451 (1981).

(7) What of letting the jurors ask questions of the trial judge and, through the judge, of witnesses and counsel? See Edises, Giving Juries New Rights and New Answers, Barrister, Winter 1975, at 18; Withrow & Suggs, Procedures for Improving Jury Trials of Complex Litigation, 25 Antitrust Bull. 493, 508 (1980).

In order to preserve alleged error for appellate review, objection must be made to the giving of an instruction or the failure to give one before the jury retires. In some states there must still be a formal "exception" taken. In the federal courts and the states following the federal pattern a specific objection is sufficient, but a party must state "distinctly" his objection and the grounds for it. Rule 51; see Rule 46. The purpose of requiring the objection, which is made out of the hearing of the jury, is to give the judge a fair opportunity to correct any error he may have made. It follows that a general exception or objection "to the refusals to charge as requested" does not serve the intended purpose and is ordinarily insufficient to present any question for review. See Rogers v. Long Island Rail Road, 29 A.D.2d 47, 285 N.Y.S.2d 803 (1967), aff'd, 22 N.Y.2d 918, 242 N.E.2d 84, 295 N.Y.S.2d 47 (1968). It is a hazardous game, and one not likely to succeed, for counsel to try to make his objection specific enough to preserve error but still not so specific as to alert the judge to his error.

Finally, appellate courts reserve the right in the interest of justice to reverse for "plain error" in instructions to which no objection was made. This power is very sparingly exercised and normally will be invoked only to prevent a clear miscarriage of justice caused by the most palpable of errors. Compare Nimrod v. Sylvester, 369 F.2d 870 (1st Cir.1966), with City of Newport v. Fact Concerts, Inc., 453 U.S. 247, 101 S.Ct. 2748 (1981).

Question: (8) In an action on a life insurance policy, the jury is instructed that to establish a defense the insurer must show by a "fair preponderance of the credible evidence" that the insured's statements in applying for the policy were fraudulent. In fact, the controlling law requires "clear, precise, and indubitable" evidence. No specific objection is made to the charge as given. The jury finds that the statements were fraudulent. Should the error be considered on appeal? See Ratay v. Lincoln Nat'l Life Ins. Co., 378 F.2d 209 (3d Cir.) (yes), cert. denied, 389 U.S. 973, 88 S.Ct. 472 (1967).

JUDICIAL EFFORTS TO INDUCE UNANIMITY

Until recently it was accepted without question that the jury right preserved by the seventh amendment entitled a party in a federal civil case to a unanimous verdict of twelve jurors. See Maxwell v. Dow, 176 U.S. 581, 586, 20 S.Ct. 448, 450 (1900). As we have seen, the insistence upon twelve jurors is no longer sacrosanct. So far there has been no authority for dispensing with the unanimity requirement other than by stipulation of the parties pursuant to Rule 48. However, under more than half of the state constitutions a less than unanimous verdict in a civil case is permitted.[f]

Question: (9) What effect would you expect this disparity between state and federal courts to have on the choice of forum, either originally or by removal?

Provisions for a nonunanimous verdict reflect an awareness of the hazard of frustration of a trial by the persistent holding out by a minority of the jurors. Sometimes use of the judge's power to comment on the evidence may help to achieve unanimity. Another and more obvious means is by a supplemental charge after it appears that a disagreement is imminent. In Railway Express Agency v. Mackay, 181 F.2d 257 (8th Cir.1950), after lengthy deliberation, a rereading of the original charge, and still further deliberation, the judge gave the following additional instruction: "This is an important case. The trial has been long and expensive. Your failure to agree upon a verdict will necessitate another trial equally as expensive. The Court is of the opinion that the case cannot be again tried better or more exhaustively than it has been on either side. It is therefore very desirable that you should agree upon a verdict. The Court does not desire that any juror should surrender his or her conscientious convictions. On the other hand, each juror should perform his or her duty conscien-

---

[f] See supra pp. 105–06, 239–41. In New York, a verdict may be rendered by five-sixths of the jurors. NYCPLR § 4113. In some states, three-quarters or even two-thirds of the jurors are suffi-cient for a verdict. See Zeisel, The Verdict of Five out of Six Civil Jurors: Constitutional Problems, 1982 Am. B.Found.Research J. 141, 155.

tiously and honestly according to the law and the evidence. And although the verdict to which a juror agrees must, of course, be his or
her own verdict, the result of his or her own convictions and not a
mere acquiescence in the conclusions of his or her fellows, yet in order to bring twelve minds to a unanimous result you must examine
the questions submitted to you with candor and with a proper regard
and deference to the opinions of each other. You should consider
that the case must at some time be decided, that you are selected in
the same manner and from the same source from which any future
jury must be, and there is no reason to suppose that the case will
ever be submitted to twelve men and women more intelligent, more
impartial or more competent to decide it; or that more or clearer evidence will be produced on one side or the other. You may conduct
your deliberations as you choose, but I suggest you now retire and
carefully consider again the evidence in this case." An objection to
this instruction as coercive in character was rejected.

This type of charge, often termed the "Allen charge" because of
the approval of its use in Allen v. United States, 164 U.S. 492, 17
S.Ct. 154 (1896), and sometimes the "dynamite charge," the "third-
degree instruction," or the "shotgun instruction," has been used
much more frequently in criminal than in civil cases. It has come
under heavy criticism on the criminal side and has indeed been
banned for such purpose in some jurisdictions. See 2 Wright § 502.
However, "[t]he noisy controversy that has arisen about the use of
the Allen charge in criminal cases has not reached the civil side of the
docket." 9 Wright & Miller § 2556, at 663. The Fifth Circuit has
reapproved the Allen charge in civil cases "if it makes clear to members of the jury that (1) they are duty bound to adhere to honest opinions; (2) they are doing nothing improper by maintaining a good faith
opinion even though a mistrial may result." Brooks v. Bay State Abrasive Products, Inc., 516 F.2d 1003, 1004 (5th Cir.1975), cert. denied,
423 U.S. 1090, 96 S.Ct. 885 (1976).

A trial judge trying to produce jury unanimity and anxious to
avoid reversal is likely to quote verbatim an Allen charge that has
been sustained by an appellate court, even though that court may
have conceded that the charge approached the limits of propriety.

Questions: (10) An instruction like that in Railway Express Agency v.
Mackay is given to a jury that has already deliberated for fifty hours. After
twenty hours more, the jury returns a verdict for the plaintiff. Should the
defendant's objection to the instruction and to the action of the court in holding the jury together for the additional hours be sustained on appeal? See
Clemens v. Chicago, R.I. & P. Ry., 163 Iowa 499, 144 N.W. 354 (1913) (yes).

(11) After protracted deliberations in a personal-injury action, the trial
judge gives a supplemental charge that includes the following: "And now if
a jury is unable to reach a verdict that is satisfactory, it seems to me that
that constitutes a black eye on our system of Government. It is really an
encouragement to the Communists and the other people who would like to

overthrow our system of Government." Is this reversible error? See Weinell v. McKeesport Connecting R.R., 411 F.2d 510 (3d Cir.1969) (yes).

(12) After protracted deliberations in a personal-injury action, the trial judge for the first time uses his power to comment on the evidence. Is this reversible error? See People v. Cook, 33 Cal.3d 400, 658 P.2d 86, 189 Cal. Rptr. 159 (1983) (yes, in criminal case).

SECTION 3.   VALIDITY OF VERDICT

JORGENSEN v. YORK ICE MACHINERY CORP.

United States Circuit Court of Appeals, Second Circuit, 1947.
160 F.2d 432, cert. denied, 332 U.S. 764, 68 S.Ct. 69 (1947).

Before L. HAND, AUGUSTUS N. HAND and CLARK, CIRCUIT JUDGES.

L. HAND, CIRCUIT JUDGE. The plaintiff appeals from a judgment, entered on the verdict of a jury, dismissing his complaint in an action for personal injuries caused by the defendant's negligence; he also brings up an order denying his motion for a new trial. . . .

. . . .

On the motion for a new trial based . . . upon the misconduct of the jury, the following appeared by affidavits. One, Murphy, was foreman of the jury, and, on the morning of the last day of the trial before the summations, he received word at his home that his son, a lieutenant in the Navy, had been killed in action. He applied to the clerk of the court to have the trial postponed for a day, but the clerk told him that this could not be done; and neither counsel nor the court learned of the occurrence and the jury was sent out. Murphy and one other of the panel swore that during their deliberations the jury stood seven to five for the defendant and that this vote never changed. All the jurors learned of the death of Murphy's son and of his wish to rejoin his family as soon as possible; and, as they thought it likely that there would be a deadlock, one or more of them wished to announce to the judge their inability to agree. However, since others thought that this would only result in their being sent back, someone suggested that, as seven were for the defendant and only five for the plaintiff, they should return a verdict for the defendant. This they did; it was a compromise to avoid further discussion and to let the foreman return to his home. Murphy's affidavit also declared that he was "much upset mentally" at the time, that he thought the plaintiff should have a verdict, and that he consented to a verdict for the defendant because he felt that he ought to return home as soon as possible. The plaintiff's attorney added an affidavit saying that another of the jurors confirmed these facts to him. The judge considered the motion on its merits, but decided that the affidavits contained nothing which would justify setting aside the verdict.

. . . .

There remains the only question on the appeal which has any substance: the order denying a new trial because of the supposed misconduct of the jury. Such an order, though discretionary, is indeed at times appealable,[3] although the occasions are extremely rare.[4] The whole subject has been obscured, apparently beyond hope of clarification, by Lord Mansfield's often quoted language in Vaise v. Delaval,[5] that no evidence of misconduct was competent which came from the jurors themselves, although, as judges have repeatedly pointed out, it is impossible to see from what source better evidence could be obtained.[6] On the other hand, it would be impracticable to impose the counsel of absolute perfection that no verdict shall stand, unless every juror has been entirely without bias, and has based his vote only upon evidence he has heard in court. It is doubtful whether more than one in a hundred verdicts would stand such a test; and although absolute justice may require as much, the impossibility of achieving it has induced judges to take a middle course, for they have recognized that the institution could not survive otherwise; they would become Penelopes, forever engaged in unravelling the webs they wove. Like much else in human affairs, its defects are so deeply enmeshed in the system that wholly to disentangle them would quite kill it. The discussion of Lamar, J., in McDonald v. Pless, supra, well states the necessary compromise . . . .

All this has, however, nothing to do with what evidence shall be competent to prove the facts when the facts do require the verdict to be set aside, as concededly some facts do. The two decisions of the Supreme Court which we have cited, as well as its approach in United States v. Reid[8] and Hyde v. United States,[9] suggest it as not improbable that when the question arises in the future, the testimony of the jurors may be held competent, and that we shall no longer hear that they may not "impeach their verdict," when it is "impeachable" if what they say is true. Maybe not; judges again and again repeat the consecrated rubric which has confused the subject; it offers an easy escape from embarrassing choices. In the case at bar at any rate we shall not dispose of the appeal in that way; we shall accept what the affidavits said, as did the judge, and like him we shall decide whether it requires the relief asked. Drunkenness, bribery, receiving incom-

[3] Mattox v. United States, 146 U.S. 140, 13 S.Ct. 50, 36 L.Ed. 917.

[4] McDonald v. Pless, 238 U.S. 264, 35 S.Ct. 783, 59 L.Ed. 1300.

[5] 1 Term Rep. 11 [(K.B.1785). On a motion for a rule to set aside a verdict "upon an affidavit of two jurors, who swore that the jury, being divided in their opinion, tossed up, and that the plaintiff's friends won," the rule was refused. Chief Justice Mansfield said: "The Court cannot receive such an affidavit from any of the jurymen themselves, in all of whom such conduct is a very high misdemeanor: but in every such case the Court must derive their knowledge from some other source: such as from persons having seen the transaction through a window, or by some such other means."— Ed.]

[6] Wigmore § 2353.

[8] 12 How. 361, 366, 13 L.Ed. 1023.

[9] 225 U.S. 347, 383, 32 S.Ct. 793, 56 L.Ed. 1114, Ann.Cas.1914A, 614.

petent documents, or privately interviewing a party, do require it; but there are many irregularities, which, however proved, do not, and among them is an agreement to abide by the vote of the majority.[10] Indeed, that is a no greater impropriety than a "quotient" verdict which the Supreme Court sustained in McDonald v. Pless, supra, and the Eighth Circuit in Manhattan Oil Co. v. Mosby.[11] Not only ought we not upset the judge's discretion in refusing to grant a new trial for such a reason; but, had he granted the motion, and had his order been in some unknown way appealable, we should not have sustained it.

Judgment affirmed.

If there is a rigorous rule like that in Vaise v. Delaval excluding jurors' testimony to impeach their verdict, as there still is in some jurisdictions, what is usually the one potential source of testimony is closed. However, it is true that the testimony of an eavesdropper as to jury misconduct can be received, as can physical evidence such as documents left in the jury room.

There is a growing trend in various jurisdictions to allow some juror testimony of misconduct. Neither the flat rule of Vaise v. Delaval nor allowance of unlimited inquiry of jurors—which would supposedly impede free discussion in the jury room, invite jury tampering and harassment, endanger every verdict, and demean the jury system—is thought to be satisfactory. Authorities are virtually in total accord in excluding evidence of mental operations of jurors. As to objective misconduct, the line has frequently been drawn between misconduct inside the jury room (e.g., the toss of a coin; the advance agreement for a quotient verdict or a majority vote) and misconduct outside the jury room (e.g., taking an unauthorized view of the scene of an accident; talking with a party or counsel).

Federal Evidence Rule 606(b) draws the line between testimony as to deliberative processes, on the one hand, and testimony as to intrusion of extraneous prejudicial information or improper outside influence, on the other hand, without regard to whether the happening is within or without the jury room.

Question: (13) Under Evidence Rule 606(b), could a juror testify to the drunken condition of a fellow juror? That is, is alcohol an "outside influence"? See 3 D. Louisell & C. Mueller, Federal Evidence 94, 143–45 (1979). Could a juror testify on the role played by the racial prejudice of a fellow juror? See id. at 131.

[10] Fabris v. General Foods Corporation, 2 Cir., 152 F.2d 660.

[11] 72 F.2d 840. [The quotient method is one by which each juror indicates the damages award he favors, these amounts are totaled, and this total is divided by the number of jurors to yield the award reported out of the jury room. The point decided in the McDonald and Manhattan Oil cases was that the jurors would not be allowed to impeach their verdict by giving evidence that they had used the quotient method.—Ed.]

The Advisory Committee's note to Evidence Rule 606(b) stated: "This rule does not purport to specify the substantive grounds for setting aside verdicts for irregularity; it deals only with the competency of jurors to testify concerning those grounds." [g]

FORD MOTOR CREDIT CO. v. AMODT, 29 Wis.2d 441, 139 N.W.2d 6 (1966). A special verdict of a jury answered "no" to one of the questions. In open court the verdict was read aloud in its entirety, and the jurors agreed it was their verdict. There was no request for polling the jury. The verdict was recorded, and the jury was discharged. Subsequently the losing party moved for a new trial, submitting affidavits of eight jurors to the effect that the answer "no" was erroneously recorded in the special verdict by the foreman and that it should have been entered as "yes." The trial judge granted a new trial on the authority of Wolfgram v. Town of Schoepke, 123 Wis. 19, 100 N.W. 1054 (1904), where it had been held that jurors could impeach their verdict by showing that the words used in conveying it to the court failed to express the conclusion reached by the jurymen. The Supreme Court of Wisconsin reversed, overruling the Wolfgram decision and saying that the public policy reasons that prompted the general rule foreclosing jurors from stultifying their own verdict, by making them incompetent to testify, applied with equal validity to a claim that an answer had been improperly recorded.

FREID v. McGRATH, 135 F.2d 833 (D.C.Cir.1943). A general verdict in a personal-injury action awarded plaintiff $425 against one defendant and $425 against the other defendant. The jurors expressly confirmed their verdict in open court. Subsequently plaintiff moved to correct the verdict, offering affidavits and testimony from almost all the jurors to the effect that they intended plaintiff to recover $850. However, cross-examination revealed that they had not focused or agreed on the extent of each defendant's liability beyond $425. On that motion, the court of appeals (2–1) gave this guidance:

"The rules of law which will govern the exercise of the District Court's discretion may be stated, briefly, as follows: Where the jury's error is patent on the face of the verdict, the court should so amend the verdict as to make it conform to correct legal principles. But where the mistake is latent in and not apparent on the face of the verdict, it is sometimes proper to receive the affidavits of the jurors to ascertain their true verdict. Although great caution should be exercised in the use of such affidavits, there is no inflexible rule against their use, especially when they are offered, not for impeachment of

---

[g] A different approach is judicial exhortation or even an order aimed at preventing disclosure of jurors' deliberations in the first place. See Note, Public Disclosures of Jury Deliberations, 96 Harv.L. Rev. 886 (1983).

the verdict, but rather for ascertainment of the true verdict. . . .
If the jury actually found a verdict in the amount of $850.00, but mistakenly apportioned that amount between two defendants, the District Court, if properly convinced of that fact, would have power to correct the verdict accordingly; so that it would express the conclusion actually reached, and finally agreed upon by the jury—but mistakenly reported to the court."

THE SEALED VERDICT

The modern practice commonly allows the jury to deliver its verdict in a sealed envelope to the court officer in charge and to disperse, instead of remaining together until the judge receives the verdict.[h] The sealed verdict is opened in the presence of the jurors when the court next sits. A party may demand a poll of the individual jurors before the verdict is recorded.

In theory the verdict is not truly a verdict when sealed but only when opened.[i] All is well if the jurors then agree, but if a juror dissents, even though he admits that he agreed with the others when the verdict was sealed, the verdict cannot stand. The judge is then faced with the choice of sending the jury back for further deliberation or declaring a mistrial. Some courts hold that the latter is the lesser evil because of the hazard of improper influence or coercion. E.g., Kramer v. Kister, 187 Pa. 227, 40 A. 1008 (1898). Others quiz the jurors as to whether they have discussed the case with outsiders and may require further deliberation upon receiving appropriate answers. E.g., Dziegiel v. Town of Westford, 274 Mass. 291, 174 N.E. 495 (1931).

Question: (14) The jury returned a verdict for the defendant. The jurors were polled by the clerk. When he asked Juror No. 11 if that was her verdict, she replied: "Yes, only insofar as it had to be unanimous." The court asked the juror to explain her statement, and she said: "The verdict, as I understand, had to be one hundred per cent in favor and we had to present one statement. I was, I think, the only one that held out and there was no possibility of any change and because of that I did." Should the verdict for the defendant have been recorded? See Grace Lines v. Motley, 439 F.2d 1028 (2d Cir.1971) (yes, although preferable to interrogate juror further or to send jury back for further deliberation).

------

[h] "And it has been held, that if the jurors do not agree in their verdict before the judges are about to leave the town, though they are not to be threatened or imprisoned, the judges are not bound to wait for them, but may carry them round the circuit from town to town in a cart." 3 W. Blackstone, Commentaries *376.

[i] In Rich v. Finley, 325 Mass. 99, 89 N.E.2d 213 (1949), a juror died after the verdict was sealed and before it was opened. The eleven remaining jurors assented to the verdict. It was held to have been error to record the "verdict" because it lacked the final concurrence of the twelve jurors.

THE PROBLEM OF SURPLUSAGE

To what extent, if any, may the trial judge properly disregard as surplusage part of what the jury has included in its verdict or in a statement appended thereto? The problem is again illustrated by the not uncommon attempt of the jurors to apportion the verdict between two defendants despite proper instructions that a verdict for the plaintiff should be for the full amount of his damages against each defendant found liable. Suppose the jury returns this verdict: "We find for the plaintiff in the sum of $20,000, $15,000 to be paid by defendant *A* and $5000 to be paid by defendant *B*." Is it proper for the trial judge to disregard the apportionment as surplusage and order judgment for $20,000 against both defendants?

Questions: (15) Would the case be different if the jury had simply returned the verdict: "We find for the plaintiff against defendant *A* in the sum of $15,000 and against defendant *B* in the sum of $5000"? What should the trial judge do? See City of Fort Worth v. Williams, 55 Tex.Civ.App. 289, 119 S.W. 137 (1909); W. Prosser, Handbook of the Law of Torts 298–99 (4th ed. 1971).

(16) In an action against agents to recover a secret profit, the jury, after much obvious trouble in reaching agreement, brought in a verdict for the plaintiff for the amount demanded. Appended to the verdict was a statement signed by all the jurors: "We, the jurors, recommend that the sum of $2300.00 claimed to be recovered by this suit be donated to the American Red Cross." What, if any, action should the trial court take? See Robyn v. White, 153 Minn. 76, 189 N.W. 577 (1922) (approved striking as surplusage, but would have preferred further deliberation).

THE "IMPOSSIBLE VERDICT"

Assume an action on a $1000 note. The jury returns a verdict for $500. The judge knows without piercing the privacy of the jury room that the jury has acted improperly. The only possible verdicts were for the plaintiff for $1000 or for the defendant. Plainly the plaintiff can complain and get a new trial (if the judge has not resolved the difficulty by sending the jury out again with further instructions). But can the defendant complain? What of the argument that he is not harmed because the verdict is lower than it should have been? See Martin Realty Co. v. Garver, 116 Kan. 689, 229 P. 70 (1924) (new trial for defendant).

How is the case different if the damages are not liquidated? In Simmons v. Fish, 210 Mass. 563, 97 N.E. 102 (1912), the jury returned a verdict for $200 for loss of an eye in an accident. Should the plaintiff be able to get a new trial? Should the defendant be able to get a new trial? (Would the defendant want a new trial?)

Question: (17) With respect to allowing further deliberation by the jury, should it matter whether (a) the jury reports a disagreement upon the opening of a sealed verdict or (b) the verdict is on its face an impossible one?

SECTION 4. TYPE OF VERDICT

Federal Rule 49, in providing for both special verdicts and general verdicts accompanied by answers to interrogatories, adopted procedural devices of respectable historical origin.[j] Yet in dissenting from the submission to Congress of the 1963 amendments to the Federal Rules of Civil Procedure, which included inconsequential changes in Rule 49(b), Justices Black and Douglas expressed the view that Rule 49 should be repealed, not amplified. It was, they said, "but another means utilized by courts to weaken the constitutional power of juries and to vest judges with more power to decide cases according to their own judgments." Order of January 21, 1963, 374 U.S. 865, 868, 83 S.Ct. 43, 45.

The theoretical merits of these alternatives to a general verdict can be easily demonstrated. These special devices guide the jurors' deliberations and help restrict the jury to its proper function. A general verdict may mask the jurors' misunderstanding or willful disregard of the evidence or of the judge's instructions. Also, the way a general verdict veils the jurors' decisionmaking process often makes it hard to determine the effect of an error in, say, the judge's instructions. General verdicts are no doubt often set aside for misdirection when, if the truth could be known, the jurors' decision properly turned on a point wholly unrelated to the judge's error. For example, in Pacific Greyhound Lines v. Zane, 160 F.2d 731 (9th Cir.1947), an action for personal injuries, the judge charged correctly on so-called actual fraud in securing a release that had been pleaded as a defense and incorrectly on so-called constructive fraud. There was a general verdict for the plaintiff, signifying that the jury had found one or the other kind of fraud. The circuit court of appeals felt obliged to reverse the judgment although there was enough evidence to go to the jury on either kind of fraud. The court remarked that had a special verdict or a general verdict with interrogatories been employed, a reversal might have been obviated.

Judges, however, have taken divergent views of the value of these devices. Judge Clark in Morris v. Pennsylvania R., 187 F.2d 837 (2d

---

[j] Edith G. Henderson in The Background of the Seventh Amendment, 80 Harv.L.Rev. 289 (1966), points out the wide use of the special verdict in England long before our Revolution, and in the colonies as well. She casts substantial doubt on the frequently stated proposition that the jury in a civil action was not obliged to give a special verdict but could insist upon giving a general verdict. However, consent of both parties to the use of a special verdict was required.

The general verdict with interrogatories also has a long history. See Morgan, A Brief History of Special Verdicts and Special Interrogatories, 32 Yale L.J. 575, 591–92 (1923).

Cir.1951), where a general verdict accompanied by answers to interrogatories had been taken, cautioned that the practice should be used with discrimination and foresight. He favored it when the issues could be clearly and sharply differentiated, so as "to save on appeal at least that portion [of the verdict] which cannot be questioned," but he disapproved it in "a relatively simple factual situation." Judge Frank, concurring in the same case, disagreed. Quoting an earlier opinion of Judge Learned Hand in his support, he said: "I should like to subject a verdict, as narrowly as was practical, to a review which should make it in fact, what we very elaborately pretend that it should be: a decision based upon law." See also J. Frank, Courts on Trial 141–43 (1949).

Professor Moore stated his views thus, formerly in 5A Moore ¶ 49.05, at 2235–36:

"Also the general verdict, at times, achieves a triumph of justice over law. The jury is not, nor should it become, a scientific fact finding body. Its chief value is that it applies the 'law,' oftentimes a body of technical and refined theoretical principles and sometimes edged with harshness, in an earthy fashion that comports with 'justice' as conceived by the masses, for whom after all the law is mainly meant to serve. The general verdict is the answer from the man in the street. If on occasion the trial judge thinks the jury should be quizzed about its overall judgment as evidenced by the general verdict, this can be done by interrogatories accompanying the general verdict. But if there is sufficient evidence to get by a motion for directed verdict, then the problem is usually best solved by an overall, common judgment of the jurors—the general verdict."

Questions: (18) If the jurors return an obvious compromise verdict, as in Simmons v. Fish, supra p. 606, should this answer from the man in the street be accepted by the trial judge? See F. James & G. Hazard, Civil Procedure 327–31 (2d ed. 1977).

(19) What bearing does the nature of the verdict have on questions of issue preclusion? (This will be reconsidered in Part Six.)

It is to be noted that under Rule 49, and as a matter of general practice elsewhere, the use of a special verdict or a general verdict with interrogatories is discretionary with the court. It no longer requires the consent of the jury, if it ever did, nor the consent of the parties. There appears to have been no case where a trial judge was reversed for abuse of discretion in deciding whether to resort to Rule 49.

Be that as it may, neither part of the Federal Rule has been very extensively used except by the federal courts in Texas, Wisconsin, and North Carolina, where special verdicts [k] were firmly embedded in state practice prior to the adoption of the Federal Rules. In federal

---

[k] These are called special issues in Texas, where they are used in virtually every jury case. See 9 Wright & Miller § 2501.

court this is, nevertheless, strictly a federal matter not controlled by state law.

―――――――

SPECIAL VERDICT

Rule 49(a) sought to correct defects in the special verdict technique as manifested in the cases both ancient and modern. Upon consent of the parties at common law, the jury at nisi prius would find the facts in detail; the findings would be entered of record; and the record would go on to recite: "That they are ignorant in point of law on which side they ought upon those facts to find the issue, but if upon the whole matter the Court shall be of opinion that the issue is proved for the Plaintiff, they find for the Plaintiff accordingly, and assess the damages at such and such a sum, but if the Court are of an opposite opinion then they find for the Defendant." Upon the record so made, the court in banc would enter the judgment that it thought appropriate.[1]

The difficulties in the use of the device were summed up by Professor Sunderland in Verdicts, General and Special, 29 Yale L.J. 253, 261 (1920), in this way:

"The chief substantial objection which can be taken to the common use of the special verdict is that in practice it is difficult and hazardous to deal with. The risks are: (1) Immaterial matters may be included; (2) material matters may be omitted; (3) conclusions of law instead of facts may be found; (4) evidentiary instead of ultimate facts may be found; (5) questions may be put to the jury in such form as to be uncertain, misleading or prejudicial.

"These are very serious risks, and a historical survey of the practice relating to special verdicts will disclose a rocky road strewn with innumerable wrecks."

The special verdict was usually drawn up by the lawyers in the form of questions or alternative findings, often in the heat of trial with little opportunity for reflection or care in wording. As it was held that the judgment must be supported by the very findings embodied in the verdict, an inadvertent omission or an ambiguity in the verdict might vitiate the judgment.

Question: (20) By what means does Rule 49(a) deal with this problem?

―――――――

[1] R. Sutton, Personal Actions at Common Law 128 (1929). The special verdict device is to be distinguished from the so-called special case at common law. This entailed a statement of facts agreed to by the parties—a special case—on which the court in banc would render judgment, without real participation by the jury.

COLUMBIA HORSE & MULE COMMISSION CO. v.
AMERICAN INS. CO.

United States Court of Appeals, Sixth Circuit, 1949.
173 F.2d 773.

Before ALLEN, MARTIN, and MCALLISTER, CIRCUIT JUDGES.

ALLEN, CIRCUIT JUDGE. This action seeks recovery under an insurance policy for the loss of 43 mules destroyed in a fire near Dickson, Tennessee. By agreement of counsel the case was submitted to the jury for special verdict upon the issues:

No. 1:

"Was the fire that destroyed the barns rented by Plaintiff John Dodd caused by his own act for the purpose of collecting on the insurance policy in question?"

No. 2:

"How many mules were destroyed when plaintiff's barns burned on April 11, 1945?"

The jury found for the appellants on Issue No. 1, and on Issue No. 2 it found the number of mules destroyed to be 34.

Appellant John Dodd, in an affidavit accompanying the proof of loss and in his testimony at the trial, asserted that the number of mules lost was 43. The jury's finding that 34 mules were destroyed is based upon the testimony of several witnesses who examined the premises immediately after the fire, and is not questioned here. The court considered that the proof of loss and affidavit claiming recovery for 43 mules constituted a willful and material misrepresentation and a false swearing in violation of the policy of insurance, which contained the usual provision that the policy should be void if the insured concealed or misrepresented any material fact or circumstance concerning the insurance or the interest of the insured in the property. Upon this ground and upon the further ground that the record contains no evidence as to the value of the 34 mules found to have been lost in the fire, the court dismissed the action.

Appellants' principal contention is that the court erred in not submitting to the jury the question whether or not Dodd's sworn statement was willfully false and fraudulent, and that the court erred in deciding as a matter of law that a false statement in the affidavit as to the property destroyed by fire voided the policy. They urge that Dossett v. First National Fire Ins. Co., 138 Tenn. 551, 198 S.W. 889, a decision of the Supreme Court of Tennessee relied upon by the District Court as supporting its decision herein, was an equity case and is not controlling in this action at law. Appellants also urge that innocent or mere mistaken misrepresentation of value, sworn to in a proof of loss, will not avoid an insurance policy. Dossett v. First National Fire Ins. Co., supra, 138 Tenn. at page 554, 198 S.W. 889. They rely upon the established rule that false statements, innocently or inadvertently made, do not constitute fraud or false swearing within the forfeiture clause of the usual policy, nor result in its avoidance. Sundquist v. Camden Fire Ins. Ass'n, 7 Cir., 119 F.2d 955, 957. Hence they maintain that an issue whether Dodd willfully or fraudulently misrepresented the number of mules lost should have been submitted to the jury. [Citations omitted.]

Assuming, but not deciding, that these questions might have been resolved in favor of the appellants if they had been presented free from procedural complications, we think the case is governed squarely by Rule 49(a) of the Federal Rules [which the court here quoted].

The two issues submitted were framed after conference between court and counsel, and after ample notice. The issue now raised, namely, whether appellant Dodd's representation as to the number of mules lost was willfully or innocently false, was omitted from the special issues submitted to the jury. Under Rule 49(a), each party, including appellants, waived the right to a jury trial upon the issue omitted. Waiver on appellants' part is emphasized by the fact that the court in its preliminary charge submitting the issues to the jury, asked counsel for further requests, and later repeated the invitation to submit further requests at the close of the general charge. Appellants did not avail themselves of this opportunity.

No demand was made by either party that a question whether Dodd's misrepresentation was innocent or willful and fraudulent be submitted to the jury before its retirement. It follows that under Rule 49(a) the court was empowered to make a finding on that issue.

The judgment entered in accordance with the finding is not erroneous, and is affirmed.

Questions: (21) Why did the court and the parties likely not submit the omitted issue to the jury?

(22) What if the trial judge had made no finding whether the plaintiff's misrepresentation was willfully false and fraudulent or was innocent and merely mistaken, but had entered judgment for the defendant on the special verdict? What if the judge had made no finding on the issue because he erroneously believed that it was legally immaterial whether the misrepresentation was willful or innocent?

(23) The Minnesota Supreme Court has held that it is reversible error for the judge in his instructions to inform the jurors of the legal consequences of their answers to special questions. McCourtie v. United States Steel Corp., 253 Minn. 501, 93 N.W.2d 552 (1958); see Minn.R.Civ.P. 49.01. Appraise this position.

(24) What if, in a Minnesota state court, counsel in closing argument expressly or by clear implication tells the jury what answers he wants it to give? How can he argue effectively if he does not do this? See 9 Wright & Miller § 2509.

GENERAL VERDICT WITH INTERROGATORIES

The practice of submitting a case to the jury for a general verdict but at the same time submitting written interrogatories on one or more issues of fact was, in this country, originally identified with New England but widely copied elsewhere.

Questions: (25) What practical differences do you perceive between the operation of Rule 49(a) and that of Rule 49(b)?

(26) What, if any, is the difference in the purposes of the two procedures?

(27) Rule 49(b) presents the trial judge with various permissible courses of conduct when inconsistencies appear in the action taken by the jury. What factors should guide his discretion in making the choice?

────────

MAYER v. PETZELT

United States Court of Appeals, Seventh Circuit, 1962.
311 F.2d 601, cert. denied, 373 U.S. 936, 83 S.Ct. 1538 (1963).

Before HASTINGS, CHIEF JUDGE, and DUFFY and KILEY, CIRCUIT JUDGES.

KILEY, CIRCUIT JUDGE. This is an appeal by plaintiff following the second trial of a diversity personal injury action against a Crystal Lake, Illinois, policeman. The first trial resulted in a $25,000 verdict for plaintiff, but a new trial was granted defendant. At the second trial on liability alone, the jury returned a general verdict for plaintiff with a special interrogatory against him on the question of due care. The District Court [for the Northern District of Illinois], notwithstanding the verdict for plaintiff, entered judgment [1] for defendant.

While driving at night in Crystal Lake, plaintiff violated a traffic law. He then drove into a dark alley behind his hotel, and defendant followed on his police department motorcycle. While defendant was attempting to arrest plaintiff, the latter ran, fell in the alley, and was injured.

. . . .

The most favorable view of the evidence for plaintiff is: On the night of his injury, plaintiff had illegally crossed the center line in making a wide right turn. Afterward he drove into the dark alley behind his hotel, parked and turned out the car lights. He then recognized, standing by his car, defendant, who had, about a month before, pursued plaintiff for "telling a lie," caught him and dragged him back to the police station ripping his shirt off in the process.[8]

────────

[1] Rule 50(b), Federal Rules of Civil Procedure.

[8] The evidence of the prior incident was excluded at the trial. We think the rul-ing was erroneous because it has a bearing on plaintiff's mental state on the night of June 23. Smith v. Cornell, 59 Ill. 66 (1871), Jennings v. Murphy, 194 F.2d 35, 37 (7th Cir.1952), 2 Jones Evidence,

Defendant, then a man of 27 who weighed 190 pounds, said to plaintiff, a man of 64, "You ___ __ _ ____, now I got you where I want you, and you come out of that car and you are going to get it." Defendant did not have his flashlight or ticket book with him at the time. While "hollering" and shaking plaintiff's car, defendant tried to open the locked doors. When defendant went to the right side, plaintiff got out the left, ran down the alley and was injured. Defendant later told a fellow officer that he ". . . must have scared hell out of him because he started to run from me."

We think the jury could on this evidence draw a reasonable inference that defendant should have foreseen, as a reasonably prudent man, that his conduct on the night in question, in view of the incident the previous month, would probably cause plaintiff, in fear for his safety, to leave the automobile, run away in the dark alley and be injured while running. This inference would support the finding of negligence. Karas v. Snell, 11 Ill.2d 233, 142 N.E.2d 46, 56 (1957), Hood v. Brinson, 30 Ill.App.2d 498, 175 N.E.2d 300 (1961).

. . . .

Implicit in the general verdict for plaintiff is a finding of absence of contributory negligence. Theurer v. Holland Furnace Co., 124 F.2d 494, 497 (10th Cir.1941). But a special interrogatory answered in the negative the question: "Did the plaintiff use ordinary care and caution for his own safety on the occasion in question?" This interrogatory is not inconsistent with the general verdict because, even though the jury might believe plaintiff was guilty of lack of due care, it might also believe that plaintiff's actions were not the proximate cause of his injury.[10] Furthermore, the District Court would not be justified in deciding that plaintiff's conduct proximately caused the injury, and entering judgment on the interrogatory. . . .

We hold that the District Court erred in entering judgment notwithstanding the verdict. . . . For the reasons given, the judgment is reversed, and the cause is remanded for trial upon the issue of damages only.

————

Question: (28) In an action by the beneficiary on a life insurance policy, the insurance company offers evidence (a) that the insured committed suicide and (b) that the insured was murdered by the beneficiary, proof of either of which defenses would defeat recovery. The jury returns a general verdict for the defendant and answers "yes" to each of two accompanying written

1149 (2d ed. 1926), 18 Illinois Law & Practice, Evidence, § 61, pp. 193–194.

[10] "It is plain that the general verdict must yield when it is so clearly at variance with one or more of the [special interrogatory] answers that the two are irreconcilable in a legal sense. But every reasonable intendment in favor of the general verdict should be indulged in an effort to harmonize the two. The answers override the general verdict and warrant the entry of judgment in disregard of the latter only where the conflict on a material question is beyond reconciliation on any reasonable theory consistent with the evidence and its fair inferences." Theurer v. Holland Furnace Co., 124 F.2d 494, 498 (10th Cir.1941).

interrogatories asking (a) whether the insured committed suicide and (b) whether the beneficiary murdered him. What should the trial judge do? What effect does Rule 49(b) have on your answer?

ARKANSAS MIDLAND RAILWAY v. CANMAN
Supreme Court of Arkansas, 1890.
52 Ark. 517, 13 S.W. 280.

[Plaintiff sued for personal injuries caused by the derailment of the defendant's railway coach in which he was a passenger. The trial resulted in a verdict and judgment for the plaintiff from which the defendant appealed. The portion of the opinion holding that the judgment must be reversed because of errors in the instructions to the jury is omitted.]

BATTLE, J.

. . . .

Another question is presented for our consideration. The statutes of this State provide that the court may require the jury, "in any case in which they render a general verdict, to find specially upon particular questions of facts to be stated in writing," and that "when the special finding of facts is inconsistent with the general verdict the former controls the latter, and the court may give judgment accordingly." (Mansf.Dig., secs. 5142, 5143.) In pursuance of these statutes the court propounded interrogatories and gave instructions to the jury, on motion of the appellant, as follows:

"1. Was the derailment of the coach in which plaintiff was a passenger caused by the insufficient skill and care of the defendant in constructing its road-bed?

"2. Was the derailment of the coach in which plaintiff was a passenger caused by the want of skill and prudence of defendant in maintaining its road-bed?

"3. Was such derailment caused by the defect in the rolling stock in the defendant's train or any of its appliances?

"4. Was such derailment caused by any negligence in operating such train?

"5. If the jury find negligence in either case, they will state in what said negligence consisted.

"6. If the jury find that after the derailment of the car the track was torn up and the ties broken, they will state whether the tearing up of the track and the breaking of the ties contributed to the injury of the plaintiff, and if so, in what way and to what extent."

And against the objection of the defendant, instructed the jury as follows:

"If the jury find negligence and cannot agree what the particular negligence was which caused the derailment of the car, they may so state."

"If the jury find that the derailment was caused by a bent rail or spreading of the track, say so."

To each of the interrogatories the jury responded: "We fail to agree," and further said: "We find negligence on the part of the defendant, but fail to agree as to what particular neglect caused the derailment of the train."

The appellant contends that the court erred in instructing the jury that if they found that the appellant had been guilty of negligence, and could not agree as to what the negligence which caused the derailment was, they might so state; and insists, that before a verdict could have been legally returned against it, there must have been an agreement of the minds of the twelve jurors as to the existence of some particular fact constituting negligence, and that they must have agreed on an affirmative answer to one of the interrogatories. The correctness of this contention depends on the evidence. It is not necessary that a jury, in order to find a verdict, should, in all cases, concur in a single view of a transaction or occurrence disclosed by the evidence. If the verdict is sustained by any one of two or more interpretations of the evidence, it cannot be impeached by showing that a part of the jury proceeded upon one interpretation and a part upon the others. Murray v. New York Life Ins. Co., 96 N.Y. 614; Chicago & N.W.R. Co. v. Dunleavy, 22 N.E. 15. But if they must necessarily agree upon the answer to any particular question before they can find a verdict, they would be guilty of a violation of duty if they returned a general verdict without doing so. Ebersole v. Northern Central Railroad Co., 23 Hun 114. If they should reply to such a question, to the effect they cannot agree, the court ought not to receive their verdict, as the reply and verdict, in that case, would be in irreconcilable conflict. As to the consistency of the verdict, and the answers of the jury to the interrogatories in this case, we express no opinion.[m]

.   .   .   .

THE SPLIT TRIAL

A local rule for the Northern District of Illinois, whence came Mayer v. Petzelt, provides that the court may order, on motion of a party or on the court's own motion, a separate trial of the issues of

[m] See Ginsburg, Special Findings and Jury Unanimity in the Federal Courts, 65 Colum.L.Rev. 256 (1965). There appears to be no federal civil case raising this issue squarely.

liability, to be followed if necessary by a trial on damages. Professor Charles Alan Wright in Procedural Reform: Its Limitations and Its Future, 1 Ga.L.Rev. 563, 569–70 (1967), had this to say about the split trial pursuant to such a rule:

"In the last few years some courts have adopted rules providing that the issue of liability may be tried first in a negligence case, and a second trial on damages is held only if plaintiff prevails on liability. This has had marvelous results in terms of saving court time. A competent study has been made of experience with such a procedure. That study concludes that cases handled in this fashion take 20 percent less time than do cases tried routinely, with the liability and damage issues submitted simultaneously to the jury. A saving of 20% in trial time of negligence cases would be an important gain for the courts. The same data show, however, that while defendants win in 42% of the cases tried routinely, they win in 79% of the cases in which the liability issue is submitted alone. This certainly suggests that juries are moved by sympathy when they have heard evidence as to the extent of plaintiff's injuries, and that this influences their decision on the liability issue. Quite possibly this is a bad thing—certainly orthodox theory supposes that it is. But when it is seen that the split trial reduces by more than half the cases in which personal injury plaintiffs are successful, it is apparent that the new procedure has made a substantial change in the nature of jury trial itself."

Questions: (29) Is the local rule consistent with the seventh amendment? See Hosie v. Chicago & N.W. Ry., 282 F.2d 639 (7th Cir.1960) (yes), cert. denied, 365 U.S. 814, 81 S.Ct. 695 (1961). Is it a desirable rule? What bearing do Professor Wright's comments have on this question?

(30) In a motor-vehicle tort case, who would be more likely to seek a separate trial of the liability issues, plaintiff or defendant? Does your answer depend upon the expected nature of the evidence on liability? on damages?

TOPIC D. NEW TRIAL

SECTION 1. ERROR IN COURSE OF TRIAL

We have already seen many instances of motions for a new trial, and of reversals by appellate courts that in the ordinary course would be followed by new trials. In the present Topic a few problems under the vast rubric of "New Trial" have been selected for study. Much of this Topic relates back to questions already touched on.

Federal Rule 59(a), without undertaking to give a catalogue of all imaginable grounds for a new trial, refers to the reasons for which new trials have heretofore been granted in actions at law in the United States courts and, in respect to actions tried without a jury, refers to the reasons for which rehearings have heretofore been granted in suits in equity in such courts.

Question: (1) California has enacted a catalogue of grounds for a new trial. Cal.Civ.Proc.Code § 657. Is this preferable to Rule 59(a), with its reference to what has been done "heretofore"?

Many of the grounds for a new trial are based upon errors committed by the trial judge in the course of trial in the admission or exclusion of evidence, in giving or refusing instructions to the jury, and the like. Ordinarily, the aggrieved party must duly object when the error is committed in order successfully to complain of it later.

The aggrieved party may renew his objection after verdict by a motion for a new trial. If a party moves for a new trial relying upon such an error, the trial judge has an opportunity to reconsider his ruling, which was initially made in the heat of trial and which on reflection and study he may conclude to have been erroneous. Not to allow him to grant a new trial but instead to require the aggrieved party to appeal would be wasteful of time and money.

However, in federal court the aggrieved party is not required to renew his objection by post-verdict motion. If due objection was made at the time of the ruling, there is no necessity to assert the alleged error again as the basis for a motion for a new trial in order to preserve the point for appellate review. See Kiernan v. Van Schaik, 347 F.2d 775 (3d Cir.1965). There are some jurisdictions where the point is lost unless incorporated in a new trial motion, although it is often hard to say whether the motion is simply being made to do service as a kind of assignment of the errors that will be relied upon on appeal instead of being really intended to give the trial judge a chance to correct his error.

There are many other sorts of error in the course of trial that call for a new trial, such as misconduct by participants other than the judge. Incidentally, if an error does not come to light until after verdict—for example, it is disclosed that a party or his counsel communicated improperly with a juror or that a juror made an unauthorized private investigation during the trial—a motion after verdict is the earliest and mandatory means of raising the question.

Question: (2) If it were shown that the party claiming to be aggrieved knew of the episode of juror misconduct before the case was submitted to the jury but deferred raising the question until after suffering an adverse verdict, should he be able to upset the verdict? See Stampofski v. Steffens, 79 Ill. 303 (1875) (no).

————

HARMLESS ERROR

Not every error duly objected to during the course of trial requires a new trial or reversal. See Rule 61 and 28 U.S.C. § 2111; see also Evidence Rule 103(a).

The question of what error in the admission of evidence is deemed prejudicial was long a matter of controversy in the English courts. One attitude is illustrated in the remarks of Chief Justice Tindal in Doe dem. Lord Teynham v. Tyler, 130 Eng.Rep. 1397, 1398 (C.P.1830) (a case where questionable evidence had been admitted and where verdict went for defendant): "But the Court will not close their eyes to the rest of the evidence; and if they see that there is enough, not merely to make the scales hang even, but greatly to preponderate in favour of the Defendant, they will not send the cause to a jury again." The second attitude, originating in the Court of Exchequer, is illustrated by the statement of Baron Parke in Crease v. Barrett, 149 Eng.Rep. 1353, 1359 (Ex.1835) (a case where evidence had been erroneously excluded and where verdict went for plaintiff): "We cannot say, however strong our opinion may be on the propriety of the present verdict, that, if the lease had been received, it would have had no effect with the jury; nor that it is clear beyond all doubt, if the verdict had been for the defendant, that it would have been set aside as improper; and therefore we think that there must be a new trial." The Court of King's Bench sided with the Court of Exchequer. Frederick v. Farr, 111 Eng.Rep. 707 (K.B.1835). Eventually the "Exchequer rule" was disapproved by rules of court issued under the Supreme Court of Judicature Act, 1875, 38 & 39 Vict., ch. 77, sched. 1, O. 39, r. 3. The present similar rule, O. 59, r. 11(2), is as follows: "The Court of Appeal shall not be bound to order a new trial on the ground of misdirection, or of the improper admission or rejection of evidence, or because the verdict of the jury was not taken upon a question which the judge at the trial was not asked to leave to them, unless in the opinion of the Court of Appeal some substantial wrong or miscarriage has been thereby occasioned."

In America too a mere technical mistake not affecting a substantial right is harmless error. Otherwise, error should be reversible unless "the appellate court believes it highly probable that the error did not affect the judgment . . . .. Any test less stringent entails too great a risk of affirming a judgment that was influenced by an error. Moreover, a less stringent test may fail to deter an appellate judge from focusing his inquiry on the correctness of the result and then holding an error harmless whenever he equated the result with his own predilections." R. Traynor, The Riddle of Harmless Error 35 (1970). A more stringent test may apply to errors affecting constitutional rights.

ROJAS v. RICHARDSON

United States Court of Appeals, Fifth Circuit, 1983.
703 F.2d 186, vacated, 713 F.2d 116 (5th Cir.1983).

Before RUBIN, JOHNSON and WILLIAMS, CIRCUIT JUDGES.

JERRE S. WILLIAMS, CIRCUIT JUDGE.

[Plaintiff worked as a ranch hand for defendants. After being thrown by a horse and severely injured, he sued them for negligence and breach of contract in the Eastern District of Texas. During closing argument the defense counsel referred to plaintiff as an "illegal alien," to which plaintiff failed to object. After verdict and judgment for defendants, plaintiff appealed.]

Even if Rojas has waived his right to appeal the use of the phrase "illegal alien," however, this Court is not precluded from reviewing the use of the phrase at trial. Fed.R.Evid. 103(d) provides: "Nothing in this rule [requiring objection to preserve appealability] precludes taking notice of plain errors affecting substantial rights although they were not brought to the attention of the court." Our authority to review, we note, is limited to "plain errors," and the errors must affect "substantial rights." We find that allegations unsupported by the record that Rojas was an illegal alien might well have a serious and negative effect on his substantial right to an impartial jury. The only serious issue is whether the allegations rise to the level of "plain error."

The plain error rule is "not a run-of-the-mill remedy." United States v. Gerald, 624 F.2d 1291, 1299 (5th Cir.1980), cert. denied, 450 U.S. 920, 101 S.Ct. 1369, 67 L.Ed.2d 348 (1981). It is invoked "only in exceptional circumstances to avoid a miscarriage of justice." Eaton v. United States, 398 F.2d 485, 486 (5th Cir.), cert. denied, 393 U.S. 937, 89 S.Ct. 299, 21 L.Ed.2d 273 (1968). The exact delineation of plain error is difficult to articulate. We have defined plain error as error which is "both obvious and substantial." United States v. Gerald, 624 F.2d at 1299; Sykes v. United States, 373 F.2d 607, 612 (5th Cir.1966), cert. denied, 386 U.S. 977, 87 S.Ct. 1172, 18 L.Ed.2d 138 (1967). But such elegant phraseology yields little guidance. The determination still rests ultimately on the facts of each case.

Perhaps the most telling guidelines were laid down by Justice
Stone in 1936, when he wrote:

> In exceptional circumstances, especially in criminal cases, ap-
> pellate courts, in the public interest, may, of their motion, no-
> tice errors to which no exception has been taken, if the errors
> are obvious, or if they otherwise seriously affect the *fairness,
> integrity, or public reputation of judicial proceedings.*

United States v. Atkinson, 297 U.S. 157, 160, 56 S.Ct. 391, 392, 80
L.Ed. 555 (1936) (emphasis added). Following the clarion call of Justice Stone's words, we must hold that the "fairness, integrity, or public reputation" of the proceedings in this case were adversely affected
by the closing jury argument of defense counsel. The closing remarks included this paragraph:

> I hope—I hope—that you don't, because Mr. Rojas is an alien,
> give him any more benefit than you would any United States
> citizen who comes in this Court. If the situation were reversed
> and you or I were in Mexico—were illegal aliens in Mexico—I
> would hope Mexico would open up their Courts, would open up
> their job market, would open up their public schools, would
> open up their State hospitals, as we have in this country for
> Mr. Rojas. Certainly he is—I'm not saying we shouldn't do
> those things, but he shouldn't be entitled to any extra benefits
> because he is an illegal alien in this country than would any
> other citizen of the United States be entitled.

These remarks prejudiced the jury on two counts. First, by introducing irrelevant and unproven allegations that Rojas was an illegal
alien, the defense clearly was appealing to the prejudice and bias of
members of the jury on the basis of national origin. Although there
was justification for presenting Rojas' Mexican citizenship to the jury
to establish diversity jurisdiction, 28 U.S.C. § 1332(a)(2), his status as
an "illegal" alien was completely irrelevant to the negligence claims
the jury was to evaluate. Furthermore, the closing reference to "illegal alien" could have placed a prejudicial gloss on the many references throughout trial to Rojas as an "alien." Having laid a strong
foundation through use of the term "alien" throughout trial, even
counsel's single reference to the incendiary, derogatory expression
"illegal alien" is prejudicial. Finally, the allegation that Rojas was in
the country illegally is unsupported in the record.

. . . . .

Second, these remarks were an impermissible invocation of the
"golden rule" argument. As we recently explained,

> What every lawyer should know is that a plea to the jury that
> they "should put themselves in the shoes of the plaintiff and
> do unto him as they would have done unto them under similar
> circumstances. . . . [is] improper because it encourages
> the jury to depart from neutrality and to decide the case on the

basis of personal interest and bias rather than on the evidence."

Loose v. Offshore Navigation, Inc., 670 F.2d 493, 496 (5th Cir.1982), quoting Ivy v. Security Barge Lines, Inc., 585 F.2d 732, 741 (5th Cir. 1978), rev'd on other grounds, 606 F.2d 524 (5th Cir.1979) (en banc), cert. denied, 446 U.S. 956, 100 S.Ct. 2927, 64 L.Ed.2d 815 (1980). [Other citations omitted.] The fact that the statement in this case was an inverse incantation of this golden rule is insufficient to validate the partiality inherent in the argument. Loose, supra. The "golden rule" argument, while not plain error, is normally ground for new trial. Id.

The closing remarks of defense counsel were highly prejudicial and a blatant appeal to jury bias. Although the district court gave a jury instruction emphasizing equal access to justice, even this instruction was ambiguous. The jury was instructed:

> You are instructed that all persons are equal before the law, and this case should be considered and decided by you as an action between persons of equal standing in the community, of equal worth, and holding the same or similar stations in life. The law is no respector of persons. All persons, including partnerships, and other lawful organizations, stand equal before the law, and are to be dealt with as equals in a Court of Justice.

While its wording might have been adequate to indicate that aliens must be treated equally, it was not adequate to tell the jury that "illegal aliens" are "equal before the law." A jury could readily conclude that someone who is "illegal" is not "equal before the law" to law abiding citizens and jurors. We are not convinced that the jury instruction could rebuild the "fairness, integrity, or public reputation of jury proceedings" that Justice Stone admonished us to protect, see Atkinson, 297 U.S. at 160, 56 S.Ct. at 392. As we first noted in Dunn v. United States, 307 F.2d 883, 887 (5th Cir.1962), "if you throw a skunk into the jury box, you can't instruct the jury not to smell it." Some references are so prejudicial that it is difficult for curative instructions to resuscitate fairness. [Citation omitted.] Even assuming that a proper jury instruction could have cured prejudice, this instruction did not do so.

     .   .   .   .

We have examined other exceptions to the manner in which the trial was conducted and find no further grounds for reversal. There is substantial evidence to support the jury verdict in this case. However, on the basis of the defendants' closing references to Rojas as an "illegal alien" and their appeal to jury prejudice, we must reverse the judgment of the district court and remand for new trial.

Reversed and remanded.

ROJAS v. RICHARDSON, 713 F.2d 116 (5th Cir.1983). On rehearing, a defendant supplemented the record with the transcript of the proceedings on voir dire, which showed that for tactical reasons the plaintiff's attorney had then made known to prospective jurors the plaintiff's status as an "illegal alien." In view of the jury's knowledge, the court could no longer conclude that the defense counsel's "highly prejudicial" closing argument was so prejudicial as to be plain error. Therefore, the court set aside its earlier decision and affirmed the district court's judgment.

Questions: (3) In his closing argument, plaintiff's counsel said: "I do not ask for a verdict for my client because he is a poor man, nor because the city [defendant] is rich and powerful. I only ask for a verdict if he is entitled to one under the law and the evidence." After verdict for the plaintiff, is a new trial warranted? See Gilman v. City of Laconia, 71 N.H. 212, 51 A. 631 (1902) (no, the "disproportion in power and resource being already before the jury"); cf. Curtis Publishing Co. v. Butts, 351 F.2d 702 (5th Cir.1965), aff'd on other grounds, 388 U.S. 130, 87 S.Ct. 1975 (1967).

(4) Should incompetence of counsel, as distinguished from misconduct, be a ground for a new trial in a civil action? See Everett v. Everett, 319 Mich. 475, 29 N.W.2d 919 (1947) (counsel, apparently unaware of the Dead Man's Act and of the best evidence rule, was blocked on the first day of trial by objections on these grounds; on opening of court the next day, he consented to a dismissal of the action with prejudice; no new trial).

EVIDENCE RULINGS IN NONJURY CASES

Errors in the admission or exclusion of evidence in trials without a jury are viewed in a unique light. See McCormick's Handbook of the Law of Evidence 137–38 (2d ed. E. Cleary 1972). Consider the remarks of the court in Builders Steel Co. v. Commissioner, 179 F.2d 377, 379 (8th Cir.1950):

"In the trial of a nonjury case, it is virtually impossible for a trial judge to commit reversible error by receiving incompetent evidence, whether objected to or not. An appellate court will not reverse a judgment in a nonjury case because of the admission of incompetent evidence, unless all of the competent evidence is insufficient to support the judgment or unless it affirmatively appears that the incompetent evidence induced the court to make an essential finding which would not otherwise have been made. Thompson v. Carley, 8 Cir., 140 F.2d 656, 660; Doering v. Buechler, 8 Cir., 146 F.2d 784, 786; Grandin Grain & Seed Co. v. United States, 8 Cir., 170 F.2d 425, 427. On the other hand, a trial judge who, in the trial of a nonjury case, attempts to make strict rulings on the admissibility of evidence, can easily get his decision reversed by excluding evidence which is objected to, but which, on review, the appellate court believes should have been admitted. In the case of Donnelly Garment Co. v. National Labor Relations Board, 8 Cir., 123 F.2d 215, 224, we stated our views upon this subject as follows: ' . . . We think that experience has demonstrated that in a trial or hearing where no jury is present, more time is ordinarily lost in listening to arguments as to the admissibility of evidence and in considering offers of proof than would be consumed in taking the evidence proffered, and that, even if the trier of facts, by making close rulings upon the admissibility of evidence, does save himself some time, that saving will be more than offset by the time consumed by the reviewing court in considering the propriety of his rulings and by the consequent delay in the final determination of the controversy. One who is capable of ruling accurately upon the admissibility of evidence is equally capable of sifting it accurately after it has been received, and, since he will base his findings upon the evidence which he regards as competent, material and convincing, he cannot be injured by the presence in the record of testimony which he does not consider competent or material. Lawyers and judges frequently differ as to the admissibility of evidence, and it occasionally happens that a reviewing court regards as admissible evidence which was rejected by the judge, special master, or trial examiner. If the record on review contains not only all evidence which was clearly admissible, but also all evidence of doubtful admissibility, the court which is called upon to review the case can usually make an end of it, whereas if evidence was excluded which that court regards as having been admissible, a new trial or rehearing cannot be avoided. We say this in the hope of preventing a repetition of what occurred in the case now before us, and to obviate any misunderstanding as to what the attitude of this Court is with respect to the taking of evidence in a hearing before a special master or a trial examiner.' "

SECTION 2.   JURY'S ERROR IN WEIGHING EVIDENCE

Assuming that the state of the evidence is such as to survive a motion for a directed verdict, whatever the standard be in the jurisdiction, a party may still seek to have the resulting verdict set aside as against the weight of the evidence. The standards for the exercise of the trial judge's discretion in passing upon a motion for a new trial on this ground are not uniform. For the federal courts the formulation, from a much-cited opinion by Judge Parker, Garrison v. United States, 62 F.2d 41, 42 (4th Cir.1932), is as follows:

"Where there is substantial evidence in support of plaintiff's case, the judge may not direct a verdict against him, even though he may not believe his evidence or may think that the weight of the evidence is on the other side; for, under the constitutional guaranty of trial by jury, it is for the jury to weigh the evidence and pass upon its credibility. He may, however, set aside a verdict supported by substantial evidence where in his opinion it is contrary to the clear weight of the

[handwritten margin notes: Fed Test. / Judge can set aside verdict on even if supported by subst. evid. if aga. clear weight of evid.]

evidence, or is based upon evidence which is false; for, even though the evidence be sufficient to preclude the direction of a verdict, it is still his duty to exercise his power over the proceedings before him to prevent a miscarriage of justice. [Citation omitted.] Verdict can be directed only where there is no substantial evidence to support recovery by the party against whom it is directed or where the evidence is all against him or so overwhelmingly so as to leave no room to doubt what the fact is. [Citation omitted.] Verdict may be set aside and new trial granted when the verdict is contrary to the clear weight of the evidence, or whenever in the exercise of a sound discretion the trial judge thinks this action necessary to prevent a miscarriage of justice."

[handwritten margin notes: state cts usu. follow fed test]

The federal test as thus stated is followed in substance by most state courts. But there are two other basic patterns put thus in F. James & G. Hazard, Civil Procedure 319–20 (2d ed. 1977):

[handwritten margin notes: 2 other patterns; 1. Judge's discretion not abused if any evid. to support set aside. 2 Can't set aside if evid. presented & in pleadings jury could reason. find what they did.]

"(1) In some states, the trial court has a genuine and well-nigh unfettered discretion which will not be deemed abused 'where there is any evidence which would support a judgment in favor of the moving party.' Here the trial court is indeed invited to act as a 'thirteenth juror.' (2) In some states, the trial court is forbidden to set aside a verdict if 'on the evidence as presented and under the pleadings, the jury could reasonably have found in accordance with the verdict as rendered.' Even these jurisdictions say the trial judge has discretion to order a new trial but it is clear that if the term has any meaning here at all it is a far narrower discretion than that of the trial judge in the first group of states described. The test for new trial is phrased and administered in such a way that it very nearly approaches the test for directed verdict, though the two are perhaps not exactly equated."

Verdicts are frequently challenged as against the weight of the evidence on the issue of the amount of damages. In addition to the case where a new trial is required because of prejudicial error in the instructions on damages, the trial judge has discretion to grant a new trial because of either the excessiveness or the inadequacy of the verdict. The practice of granting new trials on the ground of excessiveness of the verdict goes far back in the common law. See, e.g., Wood v. Gunston, 82 Eng.Rep. 864 (K.B.1655). New trials because of inadequacy of the verdict were a later development in England, but the power to grant a new trial on this ground has long been settled both in England and in this country. See Wilson, The Motion for New Trial Based on Inadequacy of Damages Awarded, 39 Neb.L.Rev. 694 (1960). When the damages are unliquidated, as in the typical action in tort for personal injuries, the question is raised as to how to formulate the standard that the trial judge should apply in reviewing the decision of the jury in fixing the damages, as is also the question, discussed in the following cases, of what the trial judge may do to eliminate the need for a new trial or to limit its scope.

[handwritten: What trial judge may do to eliminate or limit need for new trial.]

DIMICK v. SCHIEDT
Supreme Court of the United States, 1935.
293 U.S. 474, 55 S.Ct. 296.

MR. JUSTICE SUTHERLAND delivered the opinion of the Court.

This is an action brought by respondent (plaintiff) against petitioner (defendant) in the federal district court for the district of Massachusetts to recover damages for a personal injury resulting from the alleged negligent operation of an automobile on a public highway in Massachusetts. The jury returned a verdict in favor of respondent for the sum of $500. Respondent moved for a new trial on the grounds that the verdict was contrary to the weight of the evidence, that it was a compromise verdict, and that the damages allowed were inadequate. The trial court ordered a new trial upon the last named ground, unless petitioner would consent to an increase of the damages to the sum of $1500. Respondent's consent was neither required nor given. Petitioner, however, consented to the increase, and in accordance with the order of the court a denial of the motion for new trial automatically followed. Respondent appealed to the circuit court of appeals, where the judgment was reversed, the court holding that the conditional order violated the Seventh Amendment of the Federal Constitution in respect of the right of trial by jury. 70 F.2d 558. That court recognized the doctrine, frequently stated by this court, that in the case of an excessive verdict, it is within the power of the trial court to grant defendant's motion for a new trial unless plaintiff remit the amount deemed to be excessive, but held that the trial court was without power to condition the allowance of plaintiff's motion for a new trial upon the refusal of defendant to consent to an increase in the amount of damages.

[handwritten margin notes: Jury for (P) $500 / (P) moves for new trial / Trial ct. says OK unless (P) agrees to ↑ to $1500 / ((P) has no choice) / (D) agrees / Motion new trial denied / App. ct.: Conditional order violate 7th Am. - right to trial by jury]

[The Court here quoted the seventh amendment and the statutory predecessor of Rule 59(a)(1).]

In order to ascertain the scope and meaning of the Seventh Amendment, resort must be had to the appropriate rules of the common law established at the time of the adoption of that constitutional provision in 1791. Thompson v. Utah, 170 U.S. 343, 350, 18 S.Ct. 620; Patton v. United States, 281 U.S. 276, 288, 50 S.Ct. 253. A careful examination of the English reports prior to that time fails to disclose any authoritative decision sustaining the power of an English court to increase, either absolutely or conditionally, the amount fixed by the verdict of a jury in an action at law, with certain exceptions.

[handwritten margin note: To see meaning of 7th, look at CL at 1791]

[The Court's discussion of the English cases is omitted.]

From the foregoing and from many other English authorities which we have examined but deem it unnecessary to cite, we conclude that, while there was some practice to the contrary in respect of _decreasing_ damages, the established practice and the rule of the com-

[handwritten margin notes: Eng. Then: CL said sometimes could ↓ damages — forbid ↑ damages]

mon law, as it existed in England at the time of the adoption of the Constitution, forbade the court to *increase* the amount of damages awarded by a jury in actions such as that here under consideration.

[handwritten margin notes: Our CL: deny new trial if (P) agrees to ↓ damages decision by Story]

We could well rest this opinion upon that conclusion, were it not for the contention that our federal courts from a very early day have upheld the authority of a trial court to deny a motion for new trial because damages were found to be excessive, if plaintiff would consent to remit the excessive amount, and that this holding requires us to recognize a similar rule in respect of increasing damages found to be grossly inadequate. There is a decision by Mr. Justice Story, sitting on circuit, authorizing such a remittitur, as early as 1822. Blunt v. Little, Fed.Cas. No. 1,578, 3 Mason 102. There, the jury returned a verdict for $2,000 damages, suffered as a result of a malicious arrest. Defendant moved for a new trial on the ground that the damages were excessive. The court asserted its power to grant a new trial upon that ground, but directed that the cause should be submitted to another jury unless plaintiff was willing to remit $500 of the damages. This view of the matter was accepted by this Court in Northern Pacific R. Co. v. Herbert, 116 U.S. 642, 646–7, 6 S.Ct. 590, and has been many times reiterated. [Citations omitted.]

Since the decision of Mr. Justice Story in 1822, this court has never expressed doubt in respect of the rule, and it has been uniformly applied by the lower federal courts. It is, however, remarkable that in none of these cases was there any real attempt to ascertain the common law rule on the subject. . . .

. . . . .

In the last analysis, the sole support for the decisions of this court and that of Mr. Justice Story, so far as they are pertinent to cases like that now in hand, must rest upon the practice of some of the English judges—a practice which has been condemned as opposed to the principles of the common law by every reasoned English decision, both before and after the adoption of the Federal Constitution, which we have been able to find.

[handwritten margin notes: Will still allow ↓ damages today]

In the light reflected by the foregoing review of the English decisions and commentators, it, therefore, may be that if the question of remittitur were now before us for the first time, it would be decided otherwise. But, first announced by Mr. Justice Story in 1822, the doctrine has been accepted as the law for more than a hundred years and uniformly applied in the federal courts during that time. And, as it finds some support in the practice of the English courts prior to the adoption of the Constitution, we may assume that in a case involving a remittitur, which this case does not, the doctrine would not be reconsidered or disturbed at this late day.

Nevertheless, this court in a very special sense is charged with the duty of construing and upholding the Constitution; and in the discharge of that important duty, it ever must be alert to see that a doubtful precedent be not extended by mere analogy to a different case if the result will be to weaken or subvert what it conceives to be a principle of the fundamental law of the land. Compare Judson v. Gray, 11 N.Y. 408, 412.

. . . .

The controlling distinction between the power of the court and that of the jury is that the former is the power to determine the law and the latter to determine the facts. In dealing with questions like the one now under consideration, that distinction must be borne steadily in mind. Where the verdict returned by a jury is palpably and grossly inadequate or excessive, it should not be permitted to stand; but in that event, both parties remain entitled, as they were entitled in the first instance, to have a jury properly determine the question of liability and the extent of the injury by an assessment of damages. Both are questions of fact. Where the verdict is excessive, the practice of substituting a remission of the excess for a new trial is not without plausible support in the view that what remains is included in the verdict along with the unlawful excess—in that sense that it has been found by the jury—and that the remittitur has the effect of merely lopping off an excrescence. But where the verdict is too small, an increase by the court is a bald addition of something which in no sense can be said to be included in the verdict. When, therefore, the trial court here found that the damages awarded by the jury were so inadequate as to entitle plaintiff to a new trial, how can it be held, with any semblance of reason, that the court, with the consent of the defendant only, may, by assessing an additional amount of damages, bring the constitutional right of the plaintiff to a jury trial to an end in respect of a matter of fact which no jury has ever passed upon either explicitly or by implication? To so hold is obviously to compel the plaintiff to forego his constitutional right to the verdict of a jury and accept "an assessment partly made by a jury which has acted improperly, and partly by a tribunal which has no power to assess." [a]

It is said that the common law is susceptible of growth and adaptation to new circumstances and situations, and that the courts have power to declare and effectuate what is the present rule in respect of a given subject without regard to the old rule; and some attempt is made to apply that principle here. The common law is not immutable, but flexible, and upon its own principles adapts itself to varying conditions. Funk v. United States, 290 U.S. 371, 54 S.Ct. 212. But here, we are dealing with a constitutional provision which has in effect adopted the rules of the common law, in respect of trial by jury, as these rules existed in 1791. To effectuate any change in these rules is not to deal with the common law, qua common law, but to alter the Constitution. The distinction is fundamental, and has been

[a] The Court was here repeating a quotation from Lionel Barber & Co. v. Deutsche Bank, [1919] A.C. 304, 335, which was set forth in the omitted portion of the opinion.

clearly pointed out by Judge Cooley in 1 Const.Limitations, 8th ed., 124.

It is worthy of note that while for more than a century the federal courts have followed the approved practice of conditioning the allowance of a new trial on the consent of plaintiff to remit excessive damages, no federal court, so far as we can discover, has ever undertaken similarly to increase the damages, although there are numerous cases where motions for new trial have been made and granted on the ground that the verdict was inadequate. [Citations omitted.] This, it is true, is but negative evidence; but it is negative evidence of more than ordinary value. For, when we consider that during the great length of time mentioned, the federal courts were constantly applying the rule in respect of the remission of excessive damages, the circumstance that the practice here in question in respect of inadequate damages was never followed or, apparently, its approval even suggested, seems highly significant as indicating a lack of judicial belief in the existence of the power.

State decisions in respect of the matter have been brought to our attention and have received consideration. They embody rulings both ways. A review of them we think would serve no useful purpose.

Judgment affirmed.

MR. JUSTICE STONE, dissenting.

I think the judgment should be reversed.

What the trial court has done is to deny a motion for a new trial, for what seemed to it a good reason: that the defendant had given his binding consent to an increased recovery, which the court thought to be adequate, and thus to remove any substantial ground for awarding a new trial. . . . .

. . . . .

The decision of the Court is rested on the ground that the Constitution prohibits the trial judge from adopting the practice. Accordingly, I address myself to the question of power without stopping to comment on the generally recognized advantages of the practice as a means of securing substantial justice and bringing the litigation to a more speedy and economical conclusion than would be possible by a new trial to a jury, or the extent to which that or analogous practice has been adopted and found useful in the courts of the several states. See Correction of Damage Verdicts by Remittitur and Additur, 44 Yale Law J. 318. The question is a narrow one: whether there is anything in the Seventh Amendment or in the rules of the common law, as it had developed before the adoption of the Amendment, which would require a federal appellate court to set aside the denial of the motion merely because the particular reasons which moved the trial judge to deny it are not shown to have similarly moved any English judge before 1791.

The Seventh Amendment commands that "in suits at common law," the right to trial by jury shall be preserved and that "no fact tried by a jury shall be otherwise re-examined by any court of the United States, than according to the rules of the common law." Such a provision of a great instrument of government, intended to endure for unnumbered generations, is concerned with substance and not with form. There is nothing in its history or language to suggest that the Amendment had any purpose but to preserve the essentials of the jury trial as it was known to the common law before the adoption of the Constitution.[b] For that reason this Court has often refused to construe it as intended to perpetuate in changeless form the minutiae of trial practice as it existed in the English courts in 1791. From the beginning, its language has been regarded as but subservient to the single purpose of the Amendment, to preserve the essentials of the jury trial in actions at law, serving to distinguish them from suits in equity and admiralty, see Parsons v. Bedford, 3 Pet. 433, 446, and to safeguard the jury's function from any encroachment which the common law did not permit.

[margin handwritten notes:] 7th Am. written to preserve essentials of right to jury — not to be changeless

Thus interpreted, the Seventh Amendment guarantees that suitors in actions at law shall have the benefits of trial of issues of fact by a jury, but it does not prescribe any particular procedure by which these benefits shall be obtained, or forbid any which does not curtail the function of the jury to decide questions of fact as it did before the adoption of the Amendment. It does not restrict the court's control of the jury's verdict, as it had previously been exercised, and it does not confine the trial judge, in determining what issues are for the jury and what for the court, to the particular forms of trial practice in vogue in 1791.

Thus this Court has held that a federal court, without the consent of the parties, may constitutionally appoint auditors to hear testimony, examine books and accounts and frame and report upon issues of

[b] See Henderson, The Background of the Seventh Amendment, 80 Harv.L.Rev. 289, 336–37 (1966):

"Neither during the ratification controversy nor in the subsequent proceedings on adoption of the Bill of Rights was any specific consensus expressed on the relation of judge to jury in civil cases. On the contrary, while there was agreement that civil juries in a general way were a good thing, the great diversity of practice in the thirteen states was referred to as a reason why no uniform constitutional rule was possible. This diversity, moreover, seems unquestionably to have been a principal reason why the seventh amendment was drafted in such general terms."

One possible way of construing the constitutional provision "is the one which the Supreme Court has followed, on the whole, in preserving the substance of the common law trial by jury and particularly the jury's power to decide serious questions of fact, while allowing rational modifications of procedure in the interests of efficiency. The whole thrust of the history of jury practice, both before and after 1790, has been toward rationality of decision and economy of motion in the courtroom. It is possible to argue for or against the merits of any particular procedural change. But considering the diversity of practice that lies behind the seventh amendment, it seems both unnecessary and undesirable to read that amendment as imposing any but the most general limitations on the Court's power to make such procedural changes."

fact, as an aid to the jury in arriving at its verdict, Ex parte Peterson, 253 U.S. 300, 40 S.Ct. 543; it may require both a general and a special verdict and set aside the general verdict for the plaintiff and direct a verdict for the defendant on the basis of the facts specially found, Walker v. New Mexico & Southern Pacific R. Co., 165 U.S. 593, 17 S.Ct. 421; and it may accept so much of the verdict as declares that the plaintiff is entitled to recover, and set aside so much of it as fixes the amount of the damages, and order a new trial of that issue alone, Gasoline Products Co. v. Champlin Refining Co., 283 U.S. 494, 51 S.Ct. 513. Yet none of these procedures was known to the common law. In fact, the very practice, so firmly imbedded in federal procedure, of making a motion for a new trial directly to the trial judge, instead of to the court en banc, was never adopted by the common law. But this Court has found in the Seventh Amendment no bar to the adoption by the federal courts of these novel methods of dealing with the verdict of a jury, for they left unimpaired the function of the jury, to decide issues of fact, which it had exercised before the adoption of the Amendment. Compare Nashville, C. & St. L.R. Co. v. Wallace, 288 U.S. 249, 264, 53 S.Ct. 345.

If we apply that test to the present case it is evident that the jury's function has not been curtailed. After the issues of fact had been submitted to the jury, and its verdict taken, the trial judge was authorized to entertain a motion to set aside the verdict and, as an incident, to determine the legal limits of a proper verdict. A denial of the motion out of hand, however inadequate the verdict, was not an encroachment upon the province of the jury as the common law defined it. It would seem not to be any the more so here because the exercise of the judge's discretion was affected by his knowledge of the fact that a proper recovery had been assured to the plaintiff by the consent of the defendant. Thus the plaintiff has suffered no infringement of a right by the denial of his motion. The defendant has suffered none because he has consented to the increased recovery, of which he does not complain.

. . . .

. . . The fact that in one case the recovery is less than the amount of the verdict [remittitur], and that in the other it is greater [additur], would seem to be without significance. For in neither does the jury return a verdict for the amount actually recovered, and in both the amount of recovery was fixed, not by the verdict but by the consent of the party resisting the motion for a new trial.

The question with which we are now concerned—what considerations shall govern an appellate review of this discretionary action of the trial court—is one unknown to the common law, which provided for no such review. We are afforded but a meager and fragmentary guide if our review is to be controlled by the Seventh Amendment, read as though it had incorporated by reference the particular details of English trial practice exhibited by the law books in 1791. . . .

If our only guide is to be this scant record of the practice of controlling the jury's verdict, however fragmentary the state of its development at this period, and if we must deny any possibility of change, development or improvement, then it must be admitted that search of the legal scrap heap of a century and a half ago may commit us to the incongruous position in which we are left by the present decision: a federal trial court may deny a motion for a new trial where the plaintiff consents to decrease the judgment to a proper amount, but it is powerless to deny the motion if its judgment is influenced by the defendant's consent to a comparable increase in the recovery.

But I cannot agree that we are circumscribed by so narrow and rigid a conception of the common law. The Judiciary Act of 1789, c. 20, 1 Stat. 73, which impliedly adopted the common law rules of evidence for criminal trials in federal courts, and which gave to the federal courts jurisdiction of equity as it had then been developed in England, and the state constitutions which adopted the common law as affording rules for judicial decision, have never been construed as accepting only those rules which could then be found in the English precedents. When the Constitution was adopted, the common law was something more than a miscellaneous collection of precedents. It was a system, then a growth of some five centuries, to guide judicial decision. One of its principles, certainly as important as any other, and that which assured the possibility of the continuing vitality and usefulness of the system, was its capacity for growth and development, and its adaptability to every new situation to which it might be needful to apply it. "This flexibility and capacity for growth and adaptation is," as the Court declared in Hurtado v. California, 110 U.S. 516, 530, 4 S.Ct. 111, "the peculiar boast and excellence of the common law." [Citations omitted.]

. . . .

THE CHIEF JUSTICE, MR. JUSTICE BRANDEIS and MR. JUSTICE CARDOZO concur.[c]

AMOUNT OF THE REMITTITUR

How does the trial judge determine the amount of the remittitur? The answer to this question is not often spelled out in the cases, and the courts that have faced it have not all taken the same view.

In Glazer v. Glazer, 278 F.Supp. 476, 482 (E.D.La.1968), approved in Gorsalitz v. Olin Mathieson Chemical Corp., 429 F.2d 1033 (5th Cir. 1970), the court held that reduction of the verdict by remittitur should

[c] Remittitur is an almost universal feature of practice in the state courts. In some states additur is also recognized; of course, Dimick v. Schiedt is not controlling in the interpretation of state constitutions and laws. See, e.g., Freeman v. Wood, 379 Mass. 777, 401 N.E.2d 108 (1980) (Kaplan, J.). In England today there is a quite restrictive provision for both remittitur and additur. O. 59, r. 11(4).

Remitters:

1. Only to highest amt. jury could properly award.

be "only to the highest amount that the jury could properly have awarded." Professors Wright and Miller favor this "maximum recovery" rule. 11 Wright & Miller § 2815.

2. Ct. should be just rather than generous.

In Rosa v. American Oil Co., 129 Conn. 585, 30 A.2d 385 (1943), the trial judge ordered a remittitur of $2350 from a verdict of $6000. He said: "In my judgment, a fair verdict in this case would have been $2,500, and one of $3,650 the limit of legitimate generosity." On appeal, the Connecticut Supreme Court of Errors held that the remittitur should have been $3500, saying that "in fixing the amount a court should be just rather than generous." Similarly, Cal.Civ.Proc.Code § 662.5(b) provides for remittitur in the amount that "the court in its independent judgment determines from the evidence to be fair and reasonable." Professor Moore favors this approach. 6A Moore ¶ 59.08[7].

3. Lowest amt. properly award by jury

In Meissner v. Papas, 35 F.Supp. 676 (E.D.Wis.1940), aff'd, 124 F.2d 720 (7th Cir.1941), the court adopted the standard that the remittitur should reduce the verdict to the lowest amount that could properly be found by the jury. Does not this neglected "minimum recovery" rule—or, to reformulate, remitting on the defendant's new trial motion to the lowest amount that could withstand a new trial motion by the plaintiff—have the most to be said for it? Does it not seem fairest to both parties to offer the plaintiff the choice of a new trial or a recovery rather favorable to the defendant, most effective in encouraging the parties to settle for a just amount, and actually least intrusive on the parties' jury rights? See also Durant v. Surety Homes Corp., 582 F.2d 1081 (7th Cir.1978).

GASOLINE PRODUCTS CO. v. CHAMPLIN REFINING CO., 283 U.S. 494, 51 S.Ct. 513 (1931). In an action in the District of Maine brought to recover royalties due on a license to use certain "cross cracking units," defendant counterclaimed for breach by plaintiff of a contract to construct a "cross vapor treating tower" for treatment of the gasoline produced by the cracking units. The jury returned a verdict for the plaintiff on its claim and for the defendant on its counterclaim.

Ct. App. says new trial on damages in c'claim.

On appeal by defendant attacking the disposition of the counterclaim, the First Circuit reversed because of errors in the court's charge on the measure of damages on the counterclaim, and it directed a new trial limited to the amount of those damages. The Supreme Court granted certiorari, on plaintiff's petition, to review the question whether the court below erred in thus limiting the new trial. Regarding the constitutional problem, the Court said:

"It is true that at common law there was no practice of setting aside a verdict in part. If the verdict was erroneous with respect to any issue, a new trial was directed as to all. This continued to be the rule in some states after the adoption of the Constitution; but in many it has not been followed, notwithstanding the presence in their constitutions of provisions preserving trial by jury. The Massachusetts courts early modified it to permit a new trial of less than all the issues of fact when they were clearly separable. Bicknell v. Dorion, 16 Pick. 478; see Simmons v. Fish, 210 Mass. 563, 565, 97 N.E. 102. The rule as thus modified has been generally accepted in the New England states, see Zaleski v. Clark, 45 Conn. 397, 404; McKay v. New England Dredging Co., 93 Maine 201, 44 A. 614; Lisbon v. Lyman, 49 N.H. 553, 582 et seq.; Clark v. New York, N.H. & H.R. Co., 33 R.I. 83, 80 A. 406; Parizo v. Wilson, 101 Vt. 514, 144 A. 856, and consistently followed by the Court of Appeals for the First Circuit.

"Lord Mansfield, in applying the common law rule where the verdict, correct as to one issue, was erroneous as to another, said: '. . . for form's sake, we must set aside the whole verdict . . . .' Edie v. East India Co., 1 W.Bl. 295, 298.[d] But we are not now concerned with the form of the ancient rule. It is the Constitution which we are to interpret; and the Constitution is concerned, not with form, but with substance. All of vital significance in trial by jury is that issues of fact be submitted for determination with such instructions and guidance by the court as will afford opportunity for that consideration by the jury which was secured by the rules governing trials at common law. See Herron v. Southern Pacific Co., [283 U.S.] 91, 51 S.Ct. 383. Beyond this, the Seventh Amendment does not exact the retention of old forms of procedure. See Walker v. New Mexico & Southern Pacific R. Co., 165 U.S. 593, 596, 17 S.Ct. 421. It does not prohibit the introduction of new methods for ascertaining what facts are in issue, see Ex parte Peterson, 253 U.S. 300, 309, 40 S.Ct. 543, or require that an issue once correctly determined, in accordance with the constitutional command, be tried a second time, even though justice demands that another distinct issue, because erroneously determined, must again be passed on by a jury.

"If, in the present case, the jury has found, in accordance with the applicable legal rules, the amount due to petitioner on the contract for royalties and all the elements fixing its liability on the treating plant contract, there is no constitutional requirement that those issues should again be sent to a jury, merely because the exigencies of the litigation require that a separable issue be tried again."

However, the Court warned: "Where the practice permits a partial new trial, it may not properly be resorted to unless it clearly appears that the issue to be retried is so distinct and separable from the others that the trial of it alone may be had without injustice." As the record showed a dispute regarding the extent of the plaintiff's obligation under the contract that was the subject of the counterclaim, as well as on the dates of that contract's formation and breach which bore on the defendant's duty to minimize damages, the Court concluded that "the question of damages on the counterclaim is so interwo-

---

[d] A partial new trial is now permitted in England by rule of court. O. 59, r. 11(3).

ven with that of liability that the former cannot be submitted to the
jury independently of the latter without confusion and uncertainty,
which would amount to a denial of a fair trial. [Citation omitted.]
There should be a new trial of all the issues raised by the counterclaim."

————

Questions: (5) Is it appropriate to limit the grant of a new trial because
of an excessive verdict to the issue of damages alone (a) if there was error in
the instructions on damages? (b) if the instructions on damages were proper?

(6) Would your answers be different if a new trial is granted because of
inadequate damages? Compare Rosa v. City of Chester, 278 F.2d 876 (3d
Cir.1960), with Simmons v. Fish, 210 Mass. 563, 97 N.E. 102 (1912).

————

AKERMANIS v. SEA–LAND SERVICE, INC. 688 F.2d 898 (2d
Cir.1982), cert. denied, 103 S.Ct. 2087 (1983). An injured seaman sued
the shipowner under the Jones Act. By special verdict, the jury
found that defendant had been negligent, its negligence had been a
proximate cause of the accident, plaintiff had suffered $528,000 in
damages, and plaintiff had been contributorily negligent to the extent
of four per cent responsibility. On defendant's motion, the trial
judge found that this percentage was against the weight of the evidence and "that the lowest contributory negligence factor the evidence would support was 25 percent. He therefore ordered a new
trial on liability issues, but with the condition that the defendant's
motion for new trial would be denied if the plaintiff would accept a
'remittitur' of damages based on an increase of the contributory negligence factor from four to 25 percent. The plaintiff accepted, and
judgment was entered in favor of the plaintiff for 75% of the jury's
determination of the total amount of damages suffered." Defendant
appealed, and plaintiff cross-appealed.

The court of appeals found this use of remittitur to be unconstitutional under Dimick. It then remanded the case for the trial judge's
reconsideration of the new trial motion because it was not clear that
he had applied the correct standard, and the court indicated that a
new trial could be limited to the existence and extent of contributory
negligence.

————

SECTION 3. NEWLY DISCOVERED EVIDENCE

In Marshall's U.S. Auto Supply, Inc. v. Cashman, 111 F.2d 140,
142 (10th Cir.), cert. denied, 311 U.S. 667, 61 S.Ct. 26 (1940), the court
said: "A motion for new trial on the ground of newly discovered evidence must show that the evidence was discovered since the trial;
must show facts from which the court may infer reasonable diligence

on the part of the movant; must show that the evidence is not merely cumulative or impeaching; must show that it is material; and must show that it is of such character that on a new trial such evidence will probably produce a different result." The requirements set forth in this case, along with the implicit requirement that the evidence must pertain to facts existing at the time of trial, generally prevail in both federal and state courts.

See Rules 59(b) and 60(b) for the time limits on asking for a new trial based on newly discovered evidence. A motion under Rule 59 suspends the running of the time for appeal; a motion under Rule 60(b)(2) does not affect the finality of the judgment for purposes of appeal. However, the same standard for relief on the ground of newly discovered evidence generally applies under both Rules, although as time passes the likelihood of relief decreases.

The requirement that the evidence must be newly discovered (after the trial) is an obvious one, and the necessity of a showing of reasonable diligence by the moving party is no less so. It would be intolerable to let a party be casual and careless in his preparation for trial and then, after he has lost, grant him a new trial on the basis of post-trial effort that could readily have been made before.

Question: (7) Should a motion for a new trial be denied for lack of diligence upon a showing that the moving party could have ascertained the substance of the testimony of an opponent's witness, which surprised him at trial, if he had made full use of discovery procedures? Cf. Krock v. Electric Motor & Repair Co., 339 F.2d 73 (1st Cir.1964).

Many cases hold that a new trial should not be granted if the newly discovered evidence is merely cumulative, e.g., Johnson v. United States, 270 F.2d 488 (9th Cir.1959), or impeaching, e.g., Davis v. Yellow Cab Co., 220 F.2d 790 (5th Cir.1955), or is not material, e.g., Kodekey Electronics, Inc. v. Mechanex Corp., 486 F.2d 449 (10th Cir. 1973).

Questions: (8) Assume that the only witnesses at the trial of an automobile negligence case were the plaintiff and the defendant, who told diametrically different stories. Is the newly discovered evidence of a disinterested witness supporting the testimony of one of the parties "merely cumulative or impeaching" for the purposes of a new trial motion?

(9) At the trial of a personal-injury action, the defendant put in evidence films ostensibly showing the plaintiff doing manual labor inconsistent with his claim of disability. After verdict for the plaintiff, should a new trial motion be granted on the basis of additional film taken after the trial that showed the plaintiff engaged in heavy lifting and other types of laborious work? See Great Am. Indem. Co. v. Brown, 307 F.2d 306 (5th Cir.1962) (no).

The probability that the new trial would produce a different result is emphasized in the cases. But the mere fact that the new evidence would justify a different verdict is commonly not considered enough. As a practical matter the motion is usually denied unless the trial judge has an abiding feeling that injustice has plainly resulted.

In Wagner v. Loup River Public Power District, 150 Neb. 7, 33 N.W.2d 300 (1948), an action to recover damages to riparian lands from the diversion of water by the defendant, an expert testified as to his opinion of what would happen to the ground water level in the future. Subsequent events proving him wrong were relied upon as a basis for a new trial on the ground of newly discovered evidence. The trial judge granted the new trial motion, and the appellate court reversed for abuse of discretion.

In Louisville & Nashville Railroad v. Whitley County Court, 100 Ky. 413, 38 S.W. 678 (1897), the plaintiff recovered a $10,000 judgment against the railroad for a sliding of earth away from a highway, allegedly caused by the location of a railroad bed on the side of a hill below the highway. Evidence at trial was to the effect that the sliding could not be stopped without the expenditure of at least that amount. The railroad moved for a new trial on a showing that after the trial the plaintiff had actually cured the situation by an expenditure of $200 or $300 for laying pipes under the highway so as to conduct away the water of a spring previously hidden. The trial court denied the motion, saying that the evidence was not "newly discovered evidence." On appeal, the denial was reversed as an abuse of discretion.

Question: (10) What differences do you perceive between the two cases? Do they justify different results? Cf. Rule 60(b)(5) and (6).

In both of these cases, the action of the trial judge was upset for abuse of discretion. It should be emphasized, however, that the trial judge's discretion is very broad and reversals for abuse are rare.

SECTION 4. APPELLATE REVIEW OF GRANT OR DENIAL OF NEW TRIAL

FAIRMOUNT GLASS WORKS v. CUB FORK COAL CO.
Supreme Court of the United States, 1933.
287 U.S. 474, 53 S.Ct. 252.

Mr. Justice Brandeis delivered the opinion of the Court.

Cub Fork Coal Company and Paragon Colliery Company brought this action in the federal court for southern Indiana to recover from Fairmount Glass Works $32,417, with interest, as damages for breach of a contract to purchase 17,500 tons of coal, at $6.50 per ton f.o.b. mines, deliverable in twelve monthly installments beginning June, 1920. Jurisdiction of the federal court was invoked on the ground of diversity of citizenship. The Glass Works pleaded in bar several defenses; and it also set up a counterclaim in the sum of $2,000 as damages for failure to make delivery as provided by the contract.[e] Three trials before a jury were had. At each of the first two the verdict was for the defendant; and each time the judgment entered thereupon was reversed by the Circuit Court of Appeals with a general direction for a new trial, 19 F.2d 273; 33 F.2d 420. On the third trial the plaintiffs recovered a verdict for $1; and, after further proceedings, judgment was entered thereon with costs.

The plaintiffs appealed to the Circuit Court of Appeals "for the reasons set forth in the assignment of errors." The errors assigned were the failure to give eleven requested instructions. Nine instructions sought related solely to the question of liability. None of the instructions requested and refused related to the measure of damages. But the first asked for a directed verdict for $42,773.50, and the second asked that if a verdict were rendered for the plaintiffs the damages be set at $42,773.50. The charge given was not otherwise excepted to. It had appeared at the trial that after receiving in installments about 6,330 tons of coal, the defendant refused, on December 4, 1920, to accept further deliveries; and that there was a continuing serious decline in the market price of coal from that date to the end of the twelve months fixed by the contract for delivery. The defendant had insisted upon the several defenses pleaded in bar as well as upon the counterclaim. After the verdict the defendant was allowed to amend the counterclaim, so as to allege that the market price of coal was $11 a ton at the time plaintiffs failed to make the deliveries therein referred to, and that the defendant's damages from such failure were $10,000. The record recites that a motion for a new trial was made by the plaintiffs and overruled, and that the overruling was excepted to; but the grounds of the motion, and of the refusal to grant it, are not stated. The errors assigned do not include any reference to the motion for a new trial; or to the exception which was taken to the allowance of the amendment of the counterclaim after verdict.

The Circuit Court of Appeals deemed it unnecessary to consider the nine instructions relating to liability, since the verdict for the plaintiffs "upon the issues which determined liability was amply sustained by the evidence." Nor did it discuss the two instructions which alone referred to the amount of damages recoverable. But it made an order substantially as follows: If within thirty days the parties shall stipulate that the judgment be modified by substituting for $1 the sum of [$18,250] (or other agreed sum), with interest at the rate of 5 per cent from December 4, 1920, and costs, the judgment as so modified shall be affirmed; otherwise the judgment shall be reversed and a new trial be had "limited only to an ascertainment of

[e] During the early months of the contract, the market price was above the contract price and the plaintiffs delivered less than the contract installments, ostensibly because of inability to arrange for railroad cars. Later, the market price fell below the contract price and the defendant refused to accept further deliveries.

appellants' [plaintiffs'] recoverable damages and the amount of appellee's counterclaim, if upon a new trial it appears that appellee is entitled to any recovery or set-off on its counterclaim." 59 F.2d 539, 540. As the parties did not stipulate for the modification suggested by the Court of Appeals, it ordered that the judgment be reversed with costs, and that the cause be remanded to the District Court with direction to grant a new trial limited as stated. The defendant petitioned this Court for a writ of certiorari on the ground that the Circuit Court of Appeals, in violation of the Seventh Amendment of the Federal Constitution, re-examined the verdict of the jury otherwise than according to the rules of the common law, and reversed the judgment solely for alleged error of fact in the verdict and for the alleged error of the trial court in overruling a motion for a new trial. Certiorari was granted.

The reasons assigned by the Circuit Court of Appeals for its action were substantially these: It appears that a large sum is recoverable as damages; that the minimum recoverable may be determined with substantial accuracy by computation, for the defendant "breached its contract without justification on December 4, 1920," and "the market price of coal is shown for each day of the month, and the average price per month is also disclosed, so that the actual amount of damages is quite definitely ascertainable" despite "a slight discrepancy in the statements of witnesses." The amount shipped and the amount received are also quite definitely ascertainable, despite a discrepancy "due apparently to the fact that the railroads confiscated a small amount of the coal on several occasions." Computing plaintiffs' damages "upon the basis most favorable to the" defendant, and the defendant's damages on the counterclaim also on the basis most favorable to it, plaintiffs appear clearly to be entitled to $18,250, with interest at the rate of 5 per cent from December 4, 1920, and costs. As the jury fixed the damages at $1, the verdict should have been set aside and a new trial granted. Since in view of Slocum v. New York Life Insurance Co., 228 U.S. 364, 33 S.Ct. 523, the court is "not at liberty to direct judgment for such amount as we believe would fairly represent" plaintiff's damages,[f] the parties should be given the opportunity of disposing of the case without further litigation by entering into an agreement as to the damages. If the parties do not so agree, a new trial should be granted; limited to the ascertainment of damages, as in Gasoline Products Co. v. Champlin, 283 U.S. 494, 51 S.Ct. 513.

If the refusal to grant the motion for a new trial was deemed by the Circuit Court of Appeals plain reversible error, it was at liberty under its rules to notice the error although not assigned; and the omission from the record of the grounds of the motion would be no obstacle to a review, since the motion was obviously directed to the

[f] See infra pp. 650–52.

failure to award substantial damages. But we are of opinion that the action of the District Court was not reversible error.

First. The rule that this Court will not review the action of a federal trial court in granting or denying a motion for a new trial for error of fact has been settled by a long and unbroken line of decisions; and has been frequently applied where the ground of the motion was that the damages awarded by the jury were excessive or were inadequate. The rule precludes likewise a review of such action by a Circuit Court of Appeals. . . . Sometimes the rule has been rested on that part of the Seventh Amendment which provides that "no fact tried by a jury, shall be otherwise re-examined in any court of the United States, than according to the rules of the common law." More frequently the reason given for the denial of review is that the granting or refusing of a motion for a new trial is a matter within the discretion of the trial court.

It has been suggested that a review must be denied because of the historical limitation of the writ of error to matters within the record, of which the motion for a new trial was not a part.[g] Compare Judge Learned Hand in Miller v. Maryland Casualty Co., 40 F.2d 463. But the denial of review can no longer rest upon this ground, since the record before the appellate court has been enlarged to include in the bill of exceptions a motion for a new trial, made either before or after judgment. Compare Harrison v. United States, 7 F.2d 259, 262. Under certain circumstances the appellate court may inquire into the action of the trial court on a motion for a new trial. Thus, its denial may be reviewed if the trial court erroneously excluded from consideration matters which were appropriate to a decision on the motion, Mattox v. United States, 146 U.S. 140, 13 S.Ct. 50; Ogden v. United States, 112 F. 523; or if it acted on the mistaken view that there was no jurisdiction to grant it, or that there was no authority to grant it on the ground advanced, Felton v. Spiro, 78 F. 576, 581; Dwyer v. United States, 170 F. 160, 165; Paine v. St. Paul Union Stockyards Co., 35 F.2d 624, 626–628. It becomes necessary, therefore, to determine whether the circumstances of the case at bar justify an enquiry into the trial court's refusal to set aside the verdict.

Second. It is urged that the motion for a new trial presented an issue of law. The argument is that on the motion or on the court's own initiative the verdict should have been set aside as inconsistent on its face, since if the plaintiffs were entitled to recover at all they were entitled to substantial, not merely nominal, damages. The case, it is contended, is comparable to one in which the award of damages exceeded a statutory limit, see Southern Ry. Co. v. Bennett, 233 U.S. 80, 34 S.Ct. 566; or was less than an amount undisputed, Glenwood Irrig. Co. v. Vallery, 248 F. 483; Stetson v. Stindt, 279 F. 209; or was in pursuance of erroneous instructions on the measure of damages, Chesapeake & O. Ry. Co. v. Gainey, 241 U.S. 494, 496, 36 S.Ct. 633;

[g] See infra pp. 1216–17.

or was in clear contravention of the instructions of the trial court, United Press Ass'ns v. National Newspapers Ass'n, 254 F. 284; compare American R.R. Co. v. Santiago, 9 F.2d 753, 757–758.

To regard the verdict as inconsistent on its face is to assume that the jury found for the plaintiff and failed to perform its task of assessing damages. The trial judge was not obliged so to regard the verdict. The defendant had insisted upon several defenses and had set up a counterclaim. The plaintiffs were not entitled to a directed verdict. The evidence was voluminous; and, on some issues at least, conflicting. The instructions left the contested issues of liability to the jury. The verdict may have represented a finding for the defendant on those issues; the reason for the award of nominal damages may have been that the jury wished the costs to be taxed against the defendant. The defendant did not complain of the verdict. The record before us does not contain any explanation by the trial court of the refusal to grant a new trial, or any interpretation by it of the jury's verdict. In the absence of such expressions by the trial court in the case at bar, the refusal to grant a new trial cannot be held erroneous as a matter of law. Appellate courts should be slow to impute to juries a disregard of their duties, and to trial courts a want of diligence or perspicacity in appraising the jury's conduct. Compare Union Pacific R.R. Co. v. Hadley, 146 U.S. 330, 334, 38 S.Ct. 318; Dunn v. United States, 284 U.S. 390, 394, 52 S.Ct. 189.

Third. It is urged that the refusal to set aside the verdict was an abuse of the trial court's discretion, and hence reviewable. The Court of Appeals has not declared that the trial judge abused his discretion. Clearly the mere refusal to grant a new trial where nominal damages were awarded is not an abuse of discretion. This Court has frequently refrained from disturbing the trial court's approval of an award of damages which seemed excessive or inadequate, and the circuit courts of appeals have generally followed a similar policy. Whether refusal to set aside a verdict for failure to award substantial damages may ever be reviewed on the ground that the trial judge abused his discretion, we have no occasion to determine.

. . . .

The judgment of the Circuit Court of Appeals is reversed and that of the District Court is affirmed.

Mr. Justice Stone and Mr. Justice Cardozo, dissenting.

A verdict found in contravention of the instructions of the court may be reversed on appeal as contrary to law.

So much the prevailing opinion apparently concedes.

The verdict of $1 returned by the jury upon the trial of this cause may not be squared with their instructions and hence was properly annulled.

By the instructions of the trial judge they were required, if they found that the defendant had broken its contract, to award to the plaintiffs the difference between the contract price of the coal and its market value, after allowance for the defendant's counterclaim. The evidence most favorable to the defendant, both as to claim and counterclaim, made it necessary, if there was any breach, to return a substantial verdict, the minimum being capable of accurate computation. The distinction is not to be ignored between this case of a breach of contract and the cases cited in the prevailing opinion where the liability was in tort.[h] Here the minimum, if not the maximum, damages are fixed and definite. There the discretion of the jury was not subject to tests so determinate and exact. The question is not before us whether even in such circumstances there may be revision on appeal. Cf. Pugh v. Bluff City Excursion Co., 177 F. 399. Enough for present purposes that in the circumstances of the case at hand the verdict of $1 is a finding that the contract had been broken, and this irrespective of the motive that caused the verdict to be given. What the motive was we cannot know from anything disclosed to us by the record. Nothing there disclosed lays a basis for a holding that the nominal verdict for the plaintiffs was designed to save them from the costs which the law would have charged against them if there had been a verdict for defendant. The jury were not instructed as to the liability for costs, and for all that appears had no knowledge on the subject. Nor would such a motive, if there were reason to ascribe it, rescue them from the reproach of disobedience and error. It would merely substitute one form of misconduct for another. It would do this, moreover, in contradiction of the record. By no process of mere construction can a verdict that nominal loss has resulted from a breach be turned into a verdict that there had been no breach at all. On the face of the record, the jury found there was a wrong, and then, in contravention of instructions, refused, either through misunderstanding or through wilfulness, to assess the damages ensuing.

Justice is not promoted in its orderly administration when such conduct is condoned.

PETTINGILL v. FULLER

United States Circuit Court of Appeals, Second Circuit, 1939.
107 F.2d 933, cert. denied, 309 U.S. 669, 60 S.Ct. 609 (1940).

Before L. HAND, AUGUSTUS N. HAND, and CLARK, CIRCUIT JUDGES.

AUGUSTUS N. HAND, CIRCUIT JUDGE.

[The jury in a personal-injury case returned a verdict for the defendant. On the plaintiff's motion, the judge set the verdict aside for misconduct by the defendant's counsel during the cross-examination

---

[h] This is apparently a reference to a footnote in the majority opinion citing cases for the proposition that the verdict may have represented a finding for the defendant on the contested issues.

of a witness: in arguing an evidentiary point in the presence of the jury, counsel had said that the witness had been convicted of negligent driving in connection with the events in suit. A second trial followed at which the plaintiff won verdict and judgment. The defendant appealed, claiming as error the setting aside of the first verdict in his favor and seeking to reinstate that verdict. The court of appeals found that it had been an abuse of discretion to set that verdict aside, in view of the nature of the misconduct and the plaintiff's failure to request a curative instruction.]

The question remains whether on an appeal from the final judgment for the plaintiff we may review the interlocutory order setting aside the verdict rendered at the first trial and order that verdict reinstated.

In spite of the fact that the courts of the United States have been most loath to review orders granting or denying motions to set aside verdicts, it is implicit in the opinion of Justice Brandeis in Fairmount Glass Works v. Cub Fork Coal Co., 287 U.S. 474, 483–486, 53 S.Ct. 252, that they may do so in certain cases, one of which would seem to be an abuse of the trial judge's discretion. 287 U.S. at p. 485, 53 S.Ct. 252. There a review was declined because there was no explanation by the trial judge of his refusal to set the verdict aside and the record did not show that the verdict was clearly erroneous and arbitrary. The question whether an order granting or denying a motion for a new trial may be reviewed on appeal when not followed by a final judgment entered after a new trial is not involved in the case at bar. Here we are reviewing an interlocutory order after final judgment in the action. An attempt to review an order setting aside a verdict has rarely been made under such circumstances; indeed never within our knowledge. That such an order may be reviewed on an appeal from a final judgment is undoubted unless the exercise of judicial discretion involved in making it is beyond the correcting hand of a court of appeal, no matter how arbitrary it was. We think that Justice Brandeis in Fairmount Glass Works v. Cub Fork Coal Co., 287 U.S. 474, 485, 53 S.Ct. 252, evidently regarded such orders as reviewable. Indeed, the dissenting Justices (Stone and Cardozo, JJ.) held that the court of appeals properly reviewed and reversed an order granting a new trial where the trial court had abused its discretion in refusing to set aside a verdict for nominal damages rendered by a jury in plain disregard of the evidence.

The refusal to review the denial of a motion for a new trial on newly discovered evidence may stand on a different footing. Here the error of the trial court was in the course of one trial. It was not in declining to open the record where no fraud was shown and the case so far as the trial court was concerned had come to an end.

The judgment for the plaintiff on the second trial is reversed with costs, the order setting aside the verdict for the defendant is reversed, the verdict for the defendant is ordered reinstated and final judgment thereon shall be entered for the defendant.[i]

Question: (11) Why did not the defendant appeal immediately after the first verdict was set aside?

GRUNENTHAL v. LONG ISLAND RAIL ROAD

Supreme Court of the United States, 1968.
393 U.S. 156, 89 S.Ct. 331.

MR. JUSTICE BRENNAN delivered the opinion of the Court.

Petitioner was working for respondent as foreman of a track gang when a 300-pound railroad tie being lifted by the gang fell and severely crushed his right foot. He sued respondent for damages under the Federal Employers' Liability Act, 45 U.S.C. § 51 et seq., and a jury in the District Court for the Southern District of New York awarded him $305,000.[1] The trial judge denied the railroad's motion to set the award aside as excessive. The railroad appealed the denial to the Court of Appeals for the Second Circuit, and that court, one judge dissenting, ordered the District Court to grant the railroad a new trial unless the petitioner would agree to remit $105,000 of the award. 388 F.2d 480 (1968). We granted certiorari, 391 U.S. 902, 88 S.Ct. 1651 (1968). We reverse.

Petitioner argues that the Court of Appeals exceeded its appellate powers in reviewing the denial of the railroad's motion, either because such review is constitutionally precluded by the provision of the Seventh Amendment that "no fact tried by a jury, shall be otherwise reexamined in any Court of the United States, than according to the rules of the common law," [3] or because such review is prohibited by the Federal Employers' Liability Act itself. We have no occasion in this case to consider that argument, for assuming, without deciding, that the Court of Appeals was empowered to review the denial and invoked the correct standard of review, the action of the trial judge, as we view the evidence, should not have been disturbed. See Neese v. Southern R. Co., 350 U.S. 77, 76 S.Ct. 131 (1955).

[The Court's summary of the trial judge's opinion, 292 F.Supp. 813 (S.D.N.Y.1967), is omitted.]

---

[i] A similar standard of abuse of discretion was applied in City of Cleveland v. Peter Kiewit Sons' Co., 624 F.2d 749 (6th Cir.1980) (reversing *denial* of new trial based on misconduct of counsel).

[1] Petitioner's complaint sought damages of $250,000. This was amended with leave of the trial judge to $305,000 after the jury returned its verdict in that amount.

[3] All 11 Courts of Appeals have held that nothing in the Seventh Amendment precludes appellate review of the trial judge's denial of a motion to set aside an award as excessive. [Citations from each circuit omitted.]

The Court of Appeals regarded its inquiry as limited to determining whether the trial judge abused his discretion in denying the railroad's motion. Its guide for that determination, the court stated, was the standard of review announced in its earlier decision in Dagnello v. Long Island R. Co., 289 F.2d 797, 806 (1961): "[W]e appellate judges [are] not to decide whether we would have set aside the verdict if we were presiding at the trial, but whether the amount is so high that it would be a denial of justice to permit it to stand. We must give the benefit of every doubt to the judgment of the trial judge; but surely there must be an upper limit, and whether that has been surpassed is not a question of fact with respect to which reasonable men may differ, but a question of law." [4]

We read Dagnello, however, as requiring the Court of Appeals in applying this standard to make a detailed appraisal of the evidence bearing on damages. Indeed this re-examination led to the conclusion in Dagnello that it was not a denial of justice to permit the jury's award to stand. If the Court of Appeals made a similar appraisal of the evidence in this case, the details are not disclosed in the majority opinion. Beyond attaching unexplained significance to petitioner's failure in his complaint "to ask for damages in such a large sum as $305,000," the relevant discussion is limited to the bald statement that "giving Grunenthal the benefit of every doubt, and weighing the evidence precisely in the same manner as we did in Dagnello . . . we cannot in any rational manner consistent with the evidence arrive at a sum in excess of $200,000." 388 F.2d, at 484. We have therefore made our own independent appraisal of the evidence. We conclude that the trial judge did not abuse his discretion in finding "nothing untoward, inordinate, unreasonable or outrageous—nothing indicative of a runaway jury or one that lost its head."

[The Court's appraisal of the evidence is omitted.]

The judgment of the Court of Appeals is reversed and the case is remanded to that court with direction to enter a judgment affirming the judgment of the District Court.

It is so ordered.

MR. JUSTICE HARLAN, dissenting.

I think it clear that the only issue which might conceivably justify the presence of this case in this Court is whether a United States Court of Appeals may constitutionally review the refusal of a district court to set aside a verdict for excessiveness. The Court purports not to decide that question, preferring to rest its decision upon the alleged correctness of the District Court's action in the circumstances of this case. Like my Brother Stewart, I am at an utter loss to un-

[4] The standard has been variously phrased: "Common phrases are such as: 'grossly excessive,' 'inordinate,' 'shocking to the judicial conscience,' 'outrageously excessive,' 'so large as to shock the conscience of the court,' 'monstrous,' and many others." Dagnello v. Long Island R. Co., supra, 289 F.2d, at 802.

derstand how the Court manages to review the District Court's decision and find it proper while at the same time proclaiming that it has avoided decision of the issue whether appellate courts ever may review such actions.

Even assuming that this feat of legal gymnastics has been successfully performed, I believe that the correctness of this particular District Court decision, a matter whose proper resolution depends upon a detailed examination of the trial record and which possesses little if any general significance, is not a suitable issue for this Court. Accordingly, I think it appropriate to vote to dismiss the writ as improvidently granted, even though the case formally is here on an unlimited writ. . . . Since the Court professes not to reach the constitutional issue in this case, I consider it inappropriate for me, as an individual Justice, to express my opinion on it.

MR. JUSTICE STEWART, dissenting.

The Court professes not to consider the petitioner's argument that the Seventh Amendment and "the Federal Employers' Liability Act itself" prohibit judicial review of a district judge's order refusing to set aside a verdict as excessive. Yet by the very act of proceeding to review the district judge's order in this case, the Court necessarily, and I think quite correctly, completely rejects that argument. . . .

. . . .

While it is arguable that a fuller written factual discussion might have been in order, I can find no reason to suppose that the Court of Appeals did not apply the standard of judicial review that it said it was applying—the standard of the Dagnello case. Since I believe that standard to be the correct one, and since I further believe that review of issues of this kind in individualized personal injury cases should be left primarily to the courts of appeals, I would affirm the judgment.

———

TAYLOR v. WASHINGTON TERMINAL CO., 409 F.2d 145 (D.C. Cir.), cert. denied, 396 U.S. 835, 90 S.Ct. 93 (1969). An injured fireman sued the railroad for negligence under the FELA. The plaintiff won a verdict of $80,000. The defendant moved for a new trial based on excessive damages. The trial court granted the motion conditioned on a remittitur of $60,000. The plaintiff refused, and on retrial he received a verdict and judgment for $25,000. The plaintiff appealed.

The court of appeals ultimately set aside the lower court's new trial order and reinstated the original verdict. But first it had to fix the standard of review. It began by referring to the by-now generally accepted learning that new trial orders based on the weight of the evidence can be reversed, but only in rare cases.

"This learning has largely arisen from consideration of cases in which motions for new trial—especially on the ground of excessive verdict—have been *denied*. Two factors unite to favor very restricted review of such orders. The first of these is the deference due the trial judge, who has had the opportunity to observe the witnesses and to consider the evidence in the context of a living trial rather than upon a cold record. The second factor is the deference properly given to the jury's determination of such matters of fact as the weight of the evidence and the quantum of damages. This second factor is further weighted by the constitutional allocation to the jury of questions of fact.

"Where the jury finds a particular quantum of damages and the trial judge refuses to disturb its finding on the motion for a new trial, the two factors press in the same direction, and an appellate court should be certain indeed that the award is contrary to all reason before it orders a remittitur or a new trial. However, where, as here, the jury as primary fact-finder fixes a quantum, and the trial judge indicates his view that it is excessive by granting a remittitur, the two factors oppose each other. The judge's unique opportunity to consider the evidence in the living courtroom context must be respected. But against his judgment we must consider that the agency to whom the Constitution allocates the fact-finding function in the first instance—the jury—has evaluated the facts differently.[13]

"In this jurisdiction particularly, District Court judges have given great weight to jury verdicts. They have stated that a new trial motion will not be granted unless the 'verdict is so unreasonably high as to result in a miscarriage of justice,'[14] or, most recently, unless the verdict is 'so inordinately large as obviously to exceed the maximum limit of a reasonable range within which the jury may properly operate.'[15]

"At the appellate level, in reviewing a trial judge's grant of a new trial for excessive verdict, we should not apply the same standard. The trial judge's view that a verdict is outside the proper range deserves considerable deference. His exercise of discretion in granting

[13] In taking this approach, we follow the lead taken by the Third Circuit en banc in a similar case. In Lind v. Schenley Industries, Inc., 278 F.2d 79, cert. denied, 364 U.S. 835, 81 S.Ct. 58, 5 L.Ed.2d 60 (1960), that court reversed a trial court's grant of a new trial because the verdict was against the weight of the evidence. The court distinguished between cases where a new trial is granted because of some legal error and cases in which the trial judge simply reweighed evidence already submitted to a jury. In cases of the latter sort (in which grants of new trials for excessive general damages must be included), 'the [trial] judge takes over, if he does not usurp, the prime function of the jury as the trier of the facts. It then becomes the duty of the appellate tribunal to exercise a closer degree of scrutiny and supervision than is the case where a new trial is granted because of some undesirable or pernicious influence obtruding into the trial. Such a close scrutiny is required in order to protect the litigants' right to jury trial.' 278 F.2d at 90.

[14] Frank v. Atlantic Greyhound Corp., D.D.C., 172 F.Supp. 190, 191 (1959).

[15] Graling v. Reilly, D.D.C., 214 F.Supp. 234, 235 (1963).

the motion is reviewable only for abuse. Thus we will reverse the grant of a new trial for excessive verdict only where the quantum of damages found by the jury was *clearly* within 'the maximum limit of a reasonable range.' "

DONOVAN v. PENN SHIPPING CO.

Supreme Court of the United States, 1977.
429 U.S. 648, 97 S.Ct. 835.

PER CURIAM.

The petitioner, while employed by the respondents as a seaman on the SS Penn-Sailor, slipped on wet paint, injuring his right wrist and elbow. He sued the respondents under the Jones Act, 46 U.S.C. § 688, and obtained a $90,000 verdict at his jury trial. The respondents moved to set aside the verdict as excessive. Fed.Rules Civ.Proc. 50, 59. The District Court granted the motion, and ordered a new trial on damages unless the petitioner agreed to remit $25,000 of the $90,000 award.

After some time the petitioner submitted to the District Court a proposed order stating that he accepted "under protest" the reduced verdict of $65,000, but reserving nonetheless "his right to appeal therefrom." This language was adopted by the District Court in entering a judgment for the petitioner in the amount of $65,000.

The petitioner sought appellate review of the District Court's decision to order a conditional new trial. In so doing he asked the Court of Appeals for the Second Circuit to discard the settled rule that a plaintiff who has accepted a remittitur may not appeal to seek reinstatement of the original verdict. The Court of Appeals refused the petitioner's invitation, and dismissed the appeal. 536 F.2d 536.

. . . . .

The proper role of the trial and appellate courts in the federal system in reviewing the size of jury verdicts is . . . a matter of federal law, see Hanna v. Plumer, 380 U.S. 460, 466–469, 85 S.Ct. 1136, 1141–1142 (1965); Byrd v. Blue Ridge Rural Electric Coop., 356 U.S. 525, 78 S.Ct. 893 (1958), and that law has always prohibited appeals in the situation at bar. The Court of Appeals for the Second Circuit correctly adhered to the consistent rule established by this Court's decisions. In order to clarify whatever uncertainty might exist, we now reaffirm the longstanding rule that a plaintiff in federal court, whether prosecuting a state or federal cause of action, may not appeal from a remittitur order he has accepted.

The petition for a writ of certiorari is granted, and the judgment is affirmed.

THE CHIEF JUSTICE and MR. JUSTICE BLACKMUN would grant the petition for certiorari but would have the case argued and given plenary consideration rather than disposed of summarily.

APPELLATE REVIEW OF FACTS IN NONJURY CASES

The "clearly erroneous" test of Rule 52(a) conforms in general to the standard applied in modern equity practice. (By "modern equity practice" we mean the practice after the deposition method of taking testimony was abandoned and oral testimony of witnesses was allowed. In earlier times the scope of appellate review of facts in equity cases was more intrusive, the appellate court being in as good a position to decide issues of fact as the trial court, because the trial court did not personally observe the demeanor of witnesses.) Of the "clearly erroneous" standard of Rule 52(a) the Supreme Court said in United States v. United States Gypsum Co., 333 U.S. 364, 395, 68 S.Ct. 525, 542 (1948), that a judge's finding "is 'clearly erroneous' when although there is evidence to support it, the reviewing court on the entire evidence is left with the definite and firm conviction that a mistake has been committed." See generally C. Wright, The Law of Federal Courts § 96 (4th ed. 1983).

What bounds should be placed on the application of this relatively insulating standard of review?

1. In Orvis v. Higgins, 180 F.2d 537, 539–40 (2d Cir.), cert. denied, 340 U.S. 810, 71 S.Ct. 37 (1950), Judge Frank particularizes as follows:

"Where a trial judge sits without a jury, the rule varies with the character of the evidence: (a) If he decides a fact issue on written evidence alone, we are as able as he to determine credibility, and so we may disregard his finding. (b) Where the evidence is partly oral and the balance is written or deals with undisputed facts, then we may ignore the trial judge's finding and substitute our own, (1) if the written evidence or some undisputed fact renders the credibility of the oral testimony extremely doubtful, or (2) if the trial judge's finding must rest exclusively on the written evidence or the undisputed facts, so that his evaluation of credibility has no significance. (c) But where the evidence supporting his finding as to any fact issue is entirely oral testimony, we may disturb that finding only in the most unusual circumstances."

Compare the original note of the Advisory Committee on Rule 52(a): "[The 'clearly erroneous' test] is applicable to all classes of findings in cases tried without a jury whether the finding is of a fact concerning which there was conflict of testimony, or of a fact deduced or inferred from uncontradicted testimony." Note also the Advisory Committee's proposal in 1983 to amend Rule 52(a) to provide expressly that the "clearly erroneous" test applies to findings of fact "whether based on oral or documentary evidence."

2. In United States v. General Motors Corp., 384 U.S. 127, 141 n. 16, 86 S.Ct. 1321, 1328 n.16 (1966), the Court tries to articulate a distinction between "fact" and "legal standard" but has a hard time of it. Consider now the passage from its opinion by Justice Fortas:

"We note that, as in United States v. Parke, Davis & Co., 362 U.S. 29, 44–45, 80 S.Ct. 503, 511–512, the ultimate conclusion by the trial judge, that the defendants' conduct did not constitute a combination or conspiracy in violation of the Sherman Act, is not to be shielded by the 'clearly erroneous' test embodied in Rule 52(a) of the Federal Rules of Civil Procedure. That Rule in part provides: 'Findings of fact shall not be set aside unless clearly erroneous, and due regard shall be given to the opportunity of the trial court to judge of the credibility of the witnesses.' As in Parke, Davis, supra, the question here is not one of 'fact,' but consists rather of the legal standard required to be applied to the undisputed facts of the case. [Citations omitted.]

"Moreover, the trial court's customary opportunity to evaluate the demeanor and thus the credibility of the witnesses, which is the rationale behind Rule 52(a) (see United States v. Oregon State Medical Society, 343 U.S. 326, 331–332, 72 S.Ct. 690, 694–695), plays only a restricted role here. This was essentially a 'paper case.' It did not unfold by the testimony of 'live' witnesses. Of the 38 witnesses who gave testimony, only three appeared in person. The testimony of the other 35 witnesses was submitted either by affidavit, by deposition, or in the form of an agreed-upon narrative of testimony given in the earlier criminal proceeding before another judge. A vast number of documents were also introduced, and bear on the question for decision.

"In any event, we resort to the record not to contradict the trial court's findings of *fact*, as distinguished from its conclusory 'findings,' but to supplement the court's factual findings and to assist us in determining whether they support the court's ultimate legal conclusion that there was no conspiracy."

Compare Commissioner v. Duberstein, 363 U.S. 278, 289, 80 S.Ct. 1190, 1198 (1960), which defined "fact" to include any finding "based ultimately on the application of the fact-finding tribunal's experience with the mainsprings of human conduct."

3. The findings must be sufficiently comprehensive to indicate to the appellate court the factual basis of the ultimate conclusion. The nature of the requirement is illustrated in Dearborn Nat. Casualty Co. v. Consumers Petroleum Co., 164 F.2d 332 (7th Cir.1947). Insurer brought this action against insured for a declaratory judgment of nonliability on an insurance policy that required notice of an accident "as soon as practicable." The notice had been given 94 days after the accident, but only 10 days after the injured party had brought a

suit against the insured, who contended that this suit was his first knowledge of the accident. The trial court found simply that notice was given "as soon as practicable." The appellate court remanded for further findings because it could not tell whether the trial court meant that a delay of 94 days, unexplained, was "as soon as practicable" within the meaning of the policy or whether it found that the insured, until sued, lacked knowledge of the accident. On remand, the trial judge made detailed findings that the insured had no knowledge of any accident that would suggest any liability until suit was brought. Upon these findings, the judgment in favor of the insured was affirmed, 178 F.2d 277 (7th Cir.1949).

SECTION 5. INTERPLAY OF NEW TRIAL MOTION WITH RULE 50

Suppose the trial judge grants a motion to direct a verdict and accordingly withdraws the case from the jury. If, on appeal from the judgment, the appellate court holds that the trial judge committed error in granting the motion, the consequence is ordinarily a reversal of the judgment with an order for a new trial.

But suppose the trial judge denies a motion to direct a verdict at the close of all the evidence and accordingly submits the case to the jury, and the jury brings in a verdict against the party who made the motion. If the judge's denial of the motion was erroneous—if on the evidence he should have directed a verdict in favor of the moving party—what ought the consequence to be? It may seem natural and obvious that when the error is made manifest, the consequence should be the entry of a judgment in favor of the party for whom a verdict should have been directed. There are in fact a number of state statutes that allow the trial court to correct its own error by granting a motion for judgment notwithstanding the verdict (in effect the renewal of the motion for a directed verdict) and that allow the appellate court to correct the trial court's error by ordering the entry of such a judgment.

Before the promulgation of the Federal Rules, and while the Conformity Act applied generally to procedure in actions at law in the federal courts, the question arose whether a state statute along these lines could be constitutionally applied in the federal courts. A motion for a directed verdict at the close of all the evidence had been denied by the trial court. After a jury verdict against the party who had made the motion, the court denied that party's motion for judgment notwithstanding the verdict and entered judgment on the verdict. On appeal, the circuit court of appeals, holding that the motion for a directed verdict had been erroneously denied, reversed the judgment for the appellee entered on the verdict and ordered the entry of judgment for the appellant. On certiorari, the Supreme Court, agreeing that the directed verdict had been erroneously denied, held that the judgment entered on the verdict must indeed be reversed, but the Court held further that the circuit court of appeals might not order the entry of the opposite judgment and that the most it could do was to order a new trial. Slocum v. New York Life Insurance Co., 228 U.S. 364, 33 S.Ct. 523 (1913) (5–4 decision). The "re-examination clause" of the seventh amendment was thought to forbid the federal courts from following the practice authorized by the state statute. Measuring the requirements of the seventh amendment largely by the condition of common-law procedures in 1791, the Court found no precedent in the English courts of the proper historical vintage that would support the practice in question.[j]

Comment on the Slocum case was generally adverse. State courts continued to follow their statutory practice, finding it consonant with state guarantees of the right to trial by jury . See, e.g., Bothwell v. Boston Elevated Railway, 215 Mass. 467, 102 N.E. 665 (1913).

Twenty-three years later the Supreme Court found a way to overcome the Slocum decision. In olden times an English judge trying a case at nisi prius as a kind of delegate of one of the central courts at Westminster might, while submitting the case to the jury, reserve for decision by the court in banc a point of law that had arisen during the trial.[k] The point of law might be dispositive of the case, and there were occasions when the court upon deciding the point would go on to order judgment for the party who had lost the verdict. (Note that the court in banc was not operating as an appellate court in the modern sense.) Here was an analogy that could be used to advantage. In Baltimore & Carolina Line v. Redman, 295 U.S. 654, 55 S.Ct. 890 (1935), the Court in effect sanctioned the following practice in federal courts under the Conformity Act: if the trial judge, while denying a motion for a directed verdict and submitting the case to the jury, reserved the point whether a directed verdict should have been granted, he could thereafter grant a motion for judgment n.o.v. on being persuaded that the motion for a directed verdict should have been granted; and the appellate court, on review of a judgment entered on the verdict, could similarly act on the reserved point and order judgment n.o.v. to be entered.

It remained only to reduce to fiction the reservation of the point. This is accomplished by Rule 50(b). When in 1946 the Advisory Committee recommended the elimination of the language of fiction from Rule 50(b), the Supreme Court declined to adopt the recommendation.

Question: (12) Does this persisting requirement—that a party must have moved at the close of all the evidence for a directed verdict in order effec-

---

[j] The court rejected as analogies, inter alia, the old-style motions in arrest of judgment and for judgment n.o.v., which when granted had the effect of putting the previous jury verdict to naught and resulted in judgment for the moving party. See supra p. 349.

[k] See, e.g., Scott v. Shepherd, supra p. 321.

tively to move for judgment n.o.v.—have any practical justification today? See 5A Moore ¶ 50.08.

Thus, the basis was laid for making, after verdict, a motion for judgment n.o.v. as well as a motion for a new trial. However, the interplay of these two motions generated much confusion. Montgomery Ward & Co. v. Duncan, which follows immediately below, revolutionized this post-verdict practice. When it was decided in 1940, Rule 50(b) was substantially identical to the present Rule 50(b), but there was no Rule 50(c) or (d), both of which were added by the 1963 amendments. The opinion of Justice Roberts, much of which was unnecessary to the decision, provided the lower courts and lawyers, as doubtless it was intended to do, with much the same kind of guidance for nearly a quarter of a century that an amendment to the Rule would have done.[1]

MONTGOMERY WARD & CO. v. DUNCAN
Supreme Court of the United States, 1940.
311 U.S. 243, 61 S.Ct. 189.

[The plaintiff sued for personal injuries. At the close of all the evidence the defendant moved for a directed verdict. The motion was denied, and there was a verdict for the plaintiff upon which judgment was entered. Within ten days the defendant moved for judgment notwithstanding the verdict and "for a new trial in the alternative," the latter request being on the grounds that the verdict was against the weight of the evidence and was excessive and that the court erred in rulings on the evidence and the instructions. The motion concluded with a prayer that the verdict and judgment be set aside and judgment rendered for the defendant, and the further prayer "that in the event the Court refuses" to enter judgment for the defendant, the court set aside the verdict and judgment and grant the defendant a new trial. The trial court held that there was no evidence of negligence and ordered judgment for the defendant. The plaintiff filed a motion praying that "in order that the judgment of the appellate court may be final," the motion for a new trial be overruled. The court, however, merely entered a judgment for the defendant notwithstanding the verdict.

[On appeal by the plaintiff, it was held that the trial court erred in holding the evidence insufficient to make a case for the jury. The

---

[1] In reading this opinion, the student may well have difficulty with the terminology. Justice Roberts, infra p. 655 & n.12, says that an order denying a new trial is not "appealable" save in most exceptional circumstances. Further, infra p. 655 & n.15, he says that the granting of a motion for a new trial would not ordinarily be "reviewable." "Appealable order" properly relates to the kind of order from which an appeal may be taken, a matter of the timing of the appeal, as distinguished from "reviewable order," the kind of order the propriety of which the appellate court will consider when an appeal (typically from a final judgment) is before it. It is not clear that Justice Roberts has this distinction in mind.

case was reversed and remanded with instructions to enter judgment on the verdict for the plaintiff. The circuit court of appeals overruled the defendant's contention that the case should be remanded with leave to the trial court to dispose of the motion for a new trial. Its reasoning was that a new trial was asked only "in the event" judgment notwithstanding the verdict was denied, a condition that did not come into existence. "The order sustaining the motion for judgment notwithstanding the verdict," said the court, "was equivalent to a denial of the motion for a new trial; and the latter motion passed out of the case upon the entry of the order." The Supreme Court granted certiorari.]

MR. JUSTICE ROBERTS delivered the opinion of the Court.

In this case we are called upon to determine the appropriate procedure under Rule 50(b) of the Federal Rules of Civil Procedure.

. . . .

The defendant contends that the rule continues the existing practice respecting granting of new trials, and also regulates the procedure for rendering judgment notwithstanding a verdict; that the provision for an alternative motion for a new trial would be meaningless and nugatory if the granting of the motion for judgment operated automatically to dismiss it, since the bases of the two motions are, or may be, different, and orderly procedure requires that the court first rule on the motion for judgment, the granting of which renders unnecessary a ruling upon the motion for a new trial, which should be reserved until final disposition of the former.

The plaintiff insists that the trial court is limited to a choice of action on one motion or the other, but cannot rule upon the motion for judgment and leave that for a new trial to be disposed of only if judgment notwithstanding the verdict is denied. . . . .

. . . . .

. . . We come then to the substantial question which moved us to issue the writ, namely, whether under Rule 50(b) the District Court's grant of the motion for judgment effected an automatic denial of the alternative motion for a new trial. We hold that it did not.

The rule was adopted for the purpose of speeding litigation and preventing unnecessary retrials. . . .

. . . . It adds nothing of substance to rights of litigants heretofore existing and available through a more cumbersome procedure.

A motion for judgment notwithstanding the verdict did not, at common law, preclude a motion for a new trial. And the latter motion might be, and often was, presented after the former had been denied. The rule was not intended to alter the existing right to move for a new trial theretofore recognized and confirmed by statute. It permits the filing of a motion for judgment in the absence of a motion for a new trial or the filing of both motions jointly or a motion for a new trial in the alternative.

Each motion, as the rule recognizes, has its own office. The motion for judgment cannot be granted unless, as matter of law, the opponent of the movant failed to make a case and, therefore, a verdict in movant's favor should have been directed. The motion for a new trial may invoke the discretion of the court in so far as it is bottomed on the claim that the verdict is against the weight of the evidence, that the damages are excessive, or that, for other reasons, the trial was not fair to the party moving; and may raise questions of law arising out of alleged substantial errors in admission or rejection of evidence or instructions to the jury.

We are of opinion that the provision of the rule,—"A motion for a new trial may be joined with this motion, or a new trial may be prayed for in the alternative"—does not confine the trial judge to an initial choice of disposing of either motion, the exercise of which choice precludes consideration of the remaining motion. We hold that the phrase "in the alternative" means that the things to which it refers are to be taken not together but one in the place of the other.[10]

The rule contemplates that either party to the action is entitled to the trial judge's decision on both motions, if both are presented. A decision in favor of the moving party upon the motion for judgment ends the litigation and often makes it possible for an appellate court to dispose of the case without remanding it for a new trial. If, however, as in the present instance, the trial court erred in granting the motion the party against whom the verdict went is entitled to have his motion for a new trial considered in respect of asserted substantial trial errors and matters appealing to the discretion of the judge. In this case the reasons assigned in support of the motion for a new trial were in both categories. The grounds assigned for a new trial have not been considered by the court. In the circumstances here disclosed the uniform practice in state appellate courts has been to remand the case to the trial court with leave to pass upon the motion for new trial.

[margin note: If JNOV given wrongly — can still have N/Tr. considered if looking at substantial trial errors & judge's discretion]

The plaintiff urges that, whereas the rule was intended to expedite litigation, to prevent unnecessary trials, and to save the time of courts and litigants, the course urged by the defendant tends to extend the duration of litigation, to create unnecessary hardship, and to defeat the purpose of the rule.

We are of opinion that the position is untenable. This case well illustrates the efficacy of the procedure sanctioned by the rule. In view of the trial judge's conclusion that the plaintiff failed to make out a case for the jury he would, under the earlier practice, simply have granted a new trial. Upon the new trial, the judge, if his view as to the law remained unchanged, would have directed a verdict for the defendant. The only recourse of the plaintiff would have been an

[margin note: Rule does speed up litig.]

---

[10] The word "alternative" may be used properly in this sense. See Webster's International Dictionary, Second Edition.

appeal from this second judgment. If the appellate court had been of the view it here expressed, it would have reversed that judgment and remanded the cause for a third trial. Upon such third trial, if the trial court had ruled upon the evidence and given the instructions to which the defendant objects a judgment for the plaintiff would have been the subject of a third appeal and, if the defendant's position were sustained by the appellate court, the cause would be remanded for a fourth trial at which proper rulings would be rendered and proper instructions given.

Much of the delay formerly encountered may be avoided by pursuing the course for which the defendant contends. But the courts should so administer the rule as to accomplish all that is permissible under its terms. Is it necessary, if the trial judge's order for judgment be reversed on appeal, that only thereafter he deal with the alternative motion? If so, and he then refuses to set aside the original judgment, a second appeal will lie,—not from his order denying a new trial, for that order, save in most exceptional circumstances, is not appealable,[12] but from the judgment entered on the verdict, for errors of law committed on the trial. Can such a second appeal be avoided in the interest of speeding litigation? We think so.

If alternative prayers or motions are presented, as here, we hold that the trial judge should rule on the motion for judgment. Whatever his ruling thereon he should also rule on the motion for a new trial, indicating the grounds of his decision. If he denies a judgment n.o.v. and also denies a new trial the judgment on the verdict stands, and the losing party may appeal from the judgment entered upon it, assigning as error both the refusal of judgment n.o.v. and errors of law in the trial, as heretofore. The appellate court may reverse the former action and itself enter judgment n.o.v. or it may reverse and remand for a new trial for errors of law. If the trial judge, as he did here, grants judgment n.o.v. and denies the motion for a new trial, the party who obtained the verdict may, as he did here, appeal from that judgment. Essentially, since his action is subject to review, the trial judge's order is an order nisi. The judgment on the verdict may still stand, because the appellate court may reverse the trial judge's action. This being so, we see no reason why the appellee may not, and should not, cross-assign error, in the appellant's appeal, to rulings of law at the trial, so that if the appellate court reverses the order for judgment n.o.v., it may pass on the errors of law which the appellee asserts nullify the judgment on the verdict.

Should the trial judge enter judgment n.o.v. and, in the alternative, grant a new trial on any of the grounds assigned therefor, his disposition of the motion for a new trial would not ordinarily be reviewable,[15] and only his action in entering judgment would be ground

[Handwritten margin notes:]
Trial Judge should rule on both, JNOV & N/Tr.
① JNOV, N/Tr denied: D may app. App ct: rev. or rev. & remand
② JNOV grant, N/Tr denies: P App & D App for errors why orig. verd. no good
③ JNOV granted, N/Tr. grant. only JNOV appealable. If App ct reverses N/Tr. given

---

[12] See Fairmount Glass Works v. Cub Fork Coal Co., 287 U.S. 474, 481–85, 53 S.Ct. 252, 254–55.

[15] United States v. Young, 94 U.S. 258; Young v. United States, 95 U.S. 641; Phillips v. Negley, 117 U.S. 665, 671, 6

of appeal. If the judgment were reversed, the case, on remand, would be governed by the trial judge's award of a new trial.

We might reverse and direct that the cause be remanded to the District Court to pass on both motions. But that course would, in the circumstances, be neither fair nor practical. As respects federal courts, the procedure permitted by the rule is novel. The provision which is involved in this case substantially follows the first state statute to authorize such procedure.[16] The Supreme Court of that State has construed the statute to permit the trial judge to pass on the motion for judgment, leaving the motion for a new trial for later disposition. In the event that his decision is reversed, the practice is to remand the cause with leave to the trial judge to pass upon the motion for a new trial. It was therefore not unnatural for the defendant to advocate that course, or for the trial judge to follow it.

In the circumstances, we think the failure of the District Court to rule in the alternative on both matters can be cured without depriving the defendant of opportunity to have its motion for a new trial heard and decided by the trial court, by modifying the judgment below to provide that the cause be remanded to the District Court to hear and rule upon that motion.

Modified.

Questions: (13) Assume that the losing party has moved for judgment n.o.v. and in the alternative for a new trial, the latter request being on the sole ground that the court erred in ruling on the instructions. Construct four hypothetical cases demonstrating that each of the four conceivable dispositions—grant or denial of each of the two motions—can properly be made by the trial judge. Now do the same assuming instead that the motion for a new trial is on the sole ground that the verdict was against the weight of the evidence.

(14) In Momand v. Universal Film Exchange, Inc., 72 F.Supp. 469 (D.Mass.1947), aff'd, 172 F.2d 37 (1st Cir.1948), cert. denied, 336 U.S. 967, 69 S.Ct. 939 (1949), Judge Wyzanski, after granting defendants' motion for judgment n.o.v., said, in passing upon defendants' accompanying motion for a new trial: "It is doubtful whether the draftsmen of the rules and the Justices who participated in the Montgomery Ward case realized in what a dilemma their rule might in some cases place a trial judge and what foresight, abnegation and stultification it might require of him." Do you see the nature of the dilemma in which a trial judge may be placed?

---

16 2 Mason's Minnesota Statutes (1927) § 9495.

S.Ct. 901, 903; Hume v. Bowie, 148 U.S. 245, 13 S.Ct. 582; Fairmount Glass Works v. Cub Fork Coal Co., supra.

MARSH v. ILLINOIS CENT. R.

United States Court of Appeals, Fifth Circuit, 1949.
175 F.2d 498.

Before HUTCHESON, SIBLEY and WALLER, CIRCUIT JUDGES.

SIBLEY, CIRCUIT JUDGE.   Marsh, called herein appellant, a fireman on a switch engine, sued for a personal injury alleged to have been caused by negligence in maintaining the switching track and the apron covering the coupling between the engine and tender, on which apron he stood in firing.   At the conclusion of the evidence the defendant's motion for an instructed verdict was denied, and a verdict for plaintiff was returned.   The defendant then moved for a judgment notwithstanding the verdict, or . . . for a new trial on the ground, among others, that the verdict was against the overwhelming weight of the evidence.   The judge held: "The weight of the evidence is so overwhelmingly against the plaintiff that as a matter of law it becomes the duty of the court to withdraw the case from the jury and enter a judgment for the defendant.   The motion . . . for a judgment notwithstanding the verdict of the jury will be entered for the reason that the motion for a directed verdict should have been sustained. . . .   It is my judgment that the evidence was insufficient to go to the jury, but if I am wrong in that, then I do not think a new trial should be granted as there were no other errors of law."   Appeal is taken by plaintiff from the judgment notwithstanding the verdict, and a cross-appeal by the defendant from the refusal of a new trial.

1. . . .   A motion for a directed verdict, or for a judgment notwithstanding the verdict under Rule of Civil Procedure 50, 28 U.S. C.A., raises a question of law only: Whether there is any evidence which, if believed, would authorize a verdict against movant.   The trial judge in considering those motions does not exercise discretion, but makes a ruling of law, and if he errs the appellate court may reverse.   A motion for new trial is addressed to the trial judge's discretion.   He may grant a new trial if he thinks he has committed error; and he may grant one (and he alone can) because he thinks the verdict is wrong, though supported by some evidence.   The exercise of his discretion is not ordinarily reviewable on appeal, though a failure to exercise discretion, or an abuse of it, may be corrected.   The motion for a new trial is entirely independent of the other two motions and is governed by different principles, and has a different result.   It never supersedes the jury, but as its name states, it results in another jury trial, perhaps with different evidence produced.   But the motion for directed verdict or for judgment notwithstanding the verdict if granted, ends the case.

Rule of Civil Procedure 50, while altering the procedure in federal courts, did not alter the nature and effect of these motions, and each is entitled to be decided according to the principles applicable to it .

without confusing them. Montgomery Ward & Co. v. Duncan, 311 U.S. 243, 61 S.Ct. 189, 85 L.Ed. 147.

2. While it is not our function to weigh the evidence, we do agree with the trial judge's first expressed opinion that the weight of the evidence is "overwhelmingly against the plaintiff". But we do not agree that the grant of a judgment notwithstanding the verdict was therefore justified. There was evidence of the appellant, not very explicit or positive, which if believed might authorize a jury to conclude he was hurt in the manner he claims. Because the trial judge does not believe it, because of appellant's own contradictions and conduct and of opposing evidence which seem to overwhelm it, is not ground for a judgment notwithstanding the verdict, and we must reverse that judgment. Howard v. Louisiana & A.R. Co., 5 Cir., 49 F.2d 571.

3. But it is ground for the trial judge to grant a new trial, though the trial was free of other error. He has in strong terms disapproved the verdict as contrary to the evidence, so much as to warrant setting the verdict aside and entering judgment for the defendant. We have reversed the entering of a final judgment, but it is evident that the new trial ought to be granted and would have been except for the misconception that absence of other error prevented it. The full discretion vested in the trial judge not having been exercised, we will remand the case with direction to the judge to grant a new trial instead of a judgment notwithstanding the verdict if he continues to think the verdict to be against the overwhelming weight of the evidence.

The judgment is reversed on both appeals and the cause remanded for further proceedings not inconsistent with this opinion. Reversed.

Questions: (15) Consider what the court of appeals may do in each of the situations discussed by Justice Roberts in the Montgomery Ward case, taking into account the possibility that each of the alternative rulings may have been either correct or incorrect: (a) both n.o.v. and new trial denied; (b) n.o.v. granted, new trial denied; and (c) both n.o.v. and new trial granted.

(16) What of the situation omitted by Justice Roberts—denial of n.o.v. and grant of new trial? Why did Justice Roberts omit it? Imagine that *P* sues *D* for breach of contract. *D*'s motion for a directed verdict at the close of all the evidence is denied. The jury returns a verdict for *P* for $20,000. *D* moves for judgment n.o.v. and for a new trial, urging that there was no, or insufficient, evidence to support a finding of breach of contract. *D*'s motion for judgment n.o.v. is denied, but his motion for a new trial is granted. On retrial, there is a verdict and judgment for *P* for $30,000 after a trial admittedly free of error. *D* appeals, contending that there was error in denial of the motion for judgment n.o.v. after the first trial. Assume that *P* believes that the court of appeals would find such error. What position should *P* take on the appeal, and what disposition should the court of appeals make if indeed it believes there was error in the denial of *D*'s motion? Is Pettingill v. Fuller, supra p. 641, controlling? Compare Basciano v. Rei-

necke, 313 F.2d 542 (2d Cir.1963), with Ford Motor Co. v. Busam Motor Sales, Inc., 185 F.2d 531 (6th Cir.1950).

CONE v. WEST VIRGINIA PULP & PAPER CO.

Supreme Court of the United States, 1947.
330 U.S. 212, 67 S.Ct. 752.

MR. JUSTICE BLACK delivered the opinion of the Court.

The petitioner brought this action in a South Carolina state court. Upon motion of respondent, it was removed to the Federal District Court because of diversity of citizenship of the parties. The complaint claimed $25,000 damages upon allegations that the respondent's agents had trespassed upon and cut timber from lands owned by and in the possession of the petitioner. Respondent's answer denied that the petitioner had title or possession of the lands and timber. Both title and possession became crucial issues in the trial. The burden of proving them rested on the petitioner.[1] When all the evidence of both parties had been introduced, the respondent moved for a directed verdict in its favor on the ground that the petitioner had failed to prove that he either owned or was in possession of the land. This motion was denied. The jury returned a verdict for petitioner for $15,000, and the court entered judgment on the verdict. The respondent moved for a new trial on the ground of newly discovered evidence. The motion was denied. Respondent did not move for judgment notwithstanding the verdict as it might have done under Rule 50(b) of the Federal Rules of Civil Procedure . . . .

The Circuit Court of Appeals decided that the admission of certain evidence offered by the petitioner to prove legal title was prejudicial error. It held that without this improperly admitted evidence petitioner's proof was not sufficient to submit the question of title to the jury. That court also held that petitioner's evidence showing possession was insufficient to go to the jury. It therefore reversed the case. But instead of remanding it to the District Court for a new trial, the Circuit Court of Appeals directed that judgment be entered for respondent. 153 F.2d 576. That court has thus construed Rule 50(b) as authorizing an appellate court to direct a judgment notwithstanding the verdict, even though no motion for such a judgment had been made in the District Court within ten days after the jury's discharge.

The petition for certiorari challenged the power of an appellate court to direct entry of a judgment notwithstanding the verdict where timely motion for such a judgment had not been made in the District

---

[1] Under governing South Carolina law an action such as this is not one to try title but "to recover damages for trespass to property of which the plaintiff was in possession." [Citation omitted.] But possession may be presumed from proof of legal title. [Citations omitted.] Petitioner here undertook to prove possession both by showing that he had legal title and by showing that he had openly and notoriously exercised acts of dominion, possession, and ownership over a long period of years.

Court. On three previous occasions we have granted certiorari to
consider this point but failed to reach it because, upon examination of
the evidence, we found it sufficient to justify submission of all three
cases to the jury. Conway v. O'Brien, 312 U.S. 492, 61 S.Ct. 634;
Berry v. United States, 312 U.S. 450, 61 S.Ct. 637; Halliday v. United
States, 315 U.S. 94, 62 S.Ct. 438. In this case we granted certiorari
"limited to the questions of federal procedure raised by the petition
for the writ." 329 U.S. 701. The point we had in mind was whether
a party's failure to make a motion in the District Court for judgment
notwithstanding the verdict, as permitted in Rule 50(b), precludes an
appellate court from directing entry of such a judgment. Other questions have been discussed here, but we do not consider them. Consequently, we accept, without approving or disapproving, the Circuit
Court of Appeals' holding that there was prejudicial error in the admission of evidence and in the submission of the case to the jury.

Rule 50(b) contains no language which absolutely requires a trial
court to enter judgment notwithstanding the verdict even though that
court is persuaded that it erred in failing to direct a verdict for the
losing party. The rule provides that the trial court "may reopen the
judgment and either order a new trial or direct the entry of judgment
as if the requested verdict had been directed." This "either-or" language means what it seems to mean, namely, that there are circumstances which might lead the trial court to believe that a new trial
rather than a final termination of the trial stage of the controversy
would better serve the ends of justice. In short, the rule does not
compel a trial judge to enter a judgment notwithstanding the verdict
instead of ordering a new trial; it permits him to exercise a discretion
to choose between the two alternatives. See Berry v. United States,
supra, 312 U.S. at 452–453, 61 S.Ct. at 638. And he can exercise this
discretion with a fresh personal knowledge of the issues involved, the
kind of evidence given, and the impression made by witnesses. His
appraisal of the bona fides of the claims asserted by the litigants is of
great value in reaching a conclusion as to whether a new trial should
be granted. Determination of whether a new trial should be granted
or a judgment entered under Rule 50(b) calls for the judgment in the
first instance of the judge who saw and heard the witnesses and has
the feel of the case which no appellate printed transcript can impart.
[Citations omitted.] Exercise of this discretion presents to the trial
judge an opportunity, after all his rulings have been made and all the
evidence has been evaluated, to view the proceedings in a perspective
peculiarly available to him alone. He is thus afforded "a last chance
to correct his own errors without the delay, expense or other hardships of an appeal." See Greer v. Carpenter, 323 Mo. 878, 882, 19
S.W.2d 1046, 1047. Cf. United States v. Johnson, 327 U.S. 106, 112,
66 S.Ct. 464, 466.

There are other practical reasons why a litigant should not have
his right to a new trial foreclosed without having had the benefit of
the trial court's judgment on the question. Take the case where a

trial court is about to direct a verdict because of failure of proof in a certain aspect of the case. At that time a litigant might know or have reason to believe that he could fill the crucial gap in the evidence. Traditionally, a plaintiff in such a dilemma has had an unqualified right, upon payments of costs, to take a nonsuit in order to file a new action after further preparation, unless the defendant would suffer some plain legal prejudice other than the mere prospect of a second lawsuit. Pleasants v. Fant, 22 Wall. 116, 122; Jones v. S.E.C., 298 U.S. 1, 19–20, 56 S.Ct. 654, 659, and cases cited. Rule 41(a)(1) preserves this unqualified right of the plaintiff to a dismissal without prejudice prior to the filing of defendant's answer. And after the filing of an answer, Rule 41(a)(2) still permits a trial court to grant a dismissal without prejudice "upon such terms and conditions as the court deems proper."

In this case had respondents made a timely motion for judgment notwithstanding the verdict, the petitioner could have either presented reasons to show why he should have a new trial, or at least asked the court for permission to dismiss. If satisfied from the knowledge acquired from the trial and because of the reasons urged that the ends of justice would best be served by allowing petitioner another chance, the judge could have so provided in his discretion. The respondent failed to submit a motion for judgment notwithstanding the verdict to the trial judge in order that he might exercise his discretionary power to determine whether there should be such a judgment, a dismissal or a new trial. In the absence of such a motion, we think the appellate court was without power to direct the District Court to enter judgment contrary to the one it had permitted to stand.

It has been suggested that the petitioner could have presented affidavits to the Circuit Court of Appeals to support his claim for a new trial, and that that court could thereupon have remanded the question to the District Court to pass upon it. Such a circuitous method of determining the question cannot be approved. For Rule 50(b) specifically prescribes a period of ten days for making a motion for judgment notwithstanding the verdict. Yet the method here suggested would enable litigants to extend indefinitely the prescribed ten-day period simply by adoption of the expedient of an appeal. Furthermore, it would present the question initially to the appellate court when the primary discretionary responsibility for its decision rests on the District Court.

Reversed.[m]

Questions: (17) Johnson sued the railroad in district court under the Jones Act for the wrongful death of her husband. When all the evidence

---

[m] On remand, the district court interpreted the Supreme Court's opinion to require a new trial, at which the defendant ultimately prevailed by means of judgment n.o.v. This was affirmed, 170 F.2d 770 (4th Cir.1948), cert. denied, 337 U.S. 920, 69 S.Ct. 1149 (1949).

was in, the railroad moved for a directed verdict in its favor on the ground that no negligence of the railroad had been shown and that the deceased had been responsible for his own death. The court reserved decision on the motion and submitted the case to the jury, which returned a verdict for the plaintiff on which judgment was entered. Within ten days the railroad moved to set aside the verdict and judgment as excessive and contrary to the law, to the evidence, and to the weight of the evidence. It did not expressly move for judgment n.o.v. The court denied the motion to set aside the verdict and judgment and, at the same time, denied the motion for a directed verdict on which it had reserved decision. Holding that the motion for a directed verdict should have been granted, the court of appeals directed the entry of judgment for the railroad. Was this action by the court of appeals proper? See Johnson v. New York, N.H. & H.R.R., 344 U.S. 48, 73 S.Ct. 125 (1952) (Rule "forbids the trial judge or an appellate court to enter such a judgment").

(18) Assume that the railroad had instead moved for judgment n.o.v. but not for a new trial. The trial court denied the motion. Holding that the verdict was against the weight of the evidence, the court of appeals ordered a new trial. Was this action by the court of appeals proper? Cf. Jackson v. Wilson Trucking Corp., 243 F.2d 212 (D.C.Cir.1957) (suggesting that neither the trial judge nor an appellate court could so act, unless the trial judge was acting pursuant to Rule 59(d), because the issue of weight of the evidence had not been timely raised).

(19) Assume instead that the railroad had moved neither for judgment n.o.v. nor for a new trial. If Johnson's case had been very weak, what action could the court of appeals (or the trial judge) properly take? See 9 Wright & Miller §§ 2536–2537; 11 id. § 2813.

NEELY v. MARTIN K. EBY CONSTRUCTION CO., 386 U.S. 317, 87 S.Ct. 1072 (1967). Plaintiff brought a diversity action claiming that defendant's negligence caused her decedent's death. Defendant's motion for a directed verdict at the close of all the evidence was denied. After a verdict for plaintiff, defendant moved for judgment n.o.v. and in the alternative for a new trial. Both motions were denied, and judgment was entered for plaintiff. Defendant appealed. The court of appeals held that the evidence was insufficient to go to the jury and reversed "with instructions to dismiss the action." Without seeking a rehearing in the court of appeals, plaintiff sought certiorari, presenting the question whether the court of appeals could, consistent with the Federal Rules (principally Rule 50(c) and (d), added by the 1963 amendments) and with the seventh amendment, direct the trial court to dismiss the action. Certiorari was granted. The Supreme Court, in an opinion by Justice White, affirmed, holding that the court of appeals had power to order final judgment. Only Justice Black dissented on this point. Justices Douglas and Fortas agreed with the Court's construction of Rule 50 as amended, but they believed, as also did Justice Black, that the evidence was sufficient to go to the jury.

Questions: (20) Is Neely consistent with Cone v. West Virginia Pulp & Paper Co.? See Louis, Post-Verdict Rulings on the Sufficiency of the Evidence: Neely v. Martin K. Eby Construction Co. Revisited, 1975 Wis.L.Rev. 503.

(21) In the fact situation of Neely, what may the court of appeals do if it decides that the ruling below on the motion for judgment n.o.v. was erroneous? Cf. 28 U.S.C. § 2106. What factors should influence its exercise of discretion?

(22) Plaintiff brought a diversity action for her husband's death, claiming that defendant had negligently designed a "skip hoist." Defendant's motion for a directed verdict at the close of all the evidence was denied. By special verdict the jury found negligent design; but being asked, if it found negligent design, to "please indicate" which, if any, of five specified design aspects of the hoist had been found unsafe, the jury answered "yes" to one and left the other four unanswered. The trial judge ordered judgment for plaintiff on the verdict and denied defendant's motion for judgment n.o.v. The court of appeals reversed, holding that the evidence did not warrant the jury's finding of negligence in the aspect of design it had found to be unsafe. Upon plaintiff's petition for rehearing, what disposition should it then have made of the case? See Iacurci v. Lummus Co., 387 U.S. 86, 87 S.Ct. 1423 (1967) (in accordance with Rule 50(d), remand to trial judge to decide whether plaintiff is entitled to new trial).

———

O'HARE v. MERCK & CO., 381 F.2d 286 (8th Cir.1967). In this product liability case, after the denial of defendant's motion for a directed verdict at the close of all the evidence and then a verdict for plaintiff, the trial judge granted defendant's motion for judgment n.o.v. because of insufficient proof of negligence. The court of appeals affirmed, and it later denied plaintiff's petition for rehearing without explanation.

In dissent, Judge Lay would have remanded to the district court for decision on plaintiff's motion for a new trial, made in her petition for rehearing and based on allegedly erroneous jury instructions, or at least would have fully considered the motion at the appellate level.

Judge Lay first faced the argument that plaintiff had waived the point by not moving in the trial court under Rule 50(c)(2). After quoting the 1963 Advisory Committee's note thereon and the Neely case, he said:

"Therefore, it is clear that appellant has not waived any rights by failing to [move] for new trial in the court below. There are practical and cogent reasons for this rule of non-waiver, in that a verdict-winner appealing from a judgment n.o.v. primarily desires a review of that judgment and a reinstatement of the verdict. He is generally not interested in pursuing an immediate new trial order, which, if granted by the trial court, could supersede the appealable judgment. If a new trial would be granted the verdict-winner is left with no opportunity to obtain review of his original judgment. Of course, the trial court could enter a conditional order of a new trial as well as granting the n.o.v., under Fed.R.Civ.P. 50(b) and (c), but even under these circumstances the plaintiff may be reluctant to move for a new trial because of the uncertainty that the order will be conditional."

Judge Lay further concluded, in questionable reliance on Neely, that plaintiff did not have to raise the issue of a new trial in her original appellate brief. He said:

"Until the court of appeals has finally ruled on the granting of defendant's motion for judgment n.o.v., the verdict-holder's single purpose is to reinstate the verdict he obtained below from the jury. Until he sees finality in the judgment invalidating that verdict, again, he is not interested in even suggesting a new trial. In fact, in the court of appeals in many instances his argument that the jury verdict was proper under the record could be vitiated by his simultaneous emphasis on errors in the trial. Inconsistent pleas and alternative motions in his original briefs would add to his already heavy burden of persuasion. This would, of course, not always be true since frequently similar grounds could underlie both his appeal and his motion for new trial."

Question: (23) Under Rule 50 as amended, what may each party do in the trial court and in the court of appeals in order fully to protect his position against all contingencies?

TOPIC E. THE CONSTITUTIONAL GUARANTEE OF JURY TRIAL

SECTION 1. CONSTITUTIONAL AND STATUTORY FRAMEWORK

NEW YORK CONSTITUTION art. I, § 2 (1938): "Trial by jury in all cases in which it has heretofore been guaranteed by constitutional provision shall remain inviolate forever;[a] but a jury trial may be waived by the parties in all civil cases in the manner to be prescribed by law. . . ."

NEW YORK CIVIL PRACTICE LAW AND RULES § 4101: "In the following actions, the issues of fact shall be tried by a jury unless a jury trial is waived or a reference is directed under section 4317 [trial by a referee], except that equitable defenses and equitable counterclaims shall be tried by the court:

1. an action in which a party demands and sets forth facts which would permit a judgment for a sum of money only;

2. an action of ejectment; for dower; for waste; for abatement of and damages for a nuisance; to recover a chattel; or for determination of a claim to real property under article fifteen of the real property actions and proceedings law; and

3. any other action in which a party is entitled by the constitution or by express provision of law to a trial by jury."[b]

CONNECTICUT CONSTITUTION art. I, § 19 (1965): "The right of trial by jury shall remain inviolate . . . ."[c]

CONNECTICUT GENERAL STATUTES § 52–215: ". . . The following-named classes of cases shall be entered in the docket as jury cases upon the written request of either party made to the clerk within thirty days after the return day: Appeals from probate involving the validity of a will or paper purporting to be such, appeals from the actions of commissioners on insolvent estates, and, except as

[a] This means that there is a constitutional right to trial by jury "in all cases in which it has been heretofore used," as stated in the Constitution of 1894, which was the last in a series of New York constitutions that so provided. (The first was the Constitution of 1777, which protected the jury right "in all cases in which it hath heretofore been used in the Colony of New York.") Thus, 1894 should be the critical date of historical reference in New York under its current constitution. See 4 J. Weinstein, H. Korn & A. Miller, New York Civil Practice ¶¶ 4101.07–.08 (rev. 1982).

[b] Cf. NYCPLR § 4102 (demand and waiver of trial by jury), most of which has more recent origins than § 4101.

[c] This provision first appeared in the Constitution of 1818. As a constitutional matter, 1818 is interpreted still to be the critical date of historical reference in Connecticut.

665

hereinafter provided, civil actions involving such an issue of fact as, prior to January 1, 1880, would not present a question properly cognizable in equity, except that there shall be no right to trial by jury in civil actions in which the amount, legal interest or property in demand does not exceed two hundred fifty dollars or in a summary process case. . . . All issues of fact in any such case shall be tried by the jury, provided the issues agreed by the parties to be tried by the court may be so tried. . . ." [d]

Questions: (1) Are there any significant differences between the foregoing New York and Connecticut provisions? How do they compare with the seventh amendment to the United States Constitution and Federal Rule 38?

(2) On the federal level, is there any constitutional right to trial without a jury? See Note, The Right to a Nonjury Trial, 74 Harv.L.Rev. 1176 (1961).

ADVISORY JURY

Rule 39(c) preserves the power of the court, in actions not being tried by a jury, upon motion or of its own initiative, to try an issue with the assistance of an advisory jury. This discretionary power has nothing to do with the constitutional right to jury trial. It dates back to the power of the chancellor in classical equity to send an issue for trial before a law court for the purpose of enlightening his conscience; having been enlightened, the chancellor could proceed to make his own findings contrary to those of the jury, the advisory verdict in theory being non-binding. In order to create a matter litigable in a common-law court, a wager was "feigned" over the disputed issue; the jury would then decide, by resolving the issue, whether a debt was owing on the bet. The advisory jury and the use of the "feigned issue" procedure were incorporated in American practice from the earliest days. See Guggenheim, A Note on the Advisory Jury in Federal Courts, 8 Fed.B.J. 200 (1947).

Under modern practice, of course, there is no need to shuttle a case from court to court. The trial judge can in a merged system simply impanel an advisory jury and submit such issues to it as he wishes. Rule 52(a) provides that in all actions tried with an advisory jury the court shall find the facts specially. This is particularly important if the judge proposes to enter a judgment contrary to the findings of the advisory jury. The appellate court has the same power of review of the facts in a case where an advisory jury is utilized as in any nonjury case.

Question: (3) Suppose a trial judge, uncertain as to whether a jury right exists, impanels a jury, takes its verdict, and then treats it as advisory and

---

[d] The substance of this statute dates back to the Practice Act of 1879, which merged law and equity in Connecticut and which became effective January 1, 1880.

makes his own findings inconsistent with the verdict. On appeal from a judgment entered on the findings, can the court of appeals order judgment on the verdict if it finds that there was a constitutional right to jury trial? See Hildebrand v. Board of Trustees of Michigan State University, 607 F.2d 705, 712 (6th Cir.1979) ("This case presents a procedural nightmare worthy of inclusion in a first year of law school civil procedure examination authored by the most cunning of professors.").

SECTION 2. "HISTORICAL TEST"

A constitutional provision that the right of trial by jury shall be "preserved" or "remain inviolate" suggests that a question of the jury right should be resolved by resort to the situation prevailing at the time the provision was adopted, either in 1791 when the seventh amendment was adopted or, in the case of the states, at the date of the relevant state constitution.[e]

Some difficulty in applying any such historical test is inevitable. The line of demarcation between law and equity was never a clear one. There was a continuing process of change. The law courts came to deal with matters formerly cognizable only in equity, and

[e] The right of trial by jury in civil cases, a prized common-law heritage, has been curtailed in the English High Court of Justice almost to the vanishing point. The Juries Act of 1918, enacted during World War I when manpower was short, limited the right to cases alleging fraud, libel, malicious prosecution, and the like—cases involving reputation and not merely money. Except for the years 1925 to 1933, this pattern has been continued by later legislation. Today, it is put this way by the Supreme Court Act, 1981, ch. 54, § 69(1)–(4):

"(1) Where, on the application of any party to an action to be tried in the Queen's Bench Division, the court is satisfied that there is in issue—

(a) a charge of fraud against that party; or

(b) a claim in respect of libel, slander, malicious prosecution or false imprisonment; or

(c) any question or issue of a kind prescribed for the purposes of this paragraph,

the action shall be tried with a jury, unless the court is of opinion that the trial requires any prolonged examination of documents or accounts or any scientific or local investigation which cannot conveniently be made with a jury.

(2) An application under subsection (1) must be made not later than such time before the trial as may be prescribed.

(3) An action to be tried in the Queen's Bench Division which does not by virtue of subsection (1) fall to be tried with a jury shall be tried without a jury unless the court in its discretion orders it to be tried with a jury.

(4) Nothing in subsections (1) to (3) shall affect the power of the court to order, in accordance with rules of court, that different questions of fact arising in any action be tried by different modes of trial; and where any such order is made, subsection (1) shall have effect only as respects questions relating to any such charge, claim, question or issue as is mentioned in that subsection."

See also O. 33, r. 5. Discretionary orders for trial by jury are in fact rarely made. See D. Casson & I. Dennis, Odgers' Principles of Pleading and Practice in Civil Actions in the High Court of Justice 266–67 (22d ed. 1981).

"Against the obsolescence of the English civil jury, which has come about quite casually, with a minimum of soul-searching, is to be set the robust survival of the American jury." Kaplan, An American Lawyer in the Queen's Courts: Impressions of English Civil Procedure, 69 Mich.L.Rev. 821, 830 (1971).

equity courts came to try issues that had previously been left exclusively to law. It is often very hard and sometimes impossible to determine precisely when such takeovers came to pass.

Inaptness and artificiality are also inevitable in applying any such historical test. The judges of 1791 could not know that their allocation of cases between the courts of law and equity would almost two centuries later be determinative of the right to trial by jury in a judicial system where law and equity were merged. The line dividing law and equity was to a large degree the product of historical and political influences wholly unrelated to procedural concerns. Moreover, because the right to jury trial is the one significant aspect of the law-equity allocation to survive merger, it is easy to forget that the jury right was but one of many procedural factors that affected the allocation of jurisdiction between law and equity courts in premerger days. On the one hand, there were available in equity types of specific relief and means of handling multiple parties unknown in courts of law; in addition, the testimony of parties was permitted and could be compelled in equity at a time long before this was possible at law. On the other hand, the testimony of witnesses at law was oral and subject to cross-examination, and their demeanor was observable by the trier of fact, whereas in equity evidence was taken by written depositions. Obviously, the parties' exercise of any choice of courts was also a many-factored decision. As Professors James and Hazard say: "To put it colloquially, jury trial (or court trial) was often merely the tail of the dog under a system where you had to take the whole dog."[f]

Beyond all this confusion, sharp disagreements exist as to the basic thrust of the historical test. Professor Redish argues for a very narrow reading of the seventh amendment that would protect only the jury right that actually existed in 1791, ignoring as far as possible all changed conditions and excluding any new developments. Redish, Seventh Amendment Right to Jury Trial: A Study in the Irrationality of Rational Decision Making, 70 Nw.U.L.Rev. 486 (1975). The range of disagreement will perhaps be suggested by the view of Professor Wolfram.

WOLFRAM, THE CONSTITUTIONAL HISTORY OF THE SEVENTH AMENDMENT
57 Minn.L.Rev. 639, 736, 738, 744–45 (1973).

Nor does the term "common law" necessarily require a static reference. Even if one is confined to the meaning of that phrase as understood in 1791, by that time a commonly understood concept of "common law" had become that of a process characterized by occa-

[f] F. James & G. Hazard, Civil Procedure 358 (2d ed. 1977). Their § 8.2, in which this quotation appears, is instructive as to the historical test.

sional flexibility and capacity for growth in order to respond to changing social pressures, rather than that of a fixed and immutable body of unchanging rules. . . .

If "common law" in 1791 was understood by the framers of the seventh amendment as a process, rather than as a set of perpetually static rules, then one must ask whether, with the passage of time, the historical test has caused the amendment to diverge from the original conception. . . . During the centuries of their coexistence, the jurisdictions of the law courts and the chancellor, until they were merged, were subject to an unstatic process of accretion and erosion. . . . What remains constant over the history of this process, however, is the tendency toward expansion and enrichment of the remedies provided by the law courts. While the law courts in recent centuries never attempted directly to warn the chancellor off territory that had been claimed for the law courts, it seems rather certain that between the two the equity court was destined to have its powers circumscribed. . . .

. . . .

The most appealing view of the political settlement achieved by the seventh amendment is the version suggested by the argument that the term "common law" in the seventh amendment was probably intended to refer to a process of legal development, rather than to an immutable and changeless state of the law. If that was a widely shared understanding of the nature of the "common law" at the time of the adoption of the seventh amendment, then the future development of the "common law" should also be regarded as part of the political bargain that was struck. If future development was contemplated—and if it is correct to view that development as largely one of the expansion of the remedies available at "common law"—then it would seem to follow that the "common law" of the seventh amendment was intended to have a changing meaning over time. While the day might then have been some distance in the future, it would not have been unintended to have the right extend at some future point in time to the trial by jury of what in 1791 would have been termed "equity" or "admiralty" cases.

I wish to suggest, therefore, that the seventh amendment two centuries after its adoption could justifiably be read to refer neither to the law of England nor to the law of any of the states and certainly not to an arbitrary point in time, but rather to the distinctive common-law process of adjudication and lawmaking that then and now, in England and in the United States, was recognized as flexible and changing. Principally because this process cannot with fidelity be locked into any particular point in time and in order to emphasize its characteristics as a process, this may fittingly be called the "dynamic" reading of the seventh amendment.

New cause of action.—There are, to be sure, many rights and remedies created since the adoption of the federal and state constitutions. Sometimes the statute creating a new cause of action specifies trial by jury, as in the Jones Act; sometimes it is silent as to mode of trial, but a jury right may be inferred from the statute, as under the FELA. In general, whether expressly or impliedly, the legislature not only may resolve any doubts in favor of a jury right, but also can clearly expand jury rights. See Rule 38(a).

Although there is some room for innovative argument, the still generally accepted view is that the legislature cannot cut back on the jury right otherwise protected by the constitutional provision. See Pernell v. Southall Realty, 416 U.S. 363, 94 S.Ct. 1723 (1974) (by implication) (repossession of real property; jury required by seventh amendment). Thus, a negative legislative view does not affect the outcome of the constitutional test. But this does not leave the legislature's hands completely tied. The legislature has some freedom to formulate a new cause of action so that it looks sufficiently foreign to the common law and hence falls on the nonjury side of the constitutional test. See Atlas Roofing Co. v. Occupational Safety & Health Review Commission, 430 U.S. 442, 97 S.Ct. 1261 (1977) (government claim, before an administrative agency, for civil penalties for employer's violation of OSHA; no jury required). The legislature may even abolish a common-law cause of action and replace it with something new of this sort that does not involve a jury trial. See Mountain Timber Co. v. Washington, 243 U.S. 219, 37 S.Ct. 260 (1917) (when the employee's right of action against his employer for negligence was replaced by statutes setting up a system of compensation for industrial injuries, without regard to fault, there was no infringement of the jury right in providing for an administrative tribunal to adjudicate factual disputes).

In any event, if the legislature is silent, the courts resort to historical analogy in determining the jury right.

CURTIS v. LOETHER

Supreme Court of the United States, 1974.
415 U.S. 189, 94 S.Ct. 1005.

MR. JUSTICE MARSHALL delivered the opinion of the Court.

Section 812 of the Civil Rights Act of 1968, 82 Stat. 88, 42 U.S.C. § 3612, authorizes private plaintiffs to bring civil actions to redress violations of Title VIII, the fair housing provisions of the Act, and provides that "[t]he court may grant as relief, as it deems appropriate, any permanent or temporary injunction, temporary restraining order, or other order, and may award to the plaintiff actual damages and not more than $1,000 punitive damages, together with court costs and reasonable attorney fees . . . ." The question presented in this case is whether the Civil Rights Act or the Seventh Amendment requires a jury trial upon demand by one of the parties in an action . . . under this section.

Petitioner, a Negro woman, brought this action under § 812, claiming that respondents, who are white, had refused to rent an apartment to her because of her race, in violation of § 804(a) of the Act, 42 U.S.C. § 3604(a). [She sought] actual and punitive damages.

Respondents made a timely demand for jury trial in their answer. The District Court, however, held that jury trial was neither authorized by Title VIII nor required by the Seventh Amendment, and denied the jury request. Rogers v. Loether, 312 F.Supp. 1008 (ED Wis. 1970). After trial on the merits, the District Judge found that respondents had in fact discriminated against petitioner on account of her race. Although he found no actual damages, . . . he awarded $250 in punitive damages, denying petitioner's request for attorney's fees and court costs.

The Court of Appeals reversed on the jury trial issue. Rogers v. Loether, 467 F.2d 1110 (CA7 1972). . . . In view of the importance of the jury trial issue in the administration and enforcement of Title VIII and the diversity of views in the lower courts on the question, we granted certiorari, 412 U.S. 937, 93 S.Ct. 2770 (1973). We affirm.

The legislative history on the jury trial question is sparse, and what little is available is ambiguous. . . . Both petitioner and respondents have presented plausible arguments from the wording and construction of § 812. We see no point to giving extended consideration to these arguments, however, for we think it is clear that the Seventh Amendment entitles either party to demand a jury trial in an action for damages in the federal courts under § 812.

The Seventh Amendment provides that "[i]n suits at common law, where the value in controversy shall exceed twenty dollars, the right of trial by jury shall be preserved." Although the thrust of the Amendment was to preserve the right to jury trial as it existed in 1791, it has long been settled that the right extends beyond the common-law forms of action recognized at that time. Mr. Justice Story established the basic principle in 1830:

> "The phrase 'common law,' found in this clause, is used in contradistinction to equity, and admiralty, and maritime jurisprudence. . . . By *common law*, [the Framers of the Amendment] meant . . . not merely suits, which the *common* law recognized among its old and settled proceedings, but suits in which *legal* rights were to be ascertained and determined, in contradistinction to those where equitable rights alone were recognized, and equitable remedies were administered . . . .
> In a just sense, the amendment then may well be construed to embrace all suits which are not of equity and admiralty jurisdiction, whatever might be the peculiar form which they may

assume to settle legal rights." Parsons v. Bedford, 3 Pet. 433, 446–447 (1830) (emphasis in original).

Petitioner nevertheless argues that the Amendment is inapplicable to new causes of action created by congressional enactment. . . . The Seventh Amendment does apply to actions enforcing statutory rights, and requires a jury trial upon demand, if the statute creates legal rights and remedies, enforceable in an action for damages in the ordinary courts of law.

NLRB v. Jones & Laughlin Steel Corp., 301 U.S. 1, 57 S.Ct. 615 (1937), relied on by petitioner, lends no support to her statutory-rights argument. The Court there upheld the award of back pay without jury trial in an NLRB unfair labor practice proceeding, rejecting a Seventh Amendment claim on the ground that the case involved a "statutory proceeding" and "not a suit at common law or in the nature of such a suit." Id., at 48, 57 S.Ct., at 629. Jones & Laughlin merely stands for the proposition that the Seventh Amendment is generally inapplicable in administrative proceedings, where jury trials would be incompatible with the whole concept of administrative adjudication and would substantially interfere with the NLRB's role in the statutory scheme. Katchen v. Landy, 382 U.S. 323, 86 S.Ct. 467 (1966), also relied upon by petitioner, is to like effect. There the Court upheld, over a Seventh Amendment challenge, the Bankruptcy Act's grant of summary jurisdiction to the bankruptcy court over the trustee's action to compel a claimant to surrender a voidable preference; the Court recognized that a bankruptcy court has been traditionally viewed as a court of equity, and that jury trials would "dismember" the statutory scheme of the Bankruptcy Act. Id., at 339, 86 S.Ct., at 478. See also Guthrie National Bank v. Guthrie, 173 U.S. 528, 19 S.Ct. 513 (1899). These cases uphold congressional power to entrust enforcement of statutory rights to an administrative process or specialized court of equity free from the strictures of the Seventh Amendment. But when Congress provides for enforcement of statutory rights in an ordinary civil action in the district courts, where there is obviously no functional justification for denying the jury trial right, a jury trial must be available if the action involves rights and remedies of the sort typically enforced in an action at law.

We think it is clear that a damages action under § 812 is an action to enforce "legal rights" within the meaning of our Seventh Amendment decisions. [Citations omitted.] A damages action under the statute sounds basically in tort—the statute merely defines a new legal duty, and authorizes the courts to compensate a plaintiff for the injury caused by the defendant's wrongful breach. As the Court of Appeals noted, this cause of action is analogous to a number of tort actions recognized at common law.[10] More important, the relief

[10] For example, the Court of Appeals recognized that Title VIII could be viewed as an extension of the common-law duty of innkeepers not to refuse temporary lodging to a traveler without justification, a duty enforceable in a dam-

sought here—actual and punitive damages—is the traditional form of relief offered in the courts of law.

We need not, and do not, go so far as to say that any award of monetary relief must necessarily be "legal" relief. See, e.g., Mitchell v. Robert DeMario Jewelry, Inc., 361 U.S. 288, 80 S.Ct. 332 (1960); Porter v. Warner Holding Co., 328 U.S. 395, 60 S.Ct. 1086 (1946). A comparison of Title VIII with Title VII of the Civil Rights Act of 1964, where the courts of appeals have held that jury trial is not required in an action for reinstatement and back pay, is instructive, although we of course express no view on the jury trial issue in that context. In Title VII cases the courts of appeals have characterized back pay as an integral part of an equitable remedy, a form of restitution. But the statutory language on which this characterization is based—

> "[T]he court may enjoin the respondent from engaging in such unlawful employment practice, and order such affirmative action as may be appropriate, which may include, but is not limited to, reinstatement or hiring of employees, with or without back pay . . ., or any other equitable relief as the court deems appropriate," 42 U.S.C. § 2000e–5(g) (1970 ed., Supp. II)—

contrasts sharply with § 812's simple authorization of an action for actual and punitive damages. In Title VII cases, also, the courts have relied on the fact that the decision whether to award back pay is committed to the discretion of the trial judge. There is no comparable discretion here: if a plaintiff proves unlawful discrimination and actual damages, he is entitled to judgment for that amount. Nor is there any sense in which the award here can be viewed as requiring the defendant to disgorge funds wrongfully withheld from the plaintiff. Whatever may be the merit of the "equitable" characterization in Title VII cases, there is surely no basis for characterizing the award of compensatory and punitive damages here as equitable relief.

We are not oblivious to the force of petitioner's policy arguments. Jury trials may delay to some extent the disposition of Title VIII damages actions. But Title VIII actions seeking only equitable relief will be unaffected, and preliminary injunctive relief remains available without a jury trial even in damages actions. Dairy Queen, Inc. v. Wood, [369 U.S. 469, 479 n.20, 82 S.Ct. 894, 901 n.20 (1962)]. Moreover, the statutory requirement of expedition of § 812 actions, 42 U.S.C. § 3614 (1970), applies equally to jury and nonjury trials. We

ages action triable to a jury, to those who rent apartments on a long-term basis. See 467 F.2d at 1117. An action to redress racial discrimination may also be likened to an action for defamation or intentional infliction of mental distress. Indeed, the contours of the latter tort are still developing, and it has been suggested that "under the logic of the common law development of a law of insult and indignity, racial discrimination might be treated as a dignitary tort." C. Gregory & H. Kalven, Cases and Materials on Torts 961 (2d ed. 1969).

recognize, too, the possibility that jury prejudice may deprive a victim of discrimination of the verdict to which he or she is entitled. Of course, the trial judge's power to direct a verdict, to grant judgment notwithstanding the verdict, or to grant a new trial provides substantial protection against this risk, and respondents' suggestion that jury trials will expose a broader segment of the populace to the example of the federal civil rights laws in operation has some force. More fundamentally, however, these considerations are insufficient to overcome the clear command of the Seventh Amendment. The decision of the Court of Appeals must be affirmed.

Affirmed.

This historical test is relatively easy to apply when dealing with an action involving a single claim for relief as to which an ancient analogue can be found. More serious difficulties arise, however, when an attempt must be made to fit some of the more complicated actions brought under today's procedure into a historical pigeonhole. What is to be the mode of trial when a party includes both legal and equitable issues in the same complaint, or when a legal complaint is met by an equitable defense or counterclaim (or vice versa)? If, as under Rule 38, the jury right goes by issues, not by cases, what should govern the order of trial when a contested factual issue is common to a legal claim or defense and an equitable claim or defense? The cases now to be set out show difficulties in applying the historical test and even in certain respects the possible irrelevance of history.

Joinder of legal and equitable causes.—Assume that, after merger of law and equity, the plaintiff seeks legal and equitable relief, where both are available cumulatively. Does the plaintiff have a right to trial by jury on the legal issues? Does the defendant?

FARRELL v. CITY OF ONTARIO, 39 Cal.App. 351, 178 P. 740 (1919). Plaintiff sued defendant for diverting storm waters upon his land. The prayer was for damages and for an injunction. Plaintiff claimed a right to trial by jury on the legal issues. The court said:

"According to the allegations of his complaint, plaintiff had two rights of action and was entitled to two remedies, of which he might pursue either or both at his election, the legal remedy of damages for past injuries suffered and the equitable remedy of injunction to prevent their recurrence in the future. He might have prosecuted separate actions for these two remedies concurrently. In that case the facts alleged in the two actions would have been the same, except that in the action at law he would have alleged the money value of the injuries suffered and in the suit in equity he would have alleged the facts showing a threat of future repetitions thereof. Under those circumstances it will be conceded that the plaintiff would have been entitled as of right to a trial by jury of the legal issues . . . . Instead of doing this, he accepted the invitation held out to him by our laws and joined his two actions in one. He should not be held to have thereby forfeited his right to a jury trial of the legal issues . . . . ''

The court then referred to the clean-up doctrine, which had allowed the chancellor (if the plaintiff so wished) to decide all aspects of a suit wherein compensatory damages were sought as incidental to an injunction.[g] The court observed that this doctrine had no bearing on the plaintiff's jury right. But this observation led the court to an alternative ground for decision, narrower than the one given in the above-quoted passage:

"The doctrine that equity, once having taken jurisdiction, will retain it for the purpose of disposing of the entire case was limited and safeguarded in its application under the former procedure by another rule, equally well established, namely, that where the title of the plaintiff is doubtful or the violation of his right by the defendant is not clear, he will be required to first establish his title, his right, and the violation thereof, in an action at law, before equity will entertain his application for extraordinary relief.[h] High on Injunctions, § 8; 29 Cyc. 1228, and cases cited. Under this rule, if the plaintiff had filed in a court of purely equitable jurisdiction the complaint upon which this action is based and the defendant had made answer thereto, as it did here, denying plaintiff's title to the land alleged to have been injured, denying the diversion of waters, and denying the alleged injuries to the land, the court would have said to the plaintiff, in effect:

'You must first go into a court of law and there establish these disputed claims of right upon which you are basing your claims for relief; if you succeed in establishing there your legal rights, we will then entertain and consider your petition for equitable relief.'

"And, of course, in such action at law the parties would have been entitled to a jury . . . . ''

IMPERIAL SHALE BRICK CO. v. JEWETT, 169 N.Y. 143, 62 N.E. 167 (1901). An "inland marine certificate of insurance" issued to plaintiff was stated to cover a cargo of bricks shipped by plaintiff from Cleveland, Ohio to "Waukegan, Mich." The cargo became a total loss and did not reach its destination. Plaintiff sued defendants, as joint insurers, to reform the certificate to read "Waukegan, Illinois" (there being no Waukegan, Michigan) and to recover on the certificate as reformed.[i] After disposing of various defenses, the court said:

[g] See supra pp. 380–81.   [i] See supra pp. 373–74.

[h] See supra pp. 375–76.

"The defendants complain that against their objection and exception the action was tried at the Equity Term instead of before a jury. . . . The plaintiff properly asked in its complaint to have the certificate corrected in this respect. If the defendants had admitted by their answer the statement of facts alleged in this behalf in the complaint, as they did upon the trial, the equitable issue would not have arisen, but they did not, but interposed a denial, and thus the case properly came on for trial at the Equity Term.

"The complaint does not contain separate equitable and legal causes of action, but it asks such relief in equity as would, if granted, permit a recovery, as at common law. But the complaint stated no common-law cause of action, except as conditioned upon the equitable relief, and hence the right to recovery rested primarily upon equitable grounds. The court having obtained jurisdiction in equity, may, if it grant the equitable relief, retain jurisdiction and render that further judgment which properly follows thereon."

Question: (4) Is the ruling in this case compatible with the New York statute (which was at the time of decision the same as the present statute, supra p. 665, for all purposes here relevant)?

MUTUALITY

The plaintiff thus has a jury right on the legal issues. Moreover, the plaintiff historically had the power—to the extent of the clean-up doctrine—to preclude the defendant's jury right.

Question: (5) Should this lack of mutuality affect the "chancellor's" discretion in granting clean-up relief today?

In Cogswell v. New York, New Haven & Hartford Railroad, 105 N.Y. 319, 11 N.E. 518 (1887), plaintiff, complaining of a nuisance, sought damages, abatement, and an injunction. Her demand for a jury was granted below as a matter of right, but on appeal this was held to be error. At common law, said the court, the remedies of damages and abatement were available in a legal action known as an assize of nuisance, but the law court could not grant an injunction. This, then, is not a case that as a whole "was triable by jury at the adoption of the Constitution, nor is it one where, under the present system, the plaintiff is compelled to unite her claims for both equitable and legal relief in the same action." But as plaintiff chose to bring "an action for both legal and equitable relief in respect to the same cause of action," she "submits to have the issues tried by the court, or by the court with the aid of a jury, as the court in its discretion may determine, according to the practice in equity cases." (This waiver rule has been limited by NYCPLR § 4102(c), which provides that there is no waiver by joining legal and equitable claims based upon separate transactions. See Sepinski v. Bergstol, 81 A.D.2d 860, 438 N.Y.S.2d 870 (1981) (still waiver if same transaction).)

Still another attitude was expressed in Koeper v. Town of Louisville, 109 Minn. 519, 124 N.W. 218 (1910), where the same three heads of relief were sought. The court said there was a clear distinction between a case where "two causes of action, one legal and the other equitable, are united in the same action" and a case where "the cause of action is an equitable one, in which equitable relief is sought, and also legal relief as an incident to the equitable cause of action." The present case was of the latter type, and it followed that neither party was entitled to the constitutional jury.

Order of trial.—Still assume that, after merger, the plaintiff seeks cumulatively legal and equitable relief. Once you have decided that a party has a jury right, there remains the separate question of whether the right will be protected by an appropriate order of trial when a contested factual issue is common to the legal and the equitable relief.

If the plaintiff prior to merger had the right to seek cumulatively both legal and equitable relief and if there was an issue common to both types of relief, the plaintiff generally had the choice whether to bring the legal or the equitable action first. And the first determination of the common issue would bind the parties in the second action. See Brady v. Daly, 175 U.S. 148, 20 S.Ct. 62 (1899). Hence the plaintiff could choose the mode of trial of the common issue. Under a merged system, the plaintiff may or must seek all his relief in a single action. Fidelity to history would call for letting the plaintiff preserve the substance of his option by simply claiming or not claiming a jury on the common issue in the single action. If the teachings of history were to be followed, the defendant would have no choice as to mode of trial.

BRUCKMAN v. HOLLZER, 152 F.2d 730 (9th Cir.1946). Harold Lloyd Corporation, claiming copyright infringement of its photoplay, sued in separate counts, Count 1 asking damages from the three defendants for the infringement and Count 2 asking that one of the defendants, Universal Pictures Corporation, be enjoined from future infringement. (Formerly, the legal and equitable causes could have been brought separately, and either could have been brought before the other.) The plaintiff demanded a trial by jury on the first count, and the defendants moved to strike the demand. The trial court denied the motion to strike and indicated that the equitable issues would be tried by the court without a jury simultaneously with the damages claim "to the extent practicable." The defendants then brought a mandamus petition in the court of appeals to compel the district judge to strike the demand. The defendants conceded that the claim for damages, if sued on separately, would be triable before a jury, but they contended that the plaintiff by combining the damages claim with a claim for equitable relief waived his right to jury trial. The mandamus petition was denied, the court completely rejecting the waiver theory. Judge Denman pointed out that the issue of infringement, common to the legal and equitable claims for relief, might be decided one way by the jury on conflicting evidence and the opposite way by the judge, and that the first determination would be binding. Hence, he concluded, the right to trial by jury as declared by the seventh amendment could be preserved only if the court tried the common issue so that judgment would be rendered on the verdict before the equitable claim was decided.

RALPH BLECHMAN, INC. v. I.B. KLEINERT RUBBER CO., 98 F.Supp. 1005 (S.D.N.Y.1951). The plaintiffs sued under the antitrust laws for treble damages and injunctive relief. (Formerly, a claim for treble damages for violation of the antitrust laws could not be joined with a claim for equitable relief, because equity could not award damages penal in character. Hence separate actions at law and in equity were necessary, and either could be brought before the other.) Defendants moved to strike plaintiffs' jury demand on the ground that the action was essentially equitable in nature. The court denied the motion, saying that where the same claim is made the basis for both legal and equitable relief, it is of little aid to determine whether the issues are essentially legal or essentially equitable in their nature. The court also said: "Whether or not this question [the right of the plaintiffs to injunctive relief] should be separately tried by the court, and, if so, whether or not it should be tried before the legal issues, are questions not presented by the instant motion, and are matters within the discretion of the trial judge."

JUDICIAL DISCRETION

The plaintiff thus generally could control the mode of trial on the common issue. There were, however, two historical exceptions to this rule. In certain kinds of actions, represented by the Imperial Shale case, the equitable issues had to be tried first; neither the parties nor the court had any choice as to this. In certain other kinds of actions, represented by the Farrell case, the legal issues had to be tried first; again, there was no choice.

As a historical matter, both in the general situation and in the two exceptional situations, the court had no discretion as to the mode of trial on the common issue. Yet a number of cases held that judicial discretion with respect to order of trial could be invoked in a way that would dictate mode of trial. See, e.g., Orenstein v. United States, 191 F.2d 184 (1st Cir.1951). This position had no historical support.

Alternative remedies.—Now assume that, after merger, the plaintiff seeks legal and equitable remedies that are available only alternatively. What happens to the jury right?

FRASER v. GEIST, 1 F.R.D. 267 (E.D.Pa.1940). Fraser, an expert golfer, sued the executors of the estate of Geist, a wealthy golf devotee, alleging that Geist "induced" plaintiff to leave high school prior to graduation to become his golf companion by promising to set up a trust fund of at least $100,000 for plaintiff in his will. The complaint further alleged that plaintiff performed his part of the arrangement for more than five years until Geist's death, that Geist made no provision in his will for the promised trust fund, and that the executors of his estate refused to recognize any obligation. Plaintiff prayed that the executors be ordered either (1) to set up a $100,000 trust fund and pay the income to plaintiff for life or (2) to pay plaintiff a lump sum in lieu thereof as damages. The defendants denied the making of the contract. The plaintiff demanded a jury trial. The defendants moved to stike the demand on the ground that the plaintiff's claim was cognizable only in equity. Judge Kalodner avoided the difficulties by concluding that the complaint stated no claim for legal relief and hence struck the plaintiff's demand for jury trial; his reasoning was premised on the "uncertainty as to the computation of damages." He expressed regret that Rule 39 precluded "a more desirable solution—one in which the court could try the case with a jury and, in the event that equitable relief should be granted, could treat the verdict of the jury as merely advisory; but, in the event that legal relief is appropriate, could treat the jury's verdict as binding"; his thought here was "that Rule 39 makes it incumbent upon the court to decide from the pleadings and prior to trial whether or not the action is one at law or in equity."

The question of how to resolve the jury claim if the complaint can stand on both of the alternative grounds has been a favorite subject for commentators.

Professor Moore believes that Judge Kalodner's "more desirable solution" is not precluded by Rule 39. See 5 Moore ¶ 38.18, at 38–161 n.5. Professor Moore's own solution, however, was to deny plaintiff a jury because on plaintiff's preferred theory the case is one for the court. See 3 J. Moore & J. Friedman, Moore's Federal Practice 3018 (1938). But is the equitable remedy necessarily his preference?

Professor Morris characterized Judge Kalodner's ruling that the complaint stated no claim for legal relief as "dubious substantive law." Professor Morris's solution required the plaintiff to specify at the outset which remedy he prefers, and the court to treat the jury right accordingly. See Morris, Jury Trial Under the Federal Fusion of Law and Equity, 20 Tex.L.Rev. 427, 435–36 (1942). Curiously, Professor McCoid's solution required the plaintiff to take a position at the outset on trial by jury, and the court to treat the preferred remedy accordingly. See McCoid, Right to Jury Trial in the Federal Courts, 45 Iowa L.Rev. 726, 731–34 (1960).

Questions: (6) What could the plaintiff have done under the practice prior to the Federal Rules? Does this suggest that Professor Morris's approach is superior?

(7) Under the Morris approach, if the plaintiff indicates that he prefers the equitable remedy but this request for relief fails on "purely equitable" grounds, is there a jury right on the remaining legal issues? Can Judge Kalodner's "more desirable solution" be utilized to meet this contingency?

(8) Employing the approach of Professor Morris in tandem with the "more desirable solution" of Judge Kalodner, can you construct a decision-tree that accurately reconstructs history?

(9) In light of Rule 54(c), is not the Fraser v. Geist problem present in every action?

Equitable device.—Assume that, after merger, the plaintiff uses a traditionally equitable device for getting into court in order to press what is otherwise a legal claim. Examples of such devices include class action, shareholders' derivative action, intervention, interpleader, and declaratory judgment. Is there a jury right on the legal-type issues?

RANKIN v. FREBANK CO., 47 Cal.App.3d 75, 121 Cal.Rptr. 348 (1975). Two minority stockholders brought a derivative action, seeking recovery of "secret profits" alleged to have been wrongfully diverted by two of the corporation's officers. The plaintiffs demanded a jury trial, but the trial court refused. This was affirmed on appeal, the court saying there was no right to jury trial in a shareholders' derivative action under the "historically based approach" followed in California.

Equitable defense to legal claim.—Assume that, after merger, the plaintiff brings a purely legal claim and the defendant interposes a defense, such as mutual mistake, that was formerly cognizable only in equity. What happens to the jury right?

As a historical matter, the law-defendant here would have immediately gone into equity to seek relief, such as reformation or rescission, based on mutual mistake. The equity court would as a matter of course have temporarily enjoined the law action. The equitable issues would then have been tried to the court. If these issues were decided in favor of the law-defendant, the law action would be defeated. If not, the law action would then proceed. See Liberty Oil Co. v. Condon National Bank, 260 U.S. 235, 43 S.Ct. 118 (1922); cf. City of Morgantown v. Royal Ins. Co., 169 F.2d 713 (4th Cir.1948), aff'd on other grounds, 337 U.S. 254, 69 S.Ct. 1067 (1949).

Question: (10) How can this scenario be replicated in a modern procedural system?

Equitable counterclaim to legal claim (or vice versa).—Now assume that, after merger, the plaintiff brings a purely legal claim and the defendant seeks to defeat it on some ground, such as fraud, that was formerly cognizable as a defense at law and also as a claim in equity. What happens to the jury right? What of common contested factual issues?

LIFE INSURANCE FRAUD CASES

The problem of the jury right under merged procedure when one party presents in his pleading a legal claim and the other an equitable claim, and there is a substantial question of fact common to the two, is well illustrated by life insurance cases in which the insurance company seeks to establish that the policy was obtained by fraud of the insured. Consideration of these cases is relevant to an understanding of the implications of Beacon Theatres, Inc. v. Westover, which begins the next Section.

Originally, fraud in the procurement of insurance was cognizable only in equity in a suit for cancellation by rescission; such fraud could not be shown in defense of an action to recover on the policy. In the course of time, however, fraud worked from equity over to law and came to be recognized as a defense to an action at law, triable to a jury. See Ettelson v. Metropolitan Life Ins. Co., 137 F.2d 62 (3d Cir.), cert. denied, 320 U.S. 777, 64 S.Ct. 92 (1943). But, in appropriate circumstances, cancellation could still be decreed in equity.

1. Assume that the insurer uncovers evidence of fraud while the insured is still alive. A suit to cancel the policy may be brought. The insurer does not have to wait until the insured dies and then set up the fraud as a defense to an action on the policy. The lapse of time might be extremely prejudicial to establishment of the defense. This is especially true when the policy contains, as most life insurance policies do by statutory requirement, an "incontestability clause" providing that after a prescribed period, commonly two years, the policy cannot be cancelled for any reason except nonpayment of premiums. The running of the time period is thus fatal to the claim of fraud, and the insurer must be able to protect itself by suing for cancellation before the policy becomes incontestable.

Questions: (11) Would the insured have a right to trial by jury on the issue of fraud in such an action? See Connecticut Gen. Life Ins. Co. v. Candimat Co., 83 F.Supp. 1 (D.Md.1949) (no).

(12) Would there be a right to jury trial if the insured brought an action for a declaratory judgment that the policy was valid?

2.   Assume next that the insured dies while the policy is still contestable for fraud and that the beneficiary sues on the policy. If the insurer counterclaims for cancellation, should the fraud issue be determined by the jury or the judge? Alternatively, if the insurer is the first to sue and if the beneficiary counterclaims for recovery on the policy, should the issue of fraud be for the judge or the jury? Consider the effect of Rule 13(a).

Tactically, the beneficiary will almost surely prefer a jury determination of the issue of fraud, and the insurer will prefer a court determination. Whether a jury be thought "outcome determinative" or not in the Erie-Guaranty sense, a realistic view of the probabilities leads to the conclusion that when, for instance, the bereaved spouse and children are contesting with the insurance company, they are likely to fare better with a jury than with a judge. Cf. Byrd v. Blue Ridge Rural Electric Cooperative, supra p. 217, in which the majority opinion discusses the problem of jury right upon the assumption that the outcome may be substantially affected by whether an issue is decided by a judge or a jury, but ultimately minimizes the likelihood of a different result.

A possible but unattractive solution would be to have the question of the right to a jury on the issue of fraud, common to the claim and the counterclaim, turn upon which party wins the race to the courthouse. See Prudential Ins. Co. v. Saxe, 134 F.2d 16 (D.C.Cir.), cert. denied, 319 U.S. 745, 63 S.Ct. 1033 (1943).

What does resort to history in this situation suggest? Before merger, the insurer could bring a bill in equity to cancel the policy and to restrain the beneficiary from bringing an action on the policy until the disposition of the suit. The beneficiary might soon thereafter institute a law action on the policy, before any injunction issued, and he might then contend that the insurer's remedy at law was adequate because of the availability to it of the defense of fraud in the legal action. However, equity jurisdiction was commonly determined as of the date of institution of the suit and continued even though the remedy at law later became adequate. Moreover, given an incontestability clause, the beneficiary might sue within the period of contestability, take a voluntary dismissal after the period had run, and then, still within the statute of limitations, bring another action.[j] In this situation the equity court might hold the case on its docket until the action on the policy was actually tried to a jury, so as to prevent frustration of the insurer's objective of contesting fraud by the beneficiary's dismissal of the pending law action, or it might enjoin prosecution of the law action and decide the fraud issue for itself. Professor

[j] This of course is no longer possible under Rule 41(a) or a comparable state rule.

James said: "Where *A* seeks equitable relief principally to defeat an action at law by *B* against him on grounds cognizable as a defense at law, and where *B* interposes the law action by way of counterclaim, fidelity to the historical pattern would usually require that the order of trial sequence be left to the trial court's discretion, to be guided by the kind of factors enumerated in American Life Insurance Co. v. Stewart.[k] This, it should be noted, is the only type of situation in which history warrants the use of discretion for this purpose."[l]

If the beneficiary first sued on the policy, the insurer could similarly bring a bill in equity and seek to restrain the further prosecution of the law action. A similar historical analysis applies. Here, however, "equity would typically refuse to enjoin the law action and grant relief, stating that the remedy at law was adequate." [m]

SECTION 3. NEW DIRECTIONS

BEACON THEATRES, INC. v. WESTOVER

Supreme Court of the United States, 1959.
359 U.S. 500, 79 S.Ct. 948.

MR. JUSTICE BLACK delivered the opinion of the Court.

Petitioner, Beacon Theatres, Inc., sought by mandamus to require a district judge in the Southern District of California to vacate certain orders alleged to deprive it of a jury trial of issues arising in a suit brought against it by Fox West Coast Theatres, Inc. The Court of Appeals for the Ninth Circuit refused the writ, holding that the trial judge had acted within his proper discretion in denying petitioner's request for a jury. 252 F.2d 864. We granted certiorari, 356 U.S. 956, 78 S.Ct. 996, because "Maintenance of the jury as a fact-finding body is of such importance and occupies so firm a place in our history and jurisprudence that any seeming curtailment of the right to a jury trial should be scrutinized with the utmost care." Dimick v. Schiedt, 293 U.S. 474, 486, 55 S.Ct. 296, 301.

Fox had asked for declaratory relief against Beacon alleging a controversy arising under the Sherman Antitrust Act, 26 Stat. 209, as amended, 15 U.S.C. §§ 1, 2, and under the Clayton Act, 38 Stat. 731, 15 U.S.C. § 15, which authorizes suits for treble damages against Sherman Act violators. According to the complaint Fox operates a

---

[k] 300 U.S. 203, 57 S.Ct. 377 (1937). Insurer's bill in equity to cancel for fraud was followed by beneficiaries' action at law on the policy. The Court, in discussing the appropriate factors to be taken into account for the exercise of equitable jurisdiction, said: "There would be many circumstances to be weighed, as, for instance, the condition of the court calendar, whether the insurer had been precipitate or its adversaries dilatory, as well as other factors. In the end, benefit and hardship would have to be set off, the one against the other, and a balance ascertained."

[l] F. James, Civil Procedure 371 (1965).

[m] Id. at 365.

movie theatre in San Bernardino, California, and has long been exhibiting films under contracts with movie distributors. These contracts grant it the exclusive right to show "first run" pictures in the "San Bernardino competitive area" and provide for "clearance"—a period of time during which no other theatre can exhibit the same pictures. After building a drive-in theatre about 11 miles from San Bernardino, Beacon notified Fox that it considered contracts barring simultaneous exhibitions of first-run films in the two theatres to be overt acts in violation of the antitrust laws.[1] Fox's complaint alleged that this notification, together with threats of treble damage suits against Fox and its distributors, gave rise to "duress and coercion" which deprived Fox of a valuable property right, the right to negotiate for exclusive first-run contracts. Unless Beacon was restrained, the complaint continued, irreparable harm would result. Accordingly, while its pleading was styled a "Complaint for Declaratory Relief," Fox prayed both for a declaration that a grant of clearance between the Fox and Beacon theatres is reasonable and not in violation of the antitrust laws, and for an injunction, pending final resolution of the litigation, to prevent Beacon from instituting any action under the antitrust laws against Fox and its distributors arising out of the controversy alleged in the complaint. Beacon filed an answer, a counterclaim against Fox, and a cross-claim against an exhibitor who had intervened. These denied the threats and asserted that there was no substantial competition between the two theatres, that the clearances granted were therefore unreasonable, and that a conspiracy existed between Fox and its distributors to manipulate contracts and clearances so as to restrain trade and monopolize first-run pictures in violation of the antitrust laws. Treble damages were asked.

Beacon demanded a jury trial of the factual issues in the case as provided by Federal Rule of Civil Procedure 38(b). The District Court, however, viewed the issues raised by the "Complaint for Declaratory Relief," including the question of competition between the two theatres, as essentially equitable. Acting under the purported authority of Rules 42(b) and 57 it directed that these issues be tried to the court before jury determination of the validity of the charges of antitrust violations made in the counterclaim and cross-claim. A common issue of the "Complaint for Declaratory Relief," the counterclaim, and the cross-claim was the reasonableness of the clearances granted to Fox, which depended, in part, on the existence of competition between the two theatres. Thus the effect of the action of the

[1] Beacon allegedly stated that the clearances granted violated both the antitrust laws and the decrees issued in United States v. Paramount Pictures, Inc., D.C., 66 F.Supp. 323, 70 F.Supp. 53, affirmed in part and reversed in part, 334 U.S. 131, 68 S.Ct. 915, subsequent proceedings in the District Court, 85 F.Supp. 881. The decrees in that case set limits on what clearances could be given when theatres were in competition with each other and held that there should be no clearances between theatres not in substantial competition. Neither Beacon nor Fox, however, appears to have been a party to those decrees. Their relevance, therefore, seems to be only that of significant precedents.

This limits Beac. right to jury on every issue that effects damages suit

District Court could be, as the Court of Appeals believed, "to limit the petitioner's opportunity fully to try to a jury every issue which has a bearing upon its treble damage suit," for determination of the issue of clearances by the judge might "operate either by way of res judicata or collateral estoppel so as to conclude both parties with respect thereto at the subsequent trial of the treble damage claim." 252 F.2d at page 874.

"essentially equitable"- no support from DJA, R57

The District Court's finding that the Complaint for Declaratory Relief presented basically equitable issues draws no support from the Declaratory Judgment Act, 28 U.S.C. §§ 2201, 2202; Fed.Rules Civ. Proc., 57. See also 48 Stat. 955, 28 U.S.C. (1940 ed.) § 400. That statute, while allowing prospective defendants to sue to establish their nonliability, specifically preserves the right to jury trial for both parties. It follows that if Beacon would have been entitled to a jury trial in a treble damage suit against Fox it cannot be deprived of that right merely because Fox took advantage of the availability of declaratory relief to sue Beacon first. Since the right to trial by jury applies to treble damage suits under the antitrust laws, and is, in fact, an essential part of the congressional plan for making competition rather than monopoly the rule of trade, see Fleitmann v. Welsbach Street Lighting Co., 240 U.S. 27, 29, 36 S.Ct. 233, 234, the Sherman and Clayton Act issues on which Fox sought a declaration were essentially jury questions.

B/c has jury applies to damages under Sherman issues which Fox wanted Decl. Jud. w/ jury?

Nevertheless the Court of Appeals refused to upset the order of the district judge. It held that the question of whether a right to jury trial existed was to be judged by Fox's complaint read as a whole. In addition to seeking a declaratory judgment, the court said, Fox's complaint can be read as making out a valid plea for injunctive relief, thus stating a claim traditionally cognizable in equity. A party who is entitled to maintain a suit in equity for an injunction, said the court, may have all the issues in his suit determined by the judge without a jury regardless of whether legal rights are involved. The court then rejected the argument that equitable relief, traditionally available only when legal remedies are inadequate, was rendered unnecessary in this case by the filing of the counterclaim and cross-claim which presented all the issues necessary to a determination of the right to injunctive relief. Relying on American Life Ins. Co. v. Stewart, 300 U.S. 203, 215, 57 S.Ct. 377, 380, decided before the enactment of the Federal Rules of Civil Procedure, it invoked the principle that a court sitting in equity could retain jurisdiction even though later a legal remedy became available. In such instances the equity court had discretion to enjoin the later lawsuit in order to allow the whole dispute to be determined in one case in one court. Reasoning by analogy, the Court of Appeals held it was not an abuse of discretion for the district judge, acting under Federal Rule of Civil Procedure 42(b), to try the equitable cause first even though this might, through collateral estoppel, prevent a full jury trial of the counter-

Ct. Apps says that complaint as whole → also plea for injunct → equity

Am. Life Ins. Co. → ct. in equity could keep juris. even tho legal remedy becomes avail'y, equity can enjoin legal case

under R42b Equity can separate & try equitable case 1st

claim and cross-claim which were as effectively stopped as by an equity injunction.[6]

Beac. says no claim for equit. relief stated,

Beacon takes issue with the holding of the Court of Appeals that the complaint stated a claim upon which equitable relief could be granted. As initially filed the complaint alleged that threats of lawsuits by petitioner against Fox and its distributors were causing irreparable harm to Fox's business relationships. The prayer for re-

Ct. Apps. construes complaint to include injunction against threats

lief, however, made no mention of the threats but asked only that pending litigation of the claim for declaratory judgment, Beacon be enjoined from beginning any lawsuits under the antitrust laws against Fox and its distributors arising out of the controversy alleged in the complaint. Evidently of the opinion that this prayer did not state a good claim for equitable relief, the Court of Appeals construed it to include a request for an injunction against threats of lawsuits. This liberal construction of a pleading is in line with Rule 8 of

R8f

the Federal Rules of Civil Procedure. See Conley v. Gibson, 355 U.S. 41, 47–48, 78 S.Ct. 99, 102–103. But this fact does not solve our problem. Assuming that the pleadings can be construed to support such a request and assuming additionally that the complaint can be read as alleging the kind of harassment by a multiplicity of lawsuits which would *traditionally* have justified equity to take jurisdiction and set-

But neither claim can deny Beac. of jury

tle the case in one suit, we are nevertheless of the opinion that, under the Declaratory Judgment Act and the Federal Rules of Civil Procedure, neither claim can justify denying Beacon a trial by jury of all the issues in the antitrust controversy.

To justify cts. discretion of no jury must at least be irreparable harm & inad. of legal remedy

The basis of injunctive relief in the federal courts has always been irreparable harm and inadequacy of legal remedies. At least as much is required to justify a trial court in using its discretion under the Federal Rules to allow claims of equitable origins to be tried ahead of legal ones, since this has the same effect as an equitable injunction of the legal claims. And it is immaterial, in judging if that discretion is properly employed, that before the Federal Rules and the Declaratory Judgment Act were passed, courts of equity, exercising a jurisdiction separate from courts of law, were, in some cases, allowed to enjoin subsequent legal actions between the same parties involving the same controversy. This was because the subsequent legal action, though providing an opportunity to try the case to a jury, might not protect the right of the equity plaintiff to a fair and orderly adjudication of the controversy. See, e.g., New York Life Ins. Co. v. Seymour, 6 Cir., 45 F.2d 47. Under such circumstances the legal remedy could quite naturally be deemed inadequate. Inade-

---

[6] 252 F.2d at page 874. In Ettelson v. Metropolitan Life Ins. Co., 317 U.S. 188, 192, 63 S.Ct. 163, 164, this Court recognized that orders enabling equitable causes to be tried before legal ones had the same effect as injunctions. In City of Morgantown, W. Va. v. Royal Ins. Co., 337 U.S. 254, 69 S.Ct. 1067, the Court de-nied at least some such orders the status of injunctions for the purposes of appealability. It did not, of course, imply that when the orders came to be reviewed they would be examined any less strictly than injunctions. 337 U.S. at page 258, 69 S.Ct. at page 1069.

quacy of remedy and irreparable harm are practical terms, however. As such their existence today must be determined, not by precedents decided under discarded procedures, but in the light of the remedies now made available by the Declaratory Judgment Act and the Federal Rules.

Viewed in this manner, the use of discretion by the trial court under Rule 42(b) to deprive Beacon of a full jury trial on its counterclaim and cross-claim, as well as on Fox's plea for declaratory relief, cannot be justified. Under the Federal Rules the same court may try both legal and equitable causes in the same action. Fed.Rules Civ. Proc., 1, 2, 18. Thus any defenses, equitable or legal, Fox may have to charges of antitrust violations can be raised either in its suit for declaratory relief or in answer to Beacon's counterclaim. On proper showing, harassment by threats of other suits, or other suits actually brought, involving the issues being tried in this case, could be temporarily enjoined pending the outcome of this litigation. Whatever permanent injunctive relief Fox might be entitled to on the basis of the decision in this case could, of course, be given by the court after the jury renders its verdict. In this way the issues between these parties could be settled in one suit giving Beacon a full jury trial of every antitrust issue. Cf. Ring v. Spina, 2 Cir., 166 F.2d 546. By contrast, the holding of the court below while granting Fox no additional protection unless the avoidance of jury trial be considered as such, would compel Beacon to split his antitrust case, trying part to a judge and part to a jury.[10] Such a result, which involves the postponement and subordination of Fox's own legal claim for declaratory relief as well as of the counterclaim which Beacon was compelled by the Federal Rules to bring, is not permissible.

Our decision is consistent with the plan of the Federal Rules and the Declaratory Judgment Act to effect substantial procedural reform while retaining a distinction between jury and nonjury issues and leaving substantive rights unchanged. Since in the federal courts equity has always acted only when legal remedies were inadequate, the expansion of adequate legal remedies provided by the Declaratory Judgment Act and the Federal Rules necessarily affects the scope of equity. Thus, the justification for equity's deciding legal issues once it obtains jurisdiction, and refusing to dismiss a case, merely because subsequently a legal remedy becomes available, must be re-evaluated in the light of the liberal joinder provisions of the Federal Rules which allow legal and equitable causes to be brought and resolved in one civil action. Similarly the need for, and therefore, the availability of such equitable remedies as Bills of Peace, Quia Timet and Injunction must be reconsidered in view of the existence of the

[10] Since the issue of violation of the antitrust laws often turns on the reasonableness of a restraint on trade in the light of all the facts, see, e.g., Standard Oil Co. of New Jersey v. United States, 221 U.S. 1, 60, 31 S.Ct. 502, 515, it is particularly undesirable to have some of the relevant considerations tried by one factfinder and some by another.

Declaratory Judgment Act as well as the liberal joinder provision of
the Rules. This is not only in accord with the spirit of the Rules and
the Act but is required by the provision in the Rules that "[t]he right
of trial by jury as declared by the Seventh Amendment to the Constitution or as given by a statute of the United States shall be preserved
. . . . inviolate."

If this can't work, then cts discretion. But ↓

If there should be cases where the availability of declaratory judgment or joinder in one suit of legal and equitable causes would not in
all respects protect the plaintiff seeking equitable relief from irreparable harm while affording a jury trial in the legal cause, the trial
court will necessarily have to use its discretion in deciding whether
the legal or equitable cause should be tried first. Since the right to
jury trial is a constitutional one, however, while no similar requirement protects trials by the court,[17] that discretion is very narrowly
limited and must, wherever possible, be exercised to preserve jury
trial. As this Court said in Scott v. Neely, 140 U.S. 106, 109–110, 11
S.Ct. 712, 714: "In the Federal courts this [jury] right cannot be dispensed with, except by the assent of the parties entitled to it; nor can
it be impaired by any blending with a claim, properly cognizable at
law, of a demand for equitable relief in aid of the legal action or during its pendency." This long-standing principle of equity dictates
that only under the most imperative circumstances, circumstances
which in view of the flexible procedures of the Federal Rules we cannot now anticipate, can the right to a jury trial of legal issues be lost
through prior determination of equitable claims. See Leimer v.
Woods, 8 Cir., 196 F.2d 828, 833–836. As we have shown, this is far
from being such a case.

Jury is Constit Right!

Respondent claims mandamus is not available under the All Writs
Act, 28 U.S.C. § 1651. Whatever differences of opinion there may be
in other types of cases, we think the right to grant mandamus to require jury trial where it has been improperly denied is settled.

The judgment of the Court of Appeals is reversed.

MR. JUSTICE FRANKFURTER took no part in the consideration or
decision of this case.

MR. JUSTICE STEWART, with whom MR. JUSTICE HARLAN and MR.
JUSTICE WHITTAKER concur, dissenting.

. . . .

Assuming the existence of a factual issue common both to the
plaintiff's original action and the defendant's counterclaim for damages, I cannot agree that the District Court must be compelled to try
the counterclaim first. It is, of course, a matter of no great moment
in what order the issues between the parties in the present litigation
are tried. What is disturbing is the process by which the Court ar-

---

[17] See Hurwitz v. Hurwitz, 78 U.S.App.
D.C. 66, 136 F.2d 796, 798–799; cf. The

Genesee Chief v. Fitzhugh, 12 How. 443,
459–460.

rives at its decision—a process which appears to disregard the historic relationship between equity and law.

I.

The Court suggests that "the expansion of adequate legal remedies provided by the Declaratory Judgment Act . . . necessarily affects the scope of equity." Does the Court mean to say that the mere availability of an action for a declaratory judgment operates to furnish "an adequate remedy at law" so as to deprive a court of equity of the power to act? That novel line of reasoning is at least implied in the Court's opinion. But the Declaratory Judgment Act did not "expand" the substantive law. That Act merely provided a new statutory remedy, neither legal nor equitable, but available in the areas of both equity and law. When declaratory relief is sought, the right to trial by jury depends upon the basic context in which the issues are presented. See Moore's Federal Practice (2d ed.) §§ 38.29, 57.30; Borchard, Declaratory Judgments (2d ed.), 399–404. If the basic issues in an action for declaratory relief are of a kind traditionally cognizable in equity, e.g., a suit for cancellation of a written instrument, the declaratory judgment is not a "remedy at law." If, on the other hand, the issues arise in a context traditionally cognizable at common law, the right to a jury trial of course remains unimpaired, even though the only relief demanded is a declaratory judgment.

[handwritten margin notes: DJA → new remedy both equit. & legal - depends on context - issues presented]

Thus, if in this case the complaint had asked merely for a judgment declaring that the plaintiff's specified manner of business dealings with distributors and other exhibitors did not render it liable to Beacon under the antitrust laws, this would have been simply a "juxtaposition of parties" case in which Beacon could have demanded a jury trial.[7] But the complaint in the present case, as the Court recognizes, presented issues of exclusively equitable cognizance, going well beyond a mere defense to any subsequent action at law. Fox sought from the court protection against Beacon's allegedly unlawful interference with its business relationships—protection which this Court seems to recognize might not have been afforded by a declaratory judgment, unsupplemented by equitable relief. The availability of a declaratory judgment did not, therefore, operate to confer upon Beacon the right to trial by jury with respect to the issues raised by the complaint.

[handwritten margin notes: Here - Fox "essent. equit." - needed protection couldn't have gotten just from declar. judg.]

II.

The Court's opinion does not, of course, hold or even suggest that a court of equity may never determine "legal rights." For indeed it is

[7] Moore's Federal Practice (2d ed.) § 57.31[2]. "Transposition of parties" would perhaps be a more accurate description. A typical such case is one in which a plaintiff uses the declaratory judgment procedure to seek a determination of nonliability to a legal claim asserted by the defendant. The defendant in such a case is, of course, entitled to a jury trial.

precisely such rights which the Chancellor, when his jurisdiction has been properly invoked, has often been called upon to decide. Issues of fact are rarely either "legal" or "equitable." All depends upon the context in which they arise. The examples cited by Chief Judge Pope in his thorough opinion in the Court of Appeals in this case are illustrative: ". . . In a suit for specific performance of a contract, the court may determine the making, validity and the terms of the contract involved. . . . " 252 F.2d 864, 874.

Though apparently not disputing these principles, the Court holds, quite apart from its reliance upon the Declaratory Judgment Act, that Beacon by filing its counterclaim and cross-claim acquired a right to trial by jury of issues which otherwise would have been properly triable to the court. Support for this position is found in the principle that, "in the federal courts equity has always acted only when legal remedies were inadequate. . . . " Yet that principle is not employed in its traditional sense as a limitation upon the exercise of power by a court of equity. This is apparent in the Court's recognition that the allegations of the complaint entitled Fox to equitable relief—relief to which Fox would not have been entitled if it had had an adequate remedy at law. Instead, the principle is employed today to mean that because it is possible under the counterclaim to have a jury trial of the factual issue of substantial competition, that issue must be tried by a jury, even though the issue was primarily presented in the original claim for equitable relief. This is a marked departure from long-settled principles.

It has been an established rule "that equitable jurisdiction existing at the filing of a bill is not destroyed because an adequate legal remedy may have become available thereafter." American Life Ins. Co. v. Stewart, 300 U.S. 203, 215, 57 S.Ct. 377, 380. See Dawson v. Kentucky Distilleries & Warehouse Co., 255 U.S. 288, 296, 41 S.Ct. 272, 275. It has also been long settled that the District Court in its discretion may order the trial of a suit in equity in advance of an action at law between the same parties, even if there is a factual issue common to both. In the words of Mr. Justice Cardozo, writing for a unanimous Court in American Life Ins. Co. v. Stewart, supra:

> "A court has control over its own docket. . . . In the exercise of a sound discretion it may hold one lawsuit in abeyance to abide the outcome of another, especially where the parties and the issues are the same. . . . If request had been made by the respondents to suspend the suits in equity till the other causes were disposed of, the District Court could have considered whether justice would not be done by pursuing such a course, the remedy in equity being exceptional and the outcome of necessity. . . . There would be many circumstances to be weighed, as, for instance, the condition of the court calendar, whether the insurer had been precipitate or its adversaries dilatory, as well as other factors. In the end, ben-

efit and hardship would have to be set off, the one against the other, and a balance ascertained." 300 U.S. 203, 215–216, 57 S.Ct. 377, 380.[9]

III.

The Court today sweeps away these basic principles as "precedents decided under discarded procedures." It suggests that the Federal Rules of Civil Procedure have somehow worked an "expansion of adequate legal remedies" so as to oust the District Courts of equitable jurisdiction, as well as to deprive them of their traditional power to control their own dockets. But obviously the Federal Rules could not and did not "expand" the substantive law one whit.

Like the Declaratory Judgment Act, the Federal Rules preserve inviolate the right to trial by jury in actions historically cognizable at common law, as under the Constitution they must. They do not create a right of trial by jury where that right "does not exist under the Constitution or statutes of the United States." Rule 39(a). Since Beacon's counterclaim was compulsory under the Rules, see Rule 13(a), it is apparent that by filing it Beacon could not be held to have waived its jury rights. Compare American Mills Co. v. American Surety Co., 260 U.S. 360, 43 S.Ct. 149. But neither can the counterclaim be held to have transformed Fox's original complaint into an action at law. See Bendix Aviation Corp. v. Glass, D.C., 81 F.Supp. 645.

The Rules make possible the trial of legal and equitable claims in the same proceeding, but they expressly affirm the power of a trial judge to determine the order in which claims shall be heard. Rule 42(b). Certainly the Federal Rules were not intended to undermine the basic structure of equity jurisprudence, developed over the centuries and explicitly recognized in the United States Constitution.

Trial judge has discret. as to order.

For these reasons I think the petition for a writ of mandamus should have been dismissed.

———

DAIRY QUEEN, INC. v. WOOD
Supreme Court of the United States, 1962.
369 U.S. 469, 82 S.Ct. 894.

McCullough owners of DQ trademark

MR. JUSTICE BLACK delivered the opinion of the Court.

The United States District Court for the Eastern District of Pennsylvania granted a motion to strike petitioner's demand for a trial by jury in an action now pending before it on the alternative grounds

———

[9] It is arguable that if a case factually similar to American Life Ins. Co. v. Stewart were to arise under the Declaratory Judgment Act, the defendant would be entitled to a jury trial. See footnote 7. But cf. 5 Moore's Federal Practice (2d ed.), p. 158.

that either the action was "purely equitable" or, if not purely equitable, whatever legal issues that were raised were "incidental" to equitable issues, and, in either case, no right to trial by jury existed. The petitioner then sought mandamus in the Court of Appeals for the Third Circuit to compel the district judge to vacate this order. When that court denied this request without opinion, we granted certiorari because the action of the Court of Appeals seemed inconsistent with protections already clearly recognized for the important constitutional right to trial by jury in our previous decisions.

At the outset, we may dispose of one of the grounds upon which the trial court acted in striking the demand for trial by jury—that based upon the view that the right to trial by jury may be lost as to legal issues where those issues are characterized as "incidental" to equitable issues—for our previous decisions make it plain that no such rule may be applied in the federal courts. In Scott v. Neely, decided in 1891, this Court held that a court of equity could not even take jurisdiction of a suit "in which a claim properly cognizable only at law is united in the same pleadings with a claim for equitable relief."[3] That holding, which was based upon both the historical separation between law and equity and the duty of the Court to insure "that the right to a trial by a jury in the legal action may be preserved intact,"[4] created considerable inconvenience in that it necessitated two separate trials in the same case whenever that case contained both legal and equitable claims. Consequently, when the procedure in the federal courts was modernized by the adoption of the Federal Rules of Civil Procedure in 1938, it was deemed advisable to abandon that part of the holding of Scott v. Neely which rested upon the separation of law and equity and to permit the joinder of legal and equitable claims in a single action. [The Court here quoted Rule 18.]

The Federal Rules did not, however, purport to change the basic holding of Scott v. Neely that the right to trial by jury of legal claims must be preserved. Quite the contrary, Rule 38(a) expressly reaffirms that constitutional principle . . . . Nonetheless, after the adoption of the Federal Rules, attempts were made indirectly to undercut that right by having federal courts in which cases involving both legal and equitable claims were filed decide the equitable claim first. The result of this procedure in those cases in which it was followed was that any issue common to both the legal and equitable claims was finally determined by the court and the party seeking trial by jury on the legal claim was deprived of that right as to these com-

---

[3] 140 U.S. 106, 117, 11 S.Ct. 712, 716. [This was a suit in equity in which the plaintiffs sought to establish a debt of the defendant to them and to set aside as fraudulent his conveyance of land to his co-defendant so as to subject it to the payment of the debt. The Court held that an action at law on the debt must precede a suit in equity to set aside the conveyance and ordered the bill in equity dismissed. The Court further held that the defendant was entitled to trial by jury on the debt claim.—Ed.]

[4] Id., 140 U.S. at 110, 11 S.Ct. at 714.

mon issues. This procedure finally came before us in Beacon Theatres, Inc. v. Westover, a case which, like this one, arose from the denial of a petition for mandamus to compel a district judge to vacate his order striking a demand for trial by jury.

Our decision reversing that case not only emphasizes the responsibility of the Federal Courts of Appeals to grant mandamus where necessary to protect the constitutional right to trial by jury but also limits the issues open for determination here by defining the protection to which that right is entitled in cases involving both legal and equitable claims. The holding in Beacon Theatres was that where both legal and equitable issues are presented in a single case, "only under the most imperative circumstances, circumstances which in view of the flexible procedures of the Federal Rules we cannot now anticipate, can the right to a jury trial of legal issues be lost through prior determination of equitable claims." That holding, of course, applies whether the trial judge chooses to characterize the legal issues presented as "incidental" to equitable issues or not.[8] Consequently, in a case such as this where there cannot even be a contention of such "imperative circumstances," Beacon Theatres requires that any legal issues for which a trial by jury is timely and properly demanded be submitted to a jury. There being no question of the timeliness or correctness of the demand involved here, the sole question which we must decide is whether the action now pending before the District Court contains legal issues.

The District Court proceeding arises out of a controversy between petitioner and the respondent owners of the trademark "DAIRY QUEEN" [n] with regard to a written licensing contract made by them in December 1949, under which petitioner agreed to pay some $150,000 for the exclusive right to use that trademark in certain portions of Pennsylvania. The terms of the contract provided for a small initial payment with the remaining payments to be made at the rate of 50% of all amounts received by petitioner on sales and franchises to deal with the trademark and, in order to make certain that the $150,000 payment would be completed within a specified period of time, further provided for minimum annual payments regardless of petitioner's receipts. In August 1960, the respondents wrote petitioner a letter in which they claimed that petitioner had committed "a material breach of that contract" by defaulting on the contract's payment provisions and notified petitioner of the termination

---

[8] "It is therefore immaterial that the case at bar contains a stronger basis for equitable relief than was present in Beacon Theatres. It would make no difference if the equitable cause clearly outweighed the legal cause so that the basic issue of the case taken as a whole is equitable. As long as any legal cause is involved the jury rights it creates control. This is the teaching of Beacon Theatres, as we construe it." Thermo–Stitch, Inc. v. Chemi-Cord Processing Corp., 5 Cir., 294 F.2d 486, 491.

[n] H.A. McCullough and H.F. McCullough, doing business as McCullough's Dairy Queen, were the owners of the trademark, plaintiffs in this action, and respondents (in addition to the district judge) in the Supreme Court.

of the contract and the cancellation of petitioner's right to use the trademark unless this claimed default was remedied immediately. When petitioner continued to deal with the trademark despite the notice of termination, the respondents brought an action based upon their view that a material breach of contract had occurred.

The complaint filed in the District Court alleged, among other things, that petitioner had "ceased paying . . . as required in the contract;" that the default "under the said contract . . . [was] in excess of $60,000.00;" that this default constituted a "material breach" of that contract; that petitioner had been notified by letter that its failure to pay as alleged made it guilty of a material breach of contract which if not "cured" would result in an immediate cancellation of the contract; that the breach had not been cured but that petitioner was contesting the cancellation and continuing to conduct business as an authorized dealer; that to continue such business after the cancellation of the contract constituted an infringement of the respondents' trademark; that petitioner's financial condition was unstable; and that because of the foregoing allegations, respondents were threatened with irreparable injury for which they had no adequate remedy at law. The complaint then prayed for both temporary and permanent relief, including: ① temporary and permanent injunctions to restrain petitioner from any future use of or dealing in the franchise and the trademark; ② an accounting to determine the exact amount of money owing by petitioner and a judgment for that amount; and ③ an injunction pending accounting to prevent petitioner from collecting any money from "Dairy Queen" stores in the territory.

In its answer to this complaint, petitioner raised a number of defenses, including: ① a denial that there had been any breach of contract, apparently based chiefly upon its allegation that in January 1955 the parties had entered into an oral agreement modifying the original written contract by removing the provision requiring minimum annual payments regardless of petitioner's receipts thus leaving petitioner's only obligation that of turning over 50% of all its receipts; ② laches and estoppel arising from respondents' failure to assert their claim promptly, thus permitting petitioner to expend large amounts of money in the development of its right to use the trademark; and ③ alleged violations of the antitrust laws by respondents in connection with their dealings with the trademark. Petitioner indorsed upon this answer a demand for trial by jury in accordance with Rule 38(b) of the Federal Rules of Civil Procedure.

Petitioner's contention, as set forth in its petition for mandamus to the Court of Appeals and reiterated in its briefs before this Court, is that insofar as the complaint requests a money judgment it presents a claim which is unquestionably legal. We agree with that contention. The most natural construction of the respondents' claim for a money judgment would seem to be that it is a claim that they are entitled to recover whatever was owed them under the contract as of the date of its purported termination plus damages for infringement of their trademark since that date. Alternatively, the complaint could be construed to set forth a full claim based upon both of these theories—that is, a claim that the respondents were entitled to recover both the debt due under the contract and damages for trademark infringement for the entire period of the alleged breach including that before the termination of the contract. Or it might possibly be construed to set forth a claim for recovery based completely on either one of these two theories—that is, a claim based solely upon the contract for the entire period both before and after the attempted termination on the theory that the termination, having been ignored, was of no consequence, or a claim based solely upon the charge of infringement on the theory that the contract, having been breached, could not be used as a defense to an infringement action even for the period prior to its termination. We find it unnecessary to resolve this ambiguity in the respondents' complaint because we think it plain that their claim for a money judgment is a claim wholly legal in its nature however the complaint is construed. As an action on a debt allegedly due under a contract, it would be difficult to conceive of an action of a more traditionally legal character. And as an action for damages based upon a charge of trademark infringement, it would be no less subject to cognizance by a court of law.

The respondents' contention that this money claim is "purely equitable" is based primarily upon the fact that their complaint is cast in terms of an "accounting," rather than in terms of an action for "debt" or "damages." But the constitutional right to trial by jury cannot be made to depend upon the choice of words used in the pleadings. The necessary prerequisite to the right to maintain a suit for an equitable accounting, like all other equitable remedies, is, as we pointed out in Beacon Theatres, the absence of an adequate remedy at law. Consequently, in order to maintain such a suit on a cause of action cognizable at law, as this one is, the plaintiff must be able to show that the "accounts between the parties" are of such a "complicated nature" that only a court of equity can satisfactorily unravel them. In view of the powers given to District Courts by Federal Rule of Civil Procedure 53(b) to appoint masters to assist the jury in those exceptional cases where the legal issues are too complicated for the jury adequately to handle alone,[18] the burden of such a showing is considerably increased and it will indeed be a rare case in which it can be met. But be that as it may, this is certainly not such a case. A jury, under proper instructions from the court, could readily determine the recovery, if any, to be had here, whether the theory finally settled upon is that of breach of contract, that of trademark infringe-

---

[18] Even this limited inroad upon the right to trial by jury " 'should seldom be made, and if at all only when unusual circumstances exist.' " La Buy v. Howes Leather Co., 352 U.S. 249, 258, 77 S.Ct. 309, 314. See also In re Watkins, 5 Cir., 271 F.2d 771.

Novation: substit. of parties → old k end, new k
Reformation: @ Equit. = rewriting of k

ment, or any combination of the two. The legal remedy cannot be characterized as inadequate merely because the measure of damages may necessitate a look into petitioner's business records.

Nor is the legal claim here rendered "purely equitable" by the nature of the defenses interposed by petitioner. Petitioner's primary defense to the charge of breach of contract—that is, that the contract was modified by a subsequent oral agreement—presents a purely legal question having nothing whatever to do either with novation, as the district judge suggested, or reformation, as suggested by the respondents here. Such a defense goes to the question of just what, under the law, the contract between the respondents and petitioner is and, in an action to collect a debt for breach of a contract between these parties, petitioner has a right to have the jury determine not only whether the contract has been breached and the extent of the damages if any but also just what the contract is.

What is the k?
Jury decide

We conclude therefore that the district judge erred in refusing to grant petitioner's demand for a trial by jury on the factual issues related to the question of whether there has been a breach of contract. Since these issues are common with those upon which respondents' claim to equitable relief is based, the legal claims involved in the action must be determined prior to any final court determination of respondents' equitable claims.[20] The Court of Appeals should have corrected the error of the district judge by granting the petition for mandamus. The judgment is therefore reversed and the cause remanded for further proceedings consistent with this opinion.

ISSUE IN
Common:
Was there
breach of
k?

Holding

Reversed and remanded.

MR. JUSTICE STEWART concurs in the result.

MR. JUSTICE FRANKFURTER took no part in the decision of this case.

MR. JUSTICE WHITE took no part in the consideration or decision of this case.

MR. JUSTICE HARLAN, whom MR. JUSTICE DOUGLAS joins, concurring.

I am disposed to accept the view, strongly pressed at the bar, that this complaint seeks an accounting for alleged trademark infringement, rather than contract damages. Even though this leaves the complaint as formally asking only for equitable relief, this does not end the inquiry. The fact that an "accounting" is sought is not of itself dispositive of the jury trial issue. To render this aspect of the complaint truly "equitable" it must appear that the substantive claim is one cognizable only in equity or that the "accounts between the parties" are of such a "complicated nature" that they can be satisfactorily unraveled only by a court of equity. Kirby v. Lake Shore &

[20] This does not, of course, interfere with the District Court's power to grant temporary relief pending a final adjudication on the merits. . . .

Michigan Southern R. Co., 120 U.S. 130, 134, 7 S.Ct. 430, 432. See 5 Moore, Federal Practice (1951), 198–202. It is manifest from the face of the complaint that the "accounting" sought in this instance is not of either variety. A jury, under proper instructions from the court, could readily calculate the damages flowing from this alleged trademark infringement, just as courts of law often do in copyright and patent cases. Cf., e.g., Hartell v. Tilghman, 99 U.S. 547, 555; Arnstein v. Porter, 2 Cir., 154 F.2d 464; Bruckman v. Hollzer, 9 Cir., 152 F.2d 730.

Consequently what is involved in this case is nothing more than a joinder in one complaint of prayers for both legal and equitable relief. In such circumstances, under principles long since established, Scott v. Neely, 140 U.S. 106, 110, 11 S.Ct. 712, 714, the petitioner cannot be deprived of his constitutional right to a jury trial on the "legal" claim contained in the complaint.

On this basis I concur in the judgment of the Court.

Question: (13) If there is a jurisdictional challenge that involves factual issues also involved in the merits of the claim, which is legal in nature, may the judge decide the jurisdictional challenge on his own and at the outset of the action? See Note, Trial by Jury of Preliminary Jurisdictional Facts in Federal Courts, 48 Iowa L.Rev. 471 (1963).

SIMLER v. CONNER, 372 U.S. 221, 83 S.Ct. 609 (1963). The plaintiff brought a diversity action in the Western District of Oklahoma for a declaratory judgment as to the extent of his liability to the defendant, an attorney, for legal services in a will contest. There was originally a written contract for a "reasonable" attorney's fee. Two months later the parties again discussed fees, and the plaintiff wrote a confirmatory letter to the defendant agreeing that the reasonable fee was to be contingent upon recovery and fixed on the basis of specified percentages of any recovery. The defendant's work in the will action resulted in a substantial recovery for the plaintiff, and under the terms of the letter the defendant was entitled to 50 per cent thereof. In the declaratory action the plaintiff contended that this letter was the product of fraud and overreaching by the lawyer. The plaintiff's demand for a jury trial was denied, and summary judgment was later rendered to the effect that the defendant was entitled to the 50 per cent fee. The court of appeals reversed and remanded for a jury trial on the question whether the contingent fee contract was just, equitable, and free from fraud and, if it was not, then also on the question of a reasonable fee, 282 F.2d 382 (10th Cir.1960). On certiorari, the Supreme Court, without citing Byrd v. Blue Ridge Rural Electric Cooperative, supra p. 217, and with Chief Justice Warren and Justices Black and Douglas dissenting, remanded the case for reconsideration in the light of an Oklahoma decison that where the cancellation of a contingent fee contract is the basic relief sought and is necessary before any other relief can be granted, the suit is a purely equitable matter as to which neither party is entitled to a jury, 367 U.S. 486, 81 S.Ct. 1679 (1961) (per curiam). Thereupon, the court of appeals on reconsideration remanded for a trial without jury, 295 F.2d 534 (10th Cir.1961). Certiorari was again granted.

The Supreme Court now unanimously held, in another per curiam opinion, that the right to a jury trial in the federal courts is to be determined as a matter of federal law in diversity as well as other actions and that, although the substantive dimension of the claim is established by state law, its characterization as legal or equitable for purposes of the right to jury must be by recourse to federal law. The fact that the action was in form a declaratory judgment case should not, the Court said, obscure the essentially legal nature of this action to determine the fee owing. The questions involved were "traditional common-law issues," which should be submitted to a jury. The Court then said: "Accordingly, the courts below erred in denying petitioner the jury trial guaranteed him by the Seventh Amendment and the judgment is reversed."

Question: (14) In a federal diversity action, should there be a right to jury trial on an issue of a kind that state law would give to the jury but that in a federal court would normally be decided by the judge?

INDIANHEAD TRUCK LINE v. HVIDSTEN TRANSPORT, INC., 268 Minn. 176, 128 N.W.2d 334 (1964). Plaintiff sued for specific performance of an agreement for the sale and transfer by the defendant trucking company of certain operating rights, equipment, real estate, and other property and, in addition, for monetary damages for the period between the time that performance was due and the time of trial. A jury was impanelled on defendant's demand, but at the close of the evidence the trial judge dismissed the jury on the ground that neither of the parties was entitled to a jury trial as a matter of right. The judge then decreed specific performance and awarded damages for the delayed performance. On appeal, the defendant contended that this was a violation of its right to trial by jury. The judgment was affirmed with a modification not here relevant. The court said that the award of interim damages was not to be classed as an award of damages for breach of contract, and added, quoting from an annotation in 7 A.L.R.2d 1204, 1206 (1949):

"The compensation awarded as incident to a decree for specific performance is not for breach of contract and is therefore not legal damages. The complainant affirms the contract as being still in force and asks that it be performed. He cannot have it both ways, performed and broken. The situation is simply that, if the court orders it to be performed, the decree must as nearly as possible order it to be performed according to its terms, and one of those terms is the date fixed by it for its completion. This date having passed, the court, in order to relate the performance back to it, equalizes any losses occasioned by the delay by offsetting them with money payments. Often the result is more like an accounting between the parties than like an assessment of damages."

Question: (15) The court in the above case referred to federal decisions cited by the defendant and said that they "arose under constitutional . . . provisions different from those of Minnesota and therefore appear to have no bearing upon the scope of a jury trial in this state." The Minnesota Constitution provides: "The right of trial by jury shall remain inviolate, and shall extend to all cases at law without regard to the amount in controversy." What result would you expect if the case came before a federal court after Dairy Queen, Inc. v. Wood? Reconsider the discussion in Curtis v. Loether, supra p. 673, concerning the reinstatement and back-pay remedy under Title VII.

FEDERAL DOCTRINE IN STATE COURTS

The federal developments beginning with the Beacon Theatres decision have not had a pronounced effect upon state-court decisions dealing with the jury right when legal and equitable elements appear in the same case. They have been infrequently cited and less frequently followed. For example, the New York Court of Appeals had for decision a life insurance case in which the policy, containing a two-year incontestability clause, was taken out in October 1959, the insured died in July 1960, and in September 1960 the insurer notified the beneficiaries that it was rescinding the policy for fraud and tendered return of the premiums. Finally the insurer sued to cancel and the beneficiaries were served with process, seven months after notice of the alleged fraud and eighteen months after issuance of the policy. The beneficiaries then counterclaimed for recovery under the policy and moved for a prior jury trial on the fraud issue. The Court of Appeals unanimously affirmed denial of the motion, holding that the beneficiaries were not entitled as a matter of law to their claimed jury trial, that the question was one of discretion, and that the timing of the events justified the conclusion that the beneficiaries were seeking to outmaneuver the insurer. It relied upon American Life Insurance Co. v. Stewart and then added, somewhat enigmatically, "cf. Beacon Theatres v. Westover." Phoenix Mutual Life Insurance Co. v. Conway, 11 N.Y.2d 367, 183 N.E.2d 754, 229 N.Y.S.2d 740 (1962). (Reconsider Rankin v. Frebank Co., supra p. 680.)

ROSS v. BERNHARD

Supreme Court of the United States, 1970.
396 U.S. 531, 90 S.Ct. 733.

[Shareholders brought a derivative suit in federal court against the directors of their closed-end investment company, the Lehman Corporation, and against its broker, Lehman Brothers, contending that the broker controlled the corporation through an illegally large representation on its board of directors in violation of the Investment Company Act of 1940, 15 U.S.C. §§ 80a–1 to –52, and used this control to extract excessive brokerage fees from the corporation. The plaintiffs demanded a jury on the corporation's claims. The district court refused to strike the jury demand. On interlocutory appeal under 28 U.S.C. § 1292(b), the Court of Appeals for the Second Circuit reversed, holding that a derivative action was entirely equitable in nature with no jury right as to any part of it. The Supreme Court granted certiorari to resolve a conflict of circuits.]

MR. JUSTICE WHITE delivered the opinion of the Court.

. . . .

We reverse the holding of the Court of Appeals that in no event does the right to a jury trial preserved by the Seventh Amendment extend to derivative actions brought by the stockholders of a corporation. We hold that the right to jury trial attaches to those issues in derivative actions as to which the corporation, if it had been suing in its own right, would have been entitled to a jury.

The common law refused . . . to permit stockholders to call corporate managers to account in actions at law. The possibilities for abuse, thus presented, were not ignored by corporate officers and directors. Early in the 19th century, equity provided relief both in this country and in England. Without detailing these developments, it suffices to say that the remedy in this country, first dealt with by this Court in Dodge v. Woolsey, 18 How. 331 (1856), provided redress not only against faithless officers and directors but also against third parties who had damaged or threatened the corporate properties and whom the corporation through its managers refused to pursue. The remedy made available in equity was the derivative suit, viewed in this country as a suit to enforce a *corporate* cause of action against officers, directors, and third parties. As elaborated in the cases, one precondition for the suit was a valid claim on which the corporation could have sued; another was that the corporation itself had refused to proceed after suitable demand, unless excused by extraordinary conditions. Thus the dual nature of the stockholder's action: first, the plaintiff's right to sue on behalf of the corporation and, second, the merits of the corporation's claim itself.

Derivative suits posed no Seventh Amendment problems where the action against the directors and third parties would have been by a bill in equity had the corporation brought the suit. Our concern is with cases based upon a legal claim of the corporation against directors or third parties. Does the trial of such claims at the suit of a stockholder and without a jury violate the Seventh Amendment?

. . . . .

. . . What can be gleaned from this Court's opinions is not inconsistent with the general understanding, reflected by the state court decisions and secondary sources, that equity could properly resolve corporate claims of any kind without a jury when properly pleaded in derivative suits complying with the equity rules.

Such was the prevailing opinion when the Federal Rules of Civil Procedure were adopted in 1938. It continued until 1963 when the Court of Appeals for the Ninth Circuit, relying on the Federal Rules as construed and applied in Beacon Theatres, Inc. v. Westover, 359 U.S. 500, 79 S.Ct. 948 (1959), and Dairy Queen, Inc. v. Wood, 369 U.S. 469, 82 S.Ct. 894 (1962), required the legal issues in a derivative suit to be tried to a jury. DePinto v. Provident Security Life Ins. Co., 323 F.2d 826. It was this decision that the District Court followed in the case before us and that the Court of Appeals rejected.

Beacon and Dairy Queen presaged DePinto. Under those cases, where equitable and legal claims are joined in the same action, there is a right to jury trial on the legal claims which must not be infringed either by trying the legal issues as incidental to the equitable ones or by a court trial of a common issue existing between the claims. The Seventh Amendment question depends on the nature of the issue to be tried rather than the character of the overall action.[10] See Simler v. Conner, 372 U.S. 221, 83 S.Ct. 609 (1963). The principle of these cases bears heavily on derivative actions.

We have noted that the derivative suit has dual aspects: first, the stockholder's right to sue on behalf of the corporation, historically an equitable matter; second, the claim of the corporation against directors or third parties on which, if the corporation had sued and the claim presented legal issues, the company could demand a jury trial. . . . [L]egal claims are not magically converted into equitable issues by their presentation to a court of equity in a derivative suit. The claim pressed by the stockholder against directors or third parties "is not his own but the corporation's." Koster v. Lumbermens Mut. Cas. Co., 330 U.S. 518, 522, 67 S.Ct. 828, 831 (1947). The corporation is a necessary party to the action; without it the case cannot

---

[10] As our cases indicate, the "legal" nature of an issue is determined by considering, first, the pre-merger custom with reference to such questions; second, the remedy sought; and, third, the practical abilities and limitations of juries. Of these factors, the first, requiring extensive and possibly abstruse historical inquiry, is obviously the most difficult to apply. See James, Right to a Jury Trial in Civil Actions, 72 Yale L.J. 655 (1963).

proceed. Although named a defendant, it is the real party in interest, the stockholder being at best the nominal plaintiff. The proceeds of the action belong to the corporation and it is bound by the result of the suit. The heart of the action is the corporate claim. If it presents a legal issue, one entitling the corporation to a jury trial under the Seventh Amendment, the right to a jury is not forfeited merely because the stockholder's right to sue must first be adjudicated as an equitable issue triable to the court. Beacon and Dairy Queen require no less.

If under older procedures, now discarded, a court of equity could properly try the legal claims of the corporation presented in a derivative suit, it was because irreparable injury was threatened and no remedy at law existed as long as the stockholder was without standing to sue and the corporation itself refused to pursue its own remedies. Indeed, from 1789 until 1938, the judicial code expressly forbade courts of equity from entertaining any suit for which there was an adequate remedy at law. This provision served "to guard the right of trial by jury preserved by the Seventh Amendment and to that end it should be liberally construed." Schoenthal v. Irving Trust Co., 287 U.S. 92, 94, 53 S.Ct. 50, 51 (1932). If, before 1938, the law had borrowed from equity, as it borrowed other things, the idea that stockholders could litigate for their recalcitrant corporation, the corporate claim, if legal, would undoubtedly have been tried to a jury.

Of course, this did not occur, but the Federal Rules had a similar impact. Actions are no longer brought as actions at law or suits in equity. Under the Rules there is only one action—a "civil action"—in which all claims may be joined and all remedies are available. Purely procedural impediments to the presentation of any issue by any party, based on the difference between law and equity, were destroyed. In a civil action presenting a stockholder's derivative claim, the court after passing upon the plaintiff's right to sue on behalf of the corporation is now able to try the corporate claim for damages with the aid of a jury. Separable claims may be tried separately, Fed.Rule Civ. Proc. 42(b), or legal and equitable issues may be handled in the same trial. Fanchon & Marco, Inc. v. Paramount Pictures, Inc., 202 F.2d 731 (C.A.2d Cir. 1953). The historical rule preventing a court of law from entertaining a shareholder's suit on behalf of the corporation is obsolete; it is no longer tenable for a district court, administering both law and equity in the same action, to deny legal remedies to a corporation, merely because the corporation's spokesmen are its shareholders rather than its directors. Under the rules, law and equity are procedurally combined; nothing turns now upon the form of the action or the procedural devices by which the parties happen to come before the court. The "expansion of adequate legal remedies provided by . . . the Federal Rules necessarily affects the scope of equity." Beacon Theatres, Inc. v. Westover, 359 U.S., at 509, 79 S.Ct., at 956.

Thus, for example, before-merger class actions were largely a device of equity, and there was no right to a jury even on issues that might, under other circumstances, have been tried to a jury. 5 J. Moore, Federal Practice ¶ 38.38[2] (2d ed. 1969); 3B id., ¶ 23.02[1]. Although at least one post-merger court held that the device was not available to try legal issues, it now seems settled in the lower federal courts that class action plaintiffs may obtain a jury trial on any legal issues they present. [Citations omitted.]

Derivative suits have been described as one kind of "true" class action. [2 W. Barron & A. Holtzoff, Federal Practice and Procedure § 562.1 (C. Wright ed. 1961).] We are inclined to agree with the description, at least to the extent it recognizes that the derivative suit and the class action were both ways of allowing parties to be heard in equity who could not speak at law.[15] 3B J. Moore, Federal Practice ¶¶ 23.02[1], 23.1.16[1] (2d ed. 1969). After adoption of the rules there is no longer any procedural obstacle to the assertion of legal rights before juries, however the party may have acquired standing to assert those rights. Given the availability in a derivative action of both legal and equitable remedies, we think the Seventh Amendment preserves to the parties in a stockholder's suit the same right to a jury trial that historically belonged to the corporation and to those against whom the corporation pressed its legal claims.

In the instant case we have no doubt that the corporation's claim is, at least in part, a legal one. The relief sought is money damages. There are allegations in the complaint of a breach of fiduciary duty, but there are also allegations of ordinary breach of contract and gross negligence. The corporation, had it sued on its own behalf, would have been entitled to a jury's determination, at a minimum, of its damages against its broker under the brokerage contract and of its rights against its own directors because of their negligence. Under these circumstances it is unnecessary to decide whether the corporation's other claims are also properly triable to a jury. Dairy Queen, Inc. v. Wood, 369 U.S. 469, 82 S.Ct. 894 (1962). The decision of the Court of Appeals is reversed.

It is so ordered.

MR. JUSTICE STEWART, with whom THE CHIEF JUSTICE and MR. JUSTICE HARLAN join, dissenting.

In holding as it does that the plaintiff in a shareholder's derivative suit is constitutionally entitled to a jury trial, the Court today seems to rely upon some sort of ill-defined combination of the Seventh Amendment and the Federal Rules of Civil Procedure. Somehow the Amendment and the Rules magically interact to do what each separately was expressly intended not to do, namely, to enlarge the right

[15] Other equitable devices are used under the rules without depriving the parties employing them of the right to a jury trial on legal issues. [The Court here cited lower court cases allowing a jury right on legal issues to intervenors under Rule 24 and in interpleader actions.]

to a jury trial in civil actions brought in the courts of the United States.

The Seventh Amendment, by its terms, does not extend, but merely *preserves* the right to a jury trial "[i]n Suits at common law." All agree that this means the reach of the Amendment is limited to those actions that were tried to the jury in 1791 when the Amendment was adopted.[1] Suits in equity, which were historically tried to the court, were therefore unaffected by it. Similarly, Rule 38 of the Federal Rules has no bearing on the right to a jury trial in suits in equity, for it simply preserves inviolate "[t]he right of trial by jury as declared by the Seventh Amendment." Thus this Rule, like the Amendment itself, neither restricts nor enlarges the right to jury trial. Indeed nothing in the Federal Rules can rightly be construed to enlarge the right of jury trial, for in the legislation authorizing the Rules, Congress expressly provided that they "shall neither abridge, enlarge, nor modify the substantive rights of any litigant." 48 Stat. 1064. See 28 U.S.C. § 2072. I take this plain, simple, and straightforward language to mean that after the promulgation of the Federal Rules, as before, the constitutional right to a jury trial attaches only to suits at common law. So, apparently, has every federal court that has discussed the issue. Since, as the Court concedes, a shareholder's derivative suit could be brought only in equity, it would seem to me to follow by the most elementary logic that in such suits there is no constitutional right to a trial by jury. Today the Court tosses aside history, logic, and over 100 years of firm precedent to hold that the plaintiff in a shareholder's derivative suit does indeed have a constitutional right to a trial by jury. This holding has a questionable basis in policy[5] and no basis whatever in the Constitution.

The Court begins by assuming the "dual nature" of the shareholder's action. While the plaintiff's right to get into court at all is conceded to be equitable, once he is there the Court says his claim is to be viewed as though it were the claim of the corporation itself. If the corporation would have been entitled to a jury trial on such a claim, then, it is said, so would the shareholder. This conceptualization is without any historical basis. For the fact is that a shareholder's suit was not originally viewed in this country, or in England, as a suit to enforce a *corporate* cause of action. Rather, the shareholder's suit was initially permitted only against the managers of the corporation—not third parties—and it was conceived of as an equitable

[1] Where a new cause of action is created by Congress, and nothing is said about how it is to be tried, the jury trial issue is determined by fitting the cause into its nearest historical analogy. Luria v. United States, 231 U.S. 9, 34 S.Ct. 10; see James, Right to a Jury Trial in Civil Actions, 72 Yale L.J. 655.

[5] See, e.g., J. Frank, Courts on Trial 110–111 (1949). Certainly there is no consensus among commentators on the desirability of jury trials in civil actions generally. Particularly where the issues in the case are complex—as they are likely to be in a derivative suit—much can be said for allowing the court discretion to try the case itself. See discussion in 5 J. Moore, Federal Practice ¶ 38.02[1].

action to enforce the right of a beneficiary against his trustee. The shareholder was not, therefore, in court to enforce indirectly the corporate right of action, but to enforce directly his own equitable right of action against an unfaithful fiduciary. Later the rights of the shareholder were enlarged to encompass suits against third parties harming the corporation, but "the postulated 'corporate cause of action' has never been thought to describe an actual historical class of suit which was recognized by courts of law."[7] Indeed the commentators . . . recognize that historically the suit has in practice always been treated as a single cause tried exclusively in equity. They agree that there is therefore no constitutional right to a jury trial even where there might have been one had the corporation itself brought the suit.

[A discussion of prior decisions is omitted.]

These pre-1938 cases, then, firmly establish the unitary, equitable basis of shareholders' derivative suits and in no way support the Court's holding here. But, the Court says, whatever the situation may have been before 1938, the Federal Rules of Civil Procedure of that year, at least as construed in our decisions more than 20 years later in Beacon Theatres, Inc. v. Westover, 359 U.S. 500, 79 S.Ct. 948, and Dairy Queen, Inc. v. Wood, 369 U.S. 469, 82 S.Ct. 894, in any event require the conclusion reached today. I can find nothing in either of these cases that leads to that conclusion.

. . . . . .

It is true that in Beacon Theatres it was stated that the 1938 Rules did diminish the scope of federal equity jurisdiction in certain particulars. But the Court's effort to force the facts of this case into the mold of Beacon Theatres and Dairy Queen simply does not succeed. Those cases involved a combination of historically separable suits, one in law and one in equity. Their facts fit the pattern of cases where, before the Rules, the equity court would have disposed of the equitable claim and would then have either retained jurisdiction over the suit, despite the availability of adequate legal remedies, or enjoined a subsequent legal action between the same parties involving the same controversy.

But the present case is not one involving traditionally equitable claims by one party, and traditionally legal claims by the other. Nor is it a suit in which the plaintiff is asserting a combination of legal and equitable claims. For, as we have seen, a derivative suit has always been conceived of as a single, unitary, equitable cause of action. It is for this reason, and not because of "procedural impediments," that the courts of equity did not transfer derivative suits to the law side. In short, the cause of action is wholly a creature of equity. And whatever else can be said of Beacon Theatres and Dairy Queen,

[7] Note, The Right to a Jury Trial in a Stockholder's Derivative Action, 74 Yale L.J. 725, 730.

they did not cast aside altogether the historic division between equity and law.

If history is to be so cavalierly dismissed, the derivative suit can, of course, be artificially broken down into separable elements. But so then can any traditionally equitable cause of action, and the logic of the Court's position would lead to the virtual elimination of all equity jurisdiction. An equitable suit for an injunction, for instance, often involves issues of fact which, if damages had been sought, would have been triable to a jury. Does this mean that in a suit asking only for injunctive relief these factual issues *must* be tried to the jury, with the judge left to decide only whether, given the jury's findings, an injunction is the appropriate remedy? Certainly the Federal Rules make it *possible* to try a suit for an injunction in that way, but even more certainly they were not intended to have any such effect. Yet the Court's approach, it seems, would require that if any "legal issue" procedurally *could* be tried to a jury, it constitutionally *must* be tried to a jury.

The fact is, of course, that there are, for the most part, no such things as inherently "legal issues" or inherently "equitable issues." There are only factual issues, and, "like chameleons [they] take their color from surrounding circumstances."[12] Thus the Court's "nature of the issue" approach is hardly meaningful.

. . . .

The Court's decision today can perhaps be explained as a reflection of an unarticulated but apparently overpowering bias in favor of jury trials in civil actions. It certainly cannot be explained in terms of either the Federal Rules or the Constitution.

JOHNS HOPKINS UNIVERSITY v. HUTTON, 488 F.2d 912 (4th Cir.1973), cert. denied, 416 U.S. 916, 94 S.Ct. 1622, 1623 (1974). The university sued under the antifraud provisions of the securities laws, asking damages. The court on its own explored the possibility of the equitable remedy of rescission. In response to the court's inquiry, the plaintiff by letter said that it was "primarily seeking rescission" and asking damages "only if [it] is not entitled to rescission." The complaint was later amended to add a request for rescission. The trial court ruled that the defendant was "entitled to a jury trial in connection with any and all triable fact issues" that were common to the legal and equitable remedies or that related only to the legal remedy "so long as Hopkins continues to hold in reserve, in the event Hopkins is held not entitled to rescission, its claim for damages." Later, however, the trial court granted summary judgment that the plaintiff was entitled to rescission. The court of appeals reversed the summary judgment, remanding for trial; but the appellate court agreed with the trial judge as to the jury right, simply stating that

[12] James, supra, n. 1, at 692. . . .

this followed from the rationale of Ross, Dairy Queen, and Beacon Theatres.

IN RE BOISE CASCADE SECURITIES LITIGATION
United States District Court, Western District of Washington, 1976.
420 F.Supp. 99.

MORELL E. SHARP, DISTRICT JUDGE.   Before the Court are defendants' motions to strike plaintiffs' jury demands in this securities fraud litigation.   The question before the Court is whether these jury demands may be stricken without conflicting with the Seventh Amendment.   The Court is of the opinion that the answer is in the affirmative.

[In part I of its opinion, the court explained that the five consolidated cases before it arose from the acquisition of two companies by Boise Cascade.   When the deals went sour, these actions were brought against Boise, its officers and directors, and its accountant for various alleged violations of federal and state securities laws. Extensive discovery ensued.   Thus far more than 50,000 lawyer-hours had been expended and more than 900,000 documents produced.

[In part II, the court described in detail the highly complex issues of financial accounting and the problems of proof presented by this litigation.]

In sum, it appears to this Court that the scope of the problems presented by this case is immense.   The factual issues, the complexity of the evidence that will be required to explore those issues, and the time required to do so leads to the conclusion that a jury would not be a rational and capable fact finder.

III

There can be no doubt that jury trials are favored in civil litigation in this country.   The combination of the Seventh Amendment and the merger of actions at law and in equity into a single civil action under the Federal Rules of Civil Procedure encourages the use of juries to determine facts.   See Ross v. Bernard [sic], 396 U.S. 531, 539–40, 90 S.Ct. 733, 24 L.Ed.2d 729 and Opinion of Stewart, J., dissenting, see also 28 U.S.C.A. § 1861 and Redish, Seventh Amendment Right to Jury Trial: A Study in the Irrationality of Rational Decision Making, 70 Nw.U.L.Rev. 486, 490–98.

However broad this policy may be, the Supreme Court has recognized that the use of juries is not without limits.   In Ross v. Bernard, supra, the Court set forth three factors which determine the susceptibility of a claim to trial by jury:

> [F]irst, the pre-merger custom with reference to such questions; second the remedy sought; and third, the practical abilities and limitations of juries. Id. at 538 n. 10, 90 S.Ct. at 738.

No authority was cited for these three factors. As for the first two, Supreme Court precedent appears so clear as to be obvious. See e.g., Parsons v. Bedford, 28 U.S. (3 Pet.) 443, 447, 7 L.Ed. 732 (1830) (Story, J.). The third part is not explicit from previous opinions.

The procedural safeguards inherent in our legal system provide the impression and fact of fairness to the litigants and society. This is necessary in order to assure obedience to judgments and resort to the legal system as the only sanctioned means of settling disputes in a complex civilized society. Indeed, under the Fifth and Fourteenth Amendments, the legitimacy of government action is measured in terms of fairness.

Central to the fairness which must attend the resolution of a civil action is an impartial and capable fact finder. A properly selected panel of veniremen must generally be presumed to yield an impartial and capable jury. However, at some point, it must be recognized that the complexity of a case may exceed the ability of a jury to decide the facts in an informed and capable manner. When that occurs, the question arises as to whether the right and necessity of fairness is defeated by relegating fact finding to a body not qualified to determine the facts. The third part of the analysis in footnote 10 to the majority opinion in Ross v. Bernard, supra, directly recognizes this. See also Kirkham, Complex Civil Litigation—Have Good Intentions Gone Awry? 70 F.R.D. 199, 208 (1976).

Of course, the point at which a jury's limitations exceed its abilities is not precise nor is it easy of definition. No single factor alone can dictate that a jury should not hear a case. As in this case, a number of factors must combine to convince the Court that a jury would be incapable of fairly deciding the case.

IV

It must be apparent that any jury chosen to hear this case will not be a fair cross section of the community at large because of the estimated trial time of four to six months. It would not be unreasonable to excuse prospective jurors from serving in this civil case if they believe that service for that period of time would impair their employment. At the outset, then, the availability of employed persons to serve on this jury is limited. This suggests that at least the appearance of fairness would be diminished, if not eliminated, when a lengthy civil action involving millions of dollars in potential damages in a commercial setting would be heard by jurors who have not had exposure to a contemporary commercial or business environment.

This should not be taken to mean that a non-employed person is somehow less able to determine facts. Rather, a basic purpose of the jury, the determination of facts by impartial minds of diverse backgrounds, is defeated if a sizable and significant portion of the community must be excluded from service.

Pointing out the limits of a jury to hear an extended civil action does not answer the problems presented by a particular case unless it can be shown that trial to the Court would be superior.

In addition to the Court's experience in presiding over other complicated cases involving commercial matters, the Court has available to it tools that are unwieldy in the possession of a jury. Among these tools are review of daily transcripts; admission of depositions into evidence instead of reading relevant portions aloud; review of selected portions of testimony from the reporter's notes and flexibility in scheduling trial activities. In addition, the Court is able to study exhibits in depth and carry on colloquies with witnesses, expert and non-expert alike, in an orderly and systematic manner. Of course, this is in addition to the Court's knowledge of the litigation resulting from its review of the record since the cases were filed.

In the light of the limitation of a jury to determine the facts in an informed manner and the ability of the Court to hear and review the evidence in an efficient and effective manner, the Court believes that it would be more capable of fairly deciding the facts.

V

The Court is of the opinion that the third part to footnote 10 in Ross v. Bernard, supra, is of constitutional dimensions. It must be seen as a limitation to or interpretation of the Seventh Amendment. Furthermore, the Court is of the opinion that there is no conflict in this case with any statutory policy favoring trial by jury, 28 U.S.C.A. § 1861, or the Federal Rules of Civil Procedure.

The explosion of litigation in the past two decades in terms both of number of filings and the complexity and scope of many of those cases has led thoughtful minds to wonder whether the judicial system as we now know it can cope with some of these cases. See e.g., Rifkind, Are We Asking Too Much of Our Courts? 70 F.R.D. 96 (1976).

Similarly, thoughtful minds have questioned the expansion of the right to jury trial in complex commercial civil actions. See Redish, supra, at 514–530. It has been observed that:

> Any close question—and sometimes one that is not so close—is resolved in favor of the jury trial right without serious analysis of history, precedent, or policy. Shapiro and Coquillette, The Fetish of Jury Trial in Civil Cases: A Comment on Rachal v. Hill, 85 Harv.L.Rev. 442 (1971).

While it is true that the Supreme Court has favored jury trial in the cases where it has reviewed the issue, the opinions are not totally consistent. Compare Ross v. Bernard, supra, with Katchen v. Landy, 382 U.S. 323, 339, 86 S.Ct. 467, 15 L.Ed.2d 391 (1966).

With these thoughts in mind, the necessity for the appearance and fact of fairness dictate that the motions now before the Court be granted.

. . . . .

IN RE U.S. FINANCIAL SECURITIES LITIGATION, 609 F.2d 411 (9th Cir.1979) (2–1 decision), cert. denied, 446 U.S. 929, 100 S.Ct. 1866 (1980). In this mass of consolidated cases, plaintiffs sought damages under the securities laws and for common-law fraud and negligence. The factual and legal issues were highly complex, and they would apparently have required the fact-finder to decipher many financial statements and to read over 100,000 pages ("which would be the equivalent of reading the first 90 volumes of the Federal Reporter, 2d Series") during a trial lasting at least two years. The trial judge struck the demands by some plaintiffs and some defendants for jury trial. On interlocutory appeal under 28 U.S.C. § 1292(b), the court of appeals reversed, rejecting any "complexity exception" to the seventh amendment. First, with little explanation, the appellate court ruled that complexity did not serve to transform this action into the "narrow and little-used" equitable suit for an accounting. Second, it held that the famous Ross footnote should not be read as introducing some new "functional" interpretation of the seventh amendment. Third, it concluded that trial by jury in a complex case does not deny due process; an intelligent procedural approach can greatly reduce complexity,[a] and even in a complex case jurors are as competent as a judge in fact-finding. Moreover, the judge's power to grant a new trial or judgment n.o.v. protects litigants from an "irrational" verdict. In sum, "the Seventh Amendment requires a jury trial in even the most complex cases at law."

IN RE JAPANESE ELECTRONIC PRODUCTS ANTITRUST LITIGATION, 631 F.2d 1069 (3d Cir.1980) (2–1 decision). These complex consolidated cases essentially involved American television manufacturers suing their Japanese counterparts for treble damages under the antitrust laws. The trial judge refused to strike plaintiffs' demands for jury trial, rejecting any complexity exception to the seventh amendment. On interlocutory appeal under 28 U.S.C. § 1292(b), the court of appeals reversed. The appellate court ruled that in 1791 mere complexity did not make an action equitable, noting in particu-

---

[a] See Note, Court-Sanctioned Means of Improving Jury Competence in Complex Civil Litigation, 24 Ariz.L.Rev. 715 (1982). See generally Sperlich, The Case for Preserving Trial by Jury in Complex Civil Litigation, 65 Judicature 394 (1982).

lar that an equitable suit for an accounting required some relationship between the parties greater than that between an ordinary tortfeasor and victim.   It also conceded that the Ross footnote is too weak a foundation on which to build a new interpretation of the seventh amendment.   It concluded, however, that trial by jury of a case too complex for jurors to decide by rational means, with a fair and reasonable understanding of the evidence and applicable law, violates the due process clause of the fifth amendment, which thus overrides the seventh amendment.   Accordingly, the court of appeals remanded this case for careful consideration of its complexity, cautioning nevertheless that "[d]ue process should allow denials of jury trials only in exceptional cases."

Part Five

AUTHORITY TO ADJUDICATE: HEREIN OF JURISDICTION AND DUE PROCESS

TOPIC A.   JURISDICTION OVER SUBJECT MATTER

SECTION 1.   GENERAL OBSERVATIONS

Restatement of Judgments (1942) used the expression "competency of the court" more or less interchangeably with "the court's jurisdiction over the subject matter." We propose to use these two catch phrases interchangeably. The general notion underlying both may be conveyed, although imperfectly, by this question: has the sovereign properly given this court power to entertain this type of action?

As examples of lack of competence, Restatement of Judgments § 7 comment b (1942) gave the following:

"There are many situations in which a court lacks competency to render a judgment. Thus, although a State has jurisdiction to grant a divorce of parties domiciled within the State, a decree of divorce rendered by a court which is not empowered to entertain suits for divorce is void. Similarly, a judgment rendered by a justice of the peace is void if under the law of the State such justices are not empowered to deal with the subject matter of the action; as, for example, where the action is one for tort and justices of the peace are given no power except in actions of contract. So also, where a court is given power to deal with actions involving no more than a designated amount, the statute limiting the amount is ordinarily construed not merely to make erroneous a judgment rendered by such a court in excess of its power, but to make such judgment void."

Further elaborating subject-matter jurisdiction, Restatement (Second) of Judgments § 11 comment b (1980) notes:

"The rules of subject matter jurisdiction of a court are generally prescribed by the political authority that has created the court. (However, a superior political authority may impose limits on that authority. Thus, state law rather than federal law invests a state's courts with authority to adjudicate particular types of controversies, but federal law through preemption may supersede that authority). The prescriptions of subject matter jurisdiction express divisions of functions among the organs of that government, separating courts from other branches of government and differentiating one court from another."

The federal courts are particularly sensitive to questions of their own competency. Thus, it is possible for either party to raise, or for the court on its own motion to consider, a question of jurisdiction

712

over the subject matter at any stage of the federal litigation. Rule 12(h)(3) makes this explicit statement: "*Whenever* it appears by suggestion of the parties *or otherwise* that the court lacks jurisdiction of the subject matter, the court shall dismiss the action." (Emphasis added.) Dismissal for want of such jurisdiction might come in the trial court or in an appellate court. Recall Louisville & Nashville Railroad v. Mottley, supra p. 163, where the Supreme Court dismissed, even though the federal issue in the case might reappear on review of an action on the same claim initiated in a state court (as indeed it did, supra p. 176).

The proposition that a federal court is bound to consider its own jurisdiction regardless of the attitude or conduct of the parties has been said to spring from the limited nature of the judicial power of the United States under article III, section 2 of the Constitution. Mansfield, Coldwater & Lake Michigan Railway v. Swan, 111 U.S. 379, 4 S.Ct. 510 (1884). In that case the Supreme Court, noting that the record showed lack of diversity jurisdiction, ordered the action remanded to state court, although the only asserted grounds of appeal were alleged errors at trial. This worked to the benefit of the defendants-appellants, who had themselves invoked federal jurisdiction by removal from state court.

Many cases declare that the parties cannot confer jurisdiction over the subject matter by consent or collusion. For instance, in Jackson v. Ashton, 33 U.S. (8 Pet.) 148 (1834), the Supreme Court dismissed for lack of diversity jurisdiction where both sides were eager for the appeal to be heard, and where counsel for the plaintiffs-appellants argued that jurisdiction existed and counsel for the defendant-appellee expressly renounced any objection to jurisdiction.

Similarly, any party—even the party who invoked federal jurisdiction in the first place—will at any stage be heard to say that the case should be dismissed for want of competency. In American Fire & Casualty Co. v. Finn, 341 U.S. 6, 71 S.Ct. 534 (1951), a defendant who had invoked federal jurisdiction by removal and had resisted a motion to remand was allowed to challenge subject-matter jurisdiction after an adverse judgment. That is to say, there is no doctrine of waiver in connection with objections to federal jurisdiction.

Next suppose that *A* sues *B* in federal court, alleging himself to be a citizen of State *X* and *B* to be a citizen of State *Y*. *B*'s answer admits these allegations. After the running of the statute of limitations so as to bar a new action, *B* moves to dismiss for lack of subject-matter jurisdiction and satisfies the court that the parties were in fact both citizens of State *X* when suit was brought. Is the court bound to dismiss for lack of competency? Compare Page v. Wright, 116 F.2d 449 (7th Cir.1940), with Di Frischia v. New York Central Railroad, 279 F.2d 141 (3d Cir.1960).

Questions: (1) What would you think of the desirability and constitutionality of a federal statute allowing any claim, if timely brought in federal court but dismissed for lack of subject-matter jurisdiction, to be asserted in a new action in a proper state court if the now applicable statute of limitations would not have barred the original action and if the new action is commenced within thirty days after the dismissal or within such longer period as might be available under applicable state law? See ALI Study of the Division of Jurisdiction Between State and Federal Courts § 1386(b) commentary at 373–74, 453–57 (1968).

(2) What would you think of a federal statute setting up a cutoff date in any federal action after which the court could not consider, on its own motion or at the instance of any party, a newly raised question of jurisdiction over the subject matter, unless (a) a party is raising the issue and is relying upon facts he did not know, and could not be expected to have discovered in the exercise of reasonable diligence, at an earlier stage in the proceedings, or is relying on a change in jurisdictional law, or (b) there was collusion between opposing parties in concealing a known jurisdictional defect? Would it be permissible for a federal court so to proceed to adjudication of a case for which there was in fact no subject-matter jurisdiction under the congressional grants of jurisdiction? for which there was no subject-matter jurisdiction under the Constitution? See ALI Study of the Division of Jurisdiction Between State and Federal Courts § 1386(a) commentary at 366–73 (1968).

Under current law, federal or state, lack of competency may be raised not only in the ordinary course of review in the trial and appellate courts but even sometimes in subsequent litigation, as by collateral attack. What is a collateral attack? To take as examples some situations we shall soon explore, if a prior judgment is used in a new action as the basis for a claim (as where, in enforcing a judgment, suit is brought upon the judgment in another state) or as the basis for a defense (as where a defendant pleads res judicata), and if the other party in turn attacks the prior judgment to prevent its use, we have a collateral attack. The rule is that collateral attack will succeed only if the prior judgment contains certain, very serious errors.

So, suppose an action in federal court has proceeded to final judgment upon default, and suit is brought on the judgment elsewhere. The defendant now contends that the court that rendered the judgment lacked competency. If he can establish that such a defect indeed existed, the second court generally will refuse to enforce the judgment. Change the problem to this extent: suppose an action in federal court has proceeded to final judgment, but in that action the question of the court's competency was raised and litigated and the court decided that it had competency. In a suit on the judgment, is it open to the second court to reexamine the question of the first court's competency and refuse to enforce the judgment if it is convinced that the first court erred in its decision on its own competency? Generally not, because res judicata works to foreclose relitigation of a prior determination of subject-matter jurisdiction. This question is treated in Topic E of Part Six.

Courts have given varying treatment to the concept of competency in different situations. There seems to be no clear-cut all-purpose definition. Lack of competency shades off into other kinds of defects, either procedural or on the merits. To the extent that other defects entail the same consequences to the litigants as lack of competency, it may be unimportant to make sharp distinctions; but there are situations, such as collateral attack, where the court's categorization of a defect as one of competency becomes crucial.

Questions: (3) In the case of a collateral attack in a court of a different sovereign, which law should govern the question of whether there was competency in the court that rendered judgment? Should it be the law of the first court's sovereign or that of the second court's sovereign? See Restatement (Second) of Conflict of Laws § 105 comment b (1969).

(4) To what extent should one be able to go beyond the record and look to extrinsic evidence establishing a lack of competency, on either appeal or collateral attack? See Restatement (Second) of Judgments § 77 (1980).

(5) Who should have the burden of proof on competency, in either the rendering court or the collateral-attack court?

"The mechanism of law—what courts are to deal with which causes and subject to what conditions—cannot be dissociated from the ends that law subserves. So-called jurisdictional questions treated in isolation from the purposes of the legal system to which they relate become barren pedantry. After all, procedure is instrumental; it is the means of effectuating policy. Particularly true is this of the federal courts. The Judiciary Acts, the needs which urged their enactment, the compromises which they embodied, the consequences which they entailed, the changed conditions which in turn modified them, are the outcome of continuous interaction of traditional, political, social, and economic forces. In common with other courts, the federal courts are means for securing justice through law. But in addition and transcending this in importance, the legislation governing the structure and function of the federal judicial system is one means of providing the accommodations necessary to the operation of a federal government. The happy relation of States to Nation—constituting as it does our central political problem—is to no small extent dependent upon the wisdom with which the scope and limits of the federal courts are determined." F. Frankfurter & J. Landis, The Business of the Supreme Court 2 (1927).

SECTION 2. FEDERAL QUESTIONS

Federal question jurisdiction is founded on the first clause of article III, section 2 of the Constitution. What is the meaning of the term "arising under" that there appears? It was, early on, sweepingly construed to cover all cases of which a federal question forms an "ingredient." Osborn v. Bank of the United States, 22 U.S. (9 Wheat.) 738 (1824) (holding that the "arising under" language of article III authorized a statute bestowing jurisdiction on the federal courts over all actions brought by a federally chartered bank, because any such action would have as an ingredient the federal question of whether the bank under its charter has the power to sue).

The constitutional language was for the most part tracked in the Act of March 3, 1875, ch. 137, § 1, 18 Stat. 470, the statute that really for the first time gave the federal courts general original jurisdiction over federal question cases. That Act, with no changes of true substance, now appears as 28 U.S.C. § 1331. What is the meaning of the term "arising under" that there appears? It is construed much more narrowly than is the identical constitutional language. The courts have read a series of restrictions into the statutory language. In fact, we have already seen one such restriction, the well-pleaded complaint rule, in the first Louisville & Nashville Railroad v. Mottley case.

Reading article III expansively is desirable, because Congress thereby retains the power to bestow original jurisdiction over special kinds of cases that present a need for federal jurisdiction but possess merely a federal ingredient, and because the appellate jurisdiction of the Supreme Court thereby remains broad enough to cover all state cases that finally turn upon an issue of federal law. Reading § 1331 narrowly, on the other hand, is defensible in that Congress probably did not intend to inundate the lower federal courts with all the cases having a mere federal ingredient. At any rate, there is a difference in scope between the constitutional and the statutory language. Indeed, we have already observed that difference in the second Louisville & Nashville Railroad v. Mottley case, where the Supreme Court ultimately reviewed an issue of federal law decided in state court, even though it had earlier held that there was no original federal question jurisdiction.

What are these other restrictions that the courts have read into "arising under" in § 1331? One critical restriction deals with the relationship of the case to its federal element. It is clear, as already suggested, that to satisfy the statute the federal element must be more than a mere ingredient. But beyond that, it is difficult to be precise—no single definition that would encompass all the decided cases is evident. The American Law Institute, faced with the jumble of cases, did not attempt definition but instead retained the "arising under" term.[a] Others have attempted a formulation. A famous one is that of Justice Holmes, who argued: "A suit arises under the law that creates the cause of action."[b] This test yields many correct answers; for example, an action for patent infringement does arise under federal law, but an action to recover contractual royalties for use of a patent does not. However, there are problem cases, such as Smith v. Kansas City Title & Trust Co., 255 U.S. 180, 41 S.Ct. 243

---

[a] See ALI Study of the Division of Jurisdiction Between State and Federal Courts § 1311(a) commentary at 178–79 (1968).

[b] American Well Works Co. v. Layne & Bowler Co., 241 U.S. 257, 260, 36 S.Ct. 585, 586 (1916).

(1921) (federal jurisdiction exists for suit by a trust company shareholder to enjoin the trust company from investing in certain federal bonds; state law limited investment to legal securities, but plaintiff claimed that the federal statute authorizing the bonds' issuance was unconstitutional), and Shoshone Mining Co. v. Rutter, 177 U.S. 505, 20 S.Ct. 726 (1900) (federal jurisdiction does not exist for suit to determine right to possession of mining claim; a federal statute authorized this type of suit, but directed that local law should govern the rights involved). A more accurate formulation is necessarily fuzzier. Professor Mishkin's definition in the leading article on the subject is a "claim founded 'directly' upon federal law." [c]   The Supreme Court formulates the required relationship as "either that federal law creates the cause of action or that the plaintiff's right to relief necessarily depends on resolution of a substantial question of federal law." [d]

Question: (6) It has been argued that this absence of a precise definition is an advantage, because it frees the courts to determine the jurisdictional point on the basis of pragmatic considerations, such as: "the extent of the caseload increase for federal trial courts if jurisdiction is recognized; the extent to which cases of this class will, in practice, turn on issues of state or federal law; the extent of the necessity for an expert federal tribunal to handle issues of federal law that do arise; the extent of the necessity for a sympathetic federal tribunal in cases of this class." Cohen, The Broken Compass: The Requirement That a Case Arise "Directly" Under Federal Law, 115 U.Pa.L.Rev. 890, 916 (1967). What do you think of this argument?

BELL v. HOOD

Supreme Court of the United States, 1946.
327 U.S. 678, 66 S.Ct. 773.

MR. JUSTICE BLACK delivered the opinion of the Court.

Petitioners brought this suit in a federal district court to recover damages in excess of [the then jurisdictional amount of] $3,000 from the respondents who are agents of the Federal Bureau of Investigation. The complaint alleges that the Court's jurisdiction is founded upon federal questions arising under the Fourth and Fifth Amendments. It is alleged that the damages were suffered as a result of the respondents imprisoning the petitioners in violation of their Constitutional right to be free from deprivation of their liberty without due process of law, and subjecting their premises to search and their possessions to seizure, in violation of their Constitutional right to be free from unreasonable searches and seizures.[1]

---

[c] Mishkin, The Federal "Question" in the District Courts, 53 Colum.L.Rev. 157, 168 (1953).

[d] Franchise Tax Bd. v. Construction Laborers Vacation Trust, 103 S.Ct. 2841, 2856 (1983).

[1] The complaint stated in part:

"That on or about the 17th day of December, 1942, defendant R.B. Hood and each of the other defendants, unlawfully conspired with each other to act beyond their authority as said Federal Bureau of Investigation agents and police officers

Respondents moved to dismiss the complaint for failure to state a cause of action for which relief could be granted and for summary judgment on the grounds that the federal agents acted within the scope of their authority as officers of the United States and that the searches and seizures were incidental to lawful arrests and were therefore valid. Respondents filed affidavits in support of their motions and petitioners filed counter-affidavits. After hearing the motions the district judge did not pass on them but, on his own motion, dismissed the suit for want of federal jurisdiction on the ground that this action was not one that ". . . arises under the Constitution or laws of the United States . . . " as required by 28 U.S.C. § 41(1).[e] The Circuit Court of Appeals affirmed on the same ground. 9 Cir., 150 F.2d 96. At the same time it denied a motion made by petitioners asking it to direct the district court to give petitioners leave to amend their complaint in order to make it still more clearly appear that the action was directly grounded on violations of rights alleged to stem from the Fourth and Fifth Amendments. We granted certiorari because of the importance of the jurisdictional issue involved.

Respondents make the following argument in support of the district court's dismissal of the complaint for want of federal jurisdiction. (First,) they urge that the complaint states a cause of action for the common law tort of trespass made actionable by state law and that it therefore does not raise questions arising "under the Constitution or laws of the United States." [Second,] to support this contention, respondents maintain that petitioners could not recover under the Constitution or laws of the United States, since the Constitution does not expressly provide for recovery in money damages for violations of the Fourth and Fifth Amendments and Congress has not enacted a statute that does so provide. A mere reading of the com-

respectively, and agreed that they would abridge the Constitutional rights of the plaintiffs as guaranteed by the Fourth and Fifth Amendments to the Constitution of the United States to be free from the deprivation of liberty and property without due process of law, and to be free from unreasonable searches and seizures, and agreed unlawfully to simultaneously, in the early morning of December 18th, 1942, search the homes of the individual plaintiffs herein without any warrants of search or seizure, and unlawfully to seize the papers, documents and effects of said plaintiffs and of 'Mankind United,' and falsely to imprison the individual plaintiffs by unlawfully arresting some of the individual plaintiffs without a warrant of arrest and unreasonably to delay the taking of all the individual plaintiffs before a committing officer, in order to effectuate the unlawful searches and seizures aforesaid.

"That thereafter, and on the 18th day of December, 1942, . . . the defendants and each of them, in order to carry out the terms and conditions of the illegal conspiracy aforesaid, and solely for the purpose of carrying out said terms and conditions, did arrest and imprison the individual plaintiffs herein, and did search the homes of said plaintiffs, and seize and carry away books, papers and effects of said individual plaintiffs and of said 'Mankind United.'"

". . . . by reason of the deprivation of . . . [their] Constitutional rights . . . [plaintiffs had] suffered damages." [For further development of the factual background, see United States v. Bell, 48 F.Supp. 986 (S.D.Cal.1943).—Ed.]

[e] Now 28 U.S.C. § 1331.

plaint refutes the first contention and, as will be seen, the second one is not decisive on the question of jurisdiction of the federal court.

Whether or not the complaint as drafted states a common law action in trespass made actionable by state law, it is clear from the way it was drawn that petitioners seek recovery squarely on the ground that respondents violated the Fourth and Fifth Amendments. It charges that the respondents conspired to do acts prohibited by these amendments and alleges that respondents' conduct pursuant to the conspiracy resulted in damages in excess of $3,000. It cannot be doubted therefore that it was the pleaders' purpose to make violation of these Constitutional provisions the basis of this suit. Before deciding that there is no jurisdiction, the district court must look to the way the complaint is drawn to see if it is drawn so as to claim a right to recover under the Constitution and laws of the United States. For to that extent "the party who brings a suit is master to decide what law he will rely upon, and . . . does determine whether he will bring a 'suit arising under' the . . . [Constitution or laws] of the United States by his declaration or bill." The Fair v. Kohler Die & Specialty Co., 228 U.S. 22, 25, 33 S.Ct. 410, 411. Though the mere failure to set out the federal or Constitutional claims as specifically as petitioners have done would not always be conclusive against the party bringing the suit, where the complaint, as here, is so drawn as to seek recovery directly under the Constitution or laws of the United States, the federal court, but for two possible exceptions later noted, must entertain the suit. Thus allegations far less specific than the ones in the complaint before us have been held adequate to show that the matter in controversy arose under the Constitution of the United States. Wiley v. Sinkler, 179 U.S. 58, 64, 65, 21 S.Ct. 17, 20; Swafford v. Templeton, 185 U.S. 487, 491, 492, 22 S.Ct. 783, 784, 785. The reason for this is that the court must assume jurisdiction to decide whether the allegations state a cause of action on which the court can grant relief as well as to determine issues of fact arising in the controversy.

Jurisdiction, therefore, is not defeated as respondents seem to contend, by the possibility that the averments might fail to state a cause of action on which petitioners could actually recover. For it is well settled that the failure to state a proper cause of action calls for a judgment on the merits and not for a dismissal for want of jurisdiction. Whether the complaint states a cause of action on which relief could be granted is a question of law and just as issues of fact it must be decided after and not before the court has assumed jurisdiction over the controversy. If the court does later exercise its jurisdiction to determine that the allegations in the complaint do not state a ground for relief, then dismissal of the case would be on the merits, not for want of jurisdiction. Swafford v. Templeton, 185 U.S. 487, 493, 494, 22 S.Ct. 783, 785, 786; Binderup v. Pathe Exchange, 263 U.S. 291, 305–308, 44 S.Ct. 96, 98–99. The previously carved out exceptions are that a suit may sometimes be dismissed for want of ju-

Exceptions: where claim under Const. clearly appears immaterial solely for getting s.mj. or where claim is insubstan. or frivolous.

risdiction where the alleged claim under the Constitution or federal statutes clearly appears to be immaterial and made solely for the purpose of obtaining jurisdiction or where such a claim is wholly insubstantial and frivolous. The accuracy of calling these dismissals jurisdictional has been questioned. The Fair v. Kohler Die & Specialty Co., supra, 228 U.S. at page 25, 33 S.Ct. at page 411. But cf. Swafford v. Templeton, supra.

But as we have already pointed out the alleged violations of the Constitution here are not immaterial but form rather the sole basis of the relief sought. Nor can we say that the cause of action alleged is so patently without merit as to justify, even under the qualifications noted, the court's dismissal for want of jurisdiction. The Circuit Court of Appeals correctly stated that "the complaint states strong cases, and if the allegations have any foundation in truth, the plaintiffs' legal rights have been ruthlessly violated." Petitioners' complaint asserts that the Fourth and Fifth Amendments guarantee their rights to be free from unauthorized and unjustified imprisonment and from unreasonable searches and seizures. They claim that respondents' invasion of these rights caused the damages for which they seek to recover and point further to 28 U.S.C. § 41(1), which authorizes the federal district courts to try "suits of a civil nature" where the matter in controversy "arises under the Constitution or laws of the United States," whether these are suits in "equity" or at "law."[f] Petitioners argue that this statute authorizes the Court to entertain this action at law and to grant recovery for the damages allegedly sustained. Respondents contend that the Constitutional provisions here involved are prohibitions against the federal government as a government and that 28 U.S.C. § 41(1) does not authorize recovery in money damages in suits against unauthorized officials who according to respondents are in the same position as individual trespassers.

Dis. ct. must decide if can recover or not

Respondents' contention does not show that petitioners' cause is insubstantial or frivolous, and the complaint does in fact raise serious questions, both of law and fact, which the district court can decide only after it has assumed jurisdiction over the controversy. The issue of law is whether federal courts can grant money recovery for damages said to have been suffered as a result of federal officers violating the Fourth and Fifth Amendments. That question has never been specifically decided by this Court. That the issue thus raised has sufficient merit to warrant exercise of federal jurisdiction for purposes of adjudicating it can be seen from the cases where this Court has sustained the jurisdiction of the district courts in suits brought to recover damages for depriving a citizen of the right to vote in violation of the Constitution. And it is established practice for this Court to sustain the jurisdiction of federal courts to issue injunctions to protect rights safeguarded by the Constitution and to

[f] Compare the language of the present provision, § 1331.

restrain individual state officers from doing what the 14th Amendment forbids the state to do.   Moreover, where federally protected rights have been invaded, it has been the rule from the beginning that courts will be alert to adjust their remedies so as to grant the necessary relief. And it is also well settled that where legal rights have been invaded, and a federal statute provides for a general right to sue for such invasion, federal courts may use any available remedy to make good the wrong done.   Whether the petitioners are entitled to recover depends upon an interpretation of 28 U.S.C. § 41(1), and on a determination of the scope of the Fourth and Fifth Amendments' protection from unreasonable searches and deprivations of liberty without due process of law. Thus, the right of the petitioners to recover under their complaint will be sustained if the Constitution and laws of the United States are given one construction and will be defeated if they are given another. For this reason the district court has jurisdiction. Gully v. First National Bank, 299 U.S. 109, 112, 113, 57 S.Ct. 96, 97; Smith v. Kansas City Title & Trust Co., 255 U.S. 180, 199, 200, 41 S.Ct. 243, 244, 245.

Reversed.

[The concurring opinion of Justice Reed is omitted.]

MR. JUSTICE JACKSON took no part in the consideration or decision of this case.

MR. CHIEF JUSTICE STONE and MR. JUSTICE BURTON, dissenting.

The district court is without jurisdiction as a federal court unless the complaint states a cause of action arising under the Constitution or laws of the United States. Whether the complaint states such a cause of action is for the court, not the pleader, to say. When the provision of the Constitution or federal statute affords a remedy which may in some circumstances be availed of by a plaintiff, the fact that his pleading does not bring him within that class as one entitled to the remedy, goes to the sufficiency of the pleading and not to the jurisdiction. The Fair v. Kohler Die & Specialty Co., 228 U.S. 22, 25, 33 S.Ct. 410, 411; Binderup v. Pathe Exchange, 263 U.S. 291, 306- 308, 44 S.Ct. 96, 98–99, and cases cited. But where as here, neither the constitutional provision nor any act of Congress affords a remedy to any person, the mere assertion by a plaintiff that he is entitled to such a remedy cannot be said to satisfy jurisdictional requirements. Hence we think that the courts below rightly decided that the district court was without jurisdiction because no cause of action under the Constitution or laws of the United States was stated.

The only effect of holding, as the Court does, that jurisdiction is conferred by the pleader's unfounded assertion that he is one who can have a remedy for damages arising under the Fourth and Fifth Amendments is to transfer to the federal court the trial of the allegations of trespass to person and property, which is a cause of action arising wholly under state law. For even though it be decided that petitioners have no right to damages under the Constitution, the district court will be required to pass upon the question whether the facts stated by petitioners give rise to a cause of action for trespass under state law. See Hurn v. Oursler, 289 U.S. 238, 53 S.Ct. 586.

Questions: (7) An action is brought in federal district court by a building contractor against certain unions, alleging that their strike aimed at compelling him to employ union labor is a conspiracy to restrain interstate commerce in violation of the antitrust laws. This contention, once an open question, has been squarely rejected by two prior Supreme Court cases. The plaintiff invokes jurisdiction on the ground that the case arises under federal antitrust law, but the defendants move for dismissal under Rule 12(b)(1). What decision on the motion? See Levering & Garrigues Co. v. Morrin, 289 U.S. 103, 53 S.Ct. 549 (1933) (grant).

(8) In a case such as Bell v. Hood, what difference does it make whether a defendant faced with a meritless federal claim wins on Rule 12(b)(1) grounds or by means of Rule 12(b)(6)?

SECTION 3. PENDENT JURISDICTION

It is clear that if federal question jurisdiction exists for a "claim," the district court has the power to decide not only the federal question but also any other questions, be they federal or state in nature, the resolution of which is necessary to decision on the claim. After all, a court of original jurisdiction must have this power to function practically; as recognized in the constitutional reference to "cases" and in the statutory references to "civil actions," such a court decides whole cases and not just isolated questions. So, for example, the Osborn case indicated that if the Bank of the United States brought a claim on an ordinary contract, federal question jurisdiction would exist, and moreover the federal court would be empowered to decide all state-law questions it ran into when disposing of the contract claim on the merits.

Hurn v. Oursler, 289 U.S. 238, 53 S.Ct. 586 (1933), is the wellspring case concerning a rather different doctrine called pendent jurisdiction. The plaintiffs in that case joined three claims in the same complaint: (1) for infringement of the copyright in a play, a claim arising under a federal statute; (2) for unfair competition in unauthorized use of the same play, a claim arising under state law; and (3) for unfair competition through interference with the plaintiffs' rights in an uncopyrighted, revised version of the play, a claim also arising under state law. At the close of the evidence on the copyright claim in a bench trial, the trial court dismissed that claim for failure of proof of infringement and the other two claims for lack of jurisdiction. The Supreme Court held that it was error so to dismiss the second claim, saying: "The distinction to be observed is between a case where two distinct grounds in support of a single cause of action are alleged, one only of which presents a federal question, and a case where two separate and distinct causes of action are alleged, one only of which is federal in character." On this test the claim of unfair competition with regard to the copyrighted play was held to arise from the same cause of action as the copyright infringement claim, but the claim as to the uncopyrighted revision of the play was a separate and distinct cause of action and hence properly dismissed.

[margin handwritten notes: When 2 grounds in support of single c.of.a — pend. juris. When 2 sep. distinct c.of.as — no pend. juris.]

Question: (9) Upon remand, the district court in Bell v. Hood granted defendants' motion to dismiss the complaint on the ground that it failed to state a claim upon which relief could be granted, 71 F.Supp. 813 (S.D.Cal. 1947). It first decided that no federal claim was stated[g] and then concluded that consequently the pendent state claim now being urged should also be dismissed. Was this latter holding consistent with Hurn v. Oursler?

The lower courts had trouble in applying the Hurn "single cause of action" test. Although the desirability of the Hurn extension of jurisdiction seems fairly apparent, some courts would take jurisdiction of the state claim only when there was a virtually complete identity of the facts in the two claims.

In 1948 the Hurn doctrine was purportedly codified in § 1338(b) of title 28. The codification aggravated the difficulties instead of solving them. In the first place, the statute refers to a state "claim . . . when joined with a substantial and related [federal] claim." So the statute, like the Federal Rules, avoids the term "cause of action," which was the touchstone of the Hurn test. But does "claim" in the statute mean the same as "cause of action"? What meaning is to be given to "substantial"? to "related"? The statutory formulation is broader than Hurn, but how much broader? In the second place, the statute refers only to a claim of unfair competition joined to a claim under certain federal laws. Here, the subsequent cases clearly established that the statute did not abolish pendent jurisdiction in other areas of law.

UNITED MINE WORKERS v. GIBBS, 383 U.S. 715, 86 S.Ct. 1130 (1966). Plaintiff sued the union in a federal district court, alleging that the union improperly interfered in his contractual relations with

[g] The Supreme Court has since decided, contrary to the district court in Bell v. Hood, that violation of the fourth amendment by a federal agent acting under the color of his authority does give rise to a federal cause of action within 28 U.S.C. § 1331 for damages resulting from his unconstitutional conduct. Bivens v. Six Unknown Named Agents of Fed. Bureau of Narcotics, 403 U.S. 388, 91 S.Ct. 1999 (1971). Justice Black, who wrote the opinion in Bell v. Hood, dissented, along with Chief Justice Burger and Justice Blackmun.

More recently, the Supreme Court decided that violation of the due process clause of the fifth amendment similarly gives rise to a federal cause of action for damages within § 1331. Davis v. Passman, 442 U.S. 228, 99 S.Ct. 2264 (1979).

the coal company that employed him.   He claimed damage from secondary boycotts under § 303 of the Labor Management Relations Act, 29 U.S.C. § 187, and also damage from the same unlawful acts under the common law of the state. The trial court dismissed the federal claim on judgment n.o.v., but it allowed the plaintiff's verdict on the state claim to stand.

In holding that jurisdiction over the pendent state claim was properly entertained, Justice Brennan for the Supreme Court first characterized the prevailing approach of lower courts to pendent jurisdiction as "unnecessarily grudging." Rephrasing the inquiry as whether the relationship between the federal question claim and the state claim was close enough to permit "the conclusion that the entire action before the court comprises but one constitutional 'case,'" he then explained:

> "The state and federal claims must derive from a common nucleus of operative fact. But if, considered without regard for their federal or state character, a plaintiff's claims are such that he would ordinarily be expected to try them all in one judicial proceeding, then, assuming substantiality of the federal issues, there is *power* in federal courts to hear the whole.

> "That power need not be exercised in every case in which it is found to exist. It has consistently been recognized that pendent jurisdiction is a doctrine of discretion, not of plaintiff's right. Its justification lies in considerations of judicial economy, convenience and fairness to litigants; if these are not present a federal court should hesitate to exercise jurisdiction over state claims, even though bound to apply state law to them, Erie R. Co. v. Tompkins, 304 U.S. 64, 58 S.Ct. 817. Needless decisions of state law should be avoided both as a matter of comity and to promote justice between the parties, by procuring for them a surer-footed reading of applicable law. . . . [I]f it appears that the state issues substantially predominate, whether in terms of proof, of the scope of the issues raised, or of the comprehensiveness of the remedy sought, the state claims may be dismissed without prejudice and left for resolution to state tribunals. There may, on the other hand, be situations in which the state claim is so closely tied to questions of federal policy that the argument for exercise of pendent jurisdiction is particularly strong. In the present case, for example, the allowable scope of the state claim implicates the federal doctrine of pre-emption; while this interrelationship does not create statutory federal question jurisdiction, Louisville & N.R. Co. v. Mottley, 211 U.S. 149, 29 S.Ct. 42, its existence is relevant to the exercise of discretion. Finally, there may be reasons independent of jurisdictional considerations, such as the likelihood of jury confusion in treating divergent legal theories of relief, that would justify separating state and federal claims for trial, Fed.Rule Civ.Proc. 42(b). If so, jurisdiction should ordinarily be refused.

"The question of power will ordinarily be resolved on the pleadings. But the issue whether pendent jurisdiction has been properly assumed is one which remains open throughout the litigation."

Questions: (10) Considering the *power* of a federal court under Gibbs to hear a state claim pendent to a claim arising under federal law, what constitutional arguments could be made against the existence of such power? What arguments could be made on the basis of the various congressional grants of federal question jurisdiction?

(11) Considering the role of *discretion* in deciding under Gibbs whether or not such a state claim will be heard, is it desirable that the federal courts should have discretion so to define their own jurisdiction?

(12) *P* sues *D–1* in a federal district court on a claim for which there is federal question jurisdiction. Does the federal court have discretion to hear a closely related state-law claim that *P* has against *D–2*? Compare Boudreaux v. Puckett, 611 F.2d 1028 (5th Cir.1980), with Aldinger v. Howard, 427 U.S. 1, 96 S.Ct. 2413 (1976).

SECTION 4. ANCILLARY JURISDICTION

Ancillary jurisdiction is a judge-made doctrine under which a district court may, as an incident to deciding a claim within its jurisdiction, decide other claims that, if separately presented, would not be within the court's jurisdiction. [# Def.]

This concept was born as a doctrine of necessity. A federal court of original jurisdiction must have the power to handle certain incidental matters in order to function as a court of justice. For example, in Freeman v. Howe, 65 U.S. (24 How.) 450 (1861), it was said that a federal court had jurisdiction over a claim by mortgagees to the mortgaged property—where that property had previously been brought under the court's control by attachment in a diversity action to which the mortgagees were not parties—even though there was no independent jurisdictional ground for the mortgagees' claim. The reasoning was that a state court could not be allowed to interfere with the federal control of the property, and this in turn necessitated a federal forum for the mortgagees in order not to leave them remediless. Their claim would be heard under the theory that it was "ancillary and dependent, supplementary merely to the original suit."

The doctrine shifted gears in Moore v. New York Cotton Exchange, 270 U.S. 593, 46 S.Ct. 367 (1926), where the Court seemed to move toward a doctrine of convenience. It was there held that in a federal antitrust suit complaining of the Exchange's restrictions on access to cotton price quotations, the federal court had jurisdiction over the Exchange's counterclaim seeking an injunction against the plaintiff's wrongfully obtaining those quotations; the counterclaim fell within the compulsory counterclaim provision of the Equity Rules [c" claims OK for fed. ct. (here a compuls. Claim)] of 1912, but there was no independent jurisdictional ground for that counterclaim.

The utility of ancillary jurisdiction has been greatly increased by the broadened provisions for joinder of claims and parties under the Federal Rules.

REVERE COPPER & BRASS INC. v. AETNA CASUALTY & SURETY CO.

United States Court of Appeals, Fifth Circuit, 1970.
426 F.2d 709.

[*Prior Hist*]

[Revere Copper & Brass, a Maryland corporation, brought suit in federal court against Aetna, surety on performance bonds on construction contracts, alleging that Aetna's principal, a Maryland corporation named Fuller, had failed to perform its obligations under the contracts. There was diversity of citizenship between Revere and Aetna, and Revere sought to recover $2,045,000. Aetna denied Revere's allegations and impleaded Fuller under Rule 14(a), alleging that Fuller had agreed to indemnify Aetna for all losses from its suretyship. Fuller admitted Aetna's allegations, but denied the allegations in Revere's complaint and made claim against Revere, seeking to recover $1,328,880 on the basis of the same disputed contracts. Revere moved to dismiss Fuller's claim against it on the ground that there was no diversity of citizenship between them. The district court found the claim to be within its ancillary jurisdiction, and it therefore denied Revere's motion. An interlocutory appeal under 28 U.S.C. § 1292(b) followed.]

Before SIMPSON, MORGAN and INGRAHAM, CIRCUIT JUDGES.

MORGAN, CIRCUIT JUDGE.

. . . .

The theoretical basis which underlies the modern doctrine of ancillary jurisdiction appears to be fairly well settled. . . .

The exact criteria to be used to detect the presence of ancillary jurisdiction, however, is more elusive. The leading case on the modern doctrine of ancillarity is Moore v. New York Cotton Exchange, 270 U.S. 593, 46 S.Ct. 367, 78 L.Ed. 756 (1926), which held that a compulsory counterclaim under old Equity Rule 30 need not be supported by an independent basis of federal jurisdiction, but was ancillary to the main cause of action since it arose out of the transaction which was the subject matter of the original suit. In defining what it meant by the word "transaction", the Court said:

[*Compuls. C'claim OK if out of same trans-action*]

> "Transaction" is a word of flexible meaning. It may comprehend a series of many occurrences, depending not so much upon the immediateness of their connection as upon their *logical relationship*.

. . . .

It would be fair to say, therefore, that a claim is ancillary when it bears a logical relationship to the aggregate core of operative facts which constitutes the main claim over which the court has an independent basis of federal jurisdiction. However, the type of relationship contemplated by the phrase "logical relationship" remains somewhat clouded. Perhaps the simplest way to determine the type of the nexus that must necessarily exist between the main claim and another claim for the other claim to be considered ancillary is to examine the present extent of the application of the doctrine to the various devices of the Federal Rules allowing joinder of claims.

While it is well established that a compulsory counterclaim under Rule 13(a) is within the ancillary jurisdiction since it necessarily arises out of the same transaction or occurrence as the original claim, Moore v. New York Cotton Exchange, supra, a permissive counterclaim under Rule 13(b) requires an independent ground of federal jurisdiction since it does not arise out of the same transaction or occurrence as the original claim, Camper & Nicholsons, Ltd. v. Yacht "Fontainebleau II" S.D.Fla., 1968, 292 F.Supp. 734, except where a setoff is involved. Fraser v. Astra Steamship Corp., S.D.N.Y., 1955, 18 F.R.D. 240; see 3 Moore . . . ¶ 13.19. Contra, Robinson Bros. & Co. v. Tygart Steel Products Co., W.D.Pa., 1949, 9 F.R.D. 468.[7] Crossclaims under Rule 13(g) are considered ancillary since, under the Rule, they must arise "out of the transaction or occurrence that is the subject matter either of the original action or of a counterclaim therein or relating to any property that is the subject matter of the original action." Childress v. Cook, 5 Cir., 1957, 245 F.2d 798. An impleader action under Rule 14(a) is considered ancillary even though such an action does not, as a general rule, directly involve the aggregate of operative facts upon which the original claim is based, but arises out of that claim in the sense that the impleader action, such as the action for indemnity here brought by Aetna against Fuller, would not exist without the threat of liability arising out of the original claim. Waylander-Peterson Co. v. Great Northern Ry. Co., 8 Cir. 1953, 201 F.2d 408; Lesnik v. Public Industrials Corp., 2 Cir., 1944, 144 F.2d 968. Likewise, intervention as of right under Rule 24(a), available "when the applicant claims an interest relating to the property or transaction which is the subject of the action and he is so situated that the disposition of the action may as a practical matter impair or impede his ability to protect that interest, unless the applicant's interest is adequately represented by existing parties," is re-

---

[7] The treatment of permissive counterclaims involving set-offs is an exception to the logical relationship test in that they are independent from the original claim and can be said to be ancillary only in the sense that they are limited by the amount of the original claim. The ancillary status given set-offs is best explained historically from their source in English statute, 2 Geo. 2, c. 22, § 13 (1729). See, Note "Diversity Requirements In Multiparty Litigation", [58 Colum.L.Rev. 548, 553–55 (1958)].

garded as ancillary to the original claim and need not be supported by an independent ground of federal jurisdiction. Formulabs, Incorporated v. Hartley Pen Company, 9 Cir., 1963, 318 F.2d 485, 492, cert. den. 375 U.S. 945, 84 S.Ct. 352, 11 L.Ed.2d 275.

From the application of the doctrine of ancillary jurisdiction to these joinder devices, it appears that a claim has a logical relationship to the original claim if it *arises* out of the same aggregate of operative facts as the original claim in two senses: (1) that the same aggregate of operative facts serves as the basis of both claims; or (2) that the aggregate core of facts upon which the original claim rests activates additional legal rights in a party defendant that would otherwise remain dormant.

Before proceeding, another aspect of the Moore decision, supra, must be mentioned, and that is the Court's concern with the need to provide complete relief to the counterclaiming defendant. 270 U.S. at 610, 46 S.Ct. 367, 70 L.Ed. 750. A cursory review of the joinder situations to which ancillary jurisdiction is applied reveals that, generally, it is made available to litigants in a defensive posture, who would otherwise be prevented or greatly burdened in adequately protecting their interests. There is much to be said for allowing parties who are involuntarily brought into federal court to defend against a claim, or who must be allowed to intervene in a federal action as a defendant to secure their interests, to assert all their claims arising out of the controversy in one proceeding and that this is, or ought to be, one of the factors to be considered in determining the existence of ancillary jurisdiction. See, Note, "Diversity Requirements in Multiparty Litigation", supra, n. [7], at 561.

It is easily seen that Fuller's claim arises out of the aggregate of operative facts which forms the basis of Revere's claim in such a way to put their logical relationship beyond doubt. The two claims are but two sides of the same coin. The construction was not completed before the time provided in the two contracts. If Revere is not responsible for the delay, as Fuller alleges, Fuller must at least be guilty of breach of contract, not to mention the other allegations of fault in Revere's complaint. To paraphrase the Supreme Court in Moore v. New York Cotton Exchange, supra: so close is the connection between the case sought to be stated in Revere's complaint and that set up in Fuller's Rule 14(a) counterclaim that it only needs the failure of the former to establish the foundation for the latter.

Not only is the parallel between a Rule 14(a) counterclaim and a compulsory counterclaim under Rule 13(a) so close as to be persuasive on the question of ancillarity, the parallel between the instant case and cases dealing with the ability of an intervenor of right under Rule 24(a) to counterclaim against the original plaintiff without an independent basis of federal jurisdiction removes any substantial doubt. It is well established that a contractor who has agreed to indemnify his surety on a performance bond can intervene as a party defendant as of right in a suit on the performance bond against the surety and then assert his counterclaim against the plaintiff, even in the absence of an independent ground of federal jurisdiction. United States, to Use and Benefit of Foster Wheeler Corp. v. American Surety Co., 2 Cir., 1944, 142 F.2d 726; Coleman Capital Corp. v. Fidelity & Deposit Co. of Md., S.D.N.Y., 1967, 43 F.R.D. 407. It would be anomalous to hold that Fuller could have asserted its counterclaim against Revere free of any jurisdictional impediment if it had taken the initiative of intervening, and yet hold that since Fuller was brought into this action involuntarily as a third-party defendant, its counterclaim must satisfy the requirements of strict diversity and thus fail.

Revere also argues that the recognition of ancillary jurisdiction in the present situation would be an unwarranted extension of federal diversity jurisdiction in contravention of Rule 82, F.R.C.P., and the general trend to restrict this head or [sic] jurisdiction. See, ALI, Study of the Division of Jurisdiction between State and Federal Courts (Proposed Final Draft No. 1, 1965); Field, "Proposals on Federal Diversity Jurisdiction", 17 S.Car.L.R. 685 (1965). In answer to this argument, it should be noted that the Federal Rules do not expand ancillary jurisdiction, but provide opportunities for involving the doctrine, which, as has been seen, was already well established when the rules became effective, in additional situations. [Citations omitted.]

. . . .

Affirmed and remanded.

Question: (13) What should happen to an ancillary claim if the original claim on which federal jurisdiction is based is disposed of by settlement? by summary judgment? by dismissal for failure to state a claim upon which relief can be granted? by dismissal for lack of subject-matter jurisdiction? See Dery v. Wyer, 265 F.2d 804 (2d Cir.1959).

OWEN EQUIPMENT & ERECTION CO. v. KROGER

Supreme Court of the United States, 1978.
437 U.S. 365, 98 S.Ct. 2396.

MR. JUSTICE STEWART delivered the opinion of the Court.

In an action in which federal jurisdiction is based on diversity of citizenship, may the plaintiff assert a claim against a third-party defendant when there is no independent basis for federal jurisdiction over that claim? The Court of Appeals for the Eighth Circuit held in this case that such a claim is within the ancillary jurisdiction of the federal courts. We granted certiorari, 434 U.S. 1008, 98 S.Ct. 715, because this decision conflicts with several recent decisions of other Courts of Appeals.

I

FACTS

On January 18, 1972, James Kroger was electrocuted when the boom of a steel crane next to which he was walking came too close to a high tension electric power line. The respondent (his widow, who is the administratrix of his estate) filed a wrongful death action in the United States District Court for the District of Nebraska against the Omaha Public Power District (OPPD). Her complaint alleged that OPPD's negligent construction, maintenance and operation of the power line had caused Kroger's death. Federal jurisdiction was based on diversity of citizenship, since the respondent was a citizen of Iowa and OPPD was a Nebraska corporation.

OPPD then filed a third-party complaint pursuant to Fed. Rule Civ. Proc. 14(a) against the petitioner, Owen Equipment and Erection Company (Owen), alleging that the crane was owned and operated by Owen, and that Owen's negligence had been the proximate cause of Kroger's death.[3] OPPD later moved for summary judgment on the respondent's complaint against it. While this motion was pending, the respondent was granted leave to file an amended complaint naming Owen as an additional defendant. Thereafter, the District Court granted OPPD's motion for summary judgment in an unreported opinion. The case thus went to trial between the respondent and the petitioner alone.

The respondent's amended complaint alleged that Owen was "a Nebraska corporation with its principal place of business in Nebraska." Owen's answer admitted that it was "a corporation organized and existing under the Laws of the State of Nebraska," and denied every other allegation of the complaint. On the third day of trial, however, it was disclosed that the petitioner's principal place of business was in Iowa, not Nebraska,[5] and that the petitioner and the respondent were thus both citizens of Iowa. The petitioner then moved to dismiss the complaint for lack of jurisdiction. The District Court reserved decision on the motion, and the jury thereafter returned a verdict in favor of the respondent. In an unreported opinion issued

[3] Under Rule 14(a), a third-party defendant may not be impleaded merely because he may be liable to the *plaintiff*. [Citations omitted.] While the third-party complaint in this case alleged merely that Owen's negligence caused Kroger's death, and the basis of Owen's alleged liability *to OPPD* is nowhere spelled out, OPPD evidently relied upon the state common-law right of contribution among joint tortfeasors. See Dairyland Ins. Co. v. Mumert, 212 N.W.2d 436, 438 (Iowa); Best v. Yerkes, 247 Iowa 800, 77 N.W.2d 23. The petitioner has never challenged the propriety of the third-party complaint as such.

[5] The problem apparently was one of geography. Although the Missouri River generally marks the boundary between Iowa and Nebraska, Carter Lake, Iowa, where the accident occurred and where Owen had its main office, lies west of the river, adjacent to Omaha, Neb. Apparently the river once avulsed at one of its bends, cutting Carter Lake off from the rest of Iowa.

after the trial, the District Court denied the petitioner's motion to dismiss the complaint.

The judgment was affirmed on appeal, 558 F.2d 417. The Court of Appeals held that under this Court's decision in Mine Workers v. Gibbs, 383 U.S. 715, 86 S.Ct. 1130, the District Court had jurisdictional power, in its discretion, to adjudicate the respondent's claim against the petitioner because that claim arose from the "core of 'operative facts' giving rise to both [respondent's] claim against OPPD and OPPD's claim against Owen." 558 F.2d at 424. It further held that the District Court had properly exercised its discretion in proceeding to decide the case even after summary judgment had been granted to OPPD, because the petitioner had concealed its Iowa citizenship from the respondent. . . .

II

It is undisputed that there was no independent basis of federal jurisdiction over the respondent's state-law tort action against the petitioner, since both are citizens of Iowa. And although Fed.Rule Civ. Proc. 14(a) permits a plaintiff to assert a claim against a third-party defendant, . . . it does not purport to say whether or not such a claim requires an independent basis of federal jurisdiction. Indeed, it could not determine that question, since it is axiomatic that the Federal Rules of Civil Procedure do not create or withdraw federal jurisdiction.

In affirming the District Court's judgment, the Court of Appeals relied upon the doctrine of ancillary jurisdiction, whose contours it believed were defined by this Court's holding in Mine Workers v. Gibbs, supra. The Gibbs case differed from this one in that it involved pendent jurisdiction, which concerns the resolution of a plaintiff's federal and state law claims against a single defendant in one action. By contrast, in this case there was no claim based upon substantive federal law, but rather state-law tort claims against two different defendants. Nonetheless, the Court of Appeals was correct in perceiving that Gibbs and this case are two species of the same generic problem: Under what circumstances may a federal court hear and decide a state-law claim arising between citizens of the same State?[8] But we believe that the Court of Appeals failed to understand the scope of the doctrine of the Gibbs case.

. . . .

It is apparent that Gibbs delineated the constitutional limits of federal judicial power. But even if it be assumed that the District Court in the present case had constitutional power to decide the re-

---

[8] No more than in Aldinger v. Howard, 427 U.S. 1, 96 S.Ct. 2413, is it necessary to determine here "whether there are any 'principled' differences between pen- dent and ancillary jurisdiction; or, if there are, what effect Gibbs had on such differences." Id., at 13, 96 S.Ct., at 2420.

spondent's lawsuit against the petitioner,[10] it does not follow that the decision of the Court of Appeals was correct. Constitutional power is merely the first hurdle that must be overcome in determining that a federal court has jurisdiction over a particular controversy. For the jurisdiction of the federal courts is limited not only by the provisions of Art. III of the Constitution, but by Acts of Congress. [Citations omitted.]

That statutory law as well as the Constitution may limit a federal court's jurisdiction over nonfederal claims[11] is well illustrated by . . . . Aldinger v. Howard, 427 U.S. 1, 96 S.Ct. 2413 . . . . In Aldinger the Court held that a federal district court lacked jurisdiction over a state-law claim against a county, even if that claim was alleged to be pendent to one against county officials under 42 U.S.C. § 1983. . . . . [D]espite the fact that federal and nonfederal claims arose from a "common nucleus of operative fact," the Court held that the statute [28 U.S.C. § 1343(3)] conferring jurisdiction over the federal claim did not allow the exercise of jurisdiction over the nonfederal claim.

. . . Aldinger . . . thus make[s] clear that a finding that federal and nonfederal claims arise from a "common nucleus of operative fact," the test of Gibbs, does not end the inquiry into whether a federal court has power to hear the nonfederal claims along with the federal ones. Beyond this constitutional minimum, there must be an examination of the posture in which the nonfederal claim is asserted and of the specific statute that confers jurisdiction over the federal claim, in order to determine whether "Congress in [that statute] has . . . expressly or by implication negated" the exercise of jurisdiction over the particular nonfederal claim. Aldinger v. Howard, supra, 427 U.S., at 18, 96 S.Ct., at 2422.

III

The relevant statute in this case, 28 U.S.C. § 1332(a)(1), confers upon federal courts jurisdiction over "civil actions where the matter in controversy exceeds the sum or value of $10,000 . . . and is between . . . citizens of different States." This statute and its predecessors have consistently been held to require complete diversity of citizenship.[13] That is, diversity jurisdiction does not exist unless

---

[10] Federal jurisdiction in Gibbs was based upon the existence of a question of federal law. The Court of Appeals in the present case believed that the "common nucleus of operative fact" test also determines the outer boundaries of constitutionally permissible federal jurisdiction when that jurisdiction is based upon diversity of citizenship. We may assume without deciding that the Court of Appeals was correct in this regard. See also n. 13, infra.

[11] As used in this opinion, the term "nonfederal claim" means one as to which there is no independent basis for federal jurisdiction. Conversely, a "federal claim" means one as to which an independent basis for federal jurisdiction exists.

[13] E.g., Strawbridge v. Curtiss, 3 Cranch 267; Coal Company v. Blatchford, 11 Wall. 172; Indianapolis v. Chase National Bank, 314 U.S. 63, 69, 62 S.Ct. 15, 16; American Fire & Cas. Co. v. Finn,

each defendant is a citizen of a different State from *each* plaintiff. Over the years Congress has repeatedly re-enacted or amended the statute conferring diversity jurisdiction, leaving intact this rule of complete diversity. Whatever may have been the original purposes of diversity of citizenship jurisdiction, this subsequent history clearly demonstrates a congressional mandate that diversity jurisdiction is not to be available when any plaintiff is a citizen of the same State as any defendant. Cf. Snyder v. Harris, 394 U.S. 332, 338–339, 89 S.Ct. 1053, 1057–1058.[16]

Thus it is clear that the respondent could not originally have brought suit in federal court naming Owen and OPPD as codefendants, since citizens of Iowa would have been on both sides of the litigation. Yet the identical lawsuit resulted when she amended her complaint. Complete diversity was destroyed just as surely as if she had sued Owen initially. In either situation, in the plain language of the statute, the "matter in controversy" could not be "between . . . citizens of different States."

It is a fundamental precept that federal courts are courts of limited jurisdiction. The limits upon federal jurisdiction, whether imposed by the Constitution or by Congress, must be neither disregarded nor evaded. Yet under the reasoning of the Court of Appeals in this case, a plaintiff could defeat the statutory requirement of complete diversity by the simple expedient of suing only those defendants who were of diverse citizenship and waiting for them to implead nondiverse defendants.[17] If, as the Court of Appeals thought, a "common nucleus of operative fact" were the only requirement for ancillary jurisdiction in a diversity case, there would be no principled reason

341 U.S. 6, 17, 71 S.Ct. 534, 541. It is settled that complete diversity is not a constitutional requirement. State Farm Fire & Cas. Co. v. Tashire, 386 U.S. 523, 530–531, 87 S.Ct. 1199, 1203–1204.

[16] Notably, Congress enacted § 1332 as part of the Judicial Code of 1948, 62 Stat. 930, shortly after Rule 14 was amended in 1946. When the Rule was amended, the Advisory Committee noted that "in any case where the plaintiff could not have joined the third party originally because of jurisdictional limitations such as lack of diversity of citizenship, the majority view is that any attempt by the plaintiff to amend his complaint and assert a claim against the impleaded third party would be unavailing." 28 U.S.C.App., p. 7752. The subsequent re-enactment without relevant change of the diversity statute may thus be seen as evidence of congressional approval of that "majority view."

[17] This is not an unlikely hypothesis, since a defendant in a tort suit such as

this one would surely try to limit his liability by impleading any joint tortfeasors for indemnity or contribution. Some commentators have suggested that the possible abuse of third-party practice could be dealt with under 28 U.S.C. § 1359, which forbids collusive attempts to create federal jurisdiction. See, e.g., 3 Moore's Federal Practice ¶ 14.27[1], at 14–571 (2d ed. 1974); 6 C. Wright & A. Miller, Federal Practice and Procedure § 1444, at 231–232 (1971); Note, Rule 14 Claims and Ancillary Jurisdiction, 57 Va. L.Rev. 265, 274–275 (1971). The dissenting opinion today also expresses this view. . . . But there is nothing necessarily collusive about a plaintiff selectively suing only those tortfeasors of diverse citizenship, or about the named defendants' desire to implead joint tortfeasors. Nonetheless, the requirement of complete diversity would be eviscerated by such a course of events.

[handwritten margin notes:] If only need COF to be anc. ① could join Cofa aga. Owen in orig complaint as anc.

why the respondent in this case could not have joined her cause of action against Owen in her original complaint as ancillary to her claim against OPPD. Congress' requirement of complete diversity would thus have been evaded completely.

It is true, as the Court of Appeals noted, that the exercise of ancillary jurisdiction over nonfederal claims has often been upheld in situations involving impleader, cross-claims or counterclaims.[18] But in determining whether jurisdiction over a nonfederal claim exists, the context in which the nonfederal claim is asserted is crucial. See Aldinger v. Howard, 427 U.S., at 14, 96 S.Ct., at 2420. And the claim here arises in a setting quite different from the kinds of nonfederal claim that have been viewed in other cases as falling within the ancillary jurisdiction of the federal courts.

First, the nonfederal claim in this case was simply not ancillary to the federal one in the same sense that, for example, the impleader by a defendant of a third-party defendant always is. A third-party complaint depends at least in part upon the resolution of the primary lawsuit. See n. 3, supra. Its relation to the original complaint is thus not mere factual similarity but logical dependence. Cf. Moore v. New York Cotton Exchange, 270 U.S. 593, 610, 46 S.Ct. 367, 371. The respondent's claim against the petitioner, however, was entirely separate from her original claim against OPPD, since the petitioner's liability to her depended not at all upon whether or not OPPD was also liable. Far from being an ancillary and dependent claim, it was a new and independent one.

Second, the nonfederal claim here was asserted by the plaintiff, who voluntarily chose to bring suit upon a state-law claim in a federal court. By contrast, ancillary jurisdiction typically involves claims by a defending party haled into court against his will, or by another person whose rights might be irretrievably lost unless he could assert them in an ongoing action in a federal court. A plaintiff cannot complain if ancillary jurisdiction does not encompass all of his possible claims in a case such as this one, since it is he who has chosen the federal rather than the state forum and must thus accept its limitations. "[T]he efficiency plaintiff seeks so avidly is available without

---

[18] The ancillary jurisdiction of the federal courts derives originally from cases such as Freeman v. Howe, 24 How. 450, which held that when federal jurisdiction "effectively controls the property or fund under dispute, other claimants thereto should be allowed to intervene in order to protect their interests, without regard to jurisdiction." Aldinger v. Howard, 427 U.S., at 11, 96 S.Ct., at 2419. More recently, it has been said to include cases that involve multiparty practice, such as compulsory counterclaims, e.g., Moore v. New York Cotton Exchange, 270 U.S. 593, 46 S.Ct. 367; impleader, e.g., H.L. Peterson Co. v. Applewhite, 383 F.2d 430, 433 (CA5); Dery v. Wyer, 265 F.2d 804 (CA2); cross-claims, e.g., LASA Per L'Industria Del Marmo Soc. Per Azioni v. Alexander, 414 F.2d 143 (CA6); Scott v. Fancher, 369 F.2d 842, 844 (CA5); Glen Falls Indemnity Co. v. United States ex rel. Westinghouse Electric Supply Co., 229 F.2d 370, 373–374 (CA9); or intervention as of right, e.g., Phelps v. Oaks, 117 U.S. 236, 241, 6 S.Ct. 714, 716; Smith Petroleum Service, Inc. v. Monsanto Chemical Co., 420 F.2d 1103, 1113–1115 (CA5).

question in the state courts." Kenrose Mfg. Co. v. Fred Whitaker Co., 512 F.2d 890, 894 (CA4).[20]

It is not unreasonable to assume that, in generally requiring complete diversity, Congress did not intend to confine the jurisdiction of federal courts so inflexibly that they are unable to protect legal rights or effectively to resolve an entire, logically entwined lawsuit. Those practical needs are the basis of the doctrine of ancillary jurisdiction. But neither the convenience of litigants nor considerations of judicial economy can suffice to justify extension of the doctrine of ancillary jurisdiction to a plaintiff's cause of action against a citizen of the same State in a diversity case. Congress has established the basic rule that diversity jurisdiction exists under 28 U.S.C. § 1332 only when there is complete diversity of citizenship. "The policy of the statute calls for its strict construction." Healy v. Ratta, 292 U.S. 263, 270, 54 S.Ct. 700, 703; [other citations omitted]. To allow the requirement of complete diversity to be circumvented as it was in this case would simply flout the congressional command.[21]

Accordingly, the judgment of the Court of Appeals is reversed.

It is so ordered.

MR. JUSTICE WHITE, with whom MR. JUSTICE BRENNAN joins, dissenting.

The Court today states that "[i]t is not unreasonable to assume that, in generally requiring complete diversity, Congress did not intend to confine the jurisdiction of federal courts so inflexibly that they are unable . . . effectively to resolve an entire, logically entwined lawsuit." . . . In spite of this recognition, the majority goes on to hold that in diversity suits federal courts do not have the jurisdictional power to entertain a claim asserted by a plaintiff against a third-party defendant, no matter how entwined it is with the matter already before the court, unless there is an independent basis for jurisdiction over that claim. Because I find no support for such a requirement in either Art. III of the Constitution or in any statutory law, I dissent from the Court's "unnecessarily grudging"[1] approach.

. . . .

. . . [Gibbs'] language and reasoning were broad enough to cover the instant factual situation . . . . Accordingly, as far as

[20] Whether Iowa's statute of limitations would now bar an action by the respondent in an Iowa court is, of course, entirely a matter of state law. See Iowa Code § 614.10. Compare 558 F.2d, at 420, with id., at 432 n. 42 (Bright, J., dissenting); cf. Burnett v. New York Central R. Co., 380 U.S. 424, 431–432, and n. 9, 85 S.Ct. 1050, 1056–1057, and n. 9.

respondent's lawsuit against the petitioner. Thus, the asserted inequity in the respondent's alleged concealment of its citizenship is irrelevant. Federal judicial power does not depend upon "prior action or consent of the parties." American Fire & Cas. Co. v. Finn, 341 U.S. 6, 18, 71 S.Ct. 534, 542.

[21] Our holding is that the District Court lacked power to entertain the

[1] See Mine Workers v. Gibbs, 383 U.S. 715, 725, 86 S.Ct. 1130, 1138 (1966).

Art. III of the Constitution is concerned, the District Court had power to entertain Mrs. Kroger's claim against Owen.

The majority correctly points out, however, that the analysis cannot stop here. As Aldinger v. Howard, 427 U.S. 1, 96 S.Ct. 2413 (1976), teaches, the jurisdictional power of the federal courts may be limited by Congress, as well as by the Constitution. In Aldinger, although the plaintiff's state claim against Spokane County was closely connected with her § 1983 claim against the county treasurer, the Court held that the District Court did not have pendent jurisdiction over the state claim, for, under the Court's precedents at that time, it was thought that Congress had specifically determined not to confer on the federal courts jurisdiction over civil rights claims against cities and counties. That being so, the Court refused to allow "the federal courts to fashion a jurisdictional doctrine under the general language of Art. III enabling them to circumvent this exclusion . . . ." Id., at 16, 96 S.Ct., at 2421.[3]

In the present case, the only indication of congressional intent that the Court can find is that contained in the diversity jurisdictional statute . . . . Because this statute has been interpreted as requiring complete diversity of citizenship between each plaintiff and each defendant, Strawbridge v. Curtiss, 3 Cranch 267 (1806), the Court holds that the District Court did not have ancillary jurisdiction over Mrs. Kroger's claim against Owen. In so holding, the Court unnecessarily expands the scope of the complete-diversity requirement while substantially limiting the doctrine of ancillary jurisdiction.

The complete-diversity requirement, of course, could be viewed as meaning that in a diversity case, a federal district court may adjudicate only those claims that are between parties of different States. Thus, in order for a defendant to implead a third-party defendant, there would have to be diversity of citizenship; the same would also be true for cross-claims between defendants and for a third-party defendant's claim against a plaintiff. Even the majority, however, refuses to read the complete-diversity requirement so broadly; it recognizes with seeming approval the exercise of ancillary jurisdiction over nonfederal claims in situations involving impleader, cross-claims and counterclaims. . . . Given the Court's willingness to recognize ancillary jurisdiction in these contexts, despite the requirements of § 1332(a), I see no justification for the Court's refusal to approve the District Court's exercise of ancillary jurisdiction in the present case.

It is significant that a plaintiff who asserts a claim against a third-party defendant is not seeking to add a new party to the lawsuit. In

---

[3] We were careful in Aldinger to point out the limited nature of our holding:

"There are, of course, many variations in the language which Congress has employed to confer jurisdiction upon the federal courts, and we decide here only the issue of so-called 'pendent party' jurisdiction with respect to a claim brought under §§ 1343(3) and 1983. Other statutory grants and other alignments of parties and claims might call for a different result." 427 U.S., at 18, 96 S.Ct., at 2422.

the present case, for example, Owen had already been brought into the suit by OPPD, and, that having been done, Mrs. Kroger merely sought to assert against Owen a claim arising out of the same transaction that was already before the court. Thus the situation presented here is unlike that in Aldinger, supra . . . .

Because in the instant case Mrs. Kroger merely sought to assert a claim against someone already a party to the suit, considerations of judicial economy, convenience, and fairness to the litigants—the factors relied upon in Gibbs, supra—support the recognition of ancillary jurisdiction here. Already before the court was the whole question of the cause of Mr. Kroger's death. Mrs. Kroger initially contended that OPPD was responsible; OPPD in turn contended that Owen's negligence had been the proximate cause of Mr. Kroger's death. In spite of the fact that the question of Owen's negligence was already before the District Court, the majority requires Mrs. Kroger to bring a separate action in state court in order to assert that very claim. Even if the Iowa Statute of Limitations will still permit such a suit, . . . considerations of judicial economy are certainly not served by requiring such duplicative litigation.

The majority, however, brushes aside such considerations of convenience, judicial economy, and fairness because it concludes that recognizing ancillary jurisdiction over a plaintiff's claim against a third-party defendant would permit the plaintiff to circumvent the complete-diversity requirement and thereby "flout the congressional command." Since the plaintiff in such a case does not bring the third-party defendant into the suit, however, there is no occasion for deliberate circumvention of the diversity requirement, absent collusion with the defendant. In the case of such collusion, of which there is absolutely no indication here,[5] the court can dismiss the action under the authority of 28 U.S.C. § 1359. In the absence of such collusion, there is no reason to adopt an absolute rule prohibiting the plaintiff from asserting those claims that he may properly assert against the third-party defendant pursuant to Fed.Rule Civ.Proc. 14(a). The plaintiff in such a situation brings suit against the defendant only with absolutely no assurance that the defendant will decide or be able to implead a particular third-party defendant. Since the plaintiff has no control over the defendant's decision to implead a third party, the fact that he could not have originally sued that party in federal court should be irrelevant. Moreover, the fact that a plaintiff in some cases may be able to foresee the subsequent chain of events leading to the impleader does not seem to me to be a sufficient reason to declare that a district court does not have the *power* to exercise ancil-

[5] When Mrs. Kroger brought suit, it was believed that Owen was a citizen of Nebraska, not Iowa. Therefore, had she desired at that time to make Owen a party to the suit, she would have done so directly by naming Owen as a defendant.

lary jurisdiction over the plaintiff's claims against the third-party defendant.[7]

We have previously noted that "[s]ubsequent decisions of this Court indicate that Strawbridge is not to be given an expansive reading." State Farm Fire & Cas. Co. v. Tashire, 386 U.S. 523, 531 n. 6, 87 S.Ct. 1199, 1203 n. 6 (1967). In light of this teaching, it seems to me appropriate to view § 1332 as requiring complete diversity only between the plaintiff and those parties he actually brings into the suit. Beyond that, I would hold that in a diversity case the District Court has power, both constitutional and statutory, to entertain all claims among the parties arising from the same nucleus of operative fact as the plaintiff's original, jurisdiction-conferring claim against the defendant. Accordingly, I dissent from the Court's disposition of the present case.

Questions: (14) *P* of State *A* sues *D–1* of State *B* in a federal district court on a $20,000 claim for which diversity of citizenship is the only basis of jurisdiction. Does the federal court have discretion to hear a closely related nonfederal claim for $30,000 that *P* has against *D–2* of State *A*? Is this an easier or harder case for extending federal jurisdiction than the case posed in question (12), from constitutional, statutory, and discretionary points of view?

(15) *P* of State *A* sues *D* of State *B* in a federal district court on a $20,000 claim for which diversity of citizenship is the only basis of jurisdiction. *D* impleads *T* of State *A*. Then *T* asserts a nonfederal claim against *P* under the sixth sentence of Rule 14(a), which prompts a nonfederal counterclaim by *P* against *T* under Rule 13(a). Is there ancillary jurisdiction for this counterclaim? Compare Evra Corp. v. Swiss Bank Corp., 673 F.2d 951 (7th Cir.) (yes), cert. denied, 103 S.Ct. 377 (1982), with Home Ins. Co. v. Ballenger Corp., 74 F.R.D. 93, 100 n.3 (N.D.Ga.1977) (no).

ORTIZ v. UNITED STATES GOVERNMENT, 595 F.2d 65 (1st Cir.1979). Puerto Rican plaintiffs sued the United States in a federal district court for negligence under 28 U.S.C. § 1346(b), a claim within exclusive federal jurisdiction. The United States impleaded a Puerto Rican hospital. Then plaintiffs attempted to assert a nonfederal claim against the hospital under the seventh sentence of Rule 14(a).

---

[7] Under the Gibbs analysis, recognition of the District Court's power to hear a plaintiff's nonfederal claim against a third-party defendant in a diversity suit would not mean that the court would be required to entertain such claims in all cases. The District Court would have the discretion to dismiss the nonfederal claim if it concluded that the interests of judicial economy, convenience, and fairness would not be served by the retention of the claim in the federal lawsuit. See Gibbs, 383 U.S., at 726, 86 S.Ct., at 1139. Accordingly, the majority's concerns that lead it to conclude that ancillary jurisdiction should not be recognized in the present situation could be met on a case-by-case basis, rather than by the absolute rule it adopts.

On interlocutory appeal, the court of appeals held that pendent jurisdiction could be exercised over such a claim.

***

Questions: (16) *P–1* of State *A* and *P–2* of State *B* separately buy from businessman *D* of State *A* certain securities, which turn out to be worthless. When all three meet to discuss the soured deal at their club, *P–1* loudly and crudely accuses *D* of fraud, which results in a fight. *P–1* and *P–2* pound *D* to the tune of $100,000, but *D* nevertheless manages to inflict some slight damage on *P–1*. Later *P–1* sues *D* for securities fraud in a federal district court, a claim within exclusive federal jurisdiction.

(a) If *D* fails to counterclaim, can he later bring an independent action for slander or battery? Cf. Williams v. Robinson, supra p. 49.

(b) If *D* does attempt to counterclaim for slander, does federal jurisdiction exist for that counterclaim? Cf. Albright v. Gates, 362 F.2d 928 (9th Cir.1966) (ancillary jurisdiction exists). Is there federal jurisdiction for *D*'s counterclaim for battery, whether asserted with a slander counterclaim or alone? May or must *P–1* counterclaim in reply to any such counterclaim?

(c) Could *P–1* have originally joined his claim for battery with his securities claim? If so, would that affect *D*'s ability to counterclaim?

(d) If instead *P–2* had sued *D* for securities fraud in a federal district court and *D* had counterclaimed for battery, could *D* join *P–1* as an additional party to that counterclaim? See Rule 13(h).

(e) If instead *P–2* had sued *D* for securities fraud in a federal district court, *D* had counterclaimed for battery against only *P–2*, and *P–2* had impleaded *P–1* for statutory contribution, could *D* now assert a direct claim for battery against *P–1*? See Home Ins. Co. v. Ballenger Corp., 74 F.R.D. 93 (N.D.Ga.1977) (deciding before Owen that court has discretion to hear claim by defendant against third party impleaded by plaintiff where "claim derives from a common nucleus of operative facts with the other claims and, in the interest of a complete and final resolution of the case, should be resolved along with the other claims").

(17) What is, after all, the difference between pendent and ancillary jurisdiction? See Comment, Pendent and Ancillary Jurisdiction: Towards a Synthesis of Two Doctrines, 22 UCLA L.Rev. 1263 (1975).

***

SECTION 5. DIVERSITY OF CITIZENSHIP

KRAMER v. CARIBBEAN MILLS, INC.

Supreme Court of the United States, 1969.
394 U.S. 823, 89 S.Ct. 1487.

MR. JUSTICE HARLAN delivered the opinion of the Court.

The sole question presented by this case is whether the Federal District Court in which it was brought had jurisdiction over the cause, or whether that court was deprived of jurisdiction by 28 U.S.C. § 1359. . . .

The facts were these. Respondent Caribbean Mills, Inc. ("Caribbean") is a Haitian corporation. In May 1959 it entered into a contract with an individual named Kelly and the Panama and Venezuela Finance Company ("Panama"), a Panamanian corporation. The agreement provided that Caribbean would purchase from Panama 125 shares of corporate stock, in return for payment of $85,000 down and an additional $165,000 in 12 annual installments.

No installment payments ever were made, despite requests for payment by Panama. In 1964, Panama assigned its entire interest in the 1959 contract to petitioner Kramer, an attorney in Wichita Falls, Texas. The stated consideration was $1. By a separate agreement dated the same day, Kramer promised to pay back to Panama 95% of any net recovery on the assigned cause of action, "solely as a Bonus."

Kramer soon thereafter brought suit against Caribbean for $165,000 in the United States District Court for the Northern District of Texas, alleging diversity of citizenship between himself and Caribbean. The District Court denied Caribbean's motion to dismiss for want of jurisdiction. The case proceeded to trial, and a jury returned a $165,000 verdict in favor of Kramer.

On appeal, the Court of Appeals for the Fifth Circuit reversed, holding that the assignment was "improperly or collusively made" within the meaning of 28 U.S.C. § 1359, and that in consequence the District Court lacked jurisdiction. We granted certiorari, 393 U.S. 819, 89 S.Ct. 99 (1968). For reasons which follow, we affirm the judgment of the Court of Appeals.

[A discussion of statutory predecessors and judicial precedent is omitted.]

. . . When the assignment to Kramer is considered together with his total lack of previous connection with the matter and his simultaneous reassignment of a 95% interest back to Panama, there can be little doubt that the assignment was for purposes of collection, with Kramer to retain 5% of the net proceeds "for the use of his name and his trouble in collecting." [9] If the suit had been unsuccessful, Kramer would have been out only $1, plus costs. Moreover, Kramer candidly admits that "the assignment was in substantial part motivated by a desire by [Panama's] counsel to make diversity jurisdiction available . . . ."

The conclusion that this assignment was "improperly or collusively made" within the meaning of § 1359 is supported not only by pre-

---

[9] Hence, we have no occasion to re-examine the cases in which this Court has held that where the transfer of a claim is absolute, with the transferor retaining no interest in the subject matter, then the transfer is not "improperly or collusively made," regardless of the transferor's motive. . . .

Nor is it necessary to consider whether, in cases in which suit is required to be brought by an administrator or guardian, a motive to create diversity jurisdiction renders the appointment of an out-of-state representative "improper" or "collusive." . . .

cedent but by consideration of the statute's purpose. If federal jurisdiction could be created by assignments of this kind, which are easy to arrange and involve few disadvantages for the assignor, then a vast quantity of ordinary contract and tort litigation could be channeled into the federal courts at the will of one of the parties. Such "manufacture of Federal jurisdiction" was the very thing which Congress intended to prevent when it enacted § 1359 and its predecessors.

Kramer nevertheless argues that the assignment to him was not "improperly or collusively made" within the meaning of § 1359, for two main reasons. First, he suggests that the undisputed legality of the assignment under Texas law necessarily rendered it valid for purposes of federal jurisdiction. We cannot accept this contention. The existence of federal jurisdiction is a matter of federal, not state, law. See, e.g., Missouri P.R. Co. v. Fitzgerald, 160 U.S. 556, 582, 16 S.Ct. 389, 396 (1896). Nothing in the language or legislative history of § 1359 suggests that an assignment cannot be "improperly or collusively made" even though binding under state law, and this Court several times has held to the contrary under [a predecessor of § 1359]. Moreover, to accept this argument would render § 1359 largely incapable of accomplishing its purpose; this very case demonstrates the ease with which a party may "manufacture" federal jurisdiction by an assignment which meets the requirements of state law.

Second, Kramer urges that this case is significantly distinguishable from earlier decisions because it involves diversity jurisdiction under 28 U.S.C. § 1332(a)(2), arising from the alienage of one of the parties, rather than the more common diversity jurisdiction based upon the parties' residence in different States. We can perceive no substance in this argument: by its terms, § 1359 applies equally to both types of diversity jurisdiction, and there is no indication that Congress intended them to be treated differently.

In short, we find that this assignment not only falls within the scope of § 1359 but within its very core. It follows that the District Court lacked jurisdiction to hear this action, and that petitioner must seek his remedy in the state courts. The judgment of the Court of Appeals is affirmed.

MR. JUSTICE FORTAS took no part in the consideration or decision of this case.

Questions: (18) *P*, a citizen of Maine, sued *D*, an Oregon citizen, in a Maine state court for breach of contract. Before bringing his action *P* had assigned $^1/_{100}$ of his claim to an Oregon citizen, a law-school classmate of *P*'s attorney, for a consideration of $9. The potential value of the claim was about $300,000. The Oregon assignee joined with *P* as co-plaintiff. *P*'s attorney conceded that the sole purpose of the assignment was to defeat an anticipated removal by destroying complete diversity of citizenship. *D* removes under 28 U.S.C. § 1441. *P* moves to remand. What decision on that motion? How is this different from the Kramer case? See Ridgeland Box Mfg. Co. v. Sinclair Ref. Co., 82 F.Supp. 274 (E.D.S.C.1949) (remand). But see Gentle v. Lamb-Weston, Inc., 302 F.Supp. 161 (D.Me.1969). See generally ALI Study of the Division of Jurisdiction Between State and Federal Courts § 1307(b) commentary at 160–61 (1968).

(19) Recall the Black & White Taxicab case, supra p. 200. Why did the Supreme Court not avoid, by application of the predecessor of § 1359, that unpopular decision upholding diversity jurisdiction?

LESTER v. McFADDON
United States Court of Appeals, Fourth Circuit, 1969.
415 F.2d 1101.

Before HAYNSWORTH, CHIEF JUDGE, and BOREMAN and BUTZNER, CIRCUIT JUDGES.

HAYNSWORTH, CHIEF JUDGE.

. . . .

In a rural section of South Carolina one foggy evening not very long after sunset, Flossie Mae Garner Brown, with her seven year old daughter, was walking along the shoulder of a highway returning to her own home from her mother's. They were struck by a truck owned by a local lumber company and driven by a local man. The mother was killed; the daughter injured.

The young girl's action for personal injury was tried before a jury in the state court. The jury found for the defendant, evidently disbelieving the plaintiff's theory that the truck left the main portion of the highway to strike mother and child on the shoulder. The lawyers for the child and the mother's statutory beneficiaries then procured the appointment of James L. Lester, an attorney of Augusta, Georgia, as administrator of the estate for the purpose of bringing an action for wrongful death in the federal court's diversity jurisdiction.

By procuring the appointment as administrator of a citizen of Georgia this local controversy between citizens of South Carolina [2] was superficially converted into a dispute between citizens of different states. The conversion was purely superficial, of course, because the administrator has done little more than lend the use of his name. Nevertheless, there was no objection to the jurisdiction of the District Court [in South Carolina] on the basis of 28 U.S.C.A. § 1359 which withdraws jurisdiction when "any party has been improperly or collusively made or joined to invoke the jurisdiction of such court."

The absence of objection was apparently the product of the prevalence of an emasculating interpretation of the statute exemplified by such cases as Corabi v. Auto Racing, Inc., 3 Cir., 264 F.2d 784. By

---

[2] The decedent's statutory beneficiaries, as was the decedent, are residents of South Carolina, as are the defendants. They all reside in the same county.

the time the case reached this court, however, Corabi had been overruled by McSparran v. Weist, 3 Cir., 402 F.2d 867, and we were prompted to raise the question. We requested and received supplemental briefs and held the case pending action by the Supreme Court upon a petition for certiorari in McSparran, which was denied on May 19, 1969, and its decision in Kramer v. Caribbean Mills, Inc., 394 U.S. 823, 89 S.Ct. 1487, 23 L.Ed.2d 9, decided on May 5, 1969.

In the circumstances of this case the administrator has no stake in the litigation. In South Carolina an action for wrongful death may be maintained only by an executor or administrator of the decedent's estate. The cause of action inheres in the personal representative, and the statutory beneficiaries cannot proceed in their own names. Any amount recovered, however, does not go into the decedent's general estate but is payable, upon receipt by the personal representative, directly to the statutory beneficiaries, here the decedent's numerous children. Had there been assets in the general estate of the decedent, the administrator would have been required to administer them, but there were no such assets here so that this administrator has as yet had no duties to perform.

Unless there is a recovery of some damages in the wrongful death action, the administrator here would never have anything to do; if there is a recovery, his duty is limited to receipt of the funds and their disbursement to a guardian of the statutory beneficiaries. He, of course, has a fiduciary duty to see that the litigation is pressed to a conclusion as long as there is any reasonable expectation of a recovery, but when the foreign administrator is procured by the lawyers handling the litigation he can hardly be expected to ride herd upon them or exercise any effective supervision of their conduct of the litigation. Except that he acquired his authority from the South Carolina Probate Court, he has no greater standing than the next friend of a minor or incompetent or a guardian ad litem whose residence has not been thought to be controlling of the question of diversity.

Such a person is indeed a "straw party" as the McSparran court characterized the administrator there. We think his appointment for the purpose of creating apparent diversity of citizenship was an improper manufacture of jurisdiction within the meaning of § 1359. Any other interpretation would render a portion of the statute impotent [8] because it was clearly intended for the statute to apply to manufactured situations created by other means than assignments. We need not give the statute a reading which would frustrate the congressional intention to exclude from the diversity jurisdiction purely

[8] 28 U.S.C.A. § 1359 forbids collusive or improper manufacture of jurisdiction "by assignment *or otherwise.*" The italicized portion is virtually without meaning if it does not apply to a situation such as this. Presumably it would still apply to a sham incorporation within a particular state to create diversity. See, e.g., Lehigh Mining & Mfg. Co. v. Kelly, 160 U.S. 327, 16 S.Ct. 307, 40 L.Ed. 444. . . .

local controversies with no more than a contrived interstate appearance.

. . . .

The decisions of the Supreme Court in Black & White Taxicab & Transfer Co. v. Brown & Yellow Taxicab & Transfer Co., 276 U.S. 518, 48 S.Ct. 404, 72 L.Ed. 681, and Mecom v. Fitzsimmons Co., 284 U.S. 183, 52 S.Ct. 84, 76 L.Ed. 233, have no direct bearing upon the problem, though both opinions contain dicta which substantially influenced the lower courts to give to § 1359 a very restrictive reading. In the former case, a Kentucky corporation had been reincorporated in Tennessee in an attempt to create diversity of citizenship between it and the defendant, a Kentucky corporation. Earlier the Supreme Court had held purely pretensive incorporations insufficient to create diversity of citizenship, but the reincorporation of Black & White Taxicab was real. At the time the action was commenced there was no longer a Kentucky corporation. All of the assets of the former Kentucky corporation were vested in the Tennessee corporation, and the Tennessee corporation, the plaintiff, was the one entitled to enjoy the fruits of the litigation. In Mecom the Court held there was no diversity jurisdiction in an action for wrongful death when, for the purpose of defeating federal jurisdiction the action was brought by an administrator having the same citizenship as the defendant. Section 1359, of course, does not apply to the Mecom situation since it attempts only to limit federal jurisdiction and not to protect it.

In both Black & White Taxicab and Mecom, however, the Court used language indicating that it is enough if the action be brought by the real party in interest and that the courts should not inquire into the motives underlying their creation or appointment. It is that language which largely influenced the course of decision in the lower courts until McSparran.

In Kramer v. Caribbean Mills, Inc., 394 U.S. 823, 89 S.Ct. 1487, the Supreme Court held that an assignment of a claim for the purpose of creating diversity jurisdiction was improper or collusive within the meaning of the statute. It reserved the question "whether in cases in which suit is required to be brought by an administrator or guardian, a motive to create diversity jurisdiction renders the appointment of an out-of-state representative 'improper' or 'collusive'" within the meaning of § 1359. It pointed out certain differences in the situations, stating that in cases involving personal representatives someone must be appointed before suit can be brought and he owes his appointment and his authority to a decree of a state court, and that, depending on the kind of guardian or administrator he is, his powers and his authority may vary over a considerable range.

These differences, of course, are obvious, but the fact that the beneficiaries of the action may not proceed in their own name, hardly amounts to a distinction when they or their legal advisers procure the appointment of an out-of-state administrator who had no former connections with the decedent solely for the purpose of creating diversity of citizenship. The act is as voluntary and deliberate as is that of an assignor in the Kramer v. Caribbean Mills situation. Nor does it seem to us to matter in the least that the administrator owes his appointment to the decree of a probate court in South Carolina. That decree is not under attack. The appointment may be assumed to be valid in every respect and the administrator perfectly free to prosecute the action in the state court. The question here is simply whether from the circumstances of his appointment after consideration of his authority and his duties, the statute proscribes his proceeding in the federal courts rather than in the state courts. That seems clearly a federal question, the answer to which need not be influenced by the fact that the state court has authorized him to proceed in the litigation in a proper manner in a proper court, the state court being unquestionably a proper one.

As we have outlined them above, the duties of the administrator and his authority are no greater than those of the assignee in the Kramer v. Caribbean Mills situation. Each is authorized nominally, at least, to prosecute the action in his own name and is obligated to remit the net proceeds after payment of all expenses, including compensation to the assignee or administrator, to the beneficiary.

We thus find no distinction between this situation and that of the assignee which the Supreme Court considered in Kramer v. Caribbean Mills. After the Supreme Court's reservation of this question in Kramer v. Caribbean Mills the substantive similarity between this situation and that considered in Kramer, leads us to follow Kramer rather than the dicta in Black & White Taxicab and Mecom.

Under Rule 17, Federal Rules of Civil Procedure, the administrator is expressly authorized to bring suit in his own name without joining his beneficiaries. Procedurally he is the real party in interest. The rule is but a restatement of a well established doctrine, for it was held very early that an administrator was the real party in interest in the sense of entitlement to proceed in his own name. [Citations omitted.] It was in that sense that Mecom held that the administrator was the real party in interest entitled to maintain the action in his own name, though the court recognized that the beneficiaries were the "parties in interest." The plaintiff in Black & White Taxicab was the real party in interest in a much larger sense than the procedural one, however, for it was the only one on the plaintiff's side of the litigation who had a substantial stake in its outcome.

If the nominal plaintiff is a real party in interest in that latter sense, if his interest in the litigation is substantive rather than procedural only, § 1359 well may have no application.[11] If he has no stake

---

[11] It is the lack of a stake in the outcome coupled with the motive to bring into a federal court a local action normally triable only in a state court which is the common thread of the cases holding actions collusively or improperly brought. [Citations omitted.] If either factor is missing, the suit is not collusive or im-

in the outcome, if he is a real party in interest only in the narrow procedural sense of those words and his appointment was secured solely for the purpose of creating diversity of citizenship, the apparent diversity is pretensive. The pretensive making of a party is improper within the meaning of § 1359.

The American Law Institute has a better solution, one much more easily administered. Under its proposed § 1301, the citizenship of a decedent, a minor or an incompetent would be attributed to his representative.[12] That proposal requires congressional action. Meanwhile, however, no sound reason appears why the courts should continue to read existing § 1359 so ungenerously as largely to deprive it of its intended meaning.

Although we decide that a district court has no jurisdiction in a case of this kind, we apply the new rule prospectively. Equitable considerations require the exemption of the present case and of any other case now pending in the Fourth Circuit if dismissal would not leave the plaintiff a reasonable opportunity to refile a timely action in a state court or if dismissal would impose an undue burden in requiring the relitigation of issues already fully litigated.

[The court thus affirmed the $15,000 judgment for plaintiff.]

Questions: (20) What result if the facts of Lester are changed so that the administrator has many other duties besides bringing this suit, there being a large and complex estate to administer and distribute, but still he was chosen because of his diverse citizenship? See Hackney v. Newman Memorial Hosp., 621 F.2d 1069 (10th Cir.) (suggesting jurisdiction exists), cert. denied, 449 U.S. 982, 101 S.Ct. 397 (1980).

(21) What result if the facts of Lester are changed so that the out-of-state administrator of the simple Brown estate was chosen because he is an uncle of the decedent, because his nonresidence is thought to free him from close contact with the decedent's family problems, and because he is experienced in financial affairs? Compare Joyce v. Seigel, 429 F.2d 128 (3d Cir. 1970), with Bishop v. Hendricks, 495 F.2d 289 (4th Cir.), cert. denied, 419 U.S. 1056, 95 S.Ct. 639 (1974).

(22) Now imagine the facts of Lester changed so that the accident took place in North Carolina, a South Carolina administrator was appointed, and the administrator with good reason determined that the wrongful-death action could be brought most conveniently in North Carolina. Because North Carolina law then required a resident ancillary administrator to bring such an action, a North Carolina attorney was appointed ancillary administrator of the estate. Thus, it is a North Carolina plaintiff against a South Carolina

proper. See, e.g., Crawford v. Neal, 144 U.S. 585, 12 S.Ct. 759, 36 L.Ed. 552 (transferee had substantial interest); Manhattan Life Ins. Co. v. Broughton, 109 U.S. 121, 3 S.Ct. 99, 27 L.Ed. 878 (no improper motive to bring action in federal court since transferor herself was of diverse citizenship).

[12] The American Law Institute: Study of the Division of Jurisdiction between State and Federal Courts, § 1301(b)(4). See 46 F.R.D. 141, 143. Under this proposal no preliminary question of motivation for the appointment of the out-of-state administrator need be examined in determining whether jurisdiction exists.

defendant in a North Carolina federal district court. Will diversity jurisdiction be upheld? See Vaughan v. Southern Ry., 542 F.2d 641 (4th Cir.1976) (suggesting jurisdiction does not exist).

SECTION 6. JURISDICTIONAL AMOUNT

How is the district court to determine whether any applicable jurisdictional amount requirement is met? Why not wait until the end of trial to see how much is recovered? If instead it is deemed desirable to apply the test at the outset of the case, why not have a hearing to determine the probable recovery? If instead it is deemed desirable to avoid holding a hearing, why not take the plaintiff at his word, as spoken in his ad damnum clause?

SAINT PAUL MERCURY INDEMNITY CO. v. RED CAB CO., 303 U.S. 283, 58 S.Ct. 586 (1938). Red Cab Co. sued St. Paul Mercury Indemnity Co. for failure to pay workers' compensation claims as required by its contract of insurance with Red Cab covering injuries to Red Cab's employees, as a result of which Red Cab was allegedly compelled to pay or obligate itself to pay the sum of $4000. St. Paul removed the case to the federal district court on the basis of diversity of citizenship. Thereafter Red Cab filed an amended complaint still claiming $4000 in damages, but with an attached exhibit that listed the names of the injured employees and the amounts expended totaling $1380.89. On a trial without jury, judgment was entered for Red Cab for $1162.98. St. Paul appealed on the merits. The court of appeals refused to decide the merits on the ground that, as the record showed Red Cab's claim did not exceed the jurisdictional amount of $3000, the case should have been remanded to the state court.

On certiorari, the Supreme Court reversed. Justice Roberts said:

"The intent of Congress drastically to restrict federal jurisdiction in controversies between citizens of different states has always been rigorously enforced by the courts. The rule governing dismissal for want of jurisdiction in cases brought in the federal court is that, unless the law gives a different rule, the sum claimed by the plaintiff controls if the claim is apparently made in good faith. It must appear to a legal certainty that the claim is really for less than the jurisdictional amount to justify dismissal. The inability of plaintiff to recover an amount adequate to give the court jurisdiction does not show his bad faith or oust the jurisdiction. Nor does the fact that the complaint discloses the existence of a valid defense to the claim. But if, from the face of the pleadings, it is apparent, to a legal certainty, that the plaintiff cannot recover the amount claimed, or if, from the proofs, the court is satisfied to a like certainty that the plaintiff never was entitled to recover that amount, and that his claim was therefore colorable for the purpose of conferring jurisdiction, the suit will be dismissed. Events occurring subsequent to the institution of suit which reduce the amount recoverable below the statutory limit do not oust jurisdiction.

. . . .

"The present case well illustrates the propriety of the rule that subsequent reduction of the amount claimed cannot oust the district court's jurisdiction. Suit was instituted in the state court June 5, 1934. The lump sum claimed was largely in excess of $3,000, exclusive of interest and costs. The items which went to make up the respondent's demand for indemnity were numerous and each, in turn, was itself the total of several items of expenditure or liability. There is nothing to indicate that all of the sums for which reimbursement was claimed had actually been expended prior to the beginning of suit or that the sums thereafter to be expended had been ascertained. Not until the . . . amended complaint was filed in the United States court, in November 1934, did the respondent furnish a statement of the particulars of its claim. That statement is not inconsistent with the making of a claim in good faith for over $3,000 when the suit was instituted. Nor is there evidence that the petitioner when it removed the cause knew, or had reason to believe, that the respondent's claim, whether well or ill founded in law or fact, involved less than $3,000. On the face of the pleadings petitioner was entitled to invoke the jurisdiction of the federal court, and a reduction of the amount claimed, after removal, did not take away that privilege."

Question: (23) What difference should there be between a suit brought originally in the federal court and a removed case in considering the amount claimed by the plaintiff? See Albright v. R.J. Reynolds Tobacco Co., 531 F.2d 132 (3d Cir.), cert. denied, 426 U.S. 907, 96 S.Ct. 2229 (1976).

The much-quoted words of Justice Roberts, and subsequent decisions of the courts pursuant thereto, have made it clear that in a claim for unliquidated damages, most typically a personal-injury case involving pain and suffering, the amount claimed by the plaintiff will be controlling except in really flagrant circumstances. The "legal certainty" test therefore poses little problem for the plaintiff seeking to invoke federal jurisdiction.[h]

Accordingly, claims for relief have often been greatly inflated in order to circumvent the jurisdictional amount requirement. When Congress increased this amount for diversity cases from $3000 to $10,000 in 1958, it also provided a costs sanction giving the court discretionary power to deny costs to the plaintiff and in addition to impose costs upon him if he recovered less than $10,000. 28 U.S.C.

---

[h] "The test of the plaintiff's 'good faith' is not his subjective state of mind but a very strict objective standard. . . . Thus, there is but one test; good faith and legal certainty are equivalents rather than two separate tests." Jones v. Landry, 387 F.2d 102, 104 (5th Cir.1967).

[handwritten margin notes: Costs, Sanction, § 1332(b)]

§ 1332(b). Because this power has been used very rarely and because costs are not likely to be sizable, this provision has plainly not
deterred plaintiffs from making excessive claims in order to get into
a federal forum. "The records of the Administrative Office of judgments after trial in diversity cases terminated in the fiscal year 1961
(some few of which were probably filed before the 1958 increase in
jurisdictional amount from $3,000 to $10,000 became effective) show
that 614 out of 1,268 reported judgments [for plaintiff], 48 per cent of
the total, were for less than $10,000, and that the amount of the medi-
an judgment in these cases was $3,793. The amount of the median
claim in these same cases was $32,200. While it is obvious that there
are a good many cases where counsel might reasonably hope for a
judgment over $10,000 and obtain one for substantially less than that,
it seems clear that the jurisdiction is being abused." ALI Study of
the Division of Jurisdiction Between State and Federal Courts 120
(1968).

Question: (24) Would you expect Rule 11 to be effective in this regard?

The case below reflects the widely held concern over the inflation
of the claimed amount in controversy. Although it is not an isolated
example, we should emphasize that it applies the St. Paul test with
much more rigor than the general run of personal-injury actions.

NELSON v. KEEFER

United States Court of Appeals, Third Circuit, 1971.
451 F.2d 289.

Before VAN DUSEN, ALDISERT and GIBBONS, CIRCUIT JUDGES.

ALDISERT, CIRCUIT JUDGE. These appeals question the propriety
of dismissing a personal injury diversity action at pre-trial because
the district court concluded that it appeared "to a legal certainty"
that the claims were "really for less than the jurisdictional amount"
of $10,000.

[The court summarized the damage claims of the three plaintiffs,
husband, wife, and minor son, based on the automobile accident. The
claims were mostly for injuries such as whiplash, the most substantial claim being the husband's which included questionably related
medical bills of $603.50 and also property damage of $727.69.]

It is our intention to require removal from the trial list of those
"flagrant" cases where it can be determined in advance "with legal
certainty" that the congressional mandate of a $10,000 minimum was
not satisfied. . . .

We are not persuaded by the argument that a termination prior to
trial deprives a "plaintiff of his present statutory right to a jury trial." See Deutsch v. Hewes Street Realty Corp., [359 F.2d 96, 100 (2d
Cir.1966)]. Indeed, such an argument begs the question, for the pre-

[handwritten margin note: Dismissal doesn't deprive of right to jury trial]

cise issue is whether plaintiff has a statutory right to enter the court-room for any trial, jury or otherwise. The corollary suggestion that the remedy lies with Congress is similarly specious, for the reality is that Congress *did* act in 1958 in raising the amount in controversy from $3,000 to $10,000.

. . . .

Given the congressional intention to eliminate trials of unsubstantial diversity cases, and mindful that personal injury actions comprise a majority—at least 60 per cent—of diversity controversies, and that the intangible factor of pain, suffering, and inconvenience usually constitutes the largest single item of damages in personal injury claims, we have no difficulty in concluding that Congress intended that trial judges exercise permissible discretion prior to trial in adjudicating challenges to jurisdiction.

. . . .

Analogizing the authority of the court to reject a jury's verdict [as excessive], we have no difficulty in recognizing a corollary power in that same court to evaluate a case prior to trial where sufficient information has been made available through pre-trial discovery and comprehensive pre-trial narrative statements which disclose medical reports. Assuming that claimed tangible items of damage legally related to the cause of action will be taken as true, the court should be able to determine . . . the "upper limit" of a permissible award that includes tangible recoverable items such as medical special and lost wages damage items as well as the intangibles of pain, suffering, and inconvenience. If this "upper limit" does not bear a reasonable relation to the minimum jurisdictional floor, utilizing the test of St. Paul Mercury Indemnity Co., we perceive no legal obstacle to a pre-trial determination that a personal injury action does not satisfy federal jurisdictional requirements.

. . . .

Our scope of review under these circumstances is similar to that which is utilized in review of a trial court's determination that a verdict is "excessive" or "capricious." [Citations omitted.] Accordingly, although we must "give the benefit of every doubt to the judgment of the trial judge," we must "make a detailed appraisal of the evidence bearing on damages." Having done so, we find that the district court gave plaintiffs ample opportunity, at the pre-trial stage, to justify their jurisdictional claim. Convinced to a legal certainty that the evidence would not permit it to sustain a verdict for plaintiffs of $10,000 or more, the district court did not—and indeed could not—allow the case to proceed to trial.

. . . And since plaintiffs' legally recoverable ceiling did not at its apex reach the federal jurisdictional floor, the judgment of the district court will be affirmed.

Question: (25) *P* seeks an injunction against *D* in a federal district court on the basis of diversity of citizenship. Normally, the amount in controversy in such an action is the value of the relief requested. But what if it is stipulated that the benefit to *P* will be worth less than $10,000, but the cost to *D* of complying with the requested relief will be greatly in excess of that figure: is the jurisdictional amount requirement met? What if the benefit to the plaintiff is more than $10,000, but the cost to the defendant less? Should it matter whether *P* institutes the action in federal court or *D* brings it there by removal? See C. Wright, The Law of Federal Courts § 34 (4th ed. 1983).

SNYDER v. HARRIS

GAS SERVICE CO. v. COBURN

Supreme Court of the United States, 1969.
394 U.S. 332, 89 S.Ct. 1053.

[In order to resolve a conflict among the courts of appeals, the Supreme Court granted certiorari in two cases.

[In Snyder v. Harris, 390 F.2d 204 (8th Cir.1968), plaintiff brought a class action, grounded on diversity of citizenship, for herself and all others similarly situated, against members of the board of directors of Missouri Fidelity Union Trust Life Insurance Co., alleging that the defendants had sold their shares of the company's stock far in excess of fair market value, the excess representing payment to obtain control of the company, and that under Missouri law this excess should be distributed among all the shareholders. Plaintiff's own claim was for $8740 in damages; the total claim of all the 4000-odd shareholders would be about $1,200,000. The district court and the court of appeals refused to permit aggregation.

[In Gas Service Co. v. Coburn, 389 F.2d 831 (10th Cir.1968), also a diversity action, Coburn brought a class action alleging that Gas Service Co. had billed and illegally collected a city franchise tax from him and others living outside city limits. Plaintiff alleged damages to himself of $7.81; the total claim of about 18,000 customers living outside city limits was alleged to be over $10,000. The district court and the court of appeals permitted aggregation, relying on the 1966 amendment to Rule 23.]

Mr. Justice Black delivered the opinion of the Court.

. . . The issue presented by these two cases is whether separate and distinct claims presented by and for various claimants in a class action may be added together to provide the $10,000 jurisdictional amount in controversy.

. . . .

The first congressional grant to district courts to take suits between citizens of different States fixed the requirement for the jurisdictional amount in controversy at $500. In 1887 this jurisdictional amount was increased to $2,000; in 1911 to $3,000; and in 1958 to $10,000. The traditional judicial interpretation under all of these statutes has been from the beginning that the separate and distinct claims of two or more plaintiffs cannot be aggregated in order to satisfy the jurisdictional amount requirement. Aggregation has been permitted only (1) in cases in which a single plaintiff seeks to aggregate two or more of his own claims against a single defendant and (2) in cases in which two or more plaintiffs unite to enforce a single title or right in which they have a common and undivided interest. It is contended, however, that the adoption of a 1966 amendment to Rule 23 effectuated a change in this jurisdictional doctrine. . . .

The doctrine that separate and distinct claims could not be aggregated was never, and is not now, based upon . . . any rule of procedure. That doctrine is based rather upon this Court's interpretation of the statutory phrase "matter in controversy." . . . Nothing in the amended Rule 23 changes this doctrine. The class action plaintiffs in the two cases before us argue that since the new Rule will include in the judgment all members of the class who do not ask to be out by a certain date, the "matter in controversy" now encompasses all the claims of the entire class. But it is equally true that where two or more plaintiffs join their claims under the joinder provisions of Rule 20, each and every joined plaintiff is bound by the judgment. And it was in joinder cases of this very kind that the doctrine that distinct claims could not be aggregated was originally enunciated. Troy Bank v. G.A. Whitehead & Co., 222 U.S. 39, 32 S.Ct. 9 (1911); Pinel v. Pinel, 240 U.S. 594, 36 S.Ct. 416 (1916).[i]

. . . .

    . . . It is urged, however, that this Court should now overrule its established statutory interpretation and hold that "matter in controversy" encompasses the aggregation of all claims that can be brought together in a single suit, regardless of whether any single plaintiff has a claim that exceeds the required jurisdictional amount. It is argued in behalf of this position that (1) the determination of whether claims are "separate and distinct" is a troublesome question that breeds uncertainty and needless litigation, and (2) the inability of parties to aggregate numerous small claims will prevent some important questions from being litigated in federal courts. And both of these factors, it is argued, will tend to undercut the attempt of the Judicial Conference to promulgate efficient and modernized class ac-

---

[i] Pinel held that there could be no aggregation of claims by two children seeking to establish their interests in their father's estate, where the children were alleging that they had been unintentionally omitted from his will. Contrast this with the holding of Shields v. Thomas, 58 U.S. (17 How.) 3 (1855), that an estate's distributees, such as children of the decedent, could aggregate their claims against one who was alleged to have converted the estate, because they had a common and undivided interest in a single title or right.

tion procedures. We think that whatever the merit of these contentions, they are not sufficient to justify our abandonment of a judicial interpretation of congressional language that has stood for more than a century and a half.

.   .   .   .

. . .   Moreover, while the class action device serves a useful function across the entire range of legal questions, the jurisdictional amount requirement applies almost exclusively to controversies based upon diversity of citizenship. A large part of those matters involving federal questions can be brought, by way of class actions or otherwise, without regard to the amount in controversy. Suits involving issues of state law and brought on the basis of diversity of citizenship can often be most appropriately tried in state courts. . . .   There is no compelling reason for this Court to overturn a settled interpretation of an important congressional statute in order to add to the burdens of an already overloaded federal court system. Nor can we overlook the fact that the Congress that permitted the federal rules to go into effect was assured before doing so that none of the rules would either expand or contract the jurisdiction of federal courts. If there is a present need to expand the jurisdiction of those courts we cannot overlook the fact that the Constitution specifically vests that power in the Congress, not in the courts.

.   .   .   .

Mr. Justice Fortas, with whom Mr. Justice Douglas joins, dissenting.

The Court today refuses to conform the judge-made formula for computing the amount in controversy in class actions with the 1966 amendment to Rule 23 of the Federal Rules of Civil Procedure. The effect of this refusal is substantially to undermine a generally welcomed and long-needed reform in federal procedure.

.   .   .   .

Permitting aggregation in class action cases does not involve any violation of the principle, expressed in Rule 82 and inherent in the whole procedure for the promulgation and amendment of the Federal Rules, that the courts cannot by rule expand their own jurisdictions. While the Rules cannot change subject-matter jurisdiction, changes in the forms and practices of the federal courts through changes in the Rules frequently and necessarily will affect the occasions on which subject-matter jurisdiction is exercised because they will in some cases make a difference in what cases the federal courts will hear and who will be authoritatively bound by the judgment. For example, the development of the law of joinder and ancillary jurisdiction under the Federal Rules has influenced the "jurisdiction" of the federal courts in this broader sense. .   .   .   Making judicial rules for calculating jurisdictional amount responsive to the new structure of class actions is not an extension of the jurisdiction of the federal courts, but a recognition that the procedural framework in which the courts operate has been changed by a provision having the effect of law.

　. 　. 　. 　.

The new Rule 23, by redefining the law of class actions, has, with the effect of statute, provided for a decision by the district courts that the nominally separate and legally "several" claims of individuals may be so much alike that they can be tried all at once, as if there were just one claim, in a single proceeding in which most members of the class asserting the claim will not be personally present at all. When that determination has been made in accordance with the painstaking demands of Rule 23, there is authorized to be brought in the federal courts a single litigation, in which, both practically and in legal theory, the thing at stake, the "matter in controversy," is the total, combined, aggregated claim of the whole class. When that happens the courts do not obey, but violate, the jurisdictional statutes if they continue to impose an ancient and artificial judicial doctrine to fragment what is in every other respect a single claim, which the courts are commanded to stand ready to hear.

For these reasons, I would measure the value of the "matter in controversy" in a class action found otherwise proper under the amended Rule 23 by the monetary value of the claim of the whole class.

Question: (26) Does it seem wise to you to allow *P* of State *A* to sue *D* of State *B* in federal court upon two wholly unrelated claims for $4000 and $8000 respectively, but not to allow *P–1* and *P–2* of State *A* to aggregate their separate and distinct claims against *D* for $4000 and $8000 respectively arising out of the same transaction or occurrence, such as an automobile accident?

ZAHN v. INTERNATIONAL PAPER CO., 414 U.S. 291, 94 S.Ct. 505 (1973). Plaintiffs brought a class action, grounded on diversity of citizenship, on behalf of certain lake-front property owners and lessees, against an alleged polluter. The named plaintiffs' claims each exceeded $10,000. However, the district court and the court of appeals ruled that jurisdiction did not extend to absentees whose claims did not individually satisfy the jurisdictional amount requirement.

On certiorari, the Supreme Court affirmed. Justice White explained that the aggregation rules require "dismissal of those litigants whose [separate and distinct] claims do not satisfy the jurisdictional amount, even though other litigants assert claims sufficient to invoke the jurisdiction of the federal court."

[handwritten margin note: No juris for absentees whose claims not >10,000]

Justice Brennan, joined by Justices Douglas and Marshall, dissented. He argued that ancillary jurisdiction should apply here.

————

Questions: (27) *P* of State *A* sues *D* of State *B* in federal court on a claim for $800. *D* counterclaims for more than $10,000. The district court raises the question of subject-matter jurisdiction. The only possible basis of federal jurisdiction is diversity of citizenship. Should the court dismiss? Should it matter whether or not *D*'s counterclaim arises out of the same transaction or occurrence as *P*'s claim?

(28) Instead, *P* sues *D* in a court of State *A* for the $800. *D* counterclaims for more than $10,000. *D* removes to the federal court under 28 U.S.C. § 1441. *P* moves to remand. What decision on that motion? Should it matter whether or not *D*'s counterclaim arises out of the same transaction or occurrence? If so, should it matter whether or not State *A* has a compulsory counterclaim provision like Rule 13(a)? See C. Wright, The Law of Federal Courts § 37 (4th ed. 1983).

————

SECTION 7. REMOVAL

SHAMROCK OIL & GAS CORP. v. SHEETS, 313 U.S. 100, 61 S.Ct. 868 (1941). *P* of Delaware sued *D* of Texas in a Texas state court on a contract claim for more than the federal jurisdictional amount. As was permitted by Texas law, *D* counterclaimed on a wholly unrelated contract claim also in excess of the jurisdictional amount. *P* removed to the federal district court on the basis of diversity of citizenship. *D* moved to remand. The district court denied that motion, and after trial gave judgment for *P* on the claim and the counterclaim. The Fifth Circuit reversed, ordering the case remanded to state court.

On certiorari the Supreme Court affirmed the court of appeals' decision, on the basis that 28 U.S.C. § 1441(a) speaks of removal "by the defendant or the defendants" and it means what it says. The Court implied that it was irrelevant whether the counterclaim was compulsory or permissive under state law, and whether or not the counterclaim was factually related to the main claim. Indeed, the Court went out of its way to say that it mattered not whether the main claim was for more or less than the jurisdictional amount.

————

Question: (29) Does this reading of § 1441(a) make any sense? See ALI Study of the Division of Jurisdiction Between State and Federal Courts §§ 1304(c), 1312(a)(3) commentary at 147–48, 196–97 (1968).

————

AMERICAN FIRE & CASUALTY CO. v. FINN
Supreme Court of the United States, 1951.
341 U.S. 6, 71 S.Ct. 534.

MR. JUSTICE REED delivered the opinion of the Court.

These proceedings present for determination the proper federal rule to be followed on a motion by a defendant to vacate a United States District Court judgment, obtained by a plaintiff after removal from a state court by defendant, and to remand the suit to the state court. Petitioner, the movant, urges that 28 U.S.C. § 1441 did not permit this removal and therefore the District Court was without jurisdiction to render the judgment which respondent, the plaintiff below, seeks to retain. The issue arose in this way:

Petitioner, the American Fire and Casualty Company, a Florida corporation, and its codefendant, the Indiana Lumbermens Mutual Insurance Company, an Indiana corporation, removed, in accordance with 28 U.S.C. § 1446, a suit brought by respondent Finn in a Texas state court against the two corporations and an individual, Reiss, local agent of both corporations and a resident of Texas. The suit was for a fire loss on Texas property suffered by respondent, a resident of Texas. Respondent tried to have the case remanded before trial but was unsuccessful. After special issues were found by the jury, judgment was entered against petitioner for the amount of insurance claimed and costs, and in favor of the other two defendants. The District Court denied the motion to vacate the judgment and the Court of Appeals affirmed. 181 F.2d 845. The latter court concluded there were causes of action against the foreign insurance companies "separate and independent" from that stated against the resident individual. Since the causes against the companies would have been removable if sued on alone, the entire suit was removable. 28 U.S.C. § 1441(c). . . .

. . . As prompt, economical and sound administration of justice depends to a large degree upon definite and finally accepted principles governing important areas of litigation, such as the respective jurisdictions of federal and state courts, we granted certiorari. 340 U.S. 849, 71 S.Ct. 79. . . .

[The Court reviewed the legislative history of § 1441(c), adopted in the 1948 revision of title 28. The conclusion was that Congress's intent was to simplify the predecessor provision and "to limit removal from state courts."]

. . . Congress has authorized removal now under § 1441(c) only when there is a separate and independent claim or cause of action.[5] . . . The addition of the word "independent" gives emphasis to

---

[5] We think the "claim" set out in a petition states the facts upon which the "cause of action" rests. For the purpose of removal, the words cover the same allegations.

. . . . .

congressional intention to require more complete disassociation between the federally cognizable proceedings and those cognizable only in state courts before allowing removal.

. . . We are not unmindful that the phrase "cause of action" has many meanings. To accomplish its purpose of limiting and simplifying removal, Congress used the phrase "cause of action" in an accepted meaning to obtain that result. By interpretation we should not defeat that purpose.

In a suit turning on the meaning of "cause of action," this Court announced an accepted description. Baltimore S.S. Co. v. Phillips, 274 U.S. 316, 47 S.Ct. 600.[10] This Court said, 274 U.S. at page 321, 47 S.Ct. at page 602:

> "Upon principle, it is perfectly plain that the respondent suffered but one actionable wrong and was entitled to but one recovery, whether his injury was due to one or the other of several distinct acts of alleged negligence or to a combination of some or all of them. In either view, there would be but a single wrongful invasion of a single primary right of the plaintiff, namely, the right of bodily safety, whether the acts constituting such invasion were one or many, simple or complex.

> "A cause of action does not consist of facts, but of the unlawful violation of a right which the facts show."

See Magnolia Petroleum Co. v. Hunt, 320 U.S. 430, 443, 64 S.Ct. 208, 215.[11] . . . [W]e conclude that where there is a single wrong to plaintiff, for which relief is sought, arising from an interlocked series of transactions, there is no separate and independent claim or cause of action under § 1441(c).[12]

In making this determination we look to the plaintiff's pleading, which controls. Pullman Co. v. Jenkins, 305 U.S. 534, 538, 59 S.Ct. 347, 349. The single wrong for which relief is sought is the failure to pay compensation for the loss on the property. Liability lay among three parties, but it was uncertain which one was responsible. There-

---

[10] There a sailor filed a libel in admiralty and recovered for negligence in failing to provide a safe place to work, in failing to use reasonable care to avoid striking libellant, for unseaworthiness, incompetency of officers and failure to instruct plaintiff, an inexperienced sailor, in his duties. Later he sought further damages for the same accident, for negligence of officers and employees in the operation of the vessel. Recovery was denied in the second suit on the ground that it was the same cause of action as the first.

[11] . . . So in Hurn v. Oursler, 289 U.S. 238, 246, 53 S.Ct. 586, 590: "The bill alleges the violation of a single right, namely, the right to protection of the copyrighted play. And it is this violation which constitutes the cause of action. Indeed, the claims of infringement and unfair competition so precisely rest upon identical facts as to be little more than the equivalent of different epithets to characterize the same group of circumstances. The primary relief sought is an injunction to put an end to an essentially single wrong, however differently characterized, not to enjoin distinct wrongs constituting the basis for independent causes of action." [Other citations omitted.]

[12] See a discussion of cause of action in code pleading. Clark on Code Pleading (2d ed.), 137 et seq.

fore, all were joined as defendants in one petition. First, facts were
stated that made the petitioner, American Fire and Casualty Company, liable. It was alleged that the company, through its agent Reiss,
insured the property destroyed for the amount claimed, that Reiss
gave plaintiff credit for the premium, controlled her insurance,
agreed to keep the property insured at all times. She further alleged
that the Company issued the policy but Reiss retained the document
in his possession and refused to deliver it after the fire. Then followed a prayer for judgment against the Company.

The next portion of the complaint stated, in the alternative, an obligation by the Indiana Lumbermens Insurance Company to pay the
same loss. The policy with Lumbermens was attached as an exhibit,
and allegations concerning Reiss similar to those in the first portion
were made. A second prayer was added for recovery against Lumbermens.

The last portion of the complaint, alternative to both the preceding, alleged that Reiss, American Fire and Casualty Company and Indiana Lumbermens Insurance Company were jointly and severally liable for the loss. Reiss was said to be plaintiff's insurance broker,
responsible for keeping her house insured. Plaintiff alleged Reiss insured her property with Lumbermens and never notified her of any
cancellation or expiration. Reiss was alleged to have agreed later to
insure her property with American, to have promised after the fire to
deliver the policy, to have failed to make the promised delivery. She
claimed that Reiss was responsible for "anything that results in the
defeat of her recovery on either one of said policies" and that he was
"the direct cause of the condition, of said insurance, and the proximate cause of all of plaintiff's troubles and confusion." The pleader
then asserted:

"That such acts and conduct on the part of said Joe Reiss as agent
for the said two insurance companies, renders said Joe Reiss, agent,
the Joe Reiss Insurance Agency and the American Fire and Casualty
Insurance Company of Orlando, Florida, and the Indiana Lumbermens Mutual Insurance Company of Indianapolis, Indiana, jointly and
severally liable for the full amount of the damages that plaintiff has
suffered by reason of said fire in the amount of Five Thousand Dollars."

The petition concluded with a prayer for joint and several judgment against all three defendants, based on the third set of allegations.

. . . The facts in each portion of the complaint involve Reiss,
the damage comes from a single incident. The allegations in which
Reiss is a defendant involve substantially the same facts and transactions as do the allegations in the first portion of the complaint against
the foreign insurance companies. It cannot be said that there are

separate and independent claims for relief as § 1441(c) requires. Therefore, we conclude there was no right to removal.

. . . .

The judgment of the Court of Appeals must be reversed and the cause remanded to the District Court with directions to vacate the judgment entered and, if no further steps are taken by any party to affect its jurisdiction,[18] to remand the case to the District Court of Harris County, Texas, with costs against petitioner. State of Tennessee v. Union & Planters Bank, 152 U.S. 454, 464, 14 S.Ct. 654, 657.

It is so ordered.

MR. JUSTICE DOUGLAS, with whom MR. JUSTICE BLACK and MR. JUSTICE MINTON concur, dissenting.

I think petitioner, having asked for and obtained the removal of the case to the Federal District Court, and having lost its case in that court, is now estopped from having it remanded to the state court.

. . . .

———

Questions: (30) Assume you are in a state court that has rules of procedure identical in all relevant respects to the Federal Rules. Construct a case consisting of two separate and independent claims such that § 1441(c) applies by virtue of diversity jurisdiction existing as to one of those claims.

(31) Adopting the same assumption, construct a case consisting of two separate and independent claims such that § 1441(c) applies by virtue of federal question jurisdiction existing as to one of those claims. Do you see any constitutional problems in this application of § 1441(c)?

(32) Still adopting the same assumption, construct a case consisting of a federal question claim and a state claim asserted by a single plaintiff against a single defendant such that the case is not properly removable, either under § 1441(a) or under § 1441(c).

(33) Does the adoption of § 1441(c) in 1948 offer a plaintiff in a case like Shamrock the right to remove? See Lee Foods Div., Consol. Grocers Corp. v. Bucy, 105 F.Supp. 402 (W.D.Mo.1952) (no).

———

LUEBBE v. PRESBYTERIAN HOSPITAL, 526 F.Supp. 1162 (S.D.N.Y.1981). *P* of State *A* sued Dr. *D* of State *A* in a State *A* court for alleged medical malpractice resulting in serious injury. As was permitted by state law, Dr. *D* impleaded a surgical instrument's manufacturer, *T* of State *B*. Then *T* removed the entire lawsuit to

———

[18] Issues not raised in the records or briefs are not passed upon, such as the propriety of the District Court's allowing, after vacation of judgment, a motion to dismiss Reiss, the resident defendant; or the associated problem: whether, if such a dismissal is allowed, a new judgment can be entered on the old verdict without a new trial. These questions and like matters are for the consideration and decision of the District Court. [Citations omitted. On remand, both these suggestions were eventually followed, making the insurer's victory here only a temporary one, 207 F.2d 113 (5th Cir.1953), cert. denied, 347 U.S. 912, 74 S.Ct. 476 (1954).—Ed.]

the federal district court on the basis of diversity of citizenship, relying on § 1441(c). Dr. *D* moved to remand. The district court granted the motion, because a third-party defendant like *T* cannot properly remove and, anyway, this third-party claim was not separate and independent.

Question: (34) Would the result have been different if Dr. *D* had joined some wholly unrelated $20,000 claim he had against *T*?

SECTION 8. "JURISDICTION TO DETERMINE JURISDICTION"—POWER TO PUNISH DISOBEDIENCE OF COURT ORDER

UNITED STATES v. UNITED MINE WORKERS

Supreme Court of the United States, 1947.
330 U.S. 258, 67 S.Ct. 677.

[In October 1946 the United States was in possession of, and operating, most of the nation's bituminous coal mines pursuant to an Executive Order of the President issued upon his determination that labor disputes were interrupting the production of coal necessary for the operation of the economy during the transition from war to peace. Terms and conditions of employment were controlled by an agreement between Secretary of the Interior Krug, as Coal Mines Administrator, and John L. Lewis, as president of the United Mine Workers. A dispute arose as to the union's power to terminate the Krug-Lewis agreement, and Lewis gave notice to Krug on November 15 of termination as of November 20, circulating to the mine workers a copy of his letter to Krug for their "official information."

[On November 18 the United States, contending that Lewis and the union had no power unilaterally to terminate the agreement, filed a complaint against them in the United States District Court for the District of Columbia, seeking a declaratory judgment to that effect and a temporary restraining order and preliminary injunction enjoining the defendants from encouraging the mine workers to strike and from taking any action that would interfere with the court's jurisdiction and its determination of the case. Jurisdiction was based on 28 U.S.C. § 1345. A temporary restraining order was immediately issued without notice, to expire on November 27, on which day the hearing on the preliminary injunction was to be held. The complaint and restraining order were served on the defendants on November 18. A gradual walkout by the miners commenced that same day, and by midnight of November 20, consistent with the miners' "no contract, no work" policy, a full-blown strike was in progress. Mines furnishing most of the nation's bituminous coal were idle. On November 21 the United States filed a petition for a rule to show cause why the defendants should not be punished for contempt, alleging a willful violation of the restraining order. The rule issued. On November 25, the return day, the defendants denied the "jurisdiction" of the court to issue the restraining order and subsequently moved to discharge the rule to show cause. They contended that the Norris-LaGuardia Act prohibited the granting of injunctive relief. Section 4 of the Act, 29 U.S.C. § 104, provided that "[n]o court of the United States shall have jurisdiction to issue any restraining order or temporary or permanent injunction in any case involving or growing out of any labor dispute" against various specified acts including what Lewis had done. It seemed apparent that the Act would apply if the dispute were between defendants and a private employer, but the United States urged that the Act did not apply to the government as employer. On November 27 the district judge extended the restraining order, and on November 29 he overruled the motion to discharge the rule and held that the restraining order was not affected by the Norris-LaGuardia Act. The trial for contempt proceeded, and both defendants were found guilty of both criminal and civil contempt. On December 4 Lewis was fined $10,000 and the union $3,500,000, without any apportionment between criminal and civil contempt. On the same day a preliminary injunction in terms similar to those of the restraining order was issued, effective until termination of the case.

[The defendants appealed to the court of appeals, and the judgments of contempt were stayed pending appeal. The United States asked for certiorari under 28 U.S.C. § 1254(1), which allows either party to do so prior to judgment in the court of appeals, and thereafter the defendants also sought certiorari. Certiorari was granted, "[p]rompt settlement of this case being in the public interest." The Supreme Court rendered decision on March 6, 1947.]

MR. CHIEF JUSTICE VINSON delivered the opinion of the Court.

[Part I of the opinion held that the Norris-LaGuardia Act did not apply to a labor dispute with the government.]

II.

Although we have held that the Norris-LaGuardia Act did not render injunctive relief beyond the jurisdiction of the District Court, there are alternative grounds which support the power of the District Court to punish violations of its orders as criminal contempt.

. . . .

In the case before us, the District Court had the power to preserve existing conditions while it was determining its own authority to grant injunctive relief. The defendants, in making their private determination of the law, acted at their peril. Their disobedience is punishable as criminal contempt.

Although a different result would follow were the question of jurisdiction frivolous and not substantial, such contention would be idle here. The applicability of the Norris-LaGuardia Act to the United States in a case such as this had not previously received judicial consideration, and both the language of the Act and its legislative history indicated the substantial nature of the problem with which the District Court was faced.

Proceeding further, we find impressive authority for the proposition that an order issued by a court with jurisdiction over the subject matter and person must be obeyed by the parties until it is reversed by orderly and proper proceedings. This is true without regard even for the constitutionality of the Act under which the order is issued. In Howat v. Kansas, 258 U.S. 181, 189–90, 42 S.Ct. 277, 280–81 (1922), this Court said:

> "An injunction duly issuing out of a court of general jurisdiction with equity powers upon pleadings properly invoking its action, and served upon persons made parties therein and within the jurisdiction, must be obeyed by them however erroneous the action of the court may be, even if the error be in the assumption of the validity of a seeming but void law going to the merits of the case. It is for the court of first instance to determine the question of the validity of the law, and until its decision is reversed for error by orderly review, either by itself or by a higher court, its orders based on its decision are to be respected, and disobedience of them is contempt of its lawful authority, to be punished."

Violations of an order are punishable as criminal contempt even though the order is set aside on appeal, Worden v. Searls, 121 U.S. 14, 7 S.Ct. 814 (1887), or though the basic action has become moot, Gompers v. Buck's Stove & Range Co., 221 U.S. 418, 31 S.Ct. 492 (1911).

We insist upon the same duty of obedience where, as here, the subject matter of the suit, as well as the parties, was properly before the court; where the elements of federal jurisdiction were clearly shown; and where the authority of the court of first instance to issue an order ancillary to the main suit depended upon a statute, the scope and applicability of which were subject to substantial doubt. The District Court on November 29 affirmatively decided that the Norris-LaGuardia Act was of no force in this case and that injunctive relief was therefore authorized. Orders outstanding or issued after that date were to be obeyed until they expired or were set aside by appropriate proceedings, appellate or otherwise. Convictions for criminal contempt intervening before that time may stand.

[The Court then rejected the contention that procedural errors required reversal of the contempt judgments. The defendants urged that the criminal and civil contempts should not have been heard together, and that they had been deprived of their rights under Federal Rule of Criminal Procedure 42(b). The Court found that the defendants had been accorded all the rights owing to defendants in criminal contempt proceedings. The Court conceded that it might be "the better practice" to try criminal contempt alone, but found no substantial prejudice requiring reversal.

[Finally, the Court ordered the $10,000 fine imposed on Lewis to stand as punishment for criminal contempt, but found that $3,500,000 was excessive as to the union and instead imposed a $700,000 fine for criminal contempt with the balance of $2,800,000 for civil contempt being conditioned on the defendant's failure to purge itself by compliance within five days.

[The various separate opinions are omitted. Professor Chafee called this case "a masterpiece of judicial logrolling." Z. Chafee, Some Problems of Equity 366 (1950). Only Justices Reed and Burton concurred fully in the Chief Justice's opinion. Justices Frankfurter and Jackson both believed that the Norris-LaGuardia Act applied to the government and forbade the injunction; but they acquiesced in part II of the opinion, justifying punishment by criminal contempt for violation of an order made to preserve the status quo while the court was determining its own jurisdiction to grant injunctive relief. This made a shaky majority of five for resort to criminal contempt, which the Chief Justice plainly wanted. For the ultimate combination of a sanction partly criminal and partly civil, the Chief Justice needed the support of Justices Black and Douglas. Those two agreed that the Norris-LaGuardia Act was inapplicable and that a civil contempt sanction was therefore authorized; but they felt that a criminal contempt sanction here was inconsistent with the principle that in contempt proceedings courts should never exercise more than "the least possible power adequate to the end proposed," and thus they found it unnecessary to deal with the problems of part II. Justices Murphy and Rutledge dissented all the way, noting that the rule of part II authorizing punishment for disobedience of orders issued in excess of jurisdiction was contrary to the long-settled course of decision. The several opinions took up 128 pages of the U.S. Reports.]

Question: (35) As counsel for John L. Lewis, how would you have advised him before this decision? How would you have advised him if this decision were already on the books?

WALKER v. CITY OF BIRMINGHAM

Supreme Court of the United States, 1967.
388 U.S. 307, 87 S.Ct. 1824.

[In the Easter season of 1963, Rev. Martin Luther King, Jr., and a group of Birmingham, Alabama, ministers organized a campaign featuring peaceful parades and picketing to protest racial segregation. A Birmingham ordinance required that public demonstrations be licensed by the city commission, which could refuse to grant a permit only if "in its judgment the public welfare, peace, safety, health, decency, good order, morals or convenience" so required. Two attempts to obtain a permit from Commissioner "Bull" Connor were rebuffed,[j] on April 3 and April 5, but no formal written application was submitted to the full three-person commission as the ordinance stipulated.

[On Wednesday, April 10, city officials sought and obtained from a state circuit court an ex parte temporary injunction enjoining Dr. King and specified others from participating in or encouraging further mass protests without a permit. Dr. King and others who had been served with copies of the writ of injunction held a press conference the next day, declaring their intention to disobey the injunction because it was "raw tyranny under the guise of maintaining law and order." On Good Friday, April 12, Dr. King and his followers defied the injunction by holding a parade of about 50 or 60 persons with a crowd of 1000 to 1500 onlookers standing by, clapping and shouting. On Easter Sunday a crowd of 1500 to 2000 congregated. A group of about 50 started down the sidewalk two abreast. Some 300 or 400 of the onlookers followed in a crowd that occupied the entire width of the street and overflowed onto the sidewalks. Violence occurred. Members of the crowd threw rocks, which injured a newspaperman and damaged a police motorcycle.

[A week later Dr. King and other leaders were convicted by the state circuit court of criminal contempt and given the statutory maximum sentence of five days in jail and a $50 fine. The judge refused to consider contentions that the injunction and the ordinance were unconstitutional and that the ordinance had previously been administered in an arbitrary and discriminatory manner, ruling that because there had been no motion to dissolve the injunction, and no attempt to comply by applying for a permit, the only issues were whether there was jurisdiction to issue it and whether the defendants had knowingly violated it. The Supreme Court of Alabama affirmed, citing Howat v. Kansas, 258 U.S. 181, 42 S.Ct. 277 (1922). The Supreme Court of the United States granted certiorari.]

MR. JUSTICE STEWART delivered the opinion of the Court.

[The opinion quoted the same passage from Howat v. Kansas as did the Court in the United Mine Workers case, and continued:]

The rule of state law accepted and approved in Howat v. Kansas is consistent with the rule of law followed by the federal courts.[5]

In the present case, however, we are asked to hold that this rule of law, upon which the Alabama courts relied, was constitutionally

---

[j] A witness at the contempt hearing testified that Commissioner Connor said: "No, you will not get a permit in Birmingham, Alabama to picket. I will picket you over to the City Jail."

[5] [In a footnote here, after citing a number of cases, the majority made its lone citation to the United Mine Workers case.]

impermissible. We are asked to say that the Constitution compelled Alabama to allow the petitioners to violate this injunction, to organize and engage in these mass street parades and demonstrations, without any previous effort on their part to have the injunction dissolved or modified, or any attempt to secure a parade permit in accordance with its terms. Whatever the limits of Howat v. Kansas,[6] we cannot accept the petitioners' contentions in the circumstances of this case.

Without question the state court that issued the injunction had, as a court of equity, jurisdiction over the petitioners and over the subject matter of the controversy. And this is not a case where the injunction was transparently invalid or had only a frivolous pretense to validity. We have consistently recognized the strong interest of state and local governments in regulating the use of their streets and other public places. Cox v. New Hampshire, 312 U.S. 569, 61 S.Ct. 762; Poulos v. New Hampshire, 345 U.S. 395, 73 S.Ct. 760. [Other citations omitted.] When protest takes the form of mass demonstrations, parades, or picketing on public streets and sidewalks, the free passage of traffic and the prevention of public disorder and violence become important objects of legitimate state concern. . . .

The generality of the language contained in the Birmingham parade ordinance upon which the injunction was based would unquestionably raise substantial constitutional issues concerning some of its provisions. [Citations omitted.] The petitioners, however, did not even attempt to apply to the Alabama courts for an authoritative construction of the ordinance. Had they done so, those courts might have given the licensing authority granted in the ordinance a narrow and precise scope, as did the New Hampshire courts in Cox v. New Hampshire and Poulos v. New Hampshire, both supra. [Other citations omitted.] Here, just as in Cox and Poulos, it could not be assumed that this ordinance was void on its face.

The breadth and vagueness of the injunction itself would also unquestionably be subject to substantial constitutional question. But the way to raise that question was to apply to the Alabama courts to have the injunction modified or dissolved. The injunction in all events clearly prohibited mass parading without a permit, and the evidence shows that the petitioners fully understood that prohibition when they violated it.

[6] In In re Green, 369 U.S. 689, 82 S.Ct. 1114, the petitioner was convicted of criminal contempt for violating a labor injunction issued by an Ohio court. Relying on the pre-emptive command of the federal labor law, the Court held that state courts were required to hear Green's claim that the state court was *without jurisdiction* to issue the injunction. The petitioner in Green, unlike the petitioners here, had attempted to challenge the validity of the injunction *before* violating it by promptly applying to the issuing court for an order vacating the injunction. The petitioner in Green had further offered to prove that the court issuing the injunction had agreed to its violation as an appropriate means of testing its validity. [13 Wright, Miller & Cooper § 3537, at 341, observes that the briefs in Green made the point that state law did not permit appellate review of this temporary injunction.—Ed.]

The petitioners also claim that they were free to disobey the injunction because the parade ordinance on which it was based had been administered in the past in an arbitrary and discriminatory fashion. In support of this claim they sought to introduce evidence that, a few days before the injunction issued, requests for permits to picket had been made to a member of the city commission. One request had been rudely rebuffed, and this same official had later made clear that he was without power to grant the permit alone, since the issuance of such permits was the responsibility of the entire city commission. Assuming the truth of this proffered evidence, it does not follow that the parade ordinance was void on its face. The petitioners, moreover, did not apply for a permit either to the commission itself or to any commissioner after the injunction issued. Had they done so, and had the permit been refused, it is clear that their claim of arbitrary or discriminatory administration of the ordinance would have been considered by the state circuit court upon a motion to dissolve the injunction.

This case would arise in quite a different constitutional posture if the petitioners, before disobeying the injunction, had challenged it in the Alabama courts, and had been met with delay or frustration of their constitutional claims. But there is no showing that such would have been the fate of a timely motion to modify or dissolve the injunction. There was an interim of two days between the issuance of the injunction and the Good Friday march. The petitioners gave absolutely no explanation of why they did not make some application to the state court during that period. The injunction had issued ex parte; if the court had been presented with the petitioners' contentions, it might well have dissolved or at least modified its order in some respects. If it had not done so, Alabama procedure would have provided for an expedited process of appellate review. It cannot be presumed that the Alabama courts would have ignored the petitioners' constitutional claims. Indeed, these contentions were accepted in another case by an Alabama appellate court that struck down on direct review the conviction under this very ordinance of one of these same petitioners.[13]

.   .   .   .   .

The rule of law that Alabama followed in this case reflects a belief that in the fair administration of justice no man can be judge in his own case, however exalted his station, however righteous his motives, and irrespective of his race, color, politics, or religion. This Court cannot hold that the petitioners were constitutionally free to ignore all the procedures of the law and carry their battle to the streets. One may sympathize with the petitioners' impatient commitment to their cause. But respect for judicial process is a small price to pay

[13] Shuttlesworth v. City of Birmingham, 43 Ala.App. 68, 180 So.2d 114. The case is presently pending on certiorari review in the Alabama Supreme Court.

for the civilizing hand of law, which alone can give abiding meaning to constitutional freedom.

Affirmed.

. . . .

MR. CHIEF JUSTICE WARREN, whom MR. JUSTICE BRENNAN and MR. JUSTICE FORTAS join, dissenting.

. . . .

These facts lend no support to the court's charges that petitioners were presuming to act as judges in their own case, or that they had a disregard for the judicial process. They did not flee the jurisdiction or refuse to appear in the Alabama courts. Having violated the injunction, they promptly submitted themselves to the courts to test the constitutionality of the injunction and the ordinance it parroted. They were in essentially the same position as persons who challenge the constitutionality of a statute by violating it, and then defend the ensuing criminal prosecution on constitutional grounds. It has never been thought that violation of a statute indicated such a disrespect for the legislature that the violator always must be punished even if the statute was unconstitutional. On the contrary, some cases have required that persons seeking to challenge the constitutionality of a statute first violate it to establish their standing to sue. Indeed, it shows no disrespect for law to violate a statute on the ground that it is unconstitutional and then to submit one's case to the courts with the willingness to accept the penalty if the statute is held to be valid.

The Court concedes that "[t]he generality of the language contained in the Birmingham parade ordinance upon which the injunction was based would unquestionably raise substantial constitutional issues concerning some of its provisions." . . . That concession is well-founded but minimal. I believe it is patently unconstitutional on its face. Our decisions have consistently held that picketing and parading are means of expression protected by the First Amendment, and that the right to picket or parade may not be subjected to the unfettered discretion of local officials. . . . The unconstitutionality of the ordinance is compounded, of course, when there is convincing evidence that the officials have in fact used their power to deny permits to organizations whose views they dislike. . . . The only circumstance that the court can find to justify anything other than a per curiam reversal is that Commissioner Connor had the foresight to have the unconstitutional ordinance included in an ex parte injunction issued without notice or hearing or any showing that it was impossible to have notice or a hearing . . . . This injunction was such potent magic that it transformed the command of an unconstitutional statute into an impregnable barrier, challengeable only in what likely would have been protracted legal proceedings and entirely superior in the meantime even to the United States Constitution.

I do not believe that giving this Court's seal of approval to such a gross misuse of the judicial process is likely to lead to greater respect for the law any more than it is likely to lead to greater protection for First Amendment freedoms. The ex parte temporary injunction has a long and odious history in this country, and its susceptibility to misuse is all too apparent from the facts of the case. As a weapon against strikes, it proved so effective in the hands of judges friendly to employers that Congress was forced to take the drastic step of removing from federal district courts the jurisdiction to issue injunctions in labor disputes. The labor injunction fell into disrepute largely because it was abused in precisely the same way that the injunctive power was abused in this case. Judges who were not sympathetic to the union cause commonly issued, without notice or hearing, broad restraining orders addressed to large numbers of persons and forbidding them to engage in acts that were either legally permissible or, if illegal, that could better have been left to the regular course of criminal prosecution. The injunctions might later be dissolved, but in the meantime strikes would be crippled because the occasion on which concerted activity might have been effective had passed. Such injunctions, so long discredited as weapons against concerted labor activities, have now been given new life by this Court as weapons against the exercise of First Amendment freedoms. Respect for the courts and for judicial process was not increased by the history of the labor injunction.

. . . .

It is not necessary to question the continuing validity of the holding in Howat v. Kansas, however, to demonstrate that neither it nor the Mine Workers case supports the holding of the majority in this case. In Howat the subpoena and injunction were issued to enable the Kansas Court of Industrial Relations to determine an underlying labor dispute. In the Mine Workers case, the District Court issued a temporary anti-strike injunction to preserve existing conditions during the time it took to decide whether it had authority to grant the Government relief in a complex and difficult action of enormous importance to the national economy. In both cases the orders were of questionable legality, but in both cases they were reasonably necessary to enable the court or administrative tribunal to decide an underlying controversy of considerable importance before it at the time. This case involves an entirely different situation. The Alabama Circuit Court did not issue this temporary injunction to preserve existing conditions while it proceeded to decide some underlying dispute. There was no underlying dispute before it, and the court in practical effect merely added a judicial signature to a preexisting criminal ordinance. Just as the court had no need to issue the injunction to preserve its ability to decide some underlying dispute, the city had no need of an injunction to impose a criminal penalty for demonstrating on the streets without a permit. The ordinance already accomplished that. In point of fact, there is only one apparent reason why the city sought this injunction and why the court issued it: to make it possible to punish petitioners for contempt rather than for violating the ordinance, and thus to immunize the unconstitutional statute and its unconstitutional application from any attack. I regret that this strategy has been so successful.

It is not necessary in this case to decide precisely what limits should be set to the Mine Workers doctrine in cases involving violations of the First Amendment. Whatever the scope of that doctrine, it plainly was not intended to give a State the power to nullify the United States Constitution by the simple process of incorporating its unconstitutional criminal statutes into judicial decrees. I respectfully dissent.

[The dissenting opinions of Justices Douglas and Brennan, each joined in by all of the dissenting Justices, are omitted.]

SHUTTLESWORTH v. CITY OF BIRMINGHAM, 394 U.S. 147, 89 S.Ct. 935 (1969). Rev. Fred L. Shuttlesworth, one of the ministers accompanying Dr. King in the demonstrations described in Walker v. City of Birmingham and later one of the petitioners in that case, was arrested and convicted of violating the ordinance there involved, on the basis of leading the march on April 12, 1963. He was sentenced to 90 days' imprisonment at hard labor, and to an additional 48 days at hard labor in default of payment of a $75 fine and $24 costs. The Alabama Court of Appeals overturned the conviction, but that conviction was later reinstated by the Supreme Court of Alabama. The latter court rejected the contention that the ordinance was an unconstitutional censorship or prior restraint upon the exercise of first amendment freedoms. The court did so by construing the ordinance so as to limit the applicability of its broad language to protection of the public safety and convenience in the use of the streets, and thus to save it from being unconstitutional on its face. The court also ruled that there was nothing in the record tending to show that the ordinance had been applied in other than a fair and nondiscriminatory fashion. Certiorari was granted. In an opinion by Justice Stewart, who wrote the majority opinion in Walker v. City of Birmingham, the Supreme Court unanimously reversed, holding that the ordinance "as it was written" was unconstitutional and that a person could ignore it with impunity. He called the Alabama court's construction "a remarkable job of plastic surgery upon the face of the ordinance" and said that it "would have taken extraordinary clairvoyance for anyone to perceive that this language meant what the Supreme Court of Alabama was destined to find that it meant more than four years later"; in light of past understanding of and practice under the ordinance, it could not be saved by narrow and precise construction.

UNITED STATES v. RYAN, 402 U.S. 530, 91 S.Ct. 1580 (1971). This was a case holding, in accordance with Cobbledick v. United States, supra p. 515, that denial of a motion to quash a subpoena duces tecum commanding production of documents before a federal grand jury is not appealable. The Court pointed out that one who claims a subpoena is unduly burdensome or otherwise unlawful may refuse to comply, and then litigate those questions in the event contempt proceedings are brought against him; if his contentions are rejected in the trial court, they will then be ripe for appellate review; if on appeal his contentions are upheld, any contempt adjudication will then fall. At this point in the opinion the Court dropped the following footnote: "Walker v. Birmingham . . . is not to the contrary. Our holding that the claims there sought to be asserted were not open on review of petitioners' contempt convictions was based upon the availability of review of those claims at an earlier stage."

MANESS v. MEYERS, 419 U.S. 449, 95 S.Ct. 584 (1975). This was a case holding that a lawyer may not be held in criminal contempt for advising his client, a defendant in a state civil case, not to comply with a subpoena duces tecum that the court refused to quash, or with the court's follow-up order to comply, when the lawyer believes reasonably and in good faith that compliance might tend to incriminate his client in violation of the fifth amendment.

In the course of decision, the Court discussed the duty of the client to obey court orders. It began with the "basic proposition" that the "orderly and expeditious administration of justice by the courts requires" the client to comply with all court orders and then pursue review thereof. "Remedies for judicial error may be cumbersome but the injury flowing from an error generally is not irreparable . . . . When a court during trial orders a witness to reveal information, however, a different situation may be presented. Compliance could cause irreparable injury because appellate courts cannot always 'unring the bell' once the information has been released. Subsequent appellate vindication does not necessarily have its ordinary consequence of totally repairing the error." So here, although eventual review of the fifth amendment contention might be possible, there was no regular opportunity for review before compliance. And compliance constituted irreparable injury. Thus, the client could refuse to comply, and then raise his constitutional contention in any consequent contempt proceedings; if his contention were eventually upheld, any contempt adjudication would then fall.

Question: (36) Imagine a trial court has punished someone for disobedience of what it believed to be its valid order. Later the question of the validity of the order comes before an appellate court. That court finds the order to be beyond the trial court's power, but the circumstances are such that the punishment could stand under the "jurisdiction to determine jurisdiction" doctrine. Should the case be remanded for reconsideration of punishment in light of the finding of the order's invalidity? See Donovan v. City of Dallas, 377 U.S. 408, 84 S.Ct. 1579, on remand sub nom. City of Dallas v. Brown, 384 S.W.2d 724 (Tex.Civ.App.1964).

TOPIC B. TERRITORIAL AUTHORITY TO ADJUDICATE

SECTION 1. THE FRAMEWORK

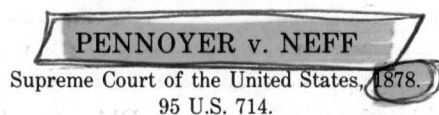

PENNOYER v. NEFF
Supreme Court of the United States, 1878.
95 U.S. 714.

Error to the Circuit Court of the United States for the District of Oregon.

. . . .

MR. JUSTICE FIELD delivered the opinion of the court.

This is an action to recover the possession of a tract of land, of the alleged value of $15,000, situated in the State of Oregon. The plaintiff asserts title to the premises by a patent of the United States issued to him in 1866 [on March 19, 1866[a]], under the act of Congress of Sept. 27, 1850, usually known as the Donation Law of Oregon. The defendant claims to have acquired the premises under a sheriff's deed, made upon a sale of the property on execution issued upon a judgment recovered against the plaintiff in one of the circuit courts of the State. The case turns upon the validity of this judgment.

It appears from the record that the judgment was rendered in February, 1866, in favor of J.H. Mitchell, for less than $300, including costs, in an action brought by him upon a demand for services as an attorney; that, at the time the action was commenced and the judgment rendered, the defendant therein, the plaintiff here, was a non-resident of the State; that he was not personally served with process, and did not appear therein; and the judgment was entered upon his default in not answering the complaint, upon a constructive service of summons by publication.

The Code of Oregon provides for such service when an action is brought against a non-resident and absent defendant, who has property within the State. It also provides, where the action is for the recovery of money or damages, for the attachment of the property of the non-resident. And it also declares that no natural person is subject to the jurisdiction of a court of the State, "unless he appear in the court, or be found within the State, or be a resident thereof, or have property therein; and, in the last case, only to the extent of

---

[a] This date appears in the reporter's digest of the facts; it does not appear in the opinions.

772

such property at the time the jurisdiction attached." Construing this latter provision to mean, that, in an action for money or damages where a defendant does not appear in the court, and is not found within the State, and is not a resident thereof, but has property therein, the jurisdiction of the court extends only over such property, the declaration expresses a principle of general, if not universal, law. The authority of every tribunal is necessarily restricted by the territorial limits of the State in which it is established. Any attempt to exercise authority beyond those limits would be deemed in every other forum, as has been said by this court, an illegitimate assumption of power, and be resisted as mere abuse. D'Arcy v. Ketchum et al., 11 How. 165. In the case against the plaintiff, the property here in controversy sold under the judgment rendered was not attached nor in any way brought under the jurisdiction of the court. Its first connection with the case was caused by a levy of the execution. It was not, therefore, disposed of pursuant to any adjudication, but only in enforcement of a personal judgment, having no relation to the property, rendered against a non-resident without service of process upon him in the action, or his appearance therein. The court below did not consider that an attachment of the property was essential to its jurisdiction or to the validity of the sale, but held that the judgment was invalid from defects in the affidavit upon which the order of publication was obtained, and in the affidavit by which the publication was proved.

There is some difference of opinion among the members of this court as to the rulings upon these alleged defects. The majority are of opinion that inasmuch as the statute requires, for an order of publication, that certain facts shall appear by affidavit *to the satisfaction of the court or judge*, defects in such affidavit can only be taken advantage of on appeal, or by some other direct proceeding, and cannot be urged to impeach the judgment collaterally.[b] The majority of the court are also of opinion that the provision of the statute requiring proof of the publication in a newspaper to be made by the "affidavit of the printer, or his foreman, or his principal clerk," is satisfied when the affidavit is made by the editor of the paper. The term "printer," in their judgment, is there used not to indicate the person who sets up the type . . . .

If, therefore, we were confined to the rulings of the court below upon the defects in the affidavits mentioned, we should be unable to uphold its decision. But it was also contended in that court, and is insisted upon here, that the judgment in the State court against the plaintiff was void for want of personal service of process on him, or of his appearance in the action in which it was rendered, and that the premises in controversy could not be subjected to the payment of the

[b] Mitchell's affidavit simply stated that the nonresident defendant "resides somewhere in the State of California, at what place affiant knows not, and he cannot be found in this State" of Oregon and "that the defendant has property in this county and State."

demand of a resident creditor except by a proceeding in rem; that is, by a direct proceeding against the property for that purpose. If these positions are sound, the ruling of the Circuit Court as to the invalidity of that judgment must be sustained, notwithstanding our dissent from the reasons upon which it was made. And that they are sound would seem to follow from two well-established principles of public law respecting the jurisdiction of an independent State over persons and property. The several States of the Union are not, it is true, in every respect independent, many of the rights and powers which originally belonged to them being now vested in the government created by the Constitution. But, except as restrained and limited by that instrument, they possess and exercise the authority of independent States, and the principles of public law to which we have referred are applicable to them. One of these principles is, that every State possesses exclusive jurisdiction and sovereignty over persons and property within its territory. As a consequence, every State has the power to determine for itself the civil status and capacities of its inhabitants; to prescribe the subjects upon which they may contract, the forms and solemnities with which their contracts shall be executed, the rights and obligations arising from them, and the mode in which their validity shall be determined and their obligations enforced; and also to regulate the manner and conditions upon which property situated within such territory, both personal and real, may be acquired, enjoyed, and transferred. The other principle of public law referred to follows from the one mentioned; that is, that no State can exercise direct jurisdiction and authority over persons or property without its territory. Story, Confl.Laws, c. 2; Wheat, Int.Law, pt. 2, c. 2. . . .

But as contracts made in one State may be enforceable only in another State, and property may be held by non-residents, the exercise of the jurisdiction which every State is admitted to possess over persons and property within its own territory will often affect persons and property without it. To any influence exerted in this way by a State affecting persons resident or property situated elsewhere, no objection can be justly taken; whilst any direct exertion of authority upon them, in an attempt to give ex-territorial operation to its laws, or to enforce an ex-territorial jurisdiction by its tribunals, would be deemed an encroachment upon the independence of the State in which the persons are domiciled or the property is situated, and be resisted as usurpation.

Thus the State, through its tribunals, may compel persons domiciled within its limits to execute, in pursuance of their contracts respecting property elsewhere situated, instruments in such form and with such solemnities as to transfer the title, so far as such formalities can be complied with; and the exercise of this jurisdiction in no manner interferes with the supreme control over the property by the State within which it is situated. Penn v. Lord Baltimore, 1 Ves. 444;

Massie v. Watts, 6 Cranch, 148; Watkins v. Holman, 16 Pet. 25; Corbett v. Nutt, 10 Wall. 464.

So the State, through its tribunals, may subject property situated within its limits owned by non-residents to the payment of the demand of its own citizens against them; and the exercise of this jurisdiction in no respect infringes upon the sovereignty of the State where the owners are domiciled. Every State owes protection to its own citizens; and, when non-residents deal with them, it is a legitimate and just exercise of authority to hold and appropriate any property owned by such non-residents to satisfy the claims of its citizens. It is in virtue of the State's jurisdiction over the property of the non-resident situated within its limits that its tribunals can inquire into that non-resident's obligations to its own citizens, and the inquiry can then be carried only to the extent necessary to control the disposition of the property. If the non-resident have no property in the State, there is nothing upon which the tribunals can adjudicate.

. . . . . If, without personal service, judgments in personam, obtained ex parte against non-residents and absent parties, upon mere publication of process, which, in the great majority of cases, would never be seen by the parties interested, could be upheld and enforced, they would be the constant instruments of fraud and oppression. Judgments for all sorts of claims upon contracts and for torts, real or pretended, would be thus obtained, under which property would be seized, when the evidence of the transactions upon which they were founded, if they ever had any existence, had perished.

Substituted service by publication, or in any other authorized form, may be sufficient to inform parties of the object of proceedings taken where property is once brought under the control of the court by seizure or some equivalent act. The law assumes that property is always in the possession of its owner, in person or by agent; and it proceeds upon the theory that its seizure will inform him, not only that it is taken into the custody of the court, but that he must look to any proceedings authorized by law upon such seizure for its condemnation and sale. Such service may also be sufficient in cases where the object of the action is to reach and dispose of property in the State, or of some interest therein, by enforcing a contract or a lien respecting the same, or to partition it among different owners, or, when the public is a party, to condemn and appropriate it for a public purpose. In other words, such service may answer in all actions which are substantially proceedings in rem. But where the entire object of the action is to determine the personal rights and obligations of the defendants; that is, where the suit is merely in personam, constructive service in this form upon a non-resident is ineffectual for any purpose. Process from the tribunals of one State cannot run into another State, and summon parties there domiciled to leave its territory and respond to proceedings against them. Publication of pro-

Publication of process isn't ok!

cess or notice within the State where the tribunal sits cannot create any greater obligation upon the non-resident to appear. Process sent to him out of the State, and process published within it, are equally unavailing in proceedings to establish his personal liability.

The want of authority of the tribunals of a State to adjudicate upon the obligations of non-residents, where they have no property within its limits, is not denied by the court below; but the position is assumed, that, where they have property within the State, it is immaterial whether the property is in the first instance brought under the control of the court by attachment or some other equivalent act, and afterwards applied by its judgment to the satisfaction of demands against its owner; or such demands be first established in a personal action, and the property of the non-resident be afterwards seized and sold on execution. But the answer to this position has already been

juris. over the prop. must come 1st b/4 juris. over the oblig's of the non-res.

given in the statement, that the jurisdiction of the court to inquire into and determine his obligations at all is only incidental to its jurisdiction over the property. Its jurisdiction in that respect cannot be made to depend upon facts to be ascertained after it has tried the cause and rendered the judgment. If the judgment be previously void, it will not become valid by the subsequent discovery of property of the defendant, or by his subsequent acquisition of it. The judgment, if void when rendered, will always remain void: it cannot occupy the doubtful position of being valid if property be found, and void if there be none. Even if the position assumed were confined to cases where the non-resident defendant possessed property in the State at the commencement of the action, it would still make the validity of the proceedings and judgment depend upon the question whether, before the levy of the execution, the defendant had or had not disposed of the property. If before the levy the property should be sold, then, according to this position, the judgment would not be binding. This doctrine would introduce a new element of uncertainty in judicial proceedings. The contrary is the law: the validity of every judgment depends upon the jurisdiction of the court before it is rendered, not upon what may occur subsequently. . . . .

The force and effect of judgments rendered against non-residents without personal service of process upon them, or their voluntary appearance, have been the subject of frequent consideration in the courts of the United States and of the several States, as attempts have been made to enforce such judgments in States other than those in which they were rendered, under the provision of the Constitution requiring that "full faith and credit shall be given in each State to the public acts, records, and judicial proceedings of every other State;" and the act of Congress providing for the mode of authenticating such acts, records, and proceedings, and declaring that, when thus authenticated, "they shall have such faith and credit given to them in every court within the United States as they have by law or usage in the courts of the State from which they are or shall be taken." In the earlier cases, it was supposed that the act gave to all judgments the same effect in other States which they had by law in the State where rendered. But this view was afterwards qualified so as to make the act applicable only when the court rendering the judgment had jurisdiction of the parties and of the subject-matter, and not to preclude an inquiry into the jurisdiction of the court in which the judgment was rendered, or the right of the State itself to exercise authority over the person or the subject-matter. . . .

. . . In all the cases brought in the State and Federal courts, where attempts have been made under the act of Congress to give effect in one State to personal judgments rendered in another State against non-residents, without service upon them, or upon substituted service by publication, or in some other form, it has been held, without an exception, so far as we are aware, that such judgments were without any binding force, except as to property, or interests in property, within the State, to reach and affect which was the object of the action in which the judgment was rendered, and which property was brought under control of the court in connection with the process against the person. The proceeding in such cases, though in the form of a personal action, has been uniformly treated, where service was not obtained, and the party did not voluntarily appear, as effectual and binding merely as a proceeding in rem, and as having no operation beyond the disposition of the property, or some interest therein. . . .

. . . In several of the cases, the decision has been accompanied with the observation that a personal judgment thus recovered has no binding force without the State in which it is rendered, implying that in such State it may be valid and binding. But if the court has no jurisdiction over the person of the defendant by reason of his non-residence, and, consequently, no authority to pass upon his personal rights and obligations; if the whole proceeding, without service upon him or his appearance, is coram non judice and void; if to hold a defendant bound by such a judgment is contrary to the first principles of justice,—it is difficult to see how the judgment can legitimately have any force within the State. The language used can be justified only on the ground that there was no mode of directly reviewing such judgment or impeaching its validity within the State where rendered; and that, therefore, it could be called in question only when its enforcement was elsewhere attempted. In later cases, this language is repeated with less frequency than formerly, it beginning to be considered, as it always ought to have been, that a judgment which can be treated in any State of this Union as contrary to the first principles of justice, and as an absolute nullity, because rendered without any jurisdiction of the tribunal over the party, is not entitled to any respect in the State where rendered. Smith v. McCutchen, 38 Mo. 415; Darrance v. Preston, 18 Iowa, 396; Hakes v. Shupe, 27 id. 465; Mitchell's Administrator v. Gray, 18 Ind. 123.

Be that as it may, the courts of the United States are not required to give effect to judgments of this character when any right is claimed under them. Whilst they are not foreign tribunals in their relations to the State courts, they are tribunals of a different sovereignty, exercising a distinct and independent jurisdiction, and are bound to give to the judgments of the State courts only the same faith and credit which the courts of another State are bound to give to them.

Since the adoption of the Fourteenth Amendment to the Federal Constitution,[c] the validity of such judgments may be directly questioned, and their enforcement in the State resisted, on the ground that proceedings in a court of justice to determine the personal rights and obligations of parties over whom that court has no jurisdiction do not constitute due process of law. Whatever difficulty may be experienced in giving to those terms a definition which will embrace every permissible exertion of power affecting private rights, and exclude such as is forbidden, there can be no doubt of their meaning when applied to judicial proceedings. They then mean a course of legal proceedings according to those rules and principles which have been established in our systems of jurisprudence for the protection and enforcement of private rights. To give such proceedings any validity, there must be a tribunal competent by its constitution—that is, by the law of its creation—to pass upon the subject-matter of the suit; and, if that involves merely a determination of the personal liability of the defendant, he must be brought within its jurisdiction by service of process within the State, or his voluntary appearance.

Except in cases affecting the personal status of the plaintiff, and cases in which that mode of service may be considered to have been assented to in advance, as hereinafter mentioned, the substituted service of process by publication, allowed by the law of Oregon and by similar laws in other States, where actions are brought against non-residents, is effectual only where, in connection with process against the person for commencing the action, property in the State is brought under the control of the court, and subjected to its disposition by a process adapted to that purpose, or where the judgment is sought as a means of reaching such property or affecting some interest therein; in other words, where the action is in the nature of a proceeding in rem. .   . .

It is true that, in a strict sense, a proceeding in rem is one taken directly against property, and has for its object the disposition of the property, without reference to the title of individual claimants; but, in a larger and more general sense, the terms are applied to actions between parties, where the direct object is to reach and dispose of property owned by them, or of some interest therein. Such are cases commenced by attachment against the property of debtors, or instituted to partition real estate, foreclose a mortgage, or enforce a lien.

[c] The concurrent resolution of Congress declaring the fourteenth amendment a part of the Constitution, following its ratification by the state legislatures, was dated July 21, 1868.

So far as they affect property in the State, they are substantially proceedings in rem in the broader sense which we have mentioned.

It is hardly necessary to observe, that in all we have said we have had reference to proceedings in courts of first instance, and to their jurisdiction, and not to proceedings in an appellate tribunal to review the action of such courts. The latter may be taken upon such notice, personal or constructive, as the State creating the tribunal may provide. They are considered as rather a continuation of the original litigation than the commencement of a new action. Nations et al. v. Johnson et al., 24 How. 195.

[margin note: Any notice ok by State is ok for App. Ct.]

It follows from the views expressed that the personal judgment recovered in the State court of Oregon against the plaintiff herein, then a non-resident of the State, was without any validity, and did not authorize a sale of the property in controversy.

[margin note: Judgement here NOT ok]

. . . . .

Neither do we mean to assert that a State may not require a nonresident entering into a partnership or association within its limits, or making contracts enforceable there, to appoint an agent or representative in the State to receive service of process and notice in legal proceedings instituted with respect to such partnership, association, or contracts, or to designate a place where such service may be made and notice given, and provide, upon their failure, to make such appointment or to designate such place that service may be made upon a public officer designated for that purpose, or in some other prescribed way, and that judgments rendered upon such service may not be binding upon the non-residents both within and without the State. As was said by the Court of Exchequer in Vallee v. Dumergue, 4 Exch. 290, "It is not contrary to natural justice that a man who has agreed to receive a particular mode of notification of legal proceedings should be bound by a judgment in which that particular mode of notification has been followed, even though he may not have actual notice of them." See also The Lafayette Insurance Co. v. French et al., 18 How. 404, and Gillespie v. Commercial Mutual Marine Insurance Co., 12 Gray (Mass.), 201. Nor do we doubt that a State, on creating corporations or other institutions for pecuniary or charitable purposes, may provide a mode in which their conduct may be investigated, their obligations enforced, or their charters revoked, which shall require other than personal service upon their officers or members. Parties becoming members of such corporations or institutions would hold their interest subject to the conditions prescribed by law. Copin v. Adamson, Law Rep. 9 Ex. 345.

[margin note: State may require non-res. entr'g partnership'i K to say how & where service can be made]

In the present case, there is no feature of this kind, and, consequently, no consideration of what would be the effect of such legislation in enforcing the contract of a non-resident can arise. The question here respects only the validity of a money judgment rendered in one State, in an action upon a simple contract against the resident of another, without service of process upon him, or his appearance therein.

Judgment affirmed.

[The dissenting opinion of Justice Hunt is omitted.]

CLOSSON v. CHASE, 158 Wis. 346, 149 N.W. 26 (1914). The relevant Wisconsin statute provided: "Service of the summons may be made without the state or by publication upon a defendant against whom a cause of action appears to exist . . . on obtaining an order therefor . . . in either of the following cases: (1) When such defendant is a nonresident of this state . . . and . . . has property within the state . . . ." In an action on promissory notes, where the plaintiff claimed no pre-existing lien on or interest in any property of the defendant, and where the nonresident defendant had been served by publication, the court said in part:

"The issuance of a writ of attachment and levy upon property thereunder is not essential to competency to make service on a defendant by publication. Gallun v. Weil, 116 Wis. 236, 92 N.W. 1091. The statutory requisite of property of the defendant within this state, existing and duly brought to the attention of the court, is all that is necessary in respect to the property feature. Such an action is regarded as one in rem. The judgment when rendered is good only against the property described in the moving papers. It is sufficient even if the property be non-attachable, if it yet be such as can be judicially reached in some way and subjected to payment of the debt sought to be collected. It is the res within the jurisdiction of the court that is essential to jurisdiction, not actual seizure of it, or even constructive seizure, unless description of the property in the moving papers and recorded purpose of the plaintiff to burden it with payment of the debt should be regarded as such seizure. Jarvis v. Barrett, 14 Wis. 591; Winner v. Fitzgerald, 19 Wis. 393; Disconto Gesellschaft v. Umbreit, 127 Wis. 651, 106 N.W. 821.

"The foregoing sufficiently answers, if any be necessary, after express and implied approval of the statute in question for more than sixty years, the suggestion that it is unconstitutional under the doctrine of Pennoyer v. Neff, 95 U.S. 714."

SECTION 2. JURISDICTION OVER THINGS— TRADITIONAL THEORY

(a) Nature of Such Jurisdiction

TYLER v. JUDGES OF THE COURT OF REGISTRATION

Supreme Judicial Court of Massachusetts, 1900.
175 Mass. 71, 55 N.E. 812, writ of error dismissed, 179 U.S. 405, 21 S.Ct. 206 (1900).

HOLMES, C.J. This is a petition for a writ of prohibition against the judges of the Court of Registration established by St.1898, c. 562, and is brought to prevent their proceeding upon an application concerning land in which the petitioner claims an interest. The ground of the petition is that the act establishing the court is unconstitutional. Two reasons are urged against the act, both of which are thought to go to the root of the statute and to make action under it impossible. The first and most important is that the original registration deprives all persons except the registered owner of any interest in the land without due process of law. There is no dispute that the object of the system, expressed in § 38, is that the decree of registration "shall bind the land and quiet the title thereto," and "shall be conclusive upon and against all persons," whether named in the proceedings or not, subject to few and immaterial exceptions. And this being admitted, it is objected that there is no sufficient process against, or notice to, persons having adverse claims, in a proceeding intended to bar their possible rights.

The application for registration is to be in writing and signed and sworn to. It is to contain an accurate description of the land, to set forth clearly other outstanding estates or interests known to the petitioner, to identify the deed by which he obtained title, to state the name and address of the occupant if there is one, and also to give the names and addresses so far as known of the occupants of all lands adjoining. § 21. As soon as it is filed, a memorandum containing a copy of the description of the land concerned is to be filed in the registry of deeds. § 20. The case is immediately referred to an examiner (appointed by the judge, § 12), who makes as full an investigation as he can and reports to the court. § 29. If in the opinion of the examiner the applicant has a good title as alleged, or if the applicant after an adverse opinion elects to proceed further, the recorder is to publish a notice by order of the court in some newspaper published in the district where any portion of the land lies. This notice is to be addressed by name to all persons known to have an adverse interest, and to the adjoining owners and occupants so far as known, and to all whom it may concern. It is to contain a description of the land, the name of the applicant, and the time and place of the hearing. § 31. A copy is to be mailed to every person named in the notice whose address is known, and a duly attested copy is to be posted in a conspicuous place on each parcel of land included in the application, by a sheriff or deputy sheriff, fourteen days at least before the return day. Further notice may be ordered by the court. § 32.

It will be seen that the notice is required to name all persons known to have an adverse interest, and this of course includes any adverse claim, whether admitted or denied, that may have been discovered by the examiner, or in any way found to exist. Taking this into account, we should construe the requirement in § 21 concerning the application, as calling upon the applicant to mention not merely outstanding interests which he admits, but equally all claims of interest set up although denied by him. We mention this here to dispose of an objection of detail urged by the petitioner, and we pass to the general objection that, however construed, the mode of notice does not satisfy the Constitution . . . . . .

If it does not satisfy the Constitution, a judicial proceeding to clear titles against all the world hardly is possible, for the very meaning of such a proceeding is to get rid of unknown as well as known claims,—indeed certainty against the unknown may be said to be its chief end,—and unknown claims cannot be dealt with by personal service upon the claimant. It seems to have been the impression of the Supreme Court of Ohio, in the case most relied upon by the petitioner, that such a judicial proceeding is impossible in this country. State v. Guilbert, 56 Ohio St. 575, 629, 47 N.E. 551. But we cannot bring ourselves to doubt that the Constitutions of the United States and of Massachusetts at least permit it as fully as did the common law. Prescription or a statute of limitations may give a title good against the world and destroy all manner of outstanding claims without any notice or judicial proceeding at all. Time and the chance which it gives the owner to find out that he is in danger of losing rights are due process of law in that case. . . .

. . . . . .

Looked at either from the point of view of history or of the necessary requirements of justice, a proceeding in rem dealing with a tangible res may be instituted and carried to judgment without personal service . . . and not encounter any provision of either Constitution. Jurisdiction is secured by the power of the court over the res. As we have said, such a proceeding would be impossible, were this not so, for it hardly would do to make a distinction between the constitutional rights of claimants who were known and those who were not known to the plaintiff, when the proceeding is to bar all. Pennoyer v. Neff, 95 U.S. 714, 727. [Other citations omitted.] In Hamilton v. Brown, 161 U.S. 256, 16 S.Ct. 585, a judgment of escheat was held conclusive upon persons notified only by advertisement to all persons interested. It is true that the statute under consideration required the petition to name all known claimants, and personal service to be made on those so named. But that did the plaintiffs no good, as they were not named. So a decree allowing or disallowing a will binds everybody, although the only notice of the proceedings given be a general notice to all persons interested. And in this case, as in that of escheat just cited, the conclusive effect of the decree is not put upon the ground that the State has an absolute power to determine the persons to whom a man's property shall go at his death, but upon the characteristics of a proceeding in rem. Bonnemort v. Gill, 167 Mass. 338, 340, 45 N.E. 768. See 161 U.S. 263, 274, 16 S.Ct. 585. Admiralty proceedings need only to be mentioned in this connection, and further citation of cases seems unnecessary.

Speaking for myself, I see no reason why what we have said as to proceedings in rem in general should not apply to such proceedings concerning land. . . .

But it is said that this is not a proceeding in rem. It is certain that no phrase has been more misused. In the past it has had little more significance than that the right alleged to have been violated was a right in rem. Austin thinks it necessary to quote Leibnitz for the sufficiently obvious remark that every right to restitution is a right in personam. So as to actions. If the technical object of the suit is to establish a claim against some particular person, with a judgment which generally, in theory at least, binds his body, or to bar some individual claim or objection, so that only certain persons are entitled to be heard in defence, the action is in personam, although it may concern the right to or possession of a tangible thing. Mankin v. Chandler, 2 Brock. 125, 127, Fed.Cas. No. 9,030. If, on the other hand, the object is to bar indifferently all who might be minded to make an objection of any sort against the right sought to be established, and if any one in the world has a right to be heard on the strength of alleging facts which, if true, show an inconsistent interest, the proceeding is in rem. Freem. Judgments, (4th ed.) § 606 ad fin. All proceedings, like all rights, are really against persons. Whether they are proceedings or rights in rem depends on the number of persons affected. Hence the res need not be personified and made a party defendant, as happens with the ship in the admiralty; it need not even be a tangible thing at all, as sufficiently appears by the case of the probate of wills. Personification and naming the res as defendant are mere symbols, not the essential matter. They are fictions, conveniently expressing the nature of the process and the result, nothing more.

.   .   .   .

Then as to seizure of the res. It is convenient in the case of a vessel, in order to secure its being on hand to abide judgment, although in the case of a suit against a man jurisdiction is regarded as established by service without the need of keeping him in prison to await judgment. It is enough that the personal service shows that he could have been seized and imprisoned. Seizure, to be sure, is said to be notice to the owner. Scott v. Shearman, 2 W.Bl. 977, 979. Mankin v. Chandler, 2 Brock. 125, 127, Fed.Cas. No. 9,030. But fastening the process or a copy to the mast would seem not necessarily to depend for its effect upon the continued custody of the vessel by the marshal. However this may be, when we come to deal with immovables there would be no sense whatever in declaring seizure to be a constitutional condition of the power of the Legislature to make a proceeding against land a proceeding in rem. Hamilton v. Brown, 161 U.S. 256, 274, 16 S.Ct. 585. The land cannot escape from the jurisdiction, and, except as security against escape, seizure is a mere form, of no especial sanctity, and of much possible inconvenience.

I do not wish to ignore the fact that seizure, when it means real dispossession, is another security for actual notice. But when it is considered how purely formal such an act may be, and that even adverse possession is possible without ever coming to the knowledge of a reasonably alert owner, I cannot think that the presence or absence of the form makes a constitutional difference; or rather, to express my view still more cautiously, I cannot but think that the immediate recording of the claim is entitled to equal effect from a constitutional point of view. I am free to confess, however, that, with the rest of my brethren, I think the act ought to be amended in the direction of still further precautions to secure actual notice before a decree is entered, and that, if it is not amended, the judges of the court ought to do all that is in their power to satisfy themselves that there has been no failure in this regard before they admit a title to registration.[d]

The quotations which we have made show the intent of the statute to bind the land, and to make the proceedings adverse to all the world, even if it were not stated in § 35, or if the amendment of 1899 did not expressly provide that they should be proceedings in rem. St. 1899, c. 131, § 1. Notice is to be posted on the land just as admiralty process is fixed to the mast. Any person claiming an interest may appear and be heard. § 34.

But perhaps the classification of the proceeding is not so important as the course of the discussion thus far might seem to imply. I have pursued that course as one which is satisfactory to my own mind, but for the purposes of decision a majority of the court prefer to assume that in cases in which, under the constitutional requirements of due process of law, it heretofore has been necessary to give to parties interested actual notice of the pending proceeding by personal service or its equivalent in order to render a valid judgment against them, it is not in the power of the Legislature, by changing the form of the proceeding from an action in personam to a suit in rem, to avoid the necessity of giving such a notice, and to assume that under this statute personal rights in property are so involved and may be so affected that effectual notice and an opportunity to be

---

[d] The present statute, Mass.Gen.Laws Ann. ch. 185, § 39, enlarges on § 32 of the 1898 Act by adding: "The court shall, so far as it considers it possible, require proof of actual notice to all adjoining owners and to all persons who appear to have any interest in or claim to the land included in the complaint. Notice to such persons by mail shall be by registered letter."

heard should be given to all claimants who are known or who by reasonable effort can be ascertained.

. . . With regard to claimants . . . remaining undiscovered, notice by publication must suffice of necessity. As to claimants . . . known, the question seems to come down to whether we can say that there is a constitutional difference between sending notice of a suit by a messenger and sending it by the post office beside publishing in a newspaper, recording in the registry, and posting on the land. It must be remembered that there is no constitutional requirement that the summons, even in a personal action, shall be served by an officer, or that the copy served shall be officially attested. Apart from local practice, it may be served by any indifferent person. It may be served on residents by leaving a copy at the last and usual place of abode. When we are considering a proceeding of this kind, it seems to us within the power of the Legislature to say that the mail, as it is managed in Massachusetts, is a sufficient messenger to convey the notice, when other means of notifying the party, like publishing and posting, also are required. We agree that such an act as this is not to be upheld without anxiety. But the difference in degree between the case at bar and one in which the constitutionality of the act would be unquestionable seems to us too small to warrant a distinction. If the statute is within the power of the Legislature, it is not for us to criticise the wisdom or expediency of what the Legislature has done.

. . . .

Petition denied.[e]

[The dissenting opinion of Justice Loring, with whom Justice Lathrop joined, is omitted.]

———

GARFEIN v. McINNIS

Court of Appeals of New York, 1928.
248 N.Y. 261, 162 N.E. 73.

LEHMAN, J. In an action for the specific performance of an alleged contract to convey real estate in the State of New York, service of the summons and complaint has been made in the State of Connecticut, upon a resident of that State. The motion of the defendant to set aside such service has been denied.

In an action "where the complaint demands judgment that the defendant be excluded from a vested or contingent interest in or lien upon specific real or personal property within the State or that such an interest or lien in favor of either party be enforced, regulated, de-

—————

[e] The Supreme Court later dismissed a writ of error because "the plaintiff in error has not the requisite interest to draw in question" the validity of the statute, 179 U.S. 405, 21 S.Ct. 206 (1900).

fined or limited, or otherwise affecting the title to such property," the summons may be served out of the State. (Sections 232 and 235, Civ. Prac.Act.) The language of the statute is sufficiently broad to cover an action for specific performance. Service without the State is sufficient to give the court jurisdiction to grant a judgment in rem binding upon a non-resident defendant so served. It does not, however, bring the non-resident defendant's person within the jurisdiction of the court. A decree in personam can be supported against a person who is not a citizen or resident of the State in which it is rendered only by actual service upon him within its jurisdiction. (Hart v. Sansom, 110 U.S. 151, 3 S.Ct. 586.) The question presented by this appeal is whether a judgment in an action for specific performance is only a decree in personam against the party who has agreed to convey property, or whether the court in such an action may grant a judgment which will operate upon the property itself and result in a transfer of the title to a successful party though the defendant fail or refuse to obey a command of the judgment directed to him.

That a court of chancery acts only upon the person is a recognized maxim of equity jurisprudence. (Ewing v. Orr Ewing, L.R. 9 App. Cas. 34. See Cook on Powers of Courts of Equity, 15 Columbia Law Review, 36.) "A decree of chancery spoke in terms of personal command to the defendant, but its directions could only be carried into effect by his personal act. . . . The decree never stood as a title in the place of an actual conveyance by the defendant; nor was it ever carried into effect by any officer acting in the defendant's name." (Pomeroy on Equity Jurisprudence, § 428.) In jurisdictions where the decrees of a court of equity still retain the traditional form and effect of a mere command, a court of equity cannot obtain jurisdiction over a non-resident by service without the State. (Hart v. Sansom, supra; Spurr v. Scoville, 3 Cush. [Mass.] 578.)

It has been doubted whether the jurisdiction of courts of equity was ever subject to any inherent limitation that its decrees must operate solely in personam, though the early chancellors adopted the "method of acting, as they said, upon the conscience of defendants." In this country "the statutes of the several states have virtually abolished the ancient doctrine that the decrees in equity can only act upon the person of a party, and have generally provided that in all cases where the ends of justice require such an effect, and where it is possible, a decree shall either operate ex proprio vigore to create, transfer, or vest the intended right, title, estate, or interest, or else that the acts required to be done in order to accomplish the object of the decree shall be performed by an officer of the court acting for and in the name of the party against whom the adjudication is made." [f] (Pomeroy's Equity Jurisprudence, § 135.) "A bill for the specific execution of a contract to convey real estate is not strictly a proceeding

---

[f] See Federal Rule 70, which is discussed supra p. 382.

in rem, in ordinary cases; but where such a procedure is authorized by statute, on publication, without personal service of process, it is, substantially, of that character." (Boswell's Lessee v. Otis, 50 U.S. 336.)

It has been held that the power of a court of equity to pronounce a judgment in rem is not dependent upon statute and may be exercised against a non-resident whenever the Legislature has authorized constructive service. (Tennant's Heirs v. Fretts, 67 West Va. 569, 68 S.E. 387.) In Silver Camp Mining Co. v. Dickert (31 Mont. 488, 78 P. 967) the court reached opposite conclusion. We need not now decide between such conflicting decisions. A court of equity, undoubtedly, may by constructive service, in accordance with statute, acquire jurisdiction over a non-resident in an action for specific performance whenever it has power, whether granted by statute or inherent, to make a decree which will result directly, or through conveyance by an officer, in the transfer of title or interest in land. (Hollander v. Central Metal & Supply Co., 109 Md. 131, 71 A. 442; Felch v. Hooper, 119 Mass. 52. See, also, 2 Story's Equity Jurisprudence [14th edition], 743.)

In this State the Legislature has provided in section 979 of the Civil Practice Act that where a "judgment directs a party . . . to convey real property, if the direction is disobeyed, the court, by order, besides punishing the disobedience as a contempt, may require the sheriff . . . to convey the real property, in conformity with the direction of the court." A decree of the court is enforceable not merely by punishment of a disobedient party but may be carried into effect by action of the sheriff operating directly upon the property. It may be that the primary purpose of the Legislature was to grant additional force to a decree in a case where the court had acquired jurisdiction of the person of a disobedient party. Its effect extends beyond such a case. It has changed the nature of the action from an action in personam, to an action substantially in rem. Though the court cannot by constructive service obtain jurisdiction of the person of a non-resident defendant and cannot compel such a defendant to obey its decree, where the court has the power to make a decree which will affect the interests of a party in property within the State, whether that party obeys the decree or not, the action is not purely in personam. The court's decree acts upon the property as well as the person of the non-resident defendant. In such case the objection that the court by constructive service obtains no jurisdiction over the person of a non-resident is without force. The Legislature has expressly provided that in an action for specific performance a court may enforce its decree by other means than direction to the defendant.

The order should be affirmed, with costs . . . . .

CARDOZO, CH. J., POUND, CRANE, ANDREWS and O'BRIEN, JJ., concur; KELLOGG, J., dissents.

Questions: (1) *B*, a resident of North Carolina, entered into a contract with *S*, a resident of South Carolina, by which *S* undertook to convey to *B* certain real estate situated in North Carolina. *S* refused to perform. What, if any, equitable relief can *B* obtain from a South Carolina court, *S* having been personally served in South Carolina and having actively contested the suit there?

(2) The decree of the South Carolina court orders *S* to convey the North Carolina land, and *S* fails to do so. Can the South Carolina court, given the existence of a South Carolina statute of either the "appointive" or the "vesting" type, give *B* title to the land? See Fall v. Eastin, 215 U.S. 1, 30 S.Ct. 3 (1909).

(3) The South Carolina court enters a decree simply ordering *S* to convey the North Carolina land, and *S* leaves South Carolina without doing so. Thereafter *B* brings an action against *S* in North Carolina on two counts: (a) for specific performance of the original contract for conveyance of the land; and (b) for enforcement of the South Carolina decree. What should be the result of the action? See Restatement (Second) of Conflict of Laws § 102 (1969).

(4) Now assume instead that *B* agreed to buy and *S* agreed to sell certain real estate situated in South Carolina. *B* refused to perform. *B* cannot be subjected to personal jurisdiction in South Carolina and has no other property there. What, if any, relief can *S* obtain from a South Carolina court? See Prudential Ins. Co. v. Berry, 153 S.C. 496, 151 S.E. 63 (1930).

HARRIS v. BALK

Supreme Court of the United States, 1905.
198 U.S. 215, 25 S.Ct. 625.

The plaintiff in error brings the case here in order to review the judgment of the Supreme Court of North Carolina, affirming a judgment of a lower court against him for $180, with interest, as stated therein. The case has been several times before the Supreme Court of that State, and is reported in 122 N.Car. 64; again, 124 N.Car. 467; the opinion delivered at the time of entering the judgment now under review, is to be found in 130 N.Car. 381; see also 132 N.Car. 10.

The facts are as follows: The plaintiff in error, Harris, was a resident of North Carolina at the time of the commencement of this action in 1896, and prior to that time was indebted to the defendant in error, Balk, also a resident of North Carolina, in the sum of $180, for money borrowed from Balk by Harris during the year 1896, which Harris verbally promised to repay, but there was no written evidence of the obligation. During the year above mentioned one Jacob Epstein, a resident of Baltimore, in the State of Maryland, asserted that Balk was indebted to him in the sum of over $300. In August, 1896, Harris visited Baltimore for the purpose of purchasing merchandise, and while he was in that city temporarily on August 6, 1896, Epstein caused to be issued out of a proper court in Baltimore a foreign or non-resident writ of attachment against Balk, attaching the debt due

Balk from Harris, which writ the sheriff at Baltimore laid in the hands of Harris, with a summons to appear in the court at a day named. With that attachment, a writ of summons and a short declaration against Balk (as provided by the Maryland statute), were also delivered to the sheriff and by him set up at the court house door, as required by the law of Maryland. Before the return day of the attachment writ Harris left Baltimore and returned to his home in North Carolina. He did not contest the garnishee process, which was issued to garnish the debt which Harris owed Balk. After his return Harris made an affidavit on August 11, 1896, that he owed Balk $180, and stated that the amount had been attached by Epstein of Baltimore, and by his counsel in the Maryland proceeding Harris consented therein to an order of condemnation against him as such garnishee for $180, the amount of his debt to Balk. Judgment was thereafter entered against the garnishee and in favor of the plaintiff, Epstein, for $180. After the entry of the garnishee judgment, condemning the $180 in the hands of the garnishee, Harris paid the amount of the judgment to one Warren, an attorney of Epstein, residing in North Carolina. On August 11, 1896, Balk commenced an action against Harris before a justice of the peace in North Carolina, to recover the $180 which he averred Harris owed him. The plaintiff in error, by way of answer to the suit, pleaded in bar the recovery of the Maryland judgment and his payment thereof, and contended that it was conclusive against the defendant in error in this action, because that judgment was a valid judgment in Maryland, and was therefore entitled to full faith and credit in the courts of North Carolina. This contention was not allowed by the trial court, and judgment was accordingly entered against Harris for the amount of his indebtedness to Balk, and that judgment was affirmed by the Supreme Court of North Carolina. The ground of such judgment was that the Maryland court obtained no jurisdiction to attach or garnish the debt due from Harris to Balk, because Harris was but temporarily in the State, and [therefore] the situs of the debt [remained] in North Carolina.

MR. JUSTICE PECKHAM, after making the foregoing statement, delivered the opinion of the court.

The state court of North Carolina has refused to give any effect in this action to the Maryland judgment; and the Federal question is, whether it did not thereby refuse the full faith and credit to such judgment which is required by the Federal Constitution. If the Maryland court had jurisdiction to award it, the judgment is valid and entitled to the same full faith and credit in North Carolina that it has in Maryland as a valid domestic judgment.

The defendant in error contends that the Maryland court obtained no jurisdiction to award the judgment of condemnation, because the garnishee, although at the time in the State of Maryland, and personally served with process therein, was a non-resident of that State, on-

ly casually or temporarily within its boundaries; that the situs of the debt due from Harris, the garnishee, to the defendant in error herein was in North Carolina, and did not accompany Harris to Maryland; that, consequently, Harris, though within the State of Maryland, had not possession of any property of Balk, and the Maryland state court therefore obtained no jurisdiction over any property of Balk in the attachment proceedings, and the consent of Harris to the entry of the judgment was immaterial. The plaintiff in error, on the contrary, insists that, though the garnishee were but temporarily in Maryland, yet the laws of that State provide for an attachment of this nature, if the debtor, the garnishee, is found in the State and the court obtains jurisdiction over him by the service of process therein; that the judgment, condemning the debt from Harris to Balk, was a valid judgment, provided Balk could himself have sued Harris for the debt in Maryland. This it is asserted, he could have done, and the judgment was therefore entitled to full faith and credit in the courts of North Carolina.

. . . .

We regard the contention of the plaintiff in error as the correct one. . . .

Attachment is the creature of the local law; that is, unless there is a law of the State providing for and permitting the attachment it cannot be levied there. If there be a law of the State providing for the attachment of the debt, then if the garnishee be found in that State, and process be personally served upon him therein, we think the court thereby acquires jurisdiction over him, and can garnish the debt due from him to the debtor of the plaintiff and condemn it, provided the garnishee could himself be sued by his creditor in that State. We do not see how the question of jurisdiction vel non can properly be made to depend upon the so-called original situs of the debt, or upon the character of the stay of the garnishee, whether temporary or permanent, in the State where the attachment is issued.

. . .

. . . .

It thus appears that Balk could have sued Harris in Maryland to recover his debt . . . .; it also appears that the municipal law of Maryland permits the debtor of the principal debtor to be garnished, and therefore if the court of the State where the garnishee is found obtains jurisdiction over him, through the service of process upon him within the State, then the judgment entered is a valid judgment.

. . .

. . . The importance of the fact of the right of the original creditor to sue his debtor in the foreign State, as affecting the right of the creditor of that creditor to sue the debtor or garnishee, lies in the nature of the attachment proceeding. The plaintiff, in such proceeding in the foreign State is able to sue out the attachment and attach the debt due from the garnishee to his (the garnishee's) creditor, because of the fact that ~~the plaintiff is really in such proceeding~~ ~~a representative of the creditor of the garnishee, and therefore if~~ ~~such creditor himself had the right to commence suit to recover the~~ ~~debt in the foreign State his representative has the same right, as~~ ~~representing him, and may garnish or attach the debt, provided the~~ ~~municipal law of the State where the attachment was sued out per-~~ ~~mits it.~~

It seems to us, therefore, that the judgment against Harris in Maryland, condemning the $180 which he owed to Balk, was a valid judgment, because the court had jurisdiction over the garnishee by personal service of process within the State of Maryland.

It ought to be and it is the object of courts to prevent the payment of any debt twice over. Thus, if Harris owing a debt to Balk, paid it under a valid judgment against him, to Epstein, he certainly ought not to be compelled to pay it a second time, but should have the right to plead his payment under the Maryland judgment. . . .

[The Court further ruled that Balk had received adequate notice of the attachment proceeding.]

Reversed.

MR. JUSTICE HARLAN and MR. JUSTICE DAY dissented.

(b) Procedural Incidents of Such Jurisdiction

Consideration of some of the procedural incidents of jurisdiction over things may help to clarify the nature of such jurisdiction, whether of the in rem variety as in Tyler or the quasi in rem varieties of Garfein and Harris. For example, consider the implications of Restatement (Second) of Judgments § 32 comment c, illustration 1 (1980):

"A brings an action against B to recover damages for breach of contract. Personal jurisdiction over B is not established, but an automobile worth $500 belonging to him is attached and he is personally notified of the proceeding. Judgment by default is rendered in favor of A for his damages to be assessed. The jury impanelled to assess the damages gives a verdict of $500 and judgment is rendered for A for $500 and $50 costs, to be paid out of the proceeds of the sale of the automobile. The automobile is sold for $500, which sum is paid to A. Of this sum $50 is applicable to the payment of the costs and $450 toward the payment of A's claim. B is not liable for the deficiency. However, in a new action brought by A against B on the original claim, A will be entitled, if successful, to recover whatever damages may be awarded in that action, which may be more or less than $500, less the sum of $450, plus the costs of the new action."

On the other hand, if B successfully defends the second action on the ground that he did not breach the contract, the prior proceeding will not be affected and A will not be directed to restore his earlier recovery.

FEDERAL ACTIONS UNDER 28 U.S.C. § 1655

Section 1655 works in some cases to authorize territorial jurisdiction. It has long been held to apply only to a lien or title existing prior to the suit, and not one created by the institution of the suit itself, as for example through attachment or garnishment. The real or personal property must be present within the district.

A defendant receives notice sufficient to satisfy procedural due process. There must in addition be jurisdiction over the subject matter—ordinarily, diversity of citizenship or a federal question.

If the absent defendant does not appear, the judgment affects only the property that is the subject of the action. The defendant can make a "special appearance" for the purpose of challenging the court's jurisdiction over the property without submitting himself to a personal judgment. Whether he can make a "limited appearance" for the purpose of defending on the merits the claim involving the property without subjecting himself to personal jurisdiction is a question addressed in the upcoming Campbell case.

FEDERAL ACTIONS UNDER RULE 4(e)(2)

For many years there was no provision for commencing an original federal action on the basis only of attachment or garnishment, that is, without personal jurisdiction over the defendant and without a pre-existing lien or title as under § 1655. See Big Vein Coal Co. v. Read, 229 U.S. 31, 33 S.Ct. 694 (1913).[g] The case of Davis v. Ensign-Bickford Co., 139 F.2d 624 (8th Cir.1944), held that Rule 64 did not effect any change; and Rosenthal v. Frankfort Distillers Corp., 193 F.2d 137 (5th Cir.1951), rejected the contention that the Erie rule required a different result to accord with state law.

In 1963, however, Rule 4(e) was amended so as to allow original quasi in rem and in rem jurisdiction to the extent authorized in the courts of the state where the federal court sits. Of course, adequate notice must be given, and jurisdiction over the subject matter must exist.

---

[g] Removal was a different matter. A suit in a state court with attachment or garnishment as the sole basis of territorial jurisdiction was removable if the usual requirements for removal were met.

JURISDICTIONAL AMOUNT

* Suppose the plaintiff's underlying claim in a quasi in rem case is for $25,000, but territorial jurisdiction exists only over a piece of property known to be worth $5000. Is any jurisdictional amount required by the federal statute governing subject-matter jurisdiction to be measured by the total claim or by the value of the property? Such case authority as there is indicates that the amount of the entire claim is controlling. But the question really must be regarded as an open one, as to which commentators disagree. Compare 2 Moore ¶ 4.32[2], at 4–355 n.22 (total claim should control), with 4 Wright & Miller § 1122, and 14 Wright, Miller & Cooper § 3632, at 26 n.5 (lesser of total claim and value of the property should control).

Questions: (5) What arguments can you make each way?

(6) Which solution is more responsive to current attitudes toward federal jurisdiction?

(7) Would your answer be different if the basis of territorial jurisdiction was an attachment of real estate, the value of which would not be known until it was sold to satisfy judgment?

CAMPBELL v. MURDOCK
United States District Court, Northern District of Ohio, 1950.
90 F.Supp. 297.

JONES, CHIEF JUDGE. This is an action to foreclose a mechanic's lien on land owned by defendant Murdock and for other relief.

It appears from the complaint that plaintiff expended considerable labor and materials in the improvement of Murdock's land pursuant to a contract between plaintiff and defendant McMahon, the duly authorized agent of Murdock. Plaintiff, even though he has joined McMahon as a party defendant, does not pray for relief as against him.

Plaintiff, Murdock and McMahon are respectively residents of Pennsylvania, South Carolina and Ohio. This Court has jurisdiction because of the diversity of citizenship and the provisions of 28 U.S. C.A. § 1655, formerly 28 U.S.C.A. § 118.

. . . Murdock, appearing specially and for the purpose of challenging this court's jurisdiction moves to dismiss the action against her, in so far as it asks for personal judgment and, appearing solely for the purpose of defending her interest in the property, moves for a more definite statement of the complaint.

. . . .

[Section 1655] provides in actions to enforce liens on property within the district for service on non-resident defendants by personal service where possible or by publication. The defendant is ordered to appear but if he does not, the final judgment can affect only the property which is the subject of the action.

Murdock claims that this section does not authorize a personal judgment against a non-resident defendant who does not make a general appearance, and she appears specially to move to dismiss the action insofar as it asks for personal judgment. The ultimate question to be decided, then, is whether Section 1655 permits personal judgments when jurisdiction is based solely on the fact that the property in controversy is located within the District.

We have been able to find only one case where the question has been squarely presented. In Bede Steam Shipping Co. v. New York Trust Co., 2 Cir., 54 F.2d 658, the court held that the non-resident defendant has but two choices. He could elect not to appear or he could make a general appearance and subject himself to the general jurisdiction of the court on all claims against him. The court specifically held that the defendant could not appear only for the purpose of defending his interest in the property.

This ruling seems reasonable and correct. The statute, it is true, limits the situations in which the court has in rem jurisdiction. But the statute does not prohibit the taking of personal judgments if the defendant appears, and it also provides, if the defendant does not appear, that the court's adjudication shall affect only the property before it. This leaves the inference that if the defendant does appear, the court may try the entire controversy between the parties.

There has been some suggestion that the personal judgment must be limited to such relief as is related to the in rem feature of the action which originally gives the court jurisdiction. The Bede case lends itself to such an interpretation. (See also 2 Cylo.Fed.Pro. 620–621) Even with this limitation a personal judgment may be had in this action. A personal judgment on the debt which gives rise to the lien in this action does not seem so incidental to the foreclosure of the lien as to defeat the jurisdiction of the court under section 1655. It is not necessary to decide what types of personal relief cannot be coupled with the actions listed in 1655, for the personal relief here is too closely related to the in rem feature of this case .   .   .   .

.   .   .   .

In the circumstances, the defendant Murdock's motion to dismiss will be overruled.

The motion for a more definite statement will be granted. It is unopposed and failure to oppose may be taken as implied consent to the court's favorable ruling on the motion.

LIMITED APPEARANCE

The same difficult problem of whether to allow a limited appearance arises in state actions, removed actions, and federal actions under Rule 4(e)(2). See generally Note, Limited Appearances, 7 Utah L.Rev. 369 (1961). In drafting Rule 4(e)(2), the rulemakers decided not to resolve the problem, but instead to remit it to "the molecular process of litigation." Kaplan, Amendments of the Federal Rules of Civil Procedure, 1961–63 (I), 77 Harv.L.Rev. 601, 628 (1964).

Contrast with Campbell the following situation: in state court, plaintiff brings a contract claim against a foreigner not subject to personal jurisdiction, with territorial jurisdiction based on the attachment of unrelated property belonging to defendant and worth less than the claim. One leading decision held that defendant could choose to (1) sacrifice his property by default, (2) make a limited appearance, or (3) enter a general appearance that would convert the jurisdiction to in personam. Cheshire National Bank v. Jaynes, 224 Mass. 14, 112 N.E. 500 (1916).

Note that the Campbell decision seems to have proceeded on the assumption that federal law governed the limited-appearance question. Some commentators disagree, and they would look instead in the circumstances of that case to state law. See, e.g., 4 Wright & Miller § 1123.

Question: (8) What arguments can you make each way?

In an action commenced on a basis other than personal jurisdiction, the defendant in federal court need not plead any counterclaims that he might happen to have. See Rule 13(a)(2), which was added by amendment in 1963. This apparently holds true even if the defendant makes a general appearance; but if the defendant chooses to assert any of his counterclaims, then the compulsory counterclaim Rule comes back into normal operation.

SECTION 3. JURISDICTION OVER PERSONS—THEORY IN EVOLUTION

(a) Presence as Basis for Jurisdiction

DARRAH v. WATSON, 36 Iowa 116 (1873). Darrah sued Watson in Iowa upon a judgment of a Virginia state court. Watson contended that the Virginia court had not acquired jurisdiction over him because, when he received in-hand service of process in Virginia, he was a citizen and resident of Pennsylvania and was in Virginia only for a few hours on business; after that service Watson had left Virginia, and a default judgment had then been rendered against him. The Iowa court held that the Virginia court had acquired jurisdiction over Watson's person, and that the Virginia judgment was entitled to full faith and credit under the Constitution and the laws of the United States.

ENFORCEMENT OF JUDGMENTS IN OTHER STATES

A money judgment for the plaintiff (or a judgment for the defendant for costs) may be enforced in the state where it is rendered. In addition, a party with a personal judgment of this kind may wish to enforce it in another state, as did Darrah. But Darrah could not simply request an Iowa sheriff to levy execution on Watson's property in Iowa in order to satisfy the Virginia judgment. The Iowa sheriff would have no authority to do so; he would be guilty of conversion if he seized the property on bare faith in a Virginia judgment. So what could Darrah do?

One way to enforce a personal judgment in another state is to bring there an action upon the judgment, with the aim being to obtain a new judgment and then to enforce that new, domestic judgment. In such an action, the forum court will, on collateral attack as in Darrah v. Watson, inquire into the possible lack of validity of the judgment of the rendering court.

If the Iowa court had decided that the Virginia judgment was not valid, it would not have allowed recovery thereon. Some broad generalizations on validity are helpful here. For a judgment to be valid and hence enforceable, first, it must be rendered by a court with competency to render it;[h] second, the court must have a sufficient basis for exercising adjudicatory authority over the defendant or other target of the action;[i] and, third, the persons to be legally affected must be given an opportunity to be heard.[j] So, for example, a personal judgment rendered by a court of a state with no basis for exercising jurisdiction over the defendant is not valid, and this is what Watson was contending.

Question: (9) Do not be led into thinking that such an issue can be raised only on collateral attack. Suppose that in the original action Watson, instead of defaulting, had challenged Virginia's jurisdiction over him. (As we shall see later, he would be permitted to appear in the Virginia court for the purpose of raising the defense of lack of jurisdiction over his person without submitting himself generally to the jurisdiction of that state.) If the trial court had rejected the contention and given judgment for Darrah, and the highest court of the state had affirmed, would Watson have a basis for review of the jurisdictional point by the Supreme Court of the United States? What of the argument that it is only the enforcement and not the rendition of the judgment that violates Watson's constitutional rights?

However, the Iowa court did find that the Virginia judgment was valid. In-hand service of process in Virginia was deemed to have au-

---

[h] See Section 1 of Topic A of this Part.

[i] The concern here is substantive due process, which gives rise to a doctrine called territorial jurisdiction, judicial jurisdiction, nexus, or amenability. This is the main focus of study for this Topic.

[j] The concern here is procedural due process. This is dealt with in passing throughout this Part and will be studied in detail in Topic C of this Part. At this stage, the student should make an effort to distinguish procedural due process from competency and especially from substantive due process.

thorized the exercise of jurisdiction over Watson (while also satisfying the demands of procedural due process). The contention of Watson thus being overcome, Iowa was required under article IV, section 1 of the Constitution to give the Virginia judgment full faith and credit. The constitutional mandate of the full faith and credit clause is that a state give the same effect to a valid judgment that it has in the state that rendered the judgment.[k] The same principle applies to all judgments as between state and federal courts. If the first judgment is from a state court and the second action is in a federal court, 28 U.S.C. § 1738 ("every court within the United States") compels this result. If the first judgment is from a federal court and the second action is in a state court, the same result of looking to the rendering sovereign's law is achieved by virtue of the federal common law of res judicata, which is applicable and binding in the state court under the supremacy clause of article VI. Finally, if both actions are in federal courts, the second court must give like respect to the judgment of the first; although other reasons have been advanced, the better view is that the result here follows from the fact that both courts are arms of the same sovereign. See Vestal, The Constitution and Preclusion/Res Judicata, 62 Mich.L.Rev. 33, 34–38 (1963).

In an action upon a judgment, the law to be applied by the forum court in determining the validity of the judgment is the law of the rendering court, but that law is subject to some very real constitutional limitations. Thus, Iowa had to look to Virginia law to see if jurisdiction over Watson had been acquired, and then inquire whether this acquisition had been consistent with due process. Similarly, in deciding the effect to be given a judgment that the forum court has determined to be valid, the law to be applied is the res judicata law of the rendering court, again subject to due process limitations. However, with respect to the method of enforcement, the forum court will apply its own law, subject to the requirement that the method not be so complex or expensive as to burden unduly the enforcement of nondomestic judgments.

There have been attempts to facilitate enforcement of nondomestic judgments by creating alternative methods of enforcement. In 1948, § 1963 was added to title 28. It dispensed with the necessity of an independent action upon a judgment by providing for registration of a district-court judgment for recovery of money or property in any other district court, with the effect of automatically converting the judgment so registered into a judgment of the court where it was registered. In addition to saving time and expense, this statute avoids the venue requirement for an independent action upon the judgment. It avoids as well the jurisdictional problems: there is no need to acquire territorial jurisdiction, and the judgment may be re-

---

[k] In Mills v. Duryee, 11 U.S. (7 Cranch) 481 (1813), Frances Scott Key, as counsel, contended unsuccessfully that full faith and credit required only that the judgment be weighed along with the evidence.

gistered even though an independent action in the registering court upon the judgment would have failed for lack of subject-matter jurisdiction.[1]

Question: (10) Does the device of registration destroy the defendant's opportunity to make a collateral attack? See 7 Moore ¶ 60.28[1].

The National Conference of Commissioners on Uniform State Laws in 1948 approved a Uniform Enforcement of Foreign Judgments Act providing for registration in the enacting state of federal or sister-state judgments. In 1964 the Commissioners approved a revision that further facilitated enforcement of such judgments by providing a procedure very similar to that in 28 U.S.C. § 1963. One or the other of these Acts has been adopted in a good number of states.

GRACE v. MacARTHUR, 170 F.Supp. 442 (E.D.Ark.1959). Arkansas citizens brought a diversity action in the Eastern District of Arkansas against three defendants on a claim arising in Arkansas. One of the defendants was served by a marshal who handed him the papers on a nonstop flight from Memphis, Tennessee, to Dallas, Texas, at a time when the plane was flying directly over the Eastern District of Arkansas. The defendant moved to quash the service on the ground that at the time he was served he was not within the territorial limits of Arkansas as required by Rule 4(f). The motion was denied.

WYMAN v. NEWHOUSE, 93 F.2d 313 (2d Cir.1937), cert. denied, 303 U.S. 664, 58 S.Ct. 831 (1938). Mr. N, a resident of New York, had had meretricious relations over a period of years with Mrs. W, a widow resident in Florida. Mrs. W wrote Mr. N stating that her mother was dying in Ireland, that she was leaving the United States to go to her mother and would not return, and that she wanted to see him once more before she left. She wrote that she loved him and entreated him to come to Florida for a last visit. These statements were essentially false. Upon his arrival at Miami airport, Mr. N was served with process in a Florida state-court action by Mrs. W for money loaned to him and for seduction under promise of marriage. Mr. N did not appear in the action, and a judgment was entered against him on his default.

In the present action upon the Florida judgment in a federal court in New York, Mr. N set up the foregoing matter as a defense. Was the defense valid? The court thought it was. The court indicated that Florida law governed. The facts showed that Mr. N had been

---

[1] Subject-matter jurisdiction is otherwise a serious concern because an action upon a federal judgment is not regarded as arising under the Constitution or laws of the United States, despite the fact that there was federal subject-matter jurisdiction for the original action in which the judgment was rendered. See Metcalf v. Watertown, 128 U.S. 586, 9 S.Ct. 173 (1888).

fraudulently enticed into the Florida jurisdiction for the sole purpose of service of process. This made the judgment invalid in the state of rendition. The judgment was thus open to attack when an effort was made to sue upon it in another jurisdiction. Mr. N was not required to assert his defense of fraud in the Florida action or to attack the judgment in Florida. Nor was he required in the present action to show that he had a defense on the merits to the Florida action.

FRAUD AND FORCE

Restatement (Second) of Conflict of Laws § 82 (1969) says: "A state will not exercise judicial jurisdiction, which has been obtained by fraud or unlawful force, over a defendant or his property."

Comment f to this section states that this prevailing rule is "not jurisdictional," that is, the rule represents only a self-imposed limitation on the state's exercise of its utmost constitutional powers. Accordingly, if a state instead chooses to exercise judicial jurisdiction in these circumstances, its action must be recognized as valid in other states.

Questions: (11) New York follows the rule of § 82. See, e.g., Terlizzi v. Brodie, 38 A.D.2d 762, 329 N.Y.S.2d 589 (1972) (New Jersey defendants were telephoned at home and falsely told that they had been chosen to receive two Broadway tickets as a promotional venture to get their opinion of the new 7:30 p.m. curtain time; they were served in the theatre by the man sitting behind them; motion to vacate service granted). But the prevailing rule, in New York and elsewhere, is that it is permissible to resort to subterfuge in order to serve a person who is voluntarily in the state. See, e.g., Gumperz v. Hofmann, 245 A.D. 622, 283 N.Y.S. 823 (1935), aff'd, 271 N.Y. 544, 2 N.E.2d 687 (1936) (defendant, an Argentine doctor sojourning in a New York City hotel, was telephoned by a process server who falsely represented himself to be a Dr. Goldman with a letter from the president of the New York County Medical Society to be personally delivered; they arranged to meet in the hotel lobby, where service was made; motion to vacate service denied). What difference accounts for the two rules?

(12) It has also been held that service is invalid in the following circumstances. Husband, an attorney, accompanied his wife to dockside; she was to sail from New York to California to visit her mother. During an affectionate farewell, he gave her a wrapped box, telling her it contained a present for her mother; in reality, it contained process for a divorce action. She sailed without opening it, and she consequently defaulted. Bulkley v. Bulkley, 6 Abb.Pr. 307 (N.Y.Sup.Ct.1858). How is this to be reconciled with Gumperz?

(13) Prospective defendant is in New York only for settlement negotiations with potential plaintiff. Negotiations break down. Plaintiff continues the conference for a few hours, not to conduct good-faith negotiations but rather as an artifice to make service on defendant in a New York state-court action by awaiting the arrival of the process server. Now there is a motion

to vacate service. What decision? Cf. Sunshine Kitchens, Inc. v. Alanthus Corp., 65 F.R.D. 4 (S.D.Fla.1974).

IMMUNITY FROM SERVICE OF PROCESS

The customary doctrine has long been that a nonresident party, witness, or counsel is immune from service of process when present in a state for attendance at litigation and for a reasonable time to go to and fro. The rule has been criticized in its entirety, see Keeffe & Roscia, Immunity and Sentimentality, 32 Cornell L.Q. 471 (1947), and has been qualified or given restrictive application, see, e.g., Wangler v. Harvey, 41 N.J. 277, 196 A.2d 513 (1963).

Questions: (14) Are the considerations different as between a witness and a party? as between counsel and a party? as between a plaintiff and a defendant?

(15) Should it matter whether the two actions involve related facts? whether the pending action for which the person comes in is criminal or civil?

(16) What, if any, effect on the immunity rule should there be if the person as to whom immunity is claimed is subject to process in the action on some other basis than his presence in the state? (Renew consideration of this question after studying the rest of this Section.)

Again, this rule is in the nature of a self-imposed limitation that the state may choose not to adopt. See Restatement (Second) of Conflict of Laws § 83 comment b (1969).

(b) Domicile as Basis for Jurisdiction

MILLIKEN v. MEYER, 311 U.S. 457, 61 S.Ct. 339 (1940). Milliken sued Meyer in a Wyoming state court to recover profits from certain Colorado oil properties. Meyer was domiciled in Wyoming at all relevant times. He received in-hand service of process in Colorado pursuant to a Wyoming statute. He did not appear in the action, and judgment was rendered against him. Subsequently Meyer sued Milliken in a Colorado state court to enjoin Milliken from enforcing the Wyoming judgment and to obtain a decree that the Wyoming judgment was invalid for want of jurisdiction over Meyer. The Colorado Supreme Court eventually granted Meyer relief. On certiorari, the Supreme Court of the United States reversed, holding that the Wyoming judgment was valid and entitled to full faith and credit in Colorado. The Court said:

"Domicile in the state is alone sufficient to bring an absent defendant within the reach of the state's jurisdiction for purposes of a personal judgment by means of appropriate substituted service. . . . That such substituted service may be wholly adequate to meet the requirements of due process was recognized by this Court in McDonald v.

Mabee, 243 U.S. 90, 37 S.Ct. 343,[m] despite earlier intimations to the contrary. See Pennoyer v. Neff, 95 U.S. 714, 733 . . . . Its adequacy so far as due process is concerned is dependent on whether or not the form of the substituted service provided for such case and employed is reasonably calculated to give him actual notice of the proceedings and an opportunity to be heard. If it is, the traditional notions of fair play and substantial justice (McDonald v. Mabee, supra) implicit in due process are satisfied. Here there can be no question on that score. . . . Certainly then Meyer's domicile in Wyoming was a sufficient basis for that extraterritorial service. As in case of the authority of the United States over its absent citizens (Blackmer v. United States, 284 U.S. 421, 52 S.Ct. 252), the authority of a state over one of its citizens is not terminated by the mere fact of his absence from the state. The state which accords him privileges and affords protection to him and his property by virtue of his domicile may also exact reciprocal duties."

[handwritten margin notes: "as long as enuf. to give actual notice of proceeding & opp. to be heard"]

Questions: (17) What if the defendant was a domiciliary when the claim arose and when the action was commenced, but ceased to be before service was made? See Allen v. Superior Court, 41 Cal.2d 306, 259 P.2d 905 (1953) (jurisdiction exists for claim arising in state).

(18) What if the defendant was a domiciliary when the claim arose, but ceased to be before the action was commenced and service was made? See Owens v. Superior Court, 52 Cal.2d 822, 345 P.2d 921 (1959) (jurisdiction exists for claim arising in state).

(19) What if, at all relevant times, the defendant was a resident but not a domiciliary? See Restatement (Second) of Conflict of Laws § 30 (1969).

Domicile was not generally recognized as a basis for personal jurisdiction at common law, and it has therefore usually been held that a court cannot exercise jurisdiction on this basis unless authorized to do so by statute. See, e.g., Duncan v. McDonough, 105 N.H. 308, 199 A.2d 104 (1964). But again, if a state's courts were authoritatively to decide that such statutory authorization was unnecessary, their judgments on this basis would be entitled to full faith and credit.

(c) Consent as Basis for Jurisdiction

Consent to personal jurisdiction before action is brought, typically as part of a contract the breach of which is the subject of the action, is generally effective. Sometimes such consent poses serious prob-

---

[m] This 1917 case is much cited, chiefly for the statement of Justice Holmes: "The foundation of jurisdiction is physical power . . . ." It held that service by publication would not yield a valid personal judgment against a person who, although technically domiciled in the state, had left it intending to establish his home elsewhere. The Court apparently believed that the notice given, and not necessarily the nexus, was fatally defective. In this connection, Justice Holmes for the Court said: "To dispense with personal service the substitute that is most likely to reach the defendant is the least that ought to be required if substantial justice is to be done."

Consent OK b/4 or after fact when accept service or waive service

lems, turning in part on whether it was voluntarily, intelligently, and knowingly given; but these problems are reserved for consideration in Topic C of this Part.

A defendant may also effectively consent to personal jurisdiction after the fact. This may be done by accepting or waiving service even though he could not otherwise have been subjected to jurisdiction and even though he is physically outside the state when he does the acts constituting the acceptance or waiver.[n] Or jurisdiction over the person may be conferred by the entry of a general appearance in an action by the defendant in person or by his authorized attorney.

Question: (20) What other action by the defendant or his authorized attorney would be effective in a federal court to confer jurisdiction over his person?

HESS v. PAWLOSKI, 274 U.S. 352, 47 S.Ct. 632 (1927). In 1923 Massachusetts enacted a statute, the material parts of which follow:

"[T]he operation by a non-resident of a motor vehicle on a public way in the commonwealth . . . shall be deemed equivalent to an appointment by such non-resident of the registrar [of motor vehicles], or his successor in office, to be his true and lawful attorney upon whom may be served all lawful processes in any action or proceeding against him, growing out of any accident or collision in which said non-resident may be involved while operating a motor vehicle on such a way, and said . . . operation shall be a signification of his agreement that any such process against him which is so served shall be of the same legal force and validity as if served on him personally. Service of such process shall be made by leaving a copy of the process with a fee of two dollars in the hands of the registrar, or in his office, and such service shall be sufficient service upon the said non-resident; provided, that notice of such service and a copy of the process are forthwith sent by registered mail by the plaintiff to the defendant, and the defendant's return receipt and the plaintiff's affidavit of compliance herewith are appended to the writ and entered with the declaration. The court in which the action is pending may order such continuances as may be necessary to afford the defendant reasonable opportunity to defend the action."

Service made in compliance with this statute was challenged by the defendant as violative of due process. The Supreme Judicial Court of Massachusetts held the statute to be a valid exercise of the police power, and on writ of error the Supreme Court affirmed. Af-

---

[n] There may be a question of interpretation whether the defendant has accepted service or has merely admitted that process has been served upon him. For instance, if he writes on the summons, "I acknowledge that this summons was handed to me in State *Y*," this is not a consent to jurisdiction in an action commenced in State *X*. In contrast, "I acknowledge due and personal service of this summons upon me and waive further service upon me," would be a consent. See Restatement (Second) of Conflict of Laws § 32 comment d, illustrations 7–8 (1969).

ter citing Pennoyer v. Neff, McDonald v. Mabee, and other decisions, Justice Butler continued:

"Motor vehicles are dangerous machines; and, even when skillfully and carefully operated, their use is attended by serious dangers to persons and property. In the public interest the State may make and enforce regulations reasonably calculated to promote care on the part of all, residents and non-residents alike, who use its highways. The measure in question operates to require a non-resident to answer for his conduct in the State where arise causes of action alleged against him, as well as to provide for a claimant a convenient method by which he may sue to enforce his rights. Under the statute the implied consent is limited to proceedings growing out of accidents or collisions on a highway in which the non-resident may be involved. It is required that he shall actually receive and receipt for notice of the service and a copy of the process. And it contemplates such continuances as may be found necessary to give reasonable time and opportunity for defense. It makes no hostile discrimination against non-residents but tends to put them on the same footing as residents. Literal and precise equality in respect of this matter is not attainable; it is not required. Canadian Northern Ry. Co. v. Eggen, 252 U.S. 553, 561–562, 40 S.Ct. 402. The State's power to regulate the use of its highways extends to their use by non-residents as well as by residents. Hendrick v. Maryland, 235 U.S. 610, 622, 35 S.Ct. 140. And, in advance of the operation of a motor vehicle on its highway by a non-resident, the State may require him to appoint one of its officials as his agent on whom process may be served in proceedings growing out of such use. Kane v. New Jersey, 242 U.S. 160, 167, 37 S.Ct. 30.[o] That case recognizes power of the State to exclude a non-resident until the formal appointment is made. And, having the power so to exclude, the State may declare that the use of the highway by the non-resident is the equivalent of the appointment of the registrar as agent on whom process may be served. [Citations omitted.] The difference between the formal and implied appointment is not substantial so far as concerns the application of the due process clause of the Fourteenth Amendment."

Questions: (21) Suppose the statute in Hess v. Pawloski were amended so that, instead of calling for service of process to be made upon a public official within the state and for notice by registered mail to the defendant, it required only service by registered mail to the out-of-state defendant. Would it be valid?

(22) Suppose the statute in Hess v. Pawloski were amended by striking out the words "on a public way in the commonwealth" and substituting "within the commonwealth." Would it be valid as applied to a nonresident

[o] The New Jersey statute required a nonresident motorist on entering the state to sign a document appointing a state official as his agent for service of process in proceedings arising out of his use of the highway. The statute was enacted in 1906, so one need not visualize traffic on the New Jersey Turnpike.

involved in an accident on private property? See Sipe v. Moyers, 353 Pa. 75,
44 A.2d 263 (1945) (yes). Why?

(d) Acts Done in State as Basis for Jurisdiction

FLEXNER v. FARSON, 248 U.S. 289, 39 S.Ct. 97 (1919). In Kentucky, Bernard Flexner entered into a contract to purchase bonds
from Farson, Son & Company, a partnership engaged in the business
of trading in securities; one Washington Flexner acted as the agent
of the partnership during the negotiations. Bernard Flexner later
commenced suit in a Kentucky state court against the partners for
breach of the contract. The partners were domiciled and resided
outside Kentucky; service was made in Kentucky upon Washington
Flexner as their agent, in attempted compliance with the following
Kentucky statute: "In actions against an individual residing in another state, or a partnership, association, or joint stock company, the
members of which reside in another state, engaged in business in this
state, the summons may be served on the manager, or agent of, or
person in charge of, such business in this state, in the county where
the business is carried on, or in the county where the cause of action
occurred." Defendants defaulted, and plaintiff obtained a money
judgment.

In an action upon the judgment against one of the partners in a
state court of Illinois, the defendant partner urged that the Kentucky
judgment was invalid for want of jurisdiction over the partners' persons. The plaintiff argued that the quoted statute had been implicitly incorporated into the contract and that the partners had thereby
effectively consented to service in actions arising from business conducted in Kentucky. The Illinois courts held that the Kentucky judgment should be denied effect. On writ of error the Supreme Court of
the United States affirmed. The entire legal discussion in the opinion
by Justice Holmes for the Court follows:

"It is argued that the pleas tacitly admit that Washington Flexner
was agent of the firm at the time of the transaction sued upon in
Kentucky,[p] and the Kentucky statute is construed as purporting to
make him agent to receive service in suits arising out of the business
done in that State. On this construction it is said that the defendants
by doing business in the State consented to be bound by the service
prescribed. The analogy of suits against insurance companies based
upon such service is invoked. Mutual Reserve Fund Life Association
v. Phelps, 190 U.S. 147, 23 S.Ct. 707. But the consent that is said to
be implied in such cases is a mere fiction, founded upon the accepted
doctrine that the States could exclude foreign corporations altogeth-

---

[p] Plaintiff alleged in the Illinois action
that Washington Flexner was the partners' agent at the time of the transaction
and at the time of service upon him. The
defendant partner's plea, to which plaintiff demurred, alleged that Washington
Flexner was not their agent at the time
of service upon him; it did not allege that
Washington Flexner was not their agent
at the time of the transaction.

er, and therefore could establish this obligation as a condition to letting them in. Lafayette Ins. Co. v. French, 18 How. 404. Pennsylvania Fire Ins. Co. v. Gold Issue Mining & Milling Co., 243 U.S. 93, 96, 37 S.Ct. 344. The State had no power to exclude the defendants and on that ground without going farther the Supreme Court of Illinois rightly held that the analogy failed,[q] and that the Kentucky judgment was void. If the Kentucky statute purports to have the effect attributed to it, it cannot have that effect in the present case. New York Life Ins. Co. v. Dunlevy, 241 U.S. 518, 522, 523, 36 S.Ct. 613."

HENRY L. DOHERTY & CO. v. GOODMAN, 294 U.S. 623, 55 S.Ct. 553 (1935). Goodman brought suit in a state court of Iowa against Henry L. Doherty, a citizen and resident of New York, trading as Henry L. Doherty & Company and engaged in the securities business, for damages arising out of a contract for the sale of stock. The contract was negotiated in Des Moines by a salesman operating from the Des Moines office. Service was made on King, the defendant's district manager in charge of the Des Moines office, pursuant to Iowa Code § 11079 (in effect since 1851), which provided: "When a corporation, company, or individual has, for the transaction of any business, an office or agency in any county other than that in which the principal resides, service may be made on any agent or clerk employed in such office or agency, in all actions growing out of or connected with the business of that office or agency."

Doherty appeared specially and challenged on constitutional grounds the jurisdiction over his person. The Iowa court upheld the service, and Doherty made no further appearance. The Iowa Supreme Court affirmed, pointing out that the statute did not violate the privileges and immunities clause because it applied equally to residents of other counties in Iowa and to nonresidents of Iowa. On appeal the Supreme Court of the United States affirmed, with Justice McReynolds saying in part:

"Iowa treats the business of dealing in corporate securities as exceptional and subjects it to special regulation. Laws 1913, c. 137; Laws 1921, c. 189; Laws 1929, c. 10, approved Mar. 19, 1929. The last cited Act requires registration and written consent for service of process upon the Secretary of State. See Merrick v. N.W. Halsey & Co., 242 U.S. 568, 37 S.Ct. 227. Doherty voluntarily established an office in Iowa and there carried on this business. Considering this fact, and accepting the construction given to § 11079, we think to apply it as here proposed will not deprive him of any right guaranteed by the Federal Constitution.

[q] The distinction between nonresident individuals and foreign corporations was elaborated in Hess v. Pawloski, where the Court explained that a state's power to exclude from doing intrastate business differs as to the two categories because the privileges and immunities clause of article IV, section 2 applies to individuals but not to corporations.

"Flexner v. Farson, 248 U.S. 289, 39 S.Ct. 97, much relied upon, does not sustain appellant's position. There the service was made upon one not then agent for the defendants; here the situation is different. King was manager of the appellant's office when the sale contract was made; also when process was served upon him. Moreover, under the laws of Iowa, neither her citizens nor non-residents could freely engage in the business of selling securities.

"The power of the States to impose terms upon non-residents, as to activities within their borders, recently has been much discussed. Hess v. Pawloski, 274 U.S. 352, 47 S.Ct. 632; Wuchter v. Pizzutti, 276 U.S. 13, 48 S.Ct. 259; Young v. Masci, 289 U.S. 253, 53 S.Ct. 599. Under these opinions it is established doctrine that a State may rightly direct that non-residents who operate automobiles on her highways shall be deemed to have appointed the Secretary of State as agent to accept service of process, provided there is some 'provision making it reasonably probable that notice of the service on the Secretary will be communicated to the non-resident defendant who is sued.'

"So far as it affects appellant, the questioned statute goes no farther than the principle approved by those opinions permits. Only rights claimed upon the present record are determined. The limitations of § 11079 under different circumstances we do not consider."

Question: (23) What vitality remained in Flexner v. Farson after the decision in the Doherty case?

DUBIN v. CITY OF PHILADELPHIA, 34 Pa.D. & C. 61 (C.P.1938). A Pennsylvania statute provided that a nonresident owner or user of real estate, and the footways and curbs adjacent thereto, by the ownership and use thereof made the Secretary of the Commonwealth his agent for service of process in any civil action arising out of any accident or injury in which such real estate, footways, or curbs were involved. There was a provision for registered-mail notice to the defendant at his last known address, as well as service upon the Secretary. The plaintiff sued in a Pennsylvania court for injuries from a fall on a broken sidewalk in Philadelphia. The abutting owner, who lived in New Jersey, was served in accordance with the statute. Presiding Judge Bok said that the statute created "another exception to the rule of personal service in personal actions," and was "a reasonable procedural requirement of a nonresident" who elected to own real estate in Pennsylvania. He therefore held it to be constitutional.

ADAM v. SAENGER, 303 U.S. 59, 58 S.Ct. 454 (1938). *X* brought an action against *Y* in a California state court for goods sold and delivered. In accordance with the California Code of Civil Procedure, *Y* was permitted and chose to bring a "cross-action" against *X* for conversion of the said goods, serving the "cross-complaint" upon X's attorney of record in the pending action. Judgment in the cross-action was taken by default against X; subsequently the main action by X was dismissed for want of prosecution. Y then brought an action in a Texas state court to enforce his judgment. The Texas court dismissed, holding that the California judgment was invalid because California had not acquired jurisdiction over X for the purposes of the cross-action; X had no connection with California other than its institution of the action against Y. On appeal within the state system, the dismissal was affirmed. On certiorari the United States Supreme Court reversed, with Justice Stone saying:

"There is nothing in the Fourteenth Amendment to prevent a state from adopting a procedure by which a judgment in personam may be rendered in a cross-action against a plaintiff in its courts, upon service of process or of appropriate pleading upon his attorney of record. The plaintiff having, by his voluntary act in demanding justice from the defendant, submitted himself to the jurisdiction of the court, there is nothing arbitrary or unreasonable in treating him as being there for all purposes for which justice to the defendant requires his presence. It is the price which the state may exact as the condition of opening its courts to the plaintiff."

Questions: (24) Why would the doctrine of ancillary jurisdiction not suffice to reach the Adam v. Saenger holding?

(25) Why would physical presence, as a basis for personal jurisdiction, not suffice to reach the Adam v. Saenger holding?

(26) *P–1* and *P–2* bring an action against D in a court of State X, which has rules concerning counterclaims and cross-claims identical with those found in the Federal Rules. D asserts a permissive counterclaim against both plaintiffs. *P–1* then brings a cross-claim, arising out of the transaction that is the subject matter of the counterclaim, against *P–2*. *P–2* has no connection with State X other than his institution of the action against D. Is there jurisdiction over *P–2* for the purposes of the cross-claim?

APPEARANCE AS DEFENDANT

If the defendant does not want to submit to personal jurisdiction, he plainly would not enter, or authorize his attorney to enter, a general appearance. If he is confident that jurisdiction over his person is lacking, he may, in theory at least, simply ignore the lawsuit entirely. Here is an illustration. Seeking money damages, P commences an action against D in a court of State X for an alleged tort committed by D in State Y. D resides in State Y, and he has never set foot in nor had any other connection with State X. P delivers process to D in State Y. In short, State X has not acquired jurisdiction over D's person. If judgment on D's default is entered against him, and an attempt made to enforce the judgment in State *Y* or elsewhere, it is generally thought that he can then set up the lack of jurisdiction in a collateral attack.

But *D* may wish to contest State *X*'s jurisdiction over his person in the original action. He may be in genuine doubt whether State *X* has acquired jurisdiction over him, or he may not relish the prospect of an overhanging judgment against him even though he is convinced it is invalid. And note that if *D* chooses to stay away, he may on collateral attack argue only the invalidity of the judgment, not the merits of the underlying claim. So, how may *D* challenge the jurisdiction in the original action, and what procedural problems might he encounter?

A state apparently has the power to treat *any* appearance by the defendant or his authorized attorney as a conferral of jurisdiction over his person. On this idea, a Texas statute built a particularly cruel trapdoor, which was not dismantled until fairly recently.[r] Under the statute, an appearance carefully denominated as special for the purpose of challenging the jurisdiction would nevertheless constitute a submission to the jurisdiction and thus nullify what might have been a perfectly good objection to the jurisdiction. If the defendant stayed away, however, he could challenge the judgment as invalid if the plaintiff sought to enforce it in Texas or elsewhere. Accordingly, in a Texas action the defendant had to choose between (1) coming in and fighting the action on the merits and (2) staying away entirely and later challenging personal jurisdiction. The Supreme Court refused to hold that imposition of this dilemma violated the fourteenth amendment. York v. Texas, 137 U.S. 15, 11 S.Ct. 9 (1890).

Question: (27) To overcome an argument in York v. Texas that the entry of a judgment without proper service was a deprivation of liberty or property, the Court responded: "It is only when process is issued thereon or the judgment is sought to be enforced that liberty or property is in present danger." Does this constitutional point impress you as sound?

Despite the acquiescence of the Supreme Court, the Texas approach found little favor in other states. Many states permitted the device of a special appearance. The defendant would file a notice that he was appearing solely for the purpose of challenging jurisdiction over his person and not submitting generally to the jurisdiction. Moreover, he had to be careful to take no action looking like a general appearance, for such action might well be treated as evidence of waiver.[s] The details of state practice in making jurisdictional objec-

---

[r] The Texas statute was abrogated in 1962 by Tex.R.Civ.P. 120a. Mississippi, the only other state to follow it, has since given it up, doing so in Mladinich v. Kohn, 250 Miss. 138, 164 So.2d 785 (1964).

[s] An ironic example is found in Jackson v. National Grange Mut. Liab. Co., 299 N.Y. 333, 87 N.E.2d 283 (1949), where the defendant urged (1) lack of jurisdiction over his person and (2) lack of jurisdiction over the subject matter. The court held that the challenge to subject-matter jurisdiction, which was unsuccessful, constituted a waiver of the objection to personal jurisdiction, which would have been good. New York undid this result by

tions varied widely, and still do. Costly and irretrievable mistakes may result from failure to master local procedure.

Under the Federal Rules and the numerous state rules patterned upon them, there is no provision for a special appearance. But a similar result is achieved. A defendant may raise a jurisdictional defense by including it in a motion in advance of answer or by including it in his answer along with other defenses. See Rule 12. As Judge Maris said in Orange Theatre Corp. v. Rayherstz Amusement Corp., 139 F.2d 871, 874 (3d Cir.), cert. denied, 322 U.S. 740, 64 S.Ct. 1057 (1944): "He is no longer required at the door of the federal courthouse to intone that ancient abracadabra of the law, de bene esse,[t] in order by its magic power to enable himself to remain outside even while he steps within." This is not, of course, to say that a jurisdictional defense may not still be waived by failure to present it in timely fashion. See Rule 12(g) and (h).

Questions: (28) *P* sues *D* in federal district court. *D* moves successfully under Rule 6(b)(1) for an extension of time to answer or move, and then within the extended time moves to dismiss under Rule 12(b)(2). Has *D* waived this jurisdictional defense?

(29) *P* sues *D* in federal district court to enjoin appropriation of trade secrets and to recover damages. *P* moves for a preliminary injunction. *D* participates in four days of contested hearing on this motion. *D* then files a motion to dismiss under Rule 12(b)(2). This motion is filed within the time prescribed by Rule 12(a). *P* argues that participation in the hearing on the preliminary injunction waived this jurisdictional defense. Should this argument prevail? See Wyrough & Loser, Inc. v. Pelmor Laboratories, 376 F.2d 543 (3d Cir.1967) (yes).

Thus, a special appearance or a Rule 12(b) defense enables the defendant to circumvent the dilemma involved in York v. Texas. But there may be another dilemma lurking down the road. Suppose the defendant has been allowed to challenge personal jurisdiction in the original action, but his challenge has been overruled. If he then defends on the merits, does he waive his right to renew the jurisdictional challenge on appeal?

A few states have answered this question in the affirmative. Unless such a state permits an interlocutory appeal, a defendant faces a hard choice between (1) standing on his jurisdictional objection, submitting to an adverse judgment, and then appealing the jurisdictional ruling and (2) forgoing his appeal as to the jurisdiction and defending on the merits. It appears that imposition of this dilemma does not offend due process. See Western Life Indemnity Co. v. Rupp, 235 U.S. 261, 35 S.Ct. 37 (1914). In justification of this approach, it has been said that a defendant who insists he is not properly before the

---

statute two years later, but some states still adhere to it.

[t] The reference was to a practice peculiar to the courts of Pennsylvania. "The legitimate purpose of the appearance de bene esse is to enable the defendant to deny the jurisdiction of the court without submitting to it." 1 Standard Pennsylvania Practice 410 (1935).

court should be barred from doing anything inconsistent with his contention.

On the other hand, the federal courts and most states have removed this dilemma as well. They allow the defendant to challenge the jurisdiction, defend on the merits, and then appeal the adverse decisions on the jurisdiction and on the merits. In summary, the dominant American rule is the one prescribed for the federal courts in Harkness v. Hyde, 98 U.S. 476, 479 (1879):

"The right of the defendant to insist upon the objection to the illegality of the service was not waived by the special appearance of counsel for him to move the dismissal of the action on that ground, or what we consider as intended, that the service be set aside; nor, when that motion was overruled, by their answering for him to the merits of the action. Illegality in a proceeding by which jurisdiction is to be obtained is in no case waived by the appearance of the defendant for the purpose of calling the attention of the court to such irregularity; nor is the objection waived when being urged it is overruled, and the defendant is thereby compelled to answer. He is not considered as abandoning his objection because he does not submit to further proceedings without contestation. It is only where he pleads to the merits in the first instance, without insisting upon the illegality, that the objection is deemed to be waived."

Question: (30) *P* sues *D* in federal district court. *D* moves to dismiss under Rule 12(b)(2), but his challenge is overruled. *D* then answers, including a counterclaim for which there is independent subject-matter jurisdiction. Claim and counterclaim are litigated and decided. If *D* loses on the main claim, may he on appeal from that judgment still assert lack of jurisdiction over his person? Does it matter whether the counterclaim was compulsory or permissive? If such appellate review were available and if the judgment on the main claim were reversed on the Rule 12(b)(2) defense, what consequence if any should this have for the judgment on the counterclaim? Does it matter whether *D* won or lost on the counterclaim? See Dragor Shipping Corp. v. Union Tank Car Co., 378 F.2d 241 (9th Cir.1967).

So, the defendant usually has a choice between coming into the original action to challenge personal jurisdiction and staying away to await raising the point on collateral attack. But he cannot raise jurisdiction both ways. If he loses his challenge in the original action and fails to upset the result on appeal, then the doctrine of res judicata will preclude his relitigating the point on collateral attack. This rule is further explored in Topic E of Part Six.

Question: (31) *P* brings an action against *D–1* and *D–2* in a court of State *X*, which has rules concerning cross-claims identical with those found in the Federal Rules. *D–2* makes a general appearance. *D–1* then appears, and he brings a cross-claim against *D–2*. *D–2* has no connection with State *X* other than his general appearance in *P*'s action against him. Is there jurisdiction over *D–2* for the purposes of the cross-claim? See Restatement (Second) of Judgments § 9 (1980).

————

HESS v. PAWLOSKI, 274 U.S. 352, 47 S.Ct. 632 (1927). This case was included in the preceding Subsection because the Massachusetts legislature drew the statute in terms of implied consent. This transparent fiction was a useful first step in escaping the rigors of Pennoyer v. Neff, but it proved troublesome in other contexts. For instance, some cases held that "consent" to suit in a state under a nonresident motorist statute was a waiver of objection to improper venue in a federal court. (This was before the general venue statute was amended to make the district in which the claim arose a proper venue.) Finally, in Olberding v. Illinois Central Railroad, 346 U.S. 338, 340–41, 74 S.Ct. 83, 85 (1953), Justice Frankfurter, observing that this venue problem "is a horse soon curried," [u] put the fiction to rest in these words:

"It is true that in order to ease the process by which new decisions are fitted into pre-existing modes of analysis there has been some fictive talk to the effect that the reason why a non-resident can be subjected to a state's jurisdiction is that the non-resident has 'impliedly' consented to be sued there. In point of fact, however, jurisdiction in these cases does not rest on consent at all. See Scott, Jurisdiction over Nonresident Motorists, 39 Harv.L.Rev. 563. The defendant may protest to high heaven his unwillingness to be sued and it avails him not. The liability rests on the inroad which the automobile has made on the decision of Pennoyer v. Neff, 95 U.S. 714, as it has on so many aspects of our social scene. . . . But to conclude from [Hess v. Pawloski] that the motorist, who never consented to anything and whose consent is altogether immaterial, has actually agreed to be sued and has thus waived his federal venue rights is surely to move in the world of Alice in Wonderland."

————

(e) Jurisdiction over Corporations

DOMESTIC CORPORATIONS

Having examined four bases of personal jurisdiction, we now consider how these bases translate into the corporate setting. To begin, incorporation in a state gives that state a basis for the exercise of jurisdiction over the corporation in any action that may be brought against it there, regardless of where the claim arose. This basis of jurisdiction assures that there is always a place at which a corporation is amenable to suit. Due process requires, however, that an adequate method be employed to give the corporation notice of the action.

————

[u] For a metric comment on Justice Frankfurter's fondness for unusual words and phrases, see Field, Frankfurter, J., Concurring . . . , 71 Harv.L. Rev. 77 (1957).

RIVERSIDE & DAN RIVER COTTON MILLS v. MENEFEE, 237 U.S. 189, 35 S.Ct. 579 (1915). Plaintiff, a citizen of North Carolina, sued defendant, a Virginia corporation, in a North Carolina state court for injuries sustained while working as defendant's employee in its Virginia cotton mill. Defendant had never transacted any business in North Carolina and had no property there. In-hand service was made in North Carolina on one of defendant's directors, who resided in North Carolina but had never transacted any business in that state for defendant. Defendant's challenge to the propriety of the service was overruled by the North Carolina state courts. On writ of error the Supreme Court reversed, holding that a judgment based on such service entailed a denial of due process. The argument that it was only the enforcement and not the rendition of the judgment that would violate the due process clause was expressly rejected.

PROBLEM OF FOREIGN CORPORATIONS: BACKGROUND OF THE INTERNATIONAL SHOE CASE

Originally no action looking to a personal judgment could be successfully maintained against a corporation outside the state of its incorporation—unless, perhaps, the corporation actually consented. The notion on which this doctrine went appears from Chief Justice Taney's statement in Bank of Augusta v. Earle, 38 U.S. (13 Pet.) 519, 588 (1839): "It is very true that a corporation can have no legal existence out of the boundaries of the sovereignty by which it is created."

This restrictive doctrine did not meet modern needs and had to be overcome. It was first overcome in the nineteenth century by manipulating the idea of "consent." If a state could exclude a foreign corporation from doing local, as distinguished from interstate, business in the state, why could it not authorize the foreign corporation to do local business on the condition that the corporation explicitly consent to be sued in the courts of the state? This device, a kind of forced consent, worked, and still works at the present time, like this: if the state requires the foreign corporation, as a condition of doing local business in the state, to appoint an agent upon whom service of process may be made, and if the corporation does appoint such an agent, this consent provides a basis for the state's rendering valid personal judgments against the corporation. This consent is none the less effective because coerced. Nor is it material that the agent so appointed is a public official, such as the Secretary of State or Commissioner of Corporations, as long as the corporation receives due process notice. There may be a question of statutory interpretation as to whether this consent, and hence jurisdiction over the corporation, comprehends only those actions arising from business done within the state or is broad enough to cover all personal actions. (On familiar principles, the highest court of the state is the final authority on this question of interpretation.) But if the latter construction is given to the statute, it does not exceed permissible constitutional limits. See Pennsylvania Fire Ins. Co. v. Gold Issue Mining & Milling Co., 243 U.S. 93, 37 S.Ct. 344 (1917).

But the foreign corporation might refuse to signify its consent in this explicit manner. The next step was to provide that if the foreign corporation did local business within the state, personal actions might be brought against it (by service of process in a prescribed manner) irrespective of any explicit indication of consent. The cases held that this provided a basis at least for the state's assuming jurisdiction in actions on claims arising from business done within the state. Thus the consent idea was further attenuated. Suppose now that the foreign corporation in question was doing only interstate business within the state. The cases held that actions growing out of that business done in the state could nevertheless be maintained against the corporation. Here the implied consent fiction was pushed to the breaking point, for the state did not have the power to exclude the corporation from doing such business. Reconsider Flexner v. Farson.

In the face of these difficulties, a nominally different idea, that of corporate "presence," was formulated. In Philadelphia & Reading Railway v. McKibbin, 243 U.S. 264, 265, 37 S.Ct. 280, 280 (1917), Justice Brandeis for the Court said: "A foreign corporation is amenable to process to enforce a personal liability, in the absence of consent, only if it is doing business within the State in such manner and to such extent as to warrant the inference that it is present there." Again, this theory presented the promise of providing nexus at least in actions on claims arising from business done within the state.

The question of how far a foreign corporation doing business in a state could be subjected, in the absence of some actual consent, to personal actions on claims not arising from business done within the state was not clearly answered by the cases. Old Wayne Mutual Life Ass'n v. McDonough, 204 U.S. 8, 27 S.Ct. 236 (1907), and Simon v. Southern Railway, 236 U.S. 115, 35 S.Ct. 255 (1915), were frequently cited for the proposition that it was not constitutionally permissible to hold a foreign corporation amenable to suit without its actual consent in the courts of a state for a cause of action unconnected with the business done in the state. Both of these cases, which are discussed in the International Shoe and the Perkins cases below, involved statutes providing that if a foreign corporation doing business in the state failed to designate an agent for service of process, service might be made upon a public official. In each case service upon a public official, no designation of an agent having been made, was held insufficient to subject the corporation to suit for a claim arising elsewhere. It is not wholly clear whether the decisions turned upon statutory interpretation or constitutional power. Moreover, mention was made in both cases of the fact that no notice to the corporation was given or required. On the other hand, Tauza v. Susquehanna Coal Co., 220 N.Y. 259, 115 N.E. 915 (1917) (Cardozo, J.), and certain

Supreme Court cases tended to affirm a state's authority over a foreign corporation doing business in the state as to a claim unconnected with that business, when service of process was made with statutory authorization upon an appropriate corporate official or agent. In Tauza, the defendant coal company was incorporated in Pennsylvania, but it had a branch office in New York City headed by a sales agent who had under him eight salesmen and also other stenographic and clerical personnel. Sales in New York were subject to confirmation by the home office in Pennsylvania, customer payments were made to the treasurer in Pennsylvania, and shipments were made from Pennsylvania. This activity was held to constitute doing business in New York and to make the corporation amenable to suit in New York on a cause of action having no relation to its New York business. Service on the sales agent in accordance with New York law was therefore upheld.

So, although the limits imposed by substantive due process were unclear, the consent and presence theories seemed to be running up against those limits. Indeed, in the early twentieth century the growing tendency to look directly at "doing business" as the relevant due process test facilitated the courts' restricting conservatively the states' powers over foreign corporations, a restriction that could be augmented simply by raising the threshold of necessary in-state activity. See generally Kalo, Jurisdiction as an Evolutionary Process: The Development of Quasi In Rem and In Personam Principles, 1978 Duke L.J. 1147.

INTERNATIONAL SHOE CO. v. WASHINGTON

Supreme Court of the United States, 1945.
326 U.S. 310, 66 S.Ct. 154.

MR. CHIEF JUSTICE STONE delivered the opinion of the Court.

The questions for decision are (1) whether, within the limitations of the due process clause of the Fourteenth Amendment, appellant, a Delaware corporation, has by its activities in the State of Washington rendered itself amenable to proceedings in the courts of that state to recover unpaid contributions to the state unemployment compensation fund exacted by state statutes, Washington Unemployment Compensation Act, Washington Revised Statutes, § 9998–103a through § 9998–123a, 1941 Supp., and (2) whether the state can exact those contributions consistently with the due process clause of the Fourteenth Amendment.

The statutes in question set up a comprehensive scheme of unemployment compensation, the costs of which are defrayed by contributions required to be made by employers to a state unemployment compensation fund. The contributions are a specified percentage of the wages payable annually by each employer for his employees' services in the state. The assessment and collection of the contributions and the fund are administered by appellees. Section 14(c) of the Act . . . authorizes appellee Commissioner to issue an order and notice of assessment of delinquent contributions upon prescribed personal service of the notice upon the employer if found within the state, or, if not so found, by mailing the notice to the employer by registered mail at his last known address.[v] That section also authorizes the Commissioner to collect the assessment by distraint if it is not paid within ten days after service of the notice. By §§ 14e and 6b the order of assessment may be administratively reviewed by an appeal tribunal within the office of unemployment upon petition of the employer, and this determination is by § 6i made subject to judicial review on questions of law by the state Superior Court, with further right of appeal in the state Supreme Court as in other civil cases.

In this case notice of assessment for the years in question was personally served upon a sales solicitor employed by appellant in the State of Washington, and a copy of the notice was mailed by registered mail to appellant at its address in St. Louis, Missouri. Appellant appeared specially before the office of unemployment and moved to set aside the order and notice of assessment on the ground that the service upon appellant's salesman was not proper service upon appellant; that appellant was not a corporation of the State of Washington and was not doing business within the state; that it had no agent within the state upon whom service could be made; and that appellant is not an employer and does not furnish employment within the meaning of the statute.

[margin note: Appellant arg.]

The motion was heard on evidence and stipulation of facts by the appeal tribunal which denied the motion and ruled that appellee Commissioner was entitled to recover the unpaid contributions. That action was affirmed by the Commissioner; both the Superior Court and the Supreme Court affirmed. 22 Wash.2d 146, 154 P.2d 801. Appellant in each of these courts assailed the statute as applied, as a violation of the due process clause of the Fourteenth Amendment, and as imposing a constitutionally prohibited burden on interstate commerce. The cause comes here on appeal under § 237(a) of the Judicial Code, 28 U.S.C. § 344(a),[w] appellant assigning as error that the challenged

[margin note: Prior Hist.]

---

[v] Section 14(c) of the Act stated: "At any time after the Commissioner shall find that any contribution or the interest thereon have become delinquent, the Commissioner may issue a notice of assessment specifying the amount due, which notice of assessment shall be served upon the delinquent employer in the manner prescribed for the service of summons in a civil action, except that if the employer cannot be found within the state, said notice will be deemed served when mailed to the delinquent employer at his last known address by registered mail." The Washington statute governing service of summons in a civil action upon a foreign corporation doing business in the state provided that the summons be served by delivery of a copy to any in-state agent, cashier, or secretary thereof. It will be observed that both methods of service referred to in § 14(c) were followed in the present case. See International Shoe Co. v. State, 22 Wash.2d 146, 151, 154 P.2d 801, 803 (1945).

[w] Now 28 U.S.C. § 1257(2).

statutes as applied infringe the due process clause of the Fourteenth Amendment and the commerce clause.

FACTS

The facts as found by the appeal tribunal and accepted by the state Superior Court and the Supreme Court, are not in dispute. Appellant is a Delaware corporation, having its principal place of business in St. Louis, Missouri, and is engaged in the manufacture and sale of shoes and other footwear. It maintains places of business in several states, other than Washington, at which its manufacturing is carried on and from which its merchandise is distributed interstate through several sales units or branches located outside the State of Washington.

Appellant has no office in Washington and makes no contracts either for sale or purchase of merchandise there. It maintains no stock of merchandise in that state and makes there no deliveries of goods in intrastate commerce. During the years from 1937 to 1940, now in question, appellant employed eleven to thirteen salesmen under direct supervision and control of sales managers located in St. Louis. These salesmen resided in Washington; their principal activities were confined to that state; and they were compensated by commissions based upon the amount of their sales. The commissions for each year totaled more than $31,000. Appellant supplies its salesmen with a line of samples, each consisting of one shoe of a pair, which they display to prospective purchasers. On occasion they rent permanent sample rooms, for exhibiting samples, in business buildings, or rent rooms in hotels or business buildings temporarily for that purpose. The cost of such rentals is reimbursed by appellant.

The authority of the salesmen is limited to exhibiting their samples and soliciting orders from prospective buyers, at prices and on terms fixed by appellant. The salesmen transmit the orders to appellant's office in St. Louis for acceptance or rejection, and when accepted the merchandise for filling the orders is shipped f.o.b. from points outside Washington to the purchasers within the state. All the merchandise shipped into Washington is invoiced at the place of shipment from which collections are made. No salesman has authority to enter into contracts or to make collections.

S ct. of wash: taking off orders off what to mean doing business in State

The Supreme Court of Washington was of opinion that the regular and systematic solicitation of orders in the state by appellant's salesmen, resulting in a continuous flow of appellant's product into the state, was sufficient to constitute doing business in the state so as to make appellant amenable to suit in its courts. But it was also of opinion that there were sufficient additional activities shown to bring the case within the rule frequently stated, that solicitation within a state by the agents of a foreign corporation plus some additional activities there are sufficient to render the corporation amenable to suit brought in the courts of the state to enforce an obligation arising out of its activities there. International Harvester Co. v. Kentucky, 234 U.S. 579, 587, 34 S.Ct. 944, 946; People's Tobacco Co. v. American

Tobacco Co., 246 U.S. 79, 87, 38 S.Ct. 233, 235; Frene v. Louisville Cement Co., 77 U.S.App.D.C. 129, 134 F.2d 511, 516. The court found such additional activities in the salesmen's display of samples sometimes in permanent display rooms, and the salesmen's residence within the state, continued over a period of years, all resulting in a substantial volume of merchandise regularly shipped by appellant to purchasers within the state. The court also held that the statute as applied did not invade the constitutional power of Congress to regulate interstate commerce and did not impose a prohibited burden on such commerce.

Appellant's argument, renewed here, that the statute imposes an unconstitutional burden on interstate commerce need not detain us. For 53 Stat. 1391, 26 U.S.C. § 1606(a) provides that "No person required under a State law to make payments to an unemployment fund shall be relieved from compliance therewith on the ground that he is engaged in interstate or foreign commerce, or that the State law does not distinguish between employees engaged in interstate or foreign commerce and those engaged in intrastate commerce." It is no longer debatable that Congress, in the exercise of the commerce power, may authorize the states, in specified ways, to regulate interstate commerce or impose burdens upon it. [Citations omitted.]

Appellant also insists that its activities within the state were not sufficient to manifest its "presence" there and that in its absence the state courts were without jurisdiction, that consequently it was a denial of due process for the state to subject appellant to suit. It refers to those cases in which it was said that the mere solicitation of orders for the purchase of goods within a state, to be accepted without the state and filled by shipment of the purchased goods interstate, does not render the corporation seller amenable to suit within the state. See Green v. Chicago, B. & Q.R. Co., 205 U.S. 530, 533, 27 S.Ct. 595, 596; International Harvester Co. v. Kentucky, supra, 234 U.S. 586, 587, 34 S.Ct. 946; Philadelphia & Reading R. Co. v. McKibbin, 243 U.S. 264, 268, 37 S.Ct. 280; People's Tobacco Co. v. American Tobacco Co., supra, 246 U.S. 87, 38 S.Ct. 235. And appellant further argues that since it was not present within the state, it is a denial of due process to subject it to taxation or other money exaction. It thus denies the power of the state to lay the tax or to subject appellant to a suit for its collection.

Historically the jurisdiction of courts to render judgment in personam is grounded on their de facto power over the defendant's person. Hence his presence within the territorial jurisdiction of a court was prerequisite to its rendition of a judgment personally binding him. Pennoyer v. Neff, 95 U.S. 714, 733. But now that the capias ad respondendum has given way to personal service of summons or other form of notice, due process requires only that in order to subject a defendant to a judgment in personam, if he be not present within the territory of the forum, he have certain minimum contacts with it such that the maintenance of the suit does not offend "traditional notions of fair play and substantial justice." Milliken v. Meyer, 311 U.S. 457, 463, 61 S.Ct. 339, 343. See Holmes, J., in McDonald v. Mabee, 243 U.S. 90, 91, 37 S.Ct. 343. Compare Hoopeston Canning Co. v. Cullen, 318 U.S. 313, 316, 319, 63 S.Ct. 602, 604, 606. See Blackmer v. United States, 284 U.S. 421, 52 S.Ct. 252; Hess v. Pawloski, 274 U.S. 352, 47 S.Ct. 632; Young v. Masci, 289 U.S. 253, 53 S.Ct. 599.

Since the corporate personality is a fiction, although a fiction intended to be acted upon as though it were a fact, Klein v. Board of Supervisors, 282 U.S. 19, 24, 51 S.Ct. 15, 16, it is clear that unlike an individual its "presence" without, as well as within, the state of its origin can be manifested only by activities carried on in its behalf by those who are authorized to act for it. To say that the corporation is so far "present" there as to satisfy due process requirements, for purposes of taxation or the maintenance of suits against it in the courts of the state, is to beg the question to be decided. For the terms "present" or "presence" are used merely to symbolize those activities of the corporation's agent within the state which courts will deem to be sufficient to satisfy the demands of due process. L. Hand, J., in Hutchinson v. Chase & Gilbert, 45 F.2d 139, 141. Those demands may be met by such contacts of the corporation with the state of the forum as make it reasonable, in the context of our federal system of government, to require the corporation to defend the particular suit which is brought there. An "estimate of the inconveniences" which would result to the corporation from a trial away from its "home" or principal place of business is relevant in this connection. Hutchinson v. Chase & Gilbert, supra, 45 F.2d 141.

"Presence" in the state in this sense has never been doubted when the activities of the corporation there have not only been continuous and systematic, but also give rise to the liabilities sued on, even though no consent to be sued or authorization to an agent to accept service of process has been given. St. Clair v. Cox, 106 U.S. 350, 355, 1 S.Ct. 354, 359; Connecticut Mutual Life Ins. Co. v. Spratley, 172 U.S. 602, 610–11, 19 S.Ct. 308, 311–12; Pennsylvania Lumbermen's Mut. Fire Ins. Co. v. Meyer, 197 U.S. 407, 414–415, 25 S.Ct. 483, 484–85; Commercial Mutual Accident Co. v. Davis, 213 U.S. 245, 255–256, 29 S.Ct. 445, 448; International Harvester Co. v. Kentucky, supra; cf. St. Louis S.W.R. Co. v. Alexander, 227 U.S. 218, 33 S.Ct. 245. Conversely it has been generally recognized that the casual presence of the corporate agent or even his conduct of single or isolated items of activities in a state in the corporation's behalf are not enough to subject it to suit on causes of action unconnected with the activities there. St. Clair v. Cox, supra, 106 U.S. 359, 360, 1 S.Ct. 362, 363; Old Wayne Mut. Life Ass'n v. McDonough, 204 U.S. 8, 21, 27 S.Ct. 236, 240; Frene v. Louisville Cement Co., supra, 134 F.2d 515, and cases cited. To require the corporation in such circumstances to defend the suit away from its home or other jurisdiction where it carries on more substantial activities has been thought to lay too great and unreasonable a burden on the corporation to comport with due process.

While it has been held, in cases on which appellant relies, that continuous activity of some sort within a state is not enough to support the demand that the corporation be amenable to suits unrelated to that activity, Old Wayne Mut. Life Ass'n v. McDonough, supra; Green v. Chicago, B. & Q.R. Co., supra; Simon v. Southern R. Co., 236 U.S. 115, 35 S.Ct. 255; People's Tobacco Co. v. American Tobacco Co., supra; cf. Davis v. Farmers Co-operative Co., 262 U.S. 312, 317, 43 S.Ct. 556, 558, there have been instances in which the continuous corporate operations within a state were thought so substantial and of such a nature as to justify suit against it on causes of action arising from dealings entirely distinct from those activities. See Missouri, K. & T.R. Co. v. Reynolds, 255 U.S. 565, 41 S.Ct. 446; Tauza v. Susquehanna Coal Co., 220 N.Y. 259, 115 N.E. 915; cf. St. Louis S.W.R. Co. v. Alexander, supra.

Finally, although the commission of some single or occasional acts of the corporate agent in a state sufficient to impose an obligation or liability on the corporation has not been thought to confer upon the state authority to enforce it, Rosenberg Bros. & Co. v. Curtis Brown Co., 260 U.S. 516, 43 S.Ct. 170, other such acts, because of their nature and quality and the circumstances of their commission, may be deemed sufficient to render the corporation liable to suit. Cf. Kane v. New Jersey, 242 U.S. 160, 37 S.Ct. 30; Hess v. Pawloski, supra; Young v. Masci, supra. True, some of the decisions holding the corporation amenable to suit have been supported by resort to the legal fiction that it has given its consent to service and suit, consent being implied from its presence in the state through the acts of its authorized agents. Lafayette Insurance Co. v. French, 18 How. 404, 407; St. Clair v. Cox, supra, 106 U.S. 356, 1 S.Ct. 359; Commercial Mutual Co. v. Davis, supra, 213 U.S. 254, 29 S.Ct. 447; Washington v. Superior Court, 289 U.S. 361, 364–365, 53 S.Ct. 624, 626–627. But more realistically it may be said that those authorized acts were of such a nature as to justify the fiction. Smolik v. Philadelphia & Reading Co., 222 F. 148, 151. Henderson, The Position of Foreign Corporations in American Constitutional Law, 94–95.

It is evident that the criteria by which we mark the boundary line between those activities which justify the subjection of a corporation to suit, and those which do not, cannot be simply mechanical or quantitative. The test is not merely, as has sometimes been suggested, whether the activity, which the corporation has seen fit to procure through its agents in another state, is a little more or a little less. St. Louis S.W.R. Co. v. Alexander, supra, 227 U.S. 228, 33 S.Ct. 248; International Harvester Co. v. Kentucky, supra, 234 U.S. 587, 34 S.Ct. 946. Whether due process is satisfied must depend rather upon the *Rule* quality and nature of the activity in relation to the fair and orderly administration of the laws which it was the purpose of the due process clause to insure.) That clause does not contemplate that a state may make binding a judgment in personam against an individual or corporate defendant with which the state has no contacts, ties, or relations.   Cf. Pennoyer v. Neff, supra; Minnesota Commercial Ass'n v. Benn, 261 U.S. 140, 43 S.Ct. 293.

But to the extent that a corporation exercises the privilege of conducting activities within a state, it enjoys the benefits and protection of the laws of that state. The exercise of that privilege may give rise to obligations, and, so far as those obligations arise out of or are connected with the activities within the state, a procedure which requires the corporation to respond to a suit brought to enforce them can, in most instances, hardly be said to be undue. Compare International Harvester Co. v. Kentucky, supra, with Green v. Chicago, B. & Q.R. Co., supra, and People's Tobacco Co. v. American Tobacco Co., supra. Compare Connecticut Mutual Life Ins. Co. v. Spratley, supra, 172 U.S. 619, 620, 19 S.Ct. 314, 315 and Commercial Mutual Accident Co. v. Davis, supra, with Old Wayne Life Ass'n v. McDonough, supra. See 29 Columbia Law Review, 187–195.

Applying these standards, the activities carried on in behalf of appellant in the State of Washington were neither irregular nor casual. They were systematic and continuous throughout the years in question. They resulted in a large volume of interstate business, in the course of which appellant received the benefits and protection of the laws of the state, including the right to resort to the courts for the enforcement of its rights. The obligation which is here sued upon arose out of those very activities. It is evident that these operations establish sufficient contacts or ties with the state of the forum to make it reasonable and just, according to our traditional conception of fair play and substantial justice, to permit the state to enforce the obligations which appellant has incurred there. Hence we cannot say that the maintenance of the present suit in the State of Washington involves an unreasonable or undue procedure.

We are likewise unable to conclude that the service of the process within the state upon an agent whose activities establish appellant's "presence" there was not sufficient notice of the suit, or that the suit was so unrelated to those activities as to make the agent an inappropriate vehicle for communicating the notice. It is enough that appellant has established such contacts with the state that the particular form of substituted service adopted there gives reasonable assurance that the notice will be actual. Connecticut Mutual Life Ins. Co. v. Spratley, supra, 172 U.S. 618, 619, 19 S.Ct. 314, 315; Board of Trade v. Hammond Elevator Co., 198 U.S. 424, 437–438, 25 S.Ct. 740, 743– 744; Commercial Mutual Accident Co. v. Davis, supra, 213 U.S. 254– 255, 29 S.Ct. 447–448. Cf. Riverside & Dan River Cotton Mills v. Menefee, 237 U.S. 189, 194, 195, 35 S.Ct. 579, 580, 581; see Knowles v. Gaslight & Coke Co., 19 Wall. 58, 61; McDonald v. Mabee, supra; Milliken v. Meyer, supra. Nor can we say that the mailing of the notice of suit to appellant by registered mail at its home office was not reasonably calculated to apprise appellant of the suit. Compare Hess v. Pawloski, supra, with McDonald v. Mabee, supra, 243 U.S. 92, 37 S.Ct. 344, and Wuchter v. Pizzutti, 276 U.S. 13, 19, 24, 48 S.Ct. 259, 260, 262; cf. Becquet v. MacCarthy, 2 B. & Ad. 951; Maubourquet v. Wyse, 1 Ir.Rep.C.L. 471. See Washington v. Superior Court, supra, 289 U.S. 365, 53 S.Ct. 626.

Only a word need be said of appellant's liability for the demanded contributions to the state unemployment fund. The Supreme Court of Washington, construing and applying the statute, has held that it imposes a tax on the privilege of employing appellant's salesmen within the state measured by a percentage of the wages, here the commissions payable to the salesmen. This construction we accept for purposes of determining the constitutional validity of the statute. The right to employ labor has been deemed an appropriate subject of taxation in this country and England, both before and since the adoption of the Constitution. Steward Machine Co. v. Davis, 301 U.S. 548, 579 et seq., 57 S.Ct. 883, 887 et seq. And such a tax imposed upon the employer for unemployment benefits is within the constitutional power of the states. Carmichael v. Southern Coal & Coke Co., 301 U.S. 495, 508 et seq., 57 S.Ct. 868, 871 et seq.

Appellant having rendered itself amenable to suit upon obligations arising out of the activities of its salesmen in Washington, the state may maintain the present suit in personam to collect the tax laid upon the exercise of the privilege of employing appellant's salesmen within the state. For Washington has made one of those activities, which taken together establish appellant's "presence" there for purposes of suit, the taxable event by which the state brings appellant within the reach of its taxing power. The state thus has constitutional power to lay the tax and to subject appellant to a suit to recover it. The activities which establish its "presence" subject it alike to taxation by the state and to suit to recover the tax. [Citations omitted.]

Affirmed.

MR. JUSTICE JACKSON took no part in the consideration or decision of this case.

MR. JUSTICE BLACK delivered the following opinion.

. . . Nor is the further ground advanced on this appeal, that the State of Washington has denied appellant due process of law, any less devoid of substance [than the claim that imposition of the tax violates the commerce clause]. It is my view, therefore, that we should dismiss the appeal as unsubstantial, Seaboard Air Line R. Co. v. Watson, 287 U.S. 86, 90, 92, 53 S.Ct. 32, 34, 35, and decline the invitation to formulate broad rules as to the meaning of due process, which here would amount to deciding a constitutional question "in advance of the necessity for its decision." Alabama State Federation of Labor v. McAdory, 325 U.S. 450, 461, 65 S.Ct. 1384, 1389.

Certainly appellant cannot in the light of our past decisions meritoriously claim that notice by registered mail and by personal service on its sales solicitors in Washington did not meet the requirements of procedural due process. And the due process clause is not brought in issue any more by appellant's further conceptualistic contention that Washington could not levy a tax or bring suit against the corporation because it did not honor that State with its mystical "presence." For it is unthinkable that the vague due process clause was ever intended to prohibit a State from regulating or taxing a business carried on within its boundaries simply because this is done by agents of a corporation organized and having its headquarters elsewhere. To read this into the due process clause would in fact result in depriving a State's citizens of due process by taking from the State the power to protect them in their business dealings within its boundaries with representatives of a foreign corporation. Nothing could be more irrational or more designed to defeat the function of our federative system of government. Certainly a State, at the very least, has power to tax and sue those dealing with its citizens within its boundaries, as we have held before. Hoopeston Canning Co. v. Cullen, 318 U.S. 313, 63 S.Ct. 602. Were the Court to follow this principle, it would provide a workable standard for cases where, as here, no other questions are involved. The Court has not chosen to do so, but instead had engaged in an unnecessary discussion in the course of which it has announced vague Constitutional criteria applied for the first time to the issue before us. It has thus introduced uncertain elements confusing the simple pattern and tending to curtail the exercise of State powers to an extent not justified by the Constitution.

Majority Rule

The criteria adopted insofar as they can be identified read as follows: Due Process does permit State courts to "enforce the obligations which appellant has incurred" if it be found "reasonable and just according to our traditional conception of fair play and substantial justice." And this in turn means that we will "permit" the State to act if upon "an 'estimate of the inconveniences' which would result to the corporation from a trial away from its 'home' or principal place of business," we conclude that it is "reasonable" to subject it to suit in a State where it is doing business.

It is true that this Court did use the terms "fair play" and "substantial justice" in explaining the philosophy underlying the holding that it could not be "due process of law" to render a personal judgment against a defendant without notice and an opportunity to be heard. Milliken v. Meyer, 311 U.S. 457, 61 S.Ct. 339. In McDonald v. Mabee, 243 U.S. 90, 91, 37 S.Ct. 343, cited in the Milliken case, Mr. Justice Holmes, speaking for the Court, warned against judicial curtailment of this opportunity to be heard and referred to such a curtailment as a denial of "fair play," which even the common law would have deemed "contrary to natural justice." And previous cases had indicated that the ancient rule against judgments without notice had stemmed from "natural justice" concepts. These cases, while giving additional reasons why notice under particular circumstances is inadequate, did not mean thereby that all legislative enactments which this Court might deem to be contrary to natural justice ought to be held invalid under the due process clause. None of the cases purport to support or could support a holding that a State can tax and sue corporations only if its action comports with this Court's notions of "natural justice." I should have thought the Tenth Amendment settled that.

I believe that the Federal Constitution leaves to each State, without any "ifs" or "buts," a power to tax and to open the doors of its courts for its citizens to sue corporations whose agents do business in those States. Believing that the Constitution gave the States that power, I think it a judicial deprivation to condition its exercise upon this Court's notion of "fair play," however appealing that term may be. Nor can I stretch the meaning of due process so far as to authorize this Court to deprive a State of the right to afford judicial protection to its citizens on the ground that it would be more "convenient" for the corporation to be sued somewhere else.

There is a strong emotional appeal in the words "fair play," "justice," [x] and "reasonable." But they were not chosen by those who wrote the original Constitution or the Fourteenth Amendment as a measuring rod for the Court to use in invalidating State or Federal laws passed by elected legislative representatives. No one, not even those who most feared a democratic government, ever formally proposed that courts should be given power to invalidate legislation under any such elastic standards. Express prohibitions against certain types of legislation are found in the Constitution, and under the long-settled practice, courts invalidate laws found to conflict with them. This requires interpretation, and interpretation, it is true, may result in extension of the Constitution's purpose. But that is no reason for reading the due process clause so as to restrict a State's power to tax and sue those whose activities affect persons and businesses within the State, provided proper service can be had. Superimposing the natural justice concept on the Constitution's specific prohibitions could operate as a drastic abridgment of democratic safeguards they embody, such as freedom of speech, press and religion, and the right to counsel. This has already happened. Betts v. Brady, 316 U.S. 455, 62 S.Ct. 1252. Compare Feldman v. United States, 322 U.S. 487, 494–503, 64 S.Ct. 1082, 1085–1089. For application of this natural law concept, whether under the terms "reasonableness," "justice," or "fair play," makes judges the supreme arbiters of the country's laws and practices. Polk Co. v. Glover, 305 U.S. 5, 17–18, 59 S.Ct. 15, 20–21; Federal Power Commission v. Natural Gas Pipeline Co., 315 U.S.

---

[x] Justice Holmes wrote to Dr. Wu on July 1, 1929, "I have said to my brethren many times that I hate justice, which means that I know if a man begins to talk about that, for one reason or another he is shirking thinking in legal terms." Justice Oliver Wendell Holmes: His Book Notices and Uncollected Letters and Papers 201 (H. Shriver ed. 1936).

575, 600, n. 4, 62 S.Ct. 736, 750, n. 4. This result, I believe, alters the form of government our Constitution provides. I cannot agree.

True, the State's power is here upheld. But the rule announced means that tomorrow's judgment may strike down a State or Federal enactment on the ground that it does not conform to this Court's idea of natural justice. I therefore find myself moved by the same fears that caused Mr. Justice Holmes to say in 1930:

"I have not yet adequately expressed the more than anxiety that I feel at the ever increasing scope given to the Fourteenth Amendment in cutting down what I believe to be the constitutional rights of the States. As the decisions now stand, I see hardly any limit but the sky to the invalidating of those rights if they happen to strike a majority of this Court as for any reason undesirable." Baldwin v. Missouri, 281 U.S. 586, 595, 50 S.Ct. 436, 439.

ADDITIONAL CONSTITUTIONAL LIMITATIONS: COMMERCE CLAUSE AND FIRST AMENDMENT

As suggested by the International Shoe case, constitutional bounds on a state's exercise of judicial authority over a foreign corporation may exist quite apart from the due process clause. In Davis v. Farmers Co-operative Equity Co., 262 U.S. 312, 43 S.Ct. 556 (1923), a Kansas plaintiff sued a Kansas railroad corporation in a Minnesota state court for a cause of action arising in Kansas. The railroad did not own or operate any lines in Minnesota, but it did maintain an agent there solely for the solicitation of traffic. The Supreme Court held that a statute authorizing service on the agent "imposes upon interstate commerce a serious and unreasonable burden which renders the statute obnoxious to the commerce clause." The commerce clause was more recently so relied on as an alternative ground for dismissal in Bryson v. Northlake Hilton, 407 F.Supp. 73 (M.D.N.C. 1976). Otherwise, the commerce clause has only very rarely been invoked for such purpose, and its continuing vitality as an independent limitation on a state's exercise of judicial authority is somewhat in doubt. It seems unlikely that the commerce clause would be invoked so to dismiss in a situation where the due process clause has been satisfied.

The first amendment also has sometimes been thought to place a limitation on a state's exercise of territorial jurisdiction over a foreign corporation, this limitation being imposed, for example, to ensure the free flow of information throughout the country. In New York Times Co. v. Connor, 365 F.2d 567, 572 (5th Cir.1966), which was a libel case against a newspaper, the Fifth Circuit described its view of the way in which the first amendment restricts a state in its exercise of territorial jurisdiction: "First Amendment considerations surrounding the law of libel require a greater showing of contact to satisfy the due process clause than is necessary in asserting jurisdiction over other types of tortious activity." While agreeing that the first amendment has a role in this area, the Second Circuit, in Buckley v. New York Post Corp., 373 F.2d 175 (2d Cir.1967), took a slightly different approach by suggesting that, with respect to a state's authority to entertain a libel case, the first amendment imposed a restriction independent of that imposed by the due process clause. Cf. Environmental Research International, Inc. v. Lockwood Greene Engineers, Inc., 355 A.2d 808 (D.C.1976) (mere dealings with a federal regulatory agency do not expose defendant to a related private contract action brought at capital, in view of first amendment right to petition for redress of grievances). However, the Supreme Court now has put a halt to such approaches, at least in libel cases. Calder v. Jones, 104 S.Ct. 1482 (1984) ("We . . . reject the suggestion that First Amendment concerns enter into the jurisdictional analysis. The infusion of such considerations would needlessly complicate an already imprecise inquiry. [Citation omitted.] Moreover, the potential chill on protected First Amendment activity stemming from libel and defamation actions is already taken into account in the constitutional limitations on the substantive law governing such suits."); see also Keeton v. Hustler Magazine, Inc., 104 S.Ct. 1473 (1984) (nonresident individual can bring a libel action against nonresident magazine in New Hampshire, where there is a uniquely long statute of limitations but where sales of magazine are only ten to fifteen thousand per month).

PERKINS v. BENGUET CONSOLIDATED MINING CO.

Supreme Court of the United States, 1952.
342 U.S. 437, 72 S.Ct. 413.

MR. JUSTICE BURTON delivered the opinion of the Court.

This case calls for an answer to the question whether the Due Process Clause of the Fourteenth Amendment to the Constitution of the United States precludes Ohio from subjecting a foreign corporation to the jurisdiction of its courts in this action in personam. The corporation has been carrying on in Ohio a continuous and systematic, but limited, part of its general business. Its president, while engaged in doing such business in Ohio, has been served with summons in this proceeding. The cause of action sued upon did not arise in Ohio and does not relate to the corporation's activities there. For the reasons hereafter stated, we hold that the Fourteenth Amendment leaves Ohio free to take or decline jurisdiction over the corporation.

After extended litigation elsewhere petitioner, Idonah Slade Perkins, a non-resident of Ohio, filed two actions in personam in the Court of Common Pleas of Clermont County, Ohio, against the several respondents. Among those sued is the Benguet Consolidated Min-

ing Company, here called the mining company. It is styled a "socie-
dad anonima" under the laws of the Philippine Islands, where it owns
and has operated profitable gold and silver mines. In one action petitioner seeks approximately $68,400 in dividends claimed to be due her
as a stockholder. In the other she claims $2,500,000 damages largely
because of the company's failure to issue to her certificates for
120,000 shares of its stock.[y]

In each case the trial court sustained a motion to quash the service of summons on the mining company. Ohio Com.Pl., 99 N.E.2d
515. The Court of Appeals of Ohio affirmed that decision, 88 Ohio
App. 118, 95 N.E.2d 5, as did the Supreme Court of Ohio, 155 Ohio St.
116, 98 N.E.2d 33. The cases were consolidated and we granted certiorari . . . . 342 U.S. 808, 72 S.Ct. 33.

We start with the holding of the Supreme Court of Ohio, not contested here, that, under Ohio law, the mining company is to be treated as a foreign corporation. Actual notice of the proceeding was giv-
en to the corporation in the instant case through regular service of
summons upon its president while he was in Ohio acting in that capacity. Accordingly, there can be no jurisdictional objection based
upon a lack of notice to a responsible representative of the corporation.

The answer to the question of whether the state courts of Ohio
are open to a proceeding in personam, against an amply notified foreign corporation, to enforce a cause of action not arising in Ohio and
not related to the business or activities of the corporation in that
State rests entirely upon the law of Ohio, unless the Due Process
Clause of the Fourteenth Amendment compels a decision either way.

The suggestion that federal due process *compels* the State to
open its courts to such a case has no substance.

"Provisions for making foreign corporations subject to service in
the state is a matter of legislative discretion, and a failure to provide for such service is not a denial of due process. Still less is it
incumbent upon a state in furnishing such process to make the
jurisdiction over the foreign corporation wide enough to include
the adjudication of transitory actions not arising in the state."
Missouri P.R. Co. v. Clarendon Co., 257 U.S. 533, 535, 42 S.Ct. 210,
211.

Also without merit is the argument that merely because Ohio permits
a complainant to maintain a proceeding in personam in its courts
against a properly served non-resident natural person to enforce a
cause of action which does not arise out of anything done in Ohio,
therefore, the Constitution of the United States *compels* Ohio to provide like relief against a foreign corporation.

[y] The briefs explain that behind these
two actions lay a marital dispute. Essentially, Mrs. Perkins was claiming that the
mining company should have paid certain
cash and stock dividends, when declared
before World War II, to her rather than
to her husband.

A more serious question is presented by the claim that the Due Process Clause of the Fourteenth Amendment *prohibits* Ohio from granting such relief against a foreign corporation. The . . . report of the case below, while denying the relief sought, does not indicate whether the Supreme Court of Ohio rested its decision on Ohio law or on the Fourteenth Amendment. . . .

. . . .

. . . Accordingly, for us to allow the judgment to stand as it is would risk an affirmance of a decision which might have been decided differently if the court below had felt free, under our decisions, to do so.

The cases [supporting the result] below are Old Wayne Life Ass'n v. McDonough, 204 U.S. 8, 27 S.Ct. 236, and Simon v. Southern R. Co., 236 U.S. 115, 35 S.Ct. 255. Unlike the case at bar, no actual notice of the proceedings was received in those cases by a responsible representative of the foreign corporation. In each case, the public official who was served with process in an attempt to bind the foreign corporation was held to lack the necessary authority to accept service so as to bind it in a proceeding to enforce a cause of action arising outside of the state of the forum. See 204 U.S. at pages 22–23, 27 S.Ct. at pages 240–241, and 236 U.S. at page 130, 35 S.Ct. at page 260. The necessary result was a finding of inadequate service in each case and a conclusion that the foreign corporation was not bound by it. The same would be true today in a like proceeding where the only service had and the only notice given was that directed to a public official who had no authority, by statute or otherwise, to accept it in that kind of a proceeding. At the time of rendering the above decisions this Court was aided, in reaching its conclusion as to the limited scope of the statutory authority of the public officials, by this Court's conception that the Due Process Clause of the Fourteenth Amendment precluded a state from giving its public officials authority to accept service in terms broad enough to bind a foreign corporation in proceedings against it to enforce an obligation arising outside of the state of the forum. That conception now has been modified by the rationale adopted in later decisions and particularly in International Shoe Co. v. Washington, 326 U.S. 310, 66 S.Ct. 154.

[Today if an authorized representative of a foreign corporation be physically present in the state of the forum and be there engaged in activities appropriate to accepting service or receiving notice on its behalf, we recognize that there is no unfairness in subjecting that corporation to the jurisdiction of the courts of that state through such service of process upon that representative. This has been squarely held to be so in a proceeding in personam against such a corporation, at least in relation to a cause of action arising out of the corporation's activities within the state of the forum.]

The essence of the issue here, at the constitutional level, is a like one of general fairness to the corporation. Appropriate tests for that are discussed in International Shoe Co. v. Washington, supra, 326 U.S. at pages 317–320, 66 S.Ct. at pages 158–160. The amount and kind of activities which must be carried on by the foreign corporation in the state of the forum so as to make it reasonable and just to subject the corporation to the jurisdiction of that state are to be determined in each case. The corporate activities of a foreign corporation which, under state statute, make it necessary for it to secure a license and to designate a statutory agent upon whom process may be served provide a helpful but not a conclusive test. For example, the state of the forum may by statute require a foreign mining corporation to secure a license in order lawfully to carry on there such functional intrastate operations as those of mining or refining ore. On the other hand, if the same corporation carries on, in that state, other continuous and systematic corporate activities as it did here—consisting of directors' meetings, business correspondence, banking, stock transfers, payment of salaries, purchasing of machinery, etc.—those activities are enough to make it fair and reasonable to subject that corporation to proceedings in personam in that state, at least insofar as the proceedings in personam seek to enforce causes of action relating to those very activities or to other activities of the corporation within the state.

. . . .

It remains only to consider, in more detail, the issue of whether, as a matter of federal due process, the business done in Ohio by the respondent mining company was sufficiently substantial and of such a nature as to *permit* Ohio to entertain a cause of action against a foreign corporation, where the cause of action arose from activities entirely distinct from its activities in Ohio. See International Shoe Co. v. Washington, supra, 326 U.S. at page 318, 66 S.Ct. at page 159.

The Ohio Court of Appeals summarized the evidence on the subject. 88 Ohio App. at pages 119–125, 95 N.E.2d at pages 6–9. From that summary the following facts are substantially beyond controversy: The company's mining properties were in the Philippine Islands. Its operations there were completely halted during the occupation of the Islands by the Japanese. During that interim the president, who was also the general manager and principal stockholder of the company, returned to his home in Clermont County, Ohio. There he maintained an office in which he conducted his personal affairs and did many things on behalf of the company. He kept there office files of the company. He carried on there correspondence relating to the business of the company and to its employees. He drew and distributed there salary checks on behalf of the company, both in his own favor as president and in favor of two company secretaries who worked there with him. He used and maintained in Clermont County, Ohio, two active bank accounts carrying substantial balances of company funds. A bank in Hamilton County, Ohio, acted as transfer agent for the stock of the company. Several directors' meetings were held at his office or home in Clermont County. From that office he supervised policies dealing with the rehabilitation of the corporation's properties in the Philippines and he dispatched funds to cover purchases of machinery for such rehabilitation. [Thus he carried on in Ohio a continuous and systematic supervision of the necessarily limited wartime activities of the company] He there discharged his duties as president and general manager, both during the occupation of the company's properties by the Japanese and immediately thereafter. While no mining properties in Ohio were owned or operated by the company, many of its wartime activities were directed from Ohio and were being given the personal attention of its president in that State at the time he was served with summons [in 1947]. Consideration of the circumstances which, under the law of Ohio, ultimately will determine whether the courts of that State will choose to take jurisdiction over the corporation is reserved for the courts of that State. Without reaching that issue of state policy, we conclude that, under the circumstances above recited, it would not violate federal due process for Ohio either to take or decline jurisdiction of the corporation in this proceeding.] This relieves the Ohio courts of the restriction . . . which may have influenced the judgment of the court below.

Accordingly, the judgment of the Supreme Court of Ohio is vacated and the cause is remanded to that court for further proceedings in the light of this opinion.

It is so ordered.[z]

MR. JUSTICE BLACK concurs in the result.

[The dissenting opinion of Justice Minton, with whom Chief Justice Vinson joined, is omitted.]

Question: (32) *P* of Florida sues *D*, a drug manufacturer incorporated in Delaware with its principal place of business in Connecticut, in a South Carolina federal court for over $10,000 on account of alleged injuries suffered from the consumption of drugs manufactured by *D*, and purchased and consumed in Florida by *P*. *D*'s activities in South Carolina are limited to solicitation by mail to South Carolina dealers and wholesalers, and the mailing of promotional literature to about 650 South Carolina doctors on its mailing lists. South Carolina has a six-year statute of limitations, which has not expired; the shorter statutes of all other states having any connection with the claim have run. *P* serves process pursuant to a South Carolina long-arm statute, which its highest court has held to go to the outer limits of due process; the long-arm statute is invoked under Rule 4(e). *D* moves to set aside the service and dismiss the complaint for lack of personal jurisdiction. What should the decision be? See Ratliff v. Cooper Laboratories, 444 F.2d 745 (4th Cir.) (grant motion), cert. denied, 404 U.S. 948, 92 S.Ct. 271 (1971); see also Helicopteros Nacionales de Colombia, S.A. v. Hall, 104 S.Ct. 1868 (1984).

---

[z] On remand the defendant's motion to quash the service of summons was de- nied, 158 Ohio St. 145, 107 N.E.2d 203 (1952).

McGEE v. INTERNATIONAL LIFE INSURANCE CO.
Supreme Court of the United States, 1957.
355 U.S. 220, 78 S.Ct. 199.

MR. JUSTICE BLACK delivered the opinion of the Court.

Petitioner, Lulu B. McGee, recovered a judgment in a California state court against respondent, International Life Insurance Company, on a contract of insurance. Respondent was not served with process in California but by registered mail at its principal place of business in Texas. The California court based its jurisdiction on a state statute which subjects foreign corporations to suit in California on insurance contracts with residents of that State even though such corporations cannot be served with process within its borders.[1] Unable to collect the judgment in California petitioner went to Texas where she filed suit on the judgment in a Texas court. But the Texas courts refused to enforce her judgment holding it was void under the Fourteenth Amendment because service of process outside California could not give the courts of that State jurisdiction over respondent. Since the case raised important questions, not only to California but to other States which have similar laws, we granted certiorari. 352 U.S. 924, 77 S.Ct. 239. It is not controverted that if the California court properly exercised jurisdiction over respondent the Texas courts erred in refusing to give its judgment full faith and credit. 28 U.S.C. § 1738.

The material facts are relatively simple. In 1944, Lowell Franklin, a resident of California, purchased a life insurance policy from the Empire Mutual Insurance Company, an Arizona corporation. In 1948 the respondent agreed with Empire Mutual to assume its insurance obligations. Respondent then mailed a reinsurance certificate to Franklin in California offering to insure him in accordance with the terms of the policy he held with Empire Mutual. He accepted this offer and from that time until his death in 1950 paid premiums by mail from his California home to respondent's Texas office. Petitioner, Franklin's mother, was the beneficiary under the policy.[a] She sent proofs of his death to the respondent but it refused to pay claiming that he had committed suicide. It appears that neither Empire Mutual nor respondent has ever had any offices or agents in California. And so far as the record before us shows, respondent has never solicited or done any insurance business in California apart from the policy involved here.

Since Pennoyer v. Neff, 95 U.S. 714, this Court has held that the Due Process Clause of the Fourteenth Amendment places some limit on the power of state courts to enter binding judgments against persons not served with process within their boundaries. But just where

---

[1] Cal.Insurance Code, West's Anno. §§ 1610–1620.

[a] She was a California resident. See McGee v. International Life Ins. Co., 288 S.W.2d 579, 580 (Tex.Ct.App.1956).

this line of limitation falls has been the subject of prolific controversy, particularly with respect to foreign corporations. In the continuing process of evolution this Court accepted and then abandoned "consent," "doing business," and "presence" as the standard for measuring the extent of state judicial power over such corporations. See Henderson, The Position of Foreign Corporations in American Constitutional Law, c. V. More recently in International Shoe Co. v. State of Washington, 326 U.S. 310, 66 S.Ct. 154, the Court decided that "due process requires only that in order to subject a defendant to a judgment in personam, if he be not present within the territory of the forum, he have certain minimum contacts with it such that the maintenance of the suit does not offend 'traditional notions of fair play and substantial justice.'" Id., 326 U.S. at page 316, 66 S.Ct. at page 158.

Looking back over this long history of litigation a trend is clearly discernible toward expanding the permissible scope of state jurisdiction over foreign corporations and other nonresidents. In part this is attributable to the fundamental transformation of our national economy over the years. Today many commercial transactions touch two or more States and may involve parties separated by the full continent. With this increasing nationalization of commerce has come a great increase in the amount of business conducted by mail across state lines. At the same time modern transportation and communication have made it much less burdensome for a party sued to defend himself in a State where he engages in economic activity.

Turning to this case we think it apparent that the Due Process Clause did not preclude the California court from entering a judgment binding on respondent. It is sufficient for purposes of due process that the suit was based on a contract which had substantial connection with that State. Cf. Hess v. Pawloski, 274 U.S. 352, 47 S.Ct. 632; Henry L. Doherty & Co. v. Goodman, 294 U.S. 623, 55 S.Ct. 553; Pennoyer v. Neff, 95 U.S. 714, 735. The contract was delivered in California, the premiums were mailed from there and the insured was a resident of that State when he died. It cannot be denied that California has a manifest interest in providing effective means of redress for its residents when their insurers refuse to pay claims. These residents would be at a severe disadvantage if they were forced to follow the insurance company to a distant State in order to hold it legally accountable. When claims were small or moderate individual claimants frequently could not afford the cost of bringing an action in a foreign forum—thus in effect making the company judgment proof. Often the crucial witnesses—as here on the company's defense of suicide—will be found in the insured's locality. Of course there may be inconvenience to the insurer if it is held amenable to suit in California where it had this contract but certainly nothing which amounts to a denial of due process. Cf. Travelers Health Ass'n v. Commonwealth of Virginia ex rel. State Corporation Comm., 339 U.S. 643, 70 S.Ct. 927. There is no contention that respondent did not have adequate notice of the suit or sufficient time to prepare its defense and appear.

. . . .

The judgment is reversed and the cause is remanded to the Court of Civil Appeals of the State of Texas, First Supreme Judicial District, for further proceedings not inconsistent with this opinion.

It is so ordered.

THE CHIEF JUSTICE took no part in the consideration or decision of this case.

Question: (33) *P*, a seaman from New York City, was discharged before his ship's voyage ended, having signed on at Beaumont, Texas, on May 16, 1970, and having been discharged at Houston, Texas, on May 18, 1970. Seeking lost wages that are protected by federal statute, he sues *D*, the shipowner, in a Pennsylvania federal court. *D*, a corporation foreign to Pennsylvania, has its offices in New York City; its only contact with Pennsylvania was when another one of its ships took on a substantial cargo in Philadelphia during June 1972. *P* chooses the place of suit for reasons of personal convenience. *P* serves process in November 1973 pursuant to a Pennsylvania long-arm statute, which is construed to go to the outer limits of due process; the long-arm statute is invoked under Rule 4(e). Upon *D*'s motion to quash service and to dismiss for lack of personal jurisdiction, what decision? See Mackensworth v. American Trading Transp. Co., 367 F.Supp. 373, 1974 A.M.C. 237 (E.D.Pa.1973) (statement of facts here supplemented by reference to the record and letters from Judge Edward R. Becker and from counsel for plaintiff, Harry Lore, Esq.), noted in Phillips, "Minimum Contacts" Reviewed or Poetic Justice Pursued, 41 Tenn.L.Rev. 683 (1974); Toll, Scratch a Lawyer, Find a Poet, 37 Shingle 74 (1974); 12 Duq.L.Rev. 717 (1974); 15 Harv.Int'l L.J. 365 (1974).

(f) Jurisdictional Statutes

The International Shoe case speaks primarily in terms of foreign corporations, although its reasoning seems equally applicable to nonresident individuals. The same is true of Perkins. The defendant in McGee was an insurance company, but Justice Black refers to the clearly discernible trend "toward expanding the permissible scope of state jurisdiction over foreign corporations and other nonresidents." Most modern jurisdictional statutes in fact cover individuals as well as corporations, and no case has been found suggesting that the standards are different in substance. In Forbes v. Wells Beach Casino, Inc., 219 A.2d 542 (Me.1966), an action for specific performance of a contract in which the moving defendant (Elias Loew of Massachusetts) had been served with process in Massachusetts pursuant to a long-arm statute, the movant argued that, at least in the case of a "human nonresident," recent Supreme Court decisions should not be read as going to the length of upholding personal jurisdiction in respect to "activities of a kind which the State of Maine has not regarded as exceptional and has not subjected to special and unique regulation." This contention the Maine court rejected.

ILLINOIS REVISED STATUTES CHAPTER 110

§ 17. *Act submitting to jurisdiction—Process* [b]

(1) Any person, whether or not a citizen or resident of this State, who in person or through an agent does any of the acts hereinafter enumerated, thereby submits said person, and, if an individual, his personal representative, to the jurisdiction of the courts of this State as to any cause of action arising from the doing of any of said acts:

cit or not is in state juris if does any of these acts

(a) The transaction of any business within this State;

(b) The commission of a tortious act within this State;

(c) The ownership, use, or possession of any real estate situated in this State;

(d) Contracting to insure any person, property or risk located within this State at the time of contracting.

(2) Service of process upon any person who is subject to the jurisdiction of the courts of this State, as provided in this section, may be made by personally serving the summons upon the defendant outside this State, as provided in this Act, with the same force and effect as though summons had been personally served within this State.

Service same out of state as if in State

(3) Only causes of action arising from acts enumerated herein may be asserted against a defendant in an action in which jurisdiction over him is based upon this section.

(4) Nothing herein contained limits or affects the right to serve any process in any other manner now or hereafter provided by law.

NELSON v. MILLER, 11 Ill.2d 378, 143 N.E.2d 673 (1957). The Illinois jurisdictional statute was upheld in an action involving alleged negligence in unloading a truck in Illinois in the course of a delivery by an out-of-state defendant. The Illinois Supreme Court said sweepingly that the entire statute reflected "a conscious purpose to assert jurisdiction over nonresident defendants to the extent permitted by the due-process clause."

Statute 1 upheld

The argument was made in this case that jurisdiction under the words "commission of a tortious act within this State" depended upon proof of all the facts necessary to spell out ultimate liability in tort. The Illinois Supreme Court rejected this contention and held that the jurisdictional requirement was met "when the defendant, personally

[b] This is the original version of the statute, enacted in 1955 as the first comprehensive long-arm statute in the nation. The statute has since been amended, but only in minor ways. It is now found at Ill.Rev.Stat. ch. 110, ¶ 2-209.

Don't have to prove tort — OK just when ① did act ② complaint states cofa from that act

or through an agent, is the author of acts or omissions within the State, and when the complaint states a cause of action in tort arising from such conduct." The rejected construction of the statute would have produced anomalous results. The preliminary hearing on jurisdiction would entail a full-dress trial on the merits as to all issues of liability. If the defendant won, he would not get a judgment on the merits but only a dismissal for lack of jurisdiction. If he defaulted, he could force a trial on all the issues of liability in his home state because these would be jurisdictional facts subject to collateral attack, and thus the statutory objective of forcing the defendant to defend his conduct in the state where it took place would be nullified.

GRAY v. AMERICAN RADIATOR & STANDARD SANITARY CORP., 22 Ill.2d 432, 176 N.E.2d 761 (1961). The plaintiff was injured by the explosion in Illinois of a hot water heater. She sued the American Radiator & Standard Sanitary Corp. and the Titan Valve Manufacturing Co. Her claim was that Titan had negligently constructed a safety valve in Ohio and sold it to American Radiator, which manufactured the heater in Pennsylvania and attached the safety valve thereto. The heater was sold to an Illinois purchaser in the course of commerce. There was no showing that Titan had had any other contact with Illinois, directly or indirectly, nor that it had any agent there. American Radiator set up a cross-claim against Titan for indemnification by reason of certain warranties made by Titan.

Titan moved to dismiss the complaint and the cross-claim for lack of jurisdiction. The trial court granted the motion, and the plaintiff appealed. The questions presented were (1) whether a tortious act was committed in Illinois within the meaning of the Illinois statute and (2) whether the statute, if so construed, was consistent with due process of law.

On the first question, the Supreme Court of Illinois said:

"The first aspect to which we must direct our attention is one of statutory construction. Under section 17(1)(b) jurisdiction is predicated on the committing of a tortious act in this State. It is not disputed, for the purpose of this appeal, that a tortious act was committed. The issue depends on whether it was committed in Illinois, so as to warrant the assertion of personal jurisdiction by service of summons in Ohio.

"The wrong in the case at bar did not originate in the conduct of a servant physically present here, but arose instead from acts performed at the place of manufacture. Only the consequences occurred in Illinois. It is well established, however, that in law the place of wrong is where the last event takes place which is necessary to render the actor liable. (Restatement, Conflict of Laws, sec. 377.) A second indication that the place of injury is the determining factor is found in rules governing the time within which an action must be brought. In applying statutes of limitation our court has computed the period from the time when the injury is done. [Citations omitted.] We think it is clear that the alleged negligence in manufacturing the valve cannot be separated from the resulting injury; and that for present purposes, like those of liability and limitations, the tort was committed in Illinois.

"Titan seeks to avoid this result by arguing that instead of using the word 'tort,' the legislature employed the term 'tortious act'; and that the latter refers only to the act or conduct, separate and apart from any consequences thereof. We cannot accept the argument. To be tortious an act must cause injury. The concept of injury is an inseparable part of the phrase. In determining legislative intention courts will read words in their ordinary and popularly understood sense. [Citations omitted.] We think the intent should be determined less from technicalities of definition than from considerations of general purpose and effect. To adopt the criteria urged by defendant would tend to promote litigation over extraneous issues concerning the elements of a tort and the territorial incidence of each, whereas the test should be concerned more with those substantial elements of convenience and justice presumably contemplated by the legislature. As we observed in Nelson v. Miller . . . , the statute contemplates the exertion of jurisdiction over nonresident defendants to the extent permitted by the due-process clause."

The court likewise answered the second question in the affirmative, after observing:

"In the case at bar defendant does not claim that the present use of its product in Illinois is an isolated instance. While the record does not disclose the volume of Titan's business or the territory in which appliances incorporating its valves are marketed, it is a reasonable inference that its commercial transactions, like those of other manufacturers, result in substantial use and consumption in this State."

The court concluded: "We construe section 17(1)(b) as providing for jurisdiction under the circumstances shown in this case, and we hold that as so construed the statute does not violate due process of law."

Question: (34) If this case had come before the Supreme Court of the United States for review, what arguments would you make for reversal? What, if any, facts in addition to those summarized above would you consider relevant?

LONGINES–WITTNAUER WATCH CO. v. BARNES & REINECKE, INC., 15 N.Y.2d 443, 209 N.E.2d 68, 261 N.Y.S.2d 8 (1965). Three cases were decided under this caption. In one of these, Feathers v. McLucas, the plaintiffs were injured by the explosion of a tractor-drawn propane gas tank, en route from Pennsylvania to Vermont, on a highway near their home in New York. They sued, among others, the Darby Corporation, which had manufactured the tank in Kansas and sold it, through an intermediary, to a Pennsylvania corporation that was an interstate carrier licensed by several states including New York. The plaintiffs charged Darby with negligence and breach of warranty in the manufacture of the tank. There was no showing that Darby had had any other contact with New York, directly or indirectly, nor that it had any agent there.

Jurisdiction over Darby was asserted under NYCPLR § 302(a)(2), which like the Illinois statute says that jurisdiction extends to a defendant who "commits a tortious act within the state." Darby's contention that no jurisdiction existed was upheld by the Court of Appeals of New York, reversing the court below.

The Court of Appeals of New York rejected the view that the legislature had intended to go to the limits of the due process clause. Looking to the wording of the statute, the court said: "The language of paragraph 2 . . . is too plain and precise to permit it to be read, as has the Appellate Division, as if it were synonymous with 'commits a tortious act *without* the state which causes injury within the state.'" The court found further support for its reading in the legislative history, before concluding that expansion of the statute's scope "is a matter for the Legislature rather than the courts."

Question: (35) *P* of Illinois has brought a paternity action against *D* of Ohio in an Illinois court. *P* alleges, in essence, that *D* sired her child out of wedlock and has failed in his duty to provide support. More specifically, she alleges that "during the time biologically certain to have been the instant of conception, your Plaintiff had sexual intercourse with your Defendant in Cook County, Illinois, and with no other person." No other connection of *D* to Illinois is alleged. *D* received in-hand service of process in Ohio pursuant to the Illinois long-arm statute. He has now, by his attorney, submitted a motion to dismiss for lack of personal jurisdiction. *D*'s papers in support deny these allegations of the complaint and further argue that, even if they were true, such facts would not sustain jurisdiction over the person. *P*'s papers just take the opposite positions. How should the motion be decided? Compare Poindexter v. Willis, 87 Ill.App.2d 213, 231 N.E.2d 1 (1967), enforced, 23 Ohio Misc. 199, 256 N.E.2d 254 (C.P.1970), with Anonymous v. Anonymous, 49 Misc.2d 675, 268 N.Y.S.2d 710 (Fam.Ct.1966). Note that some long-arm statutes would seem to reach this case. See, e.g., Wash.Rev. Code Ann. § 4.28.185(1)(e) ("act of sexual intercourse within this state with respect to which a child may have been conceived").

UNIFORM INTERSTATE AND INTERNATIONAL PROCEDURE ACT[c]

§ 1.03. *[Personal Jurisdiction Based upon Conduct]*

(a) A court may exercise personal jurisdiction over a person, who acts directly or by an agent, as to a [cause of action] [claim for relief] arising from the person's

(1) transacting any business in this state;

(2) contracting to supply services or things in this state;

(3) causing tortious injury by an act or omission in this state;

(4) causing tortious injury in this state by an act or omission outside this state if he regularly does or solicits business or engages in any other persistent course of conduct in this state or derives substantial revenue from goods or services used or consumed in this state; [or]

(5) having an interest in, using, or possessing real property in this state [; or

(6) contracting to insure any person, property, or risk located within this state at the time of contracting].

. . . . .

Questions: (36) What differences do you see between the Uniform Act and the Illinois statute? What is the significance of these differences?

(37) What would have been the result if the Gray case had arisen under the Uniform Act?

(38) Defendant makes false representations outside the state communicated by mail or telephone to plaintiff within the state, intending that they should be relied on there to plaintiff's injury. Defendant has no other connection with the state. Is there sufficient basis for jurisdiction under a statute derived from the Uniform Act? See Murphy v. Erwin-Wasey, Inc., 460 F.2d 661 (1st Cir.1972) (yes). Is there sufficient basis for jurisdiction under the Illinois statute? Cf. Southeast Guar. Trust Co. v. Rodman & Renshaw, Inc., 358 F.Supp. 1001 (N.D.Ill.1973). Is there sufficient basis for jurisdiction under NYCPLR § 302(a)(2)? Cf. Bauer Indus., Inc. v. Shannon Luminous Materials Co., 52 A.D.2d 897, 383 N.Y.S.2d 80 (1976).

---

[c] This Uniform Act, approved by the National Conference of Commissioners on Uniform State Laws in 1962, presents a comprehensive code for use in state litigation with interstate or international incidents. In addition to provisions extending personal jurisdiction over persons not within the state where the action is commenced, it supplants earlier Uniform Acts for the taking of depositions outside the state, the determination of foreign law, and the proof of official records. It has been adopted in a number of states.

The brackets generally suggest to state legislatures a choice in the form of words to conform to state usage. Section 1.03(a)(6) is in brackets because many states have similar and more explicit provisions in their insurance laws, as illustrated in McGee v. International Life Ins. Co.

CALIFORNIA CODE OF CIVIL PROCEDURE

§ 410.10   *Basis*

A court of this state may exercise jurisdiction on any basis not inconsistent with the Constitution of this state or of the United States.

Question: (39) California plaintiff brings an action in a California court against a Nebraska defendant for damages arising out of a vehicular accident, occurring in Nevada near the California border and involving plaintiff's car and defendant's truck. Defendant, an interstate trucker, was en route to California to deliver and receive cargo when the accident occurred; during the seven years preceding the accident he made about 20 trips per year into California, and he was licensed to haul freight by several states including California. Is there sufficient basis for personal jurisdiction under the California statute? See Cornelison v. Chaney, 16 Cal.3d 143, 545 P.2d 264, 127 Cal.Rptr. 352 (1976) (yes).

COOK ASSOCIATES v. LEXINGTON UNITED CORP.
Supreme Court of Illinois, 1981.
87 Ill.2d 190, 429 N.E.2d 847.

WARD, JUSTICE:

This appeal arises out of an action for breach of contract brought in the circuit court of Cook County. The plaintiff, Cook Associates, an Illinois corporation, brought the action against Lexington United Corporation, a Delaware corporation not licensed to do business in Illinois. Lexington is a dinnerware manufacturer whose principal place of business is St. Louis, Missouri. Lexington filed a special appearance to contest the court's in personam jurisdiction (Ill.Rev.Stat. 1977, ch. 110, par. 20), but its motion to quash service of process was denied. Thereafter, Lexington answered, discovery was taken, and subsequently summary judgment was granted in favor of Cook. The appellate court reversed the judgment (86 Ill.App.3d 909, 407 N.E.2d 944), holding that the circuit court lacked personal jurisdiction over Lexington. Because of the disposition it made, the appellate court did not consider the propriety of the summary judgment. We granted Cook's petition for leave to appeal.

Cook is an employment agency whose offices are in Chicago. From July 1973 to July 1976, it also maintained a branch office in Massachusetts, which was operated by Edith McIntosh. Cook specializes in the placement of executive and professional employees with employers who pay Cook a fee if a person referred by Cook is hired. On May 12, 1976, Joseph Runza, a Lexington executive, phoned McIntosh, with whom he had done business before, at Cook's

Massachusetts office. He requested assistance in filling a sales management position at Lexington. The record is unclear as to the title of the position discussed. It appears that Runza had first described it as "national sales manager" but later changed the description to "field sales manager."

On May 13, 1976, McIntosh sent Runza the names and resumes of some prospective employees, one of whom was Gregg Hoegemeir. Her accompanying letter stated: "As you know from our previous correspondence, these men, like all of our candidates, are being submitted to you upon the understanding that if they are employed, our fee will be paid by you in accordance with the enclosed schedule." Cook's fee schedule indicated its Chicago address on the letterhead, and stated that the fee would be 20% of one year's salary for positions paying $15,000 per year or more. The schedule also stated: "A fee will be due from you as to any applicant you hire within two years of our disclosure of his identity, or of our submission or referral of him, to you."

Runza communicated with Hoegemeir and arranged to meet him in Chicago. Hoegemeir's resume discloses that he was then a regional sales manager for a Chicago manufacturer and that he resided in Ballwin, Missouri. At the meeting, Runza offered Hoegemeir the position of "field sales manager" at an annual salary of $22,000. Hoegemeir rejected the offer, and the record reflects that there were no further contacts between Lexington and him for several months.

McIntosh's employment by Cook terminated in July 1976. About three months later, she opened her own employment search and placement service in Massachusetts. It appears that soon thereafter, Runza communicated with McIntosh at her home and advised he was seeking a sales manager for Lexington. This time, it appears, the position would be that of "national sales manager" at a salary in excess of $22,000. McIntosh, acting for her own agency, submitted the names of a number of candidates, including that of Hoegemeir. After several interviews with Hoegemeir, Runza offered him the position at a salary of $25,000 and Hoegemeir accepted. The record does not show whether any of the negotiations which led to Hoegemeir's employment took place in Illinois, nor does it make clear where the contract for his employment was made.

Hoegemeir began working for Lexington in December 1976, and Lexington paid McIntosh a $5,000 fee for her services. Cook later became aware of the hiring of Hoegemeir, and it demanded a $5,000 fee, representing 20% of Hoegemeir's starting salary. When Lexington refused to pay the commission, Cook filed the action for breach of contract in July 1977.

Process was served on Lexington's president, Frank Ivitch, when he was attending a trade show in Chicago. Ivitch and several other company officials were appearing in a week-long housewares exhibit of Lexington. Exhibitors were prohibited from selling merchandise at the exhibition. Less than $50,000 in orders was taken by Lexington at the exhibit, according to the answer to an interrogatory, and were later accepted at Lexington's St. Louis office. Officials of Lexington had attended two other trade shows in Chicago in 1976 and 1977. At each of them, a similar volume of orders was received and later accepted.

Lexington's other contacts with Illinois were listed in an affidavit of Ivitch, and in Lexington's answers to interrogatories. Lexington did not have an office or an employee in this State. It had no Illinois telephone number. It did not advertise in Illinois, except in connection with the trade shows held in Chicago. Lexington merchandise was sold by an independent manufacturer's representative in Illinois to his Illinois accounts. The record does not reflect the volume of those sales. The representative sold merchandise of other manufacturers as well. Working strictly on a commission basis, he received no salary from Lexington. In the year preceding the filing of this action an employee of Lexington accompanied the representative on three or four occasions, but the employee did not make any sales.

The appellate court held, on due process grounds, that the circuit court of Cook County lacked personal jurisdiction over Lexington.

When arguing before the appellate court the parties were not in agreement as to the test or standard to be applied for determining whether there was personal jurisdiction. Lexington submitted that our long-arm statute provides the only means of acquiring jurisdiction over a nonresident corporate defendant. . . . Lexington contended that the requirements of the statute were not satisfied, because the action did not arise from "the transaction of any business" by Lexington in Illinois.

Cook, on the other hand, contended that the long-arm statute does not prohibit the acquiring of jurisdiction according to the doing-business doctrine. Under that doctrine, a foreign corporation is deemed to have submitted to our jurisdiction by doing business in Illinois. The nonresident defendant becomes amenable to service as a resident corporation, under section 13.3 of the Civil Practice Act, which states:

> "A private corporation may be served (1) by leaving a copy of the process with its registered agent or any officer or agent of said corporation found anywhere in the State; or (2) in any other manner now or hereafter permitted by law. A private corporation may also be notified by publication and mail in like manner and with like effect as individuals." Ill.Rev.Stat.1977, ch. 110, par. 13.3.

Cook urged that Lexington's contacts with Illinois rendered the corporation subject to the jurisdiction of the circuit court of Cook County under the "doing business" view, or under the due process standard of "minimum contacts."

. . . . .

Under the due process clause of the fourteenth amendment there are limits to which a State is confined in asserting in personam jurisdiction over a nonresident corporate defendant. The Supreme Court in International Shoe Co. v. Washington (1945), 326 U.S. 310, 316, 66 S.Ct. 154, 158, 90 L.Ed. 95, 102, described the constitutional requirement:

"[D]ue process requires only that in order to subject a defendant to a judgment in personam, if he be not present within the territory of the forum, he have certain minimum contacts with it such that the maintenance of the suit does not offend 'traditional notions of fair play and substantial justice.' [Citations.]"

It is important to recognize that this due process standard represents only the outer limits beyond which a State may not go to acquire jurisdiction over nonresidents. A State is free to set its own limits in acquiring this jurisdiction within the perimeters allowed by the due process clause. [Citations omitted.] We recently stressed that the boundaries or limits under our statute are not to be equated with the "minimum contacts" test under the due process clause. In Green v. Advance Ross Electronics Corp. (1981), 86 Ill.2d 431, 436, 427 N.E.2d 1203, 1206, we stated, in reference to the Illinois long-arm statute:

"In Nelson v. Miller (1957), 11 Ill.2d 378, 389 [143 N.E.2d 673], this court said that the Illinois long-arm statute reflects a conscious purpose to assert jurisdiction over nonresidents to the extent permitted by the due process clause. We do not, however, regard this observation as the equivalent of declaring that the construction and application of section 17(1)(b) depend entirely upon decisions determining in what circumstances due process requirements would permit long-arm jurisdiction. Neither do we read Nelson to say that in applying section 17(1)(b) we should not construe the meaning and intent of our own statute irrespective of the due process limitations generally applicable to State long-arm statutes. *A statute worded in the way ours is should have a fixed meaning without regard to changing concepts of due process*, except, of course, that an interpretation which renders the statute unconstitutional should be avoided, if possible. Thus, instead of turning to the array of tests which have been articulated to assist in determining whether long-arm statutes as applied exceed permissible constitutional boundaries, we prefer to resolve this appeal by looking to the meaning of our statute." (Emphasis added.)

We conclude that Lexington is not amenable to the jurisdiction of our courts under either the Illinois long-arm statute or under the doctrine of submitting to jurisdiction by virtue of doing business in Illinois.

Lexington is not amenable to service under the long-arm statute because the cause of action did not arise from the transaction of business in Illinois. Cook argues, however, that a contract between Lexington and Cook was formed in Illinois at the time of Hoegemeir's interview with Lexington.   Alternatively, it says that this action arose out of Lexington's activities in Illinois because the interview with Hoegemeir in Chicago was an essential first step in a process of negotiations that culminated in the hiring of Hoegemeir.   The contentions do not persuade.   Hoegemeir rejected the offer of employment when he was interviewed in Illinois, and of course no contract was formed.   Too, it cannot be said that the Chicago interview was any part in the negotiations that led to the hiring of Hoegemeir.   The positions involved were different.   Hoegemeir rejected the position of field sales manager.   He later was hired as national sales manager, but there is no indication whatever in the record that the interview had any influence on his hiring.   It was in the fall of 1976 that Runza asked McIntosh, who was then operating her own agency, for prospects to fill the position of national sales manager.   There was no communication between Runza and Hoegemeir until McIntosh referred his name to Lexington in behalf of her own agency.

.   .   .   .

The doing-business standard, of course, continues to be used in determining questions of jurisdiction over foreign corporations not licensed in Illinois (e.g., St. Louis-San Francisco Ry. v. Gitchoff (1977), 68 Ill.2d 38, 369 N.E.2d 52), as it was early recognized that the doctrine was not preempted by the long-arm statute.   (See Lindley v. St. Louis-San Francisco Ry. Co. (7th Cir.1968), 407 F.2d 639.)   In fact, it complements the long-arm statute because if a foreign, unlicensed corporation is found to be doing business in this State, it is amenable to the jurisdiction of courts of Illinois even for causes of action not arising from the defendant's transactions of business in Illinois.   See Hertz Corp. v. Taylor (1959), 15 Ill.2d 552, 155 N.E.2d 610.

In Green v. Advance Ross Electronics Corp., from which we have quoted above, we held that the long-arm statute was not to be equated with the standard of due process.   Here we will not equate the doing-business standard with the mere satisfaction of the minimum-contacts requirement for due process.   To do so would render the long-arm statute and the doing-business standard meaningless to many corporate defendants, and it would tie our jurisdictional rules to the changing standards for due process.

Examining Lexington's activities according to the doing-business test as applied under decisions of this court, we hold that on the record before us Lexington is not amenable to jurisdiction in Illinois.

There is no all-inclusive test for determining whether a foreign corporation is doing business in this State.   In Pembleton v. Illinois Commercial Men's Association (1919), 289 Ill. 99, 104, 124 N.E. 355, appeal dismissed (1919), 253 U.S. 499, 40 S.Ct. 483, 64 L.Ed. 1032, this court stated that, in general, the term means that the corporation is conducting business in Illinois "of such a character and extent as to warrant the inference that the corporation has subjected itself to the jurisdiction and laws of the district in which it is served and in which it is bound to appear when a proper agent has been served with process." . . .

. . . .

More recently, in Connelly v. Uniroyal, Inc. (1979), 75 Ill.2d 393, 389 N.E.2d 155, cert. denied and appeal dismissed (1980), 444 U.S. 1060, 100 S.Ct. 992, 62 L.Ed.2d 738, an alien corporation was held to be amenable to Illinois jurisdiction in a product liability action, because the defendant's products regularly entered Illinois in substantial amounts. In Braband v. Beech Aircraft Corp. (1978), 72 Ill.2d 548, 382 N.E.2d 252, cert. denied (1979), 442 U.S. 928, 99 S.Ct. 2857, 61 L.Ed.2d 296, the defendant manufacturer was held to be present and doing business because it maintained a contractual relationship with an Illinois distributor who, subject to inspection by the defendant, was authorized to sell the defendant's products and required to service its products, whether or not they were sold by the distributor. The defendant co-sponsored an Illinois sales program, and its products had been advertised in this State for at least five years.

In the foregoing cases, there was a regularity of activities in Illinois that is absent in the case of Lexington. [Citations omitted.] Mr. Justice Cardozo, while serving on the New York Court of Appeals, defined "doing business" for jurisdictional purposes as the corporation's operating within the State "not occasionally or casually, but with a fair measure of permanence and continuity." Tauza v. Susquehanna Coal Co. (1917), 220 N.Y. 259, 267, 115 N.E. 915, 917. [Other New York citations omitted.]

We consider that Lexington was not doing business in Illinois through having an exhibit at three trade shows in Chicago, and its fruitless interview. We note that while Lexington received orders totaling less than $50,000 during each of those trade shows, the record does not show the size of the individual orders. There is no indication whether the persons who ordered merchandise were Illinois residents and that Lexington merchandise was introduced into Illinois. The independent manufacturer's representative resides in Illinois. The scant references to him in the record are inadequate for us to conclude that because of its association with him Lexington should be deemed to have submitted itself to our jurisdiction for all causes of action which might arise in Illinois. In essence, the record contains a statement that the representative sells Lexington's merchandise along with products of other manufacturers. The record does not show how much has been sold through him, and there is no indication of whether the representative is authorized to contract for Lexington or whether he merely transfers orders to Lexington for acceptance. There is no indication of the control, if any, Lexington has over this representative. A Lexington employee accompanied him a few times, but for what purpose the record fails to show. Nor does it disclose what the Lexington employee did on those occasions.

. . . .

Judgment affirmed.

————————

SECTION 4. A RONDEL

(a) Complex Problems of Relationship to the Forum State

MULLANE v. CENTRAL HANOVER BANK & TRUST CO.

Supreme Court of the United States, 1950.
339 U.S. 306, 70 S.Ct. 652.

MR. JUSTICE JACKSON delivered the opinion of the Court.

This controversy questions the constitutional sufficiency of notice to beneficiaries on judicial settlement of accounts by the trustee of a common trust fund established under the New York Banking Law, Consol. Laws, c. 2. The New York Court of Appeals considered and overruled objections that the statutory notice contravenes requirements of the Fourteenth Amendment and that by allowance of the account beneficiaries were deprived of property without due process of law. The case is here on appeal under 28 U.S.C. § 1257.

Common trust fund legislation is addressed to a problem appropriate for state action. Mounting overheads have made administration of small trusts undesirable to corporate trustees. In order that donors and testators of moderately sized trusts may not be denied the service of corporate fiduciaries, the District of Columbia and some thirty states other than New York have permitted pooling small trust estates into one fund for investment administration. The income, capital gains, losses and expenses of the collective trust are shared by the constituent trusts in proportion to their contribution. By this plan, diversification of risk and economy of management can be extended to those whose capital standing alone would not obtain such advantage.

Statutory authorization for the establishment of such common trust funds is provided in the New York Banking Law, § 100–c, c. 687, L.1937, as amended by c. 602, L.1943, and c. 158, L.1944. Under this Act a trust company may, with approval of the State Banking Board, establish a common fund and, within prescribed limits, invest therein the assets of an unlimited number of estates, trusts or other funds of which it is trustee. Each participating trust shares ratably in the common fund, but exclusive management and control is in the trust company as trustee, and neither a fiduciary nor any beneficiary of a participating trust is deemed to have ownership in any particular asset or investment of this common fund. The trust company must keep fund assets separate from its own, and in its fiduciary capacity may not deal with itself or any affiliate. Provisions are made for accountings twelve to fifteen months after the establishment of a fund and triennially thereafter. The decree in each such judicial settlement of accounts is made binding and conclusive as to any matter set forth in the account upon everyone having any interest in the common fund or in any participating estate, trust or fund.

In January, 1946, Central Hanover Bank and Trust Company established a common trust fund in accordance with these provisions, and in March, 1947, it petitioned the Surrogate's Court for settlement of its first account as common trustee. During the accounting period a total of 113 trusts, approximately half inter vivos and half testamentary, participated in the common trust fund, the gross capital of which was nearly three million dollars. The record does not show the number or residence of the beneficiaries, but they were many and it is clear that some of them were not residents of the State of New York.

The only notice given beneficiaries of this specific application was by publication in a local newspaper in strict compliance with the minimum requirements of N.Y. Banking Law § 100–c(12): "After filing such petition [for judicial settlement of its account] the petitioner shall cause to be issued by the court in which the petition is filed and shall publish not less than once in each week for four successive weeks in a newspaper to be designated by the court a notice or citation addressed generally without naming them to all parties interested in such common trust fund and in such estates, trusts or funds mentioned in the petition, all of which may be described in the notice or citation only in the manner set forth in said petition and without setting forth the residence of any such decedent or donor of any such estate, trust or fund." Thus the only notice required, and the only one given, was by newspaper publication setting forth merely the name and the date of establishment of the common trust fund, and a list of all participating estates, trusts or funds.

At the time the first investment in the common fund was made on behalf of each participating estate, however, the trust company, pursuant to the requirements of § 100–c(9), had notified by mail each person of full age and sound mind whose name and address was then known to it and who was "entitled to share in the income therefrom . . . [or] . . . who would be entitled to share in the principal if the event upon which such estate, trust or fund will become distributable should have occurred at the time of sending such notice." Included in the notice was a copy of those provisions of the Act relating to the sending of the notice itself and to the judicial settlement of common trust fund accounts.

Upon the filing of the petition for the settlement of accounts, appellant was, by order of the court pursuant to § 100–c(12), appointed special guardian and attorney for all persons known or unknown not otherwise appearing who had or might thereafter have any interest in the income of the common trust fund; and appellee Vaughan was appointed to represent those similarly interested in the principal. There were no other appearances on behalf of any one interested in either interest or principal.

Appellant appeared specially, objecting that notice and the statutory provisions for notice to beneficiaries were inadequate to afford due process under the Fourteenth Amendment, and therefore that the court was without jurisdiction to render a final and binding decree. Appellant's objections were entertained and overruled, the Surrogate holding that the notice required and given was sufficient. A final decree accepting the accounts has been entered, affirmed by the Appellate Division of the Supreme Court, In re Central Hanover Bank & Trust Co., 275 App.Div. 769, 88 N.Y.S.2d 907, and by the Court of Appeals of the State of New York, 299 N.Y. 697, 87 N.E.2d 73.

The effect of this decree, as held below, is to settle "all questions respecting the management of the common fund." We understand that every right which beneficiaries would otherwise have against the trust company, either as trustee of the common fund or as trustee of any individual trust, for improper management of the common trust fund during the period covered by the accounting is sealed and wholly terminated by the decree. [Citations omitted.]

We are met at the outset with a challenge to the power of the State—the right of its courts to adjudicate at all as against those beneficiaries who reside without the State of New York. It is contended that the proceeding is one in personam in that the decree affects neither title to nor possession of any res, but adjudges only personal rights of the beneficiaries to surcharge their trustee for negligence or breach of trust. Accordingly, it is said, under the strict doctrine of Pennoyer v. Neff, 95 U.S. 714, the Surrogate is without jurisdiction as to nonresidents upon whom personal service of process was not made.

Distinctions between actions in rem and those in personam are ancient and originally expressed in procedural terms what seems really to have been a distinction in the substantive law of property under a system quite unlike our own. Buckland and McNair, Roman Law and Common Law, 66; Burdick, Principles of Roman Law and Their Relation to Modern Law, 298. The legal recognition and rise in economic importance of incorporeal or intangible forms of property have upset the ancient simplicity of property law and the clarity of its distinctions, while new forms of proceedings have confused the old procedural classification. American courts have sometimes classed certain actions as in rem because personal service of process was not required, and at other times have held personal service of process not required because the action was in rem. See cases collected in Freeman on Judgments, § 1517 et seq. (5th ed.).

Judicial proceedings to settle fiduciary accounts have been sometimes termed in rem, or more indefinitely quasi in rem, or more
vaguely still, "in the nature of a proceeding in rem." It is not readily
apparent how the courts of New York did or would classify the present proceeding, which has some characteristics and is wanting in
some features of proceedings both in rem and in personam. But in
any event we think that the requirements of the Fourteenth Amendment to the Federal Constitution do not depend upon a classification
for which the standards are so elusive and confused generally and
which, being primarily for state courts to define, may and do vary
from state to state. Without disparaging the usefulness of distinctions between actions in rem and those in personam in many branches
of law, or on other issues, or the reasoning which underlies them, we
do not rest the power of the State to resort to constructive service in
this proceeding upon how its courts or this Court may regard this
historic antithesis. It is sufficient to observe that, whatever the technical definition of its chosen procedure, the interest of each state in
providing means to close trusts that exist by the grace of its laws and
are administered under the supervision of its courts is so insistent
and rooted in custom as to establish beyond doubt the right of its
courts to determine the interests of all claimants, resident or nonresident, provided its procedure accords full opportunity to appear and be
heard.

[The portion of the majority's opinion reversing for inadequacy of
notice, and Justice Burton's dissent with respect thereto, are reprinted in the next Topic. Justice Douglas did not participate.]

HANSON v. DENCKLA
Supreme Court of the United States, 1958.
357 U.S. 235, 78 S.Ct. 1228.

*Fla. judg. rev'd
Del. " aff'd*

[In 1935 Mrs. Dora Browning Donner, a Pennsylvania domiciliary,
purported to create a trust in Delaware naming the Wilmington Trust
Co., a Delaware corporation, as trustee. The corpus was composed
of securities. The trust instrument reserved a life estate to Mrs.
Donner and empowered her to appoint the remainder by will or by
inter vivos instrument. In 1944 she established her domicile in Florida, and there on December 3, 1949, she executed a will and separately
exercised her power of appointment under the trust. She died in
Florida in 1952, and her will was probated there, with her daughter
Elizabeth Hanson as executrix. The issue presented by the litigation
was whether the trust assets passed pursuant to the appointment or
in accordance with the residuary clause of the will. This in turn depended upon whether Mrs. Donner had reserved such powers over
the trust assets as to make the trust invalid. If the trust and hence
the appointment were effective, trust assets totaling $400,000 would
pass to trusts of which the Delaware Trust Co., a Delaware corpora-

tion, was trustee and of which Mrs. Hanson's children, Donner Hanson and Joseph Winsor, were the beneficiaries; several other appointees would receive minor amounts of the trust assets. Under the will, on the other hand, all these assets would pass to Mrs. Donner's two other daughters, Katherine Denckla and Dorothy Stewart, who as residuary legatees had already received over $500,000 each.

[Mrs. Denckla and Mrs. Stewart, both residents of Florida, brought a declaratory judgment action in Florida for the purpose of establishing that the assets passed under the will. Jurisdiction was secured over Mrs. Hanson, Donner Hanson, and Joseph Winsor, all Florida residents, by personal service in Florida. The Wilmington Trust Co., the Delaware Trust Co., and certain of the other appointees were also named as defendants; notice was given to these nonresidents by ordinary mail, and publication was made in a Palm Beach newspaper pursuant to Florida law; none of these nonresidents appeared. The Florida trial court held that the assets passed pursuant to the will.

[Meanwhile, Mrs. Hanson instituted a declaratory judgment action in Delaware to determine the persons who were entitled to the assets. The parties were substantially the same as in Florida. The nonresident defendants, including Mrs. Denckla and Mrs. Stewart, were notified by registered mail; only Mrs. Denckla did not appear. After the Florida decree, a guardian ad litem for Mrs. Stewart unsuccessfully urged it as res judicata. The Delaware trial court ruled that the assets passed pursuant to the appointment.

[Next the Supreme Court of Florida and then the Supreme Court of Delaware sustained the determinations of their lower courts on the merits. The Florida Supreme Court also held that the Florida courts could exercise "substantive" jurisdiction over the absent defendants; but, as the Supreme Court of the United States was later to note, "[w]hether this meant jurisdiction over the person of the defendants or jurisdiction over the trust assets is open to doubt." The Delaware Supreme Court also rejected the contention that it was bound to give full faith and credit to the Florida decree.

[These inconsistent judgments were brought to the Supreme Court of the United States.]

MR. CHIEF JUSTICE WARREN delivered the opinion of the Court.

The issues for our decision are, first, whether Florida erred in holding that it had jurisdiction over the nonresident defendants, and second, whether Delaware erred in refusing full faith and credit to the Florida decree. . . .

No. 107, The Florida Appeal. [The Court first ruled that the proper mode of review here was by petition for certiorari but that under 28 U.S.C. § 2103 the appeal would be treated as such, and the Court then granted certiorari.]

Relying upon the principle that a person cannot invoke the jurisdiction of this Court to vindicate the right of a third party, appellees urge that appellants lack standing to complain of a defect in jurisdiction over the nonresident trust companies, who have made no appearance in this action. Florida adheres to the general rule that a trustee is an indispensable party to litigation involving the validity of the trust. In the absence of such a party a Florida court may not proceed to adjudicate the controversy. Since state law required the acquisition of jurisdiction over the nonresident trust company [8] before the court was empowered to proceed with the action, any defendant affected by the court's judgment has that "direct and substantial personal interest in the outcome" that is necessary to challenge whether that jurisdiction was in fact acquired. Chicago v. Atchison, T. & S.F.R. Co., 357 U.S. 77, 78 S.Ct. 1063.

Appellants charge that this judgment is offensive to the Due Process Clause of the Fourteenth Amendment because the Florida court was without jurisdiction. There is no suggestion that the court failed to employ a means of notice reasonably calculated to inform nonresident defendants of the pending proceedings, or denied them an opportunity to be heard in defense of their interests. The alleged defect is the absence of those "affiliating circumstances" [11] without which the courts of a State may not enter a judgment imposing obligations on persons (jurisdiction in personam) or affecting interests in property (jurisdiction in rem or quasi in rem).[12] While the in rem and in personam classifications do not exhaust all the situations that give rise to jurisdiction,[13] they are adequate to describe the affiliating circumstances suggested here, and accordingly serve as a useful means of approach to this case.

In rem jurisdiction. Founded on physical power, McDonald v. Mabee, 243 U.S. 90, 91, 37 S.Ct. 343, the in rem jurisdiction of a state court is limited by the extent of its power and by the coordinate au-

[8] Hereafter the terms "trust," "trust company" and "trustee" have reference to the trust established in 1935 with the Wilmington Trust Co., the validity of which is at issue here. It is unnecessary to determine whether the Delaware Trust Co., to which the $400,000 remainder interest was appointed and was paid after Mrs. Donner's death, is also an indispensable party to this proceeding.

[11] Sunderland, The Problem of Jurisdiction, Selected Essays on Constitutional Law, 1270, 1272.

[12] A judgment in personam imposes a personal liability or obligation on one person in favor of another. A judgment in rem affects the interests of all persons in designated property. A judgment quasi in rem affects the interests of particular persons in designated property. The latter is of two types. In one the plaintiff is seeking to secure a pre-existing claim in the subject property and to extinguish or establish the nonexistence of similar interests of particular persons. In the other the plaintiff seeks to apply what he concedes to be the property of the defendant to the satisfaction of a claim against him. Restatement, Judgments, 5–9. For convenience of terminology this opinion will use "in rem" in lieu of "in rem and quasi in rem."

[13] E.g., Mullane v. Central Hanover Bank & Trust Co., 339 U.S. 306, 312, 70 S.Ct. 652, 656; Williams v. North Carolina, 317 U.S. 287, 297, 63 S.Ct. 207, 212. Fraser, Jurisdiction by Necessity, 100 U. of Pa.L.Rev. 305.

thority of sister States. The basis of the jurisdiction is the presence of the subject property within the territorial jurisdiction of the forum State. Rose v. Himely, 4 Cranch 241, 277; Overby v. Gordon, 177 U.S. 214, 221–222, 20 S.Ct. 603, 606. Tangible property poses no problem for the application of this rule, but the situs of intangibles is often a matter of controversy. In considering restrictions on the power to tax, this Court has concluded that "jurisdiction" over intangible property is not limited to a single State. State Tax Commission of Utah v. Aldrich, 316 U.S. 174, 62 S.Ct. 1008; Curry v. McCanless, 307 U.S. 357, 59 S.Ct. 900. Whether the type of "jurisdiction" with which this opinion deals may be exercised by more than one State we need not decide. The parties seem to assume that the trust assets that form the subject matter of this action [16] were located in Delaware and not in Florida. We can see nothing in the record contrary to that assumption, or sufficient to establish a situs in Florida.[17]

The Florida court held that the presence of the subject property was not essential to its jurisdiction. Authority over the probate and construction of its domiciliary's will, under which the assets might pass, was thought sufficient to confer the requisite jurisdiction. But jurisdiction cannot be predicated upon the contingent role of this Florida will. Whatever the efficacy of a so-called "in rem" jurisdiction over assets admittedly passing under a local will, a State acquires no in rem jurisdiction to adjudicate the validity of inter vivos dispositions simply because its decision might augment an estate passing under a will probated in its courts. If such a basis of jurisdiction were sustained, probate courts would enjoy nationwide service of process to adjudicate interests in property with which neither the State nor the decedent could claim any affiliation. The settlor-decedent's Florida domicile is equally unavailing as a basis for jurisdiction over the trust assets. For the purpose of jurisdiction in rem the maxim that personalty has its situs at the domicile of its owner [19] is a fiction of limited utility. Green v. Van Buskirk, 7 Wall. 139, 150. The maxim is no less suspect when the domicile is that of a decedent. In analogous

[16] This case does not concern the situs of a beneficial interest in trust property. These appellees were contesting the validity of the trust. Their concern was with the legal interest of the trustee or, if the trust was invalid, the settlor. Therefore, the relevant factor here is the situs of the stocks, bonds, and notes that make up the corpus of the trust. Properly speaking such assets are intangibles that have no "physical" location. But their embodiment in documents treated for most purposes as the assets themselves makes them partake of the nature of tangibles. Cf. Wheeler v. Sohmer, 233 U.S. 434, 439, 34 S.Ct. 607.

[17] The documents evidencing ownership of the trust property were held in Delaware, cf. Bank of Jasper v. First Nat. Bank, 258 U.S. 112, 119, 42 S.Ct. 202, 204, by a Delaware trustee who was the obligee of the credit instruments and the record owner of the stock. The location of the obligors and the domicile of the corporations do not appear. The trust instrument was executed in Delaware by a settlor then domiciled in Pennsylvania. Without expressing any opinion on the significance of these or other factors unnamed, we note that none relates to Florida.

[19] We assume arguendo for the purpose of this discussion that the trust was invalid so that Mrs. Donner was the "owner" of the subject property.

cases, this Court has rejected the suggestion that the probate decree of the State where decedent was domiciled has an in rem effect on personalty outside the forum State that could render it conclusive on the interests of nonresidents over whom there was no personal jurisdiction. Riley v. New York Trust Co., 315 U.S. 343, 353, 62 S.Ct. 608, 614; Baker v. Baker, Eccles & Co., 242 U.S. 394, 401, 37 S.Ct. 152, 154; Overby v. Gordon, 177 U.S. 214, 20 S.Ct. 603. The fact that the owner is or was domiciled within the forum State is not a sufficient affiliation with the property upon which to base jurisdiction in rem.

[margin note: No in rem juris in Fla.]

. . . .

In personam jurisdiction. Appellees' stronger argument is for in personam jurisdiction over the Delaware trustee. They urge that the circumstances of this case amount to sufficient affiliation with the State of Florida to empower its courts to exercise personal jurisdiction over this nonresident defendant. Principal reliance is placed upon McGee v. International Life Ins. Co., 355 U.S. 220, 78 S.Ct. 199. In McGee the Court noted the trend of expanding personal jurisdiction over nonresidents. As technological progress has increased the flow of commerce between States, the need for jurisdiction over nonresidents has undergone a similar increase. At the same time, progress in communications and transportation has made the defense of a suit in a foreign tribunal less burdensome. In response to these changes, the requirements for personal jurisdiction over nonresidents have evolved from the rigid rule of Pennoyer v. Neff, 95 U.S. 714, to the flexible standard of International Shoe Co. v. Washington, 326 U.S. 310, 66 S.Ct. 154. But it is a mistake to assume that this trend heralds the eventual demise of all restrictions on the personal jurisdiction of state courts. See Vanderbilt v. Vanderbilt, 354 U.S. 416, 418, 77 S.Ct. 1360, 1362. Those restrictions are more than a guarantee of immunity from inconvenient or distant litigation. They are a consequence of a territorial limitations on the power of the respective States. However minimal the burden of defending in a foreign tribunal, a defendant may not be called upon to do so unless he has had the "minimal contacts" with that State that are a prerequisite to its exercise of power over him. See International Shoe Co. v. Washington, 326 U.S. 310, 319, 66 S.Ct. 154, 159.

[margin note: Have to have minimal contacts w/ State to get in per. juris]

We fail to find such contacts in the circumstances of this case. The defendant trust company has no office in Florida, and transacts no business there. None of the trust assets has ever been held or administered in Florida, and the record discloses no solicitation of business in that State either in person or by mail. Cf. International Shoe Co. v. Washington, 326 U.S. 310, 66 S.Ct. 154; McGee v. International Life Ins. Co., 355 U.S. 220, 78 S.Ct. 199; Travelers Health Ass'n v. Virginia ex rel. State Corporation Comm., 339 U.S. 643, 70 S.Ct. 927.

[margin note: NO contact w/Fla. here]

The cause of action in this case is not one that arises out of an act done or transaction consummated in the forum State. In that respect, it differs from McGee v. International Life Ins. Co., 355 U.S. 220, 78 S.Ct. 199, and the cases there cited. In McGee, the nonresident defendant solicited a reinsurance agreement with a resident of California. The offer was accepted in that State, and the insurance premiums were mailed from there until the insured's death. Noting the interest California has in providing effective redress for its residents when nonresident insurers refuse to pay claims on insurance they have solicited in that State, the Court upheld jurisdiction because the suit "was based on a contract which had substantial connection with that State." In contrast, this action involves the validity of an agreement that was entered without any connection with the forum State. The agreement was executed in Delaware by a trust company incorporated in that State and a settlor domiciled in Pennsylvania. The first relationship Florida has to the agreement was years later when the settlor became domiciled there, and the trustee remitted the trust income to her in that State. From Florida Mrs. Donner carried on several bits of trust administration that may be compared to the mailing of premiums in McGee. But the record discloses no instance in which the *trustee* performed any acts in Florida that bear the same relationship to the agreement as the solicitation in McGee. Consequently, this suit cannot be said to be one to enforce an obligation that arose from a privilege the defendant exercised in Florida. Cf. International Shoe Co. v. Washington, 326 U.S. 310, 319, 66 S.Ct. 154, 159. This case is also different from McGee in that there the State had enacted special legislation (Unauthorized Insurers Process Act, West's Ann.Cal.Insurance Code § 1610 et seq.) to exercise what McGee called its "manifest interest" in providing effective redress for citizens who had been injured by nonresidents engaged in an activity that the State treats as exceptional and subjects to special regulation. Cf. Travelers Health Ass'n v. Virginia ex rel. State Corporation Comm., 339 U.S. 643, 647–649, 70 S.Ct. 927, 929–930; Doherty & Co. v. Goodman, 294 U.S. 623, 627, 55 S.Ct. 553, 554; Hess v. Pawloski, 274 U.S. 352, 47 S.Ct. 632.

The execution in Florida of the powers of appointment under which the beneficiaries and appointees claim does not give Florida a substantial connection with the contract on which this suit is based. It is the validity of the trust agreement, not the appointment, that is at issue here. For the purpose of applying its rule that the validity of a trust is determined by the law of the State of its creation, Florida ruled that the appointment amounted to a "republication" of the original trust instrument in Florida. For choice-of-law purposes such a ruling may be justified, but we think it an insubstantial connection with the trust agreement for purposes of determining the question of personal jurisdiction over a nonresident defendant. The unilateral activity of those who claim some relationship with a nonresident defendant cannot satisfy the requirement of contact with the forum State.

The application of that rule will vary with the quality and nature of the defendant's activity, but it is essential in each case that there be some act by which the defendant purposefully avails itself of the privilege of conducting activities within the forum State, thus invoking the benefits and protections of its laws. International Shoe Co. v. Washington, 326 U.S. 310, 319, 66 S.Ct. 154, 159. The settlor's execution in Florida of her power of appointment cannot remedy the absence of such an act in this case.

It is urged that because the settlor and most of the appointees and beneficiaries were domiciled in Florida the courts of that State should be able to exercise personal jurisdiction over the nonresident trustees. This is a non-sequitur. With personal jurisdiction over the executor, legatees, and appointees, there is nothing in federal law to prevent Florida from adjudicating concerning the respective rights and liabilities of those parties. But Florida has not chosen to do so. As we understand its law, the trustee is an indispensable party over whom the court must acquire jurisdiction before it is empowered to enter judgment in a proceeding affecting the validity of a trust. It does not acquire that jurisdiction by being the "center of gravity" of the controversy, or the most convenient location for litigation. The issue is personal jurisdiction, not choice of law. It is resolved in this case by considering acts of the trustee. As we have indicated, they are insufficient to sustain the jurisdiction.

Because it sustained jurisdiction over the nonresident trustees, the Florida Supreme Court found it unnecessary to determine whether Florida law made those defendants indispensable parties in the circumstances of this case. Our conclusion that Florida was without jurisdiction over the Delaware trustee, or over the trust corpus held in that State, requires that we make that determination in the first instance. As we have noted earlier, the Florida Supreme Court has repeatedly held that a trustee is an indispensable party without whom a Florida court has no power to adjudicate controversies affecting the validity of a trust. For that reason the Florida judgment must be reversed not only as to the nonresident trustees but also as to appellants, over whom the Florida court admittedly had jurisdiction.

No. 117, The Delaware Certiorari. The same reasons that compel reversal of the Florida judgment require affirmance of the Delaware one. Delaware is under no obligation to give full faith and credit to a Florida judgment invalid in Florida because offensive to the Due Process Clause of the Fourteenth Amendment. . . .

. . . . .

The judgment of the Delaware Supreme Court is affirmed, and the judgment of the Florida Supreme Court is reversed and the cause is remanded for proceedings not inconsistent with this opinion.

It is so ordered.

DISSENT

MR. JUSTICE BLACK, whom MR. JUSTICE BURTON and MR. JUSTICE BRENNAN join, dissenting.

I believe the courts of Florida had power to adjudicate the effectiveness of the appointment made in Florida by Mrs. Donner with respect to all those who were notified of the proceedings and given an opportunity to be heard without violating the Due Process Clause of the Fourteenth Amendment. If this is correct, it follows that the Delaware courts erred in refusing to give the prior Florida judgment full faith and credit. U.S.Const., Art. IV, § 1; 28 U.S.C. § 1738.

. . . .

Fla. can determine whether appoint. valid; . . . [I]t seems quite clear to me that there is nothing in the Due Process Clause which denies Florida the right to determine whether Mrs. Donner's appointment was valid . . . . This disposition, which was designed to take effect after her death, had very *close & substantial connections w/ Fla.* close and substantial connections with that State. Not only was the appointment made in Florida by a domiciliary of Florida, but the primary beneficiaries also lived in that State. In my view it could hardly be denied that Florida had sufficient interest so that a court with jurisdiction might properly apply Florida law, if it chose, to determine whether the appointment was effectual. Watson v. Employers Liability Assurance Corp., 348 U.S. 66, 75 S.Ct. 166; Osborn v. Ozlin, 310 U.S. 53, 60 S.Ct. 758. True, the question whether the law of a State can be applied to a transaction is different from the question whether the courts of that State have jurisdiction to enter a judgment, but the two are often closely related and to a substantial degree depend upon *When such close connect w/ a state State should have juris. unless too heavy burden on out-state D's* similar considerations. It seems to me that where a transaction has as much relationship to a State as Mrs. Donner's appointment had to Florida its courts ought to have power to adjudicate controversies arising out of that transaction, unless litigation there would impose such a heavy disproportionate burden on a nonresident defendant that it would offend what this Court has referred to as "traditional notions of fair play and substantial justice." Milliken v. Meyer, 311 U.S. 457, 463, 61 S.Ct. 339, 342, 343; International Shoe Co. v. Washington, 326 U.S. 310, 316, 66 S.Ct. 154, 158. So far as the nonresident defendants here are concerned I can see nothing which approaches that degree of unfairness. Florida, the home of the principal contenders for Mrs. Donner's largess, was a reasonably convenient forum for all.[3] Certainly there is nothing fundamentally unfair in subjecting the corporate trustee to the jurisdiction of the Florida courts. *Fair for Corp. trustee to be under Fla. juris* It chose to maintain business relations with Mrs. Donner in that State for eight years regularly communicating with her with respect to the business of the trust including the very appointment in question.

Florida's interest in the validity of Mrs. Donner's appointment is made more emphatic by the fact that her will is being administered in that State. It has traditionally been the rule that the State where a person is domiciled at the time of his death is the proper place to

---

[3] The suggestion is made that Delaware was a more suitable forum, but the plain fact is that none of the beneficiaries or legatees has ever resided in that State.

determine the validity of his will, to construe its provisions and to *Protecting the will another connection w/Fla.* marshal and distribute his personal property.] Here Florida was seriously concerned with winding up Mrs. Donner's estate and with finally determining what property was to be distributed under her will. In fact this suit was brought for that very purpose.

The Court's decision that Florida did not have jurisdiction over the trustee (and inferentially the nonresident beneficiaries) stems from principles stated the better part of a century ago in Pennoyer v. Neff, 95 U.S. 714. That landmark case was decided in 1878, at a time when business affairs were predominantly local in nature and travel between States was difficult, costly and sometimes even dangerous. There the Court laid down the broad principle that a State could not subject nonresidents to the jurisdiction of its courts unless they were served with process within its boundaries or voluntarily appeared, except to the extent they had property in the State. But as the years have passed the constantly increasing ease and rapidity of communication and the tremendous growth of interstate business activity have led to a steady and inevitable relaxation of the strict limits on state jurisdiction announced in that case. In the course of this evolution the old jurisdictional landmarks have been left far behind so that in many instances States may now properly exercise jurisdiction over nonresidents not amenable to service within their borders. Yet further relaxation seems certain. Of course we have not reached the point where state boundaries are without significance, and I do not mean to suggest such a view here. There is no need to do so. For we are dealing with litigation arising from a transaction that had an abundance of close and substantial connections with the State of Florida.]

Perhaps the decision most nearly in point is Mullane v. Central Hanover Bank & Trust Co., 339 U.S. 306, 70 S.Ct. 652. In that case the Court held that a State could enter a personal judgment in favor of a trustee against nonresident beneficiaries of a trust even though they were not served with process in that State. So far as appeared, their only connection with the State was the fact that the trust was being administered there.[5] In upholding the State's jurisdiction the Court emphasized its great interest in trusts administered within its boundaries and governed by its laws. Id., 339 U.S. at page 313, 70 S.Ct. at page 656. Also implicit in the result was a desire to avoid the necessity for multiple litigation with its accompanying waste and possibility of inconsistent results. It seems to me that the same kind of considerations are present here supporting Florida's jurisdiction over the nonresident defendants.

. . . . .

MR. JUSTICE DOUGLAS, dissenting.

. . . .

[5] There was no basis for in rem jurisdiction since the litigation concerned the personal liability of the trustee and did not involve the trust property.

Dissent

Fla. had plain & compelling relation to the trust

. . . Florida has such a plain and compelling relation to these out-of-state intangibles (cf. Curry v. McCanless, 307 U.S. 357, 59 S.Ct. 900), and the nexus between the settlor and trustee is so close, as to give Florida the right to make the controlling determination even without personal service over the trustee and those who claim under it. We must remember this is not a suit to impose liability on the Delaware trustee or on any other absent person. It is merely a suit to determine interests in those intangibles. Cf. Mullane v. Central Hanover Trust Co., supra, 339 U.S. at page 313, 70 S.Ct. at page 656. Under closely analogous facts the California Supreme Court held in Atkinson v. Superior Court, 49 Cal.2d 338, 316 P.2d 960, that California had jurisdiction over an absent trustee. I would hold the same here. . . .

SHAFFER v. HEITNER

Supreme Court of the United States, 1977.
433 U.S. 186, 97 S.Ct. 2569.

MR. JUSTICE MARSHALL delivered the opinion of the Court.

The controversy in this case concerns the constitutionality of a Delaware statute that allows a court of that State to take jurisdiction of a lawsuit by sequestering any property of the defendant that happens to be located in Delaware. Appellants contend that the sequestration statute as applied in this case violates the Due Process Clause of the Fourteenth Amendment both because it permits the state courts to exercise jurisdiction despite the absence of sufficient contacts among the defendants, the litigation, and the State of Delaware and because it authorizes the deprivation of defendants' property without providing adequate procedural safeguards. We find it necessary to consider only the first of these contentions.

I

Appellee Heitner, a nonresident of Delaware, is the owner of one share of stock in the Greyhound Corporation, a business incorporated under the laws of Delaware with its principal place of business in Phoenix, Ariz. On May 22, 1974, he filed a [multimillion dollar] shareholder's derivative suit in the Court of Chancery for New Castle County, Del., in which he named as defendants Greyhound . . . and 28 present or former officers or directors of [Greyhound].[d] In essence, Heitner alleged that the individual defendants had violated their duties to Greyhound by causing it . . . to engage in actions that resulted in [its] being held liable for substantial damages in a

[d] A subsidiary of Greyhound was also involved in this action, but nothing in the case turns on this.

private antitrust suit and a large fine in a criminal contempt action. The activities which led to these penalties took place in Oregon.

Simultaneously with his complaint, Heitner filed a motion for an order of sequestration of the Delaware property of the individual defendants pursuant to 10 Del.C. § 366.[4] This motion was accompanied by a supporting affidavit of counsel which stated that the individual defendants were nonresidents of Delaware.[e] . . . . The requested sequestration order was signed the day the motion was filed. Pursuant to that order, the sequestrator "seized" approximately 82,000 shares of Greyhound common stock belonging to 19 of the defendants,[7] and options belonging to another two defendants.[8] These seizures were accomplished by placing "stop transfer" orders or their equivalents on the books of the Greyhound Corporation. So far as the record shows, none of the certificates representing the seized property was physically present in Delaware. The stock was considered to be in Delaware, and so subject to seizure, by virtue of 8 Del. C. § 169, which makes Delaware the situs of ownership of all stock in Delaware corporations.

All 28 defendants were notified of the initiation of the suit by certified mail directed to their last known addresses and by publication in a New Castle County newspaper. The 21 defendants whose property was seized (hereafter referred to as appellants) responded by entering a special appearance for the purpose of moving to quash service of process and to vacate the sequestration order. They contended that the ex parte sequestration procedure did not accord

---

[4] 10 Del.C. § 366 provides:

"(a) If it appears in any complaint filed in the Court of Chancery that the defendant or any one or more of the defendants is a nonresident of the State, the Court may make an order directing such nonresident defendant or defendants to appear by a day certain to be designated. Such order shall be served on such nonresident defendant or defendants by mail or otherwise, if practicable, and shall be published in such manner as the Court directs, not less than once a week for 3 consecutive weeks. The Court may compel the appearance of the defendant by the seizure of all or any part of his property, which property may be sold under the order of the Court to pay the demand of the plaintiff, if the defendant does not appear, or otherwise defaults. Any defendant whose property shall have been so seized and who shall have entered a general appearance in the cause may, upon notice to the plaintiff, petition the Court for an order releasing such property or any part thereof from the seizure. The Court shall release such property unless the plaintiff shall satisfy the Court that because of other circumstances there is a reasonable possibility that such release may render it substantially less likely that plaintiff will obtain satisfaction of any judgment secured. If such petition shall not be granted, or if no such petition shall be filed, such property shall remain subject to seizure and may be sold to satisfy any judgment entered in the cause. The Court may at any time release such property or any part thereof upon the giving of sufficient security."

. . . .

[e] Nine states were represented in the affidavit's list of the individual defendants' last known addresses. However, nine of those addresses were in Arizona and eight in California.

[7] The closing price of Greyhound stock on the day the sequestration order was issued was $14\frac{3}{8}$. New York Times, May 23, 1974, at 62. Thus, the value of the sequestered stock was approximately $1.2 million.

[8] . . . .

The remaining defendants apparently owned no property subject to the sequestration order.

them due process of law and that the property seized was not capable of attachment in Delaware. In addition, appellants asserted that under the rule of International Shoe Co. v. Washington, 326 U.S. 310, 66 S.Ct. 154 (1945), they did not have sufficient contacts with Delaware to sustain the jurisdiction of that State's courts.

The Court of Chancery rejected these arguments . . . .

On appeal, the Delaware Supreme Court affirmed the judgment of the Court of Chancery. Greyhound Corp. v. Heitner, 361 A.2d 225 (1976). . . .

Appellants' claim that the Delaware courts did not have jurisdiction to adjudicate this action received . . . cursory treatment. The court's analysis of the jurisdictional issue is contained in two paragraphs:

> "There are significant constitutional questions at issue here but we say at once that we do not deem the rule of International Shoe to be one of them. . . . The reason, of course, is that jurisdiction under § 366 remains . . . quasi in rem founded on the presence of capital stock here, not on prior contact by defendants with this forum. Under 8 Del.C. § 169 the 'situs of the ownership of the capital stock of all corporations existing under the laws of this State . . . [is] in this State,' and that provides the initial basis for jurisdiction. Delaware may constitutionally establish situs of such shares here, . . . it has done so and the presence thereof provides the foundation for § 366 in this case. . . .

> "We hold that seizure of the Greyhound shares is not invalid because plaintiff has failed to meet the prior contacts tests of International Shoe." 361 A.2d, at 229.

We noted probable jurisdiction. 429 U.S. 813, 97 S.Ct. 52.[12] We reverse.

II

The Delaware courts rejected appellants' jurisdictional challenge by noting that this suit was brought as a quasi in rem proceeding. Since quasi in rem jurisdiction is traditionally based on attachment or seizure of property present in the jurisdiction, not on contacts between the defendant and the State, the courts considered appellants' claimed lack of contacts with Delaware to be unimportant. This categorical analysis assumes the continued soundness of the conceptual structure founded on the century-old case of Pennoyer v. Neff, 95 U.S. 714 (1878).

. . . .

---

[12] Under Delaware law, defendants whose property has been sequestered must enter a general appearance, thus subjecting themselves to in personam liability, before they can defend on the merits. See Greyhound Corp. v. Heitner, supra, at 235–236. . . .

From our perspective, the importance of Pennoyer is not its result, but the fact that its principles and corollaries derived from them became the basic elements of the constitutional doctrine governing state-court jurisdiction. See, e.g., Hazard, A General Theory of State-Court Jurisdiction, 1965 Sup.Ct.Rev. 241. . . . [U]nder Pennoyer state authority to adjudicate was based on the jurisdiction's power over either persons or property. This fundamental concept is embodied in the very vocabulary which we use to describe judgments. If a court's jurisdiction is based on its authority over the defendant's person, the action and judgment are denominated "in personam" and can impose a personal obligation on the defendant in favor of the plaintiff. If jurisdiction is based on the court's power over property within its territory, the action is called "in rem" or "quasi in rem." The effect of a judgment in such a case is limited to the property that supports jurisdiction and does not impose a personal liability on the property owner, since he is not before the court.[17]   In Pennoyer's terms, the owner is affected only "indirectly" by an in rem judgment adverse to his interest in the property subject to the court's disposition.

. . . . .

The Pennoyer rules generally favored nonresident defendants by making them harder to sue. This advantage was reduced, however, by the ability of a resident plaintiff to satisfy a claim against a nonresident defendant by bringing into court any property of the defendant located in the plaintiff's State. See, e.g., Zammit, Quasi-In-Rem Jurisdiction: Outmoded and Unconstitutional?, 49 St. John's L.Rev. 668, 670 (1975). For example, ... Harris v. Balk, 198 U.S. 215, 25 S.Ct. 625 (1905). . . . . .

[The Court here traced developments from Pennoyer to International Shoe, closing with extensive quotations from the latter.[f]]

. . .   Thus, the relationship among the defendant, the forum, and the litigation, rather than the mutually exclusive sovereignty of the States on which the rules of Pennoyer rest, became the central concern of the inquiry into personal jurisdiction.[20]   The immediate ef-

---

[17] [The Court here quoted from footnote 12 of Hanson v. Denckla, 357 U.S. 235, 78 S.Ct. 1228 (1958), and adopted the convention that "we will for convenience generally use the term 'in rem' in place of 'in rem and quasi in rem.' "]

[f] In the course of its discussion, the Court noted that "the International Shoe Court believed that the standard it was setting forth governed actions against natural persons as well as corporations, and we see no reason to disagree. . . . The differences between individuals and corporations may, of course, lead to the conclusion that a given set of circum-

stances establishes state jurisdiction over one type of defendant but not over the other."

[20] Nothing in Hanson v. Denckla, supra, is to the contrary. The Hanson Court's statement that restrictions on state jurisdiction "are a consequence of territorial limitations on the power of the respective States," id., 357 U.S., at 251, 78 S.Ct., at 1238, simply makes the point that the States are defined by their geographical territory. After making this point, the Court in Hanson determined that the defendant over which personal

fect of this departure from Pennoyer's conceptual apparatus was to increase the ability of the state courts to obtain personal jurisdiction over nonresident defendants. See, e.g., Green, Jurisdictional Reform in California, 21 Hastings L.J. 1219, 1231–1233 (1970); Currie, The Growth of the Long Arm: Eight Years of Extended Jurisdiction in Illinois, 1963 U.Ill.L.F. 533; Developments [in the Law—State-Court Jurisdiction, 73 Harv.L.Rev. 909, 1000–08 (1960)].

No equally dramatic change has occurred in the law governing jurisdiction in rem. There have, however, been intimations that the collapse of the in personam wing of Pennoyer has not left that decision unweakened as a foundation for in rem jurisdiction. Well-reasoned lower court opinions have questioned the proposition that the presence of property in a State gives that State jurisdiction to adjudicate rights to the property regardless of the relationship of the underlying dispute and the property owner to the forum. See, e.g., U.S. Industries, Inc. v. Gregg, 540 F.2d 142 (CA3 1976), petition for cert. pending, No. 76–359 [, cert. denied, 433 U.S. 908, 97 S.Ct. 2972 (1977)]; Jonnet v. Dollar Savings Bank, 530 F.2d 1123, 1130–1143 (CA3 1976) (Gibbons, J., concurring); Camire v. Scieszka, 358 A.2d 397 (N.H.1976); Bekins v. Huish, 1 Ariz.App. 258, 401 P.2d 743 (1965); Atkinson v. Superior Court, 49 Cal.2d 338, 316 P.2d 960 (1957), appeal dismissed and cert. denied sub nom. Columbia Broadcasting System v. Atkinson, 357 U.S. 569, 78 S.Ct. 1381 (1958). The overwhelming majority of commentators have also rejected Pennoyer's premise that a proceeding "against" property is not a proceeding against the owners of that property. Accordingly, they urge that the "traditional notions of fair play and substantial justice" that govern a State's power to adjudicate in personam should also govern its power to adjudicate personal rights to property located in the State. See, e.g., Hazard, supra; Von Mehren & Trautman, Jurisdiction to Adjudicate: A Suggested Analysis, 79 Harv.L.Rev. 1121 (1966); Traynor, Is This Conflict Really Necessary?, 37 Tex.L.Rev. 657 (1959); Ehrenzweig, The Transient Rule of Personal Jurisdiction: The 'Power' Myth and Forum Conveniens, 65 Yale L.J. 289 (1956); Developments, supra.

. . . Moreover, in Mullane [v. Central Hanover Bank & Trust Co., 339 U.S. 306, 70 S.Ct. 652 (1950),] we held that Fourteenth Amendment rights cannot depend on the classification of an action as in rem or in personam, since that is

> "a classification for which the standards are so elusive and confused generally and which, being primarily for state courts to define, may and do vary from state to state." 339 U.S., at 312, 70 S.Ct., at 656.

It is clear, therefore, that the law of state-court jurisdiction no longer stands securely on the foundation established in Pennoyer. We think that the time is ripe to consider whether the standard of

jurisdiction was claimed had not committed any acts sufficiently connected to the   State to justify jurisdiction under the International Shoe standard.

fairness and substantial justice set forth in International Shoe should be held to govern actions in rem as well as in personam.

III

The case for applying to jurisdiction in rem the same test of "fair play and substantial justice" as governs assertions of jurisdiction in personam is simple and straightforward. It is premised on recognition that "[t]he phrase, 'judicial jurisdiction over a thing,' is a customary elliptical way of referring to jurisdiction over the interests of persons in a thing." Restatement (Second) of Conflict of Laws § 56, introductory note.[22] This recognition leads to the conclusion that in order to justify an exercise of jurisdiction in rem, the basis for jurisdiction must be sufficient to justify exercising "jurisdiction over the interests of persons in a thing." [23] The standard for determining whether an exercise of jurisdiction over the interests of persons is consistent with the Due Process Clause is the minimum-contacts standard elucidated in International Shoe.

This argument, of course, does not ignore the fact that the presence of property in a State may bear on the existence of jurisdiction by providing contacts among the forum State, the defendant, and the litigation. For example, when claims to the property itself are the source of the underlying controversy between the plaintiff and the defendant,[24] it would be unusual for the State where the property is located not to have jurisdiction. In such cases, the defendant's claim to property located in the State would normally[25] indicate that he expected to benefit from the State's protection of his interest. The State's strong interests in assuring the marketability of property within its borders and in providing a procedure for peaceful resolution of disputes about the possession of that property would also support jurisdiction, as would the likelihood that important records and witnesses will be found in the State. The presence of property may also favor jurisdiction in cases, such as suits for injury suffered on the land of an absentee owner, where the defendant's ownership of

[22] "All proceedings, like all rights, are really against persons. Whether they are proceedings or rights in rem depends on the number of persons affected." Tyler v. Court of Registration, 175 Mass. 71, 76, 55 N.E. 812, 814 (Holmes, C.J.), appeal dismissed, 179 U.S. 405, 21 S.Ct. 206 (1900).

[23] It is true that the potential liability of a defendant in an in rem action is limited by the value of the property, but that limitation does not affect the argument. The fairness of subjecting a defendant to state-court jurisdiction does

not depend on the size of the claim being litigated. . . .

[24] This category includes true in rem actions and the first type of quasi in rem proceedings. See n. 17, supra.

[25] In some circumstances the presence of property in the forum State will not support the inference suggested in text. Cf., e.g., Restatement (Second) of Conflict of Laws § 60, comments c, d; Traynor, supra, at 672–673; Note, The Power of a State to Affect Title in a Chattel Atypically Removed to It, 47 Colum.L. Rev. 767 (1947).

the property is conceded but the cause of action is otherwise related to rights and duties growing out of that ownership.[29]

It appears, therefore, that jurisdiction over many types of actions which now are or might be brought in rem would not be affected by a holding that any assertion of state-court jurisdiction must satisfy the International Shoe standard. For the type of quasi in rem action typified by Harris v. Balk and the present case, however, accepting the proposed analysis would result in significant change. These are cases where the property which now serves as the basis for state-court jurisdiction is completely unrelated to the plaintiff's cause of action. Thus, although the presence of the defendant's property in a State might suggest the existence of other ties among the defendant, the State, and the litigation, the presence of the property alone would not support the State's jurisdiction. If those other ties did not exist, cases over which the State is now thought to have jurisdiction could not be brought in that forum.

Since acceptance of the International Shoe test would most affect this class of cases, we examine the arguments against adopting that standard as they relate to this category of litigation. Before doing so, however, we note that this type of case also presents the clearest illustration of the argument in favor of assessing assertions of jurisdiction by a single standard. For in cases such as Harris and this one, the only role played by the property is to provide the basis for bringing the defendant into court. Indeed, the express purpose of the Delaware sequestration procedure is to compel the defendant to enter a personal appearance. In such cases, if a direct assertion of personal jurisdiction over the defendant would violate the Constitution, it would seem that an indirect assertion of that jurisdiction should be equally impermissible.

The primary rationale for treating the presence of property as a sufficient basis for jurisdiction to adjudicate claims over which the State would not have jurisdiction if International Shoe applied is that a wrongdoer

> "should not be able to avoid payment of his obligations by the expedient of removing his assets to a place where he is not subject to an in personam suit." Restatement (Second) of Conflict of Laws § 66, comment a.

Accord, Developments, supra, at 955. This justification, however, does not explain why jurisdiction should be recognized without regard to whether the property is present in the State because of an effort to avoid the owner's obligations. Nor does it support jurisdiction to adjudicate the underlying claim. At most, it suggests that a State in which property is located should have jurisdiction to attach that property, by use of proper procedures, as security for a judg-

---

[29] Cf. Dubin v. City of Philadelphia, 34 Pa.D. & C. 61 (1938). If such an action were brought under the in rem jurisdiction rather than under a long-arm statute, it would be a quasi in rem action of the second type. See n. 17, supra.

ment being sought in a forum where the litigation can be maintained consistently with International Shoe. See, e.g., Von Mehren & Trautman, supra, at 1178; Hazard, supra, at 284–285; [other citation omitted]. Moreover, we know of nothing to justify the assumption that a debtor can avoid paying his obligations by removing his property to a State in which his creditor cannot obtain personal jurisdiction over him.[35] The Full Faith and Credit Clause, after all, makes the valid in personam judgment of one State enforceable in all other States.[36]

It might also be suggested that allowing in rem jurisdiction avoids the uncertainty inherent in the International Shoe standard and assures a plaintiff of a forum.[37] See Folk & Moyer, [Sequestration in Delaware: A Constitutional Analysis, 73 Colum.L.Rev.] 749, 767 (1973). We believe, however, that the fairness standard of International Shoe can be easily applied in the vast majority of cases. Moreover, when the existence of jurisdiction in a particular forum under International Shoe is unclear, the cost of simplifying the litigation by avoiding the jurisdictional question may be the sacrifice of "fair play and substantial justice." That cost is too high.

We are left, then, to consider the significance of the long history of jurisdiction based solely on the presence of property in a State. Although the theory that territorial power is both essential to and sufficient for jurisdiction has been undermined, we have never held that the presence of property in a State does not automatically confer jurisdiction over the owner's interest in that property. This history must be considered as supporting the proposition that jurisdiction based solely on the presence of property satisfies the demands of due process, [citation omitted], but it is not decisive. "[T]raditional notions of fair play and substantial justice" can be as readily offended by the perpetuation of ancient forms that are no longer justified as by the adoption of new procedures that are inconsistent with the basic values of our constitutional heritage. [Citations omitted.] The fiction that an assertion of jurisdiction over property is anything but an assertion of jurisdiction over the owner of the property supports an ancient form without substantial modern justification. Its continued acceptance would serve only to allow state-court jurisdiction that is fundamentally unfair to the defendant.

[35] The role of in rem jurisdiction as a means of preventing the evasion of obligations, like the usefulness of that jurisdiction to mitigate the limitations Pennoyer placed on in personam jurisdiction, may once have been more significant. Von Mehren & Trautman, supra, at 1178.

[36] Once it has been determined by a court of competent jurisdiction that the defendant is a debtor of the plaintiff, there would seem to be no unfairness in allowing an action to realize on that debt in a State where the defendant has property, whether or not that State would have jurisdiction to determine the existence of the debt as an original matter. . . .

[37] This case does not raise, and we therefore do not consider, the question whether the presence of a defendant's property in a State is a sufficient basis for jurisdiction when no other forum is available to the plaintiff.

We therefore conclude that all assertions of state-court jurisdiction must be evaluated according to the standards set forth in International Shoe and its progeny.[39]

IV

The Delaware courts based their assertion of jurisdiction in this case solely on the statutory presence of appellants' property in Delaware. Yet that property is not the subject matter of this litigation, nor is the underlying cause of action related to the property. Appellants' holdings in Greyhound do not, therefore, provide contacts with Delaware sufficient to support the jurisdiction of that State's courts over appellants. If it exists, that jurisdiction must have some other foundation.

Appellee Heitner did not allege and does not now claim that appellants have ever set foot in Delaware. Nor does he identify any act related to his cause of action as having taken place in Delaware. Nevertheless, he contends that appellants' positions as directors and officers of a corporation chartered in Delaware provide sufficient "contacts, ties, or relations," International Shoe Co. v. Washington, supra, 326 U.S., at 319, 66 S.Ct., at 160, with that State to give its courts jurisdiction over appellants in this stockholder's derivative action. This argument is based primarily on what Heitner asserts to be the strong interest of Delaware in supervising the management of a Delaware corporation. That interest is said to derive from the role of Delaware law in establishing the corporation and defining the obligations owed to it by its officers and directors. In order to protect this interest, appellee concludes, Delaware's courts must have jurisdiction over corporate fiduciaries such as appellants.

This argument is undercut by the failure of the Delaware Legislature to assert the state interest appellee finds so compelling. Delaware law bases jurisdiction not on appellants' status as corporate fiduciaries, but rather on the presence of their property in the State. Although the sequestration procedure used here may be most frequently used in derivative suits against officers and directors, Hughes Tool Co. v. Fawcett Publications, Inc., 290 A.2d 693, 695 (Del. Ch.1972), the authorizing statute evinces no specific concern with such actions. Sequestration can be used in any suit against a nonresident, see., e.g., U.S. Industries, Inc. v. Gregg, supra (breach of contract); Hughes Tool Co. v. Fawcett Publications, Inc., supra (same), and reaches corporate fiduciaries only if they happen to own interests in a Delaware corporation, or other property in the State. But as Heitner's failure to secure jurisdiction over seven of the defendants named in his complaint demonstrates, there is no necessary relation-

---

[39] It would not be fruitful for us to reexamine the facts of cases decided on the rationales of Pennoyer and Harris to determine whether jurisdiction might have been sustained under the standard we adopt today. To the extent that prior decisions are inconsistent with this standard, they are overruled.

ship between holding a position as a corporate fiduciary and owning stock or other interests in the corporation. If Delaware perceived its interest in securing jurisdiction over corporate fiduciaries to be as great as Heitner suggests, we would expect it to have enacted a statute more clearly designed to protect that interest.

Moreover, even if Heitner's assessment of the importance of Delaware's interest is accepted, his argument fails to demonstrate that Delaware is a fair forum for this litigation. The interest appellee has identified may support the application of Delaware law to resolve any controversy over appellants' actions in their capacities as officers and directors. But we have rejected the argument that if a State's law can properly be applied to a dispute, its courts necessarily have jurisdiction over the parties to that dispute.

> "[The State] does not acquire . . . jurisdiction by being the 'center of gravity' of the controversy, or the most convenient location for litigation. The issue is personal jurisdiction, not choice of law. It is resolved in this case by considering the acts of the [appellants]." Hanson v. Denckla, supra, 357 U.S., at 254, 78 S.Ct., at 1240.

Appellee suggests that by accepting positions as officers or directors of a Delaware corporation, appellants performed the acts required by Hanson v. Denckla. He notes that Delaware law provides substantial benefits to corporate officers and directors, and that these benefits were at least in part the incentive for appellants to assume their positions. It is, he says, "only fair and just" to require appellants, in return for these benefits, to respond in the State of Delaware when they are accused of misusing their powers. Brief, at 15.

But like Heitner's first argument, this line of reasoning establishes only that it is appropriate for Delaware law to govern the obligations of appellants to Greyhound and its stockholders. It does not demonstrate that appellants have "purposefully avail[ed themselves] of the privilege of conducting activities within the forum State," Hanson v. Denckla, supra, 357 U.S., at 253, 78 S.Ct., at 1240, in a way that would justify bringing them before a Delaware tribunal. Appellants have simply had nothing to do with the State of Delaware. Moreover, appellants had no reason to expect to be haled before a Delaware court. Delaware, unlike some States, has not enacted a statute that treats acceptance of a directorship as consent to jurisdiction in the State. And "[i]t strains reason . . . to suggest that anyone buying securities in a corporation formed in Delaware 'impliedly consents' to subject himself to Delaware's . . . jurisdiction on any cause of action." Folk & Moyer, supra, at 785. Appellants, who were not required to acquire interests in Greyhound in order to hold their positions, did not by acquiring those interests surrender their right to be brought to judgment only in States with which they had had "minimum contacts."

The Due Process Clause

"does not contemplate that a state may make binding a judgment . . . against an individual or corporate defendant with which the state has no contacts, ties, or relations." International Shoe Co. v. Washington, supra, 326 U.S., at 319, 66 S.Ct., at 160.

Delaware's assertion of jurisdiction over appellants in this case is inconsistent with that constitutional limitation on state power. The judgment of the Delaware Supreme Court must, therefore, be reversed.

It is so ordered.

MR. JUSTICE REHNQUIST took no part in the consideration or decision of this case.

MR. JUSTICE POWELL, concurring.

. . . .

I would explicitly reserve judgment . . . on whether the ownership of some forms of property whose situs is indisputably and permanently located within a State may, without more, provide the contacts necessary to subject a defendant to jurisdiction within the State to the extent of the value of the property. In the case of real property, in particular, preservation of the common law concept of quasi in rem jurisdiction arguably would avoid the uncertainty of the general International Shoe standard without significant cost to " 'traditional notions of fair play and substantial justice.' " . . .

Subject to the foregoing reservation, I join the opinion of the Court.

MR. JUSTICE STEVENS, concurring in the judgment.

The Due Process Clause affords protection against "judgments without notice." International Shoe Co. v. Washington, 326 U.S. 310, 324, 66 S.Ct. 154, 162 (opinion of Black, J.). . . .

The requirement of fair notice also, I believe, includes fair warning that a particular activity may subject a person to the jurisdiction of a foreign sovereign. If I visit another State, or acquire real estate or open a bank account in it, I knowingly assume some risk that the State will exercise its power over my property or my person while there. My contact with the State, though minimal, gives rise to predictable risks.

. . . .

One who purchases shares of stock on the open market can hardly be expected to know that he has thereby become subject to suit in a forum remote from his residence and unrelated to the transaction. . . . I therefore agree with the Court that on the record before us no adequate basis for jurisdiction exists and that the Delaware statute is unconstitutional on its face.

How the Court's opinion may be applied in other contexts is not entirely clear to me. I agree with Mr. Justice Powell that it should not be read to invalidate quasi in rem jurisdiction where real estate is involved. I would also not read it as invalidating other long-accepted methods of acquiring jurisdiction over persons with adequate notice of both the particular controversy and the fact that their local activities might subject them to suit. My uncertainty as to the reach of the opinion, and my fear that it purports to decide a great deal more than is necessary to dispose of this case, persuade me merely to concur in the judgment.

MR. JUSTICE BRENNAN, concurring in part and dissenting in part.

I join Parts I–III of the Court's opinion. I fully agree that the minimum contacts analysis developed in International Shoe Co. v. Washington, 326 U.S. 310, 66 S.Ct. 154 (1945), represents a far more sensible construct for the exercise of state court jurisdiction than the patchwork of legal and factual fictions that has been generated from the decision in Pennoyer v. Neff, 95 U.S. 714 (1878). It is precisely because the inquiry into minimum contacts is now of such overriding importance, however, that I must respectfully dissent from Part IV of the Court's opinion.

[Justice Brennan thought that the Court did not need to reach and should not have reached the issue in part IV.]

Nonetheless, because the Court rules on the minimum contacts question, I feel impelled to express my view. While evidence derived through discovery might satisfy me that minimum contacts are lacking in a given case, I am convinced that as a general rule a state forum has jurisdiction to adjudicate a shareholder derivative action centering on the conduct and policies of the directors and officers of a corporation chartered by that State. Unlike the Court, I therefore would not foreclose Delaware from asserting jurisdiction over appellants were it persuaded to do so on the basis of minimum contacts.

It is well settled that a derivative lawsuit as presented here does not inure primarily to the benefit of the named plaintiff. Rather, the primary beneficiaries are the corporation and its owners, the shareholders. "The cause of action which such a plaintiff brings before the court is not his own but the corporation's. . . . Such a plaintiff often may represent an important public and stockholder interest in bringing faithless managers to book." Koster v. Lumbermens Mutual Casualty Co., 330 U.S. 518, 522, 524, 67 S.Ct. 828, 831, 832 (1947).

Viewed in this light, the chartering State has an unusually powerful interest in insuring the availability of a convenient forum for litigating claims involving a possible multiplicity of defendant fiduciaries and for vindicating the State's substantive policies regarding the management of its domestic corporations. I believe that our cases fairly establish that the State's valid substantive interests are important considerations in assessing whether it constitutionally may claim jurisdiction over a given cause of action.

In this instance, Delaware can point to at least three interrelated public policies that are furthered by its assertion of jurisdiction. First, the State has a substantial interest in providing restitution for its local corporations that allegedly have been victimized by fiduciary misconduct, even if the managerial decisions occurred outside the State. . . . Second, state courts have legitimately read their jurisdiction expansively when a cause of action centers in an area in which the forum State possesses a manifest regulatory interest. . . . Finally, a State like Delaware has a recognized interest in affording a convenient forum for supervising and overseeing the affairs of an entity that is purely the creation of that State's law. . . .

To be sure, the Court is not blind to these considerations. It notes that the State's interests "may support the application of Delaware law to resolve any controversy over appellants' actions in their capacities as officers and directors." . . . But this, the Court argues, pertains to choice of law, not jurisdiction. I recognize that the jurisdictional and choice-of-law inquiries are not identical. Hanson v. Denckla, 357 U.S. 235, 254, 78 S.Ct. 1228, 1240 (1958). But I would not compartmentalize thinking in this area quite so rigidly as it seems to me the Court does today, for both inquiries "are often closely related and to a substantial degree depend upon similar considerations." Id., at 258, 78 S.Ct., at 1242 (Black, J., dissenting). In either case an important linchpin is the extent of contacts between the controversy, the parties, and the forum State. While constitutional limitations on the choice of law are by no means settled, see, e.g., Home Ins. Co. v. Dick, 281 U.S. 397, 50 S.Ct. 338 (1930), important considerations certainly include the expectancies of the parties and the fairness of governing the defendants' acts and behavior by rules of conduct created by a given jurisdiction. See, e.g., Restatement (Second) of Conflict of Laws § 6. These same factors bear upon the propriety of a State's exercising jurisdiction over a legal dispute. At the minimum, the decision that it is fair to bind a defendant by a State's laws and rules should prove to be highly relevant to the fairness of permitting that same State to accept jurisdiction for adjudicating the controversy.

Furthermore, I believe that practical considerations argue in favor of seeking to bridge the distance between the choice-of-law and jurisdictional inquiries. Even when a court would apply the law of a different forum, as a general rule it will feel less knowledgeable and comfortable in interpretation, and less interested in fostering the policies of that foreign jurisdiction, than would the courts established by the State that provides the applicable law. [Citations omitted.] Obviously, such choice-of-law problems cannot entirely be avoided in a diverse legal system such as our own. Nonetheless, when a suitor seeks to lodge a suit in a State with a substantial interest in seeing its own law applied to the transaction in question, we could wisely act to minimize conflicts, confusion, and uncertainty by adopting a liberal view of jurisdiction, unless considerations of fairness or efficiency strongly point in the opposite direction.

This case is not one where, in my judgment, this preference for jurisdiction is adequately answered. Certainly nothing said by the Court persuades me that it would be unfair to subject appellants to suit in Delaware. The fact that the record does not reveal whether they "set foot" or committed "act[s] related to [the] cause of action" in Delaware . . . is not decisive, for jurisdiction can be based strictly on out-of-state acts having foreseeable effects in the forum State. [Citations omitted.] I have little difficulty in applying this principle to nonresident fiduciaries whose alleged breaches of trust are said to have substantial damaging effect on the financial posture of a resident corporation. Further, I cannot understand how the existence of minimum contacts in a constitutional sense is at all affected by Delaware's failure statutorily to express an interest in controlling corporate fiduciaries. . . . To me this simply demonstrates that Delaware did not elect to assert jurisdiction to the extent the Constitution would allow.[5] Nor would I view as controlling or even especially meaningful Delaware's failure to exact from appellants their consent to be sued. . . . Once we have rejected the jurisdictional framework created in Pennoyer v. Neff, I see no reason to rest jurisdiction on a fictional outgrowth of that system such as the existence of a consent statute, expressed or implied.[6]

I, therefore, would approach the minimum contacts analysis differently than does the Court. Crucial to me is the fact that appellants voluntarily associated themselves with the State of Delaware, "invoking the benefits and protections of its laws," Hanson v. Denckla, supra, 357 U.S., at 253, 78 S.Ct., at 1240; International Shoe Co. v. Washington, supra, 326 U.S., at 319, 66 S.Ct., at 159, by entering into a long-term and fragile relationship with one of its domestic corpora-

---

[5] In fact, it is quite plausible that the Delaware Legislature never felt the need to assert direct jurisdiction over corporate managers precisely because the sequestration statute heretofore has served as a somewhat awkward but effective basis for achieving such personal jurisdiction. See, e.g., Hughes Tool Co. v. Fawcett Publications, Inc., 290 A.2d 693, 695 (Del.Ch.1972): "Sequestration is most frequently resorted to in suits by stockholders against corporate directors in which recoveries are sought for the benefit of the corporation on the ground of claimed breaches of fiduciary duty on the part of directors."

[6] Admittedly, when one consents to suit in a forum, his expectation is enhanced that he may be haled into that State's courts. To this extent, I agree that consent may have bearing on the fairness of accepting jurisdiction. But

whatever is the degree of personal expectation that is necessary to warrant jurisdiction should not depend on the formality of establishing a consent law. Indeed, if one's expectations are to carry such weight, then appellants here might be fairly charged with the understanding that Delaware would decide to protect its substantial interests through its own courts, for they certainly realized that in the past the sequestration law has been employed primarily as a means of securing the appearance of corporate officials in the State's courts. Supra, at n. 5. Even in the absence of such a statute, however, the close and special association between a state corporation and its managers should apprise the latter that the state may seek to offer a convenient forum for addressing claims of fiduciary breach of trust.

tions. They thereby elected to assume powers and to undertake responsibilities wholly derived from that State's rules and regulations, and to become eligible for those benefits that Delaware law makes available to its corporations' officials. E.g., 8 Del.C. §§ 143 (interest-free loans); 145 (indemnification). While it is possible that countervailing issues of judicial efficiency and the like might clearly favor a different forum, they do not appear on the meager record before us; and, of course, we are concerned solely with "minimum" contacts, not the "best" contacts. I thus do not believe that it is unfair to insist that appellants make themselves available to suit in a competent forum that Delaware might create for vindication of its important public policies directly pertaining to appellants' fiduciary associations with the State.

Question: (40) Thirteen days after the Shaffer decision the Delaware legislature had passed and the Governor had signed a bill providing that, after a certain date, a nonresident's accepting a directorship or continuing in the position of director of a Delaware corporation is to be deemed consent to the appointment of the registered agent of such corporation as his agent for service of process in connection with suits such as Shaffer; direct notice to the nonresident by registered mail is also required. See Del.Code Ann. tit. 10, § 3114. Is this statute constitutional? See Armstrong v. Pomerance, 423 A.2d 174 (Del.1980) (yes).

ATKINSON v. SUPERIOR COURT, 49 Cal.2d 338, 316 P.2d 960 (1957), appeals dismissed and cert. denied, 357 U.S. 569, 78 S.Ct. 1381 (1958). Separate class actions were brought on behalf of (1) the employees of various motion picture companies and (2) the employees of various phonograph record companies, attacking the validity of the collective bargaining agreements between their employers and the American Federation of Musicians, and also attacking certain related trust agreements. The gist of the complaints was that the A.F. of M., in violation of its duty as the employees' collective bargaining agent, agreed with the employers that certain royalty payments should be periodically turned over to a New York trustee for named trust purposes instead of to the employees, who claimed the payments as wages earned in California; it was further alleged that the employers were willing to make payment to the employees but for their agreements with the A.F. of M. to make payment to the trustee and that the officers of the A.F. of M. had wrongfully negotiated the arrangement for the selfish purpose of perpetuating themselves in office. The complaints sought a declaration of the collective bargaining agreements' invalidity and of the employees' right to the payments, and also damages from the A.F. of M.; they further asked for the appointment of a receiver to collect future royalty payments and for a preliminary injunction to prevent the employers from making payment to the trustee.

The employers, the A.F. of M., and the trustee were named as defendants. Personal jurisdiction was obtained in California over the employers and the A.F. of M. The trustee was served in New York, but did not appear. The trial court ruled the trustee an indispensable party and dismissed for lack of personal jurisdiction over the trustee. The Supreme Court of California, speaking through Justice Traynor, reversed, concluding that "service upon the trustee in New York was sufficient to give the court jurisdiction to adjudicate his right to receive payments under the contracts here involved."

Questions: (41) Appraise the Atkinson decision in the light of Mullane v. Central Hanover Bank & Trust Co., Hanson v. Denckla, and Shaffer v. Heitner.

(42) If the Atkinson case were to arise for the first time today, what position would you advise the defendant employers to take on the jurisdictional question?

(b) The Framework—Restructured or Resurrected?

KULKO v. SUPERIOR COURT, 436 U.S. 84, 98 S.Ct. 1690 (1978). Some time after a woman and first one and later the other of her children had moved to California, she sued her former husband for child support in a California court. The defendant still lived in New York but had consented to the children's living in California. Upon his special appearance, the California courts upheld personal jurisdiction as "reasonable."

On certiorari, the Supreme Court held that here jurisdiction violated due process because the defendant "did not purposefully derive benefit from any activities relating to the State" and "lacks any other relevant contact with the State." Justice Marshall, writing for the Court, cited Hanson v. Denckla liberally. He generalized that personal jurisdiction demands "a sufficient connection between the defendant and the forum State as to make it fair to require defense of the action in the forum. . . . While the interests of the forum State and of the plaintiff in proceeding with the cause in the plaintiff's forum of choice are, of course, to be considered, see McGee v. International Life Insurance Co., . . . an essential criterion in all cases is whether the "quality and nature" of the defendant's activity is such that it is "reasonable" and "fair" to require him to conduct his defense in that State. International Shoe Co. v. Washington . . . ." Justice Brennan, joined by Justices White and Powell, dissented.

RUSH v. SAVCHUK

Supreme Court of the United States, 1980.
444 U.S. 320, 100 S.Ct. 571, 580.

MR. JUSTICE MARSHALL delivered the opinion of the Court.

This appeal presents the question whether a State may constitutionally exercise quasi in rem jurisdiction over a defendant who has no forum contacts by attaching the contractual obligation of an insurer licensed to do business in the State to defend and indemnify him in connection with the suit.

I

On January 13, 1972, two Indiana residents were involved in a single-car accident in Elkhart, Ind. Appellee Savchuk, who was a passenger in the car driven by appellant Rush, was injured. The car, owned by Rush's father, was insured by appellant State Farm Mutual Automobile Insurance Co. (State Farm) under a liability insurance policy issued in Indiana. Indiana's guest statute would have barred a claim by Savchuk. Ind.Stat. § 9–3–3–1.

Savchuk moved with his parents to Minnesota in June 1973. On May 28, 1974, he commenced an action against Rush in the Minnesota state courts. As Rush had no contacts with Minnesota that would support in personam jurisdiction, Savchuk attempted to obtain quasi in rem jurisdiction by garnishing State Farm's obligation under the insurance policy to defend and indemnify Rush in connection with such a suit. [He acted pursuant to Minnesota's explicit statutory provision regarding such garnishment with respect to an insurance policy.] State Farm does business in Minnesota. Rush was personally served in Indiana. The complaint alleged negligence and sought $125,000 in damages.

. . . . Rush . . . . moved to dismiss the complaint for lack of jurisdiction over the defendant. The trial court denied the motion to dismiss . . . .

On appeal, the Minnesota Supreme Court affirmed the trial court's decision. 311 Minn. 480, 245 N.W.2d 624 (1976) (Savchuk I). It held, first, that the obligation of an insurance company to defend and indemnify a nonresident insured under an automobile liability insurance policy is a garnishable res in Minnesota for the purpose of obtaining quasi in rem jurisdiction when the incident giving rise to the action occurs outside Minnesota but the plaintiff is a Minnesota resident when the suit is filed. Second, the court held that the assertion of jurisdiction over Rush was constitutional because he had notice of the suit and an opportunity to defend, his liability was limited to the amount of the policy, and the garnishment procedure may be used only by Minnesota residents. The court expressly recognized that Rush had engaged in no voluntary activity that would justify the exercise of in personam jurisdiction. The court found, however, that considerations of fairness supported the exercise of quasi in rem jurisdiction because in accident litigation the insurer controls the defense of the case, State Farm does business in and is regulated by the State, and the State has an interest in protecting its residents and providing them with a forum in which to litigate their claims.

Rush appealed to this Court. We vacated the judgment and remanded the cause for further consideration in light of Shaffer v. Heitner, 433 U.S. 186, 97 S.Ct. 2569 (1977). 433 U.S. 902, 97 S.Ct. 2964 (1977).

On remand, the Minnesota Supreme Court held that the assertion of quasi in rem jurisdiction through garnishment of an insurer's obligation to an insured complied with the due process standards enunciated in Shaffer. 272 N.W.2d 888 (Minn.1978) (Savchuk II). The court found that the garnishment statute differed from the Delaware stock sequestration procedure held unconstitutional in Shaffer because the garnished property was intimately related to the litigation and the garnishment procedure paralleled the asserted state interest in "facilitating recoveries for resident plaintiffs." Id., at 891.[8] This appeal followed.

II

The Minnesota Supreme Court held that the Minnesota garnishment statute embodies the rule stated in Seider v. Roth, 17 N.Y.2d 111, 269 N.Y.S.2d 99, 216 N.E.2d 312 (1966), that the contractual obligation of an insurance company to its insured under a liability insurance policy is a debt subject to attachment under state law if the insurer does business in the State. Seider jurisdiction was upheld against a due process challenge in Simpson v. Loehmann, 21 N.Y.2d 305, 287 N.Y.S.2d 633, 234 N.E.2d 669 (1967), rearg. denied, 21 N.Y.2d 990, 290 N.Y.S.2d 914, 238 N.E.2d 319 (1968). The New York court relied on Harris v. Balk, 198 U.S. 215, 25 S.Ct. 625 (1905), in holding that the presence of the debt in the State was sufficient to permit quasi in rem jurisdiction over the absent defendant. The court also concluded that the exercise of jurisdiction was permissible under the Due Process Clause because, "[v]iewed realistically, the insurer in a case such as the present is in full control of the litigation" and "where the plaintiff is a resident of the forum state and the insurer is present in and regulated by it, the State has a substantial

---

[8] Minnesota would apply its own comparative negligence law, rather than Indiana's contributory negligence rule. See Schwartz v. Consolidated Freightways Corp., 300 Minn. 487, 221 N.W.2d 665 (1974). Appellants assert that Minnesota would also decline to apply the Indiana guest statute if this case were tried in Minnesota. Juris. Statement 10, n. 2; cf. Savchuk II, 272 N.W.2d, at 891–892. The constitutionality of a choice of law rule that would apply forum law in these circumstances is not before us. Cf. Home Ins. v. Dick, 281 U.S. 397, 50 S.Ct. 338 (1930).

and continuing relation with the controversy." Simpson v. Loehmann, supra, at 311, 287 N.Y.S.2d, at 637, 234 N.E.2d, at 672.

The United States Court of Appeals for the Second Circuit gave its approval to Seider in Minichiello v. Rosenberg (CA2 1968), 410 F.2d 106, adhered to en banc, 410 F.2d 117, cert. denied, 396 U.S. 844, 90 S.Ct. 69 (1969), although on a slightly different rationale. Judge Friendly construed Seider as "in effect a judicially created direct action statute. The insurer doing business in New York is considered the real party in interest and the nonresident insured is viewed simply as a conduit, who has to be named as a defendant in order to provide a conceptual basis for getting at the insurer." Id., at 109; see Donawitz v. Danek, 42 N.Y.2d 138, 142, 397 N.Y.S.2d 592, 594, 366 N.E.2d 253, 255 (1977). The court held that New York could constitutionally enact a direct action statute, and that the restriction of liability to the amount of the policy coverage made the policyholder's personal stake in the litigation so slight that the exercise of jurisdiction did not offend due process.

New York has continued to adhere to Seider. New Hampshire has followed Seider if the defendant resides in a Seider jurisdiction, but not in other cases. Minnesota is the only other State that has adopted Seider-type jurisdiction. The Second Circuit recently reaffirmed its conclusion that Seider does not violate due process after reconsidering the doctrine in light of Shaffer v. Heitner. O'Connor v. Lee-Hy Paving Corp., 579 F.2d 194 (CA2), cert. denied, 439 U.S. 1034, 99 S.Ct. 638 (1978).

III

In Shaffer v. Heitner we held that "all assertions of state-court jurisdiction must be evaluated according to the standards set forth in International Shoe and its progeny." 433 U.S., at 212, 97 S.Ct., at 2584. That is, a State may exercise jurisdiction over an absent defendant only if the defendant has "certain minimum contacts with [the forum] such that the maintenance of the suit does not offend 'traditional notions of fair play and substantial justice.' " International Shoe Co. v. Washington, 326 U.S. 310, 316, 66 S.Ct. 154, 158 (1945). In determining whether a particular exercise of state-court jurisdiction is consistent with due process, the inquiry must focus on "the relationship among the defendant, the forum, and the litigation." Shaffer v. Heitner, supra, at 204, 97 S.Ct., at 2580.

It is conceded that Rush has never had any contacts with Minnesota, and that the auto accident that is the subject of this action occurred in Indiana and also had no connection to Minnesota. The only affiliating circumstance offered to show a relationship among Rush, Minnesota, and this lawsuit is that Rush's insurance company does business in the State. Seider constructed an ingenious jurisdictional theory to permit a State to command a defendant to appear in its courts on the basis of this factor alone. State Farm's contractual obligation to defend and indemnify Rush in connection with liability claims is treated as a debt owed by State Farm to Rush. The legal fiction that assigns a situs to a debt, for garnishment purposes, wherever the debtor is found is combined with the legal fiction that a corporation is "present," for jurisdictional purposes, wherever it does business to yield the conclusion that the obligation to defend and indemnify is located in the forum for purposes of the garnishment statute. The fictional presence of the policy obligation is deemed to give the State the power to determine the policyholder's liability for the out-of-state accident.

We held in Shaffer that the mere presence of property in a State does not establish a sufficient relationship between the owner of the property and the State to support the exercise of jurisdiction over an unrelated cause of action. The ownership of property in the State is *a* contact between the defendant and the forum, and it may suggest the presence of other ties. 433 U.S., at 209, 97 S.Ct., at 2582. Jurisdiction is lacking, however, unless there are sufficient contacts to satisfy the fairness standard of International Shoe.

Here, the fact that the defendant's insurer does business in the forum State suggests no further contacts between the defendant and the forum, and the record supplies no evidence of any. State Farm's decision to do business in Minnesota was completely adventitious as far as Rush was concerned. He had no control over that decision, and it is unlikely that he would have expected that by buying insurance in Indiana he had subjected himself to suit in any State to which a potential future plaintiff might decide to move. In short, it cannot be said that the *defendant* engaged in any purposeful activity related to the forum that would make the exercise of jurisdiction fair, just, or reasonable, see Kulko v. California Superior Court, 436 U.S. 84, 93–94, 98 S.Ct. 1690, 1697–1698 (1978); Hanson v. Denckla, 357 U.S. 235, 253, 78 S.Ct. 1228, 1239 (1958), merely because his insurer does business there.

Nor are there significant contacts between the litigation and the forum. The Minnesota Supreme Court was of the view that the insurance policy was so important to the litigation that it provided contacts sufficient to satisfy due process. The insurance policy is not the subject matter of the case, however, nor is it related to the operative facts of the negligence action. The contractual arrangements between the defendant and the insurer pertain only to the conduct, not the substance, of the litigation, and accordingly do not affect the court's jurisdiction unless they demonstrate ties between the defendant and the forum.

In fact, the fictitious presence of the insurer's obligation in Minnesota does not, without more, provide a basis for concluding that there is *any* contact in the International Shoe sense between Minnesota and the insured. To say that "a debt follows the debtor" is simply to say that intangible property has no actual situs, and a debt may be sued on wherever there is jurisdiction over the debtor. State Farm is "found," in the sense of doing business, in all 50 States and the District of Columbia. Under appellee's theory, the "debt" owed to Rush would be "present" in each of those jurisdictions simultaneously. It is apparent that such a "contact" can have no jurisdictional significance.

An alternative approach for finding minimum contacts in Seider-type cases, referred to with approval by the Minnesota Supreme Court, is to attribute the insurer's forum contacts to the defendant by treating the attachment procedure as the functional equivalent of a direct action against the insurer. This approach views Seider jurisdiction as fair both to the insurer, whose forum contacts would support in personam jurisdiction even for an unrelated cause of action, and to the "nominal defendant." Because liability is limited to the policy amount, the defendant incurs no personal liability, and the judgment is satisfied from the policy proceeds which are not available to the insured for any purpose other than paying accident claims, the insured is said to have such a slight stake in the litigation as a practical matter that it is not unfair to make him a "nominal defendant" in order to obtain jurisdiction over the insurance company.

Seider actions are not equivalent to direct actions, however. The State's ability to exert its power over the "nominal defendant" is analytically prerequisite to the insurer's entry into the case as a garnishee. If the Constitution forbids the assertion of jurisdiction over the insured based on the policy, then there is no conceptual basis for bringing the "garnishee" into the action. Because the party with forum contacts can only be reached through the out-of-state party, the question of jurisdiction over the nonresident cannot be ignored.[19] Moreover, the assumption that the defendant has no real stake in the litigation is far from self-evident.[20]

---

[19] Compare the direct action statute upheld in Watson v. Employers Liability Assurance Corp., 348 U.S. 66, 75 S.Ct. 166 (1954), which was applicable only if the accident or injury occurred in the State or the insured was domiciled there and which permitted the plaintiff to sue the insurer alone, without naming the insured as a defendant. Id., at 68, n. 4, 75 S.Ct., at 168, n. 4.

[20] A party does not extinguish his legal interest in a dispute by insuring himself against having to pay an eventual judgment out of his own pocket. Moreover, the purpose of insurance is simply to make the defendant whole for the economic costs of the lawsuit; but noneconomic factors may also be important to the defendant. Professional mal-practice actions, for example, question the defendant's integrity and competence and may affect his professional standing. Cf. Donawitz v. Danek, 42 N.Y.2d 138, 397 N.Y.S.2d 592, 366 N.E.2d 253 (1977) (medical malpractice action premised on Seider jurisdiction dismissed because plaintiff was a nonresident). Further, one can easily conceive of cases in which the defendant might have a substantial economic stake in Seider litigation—if, for example, multiple plaintiffs sued in different States for an aggregate amount in excess of the policy limits, or if a successful claim would affect the policyholder's insurability. For these reasons, the defendant's interest in the adjudication of his liability cannot reasonably be characterized as de minimis.

The Minnesota court also attempted to attribute State Farm's contacts to Rush by considering the "defending parties" together and aggregating their forum contacts in determining whether it had jurisdiction. The result was the assertion of jurisdiction over Rush based solely on the activities of State Farm. Such a result is plainly unconstitutional. Naturally, the parties' relationships with each other may be significant in evaluating their ties to the forum. The requirements of International Shoe, however, must be met as to each defendant over whom a state court exercises jurisdiction.

The justifications offered in support of Seider jurisdiction share a common characteristic: they shift the focus of the inquiry from the relationship among the defendant, the forum, and the litigation to that among the plaintiff, the forum, the insurer, and the litigation. The insurer's contacts with the forum are attributed to the defendant because the policy was taken out in anticipation of such litigation. The State's interests in providing a forum for its residents and in regulating the activities of insurance companies are substituted for its contacts with the defendant and the cause of action. This subtle shift in focus from the defendant to the plaintiff is most evident in the decisions limiting Seider jurisdiction to actions by forum residents on the ground that permitting nonresidents to avail themselves of the procedure would be unconstitutional. In other words, the plaintiff's contacts with the forum are decisive in determining whether the defendant's due process rights are violated.

Such an approach is forbidden by International Shoe and its progeny. If a defendant has certain judicially cognizable ties with a State, a variety of factors relating to the particular cause of action may be relevant to the determination whether the exercise of jurisdiction would comport with "traditional notions of fair play and substantial justice." See McGee v. International Life Ins. Co., 355 U.S. 220, 78 S.Ct. 199 (1957); cf. Kulko v. California Superior Court, 436 U.S., at 98–101, 98 S.Ct., at 1700–1701. Here, however, the defendant has *no* contacts with the forum, and the Due Process Clause "does not contemplate that a state may make binding a judgment . . . against an individual or corporate defendant with which the state has no contacts, ties, or relations." International Shoe Co. v. Washington, 326 U.S., at 319, 66 S.Ct., at 160. The judgment of the Minnesota Supreme Court is, therefore,

Reversed.

[Excerpts from Justice Brennan's dissenting opinion appear after World-Wide Volkswagen Corp. v. Woodson, which follows this case. The dissenting opinion of Justice Stevens is omitted.]

Dist. Judge →

WORLD–WIDE VOLKSWAGEN CORP. v. WOODSON
Supreme Court of the United States, 1980.
444 U.S. 286, 100 S.Ct. 559, 580.

Reversed → No juris.

MR. JUSTICE WHITE delivered the opinion of the Court.

Issue: in per if only contact is NY sold to NY who was in acci. in Okla.

The issue before us is whether, consistently with the Due Process Clause of the Fourteenth Amendment, an Oklahoma court may exercise in personam jurisdiction over a nonresident automobile retailer and its wholesale distributor in a products liability action, when the defendants' only connection with Oklahoma is the fact that an automobile sold in New York to New York residents became involved in an accident in Oklahoma.

I

Facts: accident in Okla.

Respondents Harry and Kay Robinson purchased a new Audi automobile from petitioner Seaway Volkswagen, Inc. (Seaway) in Massena, N.Y., in 1976. The following year the Robinson family, who resided in New York, left that State for a new home in Arizona. As they passed through the State of Oklahoma, another car struck their Audi in the rear, causing a fire which severely burned Kay Robinson and her two children.

The Robinsons subsequently brought a products liability action in the District Court for Creek County, Okla., claiming that their injuries resulted from defective design and placement of the Audi's gas tank and fuel system. They joined as defendants the automobile's manufacturer, Audi NSU Auto Union Aktiengesellschaft (Audi); its importer, Volkswagen of America, Inc. (Volkswagen); its regional distributor, petitioner World-Wide Volkswagen Corporation (World-Wide); and its retail dealer, petitioner Seaway. Seaway and World-Wide entered special appearances,[3] claiming that Oklahoma's exercise of jurisdiction over them would offend the limitations on the State's jurisdiction imposed by the Due Process Clause of the Fourteenth Amendment.

World wide: incorp = Del Bus. off = NY sells = NY, NJ, Conn.

Seaway: incorp = NY PPB = NY

Neither does busi. in Okla at all

The facts presented to the District Court showed that World-Wide is incorporated and has its business office in New York. It distributes vehicles, parts, and accessories, under contract with Volkswagen, to retail dealers in New York, New Jersey, and Connecticut. Seaway, one of these retail dealers, is incorporated and has its place of business in New York. Insofar as the record reveals, Seaway and World-Wide are fully independent corporations whose relations with each other and with Volkswagen and Audi are contractual only. Respondents adduced no evidence that either World-Wide or Seaway does any business in Oklahoma, ships or sells any products to or in

---

[3] Volkswagen also entered a special appearance in the District Court, but unlike World-Wide and Seaway did not seek review in the Supreme Court of Oklahoma and is not a petitioner here. Both Volkswagen and Audi remain as defendants in the litigation pending before the District Court in Oklahoma.

that State, has an agent to receive process there, or purchases advertisements in any media calculated to reach Oklahoma. In fact, as respondents' counsel conceded at oral argument, Tr. of Oral Arg. 32, there was no showing that any automobile sold by World-Wide or Seaway has ever entered Oklahoma with the single exception of the vehicle involved in the present case.

[margin note: No acts in Okla.]

Despite the apparent paucity of contacts between petitioners and Oklahoma, the District Court rejected their constitutional claim and reaffirmed that ruling in denying petitioners' motion for reconsideration. Petitioners then sought a writ of prohibition in the Supreme Court of Oklahoma to restrain the District Judge, respondent Charles S. Woodson, from exercising in personam jurisdiction over them. They renewed their contention that because they had no "minimal contacts," App. 32, with the State of Oklahoma, the actions of the District Judge were in violation of their rights under the Due Process Clause.

[margin note: Dis. Ct. → yes-in per juris]

The Supreme Court of Oklahoma denied the writ, 585 P.2d 351 (1978), holding that personal jurisdiction over petitioners was authorized by Oklahoma's "Long-Arm" Statute, Okla.Stat., Tit. 12, § 1701.03(a)(4) (1971).[7] Although the Court noted that the proper approach was to test jurisdiction against both statutory and constitutional standards, its analysis did not distinguish these questions, probably because § 1701.03(a)(4) has been interpreted as conferring jurisdiction to the limits permitted by the United States Constitution. The Court's rationale was contained in the following paragraph, 585 P.2d, at 354:

[margin note: S. Ct. Okla juris b/c Long arm Stat.]

[margin note: Rationale]

> "In the case before us, the product being sold and distributed by the petitioners is by its very design and purpose so mobile that petitioners can foresee its possible use in Oklahoma. This is especially true of the distributor, who has the exclusive right to distribute such automobile [sic] in New York, New Jersey and Connecticut. The evidence presented below demonstrated that goods sold and distributed by the petitioners were used in the State of Oklahoma, and under the facts we believe it reasonable to infer, given the retail value of the automobile, that the petitioners derive substantial income from automobiles which from time to time are used in the State of Oklahoma. This being the case, we hold that under the facts presented, the trial court was justified in conclud-

---

[7] This subsection provides:

"A court may exercise personal jurisdiction over a person, who acts directly or by an agent, as to a cause of action or claim for relief arising from the person's . . . . causing tortious injury in this state by an act or omission outside this state if he regularly does or solicits business or engages in any other persistent course of conduct, or derives substantial revenue from goods used or consumed or services rendered, in this state. . . ."

The State Supreme Court rejected jurisdiction based on § 1701.03(a)(3), which authorizes jurisdiction over any person "causing tortious injury in this state by an act or omission in this state." Something in addition to the infliction of tortious injury was required.

ing that the petitioners derive substantial revenue from goods used or consumed in this State."

We granted certiorari, 440 U.S. 907, 99 S.Ct. 1212 (1979), to consider an important constitutional question with respect to state-court jurisdiction and to resolve a conflict between the Supreme Court of Oklahoma and the highest courts of at least four other States. We reverse.

II

The Due Process Clause of the Fourteenth Amendment limits the power of a state court to render a valid personal judgment against a nonresident defendant. Kulko v. Superior Court, 436 U.S. 84, 91, 98 S.Ct. 1690, 1696 (1978). A judgment rendered in violation of due process is void in the rendering State and is not entitled to full faith and credit elsewhere. Pennoyer v. Neff, 95 U.S. 714, 732–733 (1878). Due process requires that the defendant be given adequate notice of the suit, Mullane v. Central Hanover Trust Co., 339 U.S. 306, 313–314, 70 S.Ct. 652, 657 (1950), and be subject to the personal jurisdiction of the court, International Shoe Co. v. Washington, 326 U.S. 310, 66 S.Ct. 154 (1945). In the present case, it is not contended that notice was inadequate; the only question is whether these particular petitioners were subject to the jurisdiction of the Oklahoma courts.

As has long been settled, and as we reaffirm today, a state court may exercise personal jurisdiction over a nonresident defendant only so long as there exist "minimum contacts" between the defendant and the forum State. International Shoe Co. v. Washington, supra, at 316, 66 S.Ct., at 158. The concept of minimum contacts, in turn, can be seen to perform two related, but distinguishable, functions. It protects the defendant against the burdens of litigating in a distant or inconvenient forum. And it acts to ensure that the States, through their courts, do not reach out beyond the limits imposed on them by their status as coequal sovereigns in a federal system.

The protection against inconvenient litigation is typically described in terms of "reasonableness" or "fairness." We have said that the defendant's contacts with the forum State must be such that maintenance of the suit "does not offend 'traditional notions of fair play and substantial justice.'" International Shoe Co. v. Washington, supra, at 316, 66 S.Ct., at 158, quoting Milliken v. Meyer, 311 U.S. 457, 463, 61 S.Ct. 339, 342 (1940). The relationship between the defendant and the forum must be such that it is "reasonable . . . to require the corporation to defend the particular suit which is brought there." 326 U.S., at 317, 66 S.Ct., at 158. Implicit in this emphasis on reasonableness is the understanding that the burden on the defendant, while always a primary concern, will in an appropriate case be considered in light of other relevant factors, including the forum State's interest in adjudicating the dispute, see McGee v. International Life Ins. Co., 355 U.S. 220, 223, 78 S.Ct. 199, 201 (1957); the plaintiff's interest in obtaining convenient and effective relief, see Kulko v. Superior Court, supra, at 92, 98 S.Ct., at 1697, at least when that interest is not adequately protected by the plaintiff's power to choose the forum, cf. Shaffer v. Heitner, 433 U.S. 186, 211, n. 37, 97 S.Ct. 2569, 2583, n. 37 (1977); the interstate judicial system's interest in obtaining the most efficient resolution of controversies; and the shared interest of the several States in furthering fundamental substantive social policies, see Kulko v. Superior Court, supra, at 93, 98, 98 S.Ct., at 1697, 1700.

Factors con'ld

The limits imposed on state jurisdiction by the Due Process Clause, in its role as a guarantor against inconvenient litigation, have been substantially relaxed over the years. As we noted in McGee v. International Life Ins. Co., supra, at 222–223, 78 S.Ct., at 201, this trend is largely attributable to a fundamental transformation in the American economy:

Limits relaxed & But NOT gone!

> "Today many commercial transactions touch two or more States and may involve parties separated by the full continent. With this increasing nationalization of commerce has come a great increase in the amount of business conducted by mail across state lines. At the same time modern transportation and communication have made it much less burdensome for a party sued to defend himself in a State where he engages in economic activity."

The historical developments noted in McGee, of course, have only accelerated in the generation since that case was decided.

Nevertheless, we have never accepted the proposition that state lines are irrelevant for jurisdictional purposes, nor could we and remain faithful to the principles of interstate federalism embodied in the Constitution. The economic interdependence of the States was foreseen and desired by the Framers. In the Commerce Clause, they provided that the Nation was to be a common market, a "free trade unit" in which the States are debarred from acting as separable economic entities. H.P. Hood & Sons, Inc. v. Du Mond, 336 U.S. 525, 538, 69 S.Ct. 657, 665 (1949). But the Framers also intended that the States retain many essential attributes of sovereignty, including, in particular, the sovereign power to try causes in their courts. The sovereignty of each State, in turn, implied a limitation on the sovereignty of all of its sister States—a limitation express or implicit in both the original scheme of the Constitution and the Fourteenth Amendment.

Hence, even while abandoning the shibboleth that "[t]he authority of every tribunal is necessarily restricted by the territorial limits of the State in which it is established," Pennoyer v. Neff, supra, at 720, we emphasized that the reasonableness of asserting jurisdiction over the defendant must be assessed "in the context of our federal system of government," International Shoe Co. v. Washington, supra, at 317, 66 S.Ct., at 158, and stressed that the Due Process Clause ensures, not only fairness, but also the "orderly administration of the laws," id., at 319, 66 S.Ct., at 159. As we noted in Hanson v. Denckla, 357 U.S. 235, 250–251, 78 S.Ct. 1228, 1238 (1958):

> "As technological progress has increased the flow of commerce between the States, the need for jurisdiction over nonresidents has undergone a similar increase. At the same time, progress in communications and transportation has made the defense of a suit in a foreign tribunal less burdensome. In response to these changes, the requirements for personal jurisdiction over nonresidents have evolved from the rigid rule of Pennoyer v. Neff, 95 U.S. 714, to the flexible standard of International Shoe Co. v. Washington, 326 U.S. 310, 66 S.Ct. 154. But it is a mistake to assume that this trend heralds the eventual demise of all restrictions on the personal jurisdiction of state courts. [Citation omitted.] Those restrictions are more than a guarantee of immunity from inconvenient or distant litigation. They are a consequence of territorial limitations on the power of the respective States."

Thus, the Due Process Clause "does not contemplate that a state may make binding a judgment in personam against an individual or corporate defendant with which the state has no contacts, ties, or relations." International Shoe Co. v. Washington, supra, at 319, 66 S.Ct., at 159. Even if the defendant would suffer minimal or no inconvenience from being forced to litigate before the tribunals of another State; even if the forum State has a strong interest in applying its law to the controversy; even if the forum State is the most convenient location for litigation, the Due Process Clause, acting as an instrument of interstate federalism, may sometimes act to divest the State of its power to render a valid judgment. Hanson v. Denckla, supra, at 251, 254, 78 S.Ct., at 1238, 1240.

III

None of necessary min. contacts here

Applying these principles to the case at hand, we find in the record before us a total absence of those affiliating circumstances that are a necessary predicate to any exercise of state-court jurisdiction. Petitioners carry on no activity whatsoever in Oklahoma. They close no sales and perform no services there. They avail themselves of none of the privileges and benefits of Oklahoma law. They solicit no business there either through salespersons or through advertising reasonably calculated to reach the State. Nor does the record show that they regularly sell cars at wholesale or retail to Oklahoma customers or residents or that they indirectly, through others, serve or seek to serve the Oklahoma market. In short, respondents seek to base jurisdiction on one, isolated occurrence and whatever inferences can be drawn therefrom: the fortuitous circumstance that a single Audi automobile, sold in New York to New York residents, happened to suffer an accident while passing through Oklahoma.

Ps argue: cars are mobile so foreseeable that it could cause injury in Okla

It is argued, however, that because an automobile is mobile by its very design and purpose it was "foreseeable" that the Robinsons'

Audi would cause injury in Oklahoma. Yet "foreseeability" alone *Forese.* has never been a sufficient benchmark for personal jurisdiction under *Not* the Due Process Clause. In Hanson v. Denckla, supra, it was no *enuf alone* doubt foreseeable that the settlor of a Delaware trust would subse- *to give* quently move to Florida and seek to exercise a power of appointment *juris* there; yet we held that Florida courts could not constitutionally exercise jurisdiction over a Delaware trustee that had no other contacts with the forum State. In Kulko v. Superior Court, supra, it was surely "foreseeable" that a divorced wife would move to California from New York, the domicile of the marriage, and that a minor daughter would live with the mother. Yet we held that California could not exercise jurisdiction in a child-support action over the former husband who had remained in New York.

If foreseeability were the criterion, a local California tire retailer could be forced to defend in Pennsylvania when a blowout occurs there, see Erlanger Mills, Inc. v. Cohoes Fibre Mills, Inc., 239 F.2d 502, 507 (CA4 1956); a Wisconsin seller of a defective automobile jack could be haled before a distant court for damage caused in New Jersey, Reilly v. Phil Tolkan Pontiac, Inc., 372 F.Supp. 1205 (NJ 1974); or a Florida soft drink concessionaire could be summoned to Alaska to account for injuries happening there, see Uppgren v. Executive Aviation Services, Inc., 304 F.Supp. 165, 170–171 (Minn.1969). Every seller of chattels would in effect appoint the chattel his agent for service of process. His amenability to suit would travel with the chattel. We recently abandoned the outworn rule of Harris v. Balk, 198 U.S. 215, 25 S.Ct. 625 (1905), that the interest of a creditor in a debt could be extinguished or otherwise affected by any State having transitory jurisdiction over the debtor. Shaffer v. Heitner, supra, 433 U.S. 186, 97 S.Ct. 2569 (1977). Having interred the mechanical rule that a creditor's amenability to a quasi in rem action travels with his debtor, we are unwilling to endorse an analogous principle in the present case.[11]

This is not to say, of course, that foreseeability is wholly irrele- *The foresee.* vant. But the foreseeability that is critical to due process analysis is *looked at is* not the mere likelihood that a product will find its way into the forum *if (D) could* State. Rather, it is that the defendant's conduct and connection with *reasonably* the forum State are such that he should reasonably anticipate being *contemplate* haled into court there. See Kulko v. Superior Court, supra, at 97–98, *being called into ct. in that state*

---

[11] Respondents' counsel, at oral argument, see Tr. of Oral Arg. 19–22, 29, sought to limit the reach of the foreseeability standard by suggesting that there is something unique about automobiles. It is true that automobiles are uniquely mobile, see Tyson v. Whitaker & Son, Inc., 407 A.2d 1, 6, and n. 11 (Me.1979) (McKusick, C.J.), that they did play a crucial role in the expansion of personal jurisdiction through the fiction of implied consent, e.g., Hess v. Pawloski, 274 U.S. 352, 47 S.Ct. 632 (1927), and that some of the cases have treated the automobile as a "dangerous instrumentality." But today, under the regime of International Shoe, we see no difference for jurisdictional purposes between an automobile and any other chattel. The "dangerous instrumentality" concept apparently was never used to support personal jurisdiction; and to the extent it has relevance today it bears not on jurisdiction but on the possible desirability of imposing substantive principles of tort law such as strict liability.

98 S.Ct., at 1699–1700; Shaffer v. Heitner, supra, at 216, 97 S.Ct., at 2586; and see id., at 217–219, 97 S.Ct., at 2586–2587 (Stevens, J., concurring in judgment). The Due Process Clause, by ensuring the "orderly administration of the laws," International Shoe Co. v. Washington, 326 U.S., at 319, 66 S.Ct., at 159, gives a degree of predictability to the legal system that allows potential defendants to structure their primary conduct with some minimum assurance as to where that conduct will and will not render them liable to suit.

When a corporation "purposefully avails itself of the privilege of conducting activities within the forum State," Hanson v. Denckla, supra, at 253, 78 S.Ct., at 1240, it has clear notice that it is subject to suit there, and can act to alleviate the risk of burdensome litigation by procuring insurance, passing the expected costs on to customers, or, if the risks are too great, severing its connection with the State. Hence if the sale of a product of a manufacturer or distributor such as Audi or Volkswagen is not simply an isolated occurrence, but arises from the efforts of the manufacturer or distributor to serve, directly or indirectly, the market for its product in other States, it is not unreasonable to subject it to suit in one of those States if its allegedly defective merchandise has there been the source of injury to its owner or to others. The forum State does not exceed its powers under the Due Process Clause if it asserts personal jurisdiction over a corporation that delivers its products into the stream of commerce with the expectation that they will be purchased by consumers in the forum State. Compare Gray v. American Radiator & Standard Sanitary Corp., 22 Ill.2d 432, 176 N.E.2d 761 (1961).

But there is no such or similar basis for Oklahoma jurisdiction over World-Wide or Seaway in this case. Seaway's sales are made in Massena, N.Y. World-Wide's market, although substantially larger, is limited to dealers in New York, New Jersey, and Connecticut. There is no evidence of record that any automobiles distributed by World-Wide are sold to retail customers outside this tri-State area. It is foreseeable that the purchasers of automobiles sold by World-Wide and Seaway may take them to Oklahoma. But the mere "unilateral activity of those who claim some relationship with a nonresident defendant cannot satisfy the requirement of contact with the forum State." Hanson v. Denckla, supra, at 253, 78 S.Ct., at 1239–1240.

In a variant on the previous argument, it is contended that jurisdiction can be supported by the fact that petitioners earn substantial revenue from goods used in Oklahoma. The Oklahoma Supreme Court so found, 585 P.2d, at 354–355, drawing the inference that because one automobile sold by petitioners had been used in Oklahoma, others might have been used there also. While this inference seems less than compelling on the facts of the instant case, we need not question the Court's factual findings in order to reject its reasoning.

This argument seems to make the point that the purchase of automobiles in New York, from which the petitioners earn substantial revenue, would not occur *but for* the fact that the automobiles are capable of use in distant States like Oklahoma. Respondents observe that the very purpose of an automobile is to travel, and that travel of automobiles sold by petitioners is facilitated by an extensive chain of Volkswagen service centers throughout the country, including some in Oklahoma. However, financial benefits accruing to the defendant from a collateral relation to the forum State will not support jurisdiction if they do not stem from a constitutionally cognizable contact with that State. See Kulko v. Superior Court, supra, at 94–95, 98 S.Ct., at 1698–1699. In our view, whatever marginal revenues petitioners may receive by virtue of the fact that their products are capable of use in Oklahoma is far too attenuated a contact to justify that State's exercise of in personam jurisdiction over them.

Because we find that petitioners have no "contacts, ties, or relations" with the State of Oklahoma, International Shoe Co. v. Washington, supra, at 319, 66 S.Ct., at 159, the judgment of the Supreme Court of Oklahoma is

Reversed.

MR. JUSTICE BRENNAN, dissenting [in this case and in Rush v. Savchuk, which precedes this case].

The Court holds that the Due Process Clause of the Fourteenth Amendment bars the States from asserting jurisdiction over the defendants in these two cases. In each case the Court so decides because it fails to find the "minimum contacts" that have been required since International Shoe Co. v. Washington, 326 U.S. 310, 316, 66 S.Ct. 154, 158 (1945). Because I believe that the Court reads International Shoe and its progeny too narrowly, and because I believe that the standards enunciated by those cases may already be obsolete as constitutional boundaries, I dissent.

I

The Court's opinions focus tightly on the existence of contacts between the forum and the defendant. In so doing, they accord too little weight to the strength of the forum State's interest in the case and fail to explore whether there would be any actual inconvenience to the defendant. The essential inquiry in locating the constitutional limits on state-court jurisdiction over absent defendants is whether the particular exercise of jurisdiction offends "traditional notions of fair play and substantial justice." International Shoe, supra; Milliken v. Meyer, 311 U.S. 457, 463, 61 S.Ct. 339, 342 (1940). The clear focus in International Shoe was on fairness and reasonableness. Kulko v. California Superior Court, 436 U.S. 84, 92, 98 S.Ct. 1690, 1697 (1978). . . .

Surely International Shoe contemplated that the significance of the contacts necessary to support jurisdiction would diminish if some other consideration helped establish that jurisdiction would be fair

[handwritten margin note:] Int'l Shoe said less contacts needed when other consideration would juris. would be fair reas.

and reasonable. The interests of the State and other parties in proceeding with the case in a particular forum are such considerations. McGee v. International Life Insurance Co., 355 U.S. 220, 223, 78 S.Ct. 199, 201 (1957), for instance, accorded great importance to a State's "manifest interest in providing effective means of redress" for its citizens. See also Kulko v. California Superior Court, supra, at 92, 98 S.Ct., at 1697; Shaffer v. Heitner, 433 U.S. 186, 208, 97 S.Ct. 2569, 2581 (1977); Mullane v. Central Hanover Trust Co., 339 U.S. 306, 313, 70 S.Ct. 652, 657 (1950).

Another consideration is the actual burden a defendant must bear in defending the suit in the forum. McGee, supra. Because lesser burdens reduce the unfairness to the defendant, jurisdiction may be justified despite less significant contacts. . . .

. . . .

II

In each of these cases, I would find that the forum State has an interest in permitting the litigation to go forward, the litigation is connected to the forum, the defendant is linked to the forum, and the burden of defending is not unreasonable. Accordingly, I would hold that it is neither unfair nor unreasonable to require these defendants to defend in the forum State.

. . . .

In [the World-Wide case], the interest of the forum State and its connection to the litigation is strong. The automobile accident underlying the litigation occurred in Oklahoma. The plaintiffs were hospitalized in Oklahoma when they brought suit. Essential witnesses and evidence were in Oklahoma. See Shaffer v. Heitner, supra, at 208, 97 S.Ct., at 2581. The State has a legitimate interest in enforcing its laws designed to keep its highway system safe, and the trial can proceed at least as efficiently in Oklahoma as anywhere else.

The petitioners are not unconnected with the forum. Although both sell automobiles within limited sales territories, each sold the automobile which in fact was driven to Oklahoma where it was involved in an accident.[8] It may be true, as the Court suggests, that each sincerely intended to limit its commercial impact to the limited territory, and that each intended to accept the benefits and protection of the laws only of those States within the territory. But obviously these were unrealistic hopes that cannot be treated as an automatic constitutional shield.[9]

[8] On the basis of this fact the state court inferred that the petitioners derived substantial revenue from goods used in Oklahoma. The inference is not without support. Certainly, were use of goods accepted as a relevant contact, a plaintiff would not need to have an exact count of the number of petitioners' cars that are used in Oklahoma.

[9] Moreover, imposing liability in this case would not so undermine certainty as to destroy an automobile dealer's ability to do business. According jurisdiction does not expand liability except in the

An automobile simply is not a stationary item or one designed to be used in one place. An automobile is *intended* to be moved around. Someone in the business of selling large numbers of automobiles can hardly plead ignorance of their mobility or pretend that the automobiles stay put after they are sold. It is not merely that a dealer in automobiles foresees that they will move. . . . The dealer actually intends that the purchasers will use the automobiles to travel to distant States where the dealer does not directly "do business." The sale of an automobile does *purposefully* inject the vehicle into the stream of interstate commerce so that it can travel to distant States. See Kulko, supra, at 94, 98 S.Ct., at 1698; Hanson v. Denckla, 357 U.S. 235, 253, 78 S.Ct. 1228, 1239 (1958).

Cars are purposfully entered into stream of commerce

The Court accepts that a State may exercise jurisdiction over a distributor which "serves" that State "indirectly" by "deliver[ing] its products into the stream of commerce with the expectation that they will be purchased by consumers in the forum State." . . . It is difficult to see why the Constitution should distinguish between a case involving goods which reach a distant State through a chain of distribution and a case involving goods which reach the same State because a consumer, using them as the dealer knew the customer would, took them there. In each case the seller purposefully injects the goods into the stream of commerce and those goods predictably are used in the forum State.[12]

Furthermore, an automobile seller derives substantial benefits from States other than its own. A large part of the value of automobiles is the extensive, nationwide network of highways. Significant portions of that network have been constructed by and are maintained by the individual States, including Oklahoma. The States, through their highway programs, contribute in a very direct and important way to the value of petitioners' businesses. Additionally, a network of other related dealerships with their service departments operate throughout the country under the protection of the laws of the various States, including Oklahoma, and enhance the value of petitioners' businesses by facilitating their customers' traveling.

(P) *benefits from state highways*

service depts thruout US bene. (P)

Thus, the Court errs in its conclusion, . . . (emphasis added), that "petitioners have *no* 'contacts, ties, or relations' " with Oklahoma. There obviously are contacts, and, given Oklahoma's connection to the litigation, the contacts are sufficiently significant to make it

marginal case where a plaintiff cannot afford to bring an action except in the plaintiff's own State. In addition, these petitioners are represented by insurance companies. They not only could, but did, purchase insurance to protect them should they stand trial and lose the case. The costs of the insurance no doubt are passed on to customers.

[12] The manufacturer in the case cited by the Court, Gray v. American Radiator & Standard Sanitary Corp., 22 Ill.2d 432, 176 N.E.2d 761 (1961), had no more control over which States its goods would reach than did the petitioners in this case.

fair and reasonable for the petitioners to submit to Oklahoma's jurisdiction.

III

It may be that affirmance of the judgments in these cases would approach the outer limits of International Shoe's jurisdictional principle. But that principle, with its almost exclusive focus on the rights of defendants, may be outdated. . . .

International Shoe inherited its defendant focus from Pennoyer v. Neff, 95 U.S. 714 (1878), and represented the last major step this Court has taken in the long process of liberalizing the doctrine of personal jurisdiction. Though its flexible approach represented a major advance, the structure of our society has changed in many significant ways since International Shoe was decided in 1945. . . . The model of society on which the International Shoe Court based its opinion is no longer accurate. Business people, no matter how local their businesses, cannot assume that goods remain in the business' locality. Customers and goods can be anywhere else in the country usually in a matter of hours and always in a matter of a very few days.

In answering the question whether or not it is fair and reasonable to allow a particular forum to hold a trial binding on a particular defendant, the interests of the forum State and other parties loom large in today's world and surely are entitled to as much weight as are the interests of the defendant. The "orderly administration of the laws" provides a firm basis for according some protection to the interests of plaintiffs and States as well as of defendants. Certainly, I cannot see how a defendant's right to due process is violated if the defendant suffers no inconvenience. . . .

The conclusion I draw is that constitutional concepts of fairness no longer require the extreme concern for defendants that was once necessary. Rather, as I wrote in dissent from Shaffer v. Heitner, supra, at 220, 97 S.Ct., at 2588 (emphasis added), minimum contacts must exist "among the *parties*, the contested transaction, and the forum State." [15] The contacts between any two of these should not be determinative. . . .

The Court's opinion . . . suggests that the defendant ought to be subject to a State's jurisdiction only if he has contacts with the State "such that he should reasonably anticipate being haled into court there." [18] . . . There is nothing unreasonable or unfair,

---

[15] In some cases, the inquiry will resemble the inquiry commonly undertaken in determining which State's law to apply. That it is fair to apply a State's law to a nonresident defendant is clearly relevant in determining whether it is fair to subject the defendant to jurisdiction in that State. Shaffer v. Heitner, 433 U.S. 186, 225, 97 S.Ct. 2569, 2590 (1977) (Bren-

nan, J., dissenting); Hanson v. Denckla, 357 U.S. 235, 258, 78 S.Ct. 1228, 1242 (1958) (Black, J., dissenting). See n. 19, infra.

[18] The Court suggests that this is the critical foreseeability rather than the likelihood that the product will go to the forum State. But the reasoning begs the

however, about recognizing commercial reality. Given the tremendous mobility of goods and people, and the inability of businessmen to control where goods are taken by customers (or retailers), I do not think that the defendant should be in complete control of the geographical stretch of his amenability to suit. Jurisdiction is no longer premised on the notion that nonresident defendants have somehow impliedly consented to suit. People should understand that they are held responsible for the consequences of their actions and that in our society most actions have consequences affecting many States. When an action in fact causes injury in another State, the actor should be prepared to answer for it there unless defending in that State would be unfair for some reason other than that a state boundary must be crossed.[19]

In effect the Court is allowing defendants to assert the sovereign rights of their home States. The expressed fear is that otherwise all limits on personal jurisdiction would disappear. But the argument's premise is wrong. I would not abolish limits on jurisdiction or strip state boundaries of all significance, see Hanson, supra, at 260, 78 S.Ct., at 1243 (Black, J., dissenting); I would still require the plaintiff to demonstrate sufficient contacts among the parties, the forum, and the litigation to make the forum a reasonable State in which to hold the trial.[20]

I would also, however, strip the defendant of an unjustified veto power over certain very appropriate fora—a power the defendant justifiably enjoyed long ago when communication and travel over long distances was slow and unpredictable and when notions of state sovereignty were impractical and exaggerated. But I repeat that that is not today's world. If a plaintiff can show that his chosen forum State has a sufficient interest in the litigation (or sufficient contacts with the defendant), then the defendant who cannot show some real injury to a constitutionally protected interest, see O'Connor v. Lee-Hy Paving Corp., 579 F.2d 194, 201 (CA2 1978), should have no constitutional excuse not to appear.[21]

. . . .

[The dissenting opinions of Justices Marshall and Blackmun, not taking issue with the majority's approach but arguing that Seaway and World-Wide had sufficient contacts with Oklahoma to satisfy International Shoe, are omitted. Interestingly, however, Justice Blackmun began his opinion with this paragraph:]

question. A defendant cannot know if his actions will subject him to jurisdiction in another State until we have declared what the law of jurisdiction is.

[19] One consideration that might create some unfairness would be if the choice of forum also imposed on the defendant an unfavorable substantive law which the defendant could justly have assumed would not apply. See n. 15, supra.

[20] . . . I might reach a different result if the accident had not occurred in Oklahoma.

[21] Frequently, of course, the defendant will be able to influence the choice of forum through traditional doctrines, such as venue or forum non conveniens, permitting the transfer of litigation. [Citation omitted.]

I confess that I am somewhat puzzled why the plaintiffs in this litigation are so insistent that the regional distributor and the retail dealer, the petitioners here, who handled the ill-fated Audi automobile involved in this litigation, be named defendants. It would appear that the manufacturer and the importer, whose subjectability to Oklahoma jurisdiction is not challenged before this Court, ought not to be judgment-proof. It may, of course, ultimately amount to a contest between insurance companies that, once begun, is not easily brought to a termination. Having made this much of an observation, I pursue it no further.

Questions: (43) Evaluate the following argument. The restriction that emerges from the early progeny of International Shoe, especially Mullane, rests on a concept of venue in a loose sense: the multifactor determination of "reasonableness" with respect to the litigation, a standard that was pro-plaintiff in the early days but is ultimately party-neutral, puts the emphasis on *fairness* in selecting the forum. However, the restriction that emerges from the later progeny of International Shoe, beginning with Hanson, represents the current law of territorial jurisdiction in a strict sense: the conceptual concern with "power" over the target of the action, now seemingly pro-defendant in effect, puts the emphasis on governmental *structure* in limiting the states' power. Shaffer first made explicit that these two constitutional restrictions apply cumulatively, by suggesting in part III of the Court's opinion that the exercise of in rem or quasi in rem power must also be reasonable, and then by holding in part IV of the opinion that even a reasonable forum must have power in order to exercise personal jurisdiction; previously the cumulative relation of the two restrictions had sometimes gone unrecognized, as perhaps exemplified by Mullane. Incidentally, Shaffer also demonstrated that the Pennoyer tripartite construct of in rem, quasi in rem, and in personam jurisdiction is alive and well, despite the Shaffer Court's lip service to the Mullane heresy (or reform).

(44) Is that how the Court's cases are to be read? Is that how the Court should have shaped the doctrine? Are the reasonableness and power tests bound eventually to coalesce, leaving some sort of reasonableness test as the survivor? Is the tripartite categorization then doomed?

INSURANCE CORP. OF IRELAND v. COMPAGNIE DES BAUXITES DE GUINEE, 456 U.S. 694, 102 S.Ct. 2099 (1982). In December 1975, plaintiff sued a number of foreign insurance companies in a diversity action in the Western District of Pennsylvania, seeking to recover on an insurance policy. Defendants asserted a defense of lack of personal jurisdiction. Plaintiff sought discovery on that issue. After various delays by defendants and judicial rulings, the district court warned that unless defendants complied with those discovery requests or at least produced information indicating a lack of personal jurisdiction, the court would invoke Rule 37(b)(2)(A) to establish personal jurisdiction as a sanction. The court eventually did just that, in April 1979.

The Third Circuit affirmed. On certiorari granted to resolve a conflict of the circuits, the Supreme Court affirmed. Justice White for the Court began by distinguishing personal jurisdiction from subject-matter jurisdiction:

"The requirement that a court have personal jurisdiction flows not from Art. III, but from the Due Process Clause. The personal jurisdiction requirement recognizes and protects an individual liberty interest. It represents a restriction on judicial power not as a matter of sovereignty, but as a matter of individual liberty.[10] Thus, the test for personal jurisdiction requires that 'the maintenance of the suit . . . not offend "traditional notions of fair play and substantial justice." ' International Shoe v. Washington, 326 U.S. 310, 316, 66 S.Ct. 154, 158 (1945), quoting Milliken v. Meyer, 311 U.S. 457, 463, 61 S.Ct. 339, 342 (1940).

"Because the requirement of personal jurisdiction represents first of all an individual right, it can, like other such rights, be waived. . . . Furthermore, the Court has upheld state procedures which find constructive consent to the personal jurisdiction of the state court in the voluntary use of certain state procedures. See Adam v. Saenger, 303 U.S. 59, 67–68, 58 S.Ct. 454, 458 (1938) . . . .

"In sum, the requirement of personal jurisdiction may be intentionally waived, or for various reasons a defendant may be estopped from raising the issue. These characteristics portray it for what it is—a legal right protecting the individual. The plaintiff's demonstration of certain historical facts may make clear to the court that it has personal jurisdiction over the defendant as a matter of law—i.e., certain factual showings will have legal consequences—but this is not

[10] It is true that we have stated that the requirement of personal jurisdiction, as applied to state courts, reflects an element of federalism and the character of state sovereignty vis-à-vis other states. For example, in World-Wide Volkswagen Corp. v. Woodson, 444 U.S. 286, 291–293, 100 S.Ct. 559, 564–565 (1980), we stated:

'[A] state court may exercise personal jurisdiction over a nonresident defendant only so long as there exist "minimum contacts" between the defendant and the forum State. The concept of minimum contacts, in turn, can be seen to perform two related, but distinguishable, functions. It protects the defendant against the burdens of litigating in a distant or inconvenient forum. And it acts to ensure that the States, through their courts, do not reach out beyond the limits imposed on them by their status as co-equal sovereigns in a federal system.' (Citation omitted.)

Contrary to the suggestion of Justice Powell, . . . our holding today does not alter the requirement that there be 'minimum contacts' between the nonresident defendant and the forum state. Rather, our holding deals with how the facts needed to show those 'minimum contacts' can be established when a defendant fails to comply with court-ordered discovery. The restriction on state sovereign power described in World-Wide Volkswagen Corp., however, must be seen as ultimately a function of the individual liberty interest preserved by the Due Process Clause. That clause is the only source of the personal jurisdiction requirement and the clause itself makes no mention of federalism concerns. Furthermore, if the federalism concept operated as an independent restriction on the sovereign power of the court, it would not be possible to waive the personal jurisdiction requirement: Individual actions cannot change the powers of sovereignty, although the individual can subject himself to powers from which he may otherwise be protected.

the only way in which the personal jurisdiction of the court may arise. The actions of the defendant may amount to a legal submission to the jurisdiction of the court, whether voluntary or not.

. . . .

"Rule 37(b)(2)(A) itself embodies the standard established in Hammond Packing Co. v. Arkansas, 212 U.S. 322, 29 S.Ct. 370 (1909), for the Due Process limits on such rules. There the Court held that it did not violate due process for a state court to strike the answer and render a default judgment against a defendant who failed to comply with a pretrial discovery order. Such a rule was permissible as an expression of 'the undoubted right of the lawmaking power to create a presumption of fact as to the bad faith and untruth of an answer begotten from the suppression or failure to produce the proof ordered . . . . [T]he preservation of due process was secured by the presumption that the refusal to produce evidence material to the administration of due process was but an admission of the want of merit in the asserted defense.' Id., at 351, 29 S.Ct., at 380.

". . . Due process is violated only if the behavior of the defendant will not support the Hammond Packing presumption. . . . If there is no abuse of discretion in the application of the Rule 37 sanction, as we find to be the case here . . . , then the sanction is nothing more than the invocation of a legal presumption, or what is the same thing, the finding of a constructive waiver.

"Petitioners argue that a sanction consisting of a finding of personal jurisdiction differs from all other instances in which a sanction is imposed, including the default judgment in Hammond Packing, because a party need not obey the orders of a court until it is established that the court has personal jurisdiction over that party. . . .

"This argument again assumes that there is something unique about the requirement of personal jurisdiction, which prevents it from being established or waived like other rights. A defendant is always free to ignore the judicial proceedings, risk a default judgment, and then challenge that judgment on jurisdictional grounds in a collateral proceeding. See Baldwin v. Traveling Men's Ass'n, 283 U.S. 522, 525, 51 S.Ct. 517 (1931). By submitting to the jurisdiction of the court for the limited purpose of challenging jurisdiction, the defendant agrees to abide by that court's determination on the issue of jurisdiction: That decision will be res judicata on that issue in any further proceedings. Id., at 524, 51 S.Ct., at 517; American Surety Co. v. Baldwin, 287 U.S. 156, 166, 53 S.Ct. 98, 101 (1932). As demonstrated above, the manner in which the court determines whether it has personal jurisdiction may include a variety of legal rules and presumptions, as well as straightforward fact-finding."

Justice Powell concurred in the judgment, approving assertion of personal jurisdiction in this situation because plaintiff had in fact made a prima facie showing of minimum contacts. He objected to the Court's deciding on broader grounds:

"By finding that the establishment of minimum contacts is not a prerequisite to the exercise of jurisdiction to impose sanctions under Fed.Rule Civ.Proc. 37, the Court may be understood as finding that 'minimum contacts' no longer is a constitutional requirement for the exercise by a state court of personal jurisdiction over an unconsenting defendant. Whenever the Court's notions of fairness are not offended, jurisdiction apparently may be upheld.

"Before today, of course, our cases had linked minimum contacts and fair play as *jointly* defining the 'sovereign' limits on state assertions of personal jurisdiction over unconsenting defendants. See World-Wide Volkswagen Corp. v. Woodson, supra, 444 U.S., at 292–293, 100 S.Ct., at 564–565; see Hanson v. Denckla, . . . 357 U.S., at 251, 78 S.Ct., at 1238. The Court appears to abandon the rationale of these cases in a footnote. See ante at . . . n. 10. But it does not address the implications of its action. By eschewing reliance on the concept of minimum contacts as a 'sovereign' limitation on the power of States—for . . . it is the State's long-arm statute that is invoked to obtain personal jurisdiction in the District Court—the Court today effects a potentially substantial change of law. For the first time it defines personal jurisdiction solely by reference to abstract notions of fair play. And, astonishingly to me, it does so in a case in which this rationale for decision was neither argued nor briefed by the parties.

. . . .

"Alternatively, it is possible to read the Court opinion, not as affecting state jurisdiction, but simply as asserting that Rule 37 of the Federal Rules of Civil Procedure represents a congressionally approved basis for the exercise of personal jurisdiction by a federal district court. On this view Rule 37 vests the federal district courts with authority to take jurisdiction over persons not in compliance with discovery orders. This of course would be a more limited holding. Yet the Court does not cast its decision in these terms. And it provides no support for such an interpretation, either in the language or in the history of the Federal Rules."

SECTION 5. ACTIONS IN FEDERAL COURT

We have considered statutory and constitutional limitations on the exercise of territorial jurisdiction, and in doing so we have dealt with both state and federal cases. The time has come, however, to examine with a finer focus this issue of amenability to suit in the context of actions in federal court.

The federal courts can constitutionally reach much farther than can the state courts in exercising territorial jurisdiction.[g] Neverthe-

[g] See supra p. 180 note h.

less, the federal courts have decided that ordinarily they are not to assert their utmost constitutional powers of adjudication, but instead they are to act within certain limits largely derived from the interplay between the Federal Rules and the Erie doctrine. To study this subject, it is necessary to think through the provisions governing service of process, because the legislators, rulemakers, and courts have borrowed the structure of those provisions to specify amenability to federal suit.

Rule 4(e) provides that service may be made outside the forum state under the "circumstances" prescribed by any applicable federal statute.[h] This language is interpreted to mean that the particular federal service statute prescribes amenability to federal suit. For example, under 28 U.S.C. § 2361 an interpleaded party may be served anywhere in the United States, and the federal court can then exercise personal jurisdiction to the limits of fifth amendment due process.

Rule 4(e) also provides that service may be made outside the state "under the circumstances and in the manner" prescribed by the law of the state. This language is usually interpreted to mean that a party is amenable to federal suit, upon service in accordance with Rule 4(e), whenever the party would be amenable to suit in the courts of the state in which the district court sits. State law thus governs amenability to suit under this part of Rule 4(e), apparently without regard to whether the federal suit is based on a federally created claim or on a claim created by state law.

Rule 4(d), on the other hand, deals only with the "manner" in which process is served within the state, leaving open whether federal or state law should govern amenability. Here it may be necessary to distinguish suits based on a federally created claim from those based on a claim created by state law.

In a case based on a federally created claim, with service under Rule 4(d), the overwhelming federal interests in a federal determination of the bounds of territorial jurisdiction dictate that a federal standard of amenability should apply. What is this federal standard?

DeJAMES v. MAGNIFICENCE CARRIERS

United States District Court, District of New Jersey, 1980.
491 F.Supp. 1276, aff'd, 654 F.2d 280 (3d Cir.), cert.
denied, 454 U.S. 1085, 102 S.Ct. 642 (1981).

COHEN, SENIOR JUDGE:

Plaintiff, Joseph DeJames, a New Jersey citizen, has brought suit under the admiralty jurisdiction of the court, 28 U.S.C. § 1333, to recover damages for personal injuries suffered while working aboard

[h] See supra p. 179 note d.

the vessel M.V. Magnificence Venture.   The injuries allegedly occurred on January 26, 1977, while the vessel was moored at a pier in Camden, New Jersey.

According to the pleadings defendant, Hitachi Shipbuilding and Engineering Company, Ltd. (Hitachi), entered into a contract in Japan with defendants Magnificence Carriers, Inc., Venture Shipping (Managers Ltd.), and Nippon Yusen Kaisha, the charterers of the vessel, M.V. Magnificence Venture, whereby Hitachi agreed to convert the vessel into an automobile carrier.   Plaintiff alleges in his complaint that the conversion work performed by Hitachi was defective and was the direct cause of his injuries.

Presently before the court is a motion by Hitachi to dismiss the complaint against it for insufficiency of service and for lack of in personam jurisdiction.[i]   Hitachi contends that it does not maintain the requisite contacts with New Jersey to enable this court to render a binding personal judgment against it.   In support thereof, Hitachi has submitted an affidavit from Kiyoshi Ohno, manager of its ship repair business department located in Tokyo, Japan.   According to the affidavit, Hitachi completed all work on the vessel at issue in its Japanese shipyard and had no further contact or involvement with the ship once it left Osaka, Japan.   The affidavit further states that Hitachi does not maintain an office in New Jersey, nor does it have an agent of any type there or transact any business in the State.

At the outset it should be noted that when a federal court is asked to exercise personal jurisdiction over a defendant sued on a claim arising out of federal law, federal law under the due process clause of the fifth amendment is controlling.   See Honeywell, Inc. v. Metz Apparatewerke, [509] F.2d 1137, 1143 (7th Cir.1975); Fraley v. Chesapeake and Ohio Railway Company, 397 F.2d 1, 3–4 (3d Cir.1968); Alco Standard Corp. v. Benalal, 345 F.Supp. 14, 24–25 (E.D.Pa.1972).   That is not to say, however, that the analysis employed in diversity jurisdiction cases arising under the fourteenth amendment has no bearing on our decision in this case.   In this regard, the Court of Appeals for the Third Circuit has remarked that the standard of due process set forth by the Supreme Court in International Shoe Co. v. Washington, 326 U.S. 310, 66 S.Ct. 154, 90 L.Ed. 95 (1945) and its progeny is equally applicable in cases grounded on a federal claim.   See Fraley, 397 F.2d at 3; [other citations omitted].

In response to Hitachi's motion to dismiss, plaintiff argues first, that Hitachi's contacts with New Jersey are sufficient for the purposes of jurisdiction, and second, that where, as here, the court is to determine whether it has jurisdiction over a defendant who is being sued on a federal claim, it may consider not only the defendant's contacts with the forum state, but also the aggregate contacts of the

---

[i] Hitachi was served in Japan.

defendant with the United States as a whole. We take up these arguments in turn.

[The court concluded that under the International Shoe and World-Wide cases, Hitachi lacked minimum contacts with New Jersey.]

The earliest case adopting the national contacts approach is First Flight Co. v. National Carloading Corp., 209 F.Supp. 730 (E.D.Tenn. 1962). That court held that the proper inquiry in determining personal jurisdiction in a case involving federal rights is one related to the contacts with the sovereignty in question, the United States. Id. at 738. The theoretical basis behind this approach is that the restrictions of the fourteenth amendment upon state jurisdiction have no application to a cause of action arising under federal law. Instead, the argument runs, the fifth amendment due process clause controls, and a defendant's national contacts may be aggregated to satisfy that standard. [Citations omitted.] As described by one court, "it is not the territory in which a court sits that determines the extent of its jurisdiction, but rather the geographical limits of the unit of government of which the court is a part." Cryomedics, Inc. v. Spembly, Ltd., 397 F.Supp. 287, 291 (D.Conn.1975); accord, Centronics Data Computer Corp. v. Mannesmann, 432 F.Supp. 659, 663–64 & n.1 (D.N.H.1977) (quoting First Flight, 209 F.Supp. at 736–37); Holt v. Klosters Rederi A/S, 355 F.Supp. 354, 357 (W.D.Mich.1973); Alco Standard Corp. v. Benalal, 345 F.Supp. 14 (E.D.Pa.1972); Edward J. Moriarity & Co. v. General Tire & Rubber Co., 289 F.Supp. 381, 390 (S.D.Ohio 1967).

Although the fifth amendment test is sometimes expressed in more general "fairness" terms, see, e.g., Honeywell, Inc., 509 F.2d at 1143 (citing Galvan v. Press, 347 U.S. 522, 530, 74 S.Ct. 737, 742, 98 L.Ed. 911 (1954)), the International Shoe line of cases . . . provides the foundation for the test, and the analysis is substantially similar. See Honeywell, Inc., 509 F.2d at 1143; First Flight, 209 F.Supp. at 738 (E.D.Tenn.1962). Accordingly, the standard which has been applied by those courts adopting the national contacts approach is whether defendant "has such minimum contacts with the United States that the exercise of jurisdiction does not offend traditional notions of fair play and substantial justice." Holt v. Klosters Rederi A/S, 355 F.Supp. at 357 n.2 (quoting First Flight, 209 F.Supp. at 738); [other citations omitted].

. . . .

Since the First Flight opinion discussed the national contacts theory in 1962, several jurisdictions have considered the approach in federal question cases. But most courts which have analyzed the theory have refused to apply it and have instead looked solely to state contacts as a basis for jurisdiction. While these courts generally acknowledge the logic of inquiring into a defendant's contacts with the United States where the suit is based upon a federally created right, they reason that they must have a federal rule or statute authorizing nationwide or worldwide service of process before doing so. See, e.g., Wells Fargo & Co. v. Wells Fargo Exp. Co., 556 F.2d 406, 418 (9th Cir.1977) (refused to aggregate national contacts since Lanham Act did not grant the court broad service of process powers); [other citations omitted].

A review of the pertinent case law reveals that the overwhelming majority of courts which have considered the national contacts approach have rejected its application in the absence of statutory authority for service of process. After careful analysis of the rationale underlying these decisions, the court finds that it must join their ranks. We, therefore, reject plaintiff's contention in the instant matter that defendant Hitachi's national contacts may be aggregated as a basis for the exercise of jurisdiction over Hitachi.

The court's opinion in the case at bar, however, should not be construed as a total rejection of the national contacts theory. On the contrary, the court believes that it is not unfair nor unreasonable as a matter of due process to consider the nationwide contacts of an alien defendant in determining whether jurisdiction exists. As noted by Judge Wilson in his opinion in First Flight,

> One fundamental principle of the Anglo-American law of jurisdiction is that a sovereignty has personal jurisdiction over any defendant within its territorial limits, and that it may exercise that jurisdiction by any of its courts able to obtain service upon the defendant.

209 F.Supp. at 736. This court also believes that many good policy reasons exist for applying the national contacts theory, particularly in those federal question cases involving alien defendants. . . .

We also recognize, however, that the United States has by the enactment of the Federal Rules of Civil Procedure imposed restrictions upon the exercise of personal jurisdiction by its courts. One such restriction, relevant to the case at bar, is that imposed by Rule 4(e), which provides that when substituted service is made pursuant to a state's long-arm statute, the service be made "under the circumstances and in the manner prescribed in the statute." Fed.R.Civ.P. 4(e)(2). That portion of the Rule has been interpreted to mean that service under a valid state long-arm statute in a federal court is only possible in those situations where the in-state activities of the defendant would be sufficient to invoke the long-arm statute had the defendant been sued in state court. See, e.g., Hydraulics Unlimited Mfg. Co. v. B/J Manufacturing Co., 449 F.2d 775, 777 (10th Cir.1971); [other citations omitted]; see generally 4 C. Wright & A. Miller, Federal Practice and Procedure, § 1075, at 313 (2d ed. 1969). Thus, where service of process is effected by means of a state statute, a federal court is forced to look to the state in which the district is located to determine whether jurisdiction may be asserted over an out-of-state defendant.

. . . . .

Plaintiff has urged the court to exercise jurisdiction on the ground that New Jersey's long-arm rule, R. 4:4–4, N.J.Court Rules (the rule employed in the case at bar) has been construed as extending New Jersey's jurisdictional reach to its constitutional limits. See Avdel v. Mecure, 58 N.J. 264, 268, 277 A.2d 207, 209 (1971). The power of the State of New Jersey, however, is still limited by the due process requirements of the fourteenth amendment. There must still be some contact of a defendant with the forum state.

It is important to note that our rejection of the national contacts approach in the instant matter is limited to those factual situations where service of process must be made pursuant to a state statute. We believe that where service can be effected through wholly federal means, a defendant's national contacts may still be a viable basis for jurisdiction in a federal question case. Thus, for instance, where Congress has provided for nationwide service of process, we can perceive of no impediment to the application of the national contacts theory with the exception of the fifth amendment's "fairness" standard. There would be no need to make reference to any state law in making service, see Rule 4(f), and concomitantly, no need to consider any fourteenth amendment or state restrictions on that service. See, e.g., Alco Standard Corp. v. Benalal, 345 F.Supp. 14, 25 (E.D.Pa.1972) (In action brought under Securities and Exchange Act, which provides for nationwide service of process, court ruled that since the Act is national in scope, the court's jurisdictional inquiry should focus on a defendant's national contacts.) The same result would also seem appropriate when service of process is made pursuant to Rule 4(d)(3), which provides for service "[u]pon a . . . foreign corporation . . . by delivering a copy of the summons and of the complaint to . . . [an] agent authorized by appointment or by law to receive service of process". Rule 4(d)(3), like Rule 4(f), provides for a strictly federal method of service and, thus, like that Rule, does not implicate any state law limitations on jurisdiction. See First Flight, 209 F.Supp. at 735; [other citations omitted].

Since Congress has not enacted a federal statute authorizing nationwide service of process in admiralty actions, and since the district court's power in the present matter is therefore limited by the Federal Rules of Civil Procedure and, through them, the laws of New Jersey, we find the relevant jurisdictional inquiry to be the extent of the defendant Hitachi's contacts with New Jersey. And since we have determined that Hitachi lacks sufficient contacts with New Jersey to satisfy the jurisdictional standards set forth in International Shoe and its progeny, defendant Hitachi's Motion to Dismiss must be granted.[j]

---

[j] This decision was affirmed, 654 F.2d 280 (3d Cir.), cert. denied, 454 U.S. 1085, 102 S.Ct. 642 (1981). The Third Circuit made two observations of particular interest:

If the case is instead based on a state-created claim, with service under Rule 4(d), should federal or state law govern amenability? On this point there was an internecine struggle in the Second Circuit, with Judges Clark and Friendly as the protagonists. In Jaftex Corp. v. Randolph Mills, 282 F.2d 508 (2d Cir.1960), Judge Clark opted for a federal standard, over Judge Friendly's objection. The question was renewed in the Arrowsmith case below, with the court sitting in banc.

ARROWSMITH v. UNITED PRESS INTERNATIONAL

United States Court of Appeals, Second Circuit, 1963.
320 F.2d 219.

[A libel action was brought by a Maryland plaintiff against UPI, a New York corporation, in the District Court for the District of Vermont. The action was based upon a news dispatch transmitted from Georgia to UPI subscribers all over the country. The allegation was that the dispatch referred to the plaintiff, in connection with the dynamiting of an Atlanta synagogue, as a "fat cat financier" of anti-Semitic terrorist activity. Vermont was chosen because it alone had a sufficiently long statute of limitations. Service was made under Rule 4(d)(3) on UPI's "manager" in Vermont.

[The court of appeals eventually discussed the defense of lack of personal jurisdiction, for the guidance of the district court on remand.]

1. "Because this suit arises under the district court's admiralty jurisdiction, the due process clause of the fifth amendment determines whether the district court has personal jurisdiction over Hitachi. See Fraley v. Chesapeake & Ohio Railway, 397 F.2d 1, 4 (3d Cir.1968). However, [that FELA case, in which service was made under Rule 4(d)(3), applied the International Shoe standard]. This standard provides that a defendant is subject to a forum's jurisdiction only if its contacts with the forum are such that maintenance of the suit will not offend traditional notions of fair play and substantial justice. It is unclear whether the Fraley court meant that the fifth amendment requires a defendant to have minimum contacts with the forum state, or whether the court intended only that the International Shoe test be applied by analogy, so that a defendant need only have minimum contacts with the United States as a whole. In any event, even in nondiversity cases, if service of process must be made pursuant to a state long-arm statute or rule of court, the defendant's amenability to suit in federal district court is limited by that statute or rule."

2. "We will accept for purposes of this appeal DeJames' position that if service can be made by wholly federal means all of Hitachi's contacts with the United States may be aggregated to support jurisdiction in the District of New Jersey, even if these contacts are limited exclusively to Hawaii, to Alaska, or to a few states on the west coast. As we noted earlier, the Fraley court stated that the fourteenth amendment standards of due process announced in International Shoe and its progeny also apply to cases grounded on a federal claim, which is governed by fifth amendment standards. See 397 F.2d at 3. Even if this statement is not read to limit the jurisdictional inquiry to contacts with the forum state, we are not sure that some geographic limit short of the entire United States might not be incorporated into the 'fairness' component of the fifth amendment. For a discussion of possible fifth amendment limitations, see Oxford First Corp. v. PNC Liquidating Corp., 372 F.Supp. 191, 198–204 (E.D.Pa.1974)."

Before LUMBARD, CHIEF JUDGE, and CLARK, WATERMAN, MOORE, FRIENDLY, SMITH, KAUFMAN, HAYS and MARSHALL, CIRCUIT JUDGES.

FRIENDLY, CIRCUIT JUDGE.

.　.　.　.

The issue of the standard to be applied in determining whether a federal court has jurisdiction over the person of a foreign corporation in a suit where federal jurisdiction is founded solely on diversity of citizenship, 28 U.S.C. § 1332, has arisen frequently [in other courts].

.　.　.　.

There thus exists an overwhelming consensus that the amenability of a foreign corporation to suit in a federal court in a diversity action is determined in accordance with the law of the state where the court sits, with "federal law" entering the picture only for the purpose of deciding whether a state's assertion of jurisdiction contravenes a constitutional guarantee. . . . F.R.Civ.Proc. 4(d)(3) and (7) [k] both relate to the manner of service and leave open the question whether the foreign corporation was subject to service in any manner. . . .

.　.　.　.

No federal statute or Rule of Civil Procedure speaks to the issue either expressly or by fair implication. . . . No one reading the Rule would be likely to get the impression that Rule 4(d)(3) was a charter to the federal courts to make their own law as to *when* a foreign corporation is subject to suit and that the effect of Rule 4(d)(7) is to make state standards of jurisdiction *alternatively* applicable. The Advisory Committee's Notes reveal no such intention; rather they emphasize the much more limited one, which the language of the Rule indicates, of regulating the *manner* of service, saying that paragraph (3) "enumerates the officers and agents of a corporation or of a partnership or other unincorporated association upon whom service of process may be made . . . ." Eminent authority thus seems entirely justified in concluding that "Rule 4(d)(3) of the Rules of Civil Procedure tells how service of process is to be made upon a corporation which is subject to service; but it does not tell when the corporation is so subject." Hart & Wechsler, The Federal Courts and the Federal System, 959 (1953).

Despite contrary intimations as to our position in the dissent, we fully concede that the constitutional doctrine announced in Erie R.R. v. Tompkins, 304 U.S. 64, 78–80, 58 S.Ct. 817, 82 L.Ed. 1188 (1938), would not prevent Congress or its rule-making delegate from authorizing a district court to assume jurisdiction over a foreign corporation in an ordinary diversity case although the state court would not; and we reaffirm decisions of this Court that have sustained the application of certain Federal Rules of Civil Procedure differing from the rules applied by the state where the court sits. [Citations omitted.]

---

[k] Now Federal Rule 4(c)(2)(C)(i).

But we find no federal policy that should lead federal courts in diversity cases to override valid state laws as to the subjection of foreign corporations to suit, in the absence of direction by federal statute or rule. State statutes determining what foreign corporations may be sued, for what, and by whom, are not mere whimsy; like most legislation they represent a balancing of various considerations—for example, affording a forum for wrongs connected with the state and conveniencing resident plaintiffs, while avoiding the discouragement of activity within the state by foreign corporations. We see nothing in the concept of diversity jurisdiction that should lead us to read into the governing statutes a Congressional mandate, unexpressed by Congress itself, to disregard the balance thus struck by the states. . . . Thus, the present dissent points out no federal policy that makes it important to provide this Maryland plaintiff with a federal forum in Vermont, if Vermont itself would not entertain such an action, for what in every practical sense is a suit against another out-of-stater on a claim arising predominantly, if not wholly, outside the state. . . . Supreme Court decisions enforcing state "door-closing" statutes in the federal courts, and the reasons there expressed, Angel v. Bullington, 330 U.S. 183, 191–192, 67 S.Ct. 657, 91 L.Ed. 832 (1947); Woods v. Interstate Realty Co., 337 U.S. 535, 69 S.Ct. 1235, 93 L.Ed. 1524 (1949), appear to point in precisely the opposite direction from the dissent here; it seems immaterial that in such cases the state policy is expressed as a closing of the door against a particular kind of suit or plaintiff rather than as a refusal to pull a particular kind of defendant through the door. State policy is involved in one case as much as in the other, and in the absence of an overriding federal interest intimated by Congress or its delegate, should be equally respected.

Our belief that neither the federal legislature nor the federal rule-makers have had any intention to displace state statutes as to the taking of jurisdiction over foreign corporations in ordinary diversity cases is strengthened by instances where, in certain types of federal question litigation, Congress has provided for service of process outside the district. . . .

. . . .

The decision of what contacts, within the constitutionally permitted sphere, shall suffice to make a foreign corporation subject to suit is one for the state to make in the first instance; once the state has made this, there is no reason for a federal court to go further—or less far—when it is acting under a head of jurisdiction supposedly designed to protect certain suitors from possible prejudice by state courts. . . .

. . . .

Neither do we find force in the statement in Jaftex, 282 F.2d at 513, that "[t]he federal and state rules are certainly not so mutually at odds that the federal decision will seriously damage state polity."

When . . . the state standard and the supposed "federal standard" are identical or nearly so, it is hard to see what useful purpose the concept of a separate "federal standard" serves; when the "federal standard" is alleged to be significantly different from that which the state has chosen, it is equally hard to see what justification there is for it. One may agree with the premise of the dissent that the quest for uniformity between state and federal courts can be pushed too far, particularly when the issue may reasonably be denoted as one of procedure, without accepting the apparent conclusion that deliberately creating a difference in result between state and federal courts on an issue such as jurisdiction over foreign corporations in a diversity case is so demonstrable a good as to warrant federal judges in substituting their views for state legislators'. . . .

. . . . .

[The concurring opinions of Judges Smith and Waterman, and the sharp dissenting opinion of Judge Clark, are omitted.]

———

Question: (45) The Arrowsmith rule has been adopted by all the courts of appeals, but certainly not approved by all commentators. What do you think of Judge Friendly's analysis? Is Szantay v. Beech Aircraft Corp., supra p. 231, relevant to your position?

On some issues closely related to the one involved in Arrowsmith, the Erie balance is thought to come out the other way. For example, questions both of immunity from service of process and of the effect of fraud or force in the attempted acquisition of territorial jurisdiction are generally held to be governed in all federal actions by federal law. Similarly, federal law determines which acts committed in the course of litigating will confer jurisdiction over the person; thus, federal law will determine whether a defendant has made a general appearance. But there are a number of issues where it is more difficult to determine which law governs, and what that law provides. We touch upon a few of these issues here.

Questions: (46) Suit is brought against a foreign corporation in state court on a federally created claim, with service being made within the state on an officer of the defendant. The defendant removes the case to federal court and then moves to dismiss under Rule 12(b)(2). Should federal or state law govern this jurisdictional issue? Does it matter whether the defendant is served again after removal under 28 U.S.C. § 1448 and in accordance with Rule 4(d)(3)? See 4 Wright & Miller § 1082.

(47) Suit is brought on a federally created claim in a federal court located in State *A*. There is an attempt to bring in an additional corporate defendant under Rule 19, with service being made on one of its officers in State *B* in accordance with the 100-mile "bulge" provision of Rule 4(f). The additional defendant is transacting business in the "bulge" located in State *B*, but it has no connection at all with State *A*. Should federal or state law govern amenability? If a federal standard is to control, how should that standard be defined? See Kaplan, Amendments of the Federal Rules of Civil Procedure, 1961–1963 (I), 77 Harv.L.Rev. 601, 632–33 (1964).

(48) Change the facts of the preceding question so that the suit is based on a state-created claim. May the "bulge" provision operate at all in this situation? If so, should federal or state law govern amenability? If state law is to control, should the federal court look to the law of State *A* or State *B*? If the law of State *B* is to control, what happens if the facts are further changed so that the additional defendant is transacting business in State *B* but is not transacting business in and has no other connection with that part of State *B* constituting the "bulge," except the presence of its officer in the "bulge" when served?

One further aspect of the interplay between federal and state law on amenability may merit mention. Consider as an example the situation in which a federal claim and a state claim are joined in a federal action, with service being made in accordance with a federal statute providing nationwide service for the federal claim. Assuming that subject-matter jurisdiction exists for the state claim, but that the nationwide-service provision is the sole basis for exercising jurisdiction over the defendant, is there personal jurisdiction for the purposes of the state claim? The policies of judicial economy, convenience, and fairness underlying the doctrine of pendent jurisdiction suggest that some degree of "pendent service" should exist. However, a careful reading of the applicable statutes reveals no congressional intent to extend nationwide service of process to state claims. The courts have seriously split on this problem.

DIJULIO v. DIGICON, INC., 325 F.Supp. 963 (D.Md.1971). For damages allegedly caused by a misleading stock prospectus, plaintiffs sued the issuer and its officials, accountant, and underwriters.

"Jurisdiction and venue are claimed under § 22(a) of the 1933 [Securities] Act, 15 U.S.C. § 77v(a) . . . . No defendant has questioned jurisdiction or venue except William Blair & Company (Blair), one of the underwriters, which has filed a motion to quash service of process and to dismiss.

"Plaintiffs concede that their right to sue Blair in Maryland depends upon the construction and applicability of § 22(a) of the 1933 Act, which provides in pertinent part:

'The district courts of the United States, and the United States courts of any Territory, shall have jurisdiction of offenses and violations under this subchapter and under the rules and regulations promulgated by the Commission in respect thereto, and concurrent with State and Territorial courts, of all suits in equity and actions at law brought to enforce any liability or duty created by this subchapter. Any such suit or action may be brought in the district wherein the defendant is found or is an inhabitant or transacts business, or in the district where the offer or sale took place, if the defendant participated therein, and process in such cases may be served in any other district of which the defendant is an inhabitant or wherever the defendant may be found. . . .'

"Blair has not been served personally in Maryland, none of its partner-members is a citizen or resident of Maryland, it has no office in Maryland, it does not transact business in Maryland in the ordinary sense of that term, and none of the shares which were allocated to it under the Purchase Contract were sold or offered for sale by it in Maryland.

"On the other hand, Blair was listed as a member of the underwriting group in the prospectus which was made a part of the registration statement filed with the Securities and Exchange Commission, effective June 13, 1969, and filed with the Division of Securities of the State of Maryland effective on that date. Under §§ 4(3) and 5(b)(2) of the 1933 Act, 15 U.S.C. §§ 77d(3) and 77e(b)(2), any dealer selling or offering to sell Digicon stock during the next 90 days was required to deliver a copy of the prospectus to the purchaser. For the purposes of this motion, it is not disputed that sales of Digicon stock to the named plaintiffs were made in Maryland by the Baltimore office of Francis I. DuPont, A.C. Allyn, Inc. (DuPont), a dealer and one of the underwriters, during the 90 day period after June 13, 1969, and copies of the prospectus were delivered to such plaintiffs.

. . . .

"Blair argues that the Registration Statement shows that the underwriters agreed, severally and not jointly, to purchase from Digicon . . . the number of shares set opposite their respective names. That is true, but the Registration Statement, including the prospectus, was prepared and filed for the use and benefit of all the underwriters. All members of the underwriting group are subject to certain liabilities under the 1933 Act for the specified period of time regardless of which underwriter actually made the sale. It is also true, as Blair argues, that plaintiffs must satisfy the venue requirements, both statutory and constitutional.

"The industry of counsel has discovered no case precisely in point. But the courts have noted the liberal character of the venue provision with which we are dealing. [Therefore the court concluded that Blair 'participated' in the Maryland sales.]

"The maintenance of this suit against Blair 'does not offend "traditional notions of fair play and substantial justice".' International Shoe Co. v. State of Washington, 326 U.S. 310, 316, 66 S.Ct. 154, 158, 90 L.Ed. 95 (1945); Hanson v. Denckla, 357 U.S. 235, 253, 78 S.Ct. 1228, 2 L.Ed.2d 1283 (1958). Blair's motion to quash service of process and dismiss the complaint as to it is hereby denied."

SECTION 6. VENUE

FEDERAL PROVISIONS

Recall the discussion of venue in Part One. By now the nature of the subject should reappear to you with considerably greater clarity. A few additional observations should consolidate and expand your understanding.

Venue is a personal privilege of the defendant, so only the defendant as to whom venue appears improper is entitled to raise the point. *only (D)* *can raise* See Camp v. Gress, 250 U.S. 308, 39 S.Ct. 478 (1919). A defect in *issue of* venue may be waived, and it is waived if not asserted in timely fashion. *venue* See Rule 12(g) and (h). Unlike some defects in subject-matter jurisdiction, territorial jurisdiction, and opportunity to be heard, defective venue does not render a judgment invalid and subject to collateral attack.

Question: (49) How can this last sentence be explained?

Section 1391(c) of title 28 uses the term "doing business." The *venue* meaning of this term is, as are all true venue questions in federal *"doing* court, a matter of federal law. Frequently, this term is equated to *business"* the constitutional standard of amenability to suit: the defendant cor- *often =* poration is for venue purposes a resident of any district in which it is *amen.* transacting sufficient business to bring it, with respect to the particu- *to suit* lar suit, within the constitutional reach of the personal jurisdiction of the district, were the district a state. But some courts require a greater level of activity to trigger the statute.

When a plaintiff brings an action, he waives in advance any venue *When (P)* objection to counterclaims—even permissive ones. See General Elec- *brings* tric Co. v. Marvel Rare Metals Co., 287 U.S. 430, 53 S.Ct. 202 (1932). *action →* In addition, there is becoming established a doctrine of "ancillary" *waives* and "pendent" venue, which thus far is understood to mean that if a *venue* claim is within the ancillary or the pendent jurisdiction of the federal *for* court, then there is no ground for objection to venue with respect to *c'claim* that claim. See generally 15 Wright, Miller & Cooper § 3808.

STATE PROVISIONS

The place of trial of civil actions within each state is governed very largely by statute, and the statutes of the several states do not exhibit any uniform pattern. Professor Stevens, in Venue Statutes: Diagnosis and Proposed Cure, 49 Mich.L.Rev. 307 (1951), lists some thirteen items that appear in various statutory schemes as grounds of venue, including the following: where the subject of action is situated; where the cause of action arose; where "some fact" is present or happened; where defendant resides; where defendant is doing business; where defendant has a place of business; where plaintiff resides; where plaintiff is doing business; where defendant may be found; where defendant may be summoned or served; and where the seat of government is located. And provisions can be found that allow plaintiff to lay venue in any county designated in the complaint or, more simply, in any county. Professor Stevens criticizes the existing confused situation and proposes a model venue code.

Question: (50) What is, after all, the difference between territorial jurisdiction and venue? See Clermont, Restating Territorial Jurisdiction and Venue for State and Federal Courts, 66 Cornell L.Rev. 411 (1981).

(a) Local Actions

LIVINGSTON v. JEFFERSON
Circuit Court of the United States, District of Virginia, 1811.
15 F.Cas. 660 (No. 8411).

This was an action of trespass, brought in the circuit court of the United States, for the district of Virginia, by Edward Livingston, a citizen of the state of New York, against Thomas Jefferson, a citizen of the state of Virginia, and late president of the United States, for a trespass alleged to have been committed by the defendant whilst he was president, in removing him from the batture, in the city of New-Orleans, in the then territory of Orleans, now the state of Louisiana. The suit was commenced in 1810, after the expiration of Mr. Jefferson's last term of office.

The declaration contained eight counts. The first count charged that the defendant, on the 25th day of January, 1808, at the city of New-Orleans, in the district of Orleans, to wit, at Richmond, in the county of Henrico, and district of Virginia, with force and arms, a certain messuage or dwelling-house, and a close or parcel of land thereto adjoining, the said close being part of a parcel of land, known by the name of the "Batture of the Suburb St. Mary," of him, the said Edward, then and there being, did break and enter, and 200 spades, (and various other tools, planks, rails, nails, &c., specifying the number and kind,) of the proper goods and chattels of the said plaintiff, of the value of ten thousand dollars, then and there being found, did break, cut in pieces, and utterly destroy, and 20,000 cart loads of earth, (sand and clay,) of the soil of the said close, with spades, &c., did dig and raise, the said soil so dug and raised being of the value of $50,000, and with carts, &c., did carry away and convert to his own use, by which digging, the soil of the said close was greatly injured, and the said plaintiff wholly lost the said parcel thereof so dug and raised, &c. All the other counts laid the venue in the same way, "at the city of New-Orleans, &c., to wit, at Richmond, &c., &c."

. . .

The defendant demurred to the second, fifth, sixth, seventh, and eighth counts. He also pleaded the general issue, and four several pleas of justification. He justified the act as being done under a law of congress, and in his character of president of the United States, without malice. It is unnecessary to say more of these pleadings, since the question before the court turned on the third plea, which was a plea to the jurisdiction of the court. That plea was as follows: "And the said defendant in his proper person, comes and defends the force and injury, and saith that the messuage, or dwelling-house, and close or parcel of land, being a part of a parcel of land known by the name of the 'Batture of the Suburb St. Mary,' in the first and fifth counts of the plaintiff's declaration mentioned, and the several closes in the second, third, fourth, sixth, seventh, and eighth counts of the plaintiff's declaration mentioned, for the supposed breaking and entering of which said messuage, or dwelling-house, and closes, the said action is brought, are not situate, lying, and being within the Virginia district, or within the jurisdiction of this court, but are situate, lying and being in the territory of the United States of America, called the 'Territory of Orleans,' in which said territory there was, at the time of the said supposed trespasses, and long before, and at the time of the institution of the plaintiff's said action, and yet is, a court of competent jurisdiction to try and decide upon all pleas of trespass, and all causes of action arising within the said territory, wherefore since the house and lands in the declaration mentioned are not within the Virginia district, and the jurisdiction of this court, but in the said territory, the defendant prays judgment, if the court here will, or ought to have further conusance of the plea aforesaid, &c." To this plea the plaintiff replied, that ever since his cause of action, against the said defendant, accrued, "the said defendant has resided without the jurisdiction of the courts of the territory of Orleans aforesaid, to wit, within the district of Virginia, and within the jurisdiction of this court, where he now resides, by reason whereof he is not amenable to the jurisdiction of the courts of the territory of Orleans aforesaid, for the trespasses in the declaration set forth, wherefore he prays judgment, &c." To this replication the defendant demurred generally, and the plaintiff joined in demurrer.

Before MARSHALL, CIRCUIT JUSTICE, and TYLER, DISTRICT JUDGE.

[The opinion by Judge Tyler is omitted. "About the kindest thing that can be said is to attribute his entire opinion to an unhappy physical condition." 1 Moore ¶ 0.142[2.–3], at 1375 n.6.]

MARSHALL, CIRCUIT JUSTICE. The sole question now to be decided is this—Can this court take cognizance of a trespass committed on lands lying within the United States, and without the district of Virginia, in a case where the trespasser is a resident of, and is found within the district? I concur with my brother judge in the opinion that it cannot. . . . The doctrine of actions local and transitory has been traced up to its origin in the common law—and, as has been truly stated on both sides, it appears that originally all actions were local. That is, that according to the principles of the common law, every fact must be tried by a jury of the vicinage. The plain consequence of this principle is, that those courts only could take jurisdiction of a case, who were capable of directing such a jury as must try the material facts on which their judgment would depend. The jurisdiction of the courts therefore necessarily becomes local with respect to every species of action. But the superior courts of England having power to direct a jury to every part of the kingdom, their jurisdiction could be restrained by this principle only to cases arising on transactions which occurred within the realm. Being able to direct a jury either to Surrey or Middlesex, the necessity of averring in the declaration, that the cause of action arose in either county, could not be produced in order to give the court jurisdiction, but to furnish a venire. For the purpose of jurisdiction, it would unquestionably be sufficient, to aver that the transaction took place within the realm. This however being not a statutory regulation, but a principle of unwritten law, which is really human reason applied by courts, not capriciously, but in a regular train of decisions, to human affairs, according to the circumstances of the nation, the necessity of the times, and the general state of things, was thought susceptible of modification—and judges have modified it. They have not changed the old principle as to form. It is still necessary to give a venue; and where the contract exhibits on its face, evidence of the place where it was made, the party is at liberty to aver that such place lies in any county in England. This is known to be a fiction. Like an ejectment, it is the creature of the court, and is moulded to the purposes of justice, according to the view which its inventors have taken of its capacity to effect those purposes. It is however, of undeniable extent. It has not absolutely prostrated all distinctions of place, but has certain limits prescribed to it, founded in reasoning satisfactory to those who have gradually fixed these limits. It may well be doubted, whether at this day, they are to be changed by a judge not perfectly satisfied with their extent. This fiction is so far protected by its inventors, that the averment is not traversable for the purpose of defeating an action it was invented to sustain; but it is traversable whenever such traverse may be essential to the merits of the cause. It is always traversable for the purpose of contesting a jurisdiction not intended to be protected by the fiction.

In the case at bar, it is traversed for that purpose, and the question is, whether this be a case in which such traverse is sustainable; or, in other words, whether courts have so far extended their fiction as, by its aid, to take cognizance of trespasses on lands not lying within those limits which bound their process. They have, without legislative aid, applied this fiction to all personal torts, and to all contracts wherever executed. To this general rule, contracts respecting lands form no exception. It is admitted, that on a contract respecting lands, an action is sustainable wherever the defendant may be found:

yet, in such a case, every difficulty may occur which presents itself in an action of trespass. An investigation of title may become necessary. A question of boundary may arise, and a survey may be essential to the full merits of the cause: yet these difficulties have not prevailed against the jurisdiction of the court. They have been countervailed, and more than countervailed by the opposing consideration, that if the action be disallowed, the injured party may have a clear right without a remedy in a case where the person who has done the wrong, and who ought to make the compensation, is within the power of the court. That this consideration should lose its influence, where the action pursues a thing not within the reach of the court, is of inevitable necessity; but for the loss of its influence where the remedy is against the person and can be afforded by the court, I have not yet discerned a reason, other than a technical one, which can satisfy my judgment. If, however, this technical distinction be firmly established, if all other judges respect it, I cannot venture to disregard it.

The distinction taken is, that actions are deemed transitory, where transactions on which they are founded, might have taken place anywhere; but are local where their cause is in its nature necessarily local. If this distinction be established; if judges have determined to carry their innovation on the old rule, no further; if, for a long course of time, under circumstances which have not changed, they have determined this to be the limit of their fiction, it would require a hardihood which I do not possess, to pass this limit. This distinction has been repeatedly taken in the books, and recognized by the best elementary writers, especially Judge Blackstone, from whose authority no man will lightly dissent. . . .

. . . .

According to the common law of England then, the distinction taken by the defendant's counsel, between actions local and transitory, is the true distinction, and an action of quare clausum fregit, is a local action. This common law has been adopted by the legislature of Virginia. Had it not been adopted, I should have thought it in force. When our ancestors migrated to America, they brought with them the common law of their native country, so far as it was applicable to their new situation; and I do not conceive that the Revolution would, in any degree, have changed the relations of man to man, or the law which regulated those relations. In breaking our political connection with the parent state, we did not break our connection with each other. It remained subsequent to the ancient rules, until those rules should be changed by the competent authority. But it has been said, that this rule of the common law is impliedly changed by the act of assembly, which directs that a jury shall be summoned from the bystanders. Were I to discuss the effect of this act in the courts of the state, the inquiry, whether the fiction already noticed was not equivalent to it in giving jurisdiction, would present itself. There are also other regulations, as, that the jurors should be citizens, which would deserve to be taken into view. But I pass over these considerations, because I am decidedly of opinion, that the jurisdiction of the courts of the United States depends, exclusively, on the constitution and laws of the United States.

In considering the jurisdiction of the circuit courts, as defined in the judicial act [1 Stat. 73], and in the constitution which that act carries into execution, it is worthy of observation, that the jurisdiction of the court depends on the character of the parties, and that only the court of that district in which the defendant resides, or is found, can take jurisdiction of the cause.[l] In a court so constituted, the argument drawn from the total failure of justice, should a trespasser be declared to be only amenable to the court of that district in which the land lies, and in which he will never be found, appeared to me to be entitled to peculiar weight. But according to the course of the common law, the process of the court must be executed in order to give it the right to try the cause, and consequently the same defect of justice might occur. Other judges have felt the weight of this argument, and have struggled ineffectually against the distinction, which produces the inconvenience of a clear right without a remedy. I must submit to it. The law upon the demurrer is in favor of the defendant.[m]

------

[l] The Judiciary Act of September 24, 1789, ch. 20, § 11, 1 Stat. 73, declared that "the circuit courts shall have original cognizance, concurrent with the courts of the several States, of all suits of a civil nature at common law or in equity, where the matter in dispute exceeds, exclusive of costs, the sum or value of five hundred dollars, and . . . the suit is between a citizen of the State where the action is brought, and a citizen of another State. . . . And no civil suit shall be brought before . . . said courts against an inhabitant of the United States, by any original process in any other district than that whereof he is an inhabitant, or in which he shall be found at the time of serving the writ."

[m] The facts out of which this case arose are given in 4 A. Beveridge, The Life of John Marshall 100–16 (1919).

After the action of Livingston v. Jefferson was commenced, Jefferson wrote to President Madison urging the appointment of Judge Tyler to a vacancy in the court that would hear the suit. After referring to the "rancorous hatred which Marshall bears to the government of his country" and "the cunning & sophistry within which he is able to enshroud himself," Jefferson wrote: "It will be difficult to find a character of firmness enough to preserve his independence on the same bench with Marshall. Tyler, I am certain, would do it. . . . A milk & water character . . . would be seen as a calamity." He concluded what Beveridge calls "this astounding letter" in these words: "It is a little doubted that his [Livingston's] knolege [sic] of Marshall's character has induced him to bring this action. His twistifications of the law in the case of Marbury, in that of Burr, & the late Yazoo case shew how dexterously he can reconcile law to his personal biasses: and nobody seems to doubt that he is ready prepared to decide that Livingston's right to the batture is unquestionable, and that I am bound to pay for it with my private fortune."

The next day Jefferson wrote Tyler that he had "laid it down as a law" to himself "never to embarrass the President with any solicitations." Yet, in Tyler's case, wrote Jefferson, "I . . . have done it with all my heart, and in the full belief that I serve him and the public in urging the appointment."

A sequel appears in 1 L. Tyler, The Letters and Times of the Tylers 263 (1884). Jefferson prepared, for the use of his attorneys, an exhaustive brief covering his version of the facts and his views of the law. After the decision,

CASEY v. ADAMS, 102 U.S. 66 (1880). The Supreme Court here held that a special venue statute for commencement of suits against national banks did not apply to local actions, thus permitting commencement of this suit where the property was located even though the special statute was not satisfied. Chief Justice Waite explained that "no one has ever supposed that laws which prescribed generally where one should be sued, included such suits as were local in their character, either by statute or the common law, unless it was expressly so declared. Local actions are in the nature of suits in rem, and are to be prosecuted where the thing on which they are founded is situated."

ELLENWOOD v. MARIETTA CHAIR CO., 158 U.S. 105, 15 S.Ct. 771 (1895). An action was brought in the United States Circuit Court for the Southern District of Ohio by a New Jersey citizen against an Ohio citizen for a continuing trespass upon the plaintiff's land in West Virginia and the cutting and conversion of timber growing thereon. The petition contained only one count. The defendant answered, denying the allegations of the petition. The lower court ordered the case stricken from its docket on an incidental procedural point, and the Supreme Court affirmed. Justice Gray said: "Various grounds taken by the defendant in error in support of the judgment below need not be considered, because there is one decisive reason against the maintenance of the action. . . . The entire cause of action was local. The land alleged to have been trespassed upon being in West Virginia, the action could not be maintained in Ohio. The Circuit Court of the United States, sitting in Ohio, had no jurisdiction of the cause of action, and for this reason, if for no other, rightly ordered the case stricken from its docket, although no question of jurisdiction had been made by demurrer or plea."

STONE v. UNITED STATES, 167 U.S. 178, 17 S.Ct. 778 (1897). The United States brought suit in the United States District Court for

Tyler wrote to Jefferson as follows: "Judge Roane had perused it [the Jefferson brief] in manuscript and gave me some of the outlines of it, which heightened my desire to get hold of it, although I well knew you had probed the subject to its bottom. But as soon as I had received the appointment . . . (which I owe to your favor in great measure), it became my duty to shut the door against every observation which might in any way be derived from either side, lest the impudent British faction, who had enlisted on Livingston's side, might suppose an undue influence had seized upon me. It is true, I never did regard that part of the community, yet it was as well to avoid suspicion even of the devil and his imps. I wished very much to have heard the merits of the cause, but the question of jurisdiction precluded any enquiry on that part of the cause."

A view of the events that treats Jefferson more favorably is given in 3 H. Randall, The Life of Thomas Jefferson 266–69, 500, 523–24 (1858). But see W. Hatcher, Edward Livingston 137–66, 317–18 (1940).

The case is put into a broad social context by G. Dargo, Public Power and Privatization: Legal Change in the New Republic 114–70 (1980).

the District of Washington to recover the reasonable value of timber and ties manufactured from trees cut by defendant from plaintiff's land in Idaho. It was held that the action could be maintained because the gravamen was conversion, not trespass, and no judgment was sought for the trespass.

LOCAL ACTIONS IN STATE COURTS

Livingston v. Jefferson, although frequently criticized, has been followed in almost every state where the question has arisen. "Among actions that have been held to be local are those to set aside a preferential transfer of property, to foreclose or cancel a mortgage, for trespass to land, to abate a nuisance, to try title to land, and others." 15 Wright, Miller & Cooper § 3822, at 130–31. The precise scope of the doctrine, however, varies from state to state. Indeed, the Livingston doctrine has been drastically curtailed or even eliminated in a few states, either by decision as in Minnesota or by statute as in New York. See 1 Moore ¶ 0.142[2.–3].

Questions: (51) Should the United States District Court for the Southern District of New York in a diversity case now permit an action to be maintained on the facts of Livingston v. Jefferson, assuming personal service in New York? What if the case had reached the federal court by removal from a state court of New York?

(52) If, on the facts of Livingston v. Jefferson, default judgment were rendered for the plaintiff in the federal court sitting in Virginia, would the judgment be subject to collateral attack?

(53) Would 28 U.S.C. § 1655 be of any assistance, on the facts of Livingston v. Jefferson, to the plaintiff seeking recovery in the federal court sitting in Louisiana where the land lies, assuming that the defendant is not subject to personal jurisdiction?

(b) Transfer of Venue

THE INCONVENIENT FORUM

In Gulf Oil Corp. v. Gilbert, 330 U.S. 501, 67 S.Ct. 839 (1947), a diversity action in the Southern District of New York, a Virginia plaintiff sued a Pennsylvania corporation doing business in both Virginia and New York for alleged negligence in causing the plaintiff's warehouse in Lynchburg, Virginia, to burn. Defendant sought dismissal under the doctrine of forum non conveniens, claiming that Virginia was the appropriate place for trial because plaintiff lived there, defendant did business there, and all the events giving rise to the suit occurred there. The doctrine thus invoked is a discretionary one, coming into play when jurisdiction and venue are proper but the court decides that it should not hear the case because of the inconvenience of the chosen forum and because of the availability of a more convenient forum. The district court dismissed, considering itself bound under Erie by New York law. The court of appeals reversed, disagreeing as to the controlling effect of New York law and taking a restrictive view of the entire doctrine.

On certiorari, the Supreme Court, with four dissents, reversed the court of appeals and ordered dismissal. Finding no difference between New York and federal law, it did not pursue the Erie question. Justice Jackson for the majority said:

"Wisely, it has not been attempted to catalogue the circumstances which will justify or require either grant or denial of remedy. The doctrine leaves much to the discretion of the court to which plaintiff resorts, and experience has not shown a judicial tendency to renounce one's own jurisdiction so strong as to result in many abuses.

"If the combination and weight of factors requisite to given results are difficult to forecast or state, those to be considered are not difficult to name. An interest to be considered, and the one likely to be most pressed, is the private interest of the litigant. Important considerations are the relative ease of access to sources of proof; availability of compulsory process for attendance of unwilling, and the cost of obtaining attendance of willing, witnesses; possibility of view of premises, if view would be appropriate to the action; and all other practical problems that make trial of a case easy, expeditious and inexpensive. There may also be questions as to the enforcibility of a judgment if one is obtained. The court will weigh relative advantages and obstacles to fair trial. It is often said that the plaintiff may not, by choice of an inconvenient forum, 'vex,' 'harass,' or 'oppress' the defendant by inflicting upon him expense or trouble not necessary to his own right to pursue his remedy. But unless the balance is strongly in favor of the defendant, the plaintiff's choice of forum should rarely be disturbed.

"Factors of public interest also have place in applying the doctrine. Administrative difficulties follow for courts when litigation is piled up in congested centers instead of being handled at its origin. Jury duty is a burden that ought not to be imposed upon the people of a community which has no relation to the litigation. In cases which touch the affairs of many persons, there is reason for holding the trial in their view and reach rather than in remote parts of the country where they can learn of it by report only. There is a local interest in having localized controversies decided at home. There is an appropriateness, too, in having the trial of a diversity case in a forum that is at home with the state law that must govern the case, rather than having a court in some other forum untangle problems in conflict of laws, and in law foreign to itself."

THE § 1404(a) TRANSFER PROVISION

28 USC §1404(a)
same as
doctrine
forum non
conveniens

In 1948 Congress enacted 28 U.S.C. § 1404(a). It changed the remedy from dismissal of the federal action to transfer of the action to a convenient federal forum. The reviser's note explained the provision by saying: "Subsection (a) was drafted in accordance with the doctrine of forum non conveniens, permitting transfer to a more convenient forum, even though the venue is proper."

The question soon arose whether an FELA case could be transferred under § 1404(a). The Supreme Court held that such transfer was allowable, Ex parte Collett, 337 U.S. 55, 69 S.Ct. 944 (1949), although prior to 1948 it had indicated that the special venue act for FELA cases precluded dismissal on the basis of forum non conveniens, Baltimore & Ohio Railroad v. Kepner, 314 U.S. 44, 62 S.Ct. 6 (1941). In Norwood v. Kirkpatrick, 349 U.S. 29, 75 S.Ct. 544 (1955), declining to set aside transfer of three FELA cases, the Supreme Court held that § 1404(a) was intended to permit transfer upon a lesser showing of inconvenience than had been required when dismissal was the remedy. The Court added: "This is not to say that the relevant factors have changed or that the plaintiff's choice of forum is not to be considered, but only that the discretion to be exercised is broader." This appeared to give an emphasis different from Justice Jackson's statement in the Gilbert case: "But unless the balance is strongly in favor of the defendant, the plaintiff's choice of forum should rarely be disturbed." The three dissenters, in an opinion by Justice Clark, took the view that the Court's interpretation did violence to the intent of Congress and was inconsistent with the reviser's note.

§1404(a)
for both
(D) & (P)

Forum non conveniens was a defendant's remedy. With transfer substituted for dismissal, § 1404(a) became attractive to plaintiffs as well. After some early authority that "Section 1404(a) is not available to plaintiffs who voluntarily choose their own forum," Barnhart v. John B. Rogers Producing Co., 86 F.Supp. 595 (N.D.Ohio 1949), it came to be accepted that the remedy was available to any plaintiff in a proper case. (Forum non conveniens could be invoked on the court's own motion, and apparently the same is now true for § 1404(a) in rare circumstances.)

Questions: (54) What would be a proper case for transfer upon plaintiff's motion?

(55) What remains of the doctrine of forum non conveniens in federal court, after the enactment of § 1404(a)?

The hottest controversy under § 1404(a) concerned the meaning of "where it might have been brought." Could a plaintiff obtain a transfer to a district where service of process on the defendant would have been impossible? Compare Foster-Milburn Co. v. Knight, 181 F.2d 949 (2d Cir.1950), with In re Josephson, 218 F.2d 174 (1st Cir. 1954) (dictum). Since venue is a personal privilege of the defendant and since service may be consented to, could a defendant waive the "might have been brought" requirement and obtain a transfer to a district where venue would otherwise be improper as to him or where he could not otherwise be served with process?

HOFFMAN v. BLASKI, 363 U.S. 335, 80 S.Ct. 1084 (1960). In two cases the district courts ordered transfer to a more convenient district on defendants' motion. The Seventh Circuit granted mandamus, ruling that § 1404(a) did not authorize these transfers. On certiorari, the Supreme Court affirmed. Justice Whittaker explained for the Court:

7 Ct →
NO
transfer
under
§1404(a)

"Petitioners concede that these actions were properly brought in the respective transferor forums; that statutory venue did not exist over either of these actions in the respective transferee districts, and that the respective defendants were not within the reach of the process of the respective transferee courts. . . .

"Petitioners' 'thesis' and sole claim is that § 1404(a), being remedial, Ex parte Collett, 337 U.S. 55, 71, 69 S.Ct. 944, 946, should be broadly construed, and, when so construed, the phrase 'where it might have been brought' should be held to relate not only to the time of the bringing of the action, but also to the time of the transfer; and that 'if at such time the transferee forum has the power to adjudicate the issues of the action, it is a forum in which the action might *then* have been brought.' (Emphasis added.) They argue that in the interim between the bringing of the action and the filing of a motion to transfer it, the defendants may move their residence to, or, if corporations, may begin the transaction of business in, some other district, and if such is done, the phrase 'where it might have been brought' should be construed to empower the District Court to transfer the action, on motion of the defendants, to such other district; and that, similarly, if, as here, the defendants move to transfer the action to some other district and consent to submit to the jurisdiction of such other district, the latter district should be held one 'in which the action might *then* have been brought.' (Emphasis added.)

(D) asking for transfer b/c "where might have been brought" should be applied broadly & relate also to time of transfer

"We do not agree. We do not think the § 1404(a) phrase 'where it might have been brought' can be interpreted to mean, as petitioners' theory would require, 'where it may now be rebrought, with defendants' consent.' This Court has said, in a different context, that § 1404(a) is 'unambiguous, direct [and] clear,' Ex parte Collett, 337 U.S. at page 58, 69 S.Ct. at page 946, and that the 'unequivocal words of § 1404(a) and the legislative history . . . [establish] that Congress indeed meant what it said.' United States v. National City Lines, Inc., 337 U.S. 78, 84, 69 S.Ct. 955, 958. Like the Seventh Circuit, . . . we think the dissenting opinion of Judges Hastie and

S. Ct. says NO

McLaughlin in Paramount Pictures, Inc. v. Rodney, 3 Cir., 186 F.2d
111, 119, correctly answered this contention:

what ① does after suit brought doesn't matter

'But we do not see how the conduct of a defendant after suit
has been instituted can add to the forums where "it might have
been brought." In the normal meaning of words this language of
Section 1404(a) directs the attention of the judge who is considering a transfer to the situation which existed when suit was instituted.'

. . . .

If allowed this — would be discrim. asa. ℗

"The thesis urged by petitioners would not only do violence to the
plain words of § 1404(a), but would also inject gross discrimination.
That thesis, if adopted, would empower a District Court, upon a finding of convenience, to transfer an action to any district desired by the
defendants and in which they were willing to waive their statutory
defenses as to venue and jurisdiction over their persons, regardless
of the fact that such transferee district was not one in which the action 'might have been brought' by the plaintiff. Conversely, that thesis would not permit the court, upon motion of the *plaintiffs* and a
like showing of convenience, to transfer the action to the same district, without the consent and waiver of venue and personal jurisdiction defenses by the defendants. Nothing in § 1404(a), or in its legislative history, suggests such a unilateral objective and we should not,
under the guise of interpretation, ascribe to Congress any such discriminatory purpose.

. . . .

"Inasmuch as the respondents (plaintiffs) did not have a right to
bring these actions in the respective transferee districts, it follows
that the judgments of the Court of Appeals were correct and must be
affirmed."

Justice Frankfurter, joined by Justices Harlan and Brennan, dissented. He explained:

"One would have to be singularly unmindful of the treachery and
versatility of our language to deny that as a mere matter of English
the words 'where it might have been brought,' may carry more than
one meaning. For example, under Rule 3 of the Federal Rules of
Civil Procedure, civil actions are 'commenced' by filing a complaint
with the court. As a matter of English there is no reason why 'commenced' so used should not be thought to be synonymous with
'brought' as used in § 1404(a), so that an action 'might have been
brought' in any district where a complaint might have been filed, or
perhaps only in districts with jurisdiction over the subject matter of
the litigation. As a matter of English alone, the phrase might just as
well be thought to refer either to those places where the defendant 'might
have been' served with process, or to those places where the action
'might have been brought' in light of the applicable venue provision,
for those provisions speak generally of where actions 'may be
brought.' Or the phrase may be thought as a matter of English

alone to refer to those places where the action 'might have been
brought' in light of the applicable statute of limitations, or other provisions preventing a court from reaching the merits of the litigation.
On the face of its words alone the phrase may refer to any one of
these considerations, i.e., venue, amenability to service, or period of
limitations, to all of them or to none of them, or to others as well.
And to the extent that these are matters which may or may not be
raised at the defendant's election, the English of the phrase surely
does not tell whether the defendant's actual or potential waiver or
failure to raise such objections is to be taken into account in determining whether a district is one in which the action 'might have been
brought,' or whether the phrase refers only to those districts where
the plaintiff 'might have brought' the action even over a timely objection on the part of the defendant, that is, where he had 'a right' to
bring it.

. . . .

"Surely, the Court creates its own verbal prison in holding that
'the plain words' of § 1404(a) dictate that transfer may not be made
in this case although transfer concededly was in the interest of 'convenience' and 'justice.' Moreover, the Court, while finding the statutory words 'plain,' decided the case by applying, not the statutory language, but a formula of words found nowhere in the statute, namely,
whether plaintiffs had 'a right to bring these actions in the respective
transferee districts.' This is the Court's language, not that of Congress. Although it is of course a grammatically plausible interpretation of the phrase 'where it might have been brought,' it has been, I
submit, established that it is not by any means the only plausible interpretation. . . .

"In summary, then, the 'plain meaning' of § 1404(a) does not conclude the present case against the transfer, for the statute, as applied
in this case, is not 'plain' in meaning one way or another, but contains
ambiguities which must be resolved by considerations relevant to the
problem with which the statute deals. Moreover, the most obvious
significance for the set of words here in question, considered as self-
contained words, is that they have regard for the limitations contained in the regular statutory rules of venue. Those rules, it is beyond dispute, take into account the consent of the defendant to proceed in the forum, even if it is not a forum designated by statute.
And the doctrine of forum non conveniens 'in accordance with' which
§ 1404(a) was drafted, also took into account the defendant's consent
to proceed in another forum to which he was not obligated to submit.
Nor can a decision against transfer be rested upon notions of 'discrimination' or of unfairness to the plaintiff in wrenching him out of
the forum of his choice to go forward in a place to which he objects.
In the proper administration of § 1404(a), such consequences cannot
survive the necessity to find transfer to be in the interests of 'con-

venience' and 'justice,' before it can be made. On the other hand, to restrict transfer as the Court does to those very few places where the defendant was originally amenable to process and could have had no objection to the venue is drastically to restrict the number of situations in which § 1404(a) may serve the interests of justice by relieving the parties from a vexatious forum. And it is to restrict the operation of the section capriciously, for such a drastic limitation is not counseled by any legitimate interest of the plaintiff, or by any interest of the federal courts in their jurisdiction. The defendant's interest of course is not involved because he is the movant for transfer."

Question: (56) Do you think Congress should rewrite § 1404(a)? If so, how?

VAN DUSEN v. BARRACK, 376 U.S. 612, 84 S.Ct. 805 (1964). A large number of plaintiffs separately sued in the District Court for the Eastern District of Pennsylvania for wrongful deaths resulting from an air crash in Boston Harbor on takeoff of a flight to Philadelphia. (Many others brought similar actions in the District Court for the District of Massachusetts.) The defendants moved to transfer the Pennsylvania actions to Massachusetts under § 1404(a), and the court ordered the transfer. The plaintiffs brought mandamus proceedings in the Court of Appeals for the Third Circuit, in which they successfully contended that the district court's order should be vacated because Massachusetts, although venue and jurisdiction were proper there, was not a district where the actions "might have been brought": the plaintiffs, being the decedents' personal representatives who had not obtained the appointments necessary to qualify them to initiate actions in Massachusetts, were thought by the court of appeals not to have the unqualified right to bring suit there that was required by Hoffman v. Blaski.

On certiorari, the Supreme Court reversed and remanded, holding "that the words 'where it might have been brought' must be construed with reference to the federal laws delimiting the districts in which such an action 'may be brought,'" without regard to laws concerning the capacity of fiduciaries to sue.

A critical issue was what the applicable choice-of-law rule would be upon transfer. A possible difference in substantive law was at stake: Massachusetts based recovery in wrongful-death cases on the degree of the defendant's culpability and limited recovery to a $20,000 maximum, while Pennsylvania allowed compensatory damages without limitation as to amount.[n] On this aspect, the Court said

---

[n] The federal court sitting in Pennsylvania would of course apply the Pennsylvania choice-of-law rule. At that time, however, it was unclear what choice-of-law rule Pennsylvania would adopt in such an action arising in another state; but shortly afterward, it was held that Pennsylvania would apply its own rule of compensatory damages without limita-

that the transferee district court, after transfer on defendants' motion, would be obligated to apply the state law that would have been applied if there had been no change of venue.[o] The explanation in part was that there is nothing "in the language or policy of § 1404(a) to justify its use by defendants to defeat the advantages accruing to plaintiffs who have chosen a forum which, although it was inconvenient, was a proper venue." A change of venue in such circumstances, concluded Justice Goldberg, "generally should be, with respect to state law, but a change of courtrooms.[40]"

(handwritten margin note: When transfer — still use orig. state law)

Questions: (57) A diversity action by *P* against *D* for injuries to *P*, a guest passenger in *D*'s automobile, is properly brought in a federal court of State *X*, which is *D*'s residence. It is properly transferred to a federal court of State *Y*, *P*'s residence, pursuant to § 1404(a) upon *P*'s motion. The law of State *X* holds that a host driver is liable to his guest passenger for lack of ordinary care, regardless of where the accident occurred. The law of State *Y* holds that the duty of care is measured by the law of the place where the accident occurred, in this case State *Y*, where a guest passenger may recover only upon proof of gross negligence. What should be the governing law as to standard of care in this case?

(58) Change the facts of the preceding question as follows: the law of State *X* holds that a guest passenger may recover only upon proof of gross negligence, regardless of where the accident occurred; the law of State *Y* holds that the duty of care is measured by the law of the place where the accident occurred, in this case State *Y*, where a host driver is liable to his guest passenger for lack of ordinary care. What should be the governing law?

GOLDLAWR, INC. v. HEIMAN, 369 U.S. 463, 82 S.Ct. 913 (1962). Within the federal statute of limitations, plaintiff sued several defendants in the District Court for the Eastern District of Pennsylvania for treble damages and other relief under the Sherman Act, 15 U.S.C. §§ 1–2, and the Clayton Act, 15 U.S.C. § 15. On motion by two of the corporate defendants to dismiss for improper venue and

tion as to amount, Griffith v. United Air Lines, 416 Pa. 1, 203 A.2d 796 (1964).

On the other hand, the plaintiffs feared and the defendants hoped that the transferee federal court sitting in Massachusetts would, under Klaxon Co. v. Stentor Elec. Mfg. Co., 313 U.S. 487, 61 S.Ct. 1020 (1941), apply the Massachusetts choice-of-law rule and hence the Massachusetts law on damages, which, according to the plaintiffs, would be highly prejudicial to them and not "in the interest of justice."

[o] Do you think this rule would make transfer generally more likely or less likely? At any rate, after remand and the further consideration ordered by the

Supreme Court in the light of its decision, transfer of these cases was denied. Popkin v. Eastern Air Lines, 253 F.Supp. 244 (E.D.Pa.1966). See also Rapp v. Van Dusen, 350 F.2d 806 (3d Cir.1965) (holding by a divided court that Judge Van Dusen should have disqualified himself as a result of the mandamus proceedings in which he was a named party defendant).

[40] Of course the transferee District Court may apply its own rules governing the conduct and dispatch of cases in its court. We are only concerned here with those state laws of the transferor State which would significantly affect the outcome of the case.

lack of personal jurisdiction, the court, passing only on the venue contention, found venue improper as to them under 15 U.S.C. § 22 (providing for venue where defendants are inhabitants, or "found," or transacting business). By this time, the statute of limitations had run. Refusing to dismiss, the court under 28 U.S.C. § 1406(a) ordered transfer of the action as against the two defendants to the District Court for the Southern District of New York, where venue would be proper and personal jurisdiction could be obtained.

However, the transferee court then granted dismissal on the ground that the transferor court, lacking personal jurisdiction, had not had power under § 1406(a) to transfer. The Court of Appeals for the Second Circuit affirmed. On certiorari, the Supreme Court reversed (5–2). Justice Black for the majority said:

can transfer even if transferring ct. has no pers. juris. over ⒹⓈ

"The language of § 1406(a) is amply broad enough to authorize the transfer of cases, however wrong the plaintiff may have been in filing his case as to venue, whether the court in which it was filed had personal jurisdiction over the defendants or not. The section is thus in accord with the general purpose which has prompted many of the procedural changes of the past few years—that of removing whatever obstacles may impede an expeditious and orderly adjudication of cases and controversies on their merits. When a lawsuit is filed, that filing shows a desire on the part of the plaintiff to begin his case and thereby toll whatever statutes of limitation would otherwise apply."

Dissent

Justice Harlan, joined by Justice Stewart in dissent, said:

"The notion that a District Court may deal with an in personam action in such a way as possibly to affect a defendant's substantive rights without first acquiring jurisdiction over him is not a familiar one in federal jurisprudence. No one suggests that Congress was aware that 28 U.S.C. § 1406(a) might be so used when it enacted that statute."

Question: (59) A diversity action by *P* against *D* for injuries to *P*, a guest passenger in *D*'s automobile, is brought in a federal court of State *X*, which is alleged to be *D*'s residence. It is properly transferred to a federal court of State *Y*, *P*'s residence, pursuant to § 1406(a) when it appears that *D* is not a resident of State *X*. The law of State *X* holds that the duty of care is measured by the law of the defendant's residence, in this case State *Z*, where a guest passenger may recover only upon proof of gross negligence. The law of State *Y* holds that the duty of care is measured by the law of the place where the accident occurred, in this case State *Y*, where a host driver is liable to his guest passenger for lack of ordinary care. What should be the governing law?

MARTIN v. STOKES, 623 F.2d 469 (6th Cir.1980). In March 1975 a Virginia plaintiff filed a diversity action against Kentucky and California defendants in her home district, the Western District of Virginia, for injuries sustained in an automobile accident. After personal service in their home districts, defendants moved to quash process. The district court without explanation refused to quash and ordered transfer to the Western District of Kentucky, where the accident had occurred in August 1973.

However, the transferee court then granted defendants' request to dismiss on the basis of Kentucky's one-year statute of limitations, even though the transferor court would have applied Virginia's two-year statute. Plaintiff appealed.

The court of appeals ruled that (1) regardless of who moves to transfer, transferor law applies after a § 1404(a) transfer, but transferee law applies after a § 1406(a) transfer; (2) the two statutes being mutually exclusive, § 1404(a) operates only where the transferor court is a proper forum, but § 1406(a) can operate where the transferor court cannot acquire personal jurisdiction although venue is proper; and (3) this case should be remanded to make the critical determination of whether the Virginia court could have obtained personal jurisdiction.

Question: (60) Suppose that a federal court of State *A* would apply a one-year statute of limitations to a particular action if commenced there, while a federal court of State *B* would apply a two-year statute if the same case were commenced there. Can plaintiff, after transfer from an improper forum under § 1406(a), maintain that action over a statute-of-limitations defense in the following situations? (a) Federal suit is brought in forum *A* nineteen months after accrual of the cause of action; transfer to forum *B* is made one month later. (b) Federal suit is brought in forum *A* nineteen months after accrual; transfer to forum *B* is made six months later. (c) Federal suit is brought in forum *A* six months after accrual; transfer to forum *B* is made three years later. See generally Note, Choice of Law in Federal Court After Transfer of Venue, 63 Cornell L.Rev. 149 (1977).

PIPER AIRCRAFT CO. v. REYNO
Supreme Court of the United States, 1981.
454 U.S. 235, 102 S.Ct. 252.

JUSTICE MARSHALL delivered the opinion of the Court.

These cases arise out of an air crash that took place in Scotland. Respondent, acting as representative of the estates of several Scottish citizens killed in the accident, brought wrongful-death actions against petitioners that were ultimately transferred to the United States District Court for the Middle District of Pennsylvania. Petitioners moved to dismiss on the ground of forum non conveniens. After noting that an alternative forum existed in Scotland, the District Court granted their motions. 479 F.Supp. 727 (MD Pa.1979). The United States Court of Appeals for the Third Circuit reversed. 630 F.2d 149 (CA3 1980). The Court of Appeals based its decision, at least in part, on the ground that dismissal is automatically barred where the law of the alternative forum is less favorable to the plaintiff than the law of the forum chosen by the plaintiff. Because we conclude that the possibility of an unfavorable change in law should not, by itself, bar dismissal, and because we conclude that the District Court did not otherwise abuse its discretion, we reverse.

I

A

In July 1976, a small commercial aircraft crashed in the Scottish highlands during the course of a charter flight from Blackpool to Perth. The pilot and five passengers were killed instantly. The decedents were all Scottish subjects and residents, as are their heirs and next of kin. There were no eyewitnesses to the accident. At the time of the crash the plane was subject to Scottish air traffic control.

The aircraft, a twin-engine Piper Aztec, was manufactured in Pennsylvania by petitioner Piper Aircraft Company ("Piper"). The propellers were manufactured in Ohio by petitioner Hartzell Propeller, Inc. ("Hartzell"). At the time of the crash the aircraft was registered in Great Britain and was owned and maintained by Air Navigation and Trading Co., Ltd. ("Air Navigation"). It was operated by McDonald Aviation, Ltd. ("McDonald"), a Scottish air taxi service. Both Air Navigation and McDonald were organized in the United Kingdom. The wreckage of the plane is now in a hangar in Fransborough, England.

The British Department of Trade investigated the accident several months after it occurred. A preliminary report found that the plane crashed after developing a spin, and suggested that mechanical failure in the plane or the propeller was responsible. At Hartzell's request, this report was reviewed by a three-member Review Board, which held a nine-day adversary hearing attended by all interested parties. The Review Board found no evidence of defective equipment and indicated that pilot error may have contributed to the accident. The pilot, who had obtained his commercial pilot's license only three months earlier, was flying over high ground at an altitude considerably lower than the minimum height required by his company's operations manual.

In July 1977, a California probate court appointed respondent Gaynell Reyno administratrix of the estates of the five passengers. Reyno is not related to and does not know any of the decedents or their survivors; she was a legal secretary to the attorney who filed this lawsuit. Several days after her appointment, Reyno commenced separate wrongful death actions against Piper and Hartzell in the Superior Court of California, claiming negligence and strict liability. Air Navigation, McDonald, and the estate of the pilot are not parties to this litigation. The survivors of the five passengers whose estates are represented by Reyno filed a separate action in the United Kingdom against Air Navigation, McDonald, and the pilot's estate. Reyno candidly admits that the action against Piper and Hartzell was filed in the United States because its laws regarding liability, capacity to sue, and damages are more favorable to her position than are those of Scotland. Scottish law does not recognize strict liability in tort. Moreover, it permits wrongful-death actions only when brought by a decedent's relatives. The relatives may sue only for "loss of support and society."

On petitioners' motion, the suit was removed to the United States District Court for the Central District of California. Piper then moved for transfer to the United States District Court for the Middle District of Pennsylvania, pursuant to 28 U.S.C. § 1404(a). Hartzell moved to dismiss for lack of personal jurisdiction, or in the alternative, to transfer.[5] In December 1977, the District Court quashed service on Hartzell and transferred the case to the Middle District of Pennsylvania. Respondent then properly served process on Hartzell.

B

In May 1978, after the suit had been transferred, both Hartzell and Piper moved to dismiss the action on the ground of forum non conveniens.[P] The District Court granted these motions in October 1979. It relied on the balancing test set forth by this Court in Gulf Oil Corporation v. Gilbert, 330 U.S. 501, 67 S.Ct. 839 (1947), and its companion case, Koster v. Lumbermen's Mut. Cas. Co., 330 U.S. 518, 67 S.Ct. 828 (1947). . . .

After describing our decisions in Gilbert and Koster, the District Court analyzed the facts of this case. It began by observing that an alternative forum existed in Scotland; Piper and Hartzell had agreed to submit to the jurisdiction of the Scottish courts and to waive any statute of limitations defense that might be available. It then stated that plaintiff's choice of forum was entitled to little weight. The court recognized that a plaintiff's choice ordinarily deserves substantial deference. It noted, however, that Reyno "is a representative of foreign citizens and residents seeking a forum in the United States because of the more liberal rules concerning products liability law," and that "the courts have been less solicitous when the plaintiff is not an American citizen or resident, and particularly when the foreign citizens seek to benefit from the more liberal tort rules provided for the protection of citizens and residents of the United States." 479 F.Supp. at 731.

[5] The District Court concluded that it could not assert personal jurisdiction over Hartzell consistent with due process. However, it decided not to dismiss Hartzell because the corporation would be amenable to process in Pennsylvania.

[P] The defendants attributed their delay in pushing this point to delay in acquiring full knowledge of the relevant facts. In view of all the circumstances, both the Pennyslvania district court and the court of appeals refused to hold the defendants equitably estopped.

The District Court next examined several factors relating to the private interests of the litigants, and determined that these factors strongly pointed towards Scotland as the appropriate forum. Although evidence concerning the design, manufacture, and testing of the plane and propeller is located in the United States, the connections with Scotland are otherwise "overwhelming." Id., at 732. The real parties in interest are citizens of Scotland, as were all the decedents. Witnesses who could testify regarding the maintenance of the aircraft, the training of the pilot, and the investigation of the accident—all essential to the defense—are in Great Britain. Moreover, all witnesses to damages are located in Scotland. Trial would be aided by familiarity with Scottish topography, and by easy access to the wreckage.

The District Court reasoned that because crucial witnesses and evidence were beyond the reach of compulsory process, and because the defendants would not be able to implead potential Scottish third-party defendants, it would be "unfair to make Piper and Hartzell proceed to trial in this forum." Id., at 733. The survivors had brought separate actions in Scotland against the pilot, McDonald, and Air Navigation. "[I]t would be fairer to all parties and less costly if the entire case was presented to one jury with available testimony from all relevant witnesses." Ibid. Although the court recognized that if trial were held in the United States, Piper and Hartzell could file indemnity or contribution actions against the Scottish defendants, it believed that there was a significant risk of inconsistent verdicts.[7]

The District Court concluded that the relevant public interests also pointed strongly towards dismissal. The court determined that Pennsylvania law would apply to Piper and Scottish law to Hartzell if the case were tried in the Middle District of Pennsylvania.[8] As a result, "trial in this forum would be hopelessly complex and confusing for a jury." Id., at 734. In addition, the court noted that it was unfamiliar with Scottish law and thus would have to rely upon experts from that country. The court also found that the trial would be enor-

---

[7] The District Court explained that inconsistent verdicts might result if petitioners were held liable on the basis of strict liability here, and then required to prove negligence in an indemnity action in Scotland. Moreover, even if the same standard of liability applied, there was a danger that different juries would find different facts and produce inconsistent results.

[8] Under Klaxon v. Stentor Electric Manufacturing Co., 313 U.S. 487, 61 S.Ct. 1020 (1941), a court ordinarily must apply the choice-of-law rules of the state in which it sits. However, where a case is transferred pursuant to 28 U.S.C. § 1404(a), it must apply the choice-of-law rules of the state from which the case

was transferred. Van Dusen v. Barrack, 376 U.S. 612, 84 S.Ct. 805 (1964). Relying on these two cases, the District Court concluded that California choice-of-law rules would apply to Piper, and Pennsylvania choice-of-law rules would apply to Hartzell. It further concluded that California applied a "governmental interests" analysis in resolving choice-of-law problems, and that Pennsylvania employed a "significant contacts" analysis. The court used the "governmental interests" analysis to determine that Pennsylvania liability rules would apply to Piper, and the "significant contacts" analysis to determine that Scottish liability rules would apply to Hartzell.

mously costly and time-consuming; that it would be unfair to burden citizens with jury duty when the Middle District of Pennsylvania has little connection with the controversy; and that Scotland has a substantial interest in the outcome of the litigation.

In opposing the motions to dismiss, respondent contended that dismissal would be unfair because Scottish law was less favorable. The District Court explicitly rejected this claim. It reasoned that the possibility that dismissal might lead to an unfavorable change in the law did not deserve significant weight; any deficiency in the foreign law was a "matter to be dealt with in the foreign forum." Id., at 738.

C

On appeal, the United States Court of Appeals for the Third Circuit reversed and remanded for trial. The decision to reverse appears to be based on two alternative grounds. First, the Court held that the District Court abused its discretion in conducting the Gilbert analysis. Second, the Court held that dismissal is never appropriate where the law of the alternative forum is less favorable to the plaintiff.

The Court of Appeals began its review of the District Court's Gilbert analysis by noting that the plaintiff's choice of forum deserved substantial weight, even though the real parties in interest are non-residents. It then rejected the District Court's balancing of the private interests. It found that Piper and Hartzell had failed adequately to support their claim that key witnesses would be unavailable if trial were held in the United States: they had never specified the witnesses they would call and the testimony these witnesses would provide. The Court of Appeals gave little weight to the fact that Piper and Hartzell would not be able to implead potential Scottish third-party defendants, reasoning that this difficulty would be "burdensome" but not "unfair," 639 F.2d at 162. Finally, the court stated that resolution of the suit would not be significantly aided by familiarity with Scottish topography, or by viewing the wreckage.

The Court of Appeals also rejected the District Court's analysis of the public interest factors. It found that the District Court gave undue emphasis to the application of Scottish law: "the mere fact that the court is called upon to determine and apply foreign law does not present a legal problem of the sort which would justify the dismissal of a case otherwise properly before the court." Id., at 163. In any event, it believed that Scottish law need not be applied. After conducting its own choice-of-law analysis, the Court of Appeals determined that American law would govern the actions against both Piper and Hartzell.[10] The same choice-of-law analysis apparently led it to

---

[10] The Court of Appeals agreed with the District Court that California choice-of-law rules applied to Piper, and that Pennsylvania choice-of-law rules applied to Hartzell, see n. 8, supra. It did not agree, however, that California used a "governmental interests" analysis and that Pennsylvania used a "significant

conclude that Pennsylvania and Ohio, rather than Scotland, are the jurisdictions with the greatest policy interests in the dispute, and that all other public interest factors favored trial in the United States.

In any event, it appears that the Court of Appeals would have reversed even if the District Court had properly balanced the public and private interests. . . . In other words, the court decided that dismissal is automatically barred if it would lead to a change in the applicable law unfavorable to the plaintiff.

We granted certiorari in these cases to consider the questions they raise concerning the proper application of the doctrine of forum non conveniens. 450 U.S. 909, 101 S.Ct. 1346 (1981).

II

The Court of Appeals erred in holding that plaintiffs may defeat a motion to dismiss on the ground of forum non conveniens merely by showing that the substantive law that would be applied in the alternative forum is less favorable to the plaintiffs than that of the present forum. The possibility of a change in substantive law should ordinarily not be given conclusive or even substantial weight in the forum non conveniens inquiry.

We expressly rejected the position adopted by the Court of Appeals in our decision in Canada Malting Co. v. Paterson Steamships, Ltd., 285 U.S. 413, 52 S.Ct. 413 (1932). . . .

It is true that Canada Malting was decided before Gilbert, and that the doctrine of forum non conveniens was not fully crystallized until our decision in that case.[13] However, Gilbert in no way affects

contacts" analysis. Rather, it believed that both jurisdictions employed the "false conflicts" test. Applying this test, it concluded that Ohio and Pennsylvania had a greater policy interest in the dispute than Scotland, and that American law would apply to both Piper and Hartzell.

[13] The doctrine of forum non conveniens has a long history. It originated in Scotland, see Braucher, The Inconvenient Federal Forum, 60 Harv.L.Rev. 908, 909–911 (1947), and became part of the common law of many states, see id., at 911–912; Blair, The Doctrine of Forum Non Conveniens in Anglo-American Law, 29 Colum.L.Rev. 1 (1929). The doctrine was also frequently applied in federal admiralty actions. See, e.g., Canada Malting Co. v. Paterson Steamships, Ltd., 285 U.S. 413, 52 S.Ct. 413 (1932); see also Bickel, The Doctrine of Forum Non Conveniens As Applied in the Federal Courts in Matters of Admiralty, 35 Cornell L.Q. 12 (1949). In Williams v. Green Bay & Western R., 326 U.S. 549, 66 S.Ct. 284

(1946), the Court first indicated that motions to dismiss on grounds of forum non conveniens could be made in federal diversity actions. The doctrine became firmly established when Gilbert and Koster were decided one year later.

In previous forum non conveniens decisions, the Court has left unresolved the question whether under Erie R. v. Tompkins, 304 U.S. 64, 58 S.Ct. 817 (1938), state or federal law of forum non conveniens applies in a diversity case. Gilbert, supra, 330 U.S. at 509, 67 S.Ct., at 843; Koster, supra, 330 U.S. at 529, 67 S.Ct., at 834; Williams v. Green Bay & Western R., supra, 326 U.S. at 551, 558–559, 66 S.Ct., at 288–89 (1946). The Court did not decide this issue because the same result would have been reached in each case under federal or state law. The lower courts in this case reached the same conclusion: Pennsylvania and California law on forum non conveniens dismissals are virtually identical to federal law. See 630 F.2d at 158. Thus, here also, we need not resolve the Erie question.

the validity of Canada Malting. Indeed, by holding that the central focus of the forum non conveniens inquiry is convenience, Gilbert implicitly recognized that dismissal may not be barred solely because of the possibility of an unfavorable change in law.[14] Under Gilbert, dismissal will ordinarily be appropriate where trial in the plaintiff's chosen forum imposes a heavy burden on the defendant or the court, and where the plaintiff is unable to offer any specific reasons of convenience supporting his choice.[15] If substantial weight were given to the possibility of an unfavorable change in law, however, dismissal might be barred even where trial in the chosen forum was plainly inconvenient.

The Court of Appeals' decision is inconsistent with this Court's earlier forum non conveniens decisions in another respect. Those decisions have repeatedly emphasized the need to retain flexibility. . . . If central emphasis were placed on any one factor, the forum non conveniens doctrine would lose much of the very flexibility that makes it so valuable.

In fact, if conclusive or substantial weight were given to the possibility of a change in law, the forum non conveniens doctrine would become virtually useless. Jurisdiction and venue requirements are often easily satisfied. As a result, many plaintiffs are able to choose from among several forums. Ordinarily, these plaintiffs will select that forum whose choice-of-law rules are most advantageous. Thus, if the possibility of an unfavorable change in substantive law is given substantial weight in the forum non conveniens inquiry, dismissal would rarely be proper.

. . . .

The Court of Appeals' approach is not only inconsistent with the purpose of the forum non conveniens doctrine, but also poses substantial practical problems. If the possibility of a change in law were given substantial weight, deciding motions to dismiss on the ground of forum non conveniens would become quite difficult. Choice-of-law analysis would become extremely important, and the courts would frequently be required to interpret the law of foreign jurisdictions. First, the trial court would have to determine what law would apply if the case were tried in the chosen forum, and what law would apply if the case were tried in the alternative forum. It would then have to compare the rights, remedies, and procedures available under the law that would be applied in each forum. Dismissal would be appropriate only if the court concluded that the law applied by the alternative

---

[14] See also Williams v. Green Bay & Western R., supra, 326 U.S. at 555 n. 4, 66 S.Ct., at 287 n. 4 (1946) (citing with approval a Scottish case that dismissed an action on the ground of forum non conveniens despite the possibility of an unfavorable change in law).

[15] In other words, Gilbert held that dismissal may be warranted where a plaintiff chooses a particular forum, not because it is convenient, but solely in order to harass the defendant or take advantage of favorable law. This is precisely the situation in which the Court of Appeals' rule would bar dismissal.

forum is as favorable to the plaintiff as that of the chosen forum. The doctrine of forum non conveniens, however, is designed in part to help courts avoid conducting complex exercises in comparative law. As we stated in Gilbert, the public interest factors point towards dismissal where the court would be required to "untangle problems in conflict of laws, and in law foreign to itself." Gilbert, supra, 330 U.S. at 509, 67 S.Ct., at 843.

Upholding the decision of the Court of Appeals would result in other practical problems. . . . The American courts, which are already extremely attractive to foreign plaintiffs,[18] would become even more attractive. The flow of litigation into the United States would increase and further congest already crowded courts.[19]

The Court of Appeals based its decision, at least in part, on an analogy between dismissals on grounds of forum non conveniens and transfers between federal courts pursuant to § 1404(a). In Van Dusen v. Barrack, 376 U.S. 612, 84 S.Ct. 805 (1964), this Court ruled that a § 1404(a) transfer should not result in a change in the applicable law. . . . However, § 1404(a) transfers are different than dismissals on the ground of forum non conveniens.

[18] First, all but six of the 50 American states—Delaware, Massachusetts, Michigan, North Carolina, Virginia, and Wyoming—offer strict liability. 1 CCH Prod. Liab.Rep. § 4016. Rules roughly equivalent to American strict liability are effective in France, Belgium, and Luxembourg. West Germany and Japan have a strict liability statute for pharmaceuticals. However, strict liability remains primarily an American innovation. Second, the tort plaintiff may choose, at least potentially, from among 50 jurisdictions if he decides to file suit in the United States. Each of these jurisdictions applies its own set of malleable choice-of-law rules. Third, jury trials are almost always available in the United States, while they are never provided in civil law jurisdictions. G. Gloss, Comparative Law 12 (1979); J. Merryman, The Civil Law Tradition 121 (1969). Even in the United Kingdom, most civil actions are not tried before a jury. 1 G. Keeton, The United Kingdom: The Development of its Laws and Constitutions 309 (1955). Fourth, unlike most foreign jurisdictions, American courts allow contingent attorney's fees, and do not tax losing parties with their opponents' attorney's fees. R. Schlesinger, Comparative Law: Cases, Text, Materials 275–277 (3d ed. 1970); [other citation omitted]. Fifth, discovery is more extensive in American than in foreign courts. R. Schlesinger, supra, at 307, 310, and n. 33.

[19] In holding that the possibility of a change in law unfavorable to the plaintiff should not be given substantial weight, we also necessarily hold that the possibility of a change in law favorable to defendant should not be considered. Respondent suggests that Piper and Hartzell filed the motion to dismiss, not simply because trial in the United States would be inconvenient, but also because they believe the laws of Scotland are more favorable. She argues that this should be taken into account in the analysis of the private interests. We recognize, of course, that Piper and Hartzell may be engaged in reverse forum-shopping. However, this possibility ordinarily should not enter into a trial court's analysis of the private interests. If the defendant is able to overcome the presumption in favor of plaintiff by showing that trial in the chosen forum would be unnecessarily burdensome, dismissal is appropriate—regardless of the fact that defendant may also be motivated by a desire to obtain a more favorable forum. Cf. Kloeckner Reederei und Kohlenhandel v. A/S Hakedal, 210 F.2d 754, 757 (CA2), cert. dismissed by stipulation, 348 U.S. 801, 75 S.Ct. 17 (1954) (defendant not entitled to dismissal on grounds of forum non conveniens solely because the law of the original forum is less favorable to him than the law of the alternative forum).

Congress enacted § 1404(a) to permit change of venue between federal courts. Although the statute was drafted in accordance with the doctrine of forum non conveniens, see Revisor's Note, H.R.Rep. No. 308, 80th Cong., 1st Sess., A132 (1947); H.R.Rep. No. 2646, 79th Cong., 2d Sess., A127 (1946), it was intended to be a revision rather than a codification of the common law. Norwood v. Kirkpatrick, 349 U.S. 29, 75 S.Ct. 544 (1955). District courts were given more discretion to transfer under § 1404(a) than they had to dismiss on grounds of forum non conveniens. Id., at 31–32, 75 S.Ct., at 546.

The reasoning employed in Van Dusen v. Barrack is simply inapplicable to dismissals on grounds of forum non conveniens. That case did not discuss the common-law doctrine. Rather, it focused on "the construction and application" of § 1404(a). 376 U.S. at 613, 84 S.Ct., at 807–08. Emphasizing the remedial purpose of the statute, Barrack concluded that Congress could not have intended a transfer to be accompanied by a change in law. Id., at 622, 84 S.Ct., at 812. The statute was designed as a "federal housekeeping measure," allowing easy change of venue within a unified federal system. Id., at 613, 84 S.Ct., at 807–08. The Court feared that if a change in venue were accompanied by a change in law, forum-shopping parties would take unfair advantage of the relaxed standards for transfer. The rule was necessary to ensure the just and efficient operation of the statute.

We do not hold that the possibility of an unfavorable change in law should *never* be a relevant consideration in a forum non conveniens inquiry. Of course, if the remedy provided by the alternative forum is so clearly inadequate or unsatisfactory that it is no remedy at all, the unfavorable change in law may be given substantial weight; the district court may conclude that dismissal would not be in the interests of justice.[22] In these cases, however, the remedies that would be provided by the Scottish courts do not fall within this category. Although the relatives of the decedents may not be able to rely on a strict liability theory, and although their potential damages award may be smaller, there is no danger that they will be deprived of any remedy or treated unfairly.

[22] At the outset of any forum non conveniens inquiry, the court must determine whether there exists an alternative forum. Ordinarily, this requirement will be satisfied when the defendant is "amenable to process" in the other jurisdiction. Gilbert, supra, 330 U.S. at 506–507, 67 S.Ct., at 842. In rare circumstances, however, where the remedy offered by the other forum is clearly unsatisfactory, the other forum may not be an adequate alternative, and the initial requirement may not be satisfied. Thus, for example, dismissal would not be appropriate where the alternative forum does not permit litigation of the subject matter of the dispute. Cf. Phoenix Canada Oil Co. Ltd. v. Texaco, Inc., 78 F.R.D. 445 (DC Del.1978) (court refuses to dismiss, where alternative forum is Ecuador, it is unclear whether Ecuadorean tribunal will hear the case, and there is no generally codified Ecuadorean legal remedy for the unjust enrichment and tort claims asserted).

III

The Court of Appeals also erred in rejecting the District Court's Gilbert analysis. The Court of Appeals stated that more weight should have been given to the plaintiff's choice of forum, and criticized the District Court's analysis of the private and public interests. However, the District Court's decision regarding the deference due plaintiff's choice of forum was appropriate. Furthermore, we do not believe that the District Court abused its discretion in weighing the private and public interests.

A

The District Court acknowledged that there is ordinarily a strong presumption in favor of the plaintiff's choice of forum, which may be overcome only when the private and public interest factors clearly point towards trial in the alternative forum. It held, however, that the presumption applies with less force when the plaintiff or real parties in interest are foreign.

The District Court's distinction between resident or citizen plaintiffs and foreign plaintiffs is fully justified. In Koster, the Court indicated that a plaintiff's choice of forum is entitled to greater deference when the plaintiff has chosen the home forum. Koster, supra, 330 U.S. at 524, 67 S.Ct., at 831–832.[23] When the home forum has been chosen, it is reasonable to assume that this choice is convenient. When the plaintiff is foreign, however, this assumption is much less reasonable. Because the central purpose of any forum non conveniens inquiry is to ensure that the trial is convenient, a foreign plaintiff's choice deserves less deference.

B

The forum non conveniens determination is committed to the sound discretion of the trial court. It may be reversed only when there has been a clear abuse of discretion; where the court has considered all relevant public and private interest factors, and where its balancing of these factors is reasonable, its decision deserves substantial deference. Gilbert, supra, 330 U.S. at 511–512, 67 S.Ct., at 844–45; Koster, supra, 330 U.S. at 531, 67 S.Ct., at 835. Here, the Court of Appeals expressly acknowledged that the standard of review was one of abuse of discretion. In examining the District Court's

[23] . . . .

A citizen's forum choice should not be given dispositive weight, however. See Pain v. United Technologies Corp., [637 F.2d 775, 796–97 (D.C.Cir.1980)]; Mizokami Bros. v. Baychem Corp., 556 F.2d 975 (CA9 1977), cert. denied, 434 U.S. 1035, 98 S.Ct. 770 (1978). Citizens or residents deserve somewhat more deference than foreign plaintiffs, but dismissal should not be automatically barred when a plaintiff has filed suit in his home forum. As always, if the balance of conveniences suggests that trial in the chosen forum would be unnecessarily burdensome for the defendant or the court, dismissal is proper.

analysis of the public and private interests, however, the Court of Appeals seems to have lost sight of this rule, and substituted its own judgment for that of the District Court.

(1)

In analyzing the private interest factors, the District Court stated that the connections with Scotland are "overwhelming." 479 F.Supp. at 732. This characterization may be somewhat exaggerated. Particularly with respect to the question of relative ease of access to sources of proof, the private interests point in both directions. As respondent emphasizes, records concerning the design, manufacture, and testing of the propeller and plane are located in the United States. She would have greater access to sources of proof relevant to her strict liability and negligence theories if trial were held here.[25] However, the District Court did not act unreasonably in concluding that fewer evidentiary problems would be posed if the trial were held in Scotland. A large proportion of the relevant evidence is located in Great Britain.

The Court of Appeals found that the problems of proof could not be given any weight because Piper and Hartzell failed to describe with specificity the evidence they would not be able to obtain if trial were held in the United States. It suggested that defendants seeking forum non conveniens dismissal must submit affidavits identifying the witnesses they would call and the testimony these witnesses would provide if the trial were held in the alternative forum. Such detail is not necessary. Piper and Hartzell have moved for dismissal precisely because many crucial witnesses are located beyond the reach of compulsory process, and thus are difficult to identify or interview. Requiring extensive investigation would defeat the purpose of their motion. Of course, defendants must provide enough information to enable the District Court to balance the parties' interests. Our examination of the record convinces us that sufficient information was provided here. Both Piper and Hartzell submitted affidavits describing the evidentiary problems they would face if the trial were held in the United States.

The District Court correctly concluded that the problems posed by the inability to implead potential third-party defendants clearly supported holding the trial in Scotland. Joinder of the pilot's estate, Air Navigation, and McDonald is crucial to the presentation of petitioners' defense. If Piper and Hartzell can show that the accident was caused not by a design defect, but rather by the negligence of the pilot, the plane's owners, or the charter company, they will be relieved of all liability. It is true, of course, that if Hartzell and Piper were found liable after a trial in the United States, they could insti-

[25] In the future, where similar problems are presented, district courts might dismiss subject to the condition that defendant corporations agree to provide the records relevant to the plaintiff's claims.

tute an action for indemnity or contribution against these parties in Scotland. It would be far more convenient, however, to resolve all claims in one trial. The Court of Appeals rejected this argument. Forcing petitioners to rely on actions for indemnity or contributions would be "burdensome" but not "unfair." 630 F.2d at 162. Finding that trial in the plaintiff's chosen forum would be burdensome, however, is sufficient to support dismissal on grounds of forum non conveniens.

(2)

The District Court's review of the factors relating to the public interest was also reasonable. On the basis of its choice-of-law analysis, it concluded that if the case were tried in the Middle District of Pennsylvania, Pennsylvania law would apply to Piper and Scottish law to Hartzell. It stated that a trial involving two sets of laws would be confusing to the jury. It also noted its own lack of familiarity with Scottish law. Consideration of these problems was clearly appropriate under Gilbert; in that case we explicitly held that the need to apply foreign law pointed towards dismissal. The Court of Appeals found that the District Court's choice-of-law analysis was incorrect, and that American law would apply to both Hartzell and Piper. Thus, lack of familiarity with foreign law would not be a problem. Even if the Court of Appeals' conclusion is correct, however, all other public interest factors favored trial in Scotland.

Scotland has a very strong interest in this litigation. The accident occurred in its airspace. All of the decedents were Scottish. Apart from Piper and Hartzell, all potential plaintiffs and defendants are either Scottish or English. As we stated in Gilbert, there is "a local interest in having localized controversies decided at home." Gilbert, supra, 330 U.S. at 509, 67 S.Ct., at 843. Respondent argues that American citizens have an interest in ensuring that American manufacturers are deterred from producing defective products, and that additional deterrence might be obtained if Piper and Hartzell were tried in the United States, where they could be sued on the basis of both negligence and strict liability. However, the incremental deterrence that would be gained if this trial were held in an American court is likely to be insignificant. The American interest in this accident is simply not sufficient to justify the enormous commitment of judicial time and resources that would inevitably be required if the case were to be tried here.

IV

. . . Thus, the judgment of the Court of Appeals is

Reversed.

[Justice Powell took no part in the decision of this case, and Justice O'Connor took no part in its consideration or decision.

[Justice White partly concurred in the majority opinion and partly dissented. Justice Stevens, joined by Justice Brennan, dissented. These opinions—which agreed with part II of the Court's opinion, but maintained for reasons not relevant here that the Court should not have considered the issues addressed in part III—are omitted.]

TOPIC C.   OPPORTUNITY TO BE HEARD

MULLANE v. CENTRAL HANOVER BANK & TRUST CO.

Supreme Court of the United States, 1950.
339 U.S. 306, 70 S.Ct. 652.

[The facts are given in the portion of the majority's opinion reprinted supra p. 844.   After finding adequate nexus, Justice Jackson proceeded to the question of notice:]

Quite different from the question of a state's power to discharge trustees is that of the opportunity it must give beneficiaries to contest.   Many controversies have raged about the cryptic and abstract words of the Due Process Clause but there can be no doubt that at a minimum they require that deprivation of life, liberty or property by adjudication be preceded by notice and opportunity for hearing appropriate to the nature of the case.

In two ways this proceeding does or may deprive beneficiaries of property.   It may cut off their rights to have the trustee answer for negligent or illegal impairment of their interests.   Also, their interests are presumably subject to diminution in the proceeding by allowance of fees and expenses to one who, in their names but without their knowledge, may conduct a fruitless or uncompensatory contest.   Certainly the proceeding is one in which they may be deprived of property rights and hence notice and hearing must measure up to the standards of due process.

Personal service of written notice within the jurisdiction is the classic form of notice always adequate in any type of proceeding.   But the vital interest of the State in bringing any issues as to its fiduciaries to a final settlement can be served only if interests or claims of individuals who are outside of the State can somehow be determined.   A construction of the Due Process Clause which would place impossible or impractical obstacles in the way could not be justified.

Against this interest of the State we must balance the individual interest sought to be protected by the Fourteenth Amendment.   This is defined by our holding that "The fundamental requisite of due process of law is the opportunity to be heard."   Grannis v. Ordean, 234 U.S. 385, 394, 34 S.Ct. 779, 783.   This right to be heard has little reality or worth unless one is informed that the matter is pending and can choose for himself whether to appear or default, acquiesce or contest.

The Court has not committed itself to any formula achieving a balance between these interests in a particular proceeding or determining when constructive notice may be utilized or what test it must meet.   Personal service has not in all circumstances been regarded as

934

indispensable to the process due to residents, and it has more often been held unnecessary as to nonresidents. We disturb none of the established rules on these subjects. No decision constitutes a controlling or even a very illuminating precedent for the case before us. But a few general principles stand out in the books.

An elementary and fundamental requirement of due process in any proceeding which is to be accorded finality is notice reasonably calculated, under all the circumstances, to apprise interested parties of the pendency of the action and afford them an opportunity to present their objections. Milliken v. Meyer, 311 U.S. 457, 61 S.Ct. 339; Grannis v. Ordean, 234 U.S. 385, 34 S.Ct. 779; Priest v. Board of Trustees of Town of Las Vegas, 232 U.S. 604, 34 S.Ct. 443; Roller v. Holly, 176 U.S. 398, 20 S.Ct. 410. The notice must be of such nature as reasonably to convey the required information, Grannis v. Ordean, supra, and it must afford a reasonable time for those interested to make their appearance, Roller v. Holly, supra, and cf. Goodrich v. Ferris, 214 U.S. 71, 29 S.Ct. 580. But if with due regard for the practicalities and peculiarities of the case these conditions are reasonably met, the constitutional requirements are satisfied. "The criterion is not the possibility of conceivable injury, but the just and reasonable character of the requirements, having reference to the subject with which the statute deals." American Land Co. v. Zeiss, 219 U.S. 47, 67, 31 S.Ct. 200, 207; and see Blinn v. Nelson, 222 U.S. 1, 7, 32 S.Ct. 1, 2.

But when notice is a person's due, process which is a mere gesture is not due process. The means employed must be such as one desirous of actually informing the absentee might reasonably adopt to accomplish it. The reasonableness and hence the constitutional validity of any chosen method may be defended on the ground that it is in itself reasonably certain to inform those affected, compare Hess v. Pawloski, 274 U.S. 352, 47 S.Ct. 632, with Wuchter v. Pizzutti, 276 U.S. 13, 48 S.Ct. 259, or, where conditions do not reasonably permit such notice, that the form chosen is not substantially less likely to bring home notice than other of the feasible and customary substitutes.

It would be idle to pretend that publication alone, as prescribed here, is a reliable means of acquainting interested parties of the fact that their rights are before the courts. It is not an accident that the greater number of cases reaching this Court on the question of adequacy of notice have been concerned with actions founded on process constructively served through local newspapers. Chance alone brings to the attention of even a local resident an advertisement in small type inserted in the back pages of a newspaper, and if he makes his home outside the area of the newspaper's normal circulation the odds that the information will never reach him are large indeed. The chance of actual notice is further reduced when, as here, the notice required does not even name those whose attention it is supposed to attract, and does not inform acquaintances who might call it to attention. In weighing its sufficiency on the basis of equivalence with actual notice we are unable to regard this as more than a feint.

Nor is publication here reinforced by steps likely to attract the parties' attention to the proceeding. It is true that publication traditionally has been acceptable as notification supplemental to other action which in itself may reasonably be expected to convey a warning. The ways of an owner with tangible property are such that he usually arranges means to learn of any direct attack upon his possessory or proprietary rights. Hence, libel of a ship, attachment of a chattel or entry upon real estate in the name of law may reasonably be expected to come promptly to the owner's attention. When the state within which the owner has located such property seizes it for some reason, publication or posting affords an additional measure of notification. A state may indulge the assumption that one who has left tangible property in the state either has abandoned it, in which case proceedings against it deprive him of nothing, cf. Anderson National Bank v. Luckett, 321 U.S. 233, 64 S.Ct. 599; Security Savings Bank v. California, 263 U.S. 282, 44 S.Ct. 108, or that he has left some caretaker under a duty to let him know that it is being jeopardized. Ballard v. Hunter, 204 U.S. 241, 27 S.Ct. 261; Huling v. Kaw Valley Ry. & Imp. Co., 130 U.S. 559, 9 S.Ct. 503. As phrased long ago by Chief Justice Marshall in The Mary, 9 Cranch 126, 144, "It is the part of common prudence for all those who have any interest in [a thing], to guard that interest by persons who are in a situation to protect it."

In the case before us there is, of course, no abandonment. On the other hand these beneficiaries do have a resident fiduciary as caretaker of their interest in this property. But it is their caretaker who in the accounting becomes their adversary. Their trustee is released from giving notice of jeopardy, and no one else is expected to do so. Not even the special guardian is required or apparently expected to communicate with his ward and client, and, of course, if such a duty were merely transferred from the trustee to the guardian, economy would not be served and more likely the cost would be increased.

This Court has not hesitated to approve of resort to publication as a customary substitute in another class of cases where it is not reasonably possible or practicable to give more adequate warning. Thus it has been recognized that, in the case of persons missing or unknown, employment of an indirect and even a probably futile means of notification is all that the situation permits and creates no constitutional bar to a final decree foreclosing their rights. Cunnius v. Reading School District, 198 U.S. 458, 25 S.Ct. 721; Blinn v. Nelson, 222 U.S. 1, 32 S.Ct. 1; and see Jacob v. Roberts, 223 U.S. 261, 32 S.Ct. 303.

Those beneficiaries represented by appellant whose interests or whereabouts could not with due diligence be ascertained come clearly within this category. As to them the statutory notice is sufficient. However great the odds that publication will never reach the eyes of such unknown parties, it is not in the typical case much more likely to fail than any of the choices open to legislators endeavoring to prescribe the best notice practicable.

Nor do we consider it unreasonable for the State to dispense with more certain notice to those beneficiaries whose interests are either conjectural or future or, although they could be discovered upon investigation, do not in due course of business come to knowledge of the common trustee. Whatever searches might be required in another situation under ordinary standards of diligence, in view of the character of the proceedings and the nature of the interests here involved we think them unnecessary. We recognize the practical difficulties and costs that would be attendant on frequent investigations into the status of great numbers of beneficiaries, many of whose interests in the common fund are so remote as to be ephemeral; and we have no doubt that such impracticable and extended searches are not required in the name of due process. The expense of keeping informed from day to day of substitutions among even current income beneficiaries and presumptive remaindermen, to say nothing of the far greater number of contingent beneficiaries, would impose a severe burden on the plan, and would likely dissipate its advantages. These are practical matters in which we should be reluctant to disturb the judgment of the state authorities.

Accordingly we overrule appellant's constitutional objections to published notice insofar as they are urged on behalf of any beneficiaries whose interests or addresses are unknown to the trustee.

As to known present beneficiaries of known place of residence, however, notice by publication stands on a different footing. Exceptions in the name of necessity do not sweep away the rule that within the limits of practicability notice must be such as is reasonably calculated to reach interested parties. Where the names and post office addresses of those affected by a proceeding are at hand, the reasons disappear for resort to means less likely than the mails to apprise them of its pendency.

The trustee has on its books the names and addresses of the income beneficiaries represented by appellant, and we find no tenable ground for dispensing with a serious effort to inform them personally of the accounting, at least by ordinary mail to the record addresses. Cf. Wuchter v. Pizzutti, supra. Certainly sending them a copy of the statute months and perhaps years in advance does not answer this purpose. The trustee periodically remits their income to them, and we think that they might reasonably expect that with or apart from their remittances word might come to them personally that steps were being taken affecting their interests.

We need not weigh contentions that a requirement of personal service of citation on even the large number of known resident or nonresident beneficiaries would, by reasons of delay if not of expense, seriously interfere with the proper administration of the fund. Of course personal service even without the jurisdiction of the issuing authority serves the end of actual and personal notice, whatever power of compulsion it might lack. However, no such service is required under the circumstances. This type of trust presupposes a large number of small interests. The individual interest does not stand alone but is identical with that of a class. The rights of each in the integrity of the fund and the fidelity of the trustee are shared by many other beneficiaries. Therefore notice reasonably certain to reach most of those interested in objecting is likely to safeguard the interests of all, since any objections sustained would inure to the benefit of all. We think that under such circumstances reasonable risks that notice might not actually reach every beneficiary are justifiable. "Now and then an extraordinary case may turn up, but constitutional law like other mortal contrivances has to take some chances, and in the great majority of instances no doubt justice will be done." Blinn v. Nelson, supra, 222 U.S. at page 7, 32 S.Ct. at page 2.

The statutory notice to known beneficiaries is inadequate not because in fact it fails to reach everyone, but because under the circumstances it is not reasonably calculated to reach those who could easily be informed by other means at hand. However it may have been in former times, the mails today are recognized as an efficient and inexpensive means of communication. Moreover, the fact that the trust company has been able to give mailed notice to known beneficiaries at the time the common trust fund was established is persuasive that postal notification at the time of accounting would not seriously burden the plan.

In some situations the law requires greater precautions in its proceedings than the business world accepts for its own purposes. In few, if any, will it be satisfied with less. Certainly it is instructive, in determining the reasonableness of the impersonal broadcast notification here used, to ask whether it would satisfy a prudent man of business, counting his pennies but finding it in his interest to convey information to many persons whose names and addresses are in his files. We are not satisfied that it would. Publication may theoretically be available for all the world to see, but it is too much in our day to suppose that each or any individual beneficiary does or could examine all that is published to see if something may be tucked away in it that affects his property interests. We have before indicated in reference to notice by publication that, "Great caution should be used not to let fiction deny the fair play that can be secured only by a pretty close adhesion to fact." McDonald v. Mabee, 243 U.S. 90, 91, 37 S.Ct. 343.

We hold that the notice of judicial settlement of accounts required by the New York Banking Law § 100–c(12) is incompatible with the requirements of the Fourteenth Amendment as a basis for adjudication depriving known persons whose whereabouts are also known of substantial property rights. Accordingly the judgment is reversed and the cause remanded for further proceedings not inconsistent with this opinion.

Reversed.

MR. JUSTICE DOUGLAS took no part in the consideration or decision of this case.

MR. JUSTICE BURTON, dissenting.

These common trusts are available only when the instruments creating the participating trusts permit participation in the common fund. Whether or not further notice to beneficiaries should supplement the notice and representation here provided is properly within the discretion of the State. The Federal Constitution does not require it here.

———

Question: (1) What changes in the statute would you, as counsel to the appropriate committee of the New York legislature, recommend for adoption? See N.Y. Banking Law § 100–c(12), as amended by 1951 N.Y. Laws ch. 778, § 3, by which New York sought to meet the defects revealed by the Mullane case.

———

MENNONITE BOARD OF MISSIONS v. ADAMS, 103 S.Ct. 2706 (1983). In the course of lengthy proceedings to sell certain real property consequent to the owner's nonpayment of taxes, notice was posted in the county courthouse and published a number of times. Also, the county sent notice by certified mail to the owner. After title had passed, cutting off a recorded mortgage on the property, the mortgagee learned of the proceedings. The tax-sale purchaser then brought suit to quiet title, during which the mortgagee challenged the adequacy of notice of the tax sale. The Indiana courts upheld the prescribed procedure that had been employed.

On appeal, the United States Supreme Court reversed. Justice Marshall for the Court began by discussing Mullane and continued:

"In subsequent cases, this Court has adhered unwaiveringly to the principle announced in Mullane. In Walker v. City of Hutchinson, 352 U.S. 112, 77 S.Ct. 200 (1956), for example, the Court held that notice of condemnation proceedings published in a local newspaper was an inadequate means of informing a landowner whose name was known to the city and was on the official records. Similarly, in Schroeder v. City of New York, 371 U.S. 208, 83 S.Ct. 279 (1962), the Court concluded that publication in a newspaper and posted notices were inadequate to apprise a property owner of condemnation proceedings when his name and address were readily ascertainable from both deed records and tax rolls. Most recently, in Greene v. Lindsey, 456 U.S. 444, 102 S.Ct. 1874 (1982), we held that posting a summons on the door of a tenant's apartment was an inadequate means of providing notice of forcible entry and detainer actions. [Citations omitted.]

"This case is controlled by the analysis in Mullane. To begin with, a mortgagee possesses a substantial property interest that is significantly affected by a tax sale. . . .

"Since a mortgagee clearly has a legally protected property interest, he is entitled to notice reasonably calculated to apprise him of a pending tax sale. [Citation omitted.] When the mortgagee is identified in a mortgage that is publicly recorded, constructive notice by publication must be supplemented by notice mailed to the mortgagee's last known available address, or by personal service. But unless the mortgagee is not reasonably identifiable, constructive notice alone does not satisfy the mandate of Mullane.

.   .   .   .

"Personal service or mailed notice is required even though sophisticated creditors have means at their disposal to discover whether property taxes have not been paid and whether tax sale proceedings are therefore likely to be initiated. . . . It is true that particularly extensive efforts to provide notice may often be required when the State is aware of a party's inexperience or incompetence. [Citations omitted.] But it does not follow that the State may forego even the relatively modest administrative burden of providing notice by mail to parties who are particularly resourceful. [Citation omitted.] Notice by mail or other means as certain to ensure actual notice is a minimum constitutional precondition to a proceeding which will adversely affect the liberty or property interests of *any* party, whether unlettered or well versed in commercial practice, if its name and address are reasonably ascertainable."

Justice O'Connor, joined by Justices Powell and Rehnquist, dissented. She argued that the Court was departing from Mullane by adopting a rigid rule against constructive notice rather than using a balancing approach. Interestingly, in a decision five days later, these dissenters, joined by Chief Justice Burger and Justices Brennan and Stevens, formed a new majority to rule that a known putative father who had never established any relationship with his child was not entitled to notice of adoption proceedings. Lehr v. Robertson, 103 S.Ct. 2985 (1983).

————

BASIC PRINCIPLES OF PROCEDURAL DUE PROCESS

Procedural due process requires that a person or his representative be given adequate notice and opportunity to be heard before he is deprived of property or liberty by governmental action. The fourteenth amendment extends these protections to deprivations by the state governments, while the fifth amendment covers deprivations by the federal government.

In order to satisfy this constitutional prerequisite for civil adjudication, fair notice of the pendency of the action must be given to the person whose interests are to be affected or to his representative. Fair notice must be suitably formal in tenor and informative in content. Also, fair notice must be either actual notice or notice that is reasonably certain to result in actual notice. So if a reasonable method of notification is employed, the validity of a default judgment will not be affected merely by the failure to achieve actual notice. See Restatement (Second) of Judgments § 2 (1980). It should be remarked, however, that authority persists for this somewhat surprising proposition: if the method of notification prescribed by statute or rule is not reasonably certain to result in actual notice, then notice in the particular case is deemed constitutionally defective even if the person in one way or another received actual notice. See R. Casad, Jurisdiction in Civil Actions ¶ 2.03[1][c] (1983).

A reasonable opportunity to be heard is also indispensable to procedural due process. Notice to a defendant of a claim being made against him is of no value to him if he is denied the opportunity to defend the action. See Roller v. Holly, 176 U.S. 398, 20 S.Ct. 410 (1900). Indeed, it would seem that the real concern of procedural due process here is opportunity to be heard. Notice is merely the means to make possible the exercise of that right.

Descending from the constitutional level, one encounters the regulations for serving process. Local law may strictly enforce some of these nonconstitutional requirements of giving notice. However, the trend is away from an overly strict approach, with courts now tending to ignore service irregularities where there was actual notice of suitable tenor and content or where the manner of transmitting and form of notice substantially complied with the prescribed procedure. See Restatement (Second) of Judgments §§ 2–3 (1980).

How inflexible are the prescribed procedures for service? NYCPLR § 308(5) provides for what has been termed "expedient service" in cases where service cannot practicably be made in certain specified ways: service in hand; delivering process to a person of suitable age and discretion at defendant's abode or place of business, plus mailing to last known residence; or affixing process to the door of defendant's abode or place of business, plus mailing. Pursuant to this subsection, service may in this circumstance be made "in such manner as the court, upon motion without notice, directs." In Dobkin v. Chapman, 21 N.Y.2d 490, 236 N.E.2d 451, 289 N.Y.S.2d 161 (1968), the New York Court of Appeals unanimously upheld the constitutionality of service in three automobile-accident cases against the contention that the methods provided by court order did not give the absent defendants sufficient chance of receiving actual notice of the commencement of the actions (service was challenged by the uninsured motorist fund and the insurance company involved). The manner of notice ordered in the first case was ordinary mail to the address from which registered mail had been returned unclaimed; in the second case, one publication in a designated newspaper after registered mail had been returned unclaimed; and in the third case, where the defendant was known to be insured, delivery of copies of the summons and complaint to the insurance carrier plus ordinary mail to the defendant's last known New York address. The court pointed out that in these cases it was the conduct of the defendants themselves—their removal without informing anyone of their whereabouts—that prevented service of process by the usual means. Chief Judge Fuld for the court said: "Indeed, in an automobile case, no defendant need be without notice unless he chooses and wants to be; many an injured plaintiff, however, will go without recompense if, in a proper case, the standards of informative notice may not be relaxed." The court relied upon Mullane, among other cases. It also referred to NYCPLR § 317, which gives a defendant served other than by personal delivery one year after learning of entry of judgment, but in no event more than five years after such entry, to come in and defend upon a finding that he did not actually receive timely notice and has a meritorious defense. See also In re Petrol Shipping Corp., 360 F.2d 103 (2d Cir.1966) (service on foreign government not being then covered by federal or state law, service by ordinary mail upheld even without prior court authorization), cert. denied, 385 U.S. 931, 87 S.Ct. 291 (1967); Federal Rule 55(c).

———

SNIADACH v. FAMILY FINANCE CORP., 395 U.S. 337, 89 S.Ct. 1820 (1969). Plaintiff finance company sued on a $420 promissory note in a Wisconsin state court, garnishing defendant's employer. The garnishee answered, stating that it had $63.18 of the defendant's wages, earned and unpaid, and that it would pay the defendant one-half thereof as a subsistence allowance and hold the other half subject to the order of the court, as provided in a Wisconsin statute. Under that statute, the court clerk issues the garnishment summons at the request of the plaintiff's lawyer, who by serving the garnishee can then freeze the wages; the defendant must be served with the summons and complaint within ten days of service on the garnishee; if the defendant wins the main suit on the merits, the wages are restored to him, but in the interim he is deprived of them. The defendant moved to dismiss the garnishment proceedings for failure to provide procedural due process. The Wisconsin courts approved the garnishment procedure.

On certiorari, the Supreme Court reversed. After noting that wages are "a specialized type of property presenting distinct problems in our economic system," Justice Douglas for the Court held that the Wisconsin procedure violated the fourteenth amendment by failure to provide notice and opportunity to be heard before the garnishment. Justice Black was the lone dissenter.

————

FUENTES v. SHEVIN, 407 U.S. 67, 92 S.Ct. 1983 (1972). In Florida, Mrs. Fuentes purchased a stove and a stereo under conditional sales contracts that provided for monthly payments and for repossession by the seller in case of any default in payment by the buyer. Under the contracts, the seller retained a security interest in the goods pending full payment, but the buyer was entitled to possession absent default. The total cost of the stove and stereo was about $500, plus a financing charge of over $100. More than a year later, after a dispute over servicing the stove, Mrs. Fuentes stopped making payments while still owing about $200 under the contracts. The seller initiated an action for repossession in small-claims court, simultaneously obtaining a writ of replevin ordering state agents to seize the stove and stereo. The same day a deputy sheriff went with the seller's employee to Mrs. Fuentes' home, served her, and seized the disputed goods. The relevant Florida statute provides for summary issuance of a writ of replevin upon ex parte application to the court clerk by someone suing on a claim to possession of "wrongfully detained" property and upon the plaintiff's posting of a bond for double the value of the property; the property is held for three days by the agent who makes the seizure, during which time the defendant may regain possession of the property upon posting his own bond for double the property's value; if the defendant does not so act, the property then passes to the plaintiff, pending the final disposition of the underlying repossession action. Shortly after the seizure, Mrs. Fuentes sued in federal court, challenging the replevin proceedings on procedural due process grounds. Relief was denied.

On appeal, the Supreme Court reversed, holding by Justice Stewart, joined by Justices Douglas, Brennan, and Marshall, that the Florida procedure (and the similar Pennsylvania procedure involved in a companion case) violated the fourteenth amendment by failure to provide notice and opportunity to be heard before deprivation of a possessory interest in property. The required hearing would be aimed at establishing at least the probable validity of the underlying claim. Justice White, joined by Chief Justice Burger and Justice Blackmun, filed a dissenting opinion. Justices Powell and Rehnquist did not participate.

————

MITCHELL v. W.T. GRANT CO., 416 U.S. 600, 94 S.Ct. 1895 (1974). In Louisiana, Grant sold various household items to Mitchell under installment sales contracts. About a year later, Grant sued in city court for the overdue and unpaid balance of $574.17, Mitchell having paid less than one-quarter of his total principal obligation; Grant alleged having a vendor's lien on the goods securing the unpaid balance, which lien would under state law expire if Mitchell transferred possession. Grant simultaneously obtained a writ of sequestration ordering state agents to seize the goods. Soon thereafter the constable served Mitchell and, at the same time, seized the disputed goods. The relevant Louisiana statute allows sequestration where the plaintiff claims ownership or right to possession of property or a lien thereon, if it is within the defendant's power to dispose of or remove the property during the pendency of the action; the plaintiff must state specific facts by affidavit supporting issuance of the writ and must file a bond sufficient to protect the defendant against any damage resulting from wrongful issuance; issuance is accomplished by ex parte application to a judge; the defendant may immediately seek dissolution of the writ, which must then be ordered unless the plaintiff proves the grounds upon which the writ was issued—the existence of the debt, lien, and delinquency; the defendant may also regain possession upon posting his own bond for 125% of the lesser of the value of the property or the amount of the claim. Mitchell moved to dissolve the writ of sequestration for failure to provide procedural due process. The Louisiana courts approved the sequestration procedure.

On certiorari, the Supreme Court affirmed, with Justices Powell and Rehnquist joining the three Fuentes dissenters to form a new majority. Justice White delivered the opinion of the Court, which declared in part: "In our view, this statutory procedure effects a constitutional accommodation of the conflicting interests of the parties. We cannot accept petitioner's broad assertion that the Due Process Clause of the Fourteenth Amendment guaranteed to him the use and possession of the goods until all issues in the case were judicially resolved after full adversary proceedings had been completed." Justice Powell issued a concurring opinion. The former majority in Fuentes was now in dissent, arguing that the Fuentes decision controlled.

NORTH GEORGIA FINISHING, INC. v. DI–CHEM, INC.

Supreme Court of the United States, 1975.
419 U.S. 601, 95 S.Ct. 719.

MR. JUSTICE WHITE delivered the opinion of the Court.

Under the statutes of the State of Georgia, plaintiffs in pending suits are "entitled to the process of garnishment." Ga.Code Ann. § 46–101. To employ the process, plaintiff or his attorney must make an affidavit before "some officer authorized to issue an attachment, or the clerk of any court of record in which the said garnishment is being filed or in which the main case is filed, stating the amount claimed to be due in such action . . . and that he has reason to apprehend the loss of the same or some part thereof unless process of garnishment shall issue." § 46–102. To protect defendant against loss or damage in the event plaintiff fails to recover, that section also requires plaintiff to file a bond in a sum double the amount sworn to be due ["conditioned to pay said defendant all costs and damages that he may sustain in consequence of suing out said garnishment, in the event that the plaintiff shall fail to recover in the suit . . . or that the property or money sought to be garnished was not subject to process of garnishment"]. Section 46–401 permits the defendant to dissolve the garnishment by filing a bond "conditioned for the payment of any judgment that shall be rendered on said garnishment." Whether these provisions satisfy the Due Process Clause of the Fourteenth Amendment is the issue before us in this case.

On August 20, 1971, respondent filed suit against petitioner in the Superior Court of Whitfield County, Ga., alleging an indebtedness due and owing from petitioner for goods sold and delivered in the amount of $51,279.17. Simultaneously with the filing of the complaint and prior to its service on petitioner, respondent filed affidavit and bond for process of garnishment, naming the First National Bank of Dalton as garnishee. The affidavit asserted the debt and "reason to apprehend the loss of said sum or some part thereof unless process of Garnishment issues." The clerk of the Superior Court forthwith issued summons of garnishment to the bank, which was served that day. On August 23, petitioner filed a bond in the Superior Court conditioned to pay any final judgment in the main action up to the amount claimed, and the judge of that court thereupon discharged the bank as garnishee. On September 15, petitioner filed a motion to dismiss the writ of garnishment and to discharge its bond, asserting, among other things, that the statutory garnishment procedure was unconstitutional in that it violated "defendant's due process and equal protection rights guaranteed him by the Constitution of the United States and the Constitution of the State of Georgia." App. 11. The motion was heard and overruled on November 29. The Georgia Supreme Court . . . sustained the statute and rejected petitioner's claims that the statute was invalid for failure to provide notice and hearing in connection with the issuance of the writ of garnishment. 231 Ga. 260, 201 S.E.2d 321 (1973). We granted certiorari. 417 U.S. 907, 94 S.Ct. 2601 (1974). We reverse.

The Georgia court recognized that Sniadach v. Family Finance Corp., 395 U.S. 337, 89 S.Ct. 1820 (1969), had invalidated a statute permitting the garnishment of wages without notice and opportunity for hearing, but considered that case to have done nothing more than to carve out an exception, in favor of wage earners, "to the general rule of legality of garnishment statutes." 231 Ga., at 264, 201 S.E. 2d, at 323. The garnishment of other assets or properties pending the outcome of the main action, although the effect was to " 'impound [them] in the hands of the garnishee,' " id., at 263, 201 S.E.2d, at 323, was apparently thought not to implicate the Due Process Clause.

This approach failed to take account of Fuentes v. Shevin, 407 U.S. 67, 92 S.Ct. 1983 (1972), a case decided by this Court more than a year prior to the Georgia court's decision. There the Court held invalid the Florida and Pennsylvania replevin statutes which permitted a secured installment seller to repossess the goods sold, without notice or hearing and without judicial order or supervision, but with the help of the sheriff operating under a writ issued by the clerk of the court at the behest of the seller. That the debtor was deprived of only the use and possession of the property, and perhaps only temporarily, did not put the seizure beyond scrutiny under the Due Process Clause. "The Fourteenth Amendment draws no bright lines around three-day, 10-day, or 50-day deprivations of property. Any significant taking of property by the State is within the purview of the Due Process Clause." Id., at 86, 92 S.Ct., at 1997. Although the length or severity of a deprivation of use or possession would be another factor to weigh in determining the appropriate form of hearing, it was not deemed to be determinative of the right to a hearing of some sort. Because the official seizures had been carried out without notice and without opportunity for a hearing or other safeguard against mistaken repossession they were held to be in violation of the Fourteenth Amendment.

The Georgia statute is vulnerable for the same reasons. Here, a bank account, surely a form of property, was impounded and, absent a bond, put totally beyond use during the pendency of the litigation on the alleged debt, all by a writ of garnishment issued by a court clerk without notice or opportunity for an early hearing and without participation by a judicial officer.

Nor is the statute saved by the more recent decision in Mitchell v. W.T. Grant Co., 416 U.S. 600, 94 S.Ct. 1895 (1974). That case upheld the Louisiana sequestration statute which permitted the seller-creditor holding a vendor's lien to secure a writ of sequestration and, having filed a bond, to cause the sheriff to take possession of the property at issue. The writ, however, was issuable only by a judge upon the filing of an affidavit going beyond mere conclusory allegations and clearly setting out the facts entitling the creditor to sequestration. The Louisiana law also expressly entitled the debtor to an immediate hearing after seizure and to dissolution of the writ absent proof by the creditor of the grounds on which the writ was issued.

The Georgia garnishment statute has none of the saving characteristics of the Louisiana statute. The writ of garnishment is issuable on the affidavit of the creditor or his attorney, and the latter need not have personal knowledge of the facts. § 46–103. The affidavit, like the one filed in this case, need contain only conclusory allegations. The writ is issuable, as this one was, by the court clerk, without participation by a judge. Upon service of the writ, the debtor is deprived of the use of the property in the hands of the garnishee. Here a sizable bank account was frozen, and the only method discernible on the face of the statute to dissolve the garnishment was to file a bond to protect the plaintiff creditor. There is no provision for an early hearing at which the creditor would be required to demonstrate at least probable cause for the garnishment. Indeed, it would appear that without the filing of a bond the defendant debtor's challenge to the garnishment will not be entertained, whatever the grounds may be.

Respondent also argues that neither Fuentes nor Mitchell is apposite here because each of those cases dealt with the application of due process protections to consumers who are victims of contracts of adhesion and who might be irreparably damaged by temporary deprivation of household necessities, whereas this case deals with its application in the commercial setting to a case involving parties of equal bargaining power. See also Sniadach v. Family Finance Corp., 395 U.S. 337, 89 S.Ct. 1820 (1969). It is asserted in addition that the double bond posted here gives assurance to petitioner that it will be made whole in the event the garnishment turns out to be unjustified. It may be that consumers deprived of household appliances will more likely suffer irreparably than corporations deprived of bank accounts, but the probability of irreparable injury in the latter case is sufficiently great so that some procedures are necessary to guard against the risk of initial error. We are no more inclined now than we have been in the past to distinguish among different kinds of property in applying the Due Process Clause. Fuentes v. Shevin, 407 U.S., at 89–90, 92 S.Ct., at 1998–1999.

Enough has been said, we think, to require the reversal of the judgment of the Georgia Supreme Court. The case is remanded to that court for further proceedings not inconsistent with this opinion.

So ordered.

MR. JUSTICE STEWART, concurring.

It is gratifying to note that my report of the demise of Fuentes v. Shevin, 407 U.S. 67, 92 S.Ct. 1983, see Mitchell v. W.T. Grant Co., 416 U.S. 600, 629–636, 94 S.Ct. 1895, 1910–1914 (dissenting opinion), seems to have been greatly exaggerated. Cf. S. Clemens, cable from Europe to the Associated Press, quoted in 2 A. Paine, Mark Twain: A Biography 1039 (1912).

MR. JUSTICE POWELL, concurring in the judgment.

I join in the Court's judgment, but I cannot concur in the opinion as I think it sweeps more broadly than is necessary and appears to resuscitate Fuentes v. Shevin, 407 U.S. 67, 92 S.Ct. 1983 (1972). Only last term in Mitchell v. W.T. Grant Co., 416 U.S. 600, 94 S.Ct. 1895 (1974), the Court significantly narrowed the precedential scope of Fuentes. . . . The Court's opinion in this case, relying substantially on Fuentes, suggests that that decision will again be read as calling into question much of the previously settled law governing commercial transactions. I continue to doubt whether Fuentes strikes a proper balance, especially in cases where the creditor's interest in the property may be as significant or even greater than that of the debtor. Nor do I find it necessary to relegate Mitchell to its narrow factual setting in order to determine that the Georgia garnishment statutes fail to satisfy the requirements of procedural due process.

. . . .

In my view, procedural due process would be satisfied where state law requires that the garnishment be preceded by the garnishor's provision of adequate security and by his establishment before a neutral officer [3] of a factual basis of the need to resort to the remedy as a means of preventing removal or dissipation of assets required to satisfy the claim. Due process further requires that the State afford an opportunity for a prompt postgarnishment judicial hearing in which the garnishor has the burden of showing probable cause to believe there is a need to continue the garnishment for a sufficient period of time to allow proof and satisfaction of the alleged debt. Since the garnished assets may bear no relation to the controversy giving rise to the alleged debt, the State also should provide the debtor an opportunity to free those assets by posting adequate security in their place.

. . . .

. . . Quite simply, the Georgia provisions fail to afford fundamental fairness in their accommodation of the respective interests of creditor and debtor. For these reasons, I join in the judgment of the Court.

MR. JUSTICE BLACKMUN, with whom MR. JUSTICE REHNQUIST joins, dissenting.

The Court once again—for the third time in less than three years—struggles with what it regards as the due process aspects of a State's old and long-unattacked commercial statutes designed to afford a way for relief to a creditor against a delinquent debtor. On this third occasion, the Court, it seems to me, does little more than make very general and very sparse comparisons of the present case with Fuentes v. Shevin, 407 U.S. 67, 92 S.Ct. 1983 (1972), on the one hand, and with Mitchell v. W.T. Grant Co., 416 U.S. 600, 94 S.Ct. 1895 (1974), on the other; concludes that this case resembles Fuentes more than it does Mitchell; and then strikes down the Georgia statutory structure as offensive to due process. One gains the impression, par-

---

[3] I am not in accord with the Court's suggestion that the Due Process Clause might require that a *judicial* officer issue the writ of garnishment. The basic protection required for the debtor is the assurance of a prompt postgarnishment hearing before a judge. Such a hearing affords an opportunity to rectify any error in the initial decision to issue the garnishment. When combined with the availability of the garnishor's bond to compensate for any harm caused, the possibility of prompt correction of possible error suffices to satisfy the requirements of procedural due process in this context. It thus should be sufficient for a clerk or other officer of the court to issue the original writ upon the filing of a proper affidavit.

ticularly from the final paragraph of its opinion, that the Court is endeavoring to say as little as possible in explaining just why the Supreme Court of Georgia is being reversed. And, as a result, the corresponding commercial statutes of all other States, similar to but not exactly like those of Florida or Pennsylvania or Louisiana or Georgia, are left in questionable constitutional status, with little or no applicable standard by which to measure and determine their validity under the Fourteenth Amendment. This, it seems to me, is an undesirable state of affairs, and I dissent. I do so for a number of reasons:

. . . .

5. Neither do I conclude that, because this is a garnishment case, rather than a lien or vendor-vendee case, it is automatically controlled by Sniadach. Sniadach, as has been noted, concerned and reeks of wages. North Georgia Finishing is no wage earner. It is a corporation engaged in business. It was protected (a) by the fact that the garnishment procedure may be instituted in Georgia only after the primary suit has been filed or judgment obtained by the creditor, thus placing on the creditor the obligation to initiate the proceedings and the burden of proof, and assuring a full hearing to the debtor; (b) by the respondent's statutorily required and deposited double bond; and (c) by the requirement of the respondent's affidavit of apprehension of loss. It was in a position to dissolve the garnishment by the filing of a single bond. These are transactions of a day-to-day type in the commercial world. They are not situations involving contracts of adhesion or basic unfairness, imbalance, or inequality. See D.H. Overmyer Co. v. Frick Co., 405 U.S. 174, 92 S.Ct. 775 (1972); Swarb v. Lennox, 405 U.S. 191, 92 S.Ct. 767 (1972). The clerk-judge distinction, relied on by the Court, surely is of little significance so long as the court officer is not an agent of the creditor. The Georgia system, for me, affords commercial entities all the protection that is required by the Due Process Clause of the Fourteenth Amendment.

. . . .

MR. CHIEF JUSTICE BURGER dissents for the reasons stated in numbered paragraph 5 of the opinion of MR. JUSTICE BLACKMUN.

———

Question: (2) If Georgia had had a Mitchell-type statute, with which Di-Chem had complied, would the result have been different even though Di-Chem had no pre-existing interest in the bank account?

———

SCOPE OF SNIADACH'S PROGENY

The foregoing cases deal with the extension of procedural due process standards to regulate pre-judgment seizures of property for security. In this context and in others, the requirement that notice and opportunity to be heard must be given before the government deprives a person of a protected property interest, or that at least the procedures of a Mitchell-type statute must be followed, raises several problems of definition. What kind of property interest must be the subject of deprivation in order to trigger this protection? What degree of governmental involvement is necessary to trigger this protection? Once this protection is triggered, what kind of hearing will suffice?

These cases show an expansive view of the property interests the deprivation of which is regulated by the due process clauses. For example, the property involved certainly need not be a necessity of life. The interest may be only possessory. The deprivation might only be temporary.

Question: (3) *A* supplied labor to *B* in connection with the construction of *B*'s mobile home park. *A*, claiming that he had not been paid the amount due him, filed a mechanic's lien with the county recorder against the property. This lien did not disturb *B*'s possession of the property but did prevent him from alienating it freely. Does this deprivation of a property interest entail due process protection? Compare Spielman-Fond, Inc. v. Hanson's, Inc., 379 F.Supp. 997 (D.Ariz.1973), aff'd mem., 417 U.S. 901, 94 S.Ct. 2596 (1974), with Kukanskis v. Griffith, 180 Conn. 501, 430 A.2d 21 (1980).

Deprivations of significant property interests invoke the due process clauses only when they result from governmental action. However, such action need not involve direct action by government officials. Action by heavily regulated entities may qualify as governmental action if "there is a sufficiently close nexus between the State and the challenged action of the regulated entity." Jackson v. Metropolitan Edison Co., 419 U.S. 345, 351, 95 S.Ct. 449, 453 (1974). Action by private persons that the government compels or significantly encourages may also be considered governmental action. See Reitman v. Mulkey, 387 U.S. 369, 87 S.Ct. 1627 (1967). And action by private persons that is taken under authority delegated by the government and is traditionally an exclusively public function may constitute governmental action. See Evans v. Newton, 382 U.S. 296, 86 S.Ct. 486 (1966).

Question: (4) U.C.C. § 9–503 provides that upon default a secured party may repossess collateral in the debtor's possession without judicial process, as long as this can be done without breach of the peace. Would such repossession under § 9–503 constitute state action for the purposes of the fourteenth amendment? See Flagg Bros. v. Brooks, 436 U.S. 149, 98 S.Ct. 1729 (1978) (U.C.C. § 7–210 provides that a warehouseman may enforce his lien on stored goods, which lien he is given for charges due for storage, by selling the goods in a commercially reasonable manner but without judicial process; the Court held that a sale under § 7–210 does not constitute state action for the purposes of the fourteenth amendment).

Once it has been determined that due process requires a hearing, it must be decided what issues will be heard under what procedures. The courts have not been very specific on this problem, but one basic principle does emerge. Apparently the scope and nature of the hearing may be restricted or altered to reflect the importance of the interest to be affected, the need for the particular safeguard in the hearing setting, and the burden of affording that safeguard. See generally Friendly, "Some Kind of Hearing," 123 U.Pa.L.Rev. 1267 (1975).

Question: (5) What would Di-Chem have to show in the hearing required by the Supreme Court?

Sniadach and its progeny are immediately concerned with pre-judgment seizures of property for security. It is obvious, however, that they should have an influence in many other contexts, although the strength of that influence will not always be clear.

Pre-judgment attachments and garnishments of property to obtain in rem or quasi in rem jurisdiction have in the past been treated as not being subject to the procedural due process dictates of the foregoing cases. Such treatment was grounded on the theory that there is strong public interest in obtaining jurisdiction and that this consideration colors the seizure as an "extraordinary situation" beyond the reach of Sniadach's progeny. Cf. Calero-Toledo v. Pearson Yacht Leasing Co., 416 U.S. 663, 94 S.Ct. 2080 (1974) (seizure of a drug-running yacht for forfeiture proceedings is such an "extraordinary situation"). But recent cases have persuasively held that a general exception of this sort is illogical, and they have applied the Sniadach line of cases to run-of-the-mill seizures for jurisdictional purposes. E.g., Jonnet v. Dollar Savings Bank, 530 F.2d 1123 (3d Cir.1976); see Moore, Procedural Due Process in Quasi In Rem Actions After Shaffer v. Heitner, 20 Wm. & Mary L.Rev. 157 (1978).

Another context in which the Sniadach line might have an impact is that of seizures of property to enforce judgments. Here it has been held, however, that a wage garnishment need not be preceded by notice and opportunity to be heard on the propriety of the garnishment; the court reasoned that the state's interest in facilitating the enforcement of its judgments and the creditor's interest in satisfying his judgment outweighed the debtor's interests, given that the debtor had had notice and opportunity to be heard before judgment and given that the debtor would under the state law have the opportunity of a prompt post-garnishment hearing. Brown v. Liberty Loan Corp., 539 F.2d 1355 (5th Cir.1976), cert. denied, 430 U.S. 949, 97 S.Ct. 1588 (1977). But recent cases have emphasized that due process does require prompt post-seizure notice and opportunity to be heard. E.g., Finberg v. Sullivan, 634 F.2d 50 (3d Cir.1980) (en banc); see Note, Due Process, Postjudgment Garnishment, and "Brutal Need" Exemptions, 1982 Duke L.J. 192.

Question: (6) What protection does due process afford in connection with seizure of property to obtain quasi in rem jurisdiction for the purpose of enforcing an out-of-state personal judgment?

It should finally be mentioned that constitutional provisions other than the federal due process clauses may contribute to the regulation of seizure procedures. For example, in Blair v. Pitchess, 5 Cal.3d 258, 486 P.2d 1242, 96 Cal.Rptr. 42 (1971), the California Supreme Court found that the warrantless seizure of property by state agents, in a Fuentes-type situation, violated the search and seizure clause of the fourth amendment. And in Svendsen v. Smith's Moving & Trucking Co., 54 N.Y.2d 865, 429 N.E.2d 411, 444 N.Y.S.2d 904 (1981), cert. denied, 455 U.S. 927, 102 S.Ct. 1292 (1982), the New York Court of Appeals found U.C.C. § 7–210 unconstitutional under the due process clause of the state's constitution. Moreover, of course, federal and state legislative and administrative provisions may further restrict seizure procedures.

D.H. OVERMYER CO. v. FRICK CO.

Supreme Court of the United States, 1972.
405 U.S. 174, 92 S.Ct. 775.

Mr. Justice Blackmun delivered the opinion of the Court.

This case presents the issue of the constitutionality, under the Due Process Clause of the Fourteenth Amendment, of the cognovit note authorized by Ohio Rev.Code § 2323.13.

The cognovit is the ancient legal device by which the debtor consents in advance to the holder's obtaining a judgment without notice or hearing, and possibly even with the appearance, on the debtor's behalf, of an attorney designated by the holder. It was known at least as far back as Blackstone's time. 3 W. Blackstone, Commentaries *397. In a case applying Ohio law, it was said that the purpose of the cognovit is "to permit the note holder to obtain judgment without a trial of possible defenses which the signers of the notes might assert." Hadden v. Rumsey Products, Inc., 196 F.2d 92, 96 (CA2 1952). And long ago the cognovit method was described by the Chief Justice of New Jersey as "the loosest way of binding a man's property that ever was devised in any civilized country." Alderman v. Diament, 7 N.J.L. 197, 198 (1824). Mr. Dickens noted it with obvious disfavor. Pickwick Papers, c. 47. The cognovit has been the subject of comment, much of it critical.

Statutory treatment varies widely. Some States specifically authorize the cognovit. Others disallow it. Some go so far as to make its employment a misdemeanor. The majority, however, regulate its use and many prohibit the device in small loans and consumer sales.

. . . . .

The argument that a provision of this kind is offensive to current notions of Fourteenth Amendment due process is, at first glance, an appealing one. However, here, as in nearly every case, facts are important. [Overmyer was a warehousing enterprise with many warehouses in many states. It contracted with Frick for an automatic refrigeration system in a warehouse under construction in Ohio.

Overmyer fell behind in its progress payments, and Frick stopped its work. After negotiations, the work was resumed under new install-ment-payment terms and completed to Overmyer's satisfaction. Lat-er Overmyer requested additional time to make its installment pay-ments. Negotiations finally resulted in a new agreement, which included the execution of a note with a cognovit provision; there had been no such provision in the earlier agreements. As the Supreme Court was later to observe, the execution and delivery of this note "were for an adequate consideration and were the product of negotia-tions carried on by corporate parties with the advice of competent counsel." Later Overmyer ceased to make the required monthly pay-ments under the note, asserting a breach by Frick of the original con-tract. Frick caused judgment for the balance due on the note to be entered in an Ohio court without prior notice. This was effected through the appearance of an Ohio attorney, not known to Overmyer, "by virtue of the warrant of attorney" in the note. The attorney waived service of process and confessed judgment. As required by Ohio law, Overmyer was notified by the court clerk of entry of judg-ment on the cognovit note. Overmyer moved to vacate judgment, and it tendered an answer and counterclaim. The Ohio court over-ruled the motion, and the state appellate courts affirmed. Certiorari was granted.]

[Overmyer argues] that due process requires reasonable notice and an opportunity to be heard, citing Boddie v. Connecticut, 401 U.S. 371, 378, 91 S.Ct. 780, 786 (1971). It is acknowledged, however, that the question here is in a context of "contract waiver, before suit has been filed, before any dispute has arisen" and "whereby a party gives up in advance his constitutional right to defend any suit by the other, to notice and an opportunity to be heard, no matter what de-fenses he may have, and to be represented by counsel of his own choice."[9] In other words, Overmyer's position here specifically is that it is "unconstitutional to waive in advance the right to present a defense in an action on the note."[10] It is conceded that in Ohio a court has the power to open the judgment upon a proper showing. Bellows v. Bowlus, 83 Ohio App. 90, 93, 82 N.E.2d 429, 432 (1948). But it is claimed that such a move is discretionary and ordinarily will not be disturbed on appeal, and that it may not prevent execution before the debtor has notice, Griffin v. Griffin, 327 U.S. 220, 231–232, 66 S.Ct. 556, 561–562 (1946). Goldberg v. Kelly, 397 U.S. 254, 90 S.Ct. 1011 (1970), and Sniadach v. Family Finance Corp., 395 U.S. 337, 89 S.Ct. 1820 (1969), are cited.

The due process rights to notice and hearing prior to a civil judg-ment are subject to waiver. In National Equipment Rental, Ltd. v. Szukhent, 375 U.S. 311, 84 S.Ct. 411 (1964), the Court observed:

"[I]t is settled . . . that parties to a contract may agree in advance to submit to the jurisdiction of a given court, to permit

---

[9] Brief for Petitioners 16.   [10] Trans. of Oral Arg. 17.

notice to be served by the opposing party, or even to waive notice altogether." Id., at 315–316, 84 S.Ct., at 414.

And in Boddie v. Connecticut, supra, the Court acknowledged that "the hearing required by due process is subject to waiver." 401 U.S., at 378–379, 91 S.Ct., at 786.

This, of course, parallels the recognition of waiver in the criminal context where personal liberty, rather than a property right, is involved. Illinois v. Allen, 397 U.S. 337, 342–343, 90 S.Ct. 1057, 1060 (1970) (right to be present at trial); Miranda v. Arizona, 384 U.S. 436, 444, 86 S.Ct. 1602, 1612 (1966) (rights to counsel and against compulsory self-incrimination); Fay v. Noia, 372 U.S. 391, 439, 83 S.Ct. 822, 849 (1963) (habeas corpus); Rogers v. United States, 340 U.S. 367, 371, 71 S.Ct. 438, 440 (1951) (right against compulsory self-incrimination).

Even if, for present purposes, we assume that the standard for waiver in a corporate-property-right case of this kind is the same standard applicable to waiver in a criminal proceeding, that is, that it be voluntary, knowing, and intelligently made, Brady v. United States, 397 U.S. 742, 748, 90 S.Ct. 1463, 1468 (1970); Miranda v. Arizona, 384 U.S., at 444, 86 S.Ct., at 1612, or "an intentional relinquishment or abandonment of a known right or privilege," Johnson v. Zerbst, 304 U.S. 458, 464, 58 S.Ct. 1019, 1023 (1938); Fay v. Noia, 372 U.S., at 439, 83 S.Ct., at 849, and even if, as the Court has said in the civil area, "[w]e do not presume acquiescence in the loss of fundamental rights," Ohio Bell Tel. Co. v. Public Utilities Comm'n, 301 U.S. 292, 307, 57 S.Ct. 724, 731 (1937), that standard was fully satisfied here.

. . . .

We therefore hold that Overmyer, in its execution and delivery to Frick of the second installment note containing the cognovit provision, voluntarily, intelligently, and knowingly waived the rights it otherwise possessed to prejudgment notice and hearing, and that it did so with full awareness of the legal consequences.

. . . .

Some concluding comments are in order:

1. Our holding necessarily means that a cognovit clause is not, per se, violative of Fourteenth Amendment due process. Overmyer could prevail here only if the clause were constitutionally invalid. The facts of this case, as we observed above, are important, and those facts amply demonstrate that a cognovit provision may well serve a proper and useful purpose in the commercial world and at the same time not be vulnerable to constitutional attack.

2. Our holding, of course, is not controlling precedent for other facts of other cases. For example, where the contract is one of adhesion, where there is great disparity in bargaining power, and where

the debtor receives nothing for the cognovit provision, other legal consequences may ensue.

3. Overmyer, merely because of its execution of the cognovit note, is not rendered defenseless. It concedes that in Ohio the judgment court may vacate its judgment upon a showing of a valid defense and, indeed, Overmyer had a post-judgment hearing in the Ohio court. If there were defenses such as prior payment or mistaken identity, those defenses could be asserted. And there is nothing we see that prevented Overmyer from pursuing its breach-of-contract claim against Frick in a proper forum. . . .

The judgment is affirmed.

[The concurring opinion of Justice Douglas, with whom Justice Marshall joined, is omitted. Justices Powell and Rehnquist did not participate.]

Questions: (7) The Overmyer case clearly suggests that a contractual waiver of notice and opportunity to be heard may sometimes be invalid in a consumer setting, as indeed was held in Gonzalez v. County of Hidalgo, Texas, 489 F.2d 1043 (5th Cir.1973). As the attorney for a seller of consumer goods, how would you draft waiver provisions in a conditional sales contract so as to meet the requirements suggested by the Overmyer case? As the attorney for the buyer, what would you argue to establish the unconstitutionality of those provisions?

(8) As indicated by the quotation in Overmyer from National Equipment Rental, Ltd. v. Szukhent, 375 U.S. 311, 315–16, 84 S.Ct. 411, 414 (1964), the defendant can in the proper circumstances waive in advance objections to personal jurisdiction. Should the same principle be applied to venue, so that pursuant to waiver in advance an action may proceed in a place improper under the venue statute, or so that pursuant to agreement in advance an action may be brought only in a certain place despite the more permissive provisions of the venue statute? See The Bremen v. Zapata Off-Shore Co., 407 U.S. 1, 92 S.Ct. 1907 (1972).

Merger & bar = claim preclusion
collateral & direct estoppel = issue preclusion

Part Six

FORMER ADJUDICATION

TOPIC A. GENERAL OBSERVATIONS

We have already encountered a number of problems regarding rules designed to treat or prevent repetitious litigation. The purpose of this Part is to examine these problems systematically in a single place and to search out and evaluate the policies that appear to mold decision. Our primary interest will be the centrally important doctrine of res judicata.

Some questions of res judicata have not been authoritatively resolved, and there is considerable dissatisfaction with some of the solutions that have been given. Indeed, there has been a certain uneasiness in the courts with the whole doctrine, exemplified by Judge Clark's aphorism: "The defense of res judicata is universally respected, but actually not very well liked."[a] And there has been strong advocacy of drastic change.[b] Yet, as we shall see, the current Supreme Court seems to be embracing res judicata with renewed affection.

Valid judg- for ℗ = no claim → merge w/ judg

Some basic propositions.—Some basic propositions can be simply stated. If a plaintiff sues and obtains a valid and final personal judgment in his favor, generally his claim is extinguished and merged in the judgment. He cannot relitigate the claim in hopes of winning a more favorable decision against the defendant, either in the same jurisdiction or elsewhere. The judgment is substituted for the claim, and it is only the judgment that can then be enforced. (The plaintiff can sue upon the judgment in another state and obtain a fresh judgment. If he does so, the first judgment is not merged in the second. He can seek to enforce either or both, but is of course limited to one satisfaction. See Moore v. Justices of the Municipal Court, 291 Mass. 504, 197 N.E. 487 (1935).)

Judge agst ℗ no claim → bar from relit.

Similarly, if a plaintiff sues but judgment goes against him, then generally his claim is extinguished. He is barred by the judgment from relitigation of the same claim. (What is meant by these statements about "merger" and "bar" is that if the plaintiff attempts relitigation of the same claim, the defendant may successfully plead res judicata. Here is another instance where rules of law are not self-executing. What happens when the defense of res judicata is not

[a] Riordan v. Ferguson, 147 F.2d 983, 988 (2d Cir.1945) (dissenting opinion).

[b] See, e.g., Cleary, Res Judicata Reexamined, 57 Yale L.J. 339 (1948). Considering such change, Millar, The Premises of the Judgment as Res Judicata in Continental and Anglo-American Law (pts. 1–2), 39 Mich.L.Rev. 1, 238 (1940), suggested that we may draw profitably upon the experience of other legal systems.

pleaded, and a second judgment inconsistent with the first is rendered, is considered later in this Part.) [c]

How does the principle against relitigation apply to actions where the claims are different? Unlike the doctrines of merger and bar, which operate without regard to what was in fact litigated in the first suit, this aspect of res judicata makes conclusive between the parties the prior determination of an issue only if it was actually litigated and determined in the original action. Moreover, the determination of that issue must have been essential to the first judgment. This doctrine is termed "collateral estoppel" by many courts and commentators.[d] (For clarity of analysis it is useful to distinguish collateral estoppel from merger and bar, but courts too often in their thinking have lumped these quite different doctrines together. Furthermore, courts have frequently confused the picture by using idiosyncratic terminology and categorization to subdivide the subject of res judicata.[e])

Here is the basic provision, stating the three general rules along with references to the more detailed provisions, from Restatement (Second) of Judgments § 17 (1980):

> A valid and final personal judgment is conclusive between the parties, except on appeal or other direct review, to the following extent:
>
> (1) If the judgment is in favor of the plaintiff, the claim is extinguished and merged in the judgment and a new claim may arise on the judgment (see § 18);
>
> (2) If the judgment is in favor of the defendant, the claim is extinguished and the judgment bars a subsequent action on that claim (see § 19);
>
> (3) A judgment in favor of either the plaintiff or the defendant is conclusive, in a subsequent action between them on the same or a different claim, with respect to any issue actually litigated and determined if its determination was essential to that judgment (see § 27).

The rest of this Part is largely devoted to exploring the hidden depths of this basic provision on res judicata. But here, for orientation purposes, let us first take a preliminary look at some of the rather obvious implications of § 17—although several of our tentative statements require later elaboration and qualification.

[c] The two doctrines, merger and bar, now are collectively named "claim preclusion."

[d] If an exception to claim preclusion applies so that a claim may be relitigated, a doctrine identical to collateral estoppel acts to preclude relitigation of issues in any subsequent action on the same claim. This doctrine is termed "direct estoppel."

The two doctrines, collateral and direct estoppel, now are collectively named "issue preclusion."

[e] The older term "res adjudicata" is still sometimes used for "res judicata." More confusingly, many courts persist in using these two general terms to encompass only claim preclusion and not issue preclusion too.

Second action.—The doctrine of res judicata specifies certain binding effects, in subsequent litigation, of a previously rendered judgment. Generally speaking, then, res judicata can apply only when an attempt is made in a second action to foreclose relitigation of a matter already adjudicated in a previous action. Res judicata therefore has no application to an attempt in the original action to correct error in the judgment, as by motion for a new trial or by appeal.[f]

For example, compare Thompson v. Washington National Bank, 68 Wash. 42, 122 P. 606 (1912), with Louisville & Nashville Railroad v. Whitley County Court, supra p. 636. In Thompson, the plaintiff sued on a contract to lay a tile floor and lost on the ground that he had not substantially performed his contract, in that the tiled floor had been left in a discolored condition. Eight months after the judgment he sued again on the same contract, eager to show that after the first judgment the defendant had had the discoloration removed at a cost of only $12 and that therefore the contract had been substantially performed. In Whitley, post-trial events similarly showed that the judgment was erroneous, and the aggrieved party moved for a new trial on the ground of newly discovered evidence. In Thompson, res judicata was successfully pleaded; in Whitley, res judicata was not involved because the motion was made in the original action. Had Thompson moved for a new trial instead of suing again, he could have avoided the application of res judicata.

Validity.—These rules of res judicata are applicable, as we have seen, only to "valid" judgments. A judgment is treated as valid for this purpose if it is of sufficient quality to withstand any request for relief from judgment, such as a collateral attack launched in the second action. Generally speaking, a collateral attack lies on, and only on, the grounds that the court rendering the prior judgment failed to satisfy the requirement of subject-matter jurisdiction, territorial jurisdiction, or opportunity to be heard.

On the one hand, if such a defect in competence, nexus, or notice can be shown, generally the judgment will be deemed not valid and the invocation of res judicata will be defeated. Relief from judgment is thus available even by collateral attack.

On the other hand, the fact that the judgment may have been otherwise erroneous is usually immaterial with respect to res judicata. Mere error does not affect a judgment's validity. Indeed, the failure to honor an erroneous but valid judgment rendered by a court of another American jurisdiction is, in our federal system, an impermissible denial of full faith and credit. Mere error may be corrected only on direct review.

---

[f] There is a doctrine called law of the case, which stands for the sensible proposition that a court, and courts inferior to it, will normally not depart from a rule of law declared by it in a particular case if the point is again presented in the same case. See generally 1B Moore ¶ 0.404. However, this flexible and limited doctrine, although very similar to stare decisis, is distinguishable from res judicata.

Finality.—These rules of res judicata are applicable, as we have *only* also seen, only to "final" judgments. But what constitutes finality *for* for this purpose? It is not precisely the same as "final" in the stat- *FINAL* ute providing for appellate review of "final decisions of the district *Judg.s* courts." 28 U.S.C. § 1291.

First, the rules of claim preclusion stick pretty closely to the tradi- *① ct. of* tional strict formulation of finality for appellate review: the court *judg. must* rendering the judgment must ordinarily have said its last word. *have said* Compare Topic B of Part Eight, where it is shown how the strict con- *last word* cept of finality has now been stretched in the context of appealability so as to provide immediate review in situations where it is deemed necessary.

Second, when issue preclusion is involved, there is a cautious ten- *② Less* dency to be somewhat less strict in finding finality than in the case of *strict for* claim preclusion. If an issue was firmly decided after adequate hear- *issue* ing and full deliberation, a second court has discretion to give the *than.* decision preclusive effect despite its lack of finality in the strict *Claim* sense. Of course, if it were avowedly tentative, it would not be given such effect. In Lummus Co. v. Commonwealth Oil Refining Co., 297 F.2d 80, 89 (2d Cir.1961), cert. denied, 368 U.S. 986, 82 S.Ct. 601 (1962), Judge Friendly put this discretionary relaxation of the finality standard in these words: " 'Finality' in the context here relevant may mean little more than that the litigation of a particular issue has *#* reached such a stage that a court sees no really good reason for per- mitting it to be litigated again." In that case, preclusive effect on an issue of fraud in the inducement of a contract was given to a decision of the Court of Appeals for the First Circuit, by which the First Cir- cuit in litigation related to the same contract had vacated a prelimi- nary injunction staying arbitration between the parties. Restatement (Second) of Judgments § 13 (1980) adopts the view of the Lummus case.

Question: (1) For personal injuries in an automobile accident, A sues B in a jurisdiction where the issues as to liability are determined first, and the damage issues are heard later by another jury if liability is found. The jury finds for A on liability. Should this determination be controlling before the final judgment, which would have to await the assessment of damages, in a personal-injury action by B against A involving the same issues? Should this determination be controlling, by way of merger, in another action by A against B on the same claim?

Under the res judicata law of most jurisdictions, a judgment other- wise final for res judicata purposes is not deprived of finality because time still exists for attack in the trial court, as by motion for a new trial, or because a party has actually made such an attack. Likewise, the fact that the time for appeal has not expired, or that an appeal has been taken and remains pending, does not prevent a judgment from being considered final for res judicata purposes.[g] If the judg-

---

[g] Restatement of Judgments § 41 com- ment d (1942) considered loss of finality pending appeal in terms of whether tak- ing the appeal "vacates" the judgment

ment is eventually overturned, relief from a second judgment based upon it normally may be had by appropriate proceedings. See, e.g., Rule 60(b)(5).

Personal judgment.—For the moment, we are concerned only with the res judicata effects of ordinary judgments and indeed only with those effects between the parties thereto. Special rules for the effects of a judgment resting on jurisdiction over a thing are prescribed in Restatement (Second) of Judgments §§ 30, 32 (1980). Similarly, the effects of claim and issue preclusion on persons not parties to the prior judgment, and other special effects, are examined later in this Part.

Closing thoughts.—By way of illustration of the possible harshness in the operation of res judicata, we refer to a much-cited case. In Jacobson v. Mutual Benefit Health & Accident Association, 73 N.D. 108, 11 N.W.2d 442 (1943), the plaintiff had sued for $2000 on her husband's policy insuring against his accidental death. Part A of the policy entitled her to $2000 on the insured's accidental death; Part B provided that each year's renewal of the policy would add $200 to the death benefit, and there had been nine such renewals. (Plaintiff's lawyer apparently had neglected to read Part B.) That suit had resulted in judgment for the plaintiff for $2000. Later, becoming aware of the error, plaintiff brought a new suit for the additional $1800. The defendant insurer pleaded the prior judgment. The court held that plaintiff was seeking improperly to split her cause of action; that there had been but one cause of action, in solido, for the $3800; that this cause of action had been extinguished by the prior judgment; and that the second action could not be maintained. This result is not compelled by logic or by the nature of things, although it is one by which lawyers would not be surprised in the light of past decisions of the courts and by which judicial economy is arguably served; much can be said against exacting such a penalty from the plaintiff, and correspondingly giving such a windfall to the insurance company, because of counsel's failure to read the policy with care.

At any rate, the Jacobson decision shows how essential it is in applying the principle that a claim is extinguished by a judgment to determine the precise dimensions of the thing that has been extinguished. So the question of the measure of "claim," or "cause of action," reappears in a new context. This question we shall examine in the next Topic.

(as taking an appeal in equity did). That approach seems to have little relevance today, but it is still adhered to in some states. Restatement (Second) of Judgments § 13 comment f (1980) rejects it and says: "The better view is that a judgment otherwise final remains so despite the taking of an appeal unless what is called an appeal actually consists of a trial de novo . . . ." If there is to be a trial de novo in a higher court, the original decision is deprived of its finality pending the appeal.

TOPIC B. CLAIM PRECLUSION

SECTION 1. DIMENSIONS OF A CLAIM

WILLIAMSON v. COLUMBIA GAS & ELECTRIC CORP.

United States Court of Appeals, Third Circuit, 1950.
186 F.2d 464, cert. denied, 341 U.S. 921, 71 S.Ct. 743 (1951).

Before GOODRICH, KALODNER and HASTIE, CIRCUIT JUDGES.

GOODRICH, CIRCUIT JUDGE. This case involves the application of the rules of res judicata to a civil suit brought by the plaintiff, through its trustee in bankruptcy, for injuries alleged to have been sustained because of the defendant's violation of the anti-trust laws.

This action, which we shall call action No. 1, was begun on February 14, 1938. It charged that the defendant, conspiring with certain other persons, had, in violation of the provisions of the anti-trust laws, inflicted great injury upon the plaintiff. But as the complaint was amended it sought recovery against Columbia Gas and Electric Corporation alone, although other parties were named as having conspired with Columbia in the various transactions of which complaint is made.

Subsequently, on September 16, 1938, the plaintiff brought in the same court (the United States District Court for the District of Delaware) another action against the defendant charging injury in violation of the anti-trust laws. This we shall call action No. 2. In this action the charge did not read in terms of conspiracy but alleged Columbia alone as the wrongdoer.

Thus we have two actions pending by the same plaintiff against the same defendant in the same court, each involving a suit for recovery of injuries alleged to have been sustained by action on the part of the defendant in violation of the anti-trust laws of the United States. Later to be examined is the identity, or substantial identity, of these suits.

The No. 2 action came to a conclusion first. On April 29, 1939, the court ordered "That the complaint in the . . . cause be and it hereby is dismissed. . . ."

The whole question with which we have to do in this case involves the effect of this judgment for the defendant upon the plaintiff's No. 1 action. In the District Court, the defendant moved [for summary judgment in] action No. 1 because of its victory in action No. 2. The motion was granted and the plaintiff appeals. Our discussion of the main question will be divided into consideration of the several issues presented.

961

Assume for the moment that the subject-matter of action No. 1 is identical with the subject-matter No. 2 so as to amount to the same "cause of action." Then we have two questions which may be disposed of first to clear the way for the most difficult thing about the case which is the assumption of identity just stated. The two questions are: (1) Does it matter for purposes of application of res judicata that the No. 2 action, later begun, was finished first? The answer to this question is no. The point is so well settled on authority that it is not a serious matter of contention in this case. (2) The second question is, what of the fact that the recital contained in the order of dismissal . . . mentioned a stipulation between the parties and the further fact that that stipulation had to do with the time in which the alleged cause of action accrued?

Here is what had occurred. Prior to the dismissal of action No. 2 the parties had entered into a stipulation. That stipulation provided that "The alleged right of action sued upon in this cause accrued not later than January 1, 1931." It was further agreed that if the court should consider the action barred by any applicable statute of limitations the pending motion to dismiss was to be granted. The plaintiff's theory at that time was that his action was not barred by the Delaware statute of limitations, and he evidently felt sufficiently confident of his position to enter into the stipulation which posed the legal issue of its correctness.

Subsequent events proved plaintiff's theory to be incorrect. Both the District Court and this Court held that the Delaware statute was applicable and the plaintiff's suit was begun too late.[5]

Does the fact that the judgment was entered for the defendant in action No. 2 on the basis that the action was barred by lapse of time preclude the application of res judicata to action No. 1, still assuming that the causes of action are identical? The answer to this question is likewise no. The adjudication in favor of the defendant operates as a bar to another suit on the same cause of action in the same jurisdiction.[6] The fact that the case was tried upon stipulation of fact does not make it any the less a final adjudication of the plaintiff's claim.

With these minor points out of the way we now get to the main question in the case which was hypothetically assumed in the discussion just preceding. That question is whether action 1 and action 2 are substantially identical. If they are the rule of law is clear enough. "Where a valid and final personal judgment is rendered on the merits in favor of the defendant, the plaintiff cannot thereafter maintain an action on the original cause of action."[7] The general

---

[5] Williamson v. Columbia Gas & Electric Corp., D.C.Del.1939, 27 F.Supp. 198, affirmed, 3 Cir.1939, 110 F.2d 15, certiorari denied, 1940, 310 U.S. 639, 60 S.Ct. 1087, 84 L.Ed. 1407. [See supra p. 299.—Ed.]

[6] Restatement, Judgments § 49, comment a (1942) (note that it does not bar the action in another state). . . .

[7] Restatement, Judgments § 48 (1942). Cromwell v. County of Sac, 1876, 94 U.S. 351, 352, 24 L.Ed. 195.

principle is well known and undisputed. The difficulty comes in its application to varying sets of facts.

The best way to find out what is involved in the two actions is to look at the claims made by the plaintiff. Neither case went to trial on the facts so all we have is what the plaintiff charges, plus the supplementary affidavits, motions, and the like, which led up to the action of the Trial Judge dismissing plaintiff's action No. 1. The plaintiff alleges its organization and entry into the gas business. It says that the defendant, seeking to crush out a competitor, acquired the controlling shareholder interest in the plaintiff company and proceeded to manipulate its affairs to the disadvantage of the plaintiff and the advantage of the defendant. It says that after the plaintiff went into receivership the defendant named and controlled the receiver and the final result was that the plaintiff was forced into bankruptcy. This is a general statement; no attempt has been made to particularize individual charges.

The complaint in action No. 1 alleged that all this had been done as part of a continuing conspiracy in violation of Sections 1 and 2 of the Sherman Act, but, as amended, named only Columbia as defendant. The complaint in action No. 2, filed 7 months later, alleged that all that had transpired was in violation of Section 7 of the Clayton Act. The information set forth in the two complaints is substantially identical, plaintiff merely using words of conspiracy in the first action and replacing them with allegations that defendant did the same things on its own or through its agents in the second action. The wrongful acts alleged on the part of the defendant and the damages alleged to have been sustained by the plaintiff are practically identical in both suits. Indeed, the identity of the damage claims is almost startling, for except for a few figures with regard to interest the allegations of the particular items of damage are alike to the penny.

Nevertheless, plaintiff says the causes of action are different. We therefore proceed to examine the reasons stated to show the difference.

One alleged difference is that action No. 2 was a claim against Columbia as a sole tortfeasor and action No. 1 is a claim against Columbia as a conspirator. It is true that the complaint in No. 1 contains allegations of conspiracy and the complaint in action No. 2 did not. We do not think, however, that this constitutes a difference if the other elements alleged by the plaintiff are the same. Columbia was sought to be held as the party defendant in both suits. Whether Columbia is sought to be held as a sole tortfeasor or sued singly as one of several tortfeasors, assuming the injury is the same, does not matter. Several people getting together to do wrong to another do not commit a tort at the time they make their agreement, although they may commit a crime. The tort action arises when harm is done to the plaintiff. Then he may hold all the conspirators responsible for things done in pursuance of the conspiracy by any of them. But if he seeks to hold only one conspirator liable, as he may for the tort, since the liability is joint and several, he has not claimed anything substantially different from what he claims if he sues the sole conspirator as an individual tortfeasor. So we think, therefore, the presence of conspiracy allegations in action No. 1 and their absence in action No. 2 does not change the substance of the two claims.

Another difference claimed by the plaintiff in the two actions is that one suit is said to rest on the Sherman Act and the other on the Clayton Act. This argument carries no weight. While the rule may not have been clear at one time, we think it is now the law that the fact that different statutes are relied on does not render the claims different "causes of action" for purposes of res judicata. . . .

Also not in point, we think, are the cases cited by plaintiff in which the question involved was whether a plaintiff is required to state in separate counts claims based on the Sherman Act and the claims based on the Clayton Act. The purpose of the requirement of separate counts is to clarify the issues and simplify the trial, and thus the considerations in determining what are separate "causes of action" or claims for that purpose are not the same as those when the question is res judicata. As has often been said, the phrase "cause of action" means different things in different contexts.

Does action No. 1 differ from action No. 2 because the conspiracy charged in action No. 1 is alleged to be a continuing one? In a civil conspiracy suit each invasion of plaintiff's interest resulting from the conspiracy creates a new cause of action when the question is the application of the bar of the statute of limitations. This rule would be controlling if the issue here was whether the statute of limitations bars all or a part of the damages claimed by plaintiff as a result of a continuing conspiracy. But if the cause of action is the same, the principle of res judicata prevents our reaching that question, not because it was actually decided in action No. 2, but because the judgment is a final determination of not only what was actually in issue but what might have been in issue had it been raised. We do not think that the definition of "cause of action" in these cases is controlling on the question before us. The determination of the meaning of "cause of action" for purposes of deciding whether or not a person has slept on his rights is of little aid in deciding whether a prior judgment is a bar to the present action.

The purpose of the principle of res judicata is to end litigation. The theory is that parties should not have to litigate issues which they have already litigated or had a reasonable opportunity to litigate. A reading of the early cases as compared with recent ones makes it clear that the meaning of "cause of action" for res judicata purposes is much broader today than it was earlier. Formerly the whole aim in pleading, and in the elaborate system of writs, was to frame one single legal issue. That being the guiding principle, the phrase "cause of action" came to have a very narrow meaning. If the theory in the second suit was unavailable under the writ used in the first suit, the plaintiff had no opportunity to litigate it there and so plaintiff was not barred by res judicata. The force of the rule is still operative but the scope of its operation has been greatly limited by the modernization of our procedure. The principle which pervades the modern systems of pleading, especially the federal system, as exemplified by the free permissive joinder of claims, liberal amendment provisions, and compulsory counterclaims, is that the whole controversy between the parties may and often must be brought before the same court in the same action. The instant case presents an excellent example of one of the things these rules were designed to avoid. As pointed out above, the acts complained of and the demand for recovery are the same. The only thing that is different is the theory of recovery. The same witnesses and documents will be necessary in the trial in both cases. No material fact is alleged in action No. 1 that was not alleged in action No. 2, save the allegations of conspiracy. Everything that plaintiff was entitled to ask for from defendant was included in action No. 2.

Reference to the basic theory of tort liability substantiates the position taken here. To put it in rather elementary tort language, the basis of the plaintiff's recovery is liability-creating conduct on the part of defendant, the invasion of a legally protected interest of the plaintiff and the necessary causal connection between defendant's acts and plaintiff's injury. The plaintiff having alleged operative facts which state a cause of action because he tells of defendant's misconduct and his own harm has had his day in court. He does not get another day after the first lawsuit is concluded by giving a different reason than he gave in the first for recovery of damages for the same invasion of his rights. The problem of his rights against the defendant based upon the alleged wrongful acts is fully before the court whether all the reasons for recovery were stated to the court or not.

The points discussed here were all treated in the well-considered opinion of the District Judge. What we do is put in our own words our reason for thinking that he was right. The judgment will be affirmed.

Question: (1) There is a defense named "other action pending." This defense will result in dismissal if another action on the same claim between the same parties was pending in the same state, or in the same federal district, when the present action was commenced and if that other action is still pending. Why did the defendant in action No. 2 not plead immediately "other action pending"?

SMITH v. KIRKPATRICK, 305 N.Y. 66, 111 N.E.2d 209 (1953). Plaintiff originally sued defendant in New York state court for money due him under a contract of employment. His complaint alleged that the contract required him to devote his full time to soliciting export accounts for defendant; that his remuneration was to be 50% of the income derived from the business procured by him; that he procured business from which defendant derived or would derive $26,000; and that defendant failed to pay him as agreed. Defendant obtained summary judgment for the reason that the agreement pleaded did not comply with the Statute of Frauds. Plaintiff was granted leave to amend and did so, setting forth in his amended complaint two causes of action, neither of which sought recovery in quantum meruit. The first alleged an informal oral agreement terminable at will whereby plaintiff conducted some of his business through defendant's office, paying to defendant for such use of his office 50% of the gross profits of plaintiff's business so handled. The second alleged an oral agreement of joint venture substantially to the same effect. In both, plaintiff sought an accounting and other relief. A trial without jury was held, after which the trial judge dismissed the amended complaint on the merits because "plaintiff has failed to establish his causes of action by a fair preponderance of the credible evidence." He said: "It is clear to the court that the original position taken by the plaintiff correctly represented the relationship between the parties but, unfortunately for the plaintiff, that action was barred by the statute of frauds. . . . It ought to be stated, however, in fairness to the plaintiff, that the defendant was clearly guilty of overreaching the plaintiff, but the bar of the statute of frauds and the failure on the part of the plaintiff to proceed on the theory of quantum meruit have given to the defendant a windfall which in business morals and good conscience he is not entitled to."

Plaintiff took no appeal. Instead, he brought the present action seeking to recover the reasonable value of services rendered by him to defendant at defendant's request. A motion to dismiss on the ground of res judicata was denied by the trial court, but the appellate division reversed and dismissed the complaint. The New York Court of Appeals in turn reversed the appellate division and affirmed the order of the trial court.

Judge Conway for the New York Court of Appeals conceded that deciding what constitutes the "same" or "different" causes of action is difficult. Quoting with approval earlier opinions holding that the number and variety of the facts alleged do not establish more than one cause of action so long as their result is the violation of but one right by a single legal wrong, he continued:

"The two actions involve different 'rights' and 'wrongs'. The requisite elements of proof and hence the evidence necessary to sustain recovery vary materially. The causes of action are different and distinct and the rights and interests established by the previous adjudication will not be impaired by a recovery, if that be the outcome, in quantum meruit."

The court further held that the plaintiff had not, by reason of the doctrine of election of remedies,[a] lost his right to sue in quantum meruit by attempting and failing to succeed on the causes involved in the first action. The two types of remedies were not, said the court, so inconsistent or irreconcilable that the choice of the one precluded resort to the other.

———

Question: (2) Is this case consistent with Williamson? Does it reach a desirable result?

———

O'BRIEN v. CITY OF SYRACUSE, 54 N.Y.2d 353, 429 N.E.2d 1158, 445 N.Y.S.2d 687 (1981). In 1973 plaintiffs sued defendants in New York state court for de facto appropriation, alleging that in the course of urban rehabilitation the defendant city authorities had so seriously interfered with plaintiffs' property rights as to constitute a de facto taking. A 1975 nonjury trial resulted in dismissal for failure to establish a de facto taking, which was affirmed on appeal. However, the appellate division did indicate that plaintiffs had suffered serious economic loss and that defendants' acts might have constituted trespass.

In 1978 plaintiffs brought a new suit against the same defendants for trespass to the same property at various times from 1967 to 1978. Defendants moved to dismiss on grounds of res judicata and failure to serve a timely notice of claim. The trial court denied the motion. The appellate division reversed, applying res judicata to dismiss the complaint. The New York Court of Appeals affirmed the appellate division on a somewhat different basis, as Chief Judge Cooke explained:

"In analyzing the complaint, plaintiffs' allegations fall into two categories: (1) those concerning activities underlying the 1973 litigation; and (2) those asserting trespass generally. Only the claims encompassed by the first category are definitely barred by res judicata.

[a] Much of the doctrine of election of remedies is substantive law, but it is sometimes seen as bearing on res judicata. A person who originally had a choice of remedies may by his conduct before any action is brought disentitle himself to one or more of them. For instance, the remedy of rescission for fraud, involving a tender of return of the article purchased and recovery of the purchase price, may be lost by material alteration of the article after discovery of the fraud; the defrauded party is thus confined to the remedy of damages in an action for deceit. Sometimes it is held that the mere commencement of an action seeking a particular remedy is itself an election preventing resort to another remedy deemed to be inconsistent. Under the Federal Rules (and other modern procedural systems), however, a party may pursue alternative and inconsistent remedies, subject always to the obligations of Rule 11; further, he may postpone his election between them until a late stage of the action, even after findings of fact on both alternatives. See Restatement (Second) of Judgments § 25 comment m (1980); cf. Ajamian v. Schlanger, 14 N.J. 483, 103 A.2d 9 (1954). Accordingly, election of remedies, properly viewed, is readily distinguishable from res judicata.

"This State has adopted the transactional analysis approach in deciding res judicata issues (Matter of Reilly v. Reid, 45 N.Y.2d 24, 407 N.Y.S.2d 645, 379 N.E.2d 172). Under this address, once a claim is brought to a final conclusion, all other claims arising out of the same transaction or series of transactions are barred, even if based upon different theories or if seeking a different remedy (id., at pp. 29–30, 407 N.Y.S.2d 645, 648–49, 379 N.E.2d 172, 175–76). Here, all of defendants' conduct falling in the first category was also raised during the 1973 suit as the basis for that litigation. That proceeding having been brought to a final conclusion, no other claim may be predicated upon the same incidents.

"Plaintiffs, relying on Smith v. Kirkpatrick, 305 N.Y. 66, 111 N.E. 2d 209, . . . urge that de facto appropriation and trespass are actions having different theoretical bases and requiring different evidentiary proof. This contention, however, erroneously characterizes the bases of the two causes. . . . [D]e facto appropriation, in the context of physical invasion, is based on showing that the government has intruded onto the citizen's property and interfered with the owner's property rights to such a degree that the conduct amounts to a constitutional taking requiring the government to purchase the property from the owner . . . . In effect, de facto appropriation may be characterized as an aggravated form of trespass. The pertinent evidence in both actions is the same. The basic distinction lies in the egregiousness of the trespass and whether it is of such intensity as to amount to a taking.

"In any event, even if it were assumed that the two actions involved materially different elements of proof, the second suit would be barred as to the claim predicated upon the first category allegations. When alternative theories are available to recover what is essentially the same relief for harm arising out of the same or related facts such as would constitute a single 'factual grouping' (Restatement, Judgments 2d, § 61 [Tent. Draft No. 5]), the circumstance that the theories involve materially different elements of proof will not justify presenting the claim by two different actions.[1] Consequently, plaintiffs' action is barred by the doctrine of res judicata insofar as the allegations in the first category are concerned.

"Finally, the second category of allegations—the general trespass allegations—are not barred by res judicata to the extent that they describe acts occurring after the 1973 lawsuit. They are, however, barred by reason of plaintiffs' failure to serve timely a notice of claim."

The court further explained that a condition precedent to bringing a tort claim against a municipality is a timely notice of claim providing information sufficient to permit investigation of the claim, and

[1] To the extent Smith v. Kirkpatrick, 305 N.Y. 66, 111 N.E.2d 209, supra may be to the contrary, it is overruled.

that here the notice had failed to mention any trespassory acts other than those underlying the 1973 proceeding and so was ineffective with respect to the "claim" stemming from the second category of allegations.

Questions: (3) Plaintiff brought an FELA action against a railroad and lost on the ground that he was not an employee of the railroad at the time of his injury. He now sues the railroad in the same court for the same injury, basing his claim on common-law negligence, a theory available only if he was not an employee. The railroad pleads bar. What judgment? Compare Restatement (Second) of Judgments § 25 comment k (1980), with People ex rel. Chicago & E. Ill. R.R. v. Fleming, 42 Ill.2d 231, 246 N.E.2d 275 (1969).

(4) Suppose the plaintiff sues in a state court for unfair competition and loses on the merits. He then alleges the same basic wrong in a federal-court action under the federal antitrust laws, an action over which the federal courts have exclusive jurisdiction. The defendant pleads bar. What judgment? Would your answer be different if there was diversity of citizenship between the parties to the state-court action and over $10,000 was involved? See Cream Top Creamery v. Dean Milk Co., 383 F.2d 358 (6th Cir.1967) (no bar). But cf. Nash County Bd. of Educ. v. Biltmore Co., 640 F.2d 484 (4th Cir.) (bar), cert. denied, 454 U.S. 878, 102 S.Ct. 359 (1981). (Reserve for later consideration the question of issue preclusion as to issues decided in the state action.)

(5) Reverse the situation in the preceding question, assuming that the first action was in the federal court under the federal antitrust laws, with no reference to the claim of unfair competition, and the second in the state court. Should the state-court action be barred by res judicata? Would the existence of diversity jurisdiction affect your answer? What of pendent jurisdiction? Compare Restatement (Second) of Judgments § 25 comment e (1980), with 2 L. Loss, Securities Regulation 1015–16 (2d ed. 1961), and 5 id. 2976–77 (Supp.1969).

(6) Finally, assume that the plaintiff first sues in a state court for unfair competition, the suit is removed to federal court on the basis of diversity jurisdiction, and the plaintiff then loses on the merits, there never having been reference by amendment or otherwise to any federal antitrust claim. He later brings a second action in a federal court under the federal antitrust laws. Should the second action be barred by res judicata?

HENNEPIN PAPER CO. v. FORT WAYNE CORRUGATED PAPER CO.

United States Circuit Court of Appeals, Seventh Circuit, 1946.
153 F.2d 822.

[The plaintiff-seller first sued in the United States District Court for the Northern District of Indiana, alleging the defendant-buyer's failure to take and pay for 800 tons of corrugating material monthly. A written contract of July 1, 1941, provided: "Owner agrees to sell Customer, and Customer agrees to purchase, all of Customer's needs of .009 Corrugating Material that Customer will purchase monthly from the outside up to 600 tons, more or less." On the apparent assumption that this language was ambiguous and hence that evidence of contemporaneous negotiations would be admissible to clarify the meaning, plaintiff pleaded certain negotiations at about the time of the execution of the contract showing that the parties intended a commitment to buy a minimum of 600 tons per month. Plaintiff also alleged that by oral agreement during October 1941 the parties changed the minimum amount to 800 tons per month. On defendant's motion, the court struck out the allegations of the complaint regarding the negotiations contemporaneous with the written contract on the ground that the contract was unambiguous and parol evidence could not be used to vary its terms, and ruled that defendant was committed by the contract to buy only the amount it required. The case thus stood upon the written contract as allegedly modified by the oral agreement of October 1941. On this claim the defendant had verdict and judgment. No appeal was taken.

[Thereafter the plaintiff brought the present action in the United States District Court for the Northern District of Illinois to reform the written contract so as to make it correspond with the "true intent and understanding of both parties," and for recovery upon the contract as reformed. The alleged intent and understanding was that resulting from the negotiations contemporaneous with the written contract, i.e., a commitment to buy 600 tons monthly. The defendant's motion for summary judgment, supported by affidavits setting forth the proceedings in the first action, was granted. Plaintiff appealed.]

Before EVANS and SPARKS, CIRCUIT JUDGES, and BALTZELL, DISTRICT JUDGE.

BALTZELL, DISTRICT JUDGE.

. . . .

Under the Federal Rules of Civil Procedure, and under the law of Indiana, the plaintiff had the right, in the first action, to, by proper pleading, ask that the written contract of July 1, 1941, be reformed and redrawn, as it is attempting to do in the second action. It certainly knew the same facts at the time the district court struck out paragraph 5 of the complaint in the first action [the allegations concerning the contemporaneous negotiations], as it knew at the time it drafted the complaint in the second action, and it should have filed either an amended complaint or an additional count or paragraph in that action so as to have presented all issues in the same action. This it could have done "regardless of consistency and whether based on legal or on equitable grounds or on both." Rule 8(e)(2) Federal Rules of Civil Procedure. The authority to thus have joined its claims is specifically provided for in Rule 18 of the Federal Rules of Civil Procedure, as follows, "(a) Joinder of Claims. The plaintiff in his complaint . . . may join either as independent or as alternate claims as many claims either legal or equitable or both as he may have against an opposing party." [b] . . .

. . . It made its election in the first action and it cannot now, in a separate action, assume an entirely different and inconsistent position in an effort to have the same written contract reformed. As heretofore observed, such effort, if it desired a reformation of the contract, should have been undertaken in the first action.

The Supreme Court of Indiana, in the case of Royal Insurance Co. v. Stewart, 190 Ind. 444, 129 N.E. 853, 857, said, "Where a party elects to sue upon a written contract as executed, and the action proceeds to trial and judgment, he cannot thereafter bring an action to reform the contract. 2 Black on Judgments, § 632" . . . . Again, in the case of Knight v. Electric Household Utilities Corp., 133 N.J.Eq. 87, 30 A.2d 585, 588, affirmed 134 N.J.Eq. 542, 36 A.2d 201, the court said, "Whether a plaintiff is precluded by the judgment, depends upon the extent to which legal and equitable remedies have been merged in the state where the judgment is rendered. Restatement—Judgments § 66. The judgment bars the suit for reformation if the plaintiff could have obtained reformation in his original action on the contract. Royal Ins. Co. v. Stewart, Inc., 190 Ind. 444, 129 N.E. 853. But where the law court cannot give equitable relief, the judgment is not a bar. Northern Assur. Co. v. Grand View Bldg. Ass'n, 203 U.S. 106, 27 S.Ct. 27, 51 L.Ed. 109." . . .

Not only under the Federal Rules of Civil Procedure, but under the law of Indiana, the plaintiff could have, in the first action, sought a reformation of the contract, and it was its duty to have done so if it desired to litigate that question. Not having done so, and having sought an entirely different and inconsistent remedy in that action, it cannot now maintain the second action. The district court properly granted the motion of defendant for a summary judgment.

The judgment of the district court is affirmed.

SUTCLIFFE STORAGE & WAREHOUSE CO. v. UNITED STATES

United States Circuit Court of Appeals, First Circuit, 1947.
162 F.2d 849.

Before CLARK,[1] MAHONEY and WOODBURY, CIRCUIT JUDGES.

CLARK, CIRCUIT JUDGE. The present four appeals were filed in four actions instituted in the district court on February 18, 25, 26, and 28, 1946, respectively, each claiming sums due, with interest, for the use and occupancy of the same realty in Boston, over different periods of time from June 15, 1942, to December 31, 1945. The first ac-

---

[b] This was the text in force prior to July 1, 1966.

[1] Judge Clark of the Second Circuit, serving by designation.

tion covered the period from June 15, 1942, to June 30, 1943, the second and third each covered a succeeding year, and the fourth covered the final six months to the end in 1945. In all four the amounts claimed are computed at identical rates per square foot for the various parcels involved. In the latter three actions the district court has granted the defendant's motions to dismiss on the ground that they were brought for inseparable parts of the claim set forth in the first action. D.C.Mass., 68 F.Supp. 446. In the first action the defendant has made no motion and the court has entered no order.

Normally the district court would be acting quite within its discretion in taking steps to consolidate or otherwise avoid the duplication of such closely similar cases, whatever the substantive rights of the parties. Compare Rule 42(a), Federal Rules of Civil Procedure, 28 U.S.C.A. following section 723c. But the situation here is different because of the jurisdictional provisions of the Tucker Act. The first three actions claim amounts between eight and ten thousand dollars each; the last claims an amount in excess of four thousand dollars. The district court's jurisdiction of claims against the United States is limited to $10,000; for greater claims resort must be had to the Court of Claims in Washington. 28 U.S.C.A. § 41(20).ᶜ The plaintiff asserts a desire and right to sue for all amounts due in the courts of its own locality, asserting that the Tucker Act so permits and also relying on the facts alleged as showing four separate claims. And it is so entitled to sue if its contention is correct; otherwise it must either waive the excess or go to Washington to sue. The particular facts it relies upon are that on April 13, 1942, it executed a lease running until June 30, 1943, of certain premises it controlled to the United States Navy, and that this contract was renewed by separate renewal leases for periods identical with those covered by the last three actions. Plaintiff's contention—duly pleaded in each action—is that beginning about June 15, 1942, the Navy occupied and used a greater area than was designated in the lease for the period in question and that therefore the plaintiff is entitled to the reasonable value of the use and occupancy of the additional area for each period.

The defendant, however, asserts that the general rule against "splitting causes of action" applies to the Government as defendant equally with all other litigants, and that the existence of separate renewal leases for the adjoining premises does not affect the nature of the plaintiff's claims, and, indeed, is important only in connection with the defendant's own defenses. For defendant has filed answers which both claim possession of the additional premises as being actually included in the leases and alternatively assert that if this is not the case the leases failed to include the additional premises by mistake and should now be reformed to include them. In the last three actions the answers also state as a separate defense the pendency of the first action. It was this defense, made the subject of a separate

ᶜ See present 28 U.S.C. § 1346.

motion for preliminary hearing and adjudication, which was sustained by the court below.

As Professor Moore succinctly states, "The pendency of a prior pending action in the same federal court is ground for abatement of the second action." 1 Moore's Federal Practice 237; United States v. The Haytian Republic, 154 U.S. 118, 14 S.Ct. 992, 38 L.Ed. 930; Hughes v. Dundee Mortgage & Trust Inv. Co., C.C.Or., 26 F. 831; Hillgrove v. Wright Aeronautical Corp., 6 Cir., 146 F.2d 621. There is no reason why a court should be bothered or a litigant harassed with duplicating lawsuits on the same docket; it is enough if one complete adjudication of the controversy be had. As a matter of fact, it is often an advantage to the plaintiff to have the issue of double suits settled before he finds himself barred from full recovery by a partial but final judgment in one action. Thus here the plaintiff may count itself in luck to have the matter settled before a portion of its rights is irretrievably lost. For the test as ordinarily stated is whether the claims set up are legally the same so that judgment in one is a bar to the others. United States v. The Haytian Republic, supra, 154 U.S. 118, 129, 13 S.Ct. 992, 38 L.Ed. 930.

It is an ancient and well-settled legal principle that claims for amounts due on running accounts or as installment payments, such as rent under a lease, must include all amounts due at the time action is brought. [Citations omitted.] The same rule has been applied to claims for royalties under a patent, Buchanan v. General Motors Corp., 2 Cir., 158 F.2d 728, to claims affecting realty, as for continuing trespasses, Evans v. Durango Land & Coal Co., 8 Cir., 80 F. 433, 437, appeal dismissed Durango Land & Coal Co. v. Evans, 19 S.Ct. 875, 43 L.Ed. 1178, and to claims in quantum meruit for the occupancy of land, See v. See, 294 Mo. 495, 242 S.W. 949, 24 A.L.R. 880, with note collecting cases, 885–897. The doctrine is a salutary one in forcing the trial of identical matters together and affording a defendant once sued the protection of the doctrine of res judicata. Ordinarily there is no reason why a plaintiff cannot make all his claims on a running account at one time without piecemeal presentation. The fact that here involved are questions of federal jurisdiction is not a sufficient basis for departing from these usual rules as to the splitting of legal claims. The congressional policy is that all large claims must be presented in the one court in Washington, and in every practical sense there is here presented such a claim. Even though the plaintiff's own convenience might be served by adjudication in its vicinage, the congressional policy seems clearly opposed.

Nor can we see basis for varying the rule on the grounds urged by the plaintiff. There is no reason why the doctrine against splitting claims, which is thus only one application of the general doctrine of res judicata, should not apply to claims against the Government; and the cases so hold. . . .

Finally the particular facts urged by plaintiff do not vary the principle. That the plaintiff had separate leases for the adjoining property covering each fiscal year is not a sufficient basis to allow it to divide its claim for use and occupation of the particular premises here involved into four parts. In very truth its basic legal position depends upon its assertion that there were no leases covering these premises; once the existing leases are shown to affect them, the defendant has a solid basis for the assertion of its defenses. The plaintiff cannot in the same breath repudiate the leases and yet rely upon them as operating to separate its claim into parts.

The consequence of this conclusion is that there will be an affirmance of the dismissal of the latter three cases, Nos. 4238–4240 in this court. Since no action has been taken by the district court with reference to the earlier instituted action, No. 4241 in this court, there is nothing from which an appeal can be taken and we have no jurisdiction to consider it. United States v. San Geronimo Development Co., 1 Cir., 154 F.2d 78, 84, certiorari denied San Geronimo Development Co. v. United States, 329 U.S. 718, 67 S.Ct. 50. The plaintiff asks us, in the event of our affirmance of dismissal in the other three cases, to order dismissal also of this action to avoid what it terms its anomalous position in having one indivisible cause of action for an amount beyond the court's jurisdictional limit. But even if we had jurisdiction, no such action would be justified; for plaintiff has its own choice to make, whether it wishes to waive the greater amount and remain in the District Court for the District of Massachusetts, United States v. Johnson, 9 Cir., 153 F.2d 846, or now move that court for dismissal without prejudice under Rule 41(a)(2), F.R.C.P.[d] This option which it has also disposes of its claim that the defendant has waived the Tucker Act by failing to file a motion to dismiss the first action. Of course there is no such waiver in any event; the question of the binding effect of the judgment in the first action is tested only in the later actions. See authorities cited in Clark on Code Pleading, 2d Ed. 1947, 473, 479; 1 Am.Jur., Actions, § 98; Pakas v. Hollingshead, 184 N.Y. 211, 77 N.E. 40, 3 L.R.A.,N.S., 1042, 112 Am.St.Rep. 601, 6 Ann.Cas. 60.

In cases Nos. 4238–4240, the judgments are affirmed; in case No. 4241, the appeal is dismissed.

Questions: (7) Judge Clark says that "the plaintiff may count itself in luck to have the matter settled before a portion of its rights is irretrievably lost." He apparently is suggesting that the attorney for the government might have let one of the four cases go to judgment and then have pleaded res judicata to the other three. Would this be an ethically permissible course of action by the government attorney? Would your answer be the same if it were done by a privately employed attorney? Indeed, would it be ethically

[d] An additional option became available in 1960: transfer between the district court and the Court of Claims. See 28 U.S.C. § 1631.

permissible for a privately employed attorney not to use such a tactic if available?

(8) Can you make an argument that Judge Clark's suggested res judicata tactic ought not to be successful? See Todd v. Central Petroleum Co., 155 Kan. 249, 124 P.2d 704 (1942).

OTHER WAYS TO SPLIT A CLAIM

Judge Clark refers to the "ancient and well-settled legal principle that claims for amounts due on running accounts . . . must include all amounts due at the time action is brought." Suppose *D* is *P*'s tenant under a lease calling for monthly payments. *P* obtains a judgment for the May rent. He cannot, because of the "ancient and well-settled legal principle," sue later for the March or April rent. Change the facts and suppose that *D* gave *P* a series of promissory notes, one payable each month, for the rental under the lease. *P* obtains a judgment on a note falling due on May 1. Does this preclude him from suing thereafter on other notes in the series due on March 1 and April 1? Is this case different from the previous example? See Restatement (Second) of Judgments § 24 comment d (1980).

There is a conflict of authority as to whether the splitting rule precludes a person from bringing successive actions for property damage and personal injury suffered in the same automobile accident. Compare Dearden v. Hey, 304 Mass. 659, 24 N.E.2d 644 (1939) (second action precluded), with Clancey v. McBride, 338 Ill. 35, 169 N.E. 729 (1929) (second action not precluded). Which is the preferable rule?

Question: (9) Does the punishment for splitting a claim fit the crime? Professor Cleary thinks not. He would ordinarily penalize the splitter by assessment of costs for trying to make two lawsuits do the work of one rather than by complete loss of the right of recovery. See Cleary, Res Judicata Reexamined, 57 Yale L.J. 339, 349–50 (1948).

RESTATEMENT OF JUDGMENTS

The traditional approach held that more than one "cause of action" could regularly arise out of the same transaction. Harking back to the days of the forms of action and the separation of law and equity, courts tended to equate a cause of action with a single theory or ground of recovery, to allow successive actions when the court concluded that different "rights" or "primary rights" had been simultaneously infringed, or otherwise to subdivide a transaction. See, e.g., Smith v. Kirkpatrick, supra p. 965, where the court strained to manipulate the terminology so as not to deny redress to a deserving plaintiff with misguided counsel. Restatement of Judgments §§ 61–

67 (1942) reflected this prevailing judicial attitude and at the same time tried to set forth a series of black-letter rules that would bring order to a confused situation. The effort was not conspicuously successful.

Restatement (Second) of Judgments § 24 (1980) opts for a transactional view of "claim," providing that "the claim extinguished includes all rights of the plaintiff to remedies against the defendant with respect to all or any part of the transaction, or series of connected transactions, out of which the action arose" and also that the factual grouping constituting a "transaction" or a "series" is "to be determined pragmatically, giving weight to such considerations as whether the facts are related in time, space, origin, or motivation, whether they form a convenient trial unit, and whether their treatment as a unit conforms to the parties' expectations or business understanding or usage." [e] This transactional approach of the Second Restatement puts pressure on the plaintiff not to overlook or withhold from his initial complaint any grievance he has relating to the transaction in question regardless of differences in "evidence," "grounds," "theories," "remedies," or "forms of relief." Should he err in the first instance, he will, given a modern procedural system, almost certainly be allowed an opportunity to amend as the case unfolds. But failing that, he risks losing the unasserted portion of his claim.

Question: (10) Do you see any likely problems for counsel in applying the Second Restatement's definition of the factual grouping that constitutes a "transaction" or a "series"?

Finally, it should be emphasized that although there is considerable and increasing case support for the Second Restatement's approach, some courts still adhere to the older views.

COMMERCIAL BOX & LUMBER CO. v. UNIROYAL, INC., 623 F.2d 371 (5th Cir.1980). "On November 20, 1974, Commercial Box and Uniroyal entered into Purchase Contract No. 4–90145–2JB. The contract provided for Commercial Box to supply ammunition boxes to Uniroyal at the Joliet Army Ammunition Depot in Joliet, Illinois. . . . On July 21, 1975, after shipments began, Uniroyal notified Commercial Box of a change in destination. Uniroyal desired a change in its destination point from Joliet to the Kansas Army Ammunition Plant in Parsons, Kansas. Due to more rigid inspection procedures at the Kansas plant, a higher number of boxes were rejected. This required their transportation to Texarkana, Texas for correction of the defects. Upon re-delivery, they were accepted at the Kansas plant.

[e] The general rule of this section is exemplified in § 25 (along the lines of the Williamson, Hennepin, and Sutcliffe cases) and is subject to the exceptions stated in § 26 (including the exceptions suggested by Cream Top Creamery v. Dean Milk Co., supra p. 969, and Todd v. Central Petroleum Co., supra p. 975).

"After a breakdown in negotiations, Commercial Box filed a diversity suit in district court to recover its labor and lumber losses incurred in performing the contract arising out of the delivery and redelivery of boxes to Kansas. A trial by jury resulted in a monetary judgment favorable to Commercial Box. The present suit arises out of the same purchase contract but involves a different issue. The terms of payment allowed Uniroyal to deduct a discount if payment was made in ten days. . . .

"In the instant [diversity] suit, Commercial Box alleges a wrongful deduction of discounts from Uniroyal's payment prices for the period of November 1974 to January 1976. Commercial Box contends that Uniroyal had no right to the discounts since payments were made after the ten day period. Uniroyal filed a motion for summary judgment claiming that, in light of the allegations and decision in the first case, this case should be barred by res judicata . . . . The district court granted Uniroyal's motion . . . ."

After so stating the facts, the court of appeals reversed, explaining:

"The only dispute in this case as to the existence of the elements necessary to satisfy the federal res judicata rule is whether the present suit is based upon the same cause of action as the first. In comparing causes of action, the question is whether the prior right and duty and wrong are the same in each action. Kemp v. Birmingham News Company, 608 F.2d 1049, 1052 (5th Cir. 1979). A second cause of action is the same if it refers to all grounds for relief arising out of the conduct complained of in the original action. Kilgoar v. Colbert County Board of Education, 578 F.2d [1033, 1035 (5th Cir.1978)].

"Based upon the foregoing discussion of the federal law on res judicata, it is clear that the present action does not arise out of conduct complained of in the first law suit. The first cause of action was based upon losses in labor and lumber which arose from Uniroyal's unilateral decision to change the destination point for the delivery of the ammunition boxes. That was the sole issue raised in the first action. There was no mention of Uniroyal's method of payment, the time period of its payments not [sic] its taking of discounts stemming from the payment price.[2] Not only were these issues not raised but

---

[2] Because the alleged wrongful discounting occurred both prior to and during Commercial Box' prior action, the district court held that the present issue could have been tried in the first cause of action. The district court thus found that Commercial Box' failure to litigate the present issue amounted to a lack of diligence. This court cannot agree. Commercial Box could have chosen to include the present issue in its first law suit under Rule 18(a). It was not required to do so, however. Commercial Box filed suit only on the labor losses it incurred related to the change in destination. The owner and general manager of Commercial Box, Robert Torrans, stated in his deposition that the fact that the first suit was confined to the issue of increased labor and lumber costs was due to representations by Uniroyal that if claims were made solely on those issues, there would be more likelihood of payment. When Uniroyal did not pay, Torrans believed that the prior law suit had better chances of success if it was confined to those issues. In light of such alleged representations by Uniroyal and

they are in no way germane or related to the challenge made in the first suit. The issue in the present suit is based upon a different cause of action than that alleged in the first suit. Likewise, the matter involved in the present case is not one that could have been litigated in the first case in light of that case's legal and factual bases. Since this court holds that the present issue is clearly a separate and distinct action from that raised in the first suit, the district court's granting of summary judgment based upon res judicata was clearly erroneous."

Questions: (11) Does it matter whether a court proceeds (a) by defining "claim" narrowly so as to avoid claim preclusion or (b) by avoiding otherwise applicable claim preclusion through recognition of some exception thereto, such as defendant's consent to claim-splitting?

(12) In 1928 a testamentary trust was established "to produce the highest possible income consistent with reasonable security," with the further specific restriction that the bank as trustee had to invest in certain kinds of debt instruments. From 1928 to 1961 the value of the trust decreased from $400,000 to $335,000. In 1961 the beneficiaries successfully sued the trustee to lift the specific investment restriction, having alleged that the restriction was injuring the trust because of changed investment conditions. In 1972, supposedly on the basis of new information, the beneficiaries sued the trustee for mismanagement and breach of fiduciary duty during the period before 1961, seeking damages and the removal of the bank as trustee. Did the two suits arise from the same transaction? Cf. Himel v. Continental Ill. Nat'l Bank & Trust, 596 F.2d 205 (7th Cir.1979) (2–1 decision) (no claim preclusion, because suits did not arise from "same basic factual situation").

HARRINGTON v. VANDALIA–BUTLER BOARD OF EDUCATION

United States Court of Appeals, Sixth Circuit, 1981.
649 F.2d 434.

Before GEORGE CLIFTON EDWARDS, JR., CHIEF JUDGE, ENGEL and BOYCE F. MARTIN, JR., CIRCUIT JUDGES.

BOYCE F. MARTIN, JR., CIRCUIT JUDGE.

In 1974, Jeanne Harrington filed suit in the United States District Court for the Southern District of Ohio against the Vandalia-Butler Board of Education, alleging sex discrimination in employment and seeking relief under Title VII of the Civil Rights Act of 1964, 42 U.S.C. § 2000e, et seq. After a bench trial in June, 1976, the court found that she had been discriminated against in violation of Title VII and awarded compensatory damages and attorney's fees. Harrington v. Vandalia-Butler Board of Education, 418 F.Supp. 603 (S.D.Ohio

since Commercial Box was never required to include the present issue in its first complaint, we refuse to accept the   district court's finding of a lack of diligence.

1976). On appeal to this Court, the factual finding of discrimination was sustained. However, we reversed the judgment on the grounds that Title VII does not authorize compensatory damages and that the finding of discrimination, standing alone, did not support an award of attorney's fees. Harrington v. Vandalia-Butler Board of Education, 585 F.2d 192 (6th Cir. 1978), cert. denied, 441 U.S. 932, 99 S.Ct. 2058, 60 L.Ed.2d 660 (1979).

In 1978, while Harrington's appeal was pending in this court, the Supreme Court decided Monell v. Department of Social Services, 436 U.S. 658, 96 S.Ct. 2018, 56 L.Ed.2d 611 (1978). That decision overruled Monroe v. Pape, 365 U.S. 167, 81 S.Ct. 473, 5 L.Ed.2d 492 (1961), insofar as the latter held that municipalities are not "persons" subject to liability under 42 U.S.C. § 1983.[f] Immediately after Monell was decided, Harrington brought this action against the Board of Education, school principal Ralph Clay, and school superintendent Blutcher P. Gibson, alleging employment discrimination and seeking relief under § 1983.

The defendant Board of Education moved for summary judgment on the ground that the plaintiff's claim was barred by the doctrine of res judicata. On June 7, 1979, the District Court granted this motion, holding that the plaintiff had ample opportunity during the previous litigation to raise a claim for relief based on the alleged violation of § 1983.

. . . .

Harrington next contends that the defense of res judicata may not be invoked in this case because her present claim under § 1983 could not have been raised at the time the first suit was filed. She argues that the change in the law brought about by Monell precludes the availability of the defense. We disagree.

It is undisputed that appellant's earlier Title VII action and the present § 1983 suit are based on the same discriminatory acts. When two successive suits seek recovery for the same injury, "a judgment on the merits operates as a bar to the later suit, even though a different legal theory of recovery is advanced in the second suit." Cemer v. Marathon Oil Company, 583 F.2d 830, 832 (6th Cir. 1978). See also Mayer v. Distel Tool & Machine Company, 556 F.2d 798 (6th Cir. 1977); Coogan v. Cincinnati Bar Association, 431 F.2d 1209 (6th Cir. 1970). This principle applies even if an intervening decision effects a

---

[f] That statute provides: "Every person who, under color of any statute, ordinance, regulation, custom, or usage, of any State or Territory or the District of Columbia, subjects, or causes to be subjected, any citizen of the United States or other person within the jurisdiction thereof to the deprivation of any rights, privileges, or immunities secured by the Constitution and laws, shall be liable to the party injured in an action at law, suit in equity, or other proper proceeding for redress. For the purposes of this section, any Act of Congress applicable exclusively to the District of Columbia shall be considered to be a statute of the District of Columbia."

change in the law which bears directly on the legal theory advanced
in the second suit.

. . . Section 1983 was not "unavailable" to appellant when she
filed her Title VII action. She was free to challenge the validity of
Monroe v. Pape to the extent that it exempted municipalities from the
ambit of § 1983. Moreover, it is clear that if she had brought the
§ 1983 claim initially and lost it on the basis of Monroe v. Pape, she
would not be entitled to reassert the § 1983 claim in the aftermath of
Monell. She would be bound by the prior judgment on the merits.
That prior judgment is no less binding against her here merely because she elected not to advance a § 1983 claim in her first action.

. . . .

In summary, the thrust of the decisions discussed above is this:
generally, a judgment on the merits—even if erroneous—will be deprived of its conclusive effect only if it is vacated, reversed, or set
aside on direct appeal. See Moitie v. Federated Department Stores,
Inc., 611 F.2d 1267 (9th Cir. 1980); 1B Moore's Federal Practice (2d
Ed.) ¶ 0.416[2], p. 2231.

We are convinced, therefore, that the change in the law wrought
by Monell, standing alone, does not preclude the application of res
judicata to this case. That conclusion does not, however, end our inquiry, for "This court has held . . . that '[n]either collateral estoppel nor res judicata is rigidly applied. Both rules are qualified or
rejected when their application would contravene an overriding public
policy or result in manifest injustice.' Tipler v. E.I. du Pont de
Nemours and Co., 443 F.2d 125, 128 (6th Cir. 1971)." Bronson v.
Board of Education, 525 F.2d 344 (6th Cir. 1975), cert. denied, 425
U.S. 934, 96 S.Ct. 1665, 48 L.Ed.2d 175 (1976). See also United States
v. LaFatch, 565 F.2d 81 (6th Cir. 1977), cert. denied, 435 U.S. 971, 98
S.Ct. 1611, 56 L.Ed.2d 62 (1978); Ferguson v. Winn Parish Police Jury, 589 F.2d 173, 176 n.6 (5th Cir. 1979).

. . . .

In Bronson v. Board of Education, supra, we addressed the problem of res judicata in the context of school desegregation litigation.
For our purposes in the present case, it is sufficient to recall our conclusion that the strong public policy against perpetuating racial segregation in public schools does not necessarily preclude the application of res judicata and collateral estoppel to school desegregation
cases. 525 F.2d 349.

Finally, United States v. LaFatch, supra, involved an attempt by a
corporation to recover $50,000.00 it had paid to Anthony LaFatch.
According to the corporation, the money was paid in cooperation with
the FBI and under its surveillance. The transaction had provided the
basis for an extortion indictment against LaFatch. After the District
Court dismissed the extortion charge at the close of the government's
case, the corporation filed suit in an Ohio court to recover the

$50,000.00. It obtained a verdict against LaFatch for only $15,000.00. The federal District Court, which had retained custody of the money, found that the Ohio court's judgment was res judicata as to the ownership of the money and granted LaFatch's motion asking for its return. We, however, held that res judicata should not be applied for reasons of overriding public policy. We said that if the corporation's claim that it made the payment in cooperation with the FBI were true, the application of res judicata would violate the public policy of encouraging cooperation with law enforcement authorities in thwarting attempts at bribery and extortion. 565 F.2d at 84.

. . . .

. . . The policy at issue here—the availability of compensatory damages for violations of Title VII rights—does not, in our view, rise to the degree of overall importance to our society which Bronson and LaFatch suggest is necessary to avoid the preclusive effect of judgments.

We realize that in the circumstances of this case the doctrine of res judicata seems to work an unfair result. Appellant has established that she was discriminated against; the defendant's "vindication" on the merits was attributable only to the remedial limits of Title VII. Compare Bronson, supra, at 349. When she filed her Title VII action, appellant had good reason to believe that she could not successfully sue a school board under § 1983, which permits the award of damages for violations of constitutional and statutory rights. Upon learning from Monell that a municipality is now considered a "person" for the purposes of § 1983, appellant filed another suit which raised the § 1983 claim for the first time. There is undoubtedly an element of injustice in the application of res judicata to preclude that claim. However, we believe that the decisions of the Supreme Court and of this circuit, together with the policies underlying the doctrine of res judicata, compel that result.

Manifest injustice of the type necessary to except a case from the application of the doctrine is simply not present here. A mere showing that the second litigation, if allowed to proceed, would produce a different result than the first is not a showing of manifest injustice. Because the doctrine of res judicata effects a balance between competing interests, a certain degree of inequity is inevitable. Res judicata ensures the finality of judicial decisions. It encourages reliance on those decisions, thereby establishing certainty in legal relations. It bars vexatious litigation and promotes economy of judicial time and effort. Brown v. [Felsen, 442 U.S. 127, 131, 99 S.Ct. 2205, 2209 (1979)]. If the Supreme Court had decided, subsequent to appellant's Title VII suit, that compensatory damages could indeed be awarded under that statute, appellant would nevertheless be barred from reasserting her Title VII claim to collect such damages. That result would be no more or less fair than the one achieved here. The injustice inherent in either result is a necessary by-product of the general rule that judgments are final. In our opinion, that general rule must prevail here.

. . . .

SECTION 2. ADJUDICATION NOT ON THE MERITS

WATERHOUSE v. LEVINE
Supreme Judicial Court of Massachusetts, 1903.
182 Mass. 407, 65 N.E. 822.

CONTRACT for goods sold and delivered. Writ in the Municipal Court of the City of Boston dated April 13, 1901.

On appeal to the Superior Court the case was tried before Sherman, J., without a jury. The defence pleaded and relied upon was a former judgment. The judge refused to rule that the judgment was a bar to this action, and made the ruling stated by the court, admitting evidence to show the issue tried in the former action. He found for the plaintiff[s] in the sum of $336.04; and the defendant alleged exceptions.

BARKER, J. The defendant contends that the plaintiffs cannot maintain this action because judgment was rendered for the defendant upon a trial in a previous action between the same parties and for the same cause of action. Evidence was admitted in this action against the defendant's exception that the former judgment was upon the ground that the first suit was prematurely brought, the goods for the price of which both suits were brought having been sold upon a credit which had not expired when the first action was begun. The judge found as a fact that the only issue decided in the former action was whether that action was prematurely brought, and that the former judgment was entered because the action was prematurely brought and for that reason alone.

The only answer in the former action was a general denial. But under that answer the defence that the goods were bought upon a credit not expired when the suit was begun was open. Wilder v. Colby, 134 Mass. 377, 380, distinguishing Reed v. Inhabitants of Scituate, 7 Allen 141. [Other citations omitted.] Whether oral evidence would be admissible to show that a former judgment went solely upon an issue which strictly could not have been tried upon the pleadings as they stood, but was in fact tried with the assent of all parties, is a question upon which we express no opinion.

It is only when rendered upon the merits that a judgment constitutes an absolute bar to a subsequent action for the same cause and

the parties are concluded upon all issues which might have been tried.
. . .

. . . .

Exceptions overruled.

———

Questions: (13) To what extent, if any, should evidence extrinsic to the record be admissible to show that a prior judgment went solely on an issue that was not open on the pleadings but was tried by consent pursuant to Rule 15(b)?

(14) If there was evidence at the first trial on each of two issues and the trial judge's decision did not show upon which issue he relied, would his testimony on this point be admissible in the second action?

(15) Does a judgment for defendant based on the statute of limitations bar a subsequent suit on the same claim within the same jurisdiction, assuming that plaintiff has recast his suit so as to come under a limitations period that has not yet run? Does such a judgment bar a subsequent suit identical to the first, but brought in another jurisdiction that would apply a limitations period that has not yet run? See Williamson v. Columbia Gas & Elec. Corp., supra p. 962; Restatement (Second) of Judgments § 19 comment f, reporter's note (1980).

———

KEIDATZ v. ALBANY
Supreme Court of California, 1952.
39 Cal.2d 826, 249 P.2d 264.

TRAYNOR, JUSTICE. In this action to recover damages for fraud, plaintiffs alleged that they were induced to buy a newly-constructed home from defendants by certain false and fraudulent representations respecting the character of the construction of the house and its location on the described real property. They further alleged that the representations were known by defendants to be false and were made to induce plaintiffs to purchase the property and that the contract price of $6,500 exceeded the value of the property by $3,000. In their answer defendants denied the allegations of fraud and pleaded affirmatively that plaintiffs' action was barred by two former adjudications between the parties. Defendants then made a motion for summary judgment supported by affidavits setting out the following undisputed facts: In 1949, plaintiffs brought an action to rescind the contract for fraud and failure of consideration. A demurrer to the second amended complaint was sustained with leave to amend. Plaintiffs failed to amend within the time allowed, and judgment was entered for defendants for costs. Thereafter plaintiffs unsuccessfully sought relief from the judgment under section 473 of the Code of Civil Procedure. No appeal was taken, however, from the judgment or from the order denying relief under section 473. Approximately four months after the judgment in the rescission action was entered, plaintiff brought this action for damages for fraud. The trial court granted defendants' motion for summary judgment and plaintiffs have appealed.

Plaintiffs contend that their unsuccessful attempt to secure rescission of the contract does not bar their present action for damages for fraud. Defendants, on the other hand, contend that the former judgment is res judicata of all issues presented here. Since the former judgment was entered after a general demurrer had been sustained with leave to amend, it is necessary to determine the scope of the doctrine of res judicata in such circumstances. The procedural effect of such a judgment appears to be sui generis. It is a judgment on the merits to the extent that it adjudicates that the facts alleged do not constitute a cause of action, and will, accordingly, be a bar to a subsequent action alleging the same facts. [Citations omitted.] Moreover, even though different facts may be alleged in the second action, if the demurrer was sustained in the first action on a ground equally applicable to the second, the former judgment will also be a bar. [Citations omitted.] If, on the other hand, new or additional facts are alleged that cure the defects in the original pleading, it is settled that the former judgment is not a bar to the subsequent action whether or not plaintiff had an opportunity to amend his complaint. [Citations omitted]; Restatement, Judgments, § 50, Comments c and e.

In plaintiffs' first action they sought rescission of the contract. In addition to alleging certain fraudulent representations whereby they were induced to enter into the contract, they alleged that they had offered to restore everything of value they had received, and sought the return of the payments they had made. It appeared from the complaint, however, that the alleged defects in construction became apparent to plaintiffs over a year before they sought to rescind, and defendants successfully demurred on the ground that the action was barred by laches and by failure to rescind promptly. See, Civ. Code § 1691; Williams v. Marshall, 37 Cal.2d 445, 455–456, 235 P.2d 372. Whether or not the complaint stated a cause of action for rescission, the demurrer should have been overruled if a cause of action for damages was stated. Bancroft v. Woodward, 183 Cal. 99, 102, 190 P. 445; MacIsaac v. Pozzo, 26 Cal.2d 809, 815, 161 P.2d 449. Plaintiffs' complaint did not, however, allege that the property was worth less than the price they agreed to pay for it, Civ.Code § 3343, and accordingly, it did not state a cause of action for damages for fraud. Davis v. Rite-Lite Sales Co., 8 Cal.2d 675, 679, 67 P.2d 1039; Gutterman v. Gally, 131 Cal.App. 647, 651–652, 21 P.2d 1000. In the present action, plaintiffs have added this allegation that was absent from their former complaint, and accordingly, under the rule hereinabove stated, the former judgment is not a bar to this action.

Defendants contend, however, that Wulfjen v. Dolton, 24 Cal.2d 891, 151 P.2d 846, establishes the rule that a party claiming to have been defrauded must seek all the relief to which he may be entitled in one action, and that he may not, after having failed in an action to rescind a contract for fraud, thereafter bring a second action for damages.   In the Wulfjen case, however, the judgment in the rescission action had not been entered on demurrer, but had followed a full trial on the merits, and the court applied the rule that such a judgment is res judicata not only as to issues actually raised, but as to issues that could have been raised in support of the action.   See, Sutphin v. Speik, 15 Cal.2d 195, 202, 99 P.2d 652, 101 P.2d 497.   As has been pointed out above, however, it has been the settled rule in this state that a judgment entered on demurrer does not have such broad res judicata effect.   [Justice Traynor analogized this rule to the plaintiff's former right to bring a new action after suffering an involuntary nonsuit.   (This right was abrogated in 1947 by Cal.Code Civ. Proc. § 581c, providing that a judgment of nonsuit operates as an adjudication on the merits unless the court otherwise specifies.)   He conceded that there are forceful arguments, in view of the liberal rules relating to amendments to the pleadings, for requiring the plaintiff to set forth in one action all the facts relating to his dispute, citing C. Clark, Code Pleading § 84 (2d ed. 1947), and an excellent article, Von Moschzisker, Res Judicata, 38 Yale L.J. 299, 319–20 (1929).]   On the other hand less prejudice is suffered by a defendant who has had only to attack the pleadings, than by one who has been forced to go to trial until a nonsuit is granted, and the hardship suffered by being forced to defend against a new action, instead of against an amended complaint, is not materially greater.   See, Commercial Centre Realty Co. v. Superior Court, 7 Cal.2d 121, 129–130, 59 P.2d 978, 107 A.L.R. 714.   We do not feel, however, that at this time we should reweigh the conflicting arguments over the wisdom of the rule we apply.   Since it is a settled rule of procedure upon which parties are entitled to rely in conducting their litigation, any change therein should be made by the Legislature and not by this court.

.   .   .   .

The judgment is reversed.

GIBSON, C.J., and SHENK, EDMONDS, CARTER and SPENCE, JJ., concur.

SCHAUER, J., concurs in the judgment.

DISMISSAL FOR INSUFFICIENCY OF COMPLAINT

The position of Restatement of Judgments § 50 (1942) was essentially as follows:

1.   After judgment sustaining a demurrer on the ground that the facts stated were insufficient to constitute a cause of action, a new action on a complaint in which the defect has been corrected is not

barred. It does not matter that the plaintiff failed in the first action to avail himself of permission to amend.

2. However, judgment sustaining a demurrer on such ground blocks a new action alleging the same, or virtually the same, facts as alleged in the first action. This was seen as an application of direct estoppel, which precludes repetitively litigating the same issue.

3. Also, judgment sustaining a demurrer precludes a new action where the defect in the first action was "an entire failure to state a cause of action" rather than "merely the omission of an essential allegation." If, for example, the plaintiff sued for invasion of privacy and a demurrer was sustained on the ground that no such right was recognized in the state, a new action on the same cause is precluded even if the state has meanwhile altered its views on the right of privacy.

Question: (16) Should this last rule be inexorably applied, or are there extraordinary situations where relitigation ought to be allowed? Suppose, for instance, that a board of education set up plans for reduction of the teaching force as part of a school desegregation program and that a group of black teachers brought an action seeking to enjoin the plans as racially discriminatory. On demurrer, the court upheld the plans and dismissed the action. There was no appeal. Subsequently, in an identical case arising in another state, the Supreme Court of the United States declares the plans to be unconstitutional. Should those original teachers be able to maintain a new action over the defendant's plea of res judicata? See Restatement (Second) of Judgments § 26(1)(d) (1980).

There persists considerable support for the First Restatement's view, but some courts depart from it to the extent of barring a new action if, after the demurrer was sustained in the first action, the plaintiff was expressly granted leave to amend and he neglected or refused to do so. E.g., Elfman v. Glaser, 313 Mass. 370, 47 N.E.2d 925 (1943). But even this revised version of the First Restatement's position still seems inconsistent with the developing rules of pleading and especially the freedom to amend. See Osserman v. Jacobs, 369 Mass. 200, 339 N.E.2d 193 (1975) (Kaplan, J.); 1B Moore ¶ 0.409[1]; Developments in the Law—Res Judicata, 65 Harv.L.Rev. 818, 836–37 (1952).

Restatement (Second) of Judgments § 19 comment d (1980) abandons the position of the First Restatement, by providing in effect that a judgment for insufficiency of the complaint normally operates as a bar unless the court otherwise orders. In this connection, consider the effect of a rule like Rule 41(b), discussed in the following case and in 18 Wright, Miller & Cooper § 4435, at 332–38.

RINEHART v. LOCKE

United States Court of Appeals, Seventh Circuit, 1971.
454 F.2d 313.

[Plaintiff sued in 1969 under 42 U.S.C. § 1983, claiming that his arrest by the defendants—private detectives and police officers—deprived him of his constitutional rights. The Rule 12(b)(6) dismissal by the district judge was based upon the failure to allege lack of probable cause. Plaintiff sought leave to amend to include such an allegation. The judge denied leave, stating no reason. There was no appeal. More than a year later (and nearly six years after the events in suit), plaintiff brought a second action based on the same arrest, the complaint being identical in substance to the first except that it included an averment of lack of probable cause. The district court sustained the defense of res judicata and dismissed. Plaintiff appealed.]

Before SWYGERT, CHIEF JUDGE, and FAIRCHILD and STEVENS, CIRCUIT JUDGES.

FAIRCHILD, CIRCUIT JUDGE.

. . . .

Plaintiff contends that the May, 1969 dismissal did not establish that defendants were not liable to him under § 1983 on account of the 1964 arrest, but established only that he had no cause of action unless he was able to plead and prove lack of probable cause.

[The court stated that the traditional rule supported plaintiff's position, citing Gould v. Evansville & Crawfordsville R.R., 91 U.S. 526 (1876), and Restatement of Judgments § 50 comment c (1942).]

Arguably Rule 41(b), F.R.C.P., may have changed this rule where the earlier judgment, as in this case, was entered in a federal court. The Rule provides in part: "Unless the court in its order for dismissal otherwise specifies, a dismissal under this subdivision and any dismissal not provided for in this rule, other than a dismissal for lack of jurisdiction, for improper venue, or for failure to join a party under Rule 19, operates as an adjudication upon the merits."

It has been held that the list in Rule 41(b) of types of dismissal which are not presumptively adjudications on the merits is not exclusive, and that the situations where dismissals not provided for in Rule 41 are to operate as adjudication on the merits are those "in which the defendant must incur the inconvenience of preparing to meet the merits because there is no initial bar to the Court's reaching them." [2]

---

[2] Costello v. United States, 365 U.S. 265, 286, 81 S.Ct. 534, 545, 5 L.Ed.2d 551 (1961). [This case held that a dismissal of a denaturalization proceeding for failure to file a required affidavit of good cause with the complaint, where the dismissal order did not specify whether it was with or without prejudice, was not "an adjudication upon the merits" despite the wording of Rule 41(b). The Court reached this result by ruling that the term "lack of jurisdiction" appearing in the Rule is not to be read technically or narrowly, and that this dismissal was for "lack of jurisdiction."—Ed.]

The same decision indicates that a dismissal for failure to fulfill a "precondition" for consideration of the merits is not a decision on the merits.

With this gloss upon the Rule, the question remains a close one, but we are persuaded that under the Rule an order of a district court which dismisses a complaint for failure to state a claim, but which does not specify that the dismissal is without prejudice, is res judicata as to the then existing claim which it appears plaintiff was attempting to state. This view places upon a plaintiff in a case like the 1969 case in this instance the burden of persuading the district court either to include a specification that the dismissal is without prejudice or to permit an amendment. If plaintiff is unsuccessful, his recourse is to appeal. We think this view is consistent with the expedient purpose of the Rules.

[The other part of the opinion, to the effect that the action was also barred by the statute of limitations, is omitted.]

The judgment appealed from is affirmed.

———

Question: (17) May a district court specify that its dismissal for lack of jurisdiction is "with prejudice" or is "an adjudication upon the merits"? See Restatement (Second) of Judgments § 20 comment d (1980); 9 Wright & Miller § 2373.

———

DISMISSAL FOR FAILURE TO PROSECUTE OR TO OBEY A COURT ORDER OR RULE

Does a dismissal for failure to prosecute, or failure to obey a court order or rule, operate as an adjudication on the merits? There has not been in a literal sense an adjudication on the merits—there usually has been no consideration whatever of the merits—but the dismissal nevertheless operates as such an adjudication unless the court otherwise specifies. Such is the result that is prescribed by Rule 41(b), which has its counterpart in a majority of the states, and more generally by Restatement (Second) of Judgments § 19 comment e (1980). It is thought that the harsh result to the litigant who is deprived of a chance to establish his claim is justified by the interests of his opponent and those of litigants generally in having the court effectively control its docket and enforce its procedure.

Dismissal of this kind is reviewable on appeal for abuse of discretion. In most instances where abuse of discretion is the test, the appellate court strains to uphold the decision of the lower court. Here, however, the sanction of dismissal is not looked upon with favor. As the court said in Industrial Building Materials, Inc. v. Interchemical Corp., 437 F.2d 1336, 1339 (9th Cir.1970): "Application of the remedy rests within the sound discretion of the court, but since it may severely punish a party not responsible for the alleged dereliction of his counsel, the rule should only be invoked in extreme circumstances. In reviewing the propriety of dismissal under Rule 41(b) we should, we think, look to see whether the court might have first adopted other, less drastic alternatives."

"ON THE MERITS"

Restatement of Judgments § 48 (1942) stated that a valid and final personal judgment for the defendant acts as a bar only if it was "on the merits." But, over time and in response to considerations of fairness and judicial economy, the rule of bar has come to be applied more broadly, with judgments not passing directly on the substance of the claim acting as a bar. Restatement (Second) of Judgments § 19 (1980) omits the phrase "on the merits," and comment a thereto explains that this was done because the phrase is no longer descriptive of the many situations in which bar applies. But, of course, this omission does not mean that under the Second Restatement *any* valid and final personal judgment for the defendant acts as a bar: the remains of the not-on-the-merits exception are laid out in § 20.

RESTATEMENT (SECOND) OF JUDGMENTS
(1980).

§ 20. *Judgment for Defendant—Exceptions to the General Rule of Bar*

(1) A personal judgment for the defendant, although valid and final, does not bar another action by the plaintiff on the same claim:

(a) When the judgment is one of dismissal for lack of jurisdiction, for improper venue, or for nonjoinder or misjoinder of parties; or

(b) When the plaintiff agrees to or elects a nonsuit (or voluntary dismissal) without prejudice or the court directs that the plaintiff be nonsuited (or that the action be otherwise dismissed) without prejudice; or

(c) When by statute or rule of court the judgment does not operate as a bar to another action on the same claim, or does not so operate unless the court specifies, and no such specification is made.

(2) A valid and final personal judgment for the defendant, which rests on the prematurity of the action or on the plaintiff's failure to satisfy a precondition to suit, does not bar another action by the plaintiff instituted after the claim has matured, or the precondition has been satisfied, unless a second action is precluded by operation of the substantive law.

Question: (18) Should Restatement (Second) of Judgments § 20(2) (1980) apply to permit a second action even where the dismissal of the first action came not at the threshold but only after full-blown trial? Or instead should there be another exception to the exception, providing for bar where it would be "manifestly unfair" to subject the defendant to the second action? Compare Stebbins v. Nationwide Mut. Ins. Co., 528 F.2d 934 (4th Cir.1975), cert. denied, 424 U.S. 946, 96 S.Ct. 1417 (1976), with 1973 A.L.I. Proc. 307–08, 311–15, 322–23.

SECTION 3.   COUNTERCLAIM

Counterclaim pleaded.—Once a defendant pleads a counterclaim, the principles of former adjudication generally apply to it just as they apply to an original claim in a complaint. See Restatement (Second) of Judgments §§ 21(1), 23 (1980).

The one exception to this rule applies when judgment on the counterclaim is rendered in favor of the defendant, but the defendant is denied full recovery because the action was brought in a court that was not empowered to give the defendant full recovery on his counterclaim and because there were available no procedural devices (such as transferring the case to another court) by which the defendant might have obtained full recovery; in this very narrow situation, the defendant's claim is not merged in his judgment, and he may seek recovery on the remainder of his claim in a subsequent action. See id. § 21(2).

Permissive counterclaim not pleaded.—Whenever applicable law permits a counterclaim to be asserted but does not make it compulsory, a defendant has the choice between responding to the plaintiff's claim with an answer that includes the counterclaim and reserving the subject matter of the potential counterclaim for an independent action. This is usually straightforward enough, but complications ensue when the same facts constitute both a ground of defense to the plaintiff's claim and a basis for counterclaim. If these facts are not used as a defense, the main action may be lost, and therefore they will almost certainly be so used. But suppose that the defendant wishes to reserve his claim in order to bring it as an independent action, perhaps in another forum that is more convenient or might apply more favorable law. Should the defendant be free to rely on the common facts as a defense, without pleading a counterclaim, and then bring an independent action based on those same facts?

SCHWABE v. CHANTILLY, INC.
Supreme Court of Wisconsin, 1975.
67 Wis.2d 267, 226 N.W.2d 452.

WILKIE, CHIEF JUSTICE. This is a landlord-tenant case presenting a question of civil procedure. In a prior action, the landlord, Chantilly, Inc., sued the tenants, James and Mary Schwabe, for nonpayment of rent. The Schwabes set up the affirmative defense that they were fraudulently induced to sign the lease, but they did not counterclaim. Judgment was awarded to the Schwabes based upon this defense. Now in the present action they seek compensatory and punitive damages against Chantilly and Chantilly's managing officer, Abraham Wolinsky, based upon the fraud and upon malicious prosecution. Chantilly and Wolinsky moved to strike the causes of action based on fraud, arguing that by setting up the affirmative defense in the first action the Schwabes obliged themselves to also counterclaim in that action or else lose the claim completely. The trial court agreed and ordered the fraud causes of action struck from the complaint. The Schwabes appeal. We reverse.

.   .   .   .

The sole question presented here is whether plaintiffs are barred from maintaining these causes of action for fraud because they raised fraud as an affirmative defense to the prior rent-collection action brought by Chantilly, one of the defendants here. This court considered a related problem in Wm. H. Heinemann Creameries v. Milwaukee Automobile Ins. Co.[3] arising from personal injury litigation following an auto collision between A and B. In the first action where A sued B, the suit was dismissed by court order upon stipulation of the parties. Then in a subsequent action, B sued A and one question raised on appeal was whether B's action was barred on principles of res judicata because B had not counterclaimed in the first suit. Relying on sec. 263.14(1), Stats., making all counterclaims permissive, and sec. 58 of the Restatement of Judgments, the court held B's action not barred on this ground. Sec. 263.14(1), Stats., provides:

"A defendant *may* counterclaim any claim which he has against a plaintiff, upon which a judgment may be had in the action." (Emphasis supplied.)

Sec. 58 of the Restatement of Judgments provides, at page 230:

"Where the defendant does not interpose a counterclaim although he is entitled to do so, he is not precluded thereby from subsequently maintaining an action against the plaintiff on the cause of action which could have been set up as a counterclaim."

In discussing this section, the court in Heinemann particularly relied on comments b and f. However, comments c and d following this

[3] (1955), 270 Wis. 443, 71 N.W.2d 395, 72 N.W.2d 102.

section apply to the facts in the instant case where plaintiffs set up an affirmative defense but not a counterclaim in the first action.

The comments distinguish between situations where the plaintiff in the second action lost in the first case and where he won. Where he loses in the first case, he is barred from commencing a new action. As comment c to sec. 58 provides:

"Defense and counterclaim—Judgment for plaintiff—Collateral estoppel. Where the same facts constitute a ground of defense to the plaintiff's claim and also a ground for a counterclaim, and the defendant alleges these facts as a defense but not as a counterclaim, and after litigation of the defense judgment is given for the plaintiff, the defendant is precluded from maintaining an action against the plaintiff based on these facts. This is in accordance with the rule as to collateral estoppel stated in sec. 68, that where a question of fact essential to a judgment is actually litigated and determined by the judgment, the determination is conclusive between the parties in a subsequent action on a different cause of action."

However, where the party wins in the first action, based on the affirmative defense, it is permissible then to start a new action. He is then not in the position of attacking facts previously established. As comment d indicates:

"Defense and counterclaim—Judgment for defendant—Splitting Claims. Where the same facts constitute a defense to the plaintiff's claim and also a ground for counterclaim, and the defendant sets up these facts as a defense but not as a counterclaim, and after litigation of the defense judgment is given for the defendant, the defendant is not precluded from maintaining a subsequent action against the plaintiff based upon these facts. In such a case he is not improperly splitting his cause of action (compare sec. 62), although he uses the same facts first as a defense to the plaintiff's claim and later as the basis of an action against the plaintiff. In the subsequent action, the judgment in the prior action is conclusive as to the facts actually litigated and determined in the first action (see sec. 68)."

. . . Because judgment was rendered for the Schwabes in the first case they may now sue for damages caused by the fraud. Their present action does not seek to upset the determination reached in the first case and, in fact, affirms it. If they had lost, however, in the first action, under comment c a different result would be reached.

Defendants argue that plaintiffs' action is barred based primarily upon . . . Vukelic v. Upper Third Street Savings & Loan Asso.[6]
. . . .

In Vukelic, A sued B in a mortgage foreclosure action, and the court determined that approximately $15,000 was due under the mortgage. Then in a second action B sued A alleging as a "cause of action" that B had never received approximately $11,000 under the

[6] (1936), 222 Wis. 568, 269 N.W. 273.

mortgage and that the amount due should be reduced accordingly. The court held B's action barred on the grounds that the first judgment was res judicata as to the amount due. For two reasons, however, Vukelic is not persuasive in the case at bar. First, the second action commenced by B really amounted to an attack on the first judgment. In the instant case the two actions involved are completely consistent. Second, although Vukelic contains language indicating that an unused counterclaim is lost unless it is a " 'distinct cause of action,' " "one having no connection with the matters involved in the former cause of action; one not involving the same subject matter," such is no longer the law. Vukelic was decided in 1936, and in 1943 this court adopted the present version of sec. 263.14(1), Stats., making all counterclaims optional. . . . The statement in Vukelic that the only unused counterclaims that survive are those with no connection to the subject matter of the first action is thus consistent with the federal rule, but not the present rule in Wisconsin.

.   .   .   .

We conclude that the instant case seeking damages based on fraud is not barred under principles of res judicata or collateral estoppel.

.   .   .   .

Order reversed and cause remanded for further proceedings not inconsistent with this opinion.

————

Questions: (19) If the Schwabes had sought in the first action to rescind the fraudulently induced lease, would their fraud causes of action for damages have been precluded? See Restatement (Second) of Judgments § 22 comment d, illustration 6 (1980) (indicating that claim preclusion applies).

(20) Instead, if without provoking any objection the Schwabes had presented evidence in the first action of the extent of damages caused by the fraud, would their fraud causes of action for damages have been precluded?

————

ROACH v. TEAMSTERS LOCAL UNION NO. 688, 595 F.2d 446 (8th Cir.1979). First, plaintiffs unsuccessfully sued their employer and their union in a federal class action based on the loss of certain pension and seniority benefits.

Second, they unsuccessfully sued the same defendants in a federal action, Cronin v. Sears, Roebuck & Co., based on refusal to pay them witness pay for the days they had appeared as witnesses on their own behalf in that first case. They alleged that the employer had breached its collective bargaining agreement by refusing to pay and that the union had breached its duty of fair representation by failing to process properly their grievance arising from the employer's refusal. They sought actual damages for lost wages and punitive damages for mental distress. To substantiate mental distress, they offered trial evidence of their exclusion from a January 1976 union meeting. "Over defendants' objections that this meeting was totally unrelated to the witness pay dispute, [plaintiffs] were permitted to testify in considerable detail about the incident."

Third, plaintiffs sued the union in consolidated actions, seeking actual and punitive damages and alleging that they had been arbitrarily and discriminatorily prevented by union officials from attending the January 1976 meeting and that this had denied rights of free speech and assembly guaranteed by federal labor law and thus had caused damage to name and reputation, humiliation, and mental distress. The district court granted the union summary judgments, ruling that the judgment in the second action precluded the third set of actions. Plaintiffs appealed.

The court of appeals affirmed, reasoning that the critical question was whether each plaintiff was now suing on a cause of action or claim that had been adjudicated in Cronin, and resolving that question thusly:

"We have carefully reviewed again the record in Cronin, including the pleadings and the trial transcript. We are convinced that plaintiffs are attempting to recover for a wrong for which they sought recovery in Cronin. Although in Cronin plaintiffs did not plead their exclusion from the January meeting as a separate violation of their rights, a very substantial portion of the trial was devoted to that incident, and it is evident that that alleged invasion of their rights was one basis of their damage claim.

"Plaintiffs contend, however, that in Cronin they did not attempt to recover damages for their exclusion from the January meeting. They emphasize that Cronin was brought pursuant to 29 U.S.C. § 185(a) for breach of the duty of fair representation whereas their present claims are based upon 29 U.S.C. § 401 et seq., which sets forth a 'bill of rights' for members of labor organizations and specifically grants union members a cause of action for violations of these rights. They assert that the only injury for which relief was sought in Cronin and the only cause of action therein litigated was the breach of contract and the Union's breach of the duty of fair representation. The operative facts surrounding that cause of action were the events of October 1975 when the Union made the decision not to take their witness pay grievance to arbitration. Plaintiffs explain that their exclusion from the January meeting was put in evidence at the Cronin trial only for the limited purpose of demonstrating that the Union's failure to fairly represent them was malicious and in bad faith. They contend that the courts below confused mere evidence of the meeting with a cause of action.

"We recognize that the right to fair representation and the free speech and assembly rights enumerated in the bill of rights for members of labor organizations are separate and distinct statutory rights. If the Cronin trial had been strictly limited to the Union's alleged breach of the duty of fair representation the present actions may not have been barred. However, we cannot agree with plaintiffs that they did not litigate their exclusion from the January meeting in Cronin.

"In Cronin plaintiffs sought to recover damages for the mental distress they allegedly suffered as a consequence of the Union's unfair representation. At trial their evidence of mental distress consisted of testimony that plaintiffs suffered the ridicule of their coworkers and testimony about their exclusion from the January union meeting. Plaintiffs' theory was that the Union failed to represent them regarding their claims for witness pay in retaliation for their initiation of the original pension benefits suit against the Union and Sears. They contended that their exclusion from the January meeting was to prevent them from bringing the witness pay dispute before the members of the union, and that the incident demonstrated the Union was engaged in a continuing course of discriminatory treatment because of the pension benefits litigation. Plaintiffs' counsel argued vigorously to the jury that the exclusion of plaintiffs from the meeting was the type of extreme and outrageous conduct warranting punitive damages. The record thus belies plaintiffs' arguments that they did not attempt to recover in Cronin for that injury.

"Moreover, the Cronin trial court specifically held that plaintiffs' evidence about their exclusion from the meeting was inadequate to sustain an award of punitive damages. . . .

. . . . .

"In the present suits plaintiffs are asserting an alternative theory of recovery for their exclusion from the January meeting which could have and should have been raised in the previous litigation. We cannot countenance plaintiffs' attempts to split a single cause of action into multiple lawsuits. Important policy interests are served by the claim preclusion aspect of res judicata. The doctrine prevents harassment of parties by repetitive litigation, conserves judicial resources, and prevents diminishment of the prestige of the courts by minimizing inconsistent decisions. [Citations omitted.] We are satisfied that these policies will be served by applying the doctrine in the present cases. We hold plaintiffs are barred by the judgment in Cronin from relitigating their claims based on their exclusion from the January 1976 union meeting."

Question: (21) Can the Schwabe rule for defendants be reconciled with the apparent decision in Roach that a plaintiff forecloses his later claim by using evidence common to that claim?

Compulsory counterclaim not pleaded.—As conceded in Schwabe, there are two situations in which a defendant does not have a free choice between bringing a counterclaim and bringing an independent action. Whenever one of these two situations occurs, a defendant who could but does not interpose his claim as a counterclaim will be precluded from maintaining a subsequent action thereon.

One such situation occurs when the plaintiff's claim and the defendant's claim are related in such a way that if the defendant were to prevail on his claim in any subsequent action, the effect would be to nullify the prior judgment. This "common-law compulsory counterclaim rule" applies whether or not the jurisdiction has a compulsory counterclaim statute or rule of court, and whether or not the prior judgment is by default. Perhaps the scope of this somewhat imprecisely stated doctrine can be best conveyed by example. On the one hand, Restatement (Second) of Judgments § 22(2)(b) comment f, illustration 9 (1980), offers this example: "A brings an action against B for failure to pay the contract price for goods sold and delivered and recovers judgment by default. After entry of final judgment and payment of the price, B brings an action against A to rescind the contract for mutual mistake, seeking restitution of the contract price and offering to return the goods. The action is precluded." On the other hand, *D* normally may default in *P*'s personal-injury action and then bring his own action against *P* for injuries sustained in the same accident, the idea being that a judgment for *D* would not "nullify" *P*'s prior judgment. The line lies somewhere between these two examples. The doctrine's scope is also suggested by consideration of its genesis, which reveals the doctrine to be a specific aspect of a broad principle of claim preclusion: a valid and final personal judgment generally precludes the defendant from later asserting mere defenses to the claim.

The second, more common situation occurs when the potential counterclaim falls within the reach of a compulsory counterclaim statute or rule of court.

HORNE v. WOOLEVER, 170 Ohio St. 178, 163 N.E.2d 378 (1959), cert. denied, 362 U.S. 951, 80 S.Ct. 861 (1960). Woolever sued Horne in an Ohio court in February 1957, seeking $150,000 for personal injuries resulting from a collision between their two automobiles. Horne removed the action to the United States District Court for the Northern District of Ohio on diversity grounds, and he thereafter filed in the federal court an answer that was in effect a general denial. No counterclaim was pleaded. Subsequently, in August 1957, while that federal action was pending, Horne sued Woolever in an Ohio court for $65,000 for his own injuries sustained in the same accident. In March 1958, Horne paid Woolever $25,000 to settle the latter's claim; the attorneys filed a stipulation in the federal court for dismissal of Woolever's action with prejudice; and the federal judge so ordered. Thereafter, Woolever obtained judgment in Horne's Ohio action based upon the proceedings in the federal court. Ultimately, the Supreme Court of Ohio held the federal judgment to be a bar and affirmed judgment for Woolever. Judge Taft explained that Rule 13(a) had required Horne to assert his own claim as a counterclaim in Woolever's action in the federal court whether that action was originally instituted in that court or was removed from the state court, even though Ohio had no rule comparable to Rule 13(a). See Rule 81(c). He added: "To the extent to which a judgment of a federal court operates as res adjudicata in that court, it operates as res adjudicata in the courts of this state."

Question: (22) If the Horne case were decided the other way, would the Supreme Court of the United States have jurisdiction to review the final judgment of the Ohio court? Of what, if any, relevance is the fact that Rule 13 is not an act of Congress but a rule of court promulgated pursuant to the Rules Enabling Act? Of what, if any, significance is the fact that the Rules Enabling Act provides that the Rules shall govern only procedural matters and not affect substantive rights? If the Supreme Court of the United States were to hear this imagined case, how should it be decided? See 6 Wright & Miller § 1417.

DINDO v. WHITNEY

United States Court of Appeals, First Circuit, 1971.
451 F.2d 1.

Before ALDRICH, CHIEF JUDGE, McENTEE and COFFIN, CIRCUIT JUDGES.

ALDRICH, CHIEF JUDGE. Following remand of this case with our order vacating the district court's sustaining of the defense of the statute of limitations, 429 F.2d 25,ᵍ the defendant pleaded, successfully, that the action was barred by reason of plaintiff's having failed to assert it as a compulsory counterclaim, pursuant to F.R.Civ.P. 13(a), in a prior action. This question we had raised ourselves, but declined to resolve because of lack of briefing, and because of its possible

ᵍ Vermont plaintiff and New Hampshire defendant, en route to a hunting trip in northern Maine, had an accident in the Province of Quebec. When suit was brought in the New Hampshire federal court, the Quebec statute of limitations had run but the New Hampshire statute (and the Vermont statute) had not. The district court dismissed. The court of appeals reversed, saying that the relation of the parties to Quebec was most fortuitous, and that the application of the Quebec statute would further no Quebec interest but would frustrate New Hampshire's interests to some degree. For these reasons, the court of appeals was satisfied from prior decisions that the New Hampshire Supreme Court would apply the New Hampshire statute of limitations.

In 1952 the New Hampshire Supreme Court on similar facts had applied the Quebec statute. In a 1966 case, however, that court had applied New Hampshire law, which allowed a guest to recover from a host driver for ordinary negligence, instead of Vermont law, which required gross negligence; the parties in that case had had an accident in Vermont on the way from their New Hampshire home to another part of New Hampshire. The court of appeals concluded that the 1966 decision had implicitly overruled the 1952 case.

complexity. In now granting defendant's motion to dismiss on this ground, the court had before it certain testimony by way of depositions to which it made reference in its opinion, 52 F.R.D. 194. We accordingly consider the case in terms of a motion for summary judgment. This, of course, requires accepting plaintiff's version of the facts, no matter how unlikely they may seem. See Coastwise Packet Co. v. United States, 1 Cir., 1968, 398 F.2d 77, 79, cert. denied 393 U.S. 937, 89 S.Ct. 300, 21 L.Ed.2d 274.

Briefly, plaintiff Dindo alleges that defendant Whitney was a passenger in a car belonging to Whitney, but driven by Dindo; that the car went off the road, severely injuring Dindo, and that the cause of the accident was Whitney's putting his hand through the steering wheel in reaching for a flashlight on the steering shaft. Suit was brought in the district court of New Hampshire on October 29, 1968, within the New Hampshire period for suit, the accident having occurred on October 30, 1965. Dindo and Whitney had long been friends, Dindo living in Vermont and Whitney in New Hampshire. In June, 1966 Whitney sued Dindo in the district court of Vermont. Dindo gave the papers to his insurance agent, who forwarded them to Whitney's insurer which, by virtue of a clause in the policy, insured Dindo as a driver of Whitney's car with Whitney's permission. The insurer retained counsel, but informed Dindo that he should retain his own counsel as well, as the ad damnum exceeded the coverage. Dindo did not do so. In March, 1967 the insurer paid Whitney a sum within the policy limit in settlement, and an entry was made on the court docket, "Settled and discontinued." The present action is defended by the same insurer, Whitney, as the car's owner, being covered by the policy that had included coverage of Dindo.

It is clear on the record that before insurance company counsel settled the case they conferred with Dindo on a number of occasions, and apparently saw no defense to the suit. All that was said is not entirely clear. The court made findings of fact which may have been the most reasonable resolution, but which went beyond permissible bounds on a motion for summary judgment. It was proper for it to find that Dindo did not request counsel to file a counterclaim against Whitney, and that there had been time to do so, but we must accept Dindo's position that he did not realize, until he spoke with new counsel in September 1968, that he had a basis for so doing, namely, Whitney's conduct in reaching for the flashlight. Dindo, assertedly, had thought that because he was driving the car he could have no claim.

[The court here quoted from Rule 13(a).] The accident, by whomever caused, was obviously the same transaction or occurrence. Dindo claims, however, that the compulsory rule is inapplicable to him since the original case was settled, rather than pursued to final judgment on the merits. Alternatively, he says that it is inequitable to assert the rule against him when he had not realized he had a counterclaim until afterwards.

The bar arising out of Rule 13(a) has been characterized variously. Some courts have said that a judgment is res judicata of whatever could have been pleaded in a compulsory counterclaim. Dragor Shipping Corp. v. Union Tank Car Co., 9 Cir., 1967, 378 F.2d 241; United States v. Eastport S.S. Corp., 2 Cir., 1958, 255 F.2d 795. Other courts have viewed the rule not in terms of res judicata, but as creating an estoppel or waiver. Lawhorn v. Atlantic Refining Co., 5 Cir., 1962, 299 F.2d 353; Dow Chemical Co. v. Metlon Corp., 4 Cir., 1960, 281 F.2d 292. The latter approach seems more appropriate, at least when the case is settled rather than tried. The purposes of the rule are "to prevent multiplicity of actions and to achieve resolution in a single lawsuit of all disputes arising out of common matters." Southern Constr. Co. v. Pickard, 1962, 371 U.S. 57, 60, 83 S.Ct. 108, 110, 9 L.Ed. 2d 31. If a case has been tried, protection both of the court and of the parties dictates that there should be no further directly related litigation. But if the case is settled, normally the court has not been greatly burdened, and the parties can protect themselves by demanding cross-releases. In such circumstances, absent a release, better-tailored justice seems obtainable by applying principles of equitable estoppel.

If, in the case at bar, Dindo, clearly having opportunity to assert it, cf. LaFollette v. Herron, D.C.Tenn., 1962, 211 F.Supp. 919, knew of the existence of a right to counterclaim, the fact that there was no final judgment on the merits should be immaterial, and a Rule 13(a) bar would be appropriate. His conscious inaction not only created the very additional litigation the rule was designed to prevent it exposed the insurer to double liability. We are not persuaded that a final judgment is a sine qua non to invocation of the bar; there is nothing in the rule limning the term "judgment."

However, on a motion for summary judgment this factual finding could not be made on the present record. We are not prepared to say at this time what lesser facts would compel a conclusion of estoppel as a matter of law. There should be a hearing on the merits, the facts to be found by the jury. United States ex rel. Westinghouse Electric v. James Stewart Co., 9 Cir., 1964, 336 F.2d 777, subject to instructions by the court, Home Indemnity Co. of New York v. Allen, 7 Cir., 1951, 190 F.2d 490. In this connection the court may consider the effect of the cooperation clause in the policy, if there were such, since Dindo, as the insured, would be bound by such a provision. Regardless of whether he thought he had no cross-claim, Dindo's failure, presently asserted by the insurer, to give it a full and true account of the accident, might well be found by the jury to be a breach of a cooperation clause, which, in turn, might form a basis for estoppel. Or, a matter on which we do not presently express views, without such a clause estoppel might be based upon misrepresentation.

The judgment of the district court is vacated and the action remanded for further proceedings consistent herewith.

Question: (23) What did the court mean when it said that allowing this suit would expose the insurance company to "double liability"?

INSURER–INSURED CONFLICTS OF INTEREST

The Dindo case points up some of the numerous problems that exist when counsel for a liability insurance company represents its insured, as the interests of insurer and insured are likely not to be the same. Another such conflict of interest arises when the insured is interested in pressing a compulsory counterclaim, but the insurer has no interest in doing so. This kind of problem stimulated great criticism in Maine upon the adoption of a rule identical to Rule 13(a). After less than a year of experience under that rule, it was amended to except motor vehicle tort cases from its reach. See 1 R. Field, V. McKusick & L. Wroth, Maine Civil Practice 263–64 (2d ed. 1970).

Question: (24) Why should the whole doctrine of claim preclusion not be reduced to court rules similar to Rule 13(a) and somewhat analogous to the compulsory party-joinder provisions of Rule 19? See 18 Wright, Miller & Cooper § 4407, at 49–52.

TOPIC C. ISSUE PRECLUSION

SECTION 1. REQUIREMENTS OF THE RULE

LITTLE v. BLUE GOOSE MOTOR COACH CO.

Supreme Court of Illinois, 1931.
346 Ill. 266, 178 N.E. 496.

[Dr. Robert M. Little, while driving his automobile in East St. Louis, collided with a bus owned and operated by Blue Goose Motor Coach Company. Blue Goose sued Dr. Little in a justice of the peace court for damage to its bus caused by the collision and, after trial, recovered judgment for $139.35. Dr. Little's appeal to the county court was dismissed for lack of prosecution on April 2, 1926.

[During the pendency of that suit before the justice of the peace, Dr. Little commenced an action against Blue Goose in the city court of East St. Louis for personal injuries suffered by him in the collision. Dr. Little died on May 25, 1926, and his executrix was substituted as plaintiff. Her new declaration alleged in the first count that Dr. Little's death had been caused by the defendant's negligence, and in the second count that his death had been caused by the defendant's willful and wanton negligence. Blue Goose then set up as a defense the justice of the peace proceedings, contending that they constituted an "estoppel by verdict." Evidence, including testimony by the justice of the peace himself, was introduced by Blue Goose bearing on what had occurred in the proceedings before the justice of the peace. The plaintiff had verdict and judgment for $5000.

[On appeal from the judgment to the Appellate Court of Illinois, that court reversed with the following finding of fact: "The Court finds that appellant sued Dr. Robert M. Little, appellee's testate, before a Justice of the Peace for damages to its bus in the collision which occurred on November 1, 1925, and recovered a judgment therefor in the sum of $139.35; that in the rendition of said judgment it was necessarily determined that the collision and damages occasioned to the bus were due to the negligence of Dr. Little and that immediately prior to his death he could not have maintained an action for personal injuries growing out of the same collision."]

PER CURIAM.

. . . .

The first question arises on the ruling of the Appellate Court invoking against the claim of plaintiff in error the doctrine of estoppel by verdict. It is argued on behalf of plaintiff in error that where a former adjudication is relied on as a bar to a subsequent action it is essential that there be identity both of the subject matter and of the

1001

parties, and that in the instant case the subject matter is not the same, as this is the action for death by wrongful act for the benefit of the widow and next of kin, while the former suit was a claim for damages for injury to personal property. The issue on which this case is bottomed was the issue of fact which lay at the base of the judgment recovered before the justice of the peace. The allegation of the special plea is that the issue there raised was one of negligence on the part of Dr. Little on one hand and the defendant in error on the other, and that issue having been determined against Dr. Little, the fact is forever settled between these parties or their privies. Estoppel by verdict arises when a material fact in any litigation has been determined in a former suit between the same parties or between parties with whom the parties to the subsequent suit are in privity, where the fact was also material to the issue. The Appellate Court found as a matter of fact that the issue tried before the justice of the peace was an issue of negligence and was the same issue, arising on the same facts as those relied upon in the action for the wrongful death of Dr. Little, and that the issue of negligence was necessarily determined in the suit by the defendant in error against Dr. Little. That question of fact was tried before the city court in this case, and on the evidence there adduced the Appellate Court made its finding of fact. That issue of fact therefore is not open here, and we are to proceed to further consideration of the cause under the established fact that the issue of negligence, at least under the first count of the declaration, is the same issue tried before the justice of the peace.

While on appeal to the county court the trial, had there been one, would have been de novo, yet when the appeal was dismissed and a procedendo was issued to the justice of the peace, the judgment of the justice of the peace became a final determination of that issue between the parties, and is conclusive not only upon the immediate parties to that suit but also upon all persons in privity with them, and cannot be litigated again between the parties to that case or their privies in any subsequent action in the same or other court where that question arises, whether upon the same or a different cause of action or whatever may have been the nature or purpose of the action in which the judgment was rendered or of that in which the estoppel is set up. [Citations omitted.] It follows that Dr. Little could not during his lifetime maintain the action filed by him against the defendant in error, and since plaintiff in error's right to recover damages under the Injuries Act depends upon Dr. Little's right, during his lifetime, to recover damages for injuries arising out of the same collision, plaintiff in error cannot recover here. [Citation omitted.] In a suit under the Injuries Act, the cause of action is the wrongful act and not merely the death itself. [Citations omitted.] Plaintiff in error therefore was not entitled to recover under the first count of her declaration, and the Appellate Court did not err in so holding.

It is contended, however, that as the second count of the declaration charges wanton and willful negligence on the part of defendant in error, contributory negligence on the part of Dr. Little is not a defense, and that the judgment of the city court was therefore right. Contributory negligence is not a defense to willful and wanton conduct, but it does not follow that the judgment of the city court was right because of that fact. In all cases charging willful and wanton *Judg. for* negligence it is necessary to make proof of such negligence, and *D in No. 1* where there is no such proof no recovery under such charge can be *means* had. [Citation omitted.] The finding of the Appellate Court that the *no* collision was caused by the negligence of Dr. Little necessarily was a *willful* finding of fact on the willful negligence count as well as the general *neg.* negligence count. Thus the rule that contributory negligence on the part of the plaintiff is not a defense to a charge of willful negligence does not apply. Whether Dr. Little or the bus driver was responsible for the accident was, as we have seen, settled. The judgment for $139.35 necessarily decided that the bus driver was not guilty of willful negligence.[a]

.   .   .   .

Judgment affirmed.

———————

Question: (1) In Illinois it was held that two causes of action arise when a negligent act causes a person to suffer both personal injury and property damage, so that a judgment for property damage does not preclude a later action for personal injury. Clancey v. McBride, supra p. 975. Suppose Dr. Little, and not Blue Goose, had brought suit in the justice of the peace court for property damage and, after trial, judgment had been rendered in his favor. What should be the effect of these proceedings in the later city court action by the executrix?

———————

DIMENSIONS OF AN ISSUE

In applying the doctrine of issue preclusion, there predictably arises the difficult problem of defining the scope of the issue foreclosed. Restatement (Second) of Judgments § 27 comment c (1980) does not essay a precise definition of "issue," but instead proposes several factors to consider in resolving whether a matter to be presented in the second action and a matter presented in the first action constitute the same issue. Most notable among these factors is the degree of overlap, with respect to the two matters, between the evidence and legal argument advanced in the first action and that to be advanced in the second. This approach is then applied in illustrations 4 and 6:

———————

[a] Under then applicable Illinois law, the plaintiff in a negligence action had to plead and prove his own due care. See supra p. 462.

"4. A brings an action against B to recover for personal injuries in an automobile accident. A seeks to establish that B was negligent in driving at an excessive rate of speed. After trial, verdict and judgment are given for B. In a subsequent action by B against A for injuries in the same accident, A is precluded from setting up B's negligence as a defense, whether or not the alleged negligence is based on an assertion of excessive speed. It is reasonable to require A to bring forward all evidence in support of the alleged negligence in the initial proceeding. (It is assumed in this Illustration that the forum has no applicable compulsory counterclaim rule. See § 22.)

"6. A brings an action against B to recover an installment payment due under a contract. B's sole defense is that the contract is unenforceable under the statute of frauds. After trial, judgment is given for A, the court ruling that an oral contract of the kind sued upon is enforceable. In a subsequent action by A against B to recover a second installment falling due after the first action was brought, B is precluded from raising the statute of frauds as a defense, whether or not on the basis of arguments made in the prior action, but is not precluded from asserting as a defense that the installment is not owing as a matter of law on any other ground."

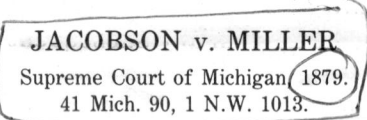

JACOBSON v. MILLER
Supreme Court of Michigan, 1879.
41 Mich. 90, 1 N.W. 1013.

[The plaintiff sued in Michigan state court for installments of rent then due under a written lease. The general issue was pleaded, but there was no denial under oath of the execution of the lease as required by court rule if execution was to be disputed. The defendant contended that he was not liable because he did not occupy the premises during the period for which rent was claimed. The plaintiff had judgment. Thereafter the plaintiff sued for subsequent installments of rent now due under the same lease. The defendant, by the requisite statement under oath, denied execution of the lease. The plaintiff offered the prior judgment as conclusive proof of execution, and the trial judge received it as such over the defendant's objection. The correctness of this ruling was the principal question presented by the appeal.]

Handwritten margin notes:
No.1 = Suit for rent; valid of lease not in ?; verd=P
No.2: Same but defense= lease not valid
Trial Ct: No estoppel

COOLEY, J.

. . . .

It is not denied by the defendant that if the execution and delivery of the lease had been disputed in the first suit, the determination of the issue would have been conclusive upon the parties in any subsequent litigation involving the right to rents under the same lease. The case would then have been within the principle of Gardner v.

Buckbee, 3 Cow. 120, where a question entirely similar in its legal aspects was considered and passed upon.

But the execution of the lease was not denied in the former suit. No issue was made upon it, and the defendant, by not denying it, suffered a default in respect to it which left it wholly outside the issue made and actually passed upon. Consequently it was not and could not have been considered by the court as a point which in that suit was open to controversy. The defendants, by their pleadings, made the actual existence of the lease an immaterial fact, and had the lease counted upon been a known forgery, the case must nevertheless have proceeded with its existence and genuineness admitted.

It is said, however, that the defendants in the first suit were at liberty to put the execution of the lease in issue, and that it was their duty to do so then if they proposed to contest it at all. This is upon the ground that public policy will not suffer the withholding of a defense with a view to further litigation, when a single suit might determine the whole controversy. This is no doubt true where the defense is sought to be made use of in the retrial of a dispute respecting the same subject matter of the former litigation. Pierce v. Kneeland, 9 Wis. 23, 31. The question now is, whether the proposition is applicable to a case where the subject matter of the second suit is different. In other words, where one is sued in respect to one subject matter, must he bring forward all his defenses, at the peril, if he fails to do so, of being debarred of them in any subsequent litigation which may involve the same questions, though relating to a different subject matter? We think not.

The precise point was before the Supreme Court of the United States in Cromwell v. County of Sac, 94 U.S. 351, 356, in which Mr. Justice Field, delivering the opinion of the court, says: "Various considerations, other than the actual merits, may govern a party in bringing forward grounds of recovery or defense in one action, which may not exist in another action upon a different demand, such as the smallness of the amount or the value of the property in controversy, the difficulty of obtaining the necessary evidence, the expense of the litigation, and his own situation at the time. A party acting upon considerations like these ought not to be precluded from contesting in a subsequent action other demands arising out of the same transaction. A judgment by default only admits for the purpose of the action the legality of the demand or claim in suit; it does not make the allegations of the declaration or complaint evidence in an action upon a different claim."

Don't have to bring up all defenses at No. 1

. . . .

The judgment must be reversed, with costs, and a new trial ordered.

[The concurring opinion of Justice Graves is omitted.]

Questions: (2) What arguments may be made that the Jacobson decision was wrong? See Denio v. City of Huntington Beach, 74 Cal.App.2d 424, 168 P.2d 785, cert. denied, 329 U.S. 773, 67 S.Ct. 191 (1946); cf. 18 Wright, Miller & Cooper § 4414, at 119–21.

(3) As the realm of issue preclusion is allowed to expand to reach some matters not really considered in the prior action—which may be done by enlarging the dimensions of the "issue" or by other means—what differences, if any, remain between the doctrines of issue preclusion and claim preclusion? See 18 Wright, Miller & Cooper § 4406, at 44 ("The distinction is one of emphasis and degree, no more."); id. § 4417, at 157 ("If different theories and consequences are to apply, care must be taken in seeking the most useful distinction possible."); cf. Currie, Res Judicata: The Neglected Defense, 45 U.Chi.L.Rev. 317, 336–42 (1978).

(4) Assuming an issue has been properly raised, by the pleadings or otherwise, should it be deemed "actually litigated and determined" if it is disposed of via directed verdict? summary judgment? demurrer? total absence of proof? stipulation? admission? default?

RES JUDICATA AND THE MECHANICS OF SETTLEMENT

When a prospective defendant settles a claim by payment of an agreed sum before action is brought, it is routine practice for him to condition his payment upon the execution by the intending plaintiff of a release of the claim. Where a suit has been brought, the defendant still insists upon a release as a part of the settlement, but there is the additional problem of disposing of the pending lawsuit. The defendant is likely to insist upon a disposition on the record that will protect him as fully as possible against further litigation on the claim. In that way, if the plaintiff does bring a later action on the same claim, the defendant may plead not only the release as a defense but also res judicata.

At common law a voluntary nonsuit or discontinuance by the plaintiff was not a bar to a new suit. However, there was a common-law device called a retraxit, a voluntary renunciation of his claim by the plaintiff in open court, which both terminated the particular action and barred relitigation of the same cause. It may be assumed that in practice such a renunciation was commonly made only when a settlement had been reached.

Under present-day practice a mere voluntary dismissal is not a bar, nor is a dismissal by stipulation of the parties, unless the notice or order of dismissal or the stipulation states otherwise. See Rule 41(a). There is, however, some authority in state courts to the effect that a dismissal shown on its face to be by agreement is a bar to a new suit. E.g., Doan v. Bush, 130 Ark. 566, 198 S.W. 261 (1917). Another way to dispose of a lawsuit that has been settled is to enter a consent judgment for the plaintiff in the agreed amount, with a further entry of "Judgment satisfied." But the parties who have adjusted their differences may prefer not to spread upon the record the details of their arrangement. They may therefore file a consent judgment for the plaintiff in a nominal amount, with a "Judgment satisfied" entry. Or the defendant may insist, as a condition of the settlement, that the entry be "Judgment for the defendant." All these forms of consent judgment terminate the pending action and normally preclude another suit upon the same claim.

A consent judgment is satisfactory enough when there is no possibility of an action upon a different claim involving the same issues. As just suggested, a consent judgment, like a judgment by default, has bar or merger effect so far as the same claim is concerned, although nothing was in fact ever litigated. But when assertion of a different claim involving the same issues is possible, one must give attention to collateral estoppel. The customary statement of the rule of collateral estoppel specifies that the issue must have been actually litigated and determined in order for there to be collateral estoppel effect. It is all very well to say, as Professor James convincingly did in Consent Judgments as Collateral Estoppel, 108 U.Pa.L.Rev. 173 (1959), that consent judgments ought not to have collateral estoppel effect; but the fact remains that in some states, apparently a minority, the law is otherwise, as shown by Annot., 91 A.L.R.3d 1170, 1183–91 (1979). Failure by counsel to take into account this risk involved in a consent judgment has produced unintended and serious consequences for his client in a later action. In Biggio v. Magee, 272 Mass. 185, 172 N.E. 336 (1930), for example, Magee's suit against Biggio for injuries from an automobile accident had been settled by Biggio's attorney, actually an attorney retained and paid by his liability insurer, with an entry on the court record of judgment for Magee in a substantial sum by agreement of the parties and with a further entry of judgment satisfied. When Biggio, this time represented by counsel of his own choosing, sued Magee for his own injuries, he was held to be collaterally estopped by the consent judgment.[b]

How, then, should the parties effectuate their agreed settlement if they wish to avoid the risk of collateral estoppel? A consent judgment is in large part a contract of the parties, acknowledged in court and ordered to be recorded. The parties are free, unless a statute or rule of court otherwise provides, to include in this contract such terms as they wish. Just as they could manifest their intention to wind up the entire controversy (i.e., give collateral estoppel effect to the judgment), see Restatement (Second) of Judgments § 27 comment e (1980), so can they stipulate that the agreement is to have no effect on any other claim. Another approach is for the parties to agree on

[b] Massachusetts promptly enacted a statute to undo the result of this decision in actions within that state's compulsory automobile insurance law, unless the settlement agreement was signed by the defendant himself. 1932 Mass.Acts ch. 130, § 1 (current version at Mass.Gen. Laws Ann. ch. 231, § 140A).

Incidentally, Massachusetts had no applicable compulsory counterclaim provision.

"Judgment for neither party, no further action to be brought on this claim." Such an entry should terminate the pending action and preclude a new suit by the plaintiff upon the same claim, but it should have no collateral estoppel effect. See Gendron v. Hovey, 98 Me. 139, 56 A. 583 (1903). But how would such an entry have affected Horne v. Woolever?

Question: (5) Might it be better for courts to analyze consent judgments in contractual terms, looking directly to the parties' intent and discarding the res judicata analysis? Compare 1B Moore ¶¶ 0.409[5], 0.444[3], with 18 Wright, Miller & Cooper § 4443.

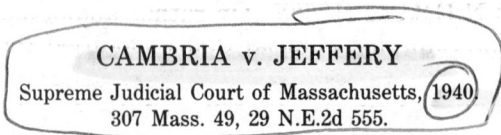

CAMBRIA v. JEFFERY
Supreme Judicial Court of Massachusetts, 1940.
307 Mass. 49, 29 N.E.2d 555.

TORT. Writ in the First District Court of Eastern Middlesex dated April 4, 1938.

No. 1 —
Dis Ct:
D was neg.
P didn't
use due
care

On removal to the Superior Court, the action was tried before Greenhalge, J. The finding of the judge of the District Court in the action of Jeffery v. Cambria was as follows: "Defendant was clearly negligent. The only question is as to the due care of the plaintiff operator. Taking all the circumstances into consideration including the fact that Concord Avenue on which defendant was driving is the more important street, I find that Ernest Jeffery did not use due care in entering the intersection."

LUMMUS, J. Two automobiles, one owned by the plaintiff Cambria and operated by his servant, the other owned and operated by the defendant Jeffery, had a collision.

No.1:
Judg =
both neg so
verdict for
D (Cam)

Jeffery brought in a District Court an action of tort for alleged negligence against Cambria to recover for bodily injury and damage to Jeffery's automobile. The judge found that the collision was caused by negligence of both operators, and therefore judgment was rendered in favor of the then defendant Cambria.

No. 2:
jury = Cam.
Judge = Jeff
b/c No.1 said
contrib neg

Afterwards the present action of tort, for alleged negligence of Jeffery causing damage to Cambria's automobile, was tried. The jury returned a verdict in favor of the plaintiff Cambria for $838.35; but the judge under leave reserved (G.L. [Ter.Ed.] c. 231, § 120) entered a verdict for the defendant Jeffery on the ground that the earlier judgment had adjudicated that the present plaintiff Cambria through his servant was guilty of contributory negligence, and reported the case.

Rule

A fact merely found in a case becomes adjudicated only when it is shown to have been a basis of the relief, denial of relief, or other ultimate right established by the judgment. [Citations omitted.]

The earlier judgment was in effect that Jeffery could not recover against Cambria. The sole basis for that judgment was the finding that Jeffery was guilty of contributory negligence. The further finding that Cambria's servant was negligent had no effect, and could have none, in producing that judgment. Therefore that judgment did not adjudicate that Cambria's servant was negligent.

No.1 only found contr. neg for Jeff → No findings on Cam's neg...

Verdict under leave reserved set aside.

Judgment upon the verdict returned by the jury.

HOME OWNERS FEDERAL SAVINGS & LOAN ASSOCIATION v. NORTHWESTERN FIRE & MARINE INSURANCE CO., 354 Mass. 448, 238 N.E.2d 55 (1968) On rather analogous facts and in a 4–3 decision, the Supreme Judicial Court modified the Cambria rule, in these words:

Modified Rule

"[O]ur holding expands the applicability of the doctrine to encompass certain findings not strictly essential to the final judgment in the prior action. Cf. Restatement, Judgments, § 68. Such findings may be relied upon if it is clear that the issues underlying them were treated as essential to the prior case by the court and the party to be bound. Stated another way, it is necessary that such findings be the product of full litigation and careful decision. Cf. Cambria v. Jeffery, 307 Mass. 49, 29 N.E.2d 555. This limited expansion of the class of findings within the ambit of the doctrine of collateral estoppel does no violence to the policies underlying the rule of the Cambria case, supra. See James, Civil Procedure, . . . at p. 583. We deem this limited extension of the rule warranted in view of the strong and oft-stated public policy of limiting each litigant to one opportunity to try his case on the merits." [c]

Questions: (6) *A* sues *B* for interest on a note. *B* alleges fraud in the execution of the note and a release of the obligation to pay interest. Upon trial, *A* gets verdict and judgment. After maturity, *A* sues *B* for the note's principal. Is the prior judgment conclusive on the question of fraud?

(7) If instead there had been a general verdict and judgment for *B* in that first action, could *B* make effective use of the judgment in the subsequent action for the principal?

ALTERNATIVE DETERMINATIONS

What if a party prevails upon the determination of each of two issues, either of which standing alone would be sufficient to support judgment in his favor? Imagine, for example, that in question (7) *B*'s victory in the first action came after trial before a judge who, sitting

[c] In Rudow v. Fogel, 376 Mass. 587, 382 N.E.2d 1046 (1978) (alternative holding) (Kaplan, J.), the Supreme Judicial Court unanimously readopted the Cambria rule.

without a jury, expressly found for *B* on both issues. Restatement of Judgments § 68 comment n (1942) took the position that the judgment is binding on both issues. The judgment is not based on one issue more than on the other, so it must be said that it is conclusive as to both issues or as to neither. The comment continued: "It seems obvious that it should not be held that neither is material, and hence both should be held to be material."

Questions: (8) Why is it obvious?

(9) How is this situation different from Cambria v. Jeffery?

In Halpern v. Schwartz, 426 F.2d 102 (2d Cir.1970), Evelyn Halpern had been involuntarily adjudicated a bankrupt on each of three different grounds, only one of which had involved a finding of actual intent to hinder, delay, or defraud creditors. In a later proceeding Mrs. Halpern sought a discharge in bankruptcy. The Bankruptcy Act provided that a discharge shall not be granted if the court finds the bankrupt acted with such intent. Mrs. Halpern was denied her discharge on the ground that the prior determination of intent was preclusive. The court of appeals reversed, holding, contrary to the First Restatement, that a judgment resting on alternative grounds (here three) is not preclusive as to any of the grounds.

Questions: (10) What arguments can you make in support of this decision?

(11) Assume that you as counsel have two alternative grounds of recovery in each of which you have confidence. What would your tactics at trial be if Halpern v. Schwartz was recognized as binding authority and you foresaw the likelihood of later litigation?

(12) Should there be, under the Halpern approach, a difference in result if there is an appeal and the appellate court expressly affirms on one of two alternative grounds? on both of the two alternative grounds?

Restatement (Second) of Judgments § 27 comments i, o (1980) takes a position contrary to the First Restatement, by providing that neither determination is preclusive unless appealed. The reporter's note thereon says that the question is a close and difficult one, but that the reasoning in Halpern v. Schwartz is highly persuasive.

Finally, in Malloy v. Trombley, 50 N.Y.2d 46, 52, 405 N.E.2d 213, 216, 427 N.Y.S.2d 969, 973 (1980) (4–3 decision), the New York Court of Appeals decided that the Halpern rule should not be applied rigidly and held "in this instance that the rule of issue preclusion is applicable notwithstanding that in a precise sense the issue precluded was the subject of only an alternative determination by the trial court. The issue was fully litigated, and the party precluded had full opportunity to be heard and was in no way, motivationally or procedurally, restricted or inhibited in the presentation of his position. Additionally, and critically in our view, the decision of the trial court gives significant internal evidence of the thorough and careful deliberation by that court, both in its consideration of the proof introduced and of the applicable law, and the determination made, although recognized to be an alternative, served a substantial operational purpose in the judicial process, thus negativing any conclusion that the trial court's resolution was casual or of any lesser quality than had the outcome of the trial depended solely on this issue."

Questions: (13) *A* sues *B* for interest on a note. *B* alleges fraud in the execution of the note and a release of the obligation to pay interest. In the trial court, *B* gets judgment upon a special verdict favorable on both issues. There is no appeal. Later, *A* sues *B* for a subsequent installment of interest on the note. Can *B* invoke issue preclusion based on the prior judgment?

(14) *A* sues *B* for a note's principal. *B* alleges prematurity of the action and also fraud in the execution of the note. In the trial court, *B* gets judgment upon a special verdict favorable on both issues. There is no appeal. After maturity, *A* sues *B* again for the note's principal. Can *B* invoke claim preclusion based on the prior judgment? issue preclusion? Compare Restatement (Second) of Judgments § 20 comment e (1980) (no bar), with Lucas, The Direct and Collateral Estoppel Effects of Alternative Holdings, 50 U.Chi.L.Rev. 701, 707–14 (1983) (bar).

INCONSISTENT JUDGMENTS

In Donald v. J.J. White Lumber Co., 68 F.2d 441 (5th Cir.1934), a taxpayer brought several successive tax actions, each action relative to a different tax year. The computation of the tax each year depended upon the determination of the depletion allowance for standing timber. This in turn depended upon the value as of March 1, 1913, the effective date of the first modern income tax law, of standing timber on land acquired by the taxpayer before that date. The higher that value was, the greater the depletion allowance and hence the lower the tax. In the first action, the Board of Tax Appeals valued the standing timber on March 1, 1913, at $5.34 per thousand feet—and the tax for the year in question was figured on that basis. In the second action, the value on March 1, 1913, was adjudged by a federal district court to be $7.00 per thousand feet—and the tax for the year involved was computed accordingly. No reference was made to the valuation of the timber in the prior action. There was no appeal from the decision in either case. In a third action, covering a third tax year, the government contended that the $5.34 valuation of the first action was binding; the taxpayer contended that the $7.00 valuation of the second action controlled. The court of appeals held that the last judgment in time is controlling.

Question: (15) Why should the rule not be that neither determination is binding?

Suppose, however, that judgments of different states are involved. The same last-in-time rule ordinarily prevails and, indeed, is compelled by the full faith and credit clause. But imagine that *A* wins on an issue against *B* in State *X* and later relies upon that judgment in a case involving the same issue in State *Y*, arguing the judgment is entitled to full faith and credit, but the court of State *Y* wrongly rejects that argument and then decides in favor of *B*. After appealing unsuccessfully in State *Y*, *A* seeks certiorari from the Supreme Court of the United States, but it is denied. Then *A* commences a third case involving the same issue in State *X*, and *B* relies upon the State *Y* judgment as preclusive. Should the State *Y* judgment be controlling? See Restatement (Second) of Conflict of Laws § 114 comment b (1969); Ginsburg, Judgments in Search of Full Faith and Credit: The Last-in-Time Rule for Conflicting Judgments, 82 Harv.L.Rev. 798 (1969).

Question: (16) Do the Federal Rules require a defendant relying upon the collateral estoppel effect of a prior judgment to set it up in his pleading? See Rule 8(c). How about a plaintiff? See 18 Wright, Miller & Cooper § 4405, at 32–38.

BERLITZ SCHOOLS OF LANGUAGES OF AMERICA v. EVEREST HOUSE
United States Court of Appeals, Second Circuit, 1980.
619 F.2d 211.

[The facts, simplified to their essence, were as follows. Berlitz Schools and Berlitz Publications had sued certain defendants, including Charles Berlitz, in New York state court for unfair competition and trademark dilution under state law. In 1974 the court, although recognizing in accord with prior litigation that Charles Berlitz could not identify himself as author of language materials unless he made clear that he was not connected with the plaintiffs in any way, had found that the following book-cover disclaimer on his "Passport" series of language books sufficed to dispel confusion: "Charles Berlitz, world-famous linguist and author of more than 100 language teaching books, is the grandson of the founder of the Berlitz Schools. Since 1967, Mr. Berlitz has not been connected with the Berlitz Schools in any way." That judgment had been affirmed on appeal.

[Later Charles Berlitz authored the new "Step-By-Step" series of language books, on the cover of which were his name and that disclaimer. Those same plaintiffs sued in the United States District Court for the Southern District of New York for trademark infringement and unfair competition under the Lanham Act, 15 U.S.C. §§ 1051–1127. In 1979 the district court granted defendants' motion for summary judgment on the basis of collateral estoppel. Plaintiffs appealed.]

Before LUMBARD, MANSFIELD and NEWMAN, CIRCUIT JUDGES.

LUMBARD, CIRCUIT JUDGE:

. . . .

. . . . The question is whether the issues finally and necessarily determined in the state proceedings are identical to those presented to the district court for determination.

The sine qua non of an action for trademark infringement, dilution of a trademark or unfair competition, is a showing by the plaintiff of the likelihood of confusion as to the origin of the goods in issue at the consumer level. [Citations omitted.] Indeed, this is precisely the claim made by plaintiffs in the district court as well as in . . . the prior state proceedings.

. . . .

Plaintiffs' principal objection to the application of [collateral estoppel] is that the facts presented herein differ substantially from those before the state court in the prior proceedings. Thus, the principal question before us is: is the legend of Charles Berlitz's name and the disclaimer on the cover of the "Step-By-Step" language books substantially different from that which was given the blessing of the New York courts? This mixed question of fact and law was decided in favor of the defendants by the district court. We cannot say that the judgment of the district court was erroneous. On the contrary, the judgment is supported by the record and the applicable law.

The appellants argue that on the "Step-By-Step" cover the name "Charles Berlitz" is larger in proportion to the disclaimer which consequently is less noticeable, and that these factual differences are sufficient to justify the relief they seek. We disagree.

It is true that the legend "Charles Berlitz" is slightly larger on the "Step-By-Step" volumes than it was on the "Passport" series, and that the disclaimer legend is slightly reduced in size. These proportional modifications are, however, so minuscule as to be hardly detectable on visual inspection. The differences are not so great as to warrant another judicial proceeding. Of course, substantially greater discrepancies in the presentation of the name "Charles Berlitz" and the disclaimer of his association with Berlitz schools may give rise to claims which might not be barred by principles of res judicata and collateral estoppel.

. . . .

Regarding plaintiffs' assertion that they are entitled to de novo determination of their federally created Lanham Act rights in a federal court [because they did not assert those rights in the state proceedings], it is enough to say that their state and federal claims all involved the issue of the likelihood of confusion. The state courts have concurrent jurisdiction to determine those claims, and having deter-

mined them adversely to the plaintiffs, that is the end of the matter.
. . . .

Accordingly, . . . the judgment which dismissed the complaint is affirmed.

Question: (17) Given such differences in circumstances between two actions, is the proper question in the second action (a) whether the same issue of law-application is involved or (b) whether the different circumstances should trigger an exception to otherwise applicable issue preclusion? Does this distinction have any significance?

SECTION 2. EXCEPTIONS TO THE RULE

UNITED STATES v. MOSER

Supreme Court of the United States, 1924.
266 U.S. 236, 45 S.Ct. 66.

[Moser was a cadet at the Naval Academy during the Civil War. Upon retirement forty years later, he sued in the Court of Claims for the difference between the pay of a captain and a rear admiral pursuant to a statute of the United States providing that "any officer of the Navy, with a creditable record, who served during the civil war shall, when retired, be retired with the rank and three-fourths the sea pay of the next higher grade." The government contended that service at the Naval Academy did not constitute service during the Civil War within the meaning of the statute, but the Court of Claims rejected the contention and decided in Moser's favor.

[Later in a suit by another claimant similarly situated, one Jasper, the Court of Claims had its attention called to another retirement statute, previously overlooked, and by reference to that statute denied Jasper recovery.

[In two subsequent actions by Moser for later installments of salary, the Court of Claims declined to follow the Jasper case, holding that by reason of its decision in the first Moser case the question was concluded as to Moser. In the present (fourth) action by Moser, the Court of Claims again held for him on the same ground. It ruled, alternatively, that its decision in the Jasper case was unsound as a matter of statutory interpretation and should be abandoned.]

MR. JUSTICE SUTHERLAND delivered the opinion of the Court.

. . . .

We find it unnecessary to consider the latter ruling, since we are of opinion that the court was clearly right in its application of the doctrine of res judicata.

The general principles are well settled, and need not be discussed. The scope of their application depends upon whether the question arises in a subsequent action between the same parties upon the same claim or demand or upon a different claim or demand. In the former case a judgment upon the merits constitutes an absolute bar to the subsequent action. In the latter case the inquiry is whether the point or question presented for determination in the subsequent action is the same as that litigated and determined in the original action. Cromwell v. County of Sac, 94 U.S. 351, 352–353. . . .

. . . . .

The suits here are upon different demands; and the point at issue is to be determined by applying the second branch of the rule. The question expressly and definitely presented in this suit is the same as that definitely and actually litigated and adjudged in favor of the claimant in the three preceding suits, viz.: whether he occupied the status of an officer who had served during the civil war.

The contention of the Government seems to be that the doctrine of res judicata does not apply to questions of law; and, in a sense, that is true. It does not apply to unmixed questions of law. Where, for example, a court in deciding a case has enunciated a rule of law, the parties in a subsequent action upon a different demand are not estopped from insisting that the law is otherwise, merely because the parties are the same in both cases. But a *fact, question* or *right* distinctly adjudged in the original action cannot be disputed in a subsequent action, even though the determination was reached upon an erroneous view or by an erroneous application of the law. That would be to affirm the principle in respect of the thing adjudged but, at the same time, deny it all efficacy by sustaining a challenge to the grounds upon which the judgment was based. [Citations omitted.] A determination in respect of the status of an individual upon which his right to recover depends is as conclusive as a decision upon any other matter. [Citations omitted.]

Affirmed.

————

Questions: (18) In an action to recover customs duties from Importer *A*, the court determines that the articles in question fall within a classification that makes them duty-free. In a later action involving Importer *B*, the court determines that articles of the same kind fall within a classification requiring payment of a substantial duty. Then Importer *A* imports additional articles of the same kind. Is the judgment in the first action preclusive on the issue of classification? See United States v. Stone & Downer Co., 274 U.S. 225, 47 S.Ct. 616 (1927) (suggesting no).

(19) Ex-cadet Moser continued for life to have his pension fixed at the higher rate dictated by the result of United States v. Moser. Ex-cadet Jasper continued for life to have his pension fixed at the lower rate, despite an ingenious effort by his administrator to alter the result by a retroactive appointment to a higher rank. Was the continued disparity of treatment of

Moser and Jasper more justifiable than allowing Importer *A* in the preceding question a permanent built-in competitive advantage?

MONTANA v. UNITED STATES, 440 U.S. 147, 99 S.Ct. 970 (1979). Montana imposed a 1% gross-receipts tax upon contractors on public, but not private, construction projects in Montana. The United States was involved in launching a state-court challenge to the tax on the ground that it discriminated against the United States in violation of the Federal Constitution. The Montana Supreme Court ultimately upheld the tax in 1973 ("Kiewit I"), and further appeal was abandoned.

Asserting a new claim that arose in connection with similar federal contracts, the United States challenged the Montana tax anew in the United States District Court for the District of Montana. The United States prevailed below. But the Supreme Court of the United States reversed, as Justice Marshall explained for the Court:

"A fundamental precept of common-law adjudication, embodied in the related doctrines of collateral estoppel and res judicata, is that a 'right, question or fact distinctly put in issue and directly determined by a court of competent jurisdiction . . . cannot be disputed in a subsequent suit between the same parties or their privies . . . .' Southern Pacific R. Co. v. United States, 168 U.S. 1, 48–49, 18 S.Ct. 18, 27 (1897). Under res judicata, a final judgment on the merits bars further claims by parties or their privies based on the same cause of action. Cromwell v. County of Sac, 94 U.S. 351, 352 (1877); Lawlor v. National Screen Service Corp., 349 U.S. 322, 326, 75 S.Ct. 865, 867 (1955); 1B J. Moore, Federal Practice ¶ 0.405[1], pp. 621–624 (2d ed. 1974) (hereinafter 1B Moore); Restatement (Second) of Judgments § 47 (Tent. Draft No. 1, Mar. 28, 1973) (merger); id., § 48 (bar). Under collateral estoppel, once an issue is actually and necessarily determined by a court of competent jurisdiction, that determination is conclusive in subsequent suits based on a different cause of action involving a party to the prior litigation. Parklane Hosiery Co. v. Shore, 439 U.S. 322, 326 n. 5, 99 S.Ct. 645, 649 n. 5 (1979); Scott, Collateral Estoppel by Judgment, 56 Harv.L.Rev. 1, 2–3 (1942); Restatement (Second) of Judgments § 68 (Tent. Draft No. 4, Apr. 15, 1977) (issue preclusion). Application of both doctrines is central to the purpose for which civil courts have been established, the conclusive resolution of disputes within their jurisdictions. Southern Pacific R. Co., supra, 168 U.S., at 49, 18 S.Ct., at 27; Hart Steel Co. v. Railroad Supply Co., 244 U.S. 294, 299, 37 S.Ct. 506, 507 (1917). To preclude parties from contesting matters that they have had a full and fair opportunity to litigate protects their adversaries from the expense and vexation attending multiple lawsuits, conserves judicial resources, and fosters reliance on judicial action by minimizing the possibility of inconsistent decisions.

. . . . .

"To determine the appropriate application of collateral estoppel in the instant case necessitates three further inquiries: first, whether the issues presented by this litigation are in substance the same as those resolved against the United States in Kiewit I; second, whether controlling facts or legal principles have changed significantly since the state-court judgment; and finally, whether other special circumstances warrant an exception to the normal rules of preclusion.

A

"A review of the record in Kiewit I dispels any doubt that the plaintiff there raised and the Montana Supreme Court there decided the precise constitutional [challenges advanced here]. . . .

. . . .

"Thus, the 'question expressly and definitely presented in this suit is the same as that definitely and actually litigated and adjudged' adversely to the Government in state court. United States v. Moser, 266 U.S. 236, 242, 45 S.Ct. 66, 67 (1924). Absent significant changes in controlling facts or legal principles since Kiewit I, or other special circumstances, the Montana Supreme Court's resolution of these issues is conclusive here.

B

"Relying on Commissioner of Internal Revenue v. Sunnen, 333 U.S. 591, 68 S.Ct. 715 (1948), the United States argues that collateral estoppel extends only to contexts in which 'the controlling facts and applicable legal rules remain unchanged.' Id., at 600, 68 S.Ct., at 720. In the Government's view, factual stasis is missing here because the contract at issue in Kiewit I contained a critical provision which the contracts involved in the instant litigation do not.

[The Court concluded that the Montana Supreme Court's opinion in Kiewit I had not been essentially predicated on the existence of that particular contractual provision and that therefore the change in facts did not suffice to avoid issue preclusion.]

"Thus, unless there have been major changes in the law governing intergovernmental tax immunity since Kiewit I, the Government's reliance on Commissioner of Internal Revenue v. Sunnen, 333 U.S. 591, 68 S.Ct. 715 (1948), is misplaced. Sunnen involved the tax status of certain income generated by a license agreement during a particular tax period. Although previous litigation had settled the status of income from the same agreement during earlier tax years, the Court declined to give collateral estoppel effect to the prior judgment because there had been a significant 'change in the legal climate.' Id., at 606, 68 S.Ct., at 723. Underlying the Sunnen decision was a concern that modifications in 'controlling legal principles,' id., at 599, 68 S.Ct., at 720, could render a previous determination inconsistent with prevailing doctrine, and that

> '[i]f such a determination is then perpetuated each succeeding year as to the taxpayer involved in the original litigation, he is accorded a tax treatment different from that given to other taxpayers of the same class. As a result, there are inequalities in the administration of the revenue laws, discriminatory distinctions in tax liability, and a fertile basis for litigious confusion. [Collateral estoppel] is not meant to create vested rights in decisions that have become obsolete or erroneous with time, thereby causing inequities among taxpayers.' Ibid. (citations omitted).

No such considerations obtain here. The Government does not contend and the District Court did not find that a change in controlling legal principles had occurred between Kiewit I and the instant suit. That the Government's amended complaint in this action replicates in substance the legal argument advanced by the . . . complaint in Kiewit I further suggests the absence of any major doctrinal shifts since the Montana Supreme Court's decision.

"Because the factual and legal context in which the issues of this case arise has not materially altered since Kiewit I, normal rules of preclusion should operate to relieve the parties of 'redundant litigation [over] the identical question of the statute's application to the taxpayer's status.' Tait v. Western Maryland R. Co., 289 U.S. 620, 624, 53 S.Ct. 706, 707 (1933). See United States v. Russel Mfg. Co., 349 F.2d 13, 18–19 (CA2 1965).

C

"The sole remaining question is whether the particular circumstances of this case justify an exception to general principles of estoppel. Of possible relevance is the exception which obtains for 'unmixed questions of law' in successive actions involving substantially unrelated claims. United States v. Moser, 266 U.S. 236, 242, 45 S.Ct. 66, 67 (1924). . . . Thus, when issues of law arise in successive actions involving unrelated subject matter, preclusion may be inappropriate. See Restatement (Second) of Judgments § 68.1, Reporter's Note, pp. 43–44 (Tent. Draft No. 4, Apr. 15, 1977); 1B Moore ¶ 0.448, p. 4235; Scott, 56 Harv.L.Rev., at 10. This exception is of particular importance in constitutional adjudication. Unreflective invocation of collateral estoppel against parties with an ongoing interest in constitutional issues could freeze doctrine in areas of the law where responsiveness to changing patterns of conduct or social mores is critical. To be sure, the scope of the Moser exception may be difficult to delineate, particularly where there is partial congruence in the subject matter of successive disputes. But the instant case poses no such conceptual difficulties. Rather, as the preceding discussion indicates, the legal 'demands' of this litigation are closely aligned in time and subject matter to those in Kiewit I.

. . . .

"Finally, the Government has not alleged unfairness or inadequacy in the state procedures to which it voluntarily submitted.[11] We must conclude therefore that it had a full and fair opportunity to press its constitutional challenges in Kiewit I. Accordingly, the Government is estopped from seeking a contrary resolution of those issues here."

Justice Rehnquist concurred in "the Court's opinion on the customary understanding that its references to . . . drafts or finally adopted versions of the Restatement of Judgments are not intended to bind the Court to the views expressed therein on issues not presented by the facts of this case."

Justice White dissented on the grounds that the change in facts sufficed to avoid issue preclusion and that the tax was unconstitutional.

————

COURTS OF LIMITED JURISDICTION

It frequently happens that issue preclusion is asserted in an action that would be outside the jurisdiction of the court that rendered the prior judgment. Should issue preclusion effect be given in such a situation? The decisions are widely divergent. Consider the illustrative cases set forth below, which are designed to suggest that a flat answer either way is an unduly rigid approach.

1. *A* sues *B* for negligently inflicted property damage in a county court with jurisdiction limited to $5000. Should a judgment holding *B* negligent and *A* in the exercise of due care be given collateral estoppel effect in *B*'s action against *A* in a court of general jurisdiction for $100,000 damages sustained in the same accident? See Gollner v. Cram, 258 Minn. 8, 102 N.W.2d 521 (1960).

2. Same as case (1) except that the first court is a small-claims court that has a $1000 limit and operates informally without pleadings, counsel, or strict rules of evidence. Is this to be distinguished from case (1)? See Sanderson v. Niemann, 17 Cal.2d 563, 110 P.2d 1025 (1941); cf. N.Y. City Civ.Ct.Act § 1808 ("A judgment obtained under this [small-claims] article may be pleaded as res judicata only as to the amount involved in the particular action and shall not otherwise be deemed an adjudication of any fact at issue or found therein in any other action or court.").

[11] Redetermination of issues is warranted if there is reason to doubt the quality, extensiveness, or fairness of procedures followed in prior litigation. See Restatement (Second) of Judgments § 68.1(c) (Tent. Draft No. 4, Apr. 15, 1977); [other citations omitted].

3. A surrogate's court—the jurisdiction of which is limited to wills, administration of estates, guardianship, and the like—decides in favor of an attorney claiming sizable fees against an estate, with the court necessarily holding that he did not commit a certain alleged fraud while administering the estate. Should this determination be given collateral estoppel effect by a court of general jurisdiction, in a suit for damages for the fraud brought against the attorney by an adverse party to the prior proceeding? See United States v. Silliman, 167 F.2d 607 (3d Cir.) (giving preclusive effect), cert. denied, 335 U.S. 825, 69 S.Ct. 48 (1948).

4. A state court in an action for license fees for use of a patent, a matter within the state court's jurisdiction, determines that the patent is invalid. Should a federal court give issue preclusion effect to this determination in a patent infringement action between the same parties and on the same patent, a matter within exclusive federal jurisdiction? What factors should be taken into account in answering this question? See 18 Wright, Miller & Cooper § 4470.

UNFORESEEABILITY OF FUTURE LITIGATION

In Evergreens v. Nunan, 141 F.2d 927, 929 (2d Cir.), cert. denied, 323 U.S. 720, 65 S.Ct. 49 (1944), Judge Learned Hand said: "Were the law to be recast, it would . . . be a pertinent inquiry whether the conclusiveness . . . of facts decided in the first [suit], might not properly be limited to future controversies which could be thought reasonably in prospect when the first suit was tried. . . . Logical relevance is of infinite possibility; there is no conceivable limit which can be put to it. Defeat in one suit might entail results beyond all calculation by either party; a trivial controversy might bring utter disaster in its train." However, Judge Hand did not feel free to recast the law in this way. Instead, in an attempt to place a reasonable restriction upon the extent to which a determination in the first suit precluded its relitigation in a second, Judge Hand drew a distinction between "ultimate facts" and "mediate data" at issue in the second suit. The latter, being merely premises from which the "ultimate facts" could be inferred, were held to be beyond the reach of issue preclusion. Only "ultimate facts" in the second suit could be conclusively established by prior determination. This distinction has received some support.

The distinction between "ultimate facts" and "mediate data" is, however, vague and difficult to apply. It has been criticized by several commentators, who have suggested that truer hazards lie in making conclusive henceforth a determination that is not seriously contested or in imposing the risk of completely unforeseeable consequences. See, e.g., F. James & G. Hazard, Civil Procedure 568–69 (2d ed. 1977). This alternative of recasting the law in terms of foreseeability has had some judicial support. In an early and prominent example, Hyman v. Regenstein, 258 F.2d 502, 511 (5th Cir.1958) (dictum), the court said that "collateral estoppel by judgment is applicable only when it is evident from the pleadings and record that determination of the fact in question was necessary to the final judgment and it was foreseeable that the fact would be of importance in possible future litigation." It seems that Judge Hand's actual decision in Evergreens will prove to be less influential than his dictum concerning foreseeability.

Question: (20) Although the foreseeability test is couched in terms of limitation, should it be used to extend collateral estoppel beyond essential issues actually litigated and determined in cases like Jacobson v. Miller where the prospect of future litigation was apparent at the time of the first action? See Developments in the Law—Res Judicata, 65 Harv.L.Rev. 818, 841 (1952).

SPILKER v. HANKIN

United States Court of Appeals, District of Columbia Circuit, 1951.
188 F.2d 35.

[Mrs. Spilker gave her attorney Hankin a series of seven notes in payment for legal services. The first was a demand note for $500; and the others, each in the amount of $250, became due at three-month intervals thereafter. Mrs. Spilker paid the demand note. When she failed to pay the second note, Hankin sued thereon in the Municipal Court for the District of Columbia. Mrs. Spilker pleaded duress, alleged that the note in suit was for an exorbitant and unconscionable fee, and further alleged that Hankin had already been overpaid. She also filed a counterclaim seeking a determination that the amount already paid was to be considered full payment for his services and asking that the remaining notes be declared void. In a trial without jury, Hankin was awarded judgment on the note, and the counterclaim was disallowed. There was no appeal.

[Later Hankin brought the present action in the same court on the five remaining notes, all of which had now become due. Mrs. Spilker's chief defense was misrepresentation, and she again urged that she had paid Hankin all his professional services were worth. The plaintiff's motion for summary judgment on the ground that the defendant was precluded by the prior judgment was denied. There was a jury trial leading to a verdict and judgment for the defendant. The Municipal Court of Appeals reversed and ordered judgment for the plaintiff. The defendant appealed.]

Before CLARK, FAHY and WASHINGTON, CIRCUIT JUDGES.

WASHINGTON, CIRCUIT JUDGE.

. . . . .

We agree with much that the learned Municipal Court of Appeals has said with regard to the principles of res judicata. We agree, for example, that in successive suits on a series of notes, defenses failing in the first suit ordinarily are foreclosed to the defendant in subsequent litigation. Restatement, Judgments § 68, Comments c, m, Illustration 5. But, with all respect to that court, we consider that weight should have been given to a factor not mentioned in its discussion of the case, that is, the fiduciary relationship of attorney and client which existed between the parties. In a very real sense attorneys are officers of the courts in which they practice; and clients are wards of the court in regard to their relationship with their attorneys. This factor is one of high significance in the present context.

The doctrine of res judicata is but the technical formulation of the "Public policy . . . that there be an end of litigation; that those who have contested an issue shall be bound by the result of the contest; and that matters once tried shall be considered forever settled as between the parties." Baldwin v. Iowa State Traveling Men's Ass'n, 283 U.S. 522, 525, 51 S.Ct. 517, 518, 75 L.Ed. 1244. This policy has long been a tenet of the common law, and even finds expression in the Constitution of the United States, in the full faith and credit clause. Experience has taught that as a general rule there is no reason why the doctrine of res judicata "should not apply in every case where one voluntarily appears, presents his case and is fully heard . . . ." [2] But rules and policies such as these must be weighed against competing necessities: situations may arise which call for exceptions. Recently this court decided a case involving such a situation, and held that "Where the application of the judicial doctrine res judicata would be inconsistent with the method devised by Congress the doctrine will not be enforced by the courts. Kalb v. Feuerstein, 1940, 308 U.S. 433, 444, 60 S.Ct. 343, 84 L.Ed. 370. It is for this reason we hold against the contention of petitioners, and not because of lack of any of the elements which usually make out a case for the application of res judicata. The doctrine is not to be used where the circumstances create a semblance of conditions for its application but to apply it would submerge the plan of Congress for the administration and enforcement of its policy." Denver Building & Construction Trades Council v. N.L.R.B., 87 U.S.App.D.C. 293, 186 F.2d 326, 332.

Other policies, not embodied in a congressional mandate, have compelled the same result. For example, while the courts of this country, as a general rule, have given res judicata effect to judgments of foreign countries, there have been situations where American courts have refused such recognition for policy reasons.[5] Decisions of this sort demonstrate that res judicata, as the embodiment of a public policy, must, at times, on occasion, yield to other policies.

---

[2] Baldwin v. Iowa State Traveling Men's Ass'n, supra.

[5] See, e.g., Hilton v. Guyot, 159 U.S. 113, 16 S.Ct. 139, 40 L.Ed. 95 . . . . [See infra p. 1080.—Ed.]

Fee contracts between attorney and client are a subject of special interest and concern to the courts. They are not to be enforced upon the same basis as ordinary commercial contracts. Especially is this true where, as in this case, a contract beneficial to the attorney is executed long after the attorney-client relationship has commenced, when the position of trust is well established, and the litigation involved is reaching its culmination. . . . When he seeks to enforce such a note the attorney cannot rely upon the usual commercial principles relative to negotiable instruments; he must rely upon the same basic considerations as if he were asking the court to enforce a fee arrangement not reflected in a note or notes.

Ordinarily the matter of a fee will be litigated but once, and the first determination will be conclusive. Were this merely a suit upon the original judgment we would, of course, consider res judicata to be applicable. But here we have a series of notes, one brought into litigation prior to the others. The original suit was for a much smaller amount, and some of the issues here in question were only indirectly involved in it. And it is the attorney who seeks further court aid with regard to his fee. The fee arrangement in question was reduced to promissory notes shortly before the termination of the litigation in which the attorney acted for the client, and appears to have been required by the attorney as a condition of his remaining in the case. While we do not mean to imply that an attorney can never protect himself with regard to his fee by making an arrangement of this sort, we consider that when under such circumstances the attorney twice brings the matter into court, the requirements of justice are better served by permitting reexamination of the merits than by treating the prior suit as foreclosing the matter. We think that the client should be permitted to make any legal or equitable defense to the remaining notes which appeals to the conscience of the court.

. . . . .

Reversed and remanded.

RESTATEMENT (SECOND) OF JUDGMENTS
(1980).

§ 28. *Exceptions to the General Rule of Issue Preclusion*

Although an issue is actually litigated and determined by a valid and final judgment, and the determination is essential to the judgment, relitigation of the issue in a subsequent action between the parties is not precluded in the following circumstances:

(1) The party against whom preclusion is sought could not, as a matter of law, have obtained review of the judgment in the initial action; or

1024

(2) The issue is one of law and (a) the two actions involve claims that are substantially unrelated, or (b) a new determination is warranted in order to take account of an intervening change in the applicable legal context or otherwise to avoid inequitable administration of the laws; or

(3) A new determination of the issue is warranted by differences in the quality or extensiveness of the procedures followed in the two courts or by factors relating to the allocation of jurisdiction between them; or

(4) The party against whom preclusion is sought had a significantly heavier burden of persuasion with respect to the issue in the initial action than in the subsequent action; the burden has shifted to his adversary; or the adversary has a significantly heavier burden than he had in the first action; or

(5) There is a clear and convincing need for a new determination of the issue (a) because of the potential adverse impact of the determination on the public interest or the interests of persons not themselves parties in the initial action, (b) because it was not sufficiently foreseeable at the time of the initial action that the issue would arise in the context of a subsequent action, or (c) because the party sought to be precluded, as a result of the conduct of his adversary or other special circumstances, did not have an adequate opportunity or incentive to obtain a full and fair adjudication in the initial action.

———

Question: (21) Should the general rule of issue preclusion be applied more flexibly, with a greater willingness to recognize exceptions, than the general rule of claim preclusion?

———

FEDERATED DEPARTMENT STORES v. MOITIE
Supreme Court of the United States, 1981.
452 U.S. 394, 101 S.Ct. 2424.

JUSTICE REHNQUIST delivered the opinion of the Court.

The only question presented in this case is whether the Court of Appeals for the Ninth Circuit validly created an exception to the doctrine of res judicata. The court held that res judicata does not bar relitigation of an unappealed adverse judgment where, as here, other plaintiffs in similar actions against common defendants successfully appealed the judgments against them. We disagree with the view taken by the Court of Appeals for the Ninth Circuit and reverse.

I

In 1976 the United States brought an antitrust action against petitioners, owners of various department stores, alleging that they had violated § 1 of the Sherman Act, 15 U.S.C. § 1, by agreeing to fix the retail price of women's clothing sold in Northern California. Seven parallel civil actions were subsequently filed by private plaintiffs seeking treble damages on behalf of proposed classes of retail purchasers, including that of respondent Moitie in state court (Moitie I) and respondent Brown (Brown I) in the United States District Court for the Northern District of California. Each of these complaints tracked almost verbatim the allegations of the Government's complaint, though the Moitie I complaint referred solely to state law. All of the actions originally filed in the District Court were assigned to a single federal judge, and the Moitie I case was removed there on the basis of diversity of citizenship and federal-question jurisdiction. The District Court dismissed all of the actions "in their entirety" on the ground that plaintiffs had not alleged an "injury" to their "business or property" within the meaning of § 4 of the Clayton Act, 15 U.S.C. § 15. Weinberg v. Federated Department Stores, 426 F.Supp. 880 (ND Cal.1977).

Plaintiffs in five of the suits appealed that judgment to the Court of Appeals for the Ninth Circuit. The single counsel representing Moitie and Brown, however, chose not to appeal and instead refiled the two actions in state court, Moitie II and Brown II.[1] Although the complaints purported to raise only state-law claims, they made allegations similar to those made in the prior complaints, including that of the Government. Petitioners removed these new actions to the District Court for the Northern District of California and moved to have them dismissed on the ground of res judicata. In a decision rendered July 8, 1977, the District Court first denied respondents' motion to remand. It held that the complaints, though artfully couched in terms of state law, were "in many respects identical" with the prior complaints, and were thus properly removed to federal court because they raised "essentially federal law" claims. The court then concluded that because Moitie II and Brown II involved the "same parties, the same alleged offenses, and the same time periods" as Moitie I and Brown I, the doctrine of res judicata required that they be dismissed. This time, Moitie and Brown appealed.

Pending that appeal, this Court on June 11, 1979 decided Reiter v. Sonotone Corp., 442 U.S. 330, 99 S.Ct. 2326, holding that retail purchasers can suffer an "injury" to their "business or property" as those terms are used in § 4 of the Clayton Act. On June 25, 1979, the Court of Appeals for the Ninth Circuit reversed and remanded the five cases which had been decided with Moitie I and Brown I, the cases that had been appealed, for further proceedings in light of Reiter.

When Moitie II and Brown II finally came before the Court of Appeals for the Ninth Circuit, the court reversed the decision of the

---

[1] Petitioners have filed a supplemental memorandum with the Court indicating that Moitie II has been voluntarily dismissed, leaving Brown II as the subject of the petition.

District Court dismissing the cases. 611 F.2d 1267.[2] Though the court recognized that a "strict application of the doctrine of res judicata would preclude our review of the instant decision," it refused to apply the doctrine to the facts of this case. It observed that the other five litigants in the Weinberg cases had successfully appealed the decision against them. It then asserted that "non-appealing parties may benefit from a reversal when their position is closely interwoven with that of appealing parties," and concluded that "because the instant dismissal rested on a case that has been effectively overruled," the doctrine of res judicata must give way to "public policy" and "simple justice." Id., at 1269–1270. We granted certiorari, 449 U.S. 991, 101 S.Ct. 526 (1980), to consider the validity of the Court of Appeals' novel exception to the doctrine of res judicata.

II

There is little to be added to the doctrine of res judicata as developed in the case law of this Court. A final judgment on the merits of an action precludes the parties or their privies from relitigating issues that were or could have been raised in that action. Commissioner v. Sunnen, 333 U.S. 591, 597, 68 S.Ct. 715, 719 (1948); Cromwell v. County of Sac, 94 U.S. 351, 352–353 (1877). Nor are the res judicata consequences of a final, unappealed judgment on the merits altered by the fact that the judgment may have been wrong or rested on a legal principle subsequently overruled in another case. Angel v. Bullington, 330 U.S. 183, 187, 67 S.Ct. 657, 659 (1947); Chicot County Drainage District v. Baxter State Bank, 308 U.S. 371, 60 S.Ct. 317 (1940); Wilson's Executor v. Deen, 121 U.S. 525, 534, 7 S.Ct. 1004, 1007 (1887). As this Court explained in Baltimore Steamship Co. v. Phillips, 274 U.S. 316, 325, 47 S.Ct. 600, 604 (1927), an "erroneous conclusion" reached by the court in the first suit does not deprive the defendants in the second action "of their right to rely upon the plea of res judicata. . . . A judgment merely voidable because based upon an erroneous view of the law is not open to collateral attack, but can be corrected only by a direct review and not by bringing another action upon the same cause of action." We have observed that "the indulgence of a contrary view would result in creating elements

---

[2] The Court of Appeals also affirmed the District Court's conclusion that Brown II was properly removed to federal court, reasoning that the claims presented were "federal in nature." We agree that at least some of the claims had a sufficient federal character to support removal. As one treatise puts it, courts "will not permit plaintiff to use artful pleading to close off defendant's right to a federal forum . . . [and that] occasionally the removal court will seek to determine whether the real nature of the claim is federal, regardless of plaintiff's characterization." 14 Wright, Miller & Cooper, Federal Practice and Procedure § 3722, at 565–566 (1976 ed.) (citing cases). The District Court applied that settled principle to the facts of this case. After "an extensive review and analysis of the origins and substance of" the two Brown complaints, it found, and the Court of Appeals expressly agreed, that respondents had attempted to avoid removal jurisdiction by "artful[ly]" casting their "essentially federal law claims" as state-law claims. We will not question here that factual finding. [Citations omitted.]

of uncertainty and confusion and in undermining the conclusive character of judgments, consequences which it was the very purpose of the doctrine of res judicata to avert." Reed v. Allen, 286 U.S. 191, 201, 52 S.Ct. 532, 534 (1932).

In this case, the Court of Appeals conceded that the "strict application of the doctrine of res judicata" required that Brown II be dismissed. By that, the court presumably meant that the "technical elements" of res judicata had been satisfied, namely, that the decision in Brown I was a final judgment on the merits and involved the same claims and the same parties as Brown II.[3] The court, however, declined to dismiss Brown II because, in its view, it would be unfair to bar respondents from relitigating a claim so "closely interwoven" with that of the successfully appealing parties. We believe that such an unprecedented departure from accepted principles of res judicata is unwarranted. Indeed, the decision below is all but foreclosed by our prior case law.

In Reed v. Allen, 286 U.S. 191, 52 S.Ct. 532 (1932), this Court addressed the issue presented here. The case involved a dispute over the rights to property left in a will. *A* won an interpleader action for rents derived from the property and, while an appeal was pending, brought an ejectment action against the rival claimant *B*. On the basis of the decree in the interpleader suit *A* won the ejectment action. *B* did not appeal this judgment, but prevailed on his earlier appeal from the interpleader decree and was awarded the rents which had been collected. When *B* sought to bring an ejectment action against *A*, the latter pleaded res judicata, based on his previous successful ejectment action. This Court held that res judicata was available as a defense and that the property belonged to *A*:

> "The judgment in the ejectment action was final and not open to assault collaterally, but subject to impeachment only through some form of direct attack. The appellate court was limited to a review of the interpleader decree; and it is hardly necessary to say that jurisdiction to review one judgment gives an appellate court no power to reverse or modify another and independent judgment. If respondent, in addition to appealing from the [interpleader] decree, had appealed from the [ejectment] judgment, the appellate court, having both cases before it, might have afforded a remedy. . . . But this course respondent neglected to follow."
> Id., at 198, 52 S.Ct., at 533.

This Court's rigorous application of res judicata in Reed, to the point of leaving one party in possession and the other party entitled to the rents, makes clear that this Court recognizes no general equitable doctrine, such as that suggested by the Court of Appeals, which countenances an exception to the finality of a party's failure to ap-

---

[3] The dismissal for failure to state a claim under Fed.Rule Civ.Proc. 12(b)(6) is a "judgment on the merits." See Angel v. Bullington, 330 U.S. 183, 190, 67 S.Ct. 657, 661 (1947); Bell v. Hood, 327 U.S. 678, 66 S.Ct. 773 (1946).

peal merely because his rights are "closely interwoven" with those of another party. Indeed, this case presents even more compelling reasons to apply the doctrine of res judicata than did Reed. Respondents here seek to be the windfall beneficiaries of an appellate reversal procured by other independent parties, who have no interest in respondents' case, not a reversal in interrelated cases procured, as in Reed, by the same affected party. Moreover, in contrast to Reed, where it was unclear why no appeal was taken, it is apparent that respondents here made a calculated choice to forgo their appeals. See also Ackermann v. United States, 340 U.S. 193, 198, 71 S.Ct. 209, 211 (1950) (holding that petitioners were not entitled to relief under Fed.R.Civ.Pro. 60(b) when they made a "free, calculated, deliberate choic[e]" not to appeal).

The Court of Appeals also rested its opinion in part on what it viewed as "simple justice." But we do not see the grave injustice which would be done by the application of accepted principles of res judicata. "Simple justice" is achieved when a complex body of law developed over a period of years is evenhandedly applied. The doctrine of res judicata serves vital public interests beyond any individual judge's ad hoc determination of the equities in a particular case. There is simply "no principle of law or equity which sanctions the rejection by a federal court of the salutary principle of res judicata." Heiser v. Woodruff, 327 U.S. 726, 733, 66 S.Ct. 853, 856 (1946). The Court of Appeals' reliance on "public policy" is similarly misplaced. This Court has long recognized that "[p]ublic policy dictates that there be an end of litigation; that those who have contested an issue shall be bound by the result of the contest, and that matters once tried shall be considered forever settled as between the parties." Baldwin v. Traveling Men's Association, 283 U.S. 522, 525, 51 S.Ct. 517, 518 (1931). We have stressed that "[the] doctrine of res judicata is not a mere matter of practice or procedure inherited from a more technical time than ours. It is a rule of fundamental and substantial justice, 'of public policy and of private peace,' which should be cordially regarded and enforced by the courts . . . ." Hart Steel Co. v. Railroad Supply Co., 244 U.S. 294, 299, 37 S.Ct. 506, 507 (1917). The language used by this Court half a century ago is even more compelling in view of today's crowded dockets:

> "The predicament in which respondent finds himself is of his own making . . . . [W]e cannot be expected, for his sole relief, to upset the general and well-established doctrine of res judicata, conceived in the light of the maxim that the interest of the state requires that there be an end to litigation—a maxim which comports with common sense as well as public policy. And the mischief which would follow the establishment of precedent for so disregarding the salutary doctrine against prolonging strife would be greater than the benefit which would result from relieving some case of individual hardship." Reed v. Allen, supra, 286 U.S., at 198–199, 52 S.Ct., at 533.

Respondents make no serious effort to defend the decision of the Court of Appeals. They do not ask that the decision below be affirmed. . . . In their view, Brown I cannot be considered res judicata as to their *state*-law claims, since Brown I raised only federal-law claims and Brown II raised additional state-law claims not decided in Brown I, such as unfair competition, fraud, and restitution.

It is unnecessary for this Court to reach that issue. It is enough for our decision here that Brown I is res judicata as to respondents' federal-law claims. Accordingly, the judgment of the Court of Appeals is reversed, and the cause remanded for proceedings consistent with this opinion.

It is so ordered.

JUSTICE BLACKMUN, with whom JUSTICE MARSHALL joins, concurring in the judgment.

While I agree with the result reached in this case, I write separately to state my views on two points.

First, I, for one, would not close the door upon the possibility that there are cases in which the doctrine of res judicata must give way to what the Court of Appeals referred to as "overriding concerns of public policy and simple justice." 611 F.2d 1267, 1269 (CA9 1980). Professor Moore has noted: "Just as res judicata is occasionally qualified by an overriding, competing principle of public policy, so occasionally it needs an equitable tempering." 1B Moore's Federal Practice ¶ 0.405[12], at 791 (1974) (footnote omitted). See also Reed v. Allen, 286 U.S. 191, 209, 52 S.Ct. 532, 537 (1932) (Cardozo, J., joined by Brandeis and Stone, JJ., dissenting) ("A system of procedure is perverted from its proper function when it multiplies impediments to justice without the warrant of clear necessity"). But this case is clearly not one in which equity requires that the doctrine give way. Unlike the nonappealing party in Reed, respondents were not "caught in a mesh of procedural complexities." Ibid. Instead, they made a deliberate tactical decision not to appeal. Nor would public policy be served by making an exception to the doctrine in this case; to the contrary, there is a special need for strict application of res judicata in complex multiple party actions of this sort so as to discourage "break-away" litigation. Cf. Reiter v. Sonotone Corp., 442 U.S. 330, 345, 99 S.Ct. 2326, 2334 (1979). Finally, this is not a case "where the rights of appealing and non-appealing parties are so interwoven or dependent upon each other as to require a reversal of the whole judgment when a part thereof is reversed." See Ford Motor Credit Co. v. Uresti, 581 S.W.2d 298, 300 (Tex.Civ.App.1979).

Second, and in contrast, I would flatly hold that Brown I is res judicata as to respondents' state-law claims. . . . [E]ven if the state and federal claims are distinct, respondents' failure to allege the state claims in Brown I manifestly bars their allegation in Brown II. The dismissal of Brown I is res judicata not only as to all claims respondents actually raised, but also as to all claims that could have

been raised. See Commissioner v. Sunnen, 333 U.S. 591, 597, 68 S.Ct.
715, 719 (1948); Restatement (Second) of Judgments § 61.1 (Tent.
Draft No. 5, Mar. 10, 1978). Since there is no reason to believe that it
was clear at the outset of this litigation that the District Court would
have declined to exercise pendent jurisdiction over state claims, respondents were obligated to plead those claims if they wished to preserve them. See id., § 61.1, Comment e. Because they did not do so,
I would hold the claims barred.

JUSTICE BRENNAN, dissenting.

In its eagerness to correct the decision of the Court of Appeals for
the Ninth Circuit, the Court today disregards statutory restrictions
on federal-court jurisdiction, and, in the process, confuses rather than
clarifies long-established principles of res judicata. I therefore respectfully dissent.

[Justice Brennan proceeded to argue strongly that Brown II was
not removable. But assuming federal jurisdiction and turning to the
res judicata problem, Justice Brennan agreed with Justice Blackmun's second point, saying that the dismissal of the federal antitrust
action in Brown I "precludes relitigation of the same claim on a state-
law theory."]

EXCEPTIONS BASED ON POSTURE OF PARTY

A party does not always come within the reach of the rules of res
judicata that we have studied so far. A party may find himself in a
special posture in the litigation so that he does not have a full and
fair opportunity to litigate certain aspects of the case, and so that to
a certain extent the application of res judicata would be inappropriate. It could be said that, to such extent, the party will be deemed a
nonparty.

For example, Restatement (Second) of Judgments § 36(2) (1980)
provides: "A party appearing in an action in one capacity, individual
or representative, is not thereby bound by or entitled to the benefits
of the rules of res judicata in a subsequent action in which he appears
in another capacity." Thus, an individual is not normally precluded
by determinations in a previous action that he litigated as a trustee.
This exception frees the fiduciary to litigate that first action without
the influence of personal interest.

On a somewhat different point, the rules of res judicata that we
have studied so far do not normally apply between parties who were
not on opposite sides of the relevant claim—although issue preclusion
can apply if they in actuality did litigate the issue fully and fairly as
adversaries to each other. See id. § 38.

Questions: (22) *W*, administratrix of *H*'s estate, sues *D* for wrongful
death of *H* in an automobile accident wherein *H* and *D* were drivers. *D*
wins, with the court finding that *D* was not negligent. *W* then sues *D* for

her own personal injuries sustained in the same accident. May *D* invoke res judicata?

(23) An automobile passenger sues Driver *A* and Driver *B*, and she recovers against both. Then Driver *A* sues Driver *B*. Is the prior judgment controlling on the issues of the two drivers' negligence? See Schwartz v. Public Administrator, 24 N.Y.2d 65, 246 N.E.2d 725, 298 N.Y.S.2d 955 (1969) (issue preclusion applies). Why?

TOPIC D. EFFECTS ON PERSONS NOT PARTIES

SECTION 1. PERSONS BOUND BY PRIOR JUDGMENT

A judgment not only will preclude the parties thereto in the various ways already considered but also will have similar effects upon persons not parties who stand in a relation of "privity" to them. "Privity" is a term of art, and it does not necessarily follow that a person who is a privy of a party for any other purpose is a privy for the purpose of res judicata. Indeed, the word "privity" in this context has been called "a short method of stating that under the circumstances and for the purpose of the case at hand [a nonparty] is bound by and entitled to the benefits of all or some of the rules of res judicata." Restatement of Judgments § 83 comment a (1942). The Second Restatement does not use the term "privity"; instead, it treats in more than twenty separate sections the specific classes of nonparties falling to some degree within the reach of the binding rules of res judicata, classifying them as persons represented by parties or as persons having substantive legal relationships with parties resulting in preclusion or as persons whose conduct justifies preclusion. Nevertheless, if the word "privity" is clearly recognized as being conclusory, it remains useful as a general descriptive term.

The premise is that there must be some substantial reason to bind a nonparty. Conventionally, privies are taken to include among others the following:

1. *Persons who are actually represented by a party to an action.* For example, beneficiaries of an express trust will normally be bound or benefited by a judgment in an action to which the trustee, in his character as trustee, was a party. This principle is not limited to formal trusts or to fiduciary relationships such as that between administrator and beneficiaries of an estate, but extends to situations of representation like principal-agent and class actions.

2. *Successors in interest to a party's property involved in an action.* For example, A brings an action to quiet title to Blackacre against an assertion by B that he holds a mortgage on the land. Judgment is given for B, adjudging the mortgage to be good. A conveys to C after judgment. The judgment is binding in a later attempt by C to quiet title. If judgment had been for A in the first action, C would similarly have been entitled to benefit from the judgment.

3. *Nonparties who control the prosecution or defense of an action.* Such a person is bound by issue preclusion as if he were himself the party whose position he espouses. For example, A brings an action against B for infringement of A's patent in connection with B's manufacturing certain goods. B has a license from O to manu-

facture the goods under O's patent. O controls the defense of the A versus B action. If A gets a judgment of infringement against B, that determination will be preclusive in a later action between A and O.

INDEMNITY

There are numerous situations where either by contract or by operation of law a person is entitled to indemnity from another person against loss. The most familiar illustration of the former is the liability insurance contract in which the insurer undertakes to pay certain kinds of judgments against its insured and his attendant expenses, up to specified policy limits. (Under the typical policy, the insurer also undertakes to defend at its own expense claims made against the insured, and the insured obligates himself to give prompt notice of any accident and to cooperate in the defense.) An instance of indemnity by operation of law, already dealt with supra p. 190, is that of an employee whose negligent conduct in carrying out his employer's business is the sole basis of the employer's liability to a third person: the employee is legally bound to indemnify the employer for his loss. (In an ordinary automobile accident in which the employer is protected by liability insurance, the protection of the policy extends to the employee as well, pursuant to a standard policy provision covering, in addition to the named insured, any person operating his motor vehicle with his express or implied consent.)

When either type of indemnity is involved, the indemnitee who is sued may "vouch in" the indemnitor, a still-available common-law device whereby the indemnitee gives the indemnitor simple notice of the action and offers him control of the defense. Once so vouched in, whether or not he accepts control of the defense, the indemnitor normally will be bound by the judgment on the questions of the indemnitee's loss. However, the indemnitor normally will be free to litigate in a later action whether and to what extent he is obligated by contract or by operation of law to indemnify.

Instead of vouching in the indemnitor, the indemnitee may, in a federal court or in a state court with a rule like Rule 14, resort to impleader. This course allows the indemnitee to retain control of the defense and also to bring the indemnitor into the action and obtain a judgment against him. The effectiveness of impleader is limited, however, by the requirement of service—whereas, according to the better view, a person vouched in need not be within the reach of the court's process.

If the indemnitee neither vouches in nor impleads the indemnitor, he does not thereby lose his right to indemnity. He must, however, establish his claim all over again without reference to the prior judgment. In a second action, the indemnitee would have to offer practically the same proof relied upon by the injured person to establish the case against the indemnitee. This may leave the indemnitee the loser because of differing views of the evidence by the two fact-finders, and in any event it is a needless expense to him.

———

RESTATEMENT (SECOND) OF JUDGMENTS
(1980).

§ 52. *Bailee and Bailor*

(1) A judgment in an action by either bailee or bailor against a third party for interference with ownership or destruction of or damage to property that is the subject of a bailment precludes a subsequent action by either, except that:

(a) Where the claim is limited to the claimant's own loss in the property it does not preclude an action by the other for his loss;

(b) If the action is by the bailee it does not preclude an action by the bailor if the judgment was based on a defense not available against the bailor;

(c) An action by the bailee against the third party for claims arising out of the transaction in which the loss occurred does not preclude an action by the bailor for his loss if the third party was on notice that the bailee's action did not seek recovery for the bailor's interest.

(2) The determination of issues in an action by either bailee or bailor is not preclusive against the other of them in a subsequent action between the latter and the third party.

———

SHOW–WORLD CENTER v. WALSH, 438 F.Supp. 642 (S.D.N.Y. 1977). A landlord (303 Corp.) unsuccessfully sued New York City officials twice in state court to challenge a safety order and later an eviction order that was enforced against only one of its many tenants, a sex shop. The landlord alleged that the orders were unconstitutional parts of a campaign to ban sex-oriented activity from the Times Square area.

Next the tenant (Show-World) sued New York City officials to challenge the eviction on similar grounds under 42 U.S.C. § 1983. The district court rejected the application of res judicata for this reason:

"During all of these proceedings . . . 303 Corp. was represented by Ralph J. Schwarz, Jr. (Schwarz) who is also general counsel to Show-World. When Schwarz perceived that the Buildings Department was acting solely against Show-World, he decided that Show-World should be separately represented and called in outside counsel on its behalf.   Mr. Herald Price Fahringer has since represented Show-World.

. . . .

"A threshold issue of critical importance to disposition of the preliminary questions in this case . . . is the nature of the relationship between Show-World, the plaintiff in this action, and 303 Corp., the plaintiff in the two State court proceedings.   The only clear, undisputed facts on this issue are that Show-World was a tenant of 303 Corp., and that both corporations have had dealings with one attorney, Ralph Schwarz.   Mr. Schwarz has been General Counsel to Show-World since 1974, when he handled that entity's incorporation and negotiated its lease with 303 Corp.   During the lease negotiation, 303 Corp. was represented in the main by its President and sole shareholder, Wallace Katz, who looked to another lawyer for legal advice on that occasion.   Mr. Katz owns no part of Show-World and 303 Corp. owns no part of Show-World.

"During the State court proceedings, Mr. Schwarz represented only 303 Corp. although, on two occasions in the State court, he did identify himself as being also the attorney for Show-World, allegedly to provide support for his assertion of personal knowledge of some of the facts there in issue.   He admitted at the hearing in the instant case that he kept his client, Show-World, informed as to the course of the [administrative] proceedings . . . .   However, he made clear in this court that he at no time represented Show-World *as a party* in the State courts.

"On the basis of these facts adduced at the hearings thus far in the case, the court finds no privity between Show-World and 303 Corp. such as to equate the interests of the two entities in the State proceedings, and, thereby, to preclude the litigation by Show-World in this court.

"Assuming, without deciding, that Show-World might have had standing to intervene in either or both of the State proceedings to date, that fact alone would not be sufficient to bar this action.   The fact that a party has a right to intervene, which it chooses not to exercise, is not enough to make it bound by a judgment in the proceeding in which it possessed such a right.   Brown v. Wright, 137 F.2d 484, 487 (4th Cir. 1943);   Western Union Telegraph Company v. Foster, 247 U.S. 105, 38 S.Ct. 438, 62 L.Ed. 1006 (1918).

"Moreover, the mere existence of a landlord-tenant (lessor-lessee) relationship is insufficient to bind the tenant to the adjudication in the prior litigation to which the landlord only was a party.   While there is language in the two cases cited to the court by defendants which would tend to indicate that under some circumstances, the 'privity of estate' between landlord and tenant may cause the latter to be bound by prior judgments to which the landlord only was a party, Kruger & Birch, Inc. v. DuBoyce, 241 F.2d 849, 854 (3rd Cir. 1957);   Fouke v. Schenewerk, 197 F.2d 234, 236 (5th Cir. 1952) (dictum), those cases appear to involve only disputes relating to either title to, or right to possession of, real property. See 50 C.J.S. Judgments § 801 and cases cited therein; cf. Weiss v. Mayflower Doughnut Corp., 1 N.Y.2d 310, 152 N.Y.S.2d 471, 474, 135 N.E.2d 208 (N.Y.1956); Traveler's Insurance Company v. United States, 283 F.Supp. 14, 31 (S.D. Tex.1968). Certainly this court has been cited no authority for the proposition that a landlord's derivative assertion of his tenant's constitutional rights in a proceeding to which the tenant was not a party should bind the tenant in a later proceeding in which the tenant seeks to raise those important rights directly. In view of the possible conflict of interest between landlord and tenant, whose rights a landlord might, at least hypothetically, be willing to sacrifice, there appears to be no basis for binding the tenant to the former adjudication on the basis of its relation to the landlord qua landlord.

"Finally, and most clearly, privity is not established from the mere fact that Show-World may happen to be 'interested' in the same question at issue in the earlier proceedings in the New York courts, whether by way of establishing a proposition of law, or by proving or disproving some state of facts. Sodak Distributing Co. v. Wayne, 77 S.D. 496, 93 N.W.2d 791, 795 (1958); Howard v. Fairmont Machinery Co., Inc., 101 F.Supp. 778, 779 (E.D.Ky.1951). Nor does the fact that the prior decision might affect Show-World's action in this court as a favorable or unfavorable judicial precedent cause Show-World to be considered a privy to 303 Corp. in the earlier proceeding. Bigelow v. Old Dominion Copper Mining & Smelting Co., 225 U.S. 111, 32 S.Ct. 641, 56 L.Ed. 1009 (1912)."

———

NEENAN v. WOODSIDE ASTORIA TRANSPORTATION CO., 261 N.Y. 159, 184 N.E. 744 (1933). Judge Crane, for the court, said in part:

"On February 7, 1929, at the corner of Seventeenth avenue and Jamaica avenue, in the borough of Queens, New York City, a collision occurred between the automobile owned and operated by John J. Huppmann and a bus of the Woodside Astoria Transportation Co., Inc. Huppmann sued the transportation company for damages [in New York state court] and proved that the collision was due solely to the negligence of its driver to which no carelessness on his part contributed. He recovered a judgment of $2,153.75 against the company.

"Later, a passenger in the bus, Mary Neenan, sued both Huppmann and the Woodside Astoria Transportation Co., Inc., for the damages due to personal injuries received in the collision and, strange as it may seem, recovered a judgment of $1,500 against both defendants. Huppmann sought to introduce the judgment roll in his action against the transportation company, but of course it was not res judicata as to the passenger, Mary Neenan, as she was not a party to that action. She was free to prove that Huppmann was also negligent. If this were not so a responsible party might by collusion shift the liability upon an irresponsible person who cared little about a judgment against him. A plaintiff may hold all joint tort feasors. There was no error in excluding the judgment roll in the action of Mary Neenan."

Questions: (1) Would a holding that Mary Neenan was bound by the prior judgment be consistent with due process of law?

(2) NYCPA § 211–a, in force at the time of the Neenan case, provided that a defendant who had paid more than his pro rata share of a judgment (i.e., the amount of the judgment divided by the number of defendants jointly liable under the judgment) could obtain contribution from the other defendants to the extent of the excess. If Woodside satisfied Mary Neenan's judgment in full and sued Huppmann for contribution, what if any effect should be given to the judgment in the prior action of Huppmann v. Woodside?

(3) Would your answer to the preceding question be different under New York's new contribution statute, NYCPLR art. 14, which provides that a defendant who has paid more than his equitable share of a judgment (i.e., a share determined in accordance with his culpability relative to that of the other wrongdoers) can obtain contribution from the other wrongdoers to the extent of the excess?

SECTION 2. PERSONS ENTITLED TO BENEFITS OF PRIOR JUDGMENT

Mutuality of estoppel.—By definition, only parties and their privies are bound by a prior judgment, although of course the categories of "privies" are susceptible to stretching. Due process does not countenance binding other nonparties, who may be termed "strangers." Parties and their privies may also benefit from a prior judgment under the rules of res judicata. But may strangers benefit from the judgment, even though they are not bound?

First of all, collateral estoppel holds the greatest promise of benefits for such a person not a party or a privy. Usually, only parties and their privies may obtain the benefits of the other rules of res judicata, as in the example already given of a successor in interest who could invoke bar based on his predecessor's successful quiet-title action against a rival claimant. So let us first think in terms of a stranger's use of collateral estoppel.

The traditional approach to collateral estoppel derived from the general rule that estoppels must be mutual—that because a stranger to a prior judgment could not be bound by it, it is unfair to let him benefit from it. The Restatement of Judgments (1942) followed the generally prevailing case law in taking this narrow approach, but tempered it with exceptions to meet exigent situations. The result was a rather grudging retreat from mutuality, which ignored a growing body of decisions espousing an even broader view.

Examine once more the problem described supra p. 190: a servant *S*, driving his master *M*'s car on *M*'s business, is in a collision with a car owned and driven by *T*. The master-servant relation makes *M* liable to *T* for *S*'s negligence, if any; as between *M* and *S*, *S* is bound (in theory at least) to make good to *M* the loss *M* suffers by *S*'s negligence. Assume that *T* sues *S* and that *S* wins. Next *T* sues *M*, relitigating the issues of *S*'s negligence and *T*'s due care, and this time *T* recovers. On the one hand, if *M* can now get indemnity from *S*, *S* is forced to pay as a result of a trial to which he was not a party when he has already been exonerated from liability in a trial to which he was a party. On the other hand, if *M* cannot recover from *S*, *M* has lost his right of indemnity as a result of a trial to which he was not a party. The natural way around this dilemma would have been to allow *M* to plead res judicata against *T* based on the prior judgment for *S*. But if *T* had won against *S*, *T* could not have used the judgment against *M*, who had never had his day in court; the mutuality rule therefore prohibited that natural solution. This was too much for the First Restatement. So an exception to the mutuality rule was created to the extent necessary to protect *S*'s victory and *M*'s right of indemnity: *M*, the indemnitee, was allowed to use the judgment in favor of *S*, the indemnitor, as a defense to a second suit by *T*. See Restatement of Judgments § 96 (1942); see also Good Health Dairy Products Corp. v. Emery, 275 N.Y. 14, 9 N.E.2d 758 (1937).[a]

But what if *T*'s first suit was against *M* for *S*'s negligence and *M* won? Because it was *S* who was bound to indemnify *M* and not the other way around, the right of indemnity was not involved when *T* next sued *S*. Here the First Restatement stuck with the mutuality requirement and refused to let *S* take advantage of the first judgment. The result was to give *T* a second chance on the same issues by merely shifting adversaries. There was already authority contrary to the First Restatement's position, e.g., Giedrewicz v. Donovan, 277 Mass. 563, 179 N.E. 246 (1931), and much more thereafter.

Question: (4) What would the Massachusetts court do, in the light of Giedrewicz v. Donovan, if *T* successfully sued *M* for *S*'s negligence (with *T* winning after a trial at which *S* testified as a witness for *M*) and then *S* sued *T* for his own injuries? See Pesce v. Brecher, 302 Mass. 211, 19 N.E.2d 36 (1939) (no res judicata). Why?

Nevertheless, Restatement of Judgments § 99 (1942) recognized another breach in the wall of mutuality, which went beyond the narrow indemnity exception and which seemed to go beyond the demands of compelling need. This broader exception is illustrated by American Button Co. v. Warsaw Button Co., 31 N.Y.S.2d 395 (Sup. Ct.1941) (alternative holding), aff'd mem., 265 A.D. 905, 38 N.Y.S.2d

---

[a] Similarly, a judgment for *T* against *S* for $200 fixed that as the maximum liability of *M* if *T*, not having satisfied his judgment against *S*, sued *M*. See Pinnix v. Griffin, 221 N.C. 348, 20 S.E.2d 366 (1942).

570 (1942). In a prior action *A* had sued *B* for breach of contract, but had lost. Then *A* sued *W* for inducing *B* so to breach that contract with *A*. The prior judgment was held to preclude *A* from recovering against *W*. The First Restatement generalized the result: a judgment in favor of a person charged with commission of a tort or with breach of a contract normally precluded recovery by the same plaintiff against another defendant who was responsible for the conduct of the former defendant.

For years almost all courts avoided a frontal attack on mutuality, living instead within its framework by an increasing recognition of such exceptions. When the challenge finally came, it precipitated great controversy and great change in the law in most jurisdictions, a process that is still not fully played out.

COCA–COLA CO. v. PEPSI–COLA CO., 36 Del. 124, 172 A. 260 (Super.Ct.1934). Pepsi-Cola offered a $10,000 reward for information leading to the detection of any dealer substituting Pepsi-Cola for any other five-cent drink. Coca-Cola sued Pepsi-Cola, claiming the reward and alleging that it had made known to the defendant instances where certain dealers had substituted Pepsi-Cola for Coca-Cola, a five-cent drink. Pepsi-Cola pleaded res judicata, asserting that the identical issues had been decided against Coca-Cola in prior actions brought by Coca-Cola against the dealers in Delaware state court. Coca-Cola demurred to this plea. The court considered res judicata to be applicable, saying: "[W]e are of the opinion that a plaintiff who deliberately selects his forum and there unsucessfully presents his proofs, is bound by such adverse judgment in a second suit involving all the identical issues already decided. The requirement of mutuality must yield to public policy."

BERNHARD v. BANK OF AMERICA NATIONAL TRUST & SAVINGS ASSOCIATION
Supreme Court of California, 1942.
19 Cal.2d 807, 122 P.2d 892.

[Mrs. Sather authorized Cook to deposit money for her in the defendant bank. Cook did so, but later withdrew it, placed it in an account of his own, and used it for his own purposes. Mrs. Sather died, appointing Cook her executor. In Cook's accounting to the probate court, no mention was made of this money. Helen Bernhard and other beneficiaries under Mrs. Sather's will filed objections to Cook's account, claiming that Cook had embezzled the money from Mrs. Sather. The probate court after hearing found that Mrs. Sather in her lifetime had made a gift to Cook of the money in question, allowed Cook's account, and discharged him as executor.

[Thereafter Helen Bernhard was appointed administratrix with the will annexed; and she brought this suit against the defendant bank, seeking to recover the deposit for the estate on the ground that Mrs. Sather had never authorized its withdrawal. The defendant pleaded that the fact that the money was paid out to Cook with the consent of Mrs. Sather was res judicata by virtue of the finding of the probate court that she made a gift of it to Cook. The trial court gave judgment for the defendant on this ground. The plaintiff appealed.]

TRAYNOR, J.

. . . .

Plaintiff contends that the doctrine of res judicata does not apply because the defendant who is asserting the plea was not a party to the previous action nor in privity with a party to that action and because there is no mutuality of estoppel.

. . . .

Many courts have stated the facile formula that the plea of res judicata is available only when there is privity and mutuality of estoppel. [Citations omitted.] Under the requirement of privity, only parties to the former judgment or their privies may take advantage of or be bound by it. Ibid. A party in this connection is one who is "directly interested in the subject matter, and had a right to make defense, or to control the proceeding, and to appeal from the judgment." [Citations omitted.] A privy is one who, after rendition of the judgment, has acquired an interest in the subject matter affected by the judgment through or under one of the parties, as by inheritance, succession, or purchase. [Citations omitted.] The estoppel is mutual if the one taking advantage of the earlier adjudication would have been bound by it, had it gone against him. [Citations omitted.]

The criteria for determining who may assert a plea of res judicata differ fundamentally from the criteria for determining against whom a plea of res judicata may be asserted. The requirements of due process of law forbid the assertion of a plea of res judicata against a party unless he was bound by the earlier litigation in which the matter was decided. [Citations omitted.] He is bound by that litigation only if he has been a party thereto or in privity with a party thereto. Ibid. There is no compelling reason, however, for requiring that the party asserting the plea of res judicata must have been a party, or in privity with a party, to the earlier litigation.

No satisfactory rationalization has been advanced for the requirement of mutuality. Just why a party who was not bound by a previous action should be precluded from asserting it as res judicata against a party who was bound by it is difficult to comprehend. (See 7 Bentham's Works (Bowring's ed.) 171.[b]) Many courts have aban-

---

[b] Bentham there attacked the rule of mutuality as "a maxim which one would suppose to have found its way from the gaming-table to the bench." See Note, A

doned the requirement of mutuality and confined the requirement of privity to the party against whom the plea of res judicata is asserted. Coca Cola Co. v. Pepsi Cola Co., [36 Del. 124, 172 A. 260 (Super.Ct. 1934)]; Liberty Mutual Ins. Co. v. George Colon & Co., 260 N.Y. 305, 183 N.E. 506; Atkinson v. White, 60 Me. 396;ᶜ Eagle, etc., Ins. Co. v. Heller, 149 Va. 82, 140 S.E. 314, 57 A.L.R. 490; Jenkins v. Atlantic Coast Line R. Co., 89 S.C. 408, 71 S.E. 1010; United States v. Wexler, 8 F.2d 880. See Good Health Dairy Food Products Corp. v. Emery, 275 N.Y. 14, 9 N.E.2d 758, 112 A.L.R. 401. The commentators are almost unanimously in accord. 35 Yale L.J. 607; 9 Va.L.Reg.,N.S., 241; 29 Ill.L.Rev. 93; 18 N.Y.U.L.Q.R. 565, 570; 12 Corn.L.Q. 92. The courts of most jurisdictions have in effect accomplished the same result by recognizing a broad exception to the requirements of mutuality and privity, namely, that they are not necessary where the liability of the defendant asserting the plea of res judicata is dependent upon or derived from the liability of one who was exonerated in an earlier suit brought by the same plaintiff upon the same facts. See cases cited in 35 Yale L.J. 607, 610; 9 Va.L.Reg.,N.S., 241, 245–247; 29 Ill.L.Rev. 93, 94; 18 N.Y.U.L.Q.R. 565, 566–567; 34 C.J. 988–989. Typical examples of such derivative liability are master and servant, principal and agent, and indemnitor and indemnitee. Thus, if a plaintiff sues a servant for injuries caused by the servant's alleged negligence within the scope of his employment, a judgment against the plaintiff on the grounds that the servant was not negligent can be pleaded by the master as res judicata if he is subsequently sued by the same plaintiff for the same injuries. Conversely, if the plaintiff first sues the master, a judgment against the plaintiff on the grounds that the servant was not negligent can be pleaded by the servant as res judicata if he is subsequently sued by the plaintiff. In each of these situations the party asserting the plea of res judicata was not a party to the previous action nor in privity with such a party under the accepted definition of a privy set forth above. Likewise, the estoppel is not mutual since the party asserting the plea, not having been a party or in privity with a party to the former action, would not have been bound by it had it been decided the other way. The cases justify this exception on the ground that it would be unjust to permit one who has had his day in court to reopen identical issues by merely switching adversaries.

In determining the validity of a plea of res judicata three questions are pertinent: Was the issue decided in the prior adjudication identical with the one presented in the action in question? Was there

Probabilistic Analysis of the Doctrine of Mutuality of Collateral Estoppel, 76 Mich.L.Rev. 612, 616 n.15 (1978).

ᶜ In this 1872 case the court said, 60 Me. at 399: "That law [that estoppels must be mutual] was adopted when parties could not be witnesses, and from a very tender care of suitors, lest by possibility injustice might be done. For it is said, and this appears to be the only reason on which the law is founded, that 'if the adverse party was not also a party to the judgment offered in evidence, it may have been obtained upon his own testimony; in which case, to allow him to derive benefit from it would be unjust.' "

a final judgment on the merits? Was the party against whom the plea is asserted a party or in privity with a party to the prior adjudication? In re Estate of Smead, 219 Cal. 572, 28 P.2d 348; Silva v. Hawkins, 152 Cal. 138, 92 P. 72, and People v. Rodgers, 118 Cal. 393, 46 P. 740, 50 P. 668, to the extent that they are inconsistent with this opinion, are overruled.

In the present case, therefore, the defendant is not precluded by lack of privity or of mutuality of estoppel from asserting the plea of res judicata against the plaintiff. Since the issue as to the ownership of the money is identical with the issue raised in the probate proceeding, and since the order of the probate court settling the executor's account was a final adjudication of this issue on the merits (Prob. Code, sec. 931 [formerly Code Civ.Proc., sec. 1637]; see cases cited in 12 Cal.Jur. 62, 63; 15 Cal.Jur. 117, 120), it remains only to determine whether the plaintiff in the present action was a party or in privity with a party to the earlier proceeding. The plaintiff has brought the present action in the capacity of administratrix of the estate. In this capacity she represents the very same persons and interests that were represented in the earlier hearing on the executor's account. In that proceeding plaintiff and the other legatees who objected to the executor's account represented the estate of the decedent. They were seeking not a personal recovery but, like the plaintiff in the present action, as administratrix, a recovery for the benefit of the legatees and creditors of the estate, all of whom were bound by the order settling the account. (Prob.Code, sec. 931. See cases cited in 12 Cal.Jur. 62, 63.) The plea of res judicata is therefore available against plaintiff as a party to the former proceeding, despite her formal change of capacity. "Where a party though appearing in two suits in different capacities is in fact litigating the same right, the judgment in one estops him in the other." (15 Cal.Jur. 189; [other citations omitted].)

The judgment is affirmed.

Decline of mutuality.—The immediate impact of Justice Traynor's root-and-branch demolition of mutuality was not significant, but it came to have widespread repercussions in many states, thanks in no small part to an influential article by Professor Brainerd Currie, Mutuality of Collateral Estoppel: Limits of the Bernhard Doctrine, 9 Stan.L.Rev. 281 (1957).

The notion that a party ought not to be allowed the luxury of a second trial on an issue he has already litigated and lost had great appeal in days of crowded dockets and mounting costs of maintaining the judicial system. But the litigation-saving aspect of the Bernhard rule is not as obvious as it superficially appears. If mutuality is completely abrogated, an adverse judgment will preclude a party on every litigated and determined issue essential to the judgment with respect to *all* persons. A prudent litigant may consequently feel bound to fight a case to the utmost in both trial and appellate courts, even though he would treat the case rather casually if its sole effects were on the immediate adversaries and their privies. See Moore & Currier, Mutuality and Conclusiveness of Judgments, 35 Tul.L.Rev. 301 (1961), which gives a stout defense of the doctrine of mutuality with "certain dispensing exceptions shown to be sound by theory and experience." The effect on the volume of litigation is not susceptible of clear proof, but in any event there remain concerns of basic fairness cutting both ways.

Most of the courts influenced by Bernhard have stopped short of accepting the full sweep of Justice Traynor's dictum. There has, however, been a contrariety of views as to where the proper stopping point is. To explore this question, the four possible situations in which the question arises deserve separate consideration. (For convenience, P = plaintiff in first action; D = defendant in first action; NP = new plaintiff, not a party or privy to first action; and ND = new defendant, not a party or privy to first action.)

1. *P* sues *D*, *D* wins. Then *P* sues *ND*. Can *ND* use collateral estoppel?

This is the strongest case for collateral estoppel. *P* chose the court (how important is this?) and the adversary. He now tries again against a new adversary, who wants to use the prior judgment defensively. This category includes Coca-Cola Co. v. Pepsi-Cola Co.

Question: (5) Is it fair to Coca-Cola to use against it in an action against Pepsi-Cola its defeat in a suit against a small dealer, who would presumably have had the fact-finder's sympathy? When a party has had a day in court, is it relevant to ask, "A day in court against whom?" Indeed, because an adjudication is traditionally a specific decision of a specific dispute involving specific litigants, where special factors off the merits may influence the outcome, could not due process be said generally to require a day in court against the present opponent?

2. *P* sues *D*, *P* wins. Then *D* sues *ND*. Can *ND* use collateral estoppel?

This situation also involves a defensive use of collateral estoppel, the difference being that here the party to the prior action did not have the initiative and so did not choose the court in that action.

Question: (6) Driver's car collides with a car driven by *T*. A passenger in Driver's car sues *T* and wins (*T* negligent). Then *T* sues Driver. Is it fair to preclude *T* on the issue of his negligence? What of the jury's likely sympathy for the first plaintiff, or indeed for any plaintiff?

3. *P* sues *D*, *D* wins. Then *NP* sues *P*. Can *NP* use collateral estoppel?

This is offensive use of collateral estoppel. Is the difference between using a prior judgment as a sword rather than as a shield significant? Note that the party against whom collateral estoppel is sought to be used chose the court in the first action. (Again, how important is this?)

Question: (7) *T* sues Driver and loses (*T* contributorily negligent). Then a passenger in Driver's car sues *T*. Is it fair to preclude *T* on the issue of his negligence? Is this a harder case than the preceding situation to justify the use of collateral estoppel?

4. *P* sues *D*, *P* wins. Then *NP* sues *D*. Can *NP* use collateral estoppel?

This is the hardest case of all. *NP* wants to use the prior judgment offensively, and here the party to the prior action did not choose the court in that action. This situation encompasses the favorite classroom hypothetical case called by Professor Currie the "multiple-claimant anomaly." Assume there are fifty passengers injured in a railroad accident. If *P–1* sues the railroad and loses, presumably no other passenger can be bound by the result (see the Neenan case). So if *P–2*, *P–3*, and *P–4* all also sue and lose, but *P–5* has the good fortune to win, does this mean that *P–6* through *P–50* can win by collateral estoppel? If so, bear in mind that plaintiffs who might normally join in a single action would have strong incentive to hang back and hope for a case with a favorable result. Bear in mind also the likely tactic of planning the first suit to be on behalf of the most appealing of the potential plaintiffs.

Question: (8) Is there a practical way to take care of this anomaly? What of denying collateral estoppel effect to a later plaintiff if the railroad has prevailed in any of the prior actions?

Even Justice Traynor balked at giving unrestricted effect to his own dictum. In Taylor v. Hawkinson, 47 Cal.2d 893, 306 P.2d 797 (1957), Mr. Taylor obtained a verdict of $63.06 for property damage, the driver of his car $65.00 for personal injuries, and Mrs. Taylor $371.94 for personal injuries. Only Mrs. Taylor moved for a new trial for insufficiency of damages, and her motion was granted. Thereafter the judgment for the other plaintiffs became final. Mrs. Taylor then sought to limit her retrial to damages on the ground that the issue of liability was governed by the Bernhard rule. The trial court submitted all issues to the jury, which returned a verdict for the defendant. The judgment was affirmed. Justice Traynor, for the court, said: "There is ample evidence to support the trial court's implied finding that the verdicts following the first trial were compromise verdicts and that the jury did not determine the issue of liability." Justice Carter, alone in dissent, said: "It is no answer to say that the judgment is not res judicata because being based on a compromise verdict the issue of liability was not determined. [Citation omitted.] If the jury did not decide that issue, it decided nothing, and the judgment entered on its verdict would not be binding on the parties thereto. To say it did not decide the issue is to ignore the pleadings, verdict and judgment, and to permit a collateral attack on the judgment which is not permitted."

Questions: (9) Does this mean that in any case the first trial is subject to reexamination to see whether the verdict appears to have been a compromise?

(10) There has been some tendency to draw the line between defensive and offensive use, allowing only the former. E.g., Albernaz v. City of Fall River, 346 Mass. 336, 191 N.E.2d 771 (1963). Is such a rule of thumb a more desirable solution than the flexibility implicit in Taylor?

BLONDER–TONGUE LABORATORIES v. UNIVERSITY OF ILLINOIS FOUNDATION

Supreme Court of the United States, 1971.
402 U.S. 313, 91 S.Ct. 1434.

[The rule in patent infringement cases in the federal courts had been, ever since Triplett v. Lowell, 297 U.S. 638, 56 S.Ct. 645 (1936), that a determination of invalidity of a patent in an action by the patentee against an alleged infringer did not preclude the patentee in a second action by him against another alleged infringer. Triplett was decided late in the heyday of the mutuality doctrine. In the present case, the lower courts allowed the Foundation to maintain a second action after losing its first, following Triplett. But, on certiorari, the Supreme Court took it upon itself to reexamine Triplett. After an extensive review of the doctrine, Justice White, speaking for a unanimous Court, said:]

The cases and authorities discussed above connect erosion of the mutuality requirement to the goal of limiting relitigation of issues where that can be achieved without compromising fairness in particular cases. The courts have often discarded the rule while commenting on crowded dockets and long delays preceding trial. Authorities differ on whether the public interest in efficient judicial administration is a sufficient ground in and of itself for abandoning mutuality, but it is clear that more than crowded dockets is involved. The broader question is whether it is any longer tenable to afford a litigant more than one full and fair opportunity for judicial resolution of the same issue. The question in these terms includes as part of the calculus the effect on judicial administration, but it also encompasses the concern exemplified by Bentham's reference to the gaming table in his attack on the principle of mutuality of estoppel. In any lawsuit where a defendant, because of the mutuality principle, is forced to present a complete defense on the merits to a claim which the plaintiff has fully litigated and lost in a prior action, there is an arguable misallocation of resources. To the extent the defendant in the second suit may not win by asserting, without contradiction, that the plaintiff had fully and fairly, but unsuccessfully, litigated the same claim in the prior suit, the defendant's time and money are diverted from alternative uses—productive or otherwise—to relitigation of a decided issue. And, still assuming that the issue was resolved correctly in the first suit, there is reason to be concerned about the plaintiff's allocation of resources. Permitting repeated litigation of the same issue as long as the supply of unrelated defendants holds out reflects either the aura of the gaming table or "a lack of discipline and of disinterestedness on the part of the lower courts, hardly a worthy or wise basis for fashioning rules of procedure." Kerotest Mfg. Co. v. C-O-Two Co., 342 U.S. 180, 185, 72 S.Ct. 219, 222 (1952). Although neither judges, the parties, nor the adversary system performs perfectly in all cases, the requirement of determining whether the party against whom an estoppel is asserted had a full and fair opportunity to litigate is a most significant safeguard.

Some litigants—those who never appeared in a prior action—may not be collaterally estopped without litigating the issue. They have never had a chance to present their evidence and arguments on the claim. Due process prohibits estopping them despite one or more existing adjudications of the identical issue which stand squarely against their position. See Hansberry v. Lee, 311 U.S. 32, 40, 61 S.Ct. 115, 117 (1940); Bernhard, 19 Cal.2d, at 811, 122 P.2d, at 984. Also, the authorities have been more willing to permit a defendant in a second suit to invoke an estoppel against a plaintiff who lost on the same claim in an earlier suit than they have been to allow a plaintiff in the second suit to use offensively a judgment obtained by a different plaintiff in a prior suit against the same defendant. But the case before us involves neither due process nor "offensive use" questions. Rather, it depends on the considerations weighing for and against permitting a patent holder to sue on his patent after it has once been held invalid following opportunity for full and fair trial.

[The Court concluded (1) that the Triplett rule was not essential to effectuate the purposes of the patent system; (2) that the economic costs of continuing adherence to Triplett were substantial in terms of (a) costs to both sides of repetitive litigation and (b) economic disruption flowing from the multiple opportunities for holders of invalid patents to exact licensing agreements from alleged infringers, who will often pay royalties under a license rather than bear the costly burden of challenging the patent; and (3) that although any burden placed on the judiciary by Triplett was an incidental matter in comparison to the other economic costs of following Triplett, its abrogation would save some judicial time if even a few relatively lengthy patent suits were fairly disposed of on pleas of collateral estoppel.[d] The Court also stated:]

Moreover, we do not suggest, without legislative guidance, that a plea of estoppel by an infringement or royalty suit defendant must automatically be accepted once the defendant in support of his plea identifies the issue in suit as the identical question finally decided against the patentee or one of his privies in previous litigation. Rather, the patentee-plaintiff must be permitted to demonstrate, if he can, that he did not have "a fair opportunity procedurally, substantively

---

[d] Prior to this decision, Judge Davis of the Court of Claims, after a sympathetic review of the trends away from mutuality in other types of litigation, gave a reasoned justification for its retention in patent infringement cases. Technograph Printed Circuits, Ltd. v. United States, 372 F.2d 969 (Ct.Cl.1967).

and evidentially to pursue his claim the first time." Eisel v. Columbia Packing Co., 181 F.Supp. 298, 301 (Mass.1960). This element in the estoppel decision will comprehend, we believe, the important concerns about the complexity of patent litigation and the posited hazard that the prior proceedings were seriously defective.

Determining whether a patentee has had a full and fair chance to litigate the validity of his patent in an earlier case is of necessity not a simple matter. In addition to the considerations of choice of forum and incentive to litigate . . . , certain other factors immediately emerge. For example, . . . appropriate inquiries would be . . . whether the opinions filed by the District Court and the reviewing court, if any, indicate that the prior case was one of those relatively rare instances where the courts wholly failed to grasp the technical subject matter and issues in suit; and whether without fault of his own the patentee was deprived of crucial evidence or witnesses in the first litigation. But as so often is the case, no one set of facts, no one collection of words or phrases, will provide an automatic formula for proper rulings on estoppel pleas. In the end, decision will necessarily rest on the trial courts' sense of justice and equity.

. . . .

It is clear that judicial decisions have tended to depart from the rigid requirements of mutuality. In accordance with this trend, there has been a corresponding development of the lower courts' ability and facility in dealing with questions of when it is appropriate and fair to impose an estoppel against a party who has already litigated an issue once and lost. As one commentator has stated:

> "Under the tests of time and subsequent developments, the Bernhard decision has proved its merit and the mettle of its author. The abrasive action of new factual configurations and of actual human controversies, disposed of in the common-law tradition by competent courts, far more than the commentaries of academicians, leaves the decision revealed for what it is, as it was written: a shining landmark of progress in justice and law administration." Currie, [Civil Procedure: The Tempest Brews, 53 Calif.L.Rev. 25, 37 (1965)].

. . . [I]t is apparent that the uncritical acceptance of the principle of mutuality of estoppel expressed in Triplett v. Lowell is today out of place. Thus, we conclude that Triplett should be overruled to the extent it forecloses a plea of estoppel by one facing a charge of infringement of a patent that has once been declared invalid.

. . . .

Res judicata and collateral estoppel are affirmative defenses that must be pleaded. Fed.Rule Civ.Proc. 8(c). The purpose of such pleading is to give the opposing party notice of the plea of estoppel and a chance to argue, if he can, why the imposition of an estoppel would be inappropriate. Because of Triplett v. Lowell, petitioner did not plead estoppel and [the Foundation] never had an opportunity to challenge the appropriateness of such a plea on the grounds [that the patentee did not have "a full and fair chance to litigate the validity of his patent" in the prior case]. Therefore, given the partial overruling of Triplett, we remand the case. Petitioner should be allowed to amend its pleadings in the District Court to assert a plea of estoppel. [The Foundation] must then be permitted to . . . supplement the record with any evidence showing why an estoppel should not be imposed in this case. If necessary, petitioner may also supplement the record. In taking this action, we intimate no views on the other issues presented in this case. The judgment of the Court of Appeals is vacated and the cause is remanded to the District Court for further proceedings consistent with this opinion.[e]

PARKLANE HOSIERY CO. v. SHORE

Supreme Court of the United States, 1979.
439 U.S. 322, 99 S.Ct. 645.

MR. JUSTICE STEWART delivered the opinion of the Court.

This case presents the question whether a party who has had issues of fact adjudicated adversely to it in an equitable action may be collaterally estopped from relitigating the same issues before a jury in a subsequent legal action brought against it by a new party.

The respondent brought this stockholder's class action against the petitioners in a federal district court. The complaint alleged that the petitioners, Parklane Hosiery Company, Inc. (Parklane) and 12 of its officers, directors, and stockholders, had issued a materially false and misleading proxy statement in connection with a merger. The proxy statement, according to the complaint, had violated [various federal securities laws]. The complaint sought damages, rescission of the merger, and recovery of costs.

Before this action came to trial, the SEC filed suit against the same defendants in a federal district court, alleging that the proxy statement that had been issued by Parklane was materially false and misleading in essentially the same respects as those that had been alleged in the respondent's complaint. Injunctive relief was requested. After a four-day trial, the District Court found that the proxy statement was materially false and misleading in the respects alleged, and entered a declaratory judgment to that effect. Securities and Exchange Commission v. Parklane Hosiery Co., 422 F.Supp. 477. The Court of Appeals for the Second Circuit affirmed this judgment. 558 F.2d 1083.

---

[e] Upon remand, the district court found that the Foundation had failed to make the requisite showing to escape the defense of estoppel and entered judgment for the defendant, 334 F.Supp. 47 (N.D. Ill.1971), aff'd, 465 F.2d 380 (7th Cir.), cert. denied, 409 U.S. 1061, 93 S.Ct. 559 (1972).

The respondent in the present case then moved for partial summary judgment against the petitioners, asserting that the petitioners were collaterally estopped from relitigating the issues that had been resolved against them in the action brought by the SEC.[2] The District Court denied the motion on the ground that such an application of collateral estoppel would deny the petitioners their Seventh Amendment right to a jury trial. The Court of Appeals for the Second Circuit reversed, holding that a party who has had issues of fact determined against him after a full and fair opportunity to litigate in a nonjury trial is collaterally estopped from obtaining a subsequent jury trial of these same issues of fact. 565 F.2d 815. The appellate court concluded that "the Seventh Amendment preserves the right to jury trial only with respect to issues of fact, [and] once those issues have been fully and fairly adjudicated in a prior proceeding, nothing remains for trial, either with or without a jury." Id., at 819. Because of an intercircuit conflict, we granted certiorari. 435 U.S. 1006, 98 S.Ct. 1875.

I

The threshold question to be considered is whether, quite apart from the right to a jury trial under the Seventh Amendment, the petitioners can be precluded from relitigating facts resolved adversely to them in a prior equitable proceeding with another party under the general law of collateral estoppel. Specifically, we must determine whether a litigant who was not a party to a prior judgment may nevertheless use that judgment "offensively" to prevent a defendant from relitigating issues resolved in the earlier proceeding.

A

[The Court here reviewed the rejection of the mutuality requirement by the Blonder-Tongue decision.]

B

The Blonder-Tongue case involved defensive use of collateral estoppel—a plaintiff was estopped from asserting a claim that the plaintiff had previously litigated and lost against another defendant. The present case, by contrast, involves offensive use of collateral estoppel—a plaintiff is seeking to estop a defendant from relitigating the issues which the defendant previously litigated and lost against another plaintiff. In both the offensive and defensive use situations,

---

[2] A private plaintiff in an action under the proxy rules is not entitled to relief simply by demonstrating that the proxy solicitation was materially false and misleading. The plaintiff must also show that he was injured and prove damages. [Citation omitted.] Since the SEC action was limited to a determination of whether the proxy statements contained materially false and misleading statements, the respondent conceded that he would still have to prove these other elements of his prima facie case in the private action. The petitioners' right to a jury trial on those remaining issues is not contested.

the party against whom estoppel is asserted has litigated and lost in an earlier action. Nevertheless, several reasons have been advanced why the two situations should be treated differently.

First, offensive use of collateral estoppel does not promote judicial economy in the same manner as defensive use does. Defensive use of collateral estoppel precludes a plaintiff from relitigating identical issues by merely "switching adversaries." Bernhard v. Bank of America Nat. Trust & Savings Assn., 19 Cal.2d 807, 813, 122 P.2d 892, 895 (1942). Thus defensive collateral estoppel gives a plaintiff a strong incentive to join all potential defendants in the first action if possible. Offensive use of collateral estoppel, on the other hand, creates precisely the opposite incentive. Since a plaintiff will be able to rely on a previous judgment against a defendant but will not be bound by that judgment if the defendant wins, the plaintiff has every incentive to adopt a "wait and see" attitude, in the hope that the first action by another plaintiff will result in a favorable judgment. [Citations omitted.] Thus offensive use of collateral estoppel will likely increase rather than decrease the total amount of litigation, since potential plaintiffs will have everything to gain and nothing to lose by not intervening in the first action.[13]

A second argument against offensive use of collateral estoppel is that it may be unfair to a defendant. If a defendant in the first action is sued for small or nominal damages, he may have little incentive to defend vigorously, particularly if future suits are not foreseeable. Evergreens v. Nunan, 141 F.2d 927, 929; cf. Berner v. British Commonwealth Pac. Airlines, 346 F.2d 532 (application of offensive collateral estoppel denied where defendant did not appeal an adverse judgment awarding damages of $35,000 and defendant was later sued for over $7 million). Allowing offensive collateral estoppel may also be unfair to a defendant if the judgment relied upon as a basis for the estoppel is itself inconsistent with one or more previous judgments in favor of the defendant.[14] Still another situation where it might be unfair to apply offensive estoppel is where the second action affords the defendant procedural opportunities unavailable in the first action that could readily cause a different result.[15]

[13] The Restatement (Second) of Judgments (Tent. Draft No. 2, 1975) § 88(3) provides that application of collateral estoppel may be denied if the party asserting it "could have effected joinder in the first action between himself and his present adversary."

[14] . . . See Restatement (Second) of Judgments (Tent. Draft No. 2, 1975) § 88(4).

[15] If, for example, the defendant in the first action was forced to defend in an inconvenient forum and therefore was unable to engage in full scale discovery or call witnesses, application of offensive collateral estoppel may be unwarranted. Indeed, differences in available procedures may sometimes justify not allowing a prior judgment to have estoppel effect in a subsequent action even between the same parties, or where defensive estoppel is asserted against a plaintiff who has litigated and lost. The problem of unfairness is particularly acute in cases of offensive estoppel, however, because the defendant against whom estoppel is asserted typically will not have chosen the forum in the first action. See Restatement (Second) of Judg-

C

We have concluded that the preferable approach for dealing with these problems in the federal courts is not to preclude the use of offensive collateral estoppel, but to grant trial courts broad discretion to determine when it should be applied.[16] The general rule should be that in cases where a plaintiff could easily have joined in the earlier action or where, either for the reasons discussed above or for other reasons, the application of offensive estoppel would be unfair to a defendant, a trial judge should not allow the use of offensive collateral estoppel.

In the present case, however, none of the circumstances that might justify reluctance to allow the offensive use of collateral estoppel is present. The application of offensive collateral estoppel will not here reward a private plaintiff who could have joined in the previous action, since the respondent probably could not have joined in the injunctive action brought by the SEC even had he so desired.[17] Similarly, there is no unfairness to the petitioners in applying offensive collateral estoppel in this case. First, in light of the serious allegations made in the SEC's complaint against the petitioners, as well as the foreseeability of subsequent private suits that typically follow a successful government judgment, the petitioners had every incentive to litigate the SEC lawsuit fully and vigorously. Second, the judgment in the Commission action was not inconsistent with any previous decision. Finally, there will in the respondent's action be no procedural opportunities available to the petitioners that were unavailable in the first action of a kind that might be likely to cause a different result.[19]

We conclude, therefore, that none of the considerations that would justify a refusal to allow the use of offensive collateral estoppel is present in this case. Since the petitioners received a "full and fair" opportunity to litigate their claims in the SEC action, the contempo-

---

ments (Tent. Draft No. 2, 1975) § 88(2) and Comment d.

[16] This is essentially the approach of the Restatement (Second) of Judgments (Tent. Draft No. 2, 1975) § 88, which recognizes that "the distinct trend if not the clear weight of recent authority is to the effect that there is no intrinsic difference between 'offensive' as distinct from 'defensive' issue preclusion, although a stronger showing that the prior opportunity was adequate may be required in the former situation than the latter." Reporter's Note, at 99.

[17] Securities and Exchange Commission v. Everest Management Corp., 475 F.2d 1236, 1240 ("the complicating effect of the additional issues and the additional parties outweighs any advantage of a single disposition of the common issues"). Moreover, consolidation of a private action with one brought by the SEC without its consent is prohibited by statute. 15 U.S.C. § 78u(g).

[19] It is true, of course, that the petitioners in the present action would be entitled to a jury trial of the issues bearing on whether the proxy statement was materially false and misleading had the SEC action never been brought—a matter to be discussed in Part II of this opinion. [And the petitioners did not have a right to a jury trial in the equitable suit brought by the SEC.—Ed.] But the presence or absence of a jury as factfinder is basically neutral, quite unlike, for example, the necessity of defending the first lawsuit in an inconvenient forum.

rary law of collateral estoppel leads inescapably to the conclusion that the petitioners are collaterally estopped from relitigating the question of whether the proxy statements were materially false and misleading.

II

The question that remains is whether, notwithstanding the law of collateral estoppel, the use of offensive collateral estoppel in this case would violate the petitioners' Seventh Amendment right to a jury trial.

[The Court here rejected the petitioners' argument and affirmed the judgment below. The Court ruled that because in 1791 an equitable determination could have collateral estoppel effect in a subsequent legal action, such estoppel by itself entails no violation of the seventh amendment. And even though the common law in 1791 permitted collateral estoppel only where there was mutuality, collateral estoppel is permissible in the circumstances of this case because the seventh amendment's protection of the fundamental elements of the jury right did not mandate the exact procedural incidents and details associated with jury trial in 1791 and so did not inhibit the subsequent evolution of collateral estoppel.

[The decision drew a passionate dissent from Justice Rehnquist. He argued that the majority was condoning a violation of the seventh amendment by permitting nonmutual collateral estoppel to destroy a jury right. Moreover, he argued that simply as a matter of res judicata law, collateral estoppel should be denied here because it "runs counter to the strong federal policy favoring jury trials" and because "the opportunity for a jury trial in the second action could easily lead to a different result from that obtained in the first action before the court and therefore . . . it is unfair to estop petitioners from relitigating the issues before a jury." He closed by observing:]

The ultimate irony of today's decision is that its potential for significantly conserving the resources of either the litigants or the judiciary is doubtful at best. . . . It is . . . probable that today's decision will have the result of coercing defendants to agree to consent orders or settlements in agency enforcement action in order to preserve their right to jury trial in the private actions. In that event, the Court, for no compelling reason, will have simply added a powerful club to the administrative agencies' arsenals that even Congress was unwilling to provide them.

Question: (11) What would have happened if the district court had instead invoked its "discretion" to determine that collateral estoppel should not apply? What should be the scope of the trial court's discretion in this context? See 18 Wright, Miller & Cooper § 4465, at 590–91.

SECOND RESTATEMENT'S APPROACH

Restatement (Second) of Judgments § 29 (1980) provides that issue preclusion, subject to all its usual exceptions, may be invoked by a nonparty against a party to the prior action, "unless the fact that he lacked full and fair opportunity to litigate the issue in the first action or other circumstances justify affording him an opportunity to relitigate the issue." The section goes on to mention some of the numerous such circumstances that should be considered, including whether the nonparty could have effected his joinder in the prior action, whether the prior determination is itself inconsistent with some other determination of the same issue, whether the prior determination seems to have been affected by relationships among the parties to the first action that are absent in the second, and whether preclusion may complicate the second action or prejudice another party thereto. Indeed, the final sentence of the reporter's note thereon states: "The ultimate question is whether there is good reason, all things considered, to allow the party to relitigate the issue."

Questions: (12) Is the purpose of res judicata in putting an end to litigation defeated by such an approach? Might one argue that we would be better off with no doctrine of res judicata than with a flexible doctrine of res judicata? See generally Holland, Modernizing Res Judicata: Reflections on the Parklane Doctrine, 55 Ind.L.J. 615 (1980).

(13) More specifically, was not the mutuality rule with certain defined exceptions preferable in terms of workability to the Second Restatement's more extensive preclusion that requires fuzzy exceptions entailing case-by-case inquiry into fairness and efficiency? Cf. Note, Nonmutuality: Taking the Fairness out of Collateral Estoppel, 13 Ind.L.Rev. 563, 596 (1980) ("Perhaps all nonmutuality runs too great a risk of unfairness because fairness cannot be unerringly determined. If fairness is the prime concern of courts, then requiring mutuality may be the best method of meeting this concern. Mutuality guarantees fairness to the party by restricting the effect of the judgment to parties with whom the original party has actually litigated. A nonparty who has not litigated has lost nothing when he is denied the use of a judgment for lack of mutuality.").

UNITED STATES v. MENDOZA, 104 S.Ct. 568 (1984). By a 1975 decision of the District Court for the Northern District of California, a number of Filipino war veterans established that the United States had denied them due process by its administration of the statute regarding the naturalization in the Philippines in 1945 and 1946 of noncitizens who had served in the American armed forces during World War II ("68 Filipinos"), a decision the United States did not appeal.

In 1978, another Filipino war veteran petitioned for naturalization. The District Court for the Central District of California and the Court of Appeals for the Ninth Circuit held that the prior decision collaterally estopped the United States on the constitutional issue. On certiorari, a unanimous Supreme Court reversed, holding that "nonmutual offensive collateral estoppel is not to be extended to the United States." Justice Rehnquist explained for the Court:

"We have long recognized that 'the Government is not in a position identical to that of a private litigant,' INS v. Hibi, 414 U.S. 5, 8, 94 S.Ct. 19, 21 (1973) (per curiam), both because of the geographic breadth of government litigation and also, most importantly, because of the nature of the issues the government litigates. It is not open to serious dispute that the government is a party to a far greater number of cases on a nationwide basis than even the most litigious private entity; in 1982, the United States was a party to more than 75,000 of the 206,193 [civil] filings in the United States District Courts. Administrative Office of the United States Courts, Annual Report of the Director 98 (1982). In the same year the United States was a party to just under 30% of the civil cases appealed from the District Courts to the Court of Appeals. Id., at 79, 82. Government litigation frequently involves legal questions of substantial public importance; indeed, because the proscriptions of the United States Constitution are so generally directed at governmental action, many constitutional questions can arise only in the context of litigation to which the government is a party. Because of those facts the government is more likely than any private party to be involved in lawsuits against different parties which nonetheless involve the same legal issues.

"A rule allowing nonmutual collateral estoppel against the government in such cases would substantially thwart the development of important questions of law by freezing the first final decision rendered on a particular legal issue. Allowing only one final adjudication would deprive this Court of the benefit it receives from permitting several courts of appeals to explore a difficult question before this Court grants certiorari. [Citations omitted.] Indeed, if nonmutual estoppel were routinely applied against the government, this Court would have to revise its practice of waiting for a conflict to develop before granting the government's petitions for certiorari. See Sup.Ct.R. 17.1.

"The Solicitor General's policy for determining when to appeal an adverse decision would also require substantial revision. The Court of Appeals faulted the government in this case for failing to appeal a decision that it now contends is erroneous. . . . But the government's litigation conduct in a case is apt to differ from that of a private litigant. Unlike a private litigant who generally does not forego an appeal if he believes that he can prevail, the Solicitor General considers a variety of factors, such as the limited resources of the government and the crowded dockets of the courts, before authorizing an appeal. Brief for the United States, at 30–31. The application of nonmutual estoppel against the government would force the Solicitor

General to abandon those prudential concerns and to appeal every adverse decision in order to avoid foreclosing further review.

"In addition to those institutional concerns traditionally considered by the Solicitor General, the panoply of important public issues raised in governmental litigation may quite properly lead successive Administrations of the Executive Branch to take differing positions with respect to the resolution of a particular issue. While the Executive Branch must of course defer to the Judicial Branch for final resolution of questions of constitutional law, the former nonetheless controls the progress of government litigation through the federal courts. It would be idle to pretend that the conduct of government litigation in all its myriad features, from the decision to file a complaint in the United States District Court to the decision to petition for certiorari to review a judgment of the Court of Appeals, is a wholly mechanical procedure which involves no policy choices whatever.

.   .   .   .   .

"The Court of Appeals did not endorse a routine application of nonmutual collateral estoppel against the government, because it recognized that the government does litigate issues of far-reaching national significance which in some cases, it concluded, might warrant relitigation. But in this case it found no 'record evidence' indicating that there was a 'crucial need' in the administration of the immigration laws for a redetermination of the due process question decided in 68 Filipinos and presented again in this case. . . . The Court of Appeals did not make clear what sort of 'record evidence' would have satisfied it that there *was* a 'crucial need' for redetermination of the question in this case, but we pretermit further discussion of that approach; we believe that the standard announced by the Court of Appeals for determining when relitigation of a legal issue is to be permitted is so wholly subjective that it affords no guidance to the courts or to the government. Such a standard leaves the government at sea because it can not possibly anticipate, in determining whether or not to appeal an adverse decision, whether a court will bar relitigation of the issue in a later case. . . .

"We hold, therefore, that nonmutual offensive collateral estoppel simply does not apply against the government in such a way as to preclude relitigation of issues such as those involved in this case. The conduct of government litigation in the courts of the United States is sufficiently different from the conduct of private civil litigation in those courts so that what might otherwise be economy interests underlying a broad application of collateral estoppel are outweighed by the constraints which peculiarly affect the government. We think that our conclusion will better allow thorough development of legal doctrine by allowing litigation in multiple forums. Indeed, a contrary result might disserve the economy interests in whose name estoppel is advanced by requiring the government to abandon virtually any exercise of discretion in seeking to review judgments unfavorable to it. . . .

"Our holding in this case is consistent with each of our prior holdings to which the parties have called our attention, and which we reaffirm. Today in a companion case we hold that the government may be estopped under certain circumstances from relitigating a question when the parties to the two lawsuits are the same. United States v. Stauffer Chemical Co., 104 S.Ct. 575 (1984); see also Montana v. United States, [440 U.S. 147, 99 S.Ct. 970 (1979)]; United States v. Moser, 266 U.S. 236, 45 S.Ct. 66 (1924). . . .

"The concerns underlying our disapproval of collateral estoppel against the government are for the most part inapplicable where mutuality is present, as in Stauffer Chemical, Montana, and Moser. The application of an estoppel when the government is litigating the same issue with the same party avoids the problem of freezing the development of the law because the government is still free to litigate that issue in the future with some other party. And, where the parties are the same, estopping the government spares a party that has already prevailed once from having to relitigate—a function it would not serve in the present circumstances. We accordingly hold that the Court of Appeals was wrong in applying nonmutual collateral estoppel against the government in this case."

―――――

Question: (14) The proposed Federal Product Liability Act, which would supplant state law, provides that there shall be no preclusion on issues of fact between different claimants' product liability actions "unless both actions were based on harm caused by the same event in which two or more persons were harmed." S. 2631, 97th Cong., 2d Sess. § 4(d) (1982). What do you think of that proposal?

―――――

NOTE, A PROBABILISTIC ANALYSIS OF THE DOCTRINE OF
MUTUALITY OF COLLATERAL ESTOPPEL
76 Mich.L.Rev. 612, 619, 622–24, 640–43, 645, 679 (1978).

Using probability theory as an aid to analysis, this Note will demonstrate that the mutuality doctrine is designed to allocate trial risks in a manner consistent with the burden of persuasion in civil litigation. Thus, the abandonment of mutuality strikes at the heart of the trial process. Where a single party (hereinafter the "common party") faces multiple opponents on a common question, the abandonment of mutuality can significantly alter the common party's probability of success. Bernhard thus amounts to little more than an instruction to the trier of fact to find against the common party simply because he is the common party, a fact entirely unrelated to the merits of the case.

.　.　.　.

. . . . [T]he burden of persuasion in civil litigation embodies a strategy designed to minimize the number of erroneous verdicts. . . . Whether the relief sought is compensatory or equitable, civil litigation is essentially a matter of loss shifting. A loss has been or will be incurred; the question is simply who should bear it. Absent some peculiar and cognizable virtue inhering in one of the parties, there is no reason to prefer an error in one direction over an error in the other. Consequently, the preponderance-of-the-evidence test instructs the factfinder to follow the error-minimizing strategy to choose the verdict most likely to be the truth. . . . The burden of persuasion is thus not merely a rule of convenience to be discarded or modified lightly. It embodies the fundamental assumption of civil litigation that, without regard to the merits, neither party is the more deserving of a favorable judgment.

. . . .

The central theme of mutuality is the fair apportionment of trial risks. By potentially precluding either party (if both would have been bound) or neither party (if either party would not have been bound), mutuality allows litigation risks to reflect only the merits of the cases. The abandonment of mutuality alters the litigation risks by forcing only one party to face the potential of preclusion in subsequent litigation, thus shifting additional risks to that party. In addition to altering the distribution of risks between the parties, the Bernhard doctrine affects the measure of trial efficacy by generally increasing the error rate.

To see more clearly and to what extent mutuality and Bernhard affect the allocation of litigation risks, consider the result in two hypothetical multiple litigation situations that differ only with respect to the presence or absence of the mutuality requirement. Because Currie initially suggested that Bernhard produces no objectionable results when the common party is the protagonist, as have other commentators, it will be assumed in both hypotheticals that a common party plaintiff seeks to assert related claims [80] against a series of defendants. As will become apparent, this assumption does not affect the alteration of trial risks produced by Bernhard.

Assume also that the plaintiff has a fifty percent probability of winning his case, that is, that if the case were tried indefinitely, the plaintiff would be successful fifty per cent of the time. . . . It is assumed that the plaintiff has ten claims, each liquidated in the amount of $100. . . .

. . . .

Finally, assume that no defendant is in privity with any other defendant, so that under the traditional mutuality doctrine, as well as under Bernhard, the common party plaintiff will not be able to use a

[80] "Related claims" denotes claims with a sufficient common basis to create a collateral estoppel problem. For the sake of simplicity, it is assumed that the common questions are dispositive of each case.

favorable judgment against one defendant to preclude any other defendant from relitigating the common issue. Given this set of assumptions, if each case is tried separately and preclusive effect is denied for lack of mutuality, all ten cases will be litigated. By hypothesis, the plaintiff can expect to win fifty percent of his cases for a total expected recovery of $500. This result is illustrated in the mutuality column of Table I.

TABLE I

		Mutuality				Bernhard	
Trial	Recovery if win trial	Probability of winning trial	Expected Recovery	Cumulative Expected Recovery	Probability of winning trial	Expected Recovery	Cumulative Expected Recovery
1	$100	.5	$50	$50	.500	$50.00	$50.00
2	$100	.5	$50	$100	.250	$25.00	$75.00
3	$100	.5	$50	$150	.125	$12.50	$87.50
4	$100	.5	$50	$200	.063	$6.30	$93.80
5	$100	.5	$50	$250	.031	$3.10	$96.90
6	$100	.5	$50	$300	.016	$1.60	$98.50
7	$100	.5	$50	$350	.008	$.80	$99.30
8	$100	.5	$50	$400	.004	$.40	$99.70
9	$100	.5	$50	$450	.002	$.20	$99.90
10	$100	.5	$50	$500	.001	$.10	$100.00

Total expected recovery $500 $100.00

On the other hand, under Bernhard, once the plaintiff loses one case, he will be precluded from litigating the remaining cases. While the probability of winning any single case that is litigated is still fifty percent, the preclusive effect of a single loss makes the probability of ever litigating a case dependent upon the outcome of previous cases. This cumulative effect reduces the common party's expected recovery from $500 to $100, as illustrated in the Bernhard column of Table I.

When the probability of winning a single case is initially assumed to be fifty percent, each successive claim under Bernhard is worth only half as much to the plaintiff as its predecessor because it is that much less likely that he will be able to recover. The presence of the preceding claims decreases the probability that the common party will recover on succeeding claims. The impact of the Bernhard doctrine is dramatic and can be evaluated in terms of expected recovery rather than mere conjecture.

. . . .

The argument advanced by one commentator—that the result produced by Bernhard is no worse than forcing a common party to litigate all claims at once so that any recovery is dependent upon that single outcome [91]—is, as Professor Currie argued, incorrect. If, in the hypotheticals, all defendants were joined in a single suit so that each would be bound by an adverse judgment as well as benefitted by a favorable one, the plaintiff's expected recovery would be $500.

[91] See Comment, [Privity and Mutuality in the Doctrine of Res Judicata, 35 Yale L.J. 607, 610–11 (1926)].

Thus, the expected recovery when all of the defendants are joined in a single action is the same as it would be if the suits were tried separately under mutuality, but it is not the same as it would be if they were tried under Bernhard. There is a vast difference between compelling a litigant to accept an all-or-nothing bet with even odds, as joinder rules do, and weighting the odds heavily in favor of his opponent, as the Bernhard doctrine does.

. . . .

This Note began by demonstrating, with the aid of probability theory, that the burden of persuasion in civil litigation embodies a strategy designed to minimize the total number of erroneous judgments and that this strategy is based on the various disutilities society attaches to the different possible outcomes of litigation. This Note then established that the abandonment of mutuality causes a statistically certain decrease in the recovery of a party facing multiple opponents on related claims. This effect of Bernhard is of concern to more than just the common party, for the mutuality doctrine is designed to allocate trial risks in a manner consistent with the burden of persuasion, that is, in a manner designed to minimize the total number of errors. Thus, the abandonment of mutuality harms the system of civil sanctions by weakening the causal link between culpable conduct and trial outcome. This Note also demonstrated that the objections to the abandonment of a mutuality requirement are not met by a requirement that the common party be precluded only if he has previously enjoyed a full and fair opportunity to litigate. Both the full and fair opportunity test and the mutuality requirement should be satisfied before the common party is precluded.

Finally, it was demonstrated that the traditional exceptions to the mutuality requirement are entirely consistent with an error minimizing strategy.

Question: (15) Evaluate the argument that "the major shortcoming with the breakdown of mutuality is that it does not go far enough to relieve court congestion and operates as a one-way street to the serious disadvantage of parties to litigation." Thus, the argument runs, there should be "a return to mutuality, but a new kind of mutuality" under which collateral estoppel expands to bind as well as benefit strangers. Berch, A Proposal to Permit Collateral Estoppel of Nonparties Seeking Affirmative Relief, 1979 Ariz.St. L.J. 511, 530–31. This change could be achieved by stretching the categories of privies or, more frankly, by abandoning the requirement of privity. Due process would be satisfied by looking to the stranger's earlier failure to intervene or, more aptly, by looking retrospectively to a party's adequate representation of the stranger. Apparent excesses could be controlled by delimiting the rule of preclusion or, similarly, by developing exceptions thereto. Taken to its logical conclusion, the new regime would give effects by collateral estoppel analogous to those of a class action. See George, Sweet Uses of Adversity: Parklane Hoisery and the Collateral Class Action, 32 Stan.L. Rev. 655 (1980). Note that there is scattered case support for this argument.

See, e.g., Cauefield v. Fidelity & Casualty Co., 378 F.2d 876 (5th Cir.), cert. denied, 389 U.S. 1009, 88 S.Ct. 571 (1967).

SPECIAL TYPES OF PROCEEDINGS

After trial, *A* is convicted of arson for having intentionally destroyed his own property by fire. Thereafter, he sues the *B* Fire Insurance Co. on its policy covering the property. Should the criminal conviction preclude *A* in the civil action? Recognizing that the customary answer to this question was in the negative, Eagle, Star & British Dominions Insurance Co. v. Heller, 149 Va. 82, 140 S.E. 314 (1927), nevertheless held that there should be preclusion, saying that the contrary result "would be a reproach to the administration of justice." The reason usually given for denying preclusion had been lack of mutuality: the parties in the two actions were not the same. Thus, the retreat from mutuality heralded by Bernhard has led many more courts to give the conviction preclusive effect, subject to the usual requirements and exceptions. E.g., Teitelbaum Furs, Inc. v. Dominion Insurance Co., 58 Cal.2d 601, 375 P.2d 439, 25 Cal.Rptr. 559 (1962). See generally Thau, Collateral Estoppel and the Reliability of Criminal Determinations: Theoretical, Practical, and Strategic Implications for Criminal and Civil Litigation, 70 Geo.L.J. 1079 (1982).

Where a criminal conviction is not so given conclusive effect in a subsequent civil action, one might ask whether it is admissible as evidence therein. As a general matter, a judgment either has conclusive effect under the rules of res judicata or has no effect at all, being inadmissible on hearsay grounds. Accordingly, where conclusive effect has been denied, the prevailing rule has been that the admission of evidence of a prior criminal conviction is reversible error. E.g., Silva v. Silva, 297 Mass. 217, 7 N.E.2d 601 (1937). But the heavier burden of proof in criminal cases would seem to make it reasonable to give a conviction at least some effect in a civil case. As a result, a number of states have adopted a half-way rule making a conviction admissible evidence but not conclusive, although there has been a tendency in those states to limit admissibility to convictions for serious offenses.

Federal Evidence Rule 803(22) makes admissible in federal court proof of conviction of a felony, demonstrating the same doubt concerning the reliability of convictions for lesser offenses. The Advisory Committee's note thereto explains that the Rule is to have no effect on the operation of res judicata.

Questions: (16) Should a conviction upon a guilty plea be conclusive in a subsequent civil action? See Haring v. Prosise, 103 S.Ct. 2368 (1983) (indicating no). Should such a conviction be admissible as evidence?

(17) Should an acquittal in a criminal case be conclusive in a subsequent civil action? Should an acquittal be admissible as evidence?

ALLEN v. McCURRY

Supreme Court of the United States, 1980.
449 U.S. 90, 101 S.Ct. 411.

JUSTICE STEWART delivered the opinion of the Court.

At a hearing before his criminal trial in a Missouri court, the respondent, Willie McCurry, invoked the Fourth and Fourteenth Amendments to suppress evidence that had been seized by the police. The trial court denied the suppression motion in part, and McCurry was subsequently convicted after a jury trial. The conviction was later affirmed on appeal. State v. McCurry, 587 S.W.2d 337 (Mo.Ct. App.). Because he did not assert that the state courts had denied him a "full and fair opportunity" to litigate his search and seizure claim, McCurry was barred by this Court's decision in Stone v. Powell, 428 U.S. 465, 96 S.Ct. 3037, from seeking a writ of habeas corpus in a federal district court. Nevertheless, he sought federal court redress for the alleged constitutional violation by bringing a damage suit under 42 U.S.C. § 1983 against the officers who had entered his home and seized the evidence in question. We granted certiorari to consider whether the unavailability of federal habeas corpus prevented the police officers from raising the state courts' partial rejection of McCurry's constitutional claim as a collateral estoppel defense to the § 1983 suit against them for damages. 444 U.S. 1070, 100 S.Ct. 1012.

I

In April 1977, several undercover police officers, following an informant's tip that McCurry was dealing in heroin, went to his house in St. Louis, Mo., to attempt a purchase. Two officers, petitioners Allen and Jacobsmeyer, knocked on the front door, while the other officers hid nearby. When McCurry opened the door, the two officers asked to buy some heroin "caps." McCurry went back into the house and returned soon thereafter, firing a pistol at and seriously wounding Allen and Jacobsmeyer. After a gun battle with the other officers and their reinforcements, McCurry retreated into the house; he emerged again when the police demanded that he surrender. Several officers then entered the house without a warrant, purportedly to search for other persons inside. One of the officers seized drugs and other contraband that lay in plain view, as well as additional contraband he found in dresser drawers and in auto tires on the porch.

McCurry was charged with possession of heroin and assault with intent to kill. At the pretrial suppression hearing, the trial judge excluded the evidence seized from the dresser drawers and tires, but denied suppression of the evidence found in plain view. McCurry was convicted of both the heroin and assault offenses.

McCurry subsequently filed the present § 1983 action for $1 million in damages against petitioners Allen and Jacobsmeyer, other unnamed individual police officers, and the city of St. Louis and its police department. The complaint alleged a conspiracy to violate McCurry's Fourth Amendment rights, an unconstitutional search and seizure of his house, and an assault on him by unknown police officers after he had been arrested and handcuffed. The petitioners moved for summary judgment. The District Court apparently understood the gist of the complaint to be the allegedly unconstitutional search and seizure and granted summary judgment, holding that collateral estoppel prevented McCurry from relitigating the search and seizure question already decided against him in the state courts. McCurry v. Allen, 466 F.Supp. 514 (ED Mo.1978).[2]

The Court of Appeals reversed the judgment and remanded the case for trial. McCurry v. Allen, 606 F.2d 795 (CA8 1979).[3] The appellate court said it was not holding that collateral estoppel was generally inapplicable in a § 1983 suit raising issues determined against the federal plaintiff in a state criminal trial. Id., at 798. But noting that Stone v. Powell, supra, barred McCurry from federal habeas corpus relief, and invoking "the special role of the federal courts in protecting civil rights," id., at 799, the court concluded that the § 1983 suit was McCurry's only route to a federal forum for his constitutional claim and directed the trial court to allow him to proceed to trial unencumbered by collateral estoppel.

II

The federal courts have traditionally adhered to the related doctrines of res judicata and collateral estoppel. Under res judicata, a final judgment on the merits of an action precludes the parties or their privies from relitigating issues that were or could have been raised in that action. Cromwell v. County of Sac, 94 U.S. 351, 352. Under collateral estoppel, once a court has decided an issue of fact or law necessary to its judgment, that decision may preclude relitigation of the issue in a suit on a different cause of action involving a party to the first case. Montana v. United States, 440 U.S. 147, 153, 99

---

[2] The merits of the Fourth Amendment claim are discussed in the opinion of the Missouri Court of Appeals. State v. McCurry, 587 S.W.2d 337 (Mo.Ct.App.). The state courts upheld the entry of the house as a reasonable response to emergency circumstances, but held illegal the seizure of any evidence discovered as a result of that entry except what was in plain view. Id., at 340. McCurry therefore argues here that even if the doctrine of collateral estoppel generally applies to this case, he should be able to proceed to trial to obtain damages for the part of the seizure declared illegal by the state courts. The petitioners contend, on the other hand, that the complaint alleged essentially an illegal entry, adding that only the entry could possibly justify the $1

million prayer. Since the state courts upheld the entry, the petitioners argue that if collateral estoppel applies here at all, it removes from trial all issues except the alleged assault. The United States Court of Appeals, however, addressed only the broad question of the applicability of collateral estoppel to § 1983 suits brought by plaintiffs in McCurry's circumstances, and questions as to the scope of collateral estoppel with respect to the particular issues in this case are not now before us.

[3] Beyond holding that collateral estoppel does not apply in this case, the Court of Appeals noted that the District Court had overlooked the conspiracy and assault charges. 606 F.2d, at 797, and n. 1.

S.Ct. 970, 973.[5]   As this Court and other courts have often recognized, res judicata and collateral estoppel relieve parties of the cost and vexation of multiple lawsuits, conserve judicial resources, and, by preventing inconsistent decisions, encourage reliance on adjudication. Id., at 153–154, 99 S.Ct., at 973–974.

In recent years, this Court has reaffirmed the benefits of collateral estoppel in particular, finding the policies underlying it to apply in contexts not formerly recognized at common law.   Thus, the Court has eliminated the requirement of mutuality in applying collateral estoppel to bar relitigation of issues decided earlier in federal court suits, Blonder-Tongue Laboratories, Inc. v. University of Illinois Foundation, 402 U.S. 313, 91 S.Ct. 1434, and has allowed a litigant who was not a party to a federal case to use collateral estoppel "offensively" in a new federal suit against the party who lost on the decided issue in the first case, Parklane Hosiery Co. v. Shore, 439 U.S. 322, 99 S.Ct. 645.[6]   But one general limitation the Court has repeatedly recognized is that the concept of collateral estoppel cannot apply when the party against whom the earlier decision is asserted did not have a "full and fair opportunity" to litigate that issue in the earlier case.   Montana v. United States, supra, 440 U.S., at 153, 99 S.Ct., at 973; Blonder-Tongue Laboratories, Inc. v. University of Illinois Foundation, supra, 402 U.S., at 328–329, 91 S.Ct., at 1443.[7]

The federal courts generally have also consistently accorded preclusive effect to issues decided by state courts.   E.g., Montana v. United States, supra; Angel v. Bullington, 330 U.S. 183, 67 S.Ct. 657. Thus, res judicata and collateral estoppel not only reduce unnecessary litigation and foster reliance on adjudication, but also promote the comity between state and federal courts that has been recognized

[5] The Restatement of Judgments now speaks of res judicata as "claim preclusion" and collateral estoppel as "issue preclusion."   Restatement of Judgments (Second) § 74 (Tent.Draft No. 3, 1976). Some courts and commentators use "res judicata" as generally meaning both forms of preclusion.

·   ·   ·   ·

[6] In Blonder-Tongue the Court noted other trends in the state and federal courts expanding the preclusive effects of judgments, such as the broadened definition of "claim" in the context of res judicata and the greater preclusive effect given criminal judgments in subsequent civil cases.   Blonder-Tongue Laboratories, Inc. v. University of Illinois Foundation, 402 U.S. 313, 326, 91 S.Ct. 1434, 1441.

[7] Other factors, of course, may require an exception to the normal rules of collateral estoppel in particular cases.   E.g.,

Montana v. United States, 440 U.S. 147, 162, 99 S.Ct. 970, 978 (unmixed questions of law in successive actions between the same parties on unrelated claims).

Contrary to the suggestion of the dissent, . . . our decision today does not "fashion" any new more stringent doctrine of collateral estoppel, nor does it hold that the collateral estoppel effect of a state-court decision turns on the single factor of whether the State gave the federal claimant a full and fair opportunity to litigate a federal question.   Our decision does not "fashion" any doctrine of collateral estoppel at all.   Rather, it construes § 1983 to determine whether the conventional doctrine of collateral estoppel applies to the case at hand.   It must be emphasized that the question whether any exceptions or qualifications within the bounds of that doctrine might ultimately defeat a collateral estoppel defense in this case is not before us.   See n. 2, supra.

as a bulwark of the federal system. See Younger v. Harris, 401 U.S. 37, 43–45, 91 S.Ct. 746, 750–51.

Indeed, though the federal courts may look to the common law or to the policies supporting res judicata and collateral estoppel in assessing the preclusive effect of decisions of other federal courts, Congress has specifically required all federal courts to give preclusive effect to state-court judgments whenever the courts of the State from which the judgments emerged would do so . . . . 28 U.S.C. § 1738 (1976); [citations omitted]. It is against this background that we examine the relationship of § 1983 and collateral estoppel, and the decision of the Court of Appeals in this case.

III

This Court has never directly decided whether the rules of res judicata and collateral estoppel are generally applicable to § 1983 actions. But in Preiser v. Rodriguez, 411 U.S. 475, 497, 93 S.Ct. 1827, 1840, the Court noted with implicit approval the view of other federal courts that res judicata principles fully apply to civil rights suits brought under that statute. See also Huffman v. Pursue, 420 U.S. 592, 606, n. 18, 95 S.Ct. 1200, 1209, n. 18; Wolff v. McDonnell, 418 U.S. 539, 554, n. 12, 94 S.Ct. 2963, 2974, n. 12.[9] And the virtually unanimous view of the Courts of Appeals since Preiser has been that § 1983 presents no categorical bar to the application of res judicata and collateral estoppel concepts. These federal appellate court decisions have spoken with little explanation or citation in assuming the compatibility of § 1983 and rules of preclusion, but the statute and its legislative history clearly support the courts' decisions.

Because the requirement of mutuality of estoppel was still alive in the federal courts until well into this century, see Blonder-Tongue Laboratories, Inc. v. University of Illinois Foundation, supra, 402 U.S., at 322–323, 91 S.Ct., at 1439–1440, the drafters of the 1871 Civil Rights Act, of which § 1983 is a part, may have had less reason to concern themselves with rules of preclusion than a modern Congress would. Nevertheless, in 1871 res judicata and collateral estoppel could certainly have applied in federal suits following state-court litigation between the same parties or their privies, and nothing in the language of § 1983 remotely expresses any congressional intent to contravene the common-law rules of preclusion or to repeal the express statutory requirements of . . . 28 U.S.C. § 1738 . . . . Section 1983 creates a new federal cause of action. It says nothing about the preclusive effect of state-court judgments.[12]

---

[9] The cases noted in Preiser applied res judicata to issues decided both in state civil proceedings, e.g., Coogan v. Cincinnati Bar Assn., 431 F.2d 1209, 1211 (CA6 1970), and state criminal proceedings, e.g., Goss v. Illinois, 312 F.2d 257, 259 (CA7 1963).

[12] By contrast, the roughly contemporaneous statute extending the federal writ of habeas corpus to state prisoners expressly rendered "null and void" any state-court proceeding inconsistent with the decision of a federal habeas court, Act of Feb. 5, 1867, ch. 28, § 1, 14 Stat.

Moreover, the legislative history of § 1983 does not in any clear way suggest that Congress intended to repeal or restrict the traditional doctrines of preclusion. The main goal of the Act was to override the corrupting influence of the Ku Klux Klan and its sympathizers on the governments and law enforcement agencies of the Southern States, see Monroe v. Pape, 365 U.S. 167, 174, 81 S.Ct. 473, 477, and of course the debates show that one strong motive behind its enactment was grave congressional concern that the state courts had been deficient in protecting federal rights, Mitchum v. Foster, 407 U.S. 225, 241–242, 92 S.Ct. 2151, 2161–2162; Monroe v. Pape, supra, 365 U.S., at 180, 81 S.Ct., at 480. But in the context of the legislative history as a whole, this congressional concern lends only the most equivocal support to any argument that, in cases where the state courts have recognized the constitutional claims asserted and provided fair procedures for determining them, Congress intended to override § 1738 or the common-law rules of collateral estoppel and res judicata. Since repeals by implication are disfavored, Radzanower v. Touche Ross & Co., 426 U.S. 148, 154, 96 S.Ct. 1989, 1993, much clearer support than this would be required to hold that § 1738 and the traditional rules of preclusion are not applicable to § 1983 suits.

As the Court has understood the history of the legislation, Congress realized that in enacting § 1983 it was altering the balance of judicial power between the state and federal courts. See Mitchum v. Foster, supra, 407 U.S., at 241, 92 S.Ct., at 2161. But in doing so, Congress was adding to the jurisdiction of the federal courts, not subtracting from that of the state courts. See Monroe v. Pape, supra, 365 U.S., at 183, 81 S.Ct., at 481 ("The federal remedy is supplementary to the state remedy . . . ."). The debates contain several references to the concurrent jurisdiction of the state courts over federal questions, and numerous suggestions that the state courts would retain their established jurisdiction so that they could, when the then current political passions abated, demonstrate a new sensitivity to federal rights.

To the extent that it did intend to change the balance of power over federal questions between the state and federal courts, the 42d Congress was acting in a way thoroughly consistent with the doctrines of preclusion. In reviewing the legislative history of § 1983 in Monroe v. Pape, supra, the Court inferred that Congress had intended a federal remedy [inter alia] . . . where state procedural law

385, 386 (1867) (current version at 28 U.S.C. § 2254), and the modern habeas statute also expressly adverts to the effect of state-court criminal judgments by requiring the applicant for the writ to exhaust his state-court remedies, 28 U.S.C. § 2254(b), and by presuming a state court resolution of a factual issue to be correct except in eight specific circumstances, id., § 2254(d). In any event, the traditional exception to res judicata for habeas corpus review, see Preiser v. Rodriguez, supra, 411 U.S., at 497, 93 S.Ct., at 1840, provides no analogy to § 1983 cases, since that exception finds its source in the unique purpose of habeas corpus—to release the applicant for the writ from unlawful confinement. Sanders v. United States, 373 U.S. 1, 8, 83 S.Ct. 1068, 1073.

was inadequate to allow full litigation of a constitutional claim, and where state procedural law, though adequate in theory, was inadequate in practice. 365 U.S., at 173–174, 81 S.Ct., at 476–477. In short, the federal courts could step in where the state courts were unable or unwilling to protect federal rights. Id., at 176, 81 S.Ct., at 478. This understanding of § 1983 might well support an exception to res judicata and collateral estoppel where state law did not provide fair procedures for the litigation of constitutional claims, or where a state court failed to even acknowledge the existence of the constitutional principle on which a litigant based his claim. Such an exception, however, would be essentially the same as the important general limit on rules of preclusion that already exists: Collateral estoppel does not apply where the party against whom an earlier court decision is asserted did not have a full and fair opportunity to litigate the claim or issue decided by the first court. . . . But the Court's view of § 1983 in Monroe lends no strength to any argument that Congress intended to allow relitigation of federal issues decided after a full and fair hearing in a state court simply because the state court's decision may have been erroneous.

. . . The Court of Appeals . . . concluded that since Stone v. Powell had removed McCurry's right to a hearing of his Fourth Amendment claim in federal habeas corpus, collateral estoppel should not deprive him of a federal judicial hearing of that claim in a § 1983 suit.

Stone v. Powell does not provide a logical doctrinal source for the court's ruling. This Court in Stone assessed the costs and benefits of the judge-made exclusionary rule within the boundaries of the federal courts' statutory power to issue writs of habeas corpus, and decided that the incremental deterrent effect that the issuance of the writ in Fourth Amendment cases might have on police conduct did not justify the cost the writ imposed upon the fair administration of criminal justice. 428 U.S., at 489–496, 96 S.Ct., at 3050–3053. The Stone decision concerns only the prudent exercise of federal court jurisdiction under 28 U.S.C. § 2254. It has no bearing on § 1983 suits or on the question of the preclusive effect of state-court judgments.

The actual basis of the Court of Appeals' holding appears to be a generally framed principle that every person asserting a federal right is entitled to one unencumbered opportunity to litigate that right in a federal district court, regardless of the legal posture in which the federal claim arises. But the authority for this principle is difficult to discern. It cannot lie in the Constitution, which makes no such guarantee, but leaves the scope of the jurisdiction of the federal district courts to the wisdom of Congress. And no such authority is to be found in § 1983 itself. For reasons already discussed at length, nothing in the language or legislative history of § 1983 proves any congressional intent to deny binding effect to a state-court judgment or decision when the state court, acting within its proper jurisdiction, has given the parties a full and fair opportunity to litigate federal claims, and thereby has shown itself willing and able to protect federal rights. And nothing in the legislative history of § 1983 reveals any purpose to afford less deference to judgments in state criminal proceedings than to those in state civil proceedings.[22] There is, in short, no reason to believe that Congress intended to provide a person claiming a federal right an unrestricted opportunity to relitigate an issue already decided in state court simply because the issue arose in a state proceeding in which he would rather not have been engaged at all.[23]

Through § 1983, the 42d Congress intended to afford an opportunity for legal and equitable relief in a federal court for certain types of injuries. It is difficult to believe that the drafters of that Act considered it a substitute for a federal writ of habeas corpus, the purpose of which is not to redress civil injury, but to release the applicant from unlawful physical confinement, Preiser v. Rodriguez, supra, 411 U.S., at 484, 93 S.Ct., at 1833; Fay v. Noia, 372 U.S. 391, 399, n. 5, 83 S.Ct. 822, 827, n. 5,[24] particularly in light of the extremely narrow scope of federal habeas relief for state prisoners in 1871.

The only other conceivable basis for finding a universal right to litigate a federal claim in a federal district court is hardly a legal basis at all, but rather a general distrust of the capacity of the state courts to render correct decisions on constitutional issues. It is ironic that Stone v. Powell provided the occasion for the expression of such an attitude in the present litigation, in view of this Court's emphatic reaffirmation in that case of the constitutional obligation of the state courts to uphold federal law, and its expression of confidence in their ability to do so. 428 U.S., at 493–494, n. 35, 96 S.Ct., at 3051–52, n. 35; see Robb v. Connolly, 111 U.S. 624, 637, 4 S.Ct. 544, 551 (Harlan, J.).

The Court of Appeals erred in holding that McCurry's inability to obtain federal habeas corpus relief upon his Fourth Amendment claim renders the doctrine of collateral estoppel inapplicable to his § 1983 suit. Accordingly, the judgment is reversed, and the case is

---

[22] . . . The Court of Appeals did not in any degree rest its holding on disagreement with the common view that judgments in criminal proceedings as well as in civil proceedings are entitled to preclusive effect. See, e.g., Emich Motors Corp. v. General Motors Corp., 340 U.S. 558, 71 S.Ct. 408.

[23] The Court of Appeals did not suggest that the prospect of collateral estoppel in a § 1983 suit would deter a defendant in a state criminal case from raising Fourth Amendment claims, and it is difficult to imagine a defendant risking conviction and imprisonment because he hoped to win a later civil judgment based upon an allegedly illegal search and seizure.

[24] Under the modern statute, federal habeas corpus is bounded by a requirement of exhaustion of state remedies and by special procedural rules, 28 U.S.C. § 2254, which have no counterparts in § 1983, and which therefore demonstrate the continuing illogic of treating federal habeas and § 1983 suits as fungible remedies for constitutional violations.

remanded to the Court of Appeals for proceedings consistent with this opinion.

It is so ordered.

JUSTICE BLACKMUN, with whom JUSTICE BRENNAN and JUSTICE MARSHALL join, dissenting.

The legal principles with which the Court is concerned in this civil case obviously far transcend the ugly facts of respondent's criminal convictions in the courts of Missouri for heroin possession and assault.

The Court today holds that notions of collateral estoppel apply with full force to this suit brought under 42 U.S.C. § 1983. In my view, the Court, in so ruling, ignores the clear import of the legislative history of that statute and disregards the important federal policies that underlie its enforcement. It also shows itself insensitive both to the significant differences between the § 1983 remedy and the exclusionary rule, and to the pressures upon a criminal defendant that make a free choice of forum illusory. I do not doubt that principles of preclusion are to be given such effect as is appropriate in a § 1983 action. In many cases, the denial of res judicata or collateral estoppel effect would serve no purpose and would harm relations between federal and state tribunals. Nonetheless, the Court's analysis in this particular case is unacceptable to me. It works injustice on this § 1983 plaintiff, and it makes more difficult the consistent protection of constitutional rights, a consideration that was at the core of the enacters' intent. Accordingly, I dissent.

. . . .

. . . Although the legislators of the 42d Congress did not expressly state whether the then-existing common-law doctrine of preclusion would survive enactment of § 1983, they plainly anticipated more than the creation of a federal statutory remedy to be administered indifferently by either a state or a federal court. The legislative intent, as expressed by supporters and understood by opponents, was to restructure relations between the state and federal courts. Congress deliberately opened the federal courts to individual citizens in response to the States' failure to provide justice in their own courts. Contrary to the view presently expressed by the Court, the 42d Congress was not concerned solely with procedural regularity. Even where there was procedural regularity, which the Court today so stresses, Congress believed that substantive justice was unobtainable. The availability of the federal forum was not meant to turn on whether, in an individual case, the state procedures were adequate. Assessing the state of affairs as a whole, Congress specifically made a determination that federal oversight of constitutional determinations through the federal courts was necessary to ensure the effective enforcement of constitutional rights.

That the new federal jurisdiction was conceived of as concurrent with state jurisdiction does not alter the significance of Congress' opening the federal courts to these claims. Congress consciously act-ed in the broadest possible manner. The legislators perceived that justice was not being done in the States then dominated by the Klan, and it seems senseless to suppose that they would have intended the federal courts to give full preclusive effect to prior state adjudica-tions. That supposition would contradict their obvious aim to right the wrongs perpetuated in those same courts.

. . . .

The Court now fashions a new doctrine of preclusion, applicable only to actions brought under § 1983, that is more strict and more confining than the federal rules of preclusion applied in other cases.

. . .

. . . [T]he Court states that the collateral estoppel effect of pri-or state adjudication should turn on only one factor, namely, what it considers the "one general limitation" inherent in the doctrine of pre-clusion: "that the concept of collateral estoppel cannot apply when the party against whom the earlier decision is asserted did not have a 'full and fair opportunity' to litigate that issue in the earlier case." . . . If that one factor is present, the Court asserts, the litigant properly should be barred from relitigating the issue in federal court.[12] One cannot deny that this factor is an important one. I do not believe, however, that the doctrine of preclusion requires the in-quiry to be so narrow, and my understanding of the policies underly-ing § 1983 would lead me to consider all relevant factors in each case before concluding that preclusion was warranted.

In this case, the police officers seek to prevent a criminal defend-ant from relitigating the constitutionality of their conduct in search-ing his house, after the state trial court had found that conduct in part violative of the defendant's Fourth Amendment rights and in part justified by the circumstances. I doubt that the police officers, now defendants in this § 1983 action, can be considered to have been in privity with the State in its role as prosecutor. Therefore, only "issue preclusion" is at stake.

The following factors persuade me to conclude that this re-spondent should not be precluded from asserting his claim in federal court. . . .

. . . [T]he process of deciding in a state criminal trial whether to exclude or admit evidence is not at all the equivalent of a § 1983 proceeding. The remedy sought in the latter is utterly different. In bringing the civil suit the criminal defendant does not seek to chal-lenge his conviction collaterally. At most, he wins damages. In con-trast, the exclusion of evidence may prevent a criminal conviction. A trial court, faced with the decision whether to exclude relevant evi-dence, confronts institutional pressures that may cause it to give a different shape to the Fourth Amendment right from what would re-

---

[12] This articulation of the preclusion doctrine of course would bar a § 1983 lit-igant from relitigating any issue he *might* have raised, as well as any issue he actually litigated in his criminal trial.

sult in civil litigation of a damages claim. Also, the issue whether to exclude evidence is subsidiary to the purpose of a criminal trial, which is to determine the guilt or innocence of the defendant, and a trial court, at least subconsciously, must weigh the potential damage to the truth-seeking process caused by excluding relevant evidence. See Stone v. Powell, 428 U.S. 465, 489–495, 96 S.Ct. 3037, 3050–3052 (1976). Cf. Bivens v. Six Unknown Federal Narcotics Agents, 403 U.S. 388, 411–424, 91 S.Ct. 1999, 2012–2018 (1971) (dissenting opinion).

A state criminal defendant cannot be held to have chosen "voluntarily" to litigate his Fourth Amendment claim in the state court. The risk of conviction puts pressure upon him to raise all possible defenses. He also faces uncertainty about the wisdom of forgoing litigation on *any* issue, for there is the possibility that he will be held to have waived his right to appeal on that issue. The "deliberate bypass" of state procedures, which the imposition of collateral estoppel under these circumstances encourages, surely is not a preferred goal. To hold that a criminal defendant who raises a Fourth Amendment claim at his criminal trial "freely and without reservation submits his federal claims for decision by the state courts," see England v. Medical Examiners, [375 U.S. 411, 419, 84 S.Ct. 461, 466 (1964)], is to deny reality. The criminal defendant is an involuntary litigant in the state tribunal, and against him all the forces of the State are arrayed. To force him to a choice between forgoing either a potential defense or a federal forum for hearing his constitutional civil claim is fundamentally unfair.

I would affirm the judgment of the Court of Appeals.

———

Beyond collateral estoppel.—There remains the question of the extent to which a stranger should be able to use the rules of res judicata other than collateral estoppel.

———

FAGNAN v. GREAT CENTRAL INSURANCE CO.

United States Court of Appeals, Seventh Circuit, 1978.
577 F.2d 418, cert. denied, 439 U.S. 1004, 99 S.Ct. 615 (1978).

Before TONE and BAUER, CIRCUIT JUDGES, and CAMPBELL, SENIOR DISTRICT JUDGE.[*]

TONE, CIRCUIT JUDGE.

The issue presented is whether the federal compulsory counterclaim rule, Rule 13(a), Fed.R.Civ.P., precludes an action against an insurance company under the Wisconsin direct action statute, when an action directly against the insured would be barred by the rule.

———

[*] The Honorable William J. Campbell, Senior District Judge of the United States District Court for the Northern District of Illinois, is sitting by designation.

The District Court answered this question in the negative and entered judgment against the insurance company. We reverse.

The collision of two automobiles in Wisconsin resulted in the death of one of the drivers, Robert Thompson, and injuries to his passenger, David Harness. The driver of the other automobile, Duane Fagnan, was also injured.

Harness, Thompson's passenger, brought an action against the administrator of Thompson's estate in the United States District Court for the District of Minnesota. The administrator filed a third party claim for contribution against Fagnan, who filed an answer to that claim. Later Harness filed a claim under Rule 14(a) against Fagnan, which Fagnan also answered. In addition, Fagnan cross-claimed against the administrator for contribution. The case was settled without a trial, and the court dismissed the action. Under the last sentence of Rule 41(b), Fed.R.Civ.P., the dismissal operated as an adjudication upon the merits.[1]

A few months after the action in Minnesota was dismissed, Duane Fagnan and his father, Raymond Fagnan, sued in a Wisconsin state court against Thompson's insurer, Great Central Insurance Company, under the Wisconsin direct action statute. Raymond Fagnan's claim was for medical expenses and care of his minor child incurred as a result of the [accident].[2] Also named as a defendant was Thompson's father, Darrold Thompson. The defendants removed the case to the United States District Court for the Western District of Wisconsin, where a trial before a jury resulted in a directed verdict in favor of Darrold Thompson, from which no appeal is taken, and verdicts in favor of both Duane Fagnan and Raymond Fagnan against the insurer, who appeals.

Relying on Rule 13(a), the insurer argues that any claim of Duane Fagnan against Robert Thompson's estate was disposed of by the judgment in the Minnesota action. The insurer now concedes that the award to Raymond Fagnan of damages for the medical expenses and care of Duane Fagnan cannot properly be challenged, since Raymond Fagnan was not a party to the Minnesota action. Accordingly, the judgment in his favor is not subject to attack.

[1] The court's order of dismissal recited that the court had been reliably informed that the case had been settled but the attorneys had "been negligent for some time in getting a stipulation of dismissal signed and filed." The court, therefore, sua sponte dismissed the action, retaining jurisdiction for 10 days, within which the parties could move to vacate. A stipulation to dismiss with prejudice had already been signed, the record before us shows, although it was apparently never filed with the court. The order of dismissal became final at the expiration of the 10 days and fell within the final category, "any dismissal not provided for in this rule," of Rule 41(b) and as such operated as an adjudication upon the merits.

[2] Under Wisconsin law a parent's liability for the medical expense and care of his minor child are separate causes of action from the child's personal injury claims and can only be asserted by the parent. Sulkowski v. Schaefer, 31 Wis. 2d 600, 143 N.W.2d 512, 515 (1966).

I.

At the time of the accident in this case, Wisconsin's direct action statutes were Wis.Stat. §§ 204.30(4) and 260.11(1). Section 204.30(4) was substantive and created "direct liability between the in[j]ured third person and the insurer," while § 260.11(1) provided the procedural vehicle by which the insurer could be made a party defendant. Miller v. Wadkins, 31 Wis.2d 281, 142 N.W.2d 855 (1966). See Koss v. Hartford Accident & Indemnity Co., 341 F.2d 472 (7th Cir. 1965). However,

> [t]he fact that a third party can sue an insurer of a motor vehicle direct . . . without first recovering a judgment against the insured defendant does not enlarge the coverage afforded by such policy or determine the insure[r]'s liability thereunder. The third party can only recover from the insurer by virtue of the contract existing between it and its insured.

Nichols v. U.S.F. & Guaranty Co., 13 Wis.2d 491, 109 N.W.2d 131, 136 (1961).

Therefore, an insurance company's liability under the Wisconsin direct action statute is derivative, i.e., the "insurer is not liable unless the assured is." Hunt v. Dollar, 224 Wis. 48, 271 N.W. 405, 409 (1937). Thus the insurer is liable in this action only if the insured, Robert Thompson's administrator, is liable.

II.

[The court here quoted Rule 13(a).] A compulsory counterclaim that is not asserted is barred by the judgment. Baker v. Gold Seal Liquors, Inc., 417 U.S. 467, 469 n.1, 94 S.Ct. 2504, 41 L.Ed.2d 243 (1974); Pipeliners Local Union No. 798, Tulsa, Okl. v. Ellerd, 503 F.2d 1193, 1198 (10th Cir. 1974).

Duane Fagnan's claim against Robert Thompson's administrator existed at the time the pleadings were served in the Minnesota action,[5] arose out of the same transaction or occurrence that was the subject of that action, and did not require for its adjudication the presence of third parties. It was therefore a compulsory counterclaim and was extinguished by the judgment in that action.

Because Duane Fagnan's claim against the administrator is barred, his claim against the insurer is also barred. The judgment in favor of Duane Fagnan against Great Central must therefore be reversed.

Affirmed in part and reversed in part. Each side will bear its own costs.

---

[5] Duane Fagnan also could have asserted his direct action against the insurer, which Minnesota law permitted him to do in view of the existence of the Wisconsin direct action statute. Myers v. Government Employees' Insurance Company, 302 Minn. 359, 225 N.W.2d 238 (1974).

TOPIC E.   CREDIT DUE TO VALID JUDGMENTS

SECTION 1. AMERICAN JUDGMENTS

FAUNTLEROY v. LUM

Supreme Court of the United States, 1908.
210 U.S. 230, 28 S.Ct. 641.

[Action was brought in a state court of Mississippi upon a Missouri judgment. The defendant pleaded that the original cause of action arose in Mississippi out of a gambling transaction in cotton futures between two Mississippi citizens, which was illegal under Mississippi law; [a] that the controversy was submitted to arbitration in Mississippi, the question of illegality not being included in the submission, and an award was made against the defendant; that the plaintiff brought suit on the award in a Missouri state court, serving the defendant with process while he was temporarily in Missouri; that the defendant was not allowed in the Missouri trial to show the nature of the transaction and hence its illegality under Mississippi law; and that verdict and judgment were entered for the plaintiff in Missouri. On demurrer, the Mississippi trial court ordered judgment for the plaintiff. The Mississippi Supreme Court reversed, ruling that the Missouri judgment was not entitled to full faith and credit. The case came to the Supreme Court of the United States on a writ of error.]

MR. JUSTICE HOLMES delivered the opinion of the court.

. . . .

The doctrine laid down by Chief Justice Marshall was "that the judgment of a state court should have the same credit, validity, and effect in every other court in the United States which it had in the state where it was pronounced, and that whatever pleas would be good to a suit thereon in such state, and none others, could be pleaded in any other court in the United States." Hampton v. M'Connel, 3 Wheat. 234. . . .

. . . .

We assume that the statement of Chief Justice Marshall is correct. It is confirmed by the act of May 26, 1790, c. 11, 1 Stat. 122 (Rev.Stat. § 905), providing that the said records and judicial proceedings "shall have such faith and credit given to them in every court within the United States as they have by law or usage in the courts of the state from whence the said records are or shall be taken." [b]

---

[a] The statutes of Mississippi made dealing in futures a misdemeanor and provided that such a contract "shall not be enforced by any court."

[b] Now 28 U.S.C. § 1738, on which see supra p. 797.

See further Tilt v. Kelsey, 207 U.S. 43, 57, 28 S.Ct. 1. Whether the award would or would not have been conclusive, and whether the ruling of the Missouri court upon that matter was right or wrong, there can be no question that the judgment was conclusive in Missouri on the validity of the cause of action. Pitts v. Fugate, 41 Mo. 405; State ex rel. Hudson v. Trammel, 106 Mo. 510, 17 S.W. 502; Re Copenhaver, 118 Mo. 377, 40 Am.St.Rep. 382, 24 S.W. 161. A judgment is conclusive as to all the media concludendi (United States v. California & O. Land Co., 192 U.S. 355, 24 S.Ct. 266); and it needs no authority to show that it cannot be impeached either in or out of the state by showing that it was based upon a mistake of law. Of course, a want of jurisdiction over either the person or the subject-matter might be shown. Andrews v. Andrews, 188 U.S. 14, 23 S.Ct. 237; Clarke v. Clarke, 178 U.S. 186, 20 S.Ct. 873. But, as the jurisdiction of the Missouri court is not open to dispute, the judgment cannot be impeached in Mississippi even if it went upon a misapprehension of the Mississippi law. [Citations omitted.]

We feel no apprehensions that painful or humiliating consequences will follow upon our decision. No court would give judgment for a plaintiff unless it believed that the facts were a cause of action by the law determining their effect. Mistakes will be rare. In this case the Missouri court no doubt supposed that the award was binding by the law of Mississippi. If it was mistaken, it made a natural mistake. The validity of its judgment, even in Mississippi, is, as we believe, the result of the Constitution as it always has been understood, and is not a matter to arouse the susceptibilities of the states, all of which are equally concerned in the question and equally on both sides.

Judgment reversed.

[The dissenting opinion of Justice White, with whom Justices Harlan, McKenna, and Day joined, is omitted.]

——————

Question: (1) Would the Supreme Court of the United States have had jurisdiction to review the Missouri judgment? If so, and the Supreme Court had heard the case, how should it have been decided?

——————

JAMES v. GRAND TRUNK WESTERN RAILROAD, 14 Ill.2d 356, 152 N.E.2d 858 (1958). The plaintiff administratrix sued the railroad in an Illinois court under the Michigan Wrongful Death Act. Thereafter a state court of Michigan, where the plaintiff in the Illinois action resided, granted the railroad an injunction restraining the plaintiff from prosecuting the Illinois action;[c] the plaintiff did not

[c] The Illinois court was to say that "the Michigan injunction was apparently issued pursuant to the policy of the State embodied in a Michigan venue statute restricting venue in suits against railroads to the county in which plaintiff resides, if the railroad lines traverse that county."

On the limited propriety of issuing such interstate injunctions in the first

appeal. Instead, she sought in Illinois a counter-injunction enjoining the railroad from enforcing the Michigan injunction. After denial of relief in the lower courts and an appeal by the plaintiff, the Illinois Supreme Court, in a 4–3 decision, restrained the enforcement of the Michigan injunction. It held that the Illinois court, having acquired jurisdiction first, was free not only to disregard an out-of-state injunction but also to protect its jurisdiction from usurpation by issuance of a counter-injunction, and that neither the full faith and credit clause nor rules of comity precluded this result. The dissenters agreed that the Michigan injunction was not entitled to full faith and credit; but they took the view that just as the first injunction sired the second, so the second might sire a third, and so forth, and that therefore the counter-injunction should be denied.

Questions: (2) Suppose the plaintiff continues to prosecute the Illinois action. What should the Michigan court do if the railroad initiates contempt proceedings? See Restatement (Second) of Conflict of Laws § 113 (1969).

(3) Would the Supreme Court of the United States have jurisdiction to review the Illinois judgment granting the injunction against the railroad? If so, and the Supreme Court were to hear the case, how should it be decided? See id. § 103 comment b.

HART v. AMERICAN AIRLINES
LANDANO v. AMERICAN AIRLINES
KIRCHSTEIN v. AMERICAN AIRLINES

Supreme Court of New York, New York County, 1969.
61 Misc.2d 41, 304 N.Y.S.2d 810.

HARRY B. FRANK, JUSTICE. Defendant American Airlines moves pursuant to CPLR, Section 602(a), for an order directing that all issues of liability in the death actions brought by plaintiffs Landano and Kirchstein be joined for trial with the 20 other American Airlines cases subject to joint trial under an order of the Appellate Division dated November 10, 1967. [See 28 A.D.2d 986.]

The actions all arise out of the crash, in Kentucky on November 8, 1965, of an American Airlines aircraft while the plane was en route from La Guardia Airport, New York to an airport in Covington, Kentucky. The crash resulted in the death of 58 out of the 62 persons aboard and, in addition to the multiple actions pending in this court, comparable actions have been instituted in other states and in various United States District Courts.

place, see Dumbauld, Judicial Interference with Litigation in Other Courts, 74 Dick.L.Rev. 369 (1970). Problems increase in the federal-state setting, as is suggested by the existence of 28 U.S.C. § 2283. See generally C. Wright, The Law of Federal Courts §§ 46–47 (4th ed. 1983).

Of the various actions instituted as a result of the crash, the first case to be tried to conclusion was that brought in the United States District Court, Northern District of Texas (Creasy v. American Airlines, Inc.), which resulted in a verdict in favor of the plaintiff therein against the defendant American Airlines. On a prior motion brought in the Hart case herein, the opinion of Mr. Justice Quinn, dated May 15, 1968, noted that in the Creasy trial, which lasted some 19 days, the Texas court applied the Kentucky wrongful death statute and submitted the question of American Airlines' liability on the basis of the substantive law of Kentucky relating to negligence. Reference to the pleadings in the two actions here sought to be joined for trial indicates that the basis for the recovery sought against defendant American Airlines is similarly predicated, and it is undisputable from the pleadings and papers herein that the issue of defendant airline's liability in these cases is identical to the issue in that regard determined in the Texas action.

In light of the Texas result which has now been affirmed on appeal, plaintiffs Landano and Kirchstein oppose defendant's motion for a joint trial by cross-moving for summary judgment on the issue of liability which, if granted, would obviate a trial on such issue and necessarily require a denial of defendant's motion.

Plaintiffs contend that while, concededly, they were not parties to the Texas action, nevertheless the determination in that action of defendant's liability for the plane crash of November 8, 1965 is, under the doctrine of collateral estoppel, conclusive on the issue of defendant's liability for such crash in the actions brought by these plaintiffs.

In its recent decision in Schwartz v. Public Administrator, 24 N.Y. 2d 65, 298 N.Y.S.2d 955, 246 N.E.2d 725, our Court of Appeals definitively crystalized the controlling considerations governing the doctrine of collateral estoppel in this State and "arrived at a modern and stable statement of the law of res judicata" grounded on "the sound principle that, where it can be fairly said that a party has had a full opportunity to litigate a particular issue, he cannot reasonably demand a second one" . . . . "There must be an identity of issue which has necessarily been decided in the prior action and is decisive of the present action, and, second, there must have been a full and fair opportunity to contest the decision now said to be controlling."

No extended discussion is necessary to demonstrate that such requirements are amply met in the instant cases. As already indicated, the issue of defendant airline's liability for the crash in which plaintiffs' decedents perished is identical to the issue of liability litigated in the Texas action where defendant was similarly charged with responsibility for that same accident. Indeed, in an airplane crash there are absent any of the problems with respect to "identity of issue" on liability which might arise in other types of accidents involving multiple participants such as automobile accident cases. With respect to the second requirement, it is in no way disputed that defendant had a full and fair opportunity to contest the issue of its liability in the course of the 19 day trial in the Texas action, and in order to defeat collateral estoppel on this ground the burden rests on the defendant to show that it had no such opportunity.

While defendant presents various arguments as to why the finding on liability should not be applied in these cases, it relies most heavily upon the prior decision of Mr. Justice Quinn in the Hart matter,[d] hereinbefore referred to, which was affirmed without opinion by the Appellate Division, 31 A.D.2d 896, 297 N.Y.S.2d 587. Although defendant concedes that such decision is not "in a strict sense" the law of the case here, it nevertheless contends that such decision compels a denial of plaintiffs' motion for summary judgment. This court disagrees. Contrary to defendant's assertions, the controlling factor in the Hart decision was the non-domicilliary status of the plaintiffs therein involved and the unwillingness of the court to apply the New York law of collateral estoppel with respect to a Texas determination on behalf of "non-domicilliary dependents of a deceased non-domicilliary 'bread winner'" having no significant contacts with New York. While such result will undoubtedly be effective to discourage possible "forum shopping" by non-residents, it does not, as defendant argues, preclude the application of the New York doctrine of collateral estoppel in an action brought by New York dependents of deceased New York residents. As was pointed out in Kilberg v. Northeast Airlines, 9 N.Y.2d 34, 39, 211 N.Y.S.2d 133, 135, 172 N.E.2d 526, 527–528, which involved a death action arising out of an airplane crash where decedent had been a New York resident, "The place of injury becomes entirely fortuitous. Our courts should if possible provide protection for our own State's people against unfair and anachronistic treatment of the lawsuits which result from these disasters." The state of Texas has no legitimate interest in imposing its rules on collateral estoppel upon these New York residents and a holding that permits such result would indeed constitute the "anachronistic treatment" warned against in Kilberg. The fact that the plaintiffs herein involved are New York domiciliaries, as were their decedents, sufficiently establishes this state's superior interest in the issue of collateral estoppel. It may be observed that these plaintiffs occupy much the same relationship to the state of Texas as the non-resident Hart plaintiffs do to New York, and the unavailability of the New York rule on collateral estoppel to the Hart plaintiffs is equally relevant in holding the instant resident plaintiffs outside the scope of the Texas rule on that issue.

[d] Unlike the cases of Landano and Kirchstein, this companion case involved only nonresidents. Justice Quinn there refused to extend collateral estoppel in favor of the nonresident plaintiffs, looking to the state law of Texas which followed the rule of mutuality of estoppel. N.Y.L.J., May 20, 1968, at 2, col. 6.

Defendant's reliance on "full faith and credit" to defeat the application of collateral estoppel herein is misplaced. This is not a situation where the judgment, as such, of the Texas court is sought to be enforced. What is here involved is a policy determination by our courts that " 'One who has had his day in court should not be permitted to litigate the question anew' " (B.R. DeWitt, Inc. v. Hall, 19 N.Y.2d 141, 144, 278 N.Y.S.2d 596, 599, 225 N.E.2d 195, 197 . . .), and, further, refusal "to tolerate a condition where, on relatively the same set of facts, one fact-finder, be it court or jury" may find a party liable while another exonerates him leading to the "inconsistent results which are always a blemish on a judicial system" (Schwartz v. Public Administrator, 24 N.Y.2d 65, 74, 298 N.Y.S.2d 955, 962, 246 N.E.2d 725, 730, supra). It is in order to carry out these policy determinations in the disposition of cases in this jurisdiction that an evidentiary use is being made of a particular issue determination made in the Texas action.

. . . .

Accordingly, plaintiffs' cross motion for summary judgment is granted and defendant's motion for a joint trial is denied. Settle order providing for an assessment of damages.

Questions: (4) Should the law of the rendering court or the law of the forum court govern the basic res judicata effects of a prior judgment? See Restatement (Second) of Conflict of Laws §§ 94–95 (1969). Should state or federal law govern the res judicata effects of a prior judgment rendered by a federal court sitting in diversity? Compare Degnan, Federalized Res Judicata, 85 Yale L.J. 741 (1976), with 18 Wright, Miller & Cooper § 4472.

(5) Should the full faith and credit clause be read to prohibit a state from giving a sister state's judgment *more* credit than it would be given where rendered? Is the giving of more credit fair to the party to be burdened?

KREMER v. CHEMICAL CONSTRUCTION CORP., 456 U.S. 461, 102 S.Ct. 1883 (1982). In this case, the Supreme Court decided that "a federal court in a Title VII case should give preclusive effect to a decision of a [New York] state court upholding a state administrative agency's rejection of an employment discrimination claim as meritless when the state court's decision would be [preclusive] in the state's own courts." After overcoming a number of the plaintiff's arguments, the Court observed:

"The more serious contention is that even though administrative proceedings and judicial review are legally sufficient to be given preclusive effect in New York, they should be deemed so fundamentally flawed as to be denied recognition under § 1738. We have previously recognized that the judicially created doctrine of collateral estoppel does not apply when the party against whom the earlier decision is asserted did not have a 'full and fair opportunity' to litigate the claim or issue . . . .

"Our previous decisions have not specified the source or defined the content of the requirement that the first adjudication offer a full and fair opportunity to litigate. But for present purposes, where we are bound by the statutory directive of § 1738, state proceedings need do no more than satisfy the minimum procedural requirements of the Fourteenth Amendment's Due Process Clause in order to qualify for the full faith and credit guaranteed by federal law. It has long been established that § 1738 does not allow federal courts to employ their own rules of res judicata in determining the effect of state judgments. Rather, it goes beyond the common law and commands a federal court to accept the rules chosen by the State from which the judgment is taken. . . .

"The State must, however, satisfy the applicable requirements of the Due Process Clause. A State may not grant preclusive effect in its own courts to a constitutionally infirm judgment, and other state and federal courts are not required to accord full faith and credit to such a judgment. Section 1738 does not suggest otherwise; other state and federal courts would still be providing a state court judgment with the 'same' preclusive effect as the courts of the State from which the judgment emerged. In such a case, there could be no constitutionally recognizable preclusion at all.

". . . We must bear in mind that no single model of procedural fairness, let alone a particular form of procedure, is dictated by the Due Process Clause. . . .

. . . .

"In our system of jurisprudence the usual rule is that merits of a legal claim once decided in a court of competent jurisdiction are not subject to redetermination in another forum. Such a fundamental departure from traditional rules of preclusion, enacted into federal law, can be justified only if plainly stated by Congress. Because there is no 'affirmative showing' of a 'clear and manifest' legislative purpose in Title VII to deny res judicata or collateral estoppel effect [in federal court] to a state court judgment affirming that a claim of employment discrimination is unproved, and because the procedures provided in New York for the determination of such claims offer a full and fair opportunity to litigate the merits, the judgment of the Court of Appeals is affirmed."

SECTION 2. JUDGMENTS OF FOREIGN NATIONS

HILTON v. GUYOT

Supreme Court of the United States, 1895.
159 U.S. 113, 16 S.Ct. 139.[e]

[French plaintiffs sued United States citizens in a circuit court of the United States upon a French judgment. The defendants denied any indebtedness and contended that the merits of the case should be examined, because the French courts would do so in a suit in France upon an American judgment against a French national. The circuit court entered judgment for the French plaintiffs without examining the merits.]

Mr. Justice Gray, after stating the case, delivered the opinion of the court.

. . . .

In view of all the authorities upon the subject, and of the trend of judicial opinion in this country and in England, following the lead of Kent and Story, we are satisfied that, where there has been opportunity for a full and fair trial abroad before a court of competent jurisdiction, conducting the trial upon regular proceedings, after due citation or voluntary appearance of the defendant, and under a system of jurisprudence likely to secure an impartial administration of justice between the citizens of its own country and those of other countries, and there is nothing to show either prejudice in the court, or in the system of laws under which it was sitting, or fraud in procuring the judgment, or any other special reason why the comity of this nation should not allow it full effect, the merits of the case should not, in an action brought in this country upon the judgment, be tried afresh, as on a new trial or an appeal, upon the mere assertion of the party that the judgment was erroneous in law or in fact. The defendants, therefore, cannot be permitted, upon that general ground, to contest the validity or the effect of the judgment sued on.

. . . .

It is next objected that in [the French] courts one of the plaintiffs was permitted to testify not under oath, and was not subjected to cross-examination by the opposite party, and that the defendants were, therefore, deprived of safeguards which are by our law considered essential to secure honesty and to detect fraud in a witness; and also that documents and papers were admitted in evidence, with which the defendants had no connection, and which would not be admissible under our own system of jurisprudence. But it having been shown by the plaintiffs, and hardly denied by the defendants, that the practice followed and the method of examining witnesses were ac-

[e] This case, covering 122 pages in the U.S. Reports, has been very drastically edited.

cording to the laws of France, we are not prepared to hold that the fact that the procedure in these respects differed from that of our own courts is, of itself, a sufficient ground for impeaching the foreign judgment.

[The Court next discussed whether a foreign judgment may be impeached on the ground that it was fraudulently obtained, and the Court cited English cases holding that it may be so impeached.]

But whether those decisions can be followed in regard to foreign judgments, consistently with our own decisions as to impeaching domestic judgments for fraud, it is unnecessary in this case to determine, because there is a distinct and independent ground upon which we are satisfied that the comity of our nation does not require us to give conclusive effect to the judgments of the courts of France; and that ground is, the want of reciprocity, on the part of France, as to the effect to be given to the judgments of this and other foreign countries.

[An extended review of the law of many countries as to the enforcement of foreign judgments is omitted.]

The reasonable, if not the necessary, conclusion appears to us to be that judgments rendered in France, or in any other foreign country, by the laws of which our own judgments are reviewable upon the merits, are not entitled to full credit and conclusive effect when sued upon in this country, but are prima facie evidence only of the justice of the plaintiffs' claim.

In holding such a judgment, for want of reciprocity, not to be conclusive evidence of the merits of the claim, we do not proceed upon any theory of retaliation upon one person by reason of injustice done to another; but upon the broad ground that international law is founded upon mutuality and reciprocity, and that by the principles of international law recognized in most civilized nations, and by the comity of our own country, which it is our judicial duty to know and to declare, the judgment is not entitled to be considered conclusive.

[The judgment was reversed. The dissenting opinion of Chief Justice Fuller, with whom Justices Harlan, Brewer, and Jackson joined, is omitted.]

Questions: (6) Should a state court, in considering whether to give conclusive effect to a French judgment in a case like Hilton v. Guyot, regard the question as one of federal law? See Moore, Federalism and Foreign Relations, 1965 Duke L.J. 248, 265.

(7) The New York courts have given conclusive effect to judgments of foreign nations without regard to any question of reciprocity, thus rejecting the rule of Hilton v. Guyot. Johnston v. Compagnie Générale Transatlantique, 242 N.Y. 381, 152 N.E. 121 (1926). In a diversity action upon a foreign judgment in a federal court in New York commenced after Erie R.R. v. Tompkins, must the New York rule be followed? See Bank of Montreal v. Kough, 612 F.2d 467 (9th Cir.1980) (yes). But cf. Reese, The Status in This

Country of Judgments Rendered Abroad, 50 Colum.L.Rev. 783, 786–88 (1950).

RESTATEMENT (SECOND) OF CONFLICT OF LAWS
(1969).

§ 98. *Recognition of Foreign Nation Judgments*

A valid judgment rendered in a foreign nation after a fair trial in a contested proceeding will be recognized in the United States so far as the immediate parties and the underlying cause of action are concerned.

Questions: (8) If Fauntleroy v. Lum had been an action to enforce a judgment of a foreign nation, rather than that of a sister state, how should the case have been decided (assuming no problem of lack of reciprocity)? See Restatement (Second) of Conflict of Laws § 117 comment c (1969).

(9) Assuming that the required circumstances for recognizing a judgment of a foreign nation exist, what is the extent of recognition? That is, should the basic res judicata effects of the prior judgment be governed by the foreign law, by the usual res judicata rules of domestic law, or by some special set of res judicata rules for international judgments? Is it significant that res judicata rules in American legal systems generally are considerably broader in effect than elsewhere? See 18 Wright, Miller & Cooper § 4473, at 745–47.

SECTION 3. VALIDITY

BANK OF MONTREAL v. OLAFSSON
United States Court of Appeals, Sixth Circuit, 1981.
648 F.2d 1078, cert. denied, 454 U.S. 1084, 102 S.Ct. 641 (1981).

Before ENGEL and MERRITT, CIRCUIT JUDGES and PHILLIPS, SENIOR CIRCUIT JUDGE.

PER CURIAM.

The plaintiff is a Canadian corporation, and the defendant a citizen of Iceland. The issue here is whether the trial court erred in setting aside a default judgment it had entered more than a year earlier. The ground for setting it aside was that it had no subject matter jurisdiction because the requisite diversity of citizenship was lacking.

The Bank of Montreal filed suit March 2, 1978 against Thorhallur G. Olafsson to recover $34,572 due it through promissory notes and an overdraft. On May 31, 1978 the District Court granted a default judgment. The Bank then filed liens on Michigan realty held in the name of Olafsson's wife, and the property was sold to the Bank in satisfaction of its judgment. On June 7, 1979 Olafsson moved to set aside the judgment on two grounds: (1) because he was never personally served with a copy of the complaint, and (2) because he had filed for bankruptcy in Canada on March 28, 1978,[2] and under Canada law it is illegal to pursue claims while bankruptcy proceedings are pending.

In argument on the motion, Olafsson raised the diversity question. The district court rendered its opinion from the bench, finding that the bank was a Canadian corporation and that Olafsson was not a citizen of the United States either. It stated that the Bank knew or should have known of the citizenship of Olafsson. It recognized that the Bank had taken action in reliance on the default but found the policy against granting judgments in cases in which the court has no jurisdiction to be overriding. It noted that it had never before addressed the jurisdictional question and concluded that the default judgment should be vacated under Fed.R.Civ.P. 60(b)(4) or 60(b)(6) because it was entered "in excess of the power of this court." The court set aside the default judgment and "all liens, writs of levy and execution, and sheriff's sales," and dismissed the suit.

The grant of motions made under rule 60(b) is a matter of discretion for the district court, and its decision is to be set aside only if it constitutes an abuse of discretion. Wright & Miller, Federal Practice and Procedure: Civil § 2872; 7 Moore's Federal Practice ¶ 60.19. The competing values implicated in the decision are on the one hand the interest in finality of judgments and on the other the interest in maintaining federal constitutional jurisdictional limitations.

[The court of appeals decided to rely on Rule 60(b)(6).] The district court also relied on rule 60(b)(6), which allows for a weighing of equities, in setting aside the judgment. See Wright & Miller, § 2864; 7 Moore's ¶ 60.27[2]. It discounted the Bank's reliance interest because of its finding that the Bank "knew or reasonably should have known" of Olafsson's citizenship. Olafsson's stated reason for not responding to the Bank's suit was that he had forwarded the complaint to his bankruptcy trustee with the understanding that he would take care of it.

. . . .

Given the lack of federal jurisdiction in the case, and considering the equities of the case under rule 60(b), we agree with the district court that the default judgment should be set aside and the case dismissed for lack of subject matter jurisdiction. The dispute between the parties over the promissory notes, overdraft, and liens can be more fairly and completely adjudicated in the Canadian bankruptcy court, in the country where the loan was made, the bank is located and Olafsson's bankruptcy is pending.

[2] In that proceeding the Bank was named as a creditor.

Accordingly, the judgment of the district court is affirmed.

———

MARSHALL v. LOCKHEAD

Court of Civil Appeals of Texas, 1952.
245 S.W.2d 307, writ of error refused n.r.e.

HALE, JUSTICE.

Appellant sued appellee [in the 134th Judicial District Court of Dallas County] to set aside a prior judgment rendered in a former suit for the collection of delinquent taxes and to recover the title and possession of a certain lot sold and conveyed to appellee under an order of sale issued on the judgment in the prior tax suit. The present case was tried before the court below without a jury and resulted in judgment that appellant take nothing.

Appellant says the judgment in the tax suit was invalid and void in so far as he is concerned, because he was not served with citation and did not enter any appearance in the former suit, and hence he insists the Court did not acquire jurisdiction over his person. On the other hand, appellee says the judgment was not void and hence is not subject to collateral attack in this suit, and that appellant, by accepting the benefits accruing to him under the same, is estopped from asserting in this suit that such judgment is void or invalid.

The record before us discloses that on May 10, 1945, a final judgment was rendered in the 44th Judicial District Court of Dallas County, whereby the court found the amount of delinquent taxes, penalties and interest due and owing to the State of Texas and certain of its political subdivisions by reason of the ownership of the two lots therein described, being hereafter referred to as Lots 6 and 18. The judgment recites that defendants, C.B. Marshall and wife, Isabelle Marshall, had been duly cited in terms of law to appear but had wholly made default. The court found the amount of taxes, penalties and interest due against each of the two lots, decreed a foreclosure of the tax lien on each lot as against the defendants and directed that an order of sale be issued for each lot.

In pursuance of an order of sale issued on the above judgment, the sheriff of Dallas County sold Lot 6 to one George A. Harnack on July 3, 1945 for the sum of $1160.00. Of this amount the sum of $530.59 was paid to the State of Texas and others in satisfaction of the taxes due on Lot 6, and the balance thereof in the sum of $626.41 was paid into the registry of the court for the former owner of said lot. Thereafter, on April 6, 1948, C.B. (Bruce) Marshall, the appellant herein, applied to the 44th Judicial District Court for an order granting him permission to withdraw such excess money from the registry of the court as the former owner of Lot 6. The court granted the application, appellant withdrew said sum of $626.41 from the registry of the court, appropriated the same to his own use and benefit, and he has not returned or offered to return the same, or any part thereof, into court. In pursuance of another order of sale issued on the above judgment, the sheriff of Dallas County sold and conveyed Lot 18 to appellee and it is this lot which appellant seeks to recover in the present suit.

In our opinion, the trial court did not err in rendering judgment that appellant take nothing by this suit. In the leading case of Crawford v. McDonald, 88 Tex. 626, 33 S.W. 325, 328, the Supreme Court of Texas said: "Where a personal judgment has been rendered against a defendant by a domestic court of general jurisdiction, and under the same his property has been seized and sold, he will not, in a contest over the title to the property, be allowed to show by evidence dehors the record that the judgment was rendered without any service whatever upon him. Logically, the judgment is, in fact, void, but on grounds of public policy the courts, in order to protect the property rights, apply the rule aforesaid, which precludes inquiry into facts dehors the record for the purpose of showing the invalidity of the judgment; and therefore, for all practical purposes, in such collateral attack, the judgment is held valid."

Furthermore, it is generally held upon sound principles of equity that one who accepts and retains the fruits of a judgment is estopped thereafter to assert its invalidity. 31 Am.Jur. 92, Sec. 432; 49 C.J.S., Judgments, § 453, p. 884; 17 T.J. p. 135, Sec. 7. This just rule applies to cases where the asserted invalidity arises from a lack of jurisdiction of the court over the person of a party to the suit. Therefore, even though the C.B. Marshall who was served with citation in the tax suit here involved was not in fact the same person as the appellant in this cause, nevertheless it appears to us that the appellant herein, by reason of his conduct in procuring and retaining the sum of $626.41 paid into the registry of the court under the judgment rendered in the tax suit, conclusively estopped himself from successfully asserting in this suit that the tax judgment or either of the sales emanating therefrom was void or invalid. [Citations omitted.]

Consequently, all of appellant's points of error are overruled and the judgment appealed from is affirmed.

BRITTON v. GANNON

Supreme Court of Oklahoma, 1955.
285 P.2d 407, cert. denied, 350 U.S. 886, 76 S.Ct. 140 (1955).

ARNOLD, JUSTICE.

Mark Gannon brought this action in the District Court of Pontotoc County against W.R. Britton on a foreign judgment rendered in favor of said Gannon against Britton in the Circuit Court of Fayette County, Illinois, in the sum of $18,000.

Defendant filed answer consisting of a general denial and allegations to the effect that Mark Gannon was only a nominal party; that the real party in interest was Roy or "Spike" Gannon, brother of Mark Gannon; that said "Spike" Gannon had advised defendant that he was filing suit to recover certain personal property owned by him and defendant which had been sold pursuant to mortgage foreclosure proceedings and that Britton was a necessary defendant, but that no judgment would be taken against him, and relying on these representations, although served with summons, Britton made no effort to defend such suit and did not know that judgment had been taken against him until the instant suit was filed. Upon motion of plaintiff and over the objections and exceptions of defendant all allegations of defendant's answer except his general denial were stricken.

[At trial, plaintiff proved his claim, but defendant's evidence was not admitted.]

The court found that under the full faith and credit clause of the Constitution of the United States, art. 4, § 1, it had no right to hear and determine the validity of the defendant's defense . . . and entered judgment in favor of plaintiff for the amount prayed for.

Defendant contends that the court erred in refusing to allow him to present evidence to the effect that the judgment in Illinois, the basis of the present suit, was procured by extrinsic fraud and therefore not entitled to full faith and credit in Oklahoma.

The general rule is that a state court is not required to recognize the judgment of a court of another state, territory, or country subject to the jurisdiction of the United States, where the court rendering the judgment was without jurisdiction or judgment was obtained by extrinsic fraud. Stephens v. Thomasson, 63 Ariz. 187, 160 P.2d 338, and cases therein cited. Whatever plea would be good in the state in which the judgment was rendered may be pleaded in suit on the judgment in any other court in the United States. Ibid. Extrinsic fraud has been defined as any fraudulent conduct of the successful party which was practiced outside of an actual adversary trial directly and affirmatively on the defeated party whereby he was prevented from presenting fully and fairly his side of the cause. Included in such definition are false representations that the defeated party is merely a nominal party against whom no relief is sought, false promises of compromise, concealment of the suit, kidnapping of witnesses, and the like. Calkin v. Wolcott, 182 Okl. 278, 77 P.2d 96. In such cases a court of equity had power to annul the decree so obtained. Ibid. See also American Ry. Express Co. v. Murphy, 234 Ill.App. 346, Village of Hartford v. First National Bank of Wood River, 307 Ill.App. 447, 30 N.E.2d 524. Some cases, as United States v. Throckmorton, 98 U.S. 61, 25 L.Ed. 93, put this on the ground that in such cases there has never been a real contest in the hearing of the case; others, such as Williams v. State of North Carolina, 325 U.S. 226, 65 S.Ct. 1092, 89 L.Ed. 1577, cited as authority in Stephens v. Thomasson, supra, on the ground that such conduct on the part of the successful party prevented the court from having jurisdiction to render the judgment which was rendered. Others, such as Levin v. Gladstein, 142 N.C. 482, 55 S.E. 371, 32 L.R.A.,N.S., 905, put it on the ground that a foreign court is not required to give greater faith and credit to the judgment than it is entitled to at home, and when the state in which the judgment was rendered would enjoin the enforcement of such judgment because of the circumstances under which it was obtained, the sister state may do likewise.

Regardless of the reason assigned for the rule, the weight of authority is overwhelming that a defense of extrinsic fraud of the nature here sought to be plead and proved may be interposed in a suit on a foreign judgment, not for the purpose of reviewing, setting aside, modifying, or annulling the judgment of the sister state, but to prevent its enforcement in the collateral court. [Citations omitted.] The trial court erred in refusing the proffered evidence of extrinsic fraud.

Reversed and remanded for a new trial.

JOHNSON, C.J., WILLIAMS, V.C.J., and CORN, BLACKBIRD and JACKSON, JJ., concur.[f]

SECTION 4. "JURISDICTION TO DETERMINE JURISDICTION"—JURISDICTIONAL FINDINGS AS RES JUDICATA

BALDWIN v. IOWA STATE TRAVELING MEN'S ASSOCIATION
Supreme Court of the United States, 1931.
283 U.S. 522, 51 S.Ct. 517.

MR. JUSTICE ROBERTS delivered the opinion of the Court.

A writ of certiorari was granted herein to review the affirmance by the Circuit Court of Appeals of a judgment for respondent rendered by the District Court for Southern Iowa. The action was upon the record of a judgment rendered in favor of the petitioner against the respondent in the United States District Court for Western Missouri.

The defense was lack of jurisdiction of the person of the respondent in the court which entered the judgment. After hearing, in which a jury was waived, this defense was sustained and the action dismissed. The first suit was begun in a Missouri state court and removed to the District Court. Respondent appeared specially and moved to quash and dismiss for want of service. The court quashed

---

[f] In a different action, relief from the same Illinois judgment was denied. Gannon v. American Airlines, 251 F.2d 476, 482 (10th Cir.1957) (2–1 decision) (judgment "not open to collateral attack in this proceeding upon the ground of fraud not going to the jurisdiction of the court"), vacated per stipulation, 251 F.2d 486 (10th Cir.1958).

the service, but refused to dismiss. An alias summons was issued and returned served, whereupon it again appeared specially, moved to set aside the service, quash the return, and dismiss the case for want of jurisdiction of its person. After a hearing on affidavits and briefs, the motion was overruled, with leave to plead within thirty days. No plea having been filed within that period, the cause proceeded and judgment was entered for the amount claimed. Respondent did not move to set aside the judgment nor sue out a writ of error.

The ground of the motion made in the first suit is the same as that relied on as a defense to this one, namely, that the respondent is an Iowa corporation, that it never was present in Missouri, and that the person served with process in the latter State was not such an agent that service on him constituted a service on the corporation. The petitioner objected to proof of these matters, asserting that the defense constituted a collateral attack and a retrial of an issue settled in the first suit. The overruling of this objection and the resulting judgment for respondent are assigned as error.

The petitioner suggests that Article IV, Section 1 of the Constitution forbade the retrial of the question determined on respondent's motion in the Missouri District Court; but the full faith and credit required by that clause is not involved, since neither of the courts concerned was a state court. (Compare Cooper v. Newell, 173 U.S. 555, 567,ᵏ 19 S.Ct. 506; Supreme Lodge, Knights of Pythias v. Meyer, 265 U.S. 30, 33,ʰ 44 S.Ct. 432.) The respondent, on the other hand, insists that to deprive it of the defense which it made in the court below, of lack of jurisdiction over it by the Missouri District Court, would be to deny the due process guaranteed by the Fourteenth Amendment; but there is involved in that doctrine no right to litigate the same question twice (Chicago Life Ins. Co. v. Cherry, 244 U.S. 25, 37 S.Ct. 492; compare York v. Texas, 137 U.S. 15, 11 S.Ct. 9).

The substantial matter for determination is whether the judgment amounts to res judicata on the question of the jurisdiction of the court which rendered it over the person of the respondent. It is of no moment that the appearance was a special one expressly saving any submission to such jurisdiction. That fact would be important upon appeal from the judgment, and would save the question of the propriety of the court's decision on the matter even though after the motion had been overruled the respondent had proceeded, subject to a reserved objection and exception, to a trial on the merits. Harkness v. Hyde, 98 U.S. 476; [other citations omitted]. The special appearance

---

ᵏ "And the courts of the United States are bound to give to the judgments of the state courts the same faith and credit that the courts of one State are bound to give to the judgments of the courts of her sister States."

ʰ "While the judicial proceedings of the federal courts are not within the terms of the constitutional provision, such proceedings, nevertheless, must be accorded the same full faith and credit by state courts as would be required in respect of the judicial proceedings of another State."

gives point to the fact that the respondent entered the Missouri court for the very purpose of litigating the question of jurisdiction over its person. It had the election not to appear at all. If, in the absence of appearance, the court had proceeded to judgment and the present suit had been brought thereon, respondent could have raised and tried out the issue in the present action, because it would never have had its day in court with respect to jurisdiction. Thompson v. Whitman, 18 Wall. 457; Pennoyer v. Neff, 95 U.S. 714; Hart v. Sansom, 110 U.S. 151, 3 S.Ct. 586; Wetmore v. Karrick, 205 U.S. 141, 27 S.Ct. 434; Bigelow v. Old Dominion Copper Co., 225 U.S. 111, 32 S.Ct. 641; McDonald v. Mabee, 243 U.S. 90, 37 S.Ct. 343. It had also the right to appeal from the decision of the Missouri District Court, as is shown by Harkness v. Hyde, supra, and the other authorities cited. It elected to follow neither of those courses, but, after having been defeated upon full hearing in its contention as to jurisdiction, it took no further steps, and the judgment in question resulted.

Public policy dictates that there be an end of litigation; that those who have contested an issue shall be bound by the result of the contest, and that matters once tried shall be considered forever settled as between the parties. We see no reason why this doctrine should not apply in every case where one voluntarily appears, presents his case and is fully heard, and why he should not, in the absence of fraud, be thereafter concluded by the judgment of the tribunal to which he has submitted his cause.

. . . .

The judgment is reversed and the cause remanded for further proceedings in conformity with this opinion.

Reversed.

Question: (10) Would the result have been different if the prior judgment against the respondent had been entered after a general appearance and the issue of personal jurisdiction had not been raised, litigated, or determined?

CHICOT COUNTY DRAINAGE DISTRICT v. BAXTER STATE BANK
Supreme Court of the United States, 1940.
308 U.S. 371, 60 S.Ct. 317.

MR. CHIEF JUSTICE HUGHES delivered the opinion of the Court.

Respondents brought this suit [on July 24, 1937] in the United States District Court for the Western Division of the Eastern District of Arkansas to recover on fourteen bonds of $1,000 each, which had been issued in 1924 by the petitioner, Chicot County Drainage District, organized under statutes of Arkansas, and had been in default since 1932.

In its answer, petitioner pleaded a decree of the same District Court in a proceeding instituted by petitioner to effect a plan of readjustment of its indebtedness under the Act of May 24, 1934, providing for "Municipal-Debt Readjustments". The decree recited that a plan of readjustment had been accepted by the holders of more than two-thirds of the outstanding indebtedness and was fair and equitable; that to consummate the plan and with the approval of the court petitioner had issued and sold new serial bonds to the Reconstruction Finance Corporation in the amount of $193,500 and that these new bonds were valid obligations; that, also with the approval of the court, the Reconstruction Finance Corporation had purchased outstanding obligations of petitioner to the amount of $705,087.06 which had been delivered in exchange for new bonds and canceled; that certain proceeds had been turned over to the clerk of the court and that the disbursing agent had filed his report showing that the Reconstruction Finance Corporation had purchased all the old bonds of petitioner other than the amount of $57,449.30. The decree provided for the application of the amount paid into court to the remaining old obligations of petitioner, that such obligations might be presented within one year, and that unless so presented they should be forever barred from participating in the plan of readjustment or in the fund paid into court. Except for the provision for such presentation, the decree canceled the old bonds and the holders were enjoined from thereafter asserting any claim thereon.

Petitioner pleaded this decree, which was entered in March, 1936, as res judicata. Respondents demurred to the answer. Thereupon the parties stipulated for trial without a jury.

The evidence showed respondents' ownership of the bonds in suit and that respondents had notice of the proceeding for debt readjustment. The record of that proceeding, including the final decree, was introduced. The District Court ruled in favor of respondents and the Circuit Court of Appeals affirmed. 8 Cir., 103 F.2d 847. The decision was placed upon the ground that the decree was void because, subsequent to its entry, this Court in a proceeding relating to a municipal district in Texas had declared the statute under which the District Court had acted to be unconstitutional. Ashton v. Cameron County District, 298 U.S. 513, 56 S.Ct. 892. In view of the importance of the question we granted certiorari. October 9, 1939. 308 U.S. 532, 60 S.Ct. 84.

. . . .

First. Apart from the contention as to the effect of the later decision as to constitutionality, all the elements necessary to constitute the defense of res judicata are present. It appears that the proceedings in the District Court to bring about a plan of readjustment were conducted in complete conformity to the statute. The Circuit Court of Appeals observed that no question had been raised as to the regularity of the court's action. The answer in the present suit alleged that the plaintiffs (respondents here) had notice of the proceeding and were parties, and the evidence was to the same effect, showing compliance with the statute in that respect. As parties, these bondholders had full opportunity to present any objections to the proceeding, not only as to its regularity, or the fairness of the proposed plan of readjustment, or the propriety of the terms of the decree, but also as to the validity of the statute under which the proceeding was brought and the plan put into effect.[i] Apparently no question of validity was raised and the cause proceeded to decree on the assumption by all parties and the court itself that the statute was valid. There was no attempt to review the decree. If the general principles governing the defense of res judicata are applicable, these bondholders, having the opportunity to raise the question of invalidity, were not the less bound by the decree because they failed to raise it. Cromwell v. County of Sac, 94 U.S. 351, 352; Case v. Beauregard, 101 U.S. 688, 692; Baltimore Steamship Co. v. Phillips, 274 U.S. 316, 319, 325, 47 S.Ct. 600, 601, 604; Grubb v. Public Utilities Commission, 281 U.S. 470, 479, 50 S.Ct. 374, 378.

Second. The argument is pressed that the District Court was sitting as a court of bankruptcy, with the limited jurisdiction conferred by statute, and that, as the statute was later declared to be invalid, the District Court was without jurisdiction to entertain the proceeding and hence its decree is open to collateral attack. We think the argument untenable. The lower federal courts are all courts of limited jurisdiction, that is, with only the jurisdiction which Congress has prescribed. But none the less they are courts with authority, when parties are brought before them in accordance with the requirements of due process, to determine whether or not they have jurisdiction to entertain the cause and for this purpose to construe and apply the statute under which they are asked to act. Their determinations of such questions, while open to direct review, may not be assailed collaterally.

. . . This rule applies equally to the decrees of the District Court sitting in bankruptcy, that is, purporting to act under a statute of Congress passed in the exercise of the bankruptcy power. The court has the authority to pass upon its own jurisdiction and its decree sustaining jurisdiction against attack, while open to direct review, is res judicata in a collateral action. Stoll v. Gottlieb, 305 U.S. 165, 171, 172, 59 S.Ct. 134, 137.

Whatever the contention as to jurisdiction may be, whether it is that the boundaries of a valid statute have been transgressed, or that the statute itself is invalid, the question of jurisdiction is still one for judical determination. If the contention is one as to validity, the question is to be considered in the light of the standing of the party who seeks to raise the question and of its particular application. In the present instance it is suggested that the situation of petitioner, Chicot County Drainage District, is different from that of the municipal district before the court in the Ashton case. Petitioner contends

---

[i] The briefs in this case indicate that while other bondholders did appear in the bankruptcy proceeding, the respondents themselves never appeared in person or by attorney. The court below likewise observed this fact, 103 F.2d at 848.

that it is not a political subdivision of the State of Arkansas but an agent of the property owners within the District. See Drainage District No. 7 of Poinsett County v. Hutchins, 184 Ark. 521, 42 S.W.2d 996. We do not refer to that phase of the case as now determinative but merely as illustrating the sort of question which the District Court might have been called upon to resolve had the validity of the Act of Congress in the present application been raised. As the question of validity was one which had to be determined by a judicial decision, if determined at all, no reason appears why it should not be regarded as determinable by the District Court like any other question affecting its jurisdiction. There can be no doubt that if the question of the constitutionality of the statute had actually been raised and decided by the District Court in the proceeding to effect a plan of debt readjustment in accordance with the statute, that determination would have been final save as it was open to direct review upon appeal. Stoll v. Gottlieb, supra.

The remaining question is simply whether respondents, having failed to raise the question in the proceeding to which they were parties and in which they could have raised it and had it finally determined, were privileged to remain quiet and raise it in a subsequent suit. Such a view is contrary to the well-settled principle that res judicata may be pleaded as a bar, not only as respects matters actually presented to sustain or defeat the right asserted in the earlier proceeding, "but also as respects any other available matter which might have been presented to that end". Grubb v. Public Utilities Commission, supra; Cromwell v. County of Sac, supra.

The judgment is reversed and the cause is remanded to the District Court with direction to dismiss the complaint.

Reversed.

Questions: (11) Would the rule of Chicot—that lack of subject-matter jurisdiction generally cannot be raised on collateral attack even though it was not actually litigated in the prior action—apply if a prior judgment were invoked merely for issue preclusion purposes? Would the rule of Chicot apply if a prior judgment were based on a complete default by all defendants? See Restatement (Second) of Judgments § 12 comment f (1980).

(12) A federal statute provides that during the pendency of bankruptcy proceedings in a federal court, the state courts shall have no jurisdiction to foreclose a mortgage on the land of a farmer. In a contested state-court proceeding, at a time when federal bankruptcy proceedings are pending, the state court erroneously assumes that it has jurisdiction and decrees foreclosure of the mortgage of K's farm. The property is sold to the mortgagee at a sheriff's foreclosure sale, and the sheriff evicts K. In a new action in the same state court, K sues the mortgagee-purchaser for cancellation of the sheriff's deed and restoration of possession. Is the foreclosure decree subject to attack in this new proceeding? See Kalb v. Feuerstein, 308 U.S. 433, 60 S.Ct. 343 (1940) (yes). Why? See Moore, Collateral Attack on Subject

Matter Jurisdiction: A Critique of the Restatement (Second) of Judgments, 66 Cornell L.Rev. 534 (1981).

DURFEE v. DUKE, 375 U.S. 106, 84 S.Ct. 242 (1963). Durfee, a Nebraska citizen, sued Duke, a Missouri citizen, in a Nebraska state court to quiet title to certain bottom land situated on the Missouri River, the main channel of which forms the boundary between Nebraska and Missouri. The Nebraska court had jurisdiction only if the land in question was in Nebraska. Whether the land was Nebraska land depended entirely upon a factual question: whether a shift in the river's course had been caused by avulsion or accretion. When the change in the channel of a river is sudden (avulsion), the state boundary remains as before; when the change is gradual (accretion), the boundary follows the channel. Duke appeared in the Nebraska court and fully litigated the issues, explicitly contesting the court's jurisdiction. The court found the land to be in Nebraska by application of the rule of avulsion, and it ordered that title to the land be quieted in Durfee. On appeal, the Supreme Court of Nebraska affirmed. Duke did not petition for certiorari. Two months later Duke sued in a Missouri state court to quiet title to the same land, alleging it to be in Missouri. The suit was removed to the federal district court by reason of diversity of citizenship. The district court, although expressing the view that on the evidence the land was in Missouri, found for Durfee on the ground that the Nebraska judgment was entitled to full faith and credit. The court of appeals reversed, and the Supreme Court of the United States granted certiorari.

The Supreme Court in turn reversed the court of appeals, holding that the Nebraska judgment was entitled to full faith and credit when the jurisdictional issue had been fully and fairly litigated by the parties and finally determined in the Nebraska courts and when Nebraska would therefore not permit collateral attack. Justice Stewart, for the Court, said that the general rule of finality of litigated jurisdictional determinations, unambiguously established in the Baldwin case with respect to jurisdiction over the person, was "no different when the claim is made that the original forum did not have jurisdiction over the subject matter."

Questions: (13) Did this case really involve a question of subject-matter jurisdiction? Compare Restatement (Second) of Judgments §§ 10, 12 (1980), with Restatement (Second) of Conflict of Laws §§ 96–97 (1969).

(14) In what circumstances should lack of opportunity to be heard survive as a ground for collateral attack?

(15) If the Nebraska court had dismissed for lack of jurisdiction because it had found the land to be in Missouri, could Duke have used this finding against Durfee in the later action in Missouri? See 18 Wright, Miller & Cooper § 4436.

Part Seven

PARTIES

TOPIC A. GENERAL JOINDER PROVISIONS

SHIELDS v. BARROW, 58 U.S. (17 How.) 130 (1855). A digest of
the facts and holding appears supra p. 187. Justice Curtis, in a passage endlessly repeated in later cases, wrote for the Court:

"The court [in Russell v. Clark's Executors, 11 U.S. (7 Cranch) 69,
98 (1812),] points out three classes of parties to a bill in equity. They
are: 1. Formal parties. 2. Persons having an interest in the controversy, and who ought to be made parties, in order that the court may
act on that rule which requires it to decide on, and finally determine
the entire controversy, and do complete justice, by adjusting all the
rights involved in it. These persons are commonly termed necessary
parties; but if their interests are separable from those of the parties
before the court, so that the court can proceed to a decree, and do
complete and final justice, without affecting other persons not before
the court, the latter are not indispensable parties. 3. Persons who
not only have an interest in the controversy, but an interest of such a
nature that a final decree cannot be made without either affecting
that interest, or leaving the controversy in such a condition that its
final termination may be wholly inconsistent with equity and good
conscience.

"A bill to rescind a contract affords an example of this kind. For,
if only a part of those interested in the contract are before the court,
a decree of rescission must either destroy the rights of those who are
absent, or leave the contract in full force as respects them; while it is
set aside, and the contracting parties restored to their former condition, as to the others. We do not say that no case can arise in which
this may be done; but it must be a case in which the rights of those
before the court are completely separable from the rights of those
absent, otherwise the latter are indispensable parties.

"Now it will be perceived, that in Russell . . . this court, after
considering the embarrassments which attend the exercise of the equity jurisdiction of the circuit courts of the United States, advanced
as far as this: They declared that formal parties may be dispensed
with when they cannot be reached; that persons having rights which
must be affected by a decree, cannot be dispensed with; and they
express a doubt concerning the other class of parties. This doubt is
solved in favor of the jurisdiction in subsequent cases, but without
infringing upon what was held in Russell . . . concerning the in-

capacity of the court to give relief, when that relief necessarily involves the rights of absent persons."

Questions: (1) Does "affect" in the quoted passage mean *legally* or *practically* affected?

(2) Try to work out the practical consequences of going ahead with only the present parties and reaching (a) a decree on the merits against Barrow or (b) a decree for Barrow, the joined defendants being good for the total amount due to Barrow under the original agreement.

(3) What arguments can the joined defendants fairly make on their own behalf against the maintenance of the present suit? on behalf of the absentees? on behalf of the public interest in a sound litigation system? With the present suit dismissed for nonjoinder, does Barrow have recourse to any other court where all interested persons can be joined?

FINDINGS OF HAZARD AND REED

The best readings on the subject of compulsory joinder are Hazard, Indispensable Party: The Historical Origin of a Procedural Phantom, 61 Colum.L.Rev. 1254 (1961), and Reed, Compulsory Joinder of Parties in Civil Actions (pts. 1–2), 55 Mich.L.Rev. 327, 483 (1957).

The ancient doctrine in this area was largely worked out in equity, where multi-party problems were most acute. In tracing the early developments, Professor Hazard contends "that until about 1780 the Court of Chancery had adhered with substantial consistency to what is presently known as the necessary party rule: all persons interested in a controversy should be made parties unless joinder is impossible or inconvenient." He says the "indispensable party rule" was invented thereafter and "rests on the principle that a court should do 'complete' justice or none at all," a principle that is, in his opinion, "impossible to follow in any workable system of judicial administration." 61 Colum.L.Rev. at 1271.

Professor Reed speaks thus of the course of decision in this country, 55 Mich.L.Rev. at 355–56:

"The result of Shields v. Barrow was to embed in American procedural law the now familiar division of required parties into categories (necessary and indispensable)—a classification not inherently bad— and a shoddy and unimaginative method of its application to individual cases. It is not surprising that other courts in picking up that classification have adopted also the Supreme Court's separability-of-rights terminology. It is one thing to determine that in the absence of some persons a case may not proceed ('indispensable' parties) and in the unavoidable absence of others a case may proceed ('necessary' parties). It is quite another to believe that certain persons, depending on the nature of their rights ('common,' 'joint,' 'united in interest'), are automatically and for all time relegated to one class or the other. That simply is not so, but it is the kind of result which the Shields v. Barrow process invites. Similarly, there is an assumption, possibly due to heavy reliance on the necessary-indispensable terminology, that a court has discretion to proceed or not to proceed in one category ('necessary') and no discretion in the other ('indispensable'). Although true when applied to a party to which the court has attached one of these labels, the assumption is basically false in failing to recognize that there is initially a broad discretion in assigning a party to the one category or other. Also, it is hard to understand, except by reference to Shields v. Barrow's misleading silence on the point, why so few courts have been aware of the availability of a less-than-absolute decree to avoid a termination of litigation without a chance to explore the merits."

Professor Reed's analysis of the decisions shows no landslide accumulation of obvious mistakes. Many of the cases reduce to standard types with the results reasonably defensible. There was, however, a tendency to shove cases into categories without attention to their differentia, to their specific facts. In some instances criticism of the cases is frustrated because the opinions, concerned with opaque terms such as "joint" and "separable," are unrevealing as to the facts.

DEFECTS IN ORIGINAL RULE 19

See Rule 19 in its original form and the Advisory Committee's note on the amended Rule in the section of the Rules pamphlet dealing with the 1966 amendments. Observe the use in original Rule 19 of the terms "joint interest" and "indispensable" to mark the boundaries of the two categories of persons falling within the compulsory joinder doctrine. The Advisory Committee drew heavily upon the findings of Hazard and Reed in its discussion of the defects in the original Rule; of particular significance was the overemphasis on labels encouraged by the old Rule, which had directed the attention of the courts to technical or abstract concepts at the expense of the pragmatic considerations that the Advisory Committee thought should be controlling.

Question: (4) In abandoning the old jurisprudence of labels, were the rulemakers justified in adopting a "non-rule" that in part just lists relevant considerations rather than drawing a precise and specific rule that would offer certainty and hence predictability and workability?

PROVIDENT TRADESMENS BANK & TRUST CO. v. PATTERSON

Supreme Court of the United States, 1968.
390 U.S. 102, 88 S.Ct. 733.

MR. JUSTICE HARLAN delivered the opinion of the Court.

This controversy, involving in its present posture the dismissal of a declaratory judgment action for nonjoinder of an "indispensable" party, began nearly 10 years ago with a traffic accident [in Pennsylvania]. An automobile owned by Edward Dutcher, who was not present when the accident occurred, was being driven by Donald Cionci, to whom Dutcher had given the keys. John Lynch and John Harris were passengers. The automobile crossed the median strip of the highway and collided with a truck being driven by Thomas Smith. Cionci, Lynch, and Smith were killed and Harris was severely injured.

Three tort actions were brought. Provident Tradesmens Bank, the administrator of the estate of passenger Lynch and petitioner here, sued the estate of the driver, Cionci, in a diversity action. The administrator of Smith, and Harris in person, each brought a state-court action against the estate of Cionci, Dutcher the owner, and the estate of Lynch [on the theory that Lynch had been in "control" of Cionci]. These Smith and Harris actions, for unknown reasons, have never gone to trial and are still pending. The Lynch action against Cionci's estate was settled for $50,000, which the estate of Cionci, being penniless, has never paid.

Dutcher, the owner of the automobile and a defendant in the as yet untried tort actions, had an automobile liability insurance policy with Lumbermens Mutual Casualty Company, respondent here. That policy had an upper limit of $100,000 for all claims arising out of a single accident. This fund was potentially subject to two different sorts of claims by the tort plaintiffs. First, Dutcher himself might be held vicariously liable as Cionci's "principal"; the likelihood of such a judgment against Dutcher is a matter of considerable doubt and dispute. Second, the policy by its terms covered the direct liability of any person driving Dutcher's car with Dutcher's "permission."

The insurance company had declined, after notice, to defend the estate of Lynch's tort action against the estate of Cionci, believing that Cionci had not had permission and hence was not covered by the policy. The facts allegedly were that Dutcher had entrusted his car to Cionci, but that Cionci had made a detour from the errand for which Dutcher allowed his car to be taken. The estate of Lynch, armed with its $50,000 liquidated claim against the estate of Cionci, brought the present diversity action [in the Eastern District of Pennsylvania] for a declaration that Cionci's use of the car had been "with permission" of Dutcher. The only named defendants were the company and the estate of Cionci [administered by Patterson]. The other two tort plaintiffs were joined as plaintiffs [on Lumbermens' motion].

Dutcher, a resident of the State of Pennsylvania as were all the plaintiffs, was not joined either as plaintiff or defendant. The failure to join him was not adverted to at the trial level.

The major question of law contested at trial was a state-law question. The District Court had ruled that, as a matter of the applicable (Pennsylvania) law, the driver of an automobile is presumed to have the permission of the owner. Hence, unless contrary evidence could be introduced, the tort plaintiffs, now declaratory judgment plaintiffs, would be entitled to a directed verdict against the insurance company. The only possible contrary evidence was testimony by Dutcher as to restrictions he had imposed on Cionci's use of the automobile. The two estate plaintiffs claimed, however, that under the Pennsylvania "Dead Man Rule" Dutcher was incompetent to testify on this matter as against them. The District Court upheld this claim. It ruled that under Pennsylvania law Dutcher was incompetent to testify against an estate if he had an "adverse" interest to that of the estate. It found such adversity in Dutcher's potential need to call upon the insurance fund to pay judgments against himself, and his consequent interest in not having part or all of the fund used to pay judgments against Cionci. The District Court, therefore, directed verdicts in favor of the two estates. Dutcher was, however, allowed to testify as against the live plaintiff, Harris. The jury, nonetheless, found that Cionci had had permission, and hence awarded a verdict to Harris also.

Lumbermens appealed the judgment to the Court of Appeals for the Third Circuit, raising various state-law questions.[1] The Court of Appeals did not reach any of these issues. Instead, after reargument en banc, it decided, 5–2, to reverse on two alternative grounds neither of which had been raised in the District Court or by the appellant.

The first of these grounds was that Dutcher was an indispensable party. The court held that the "adverse interests" that had rendered Dutcher incompetent to testify under the Pennsylvania Dead Man Rule also required him to be made a party. The court did not consider whether the fact that a verdict had already been rendered, without objection to the nonjoinder of Dutcher, affected the matter. Nor did it follow the provision of Rule 19 of the Federal Rules of Civil Procedure that findings of "indispensability" must be based on stated pragmatic considerations. It held, to the contrary, that the right of a person who "may be affected" by the judgment to be joined is a "substantive" right, unaffected by the federal rules; that a trial court "may not proceed" in the absence of such a person; and that since Dutcher could not be joined as a defendant without destroying diversity jurisdiction the action had to be dismissed.

---

[1] Appellants challenged the District Court's ruling on the Dead Man issue, the fairness of submitting the question as to Harris to a jury that had been directed to find in favor of the two estates whose position was factually indistinguishable, and certain instructions.

Since this ruling presented a serious challenge to the scope of the newly amended Rule 19, we granted certiorari. 386 U.S. 940, 87 S.Ct. 972. Concluding that the inflexible approach adopted by the Court of Appeals in this case exemplifies the kind of reasoning that the Rule was designed to avoid, we reverse.

I.

[The Court here quoted Rule 19(a) and (b).]

We may assume, at the outset, that Dutcher falls within the category of persons who, under § (a), should be "joined if feasible." The action was for an adjudication of the validity of certain claims against a fund. Dutcher, faced with the possibility of judgments against him, had an interest in having the fund preserved to cover that potential liability. Hence there existed, when this case went to trial, at least the possibility that a judgment might impede Dutcher's ability to protect his interest, or lead to later relitigation by him.

The optimum solution, an adjudication of the permission question that would be binding on all interested persons, was not "feasible," however, for Dutcher could not be made a defendant without destroying diversity. Hence the problem was the one to which Rule 19(b) appears to address itself: in the absence of a person who "should be joined if feasible," should the court dismiss the action or proceed without him? Since this problem emerged for the first time in the Court of Appeals, there were also two subsidiary questions. First, what was the effect, if any, of the failure of the defendants to raise the matter in the District Court? Second, what was the importance, if any, of the fact that a judgment, binding on the parties although not binding on Dutcher, had already been reached after extensive litigation? The three questions prove, on examination, to be interwoven.

We conclude, upon consideration of the record and applying the "equity and good conscience" test of Rule 19(b), that the Court of Appeals erred in not allowing the judgment to stand.

Rule 19(b) suggests four "interests" that must be examined in each case to determine whether, in equity and good conscience, the court should proceed without a party whose absence from the litigation is compelled. Each of these interests must, in this case, be viewed entirely from an appellate perspective since the matter of joinder was not considered in the trial court. First, the plaintiff has an interest in having a forum. Before the trial, the strength of this interest obviously depends upon whether a satisfactory alternative forum exists. On appeal, if the plaintiff has won, he has a strong additional interest in preserving his judgment. Second, the defendant may properly wish to avoid multiple litigation, or inconsistent relief, or sole responsibility for a liability he shares with another. After trial, however, if the defendant has failed to assert this interest, it is quite proper to consider it foreclosed.

Third, there is the interest of the outsider whom it would have been desirable to join. Of course, since the outsider is not before the court, he cannot be bound by the judgment rendered. This means, however, only that a judgment is not res judicata as to, or legally enforceable against, a nonparty. It obviously does not mean either (a) that a court may never issue a judgment that, in practice, affects a nonparty or (b) that (to the contrary) a court may always proceed without considering the potential effect on nonparties simply because they are not "bound" in the technical sense. Instead, as Rule 19(a) expresses it, the court must consider the extent to which the judgment may "as a practical matter impair or impede his ability to protect" his interest in the subject matter. When a case has reached the appeal stage the matter is more complex. The judgment appealed from may not in fact affect the interest of any outsider even though there existed, before trial, a possibility that a judgment affecting his interest would be rendered. When necessary, however, a court of appeals should, on its own initiative, take steps to protect the absent party, who of course had no opportunity to plead and prove his interest below.

Fourth, there remains the interest of the courts and the public in complete, consistent, and efficient settlement of controversies. We read the Rule's third criterion, whether the judgment issued in the absence of the nonjoined person will be "adequate," to refer to this public stake in settling disputes by wholes, whenever possible, for clearly the plaintiff, who himself chose both the forum and the parties defendant, will not be heard to complain about the sufficiency of the relief obtainable against them. After trial, considerations of efficiency of course include the fact that the time and expense of a trial have already been spent.

Rule 19(b) also directs a district court to consider the possibility of shaping relief to accommodate these four interests. Commentators had argued that greater attention should be paid to this potential solution to a joinder stymie, and the Rule now makes it explicit that a court should consider modification of a judgment as an alternative to dismissal. Needless to say, a court of appeals may also properly require suitable modification as a condition of affirmance.

Had the Court of Appeals applied Rule 19's criteria to the facts of the present case, it could hardly have reached the conclusion it did. We begin with the plaintiffs' viewpoint. It is difficult to decide at this stage whether they would have had an "adequate" remedy had the action been dismissed before trial for nonjoinder: we cannot here determine whether the plaintiffs could have brought the same action, against the same parties plus Dutcher, in a state court. After trial, however, the "adequacy" of this hypothetical alternative, from the plaintiffs' point of view, was obviously greatly diminished. Their interest in preserving a fully litigated judgment should be overborne only by rather greater opposing considerations than would be required at an earlier stage when the plaintiffs' only concern was for a federal rather than a state forum.

Opposing considerations in this case are hard to find. The defendants had no stake, either asserted or real, in the joinder of Dutcher. They showed no interest in joinder until the Court of Appeals took the matter into its own hands. This properly forecloses any interest of theirs, but for purposes of clarity we note that the insurance company, whose liability was limited to $100,000, had or will have full opportunity to litigate each claim on that fund against the claimant involved. Its only concern with the absence of Dutcher was and is to obtain a windfall escape from its defeat at trial.

The interest of the outsider, Dutcher, is more difficult to reckon. The Court of Appeals, concluding that it should not follow Rule 19's command to determine whether, as a practical matter, the judgment impaired the nonparty's ability to protect his rights, simply quoted the District Court's reasoning on the Dead Man issue as proof that Dutcher had a "right" to be joined .   .   .   .   There is a logical error in the Court of Appeals' appropriation of this reasoning for its own quite different purposes: Dutcher had an "adverse" interest (sufficient to invoke the Dead Man Rule) because he would have been *benefited* by a ruling *in favor of* the insurance company; the question before the Court of Appeals, however, was whether Dutcher was *harmed* by the judgment *against* the insurance company.

The two questions are not the same. If the three plaintiffs had lost to the insurance company on the permission issue, that loss would have ended the matter favorably to Dutcher. If, as has happened, the three plaintiffs obtain a judgment against the insurance company on the permission issue, Dutcher may still claim that as a nonparty he is not estopped by that judgment from relitigating the issue. At that point it might be argued that Dutcher should be bound by the previous decision because, although technically a nonparty, he had purposely bypassed an adequate opportunity to intervene. We do not now decide whether such an argument would be correct under the circumstances of this case. If, however, Dutcher is properly foreclosed by his failure to intervene in the present litigation, then the joinder issue considered in the Court of Appeals vanishes, for any rights of Dutcher's have been lost by his own inaction.

If Dutcher is not foreclosed by his failure to intervene below, then he is not "bound" by the judgment against the insurance company and, in theory, he has not been harmed. There remains, however, the practical question whether Dutcher is likely to have any need, and if so will have any opportunity, to relitigate. The only possible threat to him is that if the fund is used to pay judgments against Cionci the money may in fact have disappeared before Dutcher has an opportunity to assert his interest. Upon examination, we find this supposed threat neither large nor unavoidable.

The state-court actions against Dutcher had lain dormant for years at the pleading stage by the time the Court of Appeals acted. Petitioners assert here that under the applicable Pennsylvania vicarious liability law they have virtually no chance of recovery against Dutcher. We do not accept this assertion as fact, but the matter could have been explored below. Furthermore, even in the event of tort judgments against Dutcher, it is unlikely that he will be prejudiced by the outcome here. The potential claimants against Dutcher himself are identical with the potential claimants against Cionci's estate. Should the claimants seek to collect from Dutcher personally, he may be able to raise the permission issue defensively, making it irrelevant that the actual monies paid from the fund may have disappeared: Dutcher can assert that Cionci did not have his permission and that therefore the payments made on Cionci's behalf out of Dutcher's insurance policy should properly be credited against Dutcher's own liability. Of course, when Dutcher raises this defense he may lose, either on the merits of the permission issue or on the ground that the issue is foreclosed by Dutcher's failure to intervene in the present case, but Dutcher will not have been prejudiced by the failure of the District Court here to order him joined.

If the Court of Appeals was unconvinced that the threat to Dutcher was trivial, it could nevertheless have avoided all difficulties by proper phrasing of the decree. The District Court, for unspecified reasons, had refused to order immediate payment on the Cionci judgments. Payment could have been withheld pending the suits against Dutcher and relitigation (if that became necessary) by him. In this Court, furthermore, counsel for petitioners represented orally that they, the tort plaintiffs, would accept a limitation of all claims to the amount of the insurance policy. Obviously such a compromise could have been reached below had the Court of Appeals been willing to abandon its rigid approach and seek ways to preserve what was, as to the parties, subject to the appellant's other contentions, a perfectly valid judgment.

The suggestion of potential relitigation of the question of "permission" raises the fourth "interest" at stake in joinder cases—efficiency. It might have been preferable, at the trial level, if there were a forum available in which both the company and Dutcher could have been made defendants, to dismiss the action and force the plaintiffs to go elsewhere. Even this preference would have been highly problematical, however, for the actual threat of relitigation by Dutcher depended on there being judgments against him and on the amount of the fund, which was not revealed to the District Court. By the time the case reached the Court of Appeals, however, the problematical preference on efficiency grounds had entirely disappeared: there was no reason then to throw away a valid judgment just because it did not theoretically settle the whole controversy.

II.

Application of Rule 19(b)'s "equity and good conscience" test for determining whether to proceed or dismiss would doubtless have led to a contrary result below. The Court of Appeals' reasons for disregarding the Rule remain to be examined.[12] The majority of the court concluded that the Rule was inapplicable because "substantive" rights are involved, and substantive rights are not affected by the Federal Rules. Although the court did not articulate exactly what the substantive rights are, or what law determines them, we take it to have been making the following argument: (1) there is a category of persons called "indispensable parties" ; (2) that category is defined by substantive law and the definition cannot be modified by rule; (3) the right of a person falling within that category to participate in the lawsuit in question is also a substantive matter, and is absolute.

With this we may contrast the position that is reflected in Rule 19. Whether a person is "indispensable," that is, whether a particular lawsuit must be dismissed in the absence of that person, can only be determined in the context of particular litigation. There is a large category, whose limits are not presently in question, of persons who, in the Rule's terminology, should be "joined if feasible," and who, in the older terminology, were called either necessary or indispensable parties. Assuming the existence of a person who should be joined if feasible, the only further question arises when joinder is not possible and the court must decide whether to dismiss or to proceed without him. To use the familiar but confusing terminology, the decision to

[12] Rule 19 was completely rewritten subsequent to the proceedings in the District Court in this case. There is, however, no occasion for separate consideration of the question whether the action of the Court of Appeals would have been proper under the old version of the Rule. The new version was adopted on July 1, 1966, while the appeal, in which the joinder question first arose, was pending. The majority in the Court of Appeals did not purport to rely on the older version, but on its conclusion that the Rule, in either form, had no application to this case. The dissent below found the Rule applicable, and concluded that the District Court should not be reversed on the basis of either version.

The new text of the Rule was not intended as a change in principles. Rather, the Committee found that the old text "was defective in its phrasing and did not point clearly to the proper basis of decision." This Court, having the ultimate rule-making authority subject to congressional veto, approved the Committee's suggestions. Where the new version emphasizes the pragmatic consideration of the effects of the alternatives of proceeding or dismissing, the older version tended to emphasize classification of parties as "necessary" or "indispensable." Although the two approaches should come to the same point, since the only reason for asking whether a person is "necessary" or "indispensable" is in order to decide whether to proceed or dismiss in his absence and since that decision must be made on the basis of practical considerations, Shaughnessy v. Pedreiro, 349 U.S. 48, 75 S.Ct. 591, and not by "prescribed formula," Niles-Bement Co. v. Iron Moulders Union, 254 U.S. 77, 41 S.Ct. 39, the Committee concluded, without directly criticizing the outcome of any particular case, that there had at times been "undue preoccupation with abstract classifications of rights or obligations, as against consideration of the particular consequences of proceeding with the action and the ways by which these consequences might be ameliorated by the shaping of final relief or other precautions." . . .

proceed is a decision that the absent person is merely "necessary" while the decision to dismiss is a decision that he is "indispensable." The decision whether to dismiss (i.e., the decision whether the person missing is "indispensable") must be based on factors varying with the different cases, some such factors being substantive, some procedural, some compelling by themselves, and some subject to balancing against opposing interests. Rule 19 does not prevent the assertion of compelling substantive interests; it merely commands the courts to examine each controversy to make certain that the interests really exist. To say that a court "must" dismiss in the absence of an indispensable party and that it "cannot proceed" without him puts the matter the wrong way around: a court does not know whether a particular person is "indispensable" until it has examined the situation to determine whether it can proceed without him.

The Court of Appeals concluded, although it was the first court to hold, that the 19th century joinder cases in this Court created a federal, common-law, substantive right in a certain class of persons to be joined in the corresponding lawsuits.[16]   .   .   .

[The Court here analyzed Elmendorf v. Taylor, 23 U.S. (10 Wheat.) 152 (1825); Mallow v. Hinde, 25 U.S. (12 Wheat.) 193 (1827); Northern Indiana Railroad v. Michigan Central Railroad, 56 U.S. (15 How.) 233 (1853); and Shields v. Barrow, 58 U.S. (17 How.) 130 (1855). After quoting the famous definitions from the Shields case, the Court said:]

These generalizations are still valid today, and they are consistent with the requirements of Rule 19, but they are not a substitute for the analysis required by that Rule. Indeed, the   .   .   .   Shields definition [of indispensability] states, in rather different fashion, the criteria for decision announced in Rule 19(b). One basis for dismissal is prejudice to the rights of an absent party that *"cannot"* be avoided in issuance of a final decree. Alternatively, if the decree can be so written that it protects the interests of the absent persons, but as so written it leaves the controversy so situated that the outcome may be inconsistent with "equity and good conscience," the suit should be dismissed.

The majority of the Court of Appeals read Shields v. Barrow to say that a person whose interests "may be affected" by the decree of the court is an indispensable party, and that all indispensable parties have a "substantive right" to have suits dismissed in their absence. We are unable to read Shields as saying either. It dealt only with persons whose interests must, unavoidably, be affected by a decree

---

[16] Numerous cases in the lower federal courts have dealt with compulsory joinder, and the Court of Appeals concluded that principles enunciated in those cases required dismissal here. However, none of the cases cited here or below presented a factual situation resembling this case: the error made by the Court of Appeals was precisely its reliance on formulas extracted from their contexts rather than on pragmatic analysis.   .   .   .

.   .   .   .

and it said nothing about substantive rights.[22]   Rule 19(b), which the Court of Appeals dismissed as an ineffective attempt to change the substantive rights stated in Shields, is, on the contrary, a valid statement of the criteria for determining whether to proceed or dismiss in the forced absence of an interested person.   It takes, for aught that now appears, adequate account of the very real, very substantive claims to fairness on the part of outsiders that may arise in some cases.   This, however, simply is not such a case.

III.

[The Court here rejected the court of appeals' second alternative ground, namely, that the district court, in the exercise of discretion, should have declined jurisdiction over this action for a declaratory judgment because supposedly the same disputed issue was being presented contemporaneously in the Smith and Harris actions pending in state court.]

We think it clear that the judgment below cannot stand.   The judgment is vacated and the case is remanded to the Court of Appeals for consideration of those issues raised on appeal that have not been considered, and, should the Court of Appeals affirm the District Court as to those issues, for appropriate disposition preserving the judgment of the District Court and protecting the interests of nonjoined persons.

It is so ordered.[a]

Question: (5) What would have been the effect on federal rulemaking if the Supreme Court had adopted the Third Circuit's view that the participato-

[22] Indeed, for example, it has been clear that in a diversity case the question of joinder is one of federal law.   E.g., De Korwin v. First Nat. Bank, 156 F.2d 858, 860 (C.A.7th Cir.), citing Shields.   To be sure, state-law questions may arise in determining what interest the outsider actually has, e.g., Kroese v. General Steel Castings Corp., 179 F.2d 760 (C.A.3d Cir.), but the ultimate question whether, given those state-defined interests, a federal court may proceed without the outsider is a federal matter.

[a] On remand, the estate plaintiffs urged that the defendant insurance company was now precluded by collateral estoppel.   The argument was that the issue of permission had been settled by the verdict and judgment for Harris, against whom Dutcher had testified, and that, even if it was error not to have let him testify against the estate plaintiffs, the insurance company was not entitled to another trial of that issue.   This was offensive use against a prior defendant.

The majority of the court of appeals' panel held that collateral estoppel applied.

The majority went on to reject the other grounds urged by the insurance company for upsetting the district court's judgment.   The opinion closed by remanding "the case to the district court for further proceedings.   The district court should afford plaintiffs an opportunity to agree to the limitation to the policy limit of all their claims against the policy, whether arising out of judgments against Cionci or against Dutcher.   If no such limitation is fixed, the district court should expressly stay any execution by virtue of the declaratory judgment decree until Dutcher shall have had a full opportunity either in the court below or in the state courts to present any claims he may have to the protection of Lumbermens' policy if any judgment is rendered against him in any of the now pending state court actions."   Provident Tradesmens Bank & Trust Co. v. Lumbermens Mut. Cas. Co., 411 F.2d 88 (3d Cir.1969).

ry right of a person who may be affected by the judgment is a "substantive right" unaffected by the Federal Rules?

HAAS v. JEFFERSON NATIONAL BANK

United States Court of Appeals, Fifth Circuit, 1971.
442 F.2d 394.

Before GEWIN, AINSWORTH and ALDISERT,* CIRCUIT JUDGES.

ALDISERT, CIRCUIT JUDGE. Following a pre-trial conference, the district court entered an order finding that Charles H. Glueck was an "indispensable party" under Fed.R.Civ.Pro. 19, and dismissing the action on the ground that Glueck's presence in the case "violates the requirements of complete diversity." We must determine whether the court's action was appropriate at a pre-trial stage, and, if so, whether it abused its discretion in dismissing the action instead of proceeding without Glueck.

Invoking jurisdiction on the basis of diversity of citizenship, 28 U.S.C. § 1332, Haas, a citizen of Ohio, sought a mandatory injunction from the district court [for the Southern District of Florida] directing the Jefferson National Bank, a citizen of Florida, to issue to him 169½ shares of its common stock. Alternatively, he asked for damages reflecting the stock's value. He alleged a 1963 agreement with Glueck, also an Ohio citizen, under which they were to jointly purchase 250 shares of the bank's stock; the certificates were to issue in the name of Glueck but Haas was to have a one-half ownership of the shares. He also pleaded a similar 1966 agreement with Glueck to purchase 34 additional shares. According to Haas, he paid Glueck amounts representing one-half ownership, the bank had knowledge of his ownership interest, and the certificates and subsequent dividends were issued to Glueck.

Haas contends, however, that in 1967 he requested Glueck to order the bank to issue certificates in Haas' name, reflecting his ownership of 169½ shares, and that pursuant to this request Glueck presented to the bank properly endorsed certificates for 250 shares with instructions to reissue 170 shares to Haas and the balance to Glueck.

In its answer, the Bank explained that it had refused to make the assignment because at the time of the transfer request Glueck was indebted to it under the terms of a promissory note which required that Glueck pledge, assign, and transfer to the bank property of any kind owned by Glueck and coming into the possession of the Bank. The Bank averred that Glueck withdrew the transfer request and instead pledged the stock certificates with a second bank [in the Southern District of Florida] as collateral for a loan there.

---

* Of the Third Circuit, sitting by designation.

With these contentions forming the backdrop of the pre-trial conference, the parties stipulated to the questions of fact which remained to be litigated at trial:

(a) Did the Bank have knowledge of Haas' claimed ownership of the stock prior to Glueck's 1967 transfer request?

(b) Did Glueck withdraw the 1967 transfer request?

(c) What was the status of Glueck's obligation to the bank as represented by the promissory note?

(d) Did the second bank have possession of the stock in controversy at the time Haas filed the action?

(e) Did Haas in fact own 169½ shares of the bank stock?

Following the pre-trial conference and the entry of these stipulations, the district court entered an order directing Haas to amend his complaint to join Glueck as a party. The court then denied his motion to dismiss Glueck as a party, and granted the Bank's motion to dismiss the amended complaint on the jurisdictional ground of incomplete diversity.[1]

[The court had no difficulty in finding that the district court did not enter its joinder order prematurely and that, if it did not err in ordering the joinder of Glueck, it was obviously correct in finding the jurisdictional defect of incomplete diversity. In approaching the question whether Rule 19 required the joinder of Glueck, the court gave the classic quotation from Shields v. Barrow, referred to the Provident Tradesmens case, and set forth Rule 19.]

The Rule thus commands that we address ourselves to two broad questions: (1) Was Glueck a party "to be joined if feasible" under section (a) ? If so, (2) was the court correct, under section (b), in dismissing the action or should it have proceeded without the additional party?

It is readily apparent that Glueck "falls within the category of persons who, under § (a), should be 'joined if feasible,' " Provident Tradesmens Bank & Trust Co. v. Patterson, supra, 390 U.S. at 108, 88 S.Ct. at 737, 19 L.Ed.2d 936, for his presence is critical to the disposition of the important issues in the litigation. His evidence will either support the complaint or bolster the defense: it will affirm or refute Haas' claim to half ownership of the stock; it will substantiate or undercut Haas' contention that the Bank had knowledge of his alleged ownership interest; it will corroborate or compromise the Bank's contention that Glueck rescinded the transfer order; and it will be crucial to the determination of Glueck's obligation to the Bank under the promissory note. The essence of Haas' action against the Bank is that it "unlawfully and recklessly seized, detained, [and] exercised improper dominion" over his shares in transferring and deliv-

---

[1] Service of process was not properly effectuated because the attempted service in Ohio was beyond the territorial limits of the district court in Florida. Fed.R.Civ.Pro. 4(f).

ering them to the second bank as collateral for Glueck's loan. Thus, Glueck becomes more than a key witness whose testimony would be of inestimable value. Instead he emerges as an active participant in the alleged conversion of Haas' stock.

Applying the criterion of Rule 19(a)(2)(ii), we believe that Glueck's absence would expose the defendant Bank "to a substantial risk of incurring double, multiple, or otherwise inconsistent obligations by reason of his claimed interest." If Haas prevailed in this litigation in the absence of Glueck and were adjudicated owner of half of the stock, Glueck, not being bound by res adjudicata, could theoretically succeed in later litigation against the Bank in asserting ownership of the whole. In addition, a favorable resolution of Haas' claim against the Bank could, under (a)(2)(i), "as a practical matter impair or impede [the absent party's] ability to protect [his] interest" in all of the shares—an interest that is at least apparent since all of the stock was issued in Glueck's name.

Because Glueck cannot be made a party without destroying diversity, however, it remains to be decided whether, under Rule 19(b), his presence is so vital that "in equity and good conscience the action . . . should be dismissed, the absent person being thus regarded as indispensable." This decision is always a matter of judgment and must be exercised with sufficient knowledge of the facts in order to evaluate the exact role of the absentees. . . .

We turn now to the specific factors enumerated in Rule 19(b), as applied to the facts before us. In our view the first factor tracks the considerations of 19(a)(2)(ii) discussed above: "to what extent a judgment rendered in the person's absence might be prejudicial to him or those already parties." And based on the reasoning previously set forth, we believe this factor supplies weighty reason for a finding of indispensability.

The second factor directs the court to consider the extent to which the shaping of relief might avoid or lessen the prejudice to existing or absent parties. Because the title to the stock certificates, although not the immediate issue in this litigation, assumes such commanding importance, it is difficult to conceptualize a form of relief or protective provisions which would not require as a preliminary matter the determination of the question of title with all the resulting potential for prejudice.

In analyzing the third factor, "whether a judgment rendered in the person's absence will be adequate," . . . [i]t seems evident to us that the absence of Glueck in this litigation would, of necessity, result in less than a complete settlement of this controversy. For reasons already discussed, there is no semblance of a guarantee that a judgment on Haas' terms would settle the whole dispute generated by the facts here.

Finally Rule 19(b) requires us to consider whether the plaintiff will have an avenue for relief if the district court's dismissal for nonjoinder is affirmed. Clearly, the state courts of Ohio afford plaintiff Haas an opportunity to adjudicate his rights against Glueck.[9] They provide a ready forum to settle the question of title to the stock. Moreover assuming the disposition of the preliminary question of title in the Ohio courts, it is not difficult to conceptualize circumstances permitting the possibility of a second action against the Bank in which the problem of nonjoinder will not be so acute.

Accordingly, applying Rule 19(b)'s "equity and good conscience test", we hold that the district court did not abuse its discretion in concluding that Glueck was an indispensable party and in dismissing this action.

Affirmed.

Question: (6) The Kansas comparative negligence statute (a) provides that each tortfeasor is liable only in such proportion as his fault bears to total fault and (b) requires that, on motion of defendant, any absent person whose causal negligence is claimed to have contributed to the injury shall be joined as an additional defendant if feasible. Plaintiff, a Kansas citizen, was seriously injured as a bystander by an allegedly defective paint-sprayer manufactured by defendant, an out-of-state corporation. Plaintiff sued defendant in the Kansas federal court. Defendant moved to join the owner and the operator of the sprayer, who are insolvent Kansas citizens; and defendant also moved to dismiss, because the additional parties would destroy diversity of citizenship. What rulings?

WESTERN UNION TELEGRAPH CO. v. PENNSYLVANIA, 368 U.S. 71, 82 S.Ct. 199 (1961). Western Union, a New York corporation doing business throughout the United States and in foreign countries, carries on a telegraphic money-order business. The procedure is for the sender to pay Western Union the sum to be transmitted and the charge for doing so. If the payee is not located or fails to call for the money, the sending office is notified to make a refund to the sender. Sometimes Western Union can neither make payment to the payee nor make a refund to the sender, and sometimes neither one cashes the draft issued by Western Union in payment or refund. Pennsylvania law provides that "any real or personal property within or subject to the control of this Commonwealth . . . shall escheat to the Commonwealth" whenever it "shall be without a lawful owner" or "remain unclaimed for the period of seven successive years" or whenever "the whereabouts of such owner . . . shall be and remain unknown for the period of seven successive years."

In this Pennsylvania state-court action, Pennsylvania sought under the statute to escheat the accumulation of undisbursed money held by Western Union arising out of money orders bought in Pennsylvania. Western Union did not claim the money for itself but chal-

---

[9] In response to the court's inquiry at oral argument, Haas' counsel reported that a state action between Haas and Glueck is now pending.

lenged Pennsylvania's right to the money, urging that a judgment of escheat would not protect it from multiple liability in Pennsylvania or elsewhere. Western Union insisted that there was no "res" in Pennsylvania and that service by publication did not satisfy due process. It appeared that New York had already escheated part of the very funds claimed by Pennsylvania. The Supreme Court, in an opinion by Justice Black, reversed on the ground that Pennsylvania had no power to escheat the money, saying:

"We find it unnecessary to decide any of Western Union's contentions as to the adequacy of notice to and validity of service on the individual claimants by publication. For as we view these proceedings, there is a far more important question raised by this record—whether Pennsylvania had power at all to render a judgment of escheat which would bar New York or any other state from escheating this same property.

"Pennsylvania does not claim and could not claim that the same debts or demands could be escheated by two states. See Standard Oil Co. v. New Jersey, 341 U.S. 428, 443, 71 S.Ct. 822, 831. And our prior opinions have recognized that when a state court's jurisdiction purports to be based, as here, on the presence of property within the State, the holder of such property is deprived of due process of law if he is compelled to relinquish it without assurance that he will not be held liable again in another jurisdiction or in a suit brought by a claimant who is not bound by the first judgment. Anderson National Bank v. Luckett, 321 U.S. 233, 242–243, 64 S.Ct. 599, 604; Security Savings Bank v. California, 263 U.S. 282, 286–290, 44 S.Ct. 108, 110–111. Applying that principle, there can be no doubt that Western Union has been denied due process by the Pennsylvania judgment here unless the Pennsylvania courts had power to protect Western Union from any other claim, including the claim of the State of New York that these obligations are property 'within' New York and are therefore subject to escheat under its laws. But New York was not a party to this proceeding and could not have been made a party, and, of course, New York's claims could not be cut off where New York was not heard as a party. Moreover, the potential multi-state claims to the 'property' which is the subject of this escheat make it not unlikely that various States will claim in rem jurisdiction over it. Therefore, Western Union was not protected by the Pennsylvania judgment, for a state court judgment need not be given full faith and credit by other states as to parties or property not subject to the jurisdiction of the court that rendered it. Pennoyer v. Neff, 95 U.S. 714; Riley v. New York Trust Co., 315 U.S. 343, 62 S.Ct. 608." [b]

---

[b] In Texas v. New Jersey, 379 U.S. 674, 85 S.Ct. 626 (1965), the Court exercising its original jurisdiction developed a federal rule for escheat cases, holding generally that intangible property is subject to escheat only by the state of the last known address of the creditor, as shown by the debtor's books and records.

INVOLUNTARY PLAINTIFF

Both the original and the present versions of Rule 19(a) say that a person who should join as a plaintiff but refuses to do so may be made a defendant or, in a proper case, an involuntary plaintiff. Therefore, all parties joined under Rule 19 normally come in as defendants. A "proper case" to the contrary is one in which the recalcitrant party as a defendant would not be subject to service of process, but equitable considerations require such party to permit the use of his name as a plaintiff. The involuntary plaintiff provision is thus a narrow means of circumventing the requirement of serving process on defendants.

The Advisory Committee's note on the original Rule cited Independent Wireless Telegraph Co. v. RCA, 269 U.S. 459, 46 S.Ct. 166 (1926), as a "proper case." There RCA, exclusive licensee of a patent, wanted to bring an infringement action. Under the authorities the patentee was an indispensable party to such an action. RCA requested the patentee to join as co-plaintiff, but the patentee refused. It could not be joined as a defendant because it was not within the reach of the personal jurisdiction of the court. Thereupon RCA brought the action naming the patentee as a plaintiff without its consent and giving it notice of the suit. The Supreme Court sanctioned this procedure. In Ferrara v. Rodale Press, 54 F.R.D. 3 (E.D.Pa. 1972), the same procedure was permitted in similar circumstances in a copyright infringement action. In practice this provision of the Rule has generally been confined to such circumstances arising in patent and copyright cases, but the suggestion has been made that its use might appropriately be extended. See 3A Moore ¶ 19.06.

Questions: (7) Can you suggest a situation where such extension would be appropriate?

(8) Two Texas lawyers bring a diversity action in Texas against a Delaware defendant to recover $82,500 in owed legal fees. The defendant moves to dismiss for nonjoinder of the plaintiffs' former partner, also a Texan, who has asserted that the defendant owes him part of those fees. The court determines that the former partner should come in as a defendant under Rule 19(a). Should the court now dismiss for want of subject-matter jurisdiction? See Eikel v. States Marine Lines, 473 F.2d 959 (5th Cir.1973) (no). Why not?

PROPER PARTIES

Recall the other general Rules regarding joinder of parties, including Rules 20, 21, and 42. In particular, recall that Rule 20 establishes an outer limit on who may be joined as "proper" parties. Two other provisions in the Rules impose separate and further limits thereon. The first is Rule 17(b) and (c) treating capacity to sue or be sued, which comprises the personal qualifications legally needed by a person to litigate. The other such provision is Rule 17(a), which deserves special attention.

Rule 17(a) requires that every action be prosecuted by the real party in interest. To the student not aided by the perspective of history, the requirement may well seem either obvious or meaningless. At common law, an action had to be brought in the name of the person holding legal title to the right sued upon; so, for example, the assignee of a nonnegotiable chose in action controlled the lawsuit but had to sue in the name of his assignor; and, similarly, an insurer who had paid a loss and was therefore subrogated to the rights of his insured had to sue in the latter's name. In equity, however, a person with a beneficial or equitable interest could sue in his own name. The Field Code in merging law and equity changed the common-law rule by requiring that all actions be brought by the real party in interest, viz., the person who under the substantive law is entitled to enforce the right sued upon. Most but not all states adopted similar provisions, and Rule 17(a) followed suit, thus allowing and requiring the assignee and the subrogee to sue in their own names.

Where an assignment is total or a subrogee has paid the full amount of the loss, the only real party in interest and hence the only proper plaintiff is the assignee or subrogee. If suit is brought in the name of some other person, the defendant may challenge his right to sue. The defendant may do this by including in his answer a defense invoking Rule 17(a). If the defect appears on the face of the complaint, he may move to dismiss. If it does not so appear, as is more likely, he may raise the point by a motion for summary judgment supported by affidavits or other proof of the facts.

Question: (9) Why might the real party in interest prefer to sue in another's name? Why might the defendant want to object?

If the defendant's challenge is sustained, the defect may be corrected by substitution of the real party in interest. The present Rule, codifying the result in Link Aviation, Inc. v. Downs, 325 F.2d 613 (D.C.Cir.1963), provides that the substitution relates back to the date of commencement of the action. See the original form of the Rule, and the Advisory Committee's reasons for amending it, in the section of the Rules pamphlet dealing with the 1966 amendments.

Question: (10) Plaintiff is injured by a hit-and-run driver, unidentified except that he was driving a black Oldsmobile with an attached trailer. An investigator at a later date observes such a car passing the scene of the accident and makes note of the license-plate number. Before the limitations period expires, plaintiff's lawyer sues the owner of the observed car. After the statute has run, plaintiff's lawyer learns the identity of the true offender and moves to amend by substituting him as defendant. Should the motion be granted? Was the attorney's conduct consistent with the obligations of Rule 11?

If a subrogee has paid only part of the loss (or an assignment is partial), the subrogee is still a real party in interest, but not the only one. If either the subrogee or his creditor sues alone, the defendant may by motion seek joinder of the other. Each is a person needed for just adjudication under Rule 19(a).

Question: (11) What if such joinder is not feasible because the absentee is not subject to service of process or his joinder would destroy subject-matter jurisdiction?

It should be noted that in diversity cases state substantive law is controlling as to who is entitled to enforce the right. It is only after the identity of the real party in interest has been so determined that Rule 17(a) comes into play, telling you that suit must be brought in his name. See, e.g., McNeil Construction Co. v. Livingston State Bank, 300 F.2d 88 (9th Cir.1962). Rule 17(a), when the case is ripe for its use, is purely procedural, and it does not matter what procedural provisions the state has concerning the name in which suit is to be brought.

Finally, there are those who have advocated abolition of the real-party-in-interest rule. The argument is that the only function of a rule such as Rule 17(a), now that the common-law approach has been definitely put behind us, is to mislead: all that is correct in Rule 17(a) would still follow in its absence by the application of the remaining body of procedural and substantive law, and yet among other difficulties the uninformed might not guess that the Rule's second sentence merely gives illustrations of some usually but not universally correct applications of its first sentence. See Atkinson, The Real Party in Interest Rule: A Plea for Its Abolition, 32 N.Y.U.L.Rev. 926 (1957); Kennedy, Federal Rule 17(a): Will the Real Party in Interest Please Stand?, 51 Minn.L.Rev. 675 (1967). New York, where the rule originated, has heeded the plea and dropped it. See 2 J. Weinstein, H. Korn & A. Miller, New York Civil Practice ¶ 1004.01 (rev.1982).

TOPIC B. CLASS ACTIONS

SECTION 1. REPRESENTATIVE LITIGATION

The class action's roots seemingly trace in English equity from
the bill of peace with multiple parties, by means of which an equity
court could avoid multiplicity of litigation involving common questions of law or fact or both by a single suit in equity; it came to be a
sufficient basis for equitable jurisdiction that the court, by bringing
all the parties before it, could settle once and for all what would otherwise be a large number of actions at law.[a] From such a bill of
peace slowly evolved, by a convoluted and fitful process reflecting
various social pressures, the limited device of representative proceedings (as they are called in England) or class suits; certain absent persons were no longer deemed necessary parties, but were nevertheless
bound by judgment, thus allowing suit where otherwise no individual
action could or would be brought.[b] Given the blessing of Story, the
class suit became an accepted, albeit obscure, part of American jurisprudence at an early date.[c]

A leading case was Smith v. Swormstedt, 57 U.S. (16 How.) 288
(1853). The Methodist Episcopal Church had split over the slavery
issue. Six plaintiffs representing 1500 traveling preachers of the
Methodist Episcopal Church South sued in federal court three defendants as representatives of 3800 traveling preachers of the Methodist
Episcopal Church North, seeking a division of church property. On
objection for want of parties, the Court held that the bill could be
maintained and indicated that the decree would bind all. The Court
cited Story, who thought class-suit decrees to be ordinarily binding on
absentees; but, curiously, the Court did not cite Federal Equity Rule
48, 42 U.S. (1 How.) lvi (1842), which authorized class suits but confusingly said that "the decree shall be without prejudice to the rights
and claims of all the absent parties."

Federal Equity Rule 38, 226 U.S. 659, 33 S.Ct. xxix (1912), omitted
this qualification. In Supreme Tribe of Ben-Hur v. Cauble, 255 U.S.
356, 41 S.Ct. 338 (1921), the Court took note of the omission. There
had been a federal suit by a group of Class A certificate holders in
the Supreme Tribe, a fraternal benefit association, with the complain-

---

[a] See supra p. 375 note o.

[b] On the historical evolution, see
Yeazell, Group Litigation and Social Context: Toward a History of the Class Action, 77 Colum.L.Rev. 866 (1977) (early
period); Yeazell, From Group Litigation
to Class Action (pts. 1–2), 27 UCLA
L.Rev. 514, 1067 (1980) (1700 to present).

For a comparative perspective, see Taylor & Head, Representing Collective Interests in Civil Litigation: A Comparative Synopsis, 58 U.Det.J.Urb.L. 587
(1981).

[c] See, e.g., J. Story, Commentaries on
Equity Pleadings § 97 (Boston 1838).

ants purporting to sue on behalf of the more than 70,000 Class A holders and seeking to overturn a reorganization plan that had reclassified the certificates; the defendant Supreme Tribe had prevailed on the merits. Later, another group of Class A holders tried to raise the same issue. The Court refused to permit this, firmly saying: "The parties bringing the suit truly represented the interested class. If the decree is to be effective and conflicting judgments are to be avoided all of the class must be concluded by the decree."

See Rule 23 in its original form, and the Advisory Committee's note explaining its inadequacy as a guide to the proper extent of a class-action judgment, in the section of the Rules pamphlet dealing with the 1966 amendments. Observe particularly the three subdivisions of original Rule 23(a), which set up three kinds of class actions known familiarly as "true," "hybrid," and "spurious." (Smith v. Swormstedt and the Supreme Tribe case were examples of "true" class actions under old Rule 23(a)(1).) The most striking point about this highly conceptual classification was that although "true" and "hybrid" class actions had binding effects on all members of the class, it was generally thought that "spurious" class actions bound only the parties actually before the court and thus operated largely as a rather ordinary permissive joinder device.

HANSBERRY v. LEE
Supreme Court of the United States, 1940.
311 U.S. 32, 61 S.Ct. 115.

[Twenty-seven blocks in Chicago were subject to a restrictive agreement that none of the property should be sold to, leased to, or permitted to be occupied by blacks, the agreement to become effective when signed by owners of 95 per cent of the frontage. One of the owners had sued in an Illinois state court to enforce the agreement against four defendants involved in leasing a lot to a black man. The suit (Burke v. Kleiman) was stated to be brought on behalf of all similarly situated. It was stipulated by the parties that 95 per cent had signed the agreement, and the court found the stipulated fact to be true. The only issue raised at the trial was that of change of neighborhood. The plaintiff succeeded in the action, and an injunction issued.

[Later, other property owners brought the instant non-class suit in an Illinois state court to enforce the agreement against other defendants in respect to another lot. The defendants tried to defend on the ground that 95 per cent in truth had not signed. Though the court found as a fact that only 54 per cent had signed, it felt obliged on principles of res judicata to hold the defense to be unavailable. An injunction followed. A divided Illinois Supreme Court affirmed, viewing the present defendants as members of the plaintiff class in the first action and thus bound in the absence of fraud or collusion.[d] Certiorari was granted.]

MR. JUSTICE STONE delivered the opinion of the Court.

The question is whether the Supreme Court of Illinois, by its adjudication that petitioners in this case are bound by a judgment rendered in an earlier litigation to which they were not parties, has deprived them of the due process of law guaranteed by the Fourteenth Amendment.

. . . .

State courts are free to attach such descriptive labels to litigations before them as they may choose and to attribute to them such consequences as they think appropriate under state constitutions and laws, subject only to the requirements of the Constitution of the United States. But when the judgment of a state court, ascribing to the judgment of another court the binding force and effect of res judicata, is challenged for want of due process it becomes the duty of this Court to examine the course of procedure in both litigations to ascertain whether the litigant whose rights have thus been adjudicated has been afforded such notice and opportunity to be heard as are requisite to the due process which the Constitution prescribes. Western Life Indem. Co. v. Rupp, 235 U.S. 261, 273, 35 S.Ct. 37, 40.

It is a principle of general application in Anglo-American jurisprudence that one is not bound by a judgment in personam in a litigation in which he is not designated as a party or to which he has not been made a party by service of process. Pennoyer v. Neff, 95 U.S. 714; 1 Freeman on Judgments, 5th ed., § 407. A judgment rendered in such circumstances is not entitled to the full faith and credit which the Constitution and statute of the United States, Rev.Stat. § 905, 28 U.S.C. § 687,[e] prescribe, [citations omitted]; and judicial action enforcing it against the person or property of the absent party is not that due process which the Fifth and Fourteenth Amendments require. [Citations omitted.]

To these general rules there is a recognized exception that, to an extent not precisely defined by judicial opinion, the judgment in a "class" or "representative" suit, to which some members of the class are parties, may bind members of the class or those represented who were not made parties to it. Smith v. Swormstedt, 16 How. (57 U.S.) 288; Royal Arcanum v. Green, 237 U.S. 531, 35 S.Ct. 724; Hartford Life Ins. Co. v. Ibs, 237 U.S. 662, 35 S.Ct. 692; Hartford Life Ins. Co. v. Barber, 245 U.S. 146, 38 S.Ct. 54; Supreme Tribe of Ben-Hur v. Cauble, 255 U.S. 356, 41 S.Ct. 338; cf. Christopher v. Brusselback, 302 U.S. 500, 58 S.Ct. 350.

---

[d] The trial court in Action No. 2 had found the stipulation in Action No. 1 to be false and fraudulent, but it nevertheless held res judicata to be applicable. The Illinois Supreme Court found the stipulation to be false but not fraudulent or collusive.

[e] Now 28 U.S.C. § 1738.

The class suit was an invention of equity to enable it to proceed to a decree in suits where the number of those interested in the subject of the litigation is so great that their joinder as parties in conformity to the usual rules of procedure is impracticable. Courts are not infrequently called upon to proceed with causes in which the number of those interested in the litigation is so great as to make difficult or impossible the joinder of all because some are not within the jurisdiction or because their whereabouts is unknown or where if all were made parties to the suit its continued abatement by the death of some would prevent or unduly delay a decree. In such cases where the interests of those not joined are of the same class as the interests of those who are, and where it is considered that the latter fairly represent the former in the prosecution of the litigation of the issues in which all have a common interest, the court will proceed to a decree. Brown v. Vermuden, Ch.Cas. 272, 22 Eng.Rep. 796; London v. Richmond, 2 Vern. 421, 23 Eng.Rep. 870; Cockburn v. Thompson, 16 Ves. Jr. 321, 33 Eng.Rep. 1005; West v. Randall, C.C., 2 Mason 181, Fed. Cas. No. 17,424; Beatty v. Kurtz, 2 Pet. (27 U.S.) 566; Smith v. Swormstedt, supra; Supreme Tribe of Ben-Hur v. Cauble, supra; Story, Equity Pleadings, 2d ed., § 98.

It is evident that the considerations which may induce a court thus to proceed, despite a technical defect of parties, may differ from those which must be taken into account in determining whether the absent parties are bound by the decree or, if it is adjudged that they are, in ascertaining whether such an adjudication satisfies the requirements of due process and of full faith and credit. Nevertheless there is scope within the framework of the Constitution for holding in appropriate cases that a judgment rendered in a class suit is res judicata as to members of the class who are not formal parties to the suit. Here, as elsewhere, the Fourteenth Amendment does not compel state courts or legislatures to adopt any particular rule for establishing the conclusiveness of judgments in class suits; [citations omitted], nor does it compel the adoption of the particular rules thought by this Court to be appropriate for the federal courts. With a proper regard for divergent local institutions and interests, [citation omitted], this Court is justified in saying that there has been a failure of due process only in those cases where it cannot be said that the procedure adopted, fairly insures the protection of the interests of absent parties who are to be bound by it. [Citation omitted.]

It is familiar doctrine of the federal courts that members of a class not present as parties to the litigation may be bound by the judgment where they are in fact adequately represented by parties who are present, or where they actually participate in the conduct of the litigation in which members of the class are present as parties, Plumb v. Goodnow (Plumb v. Crane), 123 U.S. 560, 8 S.Ct. 216; Confectioners' Machinery & Mfg. Co. v. Racine Engine & Machinery Co.,

7 Cir., 163 F. 914; Id., 7 Cir., 170 F. 1021; Bryant Electric Co. v. Marshall, C.C., 169 F. 426, or where the interest of the members of the class, some of whom are present as parties, is joint, or where for any other reason the relationship between the parties present and those who are absent is such as legally to entitle the former to stand in judgment for the latter. Smith v. Swormstedt, supra; cf. Christopher v. Brusselback, supra, 302 U.S. at 503–04, 58 S.Ct. at 352, and cases cited.

In all such cases, so far as it can be said that the members of the class who are present are, by generally recognized rules of law, entitled to stand in judgment for those who are not, we may assume for the present purposes that such procedure affords a protection to the parties who are represented, though absent, which would satisfy the requirements of due process and full faith and credit. See Bernheimer v. Converse, 206 U.S. 516, 27 S.Ct. 755; Marin v. Augedahl, 247 U.S. 142, 38 S.Ct. 452; Chandler v. Peketz, 297 U.S. 609, 56 S.Ct. 602. Nor do we find it necessary for the decision of this case to say that, when the only circumstance defining the class is that the determination of the rights of its members turns upon a single issue of fact or law, a state could not constitutionally adopt a procedure whereby some of the members of the class could stand in judgment for all, provided that the procedure were so devised and applied as to insure that those present are of the same class as those absent and that the litigation is so conducted as to insure the full and fair consideration of the common issue. Compare New England Divisions Case, 261 U.S. 184, 197, 43 S.Ct. 270, 275; Taggart v. Bremner, 7 Cir., 236 F. 544. We decide only that the procedure and the course of litigation sustained here by the plea of res judicata do not satisfy these requirements.

The restrictive agreement did not purport to create a joint obligation or liability. If valid and effective its promises were the several obligations of the signers and those claiming under them. The promises ran severally to every other signer. It is plain that in such circumstances all those alleged to be bound by the agreement would not constitute a single class in any litigation brought to enforce it. Those who sought to secure its benefits by enforcing it could not be said to be in the same class with or represent those whose interest was in resisting performance, for the agreement by its terms imposes obligations and confers rights on the owner of each plot of land who signs it. If those who thus seek to secure the benefits of the agreement were rightly regarded by the state Supreme Court as constituting a class, it is evident that those signers or their successors who are interested in challenging the validity of the agreement and resisting its performance are not of the same class in the sense that their interests are identical so that any group who had elected to enforce rights conferred by the agreement could be said to be acting in the interest of any others who were free to deny its obligation.

Because of the dual and potentially conflicting interests of those who are putative parties to the agreement in compelling or resisting its performance, it is impossible to say, solely because they are parties to it, that any two of them are of the same class. Nor without more, and with the due regard for the protection of the rights of absent parties which due process exacts, can some be permitted to stand in judgment for all.

It is one thing to say that some members of a class may represent other members in a litigation where the sole and common interest of the class in the litigation is either to assert a common right or to challenge an asserted obligation. Smith v. Swormstedt, supra; Supreme Tribe of Ben-Hur v. Cauble, supra; Groves v. Farmers State Bank, 368 Ill. 35, 12 N.E.2d 618. It is quite another to hold that all those who are free alternatively either to assert rights or to challenge them are of a single class, so that any group, merely because it is of the class so constituted, may be deemed adequately to represent any others of the class in litigating their interests in either alternative. Such a selection of representatives for purposes of litigation, whose substantial interests are not necessarily or even probably the same as those whom they are deemed to represent, does not afford that protection to absent parties which due process requires. The doctrine of representation of absent parties in a class suit has not hitherto been thought to go so far. [Citations omitted.] Apart from the opportunities it would afford for the fraudulent and collusive sacrifice of the rights of absent parties, we think that the representation in this case no more satisfies the requirements of due process than a trial by a judicial officer who is in such situation that he may have an interest in the outcome of the litigation in conflict with that of the litigants. Tumey v. Ohio, 273 U.S. 510, 47 S.Ct. 437.

The plaintiffs in the Burke case sought to compel performance of the agreement in behalf of themselves and all others similarly situated. They did not designate the defendants in the suit as a class or seek any injunction or other relief against others than the named defendants, and the decree which was entered did not purport to bind others. In seeking to enforce the agreement the plaintiffs in that suit were not representing the petitioners here whose substantial interest is in resisting performance. The defendants in the first suit were not treated by the pleadings or decree as representing others or as foreclosing by their defense the rights of others; and, even though nominal defendants, it does not appear that their interest in defeating the contract outweighed their interest in establishing its validity. For a court in this situation to ascribe to either the plaintiffs or defendants the performance of such functions on behalf of petitioners here, is to attribute to them a power that it cannot be said that they had assumed to exercise, and a responsibility which, in view of their dual interests it does not appear that they could rightly discharge.

Reversed.

MR. JUSTICE MCREYNOLDS, MR. JUSTICE ROBERTS and MR. JUSTICE REED concur in the result.

Questions: (1) Where would Hansberry v. Lee fit in the tripartite classification of the 1938 formulation of Rule 23?

(2) Is Justice Stone intimating that the infirmities found in Action No. 1 could have been cured (a) by some effective form of notice to all the land owners or (b) by designating the defendants in that action as representatives of a class of dissidents? See Developments in the Law—Class Actions, 89 Harv.L.Rev. 1318, 1471–75, 1481–82 (1976). What, then, was the critical defect?

(3) Due process thus establishes a justificatory prerequisite for class actions, a ceiling that restricts class actions to constitutionally acceptable costs and so justifies our pursuit of some of the benefits of class actions. This prerequisite is termed "adequate representation." But does "adequate representation" mean that (a) presumptively, or (b) actually, the represented persons in the purported class agree with the objectives of the representative parties, who vigorously and competently pursue those objectives? And does it mean something additional, such as that (a) the absentees share common substantive interests with their representatives or (b) the former have somehow consented to representation by the latter?

FROM THE OLD RULE TO THE NEW

Rule 23 as originally written precipitated a heavy volume of litigation, apparently by directing the attention of lawyers to a hitherto unfamiliar procedural device. The issues became increasingly complex and the results, in good part because of the difficulties in the Rule, highly uncertain. Professor Chafee was led to remark: "The situation is so tangled and bewildering that I sometimes wonder whether the world would be any the worse off if the class-suit device had been left buried in the learned obscurity of Calvert on Parties to Suits in Equity." Z. Chafee, Some Problems of Equity 200 (1950).

The 1966 revision of the Rule was designed to resolve the doubts about the binding effect of the resulting judgments, to broaden the usefulness of the class-action device, and to improve the procedural management of these complex actions. It abandoned the attempt to define class actions by reference to the abstract character of the rights involved and tried to describe in more homely and pragmatic terms the situations in which class actions would be available. There is no unanimity about the degree of success of the new Rule. It has suffered from the excessive enthusiasm of its friends and the calumny of its enemies. But there is complete unanimity on the fact that, far more than did the 1938 Rule, it has witnessed a torrent of class litigation. The material that follows is aimed to give a flavor of the problems and to furnish some basis for a tentative judgment about the propriety and efficacy of the Rule.

GONZALES v. CASSIDY

United States Court of Appeals, Fifth Circuit, 1973.
474 F.2d 67.

Before DYER, CIRCUIT JUDGE, SKELTON, JUDGE,* and INGRAHAM, CIRCUIT JUDGE.

INGRAHAM, CIRCUIT JUDGE. The question in this appeal is whether plaintiff-appellant Gonzales and the class he seeks to represent are bound by the res judicata effect of a prior class suit involving the same class (represented by a different named plaintiff), the same defendants and the same issues. We agree with Gonzales that the class was inadequately represented when the class representative in the prior suit failed to appeal from the trial court's judgment. We reverse and remand.

The prior suit began in May 1969. Antonio Gaytan filed suit as a class action against Clifton Cassidy, Chairman of the Texas Department of Public Safety, in the United States District Court for the Western District of Texas, seeking a declaratory judgment that the Texas Safety Responsibility Act [2] was unconstitutional and an injunction against its enforcement. Gayton, an uninsured motorist, had been involved in an automobile accident in Texas, and pursuant to §§ 4, 5(a), 5(b) and 7 of the Act his driver's license and the registration receipt on his vehicle were suspended without a hearing on liability or fault because he did not post security—as required by the Act—for the damages claimed by the adverse party. A three-judge court was convened . . . and denied Gaytan and his class any relief by its holding that the Act was constitutional. On direct appeal to the Supreme Court, 28 U.S.C. § 1253, the district court's judgment was vacated, and the case was remanded for reconsideration in light of Bell v. Burson, 402 U.S. 535, 96 S.Ct. 1586, 29 L.Ed.2d 90 (1971), which was decided after the three-judge court's decision.

In Bell the Supreme Court held the [similar] Georgia Motor Vehicle Safety Responsibility Act unconstitutional as violative of procedural due process. . . .

On remand the three-judge court accordingly held the Texas Act unconstitutional. But, regarding the scope of relief to which Gaytan and his class were entitled, the court held:

---

* Hon. Byron G. Skelton, of the U.S. Court of Claims, sitting by designation.

[2] Tex.Rev.Civ.Stat.Ann., Art. 6701h (1969).

"This order shall apply retroactively to the Plaintiff ANTONIO R. GAYTAN, and prospectively from June 30, 1971, to all members of the class represented by said Plaintiff." [6]

Having obtained full relief for himself, Gaytan did not appeal the court's denial of retroactive relief to the other members of his class.

The present action began in the Northern District of Texas on June 24, 1971, after the Supreme Court vacated the first Gaytan decision, but before the case was heard on remand. Pedro Gonzales filed a class action against Cassidy, the defendant in Gaytan, seeking the same relief as had been sought by Gaytan in his suit. On July 1, 1971, the Gonzales court entered a temporary restraining order in favor of Gonzales and the other named plaintiffs in his action, prohibiting the defendant from suspending their licenses and vehicle registration receipts. This was before the amended order in Gaytan was rendered but only one day after the first order denying retroactive relief to all of the class except Gaytan was entered. On August 19, 1971, the Gaytan court entered its amended and final order. Then on August 25, 1971, the Gonzales court ordered a show cause hearing as to why its temporary restraining order of July 1 should not be made permanent. This hearing was held on September 28 and the court reasoned that, because Gaytan v. Cassidy was a class action and because Gonzales and the class he sought to represent were members of the Gaytan class, the principles of res judicata foreclosed their claims.[8] Gonzales appeals claiming that Gaytan's failure to appeal the final three-judge order in Gaytan v. Cassidy rendered his representation of the class inadequate, therefore precluding res judicata from attaching to that judgment.

To answer the question whether the class representative adequately represented the class so that the judgment in the class suit will bind the absent members of the class requires a two-pronged inquiry: (1) Did the trial court in the first suit correctly determine, initially, that the representative would adequately represent the class? and (2) Does it appear, after the termination of the suit, that the class representative adequately protected the interest of the class? The first question involves us in a collateral review of the Gaytan trial court's determination to permit the suit to proceed as a class action with Gaytan as the representative, while the second involves a review of the class representative's conduct of the entire suit—an inquiry

[6] Gaytan v. Cassidy, No. SA69CA153 (W.D.Tex., June 30, 1971, amended August 19, 1971). The amended order clarified the original order by explaining that it granted relief only to those persons whose effective date of suspension occurred after June 30, 1971, and to Gaytan whose suspensions occurred prior to June 30.

[8] Since Gonzales and the other named plaintiffs fell within the group to whom only prospective relief had been granted by the Gaytan court, in that their licenses had been suspended prior to June 30, 1971, they were denied relief by the application of res judicata. Plaintiff Louanner H. Edwards was granted relief, for the reason that his license had not been suspended prior to June 30. At this time the court also denied the request that the Gonzales suit be maintained as a class action.

which is not required to be made by the trial court but which is appropriate in a collateral attack on the judgment such as we have here. Our discussion will treat each question separately.

. . . .

The primary contention in this appeal is that Gaytan did not meet the requirements of 23(a)(4). Remembering that at this point we are only concerned with the court's initial determination that Gaytan would be an adequate representative, we look to the criteria on which the decision should be based. There are two: (1) the representative must have common interests with the unnamed members of the class; and (2) it must appear that the representative will vigorously prosecute the interests of the class through qualified counsel.[10] We have little difficulty in concluding that Antonio Gaytan met both of these requirements when he filed his suit in May of 1969. He was an uninsured motorist as were the members of his class; he had an automobile accident in Texas and had failed to post the necessary security under the Act as had the members of his class; his license and registration receipt were suspended without a hearing on liability or fault just as occurred to the members of his class. Likewise, he had the same basic interests in not having his license suspended or in having the suspension revoked as did the other members of his class. It is clear then that Gaytan had common interests which coincided with those of the class he sought to represent. Furthermore, there are no allegations that Gaytan's attorney was not fully qualified to handle the case, or that, initially at least, he would not vigorously prosecute the action. The fact that Gaytan's counsel appealed to the Supreme Court after the three-judge court's adverse decision and subsequently won a reversal of that decision points significantly to counsel's qualification to handle the litigation. Therefore we cannot refuse to give res judicata effect to the judgment in Gaytan v. Cassidy on the basis that the trial court in that case erroneously determined that Gaytan would be an adequate representative of the class.

The second question is whether Gaytan's conduct of the entire suit was such that due process would not be violated by giving res judicata effect to the judgment in that suit. This is the crucial issue when the judgment in a class action is under collateral attack. Our first step, however, is to examine subdivisions (b) and (c) of Rule 23 in order to establish the proper context in which to make this inquiry.

. . . Gaytan v. Cassidy obviously fits within (b)(2)—thus, to be specific, we are dealing with the res judicata effect of the judgment

---

[10] . . . In Eisen v. Carlisle and Jacquelin, 391 F.2d 555, 562 (2nd Cir., 1968), the court also noted:

"[A]n essential concomitant of adequate representation is that the party's attorney be qualified, experienced and generally able to conduct the proposed litigation. Additionally, it is necessary to eliminate so far as possible the likelihood that the litigants are involved in a collusive suit or that plaintiff has interests antagonistic to those of the remainder of the class."

in a (b)(2) type of class action.[12] Subdivision (c)(3) provides: "The judgment in an action maintained as a class action under subdivision . . . (b)(2), whether or not favorable to the class, shall include and describe those whom the court finds to be members of the class . . . ." Although the Gaytan court's opinion, neither originally nor on remand, describes the class it considered Gaytan to be representing, we agree with the lower court here that Gonzales and the class he seeks to represent were members of the Gaytan class and would at first blush appear bound by the Gaytan decision. But our inquiry into the binding effect of Gaytan does not end with Rule 23 for, "although thus declaring that the judgment in a class action includes the class, as defined, subdivision (c)(3) does not disturb the recognized principle that the court conducting the action cannot predetermine the res judicata effect of the judgment; this can be tested only in subsequent action. See Restatement, Judgments § 86, comment (h), § 116 (1942)." Advisory Committee's Notes to Rule 23 F.R.C.P., 28 U.S.C.A. at 301; Moore ¶ 23.60 at 1203. As a general rule though, a judgment in a class action will bind the absent members of the class. The exception to this general rule is grounded in due process. Due process of law would be violated for the judgment in a class suit to be res judicata to the absent members of a class unless the court applying res judicata can conclude that the class was adequately represented in the first suit. Hansberry v. Lee, 311 U.S. 32, 61 S.Ct. 115, 85 L.Ed. 22 [(1940)]. See Sam Fox Publishing Co. v. United States, 366 U.S. 683, 691, 81 S.Ct. 1309, 6 L.Ed.2d 604 (1961); Dierks v. Thompson, 414 F.2d 453 (1st Cir., 1969); Eisen v. Carlisle and Jacquelin, 391 F.2d 555 (2nd Cir., 1968); Mersay v. First Rep. Corp. of America, 43 F.R.D. 465 (S.D.N.Y., 1968).

The 1966 amendments to Rule 23 eliminated the distinctions between true, hybrid and spurious class actions and the differing res judicata effect of each type of action, thus broadening the effect of res judicata under the amended rule. It follows then that a court— whether it be the trial court making its initial 23(a)(4) determination, or a subsequent court considering a collateral attack on the judgment in a class action—must stringently apply the requirement of adequate representation. Judge Frankel has noted:

"There are, of course, some obvious limitations in any case upon the extent to which absent parties will be concluded. For one thing, as the Advisory Committee observed, such parties have a clear right in some later litigation to attack the judgment which purports to bind them. In such a later case, at least the basic considerations going to the fairness of holding them bound will be

---

[12] One distinction between members of a class in a (b)(1), (b)(2), or (b)(3) action is that absent (b)(1) and (b)(2) members do not have the privilege of opting out of the suit that is accorded to class members in a (b)(3) suit. [Citations omitted.] Also, the mandatory notice requirements of 23(c)(2) do not apply to (b)(1) and (b)(2) actions even though the discretionary notice provisions of (d)(2) are applicable. As a result of these distinctions class members in (b)(1) and (b)(2) actions must necessarily rely on the representative to protect their interests.

open for reexamination. Factors which were not brought to the attention of the first court—including, most centrally, the adequacy of representation in the first suit; [citing Hansberry v. Lee, supra]—may lead to a changed perspective."

M. Frankel, Some Preliminary Observations Concerning Civil Rule 23, 43 F.R.D. 39 (1967). And, as Justice Harlan observed: "The judgment in a class action will bind only those members of the class whose interests have been adequately represented by existing parties to the litigation." Sam Fox Publishing Co. v. United States, supra, 366 U.S. at 691, 81 S.Ct. at 1314. Our inquiry then into the adequacy of class representation for purposes of res judicata is made with the understanding that generally the class will be bound unless the party attacking the judgment can show that the class was inadequately represented.

What standards should determine whether Gaytan adequately represented the class in Gaytan v. Cassidy? In Mersay v. First Republic Corp. of America, supra, the trial court was making the 23(a)(4) determination of whether the named plaintiff would adequately represent the class when it said, "the primary criterion is the forthrightness and vigor with which the representative party can be expected to assert and defend the interests of the members of the class, so as to insure them due process." Id. 43 F.R.D. at 470. This precept is equally applicable to the determination which must be made by a court when a class action judgment is under collateral attack. We hold that the primary criterion for determining whether the class representative has adequately represented his class for purposes of res judicata is whether the representative, through qualified counsel, vigorously and tenaciously protected the interests of the class. A court must view the representative's conduct of the entire litigation with this criterion as its guidepost.

We have previously recognized that Gaytan's representation was more than adequate up to the time the three-judge court entered its final order on remand. The narrow question, therefore, is whether Gaytan's failure to appeal this order, which denied retroactive relief to all members of the class except Gaytan, constitutes inadequate representation of the class so that they are not bound by the judgment. We are compelled to hold that Gaytan's failure to prosecute an appeal on behalf of the other members of his class rendered his representation of them inadequate. For this reason, the judgment in Gaytan v. Cassidy cannot be res judicata to the class.

Gaytan, through his attorney, vigorously represented the class until he obtained individual relief. The problem is that he was representing approximately 150,000 persons, who, although having had their licenses and registration receipts suspended without due process, were denied any relief by the three-judge court's prospective only application of its decision. So long as an appeal from this decision could not be characterized as patently meritless or frivolous,

Gaytan should have prosecuted an appeal. Otherwise, it cannot be said that he vigorously and tenaciously protected the interests of the class he was purporting to represent, or that all members of the class had been afforded due process of law by having a full day in court. It is axiomatic that an appeal is a significant element in the judicial process. Gaytan's failure to prosecute an appeal deprived the members of his class, whose rights were not vindicated by the three-judge court's decision, of full participation in this process.

Appellees do not meet the argument that Gaytan's failure to appeal rendered him an inadequate representative of the class. Instead, they advance an estoppel-type argument to support the proposition that Gonzales cannot raise the inadequate representation issue. Their position is that since counsel for Gonzales was aware that on remand the Gaytan court denied retroactive relief by his June 30, 1971 order, and finally denied such relief in its amended order of August 19, Gonzales is estopped to attack the judgment collaterally because he should have intervened in Gaytan for the purposes of appeal. We reject this contention.

First, as the 1966 amendments to Rule 23 clearly illustrate, the purpose of a class action is to allow as few as one member of a class to prosecute an action for the benefit of the class if the requirements of 23(a) and (b) are met. This is one reason why the requirement of 23(a)(4) is stringently applied. The purpose of Rule 23 would be subverted by requiring a class member who learns of a pending suit involving a class of which he is a part to monitor that litigation to make certain that his interests are being protected; this is not his responsibility—it is the responsibility of the class representative to protect the interests of all class members.

Secondly, it would simply be inequitable to foreclose Gonzales from attacking the Gaytan judgment on the facts of our case. [The court here explained that the above-described chronology of events in the two actions was such as to discourage intervention.]

On remand there will be at least two issues. The first will be whether this action may be maintained as a class action. The district court denied Gonzales's motion to allow this suit to proceed as a class action. In light of our decision and for reasons of judicial economy, we think the district court should reexamine this decision, and if it concludes that Gonzales meets the prerequisites of 23(a) and (b), it would seem appropriate to allow a class action. The second issue will be the retroactivity question. We express no views on the resolution of this issue.

Reversed and remanded.

———

Questions: (4) Should Gonzales be able to collaterally attack on the ground of erroneous certification respecting Rule 23(a)(4), in addition to the ground of constitutionally inadequate representation? What precisely should be the possible grounds for an absentee's collateral attack on a class-action judgment? Compare Restatement (Second) of Judgments § 42 (1980) (broad grounds), with Note, Collateral Attack on the Binding Effect of Class Action Judgments, 87 Harv.L.Rev. 589 (1974) (narrow grounds).

(5) In a (b)(3) class action, an absent class member has a right to opt out of the class and thus to avoid any binding effect. If an absentee opts out and the class ultimately prevails (and given the demise of the doctrine of mutuality of estoppel described in Section 2 of Topic D of Part Six), may this absentee later use the class judgment as res judicata against the former adversary of the class? Compare Restatement (Second) of Judgments § 42(1)(c) comment d, illustration 6 (1980) (no), with Note, Offensive Assertion of Collateral Estoppel by Persons Opting Out of a Class Action, 31 Hastings L.J. 1189 (1980) (yes, for absentee with strong individual interest in controlling own litigation).

(6) If any person has received constitutionally adequate representation, why should the judgment not bind as well as benefit that person, whether or not a class-action judgment was rendered? In other words, why not generally treat adjudication as legislation or administration? Is the answer any more complicated than that by a cost-benefit analysis the rulemakers have chosen to give a certain scope to Rule 23 and thus marked out how far we shall permit the binding of nonparties?

SECTION 2. SCOPE OF RULE 23

GENERAL TELEPHONE CO. v. FALCON
Supreme Court of the United States, 1982.
457 U.S. 147, 102 S.Ct. 2364.

JUSTICE STEVENS delivered the opinion of the Court.

The question presented is whether respondent Falcon, who complained that petitioner did not promote him because he is a Mexican-American, was properly permitted to maintain a class action on behalf of Mexican-American applicants for employment whom petitioner did not hire.

I

In 1969 petitioner initiated a special recruitment and training program for minorities. Through that program, respondent Falcon was hired in July 1969 as a groundman, and within a year he was twice promoted, first to lineman and then to lineman-in-charge. He subsequently refused a promotion to installer-repairman. In October 1972 he applied for the job of field inspector; his application was denied even though the promotion was granted several white employees with less seniority.

Falcon thereupon filed a charge with the Equal Employment Opportunity Commission stating his belief that he had been passed over for promotion because of his national origin and that petitioner's promotion policy operated against Mexican-Americans as a class. . . . In due course he received a right to sue letter from the Commission and, in April 1975, he commenced this action under Title VII of the Civil Rights Act of 1964, 74 Stat. 253, as amended, 42 U.S.C. § 2000e et seq., in the United States District Court for the Northern District of Texas. His complaint alleged that petitioner maintained "a policy, practice, custom, or usage of: (a) discriminating against [Mexican-Americans] because of national origin and with respect to compensation, terms, conditions, and privileges of employment, and (b) . . . subjecting [Mexican-Americans] to continuous employment discrimination." Respondent claimed that as a result of this policy whites with less qualification and experience and lower evaluation scores than respondent had been promoted more rapidly. The complaint contained no factual allegations concerning petitioner's hiring practices.

Respondent brought the action "on his own behalf and on behalf of other persons similarly situated, pursuant to Rule 23(b)(2) of the Federal Rules of Civil Procedure." The class identified in the complaint was "composed of Mexican-American persons who are employed, or who might be employed, by GENERAL TELEPHONE COMPANY at its place of business located in Irving, Texas, who have been and who continue to be or might be adversely affected by the practices complained of herein." [3]

After responding to petitioner's written interrogatories,[4] respondent filed a memorandum in favor of certification of "the class of all hourly Mexican-American employees who have been employed, are employed, or may in the future be employed and all those Mexican-Americans who have applied or would have applied for employment had the Defendant not practiced racial discrimination in its employment practices." App. 46–47. His position was supported by the rul-

[3] App. 13–14. The paragraph of the complaint in which respondent alleged conformance with the requirements of Rule 23 continued:

"There are common questions of law and fact affecting the rights of the members of this class who are, and who continue to be, limited, classified, and discriminated against in ways which deprive and/or tend to deprive them of equal employment opportunities and which otherwise adversely affect their status as employees because of national origin. These persons are so numerous that joinder of all members is impracticable. A common relief is sought. The interests of said class are adequately represented by Plaintiff. Defendant has acted or refused to act on grounds generally applicable to the Plaintiff." Id., at 14.

[4] Petitioner's Interrogatory No. 8 stated:

"Identify the common questions of law and fact which affect the rights of the members of the purported class." Id., at 26.

Respondent answered that interrogatory as follows:

"The facts which affect the rights of the members of the class are the facts of their employment, the ways in which evaluations are made, the subjective rather than objective manner in which recommendations for raises and transfers and promotions are handled, and all of the facts surrounding the employment of Mexican-American persons by General Telephone Company. The questions of law specified in Interrogatory No. 8 call for a conclusion on the part of the Plaintiff." Id., at 34.

ing of the United States Court of Appeals for the Fifth Circuit in Johnson v. Georgia Highway Express, Inc., 417 F.2d 1122 (1969), that any victim of racial discrimination in employment may maintain an "across the board" attack on all unequal employment practices alleged to have been committed by the employer pursuant to a policy of racial discrimination. Without conducting an evidentiary hearing, the District Court certified a class including Mexican-American employees and Mexican-American applicants for employment who had not been hired.

Following trial of the liability issues, the District Court entered separate findings of fact and conclusions of law with respect first to respondent and then to the class. The District Court found that petitioner had not discriminated against respondent in hiring, but that it did discriminate against him in its promotion practices. App. to Pet. for Cert. 35a, 37a. The court reached converse conclusions about the class, finding no discrimination in promotion practices, but concluding that petitioner had discriminated against Mexican-Americans at its Irving facility in its hiring practices. Id., at 39a–40a.[6]

After various post-trial proceedings, the District Court ordered petitioner to furnish respondent with a list of all Mexican-Americans who had applied for employment at the Irving facility during the period between January 1, 1973, and October 18, 1976. Respondent was then ordered to give notice to those persons advising them that they might be entitled to some form of recovery. Evidence was taken concerning the applicants who responded to the notice and backpay was ultimately awarded to 13 persons, in addition to respondent Falcon. The total recovery by respondent and the entire class amounted to $67,925.49, plus costs and interest.

Both parties appealed. The Court of Appeals rejected respondent's contention that the class should have encompassed all of petitioner's operations in Texas, New Mexico, Oklahoma, and Arkansas. On the other hand, the court also rejected petitioner's argument that the class had been defined too broadly. For, under the Fifth Circuit's across-the-board rule, it is permissible for "an employee complaining of one employment practice to represent another complaining of another practice, if the plaintiff and the members of the class suffer from essentially the same injury. In this case, all of the claims are based on discrimination because of national origin." . . .

On the merits, the Court of Appeals [remanded for reconsideration of the rulings that petitioner was liable. The Supreme Court] granted certiorari to decide whether the class action was properly maintained on behalf of both employees who were denied promotion and applicants who were denied employment.

---

[6] The District Court ordered petitioner to accelerate its affirmative action plan by taking specified steps to more actively recruit and promote Mexican-Americans at its Irving facility. See id., at 41a–45a.

II

The class-action device was designed as "an exception to the usual rule that litigation is conducted by and on behalf of the individual named parties only." Califano v. Yamasaki, 442 U.S. 682, 700–701, 99 S.Ct. 2545, 2557–2558. Class relief is "peculiarly appropriate" when the "issues involved are common to the class as a whole" and when they "turn on questions of law applicable in the same manner to each member of the class." Id., at 701, 99 S.Ct., at 2557. For in such cases, "the class-action device saves the resources of both the courts and the parties by permitting an issue potentially affecting every [class member] to be litigated in an economical fashion under Rule 23." Ibid.

Title VII of the Civil Rights Act of 1964, as amended, authorizes the Equal Employment Opportunity Commission to sue in its own name to secure relief for individuals aggrieved by discriminatory practices forbidden by the Act. See 42 U.S.C. § 2000e–5(f)(1). In exercising this enforcement power, the Commission may seek relief for groups of employees or applicants for employment without complying with the strictures of Rule 23. General Telephone Co. v. EEOC, 446 U.S. 318, 100 S.Ct. 1698. Title VII, however, contains no special authorization for class suits maintained by private parties. An individual litigant seeking to maintain a class action under Title VII must meet "the prerequisites of numerosity, commonality, typicality, and adequacy of representation" specified in Rule 23(a). Id., at 330, 100 S.Ct., at 1706. These requirements effectively "limit the class claims to those fairly encompassed by the named plaintiff's claims." Ibid.

We have repeatedly held that "a class representative must be part of the class and 'possess the same interest and suffer the same injury' as the class members." East Texas Motor Freight System, Inc. v. Rodriguez, 431 U.S. 395, 403, 97 S.Ct. 1891, 1896 (quoting Schlesinger v. Reservists Committee to Stop the War, 418 U.S. 208, 216, 94 S.Ct. 2925, 2929–2930). In East Texas Motor Freight, a Title VII action brought by three Mexican-American city drivers, the Fifth Circuit certified a class consisting of the trucking company's black and Mexican-American city drivers allegedly denied on racial or ethnic grounds transfers to more desirable line-driver jobs. We held that the Court of Appeals had "plainly erred in declaring a class action." 431 U.S., at 403, 97 S.Ct., at 1896. Because at the time the class was certified it was clear that the named plaintiffs were not qualified for line-driver positions, "they could have suffered no injury as a result of the allegedly discriminatory practices, and they were, therefore, simply not eligible to represent a class of persons who did allegedly suffer injury." Id., at 403–404, 97 S.Ct., at 1897.

Our holding in East Texas Motor Freight was limited; we noted that "a different case would be presented if the District Court had certified a class and only later had it appeared that the named plaintiffs were not class members or were otherwise inappropriate class representatives." Id., at 406, n. 12, 97 S.Ct., at 1898, n. 12. . . .

We cannot disagree with the proposition underlying the across-the-board rule—that racial discrimination is by definition class discrimination. But the allegation that such discrimination has occurred neither determines whether a class action may be maintained in accordance with Rule 23 nor defines the class that may be certified. Conceptually, there is a wide gap between (a) an individual's claim that he has been denied a promotion on discriminatory grounds, and his otherwise unsupported allegation that the company has a policy of discrimination, and (b) the existence of a class of persons who have suffered the same injury as that individual, such that the individual's claim and the class claims will share common questions of law or fact and that the individual's claim will be typical of the class claims.[13] For respondent to bridge that gap, he must prove much more than the validity of his own claim. Even though evidence that he was passed over for promotion when several less deserving whites were advanced may support the conclusion that respondent was denied the promotion because of his national origin, such evidence would not necessarily justify the additional inferences (1) that this discriminatory treatment is typical of petitioner's promotion practices, (2) that petitioner's promotion practices are motivated by a policy of ethnic discrimination that pervades petitioner's Irving division, or (3) that this policy of ethnic discrimination is reflected in petitioner's other employment practices, such as hiring, in the same way it is manifested in the promotion practices. These additional inferences demonstrate the tenuous character of any presumption that the class claims are "fairly encompassed" within respondent's claim.

Respondent's complaint provided an insufficient basis for concluding that the adjudication of his claim of discrimination in promotion would require the decision of any common question concerning the failure of petitioner to hire more Mexican-Americans. Without any specific presentation identifying the questions of law or fact that

---

[13] The commonality and typicality requirements of Rule 23(a) tend to merge. Both serve as guideposts for determining whether under the particular circumstances maintenance of a class action is economical and whether the named plaintiff's claim and the class claims are so interrelated that the interests of the class members will be fairly and adequately protected in their absence. Those requirements therefore also tend to merge with the adequacy-of-representation requirement, although the latter requirement also raises concerns about the competency of class counsel and conflicts of interest. In this case, we need not address petitioner's argument that there is a conflict of interest between respondent and the class of rejected applicants because an enlargement of the pool of Mexican-American employees will decrease respondent's chances for promotion. See General Telephone Co. v. EEOC, 446 U.S. 318, 331, 100 S.Ct. 1698, 1706–1707 ("In employment discrimination litigation, conflicts might arise, for example, between employees and applicants who were denied employment and who will, if granted relief, compete with employees for fringe benefits or seniority. Under Rule 23, the same plaintiff could not represent these classes."); see also East Texas Motor Freight System, Inc. v. Rodriguez, 431 U.S. 395, 404–405, 97 S.Ct. 1891, 1897–1898.

were common to the claims of respondent and of the members of the class he sought to represent, it was error for the District Court to presume that respondent's claim was typical of other claims against petitioner by Mexican-American employees and applicants. If one allegation of specific discriminatory treatment were sufficient to support an across-the-board attack, every Title VII case would be a potential company-wide class action. We find nothing in the statute to indicate that Congress intended to authorize such a wholesale expansion of class-action litigation.[15]

The trial of this class action followed a predictable course. Instead of raising common questions of law or fact, respondent's evidentiary approaches to the individual and class claims were entirely different. He attempted to sustain his individual claim by proving intentional discrimination. He tried to prove the class claims through statistical evidence of disparate impact. Ironically, the District Court rejected the class claim of promotion discrimination, which conceptually might have borne a closer typicality and commonality relationship with respondent's individual claim, but sustained the class claim of hiring discrimination. As the District Court's bifurcated findings on liability demonstrate, the individual and class claims might as well have been tried separately. It is clear that the maintenance of respondent's action as a class action did not advance "the efficiency and economy of litigation which is a principal purpose of the procedure." American Pipe & Construction Co. v. Utah, 414 U.S. 538, 553, 94 S.Ct. 756, 766.

We do not, of course, judge the propriety of a class certification by hindsight. The District Court's error in this case, and the error inherent in the across-the-board rule, is the failure to evaluate carefully the legitimacy of the named plaintiff's plea that he is a proper class representative under Rule 23(a). As we noted in Coopers & Lybrand v. Livesay, 437 U.S. 463, 98 S.Ct. 2454, "the class determination generally involves considerations that are 'enmeshed in the factual and legal issues comprising the plaintiff's cause of action.'" Id., at 469, 98 S.Ct., at 2458 (quoting Mercantile Nat. Bank v. Langdeau, 371 U.S. 555, 558, 83 S.Ct. 520, 522). Sometimes the issues are plain enough from the pleadings to determine whether the interests of the absent parties are fairly encompassed within the named plaintiff's

---

[15] If petitioner used a biased testing procedure to evaluate both applicants for employment and incumbent employees, a class action on behalf of every applicant or employee who might have been prejudiced by the test clearly would satisfy the commonality and typicality requirements of Rule 23(a). Significant proof that an employer operated under a general policy of discrimination conceivably could justify a class of both applicants and employees if the discrimination manifested itself in hiring and promotion practices in the same general fashion, such as through entirely subjective decisionmaking processes. In this regard it is noteworthy that Title VII prohibits discriminatory employment *practices*, not an abstract policy of discrimination. The mere fact that an aggrieved private plaintiff is a member of an identifiable class of persons of the same race or national origin is insufficient to establish his standing to litigate on their behalf all possible claims of discrimination against a common employer.

claim, and sometimes it may be necessary for the court to probe behind the pleadings before coming to rest on the certification question. Even after a certification order is entered, the judge remains free to modify it in the light of subsequent developments in the litigation. For such an order, particularly during the period before any notice is sent to members of the class, "is inherently tentative." 437 U.S., at 469, n. 11, 98 S.Ct., at 2458, n. 11. This flexibility enhances the usefulness of the class-action device; actual, not presumed, conformance with Rule 23(a) remains, however, indispensable.

III

The need to carefully apply the requirements of Rule 23(a) to Title VII class actions was noticed by a member of the Fifth Circuit panel that announced the across-the-board rule. In a specially concurring opinion in Johnson v. Georgia Highway Express, Inc., supra, at 1125–1127, Judge Godbold emphasized the need for "more precise pleadings," id., at 1125, for "without reasonable specificity the court cannot define the class, cannot determine whether the representation is adequate, and the employer does not know how to defend," id., at 1126. He termed as "most significant" the potential unfairness to the class members bound by the judgment if the framing of the class is overbroad. Ibid. And he pointed out the error of the "tacit assumption" underlying the across-the-board rule that "all will be well for surely the plaintiff will win and manna will fall on all members of the class." Id., at 1127. With the same concerns in mind, we reiterate today that a Title VII class action, like any other class action, may only be certified if the trial court is satisfied, after a rigorous analysis, that the prerequisites of Rule 23(a) have been satisfied.

The judgment of the Court of Appeals affirming the certification order is reversed and the case is remanded for further proceedings consistent with this opinion.

It is so ordered.

[The opinion of Chief Justice Burger, concurring in part and dissenting in part, is omitted.]

Question: (7) "Class action procedures assist courts in giving full realization to substantive policies in two ways. First, to the extent that they open courts to claims not ordinarily litigated, class actions enable courts to enforce policies underlying causes of action in circumstances where those policies might not otherwise be effectuated. Second, to the extent that they enable courts to see the full implications of recognizing rights or remedies, class action procedures assist courts in judging precisely what outcomes of litigation would best serve the policies underlying causes of action." Developments in the Law—Class Actions, 89 Harv.L.Rev. 1318, 1353 (1976). Does not General Telephone Co. v. Falcon indicate at the least that courts in interpreting Rule 23, and possibly the rulemakers in writing and revising Rule 23 as well, should give no consideration to any effect on substantive policies more particularized than these two general effects? But see Cover, For James Wm. Moore: Some Reflections on a Reading of the Rules, 84 Yale L.J. 718, 732–39 (1975) (arguing that "trans-substantive" Rules of general application should be read in each case with some attention to particularized effect on substantive policies).

RULE 23(a) AND (b)

The new Rule 23(a) states some of the prerequisites for maintaining any class action, and these go considerably beyond the constitutional prerequisite. But it is not enough that the tests of Rule 23(a) are satisfied. A class action must also come within one of the subdivisions of Rule 23(b).

Rule 23(b)(1) has not occasioned much difficulty. The rulemakers cautiously divided it into two clauses, one looking to the effect on the party opposing the class and the other looking to the risk of prejudice to the interests of absent members of the class. Often a case will come within both of these clauses, the Supreme Tribe case offering an example. Nothing turns, however, upon which provision is controlling, because actions under these two clauses are treated the same for purposes of other parts of the Rule.

Rule 23(b)(2) was designed to reach civil-rights actions, many of which had been maintained as class actions under the original Rule. See, e.g., Potts v. Flax, 313 F.2d 284 (5th Cir.1963). It is not, however, limited to such cases. It covers situations where the defendant opposing the class has acted or refused to act on grounds generally applicable to the class, although perhaps immediately directed to only a few. It looks to final relief by way of injunction or corresponding declaratory judgment, and it does not extend to cases in which the appropriate final relief is exclusively or predominantly money damages. But a monetary award incidental to or as an element of the equitable remedy, when the primary relief is injunctive or declaratory, may be allowed under this subdivision.

Question: (8) A patentee brings an action against a defendant as representative of a class of alleged infringers of one or more of five patents. Should the action be allowed to be maintained as a class action under Rule 23(b)(1)(A) or (B) or (b)(2)? What bearing does the holding of Blonder-Tongue Laboratories v. University of Illinois Foundation, supra p. 1045, have upon this question?

Rule 23(b)(3) has been the source of many of the problems with and much of the controversy over the new Rule.

Question: (9) If a class action meets the standards of both (b)(2) and (b)(3), to which should it be assigned? Why may this assignment be crucial?

The bounds of Rule 23(a) and (b) do not completely define the scope of the class-action device. Further limiting its use are jurisdictional restrictions as well as the practical hurdles of having to comply with the procedural protections dictated by the rest of Rule 23, which we shall soon consider in greater detail.

IN RE NORTHERN DISTRICT OF CALIFORNIA, DALKON SHIELD IUD PRODUCTS LIABILITY LITIGATION

United States Court of Appeals, Ninth Circuit, 1982.
693 F.2d 847, cert. denied, 103 S.Ct. 817 (1983).

Before GOODWIN, ANDERSON and SCHROEDER, CIRCUIT JUDGES.

GOODWIN, CIRCUIT JUDGE.

Plaintiffs appeal from a district court order conditionally certifying their claims as: (1) a nationwide class action on the issue of punitive damages pursuant to Federal Rule of Civil Procedure 23(b)(1)(B); and (2) a statewide (California) class action on the issue of liability pursuant to Rule 23(b)(3). In re Northern District of California "Dalkon Shield" IUD Products Liability Litigation, 521 F.Supp. 1188 (N.D.Calif.1981); 526 F.Supp. 887 (N.D.Calif.1981).

All plaintiffs claim to have been injured by the Dalkon Shield intrauterine device. All of those plaintiffs who have joined in this appeal challenge class certification. Defendant A.H. Robins also opposes certification of the California 23(b)(3) class. Defendant Hugh J. Davis opposes certification of both classes.

Between June 1970 and June 1974, approximately 2.2 million Dalkon Shields were inserted in women in the United States. Many users sustained injuries. Complaints include uterine perforations, infections, ectopic and uterine pregnancies, spontaneous abortions, fetal injuries and birth defects, sterility, and hysterectomies. Several deaths also were reported. On June 28, 1974, Robins withdrew the Dalkon Shield from the market.

By May 31, 1981, approximately 3,258 actions relating to the Dalkon Shield had been filed, and 1,573 claims were pending. The claims are based on various theories: negligence and negligent design, strict products liability, breach of express and implied warranty, wanton and reckless conduct, conspiracy, and fraud. Most plaintiffs seek both compensatory and punitive damages.

Some plaintiffs joined Robins, Davis, and Irwin W. Lerner as defendants,[f] as well as their own doctors or medical practitioners who recommended and inserted the Dalkon Shield, and local suppliers. Many plaintiffs sued fewer defendants.

In 1975 all actions then pending in federal district courts alleging damages from the use of the Dalkon Shield were transferred by the Judicial Panel on Multidistrict Litigation to the District of Kansas for consolidated pretrial proceedings. In re A.H. Robins Co., Inc.,

[f] Davis and Lerner invented and helped to market the Dalkon Shield. Van Dyke, The Dalkon Shield: A "Primer" in IUD Liability, 6 W.St.U.L.Rev. 1, 6–7 (1978).

"Dalkon Shield" Liability Litigation, 406 F.Supp. 540 (Jud.Pan.Mult. Lit.1975), 419 F.Supp. 710 (Jud.Pan.Mult.Lit.1976), 438 F.Supp. 942 (Jud.Pan.Mult.Lit.1977). After four years of consolidated discovery, the Judicial Panel began vacating its conditional transfer orders and remanding the cases to their respective transferor courts. In re A.H. Robins Co., Inc., "Dalkon Shield" IUD Products Liability Litigation, 453 F.Supp. 108 (Jud.Pan.Mult.Lit.1978), 505 F.Supp. 221 (Jud.Pan. Mult.Lit.1981).

State courts have also received a number of Dalkon Shield cases. The results have been mixed. Some plaintiffs have recovered substantial verdicts. Others have recovered nothing. Many cases have been settled.

Approximately 166 Dalkon Shield cases were pending in the Northern District of California. After one jury trial that lasted nine weeks, Judge Williams consolidated all Dalkon Shield cases pending in that district and ordered briefing on the feasibility of a class action. All but one of California plaintiffs' counsel opposed class certification.[g] Out-of-state plaintiffs were not notified of the briefing request and did not participate in the status conferences held to discuss the class action proposal. All defendants at that time opposed class certification.

On June 25, 1981, Judge Williams entered an order conditionally certifying a nationwide class, under Fed.R.Civ.P. 23(b)(1)(B), consisting of all persons who filed actions for punitive damages against Robins.[2] The court asserted jurisdiction on the basis of diversity of citizenship, 28 U.S.C. § 1332. One stated purpose of certification was to insure the rights of all plaintiffs to a proportionate share of any punitive damages recovery from the "limited fund" of Robins' assets. Judge Williams stated:

> "At the present time, some 1,573 suits involving claims for compensatory damages well over $500 million and claimed punitive damages in excess of $2.3 billion, are pending against A.H. Robins. The potential for the constructive bankruptcy of A.H. Robins, a company whose net worth is $280,394,000.00, raises the unconscionable possibility that large numbers of plaintiffs who are not first in line at the courthouse door will be deprived of a practical means of redress."

No testimony was taken and the way in which the "fund" was limited was not specified.

Judge Williams also conditionally certified a California statewide subclass under Rule 23(b)(3) consisting of plaintiffs who have filed actions against Robins in California. This California class is limited

---

[g] The district court reported that "at least one plaintiff filed a brief in support of this court's announced decision to certify a class," 526 F.Supp. 887, 894 n.12 (N.D.Cal.1981).

[2] On the following day, June 26, Robins moved for certification of a plaintiff punitive damages class under Rule 23(b)(1)(B).

to the question of Robins' liability arising from the manufacture and sale of the Dalkon Shield. Any plaintiff may opt out of this class, whereas all plaintiffs in the nation would be bound by the determination on punitive damages.

Plaintiffs from California, Oregon, Ohio, Florida, and Kansas moved to decertify the punitive damages class. The district court denied the motion and certified the issues for an interlocutory appeal, pursuant to 28 U.S.C. § 1292(b). This court granted the interlocutory appeals and ordered them expedited.

I

The Rule 23(b)(1)(B) Nationwide Punitive Damages Class

A. *Rule 23(a) Prerequisites*

1. *Commonality.*

The district court held that the punitive damages class presented common questions about Robins' knowledge of the safety of its product at material times while the Shield was on the market. What Davis, Lerner and Robins knew about the Dalkon Shield, when they knew it, what information they withheld from the public, and what they stated in their advertising to doctors and in their product instructions during various time periods may all be common questions. These questions are not entirely common, however, to all plaintiffs.

Moreover, as the plaintiffs correctly argue, the 50 jurisdictions in which these cases arise do not apply the same punitive damages standards. Punitive damages standards can range from gross negligence to reckless disregard to various levels of wilfullness and wantonness. If commonality were the only problem in this case, it might be possible to sustain some kind of a punitive damage class. But difficulties remain with other certification requirements.

2. *Typicality.*

. . . The district court order recites that representative parties have been selected. . . . However, all of the appealing plaintiffs assert that no plaintiff has accepted the role, and that no single plaintiff or group of plaintiffs could be typical of the numerous persons who might have claims. No plaintiff has appeared in this appeal in support of class certification. Again, while typicality alone might not be an insurmountable problem, it helps make the overall situation difficult to rationalize as proper for class treatment.

3. *Adequacy of representation.*

The court designated lead counsel for the nationwide class, but he has resigned. New counsel has been designated but has not yet started to represent the class. Apparently none of the attorneys already involved in the case is willing to serve as class counsel. The district judge may well be better able to choose a good lawyer than some of the plaintiffs may be, but the right of litigants to choose their own counsel is a right not lightly to be brushed aside.

The plaintiffs argue that newly appointed, even if expert counsel, may not litigate the action as vigorously as counsel selected by plaintiffs. This court is hesitant to force unwanted counsel upon plaintiffs on the assumption that appointed counsel will be adequate. Even if the class were otherwise acceptable, it would have to be decertified if adequate lead counsel turned out to be unavailable.

We are not necessarily ruling out the class action tool as a means for expediting multi-party product liability actions in appropriate cases, but the combined difficulties overlapping from each of the elements of Rule 23(a) preclude certification in this case.

B. *The Rule 23(b)(1)(B) Requirements*

. . . .

The drafters of Rule 23 intended 23(b)(1)(B) to apply to "limited fund" cases where numerous plaintiffs claim "against a fund insufficient to satisfy all claims." Advisory Committee Note to the 1966 Revision of Rule 23, 39 F.R.D. 69, 101 (1966).

. . . .

Rule 23(b)(1)(B) certification is proper only when separate punitive damage claims necessarily will affect later claims. The district court erred by ordering certification without sufficient evidence of, or even a preliminary fact-finding inquiry concerning Robins' actual assets, insurance, settlement experience and continuing exposure.

The court's other consideration for certifying the punitive damage issue as a nationwide class action was to ensure that Robins would be punished only once. The court correctly notes, and appellants agree, that no rule of law limits the amount of punitive damages a jury may award. A class action, however, is not the only way to protect a defendant from unreasonable punitive damages. Given the difficulties in complying with the requirements of Rule 23(b)(1)(B) in this case, it was error to certify a nationwide class of punitive damages claimants.

II

The Rule 23(b)(3) California Liability Class

A. *Suitability of Class Action Litigation of Mass Products Liability Cases*

The Advisory Committee Note to the 1966 Revision of Rule 23(b)(3) (39 F.R.D. 69, 103) states:

"A 'mass accident' resulting in injuries to numerous persons is ordinarily not appropriate for a class action because of the likelihood that significant questions, not only of damages but of liability and defenses to liability, would be present, affecting the individuals in different ways. In these circumstances an action conducted nominally as a class action would degenerate in practice into multiple lawsuits separately tried. . . ."

Relying in part on that note and on the inherent obstacles to personal injury class actions, many courts have denied plaintiffs' motions for class certification in mass tort or personal injury actions, especially those alleging negligence by one or more defendants over extended periods. See Ryan v. Eli Lilly and Co., 84 F.R.D. 230 (D.S.C.1979) ("DES" action); . . . Hobbs v. Northeast Airlines, Inc., 50 F.R.D. 76 (E.D.Penn.1970) (Rule 23(b)(3) certification of airplane crash cases denied because individual plaintiffs in tort actions have an interest in controlling their own lawsuits; many other suits already were pending in other states; and Pennsylvania causes of action, under which prospective named plaintiffs were suing, might not be available to out-of-state claimants); [other citations omitted].

In Causey v. Pan American World Airways, Inc., 66 F.R.D. 392 (E.D.Va.1975), the court denied the plaintiffs' motion for class certification of airplane crash cases under Rule 23(b)(1)(A) and (B) and under Rule 23(b)(2) or (3) because most prospective plaintiffs were not United States citizens. The court noted, however, that mass accident litigation "may and probably ought to be maintained as a class action" where: (1) the class action is limited to the issue of liability; (2) class members support the action; (3) choice of law problems are minimized because the accident occurred or substantially all plaintiffs reside in the same jurisdiction; and (4) the 23(b)(3) requirement of "superiority" also is met. . . . Hernandez v. Motor Vessel Skyward, 61 F.R.D. 558 (S.D.Fla.1973), affirmed, 507 F.2d 1279 (5th Cir. 1975) . . . (Rule 23(b)(1)(A) certification on issue of defendants' negligence in preparing or making available contaminated food in suits for food poisoning on cruise ship); Bentkowski v. Marfuerza Compania Maritima, S.A., 70 F.R.D. 401 (E.D.Penn.1976) (Rule 23(b)(3) class certification in cruise ship food poisoning cases on negligence issue); [other citations omitted].

In the typical mass tort situation, such as an airplane crash or a cruise ship food poisoning, proximate cause can be determined on a class-wide basis because the cause of the common disaster is the same for each of the plaintiffs.

In products liability actions, however, individual issues may outnumber common issues. . . . No single proximate cause applies equally to each potential class member and each defendant. Furthermore, the alleged tortfeasor's affirmative defenses (such as failure to follow directions, assumption of the risk, contributory negligence, and the statute of limitations) may depend on facts peculiar to each plaintiff's case. See Rosenfeld v. A.H. Robins Co., [63 A.D.2d 11],

407 N.Y.S.2d 196 (1978) (class certification denied under New York statute patterned after Rule 23(b)(3)).

. . . .

Federal district courts recently have conditionally certified two "mass tort" class actions that involve products liability and numerous injuries caused by individual products over a long period of time. In re Agent Orange Product Liability Litigation, . . . 506 F.Supp. 762 [(E.D.N.Y.1980)], and Payton v. Abbott Labs, . . . 83 F.R.D. 382 [(D.Mass.1979)] ("DES" case). In both cases, the plaintiffs sought class status. Both cases were certified under Rule 23(b)(3).

The Agent Orange court found that Rule 23(b)(3) requirements were met because: (1) the litigation was at such an early stage that resolution of preliminary issues concerning the relationship between the government and the Agent Orange manufacturer would affect every plaintiff's claim; (2) discovery and proof in such "untested areas of law" would be so expensive and complicated that no single attorney would be likely to succeed; (3) all cases currently pending already were before that same court under multidistrict litigation procedures; and (4) facts and issues in all pending and future cases were identical or parallel. 506 F.Supp. at 790–91.

The Payton court, without distinguishing the cases prohibiting class action litigation of mass torts, certified a plaintiff class of all women who were exposed to DES in utero in Massachusetts. The court found that "over 90% of the trial time" in two individual DES suits had been devoted to "whether and when defendants knew or should have known of the dangers of DES exposure." 83 F.R.D. at 391–92. The class action was limited to resolving those issues and issues of what injuries Massachusetts law would recognize. Id. at 386–87. The Payton court partially relied upon the nonavailability in Massachusetts of offensive collateral estoppel, which in some states would prevent relitigation of decided issues. Id. at 392. Both the Payton and Agent Orange courts have recognized that neither causation nor damages may be determined in class proceedings. 83 F.R.D. at 394, 506 F.Supp. at 790.

B. *Rule 23(a) Prerequisites*

. . . .

1. *Commonality.*

. . . The district court correctly held that each California case contains common issues "of design, testing, manufacturing, labeling and inspection of the Dalkon Shields." But on the issues of negligence, strict products liability, adequacy of warnings at relevant time periods, breach of warranty, fraud and conspiracy, commonality begins to be obscured by individual case histories.

Different questions of law and fact could apply to various plaintiffs in the California class because of different representations and warnings made to each woman, different injuries suffered, and different defenses available to Robins. The commonality requirement of Rule 23(a)(2) is not, of itself, insurmountable, but problems of commonality merge into problems of management.

2. *Typicality.*

.   .   .   .

Generally, in a class action, plaintiffs who bring the action are the representative parties. They bear the burden of showing that their claims are typical, as well as the burden of demonstrating that the other Rule 23(a) elements are satisfied. Doninger v. Pacific Northwest Bell, Inc., 564 F.2d 1304, 1308–09 (9th Cir. 1977).

Appellants assert that the trial court has not designated representative parties. Named plaintiffs generally are designated parties before the class is certified and "typicality" is determined on the basis of their claims. The trial court stated in its order conditionally certifying class actions that "representative parties have been selected covering the broadest possible gamut of types of injuries . . . ." . . . This designation may require a substantial subdivision of representative subclasses and appears to offer little advantage over a few test trials that may produce more settlements than would a lengthy and complicated trial of consolidated cases.

.   .   .   .

From the large California class the court may be able to find plaintiffs whose claims are fairly representative of the varying injuries. In proving liability under a negligence theory, however, the plaintiffs have to prove not only their injuries, but that Robins and each defendant owed them a duty of care and also what those different standards of care were, if they were breached, and—most important—if the breaches proximately caused the plaintiffs' varying injuries. See generally, W. Prosser, Law of Torts, §§ 41–42 (4th ed. 1971); Restatement (Second) of Torts, ch. 16, §§ 430–461 (1965). To prove liability under a breach of warranty theory, representative plaintiffs must exist for each type of warranty, assurance, or medical advice each plaintiff received. The difficulty of meeting the typicality requirement seems obvious.

.   .   . The district court [stressed that] "plaintiffs have alleged a concerted scheme or conspiracy between defendants in the marketing, design, testing, and production of Dalkon Shields." But this generalization, while partly true, loses sight of the fact that some of the plaintiffs have not alleged that all of their defendants had so conspired. For example, some plaintiffs sued their own doctors and the local suppliers of those doctors, without planning to prove that those defendants were part of a conspiracy.

.   .   . The financial importance of common questions of law and fact cannot be used to create a class of plaintiffs who have claims against some common defendants and some separate and uncommon defendants. The complexity of issues peculiar to individual claims militates against grouping all plaintiffs into a class for only part of their recovery.

We do not decide or suggest that the typicality requirement of Rule 23(a)(3) may never be met when multiple plaintiffs sue different defendants. But the requirement is not met in this case.

3. *Adequacy of representation.*

. . . .

The trial court found that "whichever firm is chosen to represent named plaintiffs will vigorously and competently litigate the action." We assume that the plaintiffs' California counsel named in the briefs were known to the district court to be competent attorneys. And the court correctly found "no reason to suspect any antagonism between any of the absentees and the named plaintiffs."

Appellants argue, however, that adequacy is not satisfied because representative plaintiffs who do not have a cause of action against a particular defendant (such as individual doctors) cannot fairly and adequately protect the interests of those who do have such causes of action.

The counsel originally designated by the court to be lead counsel for the nationwide class and statewide class attempted to resign from both positions. The judge did not accept his resignation from the statewide class. . . .

C. *Rule 23(b)(3) Requirements*

. . . .

1. *Predominance.*

The trial judge found that a "common nucleus of operative facts" exists in this case that can be resolved in one adjudication. This common factual nucleus is "whether and when defendants knew or should have known of the dangers of the Dalkon Shield to its users . . . . [and] the facts surrounding defendants' design, production, etc. of the Dalkon Shield . . . ."

Although those are common factual questions, the court should have balanced these concerns with the greater number of questions affecting individual class members. The 23(b)(3) class is limited to the issue of liability, but Robins' overall liability, under some of the theories, cannot be proved unless each plaintiff also proves that Robins' breach of its duty proximately caused her particular injury.

For those plaintiffs who assert a breach of warranty claim, additional individual factual issues will have to be argued and determined. Robins' warranties consisted mainly of various medical journal and medical trade-show advertisements over a four-year period. Different types of advertisements were printed on different dates in different journals. Different doctors read various periodicals. The advertisements were made to and read not by plaintiffs but by their doctors.

While facts about what warranties or representations Robins made and whether Robins breached them could be determined on a class basis, these facts can also be reached in consolidated discovery proceedings, and can be expected to become standardized after a few trials.

2. *Superiority.*

Efficiency is a factor supporting class action treatment for some of the issues raised by California plaintiffs. The strongest supporting factor, however, is that by litigating portions of liability (defective or negligent design, existence of warranties) on a class basis, litigation costs of presenting evidence and expert witnesses will be greatly reduced.

A trial court can sever and try only certain issues on a class basis under Rule 23(c)(4)(A). The few issues that might be tried on a class basis in this case, balanced against issues that must be tried individually, indicate that the time saved by a class action may be relatively insignificant. A few verdicts followed by settlements might be equally efficacious.

3. *Considerations of Rule 23(b)(3)(A–D).*

In determining if common issues predominate and a class action is superior, the court should consider the factors provided in 23(b)(3)(A–D).

A. The California liability class members have a strong interest in controlling the prosecution of separate actions. Counsel for plaintiffs who have appealed have stated they will recommend that their clients opt out of the class. If a large number do so, the class will be unable to proceed.

B. Several Dalkon Shield cases already have been completed in California, and over 300 are pending.

C. The majority of California Dalkon Shield cases were not filed in the Northern District of California, although most plaintiffs' counsel are from the Northern or Central Districts.

D. Management is made difficult by the complexity and multiplicity of issues and by plaintiffs' hostility to the class action.

In addition, in this case, many plaintiffs have sued other defendants, such as their individual doctors, and the presence of these separate defendants creates additional problems of management.

CONCLUSION

The California liability class does not satisfy the typicality requirement of Rule 23(a)(3) or the Rule 23(b)(3) requirement that the class action be superior to other available means of adjudication. We do not preclude further consideration by the district court of motions to certify a more limited class or subclasses under Rule 23(b)(3).

The court erred in certifying the Rule 23(b)(1)(B) nationwide punitive damage class on its own motion without giving out-of-state plaintiffs an opportunity to participate in prior briefings or hearings, and without establishing as a fact that Robins' assets were too limited to permit conventional litigation. Even if further proceedings were had on those issues, however, the case would still fail to meet Rule 23(a)'s preliminary requirements of commonality, typicality and adequacy of representation. Moreover, separate early punitive damages awards need not inescapably affect later awards. . . . We conclude that both classes must be decertified.

. . . .

Vacated and remanded.

Question: (10) Is there and should there be provision for a compulsory class action, as where a corporation faces an endless queue of individual actions against it and wishes that they be brought together despite the unwillingness of every plaintiff, or is this and should this be the exclusive domain of Rule 19 dealing with compulsory joinder?

SECTION 3. LITIGATING CLASS ACTIONS

EISEN v. CARLISLE & JACQUELIN

Supreme Court of the United States, 1974.
417 U.S. 156, 94 S.Ct. 2140.

MR. JUSTICE POWELL delivered the opinion of the Court.

On May 2, 1966, petitioner filed a class action on behalf of himself and all other odd-lot [1] traders on the New York Stock Exchange (the Exchange). The complaint charged respondents with violations of the antitrust and securities laws and demanded damages for petitioner and his class. Eight years have elapsed, but there has been no trial on the merits of these claims. Both the parties and the courts are still wrestling with the complex questions surrounding petitioner's attempt to maintain his suit as a class action under Fed.Rule Civ. Proc. 23. We granted certiorari to resolve some of these difficulties. 414 U.S. 908, 94 S.Ct. 235 (1973).

I

Petitioner brought this class action in the United States District Court for the Southern District of New York. Originally, he sued on behalf of all buyers and sellers of odd lots on the Exchange, but sub-

---

[1] Odd lots are shares traded in lots of fewer than a hundred. Shares traded in units of a hundred or multiples thereof are round-lots.

sequently the class was limited to those who traded in odd lots during the period from May 1, 1962, through June 30, 1966. 52 F.R.D. 253, 261 (1971). Throughout this period odd-lot trading was not part of the Exchange's regular auction market but was handled exclusively by special odd-lot dealers, who bought and sold for their own accounts as principals. Respondent brokerage firms Carlisle & Jacquelin and DeCoppet & Doremus together handled 99% of the Exchange's odd-lot business. S.E.C., Report of Special Study of Securities Markets, H.R.Doc. No. 95, pt. 2, 88th Cong., 1st Sess., 172 (1963). They were compensated by the odd-lot differential, a surcharge imposed on the odd-lot investor in addition to the standard brokerage commission applicable to round-lot transactions. For the period in question the differential was $1/8$ of a point ($12^1/_2$¢) per share on stocks trading below $40 per share and $1/4$ of a point (25¢) per share on stocks trading at or above $40 per share.

Petitioner charged that respondent brokerage firms had monopolized odd-lot trading and set the differential at an excessive level in violation of §§ 1 and 2 of the Sherman Act, 15 U.S.C. §§ 1 and 2, and he demanded treble damages for the amount of the overcharge. Petitioner also demanded unspecified money damages from the Exchange for its alleged failure to regulate the differential for the protection of investors in violation of §§ 6 and 19 of the Securities Exchange Act of 1934, 15 U.S.C. §§ 78f and 78s. Finally, he requested attorneys' fees and injunctive prohibition of future excessive charges.

A critical fact in this litigation is that petitioner's individual stake in the damages award he seeks is only $70. No competent attorney would undertake this complex antitrust action to recover so inconsequential an amount. Economic reality dictates that petitioner's suit proceed as a class action or not at all. Opposing counsel have therefore engaged in prolonged combat over the various requirements of Rule 23. The result has been an exceedingly complicated series of decisions by both the District Court and the Court of Appeals for the Second Circuit. . . .

. . . .

Eisen I

As we have seen, petitioner began this action in May 1966. In September of that year [Judge Tyler of] the District Court dismissed the suit as a class action. 41 F.R.D. 147. Following denial of his motion for interlocutory review under 28 U.S.C. § 1292(b), petitioner took an appeal as of right under § 1291. Respondents then moved to dismiss on the ground that the order appealed from was not final. In Eisen I, the Court of Appeals held that the denial of class action status in this case was appealable as a final order under § 1291. 370 F.2d 119 (1966), cert. denied, 386 U.S. 1035, 87 S.Ct. 1487 (1967). This was so because, as a practical matter, the dismissal of the class action aspect of petitioner's suit was a "death knell" for the entire action. . . .

Eisen II

Nearly 18 months later the Court of Appeals reversed the dismissal of the class action in a decision known as Eisen II. 391 F.2d 555 (1968). In reaching this result the court undertook an exhaustive but ultimately inconclusive analysis of Rule 23. Subdivision (a) of the Rule sets forth four prerequisites to the maintenance of any suit as a class action . . . . The District Court had experienced little difficulty in finding that petitioner satisfied the first three prerequisites but had concluded that petitioner might not "fairly and adequately protect the interests of the class" as required by Rule 23(a)(4). The Court of Appeals indicated its disagreement with the reasoning behind the latter conclusion and directed the District Court to reconsider the point.

In addition to meeting the four conjunctive requirements of 23(a), a class action must also qualify under one of the three subdivisions of 23(b). Petitioner argued that the suit was maintainable as a class action under all three subdivisions. The Court of Appeals held the first two subdivisions inapplicable to this suit [1] and therefore turned its attention to the third subdivision, (b)(3). . . . After a detailed review . . ., the Court of Appeals concluded that the only potential barrier to maintenance of this suit as a class action was the Rule 23(b)(3)(D) directive that a court evaluate "the difficulties likely to be encountered in the management of a class action." Commonly referred to as "manageability," this consideration encompasses the whole range of practical problems that may render the class action format inappropriate for a particular suit. With reference to this litigation, the Court of Appeals noted that the difficulties of distributing any ultimate recovery to the class members would be formidable, though not necessarily insuperable, and commented that it was "reluctant to permit actions to proceed where they are not likely to benefit anyone but the lawyers who bring them." 391 F.2d, at 567. The Court therefore directed the District Court to conduct "a further inquiry . . . in order to consider the mechanics involved in the administration of the present action." Ibid.

Finally, the Court of Appeals turned to the most imposing obstacle to this class action—the notice requirement of Rule 23(c)(2). The

---

[1] Before the Court of Appeals, petitioner dropped the contention that the suit qualified under subdivision (b)(1)(B). The court held subdivision (b)(1)(A) inapplicable on the ground that the prospective class consisted entirely of small claimants, none of whom could afford to litigate this action in order to recover his individual claim and that consequently there was little chance of "inconsistent or varying adjudications with respect to individual members of the class which would establish incompatible standards of conduct for the party opposing the class . . . ." Subdivision (b)(2) was held to apply only to actions exclusively or predominantly for injunctive or declaratory relief. Advisory Committee's Note, Proposed Rules of Civil Procedure, 28 U.S.C.App., p. 7766.

District Court had held that both the Rule and the Due Process Clause of the Fifth Amendment required individual notice to all class members who could be identified. 41 F.R.D., at 151. Petitioner objected that mailed notice to the entire class would be prohibitively expensive and argued that some form of publication notice would suffice. The Court of Appeals declined to settle this issue, noting that "[o]n the record before us we cannot arrive at any rational and satisfactory conclusion on the propriety of resorting to some form of publication as a means of giving the necessary notice to all members of the class on behalf of whom the action is stated to be commenced and maintained." 391 F.2d, at 569.

The outcome of Eisen II was a remand for an evidentiary hearing on the questions of notice, manageability, adequacy of representation, and "any other matters which the District Court may consider pertinent and proper." Id., at 570. And in a ruling that aroused later controversy, the Court of Appeals expressly purported to retain appellate jurisdiction while the case was heard on remand.

Eisen III

After it held the evidentiary hearing on remand, which together with affidavits and stipulations provided the basis for extensive findings of fact, the District Court issued an opinion and order holding the suit maintainable as a class action. 52 F.R.D. 253 (1971) [(Tyler, J.)]. The court first noted that petitioner satisfied the criteria identified by the Court of Appeals for determining adequacy of representation under Rule 23(a)(4). Then it turned to the more difficult question of manageability. Under this general rubric the court dealt with problems of the computation of damages, the mechanics of administering this suit as a class action, and the distribution of any eventual recovery. The last-named problem had most troubled the Court of Appeals, prompting its remark that if "class members are not likely ever to share in an eventual judgment, we would probably not permit the class action to continue." 391 F.2d, at 567. The District Court attempted to resolve this difficulty by embracing the idea of a "fluid class" recovery whereby damages would be distributed to future odd-lot traders rather than to the specific class members who were actually injured. The court suggested that "a fund equivalent to the amount of unclaimed damages might be established and the odd-lot differential reduced in an amount determined reasonable by the court until such time as the fund is depleted." 52 F.R.D., at 265. The need to resort to this expedient of recovery by the "next best class" arose from the prohibitively high cost of computing and awarding multitudinous small damages claims on an individual basis.

Finally, the District Court took up the problem of notice. The court found that the prospective class included some six million individuals, institutions, and intermediaries of various sorts; that with reasonable effort some two million of these odd-lot investors could be identified by name and address;[5] and that the names and addresses of an additional 250,000 persons who had participated in special investment programs involving odd-lot trading[6] could also be identified with reasonable effort. Using the then current first-class postage rate of six cents, the court determined that stuffing and mailing each individual notice form would cost 10 cents. Thus individual notice to all identifiable class members would cost $225,000, and additional expense would be incurred for suitable publication notice designed to reach the other four million class members.

The District Court concluded, however, that neither Rule 23(c)(2) nor the Due Process Clause required so substantial an expenditure at the outset of this litigation. Instead, it proposed a notification scheme consisting of four elements: (1) individual notice to all member firms of the Exchange and to commercial banks with large trust departments; (2) individual notice to the approximately 2,000 identifiable class members with 10 or more odd-lot transactions during the relevant period; (3) individual notice to an additional 5,000 class members selected at random; and (4) prominent publication notice in the Wall Street Journal and in other newspapers in New York and California. The court calculated that this package would cost approximately $21,720.

The only issue not resolved by the District Court in its first opinion on remand from Eisen II was who should bear the cost of notice. Because petitioner understandably declined to pay $21,720 in order to litigate an action involving an individual stake of only $70, this question presented something of a dilemma:

"If the expense of notice is placed upon [petitioner], it would be the end of a possibly meritorious suit, frustrating both the policy behind private antitrust actions and the admonition that the new Rule 23 is to be given a liberal rather than a restrictive interpretation, Eisen II at 563. On the other hand, if costs were arbitrarily placed upon [respondents] at this point, the result might be the imposition of an unfair burden founded upon a groundless claim. In addition to the probability of encouraging frivolous class actions, such a step might also result in [respondents'] passing on to their customers, including many of the class members in this case, the expenses of defending these actions." 52 F.R.D., at 269.

[5] These two million traders dealt with brokerage firms who transmitted their odd-lot transactions to respondents Carlisle & Jacquelin and DeCoppet & Doremus via teletype. By comparing the odd-lot firms' computerized records of these teletype transactions and the general-services brokerage firms' computerized records of all customer names and addresses, the names and addresses of these two million odd-lot traders can be obtained.

[6] In the period from May 1962 through June 1968, 100,000 individuals had odd-lot transactions through participation in the Monthly Investment Plan operated by the Exchange and 150,000 persons traded in odd lots through participation in a number of payroll deduction plans operated by Merrill Lynch, Pierce, Fenner & Smith.

Analogizing to the laws of preliminary injunctions, the court decided to impose the notice cost on respondents if petitioner could show a strong likelihood of success on the merits, and it scheduled a preliminary hearing on the merits to facilitate this determination. After this hearing the District Court issued an opinion and order ruling that petitioner was "more than likely" to prevail at trial and that respondents should bear 90% of the cost of notice, or $19,548. 54 F.R.D. 565, 567 (1972) [(Tyler, J.)].

Relying on the purported retention of jurisdiction by the Court of Appeals after Eisen II, respondents on May 1, 1972, obtained an order directing the clerk of the District Court to certify and transmit the record for appellate review. Subsequently, respondents also filed a notice of appeal under 28 U.S.C. § 1291. Petitioner's motion to dismiss on the ground that the appeal had not been taken from a final order was denied by the Court of Appeals on June 29, 1972.

On May 1, 1973, the Court of Appeals issued Eisen III [by the same panel that issued Eisen II]. 479 F.2d 1005. The majority disapproved the District Court's partial reliance on publication notice, holding that Rule 23(c)(2) required individual notice to all identifiable class members. The majority further ruled that the District Court had no authority to conduct a preliminary hearing on the merits for the purpose of allocating costs and that the entire expense of notice necessarily fell on petitioner as representative plaintiff. Finally, the Court of Appeals rejected the expedient of a fluid-class recovery and concluded that the proposed class action was unmanageable under Rule 23(b)(3)(D).[h] For all of these reasons the Court of Appeals ordered

[h] The court of appeals said in part: "As soon as the evidence on the remand disclosed the true extent of the membership of the class and the fact that Eisen would not pay for individual notice to the members of the class who could be identified, and the evidence further disclosed that the class membership was of such diversity and was so dispersed that no notice by publication could be devised by the ingenuity of man that could reasonably be expected to notify more than a relatively small proportion of the class, a ruling should have been made forthwith dismissing the case as a class action. This dismissal could have saved several years of hard work by the judge and the lawyers and wholly unnecessary expense running into large figures. The fact that the cost of obtaining proofs of claim by individual members of the class and processing such claims was such as to make it clear that the amounts payable to individual claimants would be so low as to be negligible also should have been enough of itself to warrant dismissal as a class action. Other cases involving millions of diverse and unidentifiable members of an alleged class had been dismissed as unmanageable or altered in composition. And so even Eisen and his counsel conceded that the class was not manageable unless the 'fluid recovery' procedures were adopted.

. . . .

"Even if amended Rule 23 could be read so as to permit any such fantastic procedure, the courts would have to reject it as an unconstitutional violation of the requirement of due process of law. But as it now reads amended Rule 23 contemplates and provides for no such procedure. Nor can amended Rule 23 be construed or interpreted in such fashion as to permit such procedure. We hold the 'fluid recovery' concept and practice to be illegal, inadmissible as a solution of the manageability problems of class actions and wholly improper."

Fluid recovery means class-wide calculation of damages that are distributed by an individual proof-of-claim procedure plus some mechanism for indirectly applying the residue to the benefit of the class. On the subject of fluid recovery, it

the suit dismissed as a class action. One judge concurred in the result solely on the ground that the District Court had erred in imposing 90% of the notice costs on respondents. Petitioner's requests for rehearing and rehearing en banc were denied. 479 F.2d, at 1020.

Thus, after six and one-half years and three published decisions, the Court of Appeals endorsed the conclusion reached by the District Court in its original order in 1966—that petitioner's suit could not proceed as a class action. In its procedural history, at least, this litigation has lived up to Judge Lumbard's characterization of it as a "Frankenstein monster posing as a class action." Eisen II, 391 F.2d, at 572.

II

At the outset we must decide whether the Court of Appeals in Eisen III had jurisdiction to review the District Court's orders permitting the suit to proceed as a class action and allocating the cost of notice. [The Supreme Court here held that the rulings concerning notice were appealable under the collateral order doctrine, which is further discussed in the text immediately after this case. The Court reached no other questions of appealability. Moreover, the Court observed that in view of its ultimate disposition of the notice issues, it had "no occasion to consider whether the Court of Appeals correctly resolved the issues of manageability and fluid-class recovery."]

III

Turning to the merits of the case, we find that the District Court's resolution of the notice problems was erroneous in two respects. First, it failed to comply with the notice requirements of Rule 23(c)(2), and second, it imposed part of the cost of notice on respondents.

A

Rule 23(c)(2) provides that, in any class action maintained under subdivision (b)(3), each class member shall be advised that he has the right to exclude himself from the action on request or to enter an appearance through counsel, and further that the judgment, whether favorable or not, will bind all class members not requesting exclusion. To this end, the court is required to direct to class members "the best notice practicable under the circumstances, *including individual no-*

has been said that the holding of Eisen III "can be criticized as representing a mechanical and unsympathetic reading of Rule 23 and one that completely ignores the courts' discretion to fashion relief." 7A Wright & Miller § 1784. The Second Circuit's unexplained dictum that fluid recovery violates due process has likewise been criticized. See, e.g., Developments in the Law—Class Actions, 89 Harv.L.Rev. 1318, 1523–25 (1976). Can one address the desirability of fluid recovery without reaching the more fundamental question of whether the focus of class actions such as Eisen should be on compensating injured plaintiffs or sanctioning transgressive defendants? See Scott, Two Models of the Civil Process, 27 Stan.L.Rev. 937 (1975), quoted supra p. 261.

tice to all members who can be identified through reasonable effort." We think the import of this language is unmistakable. Individual notice must be sent to all class members whose names and addresses may be ascertained through reasonable effort.

The Advisory Committee's Note to Rule 23 reinforces this conclusion. See 28 U.S.C.App., p. 7765. The Advisory Committee described subdivision (c)(2) as "not merely discretionary" and added that the "mandatory notice pursuant to subdivision (c)(2) . . . is designed to fulfill requirements of due process to which the class action procedure is of course subject." Id., at 7768. The Committee explicated its incorporation of due process standards by citation to Mullane v. Central Hanover Bank & Trust Co., 339 U.S. 306, 70 S.Ct. 652 (1950), and like cases.

In Mullane the Court addressed the constitutional sufficiency of publication notice rather than mailed individual notice to known beneficiaries of a common trust fund as part of a judicial settlement of accounts. The Court observed that notice and an opportunity to be heard were fundamental requisites of the constitutional guarantee of procedural due process. It further stated that notice must be "reasonably calculated, under all the circumstances, to apprise interested parties of the pendency of the action and afford them an opportunity to present their objections." Id., at 314, 70 S.Ct., at 657. The Court continued:

> "But when notice is a person's due, process which is a mere gesture is not due process. The means employed must be such as one desirous of actually informing the absentee might reasonably adopt to accomplish it. The reasonableness and hence the constitutional validity of any chosen method may be defended on the ground that it is in itself reasonably certain to inform those affected." Id., at 315, 70 S.Ct., at 657.

The Court then held that publication notice could not satisfy due process where the names and addresses of the beneficiaries were known. In such cases, "the reasons disappear for resort to means less likely than the mails to apprise them of [an action's] pendency." Id., at 318, 70 S.Ct., at 659.

In Schroeder v. City of New York, 371 U.S. 208, 83 S.Ct. 279 (1962), decided prior to the promulgation of amended Rule 23, the Court explained that Mullane required rejection of notice by publication where the name and address of the affected person were available. The Court stated that the "general rule" is that "notice by publication is not enough with respect to a person whose name and address are known or very easily ascertainable . . . ." Id., at 212–213, 83 S.Ct., at 282. The Court also noted that notice by publication had long been recognized as a poor substitute for actual notice and that its justification was " 'difficult at best.' " Id., at 213, 83 S.Ct., at 283.

Viewed in this context, the express language and intent of Rule 23(c)(2) leave no doubt that individual notice must be provided to those class members who are identifiable through reasonable effort. In the present case, the names and addresses of 2,250,000 class members are easily ascertainable, and there is nothing to show that individual notice cannot be mailed to each. For these class members, individual notice is clearly the "best notice practicable" within the meaning of Rule 23(c)(2) and our prior decisions.

Petitioner contends, however, that we should dispense with the requirement of individual notice in this case, and he advances two reasons for our doing so. First, the prohibitively high cost of providing individual notice to 2,250,000 class members would end this suit as a class action and effectively frustrate petitioner's attempt to vindicate the policies underlying the antitrust and securities laws. Second, petitioner contends that individual notice is unnecessary in this case, because no prospective class member has a large enough stake in the matter to justify separate litigation of his individual claim. Hence, class members lack any incentive to opt out of the class action even if notified.

The short answer to these arguments is that individual notice to identifiable class members is not a discretionary consideration to be waived in a particular case. It is, rather, an unambiguous requirement of Rule 23. As the Advisory Committee's Note explained, the Rule was intended to insure that the judgment, whether favorable or not, would bind all class members who did not request exclusion from the suit. 28 U.S.C.App., pp. 7765, 7768. Accordingly, each class member who can be identified through reasonable effort must be notified that he may request exclusion from the action and thereby preserve his opportunity to press his claim separately or that he may remain in the class and perhaps participate in the management of the action. There is nothing in Rule 23 to suggest that the notice requirements can be tailored to fit the pocketbooks of particular plaintiffs.[13]

Petitioner further contends that adequate representation, rather than notice, is the touchstone of due process in a class action and therefore satisfies Rule 23. We think this view has little to commend it. To begin with, Rule 23 speaks to notice as well as to adequacy of representation and requires that both be provided. Moreover, petitioner's argument proves too much, for it quickly leads to the conclusion that no notice at all, published or otherwise, would be required in the present case. This cannot be so, for quite apart from what due process may require, the command of Rule 23 is clearly to the contra-

---

[13] Petitioner also argues that class members will not opt out because the statute of limitations has long since run out on the claims of all class members other than petitioner. This contention is disposed of by our recent decision in American Pipe & Construction Co. v. Utah, 414 U.S. 538, 94 S.Ct. 756 (1974), which established that commencement of a class action tolls the applicable statute of limitations as to all members of the class.

ry. We therefore conclude that Rule 23(c)(2) requires that individual notice be sent to all class members who can be identified with reasonable effort.[14]

B

We also agree with the Court of Appeals that petitioner must bear the cost of notice to the members of his class. . . .

We find nothing in either the language or history of Rule 23 that gives a court any authority to conduct a preliminary inquiry into the merits of a suit in order to determine whether it may be maintained as a class action. Indeed, such a procedure contravenes the Rule by allowing a representative plaintiff to secure the benefits of a class action without first satisfying the requirements for it. He is thereby allowed to obtain a determination on the merits of the claims advanced on behalf of the class without any assurance that a class action may be maintained. This procedure is directly contrary to the command of subdivision (c)(1) that the court determine whether a suit denominated a class action may be maintained as such "[a]s soon as practicable after the commencement of [the] action . . . ." In short, we agree with Judge Wisdom's conclusion in Miller v. Mackey International, 452 F.2d 424 (CA5 1971), where the court rejected a preliminary inquiry into the merits of a proposed class action:

> "In determining the propriety of a class action, the question is not whether the plaintiff or plaintiffs have stated a cause of action or will prevail on the merits, but rather whether the requirements of Rule 23 are met." Id., at 427.

Additionally, we might note that a preliminary determination of the merits may result in substantial prejudice to a defendant, since of necessity it is not accompanied by the traditional rules and procedures applicable to civil trials. The court's tentative findings, made in the absence of established safeguards, may color the subsequent proceedings and place an unfair burden on the defendant.

In the absence of any support under Rule 23, petitioner's effort to impose the cost of notice on respondents must fail. The usual rule is that a plaintiff must initially bear the cost of notice to the class. The exceptions cited by the District Court related to situations where a fiduciary duty pre-existed between the plaintiff and defendant, as in a shareholder derivative suit.[15] Where, as here, the relationship between the parties is truly adversary, the plaintiff must pay for the

---

[14] We are concerned here only with the notice requirements of subdivision (c)(2), which are applicable to class actions maintained under subdivision (b)(3). By its terms subdivision (c)(2) is inapplicable to class actions for injunctive or declaratory relief maintained under subdivision (b)(2). Petitioner's effort to qualify his suit as a class action under subdivisions (b)(1) and (b)(2) was rejected by the Court of Appeals. See n. 4, supra.

[15] See, e.g., Dolgow v. Anderson, 43 F.R.D. 472, 498–500 (EDNY 1968). We, of course, express no opinion on the proper allocation of the cost of notice in such cases.

cost of notice as part of the ordinary burden of financing his own suit.

Petitioner has consistently maintained, however, that he will not bear the cost of notice under subdivision (c)(2) to members of the class as defined in his original complaint. See 479 F.2d, at 1008; 52 F.R.D., at 269. We therefore remand the cause with instructions to dismiss the class action as so defined.[16]

The judgment of the Court of Appeals is vacated and the cause remanded for proceedings consistent with this opinion.

It is so ordered.

MR. JUSTICE DOUGLAS, with whom MR. JUSTICE BRENNAN and MR. JUSTICE MARSHALL concur, dissenting in part.

While I am in general agreement with the phases of this case touched on by the Court, I add a few words because its opinion does not fully explore the issues which will be dispositive of this case on remand to the District Court.

[Justice Douglas here explained that the subclass approach of Rule 23(c)(4)(B) would, in his view, be highly appropriate on remand.]

I agree with Professor Chafee that a class action serves not only the convenience of the parties but also prompt, efficient judicial administration.[7] I think in our society that is growing in complexity there are bound to be innumerable people in common disasters, calamities, or ventures who would go begging for justice without the class action but who could with all regard to due process be protected by it. Some of these are consumers whose claims may seem de minimis but who alone have no practical recourse for either remuneration or injunctive relief. Some may be environmentalists who have no photographic development plant about to be ruined because of air pollution by radiation but who suffer perceptibly by smoke, noxious gases, or radiation. Or the unnamed individual may be only a ratepayer being excessively charged by a utility, or a homeowner whose assessment is slowly rising beyond his ability to pay.

The class action is one of the few legal remedies the small claimant has against those who command the status quo. I would strengthen his hand with the view of creating a system of law that dispenses justice to the lowly as well as to those liberally endowed with power and wealth.

---

[16] The record does not reveal whether a smaller class of odd-lot traders could be defined, and if so, whether petitioner would be willing to pay the cost of notice to members of such a class. We intimate no view on whether any such subclass would satisfy the requirements of Rule 23. We do note, however, that our dismissal of the class action as originally defined is without prejudice to any efforts petitioner may make to redefine his class either under Rule 23(c)(4) or Fed.Rule Civ.Proc. 15.

[7] Z. Chafee, Some Problems of Equity 149 (1950).

Questions: (11) Does the notice requirement in a (b)(3) class action like Eisen arise from the due process clause or just from Rule 23(c)(2)? Is there a notice requirement in (b)(1) and (b)(2) actions? See C. Wright, The Law of Federal Courts § 72, at 482 (4th ed. 1983).

(12) Why is it that there is a duty to exert only "reasonable effort" in identifying members of the class, but there is an absolute duty to give individual notice to those so identified?

APPEALABILITY OF ORDER DENYING OR GRANTING CLASS–ACTION STATUS

Eisen I posed the question of whether an order dismissing a class action, but permitting the named plaintiff to litigate his individual claim, was appealable. Did it fall within the small class of collateral orders recognized as appealable in Cohen v. Beneficial Industrial Loan Corp., infra p. 1221, being "too important to be denied review and too independent of the cause itself to require that appellate consideration be deferred until the whole case is adjudicated"? Was it appealable under Gillespie v. United States Steel Corp., infra p. 1224, because "the inconvenience and costs of piecemeal review" were outweighed by "the danger of denying justice by delay"? The Second Circuit held it appealable as a final order, citing Cohen and Gillespie and saying that immediate review should be allowed where "a district court's order, if not reviewed, is the death knell of the action."

The Supreme Court, however, has since considered the appealability of an order denying class-action status. In Coopers & Lybrand v. Livesay, 437 U.S. 463, 98 S.Ct. 2454 (1978), the Court ruled that such an order is not appealable under 28 U.S.C. § 1291, the collateral order exception being inapplicable, Gillespie being limited to its facts, and the "death knell" rationale being here invalid. In dicta the Court observed that orders granting class certification are likewise interlocutory.

Question: (13) If rejection of the "death knell" rationale was another toll in the death knell of class actions for small consumer claims in the antitrust field and for small claims like Eisen under the federal securities statutes (where jurisdiction does not depend on amount in controversy), is this an undesirable result? Note that Snyder v. Harris, supra p. 751, and Zahn v. International Paper Co., supra p. 754, had already sounded the death knell of class actions for small claims based on diversity of citizenship.

On the same day it decided Coopers & Lybrand, the Supreme Court rejected an attempt to stretch 28 U.S.C. § 1292(a)(1) to cover an order denying class-action status to a suit seeking class-wide permanent injunctive relief. Gardner v. Westinghouse Broadcasting Co., 437 U.S. 478, 98 S.Ct. 2451 (1978).

As usual, § 1292(b) and mandamus offer possibilities of interlocutory review of class-action determinations, but § 1292(b) and especially mandamus are rarely invoked successfully here. See Comment,

Appealability of Class Action Determinations, 44 Fordham L.Rev. 548, 561–65, 568–71 (1975).

An additional discretionary route to immediate review of an order denying class-action status may lie in Rule 54(b), but the Rule's applicability to this kind of order is particularly questionable. See id. at 571–74. Perhaps somewhat more surely available but practically risky is the route whereby the disappointed named plaintiff creates a final decision by inducing a dismissal for failure to prosecute. See Comment, Rule 41(b) Dismissal as a Route to Appellate Review of an Adverse Class Determination, 48 U.Chi.L.Rev. 912 (1981).

OPPENHEIMER FUND v. SANDERS

Supreme Court of the United States, 1978.
437 U.S. 340, 98 S.Ct. 2380.

MR. JUSTICE POWELL delivered the opinion of the Court.

Respondents are the representative plaintiffs in a class action brought under Fed.Rule Civ.Proc. 23(b)(3). They sought to require petitioners, the defendants below, to help compile a list of the names and addresses of the members of the plaintiff class from records kept by the transfer agent for one of petitioners so that the individual notice required by Rule 23(c)(2) could be sent. The Court of Appeals for the Second Circuit held that the federal discovery rules, Fed.Rules Civ.Proc. 26–37, authorize the District Court to order petitioners to assist in compiling the list and to bear the $16,000 expense incident thereto. . . .

[This was a class action brought on behalf of about 121,000 purchasers of shares in the Oppenheimer Fund between 1968 and 1970, alleging violation of the federal securities laws and seeking damages that averaged about $15 per class member. The district court first held that the suit met the requirements for class-action treatment. It then imposed the task and the cost of "culling out the list of class members" on the defendants, but it put the responsibility of preparing and mailing notice to them on the plaintiffs.

[Upon defendants' appeal of this order concerning notice the Second Circuit en banc ultimately affirmed, 558 F.2d 636, 646 (2d Cir. 1977), deeming the Supreme Court's Eisen decision ("Eisen IV") to be not controlling. It thus brought itself into conflict with the Fifth Circuit's ruling in In re Nissan Motor Corp. Antitrust Litigation, 552 F.2d 1088 (5th Cir.1977). The Supreme Court granted certiorari in the instant case.]

A

Although respondents' request resembles discovery in that it seeks to obtain information, we are convinced that it more properly is handled under Rule 23(d). The critical point is that the information is sought to facilitate the sending of notice rather than to define or clarify issues in the case.

[The Court explained that Rule 26(b)(1) limits the scope of discovery to "matter that bears on, or that reasonably could lead to other matter that could bear on, any issue that is or may be in the case." Thus, "discovery often has been used to illuminate issues upon which a district court must pass in deciding whether a suit should proceed as a class action under Rule 23, such as numerosity, common questions, and adequacy of representation." But discovery was unavailable here where "respondents do not seek information because it may bear on some issue which the District Court must decide, but only for the purpose of sending notice."]

Rule 23, on the other hand, deals comprehensively with class actions, and thus is the natural place to look for authority for orders regulating the sending of notice. It is clear that Rule 23(d) vests power in the district court to order one of the parties to perform the tasks necessary to send notice.[21] Moreover, district courts sometimes have found it appropriate to order a defendant, rather than a representative plaintiff, to perform tasks other than identification that are necessary to the sending of notice.[22] Since identification simply is another task that must be performed in order to send notice, we agree with the Court of Appeals for the Fifth Circuit that Rule 23(d) also authorizes a district court in appropriate circumstances to require a defendant's cooperation in identifying the class members to whom notice must be sent. We therefore turn to a consideration of the circumstances in which such an order is appropriate and of how the cost of the defendant's complying with such an order should be allocated.

B

. . . .

[21] Although Rule 23(c)(2) states that "the court shall direct" notice to class members, it commonly is agreed that the court should order one of the parties to perform the necessary tasks. See Frankel, Some Preliminary Observations Concerning Civil Rule 23, 43 F.R.D. 39, 44 (1967); Kaplan, Continuing Work of the Civil Committee: 1966 Amendments of the Federal Rules of Civil Procedure (I), 81 Harv.L.Rev. 356, 398 n. 157 (1967). Rule 23(d) provides that in the conduct of a class action, "the court may make appropriate orders: . . . (2) requiring, for the protection of the members of the class or otherwise for the fair conduct of the action, that notice be given in such manner as the court may direct . . . ; [and] (5) dealing with similar procedural matters." The Advisory Committee apparently contemplated that the court would make orders drawing on the authority of either Rule 23(d)(2) or 23(d)(5) in order to provide the notice required by Rule 23(c)(2), for its note to Rule 23(d)(2) states, "under subdivision (c)(2), notice must *be ordered* . . . ." Advisory Committee's Notes to Fed.Rule Civ.Proc. 23, 28 U.S.C. App., p. 7768 (emphasis supplied).

[22] Thus, a number of courts have required defendants in Rule 23(b)(3) class actions to enclose class notices in their own periodic mailings to class members in order to reduce the expense of sending the notice . . . .

The first question that a district court must consider under Rule 23(d) is which party should perform particular tasks necessary to send the class notice. The general rule must be that the representative plaintiff should perform the tasks, for it is he who seeks to maintain the suit as a class action and to represent other members of his class. In Eisen IV we noted the general principle that a party must bear the "burden of financing his own suit," 417 U.S., at 179, 94 S.Ct., at 2153. Thus ordinarily there is no warrant for shifting the cost of the representative plaintiff's performance of these tasks to the defendant.

In some instances, however, the defendant may be able to perform a necessary task with less difficulty or expense than could the representative plaintiff. In such cases, we think that the District Court properly may exercise its discretion under Rule 23(d) to order the defendant to perform the task in question. As the Nissan court recognized, in identifying the instances in which such an order may be appropriate, a rough analogy might usefully be drawn to practice under Rule 33(c) of the discovery rules. Under that rule, when one party directs an interrogatory to another party which can be answered by examination of the responding party's business records, "it is a sufficient answer to such interrogatory to specify the records from which the answer may be derived or ascertained and to afford the party serving the interrogatory reasonable opportunity to" examine and copy the records, if the burden of deriving the answer would be "substantially the same" for either party. Not unlike Eisen IV, this provision is intended to place the "burden of discovery upon its potential benefitee." [25] The holding of Nissan represents application of a similar principle, for when the court concluded that the representative plaintiffs could derive the names and addresses of the class members from the defendants' records with substantially the same effort as the defendants, it required the representative plaintiffs to perform this task and hence to bear the cost. . . . But where the burden of deriving the answer would not be "substantially the same," and the task could be performed more efficiently by the responding party, the discovery rules normally require the responding party to derive the answer itself.

In those cases where a district court properly decides under Rule 23(d) that a defendant rather than the representative plaintiff should perform a task necessary to send the class notice, the question that then will arise is which party should bear the expense. On one hand, it may be argued that this should be borne by the defendant because a party ordinarily must bear the expense of complying with orders properly issued by the District Court; but Eisen IV strongly suggests that the representative plaintiff should bear this expense because it is he who seeks to maintain this suit as a class action. In

---

[25] Advisory Committee's Notes to Fed. Rule Civ.Proc. 33(c), 28 U.S.C. App., p. 7793, quoting D. Louisell, Modern California Discovery 125 (1963).

this situation, the District Court must exercise its discretion in deciding whether to leave the cost of complying with its order where it falls, on the defendant, or place it on the party that benefits, the representative plaintiff. Once again, a rough analogy might usefully be drawn to practice under the discovery rules. Under those rules, the presumption is that the responding party must bear the expense of complying with discovery requests, but he may invoke the District Court's discretion under Rule 26(c) to grant orders protecting him from "undue burden or expense" in doing so, including orders conditioning discovery on the requesting party's payment of the costs of discovery. The analogy necessarily is imperfect, however, because in the Rule 23(d) context, the defendant's own case rarely will be advanced by his having performed the tasks. . . . Thus, one of the reasons for declining to shift costs under Rule 26(c) usually will be absent in the Rule 23(d) context. For this reason, a district court exercising its discretion under Rule 23(d) should be considerably more ready to place the cost of the defendant's performing an ordered task on the representative plaintiff, who derives the benefit, than under Rule 26(c). In the usual case, the test should be whether the expense is substantial, rather than, as under Rule 26(c), whether it is "undue."

Nevertheless, in some instances, the expense involved may be so insubstantial as not to warrant the effort required to calculate it and shift it to the representative plaintiff. In Nissan, for example, the court did not find it necessary to direct the representative plaintiffs to reimburse the defendants for the expense of producing their files for inspection. In other cases, it may be appropriate to leave the cost where it falls because the task ordered is one that the defendant must perform in any event in the ordinary course of its business.[28] Although we do not attempt to catalogue the instances in which a district court might be justified in placing the expense on the defendant, we caution that courts must not stray too far from the principle underlying Eisen IV that the representative plaintiff should bear all costs relating to the sending of notice because it is he who seeks to maintain the suit as a class action.

C

In this case, we think the District Court abused its discretion in requiring petitioners to bear the expense of identifying class members. The records containing the needed information are kept by the transfer agent, not petitioners. Since petitioners apparently have the right to control these records and since the class members can be identified only by reference to them, the District Court acted within its authority under Rule 23(d) in ordering petitioners to direct the transfer agent to make the records available to respondents. The

---

[28] Thus, where defendants have been directed to enclose class notices in their own periodic mailings and the additional expense has not been substantial, representative plaintiffs have not been required to reimburse the defendants for envelopes or postage. [Citations omitted.]

preparation of the desired list requires . . . the manual sorting out of names and addresses from old records maintained on paper, the keypunching of up to 300,000 computer cards, and the creation of new computer programs for use with extant tapes and tapes that would have to be created from the paper records. It appears that neither petitioners nor respondents can perform these tasks, for both sides assume that the list can be generated only by hiring the services of a third party, the transfer agent, for a sum exceeding $16,000. As the expense of hiring the transfer agent would be no greater for respondents, who seek the information, than for petitioners, respondents should bear the expense. See Nissan, supra, at 1102–1103.

[The Supreme Court considered special circumstances that were suggested as reasons why the petitioners should pay the transfer agent. To the argument that $16,000 was a "relatively modest" amount, the Court said: "Although in some circumstances the ability of a party to bear a burden may be a consideration, the test in this respect normally should be whether the cost is substantial; not whether it is 'modest' in relation to ability to pay." To the argument that respondents had alleged petitioners to have breached a fiduciary duty to them and their class, the Court said: "A bare allegation of wrongdoing, whether by breach of fiduciary duty or otherwise, is not a fair reason for requiring a defendant to undertake financial burdens and risks to further a plaintiff's case." All other such arguments the Court likewise rejected.]

Given that respondents can obtain the information sought here by paying the transfer agent the same amount that petitioners would have to pay, that the information must be obtained to comply with respondents' obligation to provide notice to their class, and that no special circumstances have been shown to warrant requiring petitioners to bear the expense, we hold that the District Court abused its discretion in not requiring respondents to pay the transfer agent to identify the members of their own class. The judgment of the Court of Appeals is reversed, and the case is remanded for further proceedings consistent with this opinion.

It is so ordered.

———————

Question: (14) To "manage" a (b)(3) class action by means of Rule 23(d), can the district court require the absentees to opt-in by an affirmative act at an early stage of the suit if they wish to be members of the class? See 7A Wright & Miller § 1787, at 157–61.

———————

SECTION 4. TERMINATING CLASS ACTIONS

If a class action survives all these preliminary maneuvers, settlement is the most likely outcome. However, special dangers attend settlement of class actions. Accordingly, the settlement process in class actions, unlike that in ordinary litigation, is regulated. See Rule 23(e). This means that the parties' agreement may mark only the beginning of the procedural struggles.

Consider this comment from Developments in the Law—Class Actions, 89 Harv.L.Rev. 1318, 1536–37 (1976):

"Negotiation presents a serious threat to the attainment of a major purpose of class litigation—full realization of substantive policies—unless privately controlled decisions are harmonized with public interests. Even when negotiations are completely in good faith, the outcome may not reflect the range of substantive concerns underlying the regulatory statute pursuant to which suit has been brought, because the parties may not share such a broad range of interests."

Consider also this comment by an attorney experienced in class-action litigation and highly critical of the operation of the Rule in (b)(3) actions, from Simon, Class Actions—Useful Tool or Engine of Destruction, 55 F.R.D. 375, 389–90 (1973):

"The principal impetus for settlement comes from the atomic dynamics of large user class actions. When a firm with assets of, say, a billion dollars is sued in a class action with a class of several million and potential liability of, say, $2 billion, it faces the possibility of destruction. A settlement offer may then be made of $20 million—or 1% of possible exposure; with plaintiff's counsel asking $5 million in fees for himself while his clients receive miniscule recoveries. What defense lawyer can tell his client that his probable success in any jury case is better than 100 to 1; no matter how little merit there is in plaintiff's claim? This situation is not hypothetical; it happens frequently in our Federal Courts. The potential exposure in broad class actions frequently exceeds the net worth of the defendants, and corporate management naturally tends to seek insurance against whatever slight chance of success plaintiffs may have. Such insurance is usually available for a comparatively modest premium in the form of a settlement with the attorney who initiated the litigation and who purports to speak for vast numbers of people who have not retained him."

GRUNIN v. INTERNATIONAL HOUSE OF PANCAKES
United States Court of Appeals, Eighth Circuit, 1975.
513 F.2d 114, cert. denied, 423 U.S. 864, 96 S.Ct. 124 (1975).

Before VOGEL, SENIOR CIRCUIT JUDGE, and LAY and STEPHENSON, CIRCUIT JUDGES.

STEPHENSON, CIRCUIT JUDGE. These consolidated appeals arise out of the district court's approval of a proposed settlement, pursuant to Rule 23(e) of the Federal Rules of Civil Procedure, of a private antitrust national class action brought by International House of Pancakes (IHOP) franchisees against their franchisor, a division of International Industries, Inc. . . .

. . . .

On August 23, 1971, the Judicial Panel on Multi-District Litigation transferred to the Western District of Missouri nine pending actions that had been instituted by current or former franchisees of IHOP against the franchisor. In re International House of Pancakes Litigation, 331 F.Supp. 556 (Jud.Pan.Mult.Lit.1971). On October 26, 1971, the district court ordered that these actions be maintained as a class action pursuant to Fed.R.Civ.P. 23. In accordance with that order, two categories of plaintiffs were created—a class composed of current franchisees and a subclass of former franchisees. Original notice of the class action was mailed to all prospective class members on November 19, 1971. Subsequently a similar notice was sent to those parties qualifying for subclass membership.

The class action sought injunctive relief, treble damages, and attorneys' fees from IHOP on the basis that the franchise agreements and equipment leases executed between franchisor and franchisee violated the Sherman Act, 15 U.S.C. §§ 1 & 2 (1970), and the Clayton Act, 15 U.S.C. § 14 (1970). Specifically the franchisees alleged that IHOP illegally tied to the acquisition of a standard 15- or 20-year restaurant franchise the requirement that the franchisee lease or purchase a wide variety of essential products and services from IHOP or an IHOP-approved supplier. Among these "tied" items were restaurant furniture and equipment, dining room supplies, menus, food items, insurance, advertising, training, management counseling and bookkeeping services. The franchisees sought additional damages on the theory that these goods and services had been supplied at a price greatly in excess of fair market value [1] and on the grounds that the IHOP prohibition against selling any non-IHOP approved and priced food items deprived them of the opportunity to increase their individual profits.

Following the appointment of counsel for the class, extensive discovery was undertaken by the parties.[5] Within a short time serious settlement negotiations began. On April 24, 1973, a proposed settlement agreement was forwarded to the class and subclass members along with notice of a hearing to be held on June 1, 1973, in Kansas City. The agreement provided for a damage fund of $4.025 million

---

[1] For example, the pancake mix which the agreement required the franchisees to purchase from IHOP was sold to them at a markup of 100% over raw costs.

[5] According to counsel for International Industries, Inc., 20,000 pages of depositions were taken in this case and approximately 100,000 documents were produced for inspection by the parties.

(less attorneys' fees of $1.11 million) but did not amend the equipment leases in any material respect. This factor was the major subject of the objections voiced at the June hearing by a group of dissatisfied franchisees.

The district court, in a memorandum and order issued on July 12, 1973, rejected the proposed settlement. In re International House of Pancakes Litigation, 1973–2 Trade Cases ¶ 74,616 (W.D.Mo.), aff'd, 487 F.2d 303 (8th Cir.1973). The court acknowledged that the "precarious financial condition" of IHOP caused plaintiffs' counsel to conclude that "any substantial monetary judgment that might be recovered would be uncollectible, and would only result in the bankruptcy of the defendant." Nonetheless, the court stated that approval of the settlement would continue those franchise and lease provisions which allegedly violated antitrust laws, would bar class members from seeking further injunctive relief, and would provide insignificant monetary damage relief to the franchisees. The court concluded: "Certainly, they [the franchisees] are entitled to their day in court on this vital issue, and this Court will not foreclose them by approval of this settlement." The rejection was subsequently affirmed by this court in In re International House of Pancakes Litigation, 487 F.2d 303 (8th Cir.1973).

On November 7, 1973, a second settlement proposal was submitted to the court for its approval. This agreement differed from the first in that it gave each class member the option to purchase his own equipment at a rate lower than the terms of the lease or to continue to lease at a reduced rate. In addition, the settlement amended the franchise agreement in that IHOP would require its franchisees to purchase from it only their pancake flour (at a lesser markup) and coffee. The agreement also expanded and made specific the services to be provided by IHOP in exchange for the management fee and granted other concessions. Finally, the settlement created a fund of $500,000 to be shared by the subclass of former franchisees and provided for the payment of up to $1.25 million in attorneys' fees at the court's direction. Notice was sent out on November 8, 1973, and a hearing on the proposal began on November 28, 1973. In contrast to the June hearing, there were no formal objections filed with the court regarding the new proposal. However, counsel for appellant Grunin participated in the hearing and voiced his objections through cross-examination.[6] At the close of the hearings the district court approved the settlement stating simply that it was "fair, reasonable, and adequate as to said class and sub-class plaintiffs." Another order was entered on February 1, 1974, awarding attorneys' fees to respective claimants. Appeals were taken from the entry of each order.

---

[6] Appearing as amici curiae before this court are nine IHOP franchisees who object to the settlement. . . . Even if we add these nine individuals to the list of objectors, the record reveals that most IHOP franchisees favored the settlement.

I.

The initial claim set forth by appellant Grunin is that the notice sent to class and subclass members in November regarding the second proposed settlement was so inadequate as to timing, content, and means of transmission that it violated the requirements of Rule 23 and the dictates of due process. We disagree.

By virtue of the fact that an action maintained as a class suit under Rule 23 has res judicata effect on all members of the class, due process requires that notice of a proposed settlement be given to the class. See Eisen v. Carlisle & Jacquelin, 417 U.S. 156, 172–77, 94 S.Ct. 2140, 40 L.Ed.2d 732 (1974); [other citations omitted].

The notice given must be "reasonably calculated, under all of the circumstances, to apprise interested parties of the pendency of the action and afford them an opportunity to present their objections." Mullane v. Central Hanover Bank & Trust Co., 339 U.S. 306, 314, 70 S.Ct. 652, 657, 94 L.Ed. 865 (1950). In addition, the notice must "[be of such nature as] reasonably to convey the required information . . . and it must afford a reasonable time for those interested to make their appearance." Id. . . . However, Rule 23(e) provides that notice be given "in such manner as the court directs." Thus, the mechanics of the notice process are left to the discretion of the court subject only to the broad "reasonableness" standards imposed by due process. See 7A C. Wright and A. Miller, Federal Practice and Procedure, Civil § 1797 at 237 (1972).

[The court here found the notice to be adequate as to timing.]

Appellant Grunin next contends that the method of notice used in this case—mailing notice to the last known addresses of class and subclass members—was constitutionally insufficient and therefore an abuse of discretion by the district court. Relying on Lamb v. United Security Life Co., 59 F.R.D. 25 (S.D.Iowa 1972), appellant urges that, since approximately one-third of the class members were not reached by the mailing, supplemental notice by means of publication should have been ordered by the court.

We are satisfied, however, that notice by publication was unnecessary in this case for due process purposes and probably would have been of little value in alerting members of the class and subclass that were previously uninformed. In Eisen v. Carlisle & Jacquelin, 417 U.S. 156, 174–77, 94 S.Ct. 2140, 40 L.Ed.2d 732 (1974), the Supreme Court specifically held that individualized notice by mail to the last known address was the "best notice practicable" in a class action contest. The Court also reiterated its dissatisfaction with notice by publication. . . . Since the 90 to 100 class and subclass members who did not receive mailed notices were, according to their last addresses, scattered throughout the nation, the publication of notice in three or four newspapers as suggested in Lamb would have been fruitless. Under the circumstances the court properly made use of the "last known address" method and was not required to expend further time and money on less productive notice efforts.

[The court here found the content of the notice to be a fair and neutral summary of the proposed settlement's terms. The notice had also advised class members how a copy of the settlement agreement could be obtained.]

II.

The second major contention set forth by appellant Grunin is that the district court abused its discretion in approving a settlement that was not fair, reasonable, and adequate. Specifically it is alleged . . . that the benefits of the settlement to the class are illusory

. . . .

Under Rule 23(e) the district court acts as a fiduciary who must serve as a guardian of the rights of absent class members. [Citations omitted.] The court cannot accept a settlement that the proponents have not shown to be fair, reasonable, and adequate. See, e.g., City of Detroit v. Grinnell Corp., 495 F.2d 448, 455 (2d Cir.1974); [other citations omitted].

Our review of the settlement approved by the district court in this case is guided by the principle that:

> Such a determination is committed to the sound discretion of the trial judge. Great weight is accorded his views because he is exposed to the litigants, and their strategies, positions and proofs. He is aware of the expense and possible legal bars to success. Simply stated, he is on the firing line and can evaluate the action accordingly.

Ace Heating & Plumbing Co. v. Crane Co., 453 F.2d 30, 34 (3d Cir. 1971). Only upon a clear showing that the district court abused its discretion will this court intervene to set aside a judicially approved class action settlement. In re International House of Pancakes Franchise Litigation, 487 F.2d 303, 304 (8th Cir.1973). See also City of Detroit, 495 F.2d at 455. With these precepts in mind we turn to appellant's charges of error.

. . . .

The charge that the benefits of the settlement to the class are illusory calls into question the overall adequacy of the settlement. In making such an assessment "[t]he most important factor is the strength of the case for plaintiffs on the merits, balanced against the amount offered in the settlement." West Virginia v. Chas. Pfizer & Co., [440 F.2d 1079 (2d Cir.), cert. denied, 404 U.S. 871, 92 S.Ct. 81 (1971). Other citations omitted.] In addition, the court should consider such factors as the defendant's overall financial condition and ability to pay; the complexity, length and expense of further litigation; and the amount of opposition to the settlement. See City of Detroit, 495 F.2d at 463. Our evaluation of the settlement in light of these factors reveals that the agreement provided substantial benefits to the class.

. . . [T]he franchisees' probability of complete success in their suit against IHOP was by no means certain. There is evidence to suggest that a total victory, including a voiding of the equipment leases and an award of damages, would have been financially disastrous if not fatal to IHOP. Nonetheless, the district court in rejecting the first settlement proposal indicated that some revision in the equipment lease was essential. Given the court's directive and IHOP's cash flow difficulties, the parties worked out a settlement which gave valuable concessions to the franchisees yet maintained IHOP's corporate viability. It is estimated that the equipment lease options provided in the settlement were worth at least $131,000 to each class member with the total value to the class exceeding $12.5 million. Given the additional fact that any compromise involves some give and take by both sides, we feel that the district court's approval of this settlement was justified.

. . . . .

III.

The final group of issues to be decided in this appeal relates to the district court's allocation of the $1.25 million in attorneys' fees provided for in the settlement agreement. The three appeals from the award of fees assert that the trial court erred in denying fees to attorney Fichtner, in failing to compensate attorney Shapiro for his efforts in opposing the June proposal, and in employing improper standards in making the award [of $325,000] to attorney Berger and his firm. . . .

The district court's award of attorneys' fees in a class action settlement will be set aside by this court only upon a showing that the action amounted to an abuse of discretion. See City of Detroit, 495 F.2d at 468–75; Merola v. Atlantic Richfield Co., 493 F.2d 292, 295 (3d Cir.1974); Lindy Brothers Builders, Inc. v. American Radiator & Standard Sanitary Corp., 487 F.2d 161, 166 (3d Cir.1973); [other citations omitted]. We hold that the district court's denial of all or part of the fee requests made by appellants Fichtner and Shapiro was consistent with the sound exercise of that discretion. However, we feel that the award to Berger and his firm was made on the basis of insufficient specific evidence regarding the time spent on this litigation and should be remanded to the district court for reevaluation in light of the standards set forth in City of Detroit v. Grinnell Corp., supra, and related cases.

. . . . .

The formulation adopted by the Third Circuit in Lindy Brothers and reiterated in Merola provides a typical example of the factors that courts have been instructed to consider in establishing fee awards:

a) the number of hours spent in various legal activities by the individual attorneys,

b) the reasonable hourly rate for the individual attorneys.

c) the contingent nature of success, and

d) the quality of the attorneys' work.

[Citations omitted.] However, as the Second Circuit recognized in City of Detroit, the "only legitimate starting point" in establishing fees is "by merely multiplying attorney's hours and typical hourly rates. . . . It is only after such a calculation that other, less objective, factors can be introduced into the calculus." 495 F.2d at 471.

In order to insure that all necessary data is before the court, attorneys are generally required to submit detailed affidavits which itemize and explain their fee claims. Also, many courts have required that an evidentiary hearing be held at which each claimant is subject to cross-examination. See City of Detroit, 495 F.2d at 471–74. The district court in this case held such a hearing following the submission of affidavits. The record reveals that all of the attorneys involved, except Mr. Berger, furnished the court with detailed information concerning the total number of hours spent, how the time was used (e.g., research, negotiations), by whom (e.g., senior partners, associates), and what standard hourly rate was charged by each category of attorney for each type of work. At no time did Mr. Berger supply the court with *any* information relating to standard hourly rates for himself or his firm. Nor did he furnish a complete breakdown of who spent time in what endeavors. We see no reason for applying one standard to Berger and another to all other attorneys involved.

. . . .

This case is affirmed in all respects except for the award of attorneys' fees to David Berger and David Berger, P.A. On that issue we remand for reconsideration by the district court in accordance with this opinion.

———

Question: (15) Does Rule 23(e) require notice and court approval of a settlement if it is reached after the case is brought as a class action but before the class is certified under Rule 23(c)(1)? See Comment, The Applicability of Rule 23(e) to Precertification Proceedings: The Functional Approach Applied, 25 Vill.L.Rev. 487 (1980).

———

PETTWAY v. AMERICAN CAST IRON PIPE CO., 576 F.2d 1157 (5th Cir.1978), cert. denied, 439 U.S. 1115, 99 S.Ct. 1020 (1979). This was a very complex (b)(2) class action brought by black employees against their employer for employment discrimination in violation of

Title VII of the Civil Rights Act of 1964. The suit had been pending
since 1966 and produced numerous opinions both before and after
this one.

In 1974, after the previous remand by the court of appeals, the
district court encouraged the litigants to engage in settlement negotiations. The district judge played an active role in the extensive negotiations that ensued. Agreement was never really reached, and ultimately in 1975 the judge issued an injunctive decree largely based on
the defendant's final offer.

In the final stages of this process, the three named plaintiffs and
almost a third of the over two thousand other class members asked
the class attorney (Adams) to appeal, but he declined on the grounds
that the decree was fair and that an appeal would only delay implementation. They retained a new attorney (Wiggins), but the district
court denied a motion to substitute him as class counsel. A final
judgment was entered. This appeal by the named plaintiffs followed.

Rejecting appellants' contention, the court of appeals first decided
that Rule 23(e) did not apply:

"The role of an appellate court in reviewing a decree in a class
action suit varies greatly depending on whether the decree was
reached through a settlement by the litigants or whether the decree
represents the judgment of the court. [Citations omitted.] These
differing modes of review reflect a recognition of the different character of the two types of judicial resolution. The standard of review
appropriate to a court judgment is premised on the requirement that
the trial judge, following adversary presentation of the facts and law,
exercise his *independent* judgment on each of the issues presented
for decision. His ruling must be based on findings of fact supported
by evidence in the record and on conclusions of law. The role of the
trial court in arriving at an independent judgment closely parallels its
more traditional role in the non-class action context. Consequently,
review of class action judgments is patterned after the conventional
modes of review. The appellate court can review the trial court's
findings of fact to ensure that they are supported by the record and
are not clearly erroneous, while giving appropriate deference to the
trial judge's superior ability to assess demeanor and credibility. The
reviewing court is also particularly well suited to make an independent assessment of the law as applied to the facts, again giving
deference to the lower court where the law affords some measure of
latitude and discretion.

"Different problems are posed by class action settlements. Lacking a fully developed evidentiary record, both the trial court and the
appellate court would be incapable of making the independent assessment of the facts and law required in the adjudicatory context.
Moreover, a definitive judicial determination of the facts and law
would be inappropriate because compromise of legal rights is intrinsic
to the settlement process. Because of the limited control exercised

by any particular class member over the decision to engage in these compromises, however, the settlement process is more susceptible than adversarial adjudications to certain types of abuse. The interests of lawyer and class may diverge, as may the interest of different members of the class, and certain interests may be wrongfully compromised, betrayed, or 'sold out' without drawing the attention of the court. For this reason, in addition to requiring that the trial court evaluate whether a class action settlement is 'fair, adequate and reasonable and is not the product of collusion between the parties', Cotton v. Hinton, [559 F.2d 1326, 1330 (5th Cir.1977)], the law accords special protections, primarily procedural in nature, to individual class members whose interests may be compromised in the settlement process. These protections include notice, ensuring that class members know when their rights are being compromised, and an opportunity to voice objections to the settlement.

"We recognize that this neat dichotomy is in some respects oversimple. In the class action context, some of the abuses generally associated with settlements may insinuate themselves into litigation resulting in the court's own judgment. For example, in framing litigation strategy in a complex suit the class attorney and named plaintiffs might concentrate on relief for certain members of the class while ignoring the interests of others. Nevertheless, because the potential for abuse is much greater when class actions are resolved through a settlement, the procedural protections applicable to settlements are not utilized in the judgment context.[5]"

The court of appeals conceded: "Settlements and court judgments are distinguished not by different platonic essences, but by the processes of their creation." A careful examination of the record led to the conclusion that this was a court judgment.

Turning then to the defendant's contention that the named plaintiffs and Wiggins could not appeal on behalf of the class, the court said:

"In the context of individual-plaintiff litigation the roles of the attorney and the client are well defined. The A.B.A. Code of Professional Responsibility envisions the attorney as an advocate of the interests of the client. American Bar Ass'n, Code of Professional Responsibility, EC 7-1 [hereinafter cited as ABA Code]. Although the lawyer has some freedom to make tactical choices during litigation without consulting his client, the lawyer is expected to defer to the client's wishes on major litigation decisions. See ABA Code EC 7-1, EC 7-7, EC 7-9. Unfortunately, it remains unclear whether this model can be carried over to the class action context, as no clear concept of the allocation of decision-making responsibility between the attorney and the class members has yet emerged. [Citation omitted.] Certainly it is inappropriate to import the traditional understanding

---

[5] This is not to say, however, that courts should not be conscious of the possibility of similar abuses in the judgment context. . . .

of the attorney-client relationship into the class action context by simply substituting the named plaintiffs as the client. The interests of the named plaintiffs and those of other class members may diverge, and a core requirement for preventing abuse of the class action device is some means of ensuring that the interests and rights of each class member receive consideration by the court. Were the class attorney to treat the named plaintiff as the exclusive client, the interests of other class members might go unnoticed and unrepresented. See Gonzales v. Cassidy, 474 F.2d 67, 69–71, 76 (5th Cir.1973); Developments in the Law, Class Actions, 89 Harv.L.Rev. 1318, 1592–95 (1976). Thus, when a potential conflict arises between the named plaintiffs and the rest of the class, the class attorney must not allow decisions on behalf of the class to rest exclusively with the named plaintiffs. In such a situation, the attorney's duty to the class requires him to point out conflicts to the court so that the court may take appropriate steps to protect the interests of absentee class members.

"This does not mean, however, that the class attorney may ignore the wishes of the class representatives in making fundamental litigation decisions. As one court has stated, 'An attorney who prosecutes a class action with unfettered discretion becomes, in fact, the representative of the class. This is an unacceptable situation because of the possible conflicts of interest involved.' Leib v. 20th Century Corp., 61 F.R.D. 592 (M.D.Pa.1974). In the context of a shareholders' derivative action, Saylor v. Lindsley, 456 F.2d 896 (2nd Cir.1972), Judge Friendly has stressed that courts should not 'accept the view that the attorney for the plaintiff is the dominus litis and the plaintiff only a key to the courthouse door dispensable once entry has been effected':

> There can be no blinking at the fact that the interests of the plaintiff in a stockholder's derivative suit and of his attorney are by no means congruent. While, in a general sense, both are interested in maximizing the recovery this is only a half-truth. Even apart from special considerations which . . . may cause divergence of interest in cases where extremely large amounts are at stake, there is a difference in every case. The plaintiff's financial interest is in his share of the total recovery less what may be awarded to counsel, simpliciter; counsel's financial interest is in the amount of the award to him less the time and effort needed to produce it. A relatively small settlement may well produce an allowance bearing a higher ratio to the cost of the work than a much larger recovery obtained only after extensive discovery, a long trial and appeal. We say this not in criticism but in simple recognition of the facts of class action life.

456 F.2d at 900–01. The same considerations may cause a class attorney who has been awarded a substantial fee by the court to conclude that an appeal of the court's judgment might result in personally unremunerative litigation or a substantial and undesirable delay in the receipt of the fee award. When the possibility that counsel's own fervor may have been exhausted by an apparently endless legal battle is added to the equation, the potential conflict between the interests of the class and those of its attorney in an appeal cannot be ignored.

"It is, therefore, clear that the decision to appeal cannot rest entirely with either the named plaintiffs or with class counsel. Nonetheless, the Rule 23(a)(4) requirement that the trial court determine whether 'the representative parties will fairly and adequately protect the interests of the class' contemplates that the named plaintiffs will undertake a major role in the prosecution of a class action. The requirement also provides an important guarantee of a coincidence of interest between the named plaintiffs and the class.

". . . Implicit in our discussion and holding in Gonzales was the conviction that, at least under the circumstances of that case, the class plaintiff and not the class attorney, was responsible for deciding whether to appeal.

"The foregoing considerations convince us that, at least as an initial matter, the decision to appeal a class action judgment must rest with the class plaintiffs. If in making that decision the class plaintiffs arguably fail to adequately represent the interests of the class, the class attorney should point out potential inadequacies or conflicts of interest to the trial judge. Where the named plaintiffs wish to appeal, but the class attorney concludes that an appeal is not in the best interest of the class, the district court must exercise its discretion in deciding whether to substitute class counsel to allow the named plaintiffs to maintain the appeal on behalf of the class.[19] The proper exercise of the district court's discretion will depend on the facts and circumstances of each case. Among the factors that should be considered by the court are (1) the adequacy of representation of the named plaintiffs, including any apparent or potential conflicts of interest they might have with the remainder of the class, (2) the extent to which other class members support or oppose the appeal, and the extent to which an appeal may be necessary to protect the inter-

---

[19] Distinctive problems may be presented where the named plaintiffs refuse to undertake an appeal which the class attorney believes to be in the best interests of the class or where both the named plaintiffs and the class attorney decide not to appeal. If no appeal is taken and the failure to pursue an appeal constitutes inadequate representation, other members of the class may certainly pursue relief in a collateral proceeding. Gonzales v. Cassidy, supra. Whether, and how, a direct appeal may be taken absent the participation of the original named plaintiffs, or the participation of both the named plaintiffs and the class attorney, are issues we need not resolve for purposes of this appeal.

ests of absent class members, (3) the adequacy of representation provided by the class attorney and any conflicts of interest between the class attorney and the class, and (4) the reasonableness of the decision to appeal, including an assessment of the possibility of success on the merits.

. . . .

"In conclusion, we hold that under the circumstances of this case the trial judge abused his discretion by not granting appellants' motion to substitute class counsel for purposes of appealing the court's judgment. The decision to appeal rested as an initial matter with the named plaintiffs. These representatives chose to appeal, and an analysis of the factors considered above demonstrates that their choice should have been honored. The named plaintiffs have provided excellent representation in the past, and there is no indication in the record that their decision to appeal was based on any considerations other than the interests of the class. The decision received widespread support among the class. . . . While we do not question the sincerity of Mr. Adams' belief that an appeal of the injunctive decree is not in the class' interest, nothing in the record convinces us that the named plaintiffs' conclusion on this question was unreasonable. . . . Finally, the issues raised on appeal are neither frivolous nor insubstantial. We therefore shall treat this appeal of the . . . district court's decree as an appeal on behalf of the class."

The court of appeals went on to reverse and remand in an opinion of sixty-six pages, observing that they "would not substitute one hour of efficiency for one moment of justice." In essence, the court required yet greater efforts by the district judge "to remedy past employment discrimination by restructuring the multi-faceted employment practices of a large industrial concern."

SECTION 5. OVERVIEW, REVIEW, AND PREVIEW

COFFIN, THE FRONTIER OF REMEDIES: A CALL FOR EXPLORATION
67 Calif.L.Rev. 983, 988–89 (1979).

What seems to be emerging and enduring is a kind of lawsuit that differs in many facets from conventional adjudication . . .. Here is my catalogue of differences: [11]

---

[11] For a number of these perceptions, I am indebted to Abram Chayes and his article, The Role of the Judge in Public Law Litigation, 89 Harv.L.Rev. 1281, 1302 (1976). [See supra p. 279.—Ed.]

	Conventional Adjudication	*New Model*
The Issue	Likely to be of private rights and duties. If public body involved, issue likely to be procedural.	Likely to involve substantive rights and means of compelling a public body to effectuate those rights.
Parties	Likely to be one "person" suing another.	Likely to be a class of individuals suing a class of officials, public institutions, and political entities.
Critical facts	Historical (what has happened) and adjudicative (relevant to rights and liabilities of the two parties).	Predictive (situation as it is likely to exist during life of decree) and legislative (relevant to continuing decree).
Governing Principle	Legal precedents.	Strategy, tactics, and potential outcomes not informed by legal precedent.
Taking of evidence	Adversary hearing and rules of evidence.	Wide participation, relaxed standards, more expert opinions.
Relief sought	Declaration, negative injunction, damages; normally narrow, closely tied to legal injury.	Affirmative injunction, affecting many beyond parties; potentially broad.
Framing of decree	Imposed by court after hearing evidence.	Large amount of negotiation.
Impact	Confined to parties.	Affects a large segment of society.
Duration of court involvement	One-time judgment.	Continuing decree; subject to reopening and amendment.
Role of Judge	Passive: adjudicative in resolving dispute between two parties in a one time, normally self-executing, judgment.	Active: legislative in framing criteria; executive in implementing decree.
Review	Abuse of discretion and error of law; sufficiency of evidence and legal precedents important.	Contribution of appellate court to policy, strategy, and tactics more important than monitoring fact findings or legal principles.

These add up to a significant qualitative difference between conventional adjudication and the new model of litigation. New model litigation generally is brought by a broad class that enjoys wide-ranging discovery and seeks affirmative injunctive relief from public officials and institutions; under these circumstances the judge must play not only an adjudicative role, but legislative and executive roles as well.

RHODE, CLASS CONFLICTS IN CLASS ACTIONS

34 Stan.L.Rev. 1183, 1183–86, 1191–94, 1196–97, 1202, 1221, 1247, 1261–62 (1982).

A fundamental premise of American adjudicative structures is that clients, not their counsel, define litigation objectives. Thus, the American Bar Association's current and proposed ethical codes both emphasize that an attorney must defer to the client's wishes on matters affecting the merits of legal action. However, by presupposing an individual client with clearly identifiable views, these codes elide a frequent and fundamental difficulty in class action proceedings. In many such cases, the lawyer represents an aggregation of litigants with unstable, inchoate, or conflicting preferences. The more diffuse and divided the class, the greater the problems in defining its objectives.

This article examines those problems in one selected context: plaintiff class actions seeking structural reforms in public and private institutions. Such cases merit special attention on two grounds. First, the often indeterminate quality of relief available makes conflicts within plaintiff classes particularly likely. Most school desegregation, employment discrimination, prison reform, and related cases present no obvious single solution flowing ineluctably from the nature of the violation.[1] Nor will all class members alleging unlawful conduct agree on what should be done about it. Moreover, the prominence of institutional reform litigation vests these intra-class cleavages with particular significance. Such cases account for a high percentage of all class suits and an even greater proportion of legal claims attracting widespread societal concern. Thus, institutional reform litigation provides a useful paradigm for analyzing some of the most vexing issues in class representation.

In exploring these issues, this article takes one central proposition for granted. On the whole, institutional reform class actions have made and continue to make an enormous contribution to the realization of fundamental constitutional values—a contribution that no other governmental construct has proven able to duplicate. That contention has been defended at length elsewhere, and the arguments need not be recounted here.[6] Thus, the following discussion should not be taken to suggest that institutional reform class actions are misused or misconceived, or that there are preferable alternatives. The point, rather, is that the framework in which such actions proceed could benefit from both conceptual and mechanical refurbishing.

[1] See generally Chayes, The Role of the Judge in Public Law Litigation, 89 Harv.L.Rev. 1281 (1976); Fiss, The Supreme Court, 1978 Term—Foreword: The Forms of Justice, 93 Harv.L.Rev. 1 (1979); Fuller, The Forms and Limits of Adjudication, 92 Harv.L.Rev. 353 (1978).

[6] For relatively positive assessments of the courts' intervention in institutional reform litigation, see J. Handler, Social Movements and the Legal System: A Theory of Law Reform and Social Change (1978); Cavanagh & Sarat, Thinking About Courts: Toward and Beyond a Jurisprudence of Judicial Competence, 14 Law & Soc'y Rev. 371 (1980);

Chayes, supra note 4; Eisenberg & Yeazell, The Ordinary and the Extraordinary in Institutional Litigation, 93 Harv. L.Rev. 465 (1980); Fiss, supra note 4.

For more critical evaluations, see, e.g., L. Graglia, Disaster by Decree (1976); D. Horowitz, The Court and Social Policy (1977); Frug, The Judicial Power of the Purse, 126 U.Pa.L.Rev. 715 (1978); Hazard, Social Justice Through Civil Justice, 36 U.Chi.L.Rev. 699 (1969); Mishkin, Federal Courts as State Reformers, 35 Wash. & Lee L.Rev. 949, 959–61 (1978); Nagel, Separation of Powers and the Scope of Federal Equitable Remedies, 30 Stan.L. Rev. 661 (1978).

Much of the renovation required concerns our concept of class representation. In particular, we need a more coherent theory of class interests and of the role plaintiff preferences should play in defining class objectives. As a first cut at reconceptualization, this article posits a theory of representation mandating full disclosure of, although not necessarily deference to, class sentiment. A central premise is that the class as an entity has interests that may not be coextensive with the preferences of its current membership. Often those able to register views will be insufficiently disinterested or informed to speak for the entire constituency of present and future class members who will be affected by the court's decree. Nonetheless, preferences matter, not because they are conclusive of class interests, but because their disclosure is critical to the efficacy and legitimacy of judicial intervention.

. . . .

For those seeking structural reforms, class actions afford a number of obvious advantages over suits involving individual plaintiffs. By definition, class proceedings force focus on institutional practices rather than isolated grievances. Also, if a variety of allegedly unlawful practices are at issue, it can be cumbersome to seek out separate plaintiffs with standing to challenge each violation. Representing individual plaintiffs also entails some risk of mootness. School children graduate, prison inmates obtain transfers or paroles, and individual employees are subject to temptation by generous settlement offers. By contrast, once the court certifies a suit as a class action, the proceedings can continue despite the termination of individual claims, and any settlement must obtain judicial approval.[9] Thus, class representation obviates the continual need to substitute plaintiffs, and minimizes the allure of proposed settlements benefitting only named litigants. Moreover, compared with individual suits, class litigation may promise counsel greater bargaining leverage, larger attorneys' fees, and enhanced access to funding sources.

Yet by the same token, class status can also generate substantial problems in accommodating divergent client interests. . . .

. . . .

Prevailing legal doctrine offers strikingly little guidance to courts and counsel who confront intra-class schisms. Rule 23 of the Federal Rules of Civil Procedure, which governs most actions seeking structural relief, is singularly laconic. In pertinent part, the Rule requires only that "the claims or defenses of the representative parties" be "typical" of those of the class, and that the "representative parties will fairly and adequately protect the interests of the class." Once the court certifies a class, all members will be bound by the final judgment; they have no right to opt out of the action or even to receive notice of its pendency, although the court may order notice at

_____

[9] Fed.R.Civ.P. 23(e); see United States Parole Comm'n v. Geraghty, 445 U.S. 388 (1980); Goodman v. Schlesinger, 584 F.2d 1325, 1332–33 (4th Cir.1978).

its own discretion, and must do so before approving any pretrial settlement. At any time after certification, dissenting class members, opposing parties, or the court, sua sponte, may subsequently challenge the adequacy of the named plaintiffs' representation. If successful, such challenges can result in decertification of the class, restriction of the decree's res judicata effect, or some form of separate representation for plaintiffs with conflicting interests.

Given the binding consequences that attach to class status, Rule 23's mandate of adequate representation is of constitutional dimension. In essence, this requirement embodies a fundamental tenet of due process: that judicial procedure fairly protect "the interest of absent parties who are to be bound by it." [32] Yet despite the centrality of the concept to class action theory and practice, judicial pronouncements on the subject have been notably unilluminating.

The Advisory Committee that drafted Rule 23 provided no amplification of the terms "adequately protect" or "interests," and judges applying the standard have done little to fill the void. Among the primary questions left unaddressed is whether interest ever means more than preference and, if so, when and what. Do the named representative and counsel serve primarily as "instructed delegates," pursuing objectives to which a majority of class members subscribe? If so, how are those objectives to be identified, particularly if the class comprises a diffuse and changing constituency of past, present, and future claimants? Alternatively, does the representative role track Edmund Burke's notion of an "enlightened trustee," who makes an independent assessment of class concerns? Under that advocacy model, what recourse is available to individuals who do not share their trustee's vision?

. . . On the rare occasions where courts have confronted the issue, they have done little more than acknowledge the absence of any "clear principles governing the allocation of decisionmaking authority between the attorney and the class." [38] Such principles are unlikely to emerge given the constricted framework in which representation issues are currently analyzed. In general, courts have insisted only that attorneys be competent and that the claims of the named representatives be "similar," "common," or "not antagonistic" to those of the membership generally. Since few judges are inclined to engage in public ad hominems, the inquiry concerning counsel's competence is rarely a meaningful exercise. And application of the common claims requirement has yielded no coherent principles for coping with divergent preferences.

. . . . .

[32] Hansberry v. Lee, 311 U.S. 32, 42 (1940). . . .

[38] Pettway v. American Cast Iron Pipe Co., 576 F.2d 1157 (5th Cir.1978), cert. denied, 439 U.S. 1115 (1979).

Bailey v. Ryan Stevedoring Co.[51] is a case in point. There the district court denied class certification because almost all members of a black union had opposed the named plaintiffs' efforts to force integration with a white union. Opposition rested primarily on fears that minorities would lose certain beneficial employment arrangements under a consolidated structure. Plaintiffs nevertheless pursued the claim in a private suit and succeeded in obtaining merger of the unions. In contexts like Bailey, those who disagree with named plaintiffs' remedial proposals may have even less opportunity for notice and participation if the case proceeds as an individual rather than collective action. Thus, denying class certification would hardly secure, and could well impede, the protection of all interests affected by judicial decree.

On that reasoning, a federal district judge in Evans v. Buchanan [53] rejected the claim that named plaintiffs in a school desegregation case inadequately represented class members who favored different relief. Since any judicial decree would "of necessity . . . be determinative of the rights of all," the court viewed the issue as not whether interests were antagonistic but whether there had been "a full and fair presentation of all possible views on the matter." From a due process perspective, the Evans analysis makes eminent sense. In structural relief cases involving intra-class conflict, the preferable strategy is to grant certification and create sufficient procedural safeguards to ensure adequate disclosure of dissenting views.

. . . .

Formal mandates governing class adjudication assign responsibility for ensuring adequate representation to three quarters: the named plaintiffs, their attorneys, and the court. In practice, opposing parties and dissenting class members also play a role in exposing conflict. Frequently, however, none of these participants has sufficient incentive or information to respond adequately to class schisms.

. . . .

Confronted with the kinds of conflicts discussed above, courts and counsel have responded with two, not mutually exclusive, strategies. A pluralist approach is to have separate factions speak through separate representatives. A majoritarian alternative is to create opportunities for class members to express their preferences directly, through polls or public hearings.

Although useful in many instances, neither of these strategies provides anything approaching a full solution to class schisms. A generic weakness stems from the information and incentive structures discussed above. If neither the parties nor the courts are equipped or disposed to explore conflicts, then the theoretical availability of such alternatives is irrelevant. Moreover, each strategy has certain

[51] 528 F.2d 551 (5th Cir.1976), cert. denied, 429 U.S. 1052 (1977).

[53] 416 F.Supp. 328 (D.Del.), appeal dismissed, 429 U.S. 973 (1976).

practical limitations that further impair its value in addressing conflicts.

. . . .

In addressing these problems, courts and legislatures should consider two sorts of reform. One set of strategies should focus on information and incentive structures. Through amendment or interpretation of Rule 23 mandates, efforts should be made to increase judicial awareness of class schisms at an earlier stage in litigation. A second set of strategies should be directed toward improving techniques for coping with intra-class conflicts once their significance becomes apparent.

[Professor Rhode's proposals include, on the one hand, requiring the trial judge to make a factual record concerning decisions on notice and concerning the finding of adequate representation and, on the other hand, calling for more sensitive judicial attention to intervention, amici presentations, use of oversight committees of class members, and appointment of neutral advisors as experts or masters.]

To be sure, none of the proposals outlined here can guarantee better results in [every case]. But that conclusion, if disconcerting, is not necessarily damning. Given the values at issue in institutional reform cases, conflicts are an ineradicable feature of the legal landscape. Virtually all of the pluralist and majoritarian deficiencies that impede judicial management of such conflicts would arise with equal force if the underlying issues were addressed in legislative or bureaucratic settings. Indeed, one of the strongest justifications for those governance structures is equally available to class actions: While we cannot depend on disinterested and informed judgment by any single group of decisionmakers, we can at least create sufficient procedural checks and balances to prevent the worst abuses.

Moreover, to acknowledge that the formal mandates governing class actions promise far more than they deliver is not to condemn the pretense. No hypothesized procedures can insure that all class interests will be "adequately represented" or that counsel will singlemindedly pursue his "client's" objectives. But the risks of abandoning either fiction may be too great.

No matter how faulty the enforcement mechanism, such mandates serve important legitimating functions. Broad injunctions concerning client autonomy and adequate representation allow us to affirm the individual's right to be heard without in fact paying the entire price. Giving overly fixed content to those terms could propel us toward some generic prescription that raises more difficulties than it resolves. An unqualified embrace of pluralism would entail problems of increased expense and diminished effectiveness. To totter towards majoritarianism would require confrontation with the awkward fact that paternalism is often offensive in principle but desirable in practice. Like other "white lies" of the law,[297] those governing class adjudication have spared us such discomfitting choices by masking certain "weak spots in our intellectual structure."[298] But shoring up is generally preferable to papering over. And no durable renovation can proceed without more searching scrutiny of what adequate representation means in instances of conflict, and what mechanisms we might devise to nudge reality somewhat closer to fiction.

Question: (16) How does General Telephone Co. v. Falcon fit into the author's scheme?

CHAYES, THE SUPREME COURT, 1981 TERM—FOREWORD: PUBLIC LAW LITIGATION AND THE BURGER COURT

96 Harv.L.Rev. 4, 26–29, 32, 34–37 (1982).

For classical legal theory, the main problem posed by the class action was that the judgment determined the rights of absent members of the class who had not had their day in court. Today, there is a more pragmatic engagement over whether and how the class action device is to be shaped as an instrument for the vindication of group interests when they are infringed by the action of government or corporate bureaucracies. In 1966 the Federal Rules of Civil Procedure were amended, in part with a view toward improving the capacity of the class action to serve this end. The revisions coincided almost exactly with the invention of "public interest law" in the late 1960's and with the general surge of reformist zeal into the courts.

The class action seemed perfectly adapted to the social, political, and even stylistic objectives of the reformist litigators, whether in school desegregation, civil rights, apportionment, environmental, consumer, or other lawsuits challenging far-reaching government or corporate actions. Indeed, in many of these cases—for example, school desegregation or environmental suits—it is hard to conceive of individual relief apart from class relief. And in many more, the only practical way of getting into court is by way of class action. The effect of the conduct under attack on any single individual is too small to justify a traditional lawsuit seeking compensation. But in the aggregate the impact is substantial enough to be a target for redress, whether the underlying justification is compensatory, deterrent, or punitive.

The availability of the class action, in my view, had not a little to do with the burgeoning of theories about groups (as opposed to individuals) as right bearers. In any case, it emphasized the vision enun-

---

[297] L. Fuller, Legal Fictions 5 (1967)   [298] Id. at 52.
(quoting R. von Ihering).

ciated in NAACP v. Button [137] of the lawsuit as a form of political
expression and a vehicle for vindicating political and social rights.
And the class action device confirmed the self-image of public interest lawyers as spokesmen for large groupings toward which they had
duties and responsibilities different from those of the ordinary law-
yer-client relationship.

The traditional justification for the class action stresses the potential economies to be achieved when numerous individual claims with
similar factual or legal issues can be litigated in a single proceeding.
But the class can also be seen as a single jural entity capable of suing
and being sued, not unlike the more familiar organizational litigants—corporations, unions, government departments—save that it
is constructed ad hoc for the very purpose of conducting a particular
litigation and that its principal or only unifying characteristic is often
the legal relationship or grievance in controversy.

In its encounters with class actions, the Burger Court has clung to
the first conception of the class action as a congeries of individual
claims loosely bundled together for purposes of judicial efficiency.
For such purposes as amount in controversy, notice, [and] representative authority, . . . the Court's decisions tend to treat class representatives and members as classical individual claimants. The combined effect of these decisions has been to constrict arbitrarily
. . . the operation of the class action as a device for the enforcement of statutory and constitutional policies.

. . . .

The foregoing pattern is best displayed by the Court's decisions
concerning small claims class actions. The relevant provision is rule
23(b)(3) of the Federal Rules, which authorizes class treatment of
claims linked by any common question of law or fact. Such actions
can bring together hundreds, thousands, or even millions of persons
damaged by corporate action allegedly in violation of antitrust, securities, or consumer legislation. The claims of the individual class
members may be minuscule, but when aggregated they have generated enormous ad damnums, running to hundreds of millions—even bil-
lions—of dollars. Plaintiffs' lawyers in these cases have cast themselves as private attorneys general enforcing norms of conduct
plainly established by statutes or common law, norms that the defendants would otherwise escape. Defense attorneys have replied that
such class actions are no more than legalized blackmail.

The Court has never directly addressed the controversy over the
function and operation of the small claims class action. Instead, it
has disposed of the procedural problems it has faced by means of a
variety of seemingly unrelated doctrines, each anchored in the classical conception of the lawsuit and each having the effect, in one way

---

[137] 371 U.S. 415, 429–30 (1963).

or another, of limiting the effectiveness of the class action as an enforcement device.

.   .   .   .

Eisen is thus a triumph of form over substance. The reason for the notification requirement is to ensure that an absentee's claim is not foreclosed by litigation of which the absent party is not aware. But the precise effect of the Eisen decision is to foreclose the absentee along with all other class members in small claims cases; if the claimants cannot band together as a class, they will be unable to proceed at all.

[Professor Chayes also criticizes Snyder, Zahn, and Coopers & Lybrand.]

It is not clear what the actual impact of these class action decisions has been. On the one hand, federal judicial statistics have begun to show a reduction in class action filings.[181] The breakdown of these figures is not fine enough to locate the decline in the rule 23(b)(3) category, but it seems plausible that the decline reflects the less hospitable climate for these actions generated by the Court's rulings.

On the other hand, lower courts have found a number of ways around the stringency of the Zahn-Eisen requirements. Costs have been sharply reduced by permitting plaintiffs to stuff the required notice in defendants' regular mailings to class members. . . . In addition, plaintiffs have shown a good deal of ingenuity in converting rule 23(b)(3) actions into (b)(1) or (b)(2) actions. . . .

The variety of expedients employed by the lower courts suggests that the judiciary is responding to felt pressures for the use of the class action device and that the Supreme Court has failed to address the underlying realities that are the source of those pressures. . . . [T]he perspective of public law litigation brings significant issues into focus that are obscured or ignored in the Court's concentration on notice and other requirements drawn from the classical model.

The small claims class action enables strict enforcement of a range of what may be called consumer protection norms, violation of which has individually small but widely diffused impacts. The basic difficulty is that all of the norms invoked are not necessarily appropriate for strict enforcement. . . . [T]he Court must determine the appropriate scope of private enforcement of public norms.

In pursuing this inquiry, the Court should obviously draw whatever light it can from relevant statutory language and history. In most cases, however, these guides will be silent. The dominant considera-

---

[181] See Administrative Office of the United States Courts, 1980 Annual Report of the Director 78 table 31 (1980). Between 1974 and 1980, the number of class action filings dropped from 2717 to 1568. The decline was even more dramatic in terms of the ratio of class actions to the total number of civil cases filed. Class actions constituted 2.6% of all cases filed in 1974 and 0.9% in 1980. Id.

tion will be that to permit strict enforcement through the small claims class action is to elevate deterrent and punitive objectives over compensatory ones. Because individual damage claims are by definition very small, the interest in punishing the violation becomes stronger than the desire to compensate the victims. A nice concern for the distribution of damages in exact conformity to the harm suffered by each claimant gives way to the overriding objective of stripping the defendant of the profits of its unlawful act. In what circumstances is such a shift in emphasis appropriate? It may be possible to approach an answer to that question through careful analysis of the expectations generated by the norm the claimants seek to enforce, the clarity with which that norm is stated, and the importance of the substantive policies involved in the particular case.

. . . [T]his proposed approach is unlikely to generate dispositive criteria. But a focus on considerations that should inform the discretionary decision to certify a class under rule 23(b)(3) is far more consistent with the philosophy of the rule than is the Court's creation of rigid and arbitrary limitations on the availability of the device.

Question: (17) In determining how the class-action device is to be shaped, the legitimacy (from the points of view of jurisprudence, separation of powers, federalism, and due process) and the desirability (also from a variety of viewpoints) of public law litigation both must be considered. But in dealing with a Federal Rule, is there not an additional question on the extent to which substantive policies can be written or read into Rule 23?

CLASS–ACTION BILL

A sweeping reform of the current class-action procedures under Federal Rule 23(b)(3) emerged in 1977 from the Office for Improvements in the Administration of Justice, an office in the Justice Department then headed by Assistant Attorney General Daniel J. Meador. It reached Congress as S. 3475, 95th Cong., 2d Sess. (1978), a bill introduced in the Senate by Senator DeConcini of Arizona and cosponsored by Senator Kennedy of Massachusetts. In the next session of Congress, a revised version of the bill was introduced in the House as part of H.R. 5103, 96th Cong., 1st Sess. (1979), a bill that retained the central concepts of S. 3475 but reflected significant refinement in light of the Senate hearings. See generally Berry, Ending Substance's Indenture to Procedure: The Imperative for Comprehensive Revision of the Class Damage Action, 80 Colum.L.Rev. 299 (1980) (explaining and approving bill).

Senator DeConcini's statement originally introducing S. 3475, found at 124 Cong.Rec. 27,859 (1978), summarized this new attempt to alleviate the problems of pursuing, defending, and managing class actions:

"Mr. President, on behalf of Senator Kennedy and myself, I am introducing legislation to revise and reform the rules and procedures under which class actions are litigated in the Federal courts. Dissatisfaction with the current situation is widespread, and I believe the need for change is compelling. The proposal we are introducing, which was drafted in close consultation with the Department of Justice, contains some interesting and challenging departures from present practice. If implemented, it may go far toward rationalizing class action litigation. At the same time, I recognize that this is a subject matter of great complexity and great interest to many diverse groups. While this bill was prepared in consultation with a wide variety of interests, it is only a first step, not the last. Neither Senator Kennedy nor I are wedded to its provisions. The Subcommittee on Improvements in Judicial Machinery plans extensive hearings on the measure beginning this fall and continuing into the 96th Congress. Those hearings will focus on the broader questions associated with class actions. The need for revision of the class action rule; the legitimate purposes which class action litigation should serve; the extent to which our society should devote judicial resources to class actions; and the actual and potential abuses of this instrument.

"The bill which I am introducing repeals Federal rule 23(b)(3) and replaces it with two new procedures: First, a public action for redress of small monetary injuries (less than $300), and second, a class compensatory action for substantial monetary injuries (more than $300). In addition, the bill provides the courts with new tools to make cases under both procedures more manageable.

"The statute created by this bill reflects the recognition that there are, in fact, two distinct types of class suits which are presently litigated under rule 23(b)(3). One type arises where the economic injury is small but widespread. In these cases, it is not economically feasible for the injured parties to initiate individual actions. Nevertheless, where there has been a violation of the law, the public has a strong interest in seeing that the wrongdoer does not profit from his illegal conduct. Thus, the primary purpose of bringing suit in these cases is to prevent unjust enrichment and to deter illegal conduct rather than to compensate the injured parties. In contrast, the second type of suit arises from situations where the economic injury is more substantial and it is assumed that the parties will have sufficient incentive to form a class and secure adequate and representative counsel to assert their claims. In these cases, compensation of the parties remains the primary focus of the litigation.

"The public action created by this bill vests a single claim in the United States against a wrongdoer where, first, 200 persons have each sustained injury less than $300; second, the combined damages exceed $60,000; and third, the injuries arise out of the same transaction or occurrence and present a substantial common question of law or fact. The policy behind the public action is, as I mentioned earlier, the public interest in preventing unjust enrichment and deterring unlawful conduct.

"The public action can be brought by the United States, or on its behalf, by one or more injured persons, thereby providing a role for private enforcement of the public interest. If an action is brought by a private person, he must promptly serve notice on the Attorney General and the local U.S. attorney and provide them with all evidence in his possession supporting the claim. The United States may then either assume control of the action, permit the action to be prosecuted by the private party, refer the action to a State attorney general, or recommend to the court that the public interest would not be served by allowing the action to continue as a public action. If the United States assumes control of and prevails in an action brought initially by a private party, the party is entitled to an incentive fee. The public action thus accommodates public and private interests.

"The public action procedure also provides for a preliminary hearing, after strictly controlled discovery, within 4 months from the filing of the complaint. The court, at that time, decides if the prerequisites of the public action have been met and makes a preliminary assessment of the merits of the case. The preliminary hearing thus serves to protect all parties from open-ended discovery fishing expeditions and to screen out frivolous strike suits. It will also give the plaintiff a preliminary indication of his chances of prevailing before he invests substantial resources in pursuing the action. If a defendant is found liable, the judgment is calculated in an amount equal to either the total benefits realized by the defendant by this illegal conduct or the total damages caused by the defendant. This calculation can be made by any reasonable means.

"Judgments in public actions will be transferred to the Administrative Office of the U.S. Courts where they will be deposited into a public recovery fund. The Administrative Office is charged with the responsibility of giving notice of the judgment, processing claims and distributing the fund. A claim must be greater than $15 and submitted within 1 year. The transfer of this responsibility from the courts to the Administrative Office serves to conserve judicial resources.

"The compensatory action created by this bill is patterned on the present rule, but includes significant changes which are intended to increase the fairness of the procedure and to make it less expensive and time consuming. The compensatory action is to be used where 40 persons suffer injury exceeding $300 and the injuries arise out of the same transaction or occurrence and present a substantial common question of law or fact. The theory here is that persons injured in excess of $300 will have sufficient incentive to form a class and vindicate their claims.

"As in the public action, the trial judge in a compensatory action must hold a preliminary hearing, after strictly controlled discovery, within 4 months of the filing of the complaint. At this hearing, the court decides whether the class requirements have been met, makes a preliminary assessment of the merits, and also decides the content and the means of giving notice to the class. Where notice and proof of individual damage will be difficult and time-consuming, the court is given discretion to try the issues of liability and damage separately. If the defendant is found liable, then the cost of notice will shift to him. This provision, like many others in the bill, allows the court to divide complex cases into more manageable steps.

"Both the public action and the compensatory action would be subject to new management techniques which are intended to promote stronger judicial stewardship of these actions. For example, the bill provides for, first, the regulation of settlements; second, supervision by the circuit judicial councils of over-delayed district court rulings; and third, a precise method for computing an award of attorney fees based on hourly rates, but with provision for risk adjustments.

"This bill is by no means perfect. However, it does address in an innovative manner the problems inherent in present practice. And, unless we begin to act, the basic credibility of our justice system and access to our Federal courts will be called into question. To arbitrarily close the doors of the courts on class action claims gives the appearance of condoning illegal conduct. As Vice President Mondale has pointed out:

> Nothing is more destructive to a sense of justice than the widespread belief that it is much more risky for an ordinary citizen to take five dollars from one person at the point of a gun than it is for a corporation to take five dollars each from a million customers at the point of a pen.

"At the same time, however, we must protect honest and legitimate business interests from unwarranted attacks. The challenge is there, and I look forward to developing and further exploring the potential of the new concepts embodied in this legislation."

MILLER, OF FRANKENSTEIN MONSTERS AND SHINING KNIGHTS: MYTH, REALITY, AND THE "CLASS ACTION PROBLEM"

92 Harv.L.Rev. 664, 666–69, 676–77, 682, 684, 693–94 (1979).

The available information suggests that much of the [long and hot class-action] debate has been based on erroneous assumptions. It indicates that rule 23 is achieving some of its intended purposes and may well be providing systemwide economies in several contexts, even though small-claim, large-class damage cases have proven extremely resistant to expeditious processing. Although there have been instances of undesirable or unprofessional conduct, abuse does not appear to have been widespread. Stories about a few questionable occurrences have been repeated so often at professional meetings that they have created the impression that evils are commonplace in class action practice. The empirical evidence also implies that in settled class actions, particularly in the securities and treble damage antitrust contexts, the great bulk of the money received from the defendants actually is distributed to class members, in contrast to the widely held notion that the fund is either devoured by avaricious attorneys or consumed by administrative expenses.

. . . .

It is important in understanding the class action debate to realize that the "big case" phenomenon transcends the class action. The "big case" is an inevitable byproduct of the mass character of contemporary American society and the complexity of today's substantive regulations. It is a problem that would confront us whether or not rule 23 existed. Indeed, it is becoming increasingly obvious that the traditional notion of civil litigation as merely bilateral private dispute resolution is outmoded. Since our conception of the roles of judges and advocates is based on this traditional view, the ferocious attack on the class action may reflect anxiety over the growing challenge to the model's immutability.

This apprehension should be stated even more broadly. In my judgment, Federal Rule 23 is being used as a convenient scapegoat for grievances against our civil litigation system and trends in our society whose roots lie far deeper than the procedural aspects of practice under that rule. Our preoccupation with the so-called "class action problem" represents a misdirection of attention and energy, which might be better expended recalibrating the structure of litigation in light of contemporary conditions. Accordingly, the thesis of this essay is that drastic revision of class action practice at this time, either by legislation or rulemaking, would be tantamount to attempting a cure by treating one symptom of an ailment rather than dealing with its underlying cause. Any attempt at modification now not only runs the risk of being an overreaction to the argumentative din of the past few years, but seems particularly ill timed because, as will be developed below, class action practice under the existing rule appears to be stabilizing.

I. The 1966 Revision of Rule 23—Unjustly Accused

. . . .

The Advisory Committee's objectives in rewriting the rule were rather clear. It had few, if any, revolutionary notions about its work product. Although it was expected that the revision would operate to assist small claimants, the draftsmen conceived the procedure's primary function to be providing a mechanism for securing private remedies, rather than deterring public wrongs or enforcing broad social policies. . . .

. . . .

. . . The emergence of a vigorous body of class action litigators . . . does not lend credence to the oft-heard barb that rule 23 has modified "substantive rights" by permitting actions to be brought that either never could have or never would have been brought before. A more accurate formulation may be that because litigation resources exist today that were not hitherto available and a portion of them have been generated by an increased consciousness about various societal problems, more litigation—often class actions—is being instituted.

. . . . .

II. CLASS ACTION PRACTICE—RETROSPECTIVE AND PROSPECTIVE

. . . .

Even in its current elaborated form, rule 23 really must be thought of as a procedural skeleton requiring fleshing out by judges and lawyers experimenting with it in an ever-increasing range of circumstances and in a variety of innovative ways. The Reporter to the Advisory Committee on Civil Rules that drafted the revision, Professor Benjamin Kaplan (now a Justice of the Massachusetts Supreme Judicial Court), has remarked that it would probably take at least a full generation (1) to discover the problems with the rule's text, (2) to understand its various components, and (3) to develop an image of how it actually functions. Although the rule provides guidance on a number of matters and expressly authorizes various kinds of judicial activity, its basic operation ultimately depends on the ingenuity of district judges working cooperatively with counsel to engineer the management of complicated lawsuits. Patience has been and continues to be the watchword; it probably will take the full generation that Professor Kaplan envisioned to achieve anything approaching a common understanding of the scope, utility, and application of rule 23.

[Professor Miller divides the history of the administration of the amended Rule into three phases. During the first phase, lasting until 1969, the legal community exhibited both euphoria over the Rule's potential and lack of technical attention to the prerequisites for class-action treatment. The resultant overuse and misuse by plaintiffs induced the reactionary second phase, which was characterized by widespread criticism of class actions, defendants' intransigence, and judicial resistance as in Snyder, Zahn, and Eisen. Around 1973 or 1974, the third phase set in. It is marked by increasing sophistication, restraint, and stabilization in class-action practice. Plaintiffs are becoming more reasonable and careful, and defendants less intransigent. Judges are becoming more effective, especially in their use of the powers set out in Rule 23(c), (d), and (e).]

Thus, there is reason to be optimistic. The effect of this continuing maturation should be better administration of class actions by making certain that issues worthy of group adjudication are accorded it, that the class is adequately represented, and that class members are divided into workable subclasses that avoid internecine conflicts. This could well lead to a reduction in the transaction costs of class actions and, in the long run, to a more realistic utilization of rule 23.

III. Proposals for Change

[Professor Miller criticizes current proposals for change and, in particular, the class-action bill. He finds troublesome the governmental involvement in the proposed "public action," which he otherwise finds generally attractive from the viewpoints of social justice and efficiency. More strongly, he believes the "compensatory action" proposal to be too detailed in expression and too narrow in scope, and he sees this aspect of the bill as a legislative intrusion unnecessarily debilitating judicial rulemaking.

[However, Professor Miller notes that the Advisory Committee in 1977 decided that any modification in class-action practice should come from Congress, a decision approved by the Judicial Conference in 1978. The Committee thought that the big issues involved were best dealt with in the political arena. Also, apparently the Committee concluded that its mandate under the Rules Enabling Act did not give enough breadth for effective treatment. Finally, the Committee apparently had reached no consensus as to what to amend in Rule 23.]

IV. Conclusion

Given the emotional tone and misdirection of the class action debate during recent years, the ideological orientation of some of the proposals, and the indications of increased stabilization in the field, this is an inopportune time to attempt a major revision of class action practice. A few more years of experience under rule 23 should give us a better understanding of how well the class action can function and perhaps produce some movement toward consensus regarding the appropriate utilization of the federal courts for purposes of deterrence, public law enforcement, and small claim rectification.

TOPIC C. INTERVENTION

See Rule 24(a) in substantially its original form and the Advisory Committee's note on the amended Rule in the section of the Rules pamphlet dealing with the 1966 amendments. The former Rule allowed intervention of right to one whose representation by existing parties might be inadequate and who might be bound by the judgment. In Sam Fox Publishing Co. v. United States, 366 U.S. 683, 81 S.Ct. 1309 (1961), the Court held that this meant "legally bound" but that no one could be so bound if inadequately represented, citing Hansberry v. Lee, supra p. 1115. By thus making the dual requirements mutually contradictory, the Court's decision tended to have the effect of nullifying this portion of the Rule. The former Rule also allowed intervention of right to one who was so situated as to be adversely affected by a disposition of property subject to the control of the court. Surprisingly, this clause was interpreted so broadly as to disregard in effect the wording of the Rule. See, e.g., Formulabs, Inc. v. Hartley Pen Co., 275 F.2d 52 (9th Cir.), cert. denied, 363 U.S. 830, 80 S.Ct. 1600 (1960).[a]

Rule 24(a) was amended in 1966 to remedy these apparent problems, with a single test being put in place of those two former grounds for intervention of right. The changes in the Rule paralleled the simultaneous revision of Rules 19 and 23. Indeed, the new language in Rule 24(a)(2) defining a person who may intervene of right, unless his interest is adequately represented, now appears in substantially the same words where Rule 19(a)(2)(i) describes certain persons to be joined if feasible. Although they are not necessarily interpreted identically, both of these Rules emphasize the same pragmatic approach. Under the new Rule 24(a)(2), then, intervention of right lies where one claims an *interest* relating to the subject of the action and is so situated that disposition of the action may *as a practical matter impair* one's ability to protect that interest, and one's interest is *not adequately represented* by existing parties.

The new pragmatic approach to intervention of right under Rule 24(a)(2) has created considerable uncertainty as to the nature of the interest required. Soon after the amended Rule became effective, the Supreme Court gave it an expansive reading in Cascade Natural Gas Corp. v. El Paso Natural Gas Co., 386 U.S. 129, 87 S.Ct. 932 (1967). The Court had previously ordered divestiture of Pacific Northwest Pipeline Corp. by El Paso, after it had found that El Paso

---

[a] Both the former and the amended Rule allow intervention of right, under Rule 24(a)(1), when a federal statute confers an unconditional right to intervene. There are not many such statutes. The most significant one is 28 U.S.C. § 2403, which gives the United States or a state the right to intervene in a federal action wherein the constitutionality of one of its statutes is questioned.

had acquired Pacific Northwest in violation of the antitrust laws. After remand to the district court, the Attorney General negotiated an agreement of settlement with the companies. Cascade, a distributor of natural gas, was solely supplied by Pacific Northwest; it feared for the continuance of its supply under the settlement plan and sought to intervene for the purpose of contending that the plan did not comply with the Court's earlier mandate. Intervention was denied and the settlement approved below, but on appeal the Supreme Court held that Cascade had an interest entitling it to intervene of right. It was manifest that a majority of the Court was dissatisfied with the settlement negotiated by the Attorney General in carrying out the divestiture mandate, and the only way it could get at the issue, given that all the parties were content, was to allow intervention. Justice Stewart, joined in dissent by Justice Harlan, thought that the Court had "rushed headlong into a jurisprudential quagmire" by allowing persons to intervene whose interest was far too general and indefinite and by upsetting the long-established body of decisions denying intervention in government antitrust litigation. But that quagmire has been avoided. Subsequent cases have given Cascade the familiar alternative to overruling: a statement that the case must be limited to its facts. And the Supreme Court itself, in Donaldson v. United States, 400 U.S. 517, 91 S.Ct. 534 (1971), held, without citing Cascade, that a taxpayer being investigated by the Internal Revenue Service was not entitled to intervene of right in proceedings to enforce subpoenas against his former employer and its accountant, saying that Rule 24(a)(2) obviously requires "a significantly protectable interest." Yet Donaldson too has been limited to its facts. Meanwhile, the lower federal court cases have not exhibited any sense of clear direction either. In short, the cases offer no unequivocal guidance for interpreting the term "interest."

The required extent of impairment of the interest also remains unclear, although there has been some tendency to apply this requirement rather leniently. For example, can the stare decisis effect of a decision in the action be a sufficient impairment to warrant intervention of right? In Atlantis Development Corp. v. United States, 379 F.2d 818 (5th Cir.1967), an affirmative answer was given to this question, but the case was qualified by the fact that the would-be intervenor claimed a very direct interest in the very property and transaction that was the subject of the main action, viz., control over the outer continental shelf.

Finally, the requirement of inadequacy of representation is a relatively lenient one. In Trbovich v. United Mine Workers, 404 U.S. 528, 92 S.Ct. 630 (1972), the Court allowed a union member to intervene of right in an action by the Secretary of Labor to set aside a union election, saying that "the Rule is satisfied if the applicant shows that representation of his interest 'may be' inadequate; and the burden of making that showing should be treated as minimal." As the Secretary must represent the public interest in free union elections as well as protect the rights of the union member, "the union member may have a valid complaint about the performance of 'his lawyer.' " Nevertheless, in appropriate circumstances this third requirement can block nonstatutory intervention of right.

Questions: (1) What is the relationship between Rule 24(a) and the other party Rules, especially Rules 19 and 23? See Atlantis Dev. Corp. v. United States, supra. And what is the relationship between Rule 24(b) and the other party Rules, especially Rules 20 and 23? Indeed, what is the relationship of Rule 24(a) to Rule 24(b)?

(2) What is the extent of an intervenor's right of participation? May he assert additional claims, engage in discovery, examine witnesses, appeal from an adverse decision? Does it matter whether the intervention is permissive under Rule 24(b) or of right under Rule 24(a)? Does the question always have to be answered the same way without regard to the circumstances of the particular case? See Shapiro, Some Thoughts on Intervention Before Courts, Agencies, and Arbitrators, 81 Harv.L.Rev. 721 (1968).

JONES, LITIGATION WITHOUT REPRESENTATION:
THE NEED FOR INTERVENTION TO
AFFIRM AFFIRMATIVE ACTION
14 Harv.C.R.–C.L.L.Rev. 31, 31–34, 38–40, 42–44, 86–87 (1979).

When Allan Bakke went to court to challenge affirmative action and to secure an order for his admission to the University of California at Davis Medical School, no party in the suit directly represented the interests of minority applicants, who would be most affected by an unsuccessful defense of the University's race-conscious admission program. The University chose to defend its voluntary program as designed to serve general societal purposes without reference to its own arguably discriminatory practices. As a result, significant minority interests were imperiled.

The lack of minority participation in Regents of the University of California v. Bakke [, 438 U.S. 265, 98 S.Ct. 2733 (1978),] does not reflect a conscious effort by the University to exclude minorities from the litigation, but it does reflect a notable structural deficiency inherent in virtually all affirmative action litigation. . . .

. . . . .

Intervention was sought [unsuccessfully by the NAACP in Bakke]. Although, due to narrow application, traditional notions of intervention have thus far failed to protect minority interests, intervention retains great potential for safeguarding those interests in affirmative action litigation. However, full realization of this potential requires recognition of liberalized intervention standards in this context. The intervention question in Bakke arose under a state provision; this Article, however, will focus on current intervention doctrine in the federal courts, as developed under rule 24 of the Federal Rules of Civil Procedure. . . .

. . . .

Intervention, a relatively recent development in our civil procedure,[24] runs counter to the traditional Anglo-American view of private law litigation. In part, this tradition assumed that litigation typically consisted of two individuals asserting directly opposed interests. Moreover, the plaintiff, as the "master of his suit," was largely allowed to control who would be included in the litigation. Hence, intervention was seldom available, and where it was granted it was simply a method to augment, on either side of the controversy, what remained essentially two antagonistic interests.

. . . .

Suits which challenge affirmative action programs do not fit the traditional private litigation model. The Bakke case illustrates this proposition all too clearly. Although Allan Bakke sued as an individual and named only the Regents of the University of California as defendants, many present and future applicants to the Davis Medical School were directly affected by the results of the suit. Other persons, such as minority men and women unable to obtain proper medical care, were similarly affected by the litigation. Far more than an individual's claim to admission was at stake; the case signified a major challenge to all affirmative action programs. Constitutional and statutory provisions of vital significance were debated and interpreted in Bakke in the light of overriding public policies and constitutional principles. . . .

. . . .

Although the policies underlying intervention vary, they may be summarized as follows. First, intervention serves the goal of judicial economy by the consolidation of related issues into a single suit. Intervenors are welcomed into a pending lawsuit when to do so would prevent proliferation of similar litigation or discourage piecemeal adjudication. Of course, the possibility of increased complexity resulting from intervention may undercut the potential for real judicial economy. Second, intervention can prevent injury to nonparties whose interests bear a sufficiently close connection to the matter being litigated. Although protecting the interests of outsiders was a major theme underlying the early grants of intervention, it has become even more important today. In public law litigation, with its frequent objective of reordering prominent social policies and institutions, nonparties must be protected from the ever-widening impact of

---

[24] In early equity practice intervention not governed by statute was allowed. See Moore & Levi, Federal Intervention: I. The Right to Intervene and Reorganization, 45 Yale L.J. 565, 570–72 (1936). Moore and Levi describe the device of an examination pro interesse suo, which was granted to any third party claiming an interest in property under the control of the court. This procedure was the only method whereby such a party could secure protection during the pendency of the dispute.

such lawsuits. Finally, intervention often expands the information available to a court in its search for an equitable adjudication of the merits of the lawsuit. In particular, this third rationale would seem to justify expansive participation in the efforts to shape a suitable remedy. These reasons for permitting intervention are more compatible with public law litigation than with the private law model; accordingly, intervention should be viewed more liberally in the public law context.

Most of the current wave of challenges to affirmative action have been litigated as though they were private controversies. In the usual scenario, minority interests are excluded by default. The typical "reverse discrimination" plaintiff has no interest in pursuing the suit as a group action, preferring instead to challenge the program by asserting an individual right to the benefit in question. More important, the typical defendants are in a position of ethical and legal conflict and have no incentive to broaden the controversy. If the program was voluntarily instituted, its defense, it is reasoned, must be a defense of the right to continue such voluntary remediation of a general societal problem. To bring in minority representatives would only raise the issue of the defendant's prior discrimination with attendant embarrassment and potential liability. Finally, with both parties content to portray the dispute as a limited, private one, judges are conditioned by neither training nor experience to search for powers, which they may indeed possess, to ensure that the entire spectrum of interests affected by the action are duly represented. Paradoxically, then, an examination into the adequacy of the representation of all the interests in this type of litigation only begins when a volunteer with sufficient resources seeks to intervene. In effect, the parties are litigating a de facto class action without any of its procedural safeguards.

[Professor Jones (now Jordan) argues at length that in the circumstances of Bakke a minority applicant for admission to the medical school, or an organization representing such applicants, should henceforth be deemed to come within the terms of Rule 24(a)(2). In particular, she identifies three impaired and inadequately represented interests: (1) the interest in competing for every available admissions slot, (2) the interest in securing corrective measures to remedy past or present discrimination by the university, and (3) the interest in keeping alive the concept of voluntary affirmative action.]

Minorities must have direct representation in affirmative action litigation, and nonstatutory intervention of right under rule 24(a)(2) can serve as the vehicle by which such representation can be achieved. There are still unanswered questions: How can the representativeness of self-appointed minority intervenors be insured? Which minority groups should be represented? If intervention is permitted, should the intervenors be granted full participation rights or given a limited role? While these are important and perplexing questions, it is reasonable to expect that courts will find workable answers to them by experimentation in future cases. The fundamental message should not be obscured in the search for those answers: procedural barriers must not be erected that frustrate minorities' legitimate expectation that they will be able to participate in litigation which affects their basic interests.

What has been proposed will hopefully lay the foundation for a solution which serves as a call to bring intervention practice and theory into line with present day exigencies. Burgeoning public law litigation demands pluralistic participation in the formulation of judicial decisions on issues which affect large numbers of citizens and concern fundamental legal and political rights. What remains to be seen is whether the courts will respond appropriately to end litigation without representation.

FRIEDENTHAL, INCREASED PARTICIPATION BY NON–PARTIES: THE NEED FOR LIMITATIONS AND CONDITIONS

13 U.C.D.L.Rev. 259, 261–63 (1980).

[After observing that an expansive approach to intervention would be difficult to confine to any particular kinds of cases and that expansion of permissive intervention would seem the sounder course, Professor Friedenthal considers expanding the application of Rule 24(a)(2) in affirmative action suits:]

If new, broader rules of participation are to be adopted, more emphasis should be placed on how they are to be limited, rather than on when they should automatically apply. Just because a case is of great interest in the community, broad intervention is not justified. Only when it is clear that the rights of persons outside the case are directly at stake should the action be expanded to include them. Courts that go beyond that narrow compass are in danger of becoming quasi-legislative bodies, a development which raises a myriad of theoretical and practical questions.

Are the courts in such cases to hold "town meetings"? How can any interested citizen be excluded from presenting his or her point of view, or even from calling witnesses? . . .

The Bakke case . . . is a good example of an action in which a broad expansion could have caused serious difficulties. Virtually every applicant to medical school, regardless of his or her race, had an interest in the outcome of that suit. Indeed, every applicant or potential applicant to law school or other professional school had an important interest. In a sense, every citizen of California or even of the United States had a stake in the result.

As Professor Jones has noted, the interests of minority applicants were not represented. As her excellent article points out, their intervention would not have been proper under existing rules. But the interests of non-minority applicants were also unrepresented. Certainly Allan Bakke did not have any intention to provide such representation. From his perspective the result was ideal, but that is far from true from the perspective of other non-minority professional school applicants.

If Professor Jones is correct that minority applicants should have been permitted to intervene, wouldn't the judge also have been required to permit intervention by non-minorities? Where is the line to be drawn? Who is to be precluded from making argument or offering what he or she considers to be "vital" evidence?

The Bakke case is a particularly important example because the decision is not as broad as advertised, and does not necessarily preclude minority applicants from arguing in favor of affirmative action plans in future suits. The issue most discussed in regard to lack of representation is that of past discrimination on the part of the University of California. Bakke had no reason to raise the issue as it could only have worked against him, and the University was obviously not going to admit that it engaged in any such improper activity. So that issue, on which the decision might well have turned, was never presented.

But so what? The next person who brings a similar suit—for example a minority student who challenges rejection of his or her medical school application—can raise the issue of past discrimination and, if it is proven, can prevail regardless of Bakke. Only to the extent that issues cannot subsequently be raised, or when the result of the case will necessarily lead the parties to actions that will not be subject to subsequent challenge, should new broad rules of non-party participation be applicable.

Finally, the courts must pay careful attention to the rights of the original litigants before deciding to allow outsiders into the suit. An individual, such as Bakke, who merely wants to be accepted to medical school, and is not out to set a precedent or vindicate the rights of anyone else through use of a class action, should be given every fair chance to control his own lawsuit.

Such an individual will often have limited resources. As a result, he may enter into a number of stipulations just to reduce the potential costs and allow him to concentrate on key issues that will provide the relief he seeks. But what appears to be a very good chance of victory may be swept away if the court then allows all sorts of interested outsiders to enter the case and raise not only the issues as to which stipulations were made, but a host of others as well. The original party may have insufficient funds to engage in additional discovery, hire necessary experts, and search for evidence to meet these new issues.

It would therefore seem appropriate as an integral part of any new statute or rule allowing broad participation of non-parties to require those who enter the case to pay the additional costs and attorney fees reasonably necessary for the original parties to deal with such new issues. Not only would such a provision protect the original parties' interests, it would also help to assure that those who enter a case will not do so frivolously.

Questions: (3) To what extent, if any, does the due process clause dictate a right to intervene?

(4) Recall the suggestion, made but not passed on by the Supreme Court in the Provident Tradesmens case, supra p. 1101, that Dutcher might be bound by the decision because he had purposely bypassed an adequate opportunity to intervene. Recall also the appellees' argument in Gonzales v. Cassidy, supra p. 1126, that Gonzales should be estopped by his failure to intervene in the earlier class action. When, if ever, should the opportunity to intervene be treated as a duty? Is this the solution that will satisfy our desire to handle a mass tort in a single proceeding? Cf. Restatement (Second) of Judgments § 62 (1980).

BABCOCK & WILCOX CO. v. PARSONS CORP.
United States Court of Appeals, Eighth Circuit, 1970.
430 F.2d 531.

Before MATTHES, CHIEF JUDGE, HEANEY and BRIGHT, CIRCUIT JUDGES.

MATTHES, CHIEF JUDGE. This appeal comes to us from a judgment of the United States District Court for the District of Nebraska holding Insurance Company of North America (INA) liable to Parsons Corporation (Parsons) and The Babcock and Wilcox Corporation (Babcock) on two insurance policies issued by INA to Parsons. Jurisdiction in the district court was premised on the diverse citizenship of [all three] parties. Because of the complex and rather unique issues raised on appeal, we detail the factual setting of the litigation.

Parsons and Babcock were corporations involved in the construction of a power plant near Stanton, North Dakota. As is customary in the trade, they had agreed to perform services for each other, although they were working under independent contracts. On May 21, 1964, pursuant to the agreement, Babcock furnished its large crane to Parsons for the purpose of moving a derrick used by Parsons on the project. The operation was undertaken with an employee of Babcock operating the crane under instructions of Parsons' employees. During the lifting of the derrick, the crane boom broke and the boom and derrick fell to the ground. Both the crane and derrick were extensively damaged.

. . . . .

On March 26, 1965, Babcock filed a complaint against Parsons in the district court for [$29,657.60 in] damages to its crane. The complaint was in three counts. The first two alleged that Parsons had either borrowed or rented the crane from Babcock and had returned it in a damaged condition. The third count alleged merely that the crane had been damaged due to Parsons' negligence.

On receipt of the complaint Parsons notified INA and tendered it the defense. Parsons had two policies issued by INA—a general liability policy and a machinery floater policy. The former provided for indemnification of Parsons should it be held liable to a third party for damages. It also contained [a] defense clause . . . . The machinery floater policy was designed to protect property owned, rented, etc., by Parsons. The floater policy contained no defense clause.

INA declined to accept the defense of the lawsuit under the general liability policy on the basis of an exclusionary clause which exempted from coverage injury to property owned, occupied by or rented to Parsons, or property in the care, custody, or control of Parsons. . . .

Parsons . . . defended through its own counsel. . . . Parsons filed a counterclaim alleging damage to the derrick because of Babcock's negligence . . . . Parsons also filed a third-party complaint against INA, pursuant to Rule 14, . . . seeking two forms of relief: (1) that INA be held liable on its policies for any judgment rendered against Parsons in the primary action, and (2) that INA be held liable to Parsons for the reasonable expenses incurred in defending the primary action.

INA filed an answer and moved for a separate trial of the third-party action. With the consent of Parsons the motion for a separate trial was granted.

The claims between Babcock and Parsons were tried to a jury . . . . [By interrogatories] the jury found that the operator of the crane was acting as a servant of Parsons, that neither Babcock nor Parsons was negligent in operating the crane, that Babcock had sustained damages to its crane in the amount of $10,000, and that Parsons had sustained damages to its derrick in the amount of $8,000. The court entered an appropriate judgment on the basis of the verdicts returned, neither party recovering for damage to their respective units of equipment. This judgment terminated the litigation between Babcock and Parsons, and is final.

Thereafter, pursuant to leave, Parsons filed an amended complaint against INA in which it limited its claim to recovery of expenses incurred in defending the primary action. It alleged that INA was obligated to so defend under the liability [policy]. Thereupon, Babcock, on February 27, 1968, sought leave to intervene under Rule 24(a)(2), Fed.R.Civ.P., urging that its interests would be inadequately represented by Parsons and that it might be bound by a judgment entered in the third-party litigation. As a part of the motion to intervene, Babcock filed a complaint against INA alleging that the crane was in the possession of Parsons at the time of the accident, that Parsons was entitled to recover for the damage to the crane under the floater policy, and that Babcock as owner of the crane was a third-party beneficiary of the floater policy and therefore entitled to recover over against INA for damage sustained to the crane. The motion to intervene was apparently not challenged by either INA or Parsons, and the district court granted it.

[Both Parsons and Babcock recovered. INA appealed. After affirming the judgment for Parsons because the negligence count triggered a duty to defend, the court turned to Babcock's right to recover on the floater policy.]

We are met at the outset of this issue with the contention that the federal district court lacked subject matter jurisdiction of the claim Babcock as intervenor brought against INA. It is submitted, and we agree, that the prayer for damages "in the amount of $10,000, plus costs herein expended and a reasonable attorney fee," failed to satisfy the amount in controversy requirement of 28 U.S.C. § 1332(a). The question for decision is, then, whether Babcock's claim can be supported by some notion of ancillary jurisdiction. INA offers two reasons for its conclusion that Babcock's claim must stand on independent jurisdictional grounds or fail: (1) the motion to intervene should have been treated as a Rule 14 Fed.R.Civ.P. claim by plaintiff against third-party defendant; (2) even if intervention was the proper procedural device, Babcock was a permissive intervenor and not an intervenor as of right.

Were it not for the jurisdictional question, we would have no hesitancy in denying INA's belated challenge to Babcock's entrance into this suit. No objections were raised at the time of trial to the intervention, the case was tried and a final disposition was made of all the issues raised. However, because subject matter jurisdiction cannot be waived by the parties, conferred by consent or ignored by the court, we examine the question. Rock Island Millwork Co. v. Hedges-Gough Lumber Co., 337 F.2d 24 (8th Cir.1964).

First we conclude that invocation of Rule 24 was proper. We are not persuaded by the argument that Babcock's intervention was in reality a Rule 14 claim by "plaintiff" against "third-party defendant." Babcock did not file a claim against INA until after the primary litigation between Babcock and Parsons had been laid to rest. The jury had returned a verdict exonerating both parties of liability for damage to crane and derrick, and Babcock's complaint against Parsons had been dismissed with prejudice. Thus there was no longer any relationship between Babcock and INA (through Parsons) which would justify the invocation of Rule 14. In short, Babcock was no longer a "plaintiff" within the meaning of the Rule.

We turn then to the more troublesome question, i.e., was the intervention one of right or permission. Jurisdiction over a claim brought by an intervenor depends on the nature of the intervention. If the intervention is a permissive one the claim must be supported by independent jurisdictional grounds. [Citations omitted.] Where intervention is of right, however, the courts and authorities are in substantial agreement that there need be no independent jurisdictional grounds to support the intervenor's claim. [Citations omitted.]

. . . .

Assuming arguendo that Babcock had an "interest" in the Parsons-INA suit, that interest would not have been "impaired or impeded by disposition of the [Parsons-INA] action," as required by Rule 24(a)(2). Clearly, disposition of the Parsons claim would not have bound Babcock in the res judicata sense. Indeed, the principal issue in the Babcock suit was totally irrelevant to the Parsons claim. Nor are we directed to any fact which as a practical matter would have deprived Babcock of its claim if it were denied the right to participate in the Parsons-INA proceedings. We are well aware of the fact that the 1966 amendment to Rule 24(a)(2) relaxed the degree to which a party must be affected by disposition of the "action". However, the rule still requires that the intervenor be potentially disadvantaged by disposition of the main action. . . .

. . . .

In summary, we conclude that Babcock was, at best a permissive intervenor and its claim, lacking the requisite jurisdictional amount, was not cognizable by a federal court. Accordingly, the judgment in favor of Babcock must be and is reversed.

. . . .

Questions: (5) If in a class action a member of the class is permitted to intervene under Rule 24(b), should he be required to show independent jurisdictional grounds?

(6) To the general principle that ancillary jurisdiction extends to intervenors of right, "there is one long-established exception": for an intervenor within Rule 24(a) who is otherwise an indispensable party under Rule 19(b), "the ancillary concept cannot be invoked." 7A Wright & Miller § 1917, at 601–02; see also 7 id. § 1610. Does this exception make any sense?

TOPIC D. INTERPLEADER

Questions: (1) Bank has a deposit account in the name of X. Y says X has assigned the whole account to him and calls for payment. May Bank safely disregard Y's claim? [a]

(2) Y instead says the account consists of money that X embezzled from him (e.g., the fruit of the embezzlement was a check from Y to X, deposited in Bank by X). May Bank safely disregard Y's claim?

(3) Suppose in Case No. 1 or Case No. 2 that Bank investigates with due care and pays out to X, ignoring Y. May Bank defend successfully on that basis when sued by Y?

(4) Suppose that Bank awaits an action by Y. Y wins, and Bank pays Y. May Bank successfully assert this payment if X later demands payment?

(5) When Y sues, may Bank implead X? Instead, if Bank notifies X and offers X control of the defense, will X then be bound by the result of the action by Y versus Bank?

(6) In an action by Y versus Bank, may Bank successfully move to dismiss the action for failure to join X as a party needed for just adjudication?

(7) After Y makes demand, may Bank join X and Y in an action for declaratory judgment to determine which is entitled to the account? Upon an action by Y versus Bank, may Bank counterclaim, joining X and seeking a declaration?

(8) In an action by Y versus Bank, may Y join X as an additional party defendant?

(9) May Y commence an action for interpleader, joining Bank and X?

(10) After Y makes demand, Bank tries to commence an interpleader action in a state court. Suppose Y is a resident, but X is not. May Bank proceed?

NEW YORK LIFE INSURANCE CO. v. DUNLEVY
Supreme Court of the United States, 1916.
241 U.S. 518, 36 S.Ct. 613.

MR. JUSTICE McREYNOLDS delivered the opinion of the court.

Respondent, Effie J. Gould Dunlevy, instituted this suit in the Superior Court, Marin County, California, January 14, 1910, against petitioner and Joseph W. Gould, her father, to recover $2,479.70, the surrender value of a policy on his life which she claimed had been assigned to her in 1893, and both were duly served with process while in that State. It was removed to the United States District Court,

------

[a] For our present purpose, all questions are to be considered in the absence of statute. In fact, there is considerable legislation on the duties of banks in these situations.

1200

February 16, 1910, and there tried by the judge in May, 1912, a jury having been expressly waived. Judgment for amount claimed was affirmed by the Circuit Court of Appeals. 204 F. 670, 214 F. 1.

The insurance company by an amended answer filed December 7, 1911, set up in defense (1) that no valid assignment had been made, and (2) that Mrs. Dunlevy was concluded by certain judicial proceedings in Pennsylvania wherein it had been garnished and the policy had been adjudged to be the property of Gould. Invalidity of the assignment is not now urged; but it is earnestly insisted that the Pennsylvania proceedings constituted a bar.

In 1907 Boggs & Buhl recovered a valid personal judgment by default, after domiciliary service, against Mrs. Dunlevy, in the Common Pleas Court at Pittsburgh, where she then resided. During 1909, "the tontine dividend period" of the life policy having expired, the insurance company became liable for $2,479.70 and this sum was claimed both by Gould, a citizen of Pennsylvania, and his daughter, who had removed to California. In November, 1909, Boggs & Buhl caused issue of an execution attachment on their judgment and both the insurance company and Gould were summoned as garnishees. He appeared, denied assignment of the policy and claimed the full amount due thereon. On February 5, 1910,—after this suit was begun in California—the company answered, admitted its indebtedness, set up the conflicting claims to the fund and prayed to be advised as to its rights. At the same time it filed a petition asking for a rule upon the claimants to show cause why they should not interplead and thereby ascertain who was lawfully entitled to the proceeds and further that it might be allowed to pay amount due into court for benefit of proper party. An order granted the requested rule and directed that notice be given to Mrs. Dunlevy in California. This was done, but she made no answer and did not appear. Later the insurance company filed a second petition, and, upon leave obtained thereunder, paid $2,479.70 into court, March 21, 1910. All parties except Mrs. Dunlevy having appeared, a feigned issue was framed and tried to determine validity of alleged transfer of the policy. The jury found, October 1, 1910, there was no valid assignment and thereupon under an order of court the fund was paid over to Gould.

Beyond doubt, without the necessity of further personal service of process upon Mrs. Dunlevy, the Court of Common Pleas at Pittsburgh had ample power through garnishment proceedings to inquire whether she held a valid claim against the insurance company and if found to exist then to condemn and appropriate it so far as necessary to discharge the original judgment. Although herself outside the limits of the State such disposition of the property would have been binding on her. Chicago, R.I. & P. Ry. v. Sturn, 174 U.S. 710, 19 S.Ct. 797; Harris v. Balk, 198 U.S. 215, 226, 227, 25 S.Ct. 625, 628; Louisville & Nashville R.R. v. Deer, 200 U.S. 176, 26 S.Ct. 207; Baltimore & Ohio R.R. v. Hostetter, 240 U.S. 620, 36 S.Ct. 475; Shinn on Attachment and Garnishment, § 707. See Brigham v. Fayerweather, 140 Mass. 411, 413. But the interpleader initiated by the company was an altogether different matter. This was an attempt to bring about a final and conclusive adjudication of her personal rights, not merely to discover property and apply it to debts. And unless in contemplation of law she was before the court and required to respond to that issue, its orders and judgments in respect thereto were not binding on her. Pennoyer v. Neff, 95 U.S. 714; Shinn on Attachment and Garnishment, § 674. See Cross v. Armstrong, 44 Oh.St. 613, 623, 625.

[The Court held that in these circumstances there was no continuing jurisdiction over Mrs. Dunlevy based on the concluded 1907 action.]

It has been affirmatively held in Pennsylvania that a judgment debtor is not a party to a garnishment proceeding to condemn a claim due him from a third person and is not bound by a judgment discharging the garnishee (Ruff v. Ruff, 85 Pa. 333); and this is the generally accepted doctrine. Shinn on Attachment and Garnishment, § 725. Former opinions of this court uphold validity of such proceedings upon the theory that jurisdiction to condemn is acquired by service of effective process upon the garnishee.

The established general rule is that any personal judgment which a state court may render against one who did not voluntarily submit to its jurisdiction, and who is not a citizen of the State, nor served with process within its borders, no matter what the mode of service, is void, because the court had no jurisdiction over his person. Pennoyer v. Neff, supra; Freeman on Judgments, 4th ed., § 120a; Black on Judgments, 2d ed., §§ 904 and 905.

We are of opinion that the proceedings in the Pennsylvania court constituted no bar to the action in California and the judgment below is accordingly

Affirmed.

Question: (11) Would Dunlevy be decided in the same way today?

FEDERAL LEGISLATION

The Dunlevy decision, emphasizing the narrow limits of the power of state courts to deal with out-of-state claimants, gave impetus to federal interpleader legislation. The first federal act, applicable only to claims against insurance companies and aimed simply to override Dunlevy, came a year after the decision. The culmination, largely the work of Professor Chafee,[b] was the Federal Interpleader Act of

[b] The classic writings on interpleader are by Professor Chafee. See Modernizing Interpleader, 30 Yale L.J. 814 (1921); Interstate Interpleader, 33 Yale L.J. 685 (1924); Interpleader in the United States Courts (pts. 1–2), 41 Yale L.J. 1134

1936. That statute, with some minor changes, is now distributed in title 28 of the United States Code. Read §§ 1335, 1397, and 2361.

Also reexamine Rule 22. This provision was not intended to change the rules of jurisdiction and venue, but rather to preserve and liberalize the old equitable remedy of interpleader as a supplement to statutory interpleader in the federal courts.

STATE FARM FIRE & CASUALTY CO. v. TASHIRE

Supreme Court of the United States, 1967.
386 U.S. 523, 87 S.Ct. 1199.

MR. JUSTICE FORTAS delivered the opinion of the Court.

Early one September morning in 1964, a Greyhound bus proceeding northward through Shasta County, California, collided with a southbound pickup truck. Two of the passengers aboard the bus were killed. Thirty-three others were injured, as were the bus driver, the driver of the truck and its lone passenger. One of the dead and 10 of the injured passengers were Canadians; the rest of the individuals involved were citizens of five American States. The ensuing litigation led to the present case, which raises important questions concerning administration of the interpleader remedy in the federal courts.

The litigation began when four of the injured passengers filed suit in California state courts, seeking damages in excess of $1,000,000. Named as defendants were Greyhound Lines, Inc., a California corporation; Theron Nauta, the bus driver; Ellis Clark, who drove the truck; and Kenneth Glasgow, the passenger in the truck who was apparently its owner as well. Each of the individual defendants was a citizen and resident of Oregon. Before these cases could come to trial and before other suits were filed in California or elsewhere, petitioner, State Farm Fire & Casualty Company, an Illinois corporation, brought this action in the nature of interpleader in the United States District Court for the District of Oregon.

In its complaint State Farm asserted that at the time of the Shasta County collision it had in force an insurance policy with respect to Ellis Clark, driver of the truck, providing for bodily injury liability up to $10,000 per person and $20,000 per occurrence and for legal representation of Clark in actions covered by the policy. It asserted that actions already filed in California and others which it anticipated

(1932), 42 Yale L.J. 41 (1932); The Federal Interpleader Act of 1936 (pts. 1–2), 45 Yale L.J. 963, 1161 (1936); Federal Interpleader Since the Act of 1936, 49 Yale L.J. 377 (1940); Broadening the Second Stage of Interpleader, 56 Harv.L.Rev. 541 (1943); Broadening the Second Stage of Federal Interpleader, 56 Harv.L.Rev. 929 (1943).

would be filed far exceeded in aggregate damages sought the amount of its maximum liability under the policy. Accordingly, it paid into court the sum of $20,000 and asked the court (1) to require all claimants to establish their claims against Clark and his insurer in this single proceeding and in no other, and (2) to discharge State Farm from all further obligations under its policy—including its duty to defend Clark in lawsuits arising from the accident. Alternatively, State Farm expressed its conviction that the policy issued to Clark excluded from coverage accidents resulting from his operation of a truck which belonged to another and was being used in the business of another. The complaint, therefore, requested that the court decree that the insurer owed no duty to Clark and was not liable on the policy, and it asked the court to refund the $20,000 deposit.

Joined as defendants were Clark, Glasgow, Nauta, Greyhound Lines, and each of the prospective claimants. Jurisdiction was predicated upon 28 U.S.C. § 1335, the federal interpleader statute, and upon general diversity of citizenship, there being diversity between two or more of the claimants to the fund and between State Farm and all of the named defendants.

An order issued, requiring each of the defendants to show cause why it should not be restrained from filing or prosecuting "any proceeding in any state or United States Court affecting the property or obligation involved in this interpleader action, and specifically against the plaintiff and the defendant Ellis D. Clark." Personal service was effected on each of the American defendants, and registered mail was employed to reach the 11 Canadian claimants. Defendants Nauta, Greyhound, and several of the injured passengers responded, contending that the policy did cover this accident and advancing various arguments for the position that interpleader was either impermissible or inappropriate in the present circumstances. Greyhound, however, soon switched sides and moved that the court broaden any injunction to include Nauta and Greyhound among those who could not be sued except within the confines of the interpleader proceeding.

When a temporary injunction along the lines sought by State Farm was issued by the United States District Court for the District of Oregon, the present respondents moved to dismiss the action and, in the alternative, for a change of venue—to the Northern District of California, in which district the collision had occurred. After a hearing, the court declined to dissolve the temporary injunction, but continued the motion for a change of venue. The injunction was later broadened to include the protection sought by Greyhound, but modified to permit the filing—although not the prosecution—of suits. The injunction, therefore, provided that all suits against Clark, State Farm, Greyhound, and Nauta be prosecuted in the interpleader proceeding.

On interlocutory appeal,[2] the Court of Appeals for the Ninth Circuit reversed, 363 F.2d 7. The court found it unnecessary to reach respondents' contentions relating to service of process and the scope of the injunction, for it concluded that interpleader was not available in the circumstances of this case. It held that in States like Oregon which do not permit "direct action" suits against the insurance company until judgments are obtained against the insured, the insurance company may not invoke federal interpleader until the claims against the insured, the alleged tortfeasor, have been reduced to judgment. Until that is done, said the court, claimants with unliquidated tort claims are not "claimants" within the meaning of § 1335, nor are they "[p]ersons having claims against the plaintiff" within the meaning of Rule 22 of the Federal Rules of Civil Procedure.[3] Id., at 10. In accord with that view, it directed dissolution of the temporary injunction and dismissal of the action. Because the Court of Appeals' decision on this point conflicts with those of other federal courts, and concerns a matter of significance to the administration of federal interpleader, we granted certiorari. 385 U.S. 811, 87 S.Ct. 90 (1966). Although we reverse the decision of the Court of Appeals upon the jurisdictional question, we direct a substantial modification of the District Court's injunction for reasons which will appear.

I.

Before considering the issues presented by the petition for certiorari, we find it necessary to dispose of a question neither raised by the parties nor passed upon by the courts below. Since the matter concerns our jurisdiction, we raise it on our own motion. Treinies v. Sunshine Mining Co., 308 U.S. 66, 70, 60 S.Ct. 44, 47 (1939). The interpleader statute, 28 U.S.C. § 1335, applies where there are "Two or more adverse claimants, of diverse citizenship . . . ." This provision has been uniformly construed to require only "minimal diversity," that is, diversity of citizenship between two or more claimants, without regard to the circumstance that other rival claimants may be co-citizens. The language of the statute, the legislative purpose broadly to remedy the problems posed by multiple claimants to a single fund, and the consistent judicial interpretation tacitly accepted by Congress, persuade us that the statute requires no more. There remains, however, the question whether such a statutory construction is consistent with Article III of our Constitution, which extends the federal judicial power to "Controversies . . . between Citizens of different States . . . and between a State, or the Citizens thereof, and foreign States, Citizens or Subjects." In Strawbridge v. Curtiss, 3 Cranch 267 (1806), this Court held that the diversity of citizenship statute required "complete diversity": where co-citizens appeared on

[2] 28 U.S.C. § 1292(a)(1).

[3] We need not pass upon the Court of Appeals' conclusions with respect to the interpretation of interpleader under Rule 22 . . . . State Farm could not have invoked it in light of venue and service of process limitations. . . .

both sides of a dispute, jurisdiction was lost. But Chief Justice Marshall there purported to construe only "The words of the act of congress," not the Constitution itself. And in a variety of contexts this Court and the lower courts have concluded that Article III poses no obstacle to the legislative extension of federal jurisdiction, founded on diversity, so long as any two adverse parties are not co-citizens.[7] Accordingly, we conclude that the present case is properly in the federal courts.

II.

We do not agree with the Court of Appeals that, in the absence of a state law or contractual provision for "direct action" suits against the insurance company, the company must wait until persons asserting claims against its insured have reduced those claims to judgment before seeking to invoke the benefits of federal interpleader. That may have been a tenable position under the 1926 and 1936 interpleader statutes. These statutes did not carry forward the language in the 1917 Act authorizing interpleader where adverse claimants "may claim" benefits as well as where they "are claiming" them.[10] In 1948, however, in the revision of the Judicial Code, the "may claim" language was restored.[11] Until the decision below, every court confronted by the question has concluded that the 1948 revision removed whatever requirement there might previously have been that the insurance company wait until at least two claimants reduced their claims to judgments. The commentators are in accord.

Considerations of judicial administration demonstrate the soundness of this view which, in any event, seems compelled by the language of the present statute, which is remedial and to be liberally construed. Were an insurance company required to await reduction of claims to judgment, the first claimant to obtain such a judgment or to negotiate a settlement might appropriate all or a disproportionate slice of the fund before his fellow claimants were able to establish their claims. The difficulties such a race to judgment pose for the

[7] . . . We note that the American Law Institute's proposals for revision of the Judicial Code to deal with the problem of multiparty, multijurisdiction litigation are predicated upon the permissibility of "minimal diversity" as a jurisdictional basis.

[10] 39 Stat. 929 (1917). See Klaber v. Maryland Cas. Co., 69 F.2d 934, 938–939 (C.A.8th Cir. 1934), which held that the omission in the 1926 Act of the earlier statute's "may claim" language required the denial of interpleader in the face of unliquidated claims (alternative holding).

[11] Although the Reviser's Note did not refer to the statutory change or its purpose, we have it on good authority that it was the omission in the Note rather than the statutory change which was inadvertent. See 3 Moore, Fed.Prac. ¶ 22.08, at 3025–3026, n. 13. And it was widely assumed that restoration of the "may claim" language would have the effect of overruling the holding in Klaber, supra, that one may not invoke interpleader to protect against unliquidated claims. See, e.g., Chafee, 45 Yale L.J., at 1163–1167; Chafee, Federal Interpleader Since the Act of 1936, 49 Yale L.J. 377, 418–420 (1940). In circumstances like these, the 1948 revision of the Judicial Code worked substantive changes. Ex parte Collett, 337 U.S. 55, 69 S.Ct. 944 (1949).

insurer, and the unfairness which may result to some claimants, were among the principal evils the interpleader device was intended to remedy.[15]

III.

The fact that State Farm had properly invoked the interpleader jurisdiction under § 1335 did not, however, entitle it to an order both enjoining prosecution of suits against it outside the confines of the interpleader proceeding and also extending such protection to its insured, the alleged tortfeasor. Still less was Greyhound Lines entitled to have that order expanded so as to protect itself and its driver, also alleged to be tortfeasors, from suits brought by its passengers in various state or federal courts. Here, the scope of the litigation, in terms of parties and claims, was vastly more extensive than the confines of the "fund," the deposited proceeds of the insurance policy. In these circumstances, the mere existence of such a fund cannot, by use of interpleader, be employed to accomplish purposes that exceed the needs of orderly contest with respect to the fund.

There are situations, of a type not present here, where the effect of interpleader is to confine the total litigation to a single forum and proceeding. One such case is where a stakeholder, faced with rival claims to the fund itself, acknowledges—or denies—his liability to one or the other of the claimants.[16] In this situation, the fund itself is the target of the claimants. It marks the outer limits of the controversy. It is, therefore, reasonable and sensible that interpleader, in discharge of its office to protect the fund, should also protect the stakeholder from vexatious and multiple litigation. In this context, the suits sought to be enjoined are squarely within the language of 28 U.S.C. § 2361, which provides in part:

> "In any civil action of interpleader or in the nature of interpleader under section 1335 of this title, a district court may issue its process for all claimants and enter its order restraining them from instituting or prosecuting *any proceeding* in any State or United States court *affecting the property, instrument or obligation involved in the interpleader action* . . . ." (Emphasis added.)

But the present case is another matter. Here, an accident has happened. Thirty-five passengers or their representatives have claims which they wish to press against a variety of defendants: the bus company, its driver, the owner of the truck, and the truck driver.

---

[15] The insurance problem envisioned at the time was that of an insurer faced with conflicting but mutually exclusive claims to a policy, rather than an insurer confronted with the problem of allocating a fund among various claimants whose independent claims may exceed the amount of the fund. S.Rep. No. 558, 74th Cong., 1st Sess., 2–3, 7, 8 (1935); Chafee, Modernizing Interpleader, 30 Yale L.J. 814, 818–819 (1921).

[16] This was the classic situation envisioned by the sponsors of interpleader. See n. 15, supra.

The circumstance that one of the prospective defendants happens to have an insurance policy is a fortuitous event which should not of itself shape the nature of the ensuing litigation. For example, a resident of California, injured in California aboard a bus owned by a California corporation should not be forced to sue that corporation anywhere but in California simply because another prospective defendant carried an insurance policy. And an insurance company whose maximum interest in the case cannot exceed $20,000 and who in fact asserts that it has no interest at all, should not be allowed to determine that dozens of tort plaintiffs must be compelled to press their claims—even those claims which are not against the insured and which in no event could be satisfied out of the meager insurance fund—in a single forum of the insurance company's choosing. There is nothing in the statutory scheme, and very little in the judicial and academic commentary upon that scheme, which requires that the tail be allowed to wag the dog in this fashion.

State Farm's interest in this case, which is the fulcrum of the interpleader procedure, is confined to its $20,000 fund. That interest receives full vindication when the court restrains claimants from seeking to enforce against the insurance company any judgment obtained against its insured, except in the interpleader proceeding itself. To the extent that the District Court sought to control claimants' lawsuits against the insured and other alleged tortfeasors, it exceeded the powers granted to it by the statutory scheme.

We recognize, of course, that our view of interpleader means that it cannot be used to solve all the vexing problems of multiparty litigation arising out of a mass tort. But interpleader was never intended to perform such a function, to be an all-purpose "bill of peace." [17] Had it been so intended, careful provision would necessarily have been made to insure that a party with little or no interest in the outcome of a complex controversy should not strip truly interested parties of substantial rights—such as the right to choose the forum in which to establish their claims, subject to generally applicable rules of jurisdiction, venue, service of process, removal, and change of venue. None of the legislative and academic sponsors of a modern federal interpleader device viewed their accomplishment as a "bill of peace," capable of sweeping dozens of lawsuits out of the various

[17] There is not a word in the legislative history suggesting such a purpose. See S.Rep. No. 558, 74th Cong., 1st Sess. (1935). And Professor Chafee, upon whose work the Congress heavily depended, has written that little thought was given to the scope of the "second stage" of interpleader, to just what would be adjudicated by the interpleader court. See Chafee, Broadening the Second Stage of Federal Interpleader, 56 Harv.L.Rev. 929, 944–945 (1943). We note that in Professor Chafee's own study of the bill of peace as a device for dealing with the problem of multiparty litigation, he fails even to mention interpleader. See Chafee, Some Problems of Equity 149–198 (1950). In his writing on interpleader, Chafee assumed that the interpleader court would allocate the fund "among all the claimants who get judgment within a reasonable time . . . ." Chafee, The Federal Interpleader Act of 1936: II, 45 Yale L.J. 1161, 1165–1166 (1936). See also Chafee, 49 Yale L.J., at 420–421.

state and federal courts in which they were brought and into a single interpleader proceeding. . . .

In light of the evidence that federal interpleader was not intended to serve the function of a "bill of peace" in the context of multiparty litigation arising out of a mass tort, of the anomalous power which such a construction of the statute would give the stakeholder, and of the thrust of the statute and the purpose it was intended to serve, we hold that the interpleader statute did not authorize the injunction entered in the present case. Upon remand, the injunction is to be modified consistently with this opinion.[18]

IV.

The judgment of the Court of Appeals is reversed, and the case is remanded to the United States District Court for proceedings consistent with this opinion.

It is so ordered.

[The dissenting opinion of Justice Douglas is omitted. He agreed with the Court on parts I and III of its opinion, but he did not regard the victims as "claimants" to the fund in the statutory sense until their claims against the insured were reduced to judgment.]

JURISDICTION AND VENUE REQUIREMENTS

Taking into account the requirements of subject-matter jurisdiction, service, and venue, you should classify the actions that can be brought under Rule 22(1), under the federal interpleader statute, or under both. Note again that Rule 22(1) actions must look to the general statutes on subject-matter jurisdiction and venue and to the Federal Rules for service of process, whereas the interpleader statute has its own provisions on these matters.

[18] We find it unnecessary to pass upon respondents' contention, raised in the courts below but not passed upon by the Court of Appeals, that interpleader should have been dismissed on the ground that the 11 Canadian claimants are "indispensable parties" who have not been properly served. The argument is that 28 U.S.C. § 2361 provides the exclusive mode of effecting service of process in statutory interpleader and that § 2361—which authorizes a district court to "issue its process for all claimants" but subsequently refers to service of "such process" by marshals "for the respective districts where the claimants reside or may be found"—does not permit service of process beyond the Nation's borders. Since our decision will require basic reconsideration of the litigation by the parties as well as the lower courts, there appears neither need nor necessity to determine this question at this time. We intimate no view as to the exclusivity of § 2361, whether it authorizes service of process in foreign lands, whether in light of the limitations we have imposed on the interpleader court's injunctive powers the Canadian claimants are in fact "indispensable parties" to the interpleader proceeding itself, or whether they render themselves amenable to service of process under § 2361 when they come into an American jurisdiction to establish their rights with respect either to the alleged tortfeasors or to the insurance fund. See 2 Moore, Fed.Prac. ¶ 4.20, at 1091–1105.

Questions: (12) *A* Life Insurance Co., incorporated and having its principal place of business in State *X*, issued a life insurance policy to *B* that excluded death by suicide within the period before the policy became incontestable (see supra p. 681). *B* died within that period, and both *C* and *D* have claimed the proceeds of the policy as sole beneficiary. *A* Co. wants to defend on the ground of suicide and to determine which claimant can recover if that defense fails. Is interpleader available to *A* Co.? In what factual circumstances could *A* Co. proceed under the Rule? under the statute? under both?

(13) If interpleader could be invoked—as far as subject-matter jurisdiction, service, and venue are concerned—under both the Rule and the statute, what other factors would influence a stakeholder's choice between the two devices? See 3A Moore ¶¶ 22.04[3] (power to enjoin other proceedings), .10 (deposit in court registry).

(14) Could the defendant bank in the Haas case, supra p. 1106, have interpleaded by counterclaim, thus allowing Haas and Glueck to fight it out in the Florida federal court? Consider the application of ancillary jurisdiction and venue, or of 28 U.S.C. § 1655. See 7 Wright & Miller §§ 1710–1712; cf. 14 Wright, Miller & Cooper § 3636, at 78.

THE CLASSIC LIMITS ON INTERPLEADER

4 J. Pomeroy, Equity Jurisprudence § 1322 (5th ed. 1941): "[F]rom the whole course of authorities, it is clear that the equitable remedy of interpleader, independent of statutory regulations, depends upon and requires the existence of the four following elements, which may be regarded as its essential conditions: 1. The same thing, debt, or duty must be claimed by both or all the parties against whom the relief is demanded; 2. All their adverse titles or claims must be dependent, or be derived from a common source; 3. The person asking the relief—the plaintiff—must not have nor claim any interest in the subject-matter; 4. He must have incurred no independent liability to either of the claimants; that is, he must stand perfectly indifferent between them, in the position merely of a stakeholder." [c]

Question: (15) Which of Pomeroy's "classic limits" were abolished by the federal interpleader statute? by Rule 22(1)?

Neither the statute nor the Rule expressly does away with the requirement that the plaintiff must have incurred no independent liability to either of the claimants, i.e., that the plaintiff must not have rendered himself liable to one claimant without reference to his possi-

---

[c] On the origins of the classic limits, see the biting and highly interesting account by Hazard & Moskovitz, An Historical and Critical Analysis of Interpleader, 52 Calif.L.Rev. 706 (1964). The student should consider which of the classic limits are intrinsic to interpleader and which, in Chafee's phrase, were merely obstacles to just relief.

In addition to strict interpleader as described by Pomeroy, equity permitted "a bill in the nature of a bill of interpleader" when the stakeholder was not disinterested, but he had to have some ground for equitable relief other than the assertion of conflicting claims against him. See Killian v. Ebbinghaus, 110 U.S. 568, 4 S.Ct. 232 (1884).

ble liability to the other, as by a subsequent contract concerning the stake. It is probable that Professor Chafee, the draftsman of the statute, considered the independent-liability restriction to be only an aspect of the requirement that the claims be of common origin. Cf. Ex parte Mersey Docks & Harbour Board, [1899] 1 Q.B. 546 (C.A.). A conflict, however, developed. Compare Poland v. Atlantis Credit Corp., 179 F.Supp. 863 (S.D.N.Y.1960) (restriction still exists), with Knoll v. Socony Mobil Oil Co., 369 F.2d 425 (10th Cir.1966) (restriction no longer a bar), cert. denied, 386 U.S. 977, 87 S.Ct. 1173 (1967). ALI Study of the Division of Jurisdiction Between State and Federal Courts § 2361(b) commentary at 420–21 (1968) recommends resolution of this conflict by adding at the end of current § 1335(b) the words "or although the plaintiff may be independently liable to one or more of the claimants." A similar amendment of Rule 22(1) is probably desirable, although increasingly the cases under both the statute and the Rule are, without the benefit of amendment, reaching the conclusion that the independent-liability restriction no longer exists.

"BROADENING THE SECOND STAGE OF FEDERAL INTERPLEADER" [d]

Once it is determined that interpleader has been properly instituted (the so-called first stage of interpleader), the parties or some of them may discover that they have further claims against one another, either connected or unconnected with the subject of the interpleader. When must or may such claims be asserted in the interpleader action? What requirements, if any, of subject-matter jurisdiction, service, and venue will have to be satisfied? The answers to such questions define the scope of the second stage of interpleader.

Questions: (16) Assume that a bank of State X brings statutory interpleader in a federal court in State X to resolve conflicting claims to a bank deposit of $15,000 made by A of State Y with provision that it was to be withdrawn by B of State X upon satisfactory completion of a transaction involving a boat. Service is made upon A in State Y under 28 U.S.C. § 2361, effective personal service on A not being otherwise possible. A does not appear to claim the deposit. B serves and files a cross-claim against A for $50,000 damages allegedly arising out of A's negligence in connection with the boat. Is there jurisdiction over A's person for purposes of the cross-claim? See 7 Wright & Miller § 1715, at 449–53.

(17) In the preceding question, should it matter how closely related the cross-claim issues are to those in the interpleader? See Hallin v. C.A. Pearson, Inc., 34 F.R.D. 499 (N.D.Cal.1963) (yes). Should it matter whether A has appeared to claim the deposit? See Restatement (Second) of Judgments § 9 (1980) (yes). What if the interpleader action were under Rule 22(1) rath-

[d] See Professor Chafee's article so entitled, 56 Harv.L.Rev. 929 (1943).

er than the statute? See Dean Witter Reynolds Inc. v. Fernandez, 489 F.Supp. 434, 440 & n.6 (S.D.Fla.1979).

(18) If interpleader is allowed and the claimants proceed to the second stage, do they have a jury right on their claims to the deposit? Cf. Ross v. Bernhard, supra p. 700.

(19) Who should have the burden of proof on the claims to the deposit? See Phoenix Mut. Life Ins. Co. v. Reich, 75 F.Supp. 886 (W.D.Pa.1948) (each claimant).

LAW APPLIED IN FEDERAL INTERPLEADER

Obviously, in the first stage of interpleader the governing law should be federal. In the second stage, however, some problems of choice of law crop up.

It will be recalled that the Supreme Court in Klaxon Co. v. Stentor Electric Manufacturing Co., supra p. 206, directed the lower federal court hearing that diversity case to follow the rules of conflict of laws of the state in which it sat. On that same day the Supreme Court decided Griffin v. McCoach, 313 U.S. 498, 61 S.Ct. 1023 (1941), and there directed like obedience to the rules of conflict of laws of the forum state in a federal statutory interpleader action. Many think that whatever the merits of the Klaxon rule in the ordinary diversity action, they are much attenuated when it comes to federal statutory interpleader. Why so? The American Law Institute proposes an amendment to the federal interpleader statute, which would declare: "Whenever State law supplies the rule of decision on an issue, the district court may make its own determination as to which State rule of decision is applicable." ALI Study of the Division of Jurisdiction Between State and Federal Courts § 2363(c) (1968).

Part Eight

APPEALS

TOPIC A. GENERAL OBSERVATIONS

P. CARRINGTON, D. MEADOR & M. ROSENBERG, JUSTICE ON APPEAL
2–4 (1976).

In the received tradition, the functions of appellate adjudication are two-fold. One is to "review for correctness." It is probably true for most legal systems, and is emphatically true for this country's, that appellate courts serve as the instrument of accountability for those who make the basic decisions in trial courts and administrative agencies. The traditional appeal calls for an examination of the rulings below to assure that they are correct, or at least within the range of error the law for sufficient reasons allows the primary decision-maker. The availability of the appellate process assures the decision-makers at the first level that their correct judgments will not be, or appear to be, the unconnected actions of isolated individuals, but will have the concerted support of the legal system; and it assures litigants that the decision in their case is not prey to the failings of whichever mortal happened to render it, but bears the institutional imprimatur and approval of the whole social order as represented by its legal system. Thus, the review for correctness serves to reinforce the dignity, authority, and acceptability of the trial, and to control the adverse effects of any personal shortcomings of the basic decision-makers.

The second function in the traditional tandem is sometimes described as "institutional" review. Trial courts working independently have no self-regulating capacity to promote uniformity among their decisions. Without appellate review, such great divergences in practices and variations in results would arise between trial courts in the same system that they would jeopardize the belief that legal principles are a vital force in their decisions or provide a basis for predicting the application of official power. Accordingly, appellate courts are needed to announce, clarify, and harmonize the rules of decision employed by the legal system in which they serve. Until recent decades, it was customary to conceal, even from ourselves, the creative and political aspects of this function; we were given to proclaiming that judges do not make law. Today, such comment is seldom heard; it is widely understood that the judges who enunciate legal principles are engaged in a creative activity which can have significant social, economic, and political consequences. On the other hand, it is still

1213

true that rampant judicial free-wheeling in law-declaring may threaten the democratic ideal that representative government is designed to foster. Few would deny that there are appropriate limits to the judges' assumption of responsibility for the full range of social, economic and political ills which might conceivably be subjected to the judicial power.

Recognizing traditional duality in the functions of appellate adjudication is unquestionably helpful to understanding. It serves to illumine the contrast in both the concerns and the affects of appellate justice. On the one hand, appellate justice is preoccupied with the impact of decisions on particular litigants, but on the other it is concerned with the general principles which govern the affairs of persons other than those who are party to the cases decided. While appellate justice has impact on the realities of situations, it also affects the appearances and symbols which pervade the government. An appellate system which is unduly preoccupied with one of these functions to the neglect of the other, is inadequate to advance the purposes which appellate courts should serve.

The dual function analysis has served as the basis for several developments of recent decades, beginning at least as early as the Federal Judiciary Act of 1925, which conferred on the Supreme Court of the United States the power to refuse to hear many of the appeals which it had formerly been required to hear. It was the premise of that reform that the highest Court would continue to hear the cases which are of institutional importance, but would decline to hear cases which are of importance only to the individuals affected, thus leaving the function of review of district court decisions for correctness to the intermediate courts, the . . . Courts of Appeal. Many states now have intermediate court structures comparable to that of the federal system, and most have established, at least in some degree, a difference of function for the two levels of appellate courts, based on this duality.

F. JAMES & G. HAZARD, CIVIL PROCEDURE
677–80 (2d ed. 1977).

Appellate review is not a retrial of the case, but rather a review concerning whether prejudicial error occurred in its original determination. On this premise the rules on scope of review include the following:

Error appearing in the record. Review is limited to considering errors revealed in the record. An appellate court will not consider matter that may have been received in the trial court unless it is included in the record. Ordinarily it will also refuse to receive evidence of events outside the proceedings below—for example, evidence of jury misconduct that was not presented to the trial court through a vehicle such as a motion for new trial. This limitation on the evidentiary matter that an appellate court may consider is one reason why application for relief in the trial court is usually an essential precondition to seeking relief by way of appeal.

Error must have been asserted in trial court. Apart from the evidentiary problem just considered, the general rule is that a party may not complain to an appellate court of an occurrence in the trial court unless he had objected to the trial court at or promptly after the time of the occurrence. The underlying concept is that a party should take measures in the trial court that will avoid the commission or consequences of an error, so that an appeal will be necessary only insofar as such measures have failed.

Error must be raised in the appellate court. The principle of adversarial presentation applies in appellate review as well as in trial court proceedings. Accordingly, an appellate court ordinarily will not consider errors that are not pointed out to it in the presentation of the appeal. It will not, in other words, on its own initiative "search the record" for error.

. . . .

Prejudicial error. Erroneous determinations in the trial court, even when the error is clear, do not warrant reversal unless the appellate court concludes that they materially affected the outcome or involved an important issue of procedural justice. In general, the task of the appellate court is to determine whether the judgment can justly be allowed to stand, despite error, rather than to use reversal to admonish the trial court in its conduct of the proceedings below. For this and other reasons, it is an axiom of litigation strategy that, if at all possible, a case should be won in the trial court.

OLD MODES OF REVIEW

In actions at law instituted in any of the three superior courts in England, attacks on the pleadings prior to trial—for instance, demurrers—were heard and ruled on by the court in banc. A ruling at this stage might dispose of the case and result in judgment for one of the parties.

Where the pleadings eventuated in an issue of fact, the issue was typically tried at nisi prius by a single judge and jury. In the course of the trial, the judge made rulings on points of evidence and in the end he charged the jury, which rendered a verdict. Thereupon the record, including the jury verdict, was returned to the central court, and in due time, barring other steps by the party who had lost the verdict, judgment would be entered in accordance with the verdict.

After the trial but prior to the entry of the judgment, the party who had lost the verdict might apply to the court in banc for relief.

Technically this application might take the form of a request for the service of a rule on the opponent to show cause why an order should not be made by the court in favor of the applicant. These applications and the orders sought were of various kinds. Plaintiff or defendant who had lost the verdict might apply for a new trial on the ground that the nisi prius judge had ruled erroneously on a point of evidence or had charged the jury incorrectly or on the ground that the verdict was against the weight of the evidence. Here the notes of the trial judge would be made available to the court in banc. If the application was successful, the verdict might be set aside and a new trial ordered. Again, a losing defendant might move in arrest of judgment on the ground that the pleadings were not sufficient in law to support a judgment for plaintiff. Or a losing plaintiff might move for judgment notwithstanding the verdict on the ground that the plea in confession and avoidance, on which the jury had given a verdict in defendant's favor, was not sufficient in law.[a]

Such applications to the court in banc served in some cases as a means of securing reexamination of the actions of the trial judge, but they did not involve review by a higher court. For the trial judge had acted as a kind of agent of the court in trying the case at nisi prius; often the court was examining and, if necessary, correcting the rulings of one of its own members, not those of a judge of an inferior court.

It was only after judgment was entered, by one route or another, that proceedings in error by the higher court, the court of error, could be instituted.[b] The plaintiff-in-error (the party against whom judgment had gone below) would sue a writ of error out of the Chancery. This was an original writ directed to the court that had entered the judgment, directing it to send the record to the court of error in order that the claimed error might be there corrected. The return to the writ was the record.

It is important to bear in mind of what this record consisted, because the scope of review was naturally determined by what was laid before the court of error. The record comprised the process, the pleadings (together with rulings on the pleadings[c]), the clerk's minutes, the verdict,[d] and the judgment. In no event did the record contain the proceedings on a motion for a new trial made to the lower

[a] See supra p. 349.

[b] In the old days, the scheme was a confused one: speaking generally, the King's Bench was the court of error for the Court of Common Pleas, the House of Lords was the court of error for the King's Bench, and a special court called the Exchequer Chamber was the court of error for the Court of Exchequer. After 1830, the court of error for all three superior courts was a new Court of Exchequer Chamber, which consisted of the judges of the two superior courts that

had not been involved in the action being reviewed. Further review, as always, could be had in the House of Lords.

[c] These included rulings on demurrer, motion in arrest of judgment, and motion for judgment n.o.v. A ruling on demurrer to the evidence would also appear in the record; see supra pp. 568–69.

[d] This included a so-called special verdict, but not a so-called special case. The former device resulted in jury findings being entered of record, but the latter de-

court in banc, and the ruling below on such a motion, whether granted or denied, was accordingly not reviewable on writ of error. Indeed, except where a bill of exceptions (described below) had been employed, the record did not contain a word of the testimony given at the trial, nor did it contain the trial judge's rulings on matters of evidence or his charge to the jury.

After the Statute of Westminster II, 1285, 13 Edw., ch. 31, alleged errors of the trial judge could be brought before the court of error by bill of exceptions, as an alternative to a motion for a new trial. A party claiming error in the trial judge's rulings on points of evidence or in his charge to the jury reduced to writing the substance of the rulings or the parts of the charge excepted to. This bill of exceptions then formed a part of the record. The lower court took no further notice of it. But after judgment and upon writ of error, the court of error was thereby able to review the errors of law allegedly committed at the trial. "The advantage of this method of proceeding, instead of moving for a new trial, was that a bill of exceptions was taken to the Court of Error, . . . whereas the motion for a new trial was . . . made to the Court in which the case was started, of which court the Judge, whose ruling was objected to, might be a member, and there was no appeal from the judgment of such court to a Court of Error on a motion for a new trial." R. Sutton, Personal Actions at Common Law 126 (1929).

Review by a higher court in actions at law thus was confined substantially to claimed errors of law appearing on a bare record, and it took place only after judgment.

————

CRICK, THE FINAL JUDGMENT AS A BASIS FOR APPEAL
41 Yale L.J. 539, 545–48 (1932).

A complete picture of appellate processes in England in past years cannot be obtained merely by consideration of the common law courts. Much of the business now handled by our courts of general jurisdiction was taken care of in England by chancery, and we must, therefore, consider the procedure in those types of cases.

Taking Blackstone's time as a convenient point of departure, we find that the course of litigation in a simple case in equity went something as follows.

The pleadings having been filed and the parties at issue upon the facts, the evidence was taken down in writing and the case set for hearing before the chancellor or Master of the Rolls. There the evidence was read and such orders made from time to time as might be necessary. When everything had been heard the decree was pro-

vice's agreed statement of facts did not become part of the record and hence could not figure in proceedings in error. See supra p. 609.

nounced. Generally it was merely interlocutory, but eventually the final decree was made and the rights of the parties completely adjudicated.

We see, then, that there were three types of pronouncements made during the course of a case. First, orders, second, interlocutory decrees, and third, final decrees. Unlike the common law, however, which as we have seen, required a case to go to final judgment before the decisions of the court might be questioned, equity gave relief from all three types of pronouncements. If a party was dissatisfied by an order made during the course of the proceedings his remedy was by way of rehearing by petition to the Lord Chancellor, whether the cause had been heard before that dignitary or the Master of the Rolls. On this rehearing the evidence is reread and any additional evidence presented. From the decision on this rehearing an appeal lay to the House of Lords.

An interlocutory decree differed from an order in that it had to be signed by the chancellor before it could be enrolled, and prior to his signing it had only the force of an order. Therefore, prior to signing relief was the same as in the case of an order, namely, petition for a rehearing before the chancellor, and from there appeal to the House of Lords. After a decree was signed and enrolled, whether it was interlocutory or final, relief could be had only by bill of review for an error in judgment appearing on the face of the decree, or by special leave of the chancellor upon the discovery of new evidence. From a decision on this bill appeal might be taken to the House of Lords.

Appeal to the House of Lords, whether from an order or from an interlocutory or final decree, was by petition to that body, which, if it consented to hear the case, considered all the documents and not merely the enrolled decree.

Thus we see that equity practice never knew the rule of the common law that only final judgments were appealable. Not only could interlocutory decrees be taken to the House of Lords, but also those decisions which had not even attained the dignity of decrees, that is, orders. As to the reason for this, we may tentatively assign two factors. First, appeals to the House of Lords from the Lord Chancellor were established comparatively late in legal history. The chancery had come to be regarded as a court as early as the 14th or 15th Century, but appeals to the House of Lords did not become established until the latter half of the 17th Century. During the intervening centuries, therefore, a given case had its beginning and ending in the same court, and the only method by which a decision could be altered was by rehearing before the chancellor. That he reviewed all interlocutory decrees and orders made by masters in the chancery may be explained historically, as originally the chancellor was the sole judge in chancery, and the masters were regarded as mere clerks rather than judges. Even in Blackstone's time a decree was a decree of the chancellor and not of the master who really gave it, since before it could become effective as a decree it had to be signed by the chancellor.

When the House of Lords finally asserted appellate jurisdiction over proceedings in chancery, therefore, it found a system whereby the chancellor passed on all decrees issued, as well as on interlocutory orders, and we need not be surprised that appeals were taken to the Lords from interlocutory decrees because in chancery there was no particular magic in a final decree. All were, so as to speak, of equal dignity. We might expect, however, that while appeals from all decrees would be heard, there might be some doubt as to the appealability of mere orders. This supposition is borne out by Spence, who says that it was not until 1726 that appellate jurisdiction was established over interlocutory orders.

Second, when we consider the character of litigation handled in chancery we see how much more convenient it was to review intermediate decisions as the case progressed. Equity cases were those of which the chancellor had taken cognizance because there was no adequate remedy at law. Consequently much of its litigation was of a complicated type unsuited to the more simple common law forms of action. There was a much greater use of subordinate officials than in the common law courts, and the requirement of documentation of evidence introduced difficulties unknown to the King's courts. In equity, judgments were not compelled to follow stereotyped forms, and this made possible dealing with the case by as many orders, decrees, and modifications of the same as were necessary in the particular case. Thus, equity had a more elastic procedure, and also required a less rigid practice on appeal to review the many and varied steps taken below.

NOTE, APPEALABILITY IN THE FEDERAL COURTS
75 Harv.L.Rev. 351, 351–53 (1961).

Any judicial system that affords a right to appellate review must ensure that appeal does not come too late to be effective.   At the same time—especially when the amount of litigation is substantial— the system must be designed to promote the efficient disposition of judicial business.   The balance is almost universally struck by a general rule allowing appeal only from final judgment, with exceptions for circumscribed classes of interlocutory orders.   In regulating appeals from the district courts the federal system has followed this pattern since the original Judiciary Act of 1789.   Although both the courts and the Congress have adopted exceptions for defined classes of orders, these have proved inadequate.   Until [1948] the extraordinary writs were the only means for providing additional flexibility in the review of interlocutory orders.   At that time an amendment to the Federal Rules of Civil Procedure conferred discretion on the district courts to permit appeal from an order terminating fewer than all claims in a multiclaim litigation.   And in 1958 the Judicial Code was amended to allow appeal from a broad group of interlocutory orders at the discretion of both the trial and the appellate courts. . . .

The basic rationale of the finality rule is conservation of judicial resources.   Constant interruption of trial would follow from a general practice of interlocutory appeals and would consume trial court time, forestall the ultimate resolution of the case, and facilitate the harassment of one party by his opponent.   Since substantial time elapses before appellate determination,[5] it would be necessary for the trial court to spend extra hours refamiliarizing itself with the case and perhaps to select a new jury and begin anew.   A single appeal consolidating all alleged errors also minimizes the appellate court burden by eliminating more than one set of records, briefs, and arguments in an individual case.   And if the prejudiced party is the ultimate victor, if parties settle, or if the trial court later corrects its own error, appellate review will prove unnecessary.   The requirement of finality also helps to ensure the correct disposition of the merits.   After the proceedings below are complete, the appellate court is in position to assess the wisdom of particular interlocutory orders with

---

[5] The median time interval from filing notice of appeal to final disposition by the court of appeals is 8.3 months. [1960 Dir. Admin. Office U.S. Courts] Ann.Rep. 221. [The comparable figure was 10.4 months in fiscal 1982.—Ed.] This span may be considerably shortened in individual cases. See Shawe v. Wendy Wilson, Inc., 25 F.R.D. 1 (S.D.N.Y.), rev'd sub nom. Jaftex Corp. v. Randolph Mills, Inc., 282 F.2d 508 (2d Cir. 1960). But interlocutory appeals will on the average still require several months for appellate consideration. See Ann.Rep. 73.

heightened perspective; the lower court is apt to consider its orders with greater care, for errors not requiring reversal will never be corrected and those that warrant reversal will compel a complete retrial. Finally, to allow an appeal from every order to which an objection is lodged might reduce respect for the authority of the trial judge.

But there are frequent situations in which prompt review is urgent. Reversal of some interlocutory orders will terminate litigation or preclude subsequent retrial, thereby eliminating needless proceedings in the lower court. Fairness demands swift appeal in cases where delayed review will be of little or no avail. Certain types of frequently recurring orders, such as discovery orders, seldom require reversal and hence may never be reviewed; the absence of appellate guidance may result in inconsistent treatment by the lower courts. Finally there must be some means for immediately restraining a district judge in the rare case where his conduct exceeds all bounds of judicial propriety.

Of particular importance is the method for distinguishing those interlocutory orders that should be appealable from those that should not. A statute granting appeal as of right from a rigidly defined class of interlocutory orders obviates the need for preliminary judicial determination of the right to appeal. But the application of a statutory definition often gives rise to substantial litigation before the appellate tribunal, and sometimes permits appeal where it is not needed or, still worse, prevents appeal when immediate review is warranted. To permit appeal in the latter cases, tortuous constructions of finality have often been adopted. The consequent uncertainty as to the right to appeal is particularly undesirable, for a mistaken party may forfeit his right to review. An alternative approach is to establish broad statutory guidelines and condition the appeal of an interlocutory order upon the consent of either the trial or appellate court. Although such an approach imposes the additional burden of preliminary consideration of the desirability of appeal, it affords greater flexibility, confines appeal to appropriate cases, and avoids uncertainty as to the right of appeal.

COHEN v. BENEFICIAL INDUSTRIAL LOAN CORP.

Supreme Court of the United States, 1949.
337 U.S. 541, 69 S.Ct. 1221.

[A digest of the facts appears supra p. 211. The district court denied the corporate defendant's motion to require security under the state statute. The court of appeals entertained an appeal and reversed. The case reached the Supreme Court on certiorari.]

MR. JUSTICE JACKSON delivered the opinion of the Court.

.   .   .   .   .

At the threshold we are met with the question whether the District Court's order refusing to apply the statute was an appealable one. Title 28 U.S.C. § 1291 provides, as did its predecessors, for appeal only "from all final decisions of the district courts," except when direct appeal to this Court is provided. Section 1292 allows appeals also from certain interlocutory orders, decrees and judgments, not material to this case except as they indicate the purpose to allow appeals from orders other than final judgments when they have a final and irreparable effect on the rights of the parties. It is obvious that, if Congress had allowed appeals only from those final judgments which terminate an action, this order would not be appealable.

The effect of the statute is to disallow appeal from any decision which is tentative, informal or incomplete. Appeal gives the upper court a power of review, not one of intervention. So long as the matter remains open, unfinished or inconclusive, there may be no intrusion by appeal. But the District Court's action upon the application was concluded and closed and its decision final in that sense before the appeal was taken.

Nor does the statute permit appeals, even from fully consummated decisions, where they are but steps towards final judgment in which they will merge. The purpose is to combine in one review all stages of the proceeding that effectively may be reviewed and corrected if and when final judgment results. But this order of the District Court did not make any step toward final disposition of the merits of the case and will not be merged in final judgment. When that time comes, it will be too late effectively to review the present order, and the rights conferred by the statute, if it is applicable, will have been lost, probably irreparably. We conclude that the matters embraced in the decision appealed from are not of such an interlocutory nature as to affect, or to be affected by, decision of the merits of this case.

This decision appears to fall in that small class which finally determine claims of right separable from, and collateral to, rights asserted in the action, too important to be denied review and too independent of the cause itself to require that appellate consideration be deferred until the whole case is adjudicated. The Court has long given this provision of the statute this practical rather than a technical construction. Bank of Columbia v. Sweeny, 1 Pet. 567, 569; United States v. River Rouge Improvement Co., 269 U.S. 411, 414, 46 S.Ct. 144, 145; Cobbledick v. United States, 309 U.S. 323, 328, 60 S.Ct. 540, 542.

We hold this order appealable because it is a final disposition of a claimed right which is not an ingredient of the cause of action and does not require consideration with it. But we do not mean that every order fixing security is subject to appeal. Here it is the right to security that presents a serious and unsettled question. If the right were admitted or clear and the order involved only an exercise of discretion as to the amount of security, a matter the statute makes subject to reconsideration from time to time, appealability would present a different question.

[The remainder of the opinion, dealing with the merits, is omitted. The dissenting opinions of Justice Douglas, with whom Justice Frankfurter joined, and of Justice Rutledge did not discuss appealability and are also omitted.]

FIRESTONE TIRE & RUBBER CO. v. RISJORD, 449 U.S. 368, 101 S.Ct. 669 (1981). This case held that under 28 U.S.C. § 1291, no immediate appeal lies in a civil case from a district-court order denying a motion to disqualify opponent's counsel for conflict of interest. Quoting Coopers & Lybrand v. Livesay, 437 U.S. 463, 468, 98 S.Ct. 2454, 2458 (1978), the Court specified the requirements of the collateral order doctrine in these terms: " '[T]he order must conclusively determine the disputed question, resolve an important issue completely separate from the merits of the action, and be effectively unreviewable on appeal from a final judgment.' " An order refusing disqualification fails the third requirement, because such an order is "indeed reviewable on appeal after final judgment."

DUNCAN v. MERRILL LYNCH, PIERCE, FENNER & SMITH, INC., 646 F.2d 1020 (5th Cir.), cert. denied, 454 U.S. 895, 102 S.Ct. 394 (1981). In this civil case, the court of appeals vacated a district-court order granting the defendant's motion to disqualify the plaintiff's counsel, where the district court had acted to prevent utilization of the defendant's confidences acquired by the plaintiff's counsel in previously representing the defendant. At the threshold, the court of appeals held that an immediate appeal lay under the collateral order doctrine, making three observations of interest. First, the court indicated that the " 'serious and unsettled question' " requirement no longer has to be satisfied. Second, the court decided that a grant of a disqualification motion does " 'conclusively determine the disputed question' " and " 'resolve an important issue completely separate from the merits of the action.' " Third, the court distinguished the Firestone case by ruling that a grant of a disqualification motion, unlike a denial, is " 'effectively unreviewable' on appeal from a final judgment on the merits."

Questions: (1) In a class action for damages, does an appeal lie from an order disapproving a proposed settlement? Does the threat of irreparable harm to a claimed right mean that delayed review will come "too late effectively to review the present order"? To what degree is that claim of right "separable from, and collateral to," and "independent of the cause itself"? Compare Norman v. McKee, 431 F.2d 769 (9th Cir.1970) (appealable), cert. denied, 401 U.S. 912, 91 S.Ct. 879, 880 (1971), with Seigal v. Merrick, 590 F.2d 35 (2d Cir.1978) (nonappealable).

(2) If in Cohen the district court had granted security in the requested amount, would an appeal have lain? Was the question collateral? How serious was the threatened harm of delayed review? See 15 Wright, Miller & Cooper § 3911, at 491–94.

APPEALABILITY OF CONTEMPT ORDERS

There are several doctrines, other than the collateral order doctrine, that can also be classified as judicial attempts at creating rigidly defined exceptions to the normal finality standard. See generally id. §§ 3910 (orders transferring property), 3912 (death knell orders), 3917 (contempt orders). Among these is the set of rules concerning the appealability of contempt orders, which rules were discussed in the discovery setting supra pp. 515–16. Essentially, it was there explained that all definitive contempt orders, except an order sanctioning a *party* adjudged to be in purely *civil* contempt, are considered final and hence appealable.

Questions: (3) For a party who has been jailed until he complies with a discovery order requiring surrender of material claimed to be privileged, no appeal is ordinarily allowed under these rules. What arguments can you make against this result? Alternatively, could you argue that sometimes an appeal therefrom will lie under the collateral order doctrine? See generally André, The Final Judgment Rule and Party Appeals of Civil Contempt Orders: Time for a Change, 55 N.Y.U.L.Rev. 1041 (1980).

(4) Might one argue that, in defining an exception to the finality standard, one is inevitably forced to choose between the certainty (ensuring predictability and workability) of a rigid definition and the accuracy (permitting appeal if and only if needed) of a discretionary definition, unless one wants only the drawbacks of both? In this context, which is the more practicably attainable goal?

GILLESPIE v. UNITED STATES STEEL CORP.
Supreme Court of the United States, 1964.
379 U.S. 148, 85 S.Ct. 308.

MR. JUSTICE BLACK delivered the opinion of the Court.

The petitioner, administratrix of the estate of her son Daniel Gillespie, brought this action in federal court against the respondent shipowner-employer to recover damages for Gillespie's death, which was alleged to have occurred when he fell and was drowned while working as a seaman on respondent's ship docked in Ohio. She claimed a right to recover for the benefit of herself and of the decedent's dependent brother and sisters under the Jones Act, which subjects employers to liability if by negligence they cause a seaman's injury or death. She also claimed a right of recovery under the Ohio wrongful death statute because the vessel allegedly was not seaworthy as required by the "general maritime law." The complaint in addition sought damages for Gillespie's pain and suffering before he died, based on the Jones Act and the general maritime law, causes of action which petitioner said survived Gillespie's death by force of the Jones Act itself and the Ohio survival statute, respectively. The District Judge, holding that the Jones Act supplied the exclusive remedy, on motion of respondent struck all parts of the complaint which referred to the Ohio statutes or to unseaworthiness. He also struck all reference to recovery for the benefit of the brother and sisters of the decedent, who respondent had argued were not beneficiaries entitled to recovery under the Jones Act while their mother was living.

Petitioner immediately appealed to the Court of Appeals. Respondent moved to dismiss the appeal on the ground that the ruling appealed from was not a "final" decision of the District Court as required by 28 U.S.C. § 1291 (1958 ed.). . . . Without definitely deciding . . . the "close" question of appealability, the Court of Appeals proceeded to determine the controversy "on the merits as though it were submitted on an appeal"; this the court said it felt free to do since its resolution of the merits did not prejudice respondent in any way, because it sustained respondent's contentions by . . . affirming the District Court's order. 321 F.2d 518. Petitioner brought the case here, and we granted certiorari. 375 U.S. 962, 84 S.Ct. 487.

.   .   .   .

In this Court respondent joins petitioner in urging us to hold that 28 U.S.C. § 1291 (1958 ed.) does not require us to dismiss this case and that we can and should decide the validity of the District Court's order to strike. We agree. Under § 1291 an appeal may be taken from any "final" order of a district court. But as this Court often has pointed out, a decision "final" within the meaning of § 1291 does not necessarily mean the last order possible to be made in a case. Cohen v. Beneficial Industrial Loan Corp., 337 U.S. 541, 545, 69 S.Ct. 1221, 1225. And our cases long have recognized that whether a ruling is "final" within the meaning of § 1291 is frequently so close a question that decision of that issue either way can be supported with equally forceful arguments, and that it is impossible to devise a formula to resolve all marginal cases coming within what might well be called the "twilight zone" of finality. Because of this difficulty this Court has held that the requirement of finality is to be given a "practical rather than a technical construction." Cohen v. Beneficial Industrial Loan Corp., supra, 337 U.S., at 546, 69 S.Ct., at 1226. [Citations omitted.] Dickinson v. Petroleum Conversion Corp., 338 U.S. 507, 511, 70 S.Ct. 322, 324, pointed out that in deciding the question of finality the most important competing considerations are "the inconvenience and costs of piecemeal review on the one hand and the danger of denying justice by delay on the other." Such competing considerations are shown by the record in the case before us. It is true that the review of this case by the Court of Appeals could be called "piecemeal"; but it does not appear that the inconvenience and cost of trying this case will be greater because the Court of Appeals decided the issues raised instead of compelling the parties to go to trial with them unanswered. We cannot say that the Court of Appeals chose wrongly under the circumstances. And it seems clear now that the case is before us that the eventual costs, as all the parties recognize, will certainly be less if we now pass on the questions presented here rather than send the case back with those issues undecided. Moreover, delay of perhaps a number of years in having the brother's and sisters' rights determined might work a great injustice on them, since the claims for recovery for their benefit have been effectively cut off so long as the District Judge's ruling stands. And while their claims are not formally severable so as to make the court's order unquestionably appealable as to them, cf. Dickinson v. Petroleum Conversion Corp., supra, there certainly is ample reason to view their claims as severable in deciding the issue of finality . . . . Furthermore, in United States v. General Motors Corp., 323 U.S. 373, 377, 65 S.Ct. 357, 359, this Court contrary to its usual practice reviewed a trial court's refusal to permit proof of certain items of damages in a case not yet fully tried, because the ruling was "fundamental to the further conduct of the case." . . . And see Cohen v. Beneficial Industrial Loan Corp., supra, 337 U.S., at 545–547, 69 S.Ct., at 1225–1226. We think that the questions presented here are equally "fundamental to the further conduct of the case." It is true that if the District Judge had certified the case to the Court of Appeals under 28 U.S.C. § 1292(b) (1958 ed.), the appeal unquestionably would have been proper; in light of the circumstances we believe that the Court of Appeals properly implemented the same policy Congress sought to promote in § 1292(b) by treating this obviously marginal case as final and appealable under 28 U.S.C. § 1291 (1958 ed.). We therefore proceed to consider the correctness of the Court of Appeals' judgment.

[The Supreme Court went on to affirm on the merits in all major respects. The dissenting opinion of Justice Goldberg, who agreed with the majority on appealability but disagreed on the merits, is omitted. Also omitted is the dissenting opinion of Justice Harlan, stoutly defending the finality standard and arguing that it was not met in this case. Justice Stewart agreed with Justice Harlan on appealability and with the majority on the merits.] [a]

---

[a] In Coopers & Lybrand v. Livesay, 437 U.S. 463, 477 n.30, 98 S.Ct. 2454, 2462 n. 30 (1978), the Court noted: "If Gillespie were extended beyond the unique facts of that case, § 1291 would be stripped of all significance." Nevertheless, the Court has since cited Gillespie to uphold appealability in American Export Lines v. Alvez, 446 U.S. 274, 279, 100 S.Ct. 1673, 1676 (1980).

APPEALABILITY IN MULTI–CLAIM
AND MULTI–PARTY LITIGATION

Before the Federal Rules, a judgment had to make final disposition with regard to all claims and all parties in the action in order to qualify as appealable under the final decision rule.[b] As a result of great expansion of the potential size of a lawsuit through the liberal joinder provisions of the Federal Rules, it became desirable to permit appeal from orders disposing of some but fewer than all of the claims or parties before the entire action was terminated. It was even more important that a litigant should know just when an order became appealable, or otherwise he might forfeit his right to review by failure to take a timely appeal from an order disposing of some claims or parties. Rule 54(b) was intended to take care of this situation, but it had to be amended twice before it accomplished its purpose.[c] It permits the trial judge expressly to direct entry of a "final judgment" as to fewer than all the claims or parties, but only when he in his discretion makes an "express determination that there is no just reason for delay." If no such certification is made, a litigant is safe not to appeal; if he does file an appeal, it will be dismissed (unless the underlying order is appealable under some other provision or doctrine). If the certification is made, he is put on notice that he should appeal; however, it may occasionally happen that after a Rule 54(b) certification the court of appeals will dismiss the appeal (1) because the trial judge abused his discretion, (2) because there was in fact no final disposition of some claims or parties, or (3) because only a single claim for relief with two or more variants was involved.

Question: (5) What meaning should be given the term "claim for relief" in Rule 54(b)? See 10 Wright, Miller & Kane § 2657.

In short, under Rule 54(b) the trial judge, familiar with the case and the desirability of an immediate appeal, is to act as "dispatcher": he can refuse to allow an appeal or, as long as he stays within certain guidelines, can decide to allow an appeal.

There was controversy over the interpretation and validity of the part of Rule 54(b) that made an order appealable by reason of the trial judge's certification when it would not have been regarded as final before the Rules. The questions were how it was to be read with 28 U.S.C. § 1291 and whether it went beyond the Rules Ena-

---

[b] See Collins v. Miller, 252 U.S. 364, 40 S.Ct. 347 (1920). There were some exceptions to this generalization, but not numerous or drastic ones.

[c] The original Rule failed to provide a reliable guide for determining precisely which orders would be considered final. See Dickinson v. Petroleum Conversion Corp., 338 U.S. 507, 70 S.Ct. 322 (1950). The first amendment, in 1948, was de-signed to reduce this uncertainty by requiring a clear statement of what the trial court intended with reference to finality. After that amendment, the Rule read the same as the present Rule except that the reference to multiple parties, as distinguished from multiple claims, did not appear. The second amendment, in 1961, added the party language in order to resolve some doubts in the cases.

bling Act or the Constitution. These issues were settled, or ducked, by the Supreme Court in Sears, Roebuck & Co. v. Mackey, 351 U.S. 427, 76 S.Ct. 895 (1956), where Justice Burton said:

"[Rule 54(b)] does not supersede any statute controlling appellate jurisdiction. It scrupulously recognizes the statutory requirement of a 'final decision' under § 1291 as a basic requirement for an appeal to the Court of Appeals. It merely administers that requirement in a practical manner in multiple claims actions and does so by rule instead of by judicial decision."

APPEALABILITY OF STATE DECISIONS

With respect to review of state judgments and decrees by the Supreme Court of the United States, 28 U.S.C. § 1257 imposes a finality rule. Surprisingly enough, this has been interpreted in a manner very similar to that hammered out in the cases under § 1291. Indeed, the cases under the two statutes are often cited interchangeably.

Question: (6) Why could one properly term this similarity "surprising"? Would you have expected the § 1257 standard to be more or less hospitable to appeal than that of § 1291?

With respect to review of state decisions by a higher state court, there was, even before the emergence of the one form of action of the codes, a tendency in the states to depart from the old English system with its insistence on a final judgment rule at law and its freedom of interlocutory appeals in equity. Often the state legislation required finality both at law and in equity. The merger of law and equity under the codes seemed to accentuate the trend. But such a position worked serious hardship in long and complicated equity litigation, and the result was a series of attempts to engraft exceptions upon the statutes.

Modern state statutes also reflect both the force of the old law tradition and the dissatisfactions engendered by its strict application. Very common is the theme that the trial court must have rendered a final adjudication winding up the case before review becomes available, but very often a countertheme appears in the way of statutory exceptions. Moreover, the words of the statutes cannot be taken at face value. Judicial decision sometimes belies the statutory language.

Taking into account the several states' statutes and the decisions interpreting them, we find a range from a pretty strict insistence on finality to an extreme liberality in permitting interlocutory appeals, as has been traditional in New York.

In some states appeals are authorized only from "final judgments and orders," but the statute goes on to define final orders in such a way as to include orders that fall far short of the common-law con-

cept of finality. Elsewhere the statutes define in generalized terms
the kinds of interlocutory orders from which appeals may be taken,
such as "any intermediate order involving the merits and necessarily
affecting the judgment" or "any order affecting a substantial right
which determines the action and prevents a judgment." These
phrases are not construed in any uniform fashion and may be either a
narrow or a broad avenue to appeal. The quoted language is often
held not to authorize an appeal from an order sustaining or overruling a demurrer or motion to dismiss for insufficiency of statement,
with the result that the aggrieved party must refrain from pleading
over and submit to a judgment in order to obtain immediate appellate
review of the ruling. A number of legislatures have sought to avoid
some of the uncertainties arising under general definitions by specifying particular interlocutory orders as appealable, such as orders
granting or (less frequently) denying a new trial and orders sustaining or overruling a demurrer. But even such specificity may be
frustrated by judicial decisions invoking what the judges may think
are first principles. For instance, although Iowa had long authorized
an appeal from an "order which . . . sustains or overrules a demurrer," Iowa Code § 12823 (1927), it was held in Devoe v. Dusey,
205 Iowa 1262, 217 N.W. 625 (1928), that "a party may not appeal
from an adverse ruling on a demurrer unless he elects to stand upon
his pleading or suffers judgment for want of pleading or of amendment to his pleading." The court went on to say: "The reason for
such a rule is manifest. . . . To allow an appeal from a mere ruling by the trial court in settling the issues would open the door to
endless appeals to this court from rulings that lack finality." Other
state approaches are to permit interlocutory appeals in the discretion
of either the appellate court or the trial court.

Full appreciation of the appeal system in any state must take account of the possibilities of review by means of extraordinary writs
instead of appeal.

TOPIC C. REVIEW OF INTERLOCUTORY DECISIONS

ETTELSON v. METROPOLITAN LIFE INSURANCE CO., 317 U.S. 188, 63 S.Ct. 163 (1942). After the insured's death, the beneficiaries sued the insurer to recover on life insurance policies. Answering, the insurer alleged fraud by the insured in obtaining the policies and set up a counterclaim to cancel the policies and enjoin further prosecution of the lawsuit. The beneficiaries demanded trial by jury, and they moved to dismiss the counterclaim in order to preserve their jury right.

The district court denied that motion, ordering that the issue raised by the counterclaim should be first tried by the court sitting in equity. On appeal from this ruling, the court of appeals certified the appealability question to the Supreme Court. The Court held the district court's order to be appealable under the predecessor of 28 U.S.C. § 1292(a)(1), because the plaintiffs were "in no different position than if a state equity court had restrained them from proceeding in the law action."

CITY OF MORGANTOWN v. ROYAL INSURANCE CO., 337 U.S. 254, 69 S.Ct. 1067 (1949). After a loss by fire, the insurer brought an action against the insured to reform its fire policy for mutual mistake and to secure a declaration of no liability for the loss by fire; the insurer claimed that both parties had intended the policy to be a windstorm, not a fire, policy. Answering, the insured denied mistake and set up a counterclaim to recover on the policy as written. The insurer replied to the counterclaim by alleging the same facts as in its complaint. The insured demanded trial by jury, in essence requesting the issue posed by the counterclaim to be tried first; the insurer moved to strike the demand.

The district court granted that motion, and the case was set down for trial to the court without a jury. The court of appeals dismissed the appeal from this ruling. The Supreme Court, on certiorari, affirmed, likewise holding the district court's order to be nonappealable.[a]

Question: (1) Was Justice Black, joined in dissent in the Morgantown case by Justice Rutledge, right in saying: "The effect of the Court's holding here is to overrule Ettelson . . ., decided by a unanimous Court in 1942"?

---

[a] On the jury right in this setting, see supra pp. 681–83 and, more generally, Topic E of Part Four.

BALTIMORE CONTRACTORS, INC. v. BODINGER

Supreme Court of the United States, 1955.
348 U.S. 176, 75 S.Ct. 249.

[Under a joint venture agreement, Baltimore Contractors undertook to pay Bodinger 25% of the net profits of certain construction contracts; there was also a clause in the agreement providing that in case of dispute over the calculation of the profits one Frenkil should select one of two named accounting firms, or an accountant named by either of the firms, whose determination would be binding. This suit for an accounting of the profits was commenced by Bodinger in a state court and removed by Baltimore on the basis of diversity of citizenship. Baltimore then moved for a stay under the United States Arbitration Act, 9 U.S.C. § 3.

[The district court denied that motion on the ground that the clause was not in fact one for arbitration but instead dealt only with mathematical disputes, whereas the present complaint charged improper practices by Baltimore such as the use of dummy corporations to inflate the costs. Baltimore appealed to the court of appeals, which dismissed the appeal, citing the Morgantown case. Certiorari was granted.]

MR. JUSTICE REED delivered the opinion of the Court.

.   .   .   .

Congress has long expressed a policy against piecemeal appeals. .   .   . Section 22 of the Judiciary Act of 1789, 1 Stat. 73, 84, provided that appeals in civil actions could be taken to the circuit courts only from final decrees and judgments.[3] .   .   .

.   .   .   .

The provision for interlocutory appeals [that is now 28 U.S.C. § 1292(a)(1)] was first introduced in 1891 when the circuit courts of appeals were established as intermediate appellate courts. 26 Stat. 826. Section 7 of that Act allowed appeals from interlocutory orders in equity "granting or continuing" injunctions, but from those only. Additions to the class of appealable interlocutory orders were made from time to time until the enactment of § 1292 in its present form. No discussion of the underlying reasons for modifying the rule of finality appears in the legislative history, although the changes seem plainly to spring from a developing need to permit litigants to effectually challenge interlocutory orders of serious, perhaps irreparable, consequence. When the pressure rises to a point that influences Congress, legislative remedies are enacted. The Congress is in a position to weigh the competing interests of the dockets of the trial and appellate courts, to consider the practicability of savings in time and expense, and to give proper weight to the effect on litigants. When

---

[3] This enlarged the English rule for there interlocutory appeals were allowed .   .   . in equity, although not at common law.

countervailing considerations arise, interested parties and organizations become active in efforts to modify the appellate jurisdiction. This Court, however, is not authorized to approve or declare judicial modification. It is the responsibility of all courts to see that no unauthorized extension or reduction of jurisdiction, direct or indirect, occurs in the federal system. [Citation omitted.] Any such ad hoc decisions disorganize practice by encouraging attempts to secure or oppose appeals with a consequent waste of time and money. The choices fall in the legislative domain. They are enlargement of the allowable list of appealable interlocutory orders; abandonment of fragmentary appeals; or a general allowance of such appeals in the discretion of the trial judge upon findings of need, with or without the consent or approval of the appellate court.

A series of decisions of this Court has developed the rationale for determining the appealability of such an interlocutory order as this under § 1292 and its predecessors. The appealability of routine interlocutory injunctive orders raised few questions. See George v. Victor Talking Machine Co., 293 U.S. 377, 55 S.Ct. 229. There the statute was clear. It was when stays of proceedings, in distinction to injunctions, were appealed that the issue of jurisdiction became sharp. In Enelow v. New York Life Ins. Co., 293 U.S. 379, 55 S.Ct. 310, a case arising when federal courts had actions at law and proceedings in equity, a complaint at common law on a life insurance policy was met by an answer alleging fraud in the policy's procurement with a prayer for its cancellation and a motion to try the equitable issue first. The motion was granted, and jurisdiction on appeal from that order was approved on this reasoning:

> "The power to stay proceedings in another court appertains distinctively to equity in the enforcement of equitable principles, and the grant or refusal of such a stay by a court of equity of proceedings at law is a grant or refusal of an injunction within the meaning of § 129 [§ 1292]. And, in this aspect, it makes no difference that the two cases, the suit in equity for an injunction and the action at law in which proceedings are stayed, are both pending in the same court, in view of the established distinction between 'proceedings at law and proceedings in equity in the national courts and between the powers of those courts when sitting as courts of law and when sitting as courts of equity.' Per Van Devanter, J., in Griesa v. Mutual Life Ins. Co., 8 Cir., 165 F. 48, 50, 51." 293 U.S. at page 382, 55 S.Ct. at page 311.

After the adoption of the one form of action by the Fed.Rules Civ. Proc., rule 2, we reiterated this ruling in a like case. Ettelson v. Metropolitan Ins. Co., 317 U.S. 188, 63 S.Ct. 163, 164. We said a stay of the complaint until disposition of the fraud issue "is as effective . . . as an injunction . . . . The statute looks to the substantial effect of the order made."

The point was made in the Enelow case that power to stay mere steps within the framework of the litigation before a court differs as to appealability from an injunction prohibiting proceedings in another court. This distinction was applied in City of Morgantown v. Royal Ins. Co., 337 U.S. 254, 69 S.Ct. 1067. . . . We [held] that the Enelow rule did not apply; that since this was an equitable proceeding with a counterclaim to enforce the policy, the decision to hear the reformation issue first without a jury was only a decision as to how to try the case, and therefore was not an interlocutory order in the nature of an injunction. To the argument that the importance of a jury trial justified treating the order of trial as an interlocutory injunction, we answered:

> "Many interlocutory orders are equally important, and may determine the outcome of the litigation, but they are not for that reason converted into injunctions." 337 U.S. at page 258, 69 S.Ct. at page 1069.

The Morgantown case controls here. Whether the District Court was right or wrong in its ruling that the contract provision did not require arbitration proceedings, it was simply a ruling in the only suit pending, actual or fictional. It was a mere order and not an injunction as that word is understood through the Enelow and the Ettelson cases as a stay through equitable principles of a common-law action. This present case is to be distinguished from [Shanferoke Coal & Supply Corp. v. Westchester Service Corp., 293 U.S. 449, 55 S.Ct. 313 (1935),[b]] in the same way. There in a common-law action a motion for an interlocutory injunction on an equitable defense was refused. The order was appealable under Judicial Code § 129. This Court said:

> "For the reasons stated in Enelow v. New York Life Ins. Co., 293 U.S. 379, 55 S.Ct. 310, an order granting or denying a stay based on an equitable defense or cross-bill interposed in an action at law under § 274b,[c] is appealable under § 129." 293 U.S. at page 452, 55 S.Ct. at page 314.

The reliance on the analogy of equity power to enjoin proceedings in other courts has elements of fiction in this day of one form of action. The incongruity of taking jurisdiction from a stay in a law type and denying jurisdiction in an equity type proceeding springs from the persistence of outmoded procedural differentiations. Some simplification would follow from an assumption or denial of jurisdiction in both. The distinction has been applied for years, however, and we conclude that it is better judicial practice to follow the precedents

---

[b] This was a federal action to recover damages for breach of a contract with an arbitration clause. A motion to stay the action until arbitration had been had was denied on the ground that the arbitration clause was applicable only to litigation in the state courts of New York. The order was held appealable.

[c] Old 28 U.S.C. § 398, set out supra p. 396.

which limit appealability of interlocutory orders, leaving Congress to make such amendments as it may find proper.

It is difficult to generalize as to whether interlocutory appeals are or are not advantageous to an efficient administration of justice. A compromise has been worked out by Congress through § 1292. But that compromise does not authorize appeals to simplify litigation. This ruling was a step in controlling the litigation before the trial court, not the refusal of an interlocutory injunction.

Affirmed.

MR. JUSTICE BURTON concurs in the judgment of the Court.

MR. JUSTICE BLACK, with whom MR. JUSTICE DOUGLAS concurs, dissenting.

I think the District Court's order denying a stay is appealable because it is . . . a refusal to grant an interlocutory injunction within the meaning of § 1292. . . . [T]his Court has held that § 1292 makes all stay orders appealable that have the substantial effect of interlocutory injunction orders. Ettelson v. Metropolitan Ins. Co., 317 U.S. 188, 63 S.Ct. 163. The refusal to stay here had that effect. Indeed, the Court seems to admit that this order refusing a stay would be appealable had it been entered by another judge not presiding in this particular case. I agree with the Court that this jurisdictional "incongruity . . . springs from the persistence of outmoded procedural differentiations" that have "elements of fiction" in this modern day. I do not agree that the Court's obeisance to these incongruous fictions is required by congressional enactments.

The Court relies on a purpose of Congress to avoid a waste of time and money incident to repeated "piecemeal" appeals in the same suit. But . . . Congress, in §§ 1291 and 1292, has left the way open for the appeal of many judgments finally deciding collateral and severable issues separately adjudicated in a case. Any rigid rule to the contrary would itself guarantee useless delays and expenses. For two trials, one unnecessary, may take longer and cost more than two appeals where one would do. Take this case for example. It must now go back for a court accounting trial which could be time consuming and expensive to litigants and to the Government. And should petitioner lose on the merits it could undoubtedly appeal. On that review the first question for the appellate court would be whether the order denying arbitration, which the Court now refuses to consider, was right or wrong. If found wrong, the trial court's judgment on the merits would have to be vacated and the case again sent back for determination on the merits—this time by arbitration. In that event the trial the Court now orders will have been wholly futile—not even the litigant who now appears to be successful will have gained anything from it, unless perchance he stands to profit from delay. There is some difficulty, at least, in laying this wasteful procedure at the door of Congress.

CARSON v. AMERICAN BRANDS, INC.

Supreme Court of the United States, 1981.
450 U.S. 79, 101 S.Ct. 993.

JUSTICE BRENNAN delivered the opinion of the Court.

The question presented in this Title VII class action is whether an interlocutory order of the District Court denying a joint motion of the parties to enter a consent decree containing injunctive relief is an appealable order.

I

Petitioners, representing a class of present and former black seasonal employees and applicants for employment at the Richmond Leaf Department of the American Tobacco Company, brought this suit in the United States District Court for the Eastern District of Virginia under 42 U.S.C. § 1981 and Title VII of the Civil Rights Act of 1964, 42 U.S.C. § 2000e et seq. Alleging that respondents [1] had discriminated against them in hiring, promotion, transfer, and training opportunities, petitioners sought a declaratory judgment, preliminary and permanent injunctive relief, and money damages.

After extensive discovery had been conducted and the plaintiff class had been certified,[2] the parties negotiated a settlement and jointly moved the District Court to approve and enter their proposed consent decree. See Fed.Rules Civ.Proc. 23(e). The decree would have required respondents to give hiring and seniority preferences to black employees and to fill one-third of all supervisory positions in the Richmond Leaf Department with qualified blacks. While agreeing to the terms of the decree, respondents "expressly den[ied] any violation of . . . any . . . equal employment law, regulation, or order." Jt.App., at 25a.

The District Court denied the motion to enter the proposed decree. Carson v. American Brands, Inc., 446 F.Supp. 780 (ED Va.1977). Concluding that preferential treatment on the basis of race violated Title VII and the Constitution absent a showing of past or present discrimination, and that the facts submitted in support of the decree demonstrated no "vestiges of racial discrimination," id., at 790, the court held that the proposed decree illegally granted racial preferences to the petitioner class. It further declared that even if present or past discrimination had been shown, the decree would be illegal in

---

[1] Respondents in this case are: American Brands, Inc., which operates the Richmond Leaf Department of the American Tobacco Company; Local 182 of the Tobacco Workers International Union, the exclusive bargaining agent for all hourly paid production unit employees of the Richmond Leaf Department; and the International Union.

[2] The class was certified pursuant to Fed.Rule Civ.Proc. 23(b)(2). It consisted of black persons who were employed as seasonal employees at the Richmond Leaf Department on or after September 9, 1972, and black persons who applied for seasonal employment at the Department on or after that date.

that it would extend relief to *all* present and future black employees of the Richmond Leaf Department, not just to *actual* victims of the alleged discrimination. Id., at 789.

The United States Court of Appeals for the Fourth Circuit, sitting en banc, dismissed petitioners' appeal for want of jurisdiction. Carson v. American Brands, Inc., 606 F.2d 420 (CA4 1979). It held that the District Court's refusal to enter the consent decree was neither a "collateral order" under 28 U.S.C. § 1291, nor an interlocutory order "refusing" an "injunctio[n]" under 28 U.S.C. § 1292(a)(1). Three judges dissented, concluding that the order refusing to approve the consent decree was appealable under 28 U.S.C. § 1292(a)(1).

Noting a conflict in the circuits,[6] we granted certiorari. 447 U.S. 920, 100 S.Ct. 3009 (1980). We hold that the order is appealable under 28 U.S.C. § 1292(a)(1), and accordingly reverse the Court of Appeals.[7]

II

. . . .

Although the District Court's order declining to enter the proposed consent decree did not in terms "refus[e]" an "injunctio[n]," it nonetheless had the practical effect of doing so. Cf. General Electric Co. v. Marvel Rare Metals Co., 287 U.S. 430, 433, 53 S.Ct. 202, 203 (1932). This is because the proposed decree would have permanently enjoined respondents from discriminating against black employees at the Richmond Leaf Department, and would have directed changes in seniority and benefit systems, established hiring goals for qualified blacks in certain supervisory positions, and granted job bidding preferences for seasonal employees. Indeed, prospective relief was at the very core of the disapproved settlement.

For an interlocutory order to be immediately appealable under § 1292(a)(1), however, a litigant must show more than that the order has the practical effect of refusing an injunction. Because § 1292(a)(1) was intended to carve out only a limited exception to the final judgment rule, we have construed the statute narrowly to ensure that appeal as of right under § 1292(a)(1) will be available only in circumstances where an appeal will further the statutory purpose of "permit[ting] litigants to effectually challenge interlocutory orders of serious, perhaps irreparable, consequence." Baltimore Contrac-

[6] Compare Norman v. McKee, 431 F.2d 769 (CA9 1970), cert. denied, 401 U.S. 912, 91 S.Ct. 879 (1971) (refusal to enter consent decree appealable under § 1291), and United States v. City of Alexandria, 614 F.2d 1358 (CA5 1980) (refusal to enter consent decree appealable under § 1292(a)(1)), with Seigal v. Merrick, . . . 590 F.2d 35 [(2d Cir.1978)] (not appealable under § 1291), and Carson v. American Brands, Inc., 606 F.2d 420 (CA4 1979) (not appealable under § 1291 or § 1292(a)(1)). See also In re International House of Pancakes Franchise Litigation, 487 F.2d 303 (CA8 1973) (refusal to enter proposed settlement agreement appealable; no discussion of jurisdictional question).

[7] We therefore need not decide whether the order is also appealable under 28 U.S.C. § 1291.

tors, Inc. v. Bodinger, [348 U.S. 176, 181, 75 S.Ct. 249, 252 (1955)].
Unless a litigant can show that an interlocutory order of the District
Court might have "serious, perhaps irreparable, consequence," and
that the order can be "effectually challenged" only by immediate appeal, the general congressional policy against piecemeal review will
preclude interlocutory appeal.

In Switzerland Cheese Association, Inc. v. E. Horne's Market, Inc.,
385 U.S. 23, 87 S.Ct. 193 (1966), for example, petitioners contended
that the District Court's denial of their motion for summary judgment was appealable under § 1292(a)(1) simply because its practical
effect was to deny them the permanent injunction sought in their
summary judgment motion. Although the District Court order
seemed to fit within the statutory language of § 1292(a)(1), petitioners' contention was rejected because they did not show that the order
might cause them irreparable consequences if not immediately reviewed. The motion for summary judgment sought permanent and
not preliminary injunctive relief and petitioners did not argue that a
denial of summary judgment would cause them irreparable harm
pendente lite. Since permanent injunctive relief might have been obtained after trial, the interlocutory order lacked the "serious, perhaps
irreparable, consequence" that is a prerequisite to appealability under
§ 1292(a)(1).

Similarly, in Gardner v. Westinghouse Broadcasting Co., 437 U.S.
478, 98 S.Ct. 2451 (1978), petitioner in a Title VII sex discrimination
suit sought a permanent injunction against her prospective employer
on behalf of herself and her putative class. After the District Court
denied petitioner's motion for class certification, petitioner filed an
appeal under § 1292(a)(1). She contended that since her complaint
had requested injunctive relief, the court's order denying class certification had the effect of limiting the breadth of the available relief,
and therefore of "refus[ing] a substantial portion of the injunctive
relief requested in the complaint." 437 U.S., at 480, 98 S.Ct., at 2453.

As in Switzerland Cheese, petitioner in Gardner had not filed a
motion for a preliminary injunction and had not alleged that a denial
of her motion would cause irreparable harm. The District Court order thus had "no direct or irreparable impact on the merits of the
controversy." Id., at 482, 98 S.Ct., at 2454. Because the denial of
class certification was conditional, Fed.Rules Civ.Proc. 23(c)(1), and
because it could be effectively reviewed on appeal from final judgment, petitioner could still obtain the full permanent injunctive relief
she requested and a delayed review of the District Court order would
therefore cause no serious or irreparable harm. As Gardner stated:

"The order denying class certification in this case did not have
any such 'irreparable' effect. It could be reviewed both prior to
and after final judgment; it did not affect the merits of petitioner's own claim; and it did not pass on the legal sufficiency of any

claims for injunctive relief." 437 U.S., at 480–481, 98 S.Ct., at 2453–2454 (footnotes omitted).[11]

III

In the instant case, unless the District Court order denying the motion to enter the consent decree is immediately appealable, petitioners will lose their opportunity to "effectually challenge" an interlocutory order that denies them injunctive relief and that plainly has "serious, perhaps irreparable, consequence." First, petitioners might lose their opportunity to settle their case on the negotiated terms. . . . Settlement agreements may . . . be predicated on an express or implied condition that the parties would, by their agreement, be able to avoid the costs and uncertainties of litigation. In this case, that condition of settlement has been radically affected by the District Court. By refusing to enter the proposed consent decree, the District Court effectively ordered the parties to proceed to trial and to have their respective rights and liabilities established within limits laid down by that court. Because a party to a pending settlement might be legally justified in withdrawing its consent to the agreement once trial is held and final judgment entered, the District Court's order might thus have the "serious, perhaps irreparable, consequence" of denying the parties their right to compromise their dispute on mutually agreeable terms.[14]

[11] By contrast, General Electric Co. v. Marvel Rare Metals Co., 287 U.S. 430, 53 S.Ct. 202 (1932), a case in which respondents sought to appeal the District Court's dismissal of their counterclaim for injunctive relief on jurisdictional grounds, concluded that the District Court's order *did* have serious, perhaps irreparable, consequence and that it could not be effectually challenged unless an appeal were immediately taken. The Court noted that the District Court "necessarily decided that upon the facts alleged in the counterclaim defendants were not entitled to an injunction," 287 U.S., at 433, 53 S.Ct., at 204, and that this decision resolved "the very question that, among others, would have been presented to the court upon formal application for an interlocutory injunction." Ibid.

[14] Furthermore, such an order would also undermine one of the policies underlying Title VII. In enacting Title VII, Congress expressed a strong preference for encouraging voluntary settlement of employment discrimination claims. . . .

Moreover, post-judgment review of a District Court's refusal to enter a proposed consent decree raises additional problems. Not only might review come after the prevailing party has sought to withdraw its consent to the agreement, but even if the parties continued to support their decree, the Court of Appeals might be placed in the difficult position of having to choose between ordering the agreed-upon relief or affirming the relief granted by the trial court even when such relief rested on different facts or different judgments with respect to the parties' ultimate liability.

In addition, delaying appellate review until after final judgment would adversely affect the Court of Appeals' ability fairly to evaluate the propriety of the District Court's order. Courts judge the fairness of a proposed compromise by weighing the plaintiff's likelihood of success on the merits against the amount and form of the relief offered in the settlement. See Protective Comm. for Independent Stockholders v. Anderson, 390 U.S. 414, 424–425, 88 S.Ct. 1157, 1163–1164 (1968). They do not decide the merits of the case or resolve unsettled legal questions. Since the likely outcome of a trial is best evaluated in light of the state of facts and perceptions that existed when the proposed consent decree was considered, appellate review would be

There is a second "serious, perhaps irreparable, consequence" of the District Court order that justifies our conclusion that the order is immediately appealable under § 1292(a)(1). In seeking entry of the proposed consent decree, petitioners sought an immediate restructuring of respondents' transfer and promotional policies. They asserted in their complaint that they would suffer irreparable injury unless they obtained that injunctive relief at the earliest opportunity. Because petitioners cannot obtain that relief until the proposed consent decree is entered, any further delay in reviewing the propriety of the District Court's refusal to enter the decree might cause them serious or irreparable harm.

In sum, in refusing to approve the parties' negotiated consent decree, the District Court denied petitioners the opportunity to compromise their claim and to obtain the injunctive benefits of the settlement agreement they negotiated. These constitute "serious, perhaps irreparable, consequences" that petitioners can "effectually challenge" only by an immediate appeal. It follows that the order is an order "refusing" an "injunctio[n]" and is therefore appealable under § 1292(a)(1).

Reversed.[d]

Questions: (2) In a class action for damages, does an appeal under § 1292(a)(1) lie from an order disapproving a proposed settlement that includes an injunctive provision simply forbidding the defendant from violating particular federal laws? See New York v. Dairylea Corp., 698 F.2d 567 (2d Cir.1983) (suggesting no).

(3) Where a decision of a district court is interlocutory, but appealable under § 1292(a)(1), and the party aggrieved does not appeal from the decision, is he foreclosed from any subsequent review of it by the court of appeals? See 9 Moore ¶ 110.18; cf. 15 Wright, Miller & Cooper § 3911, at 498–99.

KRAUS v. BOARD OF COUNTY ROAD COMMISSIONERS

United States Court of Appeals, Sixth Circuit, 1966.
364 F.2d 919.

[Kraus sued the Board for wrongful death of her intestate in an automobile accident, upon the theory that the Board had failed to keep the roads where the accident occurred in reasonable repair. One of the defenses asserted was the failure to give written notice of claim within sixty days of the date of the accident as provided by a

more effective if held prior to the trial court's factfinding rather than after final judgment when the rights and liabilities of the parties have been established.

[d] On remand, the court of appeals ruled in a short opinion that the district court had abused its discretion by refusing to enter the consent decree. 654 F.2d 300 (4th Cir.1981) (in banc) (per curiam).

Michigan statute. A defense motion for summary judgment based on this defense was overruled by the district court on the ground that the statute did not apply to an action for wrongful death. The court inserted in its order a certification for immediate appeal under 28 U.S.C. § 1292(b).]

Before PHILLIPS, EDWARDS and CELEBREZZE, CIRCUIT JUDGES.

PHILLIPS, CIRCUIT JUDGE.

.   .   .   .

Section 1292(b) was enacted in 1958, following a study by a committee of the Judicial Conference of the United States, and was endorsed by the Judicial Conference. The purpose of this legislation was explained in the report of the committee, of which the late Judge Shackelford Miller, Jr., of this court was a member, as follows:

> "[W]e have given consideration to the action taken by the circuit conferences and have reached the conclusion that provision should be made for the allowance of appeals from the interlocutory orders in those exceptional cases where it is desirable that this be done to avoid unnecessary delay and expense and that the danger of opening the door to groundless appeals and piecemeal litigation can be avoided by proper limitations to be included in the amendatory statute. . . .

> "Your Committee is of the view that the appeal from interlocutory orders thus provided should and will be used only in exceptional cases where a decision of the appeal may avoid protracted and expensive litigation, as in antitrust and similar protracted cases, where a question which would be dispositive of the litigation is raised and there is serious doubt as to how it should be decided, as in the recent case of Austrian v. Williams (2 Cir., 198 F.2d 697). It is not thought that district judges would grant the certificate in ordinary litigation which could otherwise be promptly disposed of or that mere question as to the correctness of the ruling would prompt the granting of the certificate. The right of appeal given by the amendatory statute is limited both by the requirement of the certificate of the trial judge, who is familiar with the litigation and will not be disposed to countenance dilatory tactics, and by the resting of final discretion in the matter in the court of appeals, which will not permit its docket to be crowded with piecemeal or minor litigation."

.   .   .   .

Although it is not incumbent upon this court to express our reasons for granting or denying an application for permission to take an interlocutory appeal, we do so in the present case. We conclude that this case is not within the class of interlocutory appeals contemplated by the statute . . . .

The granting of an interlocutory appeal in the present case would not "materially advance the ultimate termination of the litigation."

Many months would be required before the case would be reached for argument on the congested docket of this court. If we grant the appeal and then should affirm the order of the district court based upon the opinion published in 236 F.Supp. 677, the case then would be remanded to the district court for trial on its merits.

On the other hand, it would appear that only a few days would be required for a jury trial and final disposition of the case in the district court. This procedure, which would avoid a piecemeal appeal, is preferable except in the extraordinary type of case contemplated by § 1292(b).

The application for leave to appeal is denied.

Questions: (4) "In the fiscal year 1981 26,362 appeals were taken to the . . . courts of appeals. By contrast trial court certificates under § 1292(b) are made in only about 100 cases a year and the courts of appeals allow interlocutory appeal in about half of those 100 cases." C. Wright, The Law of Federal Courts § 102, at 715–16 (4th ed. 1983). What situations can you suggest in which a § 1292(b) appeal would be appropriate?

(a) Imagine a nonjury action with a long trial in prospect in which, at the start of the testimony, the district judge sustains defendant's objection that an important line of evidence offered by plaintiff is inadmissible. Consider whether appeal under § 1292(b) should be permitted from the judge's ruling.

(b) Imagine a complex action in which, at the pretrial stage, the district judge makes what he sees as a close call in his discretion to stay proceedings on one of the counts of the federal complaint until the rather distant completion of a related state-court action. Consider whether the judge's ruling fits within the criteria specified in § 1292(b). Are any other avenues of appeal open to the plaintiff? See Note, Appellate Review of Stay Orders in the Federal Courts, 72 Colum.L.Rev. 518, 525–36 (1972).

(5) Evaluate the argument that all the foregoing exceptions to the finality standard should be scrapped, and in their place should operate a statute patterned on the "dispatcher" idea of Rule 54(b) but much more broadly applicable: for any order the trial judge, familiar with the litigation and the desirability of an interlocutory appeal, could decide to refuse an immediate appeal or, as long as he respects the statutory guidelines enforced by the appellate court's oversight, could decide to allow an immediate appeal. How, under such a scheme that aims at both accuracy and certainty, could one deal with the problem of a recalcitrant trial judge who refuses an interlocutory appeal for which there is a real need?

TOPIC D. MANDAMUS

ROCHE v. EVAPORATED MILK ASSOCIATION, 319 U.S. 21, 63 S.Ct. 938 (1943). "The question for decision is whether the Circuit Court of Appeals below rightly issued its writ of mandamus to the district court to correct that court's alleged error in striking respondent's pleas in abatement to a criminal indictment." In deciding in the negative, the Supreme Court noted:

"As the jurisdiction of the circuit court of appeals is exclusively appellate, its authority to issue writs of mandamus is restricted by statute to those cases in which the writ is in aid of that jurisdiction. [28 U.S.C. § 1651(a).] Its authority is not confined to the issuance of writs in aid of a jurisdiction already acquired by appeal but extends to those cases which are within its appellate jurisdiction although no appeal has been perfected. Otherwise the appellate jurisdiction could be defeated and the purpose of the statute authorizing the writ thwarted by unauthorized action of the district court obstructing the appeal. [Citations omitted.]

"The common-law writs, like equitable remedies, may be granted or withheld in the sound discretion of the court. [Citations omitted.] Hence the question presented on this record is not whether the court below had power to grant the writ but whether in the light of all the circumstances the case was an appropriate one for the exercise of that power. In determining what is appropriate we look to those principles which should guide judicial discretion in the use of an extraordinary remedy rather than to formal rules rigorously controlling judicial action. Considerations of importance to our answer here are that the trial court, in striking the pleas in abatement, acted within its jurisdiction as a district court; that no action or omission on its part has thwarted or tends to thwart appellate review of the ruling; and that while a function of mandamus in aid of appellate jurisdiction is to remove obstacles to appeal, it may not appropriately be used merely as a substitute for the appeal procedure prescribed by the statute.

"The traditional use of the writ in aid of appellate jurisdiction both at common law and in the federal courts has been to confine an inferior court to a lawful exercise of its prescribed jurisdiction or to compel it to exercise its authority when it is its duty to do so."

LA BUY v. HOWES LEATHER CO., 352 U.S. 249, 77 S.Ct. 309 (1957). This decision came in a large antitrust case brought in the overcrowded United States District Court for the Northern District of Illinois. Judge La Buy had conducted long preliminary proceedings with numerous pretrial motions. At a hearing to set the case for

1242

trial, it appeared that the trial would take six weeks. Judge La Buy remarked that he did not know when he could try the case if it was going to take so long. The next day the judge entered an order on his own motion referring the case to a master to take the evidence and then to report it to the court together with his findings of fact and conclusions of law; the trial before the master was ordered to start on a certain date and to continue with diligence. All parties objected to the reference. Defendants petitioned for a writ of mandamus. The Court of Appeals for the Seventh Circuit granted the writ, just as it did at the same time in an almost identical companion case that had come before Judge La Buy.

On certiorari, the Supreme Court affirmed. Justice Clark, for the Court, said that the courts of appeals had the power to issue writs of mandamus in aid of their appellate jurisdiction. "Since the Court of Appeals could at some stage of the antitrust proceedings entertain appeals in these cases, it has power in proper circumstances . . . to issue writs of mandamus reaching them." Hence, the only real question involved was whether the exercise of the power here was proper. Justice Clark observed that Judge La Buy had referred nine other cases to masters in the previous six years, and "that supervisory control of the District Courts by the Courts of Appeals is necessary to proper judicial administration in the federal system." The Court ruled:

"Under all of the circumstances, we believe the Court of Appeals was justified in finding the orders of reference were an abuse of the petitioner's power under Rule 53(b). They amounted to little less than an abdication of the judicial function depriving the parties of a trial before the court on the basic issues involved in the litigation.

"The use of masters is 'to aid judges in the performance of specific judicial duties, as they may arise in the progress of a cause,' Ex parte Peterson, 1920, 253 U.S. 300, 312, 40 S.Ct. 543, 547, and not to displace the court. The exceptional circumstances here warrant the use of the extraordinary remedy of mandamus."

After quoting Bankers Life & Casualty Co. v. Holland, 346 U.S. 379, 383, 74 S.Ct. 145, 148 (1953) (§ 1651(a) "meant to be used only in the exceptional case where there is clear abuse of discretion or 'usurpation of judicial power' "), the Court said: "Certainly, as the Court of Appeals found here, there was a clear abuse of discretion."

Justice Brennan, with whom Justices Frankfurter, Burton, and Harlan joined, dissented in a sharp opinion. He argued that this was not a case where a court had exceeded or refused to exercise its jurisdiction. Moreover, in his view the language of the majority opinion was unfortunate: it seemed to suggest that the All Writs Act, 28 U.S.C. § 1651(a), "confers an independent appellate power in the Courts of Appeals to review interlocutory orders," in effect allowing "interlocutory appeals by leave of the appellate court."

SCHLAGENHAUF v. HOLDER
Supreme Court of the United States, 1964.
379 U.S. 104, 85 S.Ct. 234.

[A digest of the facts appears supra p. 71. Judge Holder, a United States District Judge for the Southern District of Indiana, ordered defendant Schlagenhauf to submit to the examinations. Schlagenhauf thereupon sought a writ of mandamus from the Court of Appeals for the Seventh Circuit. That court denied the writ, holding that the discovery order was within the power of the district court. The case reached the Supreme Court on certiorari.]

MR. JUSTICE GOLDBERG delivered the opinion of the Court.

. . . .

A threshold problem arises due to the fact that this case was in the Court of Appeals on a petition for a writ of mandamus. Although it is not disputed that we have jurisdiction to review the judgment of the Court of Appeals, 28 U.S.C. § 1254(1) (1958 ed.), respondent urges that the judgment below dismissing the writ be affirmed on the ground that mandamus was not an appropriate remedy.

"The traditional use of the writ in aid of appellate jurisdiction both at common law and in the federal courts has been to confine an inferior court to a lawful exercise of its prescribed jurisdiction . . .," Roche v. Evaporated Milk Ass'n, 319 U.S. 21, 26, 63 S.Ct. 938, 941.

It is, of course, well settled, that the writ is not to be used as a substitute for appeal, Ex parte Fahey, 332 U.S. 258, 259–260, 67 S.Ct. 1558, 1559, even though hardship may result from delay and perhaps unnecessary trial, Bankers Life & Casualty Co. v. Holland, 346 U.S. 379, 382–383, 74 S.Ct. 145, 147–148; [other citations omitted]. The writ is appropriately issued, however, when there is "usurpation of judicial power" or a clear abuse of discretion, Bankers Life & Casualty Co. v. Holland, supra, 346 U.S., at 383, 74 S.Ct., at 148.

Here petitioner's basic allegation was lack of power in a district court to order a mental and physical examination of a defendant. That this issue was substantial is underscored by the fact that the challenged order requiring examination of a defendant appears to be the first of its kind in any reported decision in the federal courts under Rule 35, and we have found only one such modern case in the state courts.[6] The Court of Appeals recognized that it had the power to review on a petition for mandamus the basic, undecided question of whether a district court could order the mental or physical examination of a defendant. We agree that, under these unusual circumstances and in light of the authorities, the Court of Appeals had such power.

[6] Harabedian v. Superior Court, 195 Cal.App.2d 26, 15 Cal.Rptr. 420 (Dist.Ct. App.).

The petitioner, however, also alleged that, even if Rule 35 gives a district court power to order mental and physical examinations of a defendant in an appropriate case, the District Court here exceeded that power in ordering examinations when petitioner's mental and physical condition was not "in controversy" and no "good cause" was shown, both as expressly required by Rule 35. As we read its opinion, the Court of Appeals reached the "in controversy" issue and determined it adversely to petitioner. 321 F.2d, at 51. It did not, however, reach the issue of "good cause," apparently considering that it was not appropriate to do so on a petition for mandamus. Ibid.

We recognize that in the ordinary situation where the sole issue presented is the district court's determination that "good cause" has been shown for an examination, mandamus is not an appropriate remedy, absent, of course, a clear abuse of discretion. See Bankers Life & Casualty Co. v. Holland, supra, 346 U.S., at 383, 74 S.Ct., at 148. Here, however, the petition was properly before the court on a substantial allegation of usurpation of power in ordering any examination of a defendant, an issue of first impression that called for the construction and application of Rule 35 in a new context. The meaning of Rule 35's requirements of "in controversy" and "good cause" also raised issues of first impression. In our view, the Court of Appeals should have also, under these special circumstances, determined the "good cause" issue, so as to avoid piecemeal litigation and to settle new and important problems.

Thus we believe that the Court of Appeals had power to determine all of the issues presented by the petition for mandamus.[8] Normally, wise judicial administration would counsel remand of the cause to the Court of Appeals to reconsider this issue of "good cause." However, in this instance the issue concerns the construction and application of the Federal Rules of Civil Procedure. It is thus appropriate for us to determine on the merits the issues presented and to formulate the necessary guidelines in this area. See Van Dusen v. Barrack, 376 U.S. 612, 84 S.Ct. 805. As this Court stated in Los Angeles Brush Mfg. Corp. v. James, 272 U.S. 701, 706, 47 S.Ct. 286, 288:

> "[W]e think it clear that where the subject concerns the enforcement of the . . . Rules which by law it is the duty of this Court to formulate and put in force . . . it may . . . deal directly with the District Court . . . ."

See McCullough v. Cosgrave, 309 U.S. 634, 60 S.Ct. 703.

This is not to say, however, that, following the setting of guidelines in this opinion, any future allegation that the District Court was in error in applying these guidelines to a particular case makes man-

---

[8] It is not necessary to determine whether or not a refusal by the Court of Appeals to issue the writ, after consideration of the good-cause issue, would have been reversible error. The issuance of this extraordinary writ is itself generally a matter of discretion. See La Buy v. Howes Leather Co., 352 U.S. 249, 260, 77 S.Ct. 309, 315–316; Bankers Life & Casualty Co. v. Holland, supra; 6 Moore, Federal Practice, ¶ 54.10[4] (1953 ed.).

damus an appropriate remedy. The writ of mandamus is not to be used when "the most that could be claimed is that the district courts have erred in ruling on matters within their jurisdiction." Parr v. United States, 351 U.S. 513, 520, 76 S.Ct. 912, 917; see Bankers Life & Casualty Co. v. Holland, supra, 346 U.S., at 382, 74 S.Ct., at 147.

[Proceeding to the merits, the Supreme Court ultimately vacated and remanded. The dissenting opinions of Justice Black, with whom Justice Clark joined, and of Justice Douglas did not discuss the propriety of mandamus and are omitted.]

Mr. Justice Harlan, dissenting.

In my view the Court's holding that mandamus lies in this case cannot be squared with the course of decisions to which the majority at the threshold pays lip service. . . . As the Court recognizes, mandamus, like the other extraordinary writs, is available to correct only those decisions of inferior courts which involve a "usurpation of judicial power" or, what is tantamount thereto, "a clear abuse of discretion"; such a writ "is not to be used as a substitute for appeal." . . .

Mandamus is found to be an appropriate remedy in this instance, however, because (1) petitioner's challenge was based on an asserted lack of power in the District Court to issue the examination order, and (2) that being so, the Court of Appeals had the right also to inquire into the application of the "in controversy" and "good cause" requirements of Rule 35(a), particularly since those issues, like the question of "power," were matters of "first impression" which in "these special circumstances" should be determined by the Court of Appeals "so as to avoid piecemeal litigation and to settle new and important problems." . . .

For me this reasoning is unacceptable. Of course a court of appeals when confronted with a substantial challenge to the power of a district court to act in the premises may proceed to examine that question without awaiting its embodiment in a final judgment, as the Court of Appeals did here by issuing an order to show cause why a writ of mandamus should not issue. But once it is determined that the challenged power did exist, and that the district court acted within the limit of that power, an extraordinary writ should be denied. I know of no case which suggests that a court of appeals' right to consider such a question at an interlocutory stage of the litigation also draws to the court the right to consider other questions—here the "in controversy" and "good cause" issues—which otherwise would not be examinable upon a petition for an extraordinary writ. . . . And, as the Court correctly states, the fact that "hardship may result from delay and perhaps unnecessary trial," . . . is not a factor that makes for the issuance of such a writ.

Manifestly, today's procedural holding, when stripped of its sugarcoating, is born of the Court's belief that the petitioner should not be exposed to the rigors of these examinations before the proper "guidelines" have been established by this tribunal. Understandable as that point of view may be, it can only be indulged at the expense of making a deep inroad into the firmly established federal policy which, with narrow exceptions, permits appellate review only of the final judgments of district courts. To be sure the Court is at pains to warn that what is done today puts an end to future "interlocutory" review of Rule 35 questions. . . . Nevertheless, I find it hard to escape the conclusion that this decision may open the door to the extraordinary writs being used to test any question of "first impression," if it can be geared to an alleged lack of "power" in the district court. . . .

The Court of Appeals having correctly concluded, as this Court now holds and as I agree, that the District Court had power to order the physical and mental examinations of this petitioner, and since I believe that there was no clear abuse of discretion in its so acting, I think the lower court was quite right in denying mandamus, and I would affirm its judgment on that basis.

WILL v. UNITED STATES

Supreme Court of the United States, 1967.
389 U.S. 90, 88 S.Ct. 269.

[Judge Will, a United States District Judge for the Northern District of Illinois, in a pretrial order in a criminal tax-evasion case directed the government to respond to a bill of particulars through which the defendant sought information concerning any of his oral statements relied upon by the prosecution, including identification of the persons to whom they were made, whether those persons were government agents, whether the government had transcripts or memoranda of the statements, and the substance of any of the statements made to government agents. The government refused to comply and, facing dismissal of the indictment, sought a writ of mandamus to compel the judge to vacate his order. The Court of Appeals for the Seventh Circuit at first denied the writ, but on reconsideration reversed itself and issued the writ without opinion. Judge Will's petition for certiorari was granted "because of the wide implications of the decision below for the orderly administration of criminal justice in the federal courts."]

MR. CHIEF JUSTICE WARREN delivered the opinion of the Court.

. . . .

Both parties have devoted substantial argument in this Court to the propriety of petitioner's order. In our view of the case, however, it is unnecessary to reach this question.[1] The peremptory writ of

---

[1] It is likewise unnecessary for us to reach the question whether the writ in the circumstances of this case may be said to issue in aid of an exercise of the

mandamus has traditionally been used in the federal courts only "to confine an inferior court to a lawful exercise of its prescribed jurisdiction or to compel it to exercise its authority when it is its duty to do so." Roche v. Evaporated Milk Assn., 319 U.S. 21, 26, 63 S.Ct. 938, 941 (1943). While the courts have never confined themselves to an arbitrary and technical definition of "jurisdiction," it is clear that only exceptional circumstances amounting to a judicial "usurpation of power" will justify the invocation of this extraordinary remedy. DeBeers Consol. Mines, Ltd. v. United States, 325 U.S. 212, 217, 65 S.Ct. 1130, 1132 (1945). Thus the writ has been invoked where unwarranted judicial action threatened "to embarrass the executive arm of the government in conducting foreign relations," Ex parte Peru, 318 U.S. 578, 588, 63 S.Ct. 793, 799 (1943), where it was the only means of forestalling intrusion by the federal judiciary on a delicate area of federal-state relations, Maryland v. Soper, 270 U.S. 9, 46 S.Ct. 185 (1926), where it was necessary to confine a lower court to the terms of an appellate tribunal's mandate, United States v. United States Dist. Court, 334 U.S. 258, 68 S.Ct. 1035 (1948), and where a district judge displayed a persistent disregard of the Rules of Civil Procedure promulgated by this Court, La Buy v. Howes Leather Co., 352 U.S. 249, 77 S.Ct. 309 (1957); [other citations omitted]. And the party seeking mandamus has "the burden of showing that its right to issuance of the writ is 'clear and indisputable.'" Bankers Life & Cas. Co. v. Holland, 346 U.S. 379, 384, 74 S.Ct. 145, 148 (1953); [other citation omitted].

We also approach this case with an awareness of additional considerations which flow from the fact that the underlying proceeding is a criminal prosecution. . . . This general policy against piecemeal appeals takes on added weight in criminal cases . . . . It is enough to note that we approach the decision in this case with an awareness of the constitutional precepts that a man is entitled to a speedy trial and that he may not be placed twice in jeopardy for the same offense.

In light of these considerations and criteria, neither the record before us nor the cryptic order of the Court of Appeals justifies the invocation of the extraordinary writ in this case.

We do not understand the Government to argue that petitioner was in any sense without "jurisdiction" to order it to file a bill of particulars.[6] . . .

Court of Appeals' appellate jurisdiction. See 28 U.S.C. § 1651; Roche v. Evaporated Milk Assn., 319 U.S. 21, 25, 63 S.Ct. 938, 941 (1943). Compare In re United States, 348 F.2d 624 (1st Cir. 1965), with United States v. Bondy, 171 F.2d 642 (2d Cir. 1948). In our view, even assuming that the possible future appeal in this case would support the Court of Appeals' mandamus jurisdiction, it was an abuse of discretion for the court to act as it did in the circumstances of this case.

[6] Nor do we understand the Government to argue that a judge has no "power" to enter an erroneous order. Acceptance of this semantic fallacy would undermine the settled limitations upon the power of an appellate court to review interlocutory orders. Neither "jurisdiction" nor "power" can be said to "run the

The Government seeks instead to justify the employment of the writ in this instance on the ground that petitioner's conduct displays a "pattern of manifest noncompliance with the rules governing federal criminal trials."   .   .   .

The action of the Court of Appeals cannot, on the record before us, bear the weight of this justification.   There is absolutely no foundation in this record for the Government's assertions concerning petitioner's practice.   .   .   .

.   .   .   .

Even more important in our view, however, than these deficiencies in the record is the failure of the Court of Appeals to attempt to supply any reasoned justification of its action.   Had the Government in fact shown that petitioner adopted a policy in deliberate disregard of the criminal discovery rules and that this policy had proved seriously disruptive of the efficient administration of criminal justice in the Northern District of Illinois, it would have raised serious questions under this Court's decision in La Buy v. Howes Leather Co., 352 U.S. 249, 77 S.Ct. 309 (1957).[11]   .   .   .

.   .   .   .

Mandamus is not a punitive remedy.   The entire thrust of the Government's justification for mandamus in this case, moreover, is that the writ serves a vital corrective and didactic function.   While these aims lay at the core of this Court's decisions in La Buy and Schlagenhauf v. Holder, 379 U.S. 104, 85 S.Ct. 234 (1964), we fail to see how they can be served here without findings of fact by the issuing court and some statement of the court's legal reasoning.   A mandamus from the blue without rationale is tantamount to an abdication of the very expository and supervisory functions of an appellate court upon which the Government rests its attempt to justify the action below.

gauntlet of reversible errors."   Bankers Life & Cas. Co. v. Holland, 346 U.S. 379, 382, 74 S.Ct. 145, 147 (1953).   Courts faced with petitions for the peremptory writs must be careful lest they suffer themselves to be misled by labels such as "abuse of discretion" and "want of power" into interlocutory review of nonappealable orders on the mere ground that they may be erroneous.   "Certainly Congress knew that some interlocutory orders might be erroneous when it chose to make them nonreviewable."   De Beers Consol. Mines, Ltd. v. United States, 325 U.S. 212, 223, 225, 65 S.Ct. 1130, 1136 (1945) (dissenting opinion of Mr. Justice Douglas).

[11] The Government also places reliance on Schlagenhauf v. Holder, 379 U.S. 104,

85 S.Ct. 234 (1964), arguing that it "reaffirmed" La Buy.   Insofar as it did so, the case does not help the Government here, since we have no quarrel with La Buy, which is simply inapposite where there is no showing of a persistent disregard of the federal rules.   And it cannot be contended that Schlagenhauf on its facts supports an invocation of mandamus in this case.   The Court there did note that the various questions concerning the construction of Rule 35 were new and substantial, but it rested the existence of mandamus jurisdiction squarely on the fact that there was real doubt whether the District Court had any power at all to order a defendant to submit to a physical examination.

The peremptory common-law writs are among the most potent weapons in the judicial arsenal. "As extraordinary remedies, they are reserved for really extraordinary causes." Ex parte Fahey, 332 U.S. 258, 260, 67 S.Ct. 1558, 1559 (1947). There is nothing in the record here to demonstrate that this case falls into that category, and thus the judgment below cannot stand. What might be the proper decision upon a more complete record, supplemented by the findings and conclusions of the Court of Appeals, we cannot and do not say. Hence the writ is vacated and the cause is remanded to the Court of Appeals for the Seventh Circuit for further proceedings not inconsistent with this opinion.

It is so ordered.

MR. JUSTICE MARSHALL took no part in the consideration or decision of this case.

[The concurring opinion of Justice Black is omitted.]

WILL v. CALVERT FIRE INSURANCE CO., 437 U.S. 655, 98 S.Ct. 2552 (1978). The same Judge Will stayed in large part a federal action until the completion of previously commenced and substantially identical proceedings in state court. He refused to certify an interlocutory appeal pursuant to 28 U.S.C. § 1292(b). Calvert, the plaintiff, then petitioned for a writ of mandamus. The Court of Appeals for the Seventh Circuit granted the writ and directed Judge Will to proceed with the federal action. On certiorari, the Supreme Court reversed.

The question of whether the district court had the power to stay the federal action in these particular circumstances seriously split the Supreme Court. In the plurality opinion, Justice Rehnquist ruled that the abstention order was a matter committed to the discretion of the district judge.

On the other hand, there seemed to be little disagreement on the standard for granting mandamus. On this Justice Rehnquist wrote:

"The correct disposition of this case hinges in large part on the appropriate standard of inquiry to be employed by a court of appeals in determining whether to issue a writ of mandamus to a district court. On direct appeal, a court of appeals has broad authority to 'modify, vacate, set aside or reverse' an order of a district court, and it may direct such further action on remand 'as may be just under the circumstances.' 28 U.S.C. § 2106. By contrast, under the All Writs Act, 28 U.S.C. § 1651(a), courts of appeals may issue a writ of mandamus only when 'necessary or appropriate in aid of their respective jurisdictions.' Whereas a simple showing of error may suffice to obtain a reversal on direct appeal, to issue a writ of mandamus under such circumstances 'would undermine the settled limitations upon the power of an appellate court to review interlocutory orders.' Will v. United States, 389 U.S. 90, 98 n. 6, 88 S.Ct. 269, 275 n. 6 (1967).

"As we have repeatedly reaffirmed in cases such as Kerr v. United States District Court, 426 U.S. 394, 402, 96 S.Ct. 2119, 2123 (1976), and Bankers Life & Cas Co. v. Holland, 346 U.S. 379, 382, 74 S.Ct. 145, 147 (1953), the 'traditional use of the writ in aid of appellate jurisdiction both at common law and in the federal courts has been to confine an inferior court to a lawful exercise of its prescribed jurisdiction or to compel it to exercise its authority when it is its duty to do so.' Roche v. Evaporated Milk Assn., 319 U.S. 21, 26, 63 S.Ct. 938, 941 (1943). Calvert makes no contention that petitioner has exceeded the bounds of his jurisdiction. Rather, it contends that the District Court, in entering the stay order, has refused 'to exercise its authority when it is its duty to do so.' Ibid. There can be no doubt that, where a district court persistently and without reason refuses to adjudicate a case properly before it, the Court of Appeals may issue the writ 'in order that [it] may exercise the jurisdiction of review given by law.' Insurance Co. v. Comstock, 16 Wall. 258, 270 (1873). 'Otherwise the appellate jurisdiction could be defeated and the purpose of the statute authorizing the writ thwarted by unauthorized action of the district court obstructing the appeal.' Roche, supra, 319 U.S., at 25, 63 S.Ct., at 941.

"To say that a court of appeals has the power to direct a district court to proceed to judgment in a pending case 'when it is its duty to do so,' id., at 26, 63 S.Ct., at 941, states the standard but does not decide this or any other particular case. It is essential that the moving party satisfy 'the burden of showing that its right to issuance of the writ is "clear and indisputable." ' Bankers Life & Cas. Co., supra, 346 U.S., at 384, 74 S.Ct., at 148, quoting United States v. Duell, 172 U.S. 576, 582, 19 S.Ct. 286, 287 (1899). Judge Will urges that Calvert does not have a 'clear and indisputable' right to the adjudication of its claims in the District Court without regard to the concurrent state proceedings."

Justice Rehnquist then explained his view that the stay was a discretionary matter. Finally returning to the standard for granting mandamus, he concluded:

"Although the District Court's exercise of its discretion may be subject to review and modification in a proper interlocutory appeal, [citation omitted], we are convinced that it ought not to be overridden by a writ of mandamus.[7] Where a matter is committed to the discre-

---

[7] Although in at least one instance we approved the issuance of the writ upon a mere showing of abuse of discretion, La Buy v. Howes Leather Co., 352 U.S. 249, 257, 77 S.Ct. 309, 314 (1957), we warned soon thereafter against the dangers of such a practice. 'Courts faced with petitions for the peremptory writs must be careful lest they suffer themselves to be misled by labels such as "abuse of discretion" and "want of power" into interlocutory review of nonappealable orders on the mere ground that they may be erroneous.' Will, supra, 389 U.S., at 98 n. 6, 88 S.Ct., at 275 n. 6.

Beacon Theatres, Inc. v. Westover, 359 U.S. 500, 79 S.Ct. 948 (1959), is not to the contrary. Both the Court and the dissenters agreed that mandamus should issue to protect a clear right to a jury trial. Id., at 511, 79 S.Ct., at 957; ibid. (Stewart, J., dissenting). The Court simply concluded that it was 'not permissible,'

tion of a district court, it cannot be said that a litigant's right to a particular result is 'clear and indisputable.' "

Justice Blackmun wrote a cryptic opinion concurring in the judgment, but shedding no light on the subject of mandamus.

Justice Brennan, writing for a group of four dissenters, concluded that the district court had no authority to issue its stay order. On mandamus Justice Brennan wrote:

"Whether evaluated under the 'clear abuse of discretion' standard set forth in La Buy v. Howes Leather Co., 352 U.S. 249, 257, 77 S.Ct. 309, 314 (1957), or under the prong of Will v. United States, 389 U.S. 90, 95, 88 S.Ct. 269, 273 (1967), and Roche v. Evaporated Milk Assn., 319 U.S. 21, 26, 63 S.Ct. 938, 941 (1943), that permits the use of mandamus 'to compel [an inferior court] to exercise its authority when it is its duty to do so,' the issuance of the writ of mandamus by the Court of Appeals was proper . . . ."

Questions: (1) Adopting Justice Rehnquist's rationale in Will v. Calvert Fire Ins. Co., the Supreme Court summarily reversed the court of appeals' issuance of a writ of mandamus overturning the trial judge's grant of a new trial. Allied Chem. Corp. v. Daiflon, Inc., 449 U.S. 33, 101 S.Ct. 188 (1980) (per curiam) ("In short, our cases have answered the question as to the availability of mandamus in situations such as this with the refrain: 'What never? Well, *hardly* ever!' "). In what circumstances would granting a new trial warrant mandamus? See Central Microfilm Serv. Corp. v. Basic/Four Corp., 688 F.2d 1206, 1212 (8th Cir.1982) (issuing mandamus to overturn grant of new trial and observing that "a district court's action generally must be 'blatantly wrong' to justify mandamus relief"), cert. denied, 103 S.Ct. 1191 (1983).

(2) Given that mandamus is available in certain circumstances—that is, the case meets the threshold test emerging from these Supreme Court decisions—what considerations should influence the court of appeals' discretion in issuing mandamus? Should they be the benefits and costs of immediate review? Do they include considering the supervisory and advisory functions suggested by La Buy and Schlagenhauf? Will not such considerations inevitably affect the threshold decision on availability of mandamus?

Observe that mandamus was used in the following Supreme Court cases referred to earlier in this casebook: Colgrove v. Battin, p. 99; Beacon Theatres, Inc. v. Westover, p. 683; Dairy Queen, Inc. v. Wood, p. 691; Hoffman v. Blaski, p. 915; and Van Dusen v. Barrack, p. 918. Lower-court cases in which mandamus was used include: Reserve Mining Co. v. Lord, p. 275; Webster Eisenlohr, Inc. v. Kalodner, p. 276; Smoot v. Fox, p. 568; and Bruckman v. Hollzer, p. 677. Nevertheless, 16 Wright, Miller & Cooper § 3934, at 241, observes

id., at 508, 79 S.Ct., at 955, for the District Court to postpone a jury trial until after most of the relevant issues had been settled in an equitable action before the court. Here, we have repeatedly recognized that it is permissible for a district court to defer to the concurrent jurisdiction of a state court.

that "stern admonitions that the writs remain reserved for extraordinary situations have been effective in preventing a debilitating rush of petitioners. Substantial benefits have been obtained at seemingly acceptable costs. With considerable luck, this may always be so."

*

INDEX

References are to Pages

ABATEMENT
See also Defenses and Objections.
Pendency of a prior action, 965, 973.
Plea in, common-law, 347–348.

ABSTENTION
Pending state proceedings, 1241, 1250–1252.
Unsettled state law, 216.

ACCOUNTING
Equitable relief, 378, 407.
Jury right, 695–697, 710–711.

ADDITUR
Generally, 624–631.

ADJUDICATION
See also Jurisdiction.
Abandonment of, 281–291.
Authority for, 712–955.
Nature of, 253–298.

ADJUDICATION ON THE MERITS
Generally, 108, 982–990.
Dismissal for failure to prosecute or to obey court order or rule, 988–989.
Dismissal on time defense, 962, 982–983, 989–990, 1011.
Judgment on demurrer, 983–988.

ADMIRALTY RULES
Federal Rules, part of, 22–23.

ADMISSIONS
Evidence, 74–75, 122–123.
Requests for, discovery, 69, 75, 76, 490.

ADVERSARY SYSTEM
See also Case Management; Public Law Litigation.
Aims, 253–266.
Alterations and alternatives, 266–291.
Advocate, role of, 266–271.
Alternative dispute resolution, 280–291.
Judge, role of, 272–280.
Comparative study, 291–298.

ADVOCATE
See Attorney.

AFFIRMATIVE DEFENSES
Generally, 32–33, 39, 40, 42–43, 45–46, 461–463.
Contributory negligence, see Contributory Negligence.
Motion to strike a defense, 46, 84–85, 92, 451.
Pendency of a prior action, 965, 973.
Res judicata, 990–993, 1012, 1047–1048.
Statute of limitations, see Statute of Limitations.

ALL WRITS ACT
Extraordinary writs, 72, 157, 158–159, 1242–1253.

ALTERNATIVE DISPUTE RESOLUTION
See also Arbitration.
Generally, 28, 280–291, 305.

AMENDMENT OF PLEADINGS
Generally, 42–43, 52–56, 426–431.
At or after trial, 53, 84, 415–416, 426–431, 983.
Before trial, 52–53, 452–454.
Counterclaims, omitted, 47, 470.
Interplay with motion to dismiss, 452–454.
Relation back of, 53–56, 233–234, 235, 416, 470.
To conform to evidence, 53, 84, 415–416, 426–428, 430–431, 983.

AMOUNT IN CONTROVERSY
See also Subject-Matter Jurisdiction.
Costs sanction, 748–749.
Jurisdictional amount, 747–755.
Class actions, 194, 751–755, 1155.
Interpleader, 188.
Quasi in rem cases, 793.

ANCILLARY JURISDICTION
See also Subject-Matter Jurisdiction.
Generally, 725–739.
Impleader, 726–739, 1196–1199.
Interpleader, 1210.
Intervention, 1196–1199.
Jurisdictional amount, 754–755.

ANCILLARY VENUE
Generally, 905, 1210.

ANSWER
See also Counterclaims; Defenses and Objections.
Generally, 40–43, 456–464.
Reply to, see Reply.
Verification, 456.

APPEARANCES
General and special, 792, 796, 802, 807–810, 902.
Limited, 792, 793–795, 858, 872.
Restricted, 793–794, 807–808, 810, 833, 903, 1211–1212.

APPELLATE REVIEW
Generally, 16–17, 154–160, 175–176, 1213–1253.
Appealable and reviewable distinguished, 652.
Appellate jurisdiction, 162.
Certiorari, 16–17, 159–160, 176.
Change of theory on appeal, 411–419.
Class actions, 1155–1156, 1223, 1235–1239.
Collateral orders, 1221–1224.
Contempt orders, 16, 515–516, 760–771, 1224.
"Correctness review," 1213–1214.
Courts of appeals, 154–159.
Procedure, 20–21, 156.
"Death knell" rationale, 1155, 1224.
Discovery orders, 16, 514–516.
Extraordinary writs, 72, 1242–1253.
Facts in nonjury cases, 648–650.
Federal Rules of Appellate Procedure, 20–21, 156, 397.
Final decision rule, 154–155, 176, 1220–1229.
"Institutional review," 1213–1214.
Interlocutory decisions, 155, 454, 1230–1241.
Certification, 155, 1239–1241.
Injunctions, 155, 1230–1239.
Mandamus, 72, 1242–1253.
Multi-party and multi-claim litigation, 155, 1227–1228, 1241.
New trials, 636–648, 657–664, 1252.
Old modes of review,
Equity, 391, 648, 960, 1217–1219.
Law, 387–388, 1215–1217.
Reviewability, 652, 1214–1215.
State decisions, 175–176, 716, 1228–1229.
Stay pending appeal, 157–159, 160.
Supreme Court, 16–17, 21, 159–160, 175–176, 716, 1228.

ARBITRATION
Generally, 28, 212–214, 240, 283–284, 1231–1234.

ASSUMPSIT
Common counts, 343–344, 442–443.

ASSUMPSIT—Cont'd
General and special, 339–346.
Waiver of tort, 344–345, 403–407.

ATTACHMENT
Jurisdictional basis, 180, 788–791, 792, 856–870, 872–877.
Provisional remedy, 92–94.
Right to prior notice, 94, 942–952.

ATTORNEY
Communicating with adverse party, 492.
Competence, 29, 83, 622.
Confidentiality, 57, 117.
Conflict of interest, 1169–1172, 1223.
Discovering in good faith, 59, 512.
Duty of disclosure, 266–271.
Adverse facts, 266–268.
Adverse law, 268–269.
Duty to supplement responses, discovery, 72–73, 75.
Fees, 141–144, 697–698, 1021–1023, 1166–1167.
Fiduciary duty, 1021–1023.
Neglect, 988–989.
Pleading in good faith, 38, 85, 457–460, 749, 1112.
Role of advocate, 254–260, 266–271.
Work product, 58, 472–493, 495–496.
Zealousness, 83, 974–975.

BAR AND MERGER
See Res Judicata.

BILL OF PARTICULARS
Clarification of complaint, 449.

BILL OF PEACE
Equitable relief, 375, 568, 1114, 1144, 1208–1209.

BOND
Costs on appeal, 156.
Penal, equitable relief, 366–367.
Provisional remedies, 94, 943–949.
Stays pending appeal, 157, 159.
Supersedeas, 157.

BREACH OF PROMISE
See also Contracts.
Remedies for, 139–140, 337–346, 366–372.
Assumpsit, see Assumpsit.
Covenant, 338.
Debt, 333, 337–338.
Specific performance, 140, 367–372, 785–788.

BURDEN OF ALLEGATION
Generally, 32–33, 461–463.

BURDEN OF PROOF
Generally, 32–33, 107, 461–463, 539–553.
Allocation of, 541–542.

BURDEN OF PROOF—Cont'd
Degree of persuasion, see Preponderance of the Evidence.
Directed verdict, see Directed Verdict.
Diversity actions, 205–206.
England, historical development, 312–313.
Meaning of, 107, 539–541.
  Persuasion-burden, 539–541.
  Production-burden, 539–541.
Presumptions, see Presumptions.
Prima facie case, 543–548.
Standard of proof, see Preponderance of the Evidence.

CASE
Action on the, 318–331, 334, 339, 401.

CASE MANAGEMENT
  See also Adversary System.
  Generally, 517–538.
Discovery conferences, 77, 527.
Pretrial conferences, 77–84, 517–538.
Supervision of discovery, 499–516.

CAUSE OF ACTION
  See also Claim.
Meaning of, 37–38, 56, 723, 757, 966.
Pleading of, 436–443.

CERTIFICATION
Appellate review, 155, 159, 1227–1228, 1239–1241.
Questions of state law, 216–217.

CERTIORARI
Appellate review, 16–17, 159–160, 176.

CHANCERY COURT
See Equity.

CHANCERY DIVISION
See England.

CHOICE OF LAW
Controlling law, state or federal, 196–252.
  Amenability to suit, 893–904.
  Arbitration, 212–214, 240.
  Burden of proof, 205–206.
  Conflict of laws, 206–207, 234–235.
  Congressional role, 241–242.
  Determination of state law, 212–217.
  Directed verdict, 592.
  "Door-closing" statute, 211, 231–233.
  Erie doctrine, 196–241.
  Evidence rules, 116–117, 118, 241–242, 552.
  Federal adoption of state law, 93, 151–154, 244–247.
  Federal common law, 242–247.
  Federal Rules, 220–231, 233–234, 235–239.
  Interpleader, 1212.

CHOICE OF LAW—Cont'd
  Interstate waters, 247–248.
  Joinder, 1105, 1113.
  Jury trial, 217–220, 239–241, 248–250, 251–252, 592, 596, 608–609, 647–648, 697–698.
  Limited appearance, 795.
  Local action, 912.
  Pleading, 206, 250–251, 434, 447, 461–462.
  Presumptions, 552.
  Relation back of amendment, 233–234, 235.
  "Reverse" Erie, 247–252.
  Rules of Decision Act, 7, 197, 199.
  Service of process, 220–231.
  Standard of proof, 556.
  Statute of limitations, 207–211, 235–239, 244, 299–301.
  Swift doctrine, 196–197.
  Venue, 905, 912.
Methodology, 206–207, 234–235, 873, 924–926, 1075–1078.
Recognition and enforcement of judgments, 715, 797, 1078, 1082, 1088.
Transfer of venue, after, 918–919, 920–921.

CIRCUIT COURTS OF APPEALS
United States, 12, 163.

CITIZENSHIP
See Diversity of Citizenship Cases.

CIVIL ACTIONS
Distinguished from criminal action, 1.
Nature of, 1–3.
One form of, 299–305, 391–397, 407–408.

CIVIL RIGHTS ACTIONS
Appeals, 1235.
Attorneys' fees, 144.
Authority to adjudicate, 943.
Parties, 1121, 1127, 1167.
Pretrial, 504, 517.
Res judicata, 978, 987, 1034, 1061, 1078.
Section 1983, text of, 979.
Statute of limitations, 244.
Trial, 543, 670, 673.

CLAIM
  See also Complaint; "Transactional" View.
Dimensions of, 961–982.
Joinder, see Joinder of Claims.
Meaning of, 37–38, 56, 723, 757, 961–982, 1227.
Pleading of, 31–38, 436–454.
Splitting of, 961–982.

CLAIM PRECLUSION
See Res Judicata.

CLASS ACTIONS
Generally, 191–194, 1114–1188.
Adequate representation, 191–192, 1114–1127, 1173–1179.
Appealability, 1155–1156, 1223, 1235–1239.
Attorneys' fees, 1166–1167.
Background, 1114–1115.
Collateral attack, 1126–1127.
Federal Rule 23,
Mechanics of, 193, 1144–1172, 1179–1182.
1938 version, 1115–1120.
1966 revision, 1120–1121.
Scope of, 192–193, 1127–1144, 1173–1179.
Fluid recovery, 1149–1150.
Jurisdiction, 194, 751–755, 1155.
Jury right, 680, 703.
Notice, 193, 1144–1155, 1156–1160, 1164–1165, 1167, 1181.
Public law litigation, 1172–1188.
Reform, 1182–1188.
Res judicata, 191–193, 1032, 1114–1127.
Settlement, 193, 279, 1161–1172, 1223, 1235–1239.
Shareholders' derivative actions, 194.
Statute of limitations, 1152.
Unincorporated associations, actions relating to, 194.

"CLEAN–UP" DOCTRINE
Equitable relief, 380–381.
Jury right, 675, 676.

CODE OF PROFESSIONAL RESPONSIBILITY
See Attorney.

CODE PLEADING
Generally, 393–394, 420, 436–443, 447–448.

COGNOVIT NOTE
Due process, 952–955.

COLLATERAL ATTACK
Generally, 714–715, 796–798, 1082–1093.

COLLATERAL ESTOPPEL
See Issue Preclusion.

COMMENCEMENT OF ACTION
See Complaint.

COMMON COUNTS
See also Assumpsit.
Generally, 343–344, 442–443.

COMMON LAW
See also Common-Law Pleading;
Merger of Law and Equity.
Appellate review, 387–388, 1215–1217.
Attaint, 571.

COMMON LAW—Cont'd
Court system, 21, 98, 302, 306–317, 354–355, 384–388, 393, 1216.
Common Pleas, 316, 354, 385–386, 618.
Contrasted with equity system, 21, 354–356, 384–391.
Deficiencies, 355–366, 384–388.
Early courts, 306–307, 313, 315.
Exchequer Chamber, 387–388, 1216.
Exchequer Court, 316, 355, 386, 618.
House of Lords, 387, 393, 1216.
Nisi prius, 306, 315, 348, 651, 1215–1216.
Queen's Bench, 316, 354–355, 385, 618.
Superior courts, 98, 316, 393.
Demurrer to the evidence, 568–569, 1216.
Evidence of interested witnesses, 115, 379, 387, 392, 668.
Forms of action at, 299–346, 385–387, 392.
Types: real, personal, and mixed, 316–317, 385–386, 392.
Writs, see individual entries.
Nature of, 2, 795.
Procedure, 302–303, 346–353, 386–388.
Prooftaking,
Jury, 98–99, 302, 312, 314–315, 333, 338, 356, 605, 607, 666–669.
Oath, ordeal, and battle, 264, 312–314.
Reforms, 351–353, 391–393.
Relief, 139–140, 303, 379.
Retraxit, 1006.
Special case, 609, 1216–1217.

COMMON–LAW PLEADING
Generally, 346–353.
Declarations, 346–347.
Responses to, 347–348.
Demurrers, 347, 349–350, 352, 436, 463–464.
Departures, 349, 471.
Dilatory pleas, 347–348.
Pleas in abatement, 347–348.
Pleas to jurisdiction, 347.
Joinder of causes of action, 351, 386.
Motions for judgment n.o.v., 349, 651, 1216.
Motions in arrest of judgment, 349, 651, 1216.
Plea of general issue, 352–353, 459.
Pleas in bar, 348.
Confession and avoidance, 348.
Traverse, 348.
Rebutter, 349.
Recoupment, 464–465.
Reforms, 351–353, 391–392.
Formal defects, 351–352.
Hilary Rules, 353, 392.
Multiple pleas, 352.
Plea of general issue, 352–353.
Variance, correction of, 352, 422–426.
Rejoinder, 349.
Replication, 348, 352.

COMMON–LAW PLEADING—Cont'd
Separate counts, 352, 426.
Setoff, 465–466, 727.
Singleness of issue, 346, 352–353.
Subsidiary rules, 350–351, 431–432.
Surrebutter, 349.
Surrejoinder, 349.
Variances, 352, 422–426.

COMMON PLEAS COURT
See Common Law.

COMPARATIVE LAW
See also England; Germany.
Generally, 28, 296, 298.

COMPARATIVE NEGLIGENCE
See Contributory Negligence.

COMPETENCY
See Evidence; Subject-Matter Jurisdiction.

COMPLAINT
See also Claim.
Generally, 14, 31–38, 432–459.
Alternative and inconsistent pleading, 36–38.
Battery action, 2, 32–34.
Burden of allegation, 32–33, 461–463.
Clarification of, 449–450.
Bill of particulars, 449.
Motion for more definite statement, 39, 41, 43, 449–450.
Code pleading, 393–394, 420, 436–443, 447–448.
Content of, 31, 454–455.
Contract action, 438.
Elements of, 436.
Counts and paragraphs, 36–37, 448–449.
Defensive matter in, 445–448.
Demand for judgment, 139, 454–455, 748–749.
Fact pleading, 420, 436–443.
Common counts, 442–443.
Pros and cons, 438–440.
Failure to state a claim, defense of, 38–45, 84–85, 92, 451–454.
Fraud and mistake, pleading of, 33.
Issue pleading, 346, 420.
Joinder of claims, see Joinder of Claims.
Joinder of parties, see Parties.
Motion to strike, 39, 41, 43, 450–451.
Negligence action, 32, 438.
Elements of, 436.
Notice pleading, 420–422.
Service of, 179.
Slander action, 436–438.
Special damages, pleading of, 432–435.
Specificity required, 33–36, 420–422, 431–445.
"Theory of pleadings" doctrine, 408–411.
Change of theory on appeal, 411–419.

COMPLAINT—Cont'd
Time and place, allegations of, 431–432.
Verification, 456–459.

CONFLICT OF LAWS
See Choice of Law; Jurisdiction.

CONFORMITY ACT
Procedure, 7, 18–19, 395–397.

CONSENT
Basis of judicial jurisdiction, 41–42, 801–805, 811, 812–813, 865, 869–870, 891, 955.
Notice, waiver, 952–955.
Service, waiver, 41–42, 802.
Subject-matter jurisdiction, waiver, 41, 712–714.
Venue, waiver, 41–42, 905, 955.

CONSENT JUDGMENT
Res judicata effects, 1006–1008.

CONTEMPT
Generally, 15–16, 151, 381–382.
Appealability, 515–516, 1224.
Power to punish disobedience of court order, 760–771.

CONTRACTS
See also Breach of Promise.
Complaint, 438.
Elements of, 436.
Damages, 139–140.
Penal bond, 366–367.
Specific performance of, 140, 367–372, 785–788.

CONTRIBUTION
Judgments, 189, 1037, 1109.

CONTRIBUTORY NEGLIGENCE
Affirmative defense, 32–33, 107, 462–463, 1003.
Comparative negligence, 32, 175, 462, 634, 1109.

CONVERSION
See Trover.

CORPORATIONS
See also Shareholders' Derivative Actions.
Citizenship, diversity cases, 171–173.
Jurisdiction over,
Domestic, 811.
Foreign, 805, 812–833, 859.
Residence, venue, 177–178, 905.

COSTS
Awarding of, 141–144.
Direct and error, 262.
Discovery, 61, 64, 69, 75–76, 499–503, 512.

COSTS—Cont'd
Jurisdiction over things, 791.
Previously dismissed actions, 568.

COUNTERCLAIMS
Generally, 47–52, 464–470.
Compulsory, 47–48, 795, 995–1000.
Federal Tort Claims Act, 469.
Field Code, 394, 403–405, 466.
Jury right, 680–691.
Omitted, 47, 470.
Permissive, 48, 990–993.
Personal jurisdiction, 806–807, 810.
Recoupment, 464–465.
Recovery on, 52, 466.
Reply, see Reply.
Res judicata, 47, 990–1000, 1070–1072.
Responding to, 51.
Setoff, 465–466, 727.
Statute of limitations, effect on, 466–470.
Subject-matter jurisdiction, 725–727, 734, 738–739, 755, 759.
"Transaction or occurrence," 48–51, 739.
Venue, 905.

COURTS
See Federal Courts; State Courts.

COURTS OF APPEALS
See also Appellate Review.
Appellate jurisdiction, 162.
England, see England.
United States, 11–12, 16, 20–21, 154–159, 163.

COVENANT
Writ of, 338.

CRIMINAL LAW
Civil action following criminal case, 1060–1070.
Criminal contempt, see Contempt.
Degree of persuasion, 555–556.
Discovery, 491.
Distinguished from civil action, 1.
Federal Rules of Criminal Procedure, 23, 99, 397.
Grand jury, 515–516, 770.
Jury right, 99, 105–106.
Mandamus, 1242, 1247–1250.
Presumption of innocence, 548.
Standard of proof, 555–556.

CROSS–CLAIMS
Generally, 190–191.
Personal jurisdiction, 807, 810, 1211–1212.
Subject-matter jurisdiction, 727, 734.
Venue, 905.

CROSS–EXAMINATION
Nature of, 108, 119, 130–131.

CROSS–EXAMINATION—Cont'd
Scope and manner of, 131–132, 258–259.

DAMAGES
Remedy, 139–140.
Special, pleading, 432–435.

DEBT
Writ of, 333, 337–338.
Debt on a specialty, 338.
Simple debt, 333, 338.

DECLARATORY JUDGMENT
Action for, 144–151.
Historical development, 373.
Jury right, 680, 682, 683–691, 697–698.
Subject-matter jurisdiction, 165–166.

DECREES
Equity, 140.
Enforcement of, 151, 381–382, 785–788.
Flexibility of, 379–380.

DEFAULT
Failure to answer, 38, 942.
Res judicata, 807–808, 996, 1007, 1082–1087, 1092.

DEFENSES AND OBJECTIONS
Generally, 38–45, 459–464.
Affirmative, see Affirmative Defenses.
Consolidation and waiver of, 41–45.
Defensive matter in complaint, 445–448.
Denials, see Denials.
Failure to state a claim, 38–45, 84–85, 92, 451–454.
Manner of presenting, 40–41.
Motions, see Motions.
Preliminary hearing on defenses, 41.
Replying to, 45–46, 470–471.
Types, 38–40.
Waiver of, 41–45.

DEMAND FOR JUDGMENT
Generally, 139, 454–455, 748–749.

DEMURRER
Common-law pleading, 347, 349–350, 352, 436, 463–464.
Failure to state a claim, 38–45, 84–85, 92, 451–454.
Judgment on, effect of, 983–988.
Motion to strike a defense, 46, 84–85, 92, 451.
To answer, 463–464.
To the evidence, 568–569, 1216.

DENIALS
Generally, 39, 40, 42–43, 459–461.
Forms of, 459–460.
General denial, 459–460.

DEPOSITIONS
See Discovery.

DERIVATIVE ACTIONS
See Shareholders' Derivative Actions.

DETINUE
Writ of, 319, 333–334, 338.

DIRECT ACTION
Generally, 171–172, 872–877, 1070–1072.

DIRECT ESTOPPEL
See Issue Preclusion.

DIRECTED VERDICT
Generally, 108–110, 132–134, 568–593.
Against party with burden of proof, 132–134, 571–583.
Burden of proof, 539–553.
Degree of persuasion, 553–564.
For party with burden of proof, 133–134, 583–593.
Judgment n.o.v., 136–139, 650–664.
"Most favorable evidence" test, 571–572.
Mutual waiver doctrine, 570.
"Scintilla" test, 573, 578, 581.
"Set aside" test, 571–572.
Standard in diversity actions, 592.
Standard in FELA actions, 574–581, 590.
Standard of proof, 553–564.
Summary judgment, relation to, 565–566.

DISCOVERY
Generally, 56–77, 472–516.
Appellate review of orders, 16, 514–516.
Contempt orders, 515–516, 1224.
Interlocutory appeal, 514–515.
Mandamus, 515.
Attorney-client privilege, 57, 117, 484.
Compulsory, 79–82.
Conference, 77, 527.
Contentions, 56, 61–63, 66–69, 490.
Costs,
Sanctions, 61, 64, 69, 75–76, 499–500, 512.
Special master, 500–501.
Travel, 501–503.
Depositions, 59–65.
Judicial supervision of, 499–504.
Oral examination, 59–64.
Sequence of, 510–511.
Special master at, 500–501.
Subpoena, 60, 501–502.
Use in court proceedings, 73–74, 127.
Written questions, 64–65.
Documents, 60, 69–70.
Enforcement of orders, 75–76, 511–514.
Contempt, 515–516.
Sanctions, 61, 64, 69, 75–76, 499–503, 511–514.
Equitable relief, 379.
Experts, 58, 73, 493–496, 498–499.
First amendment problems, 117, 504–510.
Freedom of Information Act, 499.
General problems, 76–77.

DISCOVERY—Cont'd
"Good cause" requirement, 70–72, 483–485.
Hickman doctrine, 58, 472–493, 495–496.
Historical development, 379.
Identity and location of persons, 57–58, 73, 482.
Expert witnesses, 73, 493–496.
Impeachment evidence, 496–498.
Insurance policies, 58.
Interrogatories, 65–69, 490.
Binding effect of answers, 68, 74–75.
Supplementation of responses, 72–73, 75.
Judicial supervision of, 58, 75–77, 499–516.
Masters and magistrates, 500–501.
Person's own statement, 492–493.
Physical and mental examination, 5–27, 70–72.
Privileged matter, 57, 61, 117–118, 484, 513–514.
Production of documents and things, 60, 69–70.
Protective orders, 64, 76, 499–510.
Purposes of, 56–57.
Relevance, 57–58, 1156–1157.
Requests for admissions, 69, 75, 76, 490.
Sanctions for failure to make discovery, 61, 64, 69, 75–76, 499–503, 511–514, 515–516.
Scope of, 57–58, 472–499.
Signature requirement, 59, 512.
Supplementation of responses, 72–73, 75.
Trial preparation materials, 58, 472–493, 495–496.
Use in court proceedings, 73–75.
Witnesses, identity and location of, 57–58, 73, 482.
Expert witnesses, 73, 493–496.
Witnesses' statements, 472–493.
Work product of lawyer, 58, 472–493, 495–496.

DISMISSAL
Adjudication on the merits, see Adjudication on the Merits.
Compulsory nonsuit, 569–570, 985.
Demurrer to the evidence, 568–569, 1216.
Directed verdict, see Directed Verdict.
Involuntary,
Motion for, 108–109, 134, 541, 569–571.
Sanction of, 511–513, 988–989.
Motion to dismiss, see Motions.
Voluntary, 567–568, 989.
Nonsuit, 567–568.
Retraxit, 1006.
"Two-dismissal" rule, 567.

DISTRICT COURTS
Choice of court, 30–31, 177.
Service of process limitations, 179–182.

DISTRICT COURTS—Cont'd
Subject-matter jurisdiction limitations, 160–176.
Venue limitations, 177–179.
Controlling law, state or federal, see Choice of Law.
Procedure in, generally, 30.
Service of process, see Service.
Subject-matter jurisdiction, 160–176, 712–771.
   Ancillary jurisdiction, 725–739.
   Concurrent jurisdiction, 161.
   Diversity of citizenship cases, 12–14, 166–174, 739–747.
   Exclusive jurisdiction, 161.
   Federal question cases, 12, 162–166, 715–722.
   Jurisdictional amount, 747–755.
   Limited jurisdiction, 12, 161, 712–715.
   Original jurisdiction, 162.
   Pendent jurisdiction, 722–725.
   Removal jurisdiction, 174–175, 755–760.
Territorial jurisdiction,
   Jurisdiction over things, 180, 792–795.
   Personal jurisdiction, 179–181, 893–904.
Three-judge court, 148, 154.
United States, 11–12.
Venue, 177–179, 905.
   Local actions, 906–912.
   Transfer of cases, 181, 912–933.

DISTRICT OF COLUMBIA
Courts, 11–12, 21, 49–51.

DIVERSITY OF CITIZENSHIP CASES
   See also Subject-Matter Jurisdiction.
Generally, 12–14, 166–174, 739–747.
Administrators, 742–747.
Ancillary jurisdiction, see Ancillary Jurisdiction.
Assignment, 739–742.
Citizenship,
   Corporations, 171–173.
   Fourteenth amendment, definition of, 168.
   Individuals, 166–171.
   Students, 170–171.
   Unincorporated associations, 173.
   Wives, 171.
Class actions, 194, 751–755, 1155.
Complete diversity, 183, 188, 729–738, 1205–1206.
Controlling law, state or federal, see Choice of Law.
Desirability of, 174.
Devices to create or defeat, 712–715, 739–747.
Domicile, 166–171.
Interpleader, 188, 1203–1210.
Jurisdictional amount, see Amount in Controversy.
Multi-party, generally, 183.
Realignment, 183–184, 194, 1111.
Venue, see Venue.

DOCUMENTS
Discovery, 60, 69–70.

DOMICILE
Diversity cases, 166–171.
   Students, 170–171.
   Wives, 171.
Jurisdictional basis, 800–801.

DUE PROCESS
Procedural, 180–181, 796.
   Basic principles of, 934–942.
   Cognovit note, 952–955.
   Enforcement remedies, 154, 951–952.
   Joinder, 193, 1109–1110, 1114–1127, 1173–1179, 1196.
   Jury right, 710–711.
   Notice and opportunity to be heard, 934–955.
   Provisional remedies, 94, 942–952.
   Self-help, 950.
   Service of process, see Service.
   Sniadach doctrine, 942–952.
   Waiver of, 952–955.
Substantive, 180–181, 796.
   Territorial jurisdiction, see Territorial Jurisdiction.

EJECTMENT
Writ of, 333, 376, 386–387.

ELECTION OF REMEDIES
Generally, 967.

ELEVENTH AMENDMENT
Generally, 161.

ENABLING ACT
Federal Rules of Civil Procedure, 6, 17–25, 72, 105, 110, 118, 222–223, 397–398, 1133–1134, 1182, 1227–1228.

ENFORCEMENT OF JUDGMENTS
See Judgments.

ENGLAND
   See also Common Law.
Comparative studies, 296.
Court structure, modern, 305, 393.
Judicature Acts, 301, 304–305, 393, 618.
Jury, modern, 667.
Rules, modern, 393, 440, 618, 631, 633, 667.

ENTRY
Judgment, 139.

EQUITABLE ESTOPPEL
Compulsory counterclaim, 47, 999.
Intervention, 1035, 1059, 1196.
Subject-matter jurisdiction, 712–714.

EQUITABLE RELIEF
Generally, 140, 364–381.

EQUITABLE RELIEF—Cont'd
Accounting, see Accounting.
Administering, difficulties of, 368–369.
Bill of peace, 375, 568, 1114, 1144, 1208–1209.
Bill quia timet, 373.
"Clean hands" maxim, 371.
"Clean-up" doctrine, see "Clean-Up" Doctrine.
Complex litigation, 378–379, 710–711, 1095, 1114, 1192, 1210–1211.
Debtor-creditor relationships, 378–379.
Decrees, see Decrees.
Discovery, 379.
Discretionary character of, 369–372.
Inadequacy of legal relief, 367–368, 372.
Injunctions, see Injunctions.
Intervention for misconduct and mistake, 373–374.
Fraud, 373, 681–683.
Mistake, 373–374, 675–676, 680–681.
Maxims, 371, 380.
Mortgages, 367.
Mutuality of remedy, 372.
Penal bonds, 366–367.
Prior restraint, 377, 504–510.
Receivership, 366, 376, 378–379.
Scope of, 360, 364–366.
Setoff, 465.
Specific performance of contracts, 140, 367–372, 785–788.
Torts, against, 374–378.
Injunctions, 94–97, 377–378.
Labor, 377.
Nuisance, 376, 676–677.
Recaption or protection of personal property, 374.
Trespass, 374–376.
Unfair competition, 376–377.
Waste, 374.
Uses and trusts, 358–359.

EQUITY
See also Equitable Relief; Merger of Law and Equity.
Chancery Court, 21, 98, 317, 356–382, 384–385, 388–391, 393, 666–668, 960, 1217–1219.
Appellate review, 391, 648, 960, 1217–1219.
Contrasted with law courts, 21, 354–356, 384–391.
Deficiencies, 384–385, 388–391.
Evidence by interrogatories, 388–390, 392, 396, 648, 668.
Judges, 390–391.
Jurisdiction, scope of, 360, 364–366.
Common law jurisdiction, 357.
Jury, 98, 390, 666–668.
Advisory, 666–667.
Necessary parties, 389–390, 1095.
Procedure, 357, 388–391.
Reforms, 392–393.

EQUITY—Cont'd
Exchequer Court, 386, 390–391.
Historical development, 354–364.
Coke-Ellesmere dispute, 360–363.
United States, 21–22, 382–383, 391, 395–397.
House of Lords, 391, 393, 1218–1219.
Reforms, 392–393.
Scope of, 360, 364–366.

ERIE DOCTRINE
See Choice of Law.

ERROR
Harmless, 138, 618–619, 1215.
Plain, 598–599, 619–622.
Writ of, 387–388, 1216–1217.
Bill of exceptions, 1217.

ESTOPPEL
Collateral, see Issue Preclusion.
Direct, see Issue Preclusion.
Equitable, see Equitable Estoppel.

EVIDENCE
Generally, 110–132.
Admissions, 74–75, 122–123.
Amendment of pleadings to conform to, 53, 84, 415–416, 426–428, 430–431, 983.
Ancient writings, 128.
"Best evidence" rule, 128.
Burden of proof, see Burden of Proof.
Chancery Court, 388–390, 392, 396, 648, 668.
Circumstantial, 113.
Combating, 130–132.
Competency of witnesses, 114–117.
Dead Man's Acts, 115–117, 1097–1105.
Contradiction, 131.
Cross-examination, 108, 119, 130–132, 258–259.
Declarations against interest, 122–123.
Degree of persuasion, see Preponderance of the Evidence.
Demonstrative, 112.
Demurrer to the, 568–569, 1216.
Direct examination, 108, 132.
Disbelief and demeanor, 119, 561–564.
Discovery, use of products of, 73–75.
Dying declarations, 121–122, 127.
Entries in books or records, 127.
Exceptions to, 129.
Excited utterances, 123–127.
Exclusionary rules, 113–114.
Competency of witnesses, 114–117.
Hearsay, 73, 118–128, 131, 1060.
Privilege, 117–118, 241–242, 265–266.
Expert witnesses, 111, 272–274, 495–496.
Discovery of, 73, 493–496.
Failure to testify, 561, 587–588.
Family history, 127–128.

EVIDENCE—Cont'd
Federal Rules of Evidence, generally, 110–111.
Hearsay, 73, 118–128, 131, 1060.
  Exceptions to rule, 120–128.
  Multiple, 128.
  Rule, 118–120.
Impeachment, 130–131.
  Discovery of, 496–498.
Judge, calling and interrogation of witnesses, 274–276.
Judicial notice, 112, 443–445.
Jurisdiction, 715.
Juror misconduct, 116, 601–605.
Kinds of, 111–112.
Limited admissibility, 129–130.
Motions at close of, 132–134.
Newly discovered, 138, 634–636.
Objections to, 129–130.
Offer of proof, 130.
Opinion, 111–112.
Pleadings, relation to, 422–435.
  Amendment of pleadings, see Amendment of Pleadings.
  Variances, 422–426.
Preponderance of, see Preponderance of the Evidence.
Presumptions, see Presumptions.
Prior inconsistent statements, 130–131.
Prior statements of witnesses, discovery of, 472–493.
Prior testimony, 127.
Privilege, 117–118, 241–242, 265–266.
  Against self-incrimination, 117, 460–461, 513–514, 561, 770.
Real, 112.
Relevance, 112–113.
Remote, confusing, and prejudicial, 58, 128–129, 242.
Res gestae, 123–127.
Res judicata, 982–983.
Standard of proof, see Preponderance of the Evidence.
Statistical, 556–561.
Types of, 111–112.
Witnesses, see Witnesses.

EXCHEQUER CHAMBER
See Common Law.

EXCHEQUER COURT
See Common Law; Equity.

EXECUTION
Enforcement remedy, 152–154.
Right to prior notice, 154, 951–952.

EXPERT WITNESSES
Discovery, 73, 493–496.
Evidence, 111, 272–274, 495–496.
Role of, 272–274.

EXTRAORDINARY WRITS
All Writs Act, 72, 157, 158–159, 1242–1253.
Mandamus, 72, 1242–1253.
Prohibition, 277, 385, 879.

FEDERAL COURTS
Generally, 11–14, 30–31, 160–162, 174–176.
Abstention, 216, 1250–1252.
Circuit courts of appeals, 12, 163.
Controlling law, state or federal, see Choice of Law.
Courts of appeals, see Courts of Appeals.
District courts, see District Courts.
Federal Circuit, 12.
Map, 13.
Specialized courts, 12, 162, 971–974.
Supreme Court, see Supreme Court.

FEDERAL EMPLOYERS' LIABILITY ACT
Generally, 175.
Directed verdict, 574–581, 590.
Evidence, 74–75, 561–562.
Jury right, 248–250, 251–252, 643–645, 670.
Removal, 175.
Res judicata, 969.
"Reverse" Erie, 248–252.
Transfer of venue, 914.

FEDERAL LAW
See Choice of Law.

FEDERAL QUESTION CASES
See also Subject-Matter Jurisdiction.
Generally, 12, 162–166, 715–722.
"Arising under," 715–722.
Civil rights actions, see Civil Rights Actions.
Declaratory judgment, 165–166.
Jurisdictional amount, see Amount in Controversy.
Pendent jurisdiction, see Pendent Jurisdiction.
Venue, see Venue.
"Well-pleaded complaint," 162–166.

FEDERAL RULES
See also Procedural Rules.
Admiralty, 22–23.
Advisory committees, 19–20, 397–398.
Appellate Procedure, 20–21, 156, 397.
Civil Procedure, generally, 19–20, 30, 397–398.
  Adoption of, 19–20, 397.
  Amendments to, 20, 397–398.
Criminal Procedure, 23, 99, 397.
Enabling Act, see Enabling Act.
Equity, 21–22, 383, 396, 725–726, 1114.
Evidence, generally, 110–111.
Judicial Conference, 20, 397–398.
Local, 21, 98, 99–106.
Supreme Court, 17, 21, 159.

FIELD CODE
Generally, 301, 391–392, 393–395.
Answer, 394.
Complaint, 393–394, 436.
Counterclaim, 394, 403–405, 466.
Merger, 301, 393.

FINAL DECISIONS
See Appellate Review; Res Judicata.

FINDINGS AND CONCLUSIONS
See Nonjury Trial.

FORENSIC PROOF
See Evidence.

FORMER ADJUDICATION
See Res Judicata.

FORMS OF ACTION
Common law, 299–346, 385–387, 392.
One form of, 299–305, 391–393, 407–408.

FORUM NON CONVENIENS
Generally, 912–914, 921–933.
Transfer of venue, 181, 912–933.

FRAUD
Equitable relief, 373, 681–683.
Pleading of, 33.
Territorial jurisdiction, effect on, 798–800, 861.
Work product protection, effect on, 492.

FREEDOM OF INFORMATION
Act, 499.

FULL FAITH AND CREDIT
Generally, 797, 1073–1079, 1088.

GARNISHMENT
Jurisdictional basis, 180, 788–791, 792, 856–870, 872–877.
Provisional remedy, 92–94.
Right to prior notice, 94, 942–952.

GENERAL APPEARANCE
See Appearances.

GENERAL DENIAL
Answer to complaint, 459–460.

GENERAL VERDICT
See Verdict.

GERMANY
Comparative study, 291–298.
Appellate review, 295.
Attorneys, 295–296.
Conferences, 291–294.
Costs, 296.
Evidence, 294.
Judges, 295.
Pleadings, 292.

GERMANY—Cont'd
Prooftaking, 293–294.
Summons, 291.
Witnesses, 294.
Update, 296.

HARMLESS ERROR
Generally, 138, 618–619, 1215.

HEARSAY
See Evidence.

HICKMAN DOCTRINE
See Discovery.

HIGH COURT OF JUSTICE
See England.

HILARY RULES
See Common-Law Pleading.

HOUSE OF LORDS
England, 387, 391, 393, 1216, 1218–1219.

IMMUNITY
Service of process, 800.

IMPEACHMENT
Evidence, 130–131.
Discovery of, 496–498.

IMPLEADER
Generally, 189–190, 426–428, 1033–1034, 1070–1072.
Ancillary jurisdiction, 726–739, 1196–1199.
Removal jurisdiction, 759–760.
"Vouching in," 1033–1034.

IN REM PROCEEDINGS
See Territorial Jurisdiction.

INCONVENIENT FORUM
See Forum Non Conveniens.

INDEMNITY
Generally, 189, 1033–1034, 1038.
Impleader, see Impleader.
"Vouching in," 1033–1034.

INDISPENSABLE PARTIES
See Parties.

INJUNCTIONS
Appealability, 155, 1230–1239.
Contempt, see Contempt.
Equitable relief, 94–97, 140, 374–378.
Labor, 377.
Public law litigation, 366, 377–378, 1173.
Interstate, 1074–1075.
Preliminary, 94–97, 155, 809.
Temporary restraining order, 94, 155.

INSTRUCTIONS
See Jury Trial.

INTERLOCUTORY DECISIONS
See Appellate Review.

INTERPLEADER
Generally, 188, 1200–1212.
Classic limits, 1210–1211.
Jurisdiction, service, and venue, 188, 1200–1210.
Jury right, 680, 703, 1212.
Law applied in federal courts, 1212.
"Rule," 188, 1203, 1210.
Second stage, 1211–1212.
"Statutory," 188, 1202–1203, 1210.

INTERROGATORIES
See Discovery; Verdict.

INTERVENTION
Generally, 194–195, 1189–1199.
Ancillary jurisdiction, 727–728, 734, 1196–1199.
Duty, 1035, 1059, 1196.
Jury right, 680, 703.
Public law litigation, 1191–1196.

INVOLUNTARY DISMISSAL
See Dismissal.

INVOLUNTARY PLAINTIFF
See Parties.

ISSUE PRECLUSION
Generally, 957, 1001–1031, 1037–1070.
Actually litigated and determined, 1004–1008, 1021.
Alternative determinations, 1009–1011.
Ambiguous determinations, 1009.
Binding strangers, 1034–1036, 1037, 1059–1060, 1127, 1196.
Collateral estoppel, generally, 957.
Courts of limited jurisdiction, 1019–1020, 1024.
Cumulative determinations, 1009.
Dimensions of issue, 1003–1006, 1011, 1012–1014.
Direct estoppel, 957, 986.
Distinguished from claim preclusion, 956–957, 1006, 1024–1030.
Essential to judgment, 1008–1011.
Finality, 959–960.
Inconsistent judgments, 1011–1012.
Law, issues of, 1014–1019, 1024.
Mutuality of estoppel, 1037–1070.
Decline of, 1038–1070.
Government, 1053–1056.
Jury right, 1052.
Offensive-defensive distinction, 1043–1052, 1105.
Restatement provision, 1053.

ISSUE PRECLUSION—Cont'd
Rule of, 1037.
Special types of proceedings, 1060–1070, 1127.
Posture of party, 1030–1031.
Restatement provision, 957, 1023–1024.
Unforeseeability of future litigation, 1020–1021, 1024.

JOINDER OF CLAIMS
See also Claim.
Appellate review, 155, 1227–1228.
Consolidation and joint trials, 196.
Jury right, 674–680, 692.
Personal jurisdiction, 833, 903.
Pleading, 37, 49, 50, 182, 195.
Res judicata, 969–971.
Severance and separate trials, 195–196.
Subject-matter jurisdiction, 722–725, 738, 756–759.
Jurisdictional amount, aggregation, 751–755.

JOINDER OF PARTIES
See Parties.

JONES ACT
Generally, 175, 274, 634, 647, 661, 670, 1224.

JUDGE
Calling and interrogation of witnesses, 274–276.
Commenting on evidence, 134–135, 595–596, 601.
Division of functions with jury, 594–595.
Efforts to induce jury unanimity, 599–601.
Mandamus, 72, 1242–1253.
Public law litigation, 29, 279–280, 1173.
Role of, 29, 253–258, 272–280.
Discovery, judicial supervision of, 58, 75–77, 499–516.
Pretrial conference, 78–82, 276, 517–538.
Trial by, see Nonjury Trial.
Witness, acting as, 116, 983, 1001.

JUDGMENT N.O.V.
See also Directed Verdict; New Trial.
Generally, 136–139, 650–664.
Common law, 349, 651, 1216.

JUDGMENT ON THE MERITS
See Adjudication on the Merits.

JUDGMENTS
See also Res Judicata.
Actions upon, 796–798, 956.
Collateral attack, 714–715, 796–798, 1082–1093.

JUDGMENTS—Cont'd
Consent, 1006–1008.
Contribution, 189, 1037, 1109.
Credit due, 1073–1093.
    American judgments, 796–798, 1073–1079.
    Choice of law, 715, 797, 1078, 1082, 1088.
    Federal judgments, 567, 797, 997, 1078, 1088.
    Full faith and credit, 797, 1073–1079, 1088.
    Judgments of foreign nations, 1080–1082.
Declaratory, see Declaratory Judgment.
Decrees, see Decrees.
Demand for, 139, 454–455, 748–749.
Enforcement in other states, 796–798.
Enforcement of, 151–154, 381–382, 785–788, 951–952.
    Contempt, see Contempt.
    Execution, 152–154.
    Stay pending appeal, 157–159, 160.
    Supplementary proceedings, 152.
Entry of, 139.
Kinds of relief afforded by, 139–151.
    Costs, 141–144.
    Damages, 139–140.
    Declaratory, see Declaratory Judgment.
    Equitable, see Equitable Relief.
    Restoration of property, 140.
Pleadings, judgment on the, 84–85, 92.
Registration of, 797–798.
Summary, see Summary Judgment.
Valid, 796–797, 958, 1082–1087.

JUDICATURE ACTS
See England.

JUDICIAL BUSINESS
Allocation among states, 181–182.
Division between state and federal courts, 160–162, 174–176.
Venue, see Venue.

JUDICIAL CONFERENCE
Federal Rules, 20, 397–398.

JUDICIAL JURISDICTION
See Territorial Jurisdiction.

JUDICIAL NOTICE
Evidence, 112.
Pleading fact and law, 443–445.

JUDICIAL POWER
Cases and controversies, 145–151, 160–162, 723–725.
Federal courts, see Federal Courts.
States, 160–162, 174–176, 181–182.
United States, 12–14, 145–151, 160–176, 712–717.

JUDICIARY ACT OF 1789
All Writs Act, 72, 157, 158–159, 1242–1253.
Appellate review, 1220.
Rules of Decision Act, see Choice of Law.
Venue, 910.

JURISDICTION
See also Subject-Matter Jurisdiction; Territorial Jurisdiction.
Ancillary, see Ancillary Jurisdiction.
Appellate, 162.
Concurrent, 161.
Equity, scope of, 360, 364–366.
Exclusive, 161.
General, 161.
Jurisdiction to determine,
    Jurisdictional findings as res judicata, 1087–1093.
    Power to punish disobedience of court order, 760–771.
Limited, 12, 161, 712–715.
Local actions, 906–912.
"Long-arm," 832–844.
Original, 162.
"Over the person," see Personal Jurisdiction.
"Over the subject matter," see Subject-Matter Jurisdiction.
"Over things," see Territorial Jurisdiction.
Pendent, see Pendent Jurisdiction.

JURISDICTIONAL AMOUNT
See Amount in Controversy.

JURY TRIAL
See also Trial.
Accounting, 695–697, 710–711.
Advisory jury, 666–667.
Class actions, 680, 703.
Closing arguments, 134, 595–596, 619–622.
Commenting on evidence, 134–135, 595–596, 601.
Constitutional right to, 98, 665–711.
    "Historical test," 98, 667–683.
Controlling law, state or federal, see Choice of Law.
Criminal law, 99, 105–106.
Declaratory judgment, 680, 682, 683–691, 697–698.
Directed verdict, see Directed Verdict.
Division of functions between judge and jury, 594–595.
Fact and law, 594–595.
Historical development, 98–99, 302, 312, 314–315, 333, 338, 356, 605, 607, 666–669.
Instructions to jury, 134–136, 595–601.
    "Allen" charge, 599–601.
    Exceptions to, 129, 598.
    Guidelines, 596–598.

JURY TRIAL—Cont'd
Objections to, 135, 598–599.
  Pattern, 554–555.
Interpleader, 680, 703, 1212.
Intervention, 680, 703.
Judgment n.o.v., 136–139, 650–664.
Jurisdictional issues, 166, 697, 1087.
Juror misconduct, 116, 601–605.
Life insurance fraud cases, 681–683.
Motions, see Motions.
New trial, see New Trial.
Number of jurors, 99–106.
Res judicata, effect on, 1052.
Selection of jury, 106–107.
  Challenges, 106–107.
Shareholders' derivative actions, 680, 700–706.
Split trial, 615–616.
State courts, 99, 105–106, 665–666, 699.
Submission to jury, 134–136, 594–616.
Unanimity of jurors, 105–106, 239–241, 249, 599–601, 614–615.
Verdict, see Verdict.
Voir dire, 106–107.
  Challenges, 106–107.

KING'S COURTS
See Common Law.

LAW
See Common Law.

LAW OF THE CASE
Generally, 958.

LAWYER
See Attorney.

LIMITED APPEARANCE
See Appearances.

LOCAL ACTIONS
Generally, 906–912.

MAGISTRATE
Generally, 500–501, 519.

MANDAMUS
Extraordinary writ, 72, 1242–1253.

MASTER
Generally, 274, 276–279, 500–501, 1242–1243.

MERGER AND BAR
See Res Judicata.

MERGER OF LAW AND EQUITY
England, 393.
  Judicature Acts, see England.
Jury right, effect on, 22, 98, 301, 395, 408, 665–711.
Res judicata, effect on, 969–971.

MERGER OF LAW AND EQUITY—Cont'd
United States, 393–397.
  Enabling Act, see Enabling Act.
  Federal Rules of Civil Procedure, 22, 301, 397, 407–408.
  Field Code, 301, 393.

MISTAKE
Equitable relief, 373–374, 675–676, 680–681.
Pleading of, 33.

MODEL RULES OF PROFESSIONAL CONDUCT
See Attorney.

MORTGAGES
Equitable relief, 367.

MOTIONS
After decision, 136, 139, 1082–1084.
After verdict, 136–139.
  Joinder of, 138–139, 650–664.
  Judgment n.o.v., 136–139, 650–664.
  New trial, see New Trial.
Close of defendant's case, at, 109.
Close of evidence, at, 132–134.
Close of plaintiff's case, at, 108.
Compulsory nonsuit, 569–570, 985.
Defined, 15, 40.
Demurrer, see Demurrer.
Directed verdict, see Directed Verdict.
Failure to state a claim, 38–45, 84–85, 92, 451–454.
  Consequences of, 452–454.
  Effect of judgment on, 983–988.
Involuntary dismissal, 108–109, 134, 541, 569–571.
Judgment n.o.v., 136–139, 650–664.
  Common law, 349, 651, 1216.
Judgment on the pleadings, 84–85, 92.
More definite statement, 39, 41, 43, 449–450.
Motion to dismiss, 40.
Motion to strike,
  Evidence, 569.
  Insufficient defense, 46, 84–85, 92, 451.
  Prejudicial matter, 39, 41, 43, 450–451.
New trial, see New Trial.
Summary judgment, see Summary Judgment.
Transfer venue, 181, 912–933.

MULTI–CLAIM ACTIONS
See Joinder of Claims.

MULTI–PARTY ACTIONS
See Parties.

MUTUALITY
Estoppel, 1037–1070.
Jury right, 676–677.
Remedy, 372.

NECESSARY PARTIES
See Parties.

NEGLIGENCE ACTION
See also Case; Contributory Negligence.
Complaint, 32, 438.
Elements of, 436.
Damages, 139–140.

NEW TRIAL
Generally, 136–139, 571–573, 617–664.
Additur, 624–631.
Appellate review of grant or denial, 636–650.
Error in course of trial, 138, 617–623.
Error in verdict, 137–138, 623–634.
Harmless error, 138, 618–619, 1215.
Newly discovered evidence, 138, 634–636.
Partial, 632–634.
Plain error, 598–599, 619–622.
Remittitur, see Remittitur.
Rule 50, interplay with, 138–139, 650–664.
Standards, 137–138, 623–624.

NISI PRIUS
See Common Law.

NONJURY TRIAL
See also Trial.
Appellate review of facts, 648–650.
"Clearly erroneous" test, 648–649.
Closing arguments, 136.
Evidence rulings, 120, 622–623.
Findings and conclusions, 136, 649–650, 666–667, 1009–1010.
Involuntary dismissal, motion for, 108–109, 134, 541, 569–571.
Right to, 666.

NONSUIT
See also Dismissal.
Abandonment of action, 567–568, 989.
Compulsory, 569–570, 985.

NOTICE
Class actions, 193, 1144–1155, 1156–1160, 1164–1165, 1167, 1181.
Judicial, see Judicial Notice.
Procedural due process, see Due Process.
Service of process, see Service.
"Vouching in," 1033–1034.
Waiver of, 952–955.

NUISANCE
Equitable relief, 376, 676–677.
Legal relief, 319, 676–677.
Local actions, 912.

ORDERS
Defined, 15.
Show cause, 15.
Temporary restraining, see Injunctions.

ORIGINAL WRIT
Defined, 316–317.

OTHER ACTION PENDING
Pendency of a prior action, plea of, 965, 973.

PARTIES
Generally, 182–196, 1094–1212.
Ancillary jurisdiction, see Ancillary Jurisdiction.
Capacity, 1111–1112.
Caption of case, 5, 44.
Class actions, see Class Actions.
Classes of, 186–187, 1094.
Impleader, see Impleader.
Interpleader, see Interpleader.
Intervention, see Intervention.
Joinder for just adjudication, 39–42, 184, 186–187, 1094–1111.
Controlling law, state or federal, 1105.
Indispensable parties, 186–187, 1094–1110, 1209.
Trustees, 847–856, 871.
Involuntary plaintiff, 1111.
Necessary parties, 186–187, 389–390, 1094–1110.
Pendent, 725, 729–738.
Permissive joinder, 184–186, 1111–1112.
Personal jurisdiction, see Personal Jurisdiction.
Procedural due process aspects of joinder, 193, 1109–1110, 1114–1127, 1173–1179, 1196.
Public law litigation, 1172–1188, 1191–1196.
Real party in interest, 745–746, 1112–1113.
Third-party practice, see Impleader.

PENDENT JURISDICTION
See also Subject-Matter Jurisdiction.
Generally, 722–725, 739.
Pendent parties, 725, 729–738.
Res judicata, effect on, 969, 1029–1030.

PENDENT SERVICE
Generally, 903, 1211–1212.

PENDENT VENUE
Generally, 905.

PERSONAL JURISDICTION
See also Territorial Jurisdiction.
Generally, 179–182, 772–780, 793–904.
Acts done in state as basis, 804–811, 814–844.
Appearances, see Appearances.
Challenges to, 39–42, 796–797, 807–810, 1084–1085, 1087–1089.
Commerce clause, 824.
Consent as basis, 41–42, 801–805, 811, 812–813, 865, 869–870, 891, 955.

PERSONAL JURISDICTION—Cont'd
Corporations,
  Domestic, 811.
  Foreign, 805, 812–833, 859.
Domicile as basis, 800–801.
Federal courts, 179–181, 893–904.
First amendment, 824–825.
Interpleader, 188, 1200–1203, 1209–1210, 1211–1212.
"Long-arm," 832–844.
Natural persons, 795–811, 832–833, 859.
Presence as basis, 795–800, 813–814.
  Fraud and force, 798–800, 861.
  Immunity, 800.
Res judicata effect of finding, 1087–1089.
Residence as basis, 801.
Service of process, see Service.
Statutory treatment. 832–844.
Transfer of cases, 919–921.

PHYSICAL AND MENTAL EXAMINATION
Discovery, 5–27, 70–72.

PLAIN ERROR
Generally, 598–599, 619–622.

PLEADINGS
Generally, 31–56, 420–471.
Affirmative defenses, see Affirmative Defenses.
Alternative and inconsistent pleading, 36–38.
Amendment of, see Amendment of Pleadings.
Answer, see Answer.
Attorney's signature, effect of, 38, 85, 457–460, 749, 1112.
Burden of allegation, 32–33, 461–463.
Cause of action, see Cause of Action.
Claim, see Claim.
Code pleading, 393–394, 420, 436–443, 447–448.
Common counts, see Common Counts.
Common-law system, see Common-Law Pleading.
Complaint, see Complaint.
Counterclaims, see Counterclaims.
Counts and paragraphs, 36–37, 448–449.
Defenses and objections, see Defenses and Objections.
Defined, 46, 48, 452.
Denials, see Denials.
Fact pleading, 420, 436–443.
Foreign law, 444–445.
Issue pleading, 346, 420.
Joinder of claims, see Joinder of Claims.
Joinder of parties, see Parties.
Judgment on the, 84–85, 92.
Judicial notice of fact and law, 443–445.
Modern, objectives of, 420–422.
Motions, see Motions.
Notice pleading, 420–422.

PLEADINGS—Cont'd
Proof, relation to, 422–435.
  Amendment of pleadings, see Amendment of Pleadings.
  Variances, 422–426.
Reading or commenting on to jury, 450–451, 455.
Recital pleading, 436–437.
Reply, see Reply.
Signature requirement, 38, 85, 457–460, 749, 1112.
Special damages, 432–435.
Special matters, 33.
Specificity required, 33–36, 420–422, 431–445, 459–463.
Supplemental, 235.
"Theory of pleadings" doctrine, 408–411.
  Change of theory on appeal, 411–419.
Time and place, allegations of, 431–432.
Verification, 456–459.

PRELIMINARY HEARING
Defenses, on, 41.

PRELIMINARY INJUNCTIONS
See Injunctions.

PREPONDERANCE OF THE EVIDENCE
Generally, 107, 553–564.
Standard of proof,
  Civil cases, 553–556.
  Criminal cases, 555–556.
Statistical evidence, 556–561.

PRESUMPTIONS
Generally, 543–553.
Approaches,
  Federal Rules of Evidence, 552.
  1953 Uniform Rules of Evidence, 550–551.
  1974 Uniform Rules of Evidence, 551–552.
  Thayer-Model Code, 550.
Conclusive, 548.
Controlling law, state or federal, 552.
Innocence, of, 548.
Permissive, 549, 592.

PRETRIAL CONFERENCES
Generally, 77–84, 517–538.
"Big cases," 79, 526–528.
Case management, see Case Management.
Discovery conference, 77, 527.
Empirical work, 78, 518–524, 530.
Local court rules, 78, 82.
Pretrial orders, 82, 128, 519.
  Effect on ultimate trial, 82–84.
  Pretrial statements, 78, 82.
Role of judge, 78–82, 276, 517–538.
Sanctions, 84, 527–528.

PRETRIAL CONFERENCES—Cont'd
Scheduling order, 78, 525–526.
Settlement, 78, 519, 532–534.

PRIVILEGE
See Discovery; Evidence.

PRIVITY
Control of prosecution or defense, 1032–
   1033.
Represented by party to action, 1032.
Res judicata, 1032–1037, 1059–1060, 1127,
   1196.
Successors in interest, 1032.

PROCEDURAL RULES
  See also Federal Rules.
Conformity Act, 7, 18–19, 395–397.
England, generally, 393.
Field Code, see Field Code.
Hilary Rules, see Common-Law Pleading.
Nature of, 3–4, 25–26.
States, generally, 30, 395.
Substance-procedure distinction, 4–28,
   205–210, 226.

PROCESS
See Service.

PROCESS ACTS
Procedure, 17–18, 22, 382–383.

PROFESSIONAL RESPONSIBILITY
See Attorney.

PROOF
See Evidence.

PROTECTIVE ORDERS
Discovery, 64, 76, 499–510.

PROVISIONAL REMEDIES.
  Generally, 92–97, 942–952.
Attachment, see Attachment.
Garnishment, see Garnishment.
Preliminary injunctions, see Injunctions.
Sequestration, 856–857, 943–944.
Temporary restraining orders, see In-
   junctions.

PUBLIC LAW LITIGATION
  See also Adversary System.
Class actions, 1172–1188.
Intervention, 1191–1196.
Judge, role of, 29, 279–280, 1173.
Remedy, 366, 377–378, 1173.
Table of features, 1173.

QUASI IN REM PROCEEDINGS
See Territorial Jurisdiction.

QUEEN'S BENCH COURT
See Common Law.

QUEEN'S BENCH DIVISION
See England.

REAL PARTY IN INTEREST
Generally, 745–746, 1112–1113.

RECOUPMENT
Claim of, 464–465.

RELIEF
See Remedies.

RELITIGATION
See Res Judicata.

REMEDIES
Breach of promise, see Breach of Prom-
   ise.
Damages, see Damages.
Declaratory, see Declaratory Judgment.
Demand for judgment, 139, 454–455,
   748–749.
Election of, 967.
Equitable, see Equitable Relief.
Extraordinary writs, see Extraordinary
   Writs.
Injunctions, see Injunctions.
Kinds afforded by judgment, see Judg-
   ments.
Mandamus, 72, 1242–1253.
Negligence, see Negligence Action.
Provisional, see Provisional Remedies.
Unjust enrichment, 140, 344–345, 359,
   403–407.
Writs, see Common Law.

REMITTITUR
  Generally, 624–632, 634.
Amount, 631–632.
Appellate review, 647–648.

REMOVAL
Jurisdiction of district courts, 174–175,
   183–184, 755–760.
  Separate and independent claims, 756–
    760.
Service of process, 902.
Venue, 178–179, 912.
Verification of petition, 456.

REPLEVIN
Modern, 943.
Writ of, 332–333, 374.

REPLY
  Generally, 51, 470–471.
Defenses, to, 45–46, 470–471.

RES GESTAE
Evidence, 123–127.

RES IPSA LOQUITUR
Generally, 68, 274–275, 417–418, 549, 592.

RES JUDICATA
See also Judgments.
Generally, 2, 956–1093.
Adjudication on the merits, 108, 982–990.
Restatement provision, 989.
Affirmative defense to be pleaded, 1012, 1047–1048.
Alternative determinations, 1011.
Bar, 956–957.
Basic propositions, 956–957, 960.
Restatement provision, 957.
Binding strangers, 1034–1036, 1037, 1059–1060, 1127, 1196.
Claim preclusion, 956–957, 961–1000, 1024–1030, 1032–1037, 1070–1072.
Class actions, 191–193, 1032, 1114–1127.
Collateral attack, 714–715, 796–798, 1082–1093.
Collateral estoppel, see Issue Preclusion.
Consent judgment, 1006–1008.
Counterclaim, 47, 990–1000, 1070–1072.
Defense and counterclaim, 990–1000.
Dimensions of claim, 961–982.
Restatement provision, 975–976.
Direct estoppel, see Issue Preclusion.
Election of remedies, 967.
Evidence, extrinsic, 982–983.
Finality, 959–960.
Intervene, duty to, 1035, 1059, 1196.
Issue preclusion, see Issue Preclusion.
Judgments, credit due, 1073–1093.
American judgments, 796–798, 1073–1079.
Choice of law, 715, 797, 1078, 1082, 1088.
Federal judgments, 567, 797, 997, 1078, 1088.
Full faith and credit, 797, 1073–1079, 1088.
Judgments of foreign nations, 1080–1082.
Jurisdictional findings, 1087–1093.
Law of the case, 958.
Merger, 956–957.
Merger of law and equity, 969–971.
Nonparties, 1032–1072, 1127, 1196.
Pendency of a prior action, 965, 973.
Pendent jurisdiction, effect of, 969, 1029–1030.
Privity, 1032–1037, 1059–1060, 1127, 1196.
Res adjudicata, 957.
Settlement, mechanics of, 1006–1008.
Splitting claims, 961–982.
Stare decisis, 2, 364, 958.
Validity, 796–797, 958, 1082–1087.

RESIDENCE
Jurisdictional basis, 801.
Venue, 177.
Aliens, 178.
Corporations, 177–178, 905.
Unincorporated associations, 178, 905.

RESTRAINING ORDERS
See Injunctions.

RULES ENABLING ACT
See Enabling Act.

RULES OF DECISION ACT
See Choice of Law.

RULES OF PROCEDURE
See Procedural Rules.

SELF–INCRIMINATION
Privilege against, 117, 460–461, 513–514, 561, 770.

SEQUESTRATION
Generally, 381, 856–857, 943–944.

SERVICE
See also Due Process; Territorial Jurisdiction.
Generally, 14, 31, 179–181, 940–942.
Challenges to, 39–42.
"Expedient," 941–942.
Federal courts,
Hundred-mile bulge, 180, 902–903.
Interpleader, 188, 1202–1203, 1209–1210, 1211–1212.
Jurisdiction over the person, 179–181, 893–904.
Jurisdiction over things, 180, 792.
Nationwide service, 181, 188, 894, 903–904, 1209.
Pendent service, 903, 1211–1212.
Removal, 902.
Transfer of cases, 919–921.
Fraud and force, 798–800, 861.
Immunity, 800.
"Long-arm," 833.
Waiver of, 41–42, 802.

SETOFF
Claim of, 465–466, 727.

SETTLEMENT OF ACTIONS
Class actions, 193, 279, 1161–1172, 1223, 1235–1239.
Jurisdiction, effect on, 729.
Pretrial conference, 78, 519, 532–534.
Res judicata, 1006–1008.

SHAREHOLDERS' DERIVATIVE ACTIONS
Generally, 194.
Jury right, 680, 700–706.
Security, 211–212, 1221–1224.
Venue, 178, 194.
Verification of complaint, 456–459.

SIGNATURE
Discovery papers, 59, 512.
Pleadings, 38, 85, 457–460, 749, 1112.

SPECIAL APPEARANCE
See Appearances.

SPECIAL DAMAGES
Pleading, 432–435.

SPECIAL MATTERS
Pleading, 33.

SPECIAL VERDICT
See Verdict.

SPECIFIC PERFORMANCE
Equitable relief, 140, 367–372, 785–788.

STARE DECISIS
Generally, 2, 364, 958.

STATE COURTS
Generally, 12, 30, 160–161, 174–176.
Allocation of business among states, 181–182.
Appellate review, 175–176, 716, 1228–1229.
Division of business with federal courts, 160–162, 174–176.
"Reverse" Erie, 247–252.
Small-claims courts, 284, 289, 405–407, 1019.
Structure, 161.
Venue, 161, 905–906, 912.

STATE LAW
See Choice of Law.

STATEMENT OF CLAIM
See Complaint.

STATUTE OF LIMITATIONS
Adjudication on the merits, 962, 983.
Class actions, 1152.
Controlling law, state or federal, 207–211, 235–239, 244, 299–301.
Counterclaims, effect on, 466–470.
Federal Tort Claims Act, 469.
Raising defense, 33, 53, 431–432.
Transfer of venue, 919–921.

STAY
Pending appeal, 157–159, 160.

SUBJECT–MATTER JURISDICTION
See also Jurisdiction.
Generally, 12–14, 160–176, 712–771.
Alleging, 31, 454.
Amount in controversy, see Amount in Controversy.
Ancillary, see Ancillary Jurisdiction.
Appellate, 162.
Challenges to, 39–41, 454, 712–715, 1082–1084, 1089–1093.
Collateral attack, 714–715, 796–798, 1089–1093.
Competency, defined, 712.

SUBJECT–MATTER JURISDICTION—
　Cont'd
Concurrent, 161.
Consent, collusion, waiver, and estoppel, 41, 712–714.
District courts, see District Courts.
Diversity, see Diversity of Citizenship Cases.
Evidence, extrinsic, 715.
Exclusive, 161.
Federal question, see Federal Question Cases.
General, 161.
Interpleader, 188, 1203–1210.
Judicial power, see Judicial Power.
Jurisdictional amount, see Amount in Controversy.
Limited, 12, 161, 712–715.
Local actions, 906–912.
Original, 162.
Pendent, see Pendent Jurisdiction.
Power to punish disobedience of court order, 760–771.
Removal, see Removal.
Res judicata effect of finding, 1089–1093.

SUBPOENA
Discovery, 60, 501–502.
Grand jury, 515–516, 770.
Trial, 770.

SUBSTANTIVE LAW
Choice of law, see Choice of Law.
Nature of, 2–3, 25–26.
Substance-procedure distinction, 4–28, 205–210, 226.

SUMMARY JUDGMENT
Appealability, 154–155, 1237–1238.
Directed verdict, relation to, 565–566.
Motion for, 85–92.

SUMMONS
Service of, 179.

SUPERSEDEAS
Bond, 157.

SUPPLEMENTARY PROCEEDINGS
Enforcement remedy, 152.

SUPREME COURT
See also Appellate Review.
United States, 12, 16–17, 21, 159–160, 175–176, 716, 1228.

SUPREME COURT OF JUDICATURE
See England.

SWIFT DOCTRINE
See Choice of Law.

TEMPORARY RESTRAINING ORDERS
See Injunctions.

TERRITORIAL JURISDICTION
See also Jurisdiction.
Generally, 179–182, 772–904.
Amenability, 796.
Appearances, see Appearances.
Collateral attack, 714–715, 796–798, 1084–1085, 1087–1089, 1093.
Federal courts, jurisdiction over things, 180, 792–795.
In rem proceedings, 778, 781–785, 791–792, 844–871, 951.
Limited appearance, 792, 793–795, 858, 872.
Local actions, 906–912.
Nexus, 796.
Personal jurisdiction, see Personal Jurisdiction.
Quasi in rem proceedings, 180, 778–779, 780, 785–793, 844–871, 951.
Subtype one, 778–779, 785–788, 849, 859, 1210.
Subtype two, 778–779, 788–791, 849, 859, 872–877.
Res judicata effect of finding, 1087–1089, 1093.
Service of process, see Service.
Substantive due process, 180–181, 796.
Venue, relation to, 906.
Waiver, 41–42, 802, 891, 955.

"THEORY OF PLEADINGS"
Doctrine, generally, 408–411.
Change of theory on appeal, 411–419.

THIRD–PARTY PRACTICE
See Impleader.

"TRANSACTIONAL" VIEW
Amendments, relation back of, 53–56.
Ancillary jurisdiction, 726–728.
Claim preclusion, 975–976.
Counterclaims, 48–51, 739.
Cross-claims, 190–191.
Pendent jurisdiction, 724–725.
Removal, 757.

TRANSFER
See Venue.

TRESPASS
Equitable relief, 374–376.
Writ of, 311, 317–332, 374–376, 399–403, 659.
Forms of writ, 318.
Local actions, 906–912.
Possession requirement, 331–332.

TRIAL
Generally, 98–139, 539–711.
Burden of proof, see Burden of Proof.
Calendar, 98.
Close of evidence, motions at, 132–134.
Closing arguments, 134, 136, 595–596, 619–622.

TRIAL—Cont'd
Decision, motions after, 136, 139, 1082–1084.
Defendant's case, 108–109.
Motion at close of, 109.
Evidence, see Evidence.
Jury, see Jury Trial.
New, see New Trial.
Nonjury, see Nonjury Trial.
Opening statements, 107.
Place of, see Venue.
Plaintiff's case, 107–108.
Motion at close of, 108.
Rebuttal and rejoinder, 109–110.
Split, 615–616.

TROVER
Conversion, 335.
Waiver of tort, 344–345, 403–407.
Writ of, 333–337, 911–912.

UNFAIR COMPETITION
Equitable relief, 376–377.
Res judicata, 969, 1012–1014.

UNINCORPORATED ASSOCIATIONS
Actions relating to, 194.
Citizenship, diversity cases, 173.
Examples of, 173.
Residence, venue, 178, 905.

UNJUST ENRICHMENT
Remedy, 140, 344–345, 359, 403–407.

VARIANCE
Common law, 352.
Pleadings, 422–426.

VENUE
Generally, 177–179, 184, 905–906.
Ancillary, 905, 1210.
Federal courts, 177–179, 184, 905.
Divisions, 178.
Interpleader, 188, 1209–1210.
Removed cases, 178–179, 912.
Transfer of cases, 181, 912–933.
Forum non conveniens, 912–914, 921–933.
Local actions, 906–912.
Pendent, 905.
Residence, 177.
Aliens, 178.
Corporations, 177–178, 905.
Unincorporated associations, 178, 905.
State courts, 161, 905–906, 912.
Transitory actions, 906–912.
Waiver, 41–42, 905, 955.

VERDICT
Generally, 134–136, 594–616.
Compromise, 606–607, 608, 1044.
Directed, see Directed Verdict.
Error in, new trial, 137–138, 623–634.
Forms of, 134.
"Impossible," 606–607.

VERDICT—Cont'd
Integrity and validity of, 601–607.
Juror misconduct, 116, 601–605.
Kinds of, 125, 607–616.
  General, 125, 607–609.
  General with interrogatories, 125, 607–
    609, 612–615.
  Special, 125, 607–611, 663, 1216.
  Special issues, 608.
Motions after, 136–139.
Quotient, 603.
Return of, 136, 605.
Sealed 605, 607.
Split trial, 615–616.
Surplusage in, 606.

VERIFICATION
Pleadings, 456–459.
Removal petition, 456.

VOIR DIRE
Jury selection, 106–107.
  Challenges, 106–107.

VOLUNTARY DISMISSAL
See Dismissal.

"VOUCHING IN"
Indemnity, 1033–1034.

WAIVER
Compulsory counterclaim, 47, 999.
Defenses and objections, 41–45.
Notice, 952–955.
Service, 41–42, 802.
Subject-matter jurisdiction, 41, 712–714.
Territorial jurisdiction, 41–42, 802, 891,
  955.
Tort, of, 344–345, 403–407.
Venue, 41–42, 905, 955.
Work product of lawyer, 491–492, 495–
  496.

WASTE
Equitable relief, 374.

WITNESSES
  See also Evidence.
Calling and interrogation by judge, 274–
  276.
Competency of, 114–117.
Concealment of, 73, 266–268, 271.
Contradiction of, 131.
Discovery of identity and location, 57–58,
  73, 482, 493–496.
Examination of, 108, 130–132, 258–259,
  271.
Expert, see Expert Witnesses.
Impeachment of, 130–131, 496–498.
Statements of, 130–131, 472–493.

WRITS
See Common Law.

†